PC HARDWARE

IN A NUTSHELL

Third Edition

Robert Bruce Thompson and
Barbara Fritchman Thompson

O'REILLY®

Beijing • Cambridge • Farnham • Köln • Paris • Sebastopol • Taipei • Tokyo

PC Hardware in a Nutshell, Third Edition

by Robert Bruce Thompson and Barbara Fritchman Thompson

Copyright © 2003, 2002, 2000 O'Reilly & Associates, Inc. All rights reserved.
Printed in the United States of America.

Published by O'Reilly & Associates, Inc., 1005 Gravenstein Highway North,
Sebastopol, CA 95472.

O'Reilly & Associates books may be purchased for educational, business, or sales
promotional use. Online editions are also available for most titles (*safari.oreilly.com*). For
more information, contact our corporate/institutional sales department: 800-998-9938 or
corporate@oreilly.com.

Editor:	Brian Jepson
Production Editor:	Sarah Sherman
Cover Designer:	Hanna Dyer
Interior Designer:	David Futato

Printing History:

October 2000:	First Edition.
June 2002:	Second Edition.
July 2003:	Third Edition.

ISBN: 0-596-00513-X
[M]

Table of Contents

Foreword

My job is to persuade you to buy this book or make you feel you've made the right choice if you've already bought it.

That's easy because there's not another book like this, and if you do much with computers you need a good reference work on hardware. Of course there are massively larger books on the subject, but that's just the point: most of the time you're not looking for a long essay on the subject, you need information, and reliable judgment, both of which Robert Bruce Thompson is highly—I am tempted to say uniquely—qualified to give.

I can say this with some authority. I've never actually met Robert Bruce Thompson face to face, but we've been friends for years. Such is the way with the modern Internet. I first "met" him in the dark days after BYTE Magazine was suddenly and unexpectedly folded, and I continued my column on my web site (Shameless self-promotion: *www.jerrypournelle.com*.) One of the features of both the web site and the column was reader mail, and there soon appeared a corps of regulars, all experts in one or another field, all articulate, and all very generous with their time and effort. Robert Thompson stood out among these, and it was soon clear to me that he knew far more about computer hardware than I did. That was surprising: I've been in this business since 1978, and while no one can know everything, I thought I knew a good bit about nearly everything. I do, too, but Thompson knows more, both in depth and breadth, and that's astonishing.

He's pretty careful, too. Over the years I have found I agree with most of his conclusions, and when we disagree I have to rethink my position, because he's been right at least as often as I have been.

So. You have here a well written book by someone who understands the subject. It's about computer hardware and nearly everyone needs a good opinionated reference work on that subject, provided the opinions are sound, which in Thompson's case they certainly are. It's published by O'Reilly, which means it's well edited by editors who resist the temptation to become unacknowledged collaborators. It's really the best book you'll find on this subject. And if that doesn't persuade you to buy this book, I doubt anything else I can say would.

—Jerry Pournelle
Chaos Manor
July 2003

Preface

PC Hardware in a Nutshell. An oxymoron, as it turns out. When Robert began work on the first edition of this book in late 1998, he planned to write a 300-page book in five months. Barbara joined the project early, at first as the researcher and later as the full coauthor. After more than 18 months of working seven days a week, including last-minute rewrites to make everything as current as possible, we finally completed the first edition.

Robert decided to write the first edition because he couldn't find a good answer to what seemed to be a simple question. Robert, who has extensive PC experience, wanted to buy his first CD burner but didn't know much about them. He needed information about how to choose, install, configure, and use a CD burner. It would have been easy to check articles about CD burners in hardware-oriented magazines and enthusiast web sites, but Robert didn't trust them to provide accurate and unbiased information.

He next checked the shelf of PC hardware books he owns. What he found in those books was lots of *interesting* information, but a surprising dearth of *useful* information. For example, one very popular title devoted less than five of its 1500+ pages to CD-R and CD-RW, and most of these pages described only the history and low-level functioning of these devices. Advice on how to choose a CD burner? Advice on how to install it, configure it, use it, or troubleshoot it? Next to nothing. That same book devoted nearly 70 pages to a list of vendors—information easily accessible on the Web—so the shortage of information couldn't have been a result of page-count constraints.

We were determined to write a book filled with *useful* information. You won't find tables of drive parameters for hundreds of obsolete disk drives, instructions on how to change the interleave by low-level formatting of an XT hard drive, charts of keyboard scan codes, and so on. As *interesting* as those things might be, they fail the *useful* test. Pruning stuff that was merely interesting was painful because we like to read interesting stuff as much as the next person. But we quickly found out why there's so much interesting information and so relatively little useful information in most PC hardware books. *Interesting* is quick and easy to write. *Useful* is slow and hard, because you actually have to *do* all the stuff.

We found numerous errors repeated nearly verbatim in more than one book— things that were clearly wrong, but that an author had simply repeated instead of verifying it by taking the time to check for himself. We were guilty of that at times, too. When we listed the pinouts for a gameport, for example, we got that information from published sources. But surprisingly often, we found that these sources disagreed, and so were forced to check for ourselves.

And, boy, did we expend an incredible amount of time and effort checking things for ourselves. Rather than simply repeating what others had said about CD burners, for example, we decided to find out for ourselves. Doing that required building four computers—two IDE and two SCSI, one each with Windows 98 and Windows NT—and testing each configuration with different drive models by burning numerous CDs with each. About ten 14-hour days and 400 CD blanks later, we finally had a handle on CD burners. All that work turned into just a few pages and some specific product recommendations. But all that work was necessary if we wanted to write something more than just a me-too book.

Our efforts were rewarded. The first edition of *PC Hardware in a Nutshell* sold well, and was widely acclaimed by readers and reviewers alike. For example, Barnes & Noble had this to say:

> Here's one PC hardware book that pulls no punches. It even recommends specific brands and models, and tells you why—so you can evaluate whatever's on sale when you're ready to buy. The authors speak to you as if you're planning to build your own computer from scratch. That's the "big kahuna" PC maintenance project, so the book's easily up to any "smaller" challenges— like adding a CD burner, or maybe replacing your motherboard. And it's all new—not padded with obsolete data and techniques. Specific, comprehensive, and relentlessly useful—superb!

Given the success of the first edition, we considered doing just a quick update, but we decided that our readers deserved better. So we spent nearly a year building the second edition. We spent weeks on end doing detailed testing and comparisons of numerous products, the results of which often boiled down to a couple of paragraphs of advice or a single product recommendation. We greatly expanded both the breadth of topics covered and the level of detail presented. The second edition was, in every respect, twice the book that the first edition was.

Of the second edition, Barnes & Noble said:

> O'Reilly's straight-shootin', no-holds-barred, quality-focused PC hardware book is back, in a Second Edition that's even more indispensable than the first.

> The "Hardware Guys"—Barbara Fritchman Thompson and Robert Bruce Thompson—have updated *PC Hardware in a Nutshell* to reflect pretty much everything that's come down the pike in the two years following the first edition, including Athlon XP/MP microprocessors, USB 2.0, and the "Big Drive" initiative for ATA drives larger than 137 gigs.

> Want someone to make sense of all the DVD writable/rewritable standards and give you some decent advice about buying one? Look here. Want honest and specific advice about the latest motherboards and chipsets from both sides of

the Pacific? Look here. Want troubleshooting help? There's even more of it than in the first edition.

Want to put together your own PC? The Thompsons walk you through it in extraordinary detail (how to make sure your system's multiple fans are working together, not at cross-purposes; why you should only use three screws instead of four if you're mounting a drive in a cheap case; which add-on cards generate the most heat and should be given the most breathing room).

In the first edition, the authors ended most chapters with an "Our Picks" section offering specific hardware recommendations. But hardware changes so fast that they've revamped these sections to be a bit more general and moved the specific advice to the book's companion web site. Don't worry: The book's as opinionated as ever, and when the Thompsons don't like something (Sound Blaster Live! PCI cards, generic memory), believe us, they say so.

For this third edition, we again set to work, testing new components and updating the existing material. PC hardware changes fast. We ended up completely rewriting material we originally thought would need only minor revisions. This new edition required much more time and effort than we expected when we set out to write it, but at least we had fun doing it.

We wouldn't have started this project unless we thought we could write the best PC hardware book available. We think this third edition of *PC Hardware in a Nutshell* meets that goal, and we hope you will too.

Audience

This book is intended for anyone who buys, builds, upgrades, or repairs PCs in a corporate, small-business, or home setting. If you want to buy a PC, this book tells you what to look for—and what to look out for. If you want to build a PC, this book explains, component by component, the key parts of a PC, describes the important characteristics of each, provides buying guidelines, recommends specific products (by brand name and model), and takes you step by step through building the PC. If you have an older PC, this book tells you what you need to know to upgrade it—if it makes sense to do so—as well as when it makes more sense simply to retire it to less-demanding duties. Finally, if your PC breaks, this book tells you what you need to know to troubleshoot the problem and then choose and install replacement parts.

This book focuses on PC hardware running Windows 9X and Windows 2000/XP, which among them power the vast majority of PCs. For the first time, this edition includes limited coverage of Linux-related hardware issues. The coverage is limited not because we think Linux deserves or needs less complete coverage than Windows, but because we're still Linux newbies. Some of what we've written about Linux issues will no doubt be obvious to experienced Linux users, but may be helpful to those who, like us, are just starting to migrate to Linux. We use eight primary systems—desktops, notebooks, and servers. Three of those are now running Linux exclusively. We expect that proportion to be reversed by the time we finish the next edition of this book.

Organization

Each chapter of this book is devoted to one topic, and is self-supporting. The first two chapters provide an overview of PC hardware and standards, as well as detailed advice about buying, building, upgrading, and repairing PCs; describe the tools and software you'll need; explain basic procedures such as installing expansion cards; and detail the tips and tricks we've learned during 20 years of working on PCs. These chapters include:

Chapter 1, *Fundamentals*
Chapter 2, *Working on PCs*

The second group of chapters covers the core components of any PC—motherboards, processors, and memory. These chapters take the form used throughout the rest of the book, beginning with brief background information about the component, followed by an explanation of the important characteristics, guidelines on choosing among competing products, instructions for installing and configuring the component, troubleshooting information, if applicable, and a final "Our Picks" section, which tells you which products we recommend. This group includes the following chapters:

Chapter 3, *Motherboards*
Chapter 4, *Processors*
Chapter 5, *Memory*

The third group of chapters covers removable magnetic storage, including the pedestrian floppy disk drive, one of the few PC components that survives largely unchanged from the earliest days of PCs; "super-floppies" such as the Iomega Zip and the Imation LS-120; removable hard disk drives; and tape drives, which despite the arrival of new technologies remain the best choice for backing up data. This group includes the following chapters:

Chapter 6, *Floppy Disk Drives*
Chapter 7, *High-Capacity Floppy Disk Drives*
Chapter 8, *Removable Hard Disk Drives*
Chapter 9, *Tape Drives*

The fourth group of chapters covers optical storage, an increasingly important component in modern PCs. We detail what you need to know to choose, install, configure, and use CD-ROM, CD-R, CD-RW, DVD-ROM, and writable DVD drives. This group includes the following chapters:

Chapter 10, *CD-ROM Drives*
Chapter 11, *CD Writers*
Chapter 12, *DVD Drives*

The fifth group of chapters covers Parallel- and Serial-ATA (IDE) hard disk drives, which are ubiquitous in modern PCs, as well as SCSI models, which provide better performance at correspondingly higher prices. We explain the important characteristics of hard drives, provide guidelines for purchasing a hard drive, and explain how to install, prepare, configure, and troubleshoot hard drives. This group includes the following chapters:

Chapter 13, *Hard Disk Interfaces*
Chapter 14, *Hard Disk Drives*

The sixth group of chapters covers sight and sound. We describe the important characteristics of video adapters, monitors and LCD displays, sound cards, and speakers, and explain how to choose, install, configure, and troubleshoot them. This group includes the following chapters:

Chapter 15, *Video Adapters*
Chapter 16, *Displays*
Chapter 17, *Sound Adapters*
Chapter 18, *Speakers and Headphones*

The seventh group of chapters covers input devices—keyboards, mice, and game controllers. We explain how they work, how to choose the best ones for your needs, and (as usual) how to install, configure, and troubleshoot them. This group includes the following chapters:

Chapter 19, *Keyboards*
Chapter 20, *Mice and Trackballs*
Chapter 21, *Game Controllers*

The eighth group of chapters covers serial, parallel, and USB communications—the technologies that PCs use to connect with external peripherals and the outside world. We explain how each works, how to choose the best technology for your needs, and how to configure and troubleshoot communications. This group includes the following chapters:

Chapter 22, *Serial Communications*
Chapter 23, *Parallel Communications*
Chapter 24, *USB Communications*

The ninth group of chapters covers three components—cases, PC power supplies, and backup power supplies—that receive little attention, but are important to system reliability and usability. We detail the important characteristics of each, and provide guidelines for choosing the best case and power supplies for your system. This group includes the following chapters:

Chapter 25, *Cases*
Chapter 26, *Power Supplies*
Chapter 27, *Backup Power Supplies*

Finally, Chapter 28, *Building a PC*, puts it all together, illustrating how to turn a pile of components into a working PC.

Most chapters end with an "Our Picks" section. In the first edition of this book, we made specific recommendations in these sections. The problem with recommending specific makes and models in print, of course, is that PC hardware changes in Internet time. Products that were the hottest things on the market (or even preproduction engineering samples) when we started working with them had become mainstream when we went to press, and may even have been discontinued by the time the book reached the stores. So instead of focusing on ephemera in print, we instead concentrate here on important characteristics and guidelines, which don't change nearly as fast.

We recognize, though, that many people want specific advice by make and model—"Which motherboard/drive/monitor should I buy?" is one of the most common questions we get—so we've gone to some trouble to create and update pages on our web site that provide detailed recommendations. We still provide general recommendations in the "Our Picks" sections, but you'll now find our specific recommendations—by brand name and model—on our web site, at:

http://www.hardwareguys.com/picks/picks.html

We base these recommendations on our own experience, not after using the product for a day or a week, but after extensive day-in, day-out use under realistic conditions. If we say we found a particular DVD burner to be durable, that means we used that DVD burner extensively and burned a bunch of DVDs with it. If we say a particular motherboard is stable, that means we used it in one or more of our own systems over a period of weeks or months and found that it doesn't crash, even when performing stressful tasks such as running a full benchmark suite or compiling a Linux kernel. If we say a particular display is the best we've used, it's because we sat in front of it for many long hours while writing this book. And so on.

Conventions

This book uses the following typographical conventions:

italic

> Is used for the names of files, directories, hostnames, domain names, and URLs, and to emphasize new terms when they are first introduced.

`constant-width`

> Is used to show the contents of files, command syntax, and the output from commands.

`constant-italic`

> Is used in examples to show variables for which a context-specific substitution should be made. (The variable `filename`, for example, would be replaced by some actual filename.)

[*option*]

> When showing command syntax, we place optional parts of the command within brackets. For example, `ls [-l]` means that the `-l` option is not required.

> This is an example of a Note. Notes are short asides that convey supplemental information that may not be important to all readers.

> This is an example of a Warning. Warnings highlight dangerous procedures—those that may damage you, your hardware, or your data. Disregard warnings at your own peril.

We'd Like to Hear from You

We have tested and verified the information in this book to the best of our ability, but we don't doubt that some errors have crept in and remained hidden despite our best efforts and those of our editors and technical reviewer to find and eradicate them. Those errors are ours alone. Please tell us about any errors you find, as well as your suggestions for improving future editions, by writing or calling:

O'Reilly & Associates, Inc.
1005 Gravenstein Highway North
Sebastopol, CA 95472
(800) 998-9938 (in the United States or Canada)
(707) 829-0515 (international or local)
(707) 829-0104 (fax)

You can also send us email. To be put on our mailing list or to request a catalog, send email to:

info@oreilly.com

For comments on the book, send email to:

bookquestions@oreilly.com

To contact one of us directly, send email to:

barbara@hardwareguys.com
robert@hardwareguys.com

We read all email we receive, but we cannot respond individually to requests for help in choosing hardware, resolving problems, and so on. We do like to hear from readers, however.

We also have a web site for the book, which includes updated hardware recommendations, buying guides, and articles, as well as errata, archived older material, and so on:

http://www.hardwareguys.com

We also maintain a messageboard for the book, where you can read and post messages about PC hardware topics. You can read messages as a guest, but if you want to post messages you must register as a member of the messageboard. We keep registration information confidential, and you can choose to have your email address hidden on any messages you post.

http://forums.hardwareguys.com/

We each maintain a personal journal page, updated daily, which frequently includes references to new PC hardware we're working with, problems we've discovered, and other things we think are interesting. You can view these journal pages at:

Barbara: *http://www.fritchman.com/diaries/thisweek.html*
Robert: *http://www.ttgnet.com/thisweek.html*

Thank you for buying the third edition of *PC Hardware in a Nutshell*. We hope you enjoy reading it as much as we enjoyed writing it.

Acknowledgments

In addition to the O'Reilly production staff, who are listed individually in the Colophon, we want to thank our technical reviewer, Francisco García Maceda. Francisco knows so much about PC hardware that it's scary. He did yeoman duty in finding mistakes we made and in making numerous useful suggestions, all of which helped make this a better book.

We also want to thank our contacts at the hardware companies, who provided technical help, evaluation units, and other assistance. There are far too many to list individually, but they know who they are. We also want to thank the readers of our web sites and message boards, many of whom have taken the time to offer useful suggestions for improvements to the book. Thanks, folks. We couldn't have done it without you.

The photographs in this book were shot with Olympus digital cameras. We've used many digital cameras, and have developed a strong preference for Olympus models. Their experience as a premier maker of film cameras shows clearly in the construction quality, image quality, functionality, and ease-of-use of Olympus digital cameras.

Finally, we want to thank our editors, Robert J. Denn and Brian Jepson, and our publisher, Tim O'Reilly, all of whom contributed numerous useful comments and suggestions.

1

Fundamentals

This chapter covers a mixed bag of important fundamental information about PCs, including how PCs are defined, an overview of PC components and technologies, a brief explanation of system resources, guidelines for building, buying, and upgrading PCs, smart buying practices, and suggestions as to what to do with old PCs.

PCs Defined

Who decides what is and what is not a PC? That question is not as trivial as it sounds, because there has never been (and probably will never be) an all-embracing *de jure* standard to define the PC. IBM created the *de facto* PC standard (and trademarked the name) when it shipped the first IBM Personal Computer in 1981. For more than five years, until its introduction of the ill-fated proprietary PS/2 line in 1987, IBM defined the PC standard. For a short time thereafter, some considered that Compaq defined the standard. But the days when any PC maker defined the PC standard are far in the past.

These days, Intel and Microsoft jointly define the *de facto* PC standard. In fact, a good working definition of a PC is a computer that uses an Intel or compatible processor *and* can run a Microsoft operating system. Any computer that meets both requirements—a so-called *Wintel* computer—is a PC. A computer that does not is not. Computers based on some Intel processors cannot run any Microsoft operating system, and thus are not PCs. Conversely, some computers with non-Intel processors can run Microsoft operating systems, but do not qualify as PCs. For example, DEC Alpha minicomputers running Windows NT 4 are not PCs.

Two formal documents, described in the following sections, define the joint Intel/Microsoft standards for systems and components you are likely to be working with. These standards are *de facto* in the sense that system and peripheral makers are not required to comply with them to manufacture and sell their products. They might as well be *de jure* standards, however, because compliance is required to achieve such nearly mandatory certifications as inclusion on the Windows NT/ 2000/XP Hardware Compatibility Lists.

PC 99 System Design Guide

PC 99 System Design Guide (*PC 99*) is a book-length document that defines required, recommended, and optional (neither required nor recommended, but must meet the standard if included) characteristics for several classes of PCs, including *Basic PC 99* (further subdivided into *Consumer PC 99* and *Office PC 99*), *Workstation PC 99*, *Entertainment PC 99*, and *Mobile PC 99*.

PC 99 is the penultimate member of a series of documents, which began in 1990 with the first MPC standard, and continued with the *PC 95*, *PC 97*, and *PC 98* revisions. *PC 99* was formalized in mid-1998, took partial effect in July 1999 for systems to be delivered in Q4 1999, came into full effect January 1, 2000, and defined the standards for systems and components delivered through late 2001. In some ways, *PC 99* was unrealistically far ahead of its time—for example, in recommending Device Bay and 1394 as standard storage interfaces. In other ways, it was far behind—for example, in requiring only a 300 MHz processor and 32 MB of RAM for some configurations. Some portions are skewed to Intel CPUs (e.g., an L2 cache requirement was cut from 512 KB to 256 KB when Intel shipped Coppermine Pentium III CPUs with 256 KB L2 cache—probably not a coincidence), while many others are skewed toward Microsoft operating systems. Neither of those is surprising in the document that defines the Wintel standard. All of that said, *PC 99* was and remains an important document because it defined the direction of PC development as we entered the new millennium.

You can purchase *PC 99* in book form (Microsoft Press, 1998, ISBN: 0-7356-0518-1). You can view or download *PC 99 1.0* in Acrobat format (*http://www. pcdesguide.org/*) or *PC 99a*—the final release of *PC 99*, with minor updates and corrections—in compiled HTML help format (*http://www.microsoft.com/hwdev/ platform/pcdesign/desguide/default.asp*). The PC Design Guide home page (*http:// www.pcdesguide.org*) also contains links to these documents in various formats.

If you've ever crawled around under a desk trying to read the tiny icons on port connectors, you'll appreciate one very visible manifestation of PC 99 compliance—standard colors for port connectors, listed in Table 1-1. Nearly all PCs and peripherals shipped since Q4 1999 use these colors.

Table 1-1. PC 99 recommended connector color codes

Connector	Color	Connector	Color
Analog VGA	Blue	PS/2-compatible keyboard	Purple
Audio Line-in	Light Blue	PS/2-compatible mouse	Green
Audio Line-out	Lime	Serial	Teal/Turquoise
Digital monitor/flat panel	White	Speaker out/subwoofer	Orange
IEEE-1394	Gray	Right-to-left speaker	Brown
Microphone	Pink	USB	Black
MIDI/gameport	Gold	Video Out	Yellow
Parallel	Burgundy	SCSI, LAN, telephone, etc.	Not defined

PC 2001 System Design Guide

The *PC 2001 System Design Guide* (*PC 2001*) is, according to Intel and Microsoft, the final document in this series. In many respects, *PC 2001* is more an addendum to *PC 99* than a self-supporting document. Many PC 2001 specifications direct the reader to PC 99 and state only that the PC 2001 requirements are identical to those of PC 99, or are similar to those of PC 99 but with minor changes specified. The major differences between PC 99 and PC 2001 are:

- PC 2001 eliminates the strong emphasis of PC 99 on market classifications—Basic PC, Consumer PC, Entertainment PC, and so on—although it does specify different requirements for workstations and Mobile PCs where appropriate.

- PC 2001 no longer categorizes components and functionality as "recommended," instead specifying only those that are required. A component or function that is not required is not mentioned. Some requirements, identified as "if implemented," are conditional. If a manufacturer provides that component or feature, it must comply with the specified standard.

- PC 2001 eliminates some former requirements because Microsoft and Intel deem them no longer important to the industry or "no longer relevant in defining the optimal user experience with the Windows operating system," whatever that means.

- PC 2001 defines requirements intended to support new and forthcoming technologies implemented in recent Microsoft operating systems, including Windows 2000, Windows Me, and Windows XP.

- PC 2001 places a greatly increased emphasis on legacy-reduced and legacy-free systems. Some "legacy" items such as ISA expansion slots and device dependence on MS-DOS are forbidden entirely, while others are merely strongly discouraged.

- PC 2001 emphasizes (although it does not mandate) features that are collectively called the Easy PC Initiative, which focuses on ease of setup, use, expansion, and maintenance.

You can download a copy of *PC 2001* in Word, PDF, or Microsoft Compiled Help format from *http://www.pcdesguide.org*.

PC Components and Technologies

The following sections provide a quick overview of the components and technologies used in modern PCs.

Hardware Components

One of the great strengths of the PC architecture is that it is extensible, allowing a great variety of components to be added, thereby permitting the PC to perform functions its designers may never have envisioned. However, most PCs include a more-or-less standard set of components, including the following:

Motherboard
　　The *motherboard*, described in Chapter 3, is the heart of a PC. It serves as "Command Central" to coordinate the activities of the system. Its type largely

determines system capabilities. Motherboards include the following components:

Chipset

The chipset provides the intelligence of the motherboard, and determines which processors, memory, and other components the motherboard can use. Most chipsets are divided physically and logically into two components. The *Northbridge* controls cache and main memory and manages the host bus and PCI expansion bus (the various busses used in PCs are described in Chapter 3). The *Southbridge* manages the ISA bus, bridges the PCI and ISA busses, and incorporates a *Super I/O* controller, which provides serial and parallel ports, the IDE interface, and other I/O functions. Some recent chipsets, notably models from Intel, no longer use the old Northbridge/Southbridge terminology, although the functionality and division of tasks is similar. Other recent chipsets put all functions on one physical chip.

CPU slot(s) and/or socket(s)

The type of CPU slot or socket determines which processors the motherboard can use. The most popular CPU connectors are Socket 370 (late-model Intel Pentium III and Celeron processors), Socket A (AMD Athlon and Duron), Socket 478 (current Celeron and Pentium 4), Socket 423 (old-style Pentium 4), Slot 1 (old-style Pentium II/III and Celeron), Slot A (older-style Athlon), and the obsolete Socket 7 (Intel Pentium and AMD K6-* processors). Some motherboards have two or more CPU connectors, allowing them to support multiple processors. A few motherboards have both Slot 1 and Socket 370 connectors, allowing them to support either type of CPU (but not both at once).

 There are three versions of Socket 370, which differ in pinouts and which processors they support. Early Socket 370/PPGA motherboards support only older Mendocino-core Celeron processors. Later Socket 370/FC-PGA motherboards support Coppermine-core Pentium III FC-PGA processors and Coppermine128-core Celeron FC-PGA processors. The final Socket 370 motherboards, which Intel refers to as "Universal" models, support any Socket 370 processor, including Tualatin-core Pentium III and Celeron processors. Although Socket 370 is now obsolescent, tens of millions of Socket 370 systems remain in use. When you upgrade such a system it is important to check the documentation to determine which Socket 370 variant that system uses.

Voltage Regulator Module (VRM)

VRMs supply clean, tightly regulated voltage to the CPU. Faster CPUs draw more current. Good VRMs are expensive, so some motherboard makers use the lowest-rated VRM suitable for the fastest CPU the motherboard is designed to support. Better VRMs allow a motherboard to accept faster future CPUs with only a BIOS upgrade.

Memory slots

The type and number of memory slots (along with chipset limitations) determine the type and amount of memory you can install in a PC. Recent motherboards use 168-pin SDRAM DIMMs, 168- or 184-pin Rambus RIMMs, 184-pin DDR-SDRAM DIMMs, or some combination. Motherboards that use 30- or 72-pin SIMMs are obsolete.

Expansion bus slots

The type and number of expansion bus slots determine the type and number of expansion cards you can add to the system. Recent motherboards may have both PCI and ISA expansion slots, although many recent models have only PCI slots.

Integrated functions

Modern motherboards often include embedded functions, such as video and sound (and, less commonly, LAN and SCSI interfaces), that were formerly provided by add-on expansion cards. Embedded components reduce costs, and are better integrated and more reliable. Against those advantages, it may be difficult or impossible to upgrade embedded components, and you pay for those embedded components whether you use them or not. Integrated motherboards are often ideally suited for casual use, but most readers of this book will avoid them for high-performance systems and build *à la carte* from discrete components.

Processor

The *processor* or *CPU* (described in Chapter 4) is the engine that drives the PC. The CPU you use determines how fast the system runs and what operating systems and other software can run on it. Most PCs use processors from Intel (Pentium II/III/4 or Celeron) or AMD (Athlon or Duron). Processors vary in speed (currently 700 MHz to 3+ GHz), cost ($25 to $500+), physical connector (Socket 423, Socket 478, Socket 370, Socket A, Slot 1, Slot 2, Slot A, Socket 7, and so on), efficiency at performing various functions, and other respects. Although processors get much attention, the truth is that performance differences between a $50 processor and a $250 processor are relatively minor, typically a factor of two.

Memory

A PC uses *Random Access Memory* (*RAM*), also called simply *memory*, to store the programs and data with which it is currently working. RAM is available in many different types, speeds, and physical packages. The amount and type of RAM a system can use depends on its chipset, the type and number of RAM slots available, and other factors. The optimum amount of RAM depends on the operating system you run, how many and which programs you run simultaneously, and other considerations. Typical new PCs may have from 64 megabytes (MB)—marginally adequate for some environments—to 256 MB, which is sufficient for many people. Very few commercial desktop systems come standard with 512 MB or more, which is the amount now used by most "power users." Adding RAM is often a cost-effective upgrade for older systems, many of which have woefully inadequate RAM to run modern operating systems and programs. Memory is described in Chapter 5.

Floppy disk drive

The humble *floppy disk drive* (FDD) was formerly used for everything from booting the PC to storing data to running programs to making backups, but has now been largely relegated to such infrequent uses as making emergency boot diskettes, loading updated device drivers, running diagnostics programs, or "sneakernetting" documents to other systems. Many people don't use their FDDs from one month to the next. The FDD has been officially declared a "legacy" device, and many PCs manufactured after mid-2000 do not have one. All of that said, the FDD remains important to millions of PC users because it is the only read/write removable storage device present on most current PCs. Chapter 6 describes what you need to know about FDDs.

 Every time we have built a PC without an FDD, we later regretted doing so. We have had to tear down PCs just to install an FDD, something we should have done in the first place. FDDs are $15 items, and we think it is senseless to build a PC without one.

Optical drive

CD-ROM drives began to appear on mainstream PCs in the early 1990s, became ubiquitous, and have remained generally unchanged except for improvements in speed and reliability. CD-ROM discs store 600+ MB of data in read-only form, and because they are capacious and cheap to produce, are commonly used to distribute software and data. CD-ROM drives can also play CD-DA (audio) discs and multimedia discs, which makes them popular for listening to music and playing games. CD-ROM drives are detailed in Chapter 10. Chapter 11 covers CD-RW drives, which can write discs as well as read them. Chapter 12 describes DVD-ROM drives—which are the follow-on to CD-ROM, and may be used to watch movies or access very large data-bases—and DVD writers, which function much like CD writers but store about seven times as much data.

Hard disk drive

The *hard disk drive* (HDD) is the primary storage device on any PC. Unlike RAM, which retains data only while power remains applied, data written to an HDD remains stored there until you delete it. HDD space was formerly a scarce resource that users went to great lengths to conserve. Modern HDDs are so capacious (up to 200+ GB) and so inexpensive ($1.50/GB or less) that most people now regard disk space as essentially free. On the downside, modern HDDs can be difficult to install and configure, particularly in older systems, and their huge capacity makes some form of tape backup (Chapter 9) almost mandatory. Chapter 13 and Chapter 14 tell you everything you need to know about hard disk interfaces and hard disk drives.

Video adapter

A *video adapter*, also called a *graphics adapter*, accepts video data from the computer and converts it into a form the monitor can display. In addition to image quality, the video adapter you use determines the sharpness, number of colors, and stability of the image your monitor displays. Most recent video adapters display text and simple graphics adequately, but video adapters vary greatly in their suitability for use with graphics-intensive software, including games. Video adapters are covered in Chapter 15.

Display

The display you use ultimately determines the quality of the video you see. Most PCs use traditional CRT monitors, but flat-panel LCD displays are an increasingly popular choice. Displays are available in a wide variety of sizes, capabilities, features, and prices, and choosing the right one is not a trivial task. Displays are covered in Chapter 16.

Sound adapter and speakers

All PCs can produce basic warning sounds and audible prompts using their built-in speakers, but for listening to audio CDs, playing games, watching DVDs with full surround sound, using the Internet to make free long-distance telephone calls, using voice-recognition software, and performing other PC audio functions, you'll need a sound card (or embedded motherboard sound adapter) and speakers or headphones. Sound cards are covered in Chapter 17 and speakers in Chapter 18.

Keyboard and mouse

PCs use several types of devices to accept user input—keyboards for entering text; mice, trackballs, and other pointing devices for working in the Windows graphical environment; and game controllers for playing modern graphical computer games and simulations. Keyboards are covered in Chapter 19, Mice and trackballs in Chapter 20, and game controllers in Chapter 21.

Communications ports and devices

Communications ports allow a PC to connect to external peripherals such as printers, modems, and similar devices. Chapter 22 covers serial ports, which are obsolescent but still important for some uses. Chapter 23 covers parallel ports, which are still commonly used to connect printers. Chapter 24 covers Universal Serial Bus (USB) ports, which are replacing legacy serial and parallel ports, and will eventually be the only general-purpose external communications ports used on PCs.

Case and power supply

The *case* (or *chassis*) is the outer shell that contains the PC and all internal peripheral devices. The *power supply* provides regulated power to all system components and cooling airflow to keep components from overheating. Cases are described in Chapter 25, power supplies in Chapter 26. Chapter 27 tells you what you need to know about backup power supplies, which protect the power that runs your PC.

Software Components

Many people think of a PC as comprising solely physical hardware, but hardware is just a useless pile of silicon, metal, and plastic unless you have software to make it do something. *Software* is a set of detailed instructions that allow a computer to perform a task or group of tasks. Software is usually categorized as being one of three types:

Applications programs

Applications programs are what most people think of when they hear the word *software*. These programs are designed to perform specific user-oriented tasks, such as creating a word processing document or spreadsheet, browsing the Web, reading and replying to email, managing your schedule, creating a presentation, or recovering a deleted file. Hundreds of thousands of applications programs are available, from comprehensive office suites such as Microsoft Office, to vertical market packages such as medical office billing software, to single-purpose utilities such as WinZip. Whatever you might want a computer to do for you, you can probably locate applications software that will do it.

Operating system

An *operating system* is software that manages the PC itself, providing such basic functions as the ability to write and read data from a disk or to display images on the monitor. A PC can run any of dozens of operating systems, including DOS, Windows 95/98/98SE/Me (we use *Windows 9X* to refer to these collectively throughout the book, and *Windows 98* inclusively if we are discussing all versions of Windows 9X other than Windows 95), Windows NT, Windows 2000, Windows XP, Linux and other Unix variants, NetWare, BeOS, and many others. The operating system you use determines which applications programs you can run, which peripherals you can use (not all operating systems support all peripherals), which technologies are available to you (e.g., NT does not support Plug and Play or USB), and how reliable the system is. The vast majority of PCs run Windows 9X/2000/XP or Linux, so we focus on those operating systems in this book.

Device drivers

We said that the operating system determines which peripherals you can use. That's true, but only indirectly. Operating systems themselves natively recognize only the most basic, standardized system components—things like memory, the system clock, and so on. *Device drivers* are small programs that work at a very low level to integrate support for other devices into the operating system. Using device drivers allows an operating system to be extensible, which means that support for new devices can be added incrementally, without updating the operating system itself. For example, if you install a new video card, installing a device driver for that video card allows the operating system to recognize it and use its full capabilities. Most operating systems include "vanilla" device drivers that allow devices to be used at less than their full capabilities (e.g., the standard VGA driver in Windows) until an appropriate driver can be installed. Most operating systems also include specific device-driver support for common devices, such as popular video cards and printers, but these drivers are often old and slow, and do not take full advantage of hardware capabilities. In general, you should download the most recent device driver from the hardware manufacturer when you install new hardware.

Firmware Components and the PC BIOS

Firmware is a special class of software, so called because it is more or less permanently stored on chips. Firmware is often referred to generically as a *BIOS* (*Basic Input/Output System*) because the only firmware contained in early PCs was the main system *ROM-BIOS* (*Read-Only Memory BIOS*). That's no longer true. Nearly every component in a modern PC contains its own firmware. Disk drives, SCSI host adapters, video cards, sound cards, keyboards, and most other devices contain firmware, and nowadays that firmware is seldom read-only.

 Although few people do so, installing firmware updates is an important part of keeping a modern PC functioning at its best. For example, firmware for most CD writers is frequently updated to add support for new types of blank media. The most important firmware to keep updated is the main system BIOS. Good motherboard makers frequently release updated BIOS versions that add functionality, fix bugs, support faster processor speeds, and so on.

The two most important pieces of firmware in a PC are the chipset—which technically is intermediate between hardware and firmware—and the main system BIOS. The chipset is the heart of the PC. Its capabilities determine such fundamental issues as which processors the motherboard supports, how data is communicated between processor and memory, and so on. The BIOS manages the basic configuration information stored in nonvolatile CMOS memory, such as the list of installed devices, and controls many of the low-level configuration parameters that determine how the PC functions. Although the chipset cannot be updated, the BIOS in all modern PCs can be updated.

BIOS updates sometimes correct bugs, but BIOS code is so stable and well debugged (it has to be) that the purpose of most BIOS updates is to add support for new technologies. For example, many pre-1998 BIOS versions did not support hard disk drives larger than 8.4 GB. Installing an updated BIOS with Extended Interrupt 13 support allows the system to recognize and use larger hard disks. Another common reason for BIOS updates is to add support for new CPU types. For example, many Pentium II motherboards did not support Celerons, which use a different L2 caching method. Similarly, a motherboard manufactured when the fastest Pentium III available was 600 MHz might have no settings to allow using faster Pentium IIIs. Installing an updated BIOS fixes problems such as these. Systems with Flash BIOS (which is to say, all modern systems) can be updated simply by downloading the new BIOS and running a special installer program.

Updating Flash BIOS is a nontrivial operation. Performing the update incorrectly or losing power during the update can leave the PC incapable of booting. Read the detailed instructions supplied by the manufacturer before you attempt to update your BIOS, and if possible connect the PC to a UPS (Uninterruptible Power Supply) during the BIOS update. Some motherboards, notably recent Intel models, have a BIOS recovery function that allows correcting a failed update simply by changing a jumper and running the update procedure again. Some motherboards have a dual BIOS, which means that if you damage one BIOS during an update you can boot the system from the other and repair the corrupted BIOS. But many systems make no such provision, so be extremely careful when updating your system BIOS. If you fail to follow instructions exactly, or if you accidentally install the wrong BIOS update, or if the power fails during the update, the only solution may be to return the motherboard to the manufacturer for repair or replacement.

You configure BIOS options and chipset settings by running a special firmware program called CMOS Setup, which is usually invoked by pressing the F1, F2, or Delete keys while the system is booting. Some systems allow the administrator to password-protect access to CMOS Setup, while others make CMOS Setup a "blind" option. For example, recent Intel motherboards by default display an Intel splash screen rather than the standard BIOS boot screen. To run CMOS Setup, press the Esc key when the splash screen appears to clear it, and then press F2 to enter BIOS Setup.

CMOS Setup programs vary at the discretion of the motherboard or system maker in terms of what they allow you to access and change. Some Setup programs provide essentially complete access to all settings, while others allow changing only some settings, and some provide no access to chipset options at all. Figure 1-1 shows the Main screen of a typical BIOS Setup program.

```
                        PhoenixBIOS Setup Utility
    Main    Advanced    Security    Power    Boot    Exit
  ┌──────────────────────────────────────────┬─────────────────────────┐
  │                                          │   Item Specific Help    │
  │   System Time:        [15:24:04]         │                         │
  │   System Date:        [02/29/2000]       │                         │
  │                                          │  <Tab>, <Shift-Tab>, or │
  │   Legacy Diskette A:  [1.44/1.25 MB 3½"] │  <Enter> selects field. │
  │   Legacy Diskette B:  [Disabled]         │                         │
  │                                          │                         │
  │ ▶ Primary Master      [1572MB]           │                         │
  │ ▶ Primary Slave       [None]             │                         │
  │ ▶ Secondary Master    [CD-ROM]           │                         │
  │ ▶ Secondary Slave     [None]             │                         │
  │                                          │                         │
  │ ▶ Keyboard Features                      │                         │
  │                                          │                         │
  │   System Memory:      640 KB             │                         │
  │   Extended Memory:    64512 KB           │                         │
  │   Language:           [English (US)]     │                         │
  ├──────────────────────────────────────────┴─────────────────────────┤
  │ F1  Help   ↑↓ Select Item   -/+   Change Values    F9  Setup Defaults│
  │ Esc Exit   ←→ Select Menu   Enter Select ▶ Sub-Menu F10 Save and Exit│
  └──────────────────────────────────────────────────────────────────────┘
```

Figure 1-1. The Main screen of the Phoenix BIOS Setup Utility

There are so many different chipsets, BIOS versions, and Setup utilities that covering BIOS and chipset options in detail would require writing a separate book. Fortunately, someone already has. Phil Croucher's superb *The BIOS Companion* (*http://www.electrocution.com/biosc.htm*) documents BIOS and chipset options in great detail, including some that even we don't understand. Every PC technician should own a copy of this book. Another very useful BIOS resource is *Wim's BIOS Page* (*http://www.wimsbios.com/*).

Technologies

Here are some important technologies pertinent to current and next-generation PCs, with a brief explanation of each:

ACPI

> *Advanced Configuration and Power Interface (ACPI)* is the current standard for configuring system components under Plug and Play, monitoring the health of the system, and managing power usage. It replaces Intel's *Dynamic Power Management Architecture (DPMA)* and *Advanced Power Management (APM)*. All current PCs and motherboards include at least partial ACPI support. ACPI is one of those technologies that isn't quite "here yet." When it works as it should, which is usually, it provides power management and other functions that many find useful. When it doesn't work properly, or when it conflicts with other technologies such as USB, it can cause very subtle, intermittent problems that can have you pulling out your hair. It can also cause very nonsubtle problems, including systems that go into a coma rather than suspending, screens that refuse to unblank even though the system itself is running, and so on. In general, when we encounter a system that hangs or otherwise behaves strangely, our first suspects are the power supply or the memory. But ACPI conflicts are also high on the list.

AGP

> *Accelerated Graphics Port (AGP)* is a dedicated video port connector, introduced in 1997 by Intel and now nearly ubiquitous. In theory, AGP improves video performance by removing it from the 33 MHz PCI bus and by allowing a video adapter to use main system memory. In practice, all high-performance video cards (PCI or AGP) have a large amount of fast, local video memory. Video performance is constrained by the bandwidth between the graphics processor and video memory. These cards render images in local video memory rather than in main system memory, so the limited bandwidth of the PCI bus is not a bottleneck. AGP video cards do not fit PCI slots, or vice versa. AGP is fully supported under Linux, Windows 98, and Windows 2000 or later (but not under earlier Microsoft operating systems). Note that many motherboards now use AGP 2.0-compliant 1.5V AGP slots that do not support legacy 3.3V AGP cards, so if you're upgrading a motherboard you may also have to upgrade your video adapter.

IAPC

> *Instantly Available PC (IAPC)* is an Intel initiative that defines power-saving modes that retain the ability to respond to programmed or external triggers, such as LAN activity (*Wake-on-LAN, WOL*) or an inbound telephone call (*Wake-on-Ring, WOR*).

Plug and Play

Plug and Play is a joint Intel/Microsoft specification that allows computers and peripherals to configure themselves by negotiating for available system resources. Full implementation of Plug and Play requires that the chipset, BIOS, operating system, and devices all be Plug and Play-compliant. Ideally, adding a device in a Plug and Play environment requires only physically installing the device. Plug and Play then configures everything automatically, loading the appropriate driver and assigning nonconflicting resources (IRQ, I/O port, DMA, and memory space) to the device. In practice, Plug and Play sometimes does not work properly. Plug and Play is partially supported by early releases of Windows 95, and fully supported by Windows 95 OSR2+, Windows 98, Windows 2000 or later, and Linux.

UDMA/100 and /133

Ultra DMA/100 (*UDMA/100*) and *Ultra DMA/133* (*UDMA/133*) are recent standards that support IDE hard disk data-transfer rates up to 133 MB/s, eight times those supported under earlier *Programmed I/O* (*PIO*) modes, four times that of UDMA/33, and twice that of UDMA/66. UDMA (*Ultra Direct Memory Access*) modes have low CPU utilization under heavy disk load (typically ~1.5%, versus 80% for PIO), and high-end UDMA drives approach low-end SCSI drives in raw performance. The fastest current ATA hard drives can barely saturate a UDMA/66 interface, so the advantage of UDMA/100 and UDMA/133 over earlier UDMA standards is small for now. But we expect new-generation hard drives to ship in 2003 and 2004 that will saturate UDMA/66, so UDMA/100 is worth having. UDMA/100 is supported by most current systems and motherboards, and by many current IDE drives. Many current motherboards do not support UDMA/133, which is not yet a formal standard, although some motherboards shipping during 2003 will incorporate it. UDMA can be used with all versions of Windows 95/98/Me, by Windows NT/2000/XP, and by Linux, although configuring it is non-trivial in some of those environments.

The Big Drive Interface Initiative

The ATA standard has used 28-bit addressing since its inception. When using standard 512-byte blocks, a 28-bit address limits maximum drive size to 128 GB. Until 2001, that was so large as to be no limit at all, but the exponential growth in hard drive sizes has now put them hard against that 128 GB limitation. In 2001, a consortium of storage industry companies, led by Maxtor, introduced *The Big Drive Interface Initiative*. This initiative replaces the old ATA interface with a new version that uses 48-bit addressing, which allows drive sizes up to 128 petabytes (PB), still using standard 512-byte sectors. The new interface is backward-compatible with older drives, and the newer drives are backward-compatible with older interfaces (although, of course, you are limited to using 128 GB of the drive's capacity if it is connected to an older interface). As this is written, only motherboards based on the most recent chipsets have embedded 48-bit ATA interfaces. Nearly all new motherboards produced in 2003 and 2004 will include 48-bit ATA interfaces, although the ATA interface is being phased out in favor of the new Serial ATA interface. For more information about The Big Drive Interface Initiative, see *http://www.maxtor.com/en/technologies/big_drives/index.htm*.

USB

Universal Serial Bus (USB) is a general-purpose communications interface for connecting peripherals to PCs. USB 1.1 supports speeds up to 12 Mb/s. USB 2.0, finalized in February 2000, supports speeds 40 times faster—up to 480 Mb/s. USB 2.0-compliant interfaces and peripherals began shipping in late 2001, and are now commonplace. USB is royalty-free and strongly backed by Intel, which makes it likely to prevail over the competing, more expensive IEEE-1394 FireWire standard. USB will ultimately replace low-speed "legacy" serial, parallel, keyboard, mouse, and floppy interfaces, and may also become a standard or at least alternative interface for mid-speed devices such as video, network adapters, and optical drives. All recent systems and motherboards include at least USB 1.1 ports, and nearly all include USB 2.0 ports. USB 1.1 is fully supported by Linux, Windows 98, and Windows 2000/XP, but not by earlier versions of Windows. USB 2.0 is fully supported by Windows 2000/XP and recent Linux releases.

An exhaustive list of these and other PC technology standards is available in the *PC 2001* document and on the Web at *http://www.pcdesguide.org/pc2001/Resources.htm*.

The Strange Case of the AMR/CNR/ACR Slot

Nearly everything inside a PC is designed to be user-installable. The *Audio Modem Riser (AMR)*, *Communications and Networking Riser (CNR)*, and *Advanced Communication Riser (ACR)* slots are exceptions. Although their presence on many recent motherboards intrigues some upgraders, these slots were never intended as general-purpose expansion slots. All of them were designed to be used by OEM system builders, not by backyard mechanics. Here's what you need to know about AMR, CNR, and ACR slots:

AMR slot

Intel developed the AMR slot to provide an easy, standardized way to integrate modem and audio functions into finished systems at minimal cost, but OEM system builders ignored it in droves. Why? Mainly because the AMR slot took the place of a standard PCI slot, and most motherboard designers and system builders rightly preferred having an extra PCI slot to having an AMR slot of dubious utility. The AMR slot also had limited functionality and no support for Plug and Play. The result was that, although some motherboards included an AMR slot, very few AMR-compatible cards were ever developed and those that were achieved only limited distribution. We've seen exactly one AMR card.

CNR slot

Intel's answer to the problems of AMR was to redesign the AMR slot. The CNR slot, shown in Figure 1-2, can coexist with a standard PCI slot, allowing either a CNR card or a standard PCI card to use the slot position interchangeably. CNR also adds Plug and Play support and other features of interest to system designers. AMR and CNR are incompatible, at both the physical and electrical level. Although we have seen a few CNR cards, mostly modems and sound adapters, CNR cards are not much easier to find than AMR cards. For information about CNR, see *http://developer.intel.com/technology/cnr/qa.htm*.

Figure 1-2. A CNR slot (top) with CNR card inserted

ACR slot

AMR and CNR are both Intel technologies. AMD, VIA and the rest of the everyone-who-is-not-Intel camp came up with an alternative called the ACR slot, which is found on some Intel-free motherboards. The ACR slot is physically a standard PCI slot connector, which you can recognize because it's turned 90 degrees to the other PCI connectors on the motherboard. In theory, the ACR slot offers several advantages over the AMR/CNR slot, including its use of standard connectors and its additional flexibility because of the greater number of available pins. In practice, we've never seen or even heard of a card designed to fit that slot, so it is effectively a wasted connector.

Intel warns that the AMR and CNR interfaces are not rigidly defined, so it is quite possible that any given AMR or CNR card simply will not work in a particular AMR or CNR slot. If your motherboard has an AMR, CNR, or ACR slot, we suggest you pretend it's not there.

System Resources

PCs have four types of system resources—Interrupt Request (IRQ) lines, DMA channels, I/O ports, and memory ranges. Many system components and peripherals require one or more of these resources, which raises the twin problems of resource availability and resource conflicts. Resource availability is particularly important with regard to IRQs, which are in high demand, and of which only 16 exist. Resource conflicts can occur when two devices are assigned the same resource, in which case one or both devices may not function, or may function unpredictably. Resource conflicts may occur even with plentiful resources, such as I/O ports, where many are available and only a few are in use.

A frequent cause of problems when building or upgrading PCs is a shortage of required resources or unintentional resource conflicts that occur when a new component is installed that was inadvertently configured to use a resource that is already in use. Two technologies, PCI and Plug and Play, used in conjunction with recent versions of Microsoft operating systems (Windows 95 OSR2, Windows 98, and Windows 2000) and Linux go a long way toward extending the availability of resources and preventing conflicts. Even in such an ideal environment, however, resource conflicts sometimes occur, particularly if you are using older "legacy" hardware. The following sections describe what you need to know about PC resources and how to manage them.

Interrupt Request Line (IRQ)

When a component or peripheral, such as a network adapter or sound card, needs to get the CPU's attention, it does so by generating a signal on an *Interrupt Request Line (IRQ)*. Table 1-2 lists IRQs and the devices that typically use them.

Table 1-2. /16/32-bit ISA/PCI standard IRQ assignments

IRQ	Bus type	Typically used by
00	none	Non-maskable Interrupt (NMI); system timer
01	none	Keyboard port
02	none	Programmable Interrupt Controller (PIC); cascade to IRQ 09
03	8/16-bit	Communications Port 2 (COM2:)
04	8/16-bit	Communications Port 1 (COM1:)
05	8/16-bit	Sound card; printer port (LPT2:)
06	8/16-bit	Floppy disk controller
07	8/16-bit	Printer port (LPT1:)
08	none	System CMOS/real-time clock
09	8/16-bit	Redirected from IRQ 02; network interface
10	16-bit	Network interface; USB host controller
11	16-bit	Video adapter; SCSI host adapter
12	16-bit	PS/2 mouse port
13	none	Numeric data processor (math coprocessor)
14	16-bit	Primary IDE interface
15	16-bit	Secondary IDE interface

An 8-bit ISA slot contains physical IRQ lines only for IRQ 02 through IRQ 07 because IRQ 00 and IRQ 01 are reserved for system functions. A 16-bit ISA slot contains physical IRQ lines for IRQs 03 through 07, 09 through 12, 14, and 15. IRQ 09 is mapped to IRQ 02, allowing 8-bit ISA cards to recognize IRQ 09 as IRQ 02. IRQs 00, 01, 02, 08, and 13 are not present in any slot, and so cannot be assigned to devices.

If the processor receives two or more interrupts simultaneously, it processes them in order of priority. On 8-bit systems (PCs and XTs), the lower-numbered IRQ always takes priority. That is, IRQ 00 is the highest priority, and IRQ 07 is the lowest. 286 and higher systems use a second PIC to add a second set of eight IRQs, cascaded from IRQ02. That changes IRQ priority from the simple numerical order used by 8-bit systems. On 16-bit and higher systems, IRQ 00 is still the highest priority, followed by IRQ 01 and 02. But because IRQ 02 is the cascade IRQ, the IRQs that it supports—IRQ 08 through IRQ 15—are next in priority. IRQ 03 follows IRQ 15 in priority, and then in numerical order through IRQ 07, the lowest priority. Whenever possible, assign "important" devices to higher-priority IRQs. For example, if you have a serial mouse and a modem, assign the modem to COM2: (IRQ03) and the mouse to COM1: (IRQ04). Because the modem is on the higher-priority IRQ, it is serviced first if the modem and the mouse generate interrupts simultaneously.

Juggling ISA IRQs

ISA systems are obsolescent, to be charitable, but millions are still in use. If you have to work with an ISA system, remember that only IRQs 03, 04, 05, 06, 07, 09, 10, 11, 12, 14, and 15 are available. Six of those—03, 04, 06, 12, 14, and 15—are occupied by the serial ports, the floppy controller, the mouse, and the IDE interfaces on most ISA systems, leaving only 05, 07, 09, 10, and 11 available. If you require interrupt-based printing, you must allocate IRQ 07 to LPT1. If you have a sound card, it'll want IRQ 05. And so on. It's not surprising that many ISA systems have no free IRQs, and that allocating IRQs and resolving IRQ conflicts is a major issue for ISA systems.

If you find yourself out of IRQs on an ISA system, you may be able to reclaim one or more IRQs. Some cards and some systems allow using IRQ02 successfully, and some do not. If one or both of the serial ports is unused, disable it in BIOS to reclaim IRQ03 and/or IRQ04. If you have two serial devices that are never used at the same time (e.g., your modem and your Palm Pilot sync cradle), you can use a switch box to connect both to the same serial port and disable the other serial port. If there is no printer connected to the system, disable the printer port in BIOS (or configure it to a mode that does not use an IRQ) to free up IRQ 07. If you have only one IDE drive in the system, disable the secondary IDE interface in BIOS to reclaim IRQ 15. If you have two IDE drives, one on each interface, consider putting both drives on the primary IDE interface and disabling the secondary IDE interface to reclaim IRQ 15. Note, however, that putting some very old CD-ROM drives on the same IDE channel as the hard disk can seriously degrade hard disk performance.

ISA interrupts versus PCI interrupts

ISA and PCI handle interrupts very differently. ISA expansion cards are configured manually for IRQ, usually by setting a jumper, but sometimes by running a setup program. All ISA slots have all IRQ lines present, so it doesn't matter which card is placed in which slot. ISA cards use *edge-sensitive interrupts*, which means that an ISA device asserts a voltage on one of the interrupt lines to generate an interrupt. That in turn means that ISA devices cannot share interrupts because when the processor senses voltage on a particular interrupt line, it has no way to determine which of multiple devices might be asserting that interrupt. For ISA slots and devices, the rule is simple: *two devices cannot share an IRQ if there is any possibility that those two devices may be used simultaneously.* In practice that means that you cannot assign the same IRQ to more than one ISA device.

PCI cards use *level-sensitive interrupts*, which means that different PCI devices can assert different voltages on the same physical interrupt line, allowing the processor to determine which device generated the interrupt. PCI cards and slots manage interrupts internally. A PCI bus normally supports a maximum of four PCI slots, numbered 1 through 4. Each PCI slot can access four interrupts, labeled INT#1 through INT#4 (or INT#A through INT#D). Ordinarily, INT#1/A is used by PCI Slot 1, INT#2/B by Slot 2, and so on.

AGP cards support only INT#1/A and INT#2/B, and share with PCI Slot 1. If a PCI Slot 5 exists, it shares with Slot 4. In either case, with slots that share resources, avoid installing cards in both slots if both cards require the same shared resource. If you must use both slots, install only cards that can share an IRQ. If you encounter a conflict on a PCI system, simply moving cards to different slots often solves the problem.

Bridging circuitry within the chipset allows additional PCI or other busses to be cascaded from the primary PCI bus. For example, the PCI-to-ISA bridge present in most current chipsets allows cascading an ISA bus from the primary PCI bus. One function of the bridging circuitry is to convert PCI interrupts to ISA interrupts when a PCI device needs to get the processor's attention. PCI interrupts do not correspond directly to ISA IRQs, although an INT# can be mapped to an IRQ via the PC's interrupt handler if the card using that INT# requires an IRQ. Some configuration firmware restricts mapping PCI interrupts to IRQ 09, 10, or 11 or to Auto, while others allow mapping any INT# to any available IRQ.

In general, leave INT-IRQ mapping for all PCI slots set to Auto unless you have good reason to assign a specific IRQ. Sometimes a card with a dynamically mapped IRQ may work fine with some programs and not others. For example, many older games expect to find a sound card at IRQ 05. If you have a PCI/Plug and Play sound card installed in PCI Slot 3, you can use INT-IRQ mapping to assign IRQ 05 to that slot and card, keeping the old games happy.

PCI expansion cards are normally assigned an IRQ dynamically, either by the BIOS or by the operating system, depending on the version of Windows (or Linux) being used and the PCI/Plug and Play configuration options in effect. On bridged PCI-ISA systems, ISA IRQs 00, 01, 02, 08, and 13 are reserved for critical system functions. IRQs 03 through 07, 09 through 12, 14, and 15 can each be programmed using the CMOS Setup PCI/Plug and Play configuration utility as being owned by either the PCI bus *or* the ISA bus, but not both. The terminology for this varies. Some utilities allow you to specify each IRQ as *PCI/ISA Plug and Play* or *Legacy ISA* (or similar words). Others allow you to specify each IRQ as *Level-Sensitive* or *Edge-Sensitive* (or similar words). In either case, the effect is the same.

If you are installing a "legacy" card (i.e., a non-Plug and Play ISA card), you can use static IRQ mappings to assign a specific IRQ to that card. For example, if you install an old ISA sound card that requires IRQ 05, use the PCI/Plug and Play configuration utility to set IRQ 05 for Legacy ISA or Edge-Sensitive, thereby reserving that IRQ for that card.

 Do not confuse mapping PCI INT# interrupts to ISA IRQs with allocating IRQs to the ISA or PCI bus. The two are entirely unrelated. Use the former to "lock down" a PCI slot/card to a specific IRQ—for example, to allocate IRQ 05 to a PCI sound card. Use the latter to reserve IRQs for ISA devices—for example, to reserve IRQ 05 for an ISA sound card. Confusing these functions may cause lockups or other strange behavior. In general, the best way to prevent conflicts is to avoid installing ISA cards in PCI systems.

PCI Bus IRQ Steering

PCI Bus IRQ Steering is a function built into Windows 95 OSR2 or higher and Windows 98 (but not NT4 or Windows 2000/XP). IRQ Steering allows Windows itself to assign IRQs to PCI devices. With earlier versions of Windows 95, the BIOS assigns IRQs to PCI devices, and Windows must accept the decisions made by the BIOS IRQ Steering. If Windows IRQ Steering is enabled, Windows can override those BIOS decisions, although it seldom does so. OSR2 disables IRQ Steering by default; Windows 98 enables it by default.

Windows IRQ Steering allows Windows to reassign PCI interrupts automatically to accommodate the inflexible requirements of ISA devices. For example, assume that a PC with a BIOS that does not recognize non-Plug and Play ISA cards (that is, IRQ Steering is not implemented in BIOS) is running Windows 98 with IRQ Steering disabled. The PC is properly configured with all PCI devices, and the BIOS has assigned IRQ 11 to a Creative SoundBlaster AudioPCI 128 sound card. You then open the case and install a 3Com 3C509 network adapter (a non-Plug and Play ISA card), which is also configured for IRQ 11. When you restart the system, a conflict exists between the sound card on IRQ 11 and the network card, also on IRQ 11. If you enable Windows 98 IRQ Steering and restart the system, IRQ Steering takes the following actions during boot:

1. Detects that IRQ 11 is in use by both the PCI sound card and the ISA network card.

2. Disables the PCI sound card.

3. Maps a free IRQ—one that is not being used by an ISA device—to a PCI interrupt and assigns an IRQ holder to it. If IRQ 10 is available, for example, PCI Steering may assign it to a PCI interrupt.

4. Reprograms the sound card to use IRQ 10.

5. Resets the IRQ mapping table to specify that IRQ 11 is now assigned to ISA and removes the PCI IRQ holder for IRQ 11.

When the system restarts, the sound card is now assigned to IRQ 10, the network card is still IRQ 11, and both devices work. Note that IRQ Steering does nothing that you cannot do for yourself. It simply automates the process of resolving IRQ conflicts when ISA devices are present in a PCI system.

To view the IRQ assignments made by IRQ Steering, right-click the My Computer icon, choose Properties, click the Device Manager tab, and double-click the Computer icon at the top of the tree to display the View Resources page of the Computer Properties dialog, shown in Figure 1-3. IRQs which IRQ Steering has assigned to PCI are flagged with an entry labeled IRQ Holder for PCI Steering. This flag does not indicate that another device is assigned to the IRQ, but simply that IRQ Steering has reserved that IRQ for PCI, making it unavailable to ISA devices even if no PCI devices are currently using that IRQ.

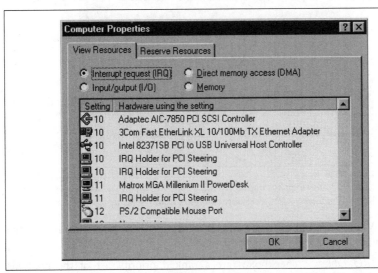

Figure 1-3. The View Resources page of the Computer Properties dialog displaying global resource allocations for IRQ, DMA, I/O ports, and memory ranges

IRQs which both the BIOS and Windows 98 have assigned to PCI are flagged twice. In Figure 1-3 IRQ Steering has assigned IRQ 10 as a PCI interrupt, which is being shared by a SCSI host adapter, a network adapter, and the USB host controller. Both BIOS IRQ Steering and Windows 98 IRQ Steering have assigned IRQ 10 to PCI. The Matrox video card on IRQ 11 is the only device assigned to that IRQ, and only BIOS IRQ Steering has assigned an IRQ Holder.

To view or change settings for IRQ Bus Steering itself, right-click the My Computer icon, choose Properties, and click the Device Manager tab. Double-click System Devices to expand the tree, and then double-click PCI Bus to display the PCI bus Properties dialog. Click the IRQ Steering tab to display the IRQ Steering page of the PCI bus Properties dialog, shown in Figure 1-4.

The IRQ Routing Status pane at the bottom of the dialog displays the current status of IRQ Steering. Windows 98 enables IRQ Steering using the defaults shown. Leaving this checkbox marked means that Windows 98 manages IRQ Steering. To disable Windows 98 IRQ Steering and allow the BIOS to manage IRQ Steering, clear the Use IRQ Steering checkbox and restart the PC. If you do

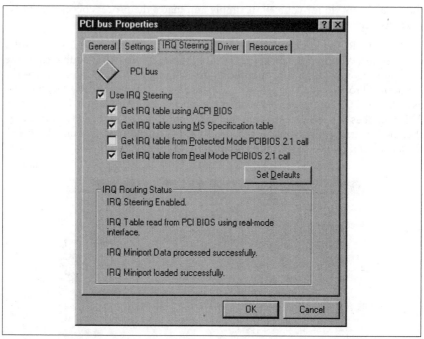

Figure 1-4. The IRQ Steering page of the PCI bus Properties dialog, which allows you to enable or disable Windows 98 IRQ Steering, configure it, and view its current status

that, the Windows Find New Hardware Wizard runs after the restart, locates the "new" devices, and installs drivers for them.

The *Get IRQ table …* checkboxes are a ranked priority list of the methods Windows can use to obtain the data it needs to manage IRQ Steering. Clearing one of these checkboxes causes Windows not to attempt that method. In Figure 1-4 Windows first attempts to obtain this data using the ACPI BIOS. That fails, so it next attempts to get the data using the MS Specification table, which also fails. The Protected Mode PCIBIOS 2.1 method is not checked, so Windows does not attempt to use that method. Finally, Windows attempts to get the data using a Real Mode PCIBIOS 2.1 call, which succeeds.

In general, leave IRQ Steering enabled. If problems occur with a PCI device being recognized or configured properly, take the following steps in order until the problem is resolved:

1. Clear the Get IRQ table using ACPI BIOS checkbox and restart the system.

2. Clear the Get IRQ table using MS Specification table checkbox and restart the system.

3. Clear the Get IRQ table using Real Mode PCIBIOS 2.1 call checkbox, mark the Get IRQ table using Protected Mode PCIBIOS 2.1 call and restart the system.

4. Clear the Use IRQ Steering checkbox and restart the system to allow the BIOS to manage IRQ steering.

If IRQ Steering cannot be enabled, the system BIOS may not support IRQ Steering (which is to say it will not allow Windows 98 IRQ Steering to change assignments), or the BIOS IRQ routing table may be missing or corrupt. In either case, contact the system or motherboard maker for an updated BIOS or additional assistance.

Direct Memory Access (DMA)

Direct Memory Access (DMA) is a means by which devices can exchange data with memory or with each other without requiring intervention by the processor. Standard DMA allows a device to exchange data with memory, but not with another device. *Bus Mastering DMA* allows two devices to communicate directly with each other. The advantage of using DMA is that it reduces the load on the processor, allowing it to perform other tasks. There are even fewer DMA channels than IRQs—eight versus 16—but DMA channels are much less in demand than IRQs, so DMA channel availability is almost never an issue. Table 1-3 lists DMA channels and the uses to which they are typically put.

Table 1-3. Standard 16-bit ISA DMA channel assignments

DMA	Bus type	Transfers	Typically used by
0	16-bit	8-bit	none
1	8/16-bit	8-bit	Some sound cards
2	8/16-bit	8-bit	Floppy disk controller
3	8/16-bit	8-bit	LPT1: in ECP mode
4	none	16-bit	DMA controller cascade
5	16-bit	16-bit	Some sound cards; ISA SCSI host adapter
6	16-bit	16-bit	ISA SCSI host adapter
7	16-bit	16-bit	Some sound cards; ISA SCSI host adapter

DMA 2 is used by nearly all systems for the floppy disk drive controller. Excluding DMA 4, which is a dedicated cascade channel (used to access the secondary DMA controller), the other DMA channels are available for use with expansion cards. DMA 0 is almost never used because, although it appears only in 16-bit slots, it supports only 8-bit transfers. Most ISA sound cards require two DMA channels, with 8-bit sound using DMA 1 and 16-bit sound using DMA 5. Note that these DMA channels pertain only to ISA cards. PCI devices do not require one of these DMA channels to use DMA. For example, if you enable DMA transfer mode on one or both of the embedded PCI IDE controllers, you will find that they operate in DMA mode without occupying ISA DMA channels.

The only time DMA conflicts are likely to arise is if you install an ISA sound card *and* an ISA SCSI host adapter. Nearly all ISA sound cards use both DMA 1 and DMA 5, and some ISA SCSI cards are configured by default to use DMA 5, which causes a conflict. The easy answer is to configure the SCSI host adapter to use DMA 6 or DMA 7. The better answer, as usual, is to avoid ISA cards whenever possible.

I/O Ports

Input/Output ports (*I/O ports*) are ranges of addresses that function like mailboxes, allowing programs and components to exchange messages and data. An I/O port has a *base address*, which is the hexadecimal address of the first byte allocated to that I/O port, and a length, which is also expressed in hexadecimal. For example, many network adapters default to base address 300h and are 20h bytes (32 decimal bytes) long, and so occupy the range 300-31Fh.

There's no shortage of I/O ports, because thousands exist. We have never seen I/O port conflicts with PCI devices operating in a Plug and Play environment, but I/O port conflicts commonly occur when two ISA devices are unintentionally assigned overlapping ranges. For example, another common base address for network adapters is 360h (range 360-37Fh). Unfortunately, that range overlaps the range of LPT1: (base address 378h), so setting a network card to 360h results in conflicts with the parallel port.

Memory Ranges

The original IBM PC used an 8088 processor, which supported up to 1 MB of physical memory, addressed as sixteen 64 KB segments. Memory locations are enumerated in hexadecimal, so the first segment includes the addresses 00000h through 0FFFFh (0 through 65,535 decimal) and the 16th includes the addresses F0000h through FFFFFh (983,040 through 1,048,575 decimal). The first 10 of those segments—00000h through 9FFFFh—comprise the base 640 KB of memory addresses that are accessible by the operating system and programs. The last six segments—A0000h through FFFFF—comprise the 384 KB of upper memory addresses (the *Upper Memory Area* or *UMA*) reserved for system use. The first two UMA segments (A0000h through BFFFFh) are reserved for video memory. The second two UMA segments (C0000h through DFFFFh) are reserved address space for ROM BIOSs that reside on some adapters, such as video cards, SCSI host adapters, and network adapters. The final two UMA segments (E0000h through FFFFF) are reserved for the motherboard BIOS.

Modern processors use a flat (unsegmented) 32-bit address space, which allows them to access up to 4 GB (4096 MB, or 4,294,967,296 bytes) of distinct memory addresses. That additional address space means that memory addresses are expressed as eight rather than five hexadecimal characters (e.g., addresses for the first MB are expressed as 00000000h through 000FFFFFh). Because few systems have anywhere near 4 GB of physical memory installed, huge ranges of unused memory addresses are available for assignment to devices that require memory ranges. Which of those ranges are used depends on how much physical memory is installed and which operating system you run.

Windows NT/2000/XP uses address ranges from the UMA of the first megabyte (000A0000h through 000FFFFFh) for the original purposes of addressing video memory, adapter ROMs, and so on. It uses address ranges at the top of its address space, F0000000h and above (up near 4 GB), to provide additional memory ranges for which there is inadequate room in UMA. Windows 98 does the same, but also uses memory ranges immediately above the end of the range occupied by physical RAM.

Memory range conflicts are seldom a problem on modern computers running recent versions of Windows.

Viewing and Reserving System Resources

Windows 9X/2000/XP and Linux all provide convenient means to view the resources that are in use. Windows 98 also allows you to reserve resources manually for non-Plug and Play ISA devices on systems with a BIOS that does not support IRQ Steering.

Viewing resources with Windows 2000 or Windows XP

To view system resources with Windows 2000 or Windows XP, use the Control Panel to display System Properties, click the Hardware tab, and then click the Device Manager button to display the dialog shown in Figure 1-5, which lists all installed devices. Clicking the + icon (or double-clicking a branch name) expands the list to show individual devices within that branch. If a problem exists with a device (a resource conflict, missing driver, etc.), Windows 2000/XP automatically expands the branch that contains that device and flags the device with an alert icon.

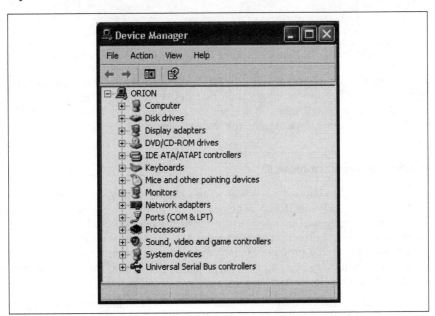

Figure 1-5. The Windows XP Device Manager displaying all installed devices

To view a global list of resources, click the View menu and select the Resources by Type option to display the Device Manager window shown in Figure 1-6. Expand the listing for the type of resource you want to view. Figure 1-6 shows that ISA IRQs 02, 05, 06, 07, 10, and 11 are available for use by new devices.

To view all resources being used by a particular device, expand the Device Manager tree (see Figure 1-5), double-click the device name to display the Properties sheet for that device, and display the Resources tab. Figure 1-7 shows the

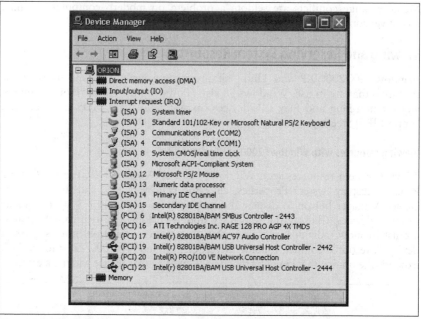

Figure 1-6. The Windows XP Device Manager displaying used and available IRQs

Properties sheet for an ATI RAGE 128 PRO AGP video card. The Resource type pane displays all resources assigned to that device, although you may have to scroll the list to see all items. If a resource conflict exists, Windows 2000/XP displays a list of other devices using the same resource(s) in the Conflicting device list pane.

Viewing resources with Windows 9X

To view system resources with Windows 98, right-click My Computer, choose Properties, and click the Device Manager tab to display the System Properties dialog shown in Figure 1-8, which lists all installed devices. Clicking the + icon (or double-clicking a branch name) expands the list to show individual devices within that branch. If a problem exists with a device (a resource conflict, missing driver, etc.), Windows 98 automatically expands the branch that contains that device and flags the device with an alert icon.

To view a global list of resources, double-click the Computer branch to display the View Resources page of the Computer Properties dialog, shown in Figure 1-9. Choosing any of the four option buttons immediately displays a global list of assignments for that resource, allowing you to determine easily which resources are unassigned. Figure 1-9 shows that IRQ 03, normally assigned to Communications Port (COM2), is available for use by a new device.

To view all resources being used by a particular device, expand the Device Manager tree (see Figure 1-8) and double-click the device name to display the Properties sheet for that device. Figure 1-10 shows the Properties sheet for a Matrox Millenium II PowerDesk video card. The Resource type pane displays all

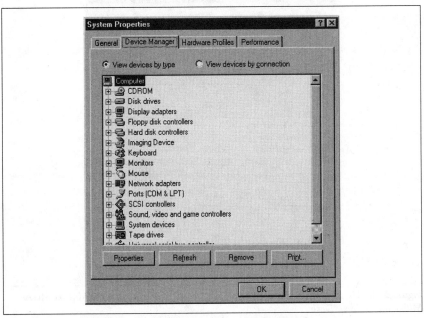

Figure 1-7. *The Properties sheet*

Figure 1-8. *Windows 98 Device Manager displaying all installed devices*

resources assigned to that device. If a resource conflict exists, Windows 98 displays a list of other devices using the same resource(s) in the Conflicting device list pane.

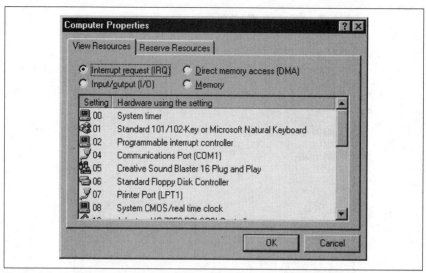

Figure 1-9. The View Resources page of the Computer Resources dialog lists resources in use

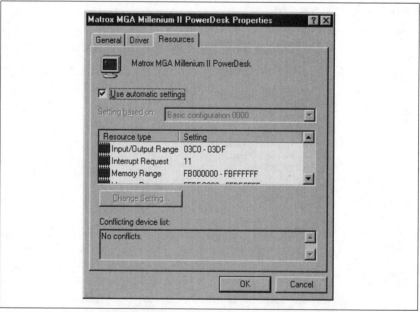

Figure 1-10. The Properties sheet listing all the resources allocated to the Matrox MGA Millenium II PowerDesk

Reserving resources with Windows 9X

If the system BIOS is up to date and all expansion cards are Plug and Play-compliant, Windows 98 and Plug and Play normally configure the system properly without further ado. However, if the system has an older BIOS and/or you need to install one or more cards that are not Plug and Play-compliant, conflicts may occur because the BIOS and Windows cannot determine which resources those older cards need. For such situations, Windows allows you to specify manually which resources these older cards require, removing them from the pool of resources that Windows manages automatically.

To reserve resources, first examine the documentation and settings for the card to determine which resources (IRQ, DMA, I/O ports, and memory ranges) it requires. Display the Device Manager and click the Reserve Resources tab to display the dialog shown in Figure 1-11. This dialog lists any resource reservations already in effect, and allows you to modify existing reservations and add new reservations. Mark one of the four option buttons to select the type of resource for which you want to add a reservation or view existing reservations.

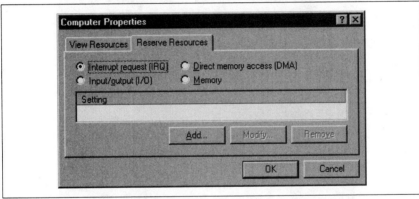

Figure 1-11. The Reserve Resources dialog, which allows you to remove resources from the pool available to Windows and assign those resources manually to legacy devices

To add a resource reservation, click Add to display the Edit Resource Setting dialog, whose appearance varies depending on the type of resource for which you are adding a reservation. Figure 1-12 shows the dialog for reserving an IRQ. Use the up and down arrows to specify a value for the resource to be reserved and click OK. You can reserve multiple resources in a single session by repeatedly selecting the resource type and adding reservations. When you finish reserving resources, click OK to store the resource reservations and then restart the system to put the changes into effect.

Device Manager initially displays reserved resources as System Reserved, as shown for IRQ03 in Figure 1-13. However, once you restart the computer, that resource will no longer be displayed in the Device Manager.

 Be very careful when reserving resources. Windows 98 allows you to reserve any resource, including ones that are already in use. Reserving an in-use resource may disable the device that is currently using that resource. If that occurs, use the Device Manager to remove the device, and then run the Add New Hardware Wizard from the Control Panel to reinstall the device.

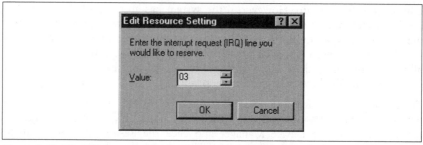

Figure 1-12. The Edit Resource Setting dialog, where you can specify the resource to be reserved

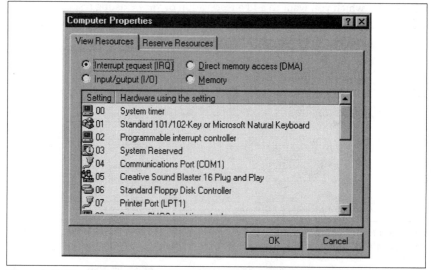

Figure 1-13. Device Manager listing reserved resources as System Reserved, as for IRQ 03

Viewing resources with Linux

Viewing resources with Linux is straightforward. If you use KDE, simply open the KDE Control Center, expand the Information branch in the left panel, and double-click an item to view the details. (If you use Gnome, simply open a terminal window and type kcontrol to start the KDE Control Center. Figure 1-14 shows the KDE Control Center displaying the I/O ports in use on this system.

If you run Linux without a GUI, do not have KDE installed, or simply prefer using a command line, change to the */proc* directory, which contains numerous descriptively named hardware configuration files. Use the cat command to display the appropriate file. For example, the command cat interrupts lists the interrupts in use. For larger files, use the more or less command to prevent data from scrolling off the screen.

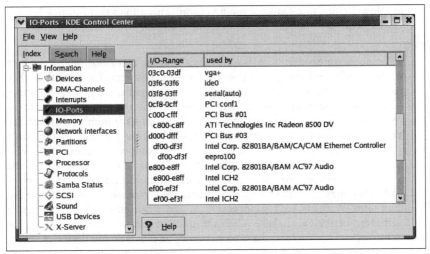

Figure 1-14. Using the KDE Control Center to list I/O ports in use

Building or Buying a PC

The make-or-buy decision is a fundamental business-school concept. Does it make more sense to make a particular item yourself or just to buy it? With entry-level PCs selling for less than $500 and fully equipped mainstream PCs for $1,200, you might wonder why anyone would bother to build a PC. After all, you can't save any money building one, can you? Well, yes you can. But that's not the only reason to build a PC. Here are some more good reasons to do so:

Choice

When you buy a PC, you get a cookie-cutter computer. You may be able to choose such options as a larger hard drive, more memory, or a better monitor, but basically you get what the vendor decides to give you. And what you get is a matter of chance. High-volume direct vendors such as Gateway and Dell often use multiple sources for components. Two supposedly identical systems ordered the same day may contain significantly different components, including such important differences as different motherboards or monitors with the same model number but made by different manufacturers. When you build a PC, you decide exactly what goes into it.

Component quality

Many computer vendors save money by using OEM versions of popular components. These may be identical to the retail version of that component, differing only in packaging. But OEM versions have several drawbacks. Many component vendors do not support OEM versions directly, instead referring you to the computer vendor. And OEM versions often differ significantly from the retail-boxed version. For example, Dell has used modified versions of standard Intel motherboards. That means owners of those systems cannot use Intel BIOS updates. Instead, they must depend on Dell to provide an updated BIOS. Dell and other major makers sometimes use downgraded versions of popular products—for example, a big-name video card that runs at a lower clock rate than the retail version. This allows them to pay less for components and still gain the cachet from using the name-brand product.

Cost

PC manufacturers aren't in business for charitable reasons. They need to make a profit, and that means they need to sell computers for more than they pay for the components and the labor to assemble them. Significantly more, in fact, because they also need to support such expensive operations as research and development departments, toll-free support numbers, and so on. But PC manufacturers get huge price breaks because they buy in very large volumes, right? Not always. The market for PC components is extremely efficient, with razor-thin margins throughout. PC manufacturers may get the hard drive that costs you $75 for only $70, but they're not going to get it for $50. They may even have to pay $80 because PC manufacturers often have long-term contracts with suppliers. That can work either to the benefit or detriment of the PC maker. When the price of memory is plummeting, for example, a PC maker may have to pay twice as much as you do for memory. Conversely, when the price of memory skyrockets, you'll pay the spot price, while the PC maker may pay only half what you do because its memory suppliers are selling on a long-term contract price. Our rule of thumb is that, on average and all other things equal, you can probably build a midrange PC yourself for about 75% to 85% of what a major manufacturer charges.

No bundled software

Most purchased PCs include Microsoft Windows, Microsoft Office, or other bundled software. If you don't need or want this software, building a PC allows you to avoid paying for it.

OEM software is one of the best-kept secrets in the direct sales channel. It isn't advertised, and no one tells you about it unless you ask. If you buy a motherboard or hard disk and need this software, ask the vendor if they can supply it. Note that, although OEM versions of Windows and Microsoft applications are often labeled "For sale only with a new PC," Microsoft has in the past taken a liberal view of what constitutes a new PC. Buying a hard drive or a motherboard may entitle you to buy an OEM version of the software you need at a greatly discounted price—less, in fact, than you'd pay for a retail upgrade version. Microsoft has tightened eligibility requirements for OEM software, though, so make sure any software offered with a motherboard or hard drive is in fact an authorized version.

OEM software prices are striking. For example, when we checked prices for a motherboard for a new system in June 2003, we could have purchased with that motherboard a full OEM version of Windows XP Home Edition (full version, not upgrade) for $68, a full OEM version of Windows XP Professional for $115, or a full OEM version of Office XP SBE for $158. Full OEM versions are generally about two-thirds the price of retail upgrade-only versions, so if you need the software, this is a cheap way to get it. Of course, Microsoft doesn't support OEM versions, which is the main reason for the low price. But then, some might argue that Microsoft doesn't support retail versions very well either.

Warranty

The retail-boxed components you'll use to build your own PC include full manufacturer warranties which may run from one to five years or more, depending on the component. PC makers use OEM components which often do not include a manufacturer warranty for the end user. If something breaks, you're at the mercy of the PC maker to repair or replace it. We've heard from readers who bought PCs from makers who went out of business shortly thereafter. When a hard drive or video card failed six months later, they contacted the maker of the item, only to find that they had OEM components which were not under manufacturer warranty.

Experience

If you buy a computer, your experience with it consists of taking it out of the box and connecting the cables. If you build the computer, you know exactly what went into it, and you're in a much better position to resolve any problems that may occur.

Although there are many advantages to building a PC, there are some offsetting advantages to buying one instead, including:

Time

Building a PC takes time, not just the time actually needed to build it, but also the time required to choose and order the components. If you're building your first PC, expect to spend at least a day selecting and ordering components and a weekend actually building it. We maintain web pages at our web site, *http://www.hardwareguys.com,* that list our picks for the best components for various types of systems, from budget to high-end.

Integration

When you build a PC, you are responsible for making sure all components are compatible, locating and installing the necessary drivers, and so on. But this isn't as onerous as it may at first appear. With very few exceptions, PC components simply plug together and work, just as any VCR works with any television.

Component availability

If you absolutely need to have the latest, greatest CPU or whatever, you may have no choice but to buy a PC that includes it. Like in any other business, component makers favor their major customers, who happen to be the large PC makers. When the Intel Pentium 4 processor first shipped, for example, you couldn't buy a retail-boxed Pentium 4 for love or money. If you wanted a Pentium 4, your only option was to buy a PC with a Pentium 4 in it because essentially 100% of Pentium 4 production was going to the PC makers. If you're considering buying a PC for this reason, we suggest you think again. It's almost never worthwhile paying a significant premium for the latest and greatest, let alone buying an entire PC to get it.

Support

If you build a PC, you become Support Central for that PC. There's no single manufacturer to call, and it's up to you to figure out where a problem lies. If you isolate the problem to, say, the motherboard, you'll have to talk to the motherboard maker directly, assuming that they'll talk to you. Some will not, notably including Intel. You also may have to deal with multiple vendors all claiming that it must be the other guy's fault. Of course, just because you bought a packaged PC doesn't guarantee that the maker provides good tech support. Some makers are famous for consistently excellent support (although, according to many of our readers, even the best manufacturers' support quality has waned as PC prices have dropped). Other makers are more variable, sometimes providing top-notch support and other times not. Some makers provide better support for corporate users than for individual buyers. Still other makers provide infamously bad support to all comers.

Bundled software

If you don't need bundled software, there's no sense in paying for it. But if you do want the software bundled with new PCs—typically Microsoft Windows and Microsoft Office—you'll be hard-pressed to find a full retail version for anything near as little as it actually costs you as part of a new PC purchase. On the other hand, as noted earlier, OEM versions of the software are often available at very low prices when you buy a disk drive or motherboard.

Upgrading a PC

Sometimes it's sensible to upgrade a PC. Other times it's not. Whether it is economically feasible to upgrade a particular PC depends largely on how old the PC is, its existing configuration, and what you expect it to do.

PCs less than a year or two old are usually easy to upgrade. Components are readily available and sell at market prices. Necessary BIOS upgrades and firmware revisions are easy to obtain. PCs more than two or three years old are harder and more expensive to upgrade. Necessary components, particularly memory and BIOS upgrades, may be difficult or impossible to obtain. Even if you can obtain them, they may be unreasonably expensive. Upgrading one item often uncovers a serious bottleneck elsewhere, and so on. In general, restrict older PCs—anything more than a couple of years old—to minor upgrades such as adding memory, replacing a hard disk or optical drive, or perhaps installing a faster processor. Although you *can* perform significant upgrades on older systems, it seldom makes economic sense to do so. If an older PC requires more than minor upgrades to meet your expected needs for the next year or so, it's probably not a good upgrade candidate.

The reason most people upgrade their PCs is to improve performance. The good news is that there are several relatively inexpensive upgrades that may yield noticeable performance increases. The bad news is that some are easier than others, and performing all of them can easily cost as much as or more than simply buying (or building) a new PC.

Processor

Upgrading the processor improves overall system performance. In general, newer systems are easy to upgrade, and older systems are more difficult (or impossible) to upgrade. Upgrade only within the same generation—for example, a Pentium 4/1.6A to a Pentium 4/2.8, or a Duron/700 to an Athlon/1800+. If you upgrade within the same generation you may have to upgrade your BIOS at the same time (usually a free download), and you may have to buy an adapter (for example, to install a Socket 370 Celeron in an older Slot 1 motherboard). Avoid upgrade kits, which are usually expensive, provide limited performance improvements, and are often plagued with compatibility problems. Replacing the motherboard, processor, *and* memory usually costs little or no more than purchasing one of these kits, and the results are much better. Upgrading processors is covered in Chapter 4. Cost: $30 to $200 (although you can spend much more). Difficulty: easy to difficult, depending on the system and the processor.

Memory

If your PC does not have at least 64 MB (Windows 95/98/Me), 128 MB (NT/2000/Linux), or 256 MB (XP) of RAM, adding RAM is the most cost-effective upgrade you can make. Additional memory improves overall system performance, sometimes dramatically. Adding memory beyond 96 MB for 95/98/Me, 128 MB for NT/2000/Linux, or 256 MB for XP results in decreasing returns. The downsides are that many older systems do not cache memory above 64 MB (check the motherboard/chipset manual), which means that increasing memory beyond 64 MB can actually *decrease* performance, and that you may be sinking money into an obsolete form of memory that cannot be migrated later to a new system. Accordingly, we do not recommend upgrading memory in systems that use any memory type older than SDRAM DIMMs. Upgrading memory is covered in Chapter 5. Cost: $25 to $150 (varies with memory size and price). Difficulty: usually easy, although physical access on some older systems is difficult and the correct memory may be hard to find and expensive to buy.

CD-ROM

If you use your CD-ROM drive only for installing software and listening to music, even an original 1X model suffices. But if you use your CD-ROM drive for playing games, accessing large databases, or ripping audio CDs to MP3 format, you'll want a better drive. Recent 32X and faster IDE models are inexpensive and easy to install. However, rather than installing a new CD-ROM drive, consider installing a CD writer and/or a DVD-ROM drive, both of which offer full CD-ROM functionality and adds additional useful capabilities. Upgrading CD-ROM drives is covered in Chapter 10. Cost: $50. Difficulty: easy.

Hard disk

Modern hard disks are huge, fast, and inexpensive. Upgrading the hard disk not only provides additional storage space, but also can dramatically increase performance if you run applications that access the disk frequently. Older systems cannot recognize large hard disks, but you can get around that problem by using a device driver (usually included with the new drive), by installing a BIOS upgrade, or by replacing the embedded IDE interface with an expansion card ($25 to $50) that supports large drives. Upgrading hard disks is covered in Chapters 13 and 14. Cost: $60 to $250. Difficulty: easy, except for problems migrating existing programs and data.

Video adapter

Video adapter technology improves almost from month to month. Even so, if you use your system primarily for word processing, email, web browsing, and similar functions, you won't get much benefit from upgrading to a new video adapter. But if you play 3D games and your video card is more than a year or so old, upgrading to a more recent model can provide dramatic performance benefits. Although it seldom makes sense to install the latest, fastest video adapter in an older system, installing a midrange current video card can boost performance at small cost. Upgrading video adapters is covered in Chapter 15. Cost: $50 to $200. Difficulty: easy to moderate.

Monitor

Although CRT monitors are a mature technology, manufacturing improvements and other factors have resulted in dramatic price reductions on larger models. Not long ago, 15-inch monitors were the norm and 17-inch monitors sold for $750. Nowadays, decent 17-inch monitors cost $150 and 19-inch monitors $250. If you spend a lot of time in front of your PC, buying a larger monitor may be the best upgrade you can make. Also, unlike most upgrades, a good monitor is a long-term asset. You can use it with your current system, your next system, and probably the next system after that. Upgrading monitors is covered in Chapter 16. Cost: $150 to $700. Difficulty: easy.

USB 2.0 ports

Most systems and motherboards made before late 2002 support only 12 Mb/s USB 1.1, which is useful only for low- and medium-speed devices such as mice, keyboards, printers, and scanners. USB 2.0 runs at 40 times the speed of USB 1.1, and supports high-speed external devices such as hard drives, tape drives, and optical drives. If you have an older system, you can add USB 2.0 support by installing an inexpensive USB 2.0 PCI adapter. Some models also include IEEE-1394 (FireWire) ports, which are useful for connecting video cameras and similar consumer devices. Upgrading USB ports is covered in Chapter 24. Cost: $25 to $100. Difficulty: easy.

Power supply

Although it may seem strange to include power supplies in the performance upgrade category, the fact is that many systems have inadequate power supplies, and replacing the original unit with a better unit can improve system performance and stability. Upgrading power supplies is covered in Chapter 26. Cost: typically $45 to $125. Difficulty: easy.

Another reason to upgrade a PC is to add missing features. Here are some common feature upgrades:

CD writer

A CD writer allows you to burn your own CDs, which can subsequently be read in any recent CD or DVD drive. CD writers are popular for making archival backups and, of course, are used by many people to copy data and audio CDs. Adding a CD writer is covered in Chapter 11. Cost: $75 to $150. Difficulty: easy.

DVD-ROM drive or a DVD writer

A DVD drive allows you to watch DVD movies on your PC and to access the increasing number of databases and games supplied on DVD. DVD drives can also read data and audio CDs, so they are a popular replacement for CD-

ROM drives. DVD writers are to DVD-ROM drives as CD writers are to CD-ROM drives. In addition to playing back video, audio, or data DVD discs, a DVD writer can write large amounts of data to a removable disc or cartridge that costs $3 to $40. Adding a DVD-ROM drive or DVD writer is covered in Chapter 12. Cost: $50 (DVD-ROM) or $200 to $300 (DVD writer). Difficulty: easy.

Tape drive

The downside of huge, cheap, modern hard disks is that there is no practical way to back them up short of installing a tape drive. Tape drives store huge amounts of data—up to 50 GB or more—on relatively inexpensive tape cartridges. Adding a tape drive is covered in Chapter 9. Cost: $200 to $900. Difficulty: easy for IDE, easy to moderate for SCSI.

Sound card and speakers

If you make no serious demands on the audio capabilities of your PC, the inexpensive sound card and speakers that probably came with it are usable. But PC audio hardware and applications are advancing faster than any component except video adapters, and there are a lot of fascinating new applications, including 3D gaming with positional audio, DVD playback, IP telephony, voice-recognition software, and so on. To use any of these new applications, you may need to replace your sound card and perhaps your speakers. Adding a sound card and speakers is covered in Chapters 17 and 18. Cost: $50 to $400. Difficulty: easy, except for potential conflicts with improperly uninstalled drivers from the original sound card.

Game controller

Years ago, people bemoaned the fact that PC games were inferior to arcade games or dedicated game consoles such as those from Sega, Sony, and others. Dramatic improvements in PC video and audio mean that nowadays the playing field is level. Many excellent games run on PCs, the Sony PlayStation series and Microsoft Xbox notwithstanding. But getting the most from those games requires adding dedicated game controller hardware, such as a joystick, wheel, or paddle. Adding a game controller is covered in Chapter 21. Cost: $10 to $150. Difficulty: easy.

The ultimate upgrade, of course, is to replace the motherboard, which in effect means building an entirely new PC. Before you undertake a motherboard upgrade, consider whether you might not do better to retire your current PC to other duties and buy or build a new system. If you do replace the motherboard, expect to pay $50 to $250 for the motherboard itself, but also plan to spend another $50 to $250 to replace processor, memory, and perhaps other components, depending on how much can be salvaged from the current system. Difficulty: easy to moderate (although it may be time-consuming) if you have some experience working on PCs, moderate to difficult if you don't.

Smart Buying Practices

Until the early 1990s, most computer products were bought in retail computer stores. Retail sales still make up a significant chunk of computer product sales—although the emphasis has shifted from computer specialty stores to mass-market resellers such as Best Buy and Costco—but the majority of computer products are now bought from direct resellers, via toll-free telephone number or the Web. Local brick-and-mortar retailers, with their high overheads, simply cannot match direct reseller prices and stay in business. Nor can they match direct reseller companies for breadth of selection or convenience. We frequently order components late in the evening. Early the next morning, our FedEx guy drops them on the front porch. All without our having to leave the house.

That said, there are some drawbacks to buying from direct resellers. You're dealing with an anonymous company, probably located far away. You must know exactly what you want, and you need to understand the pitfalls of dealing with direct resellers. Most direct resellers are reputable, but some are not. Even reputable resellers differ greatly in their business practices, so it's important to understand the rules before you play the game. We've bought hundreds of thousands of dollars worth of products from direct vendors over the last decade or so, and have learned some things from that experience. Here are some guidelines to keep in mind:

Research the product

Make sure you know exactly what you're buying before you order it. For example, a hard disk may be available in two versions, each with the same model number but with submodel numbers to designate different amounts of cache. Or you may find that a given hard disk maker manufactures two models of the same size that differ in both price and performance. Always compare using the exact manufacturer model number. Before you buy a product, research it on the manufacturer's web site and on the numerous independent web sites devoted to reviews. We use *http://www.reviewfinder. com* to locate reviews for specific products. Alternatively, you can just do a web search with the product name and "review" in the search string.

Research the vendor

Vendors vary greatly. Some we trust implicitly, and others we wouldn't order from on a bet. Some are always reliable, others always unreliable, and still others seem to vary with the phases of the moon. You can check the reputation of a vendor with the Better Business Bureau. We also check *http://www. resellerratings.com*, which maintains a database of customer-reported experiences with hundreds of vendors.

Know the market price

The list price or Suggested Retail Price (SRP) published by the manufacturer is meaningless. Many computer products normally sell for a fraction of the SRP, others sell for very near the SRP, and for still others the manufacturer has no SRP, but instead publishes an Estimated Selling Price (ESP). To do meaningful price comparisons, you need to know what different vendors actually charge for the product. Fortunately, there are many services that maintain frequently updated lists of what various vendors charge for particular products. Three such services we use are *http://www.pricewatch.com*, *http://www.pricescan.com*, and *http://www.pricegrabber.com*. These services may list 20 or more different vendors, and the prices for a particular item may vary dramatically. We tend to discard the top 25% and the bottom 25% and take an average of the middle 50% to decide what is a reasonable price for the item.

The practice of *Minimum Advertised Price* (MAP) has been common for years in some market segments (such as astronomical telescopes and aircraft avionics), but until recently has been uncommon in computer components. U.S. law prohibits manufacturers from setting minimum *selling* prices, so manufacturers have begun using MAP instead.

Under MAP, manufacturers "discourage" dealers from advertising (including via web sites) a price lower than the MAP set by the manufacturer. Dealers who comply receive co-op advertising funds from the manufacturer. A dealer that advertises a price lower than MAP receives no co-op ad funds from the manufacturer. Because co-op ad funds may make the difference between making a profit and losing money, dealers have a strong incentive to comply with MAP. But MAP determines only the lowest price at which an item can be *advertised*, not the lowest price at which it can be *sold*. Dealers are free to actually sell the product for however little they wish.

A sure sign that MAP is in effect is when you see the same item being advertised at exactly the same price by numerous resellers. A few advertising identical prices might be a coincidence, but when everyone advertises the same exact price, you can bet that MAP is in effect. Prices for computer components are nearly always negotiable, but that goes double when MAP is in effect. If you are buying a component that you believe has MAP in effect, ask the vendor some hard questions. You might be surprised at how large a discount the vendor will offer from the advertised price.

Understand retail-boxed versus OEM components

Many components are sold in both retail-boxed and OEM form. The core component is likely to be similar or identical in either case, but important details may vary. For example, Intel processors are available in retail-boxed versions that include a CPU heatsink/fan and a three-year Intel warranty. They are also available as OEM components (also called *tray packaging* or *white box*) that do not include the heatsink/fan or the three-year warranty. OEM components are not intended for retail distribution, and the manufacturer may not provide any warranty to individual purchasers. Buying OEM components is fine, as long as you understand the differences and do not attempt to compare prices between retail-boxed and OEM.

Don't buy on price alone

As our all-time-favorite, unfortunately worded ad stated, "Don't be misled by price alone." The market for PCs and components is incredibly competitive and margins are razor-thin. If a vendor advertises a component for much less than other vendors, it may be a "loss leader." More likely, though, particularly if its prices on other items are similarly low, that vendor cuts corners somewhere, whether it be by using your money to float inventory, by shipping returned product as new, by charging excessive shipping fees, or, in the ultimate case, by taking your money and not shipping the product. If you always buy from the vendor with the rock-bottom price, you'll waste a lot of time hassling with returns of defective, used, or discontinued items and dealing with your credit card company when the vendor fails to deliver at all. Ultimately, you're also likely to spend more money than you would have by buying from a reputable vendor in the first place.

Determine the real price

The actual price you pay may vary significantly from the advertised price. When you compare prices, make sure to include all charges, particularly shipping charges. Reputable vendors tell you exactly how much the total charges will be. Less reputable vendors may forget to mention shipping charges, which may be very high. It's not unheard of for vendors to break out the full manufacturer pack into individual items. For example, if a retail-boxed hard drive includes mounting hardware, some vendors will quote a price for the bare drive without making it clear that they have removed the mounting hardware and charge separately for it. Also be careful when buying products that include a rebate from the maker. Some vendors quote the net price after rebate without making it clear that they are doing so.

Watch out for web pricing versus phone pricing

Some vendors charge more for an item ordered via their 800 number than they do for the same item ordered directly from their web site. Some others add a fixed processing fee to phone orders. These charges reflect the fact that taking orders on the Web is much cheaper than doing so by phone, so this practice has become more common. But be careful. One of our readers desperately needed an $8 item that he could not find locally. He ended up paying about $68 for that item after the charges for overnight priority shipping and telephone order processing were added.

Don't be afraid to dicker

Most direct resellers are willing to sell for less than the price they advertise. All you need to do is tell your chosen vendor that you'd really rather buy from them, but not at the price they're quoting. Use lower prices you find with the price comparison services as a wedge to get a better price. But remember that reputable vendors must charge more than scum-sucking, bottom-feeder vendors if they are to make a profit and stay in business. We generally try to beat down our chosen vendor a bit on price, but we don't expect them to match the rock-bottom prices that turn up on web searches.

Always pay by credit card

Using a credit card puts the credit card company on your side if there is a problem with your order. If the vendor ships the wrong product, defective product, or no product at all, you can invoke charge-back procedures to have the credit card company refund your money. Vendors who live and die on credit card orders cannot afford to annoy credit card companies, and so tend to resolve such problems quickly. Even your threat to request a charge-back may cause a recalcitrant vendor to see reason.

Avoid vendors who place a surcharge on credit card orders

Some vendors apply a surcharge, typically 3%, to their advertised prices if you pay by credit card. Surcharges violate credit card company contracts, so some vendors instead offer a similar discount for paying cash, which amounts to the same thing. Processing credit card transactions costs money, and we're sure that some such vendors are quite reputable, but our own experience with vendors that surcharge has not been good. We always suspect that their business practices result in a high percentage of charge-back requests, and so they discourage using credit cards.

Insist on a no-questions-asked, money-back guarantee

Good vendors allow you to return a product for a full refund (often less shipping charges) within a stated period, typically 30 days. Buy only from such vendors. Note that nearly all vendors exclude some product categories, including notebook computers, monitors, printers, and opened software, either because their contracts with the manufacturer require them to do so or because some buyers commonly abuse return periods for these items, treating them as "30-day free rentals." Never buy from a vendor who uses the phrase, "All sales are final." That means exactly what it says.

Avoid vendors who charge restocking fees

Make sure to check carefully for any mention of restocking fees. Many vendors who trumpet a "no-questions-asked, money-back guarantee" mention only in the fine print that they won't refund all your money. They charge a restocking fee on returns and we've seen fees as high as 30% of the purchase price. These vendors love returns, because they make a lot more money if you return the product than if you keep it.

Get everything in writing

Don't accept verbal promises under any circumstances. Insist that the reseller confirm your order in writing, including any special terms or conditions, before charging your credit card or shipping product. The fast turnaround of web-based and 800-number ordering makes postal mail largely useless for this purpose. We're not lawyers, and don't know the legal implications of email or faxed confirmations, but we've always used them and have never encountered a problem doing so. If a reseller balks at providing written confirmation of its policies, terms, and conditions, find another vendor. Most are happy to do so.

Keep organized records

File everything related to an order step by step, including a copy of the original advertisement, email, faxed, or written confirmations provided by the reseller, copies of your credit card receipt, a copy of the packing list and invoice, and so on. When we order via the web, we print a copy of each page of the ordering process, and also use our web browser to save a copy of that page to the "never delete" folder in our data directory. We also jot down notes in our PIM regarding telephone conversations, including the date, time, telephone number and extension, person spoken to, purpose of the call, and so on. We print a copy of those to add to the folder for that order.

Accept no substitutes

Make it clear to the reseller that you expect them to ship the exact item you have ordered, not what they consider to be an "equivalent substitute." Require they provide written (or email) confirmation of the exact items they will ship, including manufacturer part numbers. Particularly when ordering a PC, leave no wiggle room. For example, if the vendor promises an ATi

RADEON 9800 Pro graphics card with 256 MB of DDR-SDRAM, make sure that the component list includes that item by name, full description, and ATi product number. Don't just specify "graphics card," "ATi graphics card", or even "ATi RADEON graphics card." Otherwise, you'll get less than you paid for—a lesser RADEON card, an OEM card with a slower processor or less than 256 MB, or even a "Powered by ATI" card, which is to say a card with an ATI processor made by another manufacturer—rather than a "Built by ATI" card. Count on it.

Verify the warranty

Ask about warranty terms. Some manufacturers provide the full specified warranty terms only for items purchased from authorized dealers in full retail packaging. For some products, the warranty period begins when the manufacturer ships the product to the distributor, which may be weeks or months before you actually receive the product. OEM products typically have much shorter warranties than retail-boxed products—sometimes as short as 90 days—and may be warranted only to the original distributor rather than to the final buyer. Better resellers may *endorse the manufacturer warranty* for some period on some products, often 30 to 90 days. That means that if the product fails, you can return the item to the reseller, who will ship you a replacement and take care of dealing with the manufacturer. Some resellers disclaim the manufacturer warranty, claiming that once they ship the item, dealing with warranty claims is your problem, even if the product arrives DOA. We've encountered that problem a couple of times. Usually, mentioning phrases such as *merchantability and fitness for a particular purpose* and *revocation of acceptance* leads them to see reason quickly. We usually demand the reseller ship us a new replacement product immediately and include a prepaid return shipping label if they want the dead item back. We don't accept or pay for dead merchandise under any circumstances, and neither should you.

Verify delivery terms

Direct resellers are required by law to ship products within the time period they promise. But that time period may be precise (e.g., "ships within 24 hours") or vague (e.g., "ships within three to six weeks"). If the vendor cannot ship by the originally promised date, it must notify you in writing and specify another date by which the item will ship. If that occurs, you have the right to cancel your order without penalty. Make sure to make clear to the reseller that you expect the item to be delivered in a timely manner, and that *time is of the essence* for the transaction. Reputable vendors ship what they say they're going to ship when they say they're going to ship it. Unfortunately, some vendors have a nasty habit of taking your money and shipping whenever they get around to it. In a practice that borders on fraud, some vendors routinely report items as "in stock" when in fact they are not. Make it clear to the vendor that you do not authorize them to charge your credit card until the item actually ships, and that if you do not receive the item when promised, you will cancel the order.

Don't expect problems to solve themselves

Even if you follow all of these guidelines, you may have a problem. Even the best resellers sometimes drop the ball. If that happens, don't expect the problem to go away by itself. If you encounter a problem, remain calm and notify the reseller first. Good resellers are anxious to resolve problems. Find out how the reseller wants to proceed, and follow their procedures, particularly for labeling returned merchandise with an RMA number. If things don't seem to be going as they should, explain to the vendor why you are dissatisfied, and tell them that you plan to request a charge-back from your credit card company. Finally, if the reseller is entirely recalcitrant and any aspect of the transaction (including, for example, a confirmation letter you wrote) took place via U.S. Postal Service, contact your postmaster about filing charges of mail fraud. That really gets a reseller's attention, but use it as a last resort.

Things to Do with Old PCs

So what do you do with an old PC that would cost too much to upgrade to current standards? We encounter that question frequently around here. We have everything from the latest multiprocessor boxes to creaking old Pentiums. Here, in no particular order, are 10 useful things to do with an old PC:

Give it to your spouse

In many households, one spouse is a PC power user and the other is much less demanding. She works at home doing serious number crunching and plays the latest 3D games to relax, while he just checks his email periodically and uses the Web to keep up with the PGA Tour results. Or vice versa. He might be happier having an older system all to himself than he would be sharing the latest, fastest PC. While you're at it, install a home network, if only to share your Internet connection. You can do so using a traditional wired Ethernet, 802.11 wireless networking, or even Home Phone Line Alliance (HPNA) or power-line networking. The cost can be as little as $50 for a couple of decent Ethernet cards and a 100BaseT cable.

Give it to your kids

Younger kids want to play educational games, some of which require a lot of PC, but many of which run just fine on a two- or three-year-old system. Older kids need word processing, web browsing, and email, but may also want to run games, some of which are quite demanding. Before you pass the old system on to the kids, consider doing one or more "$50 upgrades"—$50 for a faster processor, $50 to add RAM, $50 for a new video card, and, if necessary, $50 to replace the CD-ROM drive with a DVD-ROM drive. Before you do much more than that, remember that you can buy or build a pretty competent PC nowadays for $400 or thereabouts, not including the monitor.

Give it to an elderly neighbor or relative

An old Pentium system with a 15-inch monitor and 1 GB hard drive isn't a good upgrade candidate, but that doesn't mean it's useless. It's still good enough for web browsing, email, and light word processing, and there are many elderly people who would love to have such a machine. The stereotype that old people and computers don't mix is just wrong. One of our readers reports that his 103-year-old grandfather spends hours on the Web every day, and similar stories are common. If you ask around, what you find may surprise you. If you're going to do it, do it right. Strip the system down and reinstall Windows, Internet Explorer, Outlook Express, and Office. Carry the system over, set it up for them, connect it to their phone line, and spend a couple of hours getting them started using it. Help them get connected to the Internet, and check back periodically to make sure they're having no problems.

Give it to your church, school, or library

Many nonprofits are pathetically underequipped with PCs. You may feel guilty about offering them what you consider to be an old, slow, and relatively useless computer, but utility is in the eye of the beholder. To someone running DOS applications on a 486—which many nonprofits still do—your old Pentium may be a godsend, particularly if you're willing to spend some time helping them set it up and perhaps even network it to their other machines. Don't be surprised if a nonprofit turns down your donation, though. Many of them have strict requirements for what they're willing to accept, probably because they've been deluged by people trying to dump old XTs, 286s, and 386s for tax write-offs. If local nonprofits aren't interested, contact the National Cristina Foundation (*http://www.cristina.org*). They accept anything from Pentiums up, including individual components.

Turn it into a resource server on your home network

If you don't have a home network yet, now may be a good time to set one up. For the small cost of a couple of network cards, some cables, and perhaps an inexpensive hub, you can share peripherals such as large hard drives, tape drives, and printers among all the machines on the network. Better yet, you can use inexpensive proxy server or NAT software to share one Internet connection. Windows 98/2000/XP even has Internet Connection Sharing built in. We've retired a couple of our old systems to duties as servers. One has lots of disk space and a tape drive for system backups. The other connects to our cable modem, sharing the Internet connection with the rest of the network via a proxy server.

Use it to control your home automation and security system

Home automation, until recently the exclusive province of gear-heads, is becoming mainstream. Much still depends on obsolescent and unreliable X-10 technology, but other technologies are poised to make significant inroads. If you're not familiar with home automation, visit *http://www.home-automation.org* and check some of the web sites listed there. You might be surprised by what can be done, and an old PC can be quite useful as a central controller for a home automation system.

Use it to control your home telephone/voice mail/automated attendant system

If you work at home, consider installing a real telephone system and using your old PC to manage it. We both work at home, and until recently had a Panasonic telephone system installed. We used an old 386sx system with a Talking Technologies BigmOuth card (alas, no longer available) to provide integrated automated attendant and voice mail functions. You can do the same to project a professional, "big company" image. As they say, "On the Internet, no one knows you're a dog."

Salvage it for swappers

You may think that a 1.44 MB floppy, 1 GB hard disk, or 4X CD-ROM isn't worth much, and in one sense you're right. But if you have to troubleshoot your main system, just having a working spare of any type may save you a trip to the computer store. And that old ISA video card may be priceless if you need to install a Flash BIOS update because ISA video cards display the prompts and menus used by some Flash BIOS update programs. PCI and AGP video cards do not display the prompts, forcing you to work blind.

Keep it on your desk

If you've never tried it, you might be surprised by how useful another PC on your desk can be, particularly if you network your home PCs. Windows and multitasking are great, but nothing beats having another monitor displaying a web page or other information while you work on your main PC. Robert takes this to an extreme, working surrounded by (currently) nine PCs which share four monitors.

Install Linux

It's obvious that Linux is now a serious contender. Most people who read this book and are not running Linux now will be within a year, so it makes sense to get some experience with Linux starting now. Happily, Linux doesn't need much hardware, particularly if you're running it as a server. We've run it successfully on creaking 486 systems. It's fast on a Pentium, and it flies on older Pentium II and Celeron systems. Many people say Linux is less likely to have problems on newer hardware, and that's true to some extent. However, the problems that Linux has with older hardware are usually with unusual devices. So, although Linux may not support ancient tape drives or sound cards or network adapters, it's likely to work just fine with most of your older hardware. Our main Linux server at the moment is an elderly Pentium III/750 system that we upgraded to 256 MB of RAM and a 40 GB Seagate hard drive. It still has the original video card, sound card, and 100BaseT network adapter. Everything works for us. It probably will for you as well.

Do note that if you plan to run Linux as a desktop OS, you're not giving it a fair trial if you run it on elderly hardware. A GUI requires horsepower, whether it's running on the Linux kernel or the Windows kernel. If you have any thought of migrating to Linux as your primary desktop OS (as we did during 2002), do yourself a favor and run it on reasonable hardware—at least a 750 MHz processor and 256 MB of RAM. As with Windows, more is always better.

2

Working on PCs

Popping the lid of a PC for the first time can be pretty intimidating, but there's really no need for concern. There's nothing inside that will hurt you, other than sharp edges and those devilish solder points. There's also nothing inside that you're likely to damage, assuming you take the few simple precautions detailed in this chapter.

Some PCs—particularly those from office supply and electronics superstores—have seals that warn you the warranty is void if they're broken. This isn't so much to protect them against your ham-handedness as it is to ensure that you have to come back to them and pay their price for upgrades. We advise friends and clients to break such seals if they need to, do their own upgrades, and fight it out later if they have a problem that should be covered under warranty.

We've never heard of anyone being refused warranty service because of a broken seal, but there's always a first time. If you have a sealed PC that is still under warranty, the decision is yours. Note that hard disks are a special case. Breaking the seal on a hard disk does actually destroy it and will without question void the warranty.

Those issues aside, feel free to open your PC and tinker with it as you see fit. Far from forbidding you from working on your own PC, most mail-order and retail computer vendors actually expect you to do your own upgrades. As a matter of fact, most of them will try to talk you into doing your own warranty repairs so that they can avoid sending a technician to do them for you. This chapter explains the fundamentals you need to understand to start upgrading and repairing your PC.

Rules to Upgrade By

We've repaired, upgraded, and built hundreds of systems over the years, and learned a lot of lessons the hard way while doing it. Here are the rules we live by— some big, some small, and some more honored in the breach. We admit that we don't always take each of these steps when we're doing something simple such as swapping a video card, but you won't go far wrong following them slavishly until you have enough experience to know when it's safe to depart from them.

Back everything up

Twice. Do a verify pass, if necessary, to make sure that what is on the backup tape matches what is on the disk drive. If you're connected to a network, copy at least your data and configuration files to a network drive. It's much easier to retrieve them from there than it is to recover from tape. If there's room on the network drive, create a temporary folder and copy the entire contents of the hard disk of the machine about to undergo surgery. If you have neither a tape drive nor a network volume, but you do have a CD or DVD writer, back up at least your important data and configuration files to optical discs. About 99 times in 100 all of this will be wasted effort. The 100th time—when everything that can go wrong does go wrong—will pay you back in spades for the other 99.

 If you don't have a tape drive or a CD/DVD writer, installing one is an excellent first upgrade project. Floppy disks just aren't good enough for backup nowadays.

Make sure you have everything you need before you start

Have all of the hardware, software, and tools you'll need lined up and waiting. You don't want to have to stop in midupgrade to go off in search of a small Phillips screwdriver or to drive to the store to buy a cable. Our first rule of upgrading says you won't find the screwdriver you need and the store will be closed. If your system can boot from the CD- or DVD-ROM drive, configure it to do that and test it before proceeding. Otherwise, make sure you have a boot disk with drivers for your CD-ROM drive, and test it before you start tearing things down. Create a new emergency repair diskette immediately before you start the upgrade. Make certain you have the distribution disks for the operating system, backup software, and any special drivers you need. If you're tearing down your only PC, download any drivers you will need, and copy the unzipped or executable versions to floppies or burn them to CD *before* you take the computer apart. Just following that last piece of advice would have saved us many times from driving back to the office to download a driver we needed when upgrading a computer at another site.

Make sure you can get the answers you need

Read the manual first. A quick read-through often uncovers potential problems, hints, and tips that can make the upgrade go much more smoothly. Check the web site for any new component you are installing. You'll often find FAQs (Frequently Asked Questions), Readme's, updated drivers, and other information that can make the difference between a trouble-free upgrade and a major mess. In fact, the quality of the web site that supports a component is a large factor in our purchase decision, and we suggest that you make it one in yours. Before we even consider buying a major component, we check its web site to verify that it is likely to have answers to any questions that may arise.

Make the technology work for you

You may have a choice between a slow manual way and a quick automatic way to accomplish a given task. The latter may require spending a few bucks for a special-purpose utility program, but may save you hours of trial and error, manual labor, and aggravation. For example, if you are replacing a hard disk, you can move the contents of the existing disk to the new disk by spending hours doing a backup and restore, or you can buy a $15 utility program that does the same thing in a few minutes. In fact, most hard drives now come with software to migrate your data and programs automatically from the old hard drive to the new one. For some reason, few people use these programs or are even aware that they exist. Throughout the book, we point out utilities (many of them free) that we use to minimize manual trial-and-error work.

Record everything

During an upgrade, it's often important to be able to return to your starting point. If you've just spent an hour moving cables and changing DIP switches and jumpers, it's almost impossible to remember what went where originally. So, make sure to record each change as you make it. Some people like a visual record of what they're doing, and so use a digital camera to photograph the original state of the system and each change as they make it. In particular, if you are responsible for a large number of systems, the ability to file digital camera images by date or trouble-ticket number may be useful.

We find using a camera cumbersome, and prefer to use written or tape-recorded notes. The method we've settled on is to dictate the working details as we go along into a $30 Panasonic microcassette recorder—e.g., "pin 1 on the motherboard PS/2 keyboard connector is the red wire on the jack, with position 4 empty." Once we finish, we transfer important information—changes to jumpers and Dual Inline Pin (DIP) switches, what components we've added and removed, etc.—to the written log book for that computer. Each time we buy or build a new computer, it gets its own log book with its name on the cover. We use the black-and-white speckled hardbound composition books that Office Depot sells for a couple of bucks.

Change one thing at a time

When upgrading multiple components, do so in phases. For example, to install a new video card and a new sound card, leave the old video card in place while you install the new sound card. Restart the computer and make sure the new sound card is working properly *before* you install the new video card. If you change only one thing at a time, any problems that occur are clearly a result of that change, and are relatively easy to track down and fix. If you swap multiple components simultaneously, resulting problems are harder to troubleshoot because you're never certain whether the problem is caused by a bad or misconfigured new component, by a conflict between the new components, or by a conflict between one or more of the new components and one or more existing components.

Keep the PC grounded while you work on it

Most PC user manuals tell you to unplug the PC before working on it. They say that not because it is good practice, but to minimize the risk of being sued if someone somehow electrocutes himself while working on one of their PCs. Disregard their advice. Every experienced technician we know leaves the PC plugged in while working on it, and for good reason. Doing so keeps the PC grounded, which minimizes the very real risk of static electricity destroying sensitive chips. Best practice is to plug the PC into a power strip or surge protector that is connected to the wall receptacle, but turn the power strip off. That grounds the PC to the building ground, but also ensures that no voltage can reach the PC while you're working on it. Note that the presence of a two-to-three-prong adapter anywhere in the chain isolates the system from the dedicated ground circuit and eliminates the value of keeping the system plugged in unless the grounding wire on the adapter is connected to the building ground.

Turning off the main power switch on most older systems—those that use the AT form factor and its derivatives—removes voltage from all system components except the power supply itself, leaving the system in a safe state to work on without risk of damaging components. Many newer systems—those that use the ATX form factor and its derivatives—maintain low-voltage, low-amperage power to the motherboard *even when the main power switch is turned off*, unless that system is unplugged from the wall receptacle.

Most (but not all) such systems have a small indicator LED on the motherboard that remains lit to indicate that the system is still powered. Installing or removing an expansion card or other component on such a system without first disconnecting the power entirely may damage the motherboard and/or the component. Although some ATX power supplies have a physical power switch on the power supply itself, the safest method with such systems is either to unplug the main power cord, or to use a switched-off power strip as mentioned earlier. If in doubt, disconnect the main power cord and ground yourself by touching the power supply housing before touching other components.

Keep track of the screws and other small parts

Disassembling a PC yields an incredible number of screws and other small pieces. As you tear down a PC, organize these parts using an egg carton or old ice cube tray. As we can attest, one errant screw left on the floor can destroy a vacuum cleaner. Worse, one unnoticed screw can short out and destroy the motherboard and other components. The goal is to have all of the small parts reinstalled or accounted for when you reassemble the PC. Some people store the screws until they are needed by putting them back into the original component after removing it. This takes a bit longer, but does ensure that you use the proper screw for each component.

Some PCs use a variety of screws which look very similar but are in fact threaded differently. For example, the screws used to secure some case covers and those used to mount some disk drives may appear to be identical, but swapping them may result in stripped threads. If in doubt, keep each type of screw in a separate compartment of your organizer.

Use force when necessary, but use it cautiously

Many books tell you never to force anything, and that's good advice as far as it goes. If doing something requires excessive force, chances are a part is misaligned, you have not removed a screw, or something similar. But sometimes there is no alternative to applying force judiciously. For example, drive power cables sometimes fit so tightly that the only way to get them off is to grab them with pliers and pull hard. Some combinations of expansion card and slot fit so tightly that you must press very hard to seat the card. If you encounter such a situation, verify that everything is lined up and otherwise as it should be (and that there isn't a stray wire obstructing the slot). Then use whatever force it takes to do the job, which may be substantial.

Check and recheck before you apply power

An experienced PC technician working on a system does a quick scan of the entire PC before performing the smoke test by applying power to the PC. Don't skip this step, and don't underestimate its importance. Most PCs that fail the smoke test do so because this step was ignored. Until you gain experience, it may take several minutes to verify that all is as it should be—all components secure, all cables connected properly, no tools or other metal parts shorting anything out, and so on. Once you are comfortable working inside PCs, this step takes 15 seconds, but that may be the most important 15 seconds of the whole upgrade.

Start small for the first boot

The moment of greatest danger comes when you power up the PC for the first time. Do what's necessary to minimize damage if the smoke test fails. If the system fails catastrophically—which sometimes happens no matter how careful you are—don't smoke more than you have to. For example, we recently built a server for which we'd bought four 512 MB DIMM memory modules and two 15K Cheetah SCSI drives. A new motherboard sometimes shorts out the first time it's powered up, so rather than installing the new DIMMs and hard drives before testing, we used an old 128 MB DIMM and an old Barracuda hard disk to verify that the motherboard was good and all connections were right. Once we passed that hurdle, we installed the new DIMMs and hard disks. If the system had smoked, we'd have been out a motherboard, but our expensive new DIMMs and hard disks would be safe. We mentioned earlier another advantage to doing things this way. Limiting simultaneous changes makes it easier to get the hardware working properly. Starting small and adding components incrementally also helps you get Plug and Play configured more easily, particularly when you're installing "difficult" peripherals such as sound cards, which want to grab every free resource in sight.

Don't throw the old stuff away

Don't discard the components you pull. With new hard disks priced near $1 per gigabyte, an old 1 GB hard disk may not seem worth keeping. But you may be glad you have it the next time you need to troubleshoot your system. Despite those correspondence school ads that show a technician using an oscilloscope to troubleshoot a PC, nobody really does it that way. In the real world, you troubleshoot PCs by swapping components. Keeping old components you pull during upgrades is a convenient (and free) way to accumulate the swappers you'll need later on to troubleshoot problems with this or another PC. Label them "known good," date them, and put them on the shelf.

Leave the cover off until you're sure everything works

An easy way to tell an experienced technician from a novice is to see when he reassembles the case. Experts wait until everything is installed and tested before putting the lid back on and securing the external cables. A novice installs the component, reassembles the case, reconnects all the cables, and *then* tests it. We watched one young woman do this several times before she caught on.

 The corollary to this rule is that you should *always* put the cover back on the case once the upgrade is complete and tested. Some believe that leaving the cover off improves cooling. Wrong. Cases do not depend on convection cooling, which is the only kind you get with the cover off. Cases are designed to direct cooling air across the major heat-generating components, processors, and drives, but this engineering is useless if you run the PC uncovered. Replace the cover to avoid overheating components.

The other good reason to replace the cover is that running a system without the cover releases copious amounts of radio frequency to the surrounding environment. An uncovered system can interfere with radios, monitors, televisions, and other electronic components over a wide radius.

Tools

It's worthwhile to assemble a toolkit that contains the hand tools and software utilities that you need to work on PCs. If you work on PCs only occasionally, you can get by with a fairly Spartan set of tools. If you work on PCs frequently, devote some time, effort, and money to assembling a reasonably complete set of hand tools and utilities. The following sections detail the components that we've found worth carrying in our toolkits.

Hand Tools

You don't need many tools for routine PC upgrades and repairs. We've successfully repaired PCs using only a Swiss Army Knife, but a more complete set of tools makes jobs easier. Putting together a dedicated PC toolkit and keeping it in a fixed location avoids the hassle of looking for a tool when what you really want to do is work on your PC.

Your first thought may be to buy one of those PC toolkits available from various sources, but we suggest you avoid them. Inexpensive kits available from most mail-order vendors contain shoddy tools and are not worth even their low price. Kits available from specialty catalogs such as Specialized Products (*www. specializedproducts.com*) and Jensen (*www.jensentools.com*) are fine if you fix PCs for a living (or if your company buys the kit). Otherwise, they're overkill and much too expensive.

Instead of buying any of the prepackaged kits, head for Sears and assemble your own PC toolkit. The basic tools you need for routine PC work cost less than $50. Store these tools together, using a tool wrapper (available from auto parts stores) or a zipper case (available from specialty tool vendors or a home improvement warehouse). You can often buy sets of pliers, screwdrivers, and so forth for less than what you'd pay for each individually. We carry only the tools we need, so we usually buy the set, remove the ones we really wanted for our toolkit, and contribute the remainder to the general stock of tools around the house. Table 2-1 lists what we carry and recommend as a basic kit, with Sears part numbers in parentheses.

Table 2-1. A basic PC toolkit

Description	Description
Slotted screwdriver, 3/16" x 4" (41581)	Nutdriver, 1/4" (41971)
Slotted screwdriver, 1/4" x 4" (41583)	Nutdriver, 3/16" (41977)
Phillips screwdriver, #0 x 2 1/2" (41293)	Flashlight (twist switch)
Phillips screwdriver, #1 x 3" (41294)	Spare parts tube/organizer
Phillips screwdriver, #2 x 4" (41295)	Small brushes
Long-nose mini-pliers, 4 1/2" (45173)	Band-Aids

Even when we're not working on PCs, we always carry a Swiss Army Knife (we like the Victorinox CyberTool). If you don't routinely carry a knife, add a disposable snap-off razor blade, which is useful for opening blister-wrap packages, cutting cable ties, and so on. Also, although we prefer drivers with individual handles, you may prefer a handle with interchangeable bits. If so, get the Sears Craftsman 11-in-1 Screwdriver (41478), which includes five double-end bits and also serves as a 1/4-inch nutdriver.

If you work on PCs frequently or have special requirements, you may find useful the additions to the basic kit listed in Table 2-2. Depending on the types of PCs you work on, some of these tools may also be needed in the basic kit. For example, Compaq PCs use a lot of Torx fasteners.

Table 2-2. Supplemental tools for the basic PC toolkit

Description (source)	Description (source)
Pliers, 4" diagonal mini-pliers (Sears #45178)	Dental mirror (drugstore)
Torx driver, T10 (Sears #41473)	Hemostat (drugstore)
Torx driver, T15 (Sears #41474)	Spring-hook tool/parts retriever (auto parts store)
Screw starters (Phillips and slotted, twist-lock)	Digital voltmeter (Radio Shack, specialty vendors)
Wire stripper/crimper (Sears #82563)	

If you work on a PC in place—under a desk or wherever—you often need a third hand to hold the flashlight. For 20 years, Robert had been using the straightforward male method, holding the flashlight in his mouth and using his tongue to aim it. That works, but flashlights often taste disgusting. Barbara, being a smart woman, bought a headband-mounted flashlight, shown in Figure 2-1. That works even better, and Robert has now sworn off chewing on flashlights.

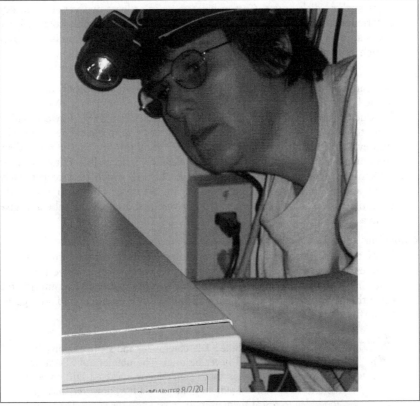

Figure 2-1. Barbara wearing a head-mounted flashlight while replacing the cover on her all-SCSI main system

In addition to the tools themselves, a good toolkit contains several consumable items, including:

Alcohol

> PC components accumulate greasy brown residue, particularly if you smoke or if you heat with gas or oil. This residue attracts and holds dust, but can be removed with rubbing alcohol. Buy isopropanol (isopropyl alcohol), which removes grease better than ethanol (ethyl alcohol), and carry a small screw-top bottle of it in your kit.

Swabs

> Keep half a dozen Q-Tips or foam swabs for cleaning mouse rollers, tape drive heads, and similar difficult-to-reach places. We prefer the foam swabs, which do not deposit stray bits of cotton.

Cotton balls

Carry a few of these as disposable cleaning aids. Moisten one with rubbing alcohol so that it is wet, but not dripping, and use it to clean larger components such as disk drives. Cotton balls come in at least two varieties. In our experience, the ones intended for medical use (which are really cotton) leave fibers all over the place. The ones Barbara uses with her nail polish remover (which appear to be a man-made fiber) don't shed nearly as much.

Freon

You can't get real Freon now because of the damage it supposedly does to the ozone layer, but everyone still calls the stuff you can buy Freon. We use Zero Residue Cleaner from Radio Shack. It comes in a pressurized spray can with a small tube that attaches to the nozzle and allows you to direct the spray. The stuff evaporates almost instantly, and does a good job of cleaning really dirty components. It's particularly useful for cleaning inaccessible things such as the fan blades inside the power supply enclosure, which tend to get really filthy and are almost impossible to clean otherwise. It's also useful for cleaning the heads on floppy and tape drives. Just stick in the tube and give them a good squirt.

Canned air

Many technicians carry a can of compressed clean, dry air to blow out dust bunnies, to evaporate cleaner residue quickly, and so on. We've never felt that air was worth paying for, so we simply blow gently to accomplish the same thing. You can use an ordinary drinking straw to direct and strengthen the airflow. Try not to spray saliva on the components.

Many PC toolkits include a DIP chip puller and a DIP chip inserter, two tools that should never be used. The ubiquity of SIMM and DIMM modules means there aren't many socketed DIP chips in modern PCs. Your system may still have a few, however, and it's a good idea to reseat them every time you pop the cover. Do a quick scan of the motherboard and expansion cards, and just press down firmly with your thumb on each socketed chip you see. If the chip has begun to walk out of its socket, you'll feel it snap back into position as you press. For more about working with DIP chips, see *http://www.hardwareguys.com/dipchip.html*.

Software Tools

In addition to hand tools, your toolkit should have an assortment of floppy diskettes and CDs that contain reporting and diagnostic utilities and essential applications. The location of the kit can vary according to your own needs. If you have only one PC, keep all this stuff near it. If you work on many PCs, carry these items with you.

Essential utilities

The contents of your software toolkit depend greatly on how many PCs you maintain, which operating systems they run, and similar factors, but a good basic assortment includes the following essential utilities:

DOS boot diskette

Even if all your computers run Windows or Linux, the most important item in your software toolkit is a DOS boot diskette with drivers for the CD-ROM drive. When the PC won't boot, this diskette allows you to install or run diagnostic and repair utilities from a CD. Without it, you may be stymied because you can't access the CD-ROM drive, even to do something as basic as reinstalling the operating system. That's true even if your system allows booting from the CD-ROM drive because not all CDs are bootable. The Windows 9X startup disk described in the following note fulfills this purpose. If you run only Windows NT/2K/XP or Linux, borrow someone's Windows 9X computer long enough to make a DOS startup diskette.

To create the Windows 95/98/Me startup diskette, open the Control Panel and double-click Add/Remove Programs. Display the Startup Disk page and click the Create Disk icon to create a startup disk. This diskette is bootable and contains the drivers needed to access most IDE CD-ROM drives. You can use a Startup Disk created on any computer to start any other computer. Floppy diskettes have a way of getting lost or damaged, and you can't get far if you can't boot a problem PC, so we generally keep several copies of the Windows 98 SE Startup Disk distributed around our work areas, in our tool-kits, and so on.

On this or another diskette, depending on free space, you'll want copies of essential utilities. At minimum, add the following files to those present on the Windows 9X startup floppy:

FORMAT.COM

Necessary to reformat the hard disk, if that becomes unavoidable.

EDIT.COM and EDIT.HLP

A standard ASCII editor that is bundled with Windows 9X and Windows 2000. Note that this is a standalone program, unlike earlier versions that required BASIC. If disk space is tight, as it may be if you need to add special drivers to the boot floppy, you can dispense with the help file. This editor uses Alt-letter commands—e.g., Alt-F to open the file menu.

All three of these "extra" files fit on a standard Windows 98 startup floppy.

The Windows 9X startup floppy contains drivers that work with nearly any IDE/ATAPI CD-ROM drive or DVD-ROM drive, and *may* work with a SCSI CD/DVD-ROM drive, depending on the type of host adapter it's connected to. If your system has a SCSI CD/DVD-ROM drive, verify that booting with the standard startup floppy allows you to access that drive. If it doesn't, download the DOS SCSI drivers from the web site of the manufacturer of your SCSI host adapter, copy them manually to the startup floppy, and make any necessary additions or changes to *autoexec.bat* and *config.sys*. Verify that the modified startup floppy will allow you to access your SCSI CD/DVD-ROM drive *before* you have a problem.

DOS diagnostics

Years ago, PCs often came with CheckIt, QAPlus, AMIDiag, or a similar diagnostic utility. Now system vendors expect people to use the bundled Windows utilities. These are fine, as far as they go, but they don't go very far. Windows (particularly NT/2K/XP) and Linux isolate users and programs from the hardware, which makes it hard for a diagnostic utility to do its job. Also, Windows-based utilities are usable only if the computer boots. You can use these bundled utilities to do things such as detecting a misconfigured component or an IRQ conflict on a bootable system, but that's not enough when you need detailed information or when the PC won't boot. For those situations, you need a DOS-based utility that provides comprehensive testing and reporting. Any of the following products will do the job. We use them all, but if you get only one, make it SmithMicro Software CheckIt.

SiSoft Sandra

SiSoft Sandra is our favorite Windows-based diagnostic utility and probably the most-used diagnostic program, not least because a free version can be downloaded from SiSoft. Although the free version is sufficient for most people's needs, SiSoft also sells the $29 Sandra Professional which includes additional functionality and technical support (*http:// www.sisoftware.demon.co.uk/sandra/*).

Symantec Norton Utilities (NU)

Almost since the first PCs shipped, most technicians have carried a copy of NU. Unfortunately, Norton discontinued the DOS version some time ago. The current Windows versions are nice desktop extenders, but provide limited hardware diagnostics. Grab a copy of a late DOS version if you can find one (*http://www.norton.com/nu*).

SmithMicro Software CheckIt

The best dedicated hardware diagnostic program is CheckIt (*http://www. checkit.com*), available in several versions. For most users, the $40 Portable Edition suffices. If you repair PCs for a living, the $296 Professional Edition provides additional tools and utilities that are worth having. Either edition can boot independent of the installed OS, and so can be used to diagnose hardware problems on a system that won't boot to Windows. The various CheckIt products are hard to find in retail stores, but can be ordered directly from the web site.

 DOS diagnostics remain a popular shareware and public-domain software category, although most are single-purpose products (e.g., a serial port tester) rather than general-purpose diagnostics. If that's all you need, though, searching a shareware library such as *http:// www.shareware.com* using the string *diagnostic* may turn up a program that does the job for free.

Emergency boot/repair diskette

Recent versions of Windows allow you to create an emergency disk that contains critical system configuration data, part or all of the registry, etc. Create or update this disk for a computer anytime you make a significant change to it.

Label and date the disk and store it near the computer or keep it with your toolkit. If you don't have a recent copy, do yourself a favor and make one right now. Use the following procedures to create an emergency disk:

Windows 95/98/Me

For Windows 9X, we recommend backing up the entire registry, which you can do simply by copying the registry files to another location. The registry comprises two files, *SYSTEM.DAT* and *USER.DAT*, which are located in the \WINDOWS folder. These files are assigned the Hidden and Read-Only attributes, so you'll need to change the default settings of Windows Explorer before you can view or copy them. To do so, from Explorer, choose View, then Folder Options, and then click the View tab. Under Files and Folders locate the Hidden Files item and mark the Show all files radio button. Once you have rendered the registry files visible, you can use Copy, then Paste to copy them to a different location. *USER.DAT* is usually only a few hundred KB, and will therefore easily fit on a floppy. *SYSTEM.DAT* may be quite large. On our test-bed system, for example, it is more than 3 MB. Fortunately, registry files are easily compressible. Using a utility such as WinZip or PKZip yields 4:1 or 5:1 compression, which allows the compressed *SYSTEM.DAT* to fit on a floppy unless the original file is huge.

 The Windows 9X Startup Disk is *not* an emergency repair disk. It is a simple boot disk which does not contain registry files or other configuration data.

Windows 2000/XP Emergency Repair Disk (ERD)

Click Start, Programs, Accessories, System Tools, and then Backup. With Backup running, click the Emergency Repair Disk icon to create the disk. In the resulting dialog, mark the Also backup the registry... checkbox to copy key system files to the repair directory on the hard disk. Like the NT ERD, the Windows 2000/XP ERD is not bootable. To repair Windows 2000/XP, you must boot either from the distribution CD or the boot floppies.

 The Windows 2000/XP ERD does not contain any registry files. Creating the ERD copies the registry files to the *%SystemRoot%\Repair* folder, where they may be lost if the hard disk crashes. To be safe, each time you create or update the ERD, copy the entire contents of that folder to another hard disk, network volume, or CD-R disc.

Linux

Use the mkbootdisk command to produce an emergency boot disk. This disk is specific to your system configuration, and should be updated anytime you make significant hardware or configuration changes. Also consider downloading a live-filesystem Linux distribution such as Knoppix. You can create a bootable disk from which Linux runs directly, allowing you to perform all sorts of diagnostic tests.

You can find various boot disks and other utilities at *http://www.bootdisk.com*. Although we are not lawyers and haven't looked into the legality of all these utilities, many of them appear to be quite useful.

Operating system distribution discs

You need the OS distribution discs to replace a failed hard disk, but you may also need them for routine upgrades and maintenance. For example, Windows prompts for the distribution disc to load drivers for a new device, and Linux distribution discs may contain hundreds of programs that weren't loaded during the initial installation. If you've updated the operating system from the initial distribution version (e.g., by applying a Windows NT/2000/XP Service Pack), also keep the Service Pack or update CD handy.

With huge hard disks costing so little, we create a separate "distribution partition" on the hard disk for most Windows systems we build. We copy the distribution CD to this partition, along with service packs, the Office CD (and any other programs the system uses), the driver CDs for installed hardware, and so on. This has several benefits, including faster installation, the fact that you don't have to locate the CD when you change options or want to install additional modules, and the fact that you can, if necessary, completely rebuild the system using only a boot floppy to get started.

Backup utility

If you use a third-party backup utility, keep a copy of the distribution disk in your kit to make sure that you can restore backup tapes after reinstalling the operating system. Few things are more frustrating than getting a failed computer up again, having a good backup tape, but not having the software at hand that you need to restore it.

Antivirus utility

If your system becomes infected by a virus, you need to have a DOS-bootable, write-protected floppy disk and a recent version of an antivirus utility. In fact, anytime a system behaves strangely, a good first step is to run a quick virus scan. The DOS-bootable floppy allows you to boot cleanly and detect and remove a virus on a DOS or Windows 9X disk, or on a Windows NT/2000/XP disk that is formatted as FAT. Because you cannot access an NTFS volume after booting from a boot floppy, the only way to remove a virus from these volumes is to boot the system from the hard disk and run an antivirus utility from a local hard disk or network drive. The big names in antivirus utilities are McAfee VirusScan from Network Associates (*http://www.nai.com*), and Norton AntiVirus from Symantec (*http://www.symantec.com*). We've used both, and either is sufficient for the task. Lately, however, we find ourselves using the free-for-personal-use AVG AntiVirus from Grisoft (*http://www.grisoft.com*).

CMOS save/restore utility

CMOS settings store the current configuration of a PC. These settings range from easily understood ones—current date/time, boot options, hard disk configuration, and so on—to ones such as advanced chipset configuration that only system designers fully understand. Although you can manually record all of the settings on paper, there's a better way—a CMOS save/restore utility. These utilities save CMOS settings to a disk file, which you can later restore to re-create the settings in one step. CheckIt Diagnostics Suite includes such a utility. If you don't have CheckIt, download a dedicated CMOS save/restore utility. There are many free and shareware alternatives available. One that we've used is Benjamin Johnston's free CMOSViewer, which runs under Windows 9X. Numerous DOS products are available from shareware archives such as *http://www.shareware.com*. Search for *CMOS*.

 Most expansion cards, modems, and disk drives come with a driver CD. Just keeping them all straight is hard enough, let alone making sure that you have the correct and most recent driver for a particular component. When we buy or build a computer, we create a folder for it on a network drive. When we buy a component that comes with a floppy diskette or CD with drivers, we copy the contents of that disk to a subfolder of that folder. If you have a CD burner, use it to make a customized CD for each computer. Collect all the drivers and other miscellany in a folder and copy them to a CD for that system. Include a change log in the root directory. When you replace a component, note that in the change log and burn a new CD with the updated and new drivers. If there's room on the CD, also include the operating system, diagnostic tools, and so forth.

Supplemental utilities

Beyond essential utilities, we carry several supplemental utilities. These tools are nice to have, but not absolutely required. Rather than doing things you can't do without them, they save you time—sometimes a lot of time. If you work on PCs frequently, every one of these commercial utilities belongs in your bag. Each of them costs money, but unless your time is worth nothing an hour, each pays for itself quickly—usually the first time you use it.

If you seldom work on PCs, these utilities probably aren't worth buying ahead of time. Instead, try to schedule your upgrades, and buy these as you need them. Note that most of these utilities are available in both inexpensive single-user/single-PC standard versions and much more expensive versions that are licensed to be used by a single technician on multiple PCs. The prices given are typical street prices for the standard versions.

Partition Magic
This $50 PowerQuest (*http://www.powerquest.com*) utility has saved us countless hours of extra work over the years. Before Partition Magic, the only way to change disk partitioning was to back up, delete the old partitions, create and format new partitions, and restore. In addition to taking hours, this process is perilous. More than once, we've been unable to restore a backup tape we made immediately before starting to repartition, even though that tape had passed a verify flawlessly. Partition Magic lets you repartition

on the fly. It takes less time and is probably safer than the old backup-and-restore method. In fact, although PowerQuest recommends backing up before repartitioning, we confess that we seldom bother to back up our own systems before repartitioning. We've never lost any data doing it that way, but if you repartition without backing up and you lose data, please don't send us any nasty messages. You have been warned.

DriveCopy

This $20 PowerQuest utility is the cheapest, easiest, and most reliable way we know to copy the contents of one hard disk to another—for example when you're replacing a hard disk. Using DriveCopy allows you to avoid the time-consuming process of backing up the old drive, installing the operating system on the new drive, and then doing a restore. Instead, you simply connect the new drive with the old drive still installed and use DriveCopy to replicate the entire contents of the old drive to the new. When you remove the old drive, the system boots from the new drive without further ado. Note that some retail-boxed hard drives come with software that performs the same function.

DriveImage

This PowerQuest utility is available in a $50 DriveImage version and a Drive-Image Pro version that is priced per user. DriveImage Pro is primarily a disk cloning product. It allows you to create an image of a master disk and then replicate that image to multiple hard disks—just the thing when you need to set up 100 identical workstations. It even has a SID editor, which allows you to get around the problem of Windows NT's unique SIDs. As a personal utility, DriveImage is useful for migrating programs and data between partitions and for disaster recovery. Unlike DriveCopy, DriveImage can copy individual partitions, can change the partition size after copying to the destination, and can automatically resize partitions to fit within a smaller drive. As useful as all this is, the really important thing about DriveImage is that it can create a compressed image of a partition. The image file typically occupies about one-quarter of the space used on the source partition, and can be stored on another partition or on removable media. If disaster strikes, you can recover the image file automatically using the bootable recovery floppies that DriveImage creates for you. Anytime we're about to do a significant software upgrade to a system, we run DriveImage first to create an image backup. That way, if the upgrade ends up causing a problem, we can immediately roll back the system to its original state.

DisplayMate

This $50 tool from Sonera Technologies (*http://www.displaymate.com*) does just one thing, but does it supremely well. It helps you optimize your video card and monitor. More than any other PC component, monitors can vary significantly between individual examples of the same model. We don't buy an expensive monitor without using DisplayMate to test it first, and neither should you. DisplayMate is also useful on an ongoing basis. Monitors change as they age. Using DisplayMate to tune them periodically results in the best possible picture. You can download a demo from the web site that is sufficient for casual testing.

The best way we've found to organize and protect CDs is to lose the jewel cases and store the CDs in one of those zippered vinyl audio CD wallets you can buy for a few dollars at Wal-Mart or Best Buy. They use plastic or Tyvek sleeves to protect the CDs, hold from a half dozen to two dozen CDs, and make it easy to find the one you want. If the CD has a serial number or init key on the original jewel case, make sure to record it on the CD, using a soft permanent marker on the *label* side.

We stock one of these wallets with essential CDs—Windows 95/98/NT/2K/XP and Red Hat Linux distribution CDs, Office, various diagnostics, and so on—and always carry it with us. We also buy a CD wallet for each PC we buy or build. New PCs usually arrive with several CDs, and even video, sound, or modem cards are likely to come with their own CDs. Storing these CDs in one place, organized by the system they belong to, makes it much easier to locate the one you need.

General Procedures

After you assemble a toolkit with the hand tools and utilities described in the preceding sections, you have everything you need to upgrade or repair a PC, except for the new components. Before you get started, take a few minutes to read through the following sections, which describe the common procedures and general knowledge you need to work on PCs. These sections describe the general tasks you perform almost anytime you work on a computer—things such as opening the case, setting jumpers and switches, manipulating cables, and adding or removing expansion cards. Instructions for specific tasks such as replacing a motherboard, disk drive, or power supply are given in the relevant chapters.

Before You Open the Case

Although you may be raring to get in there and fix something, taking the time to prepare properly before you jump in pays big dividends later. Before you open the case, do the following:

Make sure it's not a software problem
> The old saying, "If all you have is a hammer, everything looks like a nail" is nowhere truer than with PC repairs. Just as surgeons are often accused of being too ready to cut, PC technicians are always too ready to pop the lid. Before you assume that hardware is causing the problem, make sure the problem isn't being caused by an application, by Windows, or by a virus. Use your hardware diagnostic utility and virus scanner *before* you assume the hardware is at fault and start disconnecting things.

Think things through
> Inexperienced technicians dive in willy-nilly without thinking things through first. Experienced ones first decide what is the most likely cause of the problem, what can be done to resolve it, in what order they should approach the repair, and what they'll need to complete it. Medical students have a

saying: "When you hear thundering hooves, don't think about zebras." In context, that means that you should decide the most likely causes of the problem in approximate ranked order, decide which are easy to check for, and then eliminate the easy ones first. In order, check easy/likely, easy/unlikely, hard/likely, and finally hard/unlikely. Otherwise, you may find yourself tearing down a PC and removing the video card before you notice that someone unplugged the monitor.

Back up the hard disk(s)

Every time you pop the cover of a PC, there's a small but ever-present risk that something that used to work won't work when you put everything together again. One of the wires in a cable may be hanging by a thread, or the hard drive may be teetering on the edge of failure. Just opening the case may cause a marginal component to fail irreversibly. So, before you even think of doing PC surgery, make sure the hard drive is backed up.

Record CMOS settings

It's important to have a record of the CMOS settings before you open the case. Working on a PC doesn't normally affect CMOS settings, but some activities (e.g., flashing the BIOS, removing the battery, or shorting the CMOS clear jumper) can wipe out all settings. If that happens, you'll need to re-enter the settings, and you'd better have them available. Recording CMOS settings is particularly important when you're not replacing the motherboard because they're the ones you'll continue to use. If you are replacing the motherboard, the only CMOS settings you need to record are those that specify the hard disk geometry. Even if you don't plan to do anything that might affect CMOS, use your CMOS save/restore utility to save these settings to a diskette before you open the case. If you don't have such a utility, download one or record the settings with pencil and paper.

Disconnect external cables

It may seem obvious, but you need to disconnect all external cables before you can move the PC itself to the operating room. Many PCs are located under desks or are positioned so as to make it difficult to see the rear panel. If necessary, get down on the floor and crawl behind the PC with a flashlight to make sure it isn't still tethered to something. We've dragged modems, keyboards, and mice off desks because we weren't paying attention, and we once came within inches of pulling a $2,000 monitor onto the floor. Check the cables or pay the price.

Set the monitor safely aside

Monitors are not only fragile, but also can cause serious injuries if the tube implodes. A monitor on the floor is an accident waiting to happen. If you're not taking the monitor to the work area, keep it on the desk out of harm's way. If you must put it on the floor, at least turn the screen toward the wall.

Electrostatic Discharge (ESD) Precautions

You've probably been startled by a static electric shock on a dry winter day. This phenomenon—formally called *electrostatic discharge* (*ESD*)—can destroy sensitive PC components instantly. Just because you don't notice it doesn't mean it isn't there, either. Static potential must build to several thousand volts before you experience a shock, but levels of only a few hundred volts are hazardous for PCs. Worse, incremental damage may occur invisibly and is cumulative, so although any one zap may not kill a component outright, it will surely damage it and make it that much more prone to fail later on.

Although this may be off-putting, it's really no big deal. We've worked on hundreds of PCs over the years, and haven't damaged one yet, so far as we know. You can easily avoid problems with static electricity by following three rules: (1) don't wear rubber-soled shoes or synthetic clothing, (2) work in an uncarpeted area, and (3) ground yourself to dissipate the static charge each time you are about to touch a PC component.

The first generally recommended line of defense against static is an *antistatic wrist strap*. One end wraps around your wrist. The other end may have alligator clips intended to connect to the PC case or power supply, or it may have a plug intended to fit a standard power receptacle. You can buy these things for a few dollars from most mail-order places. They are sometimes included with expensive chips such as processors. We don't like these straps. They're awkward to work with, and—although we know it is safe—connecting a conductive strap to your wrist and then plugging it into the wall seems a bit outré.

We use a simpler method. It protects sensitive components just as reliably, as long as you get in the habit of following it religiously. Leave the PC you're working on plugged in, which ensures that it is grounded (although it's a good idea to use a switched-off power strip, as described earlier in this chapter). When you first sit down to work on the PC, and then each time you are about to touch a static-sensitive component, touch the chassis or power supply to dissipate the accumulated static charge. When we're working on a particularly sensitive or expensive component, like a CPU, we actually keep our left hand on the chassis the whole time we're in contact with the component. Note that ATX motherboards maintain constant low voltage, even when the system is turned off. For that reason, either disconnect the power cord before working on an ATX system or connect it to a switched-off power strip. Touching the power supply still works, however, as it provides an adequate sink for static charges.

 To minimize problems with static electricity, buy a spray/mister bottle at the hardware store or supermarket. Fill it with water and add a few drops of dishwashing liquid or fabric softener. Before you begin work, mist the work area liberally, both air and surfaces. The goal isn't to get anything wet. Just the added humidity is enough to all but eliminate static electricity.

Removing and Replacing the Cover

It sounds stupid, but it's not always immediately obvious how to get the cover off the chassis. We've worked on hundreds of different PCs from scores of manufacturers over the years, and we're still sometimes stumped. Manufacturers use an endless variety of fiendish ways to secure the cover to the chassis. Some were intended to allow tool-free access, others to prevent novice users from opening the case, and still others were apparently designed just to prove there was yet one more way to do it.

We've seen novice upgraders throw up their hands in despair, figuring that if they couldn't even get the case open they weren't destined to become PC technicians. Nothing could be further from the truth. It just sometimes takes a while to figure it out.

The most evil example we ever encountered was a mini-tower case that had no screws visible except those that secured the power supply. The cover appeared seamless and monolithic. The only clue was a 2-inch piece of silver "warranty void if removed" tape that wrapped from the top of the cover to one side, making it clear that the separation point was there. We tried everything we could think of to get that cover off. We pulled gently on the front of the case, thinking that perhaps it would pop off and reveal screws underneath. We pressed in gently on the side panels, thinking that perhaps they were secured by a spring latch or friction fit. Nothing worked.

Finally, we turned the thing upside down and examined the bottom. The bottom of computer cases is almost always unfinished metal, but this one was finished beige material that looked just like the other parts of the cover. That seemed odd, so we examined the four rubber feet closely. They had what appeared to be center inserts, so we pried gently on one of these with our small screwdriver. Sure enough, it popped off and revealed a concealed screw within the rubber foot. Once we removed those four screws, the cover slid off easily, bottom first.

The moral is that what one person can assemble, another person can disassemble. It sometimes just takes determination, so keep trying. Obviously, your first resort should be the system manual, but manuals have a way of disappearing when you need them most. Fortunately, most cases don't use such convoluted methods. Standard systems generally use one of the following methods to secure the cover to the chassis:

Classic AT-style desktop cases
> These use five screws (one per corner and one at top center) that pass through the chassis and thread into receptacles on the inside of the cover. Don't confuse the screws that secure the power supply with those that secure the cover. Cover screws are located along the edge, while power supplies are normally secured by four screws in a square pattern located at the upper- and mid-left side of the rear panel as you are viewing it. On these systems, the cover comprises the top, front, and sides of the case, and slightly overhangs the rear of the chassis when installed properly. The lower edge of each side of the cover usually has a channel that fits a rail built into the chassis. Once you remove the screws, slide the cover a few inches toward the front and then lift it off. To install the cover, place it in position with a gap of a few inches between the back edge of the cover and the rear panel. Make sure that the channels in the bottom of each side panel are aligned with the chassis rail grooves and then slide the cover toward the rear of the PC until it seats. When installing or removing the cover be careful not to snag the top center screw receptacle on any of the cables.

Late-model AT-style and low-profile desktop cases
> These use three or more screws on the back of the case, which go through an overlapping lip on the cover and thread into the chassis itself. The removable

part of the cover comprises the top and sides. To remove the cover, remove the screws from the back (make sure to remove only the cover screws, *not* the screws that secure the power supply), slide the cover back an inch or two, and then lift it clear. You may have to tilt the cover slightly by lifting the rear to allow it to come clear of the chassis. To reinstall the cover, place it over the chassis with a 1- or 2-inch gap between the front edge of the cover and the rear of the front panel, then slide the cover forward. There is a lip around the sides and top of the cover that fits inside the front cover of the case. Usually, the top will fit easily if you've put the cover on correctly, but the sides may need to be pressed in before they will fit. Also note that there may be a lip or other retaining mechanism at the bottom edge of the cover which you may need to align before the cover will seat properly. Replace the screws from the back.

Tower and mini-tower cases

These generally use three or four screws equally spaced down each side to secure the cover. The covers on most of these system cases resemble those on recent AT-style and low-profile cases. The front of the cover at the top and on both sides has an underbeveled lip that slides under the rear edge of the front bezel. The bottom edges of both side panels are channeled to fit guides that protrude vertically from the bottom of the chassis on each side. After removing the screws that secure it, remove the cover by sliding it far enough to the rear to clear the lips at the top and side front of the cover from the front panel bezel. Then lift it off.

Replacing the cover on one of these systems is often difficult because you must guide the lips on the top and both side panels of the cover under the front bezel while simultaneously making sure that the bottom of each side panel seats in the guides. The easiest way to do this is usually to lower the cover over the chassis a few inches back from its ultimate seated position. Then lift the rear of the cover an inch or two to angle the cover slightly. Make sure that the bottom edges of the cover seat in their channels, and then slide the cover toward the front while keeping the rear of the cover lifted an inch or two. Guide the top lip of the cover under the front bezel and then slowly lower the rear of the cover, making sure that the lips on the side panels slide under the sides of the front bezel.

Tool-free cases

Some of the easiest cases to work on are screwless, or nearly so. For example, one of our own favorites, the Antec KS-288 (*http://www.antec-inc.com*), has only one thumbscrew, centered at the top of the back panel. After this thumbscrew is removed, the top panel slides off to the rear. That in turn frees both side panels, which simply lift off. Reassembling the case is just as easy because it uses craftily-designed triangular slots that make it easy to align things before dropping them into place. If properly designed, a tool-free case can be just as rigid as one that uses screws. Be careful, though, about buying a cheap tool-free case. We've seen some that are incredibly flimsy.

In addition to these standard case types, you may run into one of the following:

Clamshell cases

These cases are designed to allow quick access to the inside of the PC by removing only the top portion of the case, while the sides, front, and back remain fixed. These cases divide the top down the middle from front to back. To open them, you generally remove two or four screws, which may be located on the top of the case or at the top center of the back of the case. Once you remove these screws, the two parts of the top either swing up on hinges or can be removed completely. Although never very popular with PC vendors, clamshell cases are still made, and are sometimes encountered on low-volume, custom-built systems.

Side panel cases

On these cases, all parts of the cover except the sides are semipermanently attached. Each side panel is individually secured to the chassis using thumb-screws or screws along the rear and/or bottom of the case. To remove a side panel, loosen the screws securing it and slide the panel toward the rear and/or bottom of the case, as necessary. The front and/or top of these panels are often secured using a lip that slides under an overhang on the top or rear panel. Depending on the case design, you may have to lift the panel slightly away from the chassis before it will slide clear. To reinstall the panel, reverse the process, guiding the lip into its matching channel until the panel slides easily back into the closed position and then reinsert the screws.

Managing Internal Cables and Connectors

When you pop the cover of a PC, the first thing you'll notice is cables all over the place. These cables carry power and signals between various subsystems and components of the PC. Making sure they're routed and connected properly is no small part of working on PCs.

The cables used in PCs terminate in a variety of connectors. By convention, every connector is considered either male or female. Many male connectors, also called *plugs*, have protruding pins, each of which maps to an individual wire in the cable. The corresponding female connector, also called a *jack*, has holes that match the pins on the mating male connector. Matching male and female connectors are joined to form the connection. Rather than using pins and holes, the connectors used on some cables (for example, modular telephone cables and 10BaseT Ethernet cables) use other methods to establish the connection. The connector that terminates a cable may mate with a connector on the end of another cable, or it may mate with a connector that is permanently affixed to a device, such as a hard disk or a circuit board. Such a permanently affixed connector is called a *socket*, and may be male or female.

Some cables use individual wires joined to a connector. Only three cables of this sort are common in PCs—those used to supply power to the motherboard and drives, those that connect front-panel LEDs and switches to the motherboard, and those that connect audio-out on a CD-ROM drive to a sound card.

Most PC cables contain many individual wires packaged as a *ribbon cable*, so called because individually insulated conductors are arranged side by side in a flat array that resembles a ribbon. Ribbon cables provide a way to organize the wires required to connect devices such as drives and controllers whose interfaces require many conductors. Ribbon cables are used primarily for low-voltage signals, although they are also used to conduct low-voltage/low-current power in some applications. Common ribbon cables range in size from the 10-wire cables used to extend embedded serial ports from the motherboard to the back panel, through 34-wire floppy drive cables, to 40-wire and 80-wire IDE drive cables, to 50-, 68-, and 80-wire SCSI cables. Ribbon cables are normally used only inside the case because their electrical characteristics cause them to generate considerable RF emissions, which can interfere with nearby electronic components.

System designers attempt to avoid two potential dangers with regard to PC cables. Most important is to prevent connecting a cable to the wrong device. For example, connecting a 12-volt power cable to a device that expects only 5 volts might have a catastrophic result. This goal is achieved by using unique connectors that physically prevent the cable from connecting to a device not designed to receive it. The second potential error is connecting the cable backward. Most PC cables prevent this by using asymmetrical connectors that physically fit only if oriented correctly, a process called *keying*.

Two keying methods are commonly used for PC cables, either individually or in conjunction. The first uses mating connectors whose bodies connect only one way, and is used for all power cables and some ribbon cables. The second, used for most ribbon cables, blocks one or more holes on the female connector and leaves out the corresponding pin on the male connector. Such a ribbon cable can be installed only when oriented so that missing pins correspond to blocked holes.

An ideal PC cable therefore uses unambiguous keyed connectors. You can't connect these cables to the wrong thing because the connector only fits the right thing; you can't connect it backward because the connector only fits the right way. Fortunately, most of the really dangerous cables in PCs—the ones that could damage a component or the PC itself if they were misconnected—are of this sort. Power cables for disk drives and ATX motherboards, for example, fit only the correct devices and cannot be connected backward.

Some PC cables, on the other hand, require careful attention. Their connectors may physically fit a component that they're not intended to connect to, and/or they may not be keyed, which means you can easily connect them backward if you're not paying attention. Connecting one of these cables incorrectly usually won't damage anything, but the system may not work properly, either. The cables that link front panel switches and indicator LEDs to the motherboard are of this variety. So are the power cables for old-style AT motherboards, and connecting these incorrectly *can* destroy the motherboard.

Ribbon cable fundamentals

On first glance, ribbon cables appear to be dead standard. They're nearly all light gray nowadays, although you may encounter light blue, white, or rainbow ribbon cables on older systems. All of them use a contrasting colored stripe to indicate pin 1 (brown in the case of the rainbow cables). They use only two types of connectors (described later in this section), both of which are female and only one of which is commonly used nowadays. For a ribbon cable with a given number of wires, it might seem that the only distinguishing features are how long the cable is and whether it has connectors for two devices or just one. Problems may arise, however, if incompatible keying methods are used on the two connectors that need to mate.

So-called "round" ribbon cables have recently become popular, particularly with makers that cater to gamers and other enthusiasts. A round ribbon cable is simply a standard cable that has been sliced longitudinally into smaller groups of wires. For example, a standard flat 40-wire IDE ribbon cable might be sliced into ten 4-wire segments, which are then bound with cable ties or otherwise secured into a more-or-less round package. The advantage to round ribbon cables is that they reduce clutter inside the case and improve airflow. The disadvantage is that doing this damages signal integrity on the individual wires because signal-bearing wires are put into closer proximity than intended. We recommend you avoid round ribbon cables, and replace any you find in any of your systems with flat ribbon cables. Note, however, that some round cables, such as Serial ATA cables, are designed to be round and do not need to be replaced.

Most ribbon cables use *header-pin connectors*, shown in Figure 2-2. Header-pin connectors are used on cables for hard drives, CD-ROM drives, tape drives, and similar components, as well as for connecting embedded motherboard ports to external rear panel jacks. The female header-pin connector on the cable has two parallel rows of holes that mate to a matching array of pins on the male connector on the motherboard or peripheral. On all but the least-expensive drives and other peripherals, these pins are enclosed in a plastic socket designed to accept the female connector. On inexpensive motherboards and adapter cards, the male connector may be just a naked set of pins. Even high-quality motherboards and adapter cards often use naked pins for secondary connectors (such as serial ports or feature connectors).

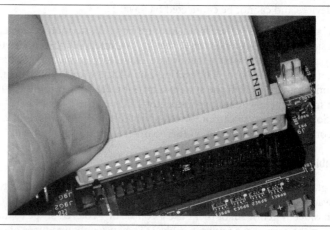

Figure 2-2. A ribbon cable with a header-pin connector

Some header-pin connectors, male and female, are not keyed. Others use connector body keying, pin/hole keying, or both. This diversity means that it is quite possible to find that you cannot use a particular header-pin cable for its intended purpose. For example, we recently installed a disk drive and attempted to use the IDE cable supplied with the drive to connect that drive to the secondary IDE header-pin connector on the motherboard. The motherboard end of that cable was keyed by a blocked hole, but the header-pin connector on the motherboard had all pins present, which prevented the cable from seating. Fortunately, the cable that came with the motherboard fit both the motherboard and the drive connectors properly, allowing us to complete the installation.

If you run into such a keying problem, there are three possible solutions:

Use an unkeyed cable
> The IDE and other header-pin cables that most computer stores sell utilize connectors that use neither connector body nor pin/hole keying. You can use one of these cables of the proper size to connect any device, but the absence of all keying means that you must be especially careful not to connect it backward.

Remove the key from the cable
> If you don't have an unkeyed cable available, you may be able to remove the key from the existing cable. Most keyed cables use a small bit of plastic to block one of the holes. You may be able to use a needle to pry the block out far enough that you can extract it with your needlenose pliers. Alternatively, try pushing a pin into the block at an angle, then bending the top of the pin over and pulling both bent pin and block with your pliers. If the key is a solid, integral part of the cable (which is rarely the case), you may be able to use a heated needle or pin to melt the key out of the hole far enough for the pin to seat.

Remove the offending pin
> Sometimes you have no choice. If the stores are closed, the only cable you have uses pin/hole keying with a solid block that you can't get out, and you must connect that cable to a header-pin connector that has all pins present, you have to go with what you have. You can use diagonal cutters to nip off the pin that prevents you from connecting the cable. Obviously, this is drastic. If you nip the wrong pin, you'll destroy the motherboard or expansion card, or at least render that interface unusable. Before you cut, see if you can swap cables within the PC to come up with an unkeyed cable for the problem connector. If not, you can sometimes bend the offending pin *slightly*—enough to allow the female connector to partially seat. This may be good enough to use as a temporary connection until you can replace the cable. If all else fails and you need to cut the pin, before doing so align the keyed female connector with the pin array and verify just which pin needs to be cut. Also, check the manual for a detailed list of signal/pin assignments on that interface. The pin you are about to remove should be labeled No Connection or N/C in that list. Use the old carpenter's maxim here— measure twice and cut once.

Connector and keying issues aside, the most common mishap with header-pin connectors occurs when you install the cable offset by a column or a row. The socketed male connectors used on most drives make this impossible to do, but the male connectors used on most motherboards and expansion cards are an unsocketed double row of pins, making it very easy to install the connector with the pins and holes misaligned. Working in a dark PC, it's very easy to slide a connector onto a set of header pins and end up with an unconnected pair of pins at one end and an unconnected pair of holes at the other. It's just as easy to misalign the connector the other way, and end up with an entire row of pins and holes unconnected.

Card-edge connectors, also called *edge-card connectors*, form a connection by sliding the female cable connector onto a formed portion of a PC circuit board which has contacts laid down on the circuit card itself to serve as the male connector. Card-edge connectors were commonly used to connect 5.25-inch floppy drives, floppy interface tape drives, and old-style ST506/412 hard drives, but are seldom used anymore because the physical and electrical connection they provide is inferior to that provided by a header-pin connector.

Card-edge connectors should be keyed on the male (circuit board) side by the presence of an off-center slot, and on the female (cable) side by the presence of a matching insert in the connector body to prevent the cable from being installed backward. However, many card-edge connectors on cables do not have this keying insert, which makes it easy to install the cable backward. Some male card-edge connectors do not have the keying slot, which makes it impossible to connect a properly keyed cable to them.

The only common problem with card-edge connectors arises when you need to connect a keyed cable to a device that has no keying slot. Male connectors without a keying slot sometimes have a prenotched area on the circuit board that you can break away with your long-nose pliers to allow the keyed cable to seat. If not, you may be able to use your pliers to remove the keying insert from the cable connector. If neither of these solutions is workable, the only solution is to replace the cable with an unkeyed version.

Locating pin 1

If you upgrade your system and it fails to boot or the new device doesn't work, chances are you connected a ribbon cable backward. This can't happen if all connectors and cables are keyed, but nearly all systems have at least some unkeyed connectors. The good news is that connecting ribbon cables backwards almost never damages anything. We're tempted to say "never" without qualification, but there's a first time for everything. If this happens to you, go back and verify the connections for each cable. Better yet, verify them before you restart the system.

One of the experienced PC technicians who reviewed the first edition of this book tells us that he has "burned up" more than one floppy disk drive by installing the cable with the pins offset. We have frequently installed FDD cables reversed, offset, and in any other combination you can imagine (it always seems easier to seat a cable by feel than it does to remove the drive and do it right) with no worse result than the system failing to boot. The FDD cable carries only signal-level voltages, so we're not sure how offsetting pins could damage a drive, but we'll certainly be more careful in the future.

To avoid connecting a ribbon cable backward, locate pin 1 on each device and then make sure that pin 1 on one device connects to pin 1 on the other. This is sometimes easier said than done. Nearly all ribbon cables use a colored stripe to indicate pin 1, so there's little chance of confusion there. However, not all devices label pin 1. Those that do usually use a silk-screened numeral 1 on the circuit board itself. If pin 1 is not labeled numerically, you can sometimes determine which is pin 1 in one of the following ways:

- Instead of a numeral, some manufacturers print a small arrow or triangle to indicate pin 1.

- The layout of some circuit boards allows no space for a label near pin 1. On these boards, the manufacturer may instead number the last pin. For example, rather than labeling pin 1 on an IDE connector, the manufacturer may label pin 40 on the other side of the connector.

- If there is no indication of pin 1 on the front of the board, turn it over (this is tough for an installed motherboard) and examine the reverse side. Some manufacturers use round solder connections for all pins other than 1, and a square solder connection for pin 1.

- If all else fails, you can make an educated guess. Many disk drives place pin 1 closest to the power supply connector. On a motherboard, pin 1 is often the one closest to the memory or processor. We freely admit that we use this method on occasion to avoid having to remove a disk drive or motherboard to locate pin 1 with certainty. We've never damaged a component using this quick-and-dirty method, but we use it only for IDE drives, rear-panel port connectors, and other cables that do not carry power. Don't try this with SCSI, particularly differential SCSI.

Once you locate an unmarked or unclearly marked pin 1, use nail polish or some other permanent means to mark it so that you won't have to repeat the process the next time.

Power supply cables

PC power supply cables are fully described in Chapter 26.

Setting Jumpers and DIP switches

Jumpers and DIP switches are two methods commonly used to set hardware options on PCs and peripherals. Although they look different, jumpers and DIP switches perform the same function—allowing you to make or break a single electrical connection, which is used to configure one aspect of a component. Jumper or switch settings may specify such things as the amount of installed memory, the base address, IRQ, and DMA assigned to a device, whether a particular function is enabled or disabled, and so on.

Older PCs and expansion cards often contain dozens of these devices, and use them to set most or all configuration options. Newer PCs typically use fewer jumpers and DIP switches, and instead use the BIOS setup program to configure components. In fact, many recent motherboards (e.g., Intel Pentium 4 boards) have only one jumper. You close this jumper when you first install the board to allow such static options as the speed of the installed processor to be configured, or to perform such infrequent actions as updating the Flash BIOS. That jumper is then opened for routine operation.

More properly called a *jumper block*, a *jumper* is a small plastic block with embedded metal contacts that may be used to bridge two pins to form an electrical connection. When a jumper block bridges two pins, that connection is called *on*, *closed*, *shorted*, or *enabled*. When the jumper block is removed, that connection is called *off*, *open*, or *disabled*. The pins themselves are also called a jumper, usually abbreviated *JPx*, where *x* is a number that identifies the jumper.

Jumpers with more than two pins may be used to select among more than two states. One common arrangement, shown in Figure 2-3, is a jumper that contains a row of three pins, numbered 1, 2, and 3. You can select among three states by shorting pins 1 and 2, or pins 2 and 3, or by removing the jumper block entirely. Note that you cannot jumper pins 1 and 3 because a jumper can be used to close only an adjacent pair of pins.

You can often use your fingers to install and remove isolated jumpers, but needle-nose pliers are usually the best tool. However, jumpers are sometimes clustered so tightly that even needlenose pliers may be too large to grab just the jumper you want to work on. When this happens, use your hemostat. When you open a jumper, don't remove the jumper block entirely. Instead, install it on just one pin. This leaves the connection open, but ensures that a jumper block will be handy if you later need to close that connection.

Jumper blocks come in at least two sizes that are not interchangeable. Standard blocks are the largest and the most commonly used, and are usually black. Mini jumper blocks are used on some disk drives and boards that use surface-mount components, and are often white or light blue. One of our technical reviewers reports that Quantum uses still a third size, which we'll deem "micro" jumper blocks, on some of its drive models. He reports that these tiny blocks disappear when dropped, cling like a burr to jumper pins, and are extremely hard to work with, even when using fine tweezers. New components always come with enough jumper blocks to configure them. If we remove one when configuring a device, we usually tape it to a convenient flat area on the device for possible future use. It's also a good idea to keep a few spares on hand, just in case you need to reconfigure

Figure 2-3. A typical PC jumper (bottom center) set to close pins 1 and 2

a component from which someone has removed all the "surplus" jumper blocks. Anytime you discard a board or disk drive, strip the jumper blocks from it first and store them in your parts tube.

A *DIP switch*, shown in Figure 2-4, is a small plastic block that contains one or more (usually four or eight) individual slide or rocker switches. Each of these individual switches performs the same function as a jumper block. Turning an individual switch on is equivalent to installing a jumper block, and turning it off to removing the jumper block. DIP switches are labeled *SWx*, where *x* is a number that identifies the switch block. Each individual switch within the block is also numbered.

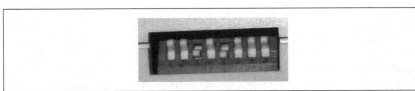

Figure 2-4. DIP switch (3 and 5 off, others on)

The "on" position may be indicated by the word *On*, *Close*, *Short*, or *Enable* printed on one side of the switch, or by an arrow pointing to the on side. Turn on a rocker switch by depressing the side of the switch or the raised nub toward the on side. Turn on a slide switch by sliding the nub toward the on side.

Installing and Removing Expansion Cards

Expansion cards are circuit boards that you install in a PC to provide functions that the PC motherboard itself does not provide. For example, many motherboards don't include video circuitry. PCs built with such motherboards use a separate video adapter expansion card to provide such circuitry. Internal modems, sound cards, network adapters, and disk controllers are other commonly used expansion cards. Figure 2-5 shows a typical expansion card.

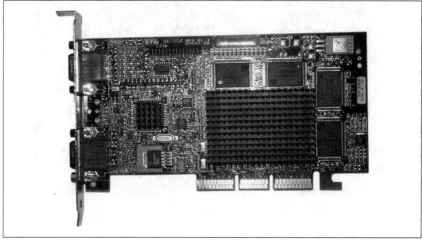

Figure 2-5. An expansion card

Each expansion card plugs into an *expansion slot* located on the motherboard or on a *riser card* that attaches to the motherboard. The rear panel of the PC chassis includes a cutout for each expansion slot, which provides external access to the card. The cutouts for vacant expansion slots are covered by thin metal *slot covers* that are secured to the chassis. These covers prevent dust from entering through the cutout and also preserve the cooling airflow provided by the power supply fan and any auxiliary fans installed in the system.

To install an expansion card, remove the slot cover, which may be secured by a small screw or may simply be die-stamped into the surrounding metal. In the latter case, carefully twist off the slot cover using a screwdriver or your needle-nose pliers. If you need to replace the slot cover later, secure it to the chassis using a small screw that fits a notch in the top portion of the slot cover. The back of the expansion card forms a bracket that resembles a slot cover and is secured to the chassis in the same way. Depending on the purpose of the card, this bracket may contain connectors that allow you to connect external cables to the card.

 Cheap cases sometimes have slot covers that must be twisted off to be removed and are destroyed in the process. If you need to cover an open slot in such a case and don't have a spare slot cover, ask your local computer store, which probably has a stack of them in its storeroom.

Installing and removing expansion cards is by far the most common activity you'll perform when working on PCs. Even if you are not working on a particular expansion card, you must sometimes remove it to provide access to the section of the PC that you do need to work on. Installing and removing expansion cards may be hard or easy, depending on the quality of the case, the motherboard, and the expansion card itself. High-quality cases, motherboards, and expansion cards are built to tight tolerances, making expansion cards easy to insert and remove. Cheap cases, motherboards, and expansion cards have such loose tolerances that you must sometimes literally bend sheet metal to force them to fit.

People often ask whether it matters which card goes into which slot. Beyond the obvious—there are different kinds of expansion slots, and a card can be installed only in a slot of the same type—there are four considerations that determine the answer to this question:

Physical restrictions

Depending on the size of the card and the design of the motherboard and case, a given card may not physically fit a particular slot. For example, a protruding drive bay, memory module, or processor may prevent a slot from accepting a full-length card. If this occurs, you may have to juggle expansion cards, moving a shorter card from a full-length slot to a short slot and then using the freed-up full-length slot for the new expansion card. Also, even if a card physically fits a particular slot, a connector protruding from that card may interfere with another card, or there may not be enough room to route a cable to it.

Technical restrictions

There are several variables, including slot type, card type, BIOS, and operating system, that determine whether a card is position-sensitive. We'll describe the different bus and slot types in Chapter 3, but for now it's enough to know that ISA cards are not slot-sensitive, but *EISA* (*Enhanced Industry Standard Architecture*) cards which are used in older servers, as well as PCI cards may be. For this reason, although it may not always be possible, it's good general practice to reinstall a card into the same slot that you removed it from.

 Although interrupt conflicts are rare with PCI motherboards and modern operating systems, they can occur. In particular, PCI motherboards with more than four PCI slots share interrupts between slots, so installing two PCI cards that require the same resource in two PCI slots that share that interrupt may cause a conflict. If that occurs, you can eliminate the conflict by relocating one of the conflicting expansion cards to another slot. Even in a system with all PC slots occupied, we have frequently eliminated a conflict just by swapping the cards around. See your motherboard manual for details.

Electrical considerations

Although it is relatively uncommon nowadays, some combinations of motherboard and power supply can provide adequate power for power-hungry expansion cards such as internal modems only if those cards are installed in the slots nearest the power supply. This was a common problem years ago, when power supplies were less robust and cards required more power than they do now, but you are unlikely to experience this problem with modern equipment. One exception to this is AGP video cards. Many recent motherboards support only AGP 2.0 1.5V and/or AGP 3.0 0.8V video cards, which means that older 3.3V AGP cards are incompatible with that slot.

Interference considerations

Another problem that is much less common with recent equipment is that some expansion cards generate enough RF to interfere with cards in adjacent slots. Years ago, the manuals for some cards (notably some disk controllers, modems, and network adapters) described this problem, and suggested that the card be installed as far as possible from other cards. We haven't seen this sort of warning on a new card in years, but you may still encounter it if your system includes older cards.

Installing expansion cards

To install an expansion card, proceed as follows:

1. Remove the cover from the chassis and examine the motherboard to determine which expansion slots are free. Locate a free expansion slot of the type required by the expansion card (expansion slot types are detailed in Chapter 3). Recent PCs may have several types of expansion slots available, including ISA, PCI, combination ISA/PCI, AGP, AMR, CNR, and ACR slots. Older PCs may have other types of unused expansion slots, including VLB (VESA Local Bus, an obsolete bus standard) and EISA. If more than one slot of the proper type is free, you can reduce the likelihood of heat-related problems by choosing one that maintains spacing between the expansion cards rather than one that clusters the cards.

2. An access hole for each expansion slot is present on the rear of the chassis. For unoccupied slots, this hole is blocked by a thin metal slot cover secured by a screw that threads downward into the chassis. Determine which slot cover corresponds to the slot you chose. This may not be as simple as it sounds. Some types of expansion slots are offset, and the slot cover that appears to line up with that slot may not be the right one. You can verify which slot cover corresponds to a slot by aligning the expansion card itself with the slot and seeing which slot cover the card bracket matches to.

3. Remove the screw that secures the slot cover, slide the slot cover out, and place it and the screw aside.

4. If an internal cable blocks access to the slot, gently move it aside or disconnect it temporarily, noting the proper connections so that you will know where to reconnect them.

5. Guide the expansion card gently into position, but do not yet seat it. Verify visually that the tongue on the bottom of the expansion card bracket will slide into the matching gap in the chassis and that the expansion card bus connector section aligns properly with the expansion slot. Figure 2-6 shows an expansion card being fitted to the motherboard in a high-quality case, with the card properly aligned and ready to be seated. Figure 2-7 shows the same card being installed in a cheap case, which doesn't allow the card to align properly with the slot if the card bracket is aligned with the chassis.

With cheap cases, you may have to use pliers to bend the card bracket slightly to make the card, chassis, and slot all line up. Rather than doing that, we prefer to replace the case.

Figure 2-6. An expansion card properly aligned and ready to seat

Figure 2-7. The same card in a cheap case, not aligning properly with the expansion slot

6. When you are sure that everything is properly aligned, position your thumbs on the top edge of the card, with one thumb at each end of the expansion slot below the card, and press gently straight down on the top of the card until it seats in the slot. Apply pressure centered on the expansion slot beneath the card, and avoid twisting or torquing the card. Some cards seat easily with little tactile feedback. Others require quite a bit of pressure and you can feel

them snap into place. Once you complete this step, the expansion card bracket should align properly with the screw hole in the chassis.

7. Replace the screw that secures the expansion card bracket, and replace any cables that you temporarily disconnected while installing the card. Connect any external cables required by the new card—don't tighten the thumb-screws quite yet—and give the system a quick once-over to make sure you haven't forgotten to do anything.

8. Turn on the PC and verify that the new card is recognized and that it functions as expected. Once you have done so, power the system down, replace the cover, and reconnect everything. Store the unused slot cover with your spares.

Removing expansion cards

To remove an expansion card, proceed as follows:

1. Remove the system cover and locate the expansion card to be removed. It's surprising how easy it is to remove the wrong card if you're not careful. No wonder surgeons occasionally get it wrong.

2. Once you're sure you've located the right card, disconnect any external cables connected to it. If the card has internal cables connected, disconnect those as well. You may also need to disconnect or reroute other unrelated cables temporarily to gain access to the card. If so, label those you disconnect.

3. Remove the screw that secures the card bracket, and place it safely aside.

4. Grasp the card firmly near both ends and pull straight up with moderate force. If the card will not release, *gently* rock it from front to back (parallel to the slot connector) to break the connection. Be careful when grasping the card. Some cards have sharp solder points that can cut you badly if you don't take precautions. If there's no safe place to grasp the card and you don't have a pair of heavy gloves handy, try using heavy corrugated cardboard between the card and your skin.

5. If you plan to save the card, place it in an antistatic bag for storage. If you are not installing a new expansion card in the vacated slot, install a slot cover to ensure proper airflow and replace the screw that secures the slot cover.

 You may encounter an expansion card that's seated so tightly that it appears to be welded to the motherboard. When this happens, it's tempting to gain some leverage by pressing upward with your thumb on a connector on the back of the card bracket. Don't do it. The edges of the chassis against which the bracket seats may be razor-sharp, and you may cut yourself badly when the card finally gives. Instead, loop two pieces of cord around the card to the front and rear of the slot itself, and use them to "walk" the card out of its slot, as shown in Figure 2-8. Your shoelaces will work if nothing else is at hand. For a card that's well and truly stuck, you may need a second pair of hands to apply downward pressure on the motherboard itself to prevent it from flexing too much and possibly cracking as you pull the card from the slot.

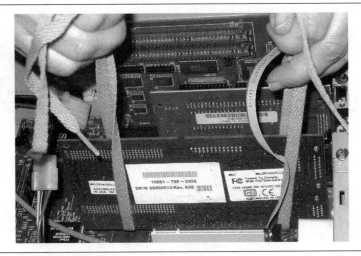

Figure 2-8. Barbara pulling a recalcitrant expansion card the safe way

Installing Drives

We attempted to write an overview section here to describe how to install and configure drives. Unfortunately, we found it impossible to condense that information to an overview level. Physical installation procedures vary significantly, and configuration procedures even more, depending on numerous factors, including:

- Drive type
- Physical drive size, both height and width
- Internal (hard drives) versus externally accessible (floppy, optical, and tape drives)
- Mounting arrangements provided by the particular case
- Drive interface (SCSI versus ATA/ATAPI)

For specific information about installing and configuring various drive types, including illustrations and examples, refer to the following chapters:

- Floppy disk drives, Chapter 6
- High-capacity floppy disk drives, Chapter 7
- Tape drives, Chapter 9
- CD-ROM drives, Chapter 10
- DVD drives, Chapter 12
- Hard disk drives, Chapter 14
- Cases, Chapter 25
- Building a PC, Chapter 28

3

Motherboards

The *motherboard* is the heart of a PC. Some manufacturers use the terms *system board*, *planar board*, *baseboard*, or *main board*, and Intel calls its motherboards *desktop boards*. No matter what you call it, the motherboard defines the PC. It provides the common link to all other components inside the PC, including the CPU, memory, disk drives, video and sound adapters, keyboard, mouse, and other peripheral components. If you are building a PC, choosing the motherboard is the most important decision you make and can be one of the most difficult. If you are upgrading a PC, replacing the motherboard is often the best and most cost-efficient means of doing so. If you are buying a PC, the motherboard it uses determines its functionality and future upgradability. This chapter describes the characteristics of motherboards, provides purchasing guidelines, and explains how to install and configure a motherboard.

Motherboard Characteristics

Several characteristics differentiate motherboards, including physical characteristics, which in combination are called the form factor; the chipset used, which defines the capabilities of the motherboard; the processors the motherboard supports; the BIOS it uses; and the internal and expansion busses that it supports. The following sections examine each of these factors.

Form Factor

Motherboards differ in size, shape, position of mounting holes, power supply connector type, and port types and locations. Together, these differences define the *form factor* of the motherboard. Form factor is a critical issue when you upgrade a system because the replacement motherboard must physically fit the case and use the existing power supply connectors. Form factor doesn't matter when you're building a new PC. You simply select the best motherboard for your needs, and then buy a case that fits it. Many motherboard manufacturers build similar motherboards in different form factors. Here are the form factors you may encounter:

AT, Baby AT (BAT), and LPX

All of these form factors are based on the motherboard used in the original 1984 IBM PC AT and are obsolete. The most recent of these motherboards use chipsets and processors that are two or more generations out of date. Although a few such motherboards remain available, they are suitable only to replace failed motherboards in obsolete systems that for some reason must remain in service. Other than that, there is no good reason to buy one of these obsolete motherboards. A system that uses this form factor is too old to be economically upgradeable.

ATX and variants

Nearly all current motherboards use the ATX form factor, or one of its smaller variants, the miniATX, µATX, FlexATX, and NLX. For a complete discussion of these form factors, including case and power supply issues, see Chapters 25 and 26.

Proprietary

Although it is much less common nowadays to find new systems that use proprietary motherboards, such boards were relatively common a few years ago, particularly in systems sold by major manufacturers such as Compaq and IBM. A cynical observer might believe that the major manufacturers did this to lock customers in. In fact, it probably had more to do with the fact that the then-current Baby AT standard had reached the end of its useful life and the ATX standard had not yet become the obvious successor. To reduce manufacturing costs and increase reliability, manufacturers that had the in-house engineering talent to do so designed their own motherboards. Some of these are actually very elegantly designed. They all share one fatal flaw, however. They aren't standard. A system that uses a proprietary motherboard form factor is effectively not upgradeable.

 Motherboards with proprietary form factors are making a comeback, at least in a limited sense. The Mini-ITX form factor advocated by VIA Technologies, although technically an open standard, is uncommon enough that it might as well be proprietary. Also, the Small Form Factor (SFF) PCs that have recently become popular use what is in effect a proprietary motherboard form factor, although such motherboards are available from a few manufacturers. We suggest you avoid both Mini-ITX and SFF. If you need a small system, use the industry-standard FlexATX form factor.

Chipsets

Just as the motherboard defines a PC, the chipset defines a motherboard. The *chipset* determines the main characteristics of the motherboard—what processors it supports, what RAM types it can use, what bus types and speeds it supports, whether it supports standards such as AGP and USB, and so on. Chipsets are so named because they usually comprise two relatively large chips. Some chipsets contain three or more chips. A few chipsets, most of which are intended for low-cost systems, have all functions on one physical chip.

Figure 3-1 shows a block diagram for the 845PE, which until July 2003 was Intel's flagship chipset for the Pentium 4 and Celeron processors. Block diagrams are helpful in understanding the functions of a chipset. Like most chipsets, the 845PE comprises a Northbridge chip, labeled GMCH, and a Southbridge chip, labeled ICH4. The Northbridge interfaces the CPU, memory, and AGP video—all of which are high-bandwidth components. The Southbridge can conveniently be thought of as a peripheral controller. The Southbridge manages low- and moderate-bandwidth components such as the PCI bus, IDE interface, USB 2.0 ports, and so on. Some motherboards supplement Southbridge functions by adding another chip, often called a Super I/O controller.

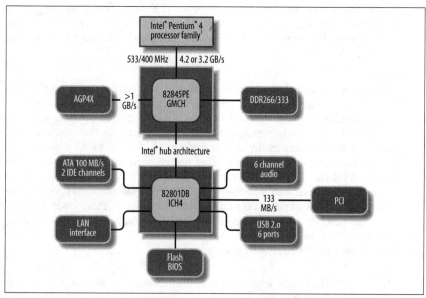

Figure 3-1. Block diagram of the Intel 845PE chipset (graphic courtesy of Intel Corporation)

Chipset makers often use one Southbridge with different Northbridges to create chipsets for different processors. For example, Intel uses the 82801DB ICH4 Southbridge in numerous Pentium 4 and Celeron chipsets. It's also possible to use the same Southbridge to create chipsets for processors from different makers. For example, VIA Technologies produces chipsets for the Intel Pentium 4 and AMD Athlon—two processors with very different architectures—by combining the same Southbridge with a Northbridge that supports the processor in question.

During transition to new technologies like USB 2.0 or Serial ATA, motherboard makers often add support for those technologies using a supplementary third-party chip. For example, the Intel 845PE chipset does not natively support Serial ATA, but Intel wanted to include that feature in its D845PEBT2 motherboard. To do so, they added an SiL S-ATA controller chip. The upside to such a solution is that it gets new technologies to market faster. The downside to such stopgap solutions relative to native support is that features, performance, and compatibility may suffer.

There are scores of motherboard manufacturers, but only a handful of chipset manufacturers. This is because designing a chipset requires significant engineering resources, but building a motherboard around that chipset is straightforward. Chipset manufacturers want motherboard manufacturers to buy their chipsets, so they provide detailed specifications, engineering drawings, and reference samples, which make building motherboards more a matter of production than design.

If you examine 20 motherboards made by 20 different manufacturers, all using the same chipset, you'll find that the similarities outweigh the differences. There may be minor variations in features and layout, but the chief differences are the quality of the components used and the quality of construction. Accordingly, it is quite possible for one manufacturer to make a terrible motherboard and another manufacturer a superb motherboard, even though both use the same chipset. The motherboard market is so competitive that price is almost invariably an excellent predictor of the quality of a motherboard.

Understanding chipset basics is important whether you are upgrading an existing PC or building a new one. If you are upgrading, understanding the chipset tells you what can and cannot be done within its limitations. If you are building or buying a new PC, its chipset is the most important factor in determining motherboard performance and future upgradability. Understanding the differences between competing chipsets lets you make rational decisions about which computer or motherboard to buy. Because chipsets are so important, we've devoted a great deal of space to explain what you need to know about them.

CPU family support

Chipsets support only one of the following CPU families, because CPU families differ greatly in how they access and manage main memory, cache, and other major system components:

- Intel Pentium Pro/Pentium II/Celeron/Pentium III sixth-generation CPUs
- Intel Pentium 4/Celeron seventh-generation CPUs
- AMD Athlon/Duron sixth-generation CPUs
- AMD Hammer-series seventh-generation CPUs

A particular chipset may support most or all CPUs within a family, or may support only one of them. For example, some chipsets support the Pentium II, Celeron, and Pentium III CPUs, while others support only one or two of those. Also, chipsets designed for late variants within a generation may not support earlier variants within that generation. For example, Intel 815-family chipsets do not support the Pentium II and early variants of the Celeron. Similarly, Intel 875-family chipsets support the current Northwood- and Prescott-core Pentium 4, and will support the forthcoming Dothan-core Pentium 4 processors, but support neither the earlier Willamette-core Pentium 4 nor the Celeron.

CPU speed support

A chipset that supports a particular CPU may support all or only some of the speeds at which that processor is available. In general, faster CPUs require faster chipsets, so you might imagine that a chipset rated to handle the fastest version of a particular CPU could also handle slower versions of that CPU. That's not always the case, however. Modern motherboards accommodate different processor speeds by varying two settings, *Front Side Bus (FSB)* speed and *CPU multiplier*:

FSB speed

FSB speed (also called host bus speed) specifies the speed at which the CPU communicates with the chipset. All sixth-generation and later chipsets support an FSB that runs at 66 MHz or faster, sometimes much faster. Early sixth-generation Intel chipsets use a 66 MHz FSB to support the Celeron and Pentium II processors. Later sixth-generation Intel chipsets use the 66 MHz and 100 MHz FSB to support Celeron, Pentium II, and Pentium III processors, and the 133 MHz FSB to support later Pentium III variants.

AMD Athlon chipsets introduced the concept of the *double-pumped FSB*, which transfers data on both the rising and falling sides of the clock pulse. Early Athlon chipsets supported the 66 MHz FSB double-pumped to 133 MHz, and the 100 MHz FSB doubled-pumped to 200 MHz. Later Athlon chipsets added support for FSB speeds of 133/266 MHz, 166/333 MHz, and 200/400 MHz.

Intel introduced the quad-pumped FSB in its seventh-generation Pentium 4 chipsets. First-generation Intel Pentium 4 chipsets used a 100 MHz FSB quad-pumped to 400 MHz. Later Intel chipsets increased the FSB to 133 MHz quad-pumped to 533 MHz, and the 200 MHz FSB quad-pumped to 800 MHz. Intel is careful to note that only data is transferred at the quad-pumped rate. Control instructions are transferred at half that rate, at 200 MHz on the 400 MHz FSB, 266 MHz on the 533 MHz FSB, and 400 MHz on the 800 MHz FSB. Still, because data comprises the vast bulk of what is transferred between processor and chipset, we consider Intel's FSB speed designations to be accurate.

For some motherboards, including many sixth-generation Intel and third-party motherboards, setting FSB speed also specifies the PCI bus speed. These motherboards, called *synchronous motherboards*, divide the FSB speed by a fixed factor to determine PCI bus speed. For a 100 MHz FSB, the divisor is 3.0, which runs the PCI bus at 33.3 MHz. A 133 MHz FSB uses a divisor of 4.0, which again runs the PCI bus at 33.3 MHz. Similarly, FSB speeds of 166 MHz and higher use divisors calculated to run the PCI bus at a standard 33.3 MHz.

Some motherboards, called *asynchronous motherboards*, allow FSB speed and PCI bus speed to be set independently, either by means of jumpers on the motherboard or by CMOS settings. They do this to allow using faster FSB speeds while limiting PCI bus speeds to 33 MHz, which is the fastest reliable setting for the standard 32-bit PCI bus. (64-bit and 66 MHz PCI slots are also available on some systems.) Otherwise, for example, overclocking a 100 MHz FSB processor by setting the FSB speed to 133 MHz would run the PCI bus at 44.4 MHz (one-third of 133), which is much too fast for reliability.

CPU multiplier

specifies the multiple of FSB speed at which the CPU runs internally. Modern chipsets may support CPU multipliers from 3.0x to 10.0x or higher. For example, a 1200 MHz Pentium III/1.2G processor with a 133.33 MHz FSB uses a 9.0 multiplier, because 9.0 x 133.33 = 1200.0. Pentium 4 processors use a multiplier calculated against the underlying bus speed (100, 133, or 200 MHz) rather than the quad-pumped bus speed (400, 533, or 800 MHz). For example, a Pentium 4/2.4G processor with a 100/400 MHz FSB uses a 24x multiplier (24 × 100 MHz = 2.4 GHz). A Pentium 4/2.4G processor with a 133/533 MHz FSB uses an 18x multiplier, and a Pentium 4/2.4G with a 200/800 MHz FSB uses a 12x multiplier.

AMD names Athlon XP processors with model numbers rather than actual processor speed, but the same principle holds true. For example, an Athlon XP 3000+, which actually operates at 2.16 GHz, uses a 166/333 MHz FSB and a 13x CPU multiplier.

All recent AMD and Intel CPUs have a locked multiplier, which means the only way to run them faster than their rated speed is to set the FSB above nominal. For example, increasing the FSB to 150 MHz from the nominal 133 MHz for a Pentium III/1.2G runs the CPU at 1350 MHz (150 x 9.0). That results in a small performance increase, but also reduces system stability because the PCI bus is running at 37.5 MHz (150/4) rather than its design speed of 33.3 MHz and because other system components are being pushed beyond their design limits.

Not all motherboards allow these parameters to be controlled manually. Some motherboards, including many early sixth-generation Intel models, allow you to set only CPU speed, which in turn selects a predetermined combination of memory bus speed and CPU multiplier. This is done to prevent *overclocking*, or running the CPU at higher than its rated speed, a practice that Intel naturally discourages. Late sixth-generation and seventh-generation Intel motherboards have no user-accessible speed settings at all, depending on the CPU to identify itself to the motherboard and setting the FSB speed and CPU multiplier accordingly. AMD, which was formerly relatively "overclocking-friendly" has also taken steps to lock down its CPUs to prevent casual overclocking.

Other motherboards, including third-party models that support Intel sixth-generation CPUs, may provide a means to set both FSB speed and CPU multiplier, either by means of a jumper setting or a menu selection in BIOS Setup. Setting CPU multipliers manually is ineffective for nearly all Intel sixth-generation and later processors, all AMD Duron processors, and all Socket A Athlon processors because they use multiplier locks.

Intel locks the CPU multiplier internally, which effectively means there's no way to change the multiplier on an Intel processor. AMD uses a method which makes the multiplier setting accessible externally. It's possible to change the CPU multiplier setting on AMD Athlon and Duron CPUs by using so-called "magic fingers" or even a graphite pencil to connect different traces on the face of the processor. We don't recommend doing that, but if you must experiment you can find detailed instructions on enthusiast sites such as AnandTech (*http://www.anandtech.com*).

FSB speeds, on the other hand, are externally determined and not locked, although Intel has recently begun efforts to lock FSB speeds as well. That means that at least for now you can change the processor speed by setting the FSB speed to some value other than nominal, assuming that the motherboard gives you that option. For example, a 1.2 GHz AMD Athlon is designed to operate with a 133 MHz FSB speed and a 9.0x multiplier. There's nothing you can do to boost the multiplier (short of getting out your pencil), but you can set the FSB speed to a faster value—say, 140 MHz. That causes the processor to run at 1260 MHz rather than 1200 MHz, a gain so minor that it will not be noticeable.

In 2001, AMD revived the hoary PR system for Athlon XP processors. Because the Athlon cannot compete with the Intel Pentium 4 on raw clock speed, AMD labels Athlon XP and MP processors with numbers that are higher than the actual clock speed but that supposedly indicate relative performance. For example, the Athlon XP 3000+ processor actually operates at 2.16 GHz. There is no danger of misconfiguring an Athlon XP system, however, because all motherboards that accept that processor configure the proper clock speed automatically.

Memory bus speed and width

One of the primary functions of a chipset is to serve as an intermediary between the processor and main memory. The memory controller portion of the chipset has two important duties. First, it reduces load on the processor by performing some memory functions without intervention from the processor, including routine housekeeping chores such as refreshing memory and managing DMA. Second, when the processor reads from or writes to main memory, it does not do so directly. Instead, the memory controller portion of the chipset works as the middleman, accepting data from the processor and transferring it to main memory, or vice versa.

Just as the FSB connects the chipset to the processor, the memory bus connects the chipset to main system memory. The speed and width of the memory bus determine how fast data can be transferred between the chipset and main

---

memory. Unless the memory bus can transfer data at least as fast as the FSB can, the processor may become starved for data. Accordingly, modern chipsets are optimized to provide a fast memory bus. The following two interrelated factors determine throughput:

Memory bus speed

Memory bus speed determines the fastest memory that can be used. For example, a chipset may be designed to support DDR-SDRAM at a maximum memory bus speed of 333 MHz, which means that the memory bus is optimized for DDR333 (PC2700) memory. Another chipset may be designed to use DDR-SDRAM at a maximum memory bus speed of 400 MHz, which means that the memory bus is optimized for DDR400 (PC3200) memory. A fast memory bus can use slower memory. For example, a chipset that supports PC3200 memory can typically use PC2700 memory instead. A slower memory bus can use faster memory, but the speed of the memory bus limits the memory to operating slower than its rated speed. For example, a system whose chipset supports at most PC2700 memory can use PC3200 memory, but treats it as though it were PC2700 memory. Sixth- and seventh-generation chipsets use memory bus speeds that range from 66 MHz to 400 MHz.

Memory bus width

Standard SDR-SDRAM and DDR-SDRAM chipsets use a 64-bit (8-byte) wide memory path. The product of bus speed and bus width determines the maximum peak throughput available. For example, a 64-bit memory bus running at 400 MHz can transfer up to 8 bytes x 400 MHz, or 3200 MB per second. Some sixth- and seventh-generation chipsets support a dual-channel memory bus, which doubles the memory bus width, thereby transferring twice as much data per clock cycle. For example, the *n*VIDIA *n*Force2 and Intel 875P chipsets support dual-channel DDR-SDRAM at 400 MHz, which provides throughput of 16 bytes per transfer at 400 MHz, or 6400 MB per second.

In an ideal system, the memory throughput matches the processor bandwidth. For example, the Pentium 4 communicates data 64 bits (8 bytes) at a time. For a Pentium 4 with an 800 MHz FSB, the processor bandwidth is (8 bytes x 800 MHz), or 6400 MB/s. Dual-channel PC3200 DDR-SDRAM also has throughput of 6400 MB/s, and is therefore an ideal match for this processor. Conversely, an AMD Athlon with a 333 MHz FSB has a bandwidth of (8 bytes x 333 MHz), or 2667 MB/s, and so is a perfect match for a single-channel PC2700 DDR-SDRAM memory controller. Table 3-1 lists the minimum memory throughput necessary for a balanced configuration at various FSB speeds.

Table 3-1. Memory bandwidth necessary at various FSB speeds

FSB speed	CPU bandwidth	Minimum balanced memory configuration
100	800 MB/s	single-channel PC100 SDR
133	1067 MB/s	single-channel PC133 SDR
200	1600 MB/s	single-channel PC1600 DDR
266	2133 MB/s	single-channel PC2100 DDR

Table 3-1. Memory bandwidth necessary at various FSB speeds (continued)

FSB speed	CPU bandwidth	Minimum balanced memory configuration
333	2667 MB/s	single-channel PC2700 DDR
400	3200 MB/s	single-channel PC3200 DDR
533	4267 MB/s	dual-channel PC2100 DDR
800	6400 MB/s	dual-channel PC3200 DDR

This balance between processor bandwidth and memory bus throughput explains why some processors benefit greatly from a faster memory bus, and others benefit little or not at all. For example, a 133 MHz FSB Pentium III has processor bandwidth of only 1067 MB/s, which means that using memory faster than PC133 SDR-SDRAM will not increase system performance because processor bandwidth becomes the bottleneck. Similarly, because no AMD Athlon processor uses an FSB faster than 400 MHz, there is little benefit in using a dual-channel memory controller with an Athlon.

Lack of balance also explains why a particular processor may perform better on one chipset than on another. For example, consider a 533 MHz FSB Pentium 4. When that processor is used with an Intel 875P chipset (dual-channel PC2700 or PC3200 DDR-SDRAM), the memory bus is more than fast enough to keep up with the 4267 MB/s bandwidth of the processor. But if that 533 MHz FSB processor is used on an Intel 845PE chipset (single-channel PC2700 DDR-SDRAM), the 4267 MB/s bandwidth of the processor is much higher than the 2667 MB/s throughput of the memory bus. Accordingly, during memory-intensive operations the processor may have to wait for memory to supply data.

The memory controllers in some chipsets link memory bus speed to FSB speed. Even though the chipset may support faster memory and you may have faster memory installed, the memory runs at the lower speed determined by the FSB speed. For example, a Pentium 4 chipset that supports PC2100, PC2700, and PC3200 DDR-SDRAM memory may allow you to use only the PC2100 memory bus speed with a 400 MHz FSB processor (regardless of the actual speed of the memory installed). With a 533 MHz FSB processor, that chipset may allow you to use either the PC2100 or PC2700 memory bus speed, and with an 800 MHz FSB processor, only the PC3200 speed.

Conversely, the memory controllers in some chipsets allow the memory bus speed to be set independently of the FSB speed. For example, the *n*VIDIA *n*Force2 chipset allows using PC3200 memory running at full speed regardless of the FSB speed of the installed processor. Although that may seem to be advantageous, the reality is that it seldom makes any difference.

When our ASUS A7N8X Deluxe motherboard sample arrived, we jumped on it because for the first time we'd be able to test the effect of different FSB and memory bus speeds, as well as the effect of dual-channel versus single-channel memory. What we found didn't surprise us. The benefit of dual-channel versus single-channel memory was nearly nil. We expected that because single-channel PC2100 or PC2700 memory is fast enough for the 266 MHz and 333 MHz Athlon FSBs, respectively.

Even with the 333 MHz FSB Athlon, dual-channel memory showed almost no improvement over single-channel, nor did PC3200 memory run any faster than PC2700, at least within the limits of error for our benchmark tests. If anything, the PC3200 memory was *slower* than PC2700 memory in this configuration, and that brings up an interesting point.

It's obviously bad to use memory that has lower throughput than the processor bandwidth because the memory can't keep up with the demands of the processor. Less obvious, but just as important, it can be bad to use memory that has a *higher* throughput than processor bandwidth. Why? Because mismatching FSB speed and memory bus speed requires the chipset to buffer transfers between main memory and the processor. Although chipset designers do everything possible to minimize the overhead costs of such buffering, there is still a price to be paid. The upshot, as we found, is that using a memory bus speed faster than what the processor requires can actually reduce memory performance.

Multiple CPU support

Some chipsets support motherboard configurations with multiple CPU sockets. These chipsets coordinate operations between the multiple processors and memory, which is necessary but not sufficient to allow *symmetric multiprocessing* (*SMP*) operation. In addition to chipset support, SMP requires:

CPU SMP support
Non-Intel CPUs other than the AMD Athlon and Duron lack the circuitry to support SMP. Intel fifth- and sixth-generation CPUs support SMP, except Coppermine128-core or later Celerons and most Coppermine-core Pentium IIIs at 1 GHz and faster. The Pentium 4 does not support SMP except in its more expensive Xeon variant. AMD produces a special version of the Athlon called the Athlon MP that supports SMP applications in conjunction with the AMD-760MP or AMD-760MPX chipset.

Operating system SMP support
DOS, Windows 3.X, and Windows 9X do not support SMP. Running one of these operating systems on an SMP PC uses only one of the CPUs. Windows NT/2000/XP Pro supports SMP, as do most Intel-based Unix implementations, including Linux. Note that Windows XP Home does *not* support SMP.

If you run an SMP-aware operating system, consider buying a motherboard that supports dual CPUs. The incremental cost is generally small, and the increased performance is significant. Prior to 2001, Intel's pricing strategy often made buying two midrange Pentium III processors less expensive than buying one top-of-the-line Pentium III. Although the AMD Athlon and Duron processors were inherently dual-capable, no SMP chipset existed for them. As a result, many enthusiasts built dual-processor Pentium III systems.

That changed when AMD shipped the dual-capable 760MP chipset, and followed not long after with the enhanced 760MPX SMP chipset. Suddenly, it became possible to build an inexpensive, fast dual-AMD system. At the same time, Intel de-emphasized entry-level SMP systems by replacing the SMP-capable i440BX chipset with newer sixth-generation chipsets that did not support SMP, and by removing SMP support from later Pentium III variants as well as from the mainstream Pentium 4 processors.

Alas, AMD has not updated the 760MPX chipset to add support for features such as USB 2.0, Serial ATA, PC2700 and PC3200 memory, and so on. Although the 760MPX platform remains a cost-effective platform with reasonably high performance, it is beginning to show its age. At the same time, Intel supports SMP only in its high-end chipsets and with Xeon processors, which makes the cost of an Intel dual-processor solution higher than it used to be.

Fortunately, the pricing gap between Intel dual-capable Xeon processors and dual-capable Athlon processors has recently narrowed, albeit in part because AMD increased the price of its dual-capable processors by introducing the Athlon MP line of processors certified for dual operation. Xeon processors are now priced competitively against Athlon MP processors, but alas, the days of using a pair of $75 processors in a dual rig are gone. Nowadays, if you want a dual-processor system, it's going to cost you. You must buy premium-priced Xeon or Athlon MP processors, or risk using uncertified Athlon XP processors for dual operation. Rats.

If you need to upgrade an existing single-processor Pentium III system to dual CPUs and the exact CPU you currently use is no longer available, see the detailed Intel Processor Specification Update (*http://developer.intel.com/design/processor/*) for a matrix of which currently available processors can be mixed and matched. In general, the safest course is to use two processors with identical S-Specs (Intel's identifying number for minor variations of a processor), but processors with different S-Specs can sometimes be used together in an SMP system, with some restrictions. For AMD systems, we recommend using only identical Athlon MP processors, although many have reported success in using identical Athlon and Athlon XP CPUs.

I/O bus support

The chipset determines what I/O bus standards the motherboard can support. The chipset manages the I/O busses, arbitrating data transfer between them, the CPU, and system memory. The chipset features determine which I/O busses the system supports, the speed at which the busses operate, and what additional related system features are supported. Depending on how you count, half a dozen or more I/O bus standards have been in common use since the first PCs. In order of their appearance, they include:

Industry Standard Architecture (ISA)
Used in 8-bit form in the PC and XT and 16-bit form in the PC/AT. Obsolete, but most motherboards made through 2000 provided at least one ISA slot for legacy cards. By late 2000, many new motherboard models shipped without ISA slots. Good riddance, we say.

MicroChannel Architecture (MCA)
An IBM standard that never caught on. Obsolete.

Extended Industry Standard Architecture (EISA)
An open standard developed by Compaq and eight other PC makers (the so-called "Gang of Nine") to compete with the proprietary MCA, but which achieved only limited acceptance, primarily in servers. Obsolete.

VESA Local Bus (VLB)
   An open standard that was widely used in 486 systems, but whose technical shortcomings made it inappropriate for Pentium and later systems. Obsolete.

Peripheral Component Interconnect (PCI)
   An open standard developed by Intel, used on late-model 486 systems and almost universally for Pentium and later systems. Older PCI systems use the PCI 2.0 standard, which limits upgrade possibilities. Newer motherboards use PCI 2.1, and current models use PCI 2.2. The PCI 2.3 Specification was approved in summer 2001, but products based on that standard are just now beginning to be deployed. PCI 3.0 was originally intended to be finalized in 2002, but various issues have delayed that standard, and we do not expect to see PCI 3.0 products until at least 2004.

Accelerated Graphics Port (AGP)
   A dedicated I/O port used on late-model fifth-generation and most sixth- and seventh-generation motherboards to provide high-performance graphics. Not technically a bus because it supports only one device, but thought of as a bus because it is implemented as an expansion slot. Note that many current motherboards support only AGP 2.0 1.5V and/or AGP 3.0 0.8V video adapters, and cannot accept legacy 3.3V AGP video adapters. For complete details about AGP, see Chapter 15.

Older motherboards provide a mix of expansion slots, usually four or five PCI slots and one shared ISA/PCI slot that can accept either type of expansion card. The chipset provides bridging functions between these I/O busses (the PC-to-ISA bridge) and between I/O busses and other system busses, including the memory bus. Current motherboards have no ISA slots at all, and contain only PCI slots and perhaps an AGP slot.

Embedded feature support

The chipset also provides various embedded low-level system functions and features. Many low-level system functions—e.g., the PIC—are well-standardized and have been so for years, so there is little to choose from among different chipsets on that basis. But features differ between chipsets, not so much between competing chipset models as between generations. Chipsets of the same generation generally implement similar features in comparable ways, so these are not issues for choosing between current chipsets. The following features are important when evaluating the upgradability of a motherboard that uses an older chipset:

ATA interface
   Any modern motherboard provides an embedded dual-channel ATA/ATAPI interface, which supports a total of four ATA/ATAPI devices, two per channel. But not all embedded ATA interfaces are equal. All current motherboards support ATA/100, and some support the ATA/133 standard, which has been rendered moot by the Serial ATA standard. The fastest current hard disks at peak throughput can barely saturate an ATA/66 interface, but choosing a chipset that supports at least ATA/100 makes hard disk upgrades easier. If you are upgrading a system with an old motherboard, the chipset should support at least PIO-4 and *independent device timing*, which allows two dissimilar

devices on one channel to both run at their optimal speed. If you are upgrading a system that uses an otherwise suitable older motherboard that does not support these features, you can disable the embedded ATA interface and install an ATA expansion card that supports recent ATA standards.

 The current ATA standard specifies 28-bit addressing, which places an absolute upper limit of 128 GB on ATA drives that use the standard 512 bytes/sector. The Maxtor Big Drive Initiative extends ATA addressing to 48 bits, which allows drive sizes of up to 128 PB, which is to say a binary million times larger than the current limit. This initiative is backed by other major industry players, including Microsoft, and has been incorporated in the new ATA standard. The most recent motherboards support 48-bit LBA natively, although some do so only for SATA ports. Motherboards based on chipsets more than a year old typically do not support 48-bit LBA for parallel ATA interfaces. However, inexpensive PCI adapters are available from vendors such as Promise Technology and SIIG that allow retrofitting 48-bit LBA PATA drives into existing systems. All SATA interfaces, embedded or add-on, support 48-bit LBA.

DMA controller and DMA mode support
Direct Memory Access (DMA) is a means to transfer data between devices without using the CPU as an intermediary, which can increase system performance. For example, a hard drive can use DMA to transfer data to and from memory without passing it through the CPU, allowing the CPU to do other things at the same time. DMA can be implemented using the DMA controller on the motherboard itself (called *first-party DMA*) or by using a DMA controller embedded on a device (called *third-party DMA* or *bus mastering DMA*). Older chipsets provide a limited selection of slower DMA modes and may make DMA available only on some expansion slots, which are typically differentiated by being a different color than non-DMA slots. Newer chipsets provide additional DMA modes, faster DMA transfers, and DMA capability on all expansion slots.

Plug and Play (PnP) support
The PnP standard is closely linked to the PCI standard. Systems that have chipsets, BIOSs, peripherals, and operating systems that are PnP-aware recognize and configure installed hardware automatically, eliminating IRQ, I/O base address, and DMA resource conflicts. A system that uses a non-PnP chipset is too old to upgrade effectively other than by replacing the motherboard.

Universal Serial Bus (USB) support
USB will eventually replace legacy I/O port standards, including serial, parallel, keyboard, and mouse ports. Most motherboards shipped since 1996 use chipsets that are USB 1.0- or 1.1-compliant. All current chipsets include USB support, and those designed from late 2002 onward support the USB 2.0 standard, which increases maximum data rates forty-fold to 480 Mb/s. To add USB 2.0 support to an older system, install an inexpensive PCI USB 2.0 card, such as those available from Adaptec, Belkin, SIIG, and many others.

You may have USB ports you don't know about. Many motherboards have "extra" USB ports that appear only as sets of header pins on the motherboard. Using these ports requires adding a port extender to route USB signals from the header pins to the outside of the case, usually to the back panel. Some newer cases have front-accessible USB connectors, which make it much easier to connect and disconnect USB devices that are moved frequently, such as cameras. We generally connect "permanent" USB devices such as printers and scanners to the USB ports on the back panel, and reserve front-panel USB ports for devices that we connect and disconnect frequently.

Accelerated Graphics Port (AGP) support

AGP provides a fast, dedicated channel between the CPU and an AGP video adapter, moving video data off the memory bus. Because AGP is implemented as an expansion slot, any AGP-capable motherboard by definition uses an AGP-capable chipset and provides an AGP slot. But the AGP standards specifies different modes, including 1X, 2X, 4X, and 8X, not all of which are implemented in all chipsets. AGP 1X is obsolete, although you can use an AGP 2X or 4X adapter in an AGP 1X motherboard. Most current motherboards support only 1.5V AGP 4X and/or 0.8V AGP 4X/8X adapters. The additional potential throughput of 4X is of little or no benefit with current video adapters, few of which can saturate even 2X AGP. Motherboards that support 8X AGP began shipping in late 2002, although once again the additional potential throughput of AGP 8X is not used by any current adapter. A few motherboards, most of which are intended for workstations, have an AGP Pro slot. AGP Pro is a backward-compatible extension of AGP that provides the additional power needed by some very high-performance video cards. Unless you plan to install an AGP Pro video adapter, you have no need for AGP Pro. When you buy a motherboard, make sure it supports at least AGP 4X. AGP 8X support is good in the sense that it means the chipset is up to date. Any motherboard that doesn't support at least 1.5V AGP 4X is out of date.

Identifying chipsets

To make upgrade decisions based on chipset, you must identify which chipset you have. If you are buying a new motherboard, this is straightforward. The motherboard specifications always list the chipset. When you upgrade an existing system, determining which chipset it uses can be difficult. You can identify the chipset in one of the following ways:

- If you have the documentation for the system board or the PC, the chipset it uses will be listed in the detailed specifications. If you do not have the documentation, but can identify the make and model of the PC or motherboard, the manufacturer's web site should list the chipset it uses.

- Use a third-party diagnostics program such as Smith Micro CheckIt or SiSoft Sandra to display system information. Figure 3-2 shows the results of running Sandra on an old Pentium III system. If you have no documentation, using a diagnostic utility is by far the easiest way to identify the chipset.

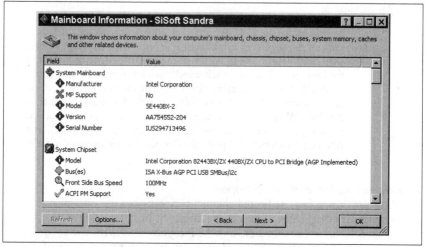

Figure 3-2. SiSoft Sandra identifying the chipset as an Intel 440BX

 Many Windows diagnostics programs do not run or have limited functionality under Windows NT/2000/XP, which limit access of applications to underlying hardware. Although Windows utilities such as Sandra provide useful information, they cannot fully test or report on low-level system hardware resources. If you need to run comprehensive testing and diagnostics on an NT/2000/XP system, the best alternative is to boot a DOS- or Linux-based diagnostic utility from floppy disk or CD.

- If you are running Linux, open a terminal, change to the */proc* directory, type the command cat pci, and examine the listing for the Host Bridge, which should be the first item. The following excerpt shows part of the */proc/pci* file for a system running an Intel 845 chipset:

```
PCI devices found:
  Bus  0, device   0, function  0:
    Host bridge: Intel Corp. 82845 845 (Brookdale) Chipset Host Bridge \
    (rev 4).
```

- Identify the chipset visually by examining the motherboard. Most chipsets have two chips, although some have only one and a few have three or more. Look for relatively large, usually square chips that are labeled with the name of a chipset manufacturer—Intel, VIA, SiS, ALi, Opti, etc. Record the string of numbers and letters that identifies each such chip. Then visit that manufacturer's web site and search for those strings to determine which chipset, if any, those chips belong to. For example, if you locate an Intel chip labeled 82438VX, a quick check of the Intel web site tells you that that chip is part of an Intel 430VX chipset (Intel calls most of its recent chipset models a *PCIset* or an *AGPset*). Note, however, that, particularly on recent systems, whose chipsets run at very high speeds, the chips that make up the chipset may have permanently installed heatsinks, which makes it impossible to read the labels.

Fifth-generation chipsets

Systems that use fifth-generation (Pentium) chipsets are too old to be economically upgradeable. Even if such a system is technically upgradeable, it is not cost-effective to do so. Instead, retire that system *in situ* to less-demanding duties, and build a new system based on current technology.

Sixth-generation Intel and Intel-compatible chipset characteristics

Intel has produced numerous sixth-generation chipsets in the 4-series and 8-series lines. Table 3-2 lists the characteristics of Intel 4-series desktop chipsets. These chipsets are obsolescent, although systems built on them may still be used productively and may even be reasonable upgrade candidates. In fact, motherboards based on the 440BX chipset were still produced as recently as late 2002, and motherboards based on i815-series chipsets were in current production as of July 2003. Although systems based on these chipsets lack modern features, they remain useful for some applications.

 Processor support varies between steppings of chipsets, CPUs, and motherboards. For example, early steppings of the 815E chipset do not support Tualatin-core Pentium III and Celeron CPUs, while later steppings do. Similarly, some sixth-generation Intel chipsets support Covington-core and Mendocino-core Celerons, but not CoppermineT-core Celerons. Even if the chipset supports a particular CPU stepping, a motherboard that uses that chipset may not support that CPU. For detailed information about CPU support, see the Intel Specification Update for the chipset (*http://developer. intel.com/design/chipsets/*) and CPU (*http://developer.intel.com/ design/processor/*) in question.

Table 3-2. Intel 4-series sixth-generation chipset characteristics

	440EX	440LX	440BX	440ZX	440ZX66
CPU support					
Pentium II (66 FSB)	●	●	●	●	●
Pentium II (100 FSB)	○	○	●	●	○
Pentium III (100 FSB)	○	○	●	●	○
Pentium III (133 FSB)	○	○	○	○	○
Celeron (66 FSB)	●	●	●	●	●
Celeron (100 FSB)	○	○	●	●	○
Number of CPUs	1	2	2	1	1
Host Bus					
66 MHz	●	●	●	●	●
100 MHz	○	○	●	●	○
133 MHz	○	○	○	○	○
Memory support					
EDO	256 MB	1 GB	○	○	○
PC66 SDRAM	256 MB	512 MB	1 GB	256 MB	256 MB

	440EX	440LX	440BX	440ZX	440ZX66
Memory Support					
PC100 SDRAM	○	○	1 GB	256 MB	○
PC133 SDRAM	○	○	○	○	○
RDRAM	○	○	○	○	○
ECC support	○	●	●	○	○
64/128/256 Mbit	●/○/○	●/○/○	●/○/○	●/○/○	●/○/○
EDO/SDRAM rows	4	6	8	4	4
RDRAM devices	○	○	○	○	○
Asynchronous setting	○	○	○	○	○
PCI					
PCI bus version	2.1	2.1	2.1	2.1	2.1
Concurrent PCI	●	●	●	●	●
Southbridge	PIIX4E	PIIX4	PIIX4E	PIIX4E	PIIX4E
ATA support	33	33	33	33	33
AGP support					
Integrated graphics	○	○	○	○	○
1X/2X/4X AGP	●/●/○	●/●/○	●/●/○	●/●/○	●/●/○

Table 3-3 lists the characteristics of obsolescent and current Intel 8-series sixth-generation desktop chipsets. Intel has produced some chipsets in two versions, one using the Integrated Controller Hub (ICH) and the other using ICH2. The major differences between these versions are that ICH2 supports ATA100 (versus ATA66 for ICH) and provides two USB controllers with four USB ports (versus one controller/two ports for ICH). The ICH2 models did not replace the ICH models immediately. ICH models continued in production because Intel sold them for a few dollars less than ICH2 models. Every penny counts (literally) to mass-market vendors, who build PCs for the lowest possible cost and sell on very slim margins.

Intel intended the ill-starred 820 chipset to be the direct replacement for the venerable (and still respected) 440BX chipset. The 820 was a miserable failure, primarily because it was designed to use expensive Rambus RDRAM memory. With the 815 and the follow-on 815E, Intel finally got it right. The 815E is a superb chipset, fully worthy of inheriting the 440BX's crown as the best sixth-generation chipset ever made. The 815 and 815E chipsets are available in two variants. The 815 and 815E include an embedded graphics adapter. The 815P and 815EP do not.

Figure 3-3 shows the Intel 815E, which is a representative Intel 8-series chipset. Intel calls the 82815 Northbridge the *Graphics and AGP Memory Controller Hub* (*GMCH*) and the 82801BA Southbridge the *I/O Controller Hub* (*ICH2*).

Intel makes the different 815 variants by mixing and matching the 82815 GMCH or the 82815EP MCH (Memory Controller Hub) with the 82801AA ICH or the 82801BA ICH2. Those variants with the MCH are designated "P" to indicate the

Figure 3-3. The Intel 815E chipset (image courtesy of Intel Corporation)

absence of embedded graphics. Those that use the 82801BA are designated "E" to indicate the presence of the enhanced ICH2 Southbridge.

The 815E has only two real limitations: first, it supports a maximum of 512 MB of memory. At the time the 815E was designed, 512 MB was a reasonable limit. Few people could afford more. But with the plummeting price of RAM, 512 MB began to look like a real limitation. Second, the 815E officially supports only one CPU (although at least one motherboard maker, Acorp, has produced a dual-CPU 815E motherboard). If the 815E supported 1 GB or more of memory and dual processors, it would have been the perfect sixth-generation chipset for Intel processors. As it was, the 815E was merely the best available.

Table 3-3. Intel 8-series sixth-generation chipset characteristics

	810	810E 810E2	820 820E	840	815 815E
CPU support					
Pentium II (100 FSB)	●	●	●	○	○
Pentium III (100 FSB)	●	●	●	○	●
Pentium III (133 FSB)	○	●	●	●	●
Celeron (66 FSB)	●	●	○	○	●
Celeron (100 FSB)	○	●	○	○	●
Number of CPUs	1	1	1-2	1-2	1
Host bus					
66 MHz	●	●	○	○	●
100 MHz	●	●	●	○	●
133 MHz	○	●	●	●	●
Memory support					
PC100 SDRAM	512 MB	512 MB	○	○	512 MB
PC133 SDRAM	○	○	○	○	512 MB
PC600 RDRAM	○	○	1 GB	8 GB	○
PC700 RDRAM	○	○	1 GB	○	○

Motherboards

Table 3-3. Intel 8-series sixth-generation chipset characteristics (continued)

	810	810E 810E2	820 820E	840	815 815E
Memory support					
PC800 RDRAM	○	○	1 GB	8 GB	○
Dual memory channel	○	○	○	●	○
ECC support	○	○	●	●	○
64/128/256 Mbit	●/●/○	●/●/○	●/●/●	●/●/●	●/●/●
SDRAM rows	4	4	○	○	6
RDRAM devices	○	○	32	32 x 2	○
Asynchronous setting	○	○	○	○	○
PCI					
PCI bus version	2.2	2.2	2.2	2.2	2.2
Concurrent PCI	●	●	●	●	●
Multiple PCI segments	○	○	○	●	○
Northbridge	82810	82810E	82820 (820) 82820E (820E)	82840	82815
Southbridge	ICH	ICH (810E) ICH2 (810E2)	ICH (820) ICH2 (820E)	ICH	ICH (815) ICH2 (815E)
ATA support	66	66 (810E) 100 (810E2)	66 (820) 100 (820E)	66	66 (815) 100 (815E)
AGP support					
Integrated graphics	82810	82810E	○	○	82815
1X/2X/4X AGP	○/○/○	○/○/○	●/●/●	●/●/●	●/●/●

 Although Intel originally claimed SDRAM support for the 820 chipset, it implemented that support via the Memory Translator Hub (MTH). After many motherboards had been shipped, Intel found that the MTH corrupted data. Intel recalled the CC820 motherboard, which was the only SDRAM 820-based motherboard it produced. Third-party motherboard makers also recalled their 820-based SDRAM motherboards. However, as with any recall, not everyone returned the boards, so you may still encounter 820-based motherboards that use SDRAM. If you discover such a board, stop using it immediately. Using it risks your data.

Other companies, including VIA Technologies, Acer Laboratories, Inc. (ALi), and Silicon Integrated Systems (SiS), make chipsets for Intel sixth-generation CPUs. In our experience, these third-party chipsets are slower, buggier, less compatible, and less stable than Intel chipsets. So why would any motherboard maker use them? Three reasons.

Price
Third-party chipsets generally sell for $5 or $10 less than Intel chipsets. If you are building a motherboard to a price point, the difference between a $40 Intel chipset and a $30 third-party chipset is huge. Although we won't say that all motherboards with non-Intel chipsets are built with cost as the only priority, it is certainly a significant issue.

Feature sets

Intel is conservative about adding support for new technologies to its chipsets. So, for example, when DDR-SDRAM became all the rage, Intel did not produce a chipset that supported it. Therefore, motherboard makers who wanted to produce DDR-SDRAM motherboards had no choice but to use a third-party chipset. Similarly, the last mainstream SMP-capable chipset Intel produced was the 440BX, which lacks support for such essentials as the 133 MHz FSB. Motherboard makers who want to produce a modern dual Pentium III board have little choice but to use a third-party chipset such as the VIA Apollo Pro133A or Apollo Pro266T.

Availability

Despite their higher costs and more limited feature sets, most motherboard makers want Intel chipsets because they perceive (rightly) that Intel chipsets are superior to those produced by other manufacturers. Intel's production capacity, while large, is not unlimited. When Intel ships a new chipset, it is often unable to meet demand. Third-party manufacturers step in with chipsets that have comparable features and are available immediately in volume.

Figure 3-4 shows the block diagram for a typical third-party chipset, in this case the VIA Apollo Pro266T, which supports Intel sixth-generation processors.

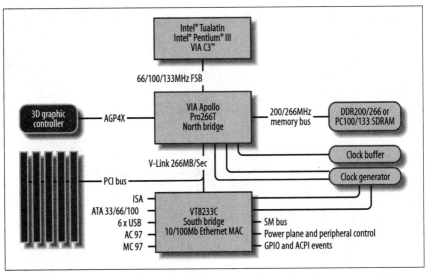

Figure 3-4. Block diagram of the VIA Apollo Pro266T chipset (graphic courtesy of VIA Technologies)

Of the third-party chipset makers, VIA Technologies is the largest and most prolific. VIA chipsets are found in motherboards made by nearly every major motherboard maker other than Intel, including such premier Taiwanese makers as ASUS, EPoX, and Gigabyte. Figure 3-5 shows the two chips that make up the VIA Apollo Pro266, a representative VIA chipset. The VT8633 chip is the Northbridge and the VT8233 is the Southbridge. As does Intel, VIA mixes and matches various

Northbridges and Southbridges from within a given family to produce related chipsets with different features.

Figure 3-5. The VIA Apollo Pro266 chipset (image courtesy of VIA Technologies)

Table 3-4 lists the characteristics of several VIA chipsets for Intel sixth-generation processors. The PM601 and Pro133 chipsets are obsolescent. The Pro133A and Pro266 are used in current motherboards. VIA produces variants of these chipsets, which differ chiefly in terms of processor support and whether embedded graphics are included. For example, the Apollo Pro133A chipset is also available as the Pro133T, which adds support for Tualatin-core Pentium III processors, and as the PM133, which adds embedded Savage video to the Pro133A chipset. Similarly, the PL133T is based on the Pro133A chipset, but includes Tualatin support and embedded Savage video. As always, the Northbridge determines which processors and memory types are supported, and the Southbridge determines which peripherals are supported.

Table 3-4. Characteristics of VIA chipsets for sixth-generation Intel processors

	PM601	Pro133	Pro133A	Pro266
CPU support				
Pentium II (66 FSB)	●	●	●	○
Pentium II (100 FSB)	●	●	●	○
Pentium III (100 FSB)	●	●	●	●
Pentium III (133 FSB)	●	●	●	●
Celeron (66 FSB)	●	●	●	●
Celeron (100 FSB)	●	●	●	●
Number of CPUs	1	1	1-2	1-2
Host bus				
66 MHz	●	●	●	●
100 MHz	●	●	●	●
133 MHz	●	●	●	●

	PM601	Pro133	Pro133A	Pro266
Memory support				
EDO	o	1.5 GB	1.5 GB	o
PC66 SDRAM	1 GB	1.5 GB	1.5 GB	4 GB
PC100 SDRAM	1 GB	1.5 GB	1.5 GB	4 GB
PC133 SDRAM	1 GB	1.5 GB	1.5 GB	4 GB
VC133 SDRAM	1 GB	1.5 GB	1.5 GB	4 GB
PC1600 DDR-SDRAM	o	o	o	4 GB
PC2100 DDR-SDRAM	o	o	o	4 GB
RDRAM	o	o	o	o
Dual memory channel	o	o	o	o
ECC support	o	●	●	●
64/128/256 Mbit	●/●/o	●/●/●	●/●/●	●/●/●
EDO/SDRAM rows	4	4	4	4
RDRAM devices	o	o	o	o
Asynchronous setting	o	●	●	●
PCI				
PCI bus version	2.2	2.2	2.2	2.2
Concurrent PCI	●	●	●	●
Multiple PCI segments	o	o	o	o
Northbridge	VT82C601	VT82C693A	VT82C694X	VT8633
Southbridge	VT82C686A	VT82C596B VT82C686A	VT82C596B VT82C686A	VT8233
ATA support	100	66	66	100
AGP support				
Integrated graphics	Blade3D	o	o	o
1X/2X/4X AGP	o/o/o	●/●/o	●/●/●	●/●/●

ALi and SiS chipsets for Intel sixth-generation processors sell in smaller numbers and are less widely used. Against Intel and VIA, which between them overwhelmingly dominate the chipset market, ALi and SiS must compete largely on price, so their chipsets are usually found in inexpensive motherboards intended for mass-market systems. For Intel processors, we recommend using motherboards based on Intel chipsets whenever possible. If you need a feature that is unavailable with an Intel chipset, choose a VIA-based motherboard. If you encounter an ALi- or SiS-based motherboard, visit *http://www.ali.com.tw/* or *http://www.sis.com/* for detailed information about their chipsets.

AMD Athlon chipset characteristics

The AMD Athlon and Duron are good sixth-generation processors that for years were hampered by mediocre chipsets. Considered in isolation, the Athlon is at least as good as the Pentium III and the Duron is in most respects better than the Celeron. But you can't use a processor without a chipset, and inferior chipsets have plagued AMD processors since their introduction.

The first Athlon chipset, the AMD-750 "Irongate," was intended by AMD as a technology demonstrator rather than as a production chipset. AMD didn't want to be in the chipset or motherboard business, although we don't understand that decision. It had always intended that production chipsets for its processors would be manufactured by VIA, ALi, and SiS. But VIA was very late to market with its first Athlon chipset, the KX133, so AMD was forced to produce the Irongate in volume for early Athlon motherboards.

The situation has improved since those early days. The majority of Athlon/Duron motherboards now use one or another VIA chipset, and the quality of subsequent VIA chipsets has improved. Current VIA chipsets are usable, if not quite up to Intel chipsets in terms of performance, compatibility, and stability. AMD produces the excellent but now aging AMD-760 series of chipsets, which we regard as equivalent in quality to Intel chipsets.

Table 3-5 lists the characteristics of three first- and second-generation VIA chipsets for the Athlon/Duron, with the AMD-750 shown for comparison. The AMD-750 and VIA KX133 are first-generation chipsets. The VIA KT133 is an early second-generation chipset. The KT133A and its derivatives such as the KM133 are late second-generation chipsets. All of these chipsets are long obsolete, but millions of motherboards that use them remain in service. The KT133A is as fast as or faster with SDR-SDRAM than the third-generation KT266 with SDR-SDRAM, and nearly as fast as the KT266A with DDR-SDRAM. ALi and SiS have also produced second-generation Athlon chipsets, but we recommend avoiding any motherboard that uses them. Note that a nominal 200 MHz FSB speed is actually a double-pumped bus running at 100 MHz, and a nominal 266 MHz FSB speed is actually 133 MHz double-pumped.

Table 3-5. Athlon/Duron SDR-SDRAM chipset characteristics

	AMD 750	VIA KX133	VIA KT133	VIA KT133A
Processor support				
Slot A / Socket A	●/○	●/●	○/●	○/●
Athlon / Duron	●/○	●/●	●/●	●/●
66/100/133 MHz FSB	○/●/○	○/●/○	○/●/●	○/●/●
Number of CPUs	1	1	1	1
Memory bus				
66 MHz	○	●	●	○
100 MHz	●	●	●	●
133 MHz	○	●	○	●
Memory support				
PC100 SDRAM	768 MB	2 GB	1.5 GB	1.5 GB
PC133 SDRAM	○	2 GB	1.5 GB	1.5 GB
VC133 SDRAM	○	2 GB	1.5 GB	1.5 GB
DDR SDRAM	○	○	○	○
ECC	●	●	○	○
64/128/256 Mbit	●/●/○	●/●/○	●/●/●	●/●/●

Table 3-5. Athlon/Duron SDR-SDRAM chipset characteristics (continued)

	AMD 750	VIA KX133	VIA KT133	VIA KT133A
Memory support				
SDRAM rows	3	4	4	4
Asynchronous setting	○	●	●	●
PCI				
PCI bus version	2.2	2.2	2.2	2.2
Concurrent PCI	●	●	●	●
Northbridge		8371	8363	8363A
Southbridge	AMD-756	82C686A	82C686A	82C686B
ATA support	66	66	100	100
AGP support				
Integrated graphics	○	○	○	○
1X/2X/4X AGP	●/●/○	●/●/●	●/●/●	●/●/●

 VIA originally named the KT133 the KZ133, but later changed the name because KZ was the abbreviation used by the Nazis for concentration camps. This change occurred just before the chipset shipped in volume, and some motherboards were produced with chipsets labeled KZ133. If you encounter such a motherboard, treat it as a KT133 model.

The availability of Double Data Rate SDRAM (DDR-SDRAM) resulted in a flurry of new Athlon/Duron chipset designs from AMD, VIA, and other makers. In fact, for sixth-generation processors such as the Athlon and Duron (as well as the Pentium III and Celeron) DDR-SDRAM is more marketing hype than substance. Sixth-generation processors are seldom bound by memory bandwidth, so doubling bandwidth results in relatively minor overall performance benefits. Still, DDR-SDRAM was the wave of the future, so all of the chipset makers jumped on board. Figure 3-6 shows a block diagram of the VIA KT266 chipset, its first chipset for AMD processors that supports DDR-SDRAM.

Table 3-6 lists the characteristics of DDR-SDRAM capable chipsets, which we define as early third-generation Athlon chipsets. Motherboards based on all of these chipsets except the AMD-760MPX began shipping in volume in summer and fall 2001. Motherboards based on the AMD-760MPX began shipping in volume in early 2002.

These chipsets differ architecturally but are similar in most functional respects. All, for example, support current Socket 462 AMD processors (although not necessarily the latest, fastest models), six PCI slots, and at least a subset of the full ACPI specification. All support six USB 1.1 ports except the AMD chipsets, which support four. None supports ATA133, Serial ATA, USB 2.0, or other recent standards promoted by Intel.

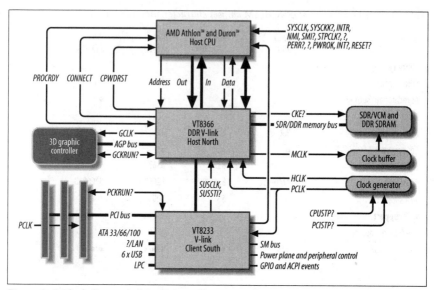

Figure 3-6. Block diagram of the VIA Apollo KT266 chipset (graphic courtesy of VIA Technologies)

Table 3-6. Early third-generation Athlon/Duron chipset characteristics

	AMD 760	AMD 760MP	AMD 760MPX	VIA KT266	VIA KT266A	ALi Magik1	SiS 735	nVIDIA nForce
General availability	2/01	6/01	12/01	4/01	9/01	2/01	5/01	9/01
Processor support								
Slot A / Socket A	○/●	○/●	○/●	○/●	○/●	○/●	○/●	○/●
Athlon / Duron	●/●	●/●	●/●	●/●	●/●	●/●	●/●	●/●
66/100/133/166 MHz FSB	○/●/●/● ○	○/●/●/ ○	○/●/●/○	○/●/●/ ○	○/●/●/○	○/●/●/ ○	●/●/●/ ●	○/●/●/ ○
Number of CPUs	1	2	2	1	1	1	1	1
Memory bus								
100 MHz	●	●	●	●	●	●	●	●
133 MHz	●	●	●	●	●	●	●	●
Memory support								
PC133 SDRAM	○	○	○	2 GB	2 GB	1 GB	1.5 GB	1.5 GB
VC133 SDRAM	○	○	○	○	○	○	○	○
PC1600 SDRAM	2 GB	3 GB	4 GB	2 GB	2 GB	1 GB	1.5 GB	1.5 GB
PC2100 SDRAM	2 GB	3 GB	4 GB	2 GB	2 GB	1 GB	1.5 GB	1.5 GB
PC2700 SDRAM	○	○	○	○	○	○	○	○
Dual memory channel	○	○	○	○	○	○	○	●

Table 3-6. Early third-generation Athlon/Duron chipset characteristics (continued)

	AMD 760	AMD 760MP	AMD 760MPX	VIA KT266	VIA KT266A	ALi Magik1	SiS 735	nVIDIA nForce
Memory support								
ECC	●	●	●	●	●	○	○	○
64/128/256 Mbit	●/●/●	●/●/●	●/●/●	●/●/●	●/●/●	●/●/●	●/●/●	●/●/●
SDRAM rows	4	4	4	4	4	4	3	3
Asynchronous setting	●	●	●	●	●	●	●	●
PCI								
PCI bus version	2.2	2.2	2.2	2.2	2.2	2.2	2.2	2.2
Concurrent PCI	●	●	●	●	●	●	●	●
Northbridge	AMD-761	AMD-762	AMD-762	VT8366	VT8366A	M1647	SiS735	IGP
Southbridge	AMD-766	AMD-766	AMD-768	VT8233	VT8233	M1535 D+	(none)	MCP
ATA support	100	100	100	100	100	100	100	100
AGP support								
Integrated graphics	○	○	○	○	○	○	○	●
1X/2X/4X AGP	●/●/●	●/●/●	●/●/●	●/●/●	●/●/●	●/●/●	●/●/●	●/●/●

The AMD-760MPX and the *n*VIDIA *n*Force are the premium chipsets in this group. Both offer high performance and stability, and the 760MPX is of course the only current chipset that supports dual AMD processors (the 760MP is discontinued). The MP and MPX chipsets differ only in the Southbridge they use. The MPX differs in two respects from the MP, one minor and one major. The minor difference is that the MPX includes embedded AC97 audio. The major difference is in their PCI busses.

The MP provides one 32/64-bit 33 MHz PCI bus. The MPX supports two PCI busses. The primary PCI bus is a 33/66 MHz, 32/64-bit bus, which is used for communications between the AMD-762 Northbridge and the AMD-768 Southbridge, and is also extended to provide one or two high-performance 64-bit PCI expansion slots. The secondary PCI bus is a 33 MHz 32-bit bus, which is used for standard 32-bit PCI peripheral cards. The primary PCI bus doubles throughput between the Northbridge and Southbridge relative to the single 33 MHz 32/64-bit PCI bus used in the AMD-760.

Be careful when configuring a system based on a motherboard with an AMD-760MPX chipset. It's possible to cripple system performance without even realizing you've done so. The primary PCI bus is a dual-speed, dual-width bus, which is really intended to operate at 66 MHz with a 64-bit bandwidth. Installing a 32-bit PCI card in one or both of the high-performance PCI slots forces the primary bus to operate in 32-bit mode rather than 64-bit mode. Similarly, installing a 33 MHz PCI card in either or both of the two high-performance slots forces the primary PCI bus to operate in 33 MHz mode rather than 66 MHz mode. Even if you never plan to install a 66 MHz 64-bit PCI card, forcing the primary PCI bus to operate more slowly halves the throughput between the Northbridge and Southbridge. Keep those 66 MHz 64-bit slots open unless you are installing a 66 MHz 64-bit expansion card in them.

In counterpoint, our technical editor, Francisco García Maceda, notes, "Because of time constraints I can't at this moment find the precise information regarding this problem and if you want, you can leave the paragraph as is. However I've just investigated this thoroughly and if I remember correctly, using a 66 MHz 32-bit card in one of the 64-bit slots doesn't cripple the bus a lot because bus width is calculated on a cycle-by-cycle basis. You're absolutely correct that using a 33 MHz PCI card (whether 32 or 64 bits) in one of the 64-bit slots forces the bus to permanently operate at 33 MHz, halving the bus throughput. That is why after several weeks of searching I chose the Promise FastTrak SX4000 IDE RAID controller for my latest workstation; although it is only 32 bits wide, it is the only IDE RAID controller currently on the market that operates at 66 MHz. Even the high-end 3Ware products (both IDE and S-ATA RAID) are 64 bits wide but operate at only 33 MHz."

Unfortunately, supplies of AMD chipsets have always been limited. For some reason, AMD prefers to leave chipset manufacturing to third parties and produces its own chipsets only to "seed" the market. Also, although dual-CPU motherboards based on the AMD-760MPX are readily available, no motherboard maker has produced a true AMD-760 uniprocessor motherboard. Some are advertised as such, but all of those in fact use only the AMD-761 Northbridge, substituting a VIA Southbridge for the AMD-766. Manufacturers do this to save a few bucks, but the resulting motherboards are not stable enough for us to recommend.

The VIA KT266 and ALi Magik1 are run-of-the-mill chipsets. There's nothing special about either of them. Both provide a standard set of features, acceptable although not outstanding performance, and reasonable stability (although early versions of the Magik1 had numerous performance and stability problems). Both are targeted squarely at the mass market, and both compete largely on price with the superior chipsets from AMD and nVIDIA. We don't consider either of them a particularly good choice. The VIA KT266A is an enhanced version of the KT266, which provides deeper internal buffers and a much-improved memory controller. Taken together, these improvements allow the KT266A to match or exceed the performance of the AMD-760 and SiS 735 chipsets, but our concerns about the stability and compatibility of VIA chipsets remain.

The real surprise is SiS. SiS chipsets do not have a reputation for high performance or stability. They're typically found in bargain-basement systems, where their low price is a fair trade-off for lower performance. With the 735 and the follow-on 745, however, SiS got it right. The 735 and 745 are actually faster than the AMD-760, and seem to be just as stable, which we frankly find astonishing.

The only problem with the SiS 735 or 745 is finding one. Just as Intel has used its clout to discourage motherboard makers from using VIA chipsets, VIA has discouraged Athlon/Duron motherboard manufacturers from using SiS chipsets. As a result, few first- or second-tier Taiwanese makers offer SiS-based motherboards. Some SiS boards are made by manufacturers whose products we wouldn't touch with a barge pole, so our favorable opinion of the SiS 735 and 745 by no means extends to all motherboards that use it.

We originally had favorable experiences with EliteGroup (ECS) motherboards based on these SiS chipsets. However, soon after we recommended those motherboards for cost-conscious users, reports of problems began to arrive. We're not sure what happened. Perhaps ECS had a bad run of motherboards (or perhaps we were lucky enough to get boards from the only good run). But, at the very least, we concluded that ECS quality control was insufficiently tight to allow us to continue recommending its products. We were unable to find another SiS-based motherboard that we felt comfortable recommending, and so withdrew our recommendation.

Sometimes it goes in the other direction. In the preceding edition of this book, we said:

> The much-hyped *n*VIDIA *n*Force chipsets turned out to be a disappointment. For example, the respected Tom's Hardware Guide concluded "KT266A Trounces nForce 420D." As of early 2002, very few motherboards based on the *n*VIDIA chipsets were shipping, and we had not yet been able to obtain any for testing. We think the high cost and mediocre performance of the *n*Force combined with the inexperience of *n*VIDIA in the chipset market dooms this chipset to failure. But we've been wrong before.

And we were wrong that time. By the time we finally got around to testing an *n*Force 220 motherboard, the original *n*Force chipset had been superseded by the *n*Force2, and original *n*Force 220 motherboards were selling at bargain prices. The board we eventually tested, an ASUS A7N266-VM, proved to be a stable motherboard with the embedded features desirable for a basic system, including GeForce2-MX video, excellent *n*VIDIA sound, and an optional LAN adapter. The obsolescent *n*Force 220 chipset certainly didn't have the bleeding-edge features of the latest and greatest *n*Force chipset, but it was more than good enough for a basic system. By the time our first *n*Force2 motherboard showed up, we were predisposed to like *n*VIDIA chipsets, and our subsequent experiences have borne that out.

Table 3-7 lists the characteristics of recent and current third-generation Athlon chipsets from VIA Technologies, which until recently was the dominant provider of Athlon chipsets. Although these later models are more stable and compatible than earlier VIA chipsets, we still consider them a step behind competing chipsets and avoid using them whenever possible.

Table 3-7. Late third-generation VIA Athlon/Duron chipset characteristics

	VIA KT333	VIA KT400	VIA KT400A	VIA KM400	VIA KT600
General availability	2/02	8/02	5/03	5/03	6/03
Processor support					
Slot A / Socket A	○/●	○/●	●/●	●/●	●/●
Athlon / Duron	●/●	●/●	●/●	●/●	●/●
100/133/166/200 MHz FSB	●/●/●/○	●/●/●/○	●/●/●/○	●/●/●/○	●/●/●/●
Number of CPUs	1	1	1	1	1
Memory bus					
100/133/166/200 MHz	●/●/●/○	●/●/●/○	●/●/●/●	●/●/●/●	●/●/●/●
Memory support					
PC133 SDRAM	○	○	○	○	○
VC133 SDRAM	○	○	○	○	○
PC1600 SDRAM	4 GB	4 GB	4 GB	4 GB	4 GB
PC2100 SDRAM	4 GB	4 GB	4 GB	4 GB	4 GB
PC2700 SDRAM	4 GB	4 GB	4 GB	4 GB	4 GB
PC3200 SDRAM	○	○	4 GB	4 GB	4 GB
Dual memory channel	○	○	○	○	○
ECC	○	○	○	○	○
64/128/256 Mbit	●/●/●	●/●/●	●/●/●	●/●/●	●/●/●
SDRAM rows	4	4	4	4	4
Asynchronous setting	●	●	●	●	●
PCI					
PCI bus version	2.2	2.2	2.2	2.2	2.2
Concurrent PCI	●	●	●	●	●
Chipset features					
Northbridge	VT8367	VT8377	VT8377A	VT8378	KT600
Southbridge	VT8235	VT8235	VT8237	VT8237	VT8237
UDMA 33/66/100/133	●/●/●/●	●/●/●/●	●/●/●/●	●/●/●/●	●/●/●/●
Serial ATA	○	○	●	●	●
USB 1.1 / 2.0 ports	0/6	0/6	0/8	0/8	0/8
AGP support					
Integrated graphics	○	○	○	●	○
1X/2X/4X/8X AGP	○/●/●/○	○/●/●/●	○/●/●/●	○/●/●/●	○/●/●/●

Table 3-8 lists the characteristics of recent and current third-generation Athlon chipsets from nVIDIA and SiS. Both of these companies, nVIDIA in particular, are successfully challenging VIA in the Athlon chipset market. The nVIDIA chipsets are in a different class from VIA and SiS chipsets. Although we have not had an opportunity to test the nForce2 400 Ultra and nForce2 400 models, we consider the original nForce2 chipset comparable to all but the most recent Intel chipsets in performance, stability, and compatibility.

	nVIDIA nForce2	nVIDIA nForce2 400 Ultra	nVIDIA nForce2 400	SiS 745	SiS 746	SiS 746FX	SiS 748
General availability	5/02	6/03	6/03	5/02	6/02	6/03	6/03
Processor support							
Slot A / Socket A	○/●	○/●	○/●	○/●	○/●	○/●	○/●
Athlon / Duron	●/●	●/●	●/●	●/●	●/●	●/●	●/●
100/133/166/200 MHz FSB	●/●/●/○	●/●/●/●	●/●/●/●	●/●/○/○	●/●/○/○	●/●/●/○	●/●/●/●
Number of CPUs	1	1	1	1	1	1	1
Memory bus							
100/133/166/200 MHz	●/●/●/●	●/●/●/●	●/●/●/●	●/●/●/○	●/●/●/○	○/●/●/●	○/●/●/●
Memory support							
PC133 SDRAM	○	○	○	○	○	○	○
VC133 SDRAM	○	○	○	○	○	○	○
PC1600 SDRAM	○	○	○	○	○	○	○
PC2100 SDRAM	3 GB	3 GB	3 GB	3 GB	3 GB	3 GB	3 GB
PC2700 SDRAM	3 GB	3 GB	3 GB	3 GB	3 GB	3 GB	3 GB
PC3200 SDRAM	3 GB	3 GB	3 GB	○	○	3 GB	3 GB
Dual memory channel	●	●	○	○	○	○	○
ECC	○	○	○	○	○	○	○
64/128/256 Mbit	●/●/●	●/●/●	●/●/●	●/●/●	●/●/●	●/●/●	●/●/●
SDRAM rows	3	3	3	3	3	3	3
Asynchronous setting	●	●	●	●	●	●	●
PCI							
PCI bus version	2.2	2.2	2.2	2.2	2.2	2.2	2.2
Concurrent PCI	●	●	●	●	●	●	●
Chipset features							
Northbridge	IGP or SPP	IGP/2U or SPP/2U	IGP/2 or SPP/2	745	746	746FX	748
Southbridge	MCP or MCP-T	MCP/2U or MCP/2U-T	MCP/2 or MCP/2-T	(none)	963L	963L	963L
UDMA 33/66/100/133	●/●/●/●	●/●/●/●	●/●/●/●	●/●/●/○	●/●/●/●	●/●/●/●	●/●/●/●
Serial ATA	○	●	●	○	○	○	
USB 1.1 / 2.0 ports	0/6	0/8	0/8	6/0	0/6	0/6	0/6
AGP Support							
Integrated graphics	IGP only	IGP/2 only	IGP/2U only	○	○	○	○
1X/2X/4X/8X AGP	○/●/●/●	○/●/●/●	○/●/●/●	○/●/●/●	●/●/●/○	○/●/●/●	○/●/●/●

Motherboards

Because bringing the Hammer-series processors to market is critical to its success, AMD began shifting resources to that project in 2002, and has since devoted little attention to the Athlon other than updating it to the Barton-core, shipping faster versions, and adding support for the 166/333 MHz and 200/400 MHz FSBs. Accordingly, chipset makers are equally disinclined to devote resources to the Athlon, so they have focused their attentions on forthcoming Hammer-series processors.

The nVIDIA nForce2 chipset, which shipped in May 2002 and began appearing in motherboards by late 2002, was the last truly new Athlon chipset. The various VIA and SiS Athlon chipsets that appeared from mid-2002 onward are really just tweaked versions of existing chipsets, modified to add support for faster DDR memory and the 166/333 MHz and 200/400 MHz FSBs. For example, the VIA KT600 chipset, code-named KT400A-CE, is pin-to-pin compatible with the KT400A, code-named KT400A-CD, and differs only in that it supports the 200/400 MHz FSB.

All of the chipsets listed in Tables 3-7 and 3-8 are competent Athlon chipsets, but we think the nVIDIA nForce2 series is by far the best choice for stability and compatibility. As we write this, in July 2003, nVIDIA has just refreshed the nForce2 chipset. The nForce2 Ultra 400 is really just a later stepping of the nForce2, with official support for the 400 MHz FSB. The nForce2 400 (no "Ultra") is a "Lite" version that lacks support for dual-channel memory.

Although many chipset makers, including VIA, Intel, and SiS, combine various Northbridges and Southbridges to create "different" chipsets, nVIDIA is the only company that markets its chipsets as "mix-and-match." nVIDIA produces two types of Northbridges. Integrated Graphics Processor (IGP) Northbridges are available in several variants, and have embedded video. System Platform Processor (SPP) Northbridges, also available in several variants, do not include embedded video. Similarly, nVIDIA produces several Southbridges, which it calls Media and Communications Processors (MCP). Because nVIDIA maintains pin compatibility for its Northbridges and Southbridges, motherboard makers can easily produce motherboards based on any mix of Northbridge and Southbridge.

For example, the nForce2 IGP includes embedded GeForce4 MX 420 video, and is intended for mainstream and corporate systems that require only basic graphics. The nForce2 SPP does not have embedded video, and is intended for high-performance systems that use discrete AGP adapters. The inexpensive nForce2 MCP provides USB 2.0, UDMA133, basic AC'97 audio without an integrated DSP, and a single nVIDIA Ethernet 100BaseT Ethernet adapter. The more expensive nForce2 MCP-T adds IEEE-1394a (FireWire) support, the nVIDIA APU (Audio Processing Unit), and a second Ethernet MAC, this one based on 3Com silicon.

In theory, then, motherboard makers can create different motherboards to sell at various price points by their choice of Northbridge/Southbridge combination. In fact, the nForce2 MCP and MCP-T Southbridges are also compatible with the earlier nForce Northbridges and the later nForce2 400 and nForce2 400 Ultra Northbridges, allowing even more flexibility.

In practice, the last thing motherboard makers want is to have a dozen or more nVIDIA models available, if only to minimize inventory problems and support nightmares and to avoid confusing buyers. Accordingly, most motherboard makers that use *n*VIDIA chipsets offer models with only one or two combinations of *n*VIDIA Northbridges and Southbridges. For example, ASUS builds only two nForce2 motherboards. It positions the A7N8X (SPP + MCP) for midrange applications and the A7N8X Deluxe (SPP + MCP-T) as a premium product.

Although we think *n*VIDIA chipsets are the best choice for an Athlon motherboard, the plethora of possible combinations of Northbridge and Southbridge means it's necessary to pay careful attention to which Northbridge and Southbridge the motherboard uses, and therefore which features it supports. Our current recommendations for *n*VIDIA-based motherboards are posted at *http:// www.hardwareguys.com/picks/motherboards.html*.

Seventh-generation Intel and Intel-compatible chipset characteristics

Although AMD tried to represent the Athlon as a seventh-generation processor, (hence the initial designation of the Athlon as the K7), the first true seventh-generation processor is the Intel Pentium 4. The Pentium 4 differs dramatically in architecture from sixth-generation processors, so chipsets designed for the Pentium 4 are not merely minor upgrades of sixth-generation chipsets. A block diagram of the first Pentium 4 chipset, the Intel 850, is shown in Figure 3-7. Later Intel chipsets use a similar hub architecture, with upgraded MCH (Northbridge) and ICH (Southbridge) components. The most recent Intel chipsets use 865- and 875-series MCH Northbridges with ICH5 or ICH5R (RAID-enabled) Southbridges.

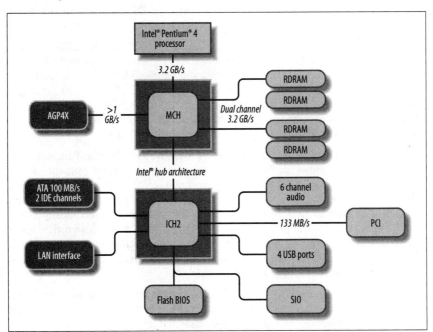

Figure 3-7. Block diagram of the Intel 850 chipset (graphic courtesy of Intel Corporation)

Current Pentium 4 chipsets are differentiated by Southbridge features, such as Serial ATA, USB 2.0, and so on, but differ primarily in the type of memory they support. Sixth-generation processors such as the Intel Pentium III do not benefit greatly from the higher bandwidth of Rambus RDRAM and DDR-SDRAM. In most circumstances, the 1067 MB/s bandwidth of PC133 SDRAM can more or less keep up with the memory bandwidth requirements of these processors.

The Pentium 4, on the other hand, can productively use much more memory bandwidth than PC133 can provide. Using PC133 with a Pentium 4 cripples it by forcing it to spend a large percentage of its time waiting for slow memory to supply data. For that reason, the Pentium 4 is better matched with a faster memory technology such as Rambus RDRAM or DDR-SDRAM.

Rambus RDRAM is available in four speeds, called PC600, PC700, PC800, and PC1066, which provide 1200 MB/s, 1400 MB/s, 1600 MB/s, and 2133 MB/s memory bandwidth, respectively. Intel 850 chipsets support two channels of PC800 or PC1066 RDRAM, for maximum throughput of 3.2 GB/s or 4.2 GB/s. Those data rates are also the design bandwidths of some models of the Pentium 4, which run a quad-pumped 100 MHz or 133 MHz FSB (for an effective 400 MHz or 533 MHz FSB) with 64-bit (8-byte) memory transfers. Transferring eight bytes 400 million or 533 million times per second translates to 3.2 GB/s or 4.2 GB/s.

Pentium 4 processors that use the 800 MHz FSB have bandwidth of 6.4 GB/s, significantly higher than the 4.2 GB/s throughput of a dual-channel PC1066 RDRAM memory subsystem. Although Rambus is developing PC1600 RDRAM to match the 6.4 GB/s bandwidth requirement of the 800 MHz FSB Pentium 4, Intel has effectively abandoned RDRAM in favor of DDR-SDRAM in its recent chipsets.

DDR-SDRAM is available in four speeds, called PC1600 (or DDR200), PC2100 (DDR266), PC2700 (DDR333), and PC3200 (DDR400), which provide 1600 MB/s, 2100 MB/s, 2700 MB/s, and 3200 MB/s memory bandwidth respectively. Although only PC3200 matches the 3.2 GB/s bandwidth of the 100/400 MHz FSB Pentium 4 and all fall short of the 4.2 GB/s bandwidth of the 133/533 MHz FSB Pentium 4, let alone the 6.4 GB/s bandwidth of the 200/800 MHz FSB Pentium 4, that's less an issue than it might at first seem.

Very few applications require the full memory bandwidth of the Pentium 4, so although PC133 bandwidth hobbles the Pentium 4 in normal operations, few applications require more bandwidth than even PC2100 DDR-SDRAM provides. Intel capitalized on this fact with its 845-series chipsets, each of which supports only single-channel DDR-SDRAM. Although these chipsets are technically imbalanced in the sense that peak memory throughput is much lower than peak processor throughput, for most applications that mismatch is a minor issue. Only when running memory-intensive applications are 845-series chipsets noticeably slower than the more balanced 850-series chipsets.

With the current 865- and 875-series chipsets, introduced in April and May 2003, Intel laid the memory bandwidth mismatch problem to rest by adding support for dual-channel DDR-SDRAM. Using dual-channel DDR technology, PC1600 DDR modules provide 3.2 GB/s, PC2100 modules 4.2 GB/s, PC2700 modules 5.4 GB/s, and PC3200 modules 6.4 GB/s. Dual-channel PC1600 memory matches the bandwidth of a 400 MHz FSB Pentium 4, dual-channel PC2100 memory that of a 533 MHz FSB Pentium 4, and dual-channel PC3200 memory that of an 800 MHz FSB Pentium 4.

The rapid progression of Pentium 4 chipsets has been interesting, to say the least. Intel has introduced new chipsets and updated versions of existing chipsets with bewildering frequency. Since the original Intel 845 chipset was introduced in late 2001, Intel has replaced its entire Pentium 4 chipset line every few months, driving motherboard makers to distraction. We'll try to sort out the confusion in this section. Table 3-9 lists the important characteristics of first-generation chipsets for the Intel Pentium 4.

Table 3-9. First-generation Pentium 4 chipset characteristics

	Intel 850	Intel 845	VIA P4X266	SiS 645	ALi ALADDiN-P4
CPU support					
PGA 423 (Willamette)	●	●	●	●	●
mPGA 478 (Willamette)	●	●	●	●	●
mPGA 478 (Celeron)	○	●	●	●	●
mPGA 478 (Northwood)	●	●	●	●	●
mPGA 478 (Prescott)	○	○	○	○	○
Number of CPUs	1-2	1	1	1	1
Host bus					
100 MHz (quad-pumped)	●	●	●	●	●
Memory support					
PC133 SDR-SDRAM	○	3 GB	4 GB	3 GB	3 GB
VC133 SDRAM	○	○	4 GB	○	○
PC1600 DDR-SDRAM	○	2 GB	4 GB	○	3 GB
PC2100 DDR-SDRAM	○	2 GB	4 GB	3 GB	3 GB
PC2700 DDR-SDRAM	○	○	○	3 GB	3 GB
PC600 RDRAM	2 GB	○	○	○	○
PC700 RDRAM	○	○	○	○	○
PC800 RDRAM	2 GB	○	○	○	○
Dual memory channel	●	○	○	○	○
ECC support	●	●	●	○	○
64/128/256/512 Mbit	○/●/●/○	●/●/●/●	●/●/●/●	●/●/●/●	●/●/●/●
SDR/DDR SDRAM rows	○	6/4	4/4	3/3	6/4
RDRAM devices	32 x 2	○	○	○	○
Asynchronous setting	○	○	●	●	●
PCI					
PCI bus version	2.2	2.2	2.2	2.2	2.2
Concurrent PCI	●	●	●	●	●
Multiple PCI segments	○	○	○	○	○
Northbridge	82850	82845	VT8753	SiS645	M1671
Southbridge	82801BA	82801BA	VT8233	SiS961	M1535D+
ATA support	100	100	100	100	100+

	Intel 850	Intel 845	VIA P4X266	SiS 645	ALi ALADDiN-P4
AGP support					
Integrated graphics	○	○	○	○	○
1X/2X/4X AGP	●/●/●	●/●/●	●/●/●	●/●/●	●/●/●

There's an odd situation that we call "the chipset that never was." Reviews and on-line PC enthusiast sites discuss the Intel 845 and "845D" chipsets as though they were two distinct products. In fact, there was only one first-generation Intel 845 chipset, and Intel never produced an "845D." Early steppings of the 845 were not certified for use with DDR-SDRAM, but later steppings can support either SDR- or DDR-SDRAM interchangeably.

Table 3-10 lists second-generation Intel chipsets for the Pentium 4. Although Intel was not expected to ship the 850E chipset, code-named Tehama-E, until fall 2002, it released that chipset in May 2002. Originally, the 850E was supposed to use the 82801DB/82801CA Southbridge (ICH4), which adds USB 2.0 support, but the 850E instead uses the same 82801BA (ICH2) Southbridge used in the original 850 chipset. The 850E is thus really not a new chipset at all, but merely a revision of the 850 chipset that Intel certifies for operation with the 533 MHz FSB. In fact, late steppings of the 850 chipset may support 533 MHz operation, although Intel does not sanction using the 850 at 533 MHz. Intel did not initially qualify the 850E for use with PC1066 RDRAM because PC1066 RDRAM was not yet shipping when the 850E was introduced. However, later steppings of the 850E add official support for PC1066 RDRAM.

Intel had also originally scheduled a fall 2002 release for several new variants of the 845 chipset, but again moved that release forward to May 2002, when it introduced the following chipsets:

845E (Brookdale-E)
> The 845E chipset differs in two major respects from the original 845 chipset. The 845E adds support for the 533 MHz FSB, and replaces the 82801BA (ICH2) Southbridge of the 845 with ICH4, which adds support for USB 2.0. Like the 845 chipset, the 845E supports PC133 SDR-SDRAM and PC1600/PC2100 DDR-SDRAM, but *not* PC2700 DDR-SDRAM.

845G (Brookdale-G)
> The 845G chipset supports the 533 MHz FSB and USB 2.0, and adds embedded graphics with 3D performance comparable to the *n*VIDIA GeForce2/MX400. In effect, the 845G is the Pentium 4 version of the popular Pentium III 815E chipset. Like the 815E, the 845G supports an AGP 4X slot, which allows the video to be upgraded by adding a standard AGP card. The 845G is the first Intel chipset that supports PC2700 DDR-SDRAM.

845GL (Brookdale-GL)
> The 845GL chipset is the "lite" version of the 845G, and is intended for budget systems that use P4-based Celeron processors. Intel introduced the 845GL chipset at $30, a very low price for an Intel chipset, and one targeted

at taking away "value segment" market share from Taiwanese chipset makers. The 845GL has the same embedded graphics as the 845G, but unlike the 845G, the 845GL does not support an external AGP connector. Nor does the 845GL support the 533 MHz FSB or PC2700 DDR-SDRAM, although it does use ICH4 and therefore supports USB 2.0.

In October 2002, Intel refreshed the 845E, 845G, and 845GL by updating the Northbridges, although the updated versions continued to use the 82801DB ICH4 Southbridge. Although it could (and probably should) have simply slipstreamed these changes as later steppings of the same chipsets rather than changing model numbers, Intel instead designated the updated 845E as the 845PE, the updated 845G as the 845GE, and the updated 845GL as the 845GV. These newer models incorporate the following major changes:

845PE

Relative to the 845E, the 845PE chipset adds support for PC2700 memory and removes support for PC1600 memory. The 845PE lacks support for ECC memory, which was present in the 845E.

845GE

Relative to the 845G, the 845GE chipset removes support for SDR-SDRAM and for PC1600 memory, and adds support for PC2700 memory.

845GV

Relative to the 845GL, the 845GV chipset adds support for the 533 MHz FSB.

The 875P chipset, introduced in April 2003, directly replaces the 850-series chipsets, and we expect those RDRAM-based chipsets to disappear quickly. The same is not true of the 845-series chipsets. Although they are superseded by the 865- and 875-series chipsets, 845-series chipsets will continue to be available well after the introduction of their replacements, chiefly because they are less expensive than the newer chipsets. The 845-series chipsets are fast and immensely stable and, like most Intel chipsets, have few compatibility problems compared to competing chipsets. If your application demands high memory performance—which few applications really do require—choose a board based on the 865- or 875-series chipsets. But for applications where midrange performance is acceptable, 845-based motherboards, as long as they remain available, are a good and less-expensive second choice.

Table 3-10. Characteristics of second-generation chipsets for the Pentium 4

	850E	845E	845PE	845G	845GE	845GL	845GV
General availability	5/02	5/02	10/02	5/02	10/02	5/02	10/02
CPU support							
PGA 423 (Willamette)	●	○	○	○	○	○	○
mPGA 478 (Willamette)	●	●	●	●	●	●	●
mPGA 478 (Celeron)	○	●	●	●	●	●	●
mPGA 478 (Northwood)	●	●	●	●	●	●	●
mPGA 478 (Prescott)	○	○	○	○	○	○	○
Number of CPUs	1	1	1	1	1	1	1

Table 3-10. Characteristics of second-generation chipsets for the Pentium 4· (continued)

	850E	845E	845PE	845G	845GE	845GL	845GV
Host bus							
400/533/800 MHz	●/●/○	●/●/○	●/●/○	●/●/○	●/●/○	●/○/○	●/●/○
Memory support							
PC133 SDR-SDRAM	○	○	○	2 GB	○	2 GB	2 GB
VC133 SDRAM	○	○	○	○	○	○	○
PC1600 DDR-SDRAM	○	2 GB	○	2 GB	○	2 GB	2 GB
PC2100 DDR-SDRAM	○	2 GB	2 GB	2 GB	2 GB	2 GB	2 GB
PC2700 DDR-SDRAM	○	○	2 GB	○	2 GB	○	○
PC3200 DDR-SDRAM	○	○	○	○	○	○	○
PC600 RDRAM	○	○	○	○	○	○	○
PC700 RDRAM	○	○	○	○	○	○	○
PC800 RDRAM (45 ns)	2 GB	○	○	○	○	○	○
PC800 RDRAM (40 ns)	2 GB	○	○	○	○	○	○
PC1066 RDRAM	●	○	○	○	○	○	○
Dual memory channel	●	○	○	○	○	○	○
ECC support	●	●	○	○	○	○	○
64/128/256/512 Mbit	○/●/●/●	○/●/●/●	○/●/●/●	○/●/●/●	○/●/●/●	○/●/●/●	○/●/●/●
SDR/DDR-SDRAM rows	○	0 / 4	0 / 4	4 / 4	0 / 4	4 / 4	4 / 4
RDRAM devices	32 x 2	○	○	○	○	○	○
Asynchronous setting	●	●	●	●	●	●	●
PCI							
PCI bus version	2.2	2.2	2.2	2.2	2.2	2.2	2.2
Concurrent PCI	●	●	●	●	●	●	●
PCI Masters	6	6	6	6	6	6	6
Multiple PCI segments	○	○	○	○	○	○	○
Chipset features							
Northbridge	82850E	82845E	82845PE	82845G	82845GE	82845GL	82845GV
Southbridge	82801BA	82801DB	82801DB	82801DB	82801DB	82801DB	82801DB
ATA 33/66/100/133	●/●/●/○	●/●/●/○	●/●/●/○	●/●/●/○	●/●/●/○	●/●/●/○	●/●/●/○
Serial ATA	○	○	○	○	○	○	○
USB 1.1 / 2.0 ports	4 / 0	0 / 6	0 / 6	0 / 6	0 / 6	0 / 6	0 / 6
AGP support							
Integrated graphics	○	○	○	●	●	●	●
1X/2X/4X/8X AGP	○/○/●/○	○/○/●/○	○/○/●/○	○/○/●/○	○/○/●/○	○/○/○/○	○/○/○/○

Table 3-10 lists native chipset capabilities. Some motherboards have additional features furnished by third-party chips. For example, the 845PE chipset supports neither Serial ATA nor RAID, but the Intel D845PEBT2 motherboard, which uses the 845PE chipset, supports Serial ATA and RAID via the Sil 3112A controller. Such external support is common during the transition to new technologies such as Serial ATA and USB 2.0 because it allows motherboard makers to provide the new features before the chipsets "catch up." Also, some combinations may be unsupported. For example, although the 845PE chipset supports PC2100 and PC2100 memory with 533 MHz FSB processors, it supports only PC2100 memory with 400 MHz FSB processors. Similar exceptions apply to the other chipset tables in this chapter.

In April 2003, Intel introduced the 875P chipset, code-named Canterwood. The 875P is based on the 845-series chipsets, but includes more than sufficient enhancements to merit a new model number. Relative to 845-series chipsets, the 875P adds support for the 800 MHz FSB and the forthcoming Prescott-core Pentium 4 processors, replaces the ICH4 Southbridge with the 82801EB ICH5 (which adds native Serial ATA support), and, last but not least, adds support for dual-channel DDR-SDRAM. The 875P is the direct replacement for the 850-series RDRAM chipsets.

In May 2003, Intel introduced the 865-series chipsets, code-named Springdale, which are variants of the 875P and are direct replacements for the 845-series chipsets. The 865-series chipsets lack the Performance Acceleration Technology (PAT) of the 875P, but are otherwise similar. Table 3-11 lists the important characteristics of 875- and 865-series chipsets.

Table 3-11. Characteristics of third-generation Intel chipsets for the Pentium 4

	875P	865P	865PE	865G
General availability	4/03	5/03	5/03	5/03
CPU support				
PGA 423 (Willamette)	○	○	○	○
mPGA 478 (Willamette)	●	●	●	●
mPGA 478 (Celeron)	○	●	●	●
mPGA 478 (Northwood)	●	●	●	●
mPGA 478 (Prescott)	●	●	●	●
Number of CPUs	1	1	1	1
Host bus				
400/533/800 MHz	○/●/●	●/●/○	●/●/●	●/●/●
Memory support				
SDR-SDRAM	○	○	○	○
PC1600 DDR-SDRAM	○	○	○	○
PC2100 DDR-SDRAM	4 GB	4 GB	4 GB	4 GB
PC2700 DDR-SDRAM	4 GB	4 GB	4 GB	4 GB

Table 3-11. Characteristics of third-generation Intel chipsets for the Pentium 4 (continued)

	875P	865P	865PE	865G
Memory support				
PC3200 DDR-SDRAM	4 GB	○	4 GB	4 GB
RDRAM	○	○	○	○
Dual memory channel	●	●	●	●
ECC support	●	○	○	○
64/128/256/512 Mbit	○/●/●/●	○/●/●/●	○/●/●/●	○/●/●/●
DDR-SDRAM rows	4	4	4	4
Asynchronous setting	●	●	●	●
PCI				
PCI bus version	2.3	2.3	2.3	2.3
Concurrent PCI	●	●	●	●
PCI Masters	6	6	6	6
Multiple PCI segments	○	○	○	○
Chipset features				
Northbridge	82875E	82865P	82865PE	82865G
Southbridge	82801EB 82801ER	82801EB 82801ER	82801EB 82801ER	82801EB 82801ER
ATA 33/66/100/133	●/●/●/○	●/●/●/○	●/●/●/○	●/●/●/○
Serial ATA	●	●	●	●
USB 1.1 / 2.0 ports	0 / 8	0 / 8	0 / 8	0 / 8
AGP support				
Integrated graphics	○	○	○	●
1X/2X/4X/8X AGP	○/○/●/●	○/○/●/●	○/○/●/●	○/○/●/●

Each of the 865- and 875-series ICH Northbridges can be coupled with the 82801EB (ICH5) Southbridge or the 82801ER (ICH5R) Southbridge, which provides native RAID support. With this chipset series, Intel seems to have reversed course on embedded video. Beginning with the 810 series, and continuing through the 815 series and the 845 series, Intel has always provided an entry-level chipset with embedded video. With the 865 series, that is no longer true. While the mainstream/performance 865G chipset includes embedded video, the entry-level 845P chipset does not. In another departure, the 875P chipset is the first Intel chipset in recent memory that does not include embedded audio. Intel targets these new chipsets as follows:

875P (Canterwood)
> Intel positions the 875P for enthusiasts and entry-level workstations. Although the 875P supports PC2700 memory and 533 MHz FSB processors, it is really intended for use with PC3200 memory and 3.2 GHz and faster Hyper-Threading Pentium 4 processors. We expect the relatively high price of the 875P chipset to limit its use to high-end motherboards such as the D875PBZ "Bonanza."

865PE (Springdale-PE)

The 865PE is essentially an 875P without PAT. Overall performance is a half-step behind the 875P, typically 3% to 10%, depending on application. Intel positions the 865PE for consumer systems that use midrange 800 MHz FSB Hyper-Threading Pentium 4 processors, such as the Pentium 4/2.40C, /2.60C, and /2.80C.

865G (Springdale-G)

The 865G is an 865PE with embedded Intel Extreme Graphics 2 video. Intel positions the 865G as a mainstream platform for consumer and corporate PCs. We expect the majority of 865-series motherboards to use this chipset. Although the embedded video performance can't touch that of even an entry-level ATI or *n*VIDIA video adapter, it is undeniably inexpensive and "good enough" for most consumer and corporate applications. Dell, Gateway, and other OEMs will sell millions of 865G-based systems.

865P (Springdale-P)

The 865P is a cut-down version of the 865PE, and lacks support for the 800 MHz FSB and PC3200 memory. Intel positions the 865P as an entry-level/mainstream chipset, targeted at mainstream consumer systems that use Celeron or low-end Pentium 4 processors. We are puzzled by the absence of embedded video in this chipset. Given its target market, embedded video is a crucial selling point. In fact, we see no market for this chipset because the cost of an 865P motherboard with even a $20 AGP adapter is likely to be higher than the cost of a similar 865G motherboard.

We think the 875P chipset is the best choice for a high-performance Pentium 4 system. For those on a budget for whom embedded video is sufficient, the 865G offers very high performance at moderate cost. If you need high video performance, an 865PE system with an ATI RADEON video adapter is the best way to go. We recommend avoiding the 865P chipset entirely.

BIOS

By themselves, the processor, memory, chipset, and other motherboard components are a useless collection of silicon, plastic, and metal. None of them individually can do much without help from other components, and none of them knows how to talk to other components. Turning this random collection of parts into a functioning computer requires a *BIOS*, or *Basic Input/Output System*.

The BIOS is a real-mode program that is more or less permanently stored on a chip that resides on the motherboard. Originally, the BIOS was stored on a ROM chip, whence the term *ROM BIOS*. The only way to upgrade a ROM BIOS is to physically remove that chip and install a new one. Nowadays, the BIOS resides on a *Programmable ROM (PROM)*, which allows the BIOS code to be updated without physically replacing the chip.

When power is applied to the system board, the CPU initializes. The final step in its hardcoded initialization routine is to jump to a predefined memory address and execute the program that it finds there. That address is the entry point for the BIOS code, so as the CPU finishes initializing, the BIOS code begins executing the system boot sequence. To begin, the BIOS initializes installed hardware and performs the power-on self test (POST). At the conclusion of the system boot sequence, the BIOS loads the operating system and passes control to it.

Once the operating system loads, the BIOS may also perform various low-level system services at the request of the operating system or applications. Operating systems such as DOS and Windows 3.X depend relatively heavily on the BIOS to provide standardized basic services. But the BIOS is a slow real-mode program, so newer operating systems such as Windows 95/98/NT/2000/XP and Linux depend less on BIOS services and more on drivers that access the hardware directly.

 Most PCs contain several BIOSs. This discussion refers to the main system BIOS, but most network adapters, video adapters, and disk host adapters contain their own specialized BIOSs. When the system boots, the main BIOS detects the presence of these specialized BIOSs and loads them, allowing the PC to support that hardware by using the program routines contained on that BIOS. Using one of these BIOSs may be automatic or optional. For example, some SCSI host adapters contain a BIOS. If you load that BIOS at boot time, you can boot from a SCSI drive attached to that adapter. If you do not load that BIOS, you cannot boot from or access the SCSI device until the operating system loads the device drivers needed to recognize it.

One major function of the BIOS is to intermediate between the chipset, the CPU, and other major system components. Full implementation of some system-level features—things such as USB, Plug and Play, Power Management, and AGP—requires support from both the chipset and the BIOS. If either lacks support for a feature, that feature is either unavailable or has limited functionality.

Most PCs and motherboards use BIOSs made by Phoenix, American Megatrends, Inc. (AMI), or Award (now a subsidiary of Phoenix). Some name-brand PCs such as IBM and Compaq use a BIOS with that manufacturer's name on it, although that BIOS is usually a relabeled Phoenix, AMI, or Award BIOS, with or without minor modifications.

When you buy a new PC or motherboard, which BIOS it uses is relatively unimportant, certainly much less so than the chipset it uses. You can safely assume that the BIOS on any new PC or motherboard will support all or most of the chipset capabilities. There may be minor exceptions—for example, some early systems with USB ports came with BIOSs that did not support USB—but such exceptions are usually unimportant to the overall functioning of the system. Also, unlike the chipset, the BIOS in a modern PC can be upgraded easily to fix bugs and to support new hardware and additional features.

Processor Support

Motherboards are designed to accept a particular processor (CPU) or CPU family. Which CPUs a motherboard supports is determined by the following:

Chipset
> Determines the CPU types the motherboard accepts. Non-Intel chipsets typically support a wide range of Intel and compatible CPUs. Officially, Intel

chipsets support only Intel CPUs. In fact, compatible CPUs such as the AMD K5/K6/K6-2, the Cyrix/IBM 6x86 (M1) and 6x86MX (M2), and the IDT WinChip run fine in motherboards with the appropriate Intel chipset. Also, although recent compatible CPUs can be installed in motherboards with older chipsets, those CPUs may not provide the highest performance of which they are capable, and some advanced features may not be supported by the chipset. The chipset also determines the fastest CPU that the motherboard can support. Intermediate speeds may or may not be supported, depending on the configuration options available for the motherboard.

CPU voltages supplied
Early Pentium-class CPUs use 5 volts. Later ones use 3.3 volts or 2.8 volts, and most later Pentium-class CPUs use dual voltage, running the internal core logic at a lower voltage than the CPU components that interface with cache, main memory, and other external components. Early fifth-generation motherboards supplied a fixed voltage to the CPU. Later ones included a *Voltage Regulator Module* (VRM) that allowed the motherboard to be configured to supply different voltages, according to the requirements of the CPU installed. Some non-Intel Socket 7 motherboards allow specifying Core voltage and I/O voltage separately, using very small increments. A motherboard like this can be tweaked to provide exactly the voltage required by a particular CPU. Sixth-generation CPUs may use 2.8 volts (e.g., Klamath-core Pentium II), 2.0 volts (e.g., Deschutes-core Pentium II), 1.6 volts (most current sixth-generation processors), or less, and seventh-generation processors are rapidly heading for the sub-1V level. As processor fabrication transitions from the 0.18μ process to 0.13μ and later 0.10μ or smaller, you can expect processor voltages to decline in lockstep. Sixth- and seventh-generation motherboards automatically detect and supply the voltage required by the processor, but you should verify that a particular motherboard can supply the voltages required by a particular processor before you install that processor.

 Just because a motherboard supplies the nominal voltage used by a given processor does not mean that processor can be used with that motherboard. Available current is also an issue. For example, early versions of the Intel SE440BX Seattle motherboard provide the 2.0 volts used by Deschutes-core Pentium IIs and Katmai-core Pentium IIIs. But the VRM on early SE440BXs cannot supply the higher current required by the Pentium III. Attempting to run a Pentium III in the motherboard may damage both motherboard and processor. Before you install or upgrade a processor in any motherboard, always check the technical documents to verify that processor is supported by that motherboard. Even if the processor appears to work initially, it may be drawing more current than the motherboard can supply, which may damage the motherboard and the processor.

Configuration options and FSB speed
A motherboard may not support the necessary settings for FSB speed and/or CPU multiplier for a particular CPU. For example, an Athlon motherboard

that offers only 200 and 266 MHz FSB speeds will not properly support an Athlon that uses the 333 or 400 MHz FSB, although it physically accepts the faster processor. Similarly, a 133 MHz FSB Pentium III may fit a Pentium II/ III motherboard that supports only 66 and 100 MHz FSB, but that processor will run at only a fraction of its rated speed.

Socket or Slot

Determines which CPU packaging styles fit the motherboard. Table 3-12 lists the socket and slot types you may encounter. Socket 370 is obsolescent. All of the others are obsolete except Socket A and Socket 478, which are used by current processors. Millions of Socket 7, Socket 8, Slot 1, and Slot A systems remain in use, however, so it is sometimes helpful to be aware of the differences.

Table 3-12. Desktop processor sockets and slots

	Pins	Voltage	Processors supported
Socket 1	169	5	486
Socket 2	238	5	486-SX; SX/2; DX; DX/2; DX/4
Socket 3	237	5 / 3.3	486-SX; SX/2; DX; DX/2; DX/4; 486 Pentium Overdrive
Socket 4	273	5	Pentium 60/66; Pentium 60/66 Overdrive
Socket 5	320	3.3	Pentium 75–300; Pentium 75+ Overdrive
Socket 6	235	3.3	(never used)
Socket 7	321	VRM	Pentium 75–300; Pentium 75+ Overdrive
Socket 8	387	VRM	Pentium Pro
Socket 370	370	VRM	PPGA Celeron, FC-PGA Pentium III
Slot 1	242	VRM	Pentium II, Celeron, Pentium III
Socket 423	423	VRM	Pentium 4 (early versions)
Socket 478	478	VRM	Pentium 4 (current versions)
Slot A	242	VRM	Athlon (slotted version)
Socket A	462	VRM	Athlon/Duron (socketed)

Identifying the socket type on an existing motherboard may or may not be simple. Most sockets are labeled, although you may have to remove the CPU to see the label. If it isn't labeled, you can identify the socket type by referring to the manual, by examining the pin layout of the socket, or—sometimes ambiguously—by determining the CPU type currently installed. Motherboard upgradability varies by socket type, as follows:

Socket 1 through Socket 8

Any system that uses one of these sockets is too old to upgrade. Replace the system.

Socket 370

Accepts a *Plastic Pin Grid Array* (PPGA) Celeron or a *Flip Chip PGA* (FC-PGA) Coppermine-core Pentium III or Coppermine128-core Celeron. Intel changed Socket 370 pinouts when it introduced the FC-PGA Pentium III. Earlier Socket 370 motherboards can accept only Celeron processors. The only direct upgrade available for these motherboards is replacing the existing

Celeron with a faster Mendocino-core Celeron. Most Coppermine-compatible Socket 370 motherboards can be upgraded with a Mendocino-core Celeron, a Coppermine128-core Celeron, or a Pentium III. The most recent Socket 370 motherboards, which Intel calls "Universal" models, can support any Socket 370 processor, including the latest Tualatin-core Pentium III and Celeron processors, which do not operate in earlier Socket 370 motherboards.

Although we've not used it, PowerLeap claims its Neo S370 PPGA to FC-PGA adapter allows some FC-PGA Pentium III and Celeron II processors to operate in some PPGA Socket 370 motherboards. The Neo S370 remaps FC-PGA pinouts to PPGA pinouts and converts the 2.0V used by PPGA processors to the 1.60/1.65V used by FC-PGA processors. This adapter works with only some motherboards, which are listed on the company's compatibility page (*http://www.powerleap.com*).

Slot 1

Accepts Pentium II, Pentium III, and/or Slot 1 Celeron CPUs. Most early Slot 1 motherboards can use either a Pentium II or a Celeron, but some support only one or the other. Later Slot 1 motherboards usually accept a Celeron, Pentium II, or Pentium III interchangeably, but again there are exceptions, which can sometimes be overcome by upgrading the BIOS. Within the limitations of the motherboard and BIOS, upgrade a Slot 1 motherboard by replacing a Celeron with a faster Celeron or Pentium III, or by replacing a Pentium II with a Pentium III. Some Slot 1 motherboards support only 66 MHz FSB CPUs. Others support both 66 MHz and 100 MHz FSB CPUs, and can be upgraded with any supported Celeron or Pentium III. However, upgrading from a 66 MHz FSB CPU to a 100 MHz FSB CPU may also require replacing existing RAM with PC100 or PC133 RAM. The most recent Slot 1 motherboards also support 133 MHz FSB processors, which is useful only for running a 133 MHz FSB Pentium III. Some Slot 1 motherboards have two CPU slots. If you run an SMP-capable operating system, you can significantly upgrade such a motherboard by adding a second CPU, which must be a Pentium II or Pentium III, and should be closely similar or identical to the original CPU. As of July 2003, new Slot 1 processors are no longer available from Intel, although they remain available from vendors as overstock or used products.

Various companies manufacture $20 "slocket" adapters, which adapt a Socket 370 processor to Slot 1. A popular use of slockets has been to run dual PPGA Celerons, a configuration that is officially unsupported by Intel, but many people have success with it. Running dual Slot 1 Celerons requires physical surgery on the CPUs themselves, but slockets allow using dual PPGA Celerons simply by setting jumpers on the slockets. Also, because Slot 1 Celerons are available only in the slower speeds and are more expensive than corresponding PPGA versions, it makes sense to upgrade a Slot 1 system by using a fast, cheap PPGA Celeron and a slocket. Note that first-generation slockets are incompatible with Coppermine128-core Celeron and Pentium III processors, and Coppermine128-core Celerons are not SMP-capable.

Slot A

Accepts the AMD Athlon processor. The only upgrade available is a faster Slot A Athlon processor. Note, however, that early Slot A motherboards (those based on the AMD-750 Irongate chipset) may support only a limited range of CPU speeds and are relatively poor upgrade candidates because of limitations in the chipset. Although AMD discontinued Slot A products some time ago, as of July 2003 Slot A processors remain available from vendors as overstock and used products.

Socket A

Accepts second- through sixth-generation AMD Athlon processors, based on the K75, Thunderbird, Palomino, Thoroughbred, and Barton cores. Early Socket A motherboards supported only the 200 MHz FSB. Most of those can accept either Athlon or Duron processors that use the 200 MHz FSB. Later Socket A motherboards support both 200 and 266 MHz FSBs, and can accept either 200 MHz FSB Athlons and Durons, or 266 MHz FSB Athlons. More recent Athlon motherboards support the 333 MHz FSB, and may accept only Athlon processors that use the Palomino or later core. The most recent Athlon motherboards support the 400 MHz FSB, and may support only Thoroughbred- and Barton-core processors. In any case, a BIOS upgrade may be needed, particularly if you are upgrading from an older core to a later core.

Socket 423

Accepts early Willamette-core Pentium 4 processors, which were made in both Socket 423 and Socket 478 versions. Socket 423 was widely regarded as a dead-end technology from the day it was introduced. The later Northwood-core Pentium 4 processors are not made in Socket 423, which limits upgrade alternatives to faster Willamette-core processors. As of July 2003, Socket 423 processors remain in limited distribution, and sell for relatively high prices. We expect Socket 423 processors to disappear entirely from the market by late 2003. Upgrading a Socket 423 system is usually a poor choice. We recommend instead replacing the motherboard and installing a current Socket 478 processor.

Socket 478

Intel's current Pentium 4 socket. Socket 478 systems can be upgraded by installing a faster Northwood-core Pentium 4 or Celeron. Upgrading from a Willamette to a current Pentium 4 or Celeron model should require only a BIOS upgrade on most Socket 478 motherboards.

Do not assume that a CPU is usable just because it fits the motherboard socket or slot. The CPU may physically fit but work improperly or not at all. For example, although the Intel SE440BX motherboard physically accepts any Slot 1 CPU—Pentium II, Celeron, or Pentium III—it works only with Pentium II CPUs. The nearly identical SE440BX2 motherboard supports various Slot 1 CPUs, including Celerons and Pentium IIIs. Similarly, an FC-PGA Pentium III processor can be physically installed in any Socket 370 motherboard, but will simply not be recognized by a Socket 370 motherboard unless that motherboard explicitly supports the Pentium III variant you are installing. Nor is it necessarily safe to upgrade to a faster model of the same processor because the VRMs on the motherboard may not be adequate for the higher current draw of the faster processor.

If you are considering a processor upgrade, our best advice is to check everything carefully. The first step is to determine exactly which motherboard you have. Even the submodel or revision may be significant. Once you determine that, visit the web page of the motherboard manufacturer to determine exactly which processor models are supported by that motherboard, and which BIOS revision a particular processor requires. Only after you have verified all of the details should you purchase a replacement processor.

 If the new processor requires a BIOS update, install the BIOS update *before* you install the new processor. Otherwise you may find yourself in a can't-get-there-from-here situation because the new processor won't boot with the old BIOS. We once fell prey to this problem. A friend needed an exact replacement for a failed Slot 1 processor in his dual-CPU system. We had exactly the processor he needed running in one of our own systems, and we also had a faster version sitting on the shelf. Being nice guys, we pulled the old processor from our system and gave it to him. He was delighted, and so were we. Until, that is, we attempted to install the faster processor in our system and found that the old BIOS didn't support it. Arrrghhh. We couldn't very well ask for the original processor back, so we ended up replacing the motherboard as well.

Bus Support

A *bus* is a shared linear pathway that connects multiple devices to provide a communication channel among them. Every bus provides access points to which devices can connect. Any device connected to the bus can communicate bidirectionally with other devices that are connected to that bus. A bus provides access points for three or more devices. A bus that connects only two devices is properly called a *port*. PC components—processor, cache, RAM, expansion cards, disks, and others—communicate using one or more of the multiple busses that exist in a modern PC. Recent PCs contain several bus types, all of which are coordinated by the chipset, as follows:

Processor bus
> Also called the *host bus* or the *Front Side Bus* (FSB), the *processor bus* is used by the processor to communicate with the chipset.

Memory bus
> The *memory bus* connects the memory subsystem to the chipset and thereby to the processor. For most systems and most applications, faster memory bus speed provides only minor performance benefits. Ideally, the speed of the memory bus should match that of the FSB.

Cache bus
> Sixth-generation and later processors use a dedicated *cache bus* (also called the *Back Side Bus* or *BSB*) to access the integrated L2 cache. This bus may operate at full processor speed (e.g., Celeron and Coppermine-core Pentium III processors), or at some integer fraction of the processor speed (e.g., Katmai-core Pentium III, K7 and later Athlon processors, and all Pentium 4 processors). Fifth-generation processors, such as Pentiums, do not have

integrated L2 cache and do not use a BSB. Instead, they use the memory bus to communicate with external L2 cache memory.

Local I/O bus

The *local I/O bus* is a high-speed bus that connects high-performance peripherals such as video adapters, disk adapters, and network adapters to the chipset, processor, and memory. Early 486 systems used *VESA Local Bus (VLB)*, which literally extended processor leads to the expansion bus slots. This tight link between processor and VLB limited the number of VLB slots that could be supported and constrained the performance of those slots. VLB systems are long obsolete. Late 486 systems and all Pentium-class and higher systems use the *Peripheral Component Interconnect (PCI)* bus for this purpose. Technically, PCI is a *mezzanine bus* rather than a true local bus because it isolates the processor electronically from PCI expansion slots. Isolating the processor from the PCI bus allows more PCI slots to be supported, and removes performance constraints on the use of those slots. Any system or motherboard you buy today should provide PCI expansion slots in adequate number for your needs.

Standard I/O bus

Older PCs and motherboards contain legacy *Industry Standard Architecture (ISA)* expansion bus slots, a design that originated in 8-bit form in 1981 with the original IBM PC and was updated to 16-bit form with the 1984 introduction of the IBM AT. Originally, the presence of these legacy ISA slots was intended to allow using older ISA expansion cards in newer systems, and ISA slots may still be used in a pinch to connect slow peripherals such as serial ports and parallel ports. However, the presence of legacy ISA devices in a system interferes with the ability of that system to configure itself under Plug and Play, and should be avoided at all costs.

Accelerated Graphics Port (AGP)

Most recent PCs and motherboards include an *Accelerated Graphics Port (AGP)* slot designed to accept an AGP video card. Although AGP is sometimes called a bus, as the name indicates it is really a port because it connects only two devices. Note that motherboards with embedded video may not include an AGP slot. That means that upgrading the video adapter in that motherboard requires using a PCI video card, which is of little concern to most users, but may be of great concern to those for whom high video performance is important.

PC expansion busses differ in two respects that determine their performance:

Bus width

Every bus is actually two separate busses. The *address bus* specifies the locations (or addresses) from and to which data is to be transferred. The *data bus* carries the actual data between the devices connected to the bus. Data busses can be of different widths, all of which are multiples of one byte (or 8 bits). All other things being equal, a wide bus communicates data faster than a narrow bus because it communicates more bytes during each transfer cycle. The original IBM PC ISA bus is 8 bits wide; the AT ISA bus that appears in older systems is 16 bits wide; the VLB and PCI local busses are 32 bits wide;

the memory, processor, and AGP busses on Pentium and later PCs are 64 bits wide. The width of the address bus and the data bus is independent. A wider address bus allows more memory locations to be accessed. For example, a 16-bit address bus can address 2^{16} or 65,536 memory locations, while a 32-bit address bus can address 2^{32} or 4,294,967,296 memory locations.

Bus speed

Busses transfer data during discrete *transfer cycles* or *clock cycles*. The clock speed of the bus determines how many transfer cycles occur each second, so a higher bus speed allows more data to be transferred per unit time. Most busses transfer one bit of data per data line per transfer cycle, so data transfer speed in bytes per second is the simple product of the bus width in bytes times the number of transfer cycles per second. For example, a PCI bus transfers 32 bits or four bytes during each cycle, and runs at 33.33 MHz, yielding throughput of (4 bytes/cycle x 33.3 million cycles/second) or 133.33 MB/s. The ISA bus requires two transfer cycles to move one byte, which halves its transfer speed relative to newer busses operating at the same speed. The AGP port running in 2X, 4X, or 8X mode transfers two, four, or eight bits of data per data line per cycle, doubling, quadrupling, or octupling its transfer rate relative to busses that transfer only one bit per data line per cycle. The Athlon uses a 100, 133, 166, or 200 MHz FSB, but transfers two bits per data line per cycle—colloquially called a *double-pumped bus*—yielding an effective FSB speed of 200, 266, 333, or 400 MHz, The Pentium 4 FSB runs at 100, 133, or 200 MHz, but transfers four bits per data line per cycle—a *quad-pumped bus*—yielding an effective FSB speed of 400, 533, or 800 MHz.

In combination, the product of bus width and bus speed determines the maximum theoretical bandwidth or throughput that the bus can provide. In practice, overhead prevents any bus from reaching its theoretical maximum. Also, some busses can run at other than their maximum speed, which further reduces throughput. Table 3-13 lists the theoretical throughput provided by common PC busses when running at the speed most commonly used in PCs.

Table 3-13. Width, speed, and throughput of common PC busses

Bus type	Width (bits)	Speed (MHz)	Bits per line per cycle	Throughput (MB/s)
ISA (XT 8-bit)	8	8.33	1	8.33
ISA (AT 16-bit)	16	8.33	1	16.66
EISA	32	8.33	1	33.33
VLB	32	33.33	1	133.33
PCI	32	33.33	1	133.33
PCI (64-bit)	64	66.66	1	533.33
AGP X1	32	66.66	1	266.66
AGP X2	32	66.66	2	533.33
AGP X4	32	66.66	4	1066.66
AGP X8	32	66.66	8	2133.33
Pentium II/Celeron FSB	64	66.66	1	533.33
Pentium II/III/Celeron FSB	64	100.00	1	800.00
Pentium III FSB	64	133.33	1	1066.66

Bus type	Width (bits)	Speed (MHz)	Bits per line per cycle	Throughput (MB/s)
Athlon/Duron FSB	64	100.00	2	1600.00
Athlon FSB	64	133.33	2	2133.33
Athlon FSB	64	166.66	2	2666.66
Athlon FSB	64	200.00	2	3200.00
Pentium 4 FSB	64	100.00	4	3200.00
Pentium 4 FSB	64	133.33	4	4266.66
Pentium 4 FSB	64	200.00	4	6400.00

Although PCI 2.1 and 2.2 allow 64-bit transfers at 66.66 MHz, very few PCs implement widths greater than 32 bits or speeds higher than 33.33 MHz. One exception is AGP, which is a modified version of PCI that provides a dedicated high-speed interface for video adapters. All AGP transfers are 32 bits wide, but use the 66.66 MHz clock speed. The initial release of AGP transferred 1 bit per data line per clock cycle, yielding 266.66 MB/s throughput. AGP 2X mode uses special encoding to transfer two bits per data line per clock cycle, doubling throughput to 533.33 MB/s. AGP 4X mode doubles throughput again to 1066.66 MB/s by transferring four bits per data line per clock cycle. AGP 8X mode redoubles throughput to 2133.33 MB/s by transferring eight bits per data line per clock cycle. AGP 8X is the last iteration of AGP. In the future, the nascent PCI Express general-purpose bus standard will replace AGP.

Various busses communicate at different widths and speeds, and using different protocols. But it's necessary for these busses to exchange data, which means that the system must have circuitry that translates between each incompatible pair of busses. This circuitry, called a *bridge*, is supplied with the chipset. There are two types of bridges:

Northbridge (or North Bridge)
> The *Northbridge* provides bridge logic for the internal system busses that link the CPU to memory and cache and provide other core functions such as PCI and power management. The Northbridge may be implemented as one or several discrete chips in the chipset.

Southbridge (or South Bridge)
> The *Southbridge* provides bridge logic for peripheral functions such as ATA, mouse, keyboard, USB, and the Super I/O serial/parallel controller. The Southbridge is usually one chip, and a particular Southbridge may be bundled with different Northbridges to create different chipsets. For example, the Intel PIIX4e PCI-to-ISA Interface Xcellerator Southbridge chip is used with minor variations on Intel chipsets that support Pentium II, Celeron, and Pentium III processors.

> If you are unfamiliar with the components and layout of a motherboard, visit *http://www.hardwareguys.com/supplement/mb-tour.html,* where you'll find an illustrated tour of a motherboard.

Choosing a Motherboard

You can sometimes upgrade a system cost effectively without replacing the motherboard. The more recent the system, the more likely this is to be true. The easiest upgrade is always replacing a processor with a faster version of the same processor. Doing that may simply mean pulling the old processor and replacing it with the faster one, although a BIOS upgrade may also be needed. Alas, there is no guarantee that a given motherboard will support a faster version of the same processor, or that a required BIOS upgrade will be available, and the rapid advances in processors mean that a faster version of your old processor may no longer be available because that series of processor has been replaced by a later series.

The next-easiest upgrade is to replace the processor with a later model from the same generation. For example, you may be able to replace a Pentium II/350 with a Pentium III/850 or, by using a slocket adapter, with a cheap, fast Celeron. When upgrading to a later-model processor, a BIOS upgrade will almost always be needed, and you should check the motherboard manufacturer's web site carefully to determine which configurations are supported.

 Faster processors may draw more current, and the VRMs on an older motherboard may be inadequate to support the new processor. Even if the processor appears to work properly at first, running it for long may damage both the motherboard and the processor. Always check to make sure that the exact processor you plan to install is supported by the motherboard.

It doesn't make sense to stretch an old motherboard too far. Just because you *can* upgrade a system without replacing the motherboard doesn't mean that you *should* do so. Motherboards are inexpensive, typically $75 to $150. Doing an in-place upgrade instead of replacing the motherboard leaves you with the limitations of the old motherboard and may limit the performance of the new processor. Before you decide to keep the motherboard, find out the costs and benefits of replacing it instead. Don't forget to factor in the supplementary benefits of a new motherboard—a better chipset and BIOS, support for the latest hard disk standards, etc. You may well decide it's worth spending the money to replace the motherboard. In fact, you may decide simply to retire the existing system to less-demanding uses and build a new system.

Use the following guidelines when choosing a motherboard:

Decide which CPU to use
> The CPU you choose determines the type of motherboard you need. Choose a Socket 478 Pentium 4 or a Socket A Athlon motherboard. With fast Socket 478 and Socket A processors available at very low prices, there is no point in buying into older technology, even though motherboards and processors using that technology may remain available.

Buy a motherboard that uses the right chipset
> For a single Pentium 4 or Celeron processor, choose a motherboard that uses an Intel 845-, 865-, or 875-series chipset, depending on your budget and

priorities. For a single Athlon processor, choose a motherboard that uses an *n*VIDIA *n*Force2-series chipset. For a dual-processor Athlon MP system, choose a motherboard that uses the AMD 760-MPX chipset. We have not tested any dual-Xeon systems, and so cannot make specific recommendations for them.

Make sure the motherboard supports the exact processor you plan to use

Just because a motherboard claims that it supports a particular processor doesn't mean that it supports all members of that processor family. For example, some motherboards support the Pentium 4 processor, but only slower models. Other motherboards support fast Pentium 4s, but not slower Pentium 4s or Celerons. Similarly, many motherboards support the Athlon with a 200 or 266 MHz FSB, but not Athlon models that use a 333 MHz or 400 MHz FSB. Make sure the motherboard supports the exact processor you plan to use, before you buy it.

Choose a board with flexible host bus speeds

Choose a motherboard that supports at least the settings you need now and expect to need for the life of the board. For example, even if you install a 400 MHz FSB Celeron initially, you should choose a motherboard that supports Pentium 4 processors using the 400, 533, and 800 MHz FSB speeds. Similarly, even if you plan to install an inexpensive 266 MHz Athlon at first, you should choose a motherboard that supports the full range of Athlon FSB speeds—200, 266, 333, and 400 MHz. Boards that offer a full range of hostbus speeds, ideally in small increments, give you the most flexibility. If you intend to overclock your system, make sure the motherboard offers multiple choices of hostbus speed (again, the smaller the increments, the better) and allows you to set CPU voltage, ideally over a wide range in 0.05-volt increments.

Make sure the board supports the type and amount of memory you need

Any new motherboard you buy should use DDR-SDRAM. PC2100 memory is still sold new, although it is now used only in the least-expensive systems. PC2700 memory is mainstream, and likely to remain so until DDR-II memory becomes widely available. PC3200 memory, which as late as early 2003 we expected to remain a technical curiosity, was legitimized by the Intel 865- and 875-series chipsets, but PC3200 memory remains difficult and expensive to produce relative to PC2700 memory, and is therefore likely to be used only in systems for which memory performance is a high priority. Even so, we recommend choosing a motherboard that supports at least PC2700 and PC3200 memory.

Do not make assumptions about how much memory a motherboard supports. A motherboard has a certain number of memory slots and the literature may state that it accepts memory modules up to a specific size, but that doesn't mean you can necessarily install the largest supported module in all of the memory slots. For example, a motherboard may have four memory slots and accept 512 MB DIMMs, but you may find that you can use all four slots only if you install 256 MB DIMMs. Memory speed may also come into play. For example, a particular motherboard may support three or four rows of PC2700 memory, but only one or two rows of PC3200 memory.

Also, chipsets and motherboards vary in terms of how much memory of different types they support. For example, the Intel 845 chipset supports up to 3 GB of SDR-SDRAM, but only up to 2 GB of DDR-SDRAM. Registered versus unbuffered memory may also be an issue. For example, although Tyan recommends (and we concur) that you use only Registered DDR-SDRAM with its S2460 Tiger MP dual-Athlon board, some have reported that the Tiger MP does work properly with unbuffered memory, but only if you limit it to one DIMM.

Nor do all motherboards necessarily support the full amount of memory that the chipset itself supports, even if there are sufficient memory sockets to do so. Always check to determine exactly what combinations of memory sizes, types, and speeds are supported by a particular motherboard.

For a general-purpose system, support for 512 MB of RAM is acceptable, and 1 GB is better. For a system that will be used for memory-intensive tasks such as professional graphics, make sure the motherboard supports at least 1 GB of RAM, and 2 GB or more is better.

 Although you may be able to find a new motherboard that supports migrating existing memory from the old motherboard, it's usually not a good idea to do so unless that older memory is current—i.e., PC2700 DDR-SDRAM or better. Memory is cheap, and it seldom makes sense to base a new motherboard purchase decision on the ability to salvage a relatively small amount of old, slow memory.

Avoid hybrid motherboards

Every time there's a change in memory technology, some manufacturers make motherboards that accept both the old and new types of memory. During the transition from SDR to DDR memory, such hybrid motherboards were common. We expect to see hybrid DDR/DDR-II motherboards when DDR-II memory begins shipping in volume. We think buying a hybrid motherboard is usually a mistake, both because we've yet to see one that worked well with both types of memory, and because hybrid motherboards are often problematic in other respects as well. Motherboards are relatively inexpensive. If you want to use DDR-SDRAM, buy a DDR-SDRAM motherboard. In a couple of years, when DDR-II memory becomes available, if you want to use DDR-II memory, buy a native DDR-II motherboard. The advantages of new memory technologies are seldom compelling enough to make it worthwhile to compromise on a hybrid. Wait until second-generation motherboards are available for the new memory technology.

Check documentation, support, and updates

Before you choose a brand or model of motherboard, check the documentation and support available for it, as well as the available BIOS and driver updates. Some people think that a motherboard that has many available patches and updates must be a bad motherboard. Not so. Frequent patch and update releases indicate that the manufacturer takes support seriously. We recommend to friends and clients that they give great weight to—and perhaps even base their buying decisions on—the quality of the web site that supports the motherboard.

Buy a motherboard with the proper form factor

If you are building a new system, choose an ATX motherboard that best meets your needs, and then buy an ATX case and power supply to hold it. For most purposes, a full-size ATX motherboard is the best choice. If system size is a major consideration, a micro-ATX or FlexATX motherboard may be a better choice, although using the smaller form factor has several drawbacks, notably giving up one or two expansion slots and making it more difficult to route cables and cool the system.

The preceding issues are always important in choosing a motherboard. But there are many other motherboard characteristics to keep in mind. Each of them may be critical for some users and of little concern to others. These characteristics include:

Expansion slots

Any motherboard you buy will provide some PCI expansion slots, but motherboards differ in how many slots they provide. Three PCI slots is marginal, four adequate, and five or more preferable. Integrated motherboards—those with embedded video, sound, and/or LAN—can get by with fewer PCI slots. Using ISA slots should be avoided at all costs, so the number of ISA slots is largely immaterial. Having an AGP 2.0 or 3.0 slot (4X or 8X) is a definite plus, even if the motherboard includes embedded video. Many recent motherboards include an *Audio-Modem Riser* (AMR) slot or *Communications and Networking Riser* (CNR) slot, the sole purpose of which is to allow system manufacturers to embed low-end audio and communications functions cheaply. Very few AMR and CNR components are commercially available, so the presence or absence of an AMR or CNR slot is immaterial, except in that the space occupied by an AMR or CNR slot is much better used to provide another PCI slot.

Warranty

It may seem strange to put something generally regarded as so important in a secondary category, but the truth is that warranty should not be a major issue for most users. Motherboards generally work or they don't. If a motherboard is going to fail, it will likely do so right out of the box or within a few days of use. In practical terms, the vendor's return policy is likely to be more important than the manufacturer's warranty policy. Look for a vendor who replaces DOA motherboards quickly, preferably by cross-shipping the replacement.

Ports, connectors, and front-panel LEDs

At a minimum, any new motherboard should provide four or more USB 2.0 ports and a dual ATA/100 or faster hard disk interface. Ideally, the motherboard should also provide least two Serial ATA connectors, and four is better. (Some motherboards that provide four S-ATA connectors include only a single parallel ATA interface, which is acceptable.) Given our druthers, we'd also like to see a serial port, an EPP/ECP parallel port, a PS/2 keyboard port, a PS/2 mouse port, and an FDD interface, but those "legacy" ports are fast disappearing.

So-called "legacy-reduced" motherboards lack serial, parallel, keyboard, mouse, and FDD ports. We avoid using those when possible because there are simply too many times when "legacy" ports are useful, but as time goes by it will be increasingly hard to avoid legacy-reduced motherboards because they'll eventually all be that way. We can live with the lack of parallel ports, because most printers nowadays use USB. Similarly, it's easy enough to use a USB keyboard and mouse if the motherboard lacks PS/2 connectors. Even serial ports are no longer critical, now that most modems and PDA cradles use USB. But we really, really resent the loss of the humble floppy drive controller. There have been times when the lack of a floppy drive controller cost us literally hours of extra work because we needed to transfer one small file or boot a system from a floppy disk, and had no way to do so. Oh, well. We guess we'll just have to get used to it.

Check the documentation to determine how the header pins for front-panel switches and indicators are arranged on the new motherboard. It's quite common to find that existing cables aren't long enough to reach the connectors on the new motherboard, or that the new motherboard uses different pin arrangements for particular connectors.

Embedded sound and video

Some motherboards include embedded sound, video, and/or LAN adapters as standard or optional equipment. In the past, such motherboards were often designed for low-end systems, and used inexpensive and relatively incapable sound and video components. But nowadays many motherboards include "name brand" sound (e.g., SoundBlaster PCI), video (e.g., nVIDIA), and LAN (e.g., Intel or 3Com) adapters, making them good choices around which to build a mainstream midrange system. Such motherboards normally cost from $0 to $25 or so more than similar motherboards without the embedded peripherals, allowing you to save $50 to $150 by buying the integrated motherboard rather than separate components. If you buy such a motherboard, make sure that the embedded devices can be disabled if you later want to replace the embedded adapters with better components.

 Embedded adapters often use the main CPU, which can reduce performance by a few percent. The speed of current processors means this is seldom an issue. However, if processor performance is critical, you may wish to use a motherboard that has few or no embedded functions.

Power management and system management

We regard power management as a useless feature and do not use it. It saves little power, increases the wear and tear on the equipment due to frequent power cycling, and tends to cause bizarre incompatibilities. We have experienced numerous problems with ACPI, with many different motherboards and operating systems, including systems that go into a coma rather than going to sleep, requiring a hard reboot to recover, and so recommend not using it at all. If for some reason you need power management, make sure the motherboard you buy supports at least a subset of the ACPI specification. Most current motherboards support some ACPI functions, but determining exactly which requires detailed examination of the technical documents for that motherboard.

System management is usually unimportant outside a corporate environment. If system management is an issue for you, look for a motherboard that supports all or some of the following features: voltage monitoring, CPU and/or system temperature sensors, chassis intrusion alarm, and fan activity monitoring for one or more fans.

Wakeup functions
Again, these features are primarily of interest to corporate IS folks rather than individual users. But if wakeup functions are important to you, you can buy a motherboard that supports "wake-on" on some or all of the following: LAN activity; modem ring-in; keyboard/mouse activity; and real-time clock.

Jumperless (or single-jumper) configuration
Older-style motherboards are configured mostly by setting jumpers. Recent motherboards use fewer (or no) jumpers, depending instead on CMOS Setup to configure motherboard settings. A board that uses CMOS Setup is marginally easier to configure than one that uses jumpers.

Boot devices supported
Any motherboard supports booting from the hard drive or a floppy drive. Most motherboards also support booting from El Torito-compliant CD-ROM drives and from floppy-replacement drives such as the LS-120 or Zip drive. Some motherboards support booting from the network. If boot support is an issue for you, make sure the motherboard you buy supports booting from your preferred device. Also make sure that CMOS Setup allows you to specify a boot sequence that allows you to make your preferred device the primary boot device.

Minor or special-purpose features
Motherboards attempt to differentiate themselves by including various minor features, such as an IRDA port or additional fan power headers (at least one is needed for the CPU fan, but some motherboards include two or three power headers to support supplemental fans).

Installing a Motherboard

Installing a motherboard for the first time intimidates most people, but it's really pretty easy if you do it by the numbers. Before you get started, prepare a well-lighted working area, ideally one with all-around access. The kitchen table (appropriately protected) or a similar surface usually works well. Have all tools and parts organized and ready to go. Open the box of each new component, verify contents against the manual or packing list to make sure no parts are missing, examine the components to ensure they appear undamaged, and do at least a quick read-through of the manual to familiarize yourself with the products.

 See also Chapter 28 for photographs of this process.

Removing the Old Motherboard

If you are replacing a motherboard, you must remove the old motherboard before installing the new one. The exact steps vary according to the motherboard and case, but use the following general steps:

1. Power down the PC and all attached devices. Disconnect all external cables other than the power cord, noting which cable connects to which port. Then move the PC to your work area and remove the cover from the case. We can attest that one wayward case screw can destroy a vacuum cleaner, so put the screws safely aside. An old egg carton or ice cube tray makes a good parts organizer.

2. If the PC power cord is connected to an outlet strip, surge suppressor, or UPS, turn off the main power switch on that device, and turn off the main PC power switch as well. This removes power from the PC, but leaves the PC grounded.

 With nearly all AT form factor power supplies and motherboards, turning off the PC power switch actually removes all power from the motherboard. With ATX (and variant) power supplies and motherboards, turning off the main PC power switch leaves some power flowing to the motherboard, which supports such features as *Wake-on-Ring (WOR)*, *Wake-on-LAN (WOL)*, and *Suspend to RAM (STR)*.

Although the voltage present is much too small to cause personal injury, working on a powered ATX motherboard may damage the motherboard, CPU, memory, or other components. Best practice when working on ATX motherboards is to use an outlet strip or other device to remove power from the PC entirely. If you must work on an ATX motherboard and have no such device, disconnect the power cord from the wall receptacle before beginning work. To avoid damaging components, touch the power supply to ground yourself before handling the motherboard, CPU, memory, or other static-sensitive components.

Even if you follow these procedures, defective wiring or other components could cause a high-voltage shock. For absolute safety, disconnect the PC power cord from the wall receptacle. (Our lawyers made us say that.)

3. Note the position and orientation of each internal cable connected to an expansion card. If necessary, sketch or photograph the connections to make sure you can reconnect the cables as they were, and then remove those cables on the expansion card. Remove the expansion cards and set them aside, preferably on an antistatic surface, although a plain tabletop also works well. Alternatively, you may be able to leave the cables connected to the expansion cards and simply place the cards out of the way, perhaps balanced on top of the power supply.

4. Label and disconnect each cable that connects to the system board, including those to the power supply, to the front panel switches and LEDs, to back

panel I/O ports, and to fans. When you complete this step, the motherboard should not have any obvious connections other than the mounting screws.

5. In most cases, the motherboard mounts directly to a fixed part of the chassis. In some cases, the motherboard mounts to a removable tray. If your motherboard uses a tray, remove the screws that secure the tray to the chassis and then lift the tray out carefully, watching for overlooked cable connections. Depending on the motherboard form factor, there may be from three to a dozen or more screws securing the motherboard to the chassis or tray. One or more screw holes may be occupied by nylon spacers that snap in from the bottom of the motherboard and slide into slots in the chassis. If the motherboard is secured only by screws, remove all of them and then attempt to remove the motherboard by lifting gently straight up. If one or more nylon spacers are present (visible as small white nubs sticking up through screw holes), rather than lift the mother board straight up, slide it gently a fraction of an inch toward the left side of the chassis and then lift straight up.

6. Place the old motherboard flat on a antistatic surface. Lacking that, put it on the tabletop. If you are salvaging the CPU or memory, ground yourself and remove those components. In any case, store the old motherboard in the antstatic bag that the new motherboard arrived in, once that bag is available.

Installing the New Motherboard

To install the motherboard, take the following steps, observing antistatic precautions throughout the process:

1. Touch the PC power supply to ground yourself, and then open the antistatic bag that contains the new motherboard. Remove the new motherboard from its antistatic bag, place the bag on a flat surface, and place the motherboard on top of the antistatic bag.

2. If you haven't done so already, read the motherboard manual to determine how to configure it. Verify each diagram in the manual against the actual motherboard to ensure that you can identify the important switches, jumpers, and connectors.

3. Configure the motherboard according to the instructions in the manual. Recent motherboards may use only one or a few configuration jumpers. Older technology motherboards may use jumpers to set numerous options, including CPU speed, host bus speed, CPU voltage, etc. Make sure to set all of these jumpers correctly, especially those that control voltage, before you apply power to the board.

4. After you have set all configuration jumpers properly, install the CPU and memory according to the instructions supplied with the motherboard and/or the components.

5. Determine how the motherboard mounts to the chassis. Old motherboards often used several snap-in nylon stand-off spacers and only a few screws to secure the motherboard. Modern motherboards use all or mostly screws, which secure to brass stand-off spacers. The important issue is whether a given hole location in the motherboard is designed to be grounded. If it is, it will mount with a screw to a conductive brass stand-off spacer. If it isn't, it

will mount using a nonconductive nylon stand-off spacer. Using a conductive brass connector where an insulating nylon connector was intended can short out and destroy the motherboard. Using a nylon connector where a brass connector was intended can cause the motherboard to operate improperly or not at all, or to radiate excessive RFI. New motherboards come with a plastic bag that contains screws and stand-off spacers of the proper type. If yours does not and you are not sure which type is required, refer to the motherboard documentation or contact technical support. If the connectors supplied with the motherboard do not include any insulating stand-offs, it's generally a safe assumption that all mounting holes are designed to be grounded to a brass stand-off connector.

6. Hold the motherboard over the chassis in the position that you will mount it. Typically all or all but one of the holes in the motherboard align with a stand-off spacer installed in the chassis. The motherboard is secured to the chassis by passing a screw through each of the motherboard screw holes and into the matching stand-off spacer. The final hole, usually the one nearest the back left corner of the motherboard, may use a slide-in spacer rather than a screw, which makes it easier to line up the motherboard with the other stand-off spacers. Most cases have many more mounting holes than are needed to secure any particular motherboard. Visually align the holes actually present in the motherboard with the chassis to determine which subset of the chassis mounting holes will actually be used. If you are building a new system, thread brass stand-off spacers into the appropriate chassis mounting holes. If you are replacing a motherboard, spacers may already be mounted in most or all of the necessary locations. Add or relocate spacers as necessary to ensure that each hole in the motherboard has a matching spacer. Don't leave any motherboard mounting holes unused. It's not that the motherboard is likely to go anywhere if you don't use all the screws. Each of those mounting holes provides support for the motherboard at a key location. If you leave one or more of the mounting holes unsupported, the motherboard may crack later when you are pressing hard to seat an expansion card, CPU, or memory module.

 When installing a Slot 1 motherboard that uses an old-style retention mechanism that must be installed before the motherboard is mounted in the case, now is the time to install it. Most new-style retention mechanisms can be installed either before or after the motherboard is mounted, and many Slot 1 motherboards come with a folding retention mechanism already installed, which requires only raising the arms to vertical and locking them in place.

7. After you've installed all necessary stand-off spacers, slide the motherboard into position, aligning all holes with their matching spacers. Secure the motherboard using the screws provided with it, or the screws that secured the original motherboard.

8. Reconnect the cables, including power supply cables, ATA cables, floppy drive cable, the cables that link the motherboard to front panel switches and LEDs, and the cables that link the motherboard I/O ports to the back panel connectors.

The motherboard package should include cables for the hard drive and floppy drive. Always use these new cables rather than the old cables. Not only are the new cables likely to be more reliable, but also they are certain to be electrically and physically compatible with the interface connectors on the new motherboard.

9. Reinstall only the expansion cards needed to test the system (usually just the video card), reconnect any cables that connect to them, and then reconnect the external cables that link the system unit to the monitor, keyboard, mouse, and so on.

10. Verify that everything that needs to be connected is connected, that everything is connected to the right thing, and that you haven't left any tools where they might short something out.

11. Time for the smoke test. Turn on the monitor and then turn on power to the system unit. The BIOS boot screen should appear on your monitor. If no video appears, or if you hear a beep sequence other than the normal single startup beep, you have something misconfigured. Turn off the power immediately (or just pull the power cord) and recheck all connections and settings you've made.

12. Once you're satisfied that the system is working properly, shut it down, remove power from it, reinstall any additional expansion cards, and restart the system.

13. When the system begins a normal boot sequence, press whatever key the BIOS boot screen prompts you to press to enter CMOS Setup. If you have jumpered the motherboard in configuration mode, special CMOS Setup options (e.g., setting CPU speed or voltages) may be available now that will no longer be available once you re-jumper the motherboard for normal operation. Configure and save the CMOS Setup options, and then turn off power to the system.

14. If necessary, re-jumper the motherboard for normal operation and then restart the system. Verify proper system operation, particularly that the system recognizes the hard drive(s) you have installed. Once you are sure that the system is working as expected, shut it down, reinstall the case cover, restart the system, and begin installing your operating system and applications.

If you replace the motherboard on a Windows system, don't try to use your current Windows installation unless you replaced a failed motherboard with an identical model. At best, if the new motherboard is similar to the old model, your existing Windows installation will almost work. If the new motherboard is significantly different, Windows may not boot. Even if it does boot, it will be unreliable. The best practice is to format the hard drive, install a fresh copy of Windows, load the chipset drivers for the new motherboard, install drivers for video, audio, and other hardware devices, reinstall all of your applications, and then restore your data. If you run Linux, you can avoid all this. Linux generally takes motherboard upgrades in stride.

Configuring CMOS

Each time a system boots, the BIOS boot screen appears momentarily. While this screen is being displayed, pressing a designated key runs the CMOS Setup program, which resides in firmware. CMOS Setup is used to configure CMOS and chipset settings ranging from those as obvious as the Date and Time to those as obscure as memory timings and bus settings.

 Recent Intel motherboards replace the standard BIOS boot screen with an Intel-logo splash screen. Display the standard BIOS boot screen on such systems by pressing the Esc key while the logo is visible.

To invoke CMOS Setup, you normally press F1 (AMI), the Delete key (Award), or F2 (Phoenix). Other BIOS manufacturers use different keys, and some system and motherboard manufacturers modify a standard BIOS to use another key. The key that invokes CMOS Setup nearly always appears on the BIOS boot screen, but if your BIOS boot screen doesn't show that key, try the Delete key, F1, F2, F10, Ctrl-Alt-S, or refer to the documentation.

The exact appearance of CMOS Setup and the available options depend on the chipset, the BIOS make and version, and changes made to the BIOS and CMOS Setup programs by manufacturers. For example, two motherboards may use the same chipset, processor, and BIOS, but one may give users complete freedom to configure chipset options, while the other allows users access to only some of the settings and uses hard-wired values for other settings.

All BIOSs default to a reasonable set of CMOS settings, one that allows the system to boot and function normally. Beyond that, it's up to you to choose settings to configure the system as you want it and to optimize its performance.

Some CMOS Setup options, the so-called basic settings, are pretty obvious— things such as time and date, hard drive parameters, power management, boot sequence, and so on. Others, particularly those segregated as advanced settings and chipset settings, are anything but obvious. The brief help descriptions provided with them are usually not much help unless you already understand the issue. The primary rule here is *if you don't understand what an option is for, don't change it.*

That's easy to say, but it ignores the fact that accepting default settings for obscure options can result in a PC that performs significantly below its potential. PC and motherboard manufacturers differ in how "aggressive" they are in choosing default settings, particularly those for such things as memory timing and wait states. Those that tend toward slower, more conservative default settings say, with some justification, that they cannot predict what components (particularly what speed and quality of memory) a user will install. Choosing conservative settings allows them to be sure that the motherboard will at least work, if not optimally. Those who are more aggressive (often, PC vendors, who have control of which memory and other components will be installed) assume that users want the highest possible performance level and use components that support those aggressive settings.

The first place to look for detailed CMOS Setup instructions is in the manual that came with the computer or motherboard. Some manufacturers provide detailed explanations of general CMOS Setup and Chipset Setup options, but many cover only basic CMOS Setup options and ignore Chipset Setup completely. If that's the case with your manual, you may be able to download detailed instructions from the BIOS manufacturer's web site.

- AMI does not provide end-user documentation, leaving that to the computer and motherboard vendors that use AMI's BIOS.

- Award Software, now a part of Phoenix Technologies, provides very detailed documentation (down to the level of different documents for different chipsets) in HMTL and *.zip* format for CMOS Setup and Chipset Setup, POST codes, beep codes, and so on (*http://www.phoenix.com/en/customer+services/bios/awardbios/*).

- Phoenix Technologies provides some information in its BIOS FAQ (*http://www.phoenix.com/en/customer+services/bios/bios+faq/*).

For a comprehensive treatment of configuring and optimizing BIOS settings, order *The BIOS Companion,* by Phil Croucher. It's available in printed form, or as a PDF file at one third the price (*http://www.electrocution.com/biosc.htm*). Another useful reference is Wim's BIOS page (*http://www.wimsbios.com/*).

Upgrading the System BIOS

When you upgrade an existing system without replacing the motherboard, the BIOS version it uses can be a critical issue. Some system features—notably support for faster or more recent processors, large hard disks, high-speed transfer modes, and AGP—are BIOS-dependent, so an in-place upgrade often requires a BIOS upgrade as well. Fortunately, recent systems use a Flash BIOS, which can be upgraded simply by downloading a later version of the BIOS to replace the existing BIOS.

Be extraordinarily careful when upgrading a Flash BIOS. Before you proceed, make *absolutely* sure that the BIOS upgrade patch you are about to apply is the *exact* one required for the current BIOS. If you apply the wrong patch, you may render your system unbootable from the floppy drive, which makes it difficult or impossible to recover by reapplying the proper patch.

Upgrading a Flash BIOS requires two files. The first is the upgraded BIOS itself in binary form. The second is the "flasher" program provided by the BIOS manufacturer, e.g., *awdflash.exe*. The exact steps you follow to upgrade a Flash BIOS vary slightly according to the BIOS manufacture—and the version of the flasher program you are using, but the following steps are typical:

1. Before proceeding, record all current BIOS settings, using either pencil and paper or a utility program that writes BIOS settings to a disk file. If you have a UPS, connect the system to it for the duration of the BIOS update. Losing power during a BIOS update can result in a motherboard that is unusable and must be returned to the maker for repair.

2. Determine the manufacturer, version, date, and identifying string of the existing BIOS. You can do this by using a third-party diagnostics program such as CheckIt, or by watching the BIOS screen that appears briefly each time the system boots. With most systems, pressing the Pause key halts the boot screen, allowing you to record the BIOS information at your leisure. With other systems, the Pause key does nothing, so you may have to reboot the system several times to record all the relevant information. It is important to record *exactly* what appears. Completely different BIOS versions are often differentiated by very minor changes in the BIOS identifying string.

3. Locate a Flash BIOS patch file that is intended to upgrade the *exact* BIOS version you have. Close isn't good enough. Begin your search on the PC manufacturer's web site. If you can't find an appropriate BIOS update there, check Wim's BIOS page (*http://www.wimsbios.com*). While you are searching for the proper BIOS update file, keep the following points in mind:

    a. Having a particular PC model is no guarantee that it uses the same BIOS as another PC with the same model number. High-volume PC manufacturers often sell systems that use different motherboards under the same model designation, and the BIOS update file intended for one motherboard used in that model cannot be used to upgrade the same model with a different motherboard.

    b. A particular motherboard and BIOS may be available in several versions that cannot use the same Flash update file. For example, Micron produced several systems using the popular Intel SE440BX Seattle motherboard, but with a slightly customized BIOS. The SE440BX Flash update available on the Intel web site can only be used to update an unaltered SE440BX, not the Micron version of that motherboard.

    c. Even a motherboard supplied directly by the manufacturer may have shipped in several revisions which require different BIOS patches. For example, one of our systems uses an EPoX KP6-BS dual-CPU motherboard, which was made in two versions, one with a 1 MB BIOS chip and the other with a 2 MB BIOS chip. The BIOS patches for these two versions are different and incompatible. Sometimes the only way to know for sure which BIOS patch you need is literally to take off the cover and examine the identifying numbers on the Flash BIOS chips themselves.

    d. BIOS patches are cumulative. That is, if your existing BIOS is version 4.003, you may find that the web site has versions 4.004, 4.005, and 4.006 available. You need not apply each of those patches sequentially. Instead, update your 4.003 BIOS directly to 4.006 in one step by applying the 4.006 patch to it.

    e. BIOS patch files are usually supplied in *.bin*, *.exe*, or *.zip* form. The *.bin* files can be used directly by the flasher utility. When run, the *.exe* files automatically extract the BIOS patch in *.bin* form. If the BIOS update is supplied as a *.zip* file, use WinZip or a similar zip utility to extract the *.bin* file.

4. Download the BIOS flasher utility, either from the motherboard manufacturer's web site or directly from the BIOS manufacturer's web site. Note

that some motherboard manufacturers supply BIOS updates as an archive file (*.zip* or *.exe*) that contains both the BIOS update *.bin* file and the flasher utility. These distributions sometimes take the form of an executable file that when run automatically creates a bootable floppy diskette and copies the *.bin* BIOS update file and the flasher utility to it.

5. Unless the BIOS update you've downloaded is one of those that automatically creates a boot floppy, format a bootable floppy disk. If you are using MS-DOS, Windows 3.X, or Windows 9X, use the command **format a: /s** to create the bootable floppy. If you are updating the BIOS on a system that runs Windows NT/2K/XP, Linux, or another non-DOS operating system, format a bootable DOS floppy on another computer. Copy the flasher utility and the *.bin* file to this floppy.

6. Enable Flash BIOS update mode on your motherboard. To prevent viruses from altering the system BIOS, most motherboards have a jumper that must be set in one position to enable Flash BIOS updates and in another position to re-enable normal system operation. Set this jumper to BIOS update mode.

7. Boot the system using the DOS boot floppy you created earlier. At the DOS prompt, type the command line specified in the documentation for your flasher utility. For example, the command to update an Abit BH-6 motherboard using the Award flasher and the *bh6_gy.bin* BIOS update file while saving a copy of the old BIOS and clearing the CMOS settings is *Awdflash bh6_gy.bin Oldbios.bin /cc*. *Oldbios.bin* specifies the filename that the old BIOS will be saved as, and the */cc* argument clears CMOS settings.

8. When the Flash BIOS update completes, restart the system and enter BIOS setup mode. Depending on the BIOS manufacturer, the flasher version you use, and the command-line arguments you specified, the CMOS settings may or may not be cleared. Even if they weren't, it's always a good idea to clear and re-enter them after a flash BIOS update, and for many BIOS updates it's mandatory. To do so, load the default BIOS settings and then enter the correct settings for time and date, hard disk type, etc., that you recorded in step 1. Once you have entered the correct settings for all values, restart the system again. It should display the updated BIOS version in the boot screen.

Although most recent systems use some variant of the method just described, some systems allow you to update the BIOS simply by copying a *.bin* file to a floppy diskette, which needn't be bootable, and restarting the system with that floppy in the drive. The obvious danger with this method is that you might unintentionally update your BIOS from a floppy disk that contains an older or hacked version. Accordingly, most recent systems require you to explicitly move a jumper to enable BIOS update mode.

Recent Intel motherboards support the Intel Express BIOS Update, which allows updating the BIOS from within Windows simply by double-clicking an executable file. Fortunately, Intel also provides floppy disk-based BIOS update routines that those of us who run Linux or other non-Windows operating systems can use to update our BIOSs.

Although updating a Flash BIOS is a pretty intimidating operation the first time you try it—or the 10th time, for that matter—BIOS updates usually complete successfully if you do everything by the numbers. But if you accidentally apply the wrong patch or if the flash update process fails through no error of your own, the PC can end up nonbootable. If this happens, there may not be an easy way to recover. Depending on the BIOS, one of the following methods to recover from a failed Flash BIOS update may be usable:

- A few motherboards have dual BIOS chips. If you corrupt one BIOS during an update, you can boot the system from the other BIOS and reflash the corrupted BIOS.

- Recent Award BIOSs have a small permanent boot-block BIOS. This portion of the BIOS is not overwritten during a Flash update, and is sufficient to allow the computer to boot to a floppy disk. Unfortunately, this BIOS supports only the floppy disk and an ISA video card. If a Flash update fails on a system with such a BIOS and a PCI or AGP video card, you can reflash the BIOS by using another system to create a bootable floppy disk that contains the *awdflash.exe* utility and the proper BIOS *.bin* file, with an *Autoexec.bat* file that automatically executes the flasher utility with the proper command-line arguments. With a PCI or AGP video card, you will not be able to view the progress of the update, but once the update completes and you restart the system, everything should operate properly. With an ISA video card, you can view the update procedure as it occurs.

- The Flash BIOS chip on some systems is socketed rather than soldered. If a failed Flash BIOS update renders such a system unbootable, you can contact the system manufacturer to request a working BIOS chip. Most manufacturers will supply a replacement chip that contains the current version of the BIOS on request. Some even do so for no charge, although they often require that you return the original nonfunctional BIOS chip. If you can get a replacement BIOS chip, simply pull the original chip, replace it with the new chip, and restart the system.

- As a last resort, if you have an identical system that works, you can temporarily install the BIOS chip from the good system into the nonworking one and reboot that system using the good BIOS chip. Once the system boots, pull the good BIOS chip and replace it with the nonworking BIOS chip without powering down the system. Then, with the system still running, execute the flasher utility from diskette to reapply the Flash BIOS update to the damaged BIOS chip. As a general rule, of course, removing and installing chips while the system is running is a good way to fry a motherboard. We've never tried this and can't guarantee that you won't fry your motherboard if you try it, but some people claim to have done it successfully. If you try it, do so at your own risk.

Because a failed Flash BIOS update may have such dire results, never flash a BIOS without first connecting the system to a UPS, if only temporarily while doing the update. The one time we violated that rule, sure enough, the lights flickered about 5 seconds after we started the update. Hoping against hope that the PC hadn't crashed—this update was one of those ones where the screen stays blank until the update is complete—we sat staring at the blank screen for another half hour before we admitted to ourselves that we'd probably just killed the motherboard. With our fingers crossed, we powered the system down and back up again, but, as expected, it was deader than King Tut. Unless your luck is better than ours, always use a UPS when flashing a BIOS.

Our Picks

Over the years, we've tested a boatload of motherboards for Intel and AMD processors, and we've come to have some pretty strong preferences. The chipset determines the features, performance, stability, and compatibility of a motherboard, but a good chipset alone does not guarantee a good motherboard. Build quality—the care with which a motherboard is constructed and the quality of supporting components such as capacitors—is also a key factor in motherboard quality. Although it is impossible to build a good motherboard using a poor chipset, it is quite possible to build a complete dog of a motherboard around an excellent chipset. For that reason, the brand name on a motherboard is as important to its quality as the chipset it uses. Here are the motherboards we recommend:

Intel Pentium 4 or Celeron system
> **Intel (D865- or D875-series).** We use Intel-branded motherboards almost exclusively for Intel processors, and on those few occasions when we must use a non-Intel motherboard for some reason, we try hard to choose a motherboard that at least uses an Intel chipset. Intel chipsets and motherboards are superb. They are the standard by which we judge other products in terms of stability, robustness, and build quality.
>
> There is a reason why Intel sells motherboards by the millions to OEM system makers. Support calls cost OEMs money, and Intel motherboards generate fewer support calls than do other brands. Intel motherboards aren't always the fastest models available and they offer few overclocking options, but their build quality, reliability, and stability make them the best choice overall. If you're building a system around an Intel processor, use an Intel-branded motherboard if at all possible.

Performance system
> If performance is a high priority, choose an Intel-branded motherboard based on the 875P chipset. Although it is similar to the 865, the 875P chipset includes Intel Performance Acceleration Technology, which boosts performance noticeably compared to the 865.

Mainstream system

For a mainstream system, choose an Intel-branded motherboard with an 865G chipset if you want embedded graphics, or an 865PE chipset if you want to use a separate AGP video adapter. The 865G and 865PE chipsets support the 800 MHz FSB, dual-channel PC3200 DDR-SDRAM, and Hyper-Threading Pentium 4 processors, which means a system built around one of these motherboards can have performance only a half-step behind an 875P-based system.

Economy system

If you are building a system on a tight budget, choose an Intel-branded motherboard with an 865G chipset. Although the 865P chipset motherboards are less expensive than 865G motherboards, 865P motherboards do not include embedded video. By the time you add even an inexpensive video card, an 865P system costs more than an 865G system, and is slower and less upgradeable.

AMD Athlon system

ASUS (*n*VIDIA chipset). For years we lamented the lack of a stable, compatible chipset for AMD Athlon processors. We have never been satisfied with the compatibility or stability of VIA chipsets, despite their popularity. The SiS 735, 745, and 746 are solid chipsets, but have been hampered by the indifferent build quality of the inexpensive motherboards that use them. We had great hopes for the *n*VIDIA nForce-series chipsets, and our experience with them has justified our optimism. The *n*VIDIA Athlon chipsets we have tested are feature-laden, stable, robust, and compatible. We were amazed because *n*VIDIA had no experience designing PC chipsets, but the company got it right the first time. With the advent of these chipsets, the Athlon can finally compete with Intel processors on a level playing field.

As is always true, using an excellent chipset does not guarantee an excellent motherboard. Fortunately, at least one motherboard maker does build excellent Athlon motherboards using *n*VIDIA chipsets. ASUS is well known for the high build quality of its motherboards, and its *n*VIDIA-based models are no exception. We tested the nForce2-based ASUS A7N8X Deluxe motherboard extensively, and found it to be fast, stable, and compatible. We expect the same to be true of ASUS motherboards that use the follow-on nForce2 400 and nForce2 400 Ultra chipsets.

AMD Athlon MP SMP system

Tyan S2466 Tiger MPX. Although the AMD 760MPX chipset is beginning to show its age—no support for PC2700 or PC3200 memory, no support for the 333 MHz or 400 MHz FSB, no USB 2.0, no AGP 8X, and so on—it remains a fast, stable, compatible foundation for a dual-processor Athlon system. Several companies produce 760MPX motherboards, but the company with the most experience in making dual-Athlon motherboards is Tyan, and its S2466 Tiger MPX motherboard is a winner. If you want to build a dual-Athlon system, build it around the Tiger MPX.

If you build a system around the Tiger MPX motherboard and a pair of Athlon MP processors, do not make the mistake of using off-brand memory or a mediocre power supply. High-quality memory and reliable power are even more important to the stability of a dual-processor system than for standard systems. Use only memory modules included on the Tyan approved memory list, and use a top-quality, high-wattage power supply, such as those sold by PC Power & Cooling for dual-processor systems. We also recommend choosing a video adapter from the Tyan approved video adapters list.

We test new chipsets and motherboards constantly. For our latest motherboard recommendations by brand name and model number, visit: *http://www. hardwareguys.com/picks/motherboards.html.*

4

Processors

The *processor*, also called the *microprocessor* or *CPU* (for *Central Processing Unit*), is the brain of the PC. It performs all general computing tasks and coordinates tasks done by memory, video, disk storage, and other system components. The CPU is a very complex chip that resides directly on the motherboard of most PCs, but may instead reside on a daughtercard that connects to the motherboard via a dedicated specialized slot.

Processor Design

A processor executes programs—including the operating system itself and user applications—all of which perform useful work. From the processor's point of view, a program is simply a group of low-level *instructions* that the processor executes more or less in sequence as it receives them. How efficiently and effectively the processor executes instructions is determined by its internal design, also called its *architecture*. The CPU architecture, in conjunction with CPU speed, determines how fast the CPU executes instructions of various types. The external design of the processor, specifically its external interfaces, determines how fast it communicates information back and forth with external cache, main memory, the chipset, and other system components.

Processor Components

Modern processors have the following internal components:

Execution unit
> The core of the CPU, the *execution unit* processes instructions.

Branch predictor
> The *branch predictor* attempts to guess where the program will jump (or branch) next, allowing the *prefetch and decode unit* to retrieve instructions

and data in advance so that they will already be available when the CPU requests them.

Floating-point unit
The *floating-point unit* (FPU) is a specialized logic unit optimized to perform noninteger calculations much faster than the general-purpose logic unit can perform them.

Primary cache
Also called *Level 1* or *L1 cache, primary cache* is a small amount of very fast memory that allows the CPU to retrieve data immediately, rather than waiting for slower main memory to respond. See Chapter 5 for more information about cache memory.

Bus interfaces
Bus interfaces are the pathways that connect the processor to memory and other components. For example, modern processors connect to the chipset Northbridge via a dedicated bus called the *frontside bus* (FSB) or *host bus.*

Processor Speed

The processor *clock* coordinates all CPU and memory operations by periodically generating a time reference signal called a *clock cycle* or *tick.* Clock frequency is specified in *megahertz* (MHz), which specifies millions of ticks per second, or *gigahertz* (GHz), which specifies billions of ticks per second. Clock speed determines how fast instructions execute. Some instructions require one tick, others multiple ticks, and some processors execute multiple instructions during one tick. The number of ticks per instruction varies according to processor architecture, its *instruction set*, and the specific instruction. *Complex Instruction Set Computer* (CISC) processors use complex instructions. Each requires many clock cycles to execute, but accomplishes a lot of work. *Reduced Instruction Set Computer* (RISC) processors use fewer, simpler instructions. Each takes few ticks but accomplishes relatively little work.

These differences in efficiency mean that one CPU cannot be directly compared to another purely on the basis of clock speed. For example, an AMD Athlon XP 3000+, which actually runs at 2.167 GHz, may be faster than an Intel Pentium 4 running at 3.06 GHz, depending on the application. The comparison is complicated because different CPUs have different strengths and weaknesses. For example, the Athlon is generally faster than the Pentium 4 clock for clock on both integer and floating-point operations (that is, it does more work per CPU tick), but the Pentium 4 has an extended instruction set that may allow it to run optimized software literally twice as fast as the Athlon. The only safe use of direct clock speed comparisons is within a single family. A 1.2 GHz Tualatin-core Pentium III, for example, is roughly 20% faster than a 1.0 GHz Tualatin-core Pentium III, but even there the relationship is not absolutely linear. And a 1.2 GHz Tualatin-core Pentium III is more than 20% faster than a 1.0 GHz Pentium III that uses the older Coppermine core. Also, even within a family, processors with similar names may differ substantially internally.

Processor Architecture

Clock speeds increase every year, but the laws of physics limit how fast CPUs can run. If designers depended only on faster clock speeds for better performance, CPU performance would have hit the wall years ago. Instead, designers have improved internal architectures while also increasing clock speeds. Recent CPUs run at more than 650 times the clock speed of the PC/XT's 8088 processor, but provide 6,500 or more times the performance. Here are some major architectural improvements that have allowed CPUs to continue to get faster every year:

Wider data busses and registers
> For a given clock speed, the amount of work done depends on the amount of data processed in one operation. Early CPUs processed data in 4-bit (*nibble*) or 8-bit (*byte*) chunks, whereas current CPUs process 32 or 64 bits per operation.

FPUs
> All CPUs work well with integers, but processing floating-point numbers to high precision on a general-purpose CPU requires a huge number of operations. All modern CPUs include a dedicated FPU that handles floating-point operations efficiently.

Pipelining
> Early CPUs took five ticks to process an instruction—one each to load the instruction, decode it, retrieve the data, execute the instruction, and write the result. Modern CPUs use *pipelining*, which dedicates a separate stage to each process and allows one full instruction to be executed per clock cycle.

Superscalar architecture
> If one pipeline is good, more are better. Using multiple pipelines allows multiple instructions to be processed in parallel, an architecture called *superscalar*. A superscalar processor processes multiple instructions per tick.

Intel Processors

Nearly all current PCs use either an Intel CPU or an Intel-compatible AMD Athlon CPU. The dominance of Intel in CPUs and Microsoft in operating systems gave rise to the hybrid term *Wintel*, which refers to systems that run Windows on an Intel or compatible CPU. Intel processors are referred to generically as *x86 processors*, based on Intel's early processor naming convention, 8086, 80186, 80286, etc. Intel has produced seven CPU generations, the first five of which are obsolete and the sixth obsolescent. They are as follows:

First generation
> The 8086 was Intel's first mainstream processor, and used 16 bits for both internal and external communications. The 8086 was first used in the late 1970s in dedicated word processors and minicomputers such as the Display-Writer and the System/23 DataMaster. When IBM shipped its first PC in 1981, it used the 8088, an 8086 variant that used 16 bits internally but only 8 bits externally, because 8-bit peripherals were more readily available and less expensive then than were 16-bit components. The 8086 achieved prominence

much later when Compaq created the DeskPro as an improved clone of the IBM PC/XT. A few early PCs, notably Radio Shack models, were also built around the 80186 and 80188 CPUs, which were enhanced versions of the 8086 and 8088 respectively. The 8088 and 8086 CPUs did not include an FPU, although an *8087* FPU, called a *math coprocessor*, was available as an optional upgrade chip. First generation Intel CPUs (or their modern equivalents) are still used in some embedded applications, but they are long obsolete as general-purpose CPUs.

Second generation

In 1982, Intel introduced the long-awaited follow-on to its first generation processors. The 80286, based on the iAPX-32 core, provided a quantum leap in processor performance, executing instructions as much as five times faster than an 808x processor running at the same clock speed. The 80286 processed instructions as fast as many mainframe processors of the time. The 80286 also increased addressable memory from 1 MB to 16 MB, and introduced *protected mode* operations. The IBM PC/AT was the first commercial implementation of the 80286. The optional *80287* FPU chip added floating-point acceleration to 80286 systems. Although long obsolete as a general-purpose CPU, the 80286 is still used in embedded controllers.

Third generation

Intel's next generation debuted in 1985 as the 80386, later shortened to just 386. The 386 was Intel's first 32-bit CPU, which communicated internally and externally with a 32-bit data bus and 32-bit address bus. The 386 was available in 16, 20, 25, and 33 MHz versions. Although 386 clock speeds were only slightly faster than those of the 80286, improved architecture resulted in significant performance increases. The optional *80387* FPU added floating-point acceleration to 386 systems. Intel later renamed the 386 to the 386DX and released a cheaper version called the 386SX, which used 32 bits internally but only 16 bits externally. The 386SX was notable as the first Intel processor that included an internal (L1) cache, although it was only 8 KB and relatively inefficient. The 386 is long obsolete as a general-purpose CPU, but it is still commonly used in embedded controllers.

Fourth generation

Intel's next generation debuted in 1989 as the 486 (there never was an 80486). The 486 was a full 32-bit CPU with 8 KB of L1 cache, included a built-in FPU, and was available in speeds from 20 MHz to 50 MHz. Intel released 486DX and 486SX versions. The 486SX was in fact a 486DX with the FPU disabled. Intel also sold the 487SX, which was actually a full-blown 486DX. Installing a 487SX in the coprocessor socket simply disabled the existing 486SX. The 486DX/2, introduced in 1992, was the first Intel processor that ran internally at a multiple of the memory bus speed. The 486DX/2 clock ran at twice bus speed, and was available in 25/50, 33/66, and 40/80 MHz versions. The 486DX/4, introduced in 1994, ran (despite its name) at thrice bus speed, doubled L1 cache to 16 KB, and was available in 25/75, 33/100, and 40/120 versions. The 486 is obsolete as a general-purpose CPU, although it is still popular in embedded applications.

Fifth generation

The Intel Pentium CPU defines the fifth generation. It provides much better performance than its 486 ancestors by incorporating several architectural improvements, most notably an increase in data bus width from 32 bits to 64 bits and an increase in CPU memory bus speed from 33 MHz to 60 and 66 MHz. Intel actually shipped several different versions of the Pentium, including:

- *Pentium P54*—the original Pentium shipped in 1993 in 50, 60, and 66 MHz versions using a 1X CPU multiplier, ran (hot) at 5.0 volts, contained a dual 8 KB + 8 KB L1 cache, and fit Socket 4 motherboards.

- *Pentium P54C*—the "Classic Pentium" first shipped in 1994, was available in speeds from 75 to 200 MHz using CPU multipliers from 1.5 to 3.0, used 3.3 volts, and contained the same dual L1 cache as the P54. P54C CPUs fit Socket 5 motherboards and most Socket 7 motherboards.

- *Pentium P55C*—the Pentium/MMX shipped in 1997, was available in speeds from 166 to 233 MHz, using CPU multipliers from 2.5 to 3.5, used 3.3 volts, and contained a dual 16 KB + 16 KB L1 cache, twice the size of earlier Pentiums. The other major change from the P54C was the addition of the MMX instruction set, a set of additional instructions that greatly improved graphics processing speed. P55C CPUs fit Socket 7 motherboards, and are still in limited distribution as of July 2003.

The Pentium and other fifth-generation processors are obsolete, although millions of Pentium systems remain in service. Any system that uses a fifth-generation processor is too old to upgrade economically.

Sixth generation

This generation began with the 1995 introduction of the Pentium Pro, and includes the Pentium II, Celeron, and Pentium III processors. Late sixth-generation Intel desktop processors had been relegated to entry-level systems by early 2002 and had been discontinued as mainstream products by mid-2002. By late 2002, only the Tualatin-core Celeron processors remained as representatives of this generation. Although it is still technically feasible to upgrade the processor in many sixth-generation systems, in practical terms it usually makes more sense to replace the motherboard and processor with seventh-generation products.

Seventh generation

This is the current generation of Intel processors, and includes Intel's flagship Pentium 4 as well as various Celeron processors based on the Pentium 4 architecture.

Intel currently manufactures several sixth-generation processors, including numerous variants and derivatives of the Celeron and Pentium III, and two seventh-generation processors, the Pentium 4 and the Celeron. The following sections describe current and recent Intel processors.

 There are times when it is essential to identify the processor a system uses. For information about identifying Intel processors, see *http://www.hardwareguys.com/supplement/cpu-id.html*.

Pentium, Pentium/MMX

Intel originally designated its processors by number rather than by name—Intel 8086, 8088, 80186, 80286, and so on. Intel dropped the "80" prefix early in the life cycle of the 80386, relabeling it as the 386. (Intel never made an "80486" processor despite what some people believe.) By the time Intel shipped its fourth-generation processors, it was tired of other makers using similar names for their compatible processors. Intel believed that these similar names could lead to confusion among customers, and so tried to trademark its X86 naming scheme. When Intel learned that part numbers cannot be trademarked, the company decided to drop the "86" naming scheme and create a made-up word to name its fifth generation processors. Intel came up with *Pentium*.

Intel has produced the following three major subgenerations of Pentium:

P54

These earliest Pentium CPUs, first shipped in March 1993, fit Socket 4 motherboards, use a 3.1 million transistor core, have 16 KB L1 cache, and use 5.0 volts for both core and I/O components. P54-based systems use a 50, 60, or 66 MHz memory bus and a fixed 1.0 CPU multiplier to yield processor speeds of 50, 60, or 66 MHz.

P54C

The so-called *Classic Pentium* CPUs, first shipped in October 1994, fit Socket 5 and most Socket 7 motherboards, use a 3.3 million transistor core, have 16 KB L1 cache, and generally use 3.3 volts for both core and I/O components. P54C-based systems use a 50, 60, or 66 MHz memory bus and CPU multipliers of 1.5, 2.0, 2.5, and 3.0x to yield processor speeds of 75, 90, 100, 120, 133, 150, 166, and 200 MHz.

P55C

The *Pentium/MMX* CPUs (shown in Figure 4-1), first shipped in January 1997, fit Socket 7 motherboards, use a 4.1 million transistor core, have a 32 KB L1 cache, feature improved branch prediction logic, and generally use a 2.8 volt core and 3.3 volt I/O components. P55C-based systems use a 60 or 66 MHz memory bus and CPU multipliers of 2.5, 3.0, 3.5, 4.0, 4.5, and 5.0x to yield processor speeds of 120, 133, 150, 166, 200, 233, 266, and 300 MHz.

The Pentium was a quantum leap from the 486 in complexity and architectural efficiency. It is a CISC processor, and was initially built on a 0.35 micron process (later 0.25 micron). Pentiums, like 486s, use 32-bit operations internally. Externally, however, the Pentium doubles the 32-bit 486 data bus to 64 bits, allowing it to access eight full bytes at a time from memory. With the Pentium, Intel also introduced new chipsets to support this wider data bus and other Pentium enhancements.

The Pentium uses a *dual-pipelined superscalar* design which, relative to the 486 and earlier CPUs, allows it to execute more instructions per clock cycle. The Pentium executes integer instructions using the same five stages as the 486—*Prefetch, Instruction Decode, Address Generate, Execute,* and *Write Back*—but the Pentium has two parallel integer pipelines versus the 486's one, which allows the Pentium to execute two integer operations simultaneously in parallel. This means

Figure 4-1. Intel Pentium/MMX processor (photo courtesy of Intel Corporation)

that, for equal clock speeds, the Pentium processes integer instructions about twice as fast as a 486.

The Pentium includes an improved 80-bit FPU that is much more efficient than the 486 FPU. The Pentium also includes a *Branch Target Buffer* to provide dynamic branch prediction, a process that greatly enhances instruction execution efficiency. Finally, the Pentium includes a *System Management Module* that can control power use by the processor and peripherals.

P54 Pentiums also improved upon 486 L1 caching. The 486 has one 8 KB L1 cache (16 KB for the 486DX/4) that uses the inefficient *write-through* algorithm. P54 and P54C Pentiums have dual 8 KB L1 caches—one for data and one for instructions—that use the much more efficient *two-way set associative write-back* algorithm. This doubling of L1 cache buffers and the improved caching algorithm combined to greatly enhance CPU performance. P55C Pentiums double L1 cache size to 16 KB, providing still more improvement.

The changes from the P54 to the P54C were relatively minor. Higher voltages and faster CPU speeds generate more heat, so Intel reduced the core and I/O voltages from 5.0/5.0V in the P54 to 3.3/3.3V in the P54C, allowing them to run the CPUs faster without excessive heating. Intel also introduced support for CPU multi-pliers, which allow the CPU to run internally at some multiple of the memory bus speed.

The changes from the P54C Classic to the P55C MMX were much more signifi-cant. In fact, had Intel not already introduced the Pentium Pro (its first sixth-generation CPU) before the P55C, the P55C might have been considered the first of a new CPU generation. In addition to doubling L1 cache size, the P55C incor-porated two major architectural enhancements:

MMX
> Although sometimes described as *MultiMedia eXtensions* or *Matrix Math eXtensions*, Intel says officially that *MMX* stands for nothing. MMX is a set of 57 added instructions that are dedicated to manipulating audio, video, and graphics data more efficiently.

SIMD
> *Single Instruction Multiple Data (SIMD)* is an architectural enhancement that allows one instruction to operate simultaneously on multiple sets of similar data.

In conjunction, MMX and SIMD greatly extend the Pentium's ability to perform parallel operations, processing 8 bytes of data per clock cycle rather than 1 byte. This is particularly important for heavily graphics-oriented operations such as video because it allows the P55C to retrieve and process eight 1-byte pixels in one operation rather than manipulating those 8 bytes as 8 separate operations. Intel estimates that MMX and SIMD used with nonoptimized software yield performance increases of as much as 20%, and can yield increases of 60% when used with MMX-aware applications.

Although the Pentium is technically obsolete, millions of Pentium systems remain in service as Linux firewalls or as dedicated appliance servers, and a significant number of them continue to be upgraded. As of July 2003 Intel still produced the Pentium/200 and /233 MMX processors in Socket 7, as well as several slower models for embedded applications. For additional information about Pentium processors, including detailed identification tables, visit *http://developer.intel.com/design/pentium/*.

Pentium Pro

Intel's first sixth-generation CPU, the Pentium Pro, was introduced in November 1995—along with the new 3.3 volt 387-pin Socket 8 motherboards required to accept it—and was discontinued in late 1998. Pentium Pro processors are no longer made, but remain available on the used market. Intel positioned the Pentium Pro for servers, a niche it never escaped, and where it continued to sell in shrinking numbers until its replacement, the Pentium II Xeon, shipped in mid-1998. The Pentium Pro predated the P55C Pentium/MMX, and never shipped in an MMX version. The Pentium Pro never sold in large numbers for two reasons:

Cost
> The Pentium Pro was a very expensive processor to build. Its core logic comprised 5.5 million transistors (versus 4.1 million in the P55C), but the real problem was that the Pentium Pro also included a large L2 cache on the same substrate as the CPU. This L2 cache required millions of additional transistors, which in turn required a much larger die size and resulted in a much lower percentage yield of usable processors, both factors that kept Pentium Pro prices very high relative to other Intel CPUs.

32-bit optimization
> The Pentium Pro was optimized to execute 32-bit operations efficiently at the expense of 16-bit performance. For servers, 32-bit optimization is ideal, but slow 16-bit operations meant that a Pentium Pro actually ran many Windows 95 client applications slower than a Pentium running at the same clock speed.

The Pentium Pro shipped in 133, 150, 166, 180, and 200 MHz versions with 256 KB, 512 KB, or 1 MB of L2 cache, and was never upgraded to a faster version. The Pentium Pro continued to sell long after the introduction of much faster Pentium II CPUs for only one reason: the first Pentium II chipsets supported only two-way

Symmetric Multiprocessing (SMP) while Pentium Pro chipsets supported four-way SMP. In some server environments, four 200 MHz Pentium Pro CPUs outperformed two 450 MHz Pentium II CPUs. The introduction of the 450NX chipset, which supports four-way SMP, and the mid-1998 introduction of the Pentium II Xeon processor, which supports eight-way SMP, removed the raison d'être for the Pentium Pro, and it died a quick death.

Pentium Pro processor architecture

Although the Pentium Pro is obsolete, it was the first Intel sixth-generation processor, and as such introduced many important architectural improvements. Understanding the Pentium Pro vis-à-vis the Pentium will help you understand current Intel CPU models. The two CPUs differ in the following major respects:

Secondary (L2) cache
Pentium-based systems may optionally be equipped with an external L2 secondary cache of any size supported by the chipset. Typical Pentium systems have a 256 KB L2 cache, but high-performance motherboards may include a 512 KB, 1 MB, or larger L2 cache. But Pentium L2 caches use a narrow (32-bit), slow (60 or 66 MHz memory bus speed) link between the processor's L1 cache and the L2 cache. The Pentium Pro L2 cache is internal, located on the CPU itself, and the Pentium Pro uses a 64-bit data path running at full processor speed to link L1 cache to L2 cache. The dedicated high-speed bus used to connect to cache is called the *Backside Bus* (*BSB*), as opposed to the traditional CPU-to-chipset bus, which is now designated the *Frontside Bus* (*FSB*). In conjunction, the BSB and FSB are called the *Dual Independent Bus* (*DIB*) architecture. DIB architecture yields dramatically improved cache performance. In effect, 256 KB of Pentium Pro L2 cache provides about the same performance boost as 2 MB or more of Pentium L2 cache.

Dynamic execution
The Pentium Pro uses a combination of techniques—including *branch prediction, data flow analysis,* and *speculative execution*—that collectively are referred to as *dynamic execution*. Using these techniques, the Pentium Pro productively uses clock cycles that would otherwise be wasted, as they are with the Pentium.

Super-pipelining
Super-pipelining is a technique that allows the Pentium Pro to use *out-of-order instruction execution*, another method to avoid wasting clock cycles. The Pentium executes instructions on a first-come, first-served basis, which means that it waits for all required data to process an earlier instruction instead of processing a later instruction for which it already has all of the data. Because it uses *linear instruction sequencing*, or *standard pipelining*, the Pentium wastes what could otherwise be productive clock cycles executing no-op instructions. The Pentium Pro is the first Intel CPU to use super-pipelining. It has a 14-stage pipeline, divided into three sections. The first section, the *in-order front end*, comprises eight stages, and decodes and issues instructions. The second section, the *out-of-order core*, comprises three stages, and executes instructions in the most efficient order possible based on available

data, regardless of the order in which it received the instructions. The third and final section, the *in-order retirement section*, receives and forwards the results of the second section.

CISC versus RISC core

The most significant architectural difference between the Pentium and the sixth-generation processors is how they handle instructions internally. Pentiums use a *Complex Instruction Set Computer (CISC)* core. CISC means that the processor understands a large number of complicated instructions, each of which accomplishes a common task in just one instruction. The Pentium Pro was the first Intel CPU to use a *Reduced Instruction Set Computer (RISC)* core. RISC means that the processor understands only a few simple instructions. Complex operations are performed by stringing together multiple simple instructions. Although RISC CPUs must perform many simple instructions to accomplish the same task that CISC CPUs do with just one or a few complex instructions, the simple RISC instructions execute much faster than CISC instructions.

The Pentium Pro translates standard Intel x86 CISC instructions into RISC instructions that the Pentium Pro microcode uses internally, and then passes those RISC instructions to the internal out-of-order execution core. This translation helps avoid limitations of the standard x86 CISC instruction set, and supports the out-of-order execution that prevents pipeline stalls, but those benefits come at a price. Although the time required is measured in nanoseconds, converting from CISC to RISC does take time, and that slows program execution. Also, 16-bit instructions convert inefficiently and frequently result in pipeline stalls in the out-of-order execution unit, which commonly result in CPU wait states of as many as seven clock cycles. The upshot is that, for pure 32-bit operations, the benefit of RISC conversion greatly outweighs the drawbacks, but for 16-bit operations, the converse is true.

For additional information about Pentium Pro processors, including detailed identification tables, visit *http://developer.intel.com/design/pro/*.

Pentium II Family

Intel's first mainstream sixth-generation CPU, the Pentium II, shipped in May 1997. Intel subsequently shipped many variants of the Pentium II, which differ chiefly in packaging, the type and amount of L2 cache they include, the processor core they use, and the FSB speeds they support. All members of the Pentium II family use the Dynamic Execution Technology and DIB architecture introduced with the Pentium Pro. Intel reduced the core voltage from the 3.3 volts used by Pentium Pro to 2.8 volts or less in Pentium II processors, which allows them to run much faster while using less power and producing less heat. In effect, you're not far wrong if you think of Pentium II, sixth-generation Celeron, and Pentium III processors as faster versions of the Pentium Pro with MMX (or the enhanced *SSE* version of MMX) added, and the following major changes:

L2 cache

The Pentium Pro taught Intel the folly of embedding the L2 cache onto the CPU substrate itself, at least for the then-current state of the technology.

Early Pentium II family processors use discrete L2 cache *Static RAM (SRAM)* chips that reside within the CPU package but are not a part of the CPU substrate. Advances in fab technology have allowed Intel again to place L2 cache directly on the processor substrate on later Pentium II family processor models. Some Pentium II family processors run L2 cache at full processor speed, while others run it at half processor speed. The least-expensive Pentium II family processors have no L2 cache at all. The L2 cache in later members of the Pentium II family is improved, not just in size and/or speed, but also in functionality. The most recent Pentium III processors, for example, use an *eight-way set associative cache*, which is more efficient than the caching schemes used on earlier variants.

Packaging

The Pentium Pro used the huge, complicated 387-pin *Dual Pattern-Staggered Pin Grid Array (DP-SPGA)* Socket 8. The extra pins provide data and power lines for the onboard L2 cache. Intel developed simplified alternative packaging methods for various members of the Pentium II family processors, which are described later in this chapter.

Improved 16-bit performance

High cost aside, the major reason the Pentium Pro was never widely used other than in servers was its poor performance with 16-bit software. Although represented as a 32-bit operating system, Windows 95/98 still contains much 16-bit code. Users quickly discovered that Windows 95 actually ran slower on a Pentium Pro than on a Pentium of the same speed. Intel solved the 16-bit problem by using the Pentium segment descriptor cache in the Pentium II.

Members of the Pentium II family include the Pentium II, Pentium II Overdrive, Pentium II Xeon, sixth-generation Celeron, Pentium III, and Pentium III Xeon. Each of these processors is described in the following sections.

Pentium II

First-generation Pentium II processors shipped in 233, 266, 300, and 333 MHz versions with the Klamath core and a 66 MHz FSB. In mid-1998, Intel shipped second-generation Pentium II processors, based on the Deschutes core, that ran at 350, 400, and 450 MHz and used a 100 MHz FSB. Pentium II processors have 512 KB of L2 cache that runs at half internal CPU speed versus 256 KB to 1 MB of full CPU speed L2 cache in the Pentium Pro. Pentium II processors use a *Single Edge Contact connector (SECC)* or *SECC2* cartridge, which contains the CPU and L2 cache (see Figure 4-2). The SECC/SECC2 package mates with a *242-contact slot connector*, formerly known as *Slot 1*, which resembles a standard expansion slot. Klamath-based processors run at 2.8 volts and are built on a 0.35μ fab. Deschutes-based processors, including all 100 MHz FSB processors and recent 66 MHz FSB processors, run at 2.0 volts and are built on a 0.25μ fab. Excepting FSB speed and fab process, all Slot 1 Pentium II processors are functionally identical. As of July 2003, Pentium II processors remain in limited distribution, but they are obsolescent.

Figure 4-2. Intel Pentium II processor in the original SECC package (photo courtesy of Intel Corporation)

For additional information about Pentium II processors, including detailed identification tables, visit *http://developer.intel.com/design/pentiumii/*. For information about the Pentium II Xeon processor, see *http://www.intel.com/support/processors/pentiumii/xeon/*.

Celeron

The sixth-generation Celeron—we keep saying "sixth-generation" because Intel also makes a seventh-generation Celeron based on the Pentium 4—was initially an inexpensive variant of the Pentium II and, in later models, an inexpensive variant of the Pentium III. Klamath-based (Covington-core) Celerons shipped in April 1998 in 266 and 300 MHz versions without L2 cache. Performance was poor, so in fall 1998 Intel began shipping modified Deschutes-based (Mendocino-core) Celerons with 128 KB L2 cache. The smaller Celeron L2 cache runs at full CPU speed, and provides L2 cache performance similar to that of the larger but slower Pentium II L2 cache for most applications. Mendocino (0.25µ) Celerons have been manufactured in 300A (to differentiate it from the cacheless 300), 333, 366, 400, 433, 466, 500, and 533 MHz versions, all of which use the 66 MHz FSB.

With the introduction of the Coppermine-core Pentium III processor, Intel also introduced Celeron processors based on a variant of the Coppermine core called the *Coppermine128* core. Celerons based on this 0.18µ, 1.6v core began shipping in 533A, 566, and 600 MHz versions soon after their announcement in May 2000, and were eventually produced in speeds as high as 1.1 GHz, which approaches the limit of the Coppermine core itself.

Coppermine128-core Celerons have half of the 256 KB on-die L2 cache disabled to bring L2 cache size to the Celeron-standard 128 KB, and use a four-way set associate L2 cache rather than the eight-way version used by the Coppermine Pentium III. Coppermine128-core Celerons through the Celeron/766, shipped in November 2000, use the 66 MHz FSB speed. Coppermine128-core Celerons that use the 100 MHz FSB speed began shipping in March 2001, beginning with 800 MHz units and eventually reaching 1.1 GHz. Other than the differences in L2 cache size and type, processor bus speed differences, and official support for SMP, Coppermine128-core Celerons support the standard Coppermine-core Pentium III features, including SSE, described later in this chapter.

 Because Coppermine128 Celerons effectively *are* Pentium IIIs, some *may* be easy to overclock. For example, a Celeron/600 (66 MHz FSB) is effectively a down-rated Pentium III/900 (100 MHz FSB). During the ramp-up of the Coppermine128-core Celerons, we believe that Intel recycled Pentium III processors that tested as unreliable at 100 MHz or 133 MHz as 66 MHz Celerons, although Intel has never confirmed this. Many early Coppermine128-core Celerons were not good overclockers, although that changed as production ramped up. Note, however, that overclocking Coppermine128-core Celerons is viable only for the slower 66 MHz FSB models—the Celeron/566 and /600. Attempting to overclock a faster Celeron by running it with a 100 MHz FSB would cause it to run near or over 1.1 GHz, which appears to be the effective limit of the Coppermine core itself.

In November 2001, Intel began shipping Celerons based on the latest Pentium III core, code-named *Tualatin*. The first Tualatin-core Celerons ran at 1.2 GHz using the 100 MHz FSB. Intel later filled in the product line by shipping 100 MHz FSB Tualatin-core Celerons at 900 MHz, 1.0 GHz, 1.1 GHz, 1.3 GHz, and finally 1.4 GHz. Tualatin-core Celerons also differ from earlier Celeron models in that they include a full 256 KB eight-way set associative L2 cache, the same as Coppermine-core Pentium III models. Tualatin-core Celerons perform like full-blown Pentium IIIs because they effectively *are* full-blown Pentium IIIs.

So why did Intel suddenly decide to uncripple the Celeron? Basically, it had devoted a lot of resources to developing the Tualatin-core Pentium III only to find itself overtaken by events. Intel needed to ship the Pentium 4 to counter fast AMD Athlons, but there was no room in Intel's lineup for two premium processors. Accordingly, the Pentium III had to go, at least as mainstream product, giving way to the new-generation Pentium 4. But that left Intel with the perfectly good, new Tualatin core, which had been developed at great expense, with no way to sell it. Talk about being all dressed up with nowhere to go.

As a way of earning back the development costs of the Tualatin core while at the same time putting the screws to AMD's low-end Duron, Intel decided to ship Pentium III processors with the Celeron name on them. The new Celerons handily outperformed Durons running at the same clock speed, and in fact were surprisingly close to the performance level of the fastest Pentium 4 and Athlon processors then available. Selling for less than $100, the Tualatin-core Celerons provided incredibly high bang for the buck. In fact, they still do today. A Celeron/1.4G running in an 815-based motherboard is slower than a fast Pentium 4 and Athlon system, certainly, but is by no means a slow system.

Celerons have been produced in four form factors:

Single Edge Processor Package cartridge
All Celerons through 433 MHz were produced in *Single Edge Processor Package (SEPP)* cartridge form, which resembles the Pentium II SECC and

SECC2 package, and is compatible with the Pentium II 242-contact slot. In mid-1999 Intel largely abandoned SEPP in favor of PPGA, and SEPP Celerons are no longer available new. Figure 4-3 shows an SEPP Celeron.

Figure 4-3. Intel Celeron processor in SEPP package (photo courtesy of Intel Corporation)

Plastic Pin Grid Array

As a cheaper alternative to SEPP, Intel developed the *Plastic Pin Grid Array* (*PPGA*). PPGA processors fit *Socket 370*, which resembles Socket 7 but accepts only PPGA Celeron and Pentium III processors. All Mendocino-core Celerons are manufactured in PPGA. The Celeron/466 was the first Celeron produced only in PPGA. PPGA processors can be used in most Socket 370 motherboards, although a few accept only Socket 370 Pentium III processors. PPGA Celerons are no longer available new. Figure 4-4 shows a PPGA Celeron.

Flip Chip Pin Grid Array

With the introduction of the Socket 370 version of the Pentium III, Intel introduced a modified version of PPGA called *Flip Chip PGA* (*FC-PGA*), which uses slightly different pinouts than PPGA. FC-PGA essentially reverses the position of the processor core from PPGA, placing the core on top (where it can make better contact with the heatsink) rather than on the bottom side with the pins. All Socket 370 Pentium III and Coppermine128-core Celerons (the 533A, 566, 600, and faster versions) require an FC-PGA compliant motherboard. FC-PGA processors physically fit older PPGA motherboards, but if you install an FC-PGA processor in a PPGA-only Socket 370 motherboard the processor doesn't work, although no harm is done. FC-PGA Celerons are no longer available new. Figure 4-5 shows an FC-PGA Celeron.

Flip Chip Pin Grid Array 2

Tualatin-core Celerons use the FC-PGA2 packaging, which is essentially FC-PGA with the addition of a flat metal plate, called an *Integrated Heat Spreader*, that covers the processor chip itself. Although these processors physically fit any Socket 370 motherboard, only very recent Socket 370 chipsets support the Tualatin core. Intel designates its own motherboard

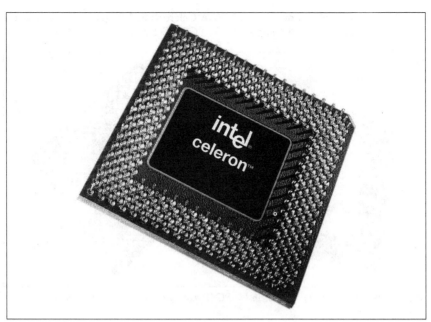

Figure 4-4. Intel Celeron processor in PPGA package (photo courtesy of Intel Corporation)

Figure 4-5. Intel Celeron processor in FC-PGA package (photo courtesy of Intel Corporation)

models that support Tualatin as "Universal" models. Other manufacturers use other terminology, but the important thing to remember is that the motherboard must explicitly support Tualatin if it is to run these processors. As of

July 2003, Intel still produces FC-PGA Celerons in 1.0, 1.1, 1.2, 1.3, and 1.4 GHz models. Figure 4-6 shows an FC-PGA2 Celeron.

Figure 4-6. Intel Celeron processor in FC-PGA2 package (photo courtesy of Intel Corporation)

Intel has produced five major variants of the Celeron, using four packages, four cores, two bus speeds, four fab sizes, and more than 20 clock speeds. Table 4-1 summarizes the major differences between these variants.

Table 4-1. Comparison of sixth-generation Celeron variants

	Covington	Mendocino	Coppermine128	Coppermine128	Tualatin
Package	SECC	SECC-2 PPGA	FC-PGA	FC-PGA	FC-PGA2
Manufacturing dates	1998	1998 – 2000	2000 – 2002	2001 – 2002	2001 –
Clock speeds (MHz)	266, 300	300A, 333, 366, 400, 433, 466, 500, 533	500A, 533A, 566, 600, 633, 667, 700, 733, 766	800, 850, 900, 950, 1000, 1100	900, 1000, 1100, 1200, 1300, 1400
L2 cache size	none	128 KB	128 KB	128 KB	256 KB
L2 cache bus width	n/a	64 bits	256 bits	256 bits	256 bits
System bus speed	66 MHz	66 MHz	66 MHz	100 MHz	100 MHz
SSE instructions	○	○	●	●	●
Dual CPU capable	●	●	○	○	○
Fabrication process	0.35μ	0.25μ	0.18μ	0.18μ	0.13μ

Dual-CPU capability deserves an explanation. Although Intel never officially supported Celerons for SMP operation, the two earliest Celeron variants did in fact support dual-CPU operation. For Covington-core and SECC-2 Mendocino-core Celerons, dual-CPU operation was impractical because enabling SMP required physical surgery on the processor package—literally drilling holes in the package and soldering wires. With PPGA Mendocino-core Celerons, dual-CPU operation was eminently practical because many dual Socket 370 motherboards were designed specifically to accept two Celerons, and no changes to the processors themselves were necessary. Beginning with the 66 MHz Coppermine128 Celerons, Intel physically disabled SMP operation in the core itself, so it is impossible to operate Coppermine- or Tualatin-core Celerons in SMP mode.

For additional information about Celeron processors, including detailed identification tables, visit *http://developer.intel.com/design/celeron/*.

Pentium III

The Pentium III, Intel's final sixth-generation processor, began shipping in February 1999. The Pentium III has been manufactured in numerous variants, including speeds from 450 MHz to 1.4 GHz (Intel defines 1 GHz as 1000 MHz), two bus speeds (100 MHz and 133 MHz), four packages (SECC, SECC2, FC-PGA, and FC-PGA2), and the following three cores:

Pentium III (Katmai core)
    Initial Pentium III variants use the *Katmai core*, essentially an enhanced Deschutes with the addition of 70 new *Streaming SIMD instructions* (formerly called *Katmai New Instructions* or *KNI* and known colloquially as *MMX/2*) that improve 3D graphics rendering and speech processing. They use the 0. 25μ process, operate at 2.0V core voltage (with some versions requiring marginally higher voltage), use a 100 or 133 MHz FSB, incorporate 512 KB four-way set associative L2 cache running at half CPU speed, and have glueless support for two-way SMP. Katmai-core processors were made in SECC2 (Slot 1/SC242) at 450, 500, 550, and 600 MHz in 100 MHz FSB variants, and at 533 and 600 MHz in 133 MHz FSB variants.

Pentium III (Coppermine core)
    Later Pentium III variants use the *Coppermine core*, which is essentially a refined version of the Katmai core. Later Coppermine processors use the updated *Coppermine-T core*. Coppermine processors use the 0.18μ process, which reduces die size, heat production, and cost. They operate at nominal 1.6V core voltage (with faster versions requiring marginally higher voltage), are available at either 100 MHz or 133 MHz FSB, and (in most variants) support SMP. Coppermine-core processors have been made in SECC2 (Slot 1/SC242) and FC-PGA (Socket 370) packaging in both 100 and 133 MHz FSB variants, running at speeds from 533 MHz to 1.13 GHz. Finally, Coppermine also incorporates the following significant improvements in L2 cache implementation and buffering:

Advanced Transfer Cache
    Advanced Transfer Cache (*ATC*) is how Intel summarizes the several important improvements in L2 cache implementation from Katmai to Coppermine. Although L2 cache size is reduced from 512 KB to 256 KB, it is now on-die (rather than discrete SRAM chips) and, like the Celeron,

operates at full CPU speed rather than half. Bandwidth is also quadrupled, from the 64-bit bus used on Katmai- and Mendocino-core Celeron processors to a 256-bit bus. Finally, Coppermine uses an eight-way set associative cache, rather than the four-way set associative cache used by earlier Pentium III and Celeron processors. Migrating L2 cache on-die increased transistor count from just under 10 million for the Katmai to nearly 30 million for Coppermine, which may account for the reported early yield problems with the Coppermine.

 When manufacturers begin producing a processor, a relatively high percentage of the processors made are unusable. In the initial phases, many of the processors on each wafer may be spoiled. As the manufacturer ramps up production and gains experience, the percentage of usable processors increases substantially, as does the percentage of processors that are usable at higher speeds. Marketing reasons aside, yield percentage is the major factor in the very high price of the fastest processors. During early production, only 1% to 10% of the processors produced may be able to run at the highest speed offered for that processor. As the yield percentage improves, manufacturers can cut processor prices. Yield percentages are one of the most closely guarded secrets in semiconductor manufacturing.

Advanced System Buffering

Advanced System Buffering (ASB) is how Intel describes the increase from Pentium III Katmai and earlier processors to the Coppermine from four to six fill buffers, four to eight queue entry buffers, and one to four write-back buffers. The increased number of buffers was primarily intended to prevent bottlenecks with 133 MHz FSB Coppermines, but also benefits those running at 100 MHz.

Pentium III (Tualatin core)

The latest Pentium III variants use the *Tualatin core*, which is the last Pentium III core Intel will ever produce. Tualatin processors use the 0.13μ process, which reduces die size, heat production, and cost, and allows considerably higher clock speeds than the Coppermine core. Had it not been for Intel's rapid transition to the Pentium 4, Tualatin-core Pentium IIIs could have been Intel's flagship processor through at least the end of 2002. Intel could have shipped Tualatins at ever-increasing clock speeds, beating the 0.18μ Palomino-core AMD Athlon on both clock speed and actual performance. Instead, Intel opted to compete using the Pentium 4. Intel has by its pricing mechanism effectively exiled Tualatin-core Pentium IIIs to niche status by selling fast Pentium 4 processors for less than Tualatin Pentium IIIs with comparable performance.

Tualatins use the 133 MHz FSB, and are available in two major variants, both of which use the FC-PGA2 packaging (with Integrated Heat Spreader). The first variant, intended for desktop systems, has the standard 256 KB L2 cache, uses the 133 MHz FSB, and was made in 1.0, 1.13, 1.2, 1.33, and 1.4 GHz models. The second variant, intended for entry-level servers and workstations, has 512 KB L2 cache, uses the 100 or 133 MHz FSB, and was made in models that run at 700, 800, 900, or 933 MHz, as well as models that run at 1.13, 1.26, and 1.4 GHz. Both variants are SMP-capable. Finally, Intel removed the much-hated Processor Serial Number from all Tualatin-core processors.

Table 4-2 summarizes the important differences between Pentium III variants as of July 2003. When necessary to differentiate processors of the same speed, Intel uses the *E* suffix to indicate support for ATC and ASB, the *B* suffix to indicate 133 MHz FSB, and the *EB* suffix to indicate both. An A suffix designates 0.13µ Tualatin-core processors. All processors faster than 600 MHz include both ATC and ASB. Note that A-step FC-PGA processors do not support SMP. B-step and higher FC-PGA and FC-PGA2 processors support SMP, except the 1B GHz processor, which is not SMP-capable in any stepping.

Table 4-2. Intel Pentium III variants

	1.40, 1.26, 1.13 GHz	1.33, 1.20, 1.13A, 1A GHz	1B GHz, 933, 866, 800EB, 733, 667, 600EB, 533EB	850, 800, 750, 700, 650, 600E, 550E	1.10G, 1G, 850, 800, 750, 700, 650, 600, 550E, 500E	1G, 933, 866, 800, 733, 667, 600EB, 533EB	600B, 533B	600, 550, 500, 450
Package	FC-PGA2	FC-PGA2	SECC2	SECC2	FC-PGA	FC-PGA	SECC2	SECC2
Process size	0.13µ	0.13µ	0.18µ	0.18µ	0.18µ	0.18µ	0.25µ	0.25µ
FSB speed (MHz)	133	133	133	100	100	133	133	100
L2 cache size (KB)	512	256	256	256	256	256	512	512
L2 cache speed	CPU	CPU	CPU	CPU	CPU	CPU	1/2 CPU	1/2 CPU
SMP support	•	•	•	•	•	•	•	•
Process or S/N	○	○	•	•	•	•	•	•

 When Intel introduced the Pentium III in FC-PGA form, it changed Socket 370 pinouts. Those changes mean that, although an FC-PGA processor physically fits any Socket 370 motherboard, it will not run in motherboards designed for the Celeron/PPGA. Motherboards designed for FC-PGA processors are nearly all backward-compatible with PPGA Celeron processors. Similarly, as with Tualatin-core Celerons, Tualatin-core Pentium IIIs operate only in late-model Socket 370 motherboards that use chipsets with explicit Tualatin support. Most motherboards designed to use PPGA Celerons or FC-PGA Coppermine-core Pentium IIIs are not compatible with Tualatin-core Pentium IIIs.

Figure 4-7 shows a Pentium III processor in the SECC2 package. Some early Pentium III models were produced in the original SECC package, which closely resembles the Pentium II SECC package shown in Figure 4-2. Figure 4-8 shows a Pentium III processor in the FC-PGA package. Other than labeling, the Pentium III processor in the FC-PGA2 package closely resembles the FC-PGA2 Celeron processor shown in Figure 4-6.

Figure 4-7. Intel Pentium III processor in SECC2 package (photo courtesy of Intel Corporation)

Figure 4-8. Intel Pentium III processor in FC-PGA package (photo courtesy of Intel Corporation)

For additional information about Pentium III processors, including detailed identification tables, visit *http://developer.intel.com/design/pentiumiii/*. For information about Pentium III Xeon processors, visit *http://developer.intel.com/design/pentiumiii/xeon/*.

Pentium 4

By late 2000, Intel found itself in a conundrum. In March of that year, AMD had forced Intel's hand by releasing an Athlon running at 1 GHz. Intel planned to release a 1.0 GHz version of its flagship processor, the Coppermine-core Pentium III, but not until much later. The Athlon/1.0G introduction was a wakeup call for Intel. It had to ship a Pentium III/1.0G immediately if it was to remain competitive on clock speed with the Athlon. One week after the Athlon/1.0G shipped, Intel shipped a Pentium III running at the magic 1.0 GHz.

The problem was that the Pentium III Coppermine core effectively topped out at about 1.0 GHz, while the Athlon Thunderbird core had plenty of headroom. For the next several months, AMD shipped faster and faster Athlons, while Intel remained stuck at 1.0 GHz. And to make matters worse, AMD could ship fast Athlons in volume, while Intel had very low yields on the fast Pentium III parts. Although 1.0 GHz Pentium IIIs were theoretically available, in reality even the 933 MHz parts were hard to come by. So Intel had to make the best of things, shipping mostly sub-900 MHz Pentium IIIs while AMD claimed the high end. Intel must have been gritting its collective teeth.

Adding insult to injury, Intel attempted unsuccessfully to ship a faster Pentium III, the ill-fated Pentium III/1.13G. These processors were available in such small volumes that many observers believed they must be almost handmade. Adding to Intel's embarrassment, popular enthusiast web sites including Tom's Hardware (*http://www.tomshardware.com*) and AnandTech (*http://www.anandtech.com*) reported that the 1.13 GHz parts did not function reliably. Intel was forced to admit this was true and withdrew the 1.13 GHz part, although it later reintroduced it successfully.

Intel had two possible responses to the growing clock speed gap. It could expedite the release of 0.13μ Tualatin-core Pentium IIIs, which have clock speed headroom at least equivalent to the Thunderbird-core and later Palomino-core Athlons, or it could introduce its seventh-generation Pentium 4 processor sooner than planned (see Figure 4-9). Intel wasn't anywhere near ready to convert its fabs to 0.13μ Tualatin-core Pentium III production, so its only real choice was to get the Pentium 4 to market quickly.

There were several problems with that course, not the least of which were that the 0.18μ Willamette-core Pentium 4 was not really ready for release and the only Pentium 4 chipsets Intel had available supported only Rambus RDRAM, which was hideously expensive at the time. But in November 2000, Intel was finally able, if only just, to ship the Pentium 4 processor running at 1.3, 1.4, and 1.5 GHz. Although many observers (including we) noted that that version of the Pentium 4 was a dead-end processor because it used Socket 423, which was due to be replaced by Socket 478 only months after the initial release, and that, despite its higher clock speed, the Pentium 4 had lower performance than Athlons or Pentium IIIs running at lower clock speeds, the Pentium 4 did at least allow Intel to regain the clock speed crown, an inestimable marketing advantage.

Processors

Figure 4-9. Intel Pentium 4 processor in mPGA478 package (photo courtesy of Intel Corporation)

AMD partisans gloated as the Athlon kicked sand in the face of the puny Socket 423 Pentium 4. But those who don't regard processors as a religious issue saw the writing on the wall. The Pentium 4 meant trouble for AMD, big trouble. The seventh-generation Pentium 4 is the most significant new Intel processor since the original Pentium Pro, which kicked off the sixth generation. The Pentium 4 has a lot of headroom, which the aging Athlon core did not.

That first Pentium 4 was significant, not so much for what it was as for what it would become. Just as Intel scaled the clock speeds of sixth-generation cores from the 120 MHz of the first Pentium Pro to the 1.4 GHz of the final Pentium III, we expect that it will scale the clock speed of the Pentium 4 by an order of magnitude or more—albeit using improved cores—eventually reaching 10 GHz to 15 GHz before introducing their next completely new core, which by that time may be named the Pentium 6, 7, or 8.

For the Pentium 4, Intel launched the fastest ramp-up in its history. In earlier generations, new processors coexisted with older processors for quite some time. Intel derived substantial revenues from the 386 long after the 486 shipped, from the 486 long after the Pentium shipped, and from the Pentium long after the Pentium II shipped. With the Pentium 4, it abandoned the idea of a staged introduction. Intel killed the market for sixth-generation processors quickly, leaving the Pentium 4 and its derivatives as the only mainstream Intel processors.

Pentium 4 processor features

Relative to sixth-generation processors, the Pentium 4 incorporates the following architectural improvements which together define the seventh generation and which Intel collectively calls NetBurst Micro-architecture.

Hyper pipelined technology
Hyper-pipelining doubles the pipeline depth compared to the Pentium III micro-architecture. The branch prediction/recovery pipeline, for example, is implemented in 20 stages in the Pentium 4, as compared to 10 stages in the Pentium III. Deep pipelines are a double-edged sword. Using a very deep

pipeline makes it possible to achieve very high clock speeds, but a deep pipeline also means that fewer instructions can be completed per clock cycle. That means the Pentium 4 can run at much higher clock speeds than the Pentium III (or Athlon), but that it needs those higher clock speeds to do the same amount of work.

Early Pentium 4 processors were roundly condemned by many observers because they were outperformed by Pentium III and Athlon processors running at much lower clock speeds, which is solely attributable to the relative inefficiency of the Pentium 4 in terms of Instructions per Cycle (IPC). Ultimately, the low IPC efficiency of the Pentium 4 doesn't matter because Intel can easily boost the clock speed until the Pentium 4 greatly outperforms the fastest Pentium III or Athlon that can be produced. What superficially appears to be a weakness of the Pentium 4 is in fact its greatest strength.

Improved branch prediction

The deep pipeline of the Pentium 4 made it mandatory to use a superior Branch Prediction Unit (BPU) because a deep pipeline with anything less than excellent branch prediction would bring the processor to its knees. When the pipeline is very deep, a pipeline clog wastes massive numbers of clock ticks, and the function of a BPU is to prevent that from happening. The Pentium 4 BPU is the most advanced available, 33% more efficient at avoiding mispredictions than the Pentium III BPU or the comparable Athlon BPU. The Pentium 4 BPU uses a more effective branch-prediction algorithm and a dedicated 4 KB branch target buffer that stores detail about branching history to achieve these results. The improved BPU is one component of the Advance Dynamic Execution (ADE) engine, Intel's name for its very deep, out-of-order speculative execution engine.

Level 1 Execution Trace Cache

In addition to the standard Level 1 8 KB data cache, the Pentium 4 includes a 12 KB L1 Execution Trace Cache. This cache stores decoded micro-op instructions in the order they will be executed, optimizing storage efficiency and performance by removing the micro-op decoded from the main execution loop and storing only those micro-op instructions that will be needed. By caching micro-op instructions before they are needed, the Execution Trace Cache ensures that the processor execution units seldom have to wait for instructions, and that the effects of branch mispredictions are minimized.

Rapid Execution Engine

Even with an excellent BPU, integer code is more likely than floating-point code to be mispredicted, and such mispredictions have a catastrophic effect on throughput. To minimize their effect, the Pentium 4 includes two *Arithmetic Logic Units (ALUs)* that operate at twice the processor core frequency. For example, the Rapid Execution Engine on a 2 GHz Pentium 4 actually runs at 4 GHz. That allows a basic integer operation (e.g., Add, Subtract, AND, OR) to execute in half a clock cycle.

400, 533, or 800 MHz system bus

One Achilles' heel of the Pentium III (and, to a lesser extent, the Athlon) is the relatively slow link between the processor and memory. For example, using PC133 SDR-SDRAM, the Pentium III achieves peak data-transfer rates of only 1067 MB/s (133 MHz times 8 bytes/transfer). In practice, sustained data-transfer rates are lower still because SDRAM is not 100% efficient and the SDRAM interface uses only minimal buffering. Conversely, the Pentium 4 has the fastest system bus available on any desktop processor. Although the bus actually operates at only 100, 133, or 200 MHz, data transfers are quad-pumped for an effective bus speed of 400, 533, or 800 MHz. Also, Intel uses elaborate buffering that ensures sustained true 400/533/800 MHz data transfers when using Rambus RDRAM or dual-channel DDR-SDRAM memory. Sustained data-transfer rates using SDR-SDRAM or DDR-SDRAM are smaller than peak transfer rates, but are still much faster than the data-transfer rates of the Pentium III or Athlon using similar memory.

Hyper-Threading technology

Finally, with the November 2002 introduction of the Pentium 4/3.06G, Intel implemented *Hyper-Threading Technology* (*HTT*) on some of its Pentium 4 processors. To understand the potential benefit of HTT, it is necessary to understand a bit about how instructions are processed in a modern processor core.

Consider a 24-hour supermarket with seven cash registers. On a Saturday afternoon, all seven of those cashiers may be busy, with customers backed up in each aisle waiting to complete their transactions. At 2:00 on a Wednesday morning, only one of the cash registers may be staffed because fewer customers are in the store. Even so, a flurry of activity may mean that a line forms at the one available cash register, leaving the remaining six unused.

The Pentium 4 has seven execution units, which are analogous to the cash registers. Two of those execution units, the double-pumped ALUs, process two operations per clock cycle. The other execution units, including the FPUs, process one operation per clock cycle. Because execution units operate independently, in theory the Pentium 4 could process a total of nine operations per clock cycle.

In practice, the Pentium 4 processes nowhere near nine operations per clock cycle because inefficiencies in matching the requirements of the running program code to the resources the processor has available mean that many of those resources go unused at any particular time. For example, typical desktop productivity software processes a lot of integer operations, loads, and stores, but leaves the floating-point execution units almost unused. Conversely, a scientific, CAD, or graphics program might use the FPUs almost exclusively, leaving the ALUs almost unused. Even programs that use integer operations almost exclusively will probably not saturate all of the ALUs. The upshot is that, during normal operations, most of the available execution units sit idle. According to Intel, the Pentium 4 typically uses only 35% of the available execution unit resources during normal operations. In effect, the CPU runs at only 35% of its potential performance.

With single-threaded programs, not much can be done to improve this situation. If, for example, the program has saturated the FPUs, all the ALUs in the world won't improve its performance. But in a multithreading environment, it's quite possible that resources not needed by one program thread might be usable by a different program thread. The problem is that a standard processor can execute only one program thread at a time. That means the second thread must wait its turn, even though the resources it needs are not being used by the currently active thread.

SMP is one solution to this problem. With multiple processors, each processor can be assigned a separate thread. These multiple threads are processed simultaneously, significantly increasing overall system performance. SMP does nothing to improve processor utilization, of course. Each of the multiple processors is still operating at only 35% or so of its potential throughput.

HTT is another solution to the problem. HTT splits each physical processor into virtual dual processors, allowing a single physical processor to process two threads simultaneously. To the extent that these two threads require different execution unit resources, they are not in conflict and can thus use a higher percentage of the available processor resources. Because each thread invariably requires resources that are also needed by the other thread, overall performance is not doubled. Performance may, however, increase by 20% or more in an HTT processor relative to a similar processor that does not support HTT.

HTT is not a panacea. If two program threads have similar resource requirements, a processor with HTT enabled may actually run those threads more slowly than the same processor with HTT disabled. For that reason, many vendors that ship HTT-capable systems turn HTT off by default. The only way to determine whether HTT will improve performance on your system is to run the system with HTT enabled and disabled and see which configuration runs faster for you. In our experience, HTT usually makes little difference either way if you are running only office applications, but if you run a mix of typical office applications and FPU-intensive applications, HTT can sometimes improve performance noticeably.

Beware of enabling HTT if you run Windows 2000, which sees an HTT processor as two physical processors, and demands licenses for twice as many processors as you actually have. Even worse, Windows 2000 uses virtual processors and ignores "extra" physical processors. For example, if you run Windows 2000 Professional, which supports two processors, on a system with two physical HTT processors, Windows 2000 recognizes only the two virtual processors on the first physical processor, and ignores the second physical processor entirely. Duh. Microsoft's "solution" for this problem is to suggest that you buy an upgrade to Windows XP. Thanks, but no thanks. We'll upgrade to Linux instead.

At its introduction in November 2002, Intel supported HTT only in the Pentium 4/3.06G, the fastest and most expensive Pentium 4 at that time. In May 2003 Intel began shipping entry-level and midrange 800 MHz FSB Pentium 4 processors with HTT support, including the 2.40C, 2.60C, and

2.80C. In June 2003, Intel began shipping HTT-enabled Pentium 4 processors at 3.2 GHz, with faster versions due later in 2003 and throughout 2004.

> Enabling HTT requires that the processor, chipset, BIOS, and operating system all support HTT. The Intel 850E, 865-, and 875-series chipsets support HTT, as do most versions of the 845-series chipsets. The 845 chipset and the 845G chipset in steppings prior to B1 do not support HTT. Windows XP supports HTT, as does Linux with a 2.4.18 or higher kernel.

In addition to its new features, the Pentium 4 also has two features that have been significantly enhanced relative to the Pentium III:

Enhanced ATC

Intel has enhanced the performance of the L2 ATC that first appeared in the Pentium III. The Pentium 4 uses a non-blocking, eight-way set associative, inclusive, full-CPU-speed, on-die, L2 cache with a 256-bit interface that transfers data during each clock cycle. Because the Pentium 4 clock is faster than that of the Pentium III, L2 cache transfers also support a much higher data rate. For example, a Pentium III operating at 1 GHz transfers L2 cache data at 16 GB/s, whereas a Pentium 4 at 1.5 GHz transfers L2 cache data at 48 GB/s (three times the transfer rate for a processor operating at 1.5 times the speed). The ATC also includes improved Data Prefetch Logic that anticipates what data will be needed by a program and loads it into cache before it is needed. Willamette-core Pentium 4 processors have a 256 KB L2 cache. Northwood-core Pentium 4 processors have a 512 KB L2 cache.

Enhanced floating-point and SSE functionality

The Pentium 4 uses 128-bit floating-point registers and adds a dedicated register for data movement. These enhancements improve performance relative to the Pentium III on floating-point and multimedia applications. The Pentium 4 also includes SSE2, an updated version of the SSE that debuted with the Pentium III. SSE, which stands for Streaming SIMD Extensions, is an acronym within an acronym. SIMD, or Single Instruction Multiple Data, allows one instruction to be applied to a multiple data set (e.g., an array), which greatly speeds performance in such applications as video/image processing, encryption, speech recognition, and heavy-duty scientific number crunching. SSE2 adds 144 new instructions to the SSE instruction set, including 128-bit SIMD integer arithmetic operations and 128-bit SIMD double-precision floating-point operations. These new instructions can greatly reduce the number of steps needed to execute some tasks, but the catch is that the application software must explicitly support SSE2. For example, an application that is not designed to use SSE2 might run at the same speed on a Pentium 4 and an Athlon, while an SSE2-capable version of that application might run literally twice as fast on the Pentium 4.

Pentium 4 processor variants

Intel has produced Pentium 4 processors using two cores, the 0.18μ Willamette core and the 0.13μ Northwood core; two form factors, the 423-pin PGA-423

(Socket 423) and the smaller 478-pin mPGA-478 (Socket 478); and three FSB speeds, 400 MHz, 533 MHz, and 800 MHz:

Willamette-core processors

Willamette-core Pentium 4 processors have 256 KB of eight-way set associative L2 cache and use the 400 MHz FSB. Intel has produced Willamette-core processors for Socket 423 and Socket 478 at core speeds of 1.30, 1.40, 1.50, 1.60, 1.70, 1.80, 1.90, and 2 GHz. Willamette-core processors have 42 million transistors and a die size of 217 square millimeters.

Northwood-core processors

Northwood-core Pentium 4 processors have 512 KB of eight-way set associative L2 cache and use the 400, 533, or 800 MHz FSB. Intel has produced Northwood-core processors only for Socket 478 at core speeds of 1.6, 1.8, 2.0, 2.2., 2.26, 2.4, 2.5, 2.53, 2.6, 2.67, 2.8, 3.0, 3.06, and 3.2 GHz, with faster variants planned for release later in 2003. Northwood-core processors have 55 million transistors. The original Northwood core used a die size of 146 square millimeters, which in July 2002 was reduced to 131 square millimeters. Although Northwood-core processors dissipate less heat than Willamette-core processors running at the same speed, the smaller die size means the heat dissipated per unit surface area is actually higher. Northwood-core processors, particularly fast ones, accordingly require careful attention to proper cooling.

The Willamette core and Socket 423 were stopgap solutions, released solely to combat AMD's clock speed lead until the "real" Pentium 4—the Socket 478 Northwood-core processor—could be shipped. Intel intended to phase out Socket 423 as a mainstream technology by late 2001, relegating Socket 423 to upgrade status only, but the demand for Socket 478 motherboards and processors caused product shortages until mid-2002. When Intel had resolved those problems, it quickly discontinued Socket 423 motherboards and processors, which are now available only from overstock vendors and as used products.

For additional information about Pentium 4 processors, including detailed identification tables, visit *http://developer.intel.com/design/pentium4/*. For information about Xeon processors, visit *http://developer.intel.com/design/xeon/prodbref/*.

Celeron (Seventh-Generation)

In May 2002, Intel shipped a new series of seventh-generation Celeron processors. Just as the original Celerons were Pentium II and Pentium III variants with smaller L2 caches and slower FSB speeds, the new Celerons are Pentium 4 variants with, you guessed it, smaller caches and slower FSB speeds.

Confusingly, Intel uses the Celeron name for two entirely different series of processors. Like the sixth-generation Celerons, seventh-generation Celerons are positioned as entry-level processors with lower performance than Intel's mainstream processors. Intel walks a fine line with these processors because they must be fast enough to satisfy the price-sensitive entry-level market and compete successfully with low-end AMD processors, yet not be fast enough to cannibalize sales of the more profitable Pentium 4 processors.

Seventh-generation Celerons fit Socket 478 motherboards. Some Socket 478 motherboards do not support the Celeron, and those that do may require a BIOS upgrade. The first seventh-generation Celeron models used a modified 0.18μ Pentium 4 Willamette core called the Willamette-128 core, which has 128 KB of eight-way set associative L2 cache, half that of the Willamette-core Pentium 4. Willamette-128 Celerons were made in 1.7 and 1.8 GHz versions, which shipped in May and June 2002.

In September 2002, Intel began producing Celerons with a modified 0.13μ Pentium 4 Northwood core called the Northwood-128 core. Intel has produced Northwood-128 Celerons running at 2.0, 2.1, 2.2, 2.3, and 2.4 GHz. Like the Willamette-128 Celerons, these processors have 128 KB of eight-way set associative L2 cache, only one-quarter that of the Northwood-core Pentium 4.

One seldom-mentioned fact is that this tiny 128 KB L2 cache greatly impairs performance of a Northwood-128 Celeron relative to that of a Northwood Pentium 4 operating at the same speed. Whereas earlier sixth- and seventh-generation Celerons often had 85% or more the performance of the corresponding Pentium III or Pentium 4, with some benchmarks a Northwood-128 Celeron shows only 65% the performance of a Northwood Pentium 4 operating at the same clock speed. In effect, that means that the fastest available Northwood-128 Celeron is noticeably slower for some tasks, especially multimedia and gaming, than the slowest available Pentium 4, which sells for only a few dollars more. Intel really shot itself in the foot that time.

The days of the Celeron as a separate processor line may be numbered, although it's possible that Intel will take the same course it did by rebranding Tualatin-core Pentium IIIs as Celerons. That is, Intel may begin using the Pentium 4 brand only for its then-current midrange and faster processors. As faster processors are introduced, Intel may simply relabel older, slower Pentium 4 processors as Celerons, without making any actual changes to the processors.

The problem Intel faces with the Celeron is the same problem AMD faced with the Duron, which AMD recently discontinued. When processor prices ranged from $100 to $1,000, it made sense to have two separate lines of processors, economy lines such as the Celeron and Duron, and premium lines such as the Pentium III, Pentium 4, and Athlon. But processor prices have fallen dramatically, and average selling price (ASP) has plummeted even more. When the least-expensive Pentium 4 sold for $300, there was plenty of pricing room for a full series of Celeron processors. Now that entry-level Pentium 4 processors are routinely available for less than $150, there's not much room for a less-expensive, slower line of processors.

Our advice is to avoid seventh-generation Celeron processors except when low system price is the highest priority. In that case, use the least-expensive Northwood-128 Celeron you can find. Otherwise, you'll find that even the least-expensive Pentium 4 significantly outperforms the fastest Celeron and costs little more.

For additional information about Celeron processors, including detailed identification tables, visit *http://developer.intel.com/design/celeron/*.

Intel has manufactured mobile variants of many of its processors, including the Pentium, Pentium II, Celeron, and Pentium III. These mobile versions are used in notebook computers and are not user-replaceable, so for all intents and purposes a notebook computer will always use the processor that was originally installed. For that reason, we have chosen to devote our available space to issues that are more likely to be important to more of our readers. For additional information about Intel mobile processors, visit *http://developer.intel.com/design/mobile/*.

AMD Processors

Until late 1999, Intel had the desktop processor market largely to itself. There were competing incompatible systems such as the Apple Mac, based on processors from Motorola, IBM, and others, but those systems sold in relatively small numbers. Some companies, including Cyrix, IDT, Harris, and AMD itself, made Intel-compatible processors, but those were invariably a step behind Intel's flagship processors. When those companies—which Intel calls "imitators"—were producing enhanced 286s, Intel was already shipping the 386 in volume. When the imitators began producing enhanced 386-compatible processors, Intel had already begun shipping the 486, and so on. Each time Cyrix, AMD, and the others got a step up, Intel would turn around and release its next-generation processor. As a result, these other companies' processors sold at low prices and were used largely in low-end systems. No one could compete with Intel in its core market.

All of that changed dramatically in late 1999, when AMD began shipping the Athlon processor. The Athlon didn't just match the best Intel processors. It was faster than the best Intel could produce, and was in many respects a more sophisticated processor. Intel had a fight on its hands, and it does to this day.

If you ever take a moment to appreciate how much processor you can get for so little money nowadays, give thanks to AMD. Without AMD, we'd all still be running sixth-generation Intel processors at 750 MHz or so. An entry-level Intel processor would cost $200 or $250, and a high-end one (that might run at 1 GHz) would probably cost $1,000 or more. The presence of AMD as a worthy competitor meant that Intel could no longer play the game of releasing faster processors in dribs and drabs at very high prices. Instead, Intel had to fight for its life by shipping faster and faster processors at lower and lower prices. We all have AMD to thank for that, and Intel should thank AMD as well. Although we're sure Intel wishes AMD would just disappear (and vice versa), the fact is that the competition has made both Intel and AMD better companies, as well as providing the obvious benefits to us, the users.

The following sections describe current and recent AMD processor models.

The AMD Athlon Family

The AMD Athlon, which was originally code-named the K7 and began shipping in August 1999, was the first Intel-compatible processor from any maker that could compete on an equal footing with mainstream Intel processors of the time.

First-generation Athlon processors matched or exceeded Katmai-core Pentium III processors in most respects, including (for the first time ever) floating-point performance. Intel finally had a real fight on its hands.

Although AMD represented the Athlon as the first seventh-generation processor, we regard the K7 Athlon as essentially an enhanced sixth-generation processor. Athlon has, in theory, several advantages relative to the aging Intel sixth-generation architecture, including the ability to perform nine operations per clock cycle (versus five for the Pentium III); more integer pipelines (three versus two); more floating-point pipelines (three versus one); a much larger L1 cache (128 KB versus 32 KB); more full x86 decoders (three versus one); and a faster FSB (100 MHz double-pumped to 200 MHz by transferring data on both the rising and falling edges of the clock cycle versus the single-pumped Intel 100/133 MHz bus, which transfers data only once during a clock cycle). While all that was very nice, tests showed that in practice the K7 Athlon and Pentium III were evenly matched at lower clock speeds, with the Pentium III sometimes showing a slight advantage in integer performance, and the Athlon a slight advantage in floating-point performance. At higher clock speeds, however, where the Pentium III L2 cache running at full CPU speed comes into play, the Coppermine Pentium III won most benchmarks handily.

AMD produced two variants of the first-generation Athlon, both in Slot A form. The earliest Athlons used the 0.25μ K7 core, but AMD transitioned within a few months to the improved 0.18μ K75 core, which was code-named Pluto for speeds lower than 1 GHz and Orion in the 1 GHz model. Although the K7 and K75 Athlons were good processors, they had the following drawbacks:

Poor chipset and motherboard support

Initial acceptance of the Athlon was hampered because the only chipset available was the AMD-750, which was originally intended as a technology demonstrator rather than as a production chipset. The VIA KX133 chipset, originally planned to ship at the same time as the Athlon, was significantly delayed, and motherboards based on the KX133 began shipping in volume only in the second quarter of 2000. Many motherboard manufacturers delayed introducing Athlon motherboards, and their first products were crude compared to the elegant motherboards available for the Pentium III. In addition to indifferent quality, stability, compatibility, performance, and features, first-generation Athlon motherboards were in short supply and relatively expensive compared to comparable models for the Pentium III. In addition, KX133-based motherboards had problems of their own, including their inability to support Slot A Thunderbird-core Athlons. AMD soon made it clear that Slot A was an interim solution and that it would quickly transition to Socket A, so manufacturers devoted little effort to improving orphaned Slot A motherboards.

Fractional CPU-speed L2 cache

Like the Deschutes-core Pentium II and the Katmai-core Pentium III, K7 Athlons run L2 cache at half CPU speed. Unlike the Coppermine Pentium III, which uses on-die L2 cache running at full CPU speed, the Athlon uses discrete L2 cache chips, which AMD had to buy from third parties. The Athlon architecture allows running L2 cache at anything from a small fraction of CPU speed to full CPU speed. AMD took advantage of this as it introduced faster versions of the Athlon by reducing the speed of L2 cache relative to processor speed, allowing the company to use less expensive L2 cache chips. The Athlon/700 and slower run L2 cache at 1/2 CPU speed; The Athlon/750, /800, and /850 run L2 cache at 2/5 CPU speed. the Athlon/900 and faster run L2 cache at 1/3 CPU speed. Unfortunately, compared to the full-speed Pentium III Coppermine L2 cache, the slow L2 cache used on fast Athlons decreases performance substantially in many applications.

High power consumption

Early Athlon processors were power-hungry, with some 0.25μ models consuming nearly 60 watts. In comparison, typical Intel processors used one-half to one-third that amount. High power consumption and the resulting heat production had many implications, including the requirement for improved system cooling and larger power supplies. In fact, for the Athlon, AMD took the unprecedented step of certifying power supplies for use with its processor. If you built a system around a first-generation Athlon, you had to make sure that both cooling and power supply were adequate to meet the extraordinarily high current draw and heat dissipation of the processor.

Lack of SMP support

Until mid-2001, no multiprocessor Athlon systems existed. Although all Athlon processors from the earliest models have been SMP-capable (and in fact use the superior point-to-point SMP method rather than Intel's shared bus method), dual-processor Athlon systems had to wait for the release of the AMD-760MP chipset (originally designated the AMD-770) in mid-2001. This early absence of SMP support hurt Athlon acceptance in the critical corporate markets, not so much because there was a huge demand for SMP but because the lack of SMP support led buyers to consider the Athlon a less advanced processor than Intel's offerings.

With the exception of SMP support, which was never lacking in the processor, these faults were corrected in the second generation of Athlon CPUs, which are based on the enhanced K75 core code-named Thunderbird. All early Athlon models used Slot A, which is physically identical to Intel's SC242 (Slot 1), but uses EV-6 electrical signaling rather than the GTL signaling used by Intel. Figure 4-10 shows a Slot A Athlon processor.

Table 4-3 lists the important characteristics of first- and second-generation Slot A Athlon variants (Model 3 is missing because it was assigned to the Duron processor). All Slot A variants use the double-pumped 100 MHz FSB, for an effective 200 MHz FSB speed. First-generation (K7- and K75-core) Athlons are characterized by their use of 512 KB L2 cache running at a fraction of CPU speed and by their use of split core and I/O voltages. Second-generation (Thunderbird-core) Athlons are characterized by their use of a smaller 256 KB L2 cache that operates at full CPU speed and by the elimination of split voltages for core and I/O. Thunderbird processors were produced in very small numbers in Slot A for OEM use, and so are included in this table for completeness, but we've never actually seen a Slot A Thunderbird and don't know anyone who has.

Figure 4-10. AMD Slot A Athlon processor

Table 4-3. Slot A Athlon variants

	Athlon	Athlon	Athlon	Athlon	Athlon	Athlon
Core	K7	K75	K75	K75	Thunderbird	Thunderbird
Model	1	2	2	2	4	4
Production dates	1999, 2000	2000	2000	2000	2000, 2001	2000, 2001
Clock speeds (MHz)	500, 550, 600, 650, 700	550, 600, 650, 700	750, 800, 850	900, 950, 1000	700, 750, 800, 850	900, 950, 1000
L2 cache size	512 KB	512 KB	512 KB	512 KB	256 KB	256 KB
L2 cache speed	1/2 CPU	1/2 CPU	2/5 CPU	1/3 CPU	CPU	CPU
L2 cache bus width	64 bits	64 bits	64 bits	64 bits	64 bits	64 bits
System bus speed	200 MHz	200 MHz	200 MHz	200 MHz	200 MHz	200 MHz
Core voltage	1.6	1.6	1.6 (750) 1.7 (800/ 850)	1.8	1.7	1.75
I/O voltage	3.3	3.3	3.3	3.3	1.7	1.75
Dual CPU-capable	m	m	m	m	m	m
Fabrication process	0.25μ	0.18μ	0.18μ	0.18μ	0.18μ	0.18μ
Interconnects	Al	Al	Al	Al	Al/Cu	Al/Cu
Die size (mm²)	184	102	102	102	120	120
Transistors (million)	22	22	22	22	37	37

Like Intel, which shifted from Slot 1 to Socket 370 for low-end processors, AMD recognized that producing cartridge-based slotted processors was needlessly expensive for the low end, and made it more difficult to compete in the value segment. Also, improvements in fabrication made it possible to embed L2 cache directly on the processor die rather than using discrete cache chips. Accordingly, AMD developed a socket technology, analogous to Socket 370, which it called Socket A. AMD had never denied that Slot A was a stopgap technology, and that Socket A was its mainstream technology of the future. AMD rapidly phased out Slot A during 2000, and by late 2000 had fully transitioned to Socket A. AMD has to date produced four major Athlon variants in Socket A. From earliest to latest, these include:

Athlon (Thunderbird core)

The *Thunderbird Athlon* was originally designated *Athlon Professional* and targeted at the mainstream desktop and entry-level workstation market, in direct competition with the Intel Pentium III and Pentium 4. The first Thunderbird processors used an 0.18μ process with aluminum interconnects, but by late 2000 AMD had transitioned to a 0.18μ process with copper interconnects. During that transition, AMD phased out Slot A Thunderbird models, and shifted entirely to Socket A. Early Thunderbirds used the 100 MHz FSB (double-pumped to 200 MHz), with later models also available in 133 MHz FSB variants. Figure 4-11 shows a Socket A Athlon Thunderbird processor.

Figure 4-11. AMD Socket A Athlon Thunderbird processor

There was to have been another variant of the Thunderbird-core Athlon, code-named Mustang and formally named Athlon Ultra, but that processor shipped only as samples. Mustang was to be a Socket A part, targeted at servers and high-performance workstations and desktops. It was to be an enhanced version of Thunderbird, with reduced core size, lower power consumption, and large, full-speed, on-die L2 cache, probably 2 MB or more. Mustang was to have used a 133 MHz DDR FSB, yielding an effective FSB of 266 MHz. It was intended to use a 0.18μ process with copper interconnects from the start, and to require the AMD-760 chipset or later. Alas, the Mustang never shipped. It would have been a wonderful processor for its time.

Athlon XP (Palomino core)

AMD originally intended to name the Palomino-core Athlon the *Athlon 4*, for obvious reasons. In fact, the first Palomino-core Athlons that shipped were the Mobile Athlon 4 and the 1.0 GHz and 1.2 GHz versions of the Athlon MP. Instead, given Microsoft's schedule for introducing Windows XP, AMD decided its new processor might tag along on the coattails of the new Windows version. Accordingly, AMD finally named the Palomino-core Athlon the Athlon XP. Various architectural changes from the Thunderbird core, detailed later in this section, allow the Athlon XP to achieve considerably higher performance at a given clock speed than a comparable Thunderbird. The Athlon XP is also the first recent AMD processor to use a model designation unrelated to its actual clock speed. All Palomino-core Athlons use the 133/266 MHz FSB. Figure 4-12 shows a Palomino-core Athlon XP processor.

Figure 4-12. AMD Athlon XP processor (image courtesy of Advanced Micro Devices, Inc.)

Athlon XP (Thoroughbred core)

The Thoroughbred core, introduced in June 2002, is really just a die shrink of the Palomino core. In reducing the fabrication process size from 0.18μ to 0.13μ, AMD was able to shrink the die from 128 mm^2 to 81mm^2 (although that increased to 84mm^2 for the XP 2200+ and faster models).

There were no significant architectural changes from the Palomino core to the Thoroughbred core, so performance did not increase with the change to the new core. Transistor count did increase somewhat, from 37.2 million to 37.5 million. AMD also increased the number of metal layers from seven in the Palomino core to eight in the Thoroughbred core, which increases manufacturing complexity and cost, but allows improved routing by optimizing electrical paths within the processor, allowing closer placement of components and faster clock speeds. (For comparison, the Intel Northwood-core Pentium 4 uses only six layers.) The die shrink also allows using lower voltages, which reduces power consumption and heat output significantly. For example, the Palomino-core Athlon XP 2100+ dissipates 72.0W maximum, while the Thoroughbred-core Athlon XP 2100+ dissipates only 62.1W. All Thoroughbred-core Athlons use the 133/266 MHz FSB.

In August 2002, AMD introduced the Thoroughbred "B" core, which increased the number of metal layers to nine, again to allow faster clock speeds. From a functional standpoint, the major change is support for the 166/333 MHz FSB, which was first used with the Athlon XP 2400+ processor. Other than FSB, the only noticeable difference between the Thoroughbred and Thoroughbred "B" cores is that the former reports a CPUID string of 680, while the later reports 681.

Athlon XP (Barton core)

The Barton core, introduced in February 2003 with the Athlon XP 3000+, uses the same 0.13μ fab size as the Thoroughbred core, but the transistor count increases from 37.5 million to 54.3 million. That boost in transistor count increases die size from 84 mm^2 to 101 mm^2. Most of the increase in transistor count and die size is a result of L2 cache size being boosted from 256 KB to 512 KB. Other than the larger cache and larger die size, the Barton core is essentially the same as the Thoroughbred B core.

Despite the doubling of L2 cache size, the Barton core is a less significant upgrade to the Thoroughbred core than one might expect. Benchmarking a Willamette-core Pentium 4 with 256 KB of L2 cache against a Northwood-core Pentium 4 with 512 KB L2 cache running at the same clock speed typically shows performance increases in the 10% to 25% range, and often more. Those who expect a similar improvement going from a 256 KB Thoroughbred-core Athlon to a 512 KB Barton-core Athlon will be disappointed. Differences in processor bandwidth and caching technologies mean that the Athlon benefits much less from the larger L2 cache than does the Pentium 4. On most benchmarks, a Barton-core Athlon shows only a 1% to 5% performance improvement relative to a Thoroughbred-core Athlon running at the same clock speed.

Barton-core processors were initially available only with a 166/333 MHz FSB. Later Barton-core processors, including the Athlon XP 3200+, will ship with the 200/400 MHz FSB.

The really significant changes took place in the upgrade to the Thunderbird and Palomino cores. Other than the reduction from 0.18μ to 0.13μ and the substitution of copper interconnects for aluminum ones, the subsequent changes to the

Athlon core, particularly those to Thoroughbred and Barton, are largely minor tweaks that allow incrementally faster processor speeds. Faced with Intel's modern Pentium 4 core, AMD has been forced to squeeze as much as possible from its aging Athlon technology in order to remain competitive.

By updating the Athlon core and using such marketing gimmicks as naming its processors with model numbers higher than their actual clock speeds, AMD has generally remained competitive. But the Barton is almost certainly the last gasp for the Athlon. In order to counter faster Pentium 4 models from Intel, AMD has no choice. It must relegate the Athlon to the entry level and grab significant market share quickly for its forthcoming Hammer-series processors. The alternative doesn't bear thinking about.

AMD actually first shipped Palomino-core Athlon processors some months before the Athlon/XP desktop processor in the Athlon 4 mobile variant and the Athlon MP/1.0G and Athlon MP/1.2G variants, all of which were designated by their actual clock speeds. Subsequent Palomino-core Athlon processors are all designated using the QuantiSpeed performance rating rather than their actual clock speeds. For example, the Athlon XP/1500+, XP/1600+, XP/1700+, XP/1800+, and XP/1900+ actually run at clock speeds of 1333, 1400, 1466, 1533, and 1600 MHz, respectively, as do the similarly badged Athlon MP SMP-capable variants.

Although Palomino-core processors use the same 0.18μ fabrication process used for Thunderbird-core processors, AMD made several improvements in layout and architecture. Relative to the Thunderbird-core Athlon, Palomino-core Athlons (including the Athlon XP, the Athlon MP, and the Mobile Athlon 4) provide 3% to 7% faster performance clock for clock, and include the following enhancements:

Improved data prefetch mechanism
> This allows the CPU, without being instructed to do so, to use otherwise unused FSB bandwidth to prefetch data that it thinks may be needed soon. This single feature accounts for most of the performance improvement in the Palomino core relative to the Thunderbird, and also increases the processor's dependence on a high-speed FSB/memory bus. Better data prefetch most benefits applications that require high memory bandwidth and have predictable memory access patterns, including video editing, 3D rendering, and database serving.

Enhanced Translation Look-aside Buffers
> *Translation Look-aside Buffers* (TLBs) cache translated memory addresses. Translation is needed for the CPU to access data in main memory. Caching translated addresses makes finding data in main memory much faster. Palomino-core Athlons include the following three enhancements to the TLBs:

> *More L1 Data TLBs*
>> Palomino-core Athlons increase the number of L1 Data TLBs from 32 to 40. The larger number of TLB entries increases the probability that the needed translated address will be cached, thereby improving performance. Even with 40 entries, though, the Palomino-core Athlon has fewer L1 TLB entries than the Intel Pentium III or Pentium 4, and the benefit of this small increase is minor.

L2 TLBs use exclusive architecture

In Thunderbird-core Athlons, the L1 and L2 TLBs are nonexclusive, which means that data cached in the L1 TLB is also cached in the L2 TLB. With the Palomino core, AMD uses an exclusive TLB architecture, which means that data cached in the L1 TLB is not replicated in the L2 TLB. The benefit of exclusive caching is that more entries can be cached in the L2 TLB. The drawback is that using exclusive caching results in additional latency when a necessary address is not cached in the L2 TLB. Overall, exclusive TLB caching again results in a minor performance increase.

TLB entries can be speculatively reloaded

Speculative reloading means that if an address is not present in the TLB, the processor can load the address into the TLB before the instruction that requested the address has finished executing, thereby making the cached address available without the latency incurred by earlier Athlon cores, which could load the TLB entry only after the requesting instruction had executed. Once again, speculative reloading provides a minor performance improvement.

SSE instruction set support

Palomino-core Athlons support the full Intel SSE instruction set, which AMD designates *3DNow! Professional*. Earlier Athlon processors supported only a subset of SSE and so could not set the processor flag to indicate full support. That meant that SSE-capable software could not use SSE on AMD processors, which in turn meant that AMD processors ran SSE-capable software much more slowly than did Intel SSE-capable processors. Palomino-core Athlons set the SSE flag to true, which allows software to use the full SSE instruction set (but *not* the SSE2 instruction set supported by Intel Pentium 4 processors). Also note that although Palomino-core Athlons support the full SSE instruction set, all that means is that they can run SSE-enabled software. It does not necessarily mean that they run SSE-enabled software as fast as a Pentium III or Pentium 4 processor does.

Reduced power consumption

Palomino-core Athlons have an improved design that reduces power consumption by 20% relative to Thunderbird, which reduces heat production and allows the Palomino core to achieve higher clock speeds than the Thunderbird core.

Rather oddly, Morgan-core Durons (based on the Athlon Palomino core) actually draw more current than the older Spitfire-core Durons (based on the Athlon Thunderbird core). In fact, Morgan-core Durons draw the same current as Palomino-core Athlons operating at the same clock speed, which leads us to believe that Morgan-core Durons are literally simply Palomino-core Athlons with part of the L2 cache disabled.

Thermal diode

Palomino-core Athlons are the first AMD processors that include a thermal diode, which is designed to prevent damage to the processor from overheating by shutting down power to the processor if it exceeds the allowable design temperature. Intel processors have included a thermal diode for years. It is nearly impossible to damage an Intel Pentium III or Pentium 4 processor by overheating, even by so extreme a step as removing the heatsink/fan from the processor while it is running. Pentium III systems crash when they overheat badly, but the processor itself is protected from damage. Pentium 4 systems don't even crash, but simply keep running, albeit at a snail's pace. The AMD thermal diode, alas, is an inferior implementation. Although the thermal diode on an AMD processor can shut down the CPU safely when heat builds gradually (as with a failed CPU fan), it does not react quickly enough to protect the processor against a catastrophic overheating event, such as the heatsink falling off.

The Godzilla-size heatsink/fan units used on modern high-speed processors cause catastrophic heatsink/fan unit failures more often than you might think. Whereas Pentium 4 processors use a heatsink/fan retention mechanism that clamps securely to the motherboard, AMD processors still depend on heatsink/fan units that clamp to the CPU socket itself, which isn't designed to support that much weight, particularly in a vertical configuration such as a minitower system. If the heatsink/fan unit comes loose, as it may do when the system is shipped or moved, an AMD processor will literally burn itself to a crisp within a fraction of a second of power being applied. We're talking smoke and flames here. This problem is one of the major causes of AMD systems arriving DOA, but may also occur anytime you move an AMD system. So, if you move an AMD system or if you've just received a new AMD system, *always* take the cover off and make sure the heatsink/fan unit is still firmly attached *before* you apply power to the system. You have been warned.

Although the Athlon XP included some significant technical enhancements over the Thunderbird-core Athlon, the change that received the most attention was AMD's decision to abandon clock speed labeling and instead designate Athlon XP models with a *Performance Rating (PR)* system

AMD K7-, K75-, and Thunderbird-core Athlon processors were labeled with their actual clock speeds. AMD Palomino-core and later Athlon XP processors use AMD's QuantiSpeed designations, which are simply a revival of the hoary PR system. Although AMD claims that these PR numbers refer to relative performance of Palomino-core processors versus Thunderbird-core processors, most observers believe that AMD hopes consumers will associate Athlon XP model numbers with Pentium 4 clock speeds. For example, although the AMD Athlon XP/2800+ processor actually runs at 2250 MHz, we think AMD believes buyers will at least subconsciously associate the 2800+ model number with the Pentium 4/2.8G, which does in fact run at a 2800 MHz clock speed.

AMD has gone to great pains to conceal the actual clock speed of Athlon MP processors from users. For example, it mandates that the actual clock speed not appear in advertisements, and has actually gone so far as to insist that system and motherboard makers modify the BIOS to ensure that it reports only the model number and not the actual clock speed. It's interesting that AMD trumpeted its faster clock speeds until Intel overtook AMD and left AMD in the dust in terms of clock speeds. Now that AMD can no longer match Intel's clock speeds, clock speeds are no longer important. Or so says AMD.

Table 4-4 lists the important characteristics of Socket A Athlon variants as of July 2003. Note that AMD has produced two Thoroughbred B processors using the same 2600+ designation. One runs at 2133 MHz on a 266 MHz FSB and the other at 2083 MHz on a 333 MHz FSB. All Socket A Athlon variants use a 64-bit backside (L2 cache) bus running at full CPU speed and use a shared voltage rail for VCORE and VI/O. For more information about these processors, see *http://www. amd.com*.

Table 4-4. AMD Socket A Athlon variants

	Athlon	Athlon XP	Athlon XP	Athlon XP	Athlon XP
Core	Thunderbird	Palomino	Thoroughbred	Thoroughbred B	Barton
Model	4	6	8 (CPUID 680)	8 (CPUID 681)	10
Production dates	2000, 2001	2001 -	2002, 2003	2002, 2003	2003 -
Clock speeds (MHz)	750, 800, 850, 900, 950, 1000, 1100, 1133, 1200, 1300, 1333, 1400	1333, 1400, 1466, 1533, 1600, 1666, 1733	1467, 1533, 1600, 1667, 1733, 1800	1667, 1800, 2000, 2083 (333), 2133 (266), 2166, 2250	1833, 2083, 2166, 2200
Model designation	n/a	1500+, 1600+, 1700+, 1800+, 1900+, 2000+, 2100+	1700+, 1800+, 1900+, 2000+, 2100+, 2200+	2000+, 2200+, 2400+, 2600+ (333), 2600+ (266), 2700+, 2800+	2500+, 2800+, 3000+ 3200+
L2 cache size	256 KB	256 KB	256 KB	256 KB	512 KB
System bus speed (MHz)	200, 266	266	266	266, 333	333
Voltage (V)	1.7, 1.75	1.75	1.5, 1.6, 1.65	1.5, 1.6, 1.65	1.65
Fabrication process	0.18μ	0.18μ	0.13μ	0.13μ	0.13μ
Interconnects	Al/Cu	Cu	Cu	Cu	Cu
Die size (mm²)	120	128	81, later 84	84	101
Transistors (million)	37	37.2	37.5	37.6	54.3

Other AMD processors

AMD has produced two special-purpose variants of the Athlon, the Duron and the SMP-certified Athlon MP:

Duron

The Duron was AMD's answer to the low-end Intel Celeron. Just as Intel introduced the Celeron in an attempt to maintain a high average selling price for its flagship Pentium III and Pentium 4 processors, AMD introduced the Duron as a "value" version of the Athlon. AMD has produced two models of the Duron:

Duron (Spitfire core)

The Duron, code-named Spitfire and for a short time designated Athlon Value, was targeted at the value desktop market, and was to be a Celeron-killer. With it AMD straddled a fine line between matching Celeron clock speeds and performance on the one hand, versus avoiding cannibalizing sales of Athlon processors on the other. Accordingly, AMD differentiated the Duron by limiting the clock speed of the fastest current Duron to one step below the clock speed of the slowest current Athlon, by using a smaller and less efficient L2 cache, and by making the Duron only in 100 MHz FSB versions (versus the 133 MHz or higher FSB available on some Athlon models). The Spitfire-core Duron was an excellent processor for its time. It unquestionably offered more bang for the buck than any other processor sold by AMD or Intel. Although it achieved reasonable sales volumes in Europe, the Duron never really took off in the U.S. because of the absence of high-quality integrated Duron motherboards.

Duron (Morgan core)

The Morgan-core Duron is simply a refresh of the Spitfire Duron to use the newer Palomino core. The advantages of the Morgan-core Duron over the Spitfire-core Duron are analogous to the advantages of the Palomino-core Athlon over the Thunderbird-core Athlon. The Morgan core is essentially a Palomino core with a smaller and less efficient L2 cache. As it did with the Spitfire, AMD carefully managed the Morgan to prevent cannibalizing sales of the Athlon XP. The fastest current Morgan was always at least one step slower than the slowest current Athlon XP. In terms of absolute performance clock for clock, the Morgan slightly outperforms the Coppermine-core Pentium III and the Tualatin-core Celeron.

The Appaloosa-core Duron, based on the Thoroughbred-core Athlon XP, was announced but later canceled. The Duron was a victim of AMD's success with the Athlon. As faster Athlons were introduced at lower prices, the Duron was simply squeezed out of its market niche. The Duron is still available as of July 2003, but is likely to disappear before year end. Figure 4-13 shows an AMD Duron processor.

Athlon MP

Even the first Athlon processors had the circuitry needed to support dual-processor operation. That feature was useless until the introduction of the

Figure 4-13. AMD Duron processor (image courtesy of Advanced Micro Devices, Inc.)

AMD-760MP chipset because no prior Athlon chipset supported dual processors. In mid-2001, Tyan shipped its 760MP-based Thunder motherboard. It supported dual Athlons, but was expensive and required a special power supply. In late 2001, Tyan shipped the inexpensive Tiger MP dual Athlon board, which used a standard power supply. Suddenly, dual Athlon systems were affordable, and many enthusiasts set out to build them.

AMD capitalized on this new market by introducing Athlon XP processors certified for dual-processor operation, which they named the Athlon MP. Athlon MP processors are binned (hand-picked and individually tested) for reliable SMP operation, or so the rumor has it. We have our doubts. We and many of our readers have run dual Athlon XPs successfully. Alas, AMD has disabled SMP operation on recent Athlon XP processors. If you want a dual Athlon system using current products, the only option is to use SMP-certified (and more expensive) Athlon MP processors. AMD has made Athlon MP processors using two cores:

Athlon MP (Palomino core)
>   The first Athlon MP models used the Palomino core. They shipped in June 2001, four months before AMD introduced the first Palomino-core Athlon XP models. At that time, AMD had not yet decided to use model numbers rather than clock speeds to designate its processors, so the first two Athlon MP models were designated the Athlon MP/1.0G and the Athlon MP/1.2G. Those numbers accurately reflect their true clock speeds of 1000 MHz and 1200 MHz, respectively. By October 2001, when AMD began rolling out the new Palomino-core Athlon XPs, it had decided to designate the first model the Athlon XP/1500+, even though

its actual clock speed was only 1333 MHz. All subsequent Athlon MP processors are designated by model number rather than clock speed. Functionally, the Palomino-core Athlon MP is identical to the Palomino-core Athlon XP.

Athlon MP (Thoroughbred core)

Functionally, the Thoroughbred-core Athlon MP is identical to the Thoroughbred-core Athlon XP. When AMD transitioned to Thoroughbred-core Athlon XPs, it did not immediately introduce Athlon MP processors based on the Thoroughbred core. Instead, AMD began the staged introduction of Athlon MP processors that continues today. For example, in June 2002, AMD introduced Thoroughbred-core Athlon XP models 1700+ through 2200+. It was not until late August that AMD introduced Thoroughbred-core Athlon MP models at 2000+ and 2200+, just days after it introduced the Athlon XP 2400+ and 2600+. AMD says the delay is needed to certify faster models for SMP operation, which seems to us a reasonable explanation.

Athlon MP (Barton core)

In May 2003 AMD shipped the Athlon MP 2800+, the first Athlon MP based on the Barton core. The 2800+ may also be the final Athlon MP model, because AMD now devotes all of its attention to the Opteron. Functionally, the Barton-core Athlon MP is identical to the Barton-core Athlon XP, including the increase from 256 KB to 512 KB of L2 cache. Interestingly, a few examples of the Athlon MP 2800+ with 333 MHz FSB have surfaced. We don't understand why AMD would produce such a processor. The 760MPX (the only Athlon chipset that supports SMP) supports a maximum FSB speed of 266 MHz, which seems to render a 333 MHz FSB Athlon MP pointless. We can only speculate that AMD plans a refresh of the 760MPX to add support for the 333 MHz FSB.

Table 4-5 lists the important characteristics of Socket A Duron and Athlon MP variants as of July 2003. For more information about these processors, see *http://www.amd.com*.

Table 4-5. Socket A Duron and Athlon MP variants

	Duron	Duron	Athlon MP	Athlon MP	Athlon MP	Athlon MP
Core	Spitfire	Morgan	Palomino	Palomino	Thorough-bred	Barton
Model	3	7	6	6	8	10
Production dates	2000 - 2001	2001 - 2003	2001 - 2002	2001 - 2002	2002 -	2003-
Clock speeds (MHz)	600, 650, 700, 750, 800, 850, 900, 950	1000, 1100, 1200, 1300	1000, 1200	1333, 1400, 1533, 1600, 1667, 1733	1667, 1800, 2000, 2133	2133
Model designation	n/a	n/a	n/a	1500+, 1600+, 1800+, 1900+, 2000+, 2100+	2000+, 2200+, 2400+, 2600+	2800+

Table 4-5. *Socket A Duron and Athlon MP variants (continued)*

	Duron	Duron	Athlon MP	Athlon MP	Athlon MP	Athlon MP
L2 cache size	64 KB	64 KB	256 KB	256 KB	256 KB	512 KB
System bus speed	200 MHz	200 MHz	266 MHz	266 MHz	266 MHz	266 MHz
Voltage (V)	1.5V, 1.6V	1.75V	1.75V	1.75V	1.6V, 1.65V	1.6V
Dual CPU-capable	○	○	●	●	●	●
Fabrication process	0.18μ	0.18μ	0.18μ	0.18μ	0.13μ	0.13μ
Interconnects	Cu	Cu	Cu	Cu	Cu	Cu
Die size (mm²)	100	106	128	128	85	101
Transistors (million)	25.00	25.18	37.2	37.2	37.5	54.3

Choosing a Processor

The processor you choose determines how fast the system runs, and how long it will provide subjectively adequate performance before you need to replace the processor or the system itself. Buying a processor just fast enough to meet current needs means that you'll have to upgrade in a few months. But processor pricing has a built-in law of diminishing returns. Spending twice as much on a processor doesn't buy twice the performance. In fact, you'll be lucky to get 25% more performance for twice the money. So although it's a mistake to buy too slow a processor, it's also a mistake to buy one that's too fast. Consider the following issues when choosing a processor:

Horizon
> What kind of applications do you run and how long do you want the system to be usable without requiring an upgrade? If you run mostly standard productivity applications and don't upgrade them frequently, a low-end processor may still be fast enough a year or more after you buy it. If you run cutting-edge games or other demanding applications, buy a midrange or faster processor initially, and expect to replace it every six months to a year. But expect to pay a price for remaining on the bleeding edge.

Hassle
> Do you mind upgrading your system frequently? If you don't mind replacing the processor every six to 12 months, you can get most of the performance of a high-end system at minimal cost by replacing the processor frequently with the then-current midrange processor. In the past, this was easier with AMD processors because AMD has used Socket A for years and had standardized on 100/200 MHz and 133/266 MHz FSBs. It was sometimes possible to install a current processor in a two-year-old motherboard with only a BIOS upgrade.

Intel made things much more difficult, replacing Socket 370 with Socket 423 and then Socket 478, and introducing faster FSB speeds frequently. Although many considered these changes as cynical planned obsolescence, in fact these changes resulted simply from Intel's much faster product development cycle. The situation is different now. Intel has stabilized around Socket 478 and the 800 MHz FSB (although the forthcoming Prescott processors will use a different socket), and AMD is in a state of flux. AMD recently introduced the 166/333 MHz and 200/400 MHz FSBs for the Athlon, which will rapidly render older motherboards obsolete. Also, AMD has deemphasized Athlon product development in favor of its forthcoming Hammer-series processors, which are entirely incompatible with the Athlon series. On balance, Intel actually offers a better upgrade path for now, although that may change depending on the decisions AMD makes with regard to Hammer-series processors.

Trade-offs

If you're working on a fixed budget, don't spend too much on the processor to the detriment of the rest of the system. Instead of spending $300 on a fast processor and compromise on the other components, you're better off spending $150 on a midrange processor and using the other $150 to buy more memory, a faster hard disk, and better video. A low-end Pentium 4 with lots of memory, a fast hard drive, and a good video adapter blows the doors off the fastest Pentium 4 with inadequate memory, a slow hard drive, and a cheesy video card every day of the week. Don't make yourself "processor-poor."

Form factor

Keep form factor in mind when you're shopping for a processor, particularly if you're also buying a motherboard:

Socket 7

Don't consider buying a Socket 7 processor, even as an inexpensive upgrade to a working system. Any money spent on Socket 7 is wasted. Retire the old system to less-demanding duties, and build or buy a new system instead.

Slot 1

Slot 1 was obsolete by the end of 2001. Although new Slot 1 processors remain in limited distribution, new Slot 1 motherboards are now almost impossible to find. An existing Slot 1 system may or may not be a good upgrade candidate depending on the motherboard characteristics. Some Slot 1 motherboards support fast Pentium III processors, and can be upgraded at reasonable expense. For example, we recently upgraded an older Pentium II server to a Pentium III using a salvaged processor. Because we used a relatively slow Pentium III processor, even if we had to buy the processor, the total upgrade cost would have been about $75. Performance more than doubled, which gives that server another two years or more of useful life.

Other Slot 1 motherboards have neither BIOS support nor adequate VRMs to support faster processors. Although it's possible to upgrade those systems with marginally faster Slot 1 processors, doing so makes no economic sense. Before you upgrade any Slot 1 system, check prices carefully. Some Slot 1 processors are very expensive relative to the performance boost they provide. You may be able to replace the motherboard, processor, *and* memory with Socket 478 Pentium 4 or Socket A Athlon components for little more than the cost of the Slot 1 processor alone.

Slot A

Like Intel processors, AMD Athlon processors were originally produced in slotted versions, which were subsequently replaced by socketed versions. Slot A motherboards and processors are now almost impossible to find, and any Slot A motherboard is now so old that it is a poor upgrade candidate. If for some reason you must replace the processor in a Slot A system, pay careful attention to the chipset it uses. Motherboards based on the AMD-750 chipset can use Slot A processors based on the K7, K75, and Thunderbird cores (although Slot A Thunderbirds are difficult to find). Motherboards based on the VIA KX133 chipset are incompatible with Slot A Thunderbird Athlon processors, but can use Athlons based on the K7 and K75 cores. As of July 2003, Slot A processors are still in limited distribution, but soon the only alternative will be the used market.

Socket 370

As of July 2003 Socket 370 is moribund. Intel pulled out all the stops to push the Pentium 4 at the expense of its sixth-generation Celeron and Pentium III processors, and by mid-2002 Socket 370 was no longer a mainstream technology. Intel still offers a limited selection of Socket 370 Celeron and Pentium III processors. Alas, Intel no longer makes Socket 370 motherboards, so third-party motherboard makers are now the only source for new Socket 370 motherboards.

Although it no longer makes economic sense to build a new Socket 370 system, existing Socket 370 systems may be economically upgradeable. When upgrading an older Socket 370 system, verify compatibility between your motherboard and the Socket 370 processor you propose to buy. There are many incompatibilities between older motherboards and newer processors. Some problems can be solved with a simple BIOS update, but many are unsolvable because the older motherboard's chipset or VRMs do not support newer Socket 370 processors.

Socket A

In the past, AMD did a much better job than Intel at maintaining backward compatibility. Intel changed sockets and FSB speeds frequently, but AMD just kept using Socket A and the standard 100/200 and 133/266 MHz FSB speeds. The Hammer-series processors, due later in 2003, will change that, but Socket A motherboards and processors will remain available for at least the next year or two. As long as you don't mind buying into an obsolescent technology, Socket A remains a good choice for a new system until Hammer-series processors and motherboards become inexpensive mainstream products.

Older Socket A systems may or may not be good upgrade candidates. In general, older-model Socket A motherboards can use newer Socket A processors, although perhaps not the fastest models. A Socket A system that supports only the 200 MHz FSB is probably too old to be economically upgradeable. For such systems, replace the motherboard, processor, and memory with current products. Most Socket A systems that support the 266 MHz FSB or higher and that support at least PC2100 DDR-SDRAM are excellent upgrade candidates. By replacing an older Duron or Athlon processor with a current low-end Athlon, you may be able to double system performance for much less than $100. Before you make such an upgrade, verify that your motherboard supports the specific processor model and speed that you plan to install. You will probably need to upgrade the BIOS as well.

If your goal is to build a dual-processor system, your best option is a pair of Socket A Athlon MP processors running in an AMD-760MPX based motherboard. As always, an older motherboard may have BIOS or VRM issues with newer processors, so you still need to verify compatibility.

 Always verify the cooling requirements of a replacement processor. The existing CPU heatsink/fan unit may fit the new processor, but that's no guarantee that it is adequate to cool the new processor adequately. We almost learned that the hard way. In late 2002, AMD sent us a preproduction sample of its new 333 MHz FSB Athlon 2600+, including just the bare CPU. We verified that the ASUS A7N8X Deluxe motherboard supported the 2600+, but we didn't think about the heatsink. We'd already squirted thermal goop onto the processor and were about to install an off-the-shelf heatsink when we remembered that we'd gotten in some sample heatsinks from DynaTron, and decided to try one of those. That was fortunate because as we were reading the DynaTron literature we realized that the heatsink we were about to use was rated only for XP 2000+ and slower Athlons. If we'd installed that heatsink and powered up the system, our shiny new 2600+ processor might have burnt itself to a crisp in seconds. Processors aren't much good if you let the smoke out.

Socket 423

Socket 423 was Intel's first socket for the Pentium 4, and was simply a stopgap solution that allowed Intel to bring Pentium 4 processors to market quickly to compete with the AMD Athlon on clock speed. Socket 423 processors and motherboards are obsolete. Socket 423 motherboards are nearly impossible to find, although Socket 423 processors remain in limited distribution. A Socket 423 system is a poor upgrade candidate because the fastest available Socket 423 processor will be little or no faster than the processor already installed. Replacing the motherboard, processor, and memory is a far better solution.

Socket 478

A Socket 478 processor is the best choice if you are building a new mainstream system. An existing Socket 478 system can easily be upgraded simply by dropping in a faster Socket 478 processor, a condition that is likely to remain true for some time. As always, it's possible that BIOS, chipset, and VRM issues may restrict the speed of the fastest Socket 478 processor that can be installed in a particular motherboard, but Socket 478 currently offers the best options for future upgradability.

When upgrading a system, the existing motherboard determines upgradability, as follows:

Socket 7 and earlier motherboards

These motherboards are simply too old to upgrade economically. We recommend retiring such ancient systems, or discarding them entirely.

Slot 1 motherboards

Slot 1 Pentium II and Celeron processors remain in limited distribution, although we expect them to disappear entirely by the end of 2003 or early 2004. Fortunately, some Slot 1 motherboards can be upgraded by using a slocket adapter, which accepts a Socket 370 processor and plugs into the motherboard Slot 1. The best candidates for such upgrades are motherboards designed for the Pentium III that support the 100 MHz or 133 MHz FSB. Even if a particular motherboard can be upgraded via slocket, it may be limited by BIOS, chipset, or VRM issues as to which particular Socket 370 processors are usable. In general, FC-PGA Celerons are the most likely to work, assuming that the motherboard supports the Celeron L2 caching method. An FC-PGA Coppermine-core Pentium III may or may not work, depending on the particular slocket/processor combination and the chipset and BIOS configuration of the motherboard. We know of no slocket that allows FC-PGA2 Celerons and Pentium IIIs to be used in Slot 1 motherboards. Before you attempt to upgrade a Slot 1 motherboard with a slocket, verify with the slocket maker that the slocket, processor, and motherboard you plan to use are compatible.

Slot A motherboards

Slot A processors are now almost impossible to find new. Slot A motherboards are now so old that it makes no sense to spend money upgrading them. Instead, replace the processor, motherboard, and memory with current products. You can buy a decent Socket A processor, motherboard, *and* memory for less than $200, which makes messing around with an obsolete processor and motherboard a complete waste of time.

Socket 370 motherboards

Upgrading a Socket 370 system *should* be easy. Unfortunately, it often isn't. The problem with upgrading Socket 370 motherboards is that there have been so many variants of the socket itself and processors intended to fit it that determining compatibility can be difficult. Any Socket 370 processor physically fits any Socket 370 socket, but there are actual pinout differences between early Socket 370 sockets and processors and later versions. Late-model Socket 370 processors—Coppermine- and Tualatin-core Celerons and Pentium IIIs—will not operate in early-model Socket 370 motherboards, and early-model Socket 370 processors—Mendocino-core Celerons and Katmai-core Pentium IIIs—may or may not operate in later-model Socket 370 motherboards. In addition, chipset issues are important with Socket 370 because early Socket 370 chipset revisions do not support later Socket 370 processors, even though the processor is otherwise compatible electrically and physically with the socket. Intel rationalized this situation in late 2001 by introducing its so-called "Universal" Socket 370 motherboards, which can accept any Socket 370 processor. If you intend to upgrade the processor in a Socket 370 system, the best advice is first to determine exactly what motherboard you have (including revision level). Once you've done that, visit the motherboard maker's web site and read the technical documentation to determine which currently available Socket 370 processors can be used in that motherboard.

Socket A, Socket 423, and Socket 478

Motherboards that use any of these sockets can be upgraded using current processors. Socket 423 is a poor upgrade candidate because only relatively slow processors are available for it. Socket A and Socket 478 motherboards are generally good upgrade candidates because there are numerous models of fast, inexpensive processors available for both of them. As always, check the documentation for the motherboard to ensure that it supports the type, FSB speed, and clock speed of the processor you plan to install. Ordinarily, such upgrades are relatively straightforward, requiring a BIOS upgrade at most.

Forthcoming AMD and Intel Processors

Intel and AMD constantly strive to out-do each other in bringing faster and more capable processors to market. In late 2003 and into 2004, each company will be ramping up its new-generation desktop processors. Although the current Athlon XP and Pentium 4 processors will continue to sell in large numbers throughout 2003 and into 2004, the future definitely belongs to these new processor lines. AMD hopes to get a foothold in the corporate market and to increase their general market share with their new desktop processors, but Intel has some plans of its own to protect its 80%+ general market share and its nearly 100% corporate market share.

 As we write this in July 2003, only the Opteron processor is shipping, and only in limited numbers. The Athlon 64 and the Prescott/Pentium 5 are not yet shipping and we have been unable to get pre-production samples from AMD and Intel. Accordingly, much of this section is speculative, based on published information that is subject to change, industry rumors, and informed speculation. However, we thought it worthwhile to include the best information we had available as we went to press, because even imperfect or incomplete information may be useful to our readers.

AMD Opteron and Athlon 64

By mid-2002, AMD was struggling to produce Athlons that could match Pentium 4 performance. By July 2003, it was obvious to nearly everyone that the Athlon XP had reached the end of the line and that the 3200+ would almost certainly be the final Athlon XP processor. AMD was able to push the Athlon core further than anyone expected, eventually reaching a core clock speed of 2.2 GHz in the Barton-core Athlon XP 3200+ model. AMD also expanded L2 cache from 256 KB on earlier cores to 512 KB on the Barton core, and increased FSB speeds from 266 MHz to 333 MHz and eventually to 400 MHz on the final Athlon XP models.

But all of these enhancements yielded only marginal performance improvements over earlier Athlon models. The real problem was that the Athlon core itself had reached its limits, while Intel's Pentium 4 core wasn't even breathing hard. AMD badly needed an entirely new processor core if they were to compete with Intel on anything like a level playing field.

In April 2003, AMD shipped their new-generation processor, code-named K8 or Sledgehammer, officially named Opteron, and ironically dubbed "Lateron" by pundits because of the repeated and lengthy delays AMD suffered in bringing this processor to market. (Nor is AMD alone in having evil nicknames applied to its processors. Some wags called the original Itanium 1 the "Itanic" because, like its namesake, it sank without a trace.)

AMD will produce two processor lines based on the K8 core. The Opteron is intended for servers, and began shipping in April 2003. The Athlon 64 is a cut-down version of the Opteron intended for desktop systems, and is to begin shipping in September 2003. The key feature of both processors is that they support both 32-bit and 64-bit instructions, and can dynamically alternate 32- and 64-bit threads.

In contrast to the 64-bit Intel Itanium, which executes 64-bit code natively but 32-bit IA-32 code only via slow translation, the Opteron and Athlon 64 are 64-bit processors that can execute 64-bit code using the AMD64 instruction set—called "long" mode—and can also execute standard 32-bit code natively, called "legacy" mode. To support 32- and 64-bit operations in one processor, AMD modified the Athlon XP core to add eight 64-bit general-purpose registers and eight 64-bit versions of the original eight 32-bit general purpose registers. These 64-bit registers are accessible only when the processor is operating in long mode. In legacy mode, the Opteron and Athlon 64 processors appear to 32-bit software as a standard 32-bit Athlon processor.

The Opteron and Athlon 64 are incompatible with current chipsets and motherboards, so using either requires buying or building a new system. As of July 2003, Opteron systems and motherboards are in limited distribution. We expect Athlon 64 products to become available in September 2003.

Opteron

The Opteron is based on the variant of the K8 core codenamed Sledgehammer. Various Opteron models support 1-, 2-, 4-, and 8-way operation and are targeted at servers. AMD plans to produce at least three Opteron series. Opteron 100-series processors support only 1-way processing, and are due in September 2003. Opteron 200-series processors support 1- and 2-way processing, and shipped in April 2003. Opteron 400-series processors support 1-, 2-, 4-, and 8-way processing, and are to ship in September 2003 and into 2004.

Rather than the clock speed designations or QuantiSpeed model numbers AMD used for earlier processors, AMD assigns each Opteron model an arbitrary number to indicate relative performance. For example, the Opteron processor roadmap includes the 140, 240, and 840 models, which operate at 1.4 GHz; the 1.6 GHz 142, 242, and 842 models; and the 1.8 GHz 144, 244, and 844 models. AMD plans to release later Opteron models operating at 2.0 GHz (presumably the 146, 246, and 846 models), as well as models operating at 2.2 GHz (148, 248, and 848).

Opteron processors use 6.4 GB/s HyperTransport Technology (HTT) channels to provide a high-speed link between the processor components themselves and to the outside world. The Opteron has three HTT channels, which may be either of two types. Coherent HTT channels link the processor to other Opteron processors. Opteron 100-series, 200-series, and 800-series processors have zero, one, or three coherent HTT channels, respectively. Standard HTT channels link the processor to I/O interfaces such as a Southbridge or PCI Express bridge.

 Do not confuse AMD HTT (HyperTransport Technology) with Intel HTT (Hyper-Threading Technology). You'd think they could come up with different TLAs. It isn't like there aren't lots of letters to choose from.

The Opteron features a 1024 KB L2 cache and a dual-channel DDR333 memory controller, which uses a 144-bit interface that requires 72-bit ECC memory. Relocating the memory controller from the chipset, where it has traditionally resided, directly onto the processor core allows memory to be more tightly integrated with the processor for higher performance. The downside is that the Opteron is limited to using memory no faster than DDR333 unless AMD changes the processor core itself, or unless a chipset maker adds an external memory controller.

 Informed sources speculate that AMD may tweak the shipping K8 core to add support for DDR400 and perhaps DDR533. Support for DDR-II will come no earlier than mid-2004, pending JEDEC approval of a final DDR-II specification.

The Opteron uses Socket 940, newly introduced by AMD for this processor. Relative to Socket 462, those extra contacts are used primarily to support the three HTT channels.

Athlon 64

The Athlon 64 processor is based on the variant of the K8 core codenamed Clawhammer. The Athlon 64 supports 1- and 2-way operation, is due in September 2003, and is targeted at desktop systems. The Athlon 64 differs from the Opteron in the following important respects:

HyperTransport Technology channels
    Rather than the three HTT channels used by the Opteron, the Athlon 64 has only one HTT channel.

Memory controller
    Rather than the 144-bit dual-channel DDR333 ECC memory controller used by the Opteron, the Athlon 64 has a 64-bit single-channel DDR333 non-ECC

memory controller. (Shipping models may include DDR400 support.) The narrower memory interface of the Athlon 64 means its memory bandwidth is half that of the Opteron. Like the Opteron, the Athlon 64 integrates the memory controller onto the processor.

Cache size

The Athlon 64 and Opteron both have the AMD-standard 128 KB L1 cache, with 64 KB allocated to instructions and 64 KB to data. Opteron processors provide 1 MB of L2 cache. Athlon 64 processors are available with either 256 KB or 1 MB L2 cache. Our moles tell us that for performance reasons, AMD may decide to ship the "small" Athlon 64 with 512 KB L2 cache rather than 256 KB.

Chipset support

Most Opteron systems will be built around the server-class AMD 8000-series chipset. Most Athlon 64 systems will use desktop-class chipsets such as the *n*VIDIA *n*Force3, the VIA K8T800/K8M800, and others. Based on our experiences with the *n*Force and *n*Force2 Athlon chipsets, we expect the *n*Force3 to be the best Athlon 64 chipset.

The Athlon 64 uses Socket 754, another new AMD socket. As with Socket 940, the additional contacts are necessary to support the single HTT channel supported by the Athlon 64. Because the Athlon 64 has only one HTT channel, it can use the smaller socket.

Table 4-6 details the important characteristics of the Opteron and Athlon 64 processors, with the Barton-core Athlon XP shown for comparison. Most of the items are self-explanatory, but a couple deserve comment.

Generation

AMD regards the Athlon XP as seventh-generation and the Opteron/Athlon 64 as eighth-generation. We consider both of those processor families to be hybrids, straddling the generational boundaries defined by Intel processors. In particular, the 64-bitness of the Opteron and Athlon 64 give them a definite claim to eighth-generation status, but architecturally they remain near relatives of the hybrid sixth/seventh-generation Athlon XP.

Fabrication process

With the Opteron and Athlon 64, AMD uses the Silicon-on-Insulator (SOI) process rather than the traditional CMOS process. SOI offers potentially huge benefits, but at a correspondingly high risk. During the first half of 2003, AMD's problems with SOI in getting high yields at fast clock speeds were widely reported in the industry press. We think the most important issue for the new AMD processors is how well and how quickly the AMD Dresden fab will be able to master SOI production. If they succeed, they will produce high yields of the new processors and be able to scale clock speeds up quickly. If they fail, the Opteron and Athlon 64 will be expensive to produce and will languish at lower clock speeds. The phrase "bet the company" is often used in the high technology field, but in this case we think AMD is indeed betting the company on the success of their SOI process.

Table 4-6. Characteristics of Opteron and Athlon 64 versus Athlon XP

	Opteron	Athlon 64	Athlon XP
Core	Sledgehammer	Clawhammer	Barton
Generation	7th/8th	7th/8th	6th/7th
CPU Socket	940	754	462
Production dates	April 2003 –	September 2003 –	February 2003 –
Clock speeds (MHz)	1400, 1600, 1800	1600, 1800, 2000	1833, 2083, 2133, 2200
Model designation	240, 242, 244	3400+, 3600+, 3800+	2500+, 2800+, 3000+, 3200+
L2 cache size	1024 KB	256, 512 (?), or 1024 KB	512 KB
External bus speed	333 MHz DDR-SDRAM 19.2 GB/s HTT (triple)	333 MHz DDR-SDRAM 6.4 GB/s HTT (single)	333, 400 MHz DDR-SDRAM EV-6
Instruction set	IA-32/AMD64	IA-32/AMD64	IA-32
Multimedia support	MMX, 3DNow!, SSE, SSE2	MMX, 3DNow!, SSE, SSE2	MMX, 3DNow!, SSE
Voltage (V)	1.55	1.55	1.65
Fabrication process	0.13 (CMOS, SOI)	0.13 (CMOS, SOI)	0.13 (CMOS)
Interconnects	Cu	Cu	Cu
Die size	193 mm^2	104 mm^2	101 mm^2
Transistors (million)	105.9+	67	54.3

Intel Pentium 5?

Intel and AMD play a constant game of leapfrog. The introduction of the Opteron/Athlon 64 almost demanded that Intel introduce a new processor of its own. That processor is the Prescott-core Pentium, due in the fourth quarter of 2003, which Intel may or may not call the Pentium 5.

On balance, we think Intel will decide to name their new processor the Pentium 5, both for marketing reasons and for technical reasons. From a marketing standpoint, Intel would clearly like to counter the Opteron and Athlon processors with a newly-named processor of their own. From a technical standpoint, the improvements in architecture and instruction set are sufficient to justify the Pentium 5 name for the Prescott-core processor.

No matter what Intel chooses to call this processor, it is a significant improvement on the current Northwood-core Pentium 4. Relative to current Northwood-core processors, the Prescott-core processors increase L1 cache size, boost L2 cache from 512 KB to 1024 KB (matching the new AMD processors), and increase pipeline depth to enable higher core frequencies.

Just those enhancements would have made life difficult for the new AMD processors. But a more significant enhancement lurks within Prescott. The Prescott New Instructions (PNI) are 13 new instructions that extend the SSE and SSE2 multimedia instruction sets used by earlier Intel processors. In particular, three of the new PNI instructions are worth noting. One adds support for AV encoding—as opposed to AV decoding, which was supported by earlier Intel processors—and two improve thread control for Hyper-Threading Technology (HTT) operations.

The new HTT thread control instructions are likely to boost performance substantially, with less sensitivity to application mix. In the past, the benefit of HTT depended largely on the specific applications being run. Some applications showed major performance improvements with HTT, most applications showed no change, and some actually ran slower with HTT enabled. The improved HTT threading support available with PNI means that HTT will become more generally useful. For more information about PNI, visit *http://cedar.intel.com/media/pdf/ PNI_LEGAL3.pdf*.

Prescott-core processors may also have a major hidden feature. We admit that this is pure speculation on our part, but we do have some historical evidence for our beliefs. Intel built Hyper-Threading Technology into Northwood-core processors, where it remained hidden until Intel chose to reveal it. We think history may repeat itself. Intel may have embedded their Yamhill technology into Prescott as a hidden feature.

Intel's world view is that 32-bit processors are sufficient for desktop systems, that only datacenters require 64-bit processors, and that 64-bit processors should operate natively in 64-bit mode rather than as 32/64-bit hybrids. But Intel always has a Plan B, and in this case Plan B is Yamhill. Yamhill is, in effect, Intel's version of AMD's hybrid AMD64 architecture. Intel would prefer to drive people to its native 64-bit Itanium architecture. But if that fails and AMD64 catches on, Intel can spring Yamhill as a nasty surprise to AMD. Don't be surprised if that happens.

Table 4-7 shows the important characteristics of the Prescott-core "Pentium 5", with the Northwood-core Pentium 4 shown for comparison.

Table 4-7. Characteristics of Prescott "Pentium 5" versus Pentium 4

	"Pentium 5"	Pentium 4
Core	Prescott	Northwood "A"
Generation	7th/8th	7th
CPU Socket	478, 775	478
Production dates	October 2003 (?) –	November 2002 –
Clock speeds (MHz)	3200, 3400, and higher	2400, 2600, 2800, 3000, 3060, 3200
L2 cache size	1024 KB	512 KB
External bus speed	800, 1066, 1200 MHz	400, 533, 800 MHz
Instruction set	IA-32/Yamhill-64 (?)	IA-32
Multimedia support	MMX, SSE, SSE2, PNI	MMX, SSE, SSE2
Voltage (V)	1.25	1.500, 1.525, 1.550
Fabrication process	0.09 (CMOS)	0.13 (CMOS)
Interconnects	Cu	Cu
Die size	109 mm^2	131 mm^2
Transistors (million)	~ 100	55

Our Thoughts

We won't comment in detail on server processors, because we don't understand that market well enough. We note, however, that IT managers are notoriously conservative in adopting new platforms, and the perception of Intel as the tried-and-true 64-bit solution, particularly with regard to chipsets, probably militates against the broad acceptance of the Opteron in the datacenter. We're sure that the Opteron will have some "wins", but overall we think that 32-bit Intel processors will continue to dominate PC-server space. Those who need the additional memory addressability and other features of 64-bit processors will probably continue using heavy iron, at least in the short term.

On the desktop side, the picture isn't much better for AMD. We think the Intel Pentium 5 (or whatever Intel chooses to call it) will walk all over the Athlon 64. Although the Athlon 64 runs 32-bit code competently—something Intel has never been able to achieve with its 64-bit processors—its forte is 64-bit operations, and for now 32-bit operations are sufficient for the desktop. The only 64-bit operating system available is Linux, although Microsoft promises a 64-bit Windows Real Soon Now. Even if that comes to pass, the dearth of 64-bit applications programs means that the Athlon 64 will be operating in 32-bit mode nearly all the time.

Considered as a 32-bit processor, the Athlon 64 is in effect a slightly enhanced Athlon XP. It operates at a severe disadvantage relative to the Prescott-core Pentium. AMD had severe teething pains getting the K8 core running faster than 1.8 GHz, and we do not expect the K8 core to scale nearly as well as the new 0.09μ Intel core. We think it likely that when the new Intel core debuts at 3.4 GHz, it will match or exceed the fastest Athlon 64 model in most 32-bit operations. And, while AMD has to work very hard for each increment in Athlon 64 clock speed, we expect the new Intel core to scale effortlessly to 5 GHz or faster.

Although we admire AMD and appreciate the results of their competition with Intel, we're forced to conclude that AMD is likely to be an also-ran in the desktop processor race throughout 2003 and well into 2004. The arrival of 64-bit Windows and 64-bit applications may help somewhat, but we think it will be insufficient to turn the tide. Certainly, 64-bit processing (and memory address-ability) will be a blessing for some people. Those who work with huge databases or do serious image processing and video work can use every bit of horsepower and memory they can get. But for the most part we think 64-bit processing for the desktop is a technology of the future, and is unlikely in the short term to create a large demand for the new 64-bit AMD processors.

Installing a Processor

The following sections describe the steps required to install and configure standard slotted and socketed processors. The steps we describe are generally applicable to any modern processor of a given type, but the details may vary slightly between different processors, particularly with regard to such things as configuring the motherboard and installing heatsink/fan units. If this is the first time you've installed a processor, or if you are in doubt about any step, refer to the documentation provided by the manufacturer of your specific processor and motherboard.

Before you install any processor, make sure that you have identified exactly both the processor itself and the motherboard you plan to install it in. If the processor is not new, you can identify it using the steps described earlier in this chapter. All high-quality motherboards have information printed on the board itself that identifies the manufacturer, model, and revision number. If the board does not contain such information, you may be able to identify the board by writing down the full BIOS string displayed by the BIOS boot screen and checking that string against one of the BIOS sites listed in Chapter 3. However, such "anonymous" boards are generally of very low quality, so it's usually better to replace such a board rather than attempt to use it.

 Before you install a processor, make absolutely sure the processor is compatible with the motherboard. It is not safe to assume merely because the processor fits the socket or slot that that processor will function properly in that motherboard. In some cases, the processor simply will not work. For example, there are many incompatibilities between Socket 370 processors and motherboards. Not all Socket 370 processors can be used in all Socket 370 motherboards, even if the processor and the motherboard were both made by Intel. In that situation, no damage is done. The processor simply doesn't work.

There are, however, two common situations in which installing an incorrect processor may damage the processor and/or the motherboard:

- Installing a fast processor in a motherboard designed to use only slower versions of that processor. For example, a Slot 1 Pentium II/III motherboard may be rated to accept processors no faster than 450 MHz. Installing a 550 MHz Slot 1 Pentium III may damage the processor or motherboard because the faster processor draws more current than the VRM on the motherboard is designed to supply.

- Installing a processor that requires low voltage in a motherboard that can supply only higher voltage. This problem arises only with Socket 7 and earlier motherboards. Slot 1 and later motherboards and processors automatically negotiate the proper voltage. If the motherboard cannot supply the voltage required by the processor, it simply does not power the processor at all. But if you are installing a late-model Socket 7 processor in an older motherboard, be very certain that that motherboard can supply the proper lower voltages required by the new processor (and that it is configured to do so). Otherwise, your new processor may literally go up in smoke the first time you apply power.

The exact sequence of steps required to install a processor depends on its packaging (slotted versus socketed) and whether it comes with a heatsink and fan installed. Regardless of processor type, always begin by laying the motherboard flat on a firm surface, padding it with the antistatic foam or bag supplied with it. Inserting the CPU (and memory) may require substantial force, so it's important to ensure that the motherboard is fully supported to avoid cracking it.

Before you install any processor, obtain and read the installation documentation for both the processor and the motherboard. Spending a few minutes doing that may well save you hours of frustration.

Installing a Socketed Processor

All modern mainstream processors are socketed rather than slotted. These include the Intel Pentium III and Celeron (Socket 370), the Intel Pentium 4 (Socket 423 and Socket 478), and the AMD Athlon and Duron (Socket A). Fifth-generation processors such as the Intel Pentium and AMD K5 use Socket 5 or Socket 7, and hybrid fifth/sixth-generation processors such as the AMD K6 series and Cyrix 686 series use Socket 7.

Installing any socketed processor is a straightforward operation if you do things by the numbers. The most important thing to remember is that processors are particularly sensitive to static shock. Take great care to observe antistatic procedures while you are handling the processor. It's a good rule of thumb to always keep one hand in contact with the PC power supply while you handle the processor.

All recent socketed motherboards have a *Zero Insertion Force* (ZIF) socket. As its name implies, the ZIF socket allows a chip with hundreds of pins to be seated easily. Older friction-fit sockets made it nearly impossible to seat a complex chip with hundreds of pins properly. If you encounter a motherboard without a ZIF socket, that in itself is a good reason to replace the motherboard before installing the new processor.

Regardless of the type of socketed processor you are installing, take the following preliminary steps:

1. If you are installing a new processor in an older system, before you begin work check to see if an updated BIOS is available for the system. The new processor may require a BIOS update to function at full capacity, or indeed to function at all. If a new BIOS is available, download it and update your PC as described in Chapter 3.

2. Move the PC or motherboard to a well-lit work area, preferably one with all-around access. Collect all of the tools, software, manuals, and upgrade components you need. Read through the processor documentation before proceeding.

3. To install a processor in a new motherboard, ground yourself, remove the motherboard from its packaging, and place it flat on its accompanying anti-static bag. If you are installing a new processor in an existing PC, you can probably do so without removing the motherboard, although you may have to reroute or temporarily disconnect cables to gain unobstructed access to the socket.

If a heatsink and/or fan are not already installed on the processor, check the instructions or examine the components to determine whether the cooling devices need to be installed before or after you install the processor in the socket. Some cooling devices are easy to install regardless of whether the processor is already in its socket. Most are designed to be installed with the processor already seated in its socket, but a few are easier to install on a loose processor. If your cooling device appears to be easy to install either way, install it after the processor is in the socket. That makes it much easier to get the processor aligned and seated correctly. When you install the cooling device, don't forget to apply thermal compound if the documentation recommends it.

Installing Socket 5 and Socket 7 processors

Socket 5 and Socket 7 motherboards must be configured properly to support the particular processor you are installing. If you are installing a Slot 1 or later processor, skip to the following section. If you are installing a Socket 5 or Socket 7 processor, take the steps described in the preceding section, and then continue as follows:

1. Use the processor and motherboard documentation to verify that the processor and motherboard are compatible, and to determine the proper settings for bus speed, CPU multiplier, core voltage, and I/O voltage. Use the motherboard manual or manufacturer's web site to locate the configuration jumpers and to determine the jumper settings that match those required by the new processor. On some systems, settings are made by a combination of jumper settings and entries in BIOS setup. There are four settings you may have to make, all of which may not be present on a given motherboard:

    Bus speed
      All Socket 5 and Socket 7 motherboards provide settings at least for 60 and 66 MHz. Some motherboards provide higher bus speeds, often including 75 and 83 MHz. These higher bus speeds are used to over-clock a 60 or 66 MHz processor—running it faster than its rated speed. Don't use these settings unless you are sure you want to overclock the processor. More recent Socket 7 motherboards, called Super7 mother-boards, also provide 95 and 100 MHz bus settings, which are the standard speeds for newer Socket 7 processors. These motherboards may also include various overclocking settings, including 103, 112, and 124 MHz. Again, avoid using overclocking unless you are making an informed decision to do so.

    CPU multiplier
      The product of the bus speed and CPU multiplier determines how fast the processor runs. For example, using a 60 MHz bus speed with a 2.5X multiplier runs the processor at 150 MHz. Note that some processors convert the chosen CPU multiplier internally to a different multiplier. For example, some processors convert a 1.5X CPU multiplier motherboard setting to an internal 4.0X multiplier. Note also that some CPUs are named with a "performance rating" rather than their actual speed. For example, the WinChip2-300 actually runs at 250 MHz (100 MHz x 2.5), but uses the "300" name to indicate its supposed performance relative to other processors. When setting the bus speed and CPU multiplier, it is important to choose settings that run the processor at its actual rated speed rather than the labeled performance equivalent.

    You can sometimes choose between two combinations of bus speed and CPU multiplier that have the same product. In this case, choose the

Processors

combination of the higher bus speed and lower multiplier, so long as the higher bus speed is supported. For example, when installing a 300 MHz processor, you can choose 66MHz/4.5X or 100MHz/3.0X. Either setting runs the processor at 300 MHz, but the latter setting provides marginally faster performance by allowing data to be communicated faster between the CPU and the external L2 cache memory.

Voltage

Different processors require different voltages. Some processors operate on a single voltage, and others (called *split rail processors*) require different values for *Core Voltage* and *I/O Voltage*. Old motherboards may support only one fixed voltage, and so may not be usable with recent low-voltage or dual-voltage CPUs. Pay close attention to voltage because installing a low-voltage CPU in a high-voltage motherboard may destroy the processor. Adapters are available to allow installing newer low-voltage processors in older motherboards, but in that situation it is better in every respect simply to replace the motherboard.

Asynchronous PCI

Systems with a 60 or 66 MHz FSB run the PCI bus at half speed—30 MHz and 33 MHz, respectively. Systems with a 100 MHz FSB run the PCI bus at one third speed—33 MHz. This process of using these fixed divisors is called synchronous PCI. But PCI devices are unreliable much above 33 MHz, and overclocking the system by using a 75, 83, or 95 MHz FSB would cause the PCI bus to run at 37.5 MHz (marginal), 41.5 MHz (unusable), or 47.5 MHz (ridiculous). So many motherboards designed to support overclocking include a jumper that allows setting the PCI bus to 33 MHz regardless of the FSB speed.

2. Once you have set and verified all jumpers, lift the ZIF lever, which is located on one side of the socket, as far as it will go. If there is a processor in the socket, grasp it firmly and lift it free. It should come away without resistance.

3. Locate Pin 1 on the new processor. Pin 1 is usually indicated by a dot or beveled edge on one corner of the processor, or by a missing pin on that corner. Locate Pin 1 on the ZIF socket, which is usually indicated by a dot or beveled edge, and sometimes by a numeral 1 silk-screened onto the motherboard itself. Orient Pin 1 on the new processor to Pin 1 on the socket and then gently press the processor into the socket, as shown in Figure 4-14. The processor should seat fully with little or no resistance, dropping into place because of its own weight. If the processor does not seat easily, remove it, verify that the pins align correctly, and try to seat it again. Avoid excessive force when seating the processor. It's easy to bend pins, and straightening them is next to impossible.

Figure 4-14. Dropping the processor into the socket, where it should seat fully by its own weight (Be sure to align the pins first)

The processor shown in Figure 4-14 is an Intel Pentium/200, which we were relocating from a system with a failed motherboard to replace a slower processor in another system. The mottling visible on the processor is the remnants of the thermal pad from the old heatsink. Good practice would have been to clean the leftover parts of the thermal pad from the processor and heatsink before proceeding, but we simply added a dollop of thermal goop, which worked fine. We certainly wouldn't do this on any processor we cared about.

4. Once the processor is fully seated, press the ZIF lever down until it is parallel to the edge of the socket, as shown in Figure 4-15. This locks the processor into the socket and makes electrical contact on all pins.

5. If you did not previously install the cooling device, do so now. Don't forget to use thermal compound to improve heat transfer between the processor and the cooling device. Most heatsinks and heatsink/fan units clip directly to the processor or to the socket. Once you have the heatsink aligned properly with the processor (most fit properly in only one orientation) align the clip and press down until it locks into place, as shown in Figure 4-16. If your cooling unit includes a fan, attach the fan power cable to a motherboard fan power header or to an available power supply connector, as appropriate.

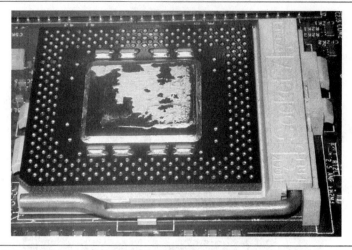

Figure 4-15. The ZIF lever pressed down and locked into place

 If no thermal compound or pad was supplied with the heatsink/fan, buy a tube of thermal goop at Radio Shack (it costs $2 or so) and use it. A processor installed without thermal compound may run 20C or more hotter than one with thermal compound, which at best may shorten the life of the processor and at worst may cause frequent system hangs or physical damage to the processor. Thermal compound is frequently omitted, sometimes even on name-brand commercial PCs, so it's worth checking any processor that you didn't install yourself. If you are installing a recent AMD processor, pay close attention to AMD's published requirements for cooling. Using anything other than a brand of phase-change media specifically approved by AMD may void your warranty.

Figure 4-16. Attaching the heatsink securely using the locking clips

If you are upgrading to a faster processor, do not assume that you can use the heatsink/fan unit from the original processor. Faster processors may generate more heat, and may require a more capable HSF unit. Running a newer, hotter processor with the old HSF may at best result in sporadic lockups and at worst in damaging the processor. We said this earlier in the chapter, but it bears repeating.

6. Install the motherboard, if necessary, connect or reroute any cables you moved, do a quick visual once-over, reconnect the monitor, keyboard, and mouse, and then apply power to the system. The system should begin a normal boot sequence. If nothing (or something strange) happens, immediately turn the power off and reverify all connections and settings.

7. Once the system boots normally, enter CMOS Setup and make whatever changes, if any, the processor documentation recommends. Once the system is working normally, turn off the power, reinstall the chassis cover, return the PC to its working location, reconnect all cables, and restart the system.

Installing modern socketed processors

Installing recent socketed processors—the Intel Pentium III/4/Celeron or the AMD Athlon/Duron—requires essentially the same steps described in the preceding section, except that recent processors do not require the motherboard be configured manually.

Most Socket 370, Socket 423, Socket 478, and Socket A motherboards are self-configuring. They detect the type and speed of processor installed and properly configure FSB speed, CPU multiplier, voltage, and other settings automatically. However, some motherboards intended for overclockers allow overriding information supplied by the processor—for example, by setting a 66 MHz FSB Celeron to run at 100 MHz FSB. Depending on the motherboard, changing such settings may require setting jumpers or altering the default BIOS settings. All such motherboards we have seen default to "Auto," which uses the settings supplied by the processor.

There are, however, several issues to be aware of when installing a modern socketed processor:

Compatibility

As we explained in some detail earlier in this chapter, compatibility between motherboard and processor is a major issue. That a processor physically fits the motherboard socket is no guarantee that it will work at all, or even that attempting to use it will not damage the processor and/or motherboard.

With Socket A, AMD has done a much better job of maintaining forward- and backward-compatibility than Intel has done with Socket 370. Even so, with either AMD or Intel processors, it's important to check that the motherboard supports the exact processor you plan to install.

In particular, make sure that the motherboard is rated for processors at least as fast as the processor you plan to install. If the motherboard documentation mentions only slower processors, don't give up hope. High-quality motherboards are often over engineered, using larger VRMs than necessary to support the processors they were designed for. It's quite possible that the motherboard maker issued updated specifications for your motherboard that include support for faster processors. Check the motherboard manufacturer's web site to make sure.

Also verify that the motherboard supports the FSB speed of the processor. If it doesn't, the processor will still operate, but at a much reduced speed. For example, installing a 133 MHz FSB Pentium III/933 in a motherboard that supports only a 100 MHz FSB causes that processor to run at only 700 MHz. Similarly, installing a 266 MHz FSB Athlon in a motherboard that supports only the 200 MHz FSB means that processor runs at only 75% of its rated speed.

BIOS revision level

The BIOS revision level can determine which processors your motherboard supports. A later BIOS may add support for faster versions of a given processor, and may also add support for an entirely new processor. For example, we have an early Slot 1 board that was designed for the cacheless Slot 1 Celeron and did not support later Slot 1 Celerons, which included embedded L2 cache. A BIOS update for that board added support for cached Celerons, and a subsequent BIOS update added support for the new features and changed caching scheme of the Pentium III. Don't assume that because you just purchased a motherboard that it necessarily has the latest BIOS. Some makers, notably Intel, issue BIOS revisions very frequently, and the motherboard you receive may have been in the pipeline for weeks or even months. Before you install a processor in any motherboard, new or old, the first thing you should do is identify the motherboard precisely, check the manufacturer's web site for the most recent BIOS update, and download that update. Once you have the system up and running, install the updated BIOS before you do anything else.

 A motherboard with an early BIOS revision may create a "can't get there from here" situation. That is, the processor you want to install may refuse to boot without a later BIOS revision than is currently installed on the motherboard. In that case, the best alternative is to install temporarily a processor that the earlier BIOS supports. That's why when we upgrade older systems, we install the latest BIOS version on the old system before we remove the original processor. That's also why we keep a stack of old processors around.

Chipset revision level

Many motherboard manufacturers, including top-notch ones such as Intel, have a nasty habit of slipstreaming revisions. Even two motherboards with identical model numbers may be significantly different. In some cases, that difference is as trivial as different BIOS versions, which is easily fixed. Other times, though, there are very real hardware differences between the boards, and those differences may determine which processors a particular board supports. For example, Intel has produced the popular D815EEA2 "Easton 2" motherboard in two distinct forms. Both versions use the 815E chipset, but the version with an early chipset revision level does not support Tualatin-core Pentium III and Celeron processors. If you have the earlier version, you're out of luck. The newer processors simply won't run in it.

If you're buying a new motherboard, check the manufacturer's web site to determine the current rev level and ask the vendor whether the motherboard he wants to sell you is the latest rev level. If not, buy your motherboard elsewhere. If you're using an older motherboard, check the manufacturer's web site to determine what variants exist and what implication those variants have for processor support.

Heatsink compatibility

Socket 370 processors are a particular problem in this respect. There are three different physical forms of Socket 370 processors you are likely to encounter. Early Socket 370 processors use PPGA packaging. These processors have a flat top, with the processor chip itself on the bottom (pin) side of the package. Pentium III and Celeron FC-PGA processors also have a flat top, but with the processor chip protruding above the surface of the processor, on the side opposite the pins, where it comes into direct contact with the heatsink. The most recent Pentium III and Celeron processors use FC-PGA2 packaging, which is similar to FC-PGA but includes a flat metal integrated heat spreader that shrouds the processor chip itself.

Each of these styles requires a physically different heatsink. Using an incorrect heatsink may damage the processor, either physically or by allowing it to overheat. For example, clamping a PPGA heatsink (which has a flat contact surface) onto an FC-PGA processor (which has a raised processor chip) may literally crush the processor. Conversely, installing an FC-PGA heatsink on a PPGA processor may allow the processor to overheat because a portion of it is not in contact with the heatsink.

Heatsink rating is another issue. Faster processors generate more heat, and require larger or more efficient heatsinks. Don't assume that just because a heatsink is designed to be used with a particular type of processor it is usable with that processor running at any arbitrary speed. For example, a particular heatsink may be designed to cool an AMD Duron running at 850 MHz or less. Using that heatsink on a 1.2 GHz Duron will likely allow the processor to overheat and perhaps damage itself.

Don't assume that all heatsink/fan units will necessarily fit your motherboard and case. Some heatsink/fan units are physically quite large and may not fit. In particular, the portion of the heatsink that overhangs the processor may come into contact with capacitors and other components that protrude above the motherboard. It's not uncommon to find that clamping the heatsink/fan unit into place crushes components that immediately surround the processor socket, so be very careful. Some case/motherboard combinations are also incompatible with some heatsink/fan units because the heatsink/fan is so tall that it cannot be installed because the power supply or portions of the chassis block the space needed by the heatsink fan. If in doubt, measure the available clearances before you order a heatsink/fan unit, and make sure you can return a unit that is incompatible with your motherboard and/or case.

Whichever processor you install, make absolutely certain that the heatsink you plan to use both fits that processor properly and is rated for the processor speed. If you buy a retail-boxed processor, it will come with a heatsink/fan unit appropriate for the processor. If you buy an OEM processor or are reinstalling a processor pulled from another system, make sure the heatsink you use is rated for that particular processor.

Power supply compatibility

Most people don't think about the power supply when they're building or upgrading a system, but the power supply can be a critical issue. Many systems, particularly mass-market systems and consumer-grade systems from major OEMs such as Gateway and Dell, have power supplies that are marginal at best, both in terms of quality and output rating. For example, we have a full-tower Gateway system that arrived with a 150W power supply, and that's *after* we paid for an upgraded power supply. How small must the standard power supply have been?

Modern fast processors have high current draws, and you cannot safely assume that the existing power supply has enough reserve capacity to power them adequately. If you're building a system or upgrading the processor speed significantly in an existing system, make sure that your power supply is up to the job. Otherwise, you may find that the system will not even boot. If the power supply is barely adequate, you may find that the system crashes frequently. We often hear from people who've upgraded their systems with first-rate motherboards and processors, only to find that the new system crashes at the drop of a hat. When that happens, it usually turns out that they've used generic memory or that they just assumed the original power supply would be good enough. Often, it wasn't.

Installing a Slotted Processor

Although mainstream slotted processors are now obsolescent, they remain in limited distribution. A faster slotted processor may be a worthwhile upgrade for an older system. Installing a faster slotted processor can greatly improve system performance and extend the useful life of an otherwise obsolescent system.

For example, until late 2001 our Internet gateway system was an older Celeron. We'd been having some problems with it locking up, which we suspected were caused by the commodity memory installed in it or by the undersized power supply. One day, after three lockups in as many hours, Robert (who is a procrastinator) finally decided to do something about it. We tore down that system and replaced the power supply with an Antec unit and the 64 MB of generic memory with a 128 MB Crucial stick.

While we had the case open for a cleaning and general upgrading, we noticed that the system still had its original Celeron/333 installed, so we decided to replace it with a Pentium II/450 that we'd pulled from another system. The faster clock speed and larger L2 cache of the Pentium II yield performance nearly twice that of the original processor, which takes that system from marginal to more than sufficient for the gateway and mail server tasks to which it is devoted. For a cost of less than $100 (even if we'd had to buy the processor), we now have a reliable Internet gateway system that we expect to continue using for several years to come.

Installing a slotted processor is in some ways easier than installing a socketed processor and in some ways harder. Intel manufactures processors for two similar but incompatible slots. The 242-pin connector, formerly called Slot 1, accepts slotted Celeron, Pentium II, and Pentium III processors. The 330-pin connector, formerly called Slot 2, accepts Pentium II/III Xeon-class processors. These various processors come in different physical packaging (SEC, SEC2, SEPP, etc.), each of which uses a different *retention mechanism*. For example, an SEC Pentium II and an SEPP Celeron both fit the same Slot 1, but use different and incompatible retention mechanisms.

To further complicate matters, Intel ships the same processor in different variants. For example, the retail-boxed version of the Pentium II processor comes with an attached fan, while the OEM version of that processor does not. If you purchase an OEM processor with an attached fan, that package may or may not fit the standard retention mechanism (although it usually does fit). So, the first rule is to make sure that the retention mechanism accepts the processor. If you purchase a cooling device that does not fit the standard retention mechanism, it should be supplied with a mechanism that fits it. Thankfully, all retention mechanisms mount to the standard set of holes in Slot 1 motherboards. Fortunately, AMD Slot A processors are a much simpler matter. All of them use the same physical mounting mechanism, and all Slot A motherboards can accept any Slot A processor. To install a Slot 1 Intel Celeron/Pentium II/Pentium III or a Slot A AMD Athlon processor, take the following steps:

1. When installing a new processor in an older system, determine if a BIOS update is available because the processor may require a later BIOS to support its new features. For example, the Intel SE440BX2-V motherboard accepts various Slot 1 processors, including some Pentium IIIs. But you must upgrade the BIOS to take advantage of the new Pentium III SIMD instructions. Installing the Pentium III without upgrading the BIOS simply makes the

Pentium III run like a faster Pentium II. If a new BIOS is available, download it and update your PC as described in the preceding chapter.

2. Move the PC or motherboard to a well-lit work area, preferably one with all-around access. Collect all of the tools, software, manuals, and upgrade components you need. Read through the processor documentation before proceeding.

3. To install a processor in a new motherboard, ground yourself, remove the motherboard from its packaging, and place it flat on its accompanying anti-static bag. If you are installing a new processor in an existing PC that uses a compatible retention mechanism, you can probably do so without removing the motherboard, although you may have to reroute or disconnect cables to gain unobstructed access to the slot. If the retention mechanism needs to be replaced—e.g., when upgrading a Celeron system to a Pentium III—you may or may not have to remove the system board to replace the retention mechanism.

4. If it is not already installed, install the retention mechanism by following the instructions supplied with it or with the motherboard. Standard retention mechanisms are notched at one end to match the notch in the Slot 1 connector on the motherboard. Align the retention mechanism and seat the four posts into the matching holes on the motherboard. Press down firmly until the retention mechanism seats. Each post has a sliding internal pin topped by a flat, circular piece of white plastic. Forcing that pin down into the post expands the bottom of the post on the far side of the motherboard, securing the post to the motherboard. Press down each of the pins until it snaps into place. Some newer Slot 1 motherboards come with the retention mechanism already installed, but with the vertical supports folded flat. If your motherboard is like this, lift the vertical supports until they snap into place.

5. If the cooling device is not already installed on the processor, install it now. Some processor packages also contain a supplementary support mechanism designed to secure the processor against the additional weight and vibration of the cooling fan. If your package contains such a supplemental support, install it on the processor according to the instructions provided with it.

6. Refer to the processor documentation to determine the proper settings for bus speed and CPU multiplier. Refer to the motherboard manual or manufacturer web site to locate configuration jumpers and to determine the jumper settings that match those required by the new processor. Some boards have separate jumpers for FSB speed and CPU multiplier, others have jumpers for CPU speed only (which implicitly sets both FSB speed and CPU multiplier), and still others use "jumperless setup" which sets FSB and CPU multiplier options in CMOS Setup. Slot 1 processors do not require voltages to be set manually. All current Slot 1 processors use 3.3 volts for external I/O. Klamath-based processors use 2.8 volts internally, and Deschutes-based processors use 2.0 volts. Voltage setting is handled completely automatically via the Voltage ID (VID) pins on the processor itself.

7. Once you have made necessary jumper changes, if any, install the processor, first removing the existing processor if necessary. Note that the card-edge

connector on the processor has a key notch, as does the slot. Slide the processor into the support bracket, making sure that the key is oriented properly, as shown in Figure 4-17.

Figure 4-17. Guiding the processor into place, while aligning the keying tab in the slot with that in the processor's card-edge connector

8. Using both thumbs, press down firmly on the processor until it seats fully, as shown in Figure 4-18. This may require applying significant pressure, but you should feel and hear the processor seat. Most support brackets have locking tabs at the top that will snap into place to secure the processor once it is fully seated.

Figure 4-18. Using both thumbs to press firmly until the processor seats fully

9. If the fan power lead is designed to connect to a motherboard power header, connect it now. If the fan power lead instead is designed to connect to a power supply power connector, you'll make that connection after the motherboard is installed in the case.

Completing the Installation

Once you have physically installed the processor and memory (as described in Chapter 5), installed the motherboard in the case, and connected all cables, you're ready to test the system. Verify that everything is connected properly and that you haven't left any tools in the patient. Connect a monitor, keyboard, and mouse to the system. With the case cover still off, apply power. Everything should spin up properly, including the processor fan if one is installed. If it doesn't, immediately turn the power off and recheck your work.

Once the processor is functioning, restart the system, enter BIOS Setup, and set the processor speed if necessary. Setting processor speed is unnecessary with modern processors. In fact, it's usually impossible to do so because the processor reports its speed to the motherboard, which automatically configures itself for that speed. Older processors may or may not require setting processor speed manually, depending on the particular processor and motherboard. Note that with some motherboards, you must move a jumper from "Normal" to "Configure" mode before you can change some settings, including processor speed. Once you have configured BIOS settings appropriately, save the changes and turn off the system.

Our Picks

Although processor makers probably hate us for saying so, the processor actually plays a relatively minor role in overall system performance. The difference in absolute processor performance between a $50 processor and a $500 processor may be a factor of two or less. Nor does buying a $500 processor make your system run twice as fast because processor speed is only one element of system performance. Before you plunk down $500 for a processor, consider instead spending that extra money on more memory, a faster video card, a SCSI hard drive, or all of those.

Inexpensive system ($750 or less)
 AMD Athlon XP. In this price range, spend $75 or so on the processor. We recommend choosing the least-expensive Athlon XP you can find in retail-boxed form. Low-end Athlon processors provide incredible bang for the-buck. Your system won't be quite as fast as one that uses a midrange or faster Athlon XP or Pentium 4, but it won't be all that much slower, either.

 Be very careful when buying inexpensive processors. A price much lower than $75 may mean that you're being quoted on discontinued inventory. That's fine if you know what you're getting and are willing to accept the older processor. A lowball price may also mean you're being quoted on an OEM version, which does not include the heatsink and fan, and may have only a short guarantee rather than the three-year guarantee on the retail-boxed model. By the time you buy a separate heatsink and fan, you'll probably spend more than you would have by buying the retail-boxed model in the first place. Caveat emptor definitely applies when you buy any processor. Ask specifically what you're getting or you may get a nasty surprise.

Mainstream system ($750 to $1,200)

Intel Pentium 4 or AMD Athlon XP. In this price range, you have a bit more room to play, and it makes sense to allocate some of that extra money to a faster processor. At the lower end of this price range, choose the fastest retail-boxed AMD Athlon XP you can find for $100 or so (the Intel Pentium 4 doesn't compete in the $100 price range). At the higher end, choose the fastest retail-boxed Intel Northwood-core Pentium 4 or AMD Athlon XP you can find for $150.

Performance system ($1,200+)

Intel Pentium 4 or AMD Athlon XP. This budget level provides considerably more options. For a system in this price range, choose the fastest retail-boxed AMD Athlon XP or Intel Pentium 4 (533 or 800 MHz FSB) you can find in the sub-$200 range.

Dual-processor system

AMD Athlon MP. If you run Windows 2000/XP, Linux, or another SMP-capable operating system, we recommend using a dual-processor system. In our experience, responsiveness in a multitasking environment is better with two midrange processors than with one fast processor. If you choose components carefully, you can build a dual-processor Athlon system for only $250 or so more than the cost of a comparable mainstream system. Your system won't run any one task as fast as it would with a faster single processor, but it won't bog down when you're running many tasks, as the fast single-processor system will.

Processor cooling solutions

TaiSol or DynaTron. A retail-boxed processor includes a heatsink/fan unit that is perfectly adequate for routine use. If you buy an OEM processor, which does not include a heatsink/fan unit, or if you overclock or otherwise push your system beyond its design limits, you'll need a high-quality third-party heatsink/fan unit. Such units vary widely in price, cooling efficiency, and noise level, but the best units overall in our opinion are those manufactured by TaiSol and DynaTron. We have used various TaiSol and DynaTron heatsink/fan models on various processors—including Celerons, Pentium IIIs, Pentium 4s, Athlons, and Durons running at various speeds—and have found them to be effective, quiet, and reasonably priced.

We constantly test and review processors. For information about which specific processors we recommend by brand and model, visit *http://www.hardwareguys. com/picks/processors.html*. We also maintain a set of system guides that detail our currently recommended system configurations for various purposes and in various price ranges. You can view the latest system guides at *http://www.hardwareguys. com/guides/guides.html*.

5

Memory

A few years ago, this book could have covered memory in a page or two. All memory came as discrete chips, and there were only a few sizes and speeds available. You bought however many chips you needed, installed them, and that was that.

Dramatic CPU speed increases over the last few years have brought designers up against one hard fact. It's difficult to design faster CPUs, but it's even harder to build faster memory. Building *affordable* fast memory is harder still. Faster processors require faster memory, so engineers have come up with various methods to increase memory speeds. One result is that memory isn't a simple issue anymore. This chapter tells you what you need to know to make good decisions about buying memory when you build or upgrade a system.

Understanding Memory

This chapter focuses on general-purpose memory, where PCs store programs and data that are currently in use, the pipeline that supplies data to and receives results from the processor. General-purpose memory, called *read-write memory* or *Random Access Memory (RAM)*, must be readable-from and writable-to. Two types of RAM are used on modern PCs:

Dynamic RAM (DRAM)
  Dynamic RAM stores data for only a tiny fraction of a second before losing it. To maintain stored data, the system must constantly *refresh* DRAM, which exacts a performance penalty and limits its speed. Typical DRAM provides 60 ns access, but is inexpensive and consumes relatively little power.

Static RAM (SRAM)
  Static RAM automatically maintains its contents as long as power is applied to it, without requiring refresh. SRAM provides access times an order of magnitude faster than DRAM, but is expensive and power-hungry.

PCs use a tiered memory architecture that takes advantage of these characteristics:

Main memory
> The bulk of a PC's memory uses DRAM and is called *main memory*. It is large—typically 64 MB to 512 MB or more—but too slow to keep up with a modern CPU. Main memory is where the CPU stores programs and data that it will soon need. Main memory functions as a buffer between the CPU and disk and stores tens to hundreds of megabytes.

Cache memory
> *Cache memory* is a small amount of fast SRAM that buffers access between the CPU and main memory.

Modern PCs have two layers of cache memory:

Primary cache memory
> Primary cache, also called *Level 1 cache* or *L1 cache*, is typically 16 to 128 KB of very fast memory on the same chip as the CPU itself. L1 cache size and efficiency are major factors in CPU performance. The amount and type of L1 cache is determined by the CPU you use, and cannot be upgraded.

Secondary cache memory
> L1 cache is not large enough to eliminate the speed disparity between processors and main memory. *Secondary cache*, also called *Level 2 cache, L2 cache*, or (on Pentium-class motherboards) *external cache*, bridges that gap with a reasonable compromise between cost and performance. L2 cache is a part of the CPU package (or of the CPU substrate itself) on all modern processors, including the Intel Celeron/Pentium II/III/4 and the AMD Athlon/Duron/Opteron. Modern processors have L2 cache memory sizes ranging from 128 KB to 2 MB.

> Pentium and earlier processors use discrete L2 cache chips on the motherboard. Although it's possible to upgrade the L2 cache on many such systems, it seldom—we're tempted to say "never"—makes sense to spend money on a system that old. If for some reason you must upgrade a Pentium-class motherboard, see the first or second edition of this book for details.
>
> Some PCs and motherboards arrive with cache disabled. Always check the Chipset Setup section of CMOS Setup to verify that L1 and L2 cache are both enabled.

Memory Access Methods

PC memory may use the following access methods:

Asynchronous
> *Asynchronous DRAM*, which was used in all PCs until the late 1990s, uses a window of fixed minimum duration to determine when operations may occur. If the CPU has transferred data while a window is open, and if a subsequent clock cycle occurs while that window remains open, the CPU cannot transfer additional data until the next window opens, thereby wasting that

clock cycle. Asynchronous operation forces the CPU to conform to a fixed schedule for transferring data, rather than doing so whenever it wishes. Asynchronous DRAM is available in the following types:

Fast Page Mode (FPM) DRAM

FPM was commonly used on 486 and earlier systems, and may be installed in early Pentium systems. FPM is not supported by recent chipsets. Although you can migrate FPM DRAM from an old Socket 5 or Socket 7 system to a newer Socket 7 system, it is good for little else. You may be able to install surplus FPM DRAM in your laser printer.

Extended Data Out (EDO) DRAM

EDO, also sometimes called *Hyper Page Mode DRAM*, is marginally faster than FPM, is still available in all common package types, and was commonly installed on new systems until late 1998. EDO DRAM now costs so much that it is often less expensive to replace the existing motherboard, processor, and memory with current products than to buy EDO memory. That said, you may be able to upgrade the memory in an EDO-based system economically. Many EDO-based systems can also use SDRAM DIMMs, which are faster, much less expensive, and much more readily available. To upgrade the memory in such systems, replace the existing EDO memory with compatible SDRAM DIMMs.

Burst Extended Data Out (BEDO) DRAM

BEDO slightly improved upon EDO, but was inferior to SDRAM, which was introduced at about the same time, and so never became popular. If you have a BEDO-based system, follow the upgrade advice given for an EDO-based system.

All forms of asynchronous DRAM are now obsolete. Although asynchronous DRAM is still available, it costs so much per megabyte that it never makes sense to buy it. For example, in July 2003, the price per megabyte of asynchronous DRAM SIMMs was five to 25 times that of SDRAM DIMMs, depending on capacity and type.

A system or motherboard that accepts only asynchronous DRAM is too old to be upgraded economically. If you have such a system, we recommend you upgrade its memory only if you can salvage compatible memory from discarded systems. If you have a late-model Pentium or Pentium Pro system that also accepts SDRAM and is still performing useful service (perhaps as a fax server or other appliance), we suggest you pull all of the asynchronous DRAM and replace it with compatible SDRAM.

Synchronous

Synchronous DRAM, also called *SDRAM*, shares a common clock reference with the CPU. No window is needed because the CPU and memory are slaved together, allowing the CPU to transfer data to and from memory whenever it wishes to do so, instead of requiring the CPU to await an arbitrary window. For links to formal SDRAM standards, see the Intel SDRAM Specifications page at *http://developer.intel.com/technology/memory/pcsdram/spec/index.htm*.

SDRAM takes one of the following forms:

JEDEC SDRAM

Ordinary SDRAM, sometimes called JEDEC SDRAM or PC66 SDRAM to differentiate it from PC100 SDRAM and PC133 SDRAM. PC66 SDRAM was formerly less expensive than PC100 or PC133 SDRAM, but as the price of those faster variants declined to near that of PC66 SDRAM, the demand for PC66 SDRAM plummeted. PC66 SDRAM is now hard to find and may cost more than PC100 or PC133 SDRAM. Because PC133 SDRAM can be used on nearly any system running a 133 MHz or slower FSB, buying JEDEC SDRAM never makes sense, even for systems that run memory at 66 MHz. PC66 SDRAM salvaged from an older system can be used in any system that runs a 66 MHz FSB, including those running older-model Celeron or Pentium II processors.

PC100 SDRAM

SDRAM that complies with the Intel PC100 specification, and is rated for use on a 100 MHz FSB. Like PC66 SDRAM, PC100 SDRAM is obsolescent, and may actually cost more than faster PC133 SDRAM.

PC133 SDRAM

SDRAM that complies with the Intel PC133 specification, and is rated for use on a 133 MHz FSB. PC133 SDRAM costs little or no more than PC100 SDRAM, operates properly—although only at the lower speed—in nearly all systems designed to use PC66 or PC100 SDRAM, and is usually the best choice when you're buying SDRAM memory, even for a 66 MHz or 100 MHz FSB system. PC133 SDRAM is commonly available in two variants which vary only in CAS latency. *CAS-3 PC133 SDRAM* is the more common form, and is what you will receive if you do not specify otherwise. *CAS-2 PC133 SDRAM* has lower latency, is therefore slightly faster in a motherboard that can take advantage of it, and costs only a few cents more per megabyte.

PC133 SDRAM is obsolescent. Even entry-level systems now use some variant of DDR-SDRAM, described in the next section, so PC133 SDRAM is now useful only to upgrade older systems. In those systems, PC133 SDRAM provides memory throughput that is well matched to the bandwidth of the processor.

Some memory packagers sell so-called PC166 SDRAM. In fact, there is no such standard, and these modules are used primarily by overclockers who run the FSB at 166 MHz rather than 133 MHz. We suggest that you avoid both running your FSB at a higher than intended speed and using PC166 SDRAM.

DDR-SDRAM

Double Data Rate SDRAM (DDR-SDRAM) doubles the amount of data transferred per clock cycle, and thereby effectively doubles peak memory bandwidth. DDR-SDRAM is an evolutionary improvement of standard SDRAM, which is now sometimes called Single Data Rate SDRAM or SDR-SDRAM to differentiate it. Because DDR-SDRAM costs essentially the same to produce as SDR-SDRAM, it sells for about the same price.

The chips used to produce DDR-SDRAM DIMMs are named for their operating speed. For example, 100 MHz chips are double-pumped to 200 MHz, and so are called PC200 (or DDR200) chips. (We use the "PCxxx" speed nomenclature rather than the "DDRxxx" nomenclature for first generation DDR memory, although "DDRxxx" is also commonly used.) Similarly, chips that operate at 133 MHz are called PC266 chips, those that operate at 166 MHz are called PC333 chips, and those that operate at 200 MHz are called PC400 chips. (In fact, only PC200 and PC266 are formal standards, although memory makers produce so-called PC333 and PC400 chips based on de facto standards.)

Unlike SDR-SDRAM DIMMs, which are designated by their chip speeds, DDR-SDRAM DIMMs are designated by their throughput. Their data path is 64 bits (8 bytes) wide. So, for example, a DDR-SDRAM DIMM that uses PC200 chips transfers 8 bytes 200 million times per second, for a total throughput of 1,600 million bytes/second and is called a PC1600 DIMM. Similarly, DDR-SDRAM DIMMs that use PC266 chips are labeled PC2100, and those that use PC333 chips are labeled PC2700. Based on chip speed, PC2700 modules are actually PC2667, but no one uses that name. Some early DIMMs built with PC333 chips were labeled PC2600, but all memory makers now use the PC2700 designation for obvious reasons. DDR-SDRAM DIMMs that use PC400 chips are labeled PC3200.

PC2700 DDR-SDRAM is now the dominant mainstream memory technology, although the April 2003 introduction of the Intel 875P chipset has kickstarted the market for PC3200 memory. All mainstream AMD and Intel processors and chipsets now support PC2700 or faster DDR-SDRAM, and there is little reason to choose any slower type of memory. PC1600 DDR-SDRAM was economically obsoleted by mid-2002, when the price of PC2100 memory fell to the same level as PC1600. By early 2003, the same fate befell PC2100 memory, as the price of PC2700 memory fell to PC2100 levels.

Used with chipsets such as the Intel 875P that are optimized for it, PC3200 memory is faster than PC2700 memory, but not as fast as one might expect. In a motherboard that matches processor bandwidth to PC3200 memory bandwidth, memory performance may increase by 5% to 8%, rather than the nominal 18.5%.

In a motherboard that mismatches processor bandwidth to PC3200 bandwidth, the performance increase is much smaller, and may even be negative. For example, in early 2003 we used an ASUS A7N8X nForce2 motherboard with dual-channel DDR memory support to test Corsair CL2 PC3200 DIMMs against Crucial CL2.5 PC2700 DIMMs. We found that, although the PC3200 DIMMs did yield slightly faster benchmark numbers than PC2700 DIMMs, the practical advantage of PC3200 was nil.

We expect PC3200 to be the fastest DDR-SDRAM that will ever be produced in volume. Mass-produced PC3200 modules push the electrical and mechanical limits of current technology. Some memory makers, notably Corsair, rigorously test chips to isolate those fast enough to operate as PC433 and use those chips to produce small runs of what amount to handcrafted PC3500 DIMMs. These PC3500 modules are very expensive and provide only minor throughput improvements relative to PC3200 modules.

DDR-II SDRAM

By early 2003, the original DDR-SDRAM technology was fast approaching its limits. As AMD and Intel transition to higher FSB speeds, DDR-SDRAM will be hard-pressed to keep pace. Current DDR technology tops out at PC3200. Dual-channel DDR chipsets using PC3200 memory limit peak throughput to 6400 MB/s. That is sufficient for now, but as FSB speeds increase from 400 MHz to 533 MHz, 800 MHz, and beyond, even dual-channel DDR-SDRAM will be challenged to keep up with increases in processor bandwidth.

The long-term solution is *DDR-II SDRAM*. DDR-II incorporates a series of evolutionary improvements on DDR-I technology, including increased performance and bandwidth, reduced cost, lower power consumption, and improved packaging. DDR-II basic device timing and page size are compatible with DDR-I, and because the DDR-II command set is a superset of the DDR-I command set, a DDR-II controller can also control DDR-I modules.

DDR-II DIMMs use a new 232-pin connector, and it is likely that DDR-I modules will be produced with that connector to facilitate the transition from DDR-I to DDR-II modules. DDR-II chips will initially ship in DDR400 and DDR533 variants, which will be used to produce PC3200 and PC4300 DDR-II DIMMs. We expect that DDR-II will eventually be produced in DDR600, DDR667, and DDR800 variants, which will be used to produce PC4800, PC5300, and PC6400 modules, respectively.

Although some high-performance video cards currently use DDR-II, we do not expect DDR-II to become standard in desktop PCs until late 2004 or 2005. We think PC2700 DDR-I modules in single- and dual-channel configurations will remain the standard until DDR-II chipsets ship in volume in 2004. DDR-II will at first be used in high-end systems, and will migrate to midrange and entry-level systems throughout 2004 and 2005.

Quad Band Memory (QBM)

On the theory that if twice as fast is good, four times as fast must be better, the QBM Alliance is developing Quad Band Memory (QBM), sometimes called Quad Data Rate SDRAM (QDR-SDRAM). The QBM Alliance roster boasts many second- and third-tier companies, including Acer Laboratories, Acuid, Avant Technology, CST, Denali Software, Integrated Circuit Systems, Kentron Technologies, Netlist, Peripheral Enhancements, PNY Technologies, SiS, SiSoft, ST Microelectronics, Terarecon, and VIA Technologies. Alas, the key first-tier chipset/

motherboard companies—notably Intel and AMD—are not QBM Alliance members. Neither have major memory companies such as Crucial/Micron, Kingston, or Samsung chosen to join the QBM Alliance. Without real support from those companies, we don't think the QBM Alliance can hope to establish a viable standard.

QBM is based on DDR-I technology, but quad-pumps rather than double-pumps the data channel. Although we have been wrong before, we expect QBM to fail for both technical and marketing reasons. Technically, QBM offers little real advantage over dual-channel PC2700 or PC3200 DDR-SDRAM, which is already widely supported by chipsets for Intel and AMD processors. That means memory makers have no incentive to produce yet another type of module that would sell in relatively small numbers, making it difficult to recoup their startup costs. From a marketing standpoint, QBM is almost doomed from the start. At best, QBM will garner support from second- and third-tier companies such as VIA Technologies and Kentron, which means that QBM will be perceived by consumers as a second-rate solution. Meanwhile, Intel and AMD will continue backing DDR-I and DDR-II, leaving only scraps for QBM.

Rambus RDRAM

SDRAM uses separate address, control, and data busses, each with many lines. Managing these wide parallel busses limits performance. Protocol-based DRAM instead uses a narrow, very fast channel with protocols that manage address, control, and data information. Rambus RDRAM, a proprietary RAM standard developed jointly by Intel and Rambus, is the sole surviving type of protocol-based RAM.

There are three types of Rambus memory, called Base Rambus, Concurrent Rambus, and Direct Rambus. The first two are obsolescent, and are used only in devices such as game consoles. All Rambus memory used in PCs is Direct Rambus memory. RDRAM is available in four speeds, designated PC600, PC700, PC800, and PC1066, although only PC800 and PC1066 are used in current systems. As with DDR-SDRAM, RDRAM modules are named according to their throughput, but with a difference. RDRAM uses a 16-bit or 18-bit data path (versus 64-bit for SDRAM) to transfer two bytes at a time. Accordingly, PC600 RDRAM provides peak throughput of 1200 million bytes/second, PC700 1400 million bytes/second, PC800 1600 million bytes/second, and PC1066 2133 million bytes/second.

 Until recently, Rambus RIMMs were supplied as 16-bit or 18-bit parts. In dual-channel RDRAM motherboards, those modules had to be installed in pairs, one per channel. PC1066 32/36-bit RDRAM modules are now available. These 32/36-bit RIMMs are in effect two RIMMs combined into a single package, and can be installed singly in dual-channel RDRAM systems.

In theory, then, it appears that PC800 RDRAM matches the throughput of PC1600 DDR-SDRAM, and PC1066 RDRAM the throughput of PC2100 DDR-SDRAM. In fact, that is true only if you are considering peak

---

throughput. In the real world, RDRAM provides higher sustained throughput because it is more efficient than SDRAM in typical applications. Whereas SDRAM efficiencies are in the 40% to 70% range, RDRAM efficiency is about 80%. Accordingly, PC800 RDRAM might deliver sustained throughput of 1280 million bytes/second, whereas PC1600 DDR-SDRAM delivers much less, and even PC2100 DDR-SDRAM may not be able to match the actual sustained throughput of PC800 RDRAM.

On that basis, RDRAM might seem the better choice, but that is seldom true for several reasons. First, the throughput advantage of RDRAM is unrealized in most applications. Although modern processors such as the Pentium 4 can in theory use very wide memory bandwidths, in practice few applications require more memory bandwidth than PC1600 DDR-SDRAM provides, let alone PC2100, PC2700, or PC3200 DDR-SDRAM. Second, RDRAM typically costs significantly more than DDR-SDRAM. Third, throughput is only one aspect of memory performance. At least as important as throughput is *latency*—the time that elapses from requesting data from memory until the memory begins delivering that data. Despite the arguments of Rambus to the contrary, real-world RDRAM implementations exhibit high latency. What's worse is that RDRAM latency is cumulative. That is, with SDRAM, latency is a property of the memory chips themselves and remains the same regardless of the number of DIMMs installed in the system. With RDRAM, installing additional memory modules increases latency linearly. Not surprisingly, all the memory performance comparisons that we have seen from Rambus are based on using one RDRAM module per channel.

One can argue theory all day, of course, but the simple fact is that in our experience Rambus RDRAM memory seldom provides a significant performance advantage over SDRAM and may, in fact, be slower in some applications than even PC133 SDR-SDRAM. We suggest avoiding RDRAM memory entirely. In the past, we recommended RDRAM for Pentium 4 systems for which memory performance was a very high priority and the additional cost of RDRAM was not a deciding factor. With the advent of dual-channel DDR-SDRAM systems, that advice is now obsolete, because dual-channel PC2700 or PC3200 memory outperforms RDRAM in every respect. Intel will soon discontinue all of their RDRAM motherboards, making the point moot.

As of July 2003, the memory landscape for PCs appears to be predictable for the next couple of years. PC133 SDR-SDRAM and PC1600/PC2100 DDR-SDRAM are useful only for upgrading older systems. PC2700 DDR-I SDRAM is the current standard, although the Intel 875P- and 865-series chipsets have made PC3200 DDR-SDRAM a mainstream technology. Inexpensive systems use single-channel PC2700 DDR-SDRAM, and mainstream or higher systems use dual-channel PC2700 or PC3200 DDR-SDRAM. This state of affairs is likely to remain unchanged for the next year or more, so PC2700 or PC3200 DDR-I SDRAM remains a "safe" purchase.

As we move into 2004, PC2700 and PC3200 DDR-I SDRAM will begin yielding its position as the mainstream memory technology to dual-channel PC3200 DDR-II SDRAM, at first in high-end systems and later in the year in midrange systems.

By late 2004, only entry-level PCs will use PC2700 or PC3200 DDR-I SDRAM. Beginning in 2005, even inexpensive systems will use PC3200 DDR-II SDRAM, and high-end systems will use faster variants of DDR-II SDRAM.

Rambus RDRAM never became a mainstream memory technology despite Intel's efforts to push it. Those efforts were particularly futile with Pentium III-class processors, which do not require the additional bandwidth available with RDRAM. Those early efforts to promote RDRAM failed miserably because people noticed that despite the hype, RDRAM provided little or no performance benefit relative to PC133 SDRAM with sixth-generation processors.

The advent of the bandwidth-hungry Pentium 4 processor should have made the advantages of RDRAM compelling, but the issue of relative memory performance has been overtaken by events. Intel's contract with Rambus has expired, its enthusiasm for RDRAM has faded, and it has now developed dual-channel DDR-SDRAM chipsets that provide more throughput than RDRAM with better latency and at a lower price. In our testing, RDRAM-based Pentium 4 systems provide better memory performance than those that use single-channel DDR-SDRAM, but worse performance than those that use dual-channel DDR-SDRAM. That leaves RDRAM as an expensive technology with no remaining market niche, and we expect it to fade quickly.

CAS Latency

CAS latency is the delay, in clock cycles, between the time the processor requests data from memory and the time the memory makes the first piece of data available to be read. SDR-SDRAM modules may have a CAS latency of 1, 2, or 3. DDR-SDRAM modules have a CAS latency of 2 or 2.5. CAS latency is often abbreviated as CAS or CL. For example, a PC133 module may be labeled CAS2, CAS-2, CAS=2, CL2, CL-2, or CL=2, all of which mean that module has a CAS latency of 2.

Current systems read memory in 32-bit chunks, comprising four 8-bit bytes. CAS latency specifies the number of clock cycles required before the first byte can be read. After that first byte is read, the remaining bytes are read without latency, in one clock cycle each. For example, CL3 memory delivers the first byte after three clock cycles and the other three bytes in one clock cycle each. This memory timing is designated 3-1-1-1 and indicates that six clock cycles (3+1+1+1) are needed to read all four bytes. CL2 memory uses a 2-1-1-1 memory timing, and therefore reads all four bytes in five clock cycles (2+1+1+1). Similarly, CL1 memory uses a 1-1-1-1 memory timing and requires only four clock cycles to complete the read.

On that basis, one might conclude that CL2 memory is 16.7% faster than CL3 memory and CL1 memory is 33.3% faster than CL3, which is a substantial difference. In fact, that differential holds only for single 32-bit reads, whereas most reads are streaming. During streaming reads, each 32-bit read after the first is performed without latency. As the number of streamed 32-bit reads per access increases, the relative significance of the CAS latency overhead incurred for the first byte diminishes.

For example, compare a streaming 32-byte read (eight sequential 32-bit reads) with CL3 versus CL2 versus CL1 memory. With CL3 memory, the first 32-bit read requires six clock cycles. Each of the following seven 32-bit reads does not incur the CAS latency penalty, and so requires only four clock cycles. The full 32-byte read therefore requires a total of 6 + (7*4) or 34 clock cycles. With CL2 memory, the first 32-bit read requires five clock cycles, and each of the following seven 32-bit reads again requires only four clock cycles, for a total of 33 clock cycles. With CL1 memory, all eight 32-bit reads require four clock cycles each, for a total of 32 clock cycles. In this (very realistic) example, CL2 memory is actually only 2.9% faster (1/34) than CL3 memory, and CL1 memory is only 5.9% (2/34) faster than CL3.

In practice, lower CAS latencies benefit highly random read operations but do little to help streaming (sequential) read operations. Typical PC read operations use sequential read operations heavily, which means that you can expect only a minor improvement in memory performance if you use memory with a lower CAS latency rating. It's worth paying a bit more for memory with faster CAS latency, but not for the reason you might expect. (See the last point in the following bulleted list.)

Keep these CL-related issues in mind:

- Most motherboards can use memory of any CL timing, although some motherboards may not take advantage of the reduced latency. A few motherboards require memory with a specific CL timing. For example, a motherboard that requires CL2 PC133 may not work properly with CL3 PC133 memory, and a motherboard that requires CL3 PC133 memory may not work properly with CL2 PC133. This is a good reason to use the memory configurator utilities provided by Crucial and other memory makers, which take CAS latency issues into account when listing compatible memory modules.

- Some motherboards allow mixing memory with different CL timings, although the faster memory almost always operates at the CAS latency of the slowest module installed. Some motherboards work properly with memory of different CL timings as long as all memory installed has the same CL timing, but misbehave if you install mixed modules of different CL timings. We suspect these problems are caused by minor electrical differences such as capacitance, but have never gotten a good explanation of why this is true. Although problems with mixed CL timings are unusual in our experience, we recommend not mixing CL timings for this reason.

- Most motherboards that support different CL timings configure themselves optimally automatically based on the information reported by the memory module itself, but some require setting memory timings manually in the Chipset Configuration section of BIOS Setup. If you install "fast" modules in a system, it's worth checking BIOS Setup to make sure the system is configured to use the faster CL timings.

- Using conservative memory timings can increase the stability and reliability of a system at a minimal cost in terms of reduced performance. For example, if a system has PC133 CL2 memory installed and crashes too frequently, you can increase the stability of that system by configuring CMOS Setup to use CL3 memory timings. CL2 memory running as CL3 is much more stable than

CL2 memory running as CL2, and probably more stable than CL3 memory running as CL3. The performance hit will be so small that you won't even notice it unless you run a memory benchmark program.

Memory Packaging

Memory is available in various physical packaging. Roughly in order of their appearance, the major types of DRAM packaging include:

DIP (Dual Inline Pin Package)
> This package comprises a rectangular chip with a row of pins down each long side, making it resemble an insect. DIP was the most common DRAM package used in PCs through early 386 models. DIP chips were produced in Page Mode and Fast Page Mode, and are long obsolete. DIP packaging was also used for L2 cache memory on most 486 and some Pentium-class motherboards. DIP DRAM is useless nowadays.

SIPP (Single Inline Pin Package)
> This package turns a DIP chip on its side and extends all leads straight out one side, parallel to the plane of the chip. SIPPs were intended to allow memory to be installed more densely, and were used in a few 386SX systems, but they never caught on. SIPPs were produced in Page Mode and Fast Page Mode form, and are long obsolete.

SIMM (Single Inline Memory Module)
> This package mounts multiple individual DRAM DIP chips on a small circuit board with a card-edge connector designed to fit a socket on the motherboard. Mainstream SIMMs have been manufactured in two form factors:

> *30-pin*
>> These SIMMs were used in a few 286 systems, most 386 systems, and some 486 systems, and were produced in Page Mode and Fast Page Mode form. Although they are still available, 30-pin SIMMs are obsolete. If you tear down an old system, any 30-pin SIMMs you salvage are too small and too slow to be useful. However, some laser printers do use them.

> *72-pin*
>> These SIMMs were used in some 386 systems, most 486 systems, and nearly all Pentium-class systems built before the advent of DIMMs. 72-pin SIMMs were produced in Fast Page Mode, EDO form, and BEDO form. When tearing down old systems, 72-pin SIMMs may be worth salvaging, as they can be used to expand the memory on a late-model Pentium or Pentium Pro system or to expand the memory in some laser printers.

Figure 5-1 shows a 72-pin SIMM (top) and a 30-pin SIMM. The 72-pin SIMM is keyed by the notch at the bottom right; the 30-pin SIMM by the notch at the bottom left. The holes on either side immediately above the bottom row of contacts are used by the slot retention mechanism to secure the SIMM in the slot. Although it may not be visible in the reproduction, the top SIMM uses gold contacts and the bottom SIMM tin contacts.

Figure 5-1. 72-pin SIMM (top) and 30-pin SIMM

DIMM (Dual Inline Memory Module)

DIMMs are dual-side modules that use connectors on both sides of the circuit board. SDR-SDRAM DIMMs have 168 pins, but SDR-SDRAM is also available in 100- and 144-pin DIMMs. DDR-SDRAM is packaged in 184-pin DIMMs, which are physically similar to standard 168-pin SDR-SDRAM DIMMs, but have additional pins and different keying notch positions to prevent them from being interchanged. DDR-II DIMMs are similar to DDR DIMMs, but use a 232-pin connector. Only SDR-SDRAM, DDR-SDRAM, and EDO are commonly packaged as DIMMs.

SODIMM (Small Outline DIMM)

A special package used in notebook computers and on some video adapters.

RIMM

A Rambus RDRAM module. RIMM is a trade name rather than an acronym. RIMMs are physically similar to standard SDRAM DIMMs, except that the keying notches are in different locations. RDRAM is available in 168-pin and 184-pin modules. Early RDRAM motherboards used 168-pin RIMMs. Most current RDRAM motherboards use 184-pin RIMMs.

Figure 5-2 shows the two most common physical packages for memory used in recent systems. The top module is a 168-pin PC133 SDRAM DIMM. The bottom module is a 184-pin PC2100 DDR-SDRAM DIMM (faster DDR-SDRAM modules use the same package). The physical dimensions of both are the same: 5.375 inches (13.6525 cm) wide by 1.375 inches (3.4925 cm) tall. The width is standardized for all memory modules to ensure they fit the standard slot. The height may vary slightly, and is a factor only in that tall modules may interfere with other components in a tightly packed system. Both of these modules use nine chips, which indicates that they are Error Checking and Correction (ECC) modules. Nonparity modules use only eight chips.

The major difference between these DIMMs, other than the number of pins, is the location of the keying notches. SDRAM DIMMs use two notches, one centered and one offset. DDR-SDRAM DIMMs use only one offset keying notch. The

Figure 5-2. PC133 SDRAM DIMM (top) and PC2100 DDR-SDRAM DIMM

number and position of these keying notches ensure that only the proper memory type can be installed in a slot and that the module is oriented correctly. Rambus RIMMs use similar physical packaging, but with the keying notches in different locations. Rambus RIMMs also cover the individual chips with a metal shroud designed to dissipate heat.

Banks versus Rows

Memory *rows* and *banks* are easily confused. Rows are physical groups and banks are logical groups. A bank comprises one or more rows, the number depending on CPU address bus width and the width of the memory, which is closely associated with its form factor.

DIP

These are 1 bit wide, and require eight chips per row (nine, if parity is used). The number of rows per bank depends on the CPU. XT-class PCs, which use an 8-bit memory bus, require one row per bank. 286s (16-bit bus) require two rows per bank. 386s and 486s (32-bit bus) require four rows per bank.

30-pin SIMM

These are 8 bits wide. 286s require two modules (rows) per bank. 386s and 486s require four modules per bank. Pentiums (64-bit bus) require eight modules per bank.

72-pin SIMMs

These are 32 bits wide. 486s require one module per bank. Pentium and higher systems require two modules per bank.

168-pin and 184-pin DIMMs

These are 64 bits wide. One DIMM always forms one bank.

168-pin and 184-pin RIMMs

Older motherboards use 168-pin RIMMs. Most newer motherboards use 184-pin RIMMs. Although most RIMMs technically use a 16- or 18-bit communications channel, a single RIMM appears to the chipset as one bank. Some motherboards have a single RDRAM channel, such as those based on the Intel 820 chipset, and allow RIMMs to be installed individually. Other motherboards, such as those based on the Intel 850 chipset, have dual RDRAM channels, and require that RIMMs be installed in pairs, one per channel. Note, however, that a 32/36-bit RIMM is physically packaged as one module, but is logically two RIMMs. That means you can populate a dual-channel Rambus motherboard with just one 32/36-bit RIMM.

 In a RIMM-based system, all memory slots must be populated, either with a RIMM module or with a *Continuity RIMM (CRIMM)*, which provides electrical continuity. If any RIMM slot is empty, the system will not boot. For those who work primarily with DIMMs, as we do, it's easy to forget this requirement. We spent an hour one day trying to figure out why a system we'd built just sat there beeping instead of booting. Turned out that we'd forgotten to install the CRIMM, which was buried deep in the motherboard packaging. All RDRAM motherboards we know of allow RIMMs and CRIMMs to be installed interchangeably. That is, it doesn't matter which slots you populate with RIMMs and which with CRIMMs.

You must install memory *at least* one full bank at a time. If you install more than one bank, you must install in full-bank increments. One 168-pin or 184-pin DIMM or 16/18-bit RIMM always equals one bank, regardless of the type of motherboard or processor. One 72-pin SIMM equals one bank in 386s and 486s. Two SIMMs equal one bank in Pentiums. Older systems, particularly 486s, may interleave banks to improve performance, which requires installing *two* banks at a time.

 Motherboards with dual-channel DDR-SDRAM memory controllers, such as the Intel D875PBZ or the ASUS A7N8X Deluxe, require adding DIMMs in pairs to enable dual-channel operation. Most such motherboards can operate with only one DIMM installed, but that disables dual-channel memory operation, which may incur a significant performance penalty. When installing DIMMs in pairs, the best practice is to use only identical DIMMs, but some motherboards allow using DIMMs with mixed speeds. See the motherboard manual for complete details.

In addition to banks, you may need to consider *rows* or *devices*, particularly if you install a large amount of memory. Each SDRAM chipset supports at most a given number of rows of memory, and this limit does not necessarily correspond with the number of physical memory slots on a motherboard that uses that chipset. A *single-sided SDRAM DIMM* has chips physically installed on only one side of the module, and appears to the chipset as one row of memory. A *double-sided SDRAM DIMM* has chips physically installed on both sides of the module, and appears to the chipset as two rows of memory.

So, for example, if a motherboard has three physical DIMM slots and its chipset supports only four rows of memory, you are restricted in terms of which DIMMs you can install. You can install single-sided DIMMs in all three memory slots because those three DIMMs total only three rows. You can install one double-sided

DIMM and two single-sided DIMMs because that totals only four rows. But if you install two double-sided DIMMs, you must leave the third slot empty because the two double-sided DIMMs total four rows, which is the maximum the chipset supports.

Two other factors may have a bearing on how many SDRAM DIMMs you can install:

Memory speed
Installing faster memory may reduce the number of DIMMs you can install. For example, a motherboard may have three DIMM slots, all of which can be populated with PC2700 DIMMs. But that motherboard may support at most two PC3200 DIMMs, forcing you to leave the third DIMM slot empty if you install PC3200 memory.

 Using too much fast memory can cause subtle memory problems. Motherboard, system, and memory manufacturers often do not publicize this problem. As a rule of thumb when installing fast memory, choose fewer high-capacity modules in preference to more lower-capacity modules. This problem is particularly likely to arise when you "push the envelope"—for example, by installing PC3200 or PC3500 memory, overclocking your system, or running dual processors.

Unbuffered versus Registered DIMMs
Unbuffered SDRAM DIMMs require the chipset memory controller to manage each chip on the DIMM individually. There is an upper limit on how many memory chips the memory controller can manage, which restricts the total number of unbuffered memory chips that the motherboard can support. *Registered SDRAM DIMMs* (sometimes called *Buffered SDRAM DIMMs*) put an additional layer of circuitry between the chipset memory controller and the actual memory chips, which in effect reduces the number of memory chips visible to the chipset memory controller to a manageable number. Registered DIMMs are uncommon in desktop systems because they cost more and are slower than unbuffered DIMMs. A CL2 registered DIMM has about the same memory performance as a CL3 unbuffered DIMM. Some motherboards support only unbuffered DIMMs, others only registered DIMMs, and some support either sort. A motherboard that supports either type may allow using one or the other, but not both at once.

RDRAM systems also limit the number of memory chips that can be installed at one time. Each RIMM comprises multiple RDRAM memory chips, each of which is called an *RDRAM device*. A typical RDRAM chipset might support at most 32 RDRAM devices per channel. If a RIMM uses 16 RDRAM chips (devices), you could install two of those RIMMs on the channel and still be within the upper limit on RDRAM devices. Attempting to install a third RIMM on that system would cause the system to fail to boot. Conversely, if you were installing RIMMs that use eight devices, three RIMMs would total only 24 devices, and so would be within the device limitation of that channel.

Chip Density

Memory modules are constructed from individual memory chips, which vary in their capacity. Chip capacities are specified in megabits (Mb or Mbit) rather than megabytes (MB). Because there are eight bits per byte, a memory module that uses eight chips can store the number of megabytes specified by the megabit size of the chip. For example, a memory module that uses eight 128-Mbit chips is a 128 MB memory module.

Recent memory modules may use 16-, 64-, 128-, 256-, or 512-Mbit chips. A memory module of a specified capacity may use fewer high-capacity chips or more low-capacity chips. For example, a 256 MB DIMM might use eight 256-Mbit chips or sixteen 128-Mbit chips. Although both DIMMs have the same 256 MB capacity, the eight-chip DIMM is a single-sided DIMM and the 16-chip DIMM is a double-sided DIMM. For a given capacity, it's generally better to install a single-sided DIMM when possible because chipsets support only so many rows of memory, and a double-sided DIMM "uses up" two rows.

However, you must not install memory that uses higher-capacity chips than your chipset supports. For example, the Intel 815 chipset supports 16-, 64-, 128-, and 256-Mbit chips, so an 815-based motherboard could use either the eight-chip or the 16-chip, 256 MB DIMM. The Intel 440BX chipset, however, supports only 16-, 64-, and 128-Mbit chips, so a 440BX-based motherboard could use only the 16-chip 256 MB DIMM. Attempting to install a DIMM that uses higher-capacity chips than the chipset supports has unpredictable consequences. Sometimes, the system will simply refuse to recognize the DIMM. Other times, the system will recognize the DIMM, but at some fraction (typically one-half or one-quarter) of its actual capacity.

You must also avoid using chips of too low a capacity. For example, the Intel 875P chipset supports 128-, 256-, and 512-Mbit chips, but not 64-Mbit chips. Installing an older DIMM that uses 64-Mbit chips in an Intel 875P-based motherboard results in the DIMM not being recognized.

 If you use Crucial memory, which we recommend, the best way to make sure that the module you choose is compatible with your system is to use the Crucial Memory Selector on the Crucial home page (*http://www.crucial.com/*). That tool allows you to specify your system or motherboard model, and displays only memory modules that are compatible with your system.

Parity and ECC Memory

Two types of memory use extra bits to store checksum information that can detect and sometimes correct memory errors. They are as follows:

Parity memory
Uses nine bits per byte to provide simple error detection, so simple as to be useless on modern PCs. Most early DIP-based PCs required parity memory, and so used nine chips per row. SIMMs, which are much more reliable than DIPs, made parity unnecessary. The Intel Triton Pentium-class chipset and

competing chipsets removed support for parity memory. Recent chipsets again support parity memory, but there is no good reason to use it.

Although parity memory is still sold, buy it only if your computer requires it. Some computers do not allow mixing parity and nonparity modules. Before buying parity memory, verify which type is already installed and whether your chipset can mix parity with nonparity memory. Identify parity modules by counting the chips on the module. If that number is evenly divisible by three, it's a parity module. If nonparity memory is installed, or if parity memory is installed but your chipset allows mixing types, buy nonparity memory. Buy parity memory only if parity memory is already present and your chipset does not allow mixing types.

ECC memory

An enhanced form of error-checking memory that can detect single- and multibit errors and correct all single- and some multibit errors. ECC originated on mainframes, migrated to minicomputers, and is now common on PC servers.

ECC memory requires five extra bits to protect an 8-bit byte, six to protect a 16-bit word, seven to protect a 32-bit word, and eight to protect a 64-bit word. A 72-bit-wide DIMM supports either parity or ECC interchangeably. Chipsets that support 168-pin DIMMs may also support ECC, although ECC is not always implemented in BIOS. If your BIOS supports it, you can use ECC by installing 72-bit DIMMs and enabling ECC in Chipset Setup. The downside, however, is that 72-bit DIMMs cost about 12.5% more than standard 64-bit DIMMs, and enabling ECC reduces memory performance, typically by about 3%. Use ECC memory on servers when constant uptime is critical. Do not use ECC memory in standard desktop PCs except those that have a large amount of memory installed.

 One common cause of "flipped bit" memory errors is, believe it or not, cosmic rays. The more memory you have installed, the more likely it is that a random cosmic ray will impact one of the memory cells in a chip on your system, causing the contents of that cell to flip from a binary zero to a one or vice versa. We don't pretend to understand this issue, but we've been told by memory experts that for systems with 512 MB of RAM using ECC versus nonparity memory is about an even trade-off in terms of extra cost and lost performance versus the likelihood of memory errors. For systems with 768+ MB, we use ECC memory exclusively, if the motherboard supports it.

How Much Memory Is Enough?

Back when memory cost $50 per megabyte, we advised people to install as much memory as they could afford. With memory now selling for pennies per megabyte, we advise people to install as much memory as their motherboards will accept.

How much memory you actually need depends on the operating system and applications you use, how many windows you keep open, which background services and processes you run, and so on. Memory is more important than processor speed when it comes to system performance. Windows XP runs faster on a slow Celeron with 256 MB than on a fast Pentium 4 with 64 MB.

Using a big swap/paging file cannot substitute for having enough RAM. Windows virtual memory allows you to run more and larger programs than fit into physical memory by temporarily swapping data from RAM to a disk file. When Windows swaps to disk, performance takes a major hit. If your hard disk clatters away every time you switch between running applications, that's a sure sign that heavy paging is going on and that your system needs more memory. RAM is cheap. Install enough of it to minimize use of the paging file.

To determine how much memory you need, choose the following category that best describes your usage pattern. If you fall between two, choose the higher. Note that newer versions of applications usually require more memory.

Light
> Web browsing, email, casual word processing and spreadsheets, checkbook management, and simple games; one or two windows open; particularly if using software one or two versions behind current releases.

Typical
> Applications listed previously, particularly current versions; three to five windows open; using more demanding applications, including casual database updates and queries, complex spreadsheets, light/moderate programming, and mainstream games. File and print sharing in small workgroups or home networks.

Heavy
> Memory-intensive applications—e.g., Photoshop; speech/pattern-recognition software; many windows open; multiple background services; graphics-intensive games such as Quake III; heavy programming, especially with an Integrated Development Environment (IDE) and doing frequent compiles and links. File and print sharing for large workgroups or departmental groups. Limited use as an application or database server.

Extreme
> Professional scientific, engineering, and statistical applications; manipulating very large data sets. Use as a consolidated file, print, application, and database server.

Table 5-1 lists the minimum amount of memory we recommend by operating system and usage. These are *ad hoc* rules based on our experience, so your mileage may vary. More is always better because using more than the recommended minimum contributes to system stability. Windows 9X is of questionable robustness for Heavy usage, let alone Extreme usage, so we do not provide recommendations for Windows 9X in Extreme usage.

As we update this table for each edition, the amount of RAM we recommend keeps growing, both because later releases of the operating systems need more memory and because new versions of applications typically want more memory. Only a couple of years ago, running 512 MB of RAM on a desktop system raised eyebrows, and 1 GB was unheard of except among graphics professionals and others with heavy demands. Nowadays, 512 MB systems are commonplace, and 1 GB systems are not unusual. We remember a time not all that long ago when we were delighted to have 1 GB of *disk space*.

Table 5-1. Recommended memory by operating system and usage pattern

Operating system	Light	Typical	Heavy	Extreme
Windows 95	24 MB	64 MB	128 MB	N/R
Windows 98/98SE	32 MB	64 MB	128 MB	N/R
Windows Me	64 MB	64 MB	128 MB	N/R
Windows NT 4 Workstation	64 MB	128 MB	256 MB	384+ MB
Windows NT 4 Server	96 MB	256 MB	512 MB	768+ MB
Windows 2000 Professional	128 MB	256 MB	512 MB	1024+ MB
Windows 2000 Server	128 MB	256 MB	512 MB	1024+ MB
Windows XP Home/Professional	128 MB	256 MB	512 MB	1024+ MB
Linux (GUI workstation)	128 MB	256 MB	512 MB	1024+ MB
Linux (text-based server)	128 MB	256 MB	512 MB	1024+ MB

Each operating system has a "sweet spot," which depends on the application mix, but is typically about midway between our recommendations for Typical and Heavy usage. Adding memory increases performance until you reach the sweet spot, but adding more than that results in decreasing returns. We generally find the sweet spot for Windows 95/98/Me to be 96 MB; for Windows NT Workstation 4.0, 192 MB; and for the remaining operating systems, 384 MB. Your mileage may vary.

In general, the best way to determine if you've reached the sweet spot for your own mix of applications and your personal working style is to keep an eye on how frequently the system pages out to the hard disk. If that happens frequently, you need more memory. If your system pages only occasionally, you probably have enough memory. Our rule is simple. If in doubt, always err on the side of having more memory rather than less.

If you're wondering whether we practice what we preach, Robert uses 1 GB of RAM on his primary Windows 2000 Professional desktop system, and 512 MB on his secondary Windows 2000 Pro systems. Barbara uses 1 GB on her Windows 2000 Pro system. (We don't use Windows XP on any of our production systems.) Our two general-purpose NT 4 servers provide file and print sharing and domain controller functions, and run happily with 128 MB each. Our main Linux server uses 512 MB, and our secondary Linux servers have 256 MB each. Our Linux desktop systems have 384 MB or 512 MB, and all supplementary and test-bed systems have at least 256 MB. Other than our legacy NT4 Server boxes, we no longer have any systems running 128 MB or less.

Memory Selection Guidelines

The following sections provide guidelines for selecting memory for a new system or to upgrade an existing system. Follow these guidelines as closely as possible to ensure the memory you select functions optimally in your system.

Upgrading Older Systems

When upgrading an older motherboard, it is sometimes impossible to match the installed memory. Some motherboards have 30-pin and 72-pin SIMM sockets, and many have both SIMM and DIMM sockets. If the installed memory occupies all available sockets of one type, you may have to add memory of a different type.

If so, consult the manual to determine supported configurations. For example, many 30/72-pin motherboards provide four 30-pin and two 72-pin sockets, but allow you to populate both 72-pin sockets only if no memory is installed in the 30-pin sockets. Similarly, motherboards with both SIMM and DIMM sockets may allow using a DIMM only if one or more SIMM sockets are vacant or populated only with single-sided SIMMs.

Mixing memory types may degrade performance. Some chipsets run all memory at the speed of the slowest module. Others, including the 430HX and 430VX, run each bank at optimum speed. Mixed-memory configurations are nonstandard and best avoided. Memory is cheap enough that it's often better to use all new memory.

Be very conscious of costs when upgrading older systems. Although older memory types are still available, the cost per MB may be very high. For the same cost as a large amount of old-style memory, you may literally be able to purchase a new motherboard, processor, *and* the same amount of modern memory. If for some reason we need to upgrade memory in a SIMM-based system, we try to scrounge compatible SIMMs from hangar queens rather than buying new modules.

Observe the following general guidelines when selecting memory:

- Verify your motherboard can cache the full amount of RAM you install. For example, the Intel 430TX chipset supports 256 MB of RAM, but caches only 64 MB. Adding RAM beyond 64 MB actually decreases system performance. Some motherboards have insufficient cache installed to cache the full amount of cacheable RAM supported by the chipset. Some of these have sockets that you can fill with additional cache. The cacheable RAM area of Slot 1 systems is determined by the processor itself. The L2 cache present on Pentium II CPUs can cache a maximum of 512 MB of system memory. Modern socketed processors from Intel and AMD can cache more main memory than can physically be installed.

- Purchase only name-brand memory, especially if you overclock your system. Motherboards vary in their tolerance for different brands of memory. Some motherboards accept and use nearly any compatible memory, but others are reliable only with some brands of memory. A name-brand memory module functions properly on nearly any motherboard designed to accept that module. We use only Crucial memory (*http://www.crucial.com*) and Kingston memory (*http://www.kingston.com*) in our systems, and have never had a problem with them.

- Don't attempt to save money by mixing newer memory with older memory. For example, if you buy two 32 MB PC133 SDRAM DIMMs for a system that currently has one 16 MB EDO DIMM installed, you may be tempted to use all three DIMMs for a system total of 80 MB rather than 64 MB. That's usually a mistake. Some systems accept mixed EDO and SDRAM memory, but most systems will run the newer, faster memory at the same speed as the older, slower memory. The same holds true for upgrading newer systems. For example, if you buy two 256 MB PC2700 DIMMs to upgrade a system that currently has one 128 MB PC1600 DIMM, settle for 512 MB of pure PC2700 memory rather than going for 640 MB of mixed-speed memory that will operate at only PC1600.

- Buy one larger-capacity module in preference to two smaller ones of the same total capacity. This is particularly important with DIMM modules. Most motherboards have only two to four DIMM sockets, so buying smaller-capacity DIMMs may later force you to replace existing memory when you want to add more memory to the system.

- Memory modules and sockets may use tin or gold contacts. Manufacturers often recommend using modules with the same contact metal as the sockets. In theory, mixing gold and tin can cause corrosion and other problems. In practice, we've never seen this happen.

Upgrading Newer Systems

Newer systems use DIMM or RIMM modules exclusively. DIMM and RIMM memory are available in many more variants than SIMM memory, so be careful to buy DIMMs or RIMMs that match your requirements. Use these guidelines when choosing DIMM or RIMM memory modules:

- For SDRAM DIMMs, get the proper voltage. All DDR-SDRAM DIMMs use 2.5V. Most SDR-SDRAM DIMMs use 3.3V. Some DIMMs, often called Macintosh DIMMs, use 5V. Some early DIMM-based PC motherboards use 5V DIMMs.

- DIMMs are available in EDO, SDR-SDRAM, and DDR-SDRAM. Some transition motherboards support two types—EDO and SDR-SDRAM, or SDR-SDRAM and DDR-SDRAM. If you have the choice of EDO or SDR-SDRAM, buy SDR-SDRAM DIMMs for future flexibility. If your motherboard supports both SDR-SDRAM and DDR-SDRAM, buy DDR-SDRAM.

- SDR-SDRAM and DDR-SDRAM DIMMs are available in *buffered* (also called *registered*) and *unbuffered* versions. Some motherboards accept only buffered DIMMs, others accept only unbuffered DIMMs, and still others will accept either buffered or unbuffered DIMMs, but do not allow mixing types. Check the motherboard or system maker's documentation or web site to verify which type(s) of module your system accepts. If you are upgrading an existing system that accepts both types, open the lid to determine which type is currently installed. Even if the motherboard accepts mixed buffered and unbuffered DIMMs, avoid mixing types if possible.

- Buy the fastest-speed memory available, which usually costs little or no more than slower versions. For SDR-SDRAM, buy nothing slower than PC133 modules, which are backward-compatible with systems that use PC100 or PC66 memory. For DDR-SDRAM, buy PC2700 or (better) PC3200 modules in preference to PC2100 modules. Like SDR-SDRAM modules, faster DDR-SDRAM modules are generally backward-compatible with motherboards designed to use slower modules. Verify backward compatibility using the Crucial Memory Configurator (*http://www.crucial.com*).

 No-name and off-brand memory may be fraudulently labeled. The manufacturer's reputation is the only guarantee that a module labeled "PC2700" or "PC3200" in fact meets the required specifications. Using substandard memory may at best cause frequent lock-ups and at worst corrupt data or cause boot failures.

- Don't mistake modules labeled "100 MHz" for true PC100 memory. PC100 memory supports 125 MHz (8 ns) operation, but 100 MHz (10 ns) memory is usable at FSB speeds no higher than 83 MHz. Some vendors label modules "LX" to indicate they work with the 66 MHz FSB 440LX chipset, and "BX" to indicate they work with the 100 MHz FSB 440BX chipset. "BX" modules *usually* run at 100 MHz FSB, but are not PC100 modules unless so labeled. Similarly, some vendors sell "133 MHz" DIMMs, hoping buyers will mistake them for PC133.

 Access time for memory modules is rated for the entire module rather than for the individual chips that comprise it, which is why a module that uses 60 ns chips can have a 10 ns access time.

- Make sure DIMMs support Serial Presence Detect (SPD), a serial EEPROM that stores DIMM parameters—including memory type, size, speed, voltage, number of row and column addresses, and so forth—which can be read by the system BIOS at boot time and used to correctly configure memory. Some motherboards won't boot with non-SPD memory. Others boot, but with a warning message. Some vendors label SPD modules "EEPROM," but a module so labeled isn't necessarily SPD-compliant. Ask.

- Purchase modules with lower CAS latency whenever possible. PC100 and PC133 DIMMs are readily available in CAS2 or CAS3 (sometimes shown as CL2 or CL3). CAS2 modules provide a small performance boost relative to CAS3 modules. More important, CAS2 modules have a bit more in reserve that allows them to function more reliably in overclocked or heavily loaded systems. CAS2 modules typically cost 2% or so more than CAS3. You may find CAS1 modules, which ordinarily sell at a high enough premium over CAS2 modules to make them a poor choice.

- When upgrading an older system, determine whether it requires two-clock or four-clock modules. Recent PCs use four-clock memory, which is now ubiquitous. If your system requires two-clock memory, you'll have to ask for it. It may be a special-order item, for which you will be charged a premium.

All 168-pin DIMMs, 184-pin DIMMs, and 184-pin RIMMs use similar sockets, but both modules and sockets are keyed to prevent using the wrong type of module. If there is such a thing as a "standard" SDR-SDRAM DIMM, it would be 3.3 volt, nonparity (x64), unbuffered, PC100, CAS3. Similarly, a "standard" DDR-SDRAM DIMM would be 2.5 volt, nonparity (x64), PC2700 or PC3200, CAS2.5.

SIMM Guidelines

Use the following guidelines when choosing SIMM memory modules:

- Unless you are upgrading an older Socket 7 system that accepts only 72-pin SIMMs, buy only 168-pin DIMM memory. Many Socket 7 motherboards have both SIMM and DIMM sockets. Buying DIMMs for such a board makes more sense than buying obsolete SIMMs. However, note that some early boards support DIMMs only with very slow memory timings.

- SIMMs are available in FPM and EDO. If your motherboard supports either type, buy EDO (assuming you can't scrounge it somewhere). Some motherboards support both FPM and EDO, but do not allow mixing types, either per bank or globally. Because FPM is obsolescent and demand for it is small, FPM often costs more than EDO. If FPM is installed and the motherboard does not allow mixing FPM with EDO, consider removing FPM SIMMs and installing all EDO SIMMs.

- Don't assume the motherboard supports large SIMMs. Check the manufacturer's web site to determine the supported SIMM capacities and memory configurations. Older motherboards often support nothing larger than 16 MB SIMMs. Conversely, don't assume the motherboard cannot support larger SIMMs than those currently installed just because the manual says so. For example, one of our technical reviewers from an earlier edition has a Compaq system whose manual lists 16 MB SIMMs as the largest supported. That was true when the manual was printed because 32 MB SIMMs were not yet available. But that system uses 32 MB SIMMs without problems.

- Some motherboards, particularly those with four or more SIMM sockets, restrict the number of double-sided SIMMs that can be used, or restrict the total number of SIMM sides that can be used. If your motherboard has such a limitation, verify that the combination of currently installed SIMMs and the SIMMs you plan to install does not exceed the limit.

Upgrading Memory in Pentium Pro and Pentium-Class Systems

Pentium Pro and P54C/P55C Pentium-class systems, including those with an AMD K6 or higher, are too old to be good upgrade candidates, but many such systems are still used as firewalls and fax servers, and for other appliance duties, where it may make sense to extend their useful lives for another year or two by installing a memory upgrade. When upgrading memory in a Pentium or Pentium Pro, note the following issues:

- Try to install the memory identical to that already installed. Early Pentiums and most Pentium Pros use 72-pin SIMMs, but either type of system may use DIMMs in addition to or instead of SIMMs. Existing memory may be FPM, EDO, or SDRAM. Many systems can use different memory types—e.g., FPM or EDO—but do not allow mixed types. If you have a choice, install SDR-SDRAM DIMMs. Even PC66 DIMMs work fine in systems this old, and most systems of this type yield better memory performance with SDRAM than with older memory styles.

- Most such systems have nonparity memory installed. Some do not support parity memory. Pentium Pro systems often have parity memory installed, and may use ECC. Some systems support parity or nonparity memory, but do not allow mixed types. Others accept parity or nonparity RAM interchangeably, but disable parity if any nonparity modules are installed. For SIMM-based systems, count chips to determine memory type. For DIMM-based systems, locate the identification number on a module and check the manufacturer's documentation to determine its type.

- These systems use a 64-bit memory bus, and therefore require adding 72-pin SIMMs in pairs. DIMMs may be added individually.

- Most SIMM-based systems use 60 or 50 ns memory. Make sure new memory is at least as fast as that already installed. Early DIMM-based systems use FPM or EDO DIMMs, which you should match as closely as possible. Later DIMM-based systems may use JEDEC (PC66) SDRAM. You can use PC66 SDRAM, but it's better to buy PC133 SDRAM, which can be recycled later into systems that will themselves be approaching their design lifetimes.

Upgrading Memory in Pentium II/III/4, Celeron, and Athlon Systems

These systems are excellent candidates for memory upgrades. Early Pentium II systems often have only 16 MB of RAM. In the price-sensitive consumer Celeron market, many early systems shipped with only 16 MB, and some Celeron systems have been sold with only 8 MB. Expanding memory to 128 MB or more is the most cost-effective upgrade you can make. When upgrading memory in one of these systems, note the following issues:

- Some early Pentium II and Celeron systems use EDO SIMMs or DIMMs, but most use 3.3 volt 168-pin unbuffered JEDEC SDR-SDRAM DIMMs.

- Conserve DIMM sockets. A few motherboards have four DIMM sockets, most have three, and some low-end systems have only two. If you have the choice, always install one larger DIMM rather than two smaller ones that total the same amount of memory. Note, however, that older systems may not recognize large-capacity DIMMs or those that use 128-megabit or larger memory chips. In that situation, a BIOS upgrade may help, but the limitation is often hardcoded into the chipset.

- Most of these systems have nonparity memory installed, but can use either parity or nonparity DIMMs interchangeably. Unless you plan to install 512 MB or more, install nonparity DIMMs. We have been told that when using very large amounts of memory—more than 512 MB—memory errors introduced by cosmic rays make it worthwhile to pay the additional cost for parity/ECC memory and to accept the small performance hit that using ECC produces.

- Memory must always be added in full banks. These systems use a 64-bit memory bus, and therefore require adding 72-pin SIMMs in pairs. DIMMs may be added individually.

- Most SIMM-based systems use 60 ns or 50 ns memory. Make sure memory you add is at least as fast as the memory that is already installed. Early DIMM-based systems use FPM or EDO DIMMs, which you should match as closely as possible. Later DIMM-based systems may use JEDEC (PC66) SDRAM. You can install PC66 SDRAM, but it usually makes more sense to buy PC133 SDRAM for these systems because it can be recycled later if you upgrade to a faster system.

Installing Memory

Installing a SIMM or DIMM module is straightforward. Most recent motherboards automatically detect installed memory modules regardless of the slot they occupy, but it is good practice to fill banks from the lowest numbered to the highest. For example, if the motherboard has three banks, fill Bank 1 only after Bank 0 is filled, and fill Bank 2 only after Banks 0 and 1 are filled.

Some motherboards require larger modules be installed in lower-numbered banks. For example, if the motherboard has three DIMM sockets, Bank 0 is currently occupied by a 32 MB DIMM, and you are installing two 64 MB DIMMs, instead of simply installing the two new 64 MB DIMMs in Banks 1 and 2, you may need to remove the 32 MB DIMM from Bank 0, install the 64 MB DIMMs in Banks 0 and 1, and then reinstall the original 32 MB DIMM in Bank 2.

That rule is not invariable, though. A few motherboards require smaller modules be installed in the lower banks. Some motherboards don't care which module you install in which bank. Best practice is to check the manual before installing memory. If no documentation is available, experiment by moving modules around. If some or all of the memory is not recognized during the boot-time memory check or in CMOS Setup, try rearranging the modules. If all memory is recognized, you can safely assume that you have the modules installed correctly.

Windows and recent Linux releases automatically recognize the full amount of memory physically installed. However, Linux kernel version 2.0.36 or earlier may not recognize more than 64 MB of RAM automatically. Some have reported this problem on older hardware even with newer kernels. If you upgrade RAM beyond 64 MB in such a system, add the line append="mem=XXXM" to the file /etc/lilo. conf, where XXX is the amount of physical RAM installed, and re-run /sbin/lilo to make the changes take effect. For example, if you install 256 MB, add append="mem=256M".

One of our editors notes that you can also usually specify this at boot time, which can be useful for experimenting with different numbers (he came across one old system in which he needed to use one less than the total installed memory, or else Linux crashed). Also, lilo may be headed for extinction in favor of bootloaders such as grub, which reads its config file at boot time rather than requiring running a utility each time you change it. The best solution is to upgrade to a more recent Linux kernel.

Installing and Removing a SIMM

To install a SIMM
Locate a free SIMM socket of the proper type (30- or 72-pin). One side of the SIMM has a notch that aligns with a matching post on the SIMM slot support bracket, which prevents the SIMM from being installed backward. Align the notch and then slide the contact edge of the SIMM into the SIMM slot at about a 45-degree angle, as shown in Figure 5-3.

Once you have the SIMM aligned properly, maintain slight pressure toward the slot and pivot the SIMM upward toward the vertical until it snaps into place, as shown in Figure 5-4. Verify that the spring connectors on each side of the SIMM slot bracket have both snapped into the matching holes on the SIMM.

To remove a SIMM
Locate the spring connectors at the top of each side of the SIMM slot bracket and press both of them lightly at the same time while simultaneously pressing the SIMM gently away from the vertical. After the spring connectors release their grip on the SIMM, pivot the SIMM gently downward to about a 45-degree angle and then pull it gently out of the slot. Locking tabs sometimes exert considerable force, so you may find it easier to press the release gently with a small screwdriver, as shown in Figure 5-5.

Figure 5-3. Inserting the SIMM at a 45-degree angle

Figure 5-4. Rotating the SIMM to vertical and making sure the locking tabs snap into place

Figure 5-5. Using a small screwdriver to press down on the locking tabs until they release, while maintaining gentle pressure on the module

 The motherboard shown in Figures 5-3 through Figure 5-5 uses metal locking tabs. Some inexpensive motherboards use plastic tabs, which are quite easy to break off. If a tab does break off, that SIMM slot is unusable because the pressure exerted by the tab is required to ensure good contact between the memory module and the slot contacts. Nearly all recent DIMM- and RIMM-based systems use plastic locking tabs, so the absence of metal tabs on these newer systems is not an indication of low quality.

Installing and Removing a DIMM or RIMM

To install a DIMM or RIMM

Locate a free socket and pivot the ejector arms on each side of the socket as far as possible toward the horizontal. The contact edge of the DIMM module is keyed with notches that correspond to protuberances in the DIMM socket. Align the notches and slide the DIMM straight down into the socket. Position your thumbs on top of the DIMM at each end and press down firmly, as shown in Figure 5-6.

Figure 5-6. Aligning the memory module and pressing straight down until it seats

The DIMM slides (sometimes snaps) into the socket, which automatically pivots the ejector arms toward the vertical. If the ejector arms are not fully vertical, press them toward the DIMM until they lock into the vertical position, as shown in Figure 5-7. Note that some DIMM sockets have minor physical variations. If the DIMM does not fit easily into the socket, do not force it. Contact the vendor who supplied the DIMM for a replacement.

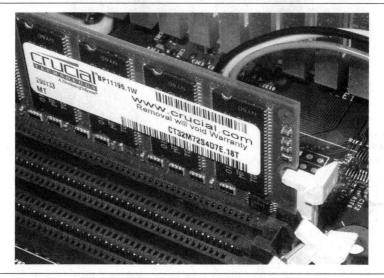

Figure 5-7. The ejector arms pivoting back to the vertical when the memory module is fully seated

 If you are installing Rambus RIMMs, also install a CRIMM in each unused memory slot. Rambus systems malfunction unless all memory slots are occupied, either by a RIMM or a CRIMM. Most Rambus motherboards have enough CRIMMs bundled with the motherboard to populate all but one memory slot. If you run short of CRIMMs, you can buy them at most computer stores.

To remove a DIMM or RIMM
Pivot both ejector arms simultaneously toward the horizontal position. The DIMM simply pops out.

Testing and Configuring Newly Installed Memory

After you install the new memory modules and verify that all is as it should be, apply power to the system. The memory self-test should increment up to the newly installed amount of memory. If it instead shows only the original amount of memory, the cause is almost always that you have not seated the new memory module completely. Power down, reseat the module, and try again.

If the memory check shows an amount of memory larger than the original amount but smaller than the expected new amount, the problem is almost always that the BIOS and/or chipset do not support memory modules of the size you've installed.

If that occurs, you may need to do one or more of the following things to resolve the problem:

- Check the Chipset Setup portion of CMOS Setup to determine how memory is configured for the newly installed bank(s). Most recent chipsets and BIOSs automatically determine the correct size and configuration parameters for installed modules. But some chipsets, BIOSs, and memory modules do not implement SPD correctly. If this occurs, you may have to set the correct size manually, if indeed the module size you have installed is an available option.

- A limitation on maximum module size may be enforced by the chipset, the BIOS, or both. Before deciding you cannot use the larger module, check the motherboard manufacturer's web site for a BIOS update. If the restriction on module size is enforced by the BIOS but not by the chipset, you may find that a later BIOS revision adds support for the larger module.

- If all else fails, the only alternative may be to return the memory module (you did make sure you had the right to return an incompatible module, didn't you?) and obtain a smaller module.

Troubleshooting Memory Installation and Operation

Once installed and configured, memory seldom causes problems. When problems do occur, they may be as obvious as a failed RAM check at boot or as subtle as a few corrupted bits in a datafile. The usual symptom of memory problems is a kernel panic under Linux or a blue-screen crash under Windows. Unfortunately, that occurs so often with Windows that it's of little use as a diagnostic aid. When troubleshooting memory problems, always do the following:

- Use standard antistatic precautions. Ground yourself before you touch a memory module.

- Remove and reinstall all memory modules to ensure they are seated properly. While you're doing that, it's a good idea to clean the contacts on the memory module. Some people gently rub the contacts with a pencil eraser. We've done that ourselves, but memory manufacturers recommend against it because of possible damage to the contacts. Also, there is always the risk of a fragment from the eraser finding its way into the memory slot, where it can block one or more contacts. Better practice is to use a fresh dollar bill, which has just the right amount of abrasiveness to clean the contacts without damaging them.

 Although we have never used it, many people whom we respect recommend using Stabilant-22, a liquid contact enhancer. You'll probably keel over from sticker shock when you see the price of this stuff, but a drop or two is all that's needed, and a tiny tube lasts most people for years (*http://www.stabilant.com/*).

- Before assuming memory is the problem, check all internal cables to ensure none is faulty or has come loose.

The next steps you should take depend on whether you have made any changes to memory recently.

... When You Have Not Added Memory

If you suspect memory problems but have not added or reconfigured memory (or been inside the case), it's unlikely that the memory itself is causing the problem. Memory does simply die sometimes, and may be killed by electrical surges, but this is uncommon because the PC power supply itself does a good job of isolating memory and other system components from electrical damage. The most likely problem is a failing power supply. Try one or both of the following:

- If you have another system, install the suspect memory in it. If it runs there, the problem is almost certainly not the memory, but the power supply.

- If you have other memory, install it in the problem system. If it works, you can safely assume that the original memory is defective. More likely is that it will also fail, which strongly indicates power supply problems.

If you have neither another system nor additional memory, and if your system has more than one bank of memory installed, use binary elimination to determine which modules are bad. For example, if you have two modules installed (one per bank), simply remove one module to see if that cures the problem. If you have four identical modules installed (one per bank), designate them A, B, C, and D. Install only A and B and restart the system. If no problems occur, A and B are known good and the problem must lie with C and/or D. Remove B and substitute C. If no problems occur, you know that D is bad. If the system fails with A and C, you know that C is bad, but you don't know whether D is bad. Substitute D for C and restart the system to determine if D is good.

If you haven't enough banks to allow binary elimination, the best solution is to remove the modules, wrap them if possible in a static-safe bag (the pink plastic that most components arrive in), and take them to a local computer store that has a memory tester.

 MS-DOS, Windows 3.X, and Windows 9X do not stress memory. If you install Windows NT/2000/XP or Linux, memory errors may appear on a PC that seemed stable. People often therefore assume that they did something while installing the new OS to cause the errors, but that is almost never the case. Such errors almost always indicate a real problem with physical memory. The memory was defective all along, but the more forgiving OS simply ignored the problem.

... When You Are Adding Memory

If you experience problems when adding memory, note the following:

- If a DIMM appears not to fit, there's good reason. SDR-SDRAM DIMMs have two notches whose placement specifies 3.3V versus 5V and buffered versus unbuffered. DDR-SDRAM DIMMs have a keying notch in a different location. If the DIMM notches don't match the socket protrusions, the DIMM is of the wrong type.

- If the system displays a memory mismatch error the first time you restart, that usually indicates no real problem. Follow the prompts to enter Setup, select Save and Exit, and restart the system. The system should then recognize the new memory. Some systems require these extra steps to update CMOS.

- Verify the modules are installed in the proper order. Unless the motherboard documentation says otherwise, fill banks sequentially from lowest number to highest. Generally, install the largest module in Bank 0, the next largest in Bank 1, and so on. A few systems require the smallest module be in Bank 0 and larger modules sequentially in higher banks.

- If the system recognizes a newly installed module as half actual size and that module has chips on both sides, the system may recognize only single-banked or single-sided modules. Some systems limit the total number of "sides" that are recognized, so if you have some existing smaller modules installed, try removing them. The system may then recognize the double-side modules. If it doesn't, return those modules and replace them with single-sided modules.

- A memory module may not be defective, but still be incompatible with your system. For example, many 486s treat three-chip and nine-chip SIMMs differently, although they should theoretically be interchangeable. Some 486s use only three-chip SIMMs or only nine-chip SIMMs. Others use either, but generate memory errors if you have both types installed.

- A memory module may not be defective, but still be incompatible with your current configuration. For example, if you install a CAS3 PC133 DIMM in a 133 MHz FSB Pentium III motherboard that is configured to use CAS2 timing, the system will almost certainly generate memory errors.

Our Picks

We use and recommend only name-brand memory. Commodity memory may not work properly in a given motherboard. Even if it appears to work properly at first, you may later experience subtle problems attributable to the memory. Name-brand memory costs little more than commodity memory, and is definitely worth the small extra cost.

We have installed Crucial or Kingston memory almost exclusively in the scores of systems we've built during the last several years, and have experienced no problems attributable to memory in those systems. That's something we can't say for other brands of memory we've tested, and certainly not for commodity memory. We frequently use the Crucial Memory Configurator on Crucial's web site, which allows you to enter the manufacturer and model of your system or motherboard and returns a list of memory modules, with prices, that are certified to be compatible with that system or motherboard.

Here are our recommendations for memory:

SIMM

If you are upgrading a SIMM-based system, tread carefully. Such systems are now so old that major upgrades make poor economic sense. SIMM modules are quite expensive per MB, and it's quite easy to spend more on large-capacity SIMMs than the cost of a new motherboard, processor, *and* memory. If it's a question of adding 16 MB or 32 MB to extend the useful life of an older system, use the Crucial Memory Configurator to determine which module(s) fit your motherboard, and buy the appropriate Crucial SIMM. (*http://www.crucial.com*).

SDR-SDRAM DIMM

For maximum flexibility when upgrading an existing system, we recommend whenever possible purchasing only PC133 SDRAM memory, even for motherboards that require only PC66 or PC100. Before you do so, however, verify on the motherboard manufacturer's web site that your motherboard functions properly with PC133 SDRAM. A few motherboards designed for PC66 or PC100 memory have problems with PC133. When we need SDR-SDRAM memory, we use Crucial or Kingston modules exclusively (*http://www.crucial. com* or *http://www.valueram.com*).

DDR-SDRAM DIMM

If you are building a new Athlon or Pentium 4 system, we recommend using DDR-SDRAM. As is the case with SDR-SDRAM, you can nearly always use a faster module than required. For future flexibility, we recommend buying PC2700 or PC3200 DDR modules. If PC3500 modules become widely available and affordable—which we do not expect to happen—buy them instead. Buying commodity memory is always a bad idea, but when it comes to DDR, buying commodity memory is a *very* bad idea. DDR really pushes the limits, and using a high-quality module from a good maker is even more important than usual. If your motherboard supports both unbuffered and buffered (registered) DDR-SDRAM, consider installing registered modules for additional stability. Note that some motherboards *require* registered modules. We have used Crucial and Kingston DDR modules with equal success, and recommend them exclusively.

Rambus RDRAM RIMM

The April and May 2003 introduction of the Intel 875P- and 865-series dual-channel DDR-SDRAM chipsets effectively rendered RDRAM obsolete. If you are building a Pentium 4 system and require the highest possible memory performance, use an Intel dual-channel DDR-SDRAM motherboard and Crucial or Kingston PC3200 DIMMs.

Whatever type of memory you install, install plenty of it. For legacy Windows 9X systems, there seems to be little benefit to having more than 128 MB. For Windows NT/2000/XP, we consider 256 MB to be a good starting point, and usually install more. With the price of memory so low, we recommend you fill all of your memory slots with the largest supported modules and be done with it. We've seldom encountered a system that was having problems because it had too much memory. If you do install a large amount of memory, use ECC modules for their error-correcting capabilities.

For updated recommendations, visit: *http://www.hardwareguys.com/picks/ memory.html*.

6

Floppy Disk Drives

The following four chapters cover standard floppy disk drives, high-capacity "super" floppy disk drive replacements, removable hard drives, and tape drives, all of which are characterized as removable magnetic storage devices. These devices use media that can be swapped in and out of the drive, versus hard disk drives, whose media are a fixed part of the drives themselves. Although they are typically slower at accessing data than hard disks—sometimes much slower—removable magnetic storage devices are useful because you can store an unlimited amount of data on additional cartridges, albeit with only a subset of the data available online at any one time. Because media are separate items, you can transfer data between computers that are not networked, if those computers are equipped with a compatible drive. Removable media also allow storing data off-site as protection against fire, theft, or other catastrophes.

A major drawback of removable magnetic storage is inherent: magnetic storage is less reliable than optical storage. Over time, zero bits and one bits stored as magnetic domains tend to become an unreadable blur. A less obvious drawback of magnetic versus optical storage is the proprietary nature of most magnetic drives and media, and the continually changing standards. Try, for example, to read data written only five years ago to a proprietary DC600 tape drive. The original drive is dead, the manufacturer no longer exists, and the software used to write the data won't run on anything later than Windows 3.1 anyway. Even something as simple as reading data from a 5.25-inch floppy diskette can turn into a major undertaking. Accordingly, the most appropriate uses of these drives are to provide supplemental working storage, to transfer large amounts of data between computers, and to make backups. They are unsuitable for long-term data archiving.

Removable magnetic storage devices differ in many respects, including drive cost, storage capacity, and access time. Perhaps the most important difference is the cost of media, both per cartridge and per megabyte stored. When selecting a removable magnetic storage device, always keep in mind that media cost over the service life of the drive may greatly exceed the cost of the drive itself, particularly for drives that use proprietary, patented, and/or licensed media. Many of these drives are marketed on the King Gillette model of giving away the razor and selling the blades. The cost of those blades can really add up.

A *floppy disk drive* (FDD) is so called because it records data on a flexible circular plastic disk coated with ferrite or some other magnetic medium. This plastic disk is enclosed within a protective sleeve or cartridge. This assembly is called a *floppy disk* or a *diskette*. FDDs have been manufactured to accept 8-, 5.25-, and 3.5-inch diskettes, although only the last is still in common use.

Diskette Types and Formats

Before a diskette can be used to store data, you must prepare it by formatting it, although many diskettes nowadays come preformatted. Formatting creates the physical tracks and sectors that the drive uses to store data (called *low-level* or *physical formatting*) and the logical structure used by the operating system to organize that data (called *logical* or *DOS formatting*). Unlike hard disks, which require two separate formatting passes, FDDs perform both physical and logical formatting in one step. Also unlike hard disks, diskettes do not need to be partitioned.

 The Quick Format option available in Windows and later versions of DOS doesn't really format the diskette. It simply "zeros out" the File Allocation Tables and Root Directory entries, giving the appearance of a freshly formatted diskette but using the original format. Because data on diskettes fades with time, your data will be much safer if you do an actual format, which does a surface test and refreshes the physical and logical format structure of the diskette. Use Quick Format only on diskettes that have recently had a full format done on them. Also, do not count on a Quick Format to wipe sensitive data from a diskette. It's trivially easy to recover such data. To wipe data, do a full format on the diskette. Better yet, use a wipe utility, or bulk-erase the diskette. You have been warned.

To format a diskette with Windows, right-click the drive icon in My Computer or Explorer, choose Format, and mark the appropriate options. At the command line, format a diskette by typing the command format a: /options, where a: is the drive letter of the FDD, and /options controls how the disk will be formatted. The available options and the required syntax vary according to the version of DOS or Windows you use. Type format /? to display available formatting options. Which options are usable depends upon both the FDD type and the diskette type. Some FDDs accept only one type of diskette, while others accept two or more.

To format a diskette with Linux, run kfloppy (the KDE Floppy Formatter, shown in Figure 6-1) or gfloppy, the Gnome equivalent. Choose the appropriate size, filesystem, and other options, and then click the Format button. If you prefer a command line, mformat is convenient for formatting DOS floppies. The mdir and mcopy utilities are Linux equivalents for the DOS dir and copy commands, but with additional features.

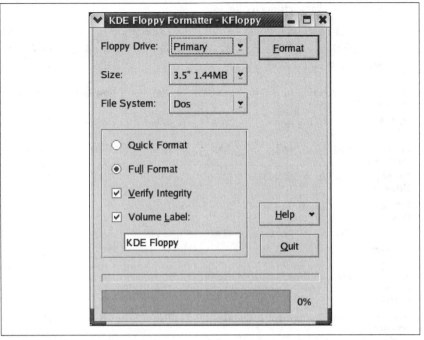

Figure 6-1. The KDE Floppy Formatter avoids having to mount the diskette or remember command-line options

For about a decade, the 3.5-inch High-Density (HD) FDD has been standard. However, you may encounter older types of FDDs and diskettes when upgrading an old machine or salvaging data, so it's worth knowing something about these obsolescent and obsolete formats. Table 6-1 lists the various diskette formats that have been supported on the IBM platform over the years.

Table 6-1. Diskette characteristics

	5.25-inch formats			3.5-inch formats		
	SSDD	DSDD	HD	DD	HD	ED
Formatted capacity (KB)	160 / 180	320 / 360	1200	720	1440	2880
Media descriptor byte	0xFE / 0xFC	0xFF / 0xFD	0xF9	0xF9	0xF0	0xF0
Bytes/ Sector	512	512	512	512	512	512
Sectors/ Track	8 / 9	8 / 9	15	9	18	36
Tracks/Side	40	40	80	80	80	80
Sides	1	2	2	2	2	2
Sectors/Disk	320 / 360	640 / 720	2,400	1,440	2,880	5,760
Available sectors/Disk	313 / 351	630 / 708	2,371	1,426	2,847	5,726

Table 6-1. Diskette characteristics (continued)

	5.25-inch formats			3.5-inch formats		
	SSDD	**DSDD**	**HD**	**DD**	**HD**	**ED**
Tracks/Inch (TPI)	48 / 48	48 / 48	96	135	135	135
Track width (inch/mm)	.0118/.300	.0118 /.300	.0061/.155	.0045/.115	.0045/.115	.0045/.115
Bits/Inch (BPI)	5,876	5,876	9,646	8,717	17,434	34,868
Media formulation	Ferrite	Ferrite	Cobalt	Cobalt	Cobalt	Barium
Coercivity (Oersteds)	300 / 300	300 / 300	600	600	720	750
Sectors/ Cluster	1	2	1	2	1	2
FAT type	12-bit	12-bit	12-bit	12-bit	12-bit	12-bit
FAT length (Sectors)	1 / 2	1 / 2	7	3	9	9
Root directory (Sectors)	4 / 4	7 / 7	14	7	14	15
Root directory entries	64 / 64	112 / 112	224	112	224	240

In addition to the standard formats described in Table 6-1, Microsoft has used the proprietary *DMF* (*Distribution Media Format*) for some distribution diskettes. DMF increases the capacity of a standard high-density 3.5-inch diskette by reducing the inter-sector gap to allow 21 sectors/track rather than the standard 18 sectors/track, thereby expanding capacity to a true 1.64 MB (usually called 1.68, 1.7, or 1.72 MB).

On most systems, you cannot read data from or write data to DMF diskettes directly because DIR, DISKCOPY, and other standard disk utilities do not recognize DMF. In fact, attempting to use DISKCOPY to copy a DMF diskette not only yields an unreadable target diskette, but also may actually damage the DMF source diskette. DMF diskettes are readable only by Setup and other Microsoft utilities designed to work with CAB files (the compressed Cabinet files used for software distribution), as well as by some third-party utilities such as WinZip (*http://www. winzip.com*), which allows you to extract data directly from compressed CAB files, and WinImage (*http://www.winimage.com*), which allows you to format and copy DMF diskettes directly.

Fortunately, most software is now distributed on CD or DVD discs, so DMF diskettes are seldom used nowadays. We say fortunately because in our experience DMF diskettes are much more likely than standard 1.44 MB diskettes to generate read errors. We have frequently found DMF diskettes that were unreadable straight out of the box, and a DMF diskette that is several years old is very likely to be unreadable. A standard diskette was simply never intended to store that much data.

If you encounter an unreadable DMF diskette, we recommend using WinImage to attempt to extract the CAB files manually to the hard disk. If one FDD consistently generates read errors, the diskette may be readable on a different drive, at least well enough to let you extract the CAB files.

Drive Types

As distinct from diskette types and formats, six drive types have been installed in PC-compatible systems:

5.25-inch 160/180 KB (SSDD)
> *Single-Sided, Double-Density (SSDD)* was the standard FDD in very early PC-class systems. These drives read and write only SSDD diskettes.

5.25-inch 320/360 KB (DSDD)
> *Double-Sided, Double-Density (DSDD)* was the standard FDD in PC-class systems, and was often found as a second FDD in early AT and 386 systems. These drives read and write single-sided (160/180 KB) and double-sided (320/360 KB) formats.

5.25-inch 1.2 MB (HD)
> *High-Density (HD)*—this and all later formats are double-sided, but that part is no longer stated—is the standard FDD in 286, 386, and some early 486 systems, and is often found as a second FDD in early systems with 3.5-inch primary FDDs. These drives read and write any 5.25-inch format. A diskette previously formatted or written to by a 5.25-inch DD drive and then written to by a 5.25-inch HD drive may not subsequently be reliably readable in any 5.25-inch DD drive.

3.5-inch 720 KB (DD)
> *Double-Density (DD)* is an interim standard, commonly found as a primary drive in early low-end 286 systems, and as a secondary drive in a few PC-class systems and many 286, 386, and 486 systems. These drives read and write only the 720 KB DD format.

3.5-inch 1.44 MB (HD)
> *High-Density (HD)* is the standard FDD on mainstream systems for the past decade. These drives read, write, and format any 3.5-inch HD or DD diskette.

3.5-inch 2.88 MB (ED)
> *Extra-Density (ED)* is a failed standard, introduced by IBM and now effectively obsolete. ED diskettes are very expensive—typically $3 each versus $0.25 for a 1.44 MB diskette—which doomed the format. These drives are difficult to find new nowadays, but can read, write, and format any 3.5-inch diskette in any format.

 5.25-inch drives and 3.5-inch drives use different methods for write-protecting diskettes. 5.25-inch diskettes have a write-enable notch. To write-protect a 5.25-inch diskette, cover that notch with opaque tape. 3.5-inch diskettes have a write-protect hole with a sliding shutter. To write-protect a 3.5-inch diskette, slide the shutter to uncover the hole.

FDD Interface and Cabling

The FDD interface and power requirements are completely standardized, as follows:

Controller

PC-class systems used a separate FDD controller card. XT- and AT-class systems and some early 386s used a combination HDD/FDD controller card. Current systems use an embedded FDD controller. These controllers differ only in their maximum data rate, which determines the FDD types they support. Early controllers run at 250 Kb/s, which supports only 360 KB 5.25-inch FDDs and 720 KB 3.5-inch FDDs. Later controllers run at 500 Kb/s, which supports any standard FDD, or at 1 Mb/s, which is required for 2.88 MB 3.5-inch FDDs. Run BIOS Setup to determine which FDD types a given system supports.

 If you must install a higher-capacity FDD than the controller supports—e.g., if you must salvage data from a hard drive in a system whose old 5.25-inch 360 KB FDD has failed and you have only a 3.5-inch HD FDD to replace it—you have two alternatives:

- Remove or disable the onboard FDD controller, and replace it with a third-party FDD controller that supports the higher-capacity FDD.

- Lie to the old system about what type of FDD you are installing. For example, install a 1.44 MB FDD, but tell the system that it is a 360 KB or 720 KB FDD. All FDDs run at 300 RPM, except 5.25-inch 1.2 MB FDDs, which run at 360 RPM. That means that any ED, HD, or DD 3.5-inch FDD can emulate any lower-capacity 3.5-inch drive, as well as the 5.25-inch 360 KB FDD. Use blank DD diskettes, and format them in the new drive. Copy data to the floppies and then attempt to read them on another system. Some systems will happily read such oddities as a 3.5-inch 360 KB diskette, but others will simply return an "unknown media type" message. If the latter occurs, use BIOS Setup on the good system to reconfigure the FDD temporarily to the same settings as those on the older system.

Data cable

FDD data cables use a standard 34-pin pinout (see Table 6-2), but connectors vary. 5.25-inch drives use a card-edge connector. 3.5-inch drives use a header-pin connector. Older standard FDD cables have at least three connectors, one for the FDD interface and two for drives. Many FDD cables have five connectors, with redundant header-pin and card-edge connectors at each of the two drive positions, allowing any type of FDD to be connected at either position. Because many newer systems support only one FDD, new data cables have only two connectors, one for the FDD interface and one for the drive itself.

Table 6-2. Floppy disk drive cable pinouts

Pin #	Signal	Pin #	Signal
Odd pins (1 – 33)	Ground	20	Step Pulse
2, 4, and 6	Not Used	22	Write Data
8	Index	24	Write Enable
10	Motor Enable A	26	Track 0
12	Drive Select B	28	Write Protect
14	Drive Select A	30	Read Data
16	Motor Enable B	32	Select Head 1
18	Direction (Stepper Motor)	34	Disk Change

Power

Obsolete 5.25-inch drives accept the larger Molex power connector. Current 3.5-inch drives accept the smaller Berg power connector, shown in Figure 6-2. A chassis that permits a 3.5-inch drive to be installed in a 5.25-inch bay typically includes a Molex-to-Berg adapter. Pinouts and voltages for both of these power connectors are covered in Chapter 26.

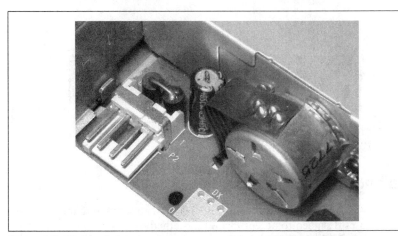

Figure 6-2. Unshrouded 4-pin power connector (labeled P2 here), used by all 3.5-inch FDDs

The BIOS identifies the drive as A: or B: based on how the drive is jumpered and by the cable position to which that drive connects. Older 5.25-inch drives have four *drive select* (DS) jumper positions, labeled DS0 through DS3 or DS1 through DS4. Later drives have only two settings, labeled DS0/DS1 or DS1/DS2. Many recent 3.5-inch drives are permanently set to the second DS position (DS1/DS2). The BIOS recognizes a drive set to the first DS position (DS0/DS1) as A: and a drive set to the second DS position (DS1/DS2) as B:, assuming that the drive is connected to the controller with a straight-through cable.

But a standard two-drive FDD cable has wires 10 through 16 twisted between the first (middle) drive connector and the second (end) drive connector, which effectively reverses the jumper setting on the drive connected to the end connector. In other words, a drive that is jumpered as the second drive (DS1/DS2 or B:) and connected to the end connector is seen by the system as the first drive (DS0/DS1 or A:) because of the twist. Because many recent chipsets support only a single FDD, many recent FDD cables have only two connectors, one for the motherboard FDD interface, and the second for the single FDD. This cable has a twist, shown in Figure 6-3, which means that a drive connected to it must be set to the second DS position if it is to be recognized as A:.

Figure 6-3. Conductors 10 through 16 are twisted before the final device connector in a standard FDD cable

Installing an FDD

Installing an FDD in all but the newest systems is straightforward. Note, however, that some cases designed to accept FlexATX motherboards have only one externally accessible 5.25-inch drive bay, intended to accept a CD or DVD drive. This is because FlexATX systems are intended to boot from CD and so eliminate "legacy" connectors, including the FDD. That means if you intend to install an FDD in a FlexATX system, you'll need a case with two or more externally accessible drive bays (assuming you also want to install an optical drive and/or tape drive in the system), and you'll need to buy a separate PCI card that provides an FDD interface because FlexATX and other "legacy-reduced" and "legacy-free" motherboards do not provide an embedded FDD interface.

FlexATX motherboards also fit standard ATX cases, so installing the FlexATX motherboard in a standard ATX case eliminates the drive bay problem, although not the lack of an FDD interface. If you really need an FDD in a system, we recommend using a motherboard that provides an embedded FDD interface.

Use the following rules when installing FDDs:

- To install one FDD in a system, standard practice is to jumper that drive as the second drive (DS1/DS2) and connect it to the end connector. Alternatively, you can jumper the drive as the first drive (DS0/DS1) and connect it to the middle connector. Either method allows the system to see that drive as A:. If your drive cable has only two connectors, jumper the drive as the second drive (DS1/DS2). Note that most current 3.5-inch FDDs are set permanently as the second drive, and have no jumper to allow changing that assignment. Such drives work properly with a two-connector data cable, and should be connected to the end connector on a three-position data cable.

- To install two FDDs in a system, jumper both drives as the second drive (DS1/DS2). Connect the A: drive to the end connector and the B: drive to the middle connector. (Note that the chipsets used in many recent systems support only one FDD.)

- Sometimes, cable constraints (length or available connector types) make it impossible to configure the drives as you want them. If this happens, check BIOS Setup to see if it allows you to exchange A: and B:, overriding the drive designations made by DS jumper settings and cable position.

To install the FDD, take the following steps:

1. Before you start, examine the drive to verify the location of Pin 1 on the data connector because it may be impossible to determine which is Pin 1 once the drive is installed in the computer. Most drives use an unshrouded and unkeyed connector, many of which are very poorly labeled. Some do not label Pin 1 at all. On all such drives we have seen, Pin 1 is located nearest the power connector. Better drives use a shrouded and/or keyed connector such as that shown in Figure 6-4, and are a better choice.

Figure 6-4. An NEC 3.5-inch FDD, which uses a shrouded cable connector rather than the typical bare pins (note the missing pin at lower left, which keys the connector)

2. Once you have located Pin 1 on the drive, connect the FDD data cable to the drive, aligning Pin 1 on the cable (the side with the red stripe) with Pin 1 on the drive. Do this before you install the FDD in the drive bay, particularly if you are using a drive with an unshrouded data connector. Otherwise, it's very easy to install the data cable offset by a column or row of pins. We know

because we've done it frequently. Be very careful when installing the cable because it's quite easy to bend pins on an unshrouded connector. Once you're sure the cable is aligned properly with the connector, place your thumb in the middle of the cable connector, as shown in Figure 6-5, and push gently on the cable connector until it seats fully.

Figure 6-5. Connecting the cable to the FDD, with Pin 1 oriented properly and all pins aligned

3. In most cases, the FDD installs from the front, but in some cases it installs from the rear. If the drive bay requires installing from the front, slide the FDD into the bay, using your free hand to feed the cable through without kinking it, as shown in Figure 6-6. In most cases, you must leave the FDD projecting half an inch or so in front of the metal chassis so that the FDD bezel will align properly with the case bezel once it is installed. Most 3.5-inch FDD bays have round screw holes positioned properly to ensure that everything aligns once the case bezel is replaced. Some, however, have elongated slots rather than round holes. On these cases, you may have to align the FDD by trial and error.

4. Once you have properly aligned the screw holes in the drive bay with those in the drive, insert the screws and tighten them until they are fully seated. Do not overtorque the screws. The number of screws required and their positions depend upon the particular FDD and case. Most FDDs and cases allow you to install as many as eight screws—two in front and two in back on each of the two sides. That's complete overkill. We generally use four screws, top-front and bottom-back on each side. Some cases make it very difficult to install screws to support the right side of the FDD (as you face the front of the case). In such cases, we generally install screws in all four positions on the left side of the drive and leave the right side unsupported. If your case is one that requires trial-and-error alignment to get the front of the FDD lined up with the front of the case, insert only two screws initially and tighten them down only enough to allow the FDD to slide in or out with some resistance. Then, replace the front system bezel, get the FDD aligned just right, tighten the two screws you already installed, and then install the remaining screws. If

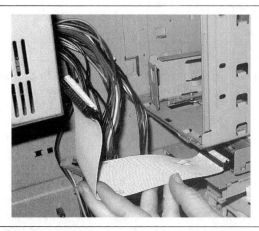

Figure 6-6. Sliding the FDD into the drive bay, making sure the cable feeds smoothly into the case interior

you're a belt-and-suspenders person, place a small dab of nail polish on each screw head to prevent it from vibrating loose.

5. With the drive securely fastened to the chassis, connect the power cable to the drive, as shown in Figure 6-7. The power cable and connector are keyed, and so can fit only in the proper orientation. But be careful to align everything properly before you press the connector into place. Some drives use fragile pins on the power connector, and we've bent more than one set when attempting to connect power to an FDD in an awkward situation, such as working under a desk in near darkness.

Figure 6-7. Connecting the power cable to the FDD, making sure the connector is aligned properly with the pins

The BIOS of all modern systems recognizes standard FDDs automatically, so no configuration is required.

Working with FDDs

Keep the following issues in mind when working with FDDs:

Choosing
3.5-inch HD FDDs are $10 commodity items made by several manufacturers. We prefer the Teac FD235HF, but there is little difference between brands. Buy whatever is offered. 5.25-inch FDDs are still available, but that won't last forever. If you need a 5.25-inch FDD to rescue data on old disks, get the drive now. If you patronize a local computer store, check there first. They may have a stack of old 5.25-inch FDDs they'd be happy to give away or sell cheaply.

Installing
5.25-inch FDDs require a 5.25-inch half-height, externally accessible drive bay. 3.5-inch FDDs can be installed in an externally accessible 3.5-inch third-height bay, or, by using an adapter, in a 5.25-inch half-height bay. The BIOS automatically detects installed FDDs, but can determine type unambiguously only for 5.25-inch HD (1.2 MB) FDDs, which spin at 360 RPM rather than 300. For other drive types, older machines assume 360 KB or 720 KB and newer systems assume 1.44 MB. Use BIOS Setup to confirm that the drive type is configured correctly.

Cabling
If you add or replace an FDD, also replace the cable, particularly if it is the original cable. Manufacturers often fold and crimp the FDD cable for improved cable routing and airflow. An old cable that has been so treated is no longer reliable, especially after you disturb it to install the new drive.

Change Line Support
All but the oldest FDD controllers use line 34 for Change Line Support. When the FDD door is opened, the FDD signals on line 34 to tell the system that the diskette may have been changed. If you install a 360 KB or 720 KB FDD, verify the Change Line setting, ordinarily set on the drive by a jumper labeled "Line 34" or "Change Line." If you install such a drive in a PC/XT-class system, leave the jumper open. On any later system, install a jumper block to connect line 34 and enable Change Line Support. Failing to do so and then writing to a diskette in that drive may destroy the data on that diskette by overwriting the FATs and root directory entries with data from the diskette that was formerly in the drive.

Cleaning
FDDs are used so little nowadays—an occasional boot or program install— that head wear and media accumulation aren't problematic. Dust needs to be removed periodically. You can buy special FDD cleaning kits, but we don't bother with them. Every few months (or when we open the case for other reasons) we vacuum out the drive and drench it down with Zero Residue Cleaner or rubbing alcohol.

Repairing
Don't. Replace the drive. Modern 3.5-inch drives are so cheap that it makes no sense to repair one, and they are often sealed units without repair access anyway. Older 5.25-inch drives often are repairable, but the cost to do so exceeds the cost of replacing the drive.

Working with Obsolete Diskette Formats

If you've been computing for a long time, it's sometimes necessary to read a diskette written in an obsolete format. You may also need to format and write a diskette in an obsolete format—e.g., to create a boot diskette for an older system whose hard drive will not boot but still contains valuable data. If you find yourself in such a position, keep the following issues in mind:

- A 3.5-inch 1.44 MB FDD can read, write, and format 720 KB (DD) and 1.44 MB (HD) diskettes. 3.5-inch 2.88 MB (ED) diskettes are readable only by an ED drive. These are difficult to find new, so your only option may be to locate someone with an ED drive who is willing to allow you to use it to transfer your data.

- A 5.25-inch 1.2 MB FDD can read any 5.25-inch diskette written with an IBM format in any 360 KB or 1.2 MB drive. A problem may arise when you exchange 360 KB diskettes between 360 KB and 1.2 MB drives. 360 KB drives write a wider track than 1.2 MB drives, which cannot completely erase or format data put down by 360 KB drives. If a 360 KB drive formats or writes to a 360 KB diskette, a 1.2 MB drive can subsequently read, write, or format that diskette, but once that diskette has been written or formatted in the 1.2 MB drive, it will no longer be reliably readable in a 360 KB drive. This problem does not arise if the 360 KB diskette has never been written to in a 360 KB drive. Accordingly, if you need to write data with a 1.2 MB drive that must subsequently be read by a 360 KB drive, use blank 360 KB diskettes (bulk-erased, if necessary), and format them to 360 KB in the 1.2 MB drive.

- Old diskettes often have errors, either because the diskette has been physically abused or simply because the magnetic domains on the diskette have gradually faded with time. Reading data from a diskette that was last written five or more years ago is very likely to yield some read errors; a diskette 10 or more years old is almost certain to have multiple read errors, and may be completely unreadable. Using the diskette rescue utilities included with Norton Utilities for DOS (*http://www.symantec.com*) and SpinRite (*http://www.spinrite.com*) can often retrieve some or all of the data from a marginal diskette.

 If the data is critical, consider sending the diskette to one of the firms that specialize in data retrieval and advertise in the back of computer magazines. These services are not cheap and cannot guarantee that the data can be salvaged, but they do offer the best hope. If the data is important enough to pay a data retrieval firm to salvage, send the diskette to the company without trying to salvage the data yourself first. Running one of the utilities mentioned previously may render what would have been salvageable data unreadable by the data retrieval company.

- You can generally install a newer FDD in an older system and use it to emulate an older FDD, with the following limitations:

  - The 5.25-inch 1.2 MB FDD spins at 360 RPM (versus 300 RPM for all other FDDs) and cannot be used in a system whose FDD controller supports only 360 KB FDDs.

  - You can install a 3.5-inch 1.44 MB FDD in nearly any 286 or later computers and some late-model XT clones, although the drive may be recognized only as 720 KB. If that occurs, use 720 KB (DD) diskettes in that drive. In theory, you should also be able to install a 3.5-inch FDD in a PC- or XT-class system and use it as a 360 KB FDD. In practice, this works on some PC- and XT-class systems, but not all. For reasons that are not clear to us, some old systems refuse to recognize the 3.5-inch drive. If that occurs, your only alternative is to locate an actual 5.25-inch 360 KB drive and use it to do the transfer.

 To use this method, you also have to temporarily reconfigure the 3.5-inch drive on the modern system to 360 KB in order to read and write 360 KB 3.5-inch diskettes. Some systems allow this, but others return a hardware error. Before you install the 3.5-inch FDD in the older system, check the newer system to make sure that it allows its 3.5-inch drive to run as a 360 KB 5.25-inch drive. To do so, run BIOS Setup on the newer machine, set the drive type to 360 KB 5.25-inch, and restart the system. If the system does not return a hardware error, insert a blank 720 KB (DD) diskette into the drive and issue the command format a:. If the diskette formats successfully to 360 KB, that drive is usable for your purposes.

Salvaging Diskette Data

If a diskette is physically damaged, you may be able to salvage the data by removing the actual diskette medium from its protective sheath. For a 5.25-inch diskette, take the following steps, which we've used successfully more than once:

1. Use a razor blade or sharp knife carefully to trim about 1/8 of an inch (3 mm) from the bottom edge of the protective sheath of another diskette that you don't care about. The bottom edge is that nearest the drive door when the diskette is inserted into the drive.

2. Gently squeeze the two edges adjoining the trimmed edge toward the center to open a gap in the trimmed edge. Grasp the plastic medium and gently slide it out of the sheath, leaving the Tyvek inner liner in place. Discard the medium and save the sheath.

3. Repeat the first step on the damaged diskette, and then remove the medium, touching it as little as possible. Put your finger in the central hub hole and gently press the medium toward the trimmed edge. If you must grasp the medium itself, do so only at the very edge. Be very careful not to bend or deform the medium while you are extracting it.

4. Gently slide the medium from the damaged diskette into the new sheath that you previously prepared, making sure that the medium is right-side up, fully inserted, and that the hub hole in the medium is centered in the hub hole on

the sheath. Rotate the medium gently by using your finger in the hub hole to ensure that it turns easily.

5. Insert the patched diskette into the drive and attempt to access it. It's not necessary to tape or otherwise secure the trimmed edge. If you can access some or all of the data on the patched diskette, immediately copy it elsewhere and then discard the diskette.

Salvaging data from a 3.5-inch diskette is usually impossible. Any damage that renders the hard plastic shell unusable normally also destroys the medium that it contains. However, if recovering the data is critical, you can attempt the following steps, which we've had much less luck with:

1. Locate a 3.5-inch diskette of the same type (DD, HD, or ED) as the damaged diskette that you are willing to destroy. Using a nail file or small screwdriver, gently pry the sliding metal shutter off the diskette and discard the shutter.

2. Gently pry open the shell. Remove and discard the medium, leaving the two Tyvek inner liners in place. Place the shell aside.

3. Repeat the first step on the damaged diskette, and then remove the medium, touching it as little as possible. If the medium is visibly damaged, as it probably will be, continuing is likely to be useless. However, we did once succeed in recovering some files from a medium that appeared to be severely damaged, so it may be worth the effort.

4. Place the medium from the damaged diskette into the new shell you prepared, making sure to orient the medium as it was in the original diskette, and snap the shell closed. Use your fingertip to make sure that the medium turns freely within the shell. Insert the repaired diskette into the drive (you need not replace the shutter first) and attempt to read the diskette.

Our Picks

Here are the FDDs we recommend:

3.5-inch FDD

Any name-brand drive. These $15 drives are commodity items, and one is about as good as another. We use whatever make happens to be most readily available or cheapest, including (alphabetically) Mitsumi, NEC, Sony, Teac, Toshiba, and probably several others we've forgotten. We use Teac 235HF units by choice, but that's probably just from habit. If you have a choice, pick an FDD that uses a shrouded connector for the data cable.

5.25-inch FDD

None. Although we keep one or two around on general principles, the 5.25-inch FDD is obsolete except to read old 5.25-inch diskettes, most of which were written so long ago that they are now probably unreadable. As of July 2003, new 5.25-inch FDDs are still sold, but few vendors stock them and they are now very hard to find. If you need to read an old 5.25-inch diskette, contact your local computer store, which probably has a stack of 5.25-inch HD (1.2 MB) FDDs in the back room and will likely give you one for the asking.

For updated recommendations, visit *http://www.hardwareguys.com/picks/fdd.html*.

7

High-Capacity Floppy
Disk Drives

Many vendors have tried and failed to establish a standard for a high-capacity FDD. All these so-called superfloppy drives have suffered from some combination of nonstandardization, incompatibility with standard diskettes, lack of boot support, expensive media, small installed base, lack of OEM acceptance, low reliability, and poor performance.

Iomega Zip Drives and, to a lesser extent, Panasonic SuperDisk (LS-120/LS-240) Drives have sold in moderate numbers, especially in some niche markets. Others, such as the fast, 200 MB Sony HiFD and the Samsung Pro-FD, had features that compared favorably to the Zip Drives and SuperDisk Drives, but either never shipped in volume or were not adopted in numbers large enough to reach critical mass. The story of high-capacity FDDs has largely been one of too little, too late, and too expensive.

The ubiquity of inexpensive, fast, reliable CD-RW drives has effectively killed the market for high-capacity FDDs except in specialized niches such as prepress graphics work, which remains a Zip Drive stronghold. In what may be the final straw, Iomega settled a class action lawsuit in spring 2001 filed on behalf of those who had purchased Zip Drives between 1995 and 2001. In settling that lawsuit, Iomega in effect admitted that Zip Drives and discs were unreliable, which doesn't bode well for the continuing existence of the Zip Drive.

All of that said, there are a (very) few applications in which high-capacity FDDs make sense, so we'll spend this short chapter talking about them. A high-capacity FDD is a reasonable choice in the following situations:

- You frequently need to transfer files larger than will fit a standard FDD between systems that are not networked and are not equipped with CD writers. For example, you need to move work files back and forth between home and office, or between a notebook system equipped with an internal high-capacity FDD and a desktop system.

- You receive files from people who have a high-capacity FDD but not a CD writer. That, of course, is increasingly uncommon, as CD writers have become ubiquitous.

- You have a "guest computer" for use by visitors who carry their work with them and need access to a computer to make on-the-fly, last-minute changes to their work. Using a high-capacity FDD on such a machine minimizes the footprint of multiple casual users and is easier to support than a CD writer.

- If your corporate mail system is slow or limits the size of file attachments, a high-capacity FDD can be used to "sneakernet" files between departments that do not share servers or mapped drives on the corporate network.

- Per Iomega's suggested uses for its Zip Drive, you can "Store encoded secret files before you hand them over to Russia." (We are not making this up.)

Table 7-1 lists the key characteristics of Iomega Zip Drives and Panasonic Super-Disk Drives with CD-R/RW shown for comparison. Transfer rates and access times are the best available, and may be inferior for some interfaces and drive models. Prices are approximate in US$ and are current as of July 2003.

Table 7-1. Key characteristics of high-capacity FDDs, with CD-R/RW shown for comparison

	Zip100	Zip250	Zip750	LS-120	LS-240	CD-R/RW
Native capacity (MB)	100	250	750	120	243	700
IDE/SCSI/ Parallel/ USB	●/●/●/●	●/●/●/●	●/○/○/●	●/●/●/●	●/○/○/●	●/●/●/●
Rotation rate (RPM)	2,945	2,945	3,676	720	1,500	variable
Average read access (ms)	39	39	37	112	65	65
Sustained transfer (MB/s)	1.4	2.4	7.3	0.2	0.4	7.2
Typical drive cost	$60	$75	$100	$100	$180	$75
Media cost (per cartridge)	~ $7	~ $9	~ $12	~ $8	~ $10	~ $0.20
Media cost (per gigabyte)	~ $70	~ $36	~ $16	~ $65	~ $40	~ $0.29
Bootable	●	●	●	●	●	●
Read / Write 1.44 MB?	○/○	○/○	○/○	●/●	●/●	○/○

CD-R/RW is clearly a better choice for most uses, particularly when media cost is an issue. Zip Drives and SuperDisk Drives do have some advantages, however:

- Zip Drives and LS-120 SuperDisk Drives are a bit more convenient to use than CD writers and slightly faster if you need to write only a few small files. A CD writer is faster if you need to write a large amount of data.

- SuperDisk Drives can read and write 1.44 MB diskettes, so a machine with a SuperDisk Drive doesn't need a standard 1.44 MB FDD, assuming the system BIOS supports booting from a SuperDisk Drive.

- LS-240 SuperDisk Drives support FD32MB technology, which allows formatting a standard 1.44 MB diskette as a write-once 32 MB diskette. Although that sounds like an attractive way to recycle old 1.44 MB diskettes, FD32MB diskettes can be read only in LS-240 drives and their reliability is questionable, particularly for long-term storage.

- Unlike a CD, a Zip disk or SuperDisk disk fits in a shirt pocket and is protected by its case and shutter.

High-Capacity FDD Types

Although many types of high-capacity FDDs have been announced, and some have even been produced in small numbers, the only high-capacity FDDs that have achieved even moderate market penetration are the Iomega Zip Drive and the Panasonic SuperDisk Drive. The following sections detail these drives.

Iomega Zip Drive

The Iomega Zip Drive is the direct descendant of the Iomega Bernoulli Box, a mass storage device that was a popular (and expensive) add-on for IBM XT/AT systems and compatibles throughout the 1980s. The first Bernoulli boxes used 8-inch 10 MB cartridges. Later models used 5.25-inch cartridges that ranged from 20 MB to 230 MB. Various single- and dual-drive Bernoulli Box models were available, but they never achieved mass-market success because the drives were very expensive and used expensive cartridges that required periodic replacement.

A Bernoulli cartridge was in effect a large floppy diskette contained in a plastic shell. As the disk rotated, differential air pressure—called the Bernoulli Principle, hence the name—pulled the disk toward the heads, with which it remained in contact while the drive was spinning. This meant that Bernoulli cartridges wore out relatively quickly, and many users spent as much on cartridges as on the drive itself. But, in the days when hard drives were slow and held only 10 or 20 MB, the Bernoulli Box was a reasonable solution for people who needed a lot of disk storage for databases and similar applications. The Bernoulli Box was as fast as a hard drive, or nearly so, and one could expand storage simply by buying additional cartridges, a revolutionary concept in those days.

By the late 1980s, as hard drives increased in size and performance, the Bernoulli Box was becoming obsolescent. But the technology was still sound, so Iomega repositioned the Bernoulli Box in a smaller, cheaper form as supplemental rather than primary storage, and named it the Zip Drive. In effect, Iomega shrunk the

Bernoulli Box and its cartridges to a standard 3.5-inch form factor. The Zip Drive was inexpensive, had large capacity and reasonably high performance for the time, and so became a popular accessory for those who needed removable, transportable storage.

As the 1990s ended, the Zip Drive had fallen prey to the march of technology, just as the Bernoulli Box had a decade earlier. Although Iomega increased the capacity and performance of the Zip Drive marginally, other technologies—notably CD writers—provided superior and less-expensive solutions in the niche formerly dominated by the Zip Drive. The Zip Drive might ultimately have replaced the standard floppy drive but for two problems: its inability to function universally as a boot floppy in standard systems, and the very high cost of Zip disks. Had those problems been addressed, the Zip Drive might have become ubiquitous. They were not, and so the Zip Drive is rapidly fading from the scene.

As the market for the Zip Drive disappears, Iomega still claims "millions of users" for the Zip Drive. That sounds impressive until one realizes it means that 1 billion or more systems have been built without Zip Drives. So, in fact, although millions of Zip Drives have been sold, they are now seldom installed in new systems and have become very much a niche product. But those millions of drives do make the Zip Drive a standard of sorts, to the extent that there can be any standard in a market as fragmented as high-capacity FDDs.

Iomega currently produces three versions of the Zip Drive, which are detailed in the following sections.

The Zip100 Drive

The Zip100 Drive has been made in numerous variants, including internal ATAPI/ IDE and SCSI models and external parallel port, SCSI, and USB models. Iomega once produced the Zip Plus model, which had both SCSI and parallel port interfaces, but that model is no longer made. In addition to the standard internal models, Iomega produces several specialized internal IDE units designed to fit particular notebook systems. Various third-party manufacturers have produced internal and PC Card models for specific notebook computers.

Unfortunately, Zip Drives cannot read, write, or boot from standard 3.5-inch 720 KB or 1.44 MB floppy disks, which makes it impractical to use them as the sole floppy drive in most systems. Zip100 drives use a 3.5-inch disk cartridge that's about twice as thick as a standard 3.5-inch floppy diskette and stores a nominal 100 MB. Zip100 disks can be read and written by Zip100 and Zip250 drives, but Zip100 drives can use only Zip100 disks. The Zip750 Drive can read Zip100 disks, but not write them.

 Some (but by no means all) recent computers and motherboards explicitly support the Zip Drive in BIOS Setup. On such systems, you can enable an ATAPI/IDE Zip Drive as a boot device. If you do so, you need not install a standard FDD in that system unless you need compatibility with standard floppy disks.

Like standard floppy disks, Zip disks must be formatted before data can be stored on them, although preformatted Zip disks are readily available. You can format a Zip disk in one of two ways. A long format requires 10 minutes or more and corresponds to a full format on a standard floppy disk. The long format actually formats the entire disk and verifies the surface. A short format requires only 10 seconds or so, and corresponds to a Quick Format on a standard floppy disk. The short format simply zeroes out the FAT and root directory without actually formatting the disk or verifying its surface. As with standard floppies, a short format can be done only on a disk that has previously had a long format done on it.

Regardless of interface, all Zip100 drives provide track-to-track, maximum, and average seek times of 4 ms, 55 ms, and 29 ms, respectively. Because all Zip100 drives spin at 2,941 RPM, average latency is about 10.2 ms, yielding average access times of about 39 milliseconds, much slower than a hard drive but noticeably faster than CD and DVD recorders. The typical start time for Zip100 drives is about three seconds, which is the delay between inserting a disk and when that disk can be read or written. Overall, regardless of the interface, Zip100 drives "feel" somewhat faster to us than standard floppy drives when reading or writing one or a few small files, and much faster when writing many (or large) files.

The sustained transfer rates, burst transfer rates, and average throughput of Zip100 drives vary according to interface:

- All Zip100 drives provide a minimum sustained transfer rate of 0.79 MB/s, which is determined by the drive mechanism.

- All Zip100 drives have a potential maximum sustained transfer rate of 1.40 MB/s, again determined by the mechanism and internal interface, but in practice only the ATAPI/IDE and SCSI models are likely to achieve anything near this rate. In our experience, parallel models provide slower sustained transfers, much slower if the parallel port is an older model or is misconfigured. USB models are limited by the USB interface to 12 Mb/s, which translates to a maximum sustained transfer rate of 1.20 MB/s.

- The burst transfer rate of Zip100 drives is limited by the internal interface to 26.7 Mb/s, but again only the ATAPI/IDE and SCSI models are likely to come close to that rate. The parallel and USB models are limited by their interfaces to less than ~20 Mb/s and 12 Mb/s, respectively.

- Iomega specifies the typical throughput for all Zip100 drives as 60 MB/minute, except the parallel model, which it specifies as 20 MB/minute. Based on our own experience, those numbers may be a bit high. Using an ATAPI/IDE or SCSI Zip100 drive, it typically takes us between two and five minutes to copy a full disk to or from a fast hard drive—noticeably slower than the rated throughput—and it takes much longer if many small files are being copied. We also find that the parallel and USB models are correspondingly slower than their rated throughput in real-world use.

The Zip250 Drive

When the Zip100 Drive was introduced, its capacity and performance were reasonable for the time. In those days of smaller hard drives, many people could back up their entire hard disks to one or two Zip100 disks. But as the years passed, faster systems with larger and faster hard drives were introduced and newer versions of applications programs continued to generate larger and larger datafiles. Iomega realized that the Zip100 Drive was fast becoming too small and too slow to be useful for many users, so it introduced the Zip250 Drive, which provides more than twice the capacity and somewhat higher performance.

The Zip250 drive has been made in the same interfaces as the Zip100 Drive: ATAPI/IDE, parallel port, SCSI, and USB. Iomega also produces PC Card and FireWire adapters that allow the USB Zip250 Drive to be used with those interfaces. Like the Zip100 Drive, the Zip250 Drive cannot read, write, or boot from standard 1.44 MB diskettes. The Zip250 Drive accepts both Zip100 disks and Zip250 disks, although we've found that using Zip100 disks negates the performance benefits of the Zip250 Drive.

The Zip250 Drive uses the same rotation rate as the Zip100 Drive, and provides comparable seek and access times with one exception. The USB Zip250 Drive specifies average seek time as less than 40 ms, noticeably slower than the other models. ATAPI/IDE, parallel port, and SCSI Zip250 Drives specify sustained transfer rates of 1.2 MB/s minimum and 2.4 MB/s maximum, although in our experience the parallel port model in fact has about half the transfer rate of the SCSI and ATAPI/IDE models. The USB Zip250 Drive provides maximum sustained throughput of 1.4 MB/s when using the USB interface, 0.9 MB/s with the PC Card adapter, and 2.3 MB/s with the FireWire adapter.

The Zip750 Drive

When the Zip250 Drive was introduced, we thought the Zip Drive had reached its limits. Iomega proved us wrong by introducing the Zip750 Drive, which triples the capacity and throughput of the Zip250 Drive.

The Zip750 drive is available with ATAPI/IDE, USB, and FireWire interfaces. Like the Zip100 and Zip250 Drives, the Zip750 Drive cannot read, write, or boot standard 1.44 MB diskettes. The Zip750 Drive reads and writes Zip750 and Zip250 disks, and reads Zip100 disks.

The Zip750 Drive spins disks 25% faster than the Zip100 or Zip250 Drive, and accordingly has an average access time (seek plus latency) of a couple of milliseconds faster than older models. The higher data density and rotation rate of the Zip750 allow a sustained transfer rate of 7.3 MB/s, three times that of the Zip250, when using the ATAPI, USB 2.0, or FireWire interface. When used with a USB 1.1 interface, the Zip750 Drive transfers data at only 0.9 MB/s, but that is a limitation of the interface rather than the drive. The difference in transfer rates between the Zip100/250 Drives and the Zip750 Drive is quite noticeable. To us, a Zip 100 or Zip250 Drive feels like a fast floppy drive, whereas a Zip750 Drive feels like a slow hard drive.

Despite the faster performance of the Zip750 Drive, we think it is likely to sell in small numbers because the Zip750 lacks compatibility with the Zip100 drive and because Zip disks remain very expensive per byte stored. If you must have a Zip Drive, the Zip750 Drive is the one to get, but we suggest you think carefully before you buy any Zip Drive at all.

From 1998 until 2002, Iomega made a miniature Zip Drive called the Clik! Drive, later renamed the PocketZip Drive. Iomega designed PocketZip for MP3 players and digital cameras, but PocketZip was never widely adopted. PocketZip Drives use the PocketZip disk, which is a smaller version of the Zip disk. It is about 2 inches square, is 3/4 of an inch thick, weighs less than half an ounce, stores about 40 MB, costs $10 or so, and has performance similar to a standard Zip Drive. PocketZip Drives sold in relatively small numbers, so continuing availability of PocketZip disks is uncertain.

SuperDisk Drive

The only serious competitor to the Zip Drive in the high-capacity floppy drive segment is the SuperDisk Drive, which was developed by Panasonic, Compaq, Imation, and others. SuperDisk Drive disks closely resemble standard 3.5-inch 1. 44 MB diskettes, but are distinguishable by their triangular media shutter and trapezoidal labeling space. SuperDisk disks can be read and written only in a SuperDisk Drive.

The SuperDisk Drive was intended to be a universal replacement for the standard 3.5-inch 1.44 MB FDD, a goal that it failed to achieve. The SuperDisk Drive was originally available only in the 120 MB LS-120 model. In 2001, Panasonic finally began shipping the long-promised 240 MB LS-240 model to OEMs. Although a few system makers, notably Compaq, bundled SuperDisk Drives with some models, the SuperDisk Drive has always been a distant second to the Zip Drive in popularity.

Although Panasonic still makes LS-120 and LS-240 SuperDisk Drives, the drives and media have very limited distribution, primarily by notebook computer OEMs. We consider the long-term viability of the SuperDisk Drive dubious. They are at best niche products, and at worst may be orphaned at any time.

Choosing a High-Capacity FDD

Use the following guidelines when choosing a high-capacity FDD:

If you need to exchange data bidirectionally with other people or computers not on your network. Buy a drive compatible with the media in use. SuperDisk Drives and Zip Drives cannot read or write each other's media. SuperDisk Drives are common on recent Compaq computers, but are seldom seen elsewhere. Zip Drives are by far the most commonly used superfloppy, so installing one allows you to exchange data with more people. In theory, the Zip750 Drive is most flexible because it reads all Zip disks and writes 750 MB and 250 MB disks. But the inability of the Zip750 to write 100 MB disks means it isn't useful if you need to exchange data with people who use Zip100 drives. In that situation, choose the Zip250 Drive.

If you need to send data to other people or computers, but will not receive data from them. Do not buy a high-capacity FDD. Buy a CD-RW drive and a supply of CD-R discs. Nearly everyone has a CD-ROM drive that can read the CDs you produce, and sending people $0.20 CD-R discs is a lot less painful than sending them $10 Zip disks.

If you will use the drive to back up and/or archive data. Do not buy a high-capacity FDD. They are unsuitable for these purposes because they are slow and use costly and relatively unreliable media. If backup is your primary need, buy a tape drive. If you need to archive data permanently, buy a CD-RW drive or DVD writer and archive the data to optical discs. If you can afford only one drive, and if 650 MB is enough capacity to back up your important data, buy a fast CD writer and some CD-RW discs, which can be reused repeatedly. If 650 MB is insufficient and your budget is somewhat larger, buy a DVD writer and a supply of rewritable discs.

 You may have the functional equivalent of a high-capacity floppy drive lurking in your camera case. Although most people use them only to store and move images, a digital camera memory card and USB card reader can be used as a high-capacity FDD. In fact, before marketers got around to renaming it, the SmartMedia Card was called the SSFDC (Solid State Floppy Disk Card). We hadn't thought about using our digital camera equipment that way until one day we desperately needed to transfer some files from a notebook system with a dead LAN interface. We were about to install a USB CD writer and software on the notebook system when we realized everything we needed to transfer the files was already installed. Duh.

You can use any memory card that allows you to read and write ordinary files. Memory cards have maximum capacities ranging from 128 MB to 1 GB or more, depending on type, so these cards can be used to transfer a large amount of data in one pass. In fact, this method is so useful for emergency data transfers that we keep a $20 USB card reader with driver CD and a 64 MB card in our kit. Memory cards cost more per megabyte capacity than SuperDisk or Zip disks, but you can use the memory card in your digital camera when you're not using it to transfer files.

Another alternative to using a high-capacity FDD for data portability is a USB Flash Memory Drive. These keyring-size devices are made by Belkin, Lexar, SanDisk, Sony, and others in capacities from 16 MB to 1 GB or more. Some have removable media, but most do not. Although these devices are relatively costly per byte stored, they have become increasingly popular as "personal data stores" because they are small, rugged, and trivially easy to move between systems.

Other than drives we install temporarily for testing purposes, we've used only two high-capacity FDDs regularly. We installed one Zip250 drive on our network, which we used only to read Zip disks that people sent us. That drive died, and we didn't bother to replace it because nowadays everyone sends us CDs. We also had an Imation LS-120 drive installed in one of our systems, but it died. We didn't bother to replace it, either, because no one had ever sent us an LS-120 disk. That's a small sample, certainly, but based on our experiences we see little point to having a high-capacity FDD at all. We actually get more use from the one 5.25-inch 1.2 MB FDD that we use occasionally to read antique 5.25-inch floppies. We now exclusively use tape drives for backup, and CD or DVD writers for archiving data or sending it to others.

Choosing a Zip Drive

If, despite our discouragement, you decide to install a Zip Drive, keep the following in mind:

Click of Death (COD)
Zip disks whose logical formatting is damaged cause the dreaded Click of Death. When this occurs, the drive repeatedly seeks unsuccessfully, making a characteristic COD clicking sound. This problem can usually be solved simply by using another disk. However, if the problem disk is physically damaged, it generates the same clicking sound but also physically damages any drive you attempt to read it in. When they experience COD, many people immediately either attempt to read the disk in another drive, which simply destroys that drive as well, or attempt to read another disk in the damaged drive, which simply destroys yet another disk. A damaged drive literally has its heads ripped loose and a damaged disk has its edge shredded. Using a good disk in a damaged drive destroys that disk, which will subsequently destroy any drive that attempts to access it. If you experience COD, always examine the disk carefully to determine if it is physically damaged before you do anything else. For details about COD, visit *http://grc.com/tip/ clickdeath.htm*. This page describes the COD in full detail and has a link to a free utility that you can use to test Zip and Iomega Jaz Drives for this problem.

Choose your interface carefully
Zip Drives have been made in IDE, SCSI, parallel port, and USB interfaces. An external SCSI, parallel, or USB model provides the most flexibility. It can be carried from computer to computer along with the data—e.g., to download a large service pack using the T1 at work and then carry the drive home to install the service pack—and used to expand the disk storage available on older laptop systems with small hard drives.

IDE/ATAPI
The IDE/ATAPI version (Zip Insider) is fast, is easy to install, and runs reliably. However, if you plan to use your Zip Drive for disaster recovery—which is not the best choice anyway—note that the Iomega IDE Zip drivers do not function under DOS. The SCSI and parallel drivers do, which means you can access data on a SCSI or parallel Zip Drive before Windows is reinstalled and running. We have had few problems when installing the ATAPI version as the Sole/Master on the Secondary ATA channel—the usual configuration on a system that has an existing Primary/Master hard disk and a Primary/Slave CD-ROM drive. We have experienced occasional problems installing the ATAPI

version as a Slave on the Primary channel with a Primary/Master hard disk. If this happens, installing the Zip as Secondary/Master usually solves the problem. We have experienced more problems when installing an ATAPI Zip Drive as either Master or Slave on the Secondary ATA channel with a CD-ROM drive jumpered to the opposite. Some systems do not function properly with the CD-ROM as Master and the Zip as Slave, but work fine with the Zip as Master and the CD-ROM as Slave. Others work properly with the drives jumpered conversely. Some systems don't work properly either way, and the only option is to swap drives around between the Primary and Secondary channels, or to substitute a different CD-ROM drive. Also note that ATAPI Zip Drives frequently conflict with CD and DVD writers, tape drives, and other ATAPI devices.

SCSI

The SCSI version is fast and runs reliably. However, to use it you must install a SCSI adapter, which adds to the expense and complexity. Note that only the final device in a SCSI chain should be terminated, and SCSI Zip Drives are terminated by default on the assumption that they will be the only SCSI device installed. If you install a SCSI Zip Drive on an existing SCSI chain, turn off termination unless the Zip Drive is the final device on the chain. In that case, make sure to turn off termination on the device that was formerly the last device.

Parallel

These are much slower than the other versions, but can be used on any computer with an available parallel port. We have occasionally encountered incompatibilities with the parallel versions, including failure to recognize the drive and inability to access the drive other than in Safe Mode under Windows 95/98. If this occurs, check BIOS Setup to determine how the parallel port is configured. Setting the port to EPP or EPP/ECP (depending on your BIOS) may resolve the problem, and will allow the Zip Drive to operate at the highest possible speed, although that is still much slower than the other versions. If the port is already configured correctly, removing and then reinstalling the drivers sometimes cures the problem.

Parallel Zip Drives may also be problematic under Windows NT. Some Windows NT systems bluescreen at boot if a parallel Zip Drive is attached. If this occurs, remove the Iomega parallel port SCSI driver, change the parallel port mode (some NT systems work properly only if configured for Standard Parallel Port mode, while others seem to prefer EPP/ECP mode), and reinstall the Iomega parallel port SCSI driver.

Parallel Zip Drives may also cause conflicts with some printer drivers, notably those for HP inkjet printers. This problem is documented with workarounds on both the Iomega and HP web sites.

USB

After a somewhat rocky start, particularly on Windows 2000 systems, we now consider USB Zip Drives to be reasonably reliable under Windows 9X and Windows 2000/XP, assuming that you install recent drivers. USB

Zip Drives, like other USB drives, may be less prone to causing trouble if connected to a root USB port rather than to a hub.

Always eject the disk properly
Although the Zip Drive has an Eject button, using it risks damaging your data. Always eject the disk by selecting My Computer, highlighting the drive icon, and choosing Eject. Alternatively, use the Iomega icon on the desktop to eject the disk. If you have just written data to the disk, a period of several seconds must pass before software Eject is enabled. During this period, data is being written to the disk. Using the Eject button on the drive may force an eject before the write is complete, which trashes your data.

Check frequently for updated drivers
Many Zip Drive problems can be solved by using the most current drivers, which Iomega updates frequently. Numerous strange things happen with Zip Drives using older drivers—e.g., exiting Excel97 SR1 causes the Zip disk to eject under some circumstances when using older drivers. If your Zip Drive begins behaving strangely, update your driver to the latest version before taking any other troubleshooting steps.

Keep the system simple
A Zip Drive usually works reliably on a system that has only a hard drive and a CD-ROM drive. On a system that also has a tape drive, CD writer, and/or DVD writer, installing a Zip Drive may cause conflicts. In particular, installing a Zip Drive may cause problems on a system with other components that use virtual drive volumes, such as a CD writer with packet-writing software or backup software that assigns a virtual drive volume to the tape drive.

Choosing a SuperDisk Drive

If, despite our discouragement, you decide to install a SuperDisk Drive, keep the following in mind:

Choose the LS-120 SuperDisk Drive
The LS-240 SuperDisk Drive is expensive. Its only advantages relative to the LS-120 are that it has twice the capacity and supports FD32MB, which allows using 1.44 MB diskettes as 32 MB write-once media. If you must have a high-capacity FDD larger than 120 MB, choose the Zip250 Drive, which is much cheaper than the LS-240 and uses readily available disks. As far as writing 32 MB to a 1.44 MB diskette, we wouldn't trust our data to such a scheme and suggest you don't either.

Choose the internal ATAPI model whenever possible
Our readers report many fewer problems with the internal ATAPI SuperDisk Drives than with USB, parallel port, and PC Card models. ATAPI models are supported natively by Windows 95B and later, and usually just work. The USB, parallel port, and PC Card models require drivers, and we've had reports of driver conflicts and other problems with them. The ATAPI model running under Windows 95A and earlier also requires drivers, so we expect similar conflicts might occur with that configuration.

Choose the USB model if you have a notebook
The external USB drive can be transferred easily between a notebook and desktop system—assuming, of course, that both systems have USB ports and a USB-aware OS—allowing you to move data back and forth in relatively large chunks. The same might be true of the parallel port model, but we've never been pleased with any parallel port drive. The PC Card model is usable only on a notebook computer, unless you happen to have a PC Card interface on your desktop system. We've found that USB drives in general are less likely to cause problems if you connect them to a root USB port rather than to a USB hub, and we suspect that is also true for USB SuperDisk Drives.

Verify that your BIOS supports the SuperDisk Drive
Although the SuperDisk Drive can be installed in nearly any computer by installing drivers for it, it works best in a computer whose BIOS natively supports it. BIOS support means that you can boot from the SuperDisk Drive, and generally also means you're less likely to have conflicts or other problems with the drive.

Don't depend on the SuperDisk Drive for backups
Of the few people we know who've installed a SuperDisk Drive, most use it for backing up. That's a mistake because the disks are expensive and relatively unreliable compared to alternatives. Although the drives themselves are inexpensive, the cost of disks quickly mounts to the point where you'd have spent less for a better backup solution, such as a CD writer, DVD writer, or tape drive. The SuperDisk Drive may make sense in special situations, such as routinely transferring moderate amounts of data between a work system and a home system. Even in such situations, however, we recommend using CD-RW drives with packet-writing software, which are much more flexible, store more data, and use much less-expensive media.

Using an ATAPI Zip or SuperDisk Drive as the Boot Device

To configure your system to boot from an ATAPI Zip Drive or SuperDisk Drive, take the following steps:

1. Restart the system and enter BIOS Setup (usually by pressing F1, F2, or the Delete key while the BIOS boot screen is visible).

2. Verify that your high-capacity FDD is displayed as a connected device in the IDE configuration section. Most recent motherboards list the drive by name, but some older motherboards may list it only as an ATAPI device.

3. In BIOS Setup, locate the Boot Sequence setting (probably in the BIOS Features or Advanced Settings section) and view the available options. If an option corresponds directly to your drive (e.g., "SuperDisk Drive" or "LS-120" for the SuperDisk Drive or "Zip Drive" for the Zip Drive), set the first boot device to that option. If the BIOS provides a named boot option only for the Zip Drive but you have a SuperDisk Drive (or vice versa), try lying to the BIOS. We've never done that, but some readers have reported success using that method.

If neither drive is listed by name, but the BIOS offers an option such as "ATAPI Device/Drive," "Floptical Drive," "Removable Device/Drive," or "UHD Floppy," set the first boot device to that option. If none of these options appears, your motherboard probably does not support booting from a high-capacity FDD. Check the motherboard maker's web site for a BIOS update. Downloading and installing that update may add extended boot support to your motherboard.

4. After you configure Boot Sequence to use the high-capacity FDD as the first boot device, use BIOS Setup to disable the embedded FDD controller and to set Floppy Drive A: and Floppy Drive B: to "Not Installed." Save all changes and power down the system.

5. Insert a blank formatted disk in the drive and use the appropriate operating system commands to transfer system files to the disk and make it bootable. For a Zip Drive, you must use a Zip disk. For a SuperDisk Drive, you may use either a standard 3.5-inch 1.44 MB floppy diskette or a SuperDisk disk. Restart the system with the bootable disk in the drive. The system should boot normally to the FDD. If it doesn't, recheck your BIOS Setup configuration. Once you have verified that the system boots properly from the FDD, don't forget to restart the system and use BIOS Setup to change the boot order if you prefer to use something other than the FDD as the primary boot device.

Drive Letter Assignment Problems

One of the most common problems users report with high-capacity FDDs is confusion over drive letter assignments. Installing a high-capacity FDD often causes other drive letter assignments to change. The presence of an optical drive such as a DVD writer further complicates matters, and even the decision to boot the system with or without disks in one or another removable drive may cause drive letter changes. In addition, different operating systems handle assigning drives and reassigning drive letters differently. The result is that it's easy to become hopelessly confused about which drive letter corresponds to which drive. How drive letters are assigned is explained in Chapter 13. If you have the opposite problem—your drive isn't assigned a drive letter at all—download and install the most recent drivers for your drive.

Our Picks

Here are the high-capacity FDD we recommend:

For general-purpose systems
None. There's seldom reason to install a high-capacity FDD in a general-purpose system. For inexpensive archiving and backing up, or for transferring moderately large files between non-networked systems, a Plextor PlexWriter CD-RW drive with Ahead Software's Nero Burning ROM software is a much superior solution in every respect—cost, performance, and reliability. For moderate-capacity removable storage with drive letter access, we recommend a Plextor PlexWriter CD-RW drive with Ahead Software's

InCD software, which makes a CD-RW disc look like a giant floppy. See Chapter 11 for more information about CD-RW drives and software.

For specialized applications

Zip250 Drive or LS-120 SuperDisk Drive, according to specific requirements. About the only good reason to install a high-capacity FDD is to transfer moderately large files between systems that are not networked and cannot read (or read/write) CDs. For example, you may have a notebook computer that has a SuperDisk installed but does not have a CD writer or a network card. In that situation, installing a SuperDisk on your desktop system may be the simplest way to exchange files between the systems. Or you may need to exchange large graphics files with a prepress graphics house that accepts only Zip disks, in which case installing a Zip250 Drive provides both reasonably high capacity and compatibility with the relatively large installed base of Zip100 and Zip250 drives.

In general, the internal ATAPI models of either the Zip Drive or the Super-Disk Drive provide high performance, the fewest compatibility problems, and the lowest cost. However, if your application requires an external drive— perhaps because you need to move the drive from machine to machine— consider your choice of interface carefully per the guidelines listed earlier in the chapter. For more information, see *http://www.iomega.com* (Zip) and *http://www.mke.panasonic.co.jp/en/device/storage/superdisk/lkm_fc34_5.html* (SuperDisk).

For updated recommendations, visit *http://www.hardwareguys.com/picks/fdd.html*.

8

Removable Hard Disk Drives

Although any hard drive can obviously be removed, the term *removable hard disk drive* refers to hard drives designed to be removed and reinstalled easily, without opening the case or disconnecting and reconnecting cables. There are two distinct types of removable hard disk drives:

Cartridge-based drives

Cartridge-based drives such as the Iomega Jaz and Castlewood ORB use a self-contained, sealed cartridge about the size of a thick 3.5-inch floppy disk. The cartridge contains only the disk itself. The head mechanism resides in the drive. You insert the disk into the drive much as you would a floppy disk. Inserting the disk causes a shutter on the disk to open, allowing the drive's head mechanism to read and write the disk. The Iomega Peerless system instead uses a cartridge that is essentially the HDA (head-disk assembly) of a standard hard drive. Cartridge-based units are available in internal and external versions, using IDE, parallel port, SCSI, USB, PC Card, or FireWire interfaces.

Cartridge-based drives have always been niche products, but are now obsolete in practical terms. Their raison d'être, transferring moderately large data sets between systems, is now better served by a DVD writer or similar industry-standard writable optical drives. For most purposes, cartridge-based drives are now too small, slow, proprietary, and expensive. The Castlewood ORB is the only cartridge-based drive that remains in production.

Frame/carrier-based drives

These drives are actually just modified drive bays that allow a standard hard drive mounted in a carrier assembly to be inserted and removed easily. The frame resides permanently in an external drive bay, and is connected permanently to power and to the IDE interface or SCSI host adapter. The carrier assembly contains power and data cables, which remain permanently attached to the hard drive. The rear of the carrier assembly contains a custom connector that routes power and data signals from the frame. The connector that mates the carrier to the frame is designed for durability, and is typically rated for 2,000 to 50,000 insertions and removals.

These devices are simply physical modifications that allow easy removal and insertion, so the system sees the drive as just another hard disk drive because it *is* just another hard disk drive. Frame/carrier assemblies are available for any hard disk interface, from IDE to Ultra320 SCSI. More sophisticated units support such functions as hot-swapping, sparing, and RAID, if your host adapter, drivers, and operating system also support those functions.

External Hard Disk Drives

External hard drives are a related class of storage device but do not qualify as true removable hard disk drives. They are similar to removable hard disk drives in that they allow large amounts of data to be moved between systems. They are dissimilar in that they do not use removable media.

External SCSI drives have been around for years, of course, but they have always been a niche product. External Plug and Play drives with USB or FireWire interfaces (or both) are becoming increasingly popular, particularly with notebooks. In effect, these devices are simply standard IDE hard drives in an external enclosure with a USB or FireWire interface.

The drives perform as you would expect a modern IDE hard drive to perform. In the past, the problem was the interface. FireWire was fast enough to use as a hard disk interface, but few computers had FireWire ports and the cost of adding FireWire to both a PC and notebook made this solution quite expensive. USB 1.1 was ubiquitous but too slow for reasonable hard drive performance. In 2002 systems began shipping with USB 2.0 interfaces, which are more than fast enough to support any current hard drive.

Pioneered by Maxtor with its Personal Storage 3000-series drives, external USB 2.0 hard drives proliferated as USB 2.0 became common. Competing models are available from Maxtor, Western Digital, Iomega, CMS, QPS, and others with capacities as high as 250 GB or more. Although these drives can be used just like any other hard drive, they are marketed as backup/archive solutions. Makers generally bundle software such as Dantz Retrospect that allows backing up your internal hard drive to the external drive with just the push of a button. As the drive fills up, it's an easy matter to delete old backup data to make room for new. We have serious concerns about using an external hard drive as your only backup solution, but it's undeniable that these drives make backing up fast and easy.

Uses for Removable and External Hard Disk Drives

Although most systems do not need a removable or external hard drive, such drives have the following uses:

Expanding storage on obsolescent laptop systems

Installing a larger hard drive in a desktop system is trivial, but on a proprietary laptop system it may be impossible or extremely expensive to upgrade the hard drive. If you're faced with this situation, using a removable or external hard drive may extend the usable life of the laptop. If the laptop has an available PC Card slot, install a USB 2.0 PC Card adapter so that you can take advantage of the much higher throughput of USB 2.0 external drives.

Transporting large amounts of data

If you need to transport large amounts of data to remote sites, a removable hard drive may be the only practical option. Cartridge-based removable hard disk drives store up to 20 GB, and frame/carrier-based removable hard disk drives are limited only by the capacity of the largest standard hard drives available. For example, one of our readers works for a company that produces digital special effects for movies, always on very short deadlines. The time needed to back up 100 GB of image data to tape—as well as the cost and complexity of installing the required $35,000 tape drives at each end—makes tape impractical. Instead, they install a frame-based removable hard disk drive system at each end, copy the huge datafiles to high-performance SCSI hard drives, and FedEx the hard drives to the movie production company. When the disk arrives, the production company staff simply plugs it into the frame and copies the data from the removable hard drive to the server. Now that USB 2.0 external hard drives with capacities of 250 GB or more are available at reasonable prices, we expect them to be used for this purpose.

Allowing one computer to boot cleanly into multiple operating systems

Software development and similar work that requires using multiple operating systems always presents a problem. You could configure one PC to multiboot different operating systems, but that is seldom entirely satisfactory. You could install a dedicated computer for each OS, but doing that is expensive, generates a lot of noise and wastes heat, and means you're soon covered up in computers. Or you could use one computer with a frame/carrier-based removable hard drive. Installing each OS on its own hard drive means you can simply insert the carrier with the appropriate OS, restart the system, and have the equivalent of a dedicated PC running that OS.

That's why we use a frame/carrier unit on our main test-bed system. We know one person who does the same on his home computer. He, his wife, and his children each have their own hard drives mounted in carriers. He uses Linux, his wife uses Windows 2000, and the kids use Windows 98. When someone wants to use the computer, he inserts his own hard drive and restarts the system to boot into his own environment, with no worries about conflicts or accidentally damaging someone else's data or configuration.

Supporting multiple very large data sets

Although it is a specialized application, some scientists, market researchers, and others need to manipulate extremely large data sets—sometimes in the 100 GB range. Although it may be possible to build a PC with sufficient disk space to store all the data sets on the main hard drive, it's often cheaper and more efficient to allow those data sets to be swapped in and out as needed. If there are many such data sets, using a frame/carrier removable hard drive may be the best option.

Specialized backup requirements

Although one or another tape technology is usually the best choice for routine backup, there are times when tape is simply not practical, either because of the time required to back up or the time required to restore. For example, assume that you have a 150 GB database stored on a mirrored set of Seagate Barracuda 180 Ultra320 hard drives. Your backup window is very short, and no tape drive is large enough and fast enough to back up that entire 150 GB in the time available. Furthermore, even if tape were workable for backup, you can't afford to have the database offline for the time it would take to restore it.

If the frame/carrier unit, the OS, and the host adapter all support hot-swapping and RAID, you can remove and insert drives as needed without downing the server. In that situation, you might install three frame/carrier-based removable hard drives, each with a Seagate Barracuda 180 hard drive. Two of those would be mirrored/duplexed to provide primary storage. The third would be used as a destination for an image of the working data set. The 160 MB/s transfer rate of Ultra160 SCSI theoretically allows you to transfer the entire 150 GB database to the target drive in about 32 minutes—with half the 160 MB/s throughput used for reads and half for writes—although in practice it might take twice that long. Still, in comparison to even a very fast tape drive, the disk-to-disk transfer takes no time at all. Also, that backup hard drive can be replicated offline on another system for redundancy. With a recent backup stored on a hard drive, if you have a catastrophic failure, you can simply insert the backup hard drive and run directly from it, without spending the time needed to recover from tape.

Securing data

If you work with extremely sensitive data, using a removable hard drive allows you to secure that data by taking it with you or by storing it in a vault. When we first encountered a removable hard disk drive many years ago, this was the reason that drive was being used. The corporation ran two payroll systems, one for executives and the other for everyone else, and was paranoid that an employee would find out just how much more the executives were paid than everyone else. The executive payroll system used a removable hard drive, which was secured in the vault immediately after the executive payroll was run. And their fears were perhaps justified. If it's any indication, when we had to troubleshoot a problem with the payroll software on the executive payroll computer, it turned out that the problem was that the field for monthly salary could not exceed $99,999!

If you use a removable hard drive to secure your data, it must be bootable and should be the only hard drive in the system. If the removable drive is configured as a secondary hard drive, the internal primary hard drive may retain temporary files, backup data files, OS swap files, and similar files that could compromise the security of your data. For absolute data security, configure the system without a permanent hard drive and always power down the system when you remove the drive.

Removable
HDDs

Cartridge-Based Removable Hard Disk Drives

Cartridge-based removable hard disk drives were an odd product category. They provided the capacity and performance of an obsolete hard disk, but in removable form. In previous editions, we covered such cartridge-based removable hard drives as the Iomega Jaz, the Iomega Peerless, and the Castlewood ORB, but we (and the market) have now declared them officially dead.

The availability of cheap, huge, fast hard disks and such technologies as CD writers and DVD writers has killed the demand for cartridge-based removable hard drives. Cartridge-based drives still find limited use for such tasks as transferring image files and other prepress material to service bureaus, but even those uses are dwindling fast. Most people are far better served by standard hard drives in internal, external USB 2.0, or frame/carrier-based removable form and by writable technologies such as CD-RW, writable DVD, and tape.

Dealing with Orphaned Cartridge-Based Drives

Even the best-selling cartridge-based removable hard drives have always been at best a niche item. Some manufacturers have used the King Gillette model—giving away the razor and selling the blades—and so have sold their drives for less than what it costs to make them, expecting to make large profits by selling high-margin proprietary disks. Unfortunately, it often hasn't worked out that way, as many manufacturers apparently greatly overestimated the number of cartridges that people would buy.

The predictable result has been bankrupt manufacturers and orphaned drives, such as the 230 MB EzFlyer, the 1 GB SparQ, and the 1.5 GB SyJet (all from SyQuest), and the 250 MB Avatar Shark. Although support, maintenance services, and media are still available for some orphaned drives, either from the original manufacturer or from a third party, these drives and disks are on their way out and it's foolish to depend on them, let alone throw good money after bad. If you have an orphaned drive, we recommend taking the following steps:

- Transfer all data from the orphaned drive to hard disk, CD-RW, writable DVD, tape, or a similar standard technology while you can still do so. Neither your drive nor your disks will last forever. Your data is rotting as you read these words.

- If you have valuable data on disks you cannot read because your drive has failed, search the Web for data recovery services that can read the type of disk you use. There are many such services, and most of them are reasonably priced. Or at least they're reasonably priced if the drive is the problem and the disks themselves are readable. For disks with read errors, expect to pay a high price to have that data recovered, if indeed it is recoverable. Alternatively, search online auction services to locate a functional drive that will read your disks. If you have many disks to transfer or if you're concerned about security, buying a working used drive is definitely the less expensive way to go.

- Once you have good copies of all your data (or all that can be recovered), stop using the orphaned drive. Do a full format of all of your disks, and put the drive and disks up for sale on one of the online auction sites. Not only can you recover some of your investment, but you may be doing a favor for someone who's searching desperately for a way to read his own disks. If you're concerned about someone recovering your data from the disks you formatted, use any of the "secure erase" utilities you can find on the Internet to overwrite your data such that it cannot be recovered.

- If you simply must be able to read orphaned disks of a particular type on an ongoing basis, stock up on spare drives that will read those disks. For example, we know of one service company that told all its clients to buy SyQuest SparQ drives. That company frequently exchanges data with its clients on SyQuest SparQ cartridges, and so has bought several used SparQ drives to guard against drive failure. Recognize, however, that those with whom you are exchanging data are also subject to drive and disk failures. Encourage them to upgrade to something sustainable and standardized, such as CD-RW, writable DVD, or DDS tape (see "Tape Technologies" in Chapter 9).

Frame/Carrier-Based Removable Hard Disk Drives

Frame/carrier-based systems are drive-bay adapters that convert a 3.5-inch hard disk drive into a removable drive. These products comprise a drive carrier into which a standard hard drive is permanently installed, and a receiving frame that installs in a standard 5.25-inch drive bay and accepts the drive carrier. You can purchase additional receiving frames separately if you need to move data between systems. Similarly, you can buy drive carriers separately if you need to use multiple hard drives in one system. Figure 8-1 shows an assembled frame/carrier unit.

Figure 8-1. StorCase Data Express DE-100 frame, with carrier partially inserted

Frame/carrier removable systems are an excellent choice for removable storage. They provide the capacity and performance of a standard hard drive because they *use* a standard hard drive. There are no compatibility or configuration issues, again because they use standard hard drives, which the computer recognizes as such.

Our Picks

Here are the removable hard disk drives we recommend:

Removable cartridge-based hard disk drive
> **None.** The day of the Iomega Peerless, Castlewood ORB, and similar cartridge-based removable hard drives has passed. They do nothing that can't be done better by writable optical drives, frame/carrier-based systems, and external USB 2.0 drives.

Removable frame/carrier-based hard disk drive
> **StorCase Data Express.** Data Express units are available in every hard drive interface from IDE to Ultra320 SCSI, and with options such as support for hot-swapping and RAID. We use a Data Express IDE unit in our main test-bed system (*http://www.storcase.com*).

 The sole disadvantage of the Data Express is that it is oriented toward VARs and system integrators, and can be hard to find at retail. If you have difficulty finding the Data Express and prefer something available from retailers, consider the Antec DataSwap series, which can be purchased directly from Antec or from numerous resellers (*http://www.antec-inc.com*).

External hard disk drive
> **Maxtor Personal Storage 5000-series.** Frame/carrier systems are the most flexible solution, but require that each system to or from which data is to be transferred have a frame installed. If you need Plug and Play connectivity and high capacity and performance, the best solution is a USB 2.0 external hard drive, and the best product we know of in that category is the Maxtor Personal Storage 5000 (*http://www.maxtor.com*).

For updated recommendations, visit: *http://www.hardwareguys.com/picks/remstore.html*.

9

Tape Drives

Although the cost and capacity of removable optical and magnetic storage devices continue to improve, tape drives remain the best choice to back up or transfer very large amounts of data. Tape drives provide a combination of high capacity, speed, low media cost, and reliability that no other technology can match.

Tape Technologies

Four tape technologies compete in the PC and small server markets:

Quarter Inch Cartridge (QIC)
Originally developed in the early 1970s, two styles of QICs have been made. The physically larger DC600 cartridge is obsolete. Recent QIC tape drives use DC2000 minicartridges, which have been made in capacities from 400 MB to 20 GB. QIC drives use *serpentine recording*, which records many parallel tracks on each tape. The drive records data from the beginning to the end of the first track, reverses direction, writes data from the end to beginning of the second track, and so on, until all tracks have been written. This means that filling a tape may require more than 100 passes of the tape through the drive, which increases wear and tear on both drive and tape. Some recent QIC drives have the extra head required for *read-while-write*, which allows the drive to back up and compare data in one pass. Doing a compare on a single-head drive doubles the number of passes required, and extends backup time significantly.

Current QIC drives use *Travan technology*, a combination of tape and drive technologies developed by 3M/Imation, and now implemented by many drive manufacturers. Travan-NS (Network Solution) drives provide *read-while-write verification* and *hardware compression*, which allows the drive to compress data as it writes it, rather than depending on compression performed by the backup software. The most recent Travan technology, called Travan 40, is targeted at desktop PCs and small servers, and does not include read-while-write verification or hardware compression. Travan drives are relatively inexpensive, provide high capacity and performance, and are available in IDE, SCSI, USB, FireWire, and parallel interfaces. Travan drives are well-supported by all major operating systems, including Linux. The major drawback of Travan is the relatively high cost of tapes—$25 to $50, depending on capacity.

Advanced Digital Recording (ADR)

Advanced Digital Recording, or *ADR*, is a proprietary technology based on a patent portfolio held by Philips, and is best known for its use in tape drives made by OnStream. ADR writes eight tracks simultaneously, which allows it to provide high throughput while running the tape very slowly. That in turn means ADR drives are quieter and minimize tape wear relative to other serpentine tape technologies such as Travan. ADR equals or betters Travan in most other respects as well, including capacity, throughput, reliability, and operating system support. Unfortunately, the price of ADR tapes is also comparable to that of Travan tapes.

Digital Data Storage (DDS)

Digital Data Storage, or *DDS*, is often incorrectly called *Digital Audio Tape (DAT)*. Actually, there is a technology called DataDAT, but it's nonstandard, and nearly all drives use the DDS standard instead. DDS drives use helical-scan recording similar to that used by a VCR. The recording head rotates at an angle relative to tape movement and lays down a series of short diagonal tracks across the full width of the tape. This means a DDS drive can theoretically fill a tape during one pass, although real-world drives may require several passes to do so. Relative to serpentine drives, the lower tape speed and smaller number of passes mean that DDS drives incur much less wear on both drive and tape during a backup pass, but the more complex tape path offsets this advantage somewhat. Nearly all DDS drives support read-while-write. DDS drives provide high capacity and performance and are well-supported by Windows and Linux, but are relatively expensive and require a SCSI interface. The major advantage of DDS drives is that they use relatively inexpensive tapes, typically $3 to $15. DDS drives are most appropriate for servers and workstations that use a tape rotation scheme that requires many tapes. We also consider DDS drives appropriate for desktop PCs that store large amounts of high-value data.

Advanced Intelligent Tape (AIT)

Advanced Intelligent Tape, or *AIT*, was developed by Sony and is a proprietary technology that uses 8mm tape in a 3.5-inch form factor cartridge. Sony and Seagate produce AIT tape drives, which are more expensive than DDS drives but provide higher capacity and sustained transfer rates, better error correction, and faster random access. AIT drives are self-cleaning, which is a significant advantage in server environments, albeit less so for desktop systems. AIT is well known in the server and workstation markets, but the relatively high cost of AIT drives limited their acceptance in the PC market until recently.

Many AIT advantages result from *MIC* (*Memory In Cassette*), a technology that is built into AIT drives and tapes. DDS and other older tape technologies store the Table of Contents (TOC) and other tape information on the tape itself, which means the tape must be rewound each time the TOC needs to be written or read. MIC is a 64 KB EEPROM embedded in the AIT tape. MIC contains the TOC, which can be read or written without moving the tape, which allows an AIT drive to load, unload, and search tapes much faster. MIC also stores data about the number of times the tape has been loaded and how frequently each area of the tape has been written, which contributes to increased reliability.

AIT is available in three variants, known as AIT-1, AIT-2, and AIT-3, that differ in capacity and throughput. AIT drives are well-supported by Windows and Linux. AIT-1 drives are now inexpensive enough that they are a reasonable choice to back up workstations, small servers, and high-end PCs if a less expensive DDS-3 or DDS-4 drive has insufficient capacity.

 Some readers point out that the cost of a tape drive and tapes may exceed the cost of a PC. That is true, but immaterial. What matters is not the cost of the PC or the tape drive, but the value of the data that tape drive protects. The key issues that determine if tape is an appropriate choice for backing up are how much data needs to be protected, how often the data changes, and the cost of reconstructing the data if it were lost. If you have relatively little data that changes infrequently and is of little value, backing up to CD-R or writable DVD is a less expensive alternative. But if you have a lot of data that changes frequently and is of high value, tape is by far the best choice. Not necessarily the cheapest, but the best.

Tables 9-1, 9-2, and 9-3 list key selection criteria for typical tape drives that use these four technologies. Capacity and sustained transfer rates are native, and assume no compression. Uncorrectable error rate is the minimum number of bits the drive is expected to read successfully before encountering an unrecoverable error. An unrecoverable error is one for which the drive cannot reconstruct the data from ECC data. When that happens, the original data is irretrievably lost. For example, a typical tape drive has an uncorrectable error rate of 10^{-15}. That means the drive on average reads 10^{15} bits (more than 100,000 GB) before it encounters a read error that cannot be corrected using the ECC data stored on the tape. For comparison, typical hard drives have an uncorrectable error rate of 10^{-14} and typical CD writers 10^{-12}. That means in the course of reading the same amount of data the hard drive generates 10 times as many uncorrectable errors as the tape drive, and the CD writer 1,000 times as many. Items listed as "NLA" are no longer readily available.

Table 9-1. Key selection criteria for Travan drives

	TR-1	TR-2	TR-3	TR-4	NS8	TR-5	NS20	Travan 40
Capacity (MB)	400	800	1600	4000	4000	10,000	10,000	20,000
Sustained transfer rate (MB/min)	3.75	3.75	7.5	30	36	60	60	120

Table 9-1. Key selection criteria for Travan drives (continued)

	TR-1	TR-2	TR-3	TR-4	NS8	TR-5	NS20	Travan 40
Uncorrectable error rate	10^{-14}	10^{-14}	10^{-14}	10^{-15}	10^{-15}	10^{-15}	10^{-15}	10^{-15}
IDE/SCSI interface	●/●	●/●	●/●	●/●	●/●	●/●	●/●	●/○
USB/Parallel interface	○/●	○/●	○/●	●/●	●/○	●/○	●/○	●/○
Read-while-write?	○	○	○	○	●	○	●	○
HW compression?	○	○	○	○	●	○	●	○
Native QIC format	3010	3020	3080	3095	3095	3220	3220	Travan 40
Can read/write QIC-40 tapes?	●/○	○/○	○/○	○/○	○/○	○/○	○/○	○/○
Can read/write QIC-80 tapes?	●/●	●/○	●/○	○/○	○/○	○/○	○/○	○/○
Can read/write QIC-3010 tapes?	●/●	●/●	●/●	○/○	○/○	○/○	○/○	○/○
Can read/write QIC-3020 tapes?	○/○	●/●	●/●	●/○	●/○	○/○	○/○	○/○
Can read/write QIC-3080 tapes?	○/○	○/○	●/●	●/●	●/●	○/○	○/○	○/○
Can read/write QIC-3095 tapes?	○/○	○/○	○/○	●/●	●/●	●/○	●/○	○/○
Can read/write QIC-3220 tapes?	○/○	○/○	○/○	○/○	○/○	●/●	●/●	●/○
Can read/write Travan 40 tapes?	○/○	○/○	○/○	○/○	○/○	○/○	○/○	●/●
Drive cost (US$)	NLA	NLA	NLA	NLA	NLA	NLA	~ 225	~ 325
Tape cost (US$)	NLA	NLA	25	24	24	35	35	50
Tape cost/GB (US$)	n/a	n/a	15.63	6.00	6.00	3.50	3.50	2.50

In the preceding edition we said we didn't expect to see Travan TR-6 drives because they would cost as much as DDS-4 drives and require very expensive tapes. Seagate proved us (partially) wrong by shipping Travan 40 tape drives in mid-2002, just as that edition hit the stores. Oh, well.

Travan 40 drives are about half the price of DDS-4 drives, and store 20 GB (40 GB compressed) on a $50 tape. The good news is that those hideously expensive tapes are guaranteed for life, although we wouldn't use any tape heavily for more than a couple of years even if our own mothers guaranteed it. Travan 40 drives are obviously targeted at high-end desktop systems rather than servers. They do not support read-while-write or hardware data compression, and are available only with an ATAPI interface.

Table 9-2 lists the key characteristics of ADR tape drives. First-generation ADR drives use the original ADR30 or ADR50 tapes. ADR30 models are still sold, targeted at price-sensitive buyers and desktop PCs. Second-generation ADR^2 drives are considerably more expensive, use higher-capacity ADR2.60C or ADR2.120C tapes, and are marketed as an inexpensive, high-capacity alternative to DDS libraries or AIT drives for network servers.

Table 9-2. Key selection criteria for ADR drives

	ADR30	ADR50	ADR2.60C	ADR2.120C
Capacity (MB)	15,000	25,000	30,000	60,000
Sustained transfer rate (MB/min)	120	120	240	480
Uncorrectable error rate	10^{-19}	10^{-19}	10^{-19}	10^{-19}
IDE/SCSI interface	●/●	○/●	●/●	○/●
USB/Parallel interface	●/●	○/○	●/○	○/○
Read-while-write?	○	○	○	○
HW compression?	○	●	○	○
Can read/write ADR30 tapes?	●/●	●/●	○/○	○/○
Can read/write ADR50 tapes?	○/○	●/●	○/○	○/○
Can read/write ADR2.60C tapes?	○/○	○/○	●/●	●/●
Can read/write ADR2.120C tapes?	○/○	○/○	○/○	●/●
Drive cost (US$)	225 - 350	NLA	400 - 650	750 - 900
Tape cost (US$)	35	50	55	80
Tape cost/GB (US$)	2.33	2.00	1.83	1.33

Table 9-3 lists the key characteristics of DDS and AIT drives. Other than one off-brand ATAPI DDS model, all DDS and AIT drives we know of use some form of SCSI interface. DDS-1 was originally designated simply DDS. When DDS-2 drives became available, DDS drives were renamed DDS-1 to differentiate them. DDS-1 drives come in two variants. The original DDS-1 drives did not support hardware compression. DDS-1 drives with hardware compression added are called DDS-DC drives. All DDS-1 drives can use 60-meter DDS-1 tapes, which store 1.3 GB natively, and 90-meter DDS-1 tapes, which store 2.0 GB natively. Other than non-DC DDS-1 drives, all DDS and AIT drives support read-while-write and hardware compression. All DDS and AIT drives can read and write tapes based on earlier standards, except that DDS-4 drives cannot use 60-meter DDS-1 tapes.

Table 9-3. Key selection criteria for DDS and AIT drives

	DDS-1	DDS-2	DDS-3	DDS-4	AIT-1	AIT-2	AIT-3
Capacity (GB)	1.3/2	4	12	20	25/35	36/50	100
Sustained transfer rate (MB/min)	36	36	72	144	240	360	720
Uncorrectable error rate	10^{-15}	10^{-15}	10^{-15}	10^{-15}	10^{-17}	10^{-17}	10^{-17}
Can read/write DDS-1 tapes?	●/●	●/●	●/●	●/●	○/○	○/○	○/○
Can read/write DDS-2 tapes?	○/○	●/●	●/●	●/●	○/○	○/○	○/○
Can read/write DDS-3 tapes?	○/○	○/○	●/●	●/●	○/○	○/○	○/○
Can read/write DDS-4 tapes?	○/○	○/○	○/○	●/●	○/○	○/○	○/○
Can read/write AIT-1 tapes?	○/○	○/○	○/○	○/○	●/●	●/●	●/●
Can read/write AIT-2 tapes?	○/○	○/○	○/○	○/○	○/○	●/●	●/●
Can read/write AIT-3 tapes?	○/○	○/○	○/○	○/○	○/○	○/○	●/●
Drive cost (US$)	NLA	NLA	~ 425	~ 550	~ 700	~ 1,000	~ 2,000
Tape cost (US$)	~ 4	~ 4	~ 6	~ 12	~ 50	~ 60	~ 75
Tape cost/GB (US$)	~ 2.00	~ 1.00	~ 0.50	~ 0.60	~ 1.43	~ 1.20	~ 0.75

Choosing a Tape Drive

Consider the following issues when choosing a tape drive:

Capacity
> The single most important consideration. Get a drive that can back up all data on one tape, allowing for some growth. If your data set exceeds the

capacity of one tape, you may find that drive is no longer usable (if no one is available to change tapes during an overnight backup) or that it has suddenly become very expensive to use (because you must buy twice as many tapes). In such a case, the only alternative to replacing the drive is to use a backup scheme that mixes full and incremental or differential partial backups, which is riskier for your data.

Most tape drive manufacturers arbitrarily rate their drives at double actual native capacity, assuming you will use software or hardware compression to double the amount of data that fits on a tape. AIT drive specifications go further still, assuming 2.6X compression. The actual compression ratio you experience depends on the data mix (e.g., documents and spreadsheets compress well; executables, images, and archives much less so), the backup software you use, and sometimes on the speed of the computer where the drive resides. We find that real-world data sets typically compress at 1.5:1 to 1.7:1, so plan accordingly.

 Having adequate tape drive capacity does not necessarily mean being able to back up your entire hard drive (or drive farm) to one tape in one pass. For example, our network contains more than a terabyte (1000 GB) of disk space with hundreds of gigabytes in use. Yet for backups we use only two DDS-3 drives that store 12 GB natively, one DDS-4 drive that stores 20 GB natively and one Travan NS-20 drive that stores 10 GB natively. We are well protected, despite our total tape drive capacity being much smaller than the amount of data we have stored. Why? Because much of that data doesn't need to be backed up frequently, if at all.

Some is archived "real" data—things such as previous editions of this book. We back up that data periodically to inexpensive DDS-3 tapes as well as CD-R and DVD+R/RW discs. We need to renew those backups only every few months when we move material from our working data directories to our archive directories. Hundreds of gigabytes of data need not be backed up at all. That comprises copies of operating systems and applications that we keep on network volumes for convenience, ISOs of numerous older Linux distributions, MP3s we ripped from our CD collection (which we plan to re-rip as OGG files anyway), movies we recorded and watched but haven't yet gotten around to deleting, and so on. In other words, stuff that we wouldn't miss if we lost it, or that we could easily reproduce if necessary. Our actual working data fits easily on one DDS-3 tape, so for us DDS-3 suffices.

Speed

This may or may not be a critical factor, depending on your own environment and practices. If you have a limited backup window available, speed may be as important as capacity. If you can simply start a backup when you finish work for the day and allow it to run overnight, speed may be a minor factor.

Actual throughput depends on the drive mechanism, the interface, the speed of the computer in which the drive is installed, and the data set being backed up, but will likely be lower than the drive manufacturer advertises. Compression may also have a significant impact on throughput, for better or worse. For example, our Seagate Scorpion 40 DDS-4 drive is rated at 165 MB/min native and 330 MB/min compressed, but we typically get only 275 MB/min with compression enabled. Similarly, our Seagate Travan NS20 SCSI drive is rated at 60 MB/min native and 120 MB/min compressed, but we actually get about 100 MB/min. The lower-than-expected throughput with compression is no fault of the drives, but results from our data being less compressible than the assumed 2:1. For these drives, compression improves throughput, albeit not to the expected extent. Conversely, when we tested an OnStream DI30 drive that is rated at 60 MB/min native and 120 MB/min with compression, we actually got 45–50 MB/min native, but only 15–17 MB/min when using the bundled Echo software with compression enabled. In that case, it turned out the compression software was poorly designed, a problem that was fixed in a later release. All of these figures are for backing up local volumes. Backing up data across a network, even a fast network, commonly cuts throughput by half or more due to operating system overhead, file-system overhead, and network latency.

 If your tape drive provides hardware compression and your backup application has software compression, don't use both methods together. Either works well by itself, but using both may actually reduce throughput, as the drive tries to compress data that's already been compressed by the backup software. In general, hardware compression is faster than software compression. There are exceptions, though, and which compression method is more efficient may depend on the drive, backup software, and mix of data being backed up. The only way to determine which method is faster is to try both, but be sure to try them one at a time.

Media cost

Travan and OnStream ADR drives are constructed with loose tolerances, and are accordingly inexpensive, but require expensive tapes built to close tolerances. DDS drives, conversely, are expensive because they are built to tight tolerances, which allows them to use inexpensive, loose-tolerance tapes. AIT drives are expensive and use expensive tapes, but their very high capacity and throughput may make them the only alternative when DDS-4 isn't large enough or fast enough. A typical tape rotation may require from four to 50 or more tapes. Tapes must be replaced periodically (on the schedule recommended by the drive and/or tape manufacturer—trying to stretch the lifetime of tapes is a foolish economy). Tape drives have a realistic service life of perhaps two to three years with heavy use, and four or five years with moderate use (by which time the drive is likely no longer adequate for your needs anyway). Expect to spend from as much to several times as much as the cost of the drive to buy tapes over the drive's life.

Interface

Internal tape drives are available with ATAPI/IDE or SCSI interfaces. External tape drives are available with SCSI, Parallel, USB 1.1, USB 2.0, or FireWire (IEEE-1394) interfaces.

ATAPI

ADR and Travan drives are available with ATAPI interfaces. ATAPI drives are typically less expensive than those using other interfaces, can use the ubiquitous IDE interface present on any modern motherboard, provide reasonably high throughput, and are easy to install. Choose an ATAPI drive for convenience, ease of installation, or when cost is an overriding issue.

SCSI

ADR, Travan, DDS, and AIT drives are available with SCSI interfaces. SCSI drives typically sell for at least a $50 to $100 premium over similar ATAPI models, require adding a $100+ SCSI interface card if the PC is not already so equipped, and are more complicated to install and configure than ATAPI models. SCSI drives typically provide much higher throughput and much lower CPU utilization than ATAPI models. The largest and most feature-laden drives are available only in SCSI. Most SCSI-only models are designed for use on servers, and are therefore better built and more reliable than ATAPI drives designed for the mass market. Choose a SCSI drive for highest capacity, performance, durability, and reliability. SCSI is the only option if there are no available ATAPI connections, or if you require capacity and/or features available only in a SCSI model.

Parallel

Drives that use the parallel interface typically have half or less the throughput of SCSI or ATAPI/IDE, but may be a reasonable choice if you must use one drive to back up local data on multiple standalone PCs that do not have recent USB ports. On a small network, it is usually better to map a drive on the server where a tape drive resides for each local workstation volume, and back up centrally to an ATAPI or SCSI drive. If you are considering a parallel drive because you have several standalone PCs that must be backed up, consider instead connecting those PCs with a simple network and using an internal server-based tape drive.

USB

USB 1.1 drives typically have between half and two-thirds the throughput of ATAPI/IDE and SCSI drives, and are a better choice than parallel port drives for backing up local data on multiple standalone PCs if all of those PCs have reasonably recent USB ports. USB 1.1 tape drives have a theoretical maximum throughput of about 90 MB/min and a typical actual throughput of 60 MB/min or less. USB 2.0 models are limited by the speed of the drive mechanism rather than the speed of the interface.

FireWire

There are a few external tape drives available that use the FireWire interface, none of which we have tested. FireWire tape drives offer Plug and
Play compatibility similar to USB models, but are much faster than USB
1.1 drives. The relatively high cost of FireWire tape drives and the fact
that few PCs have FireWire interfaces make them a poor choice for most
people. The exception is if you have desktop PCs and, particularly, notebook PCs that have a FireWire interface installed. In that case, a
FireWire tape drive may be the fastest, easiest tool for backing up.

Cross-drive compatibility

Here's a dirty little secret that drive manufacturers don't talk much about.
You might reasonably assume that a tape you created in one drive would be
readable in a similar drive, but that's not always the case. In particular, we
have found that some Travan TR-4 drives produce tapes that cannot be read
by another drive, even one of the identical make and model. We seldom
encounter that problem on AIT, DDS, Travan NS8/NS20, and OnStream
ADR drives, although we have had infrequent reports of such compatibility
problems occurring with them.

Unless you use a tape drive to transfer large quantities of data between
computers, this may seem a minor issue. It can be critical, however, if your
computer is stolen or damaged by flood or fire. Even if your backup tapes are
safely locked away, you may find that a replacement drive of the same model
is unable to read them. If your data is important enough to warrant extreme
precautions, buy two identical tape drives and verify that a tape written in
either drive is readable by the other. Repeat this verification periodically
because drives do start marching to their own drummer as they age. Alternatively, consider backing up key data frequently to CD-R or writable DVD and
verifying that the disc is readable.

Operating system compatibility

Hardware-level compatibility and application compatibility are important
issues in choosing a tape drive. At the hardware level, any current tape drive
is almost certainly compatible with all recent versions of Windows. Most
current tape drives also support Linux, but there are exceptions, so check
hardware compatibility and driver availability for your specific Linux distribution and version before you buy a tape drive. Linux drivers may be
available for a particular tape drive, but using them may require recompiling
the kernel or taking other steps that you may not be comfortable performing.

Application compatibility varies. Many tape drives are bundled with backup
software that is targeted at a specific market. For example, a drive intended
for desktop systems may include backup software that runs under Windows
9X, 2000 Professional, and XP Professional but not under Windows 2000
Server or Linux. Conversely, a tape drive targeted at servers may include
bundled backup software that runs under one or several server operating
systems. If you intend to use the tape drive with Linux or an unsupported
Windows version, you must obtain backup software separately. That software may be free, as are several Linux backup programs, or it may be
expensive enough to make a different tape drive a better choice.

Installing and Configuring a Tape Drive

External tape drives are "installed" simply by connecting them to the parallel, SCSI, USB, or FireWire port, as appropriate, and connecting power, although you may have to set jumpers to configure a SCSI drive for the proper SCSI ID and termination. Internal tape drives are 3.5- or 5.25-inch half-height devices, and require the same physical installation steps as any other externally accessible drive. The exact configuration steps required differ between ATAPI and SCSI interfaces, as described in the following sections.

Some tape drive manufacturers, including Seagate, recommend installing the backup software *before* installing the tape drive. But do not *run* the backup software before the drive is installed and recognized by the computer and operating system, or you may find that you need to reinstall the backup software in order for it to recognize the drive. Microsoft Backup has burned us this way more than once. Conversely, some tape backup software—typically that bundled with a tape drive—refuses to install unless a tape drive that it supports is already installed. Read the manual for the tape drive *and* the backup software before you begin the installation.

Installing and Configuring an ATAPI Tape Drive

ATAPI tape drives are physically installed and configured just like any other ATAPI/IDE device: set the drive's Master/Slave jumper; secure the drive in an available drive bay using four screws; connect the data cable, aligning Pin 1 on the drive connector with the colored stripe on the cable; and connect the power cable. Note the following issues when installing an ATAPI tape drive:

- Installing a tape drive on the same IDE channel as a hard disk risks data corruption. If the system has one hard disk, install it as the Primary Master and the tape drive on the Secondary channel. If the system has two hard disks, install both on the Primary channel, and install the tape drive on the Secondary channel. Do not install three ATA hard disks in a system with an ATAPI tape drive. If the system has an ATAPI CD-ROM drive, make that drive Secondary Master and the tape drive Secondary Slave. If the system has no ATAPI CD-ROM drive, make the tape drive Secondary Master.

- Some tape drives have configuration jumpers to enable such things as hardware compression, read-while-write, DMA/PIO mode, and emulation mode. If your drive has one or more of these jumpers, set them as follows:

   Hardware compression
      Ordinarily, enable this option to allow the drive itself to compress the data stream before recording it to tape, but note that software compression is sometimes more efficient than hardware compression. If you enable hardware compression, disable compression in your backup utility. Leaving both enabled results in "churning" that can actually increase the size of the data being written to tape. Some backup utilities have a configuration checkbox that allows you to select hardware compression. We've never been entirely sure of the purpose of this checkbox because hardware compression is (or should be) transparent to the backup application, but if

Tape Drives

your backup utility has such a checkbox, it's probably a good idea to mark it if you enable hardware compression on the drive.

 Although different drive models from a particular manufacturer may supposedly use compatible hardware compression, any tape made with hardware compression enabled may be unreadable except in the drive that wrote it. There is no guarantee that you will be able to read a hardware-compressed tape made on one drive with any other drive. Something as subtle as a minor difference in firmware revision may prevent reading a compressed tape even in a seemingly identical drive.

Read-while-write

If your drive has a jumper to enable read-while-write, doing so allows the drive to use its separate read head to read and verify data immediately after it is written, avoiding the need for a time-consuming second compare pass. Not all backup software supports this function. If your backup software does support it, you may need to enable support for it within the backup program.

DMA/PIO mode

DMA mode increases throughput and reduces CPU utilization, but not all tape drives can operate in DMA mode. If your drive is DMA-capable, it may have a jumper to configure the drive for DMA mode versus PIO mode. In general, if the tape drive is the only device on the ATA channel, or if the other device on that channel is also DMA-capable, enable DMA mode for the tape drive and enable DMA support for that channel in the operating system. If the tape drive shares the channel with a PIO-only device (e.g., an older CD-ROM drive), disable DMA mode for the tape drive or (better) replace the other device with a DMA-capable device.

Emulation mode

Some tape drives can emulate other drives via a jumper setting that causes the drive to return incorrect identification data to the operating system. For example, we have an old Tecmar Travan NS20 tape drive that was jumpered by default to identify itself as a Wangtek Model 51000. Removing this jumper causes the drive to identify itself as a Tecmar Travan NS20. Using emulation allows a new drive model to be used with older software that does not support the new model. Set this jumper, if present, according to the manufacturer's instructions.

- Recent BIOSes allow setting boot sequence to first attempt booting from a CD-ROM drive. What this actually tells the system is to boot from the first ATAPI device. If an ATAPI tape drive is configured as Master (even on the Secondary channel), a system so configured may attempt to boot from the tape drive, which causes the system to hang. You can avoid this problem by setting the CD-ROM drive to Secondary Master and the tape drive to Secondary Slave. This problem may also occur if the tape drive is the only device on the Secondary channel, whether it is configured as Master or Slave. If you cannot correct the configuration or disable CD-ROM boot in BIOS, boot the system with no tape in the drive.

Installing and Configuring a SCSI Tape Drive

Installing and configuring a SCSI tape drive is a bit more complicated than installing an ATAPI model. Rather than attempting to provide step-by-step instructions, which vary according to the specific drive and adapter, we've chosen to illustrate a typical installation using a Seagate Hornet NS20 drive and an Adaptec 2930 SCSI host adapter, both representative selections.

- If you have not already done so, install the SCSI host adapter. To do so, power down the system, remove the cover, and locate an available bus-mastering PCI slot. (Some older systems don't support bus mastering on all slots. Bus-mastering slots are usually white or ivory; non-bus-mastering slots are brown or black.) Remove the slot cover for the selected slot, align the bus connector with the slot, and press down firmly to seat the adapter. Use the screw that secured the slot cover to secure the adapter. If you have a spare drive activity indicator LED, connect it to J2 on the host adapter to indicate SCSI bus activity.

- The Adaptec host adapter supports *SCAM* (*SCSI Configured Auto-Magically*)—a kind of Plug and Play for SCSI that automatically configures SCSI ID and termination. (SCAM is described in "Installing and Configuring a CD-ROM Drive" in Chapter 10). Like most tape drives, the Seagate Travan NS20 does not support SCAM, so we'll have to set jumpers manually to assign SCSI ID and set termination.

Like most manually configured SCSI devices, the Seagate Travan NS20 drive has three jumpers—ID0 (SCSI ID 1), ID1 (SCSI ID 2), and ID2 (SCSI ID 4). Installing jumper blocks on zero or more of these jumpers allows you to set SCSI IDs 0 through 7. Connecting no jumpers assigns SCSI ID 0. Connecting one jumper assigns the SCSI ID associated with that jumper (e.g., ID1 assigns SCSI ID 2). Connecting two jumpers assigns the SCSI ID that is the sum of the two jumpers (e.g., ID0 and ID2 sums the SCSI IDs 1 and 4 to assign the SCSI ID 5). Connecting all three jumpers assigns SCSI ID 7. Like most SCSI tape drives that require the SCSI ID to be assigned manually, the Seagate Travan NS20 drive by default is jumpered to SCSI ID 4, which is usually not in use by other devices.

 Avoid setting a tape drive to SCSI ID 0, 1, or 7. ID 0 is reserved by convention for a bootable hard drive, ID 1 for a second hard drive, and ID 7 for the host adapter.

- The Seagate Travan NS20 drive also requires setting termination manually. Exactly two devices must be terminated on each SCSI bus, and these devices must be those at each end of the bus, as follows:
  - If the SCSI adapter has only internal devices attached to it, the adapter itself and the final device on the internal SCSI chain must be terminated.
  - If the SCSI adapter has only external devices attached to it, the adapter itself and the final device on the external SCSI chain must be terminated.
  - If the SCSI adapter has both internal and external devices attached to it, the adapter must not be terminated. Instead, terminate the final internal device and the final external device attached to the SCSI chain.

In this case, the Seagate tape drive is the final device on the internal SCSI chain, which has no external devices, so the drive and the host adapter must both be terminated. By default, Pins 3 and 4 on the drive are jumpered, which terminates it. That's the correct setting, so we leave it as is. If we were installing the Seagate Travan NS20 between two existing SCSI devices, we'd remove the jumper from Pins 3 and 4 to disable termination.

Pins 1 and 2 are also jumpered by default, which enables Termination Power. Again, that's the correct setting, so we leave it at default. Pins 5/6 and 7/8 are reserved on this drive, so we leave them unjumpered, which is the default. Pins 9/10 are jumpered, which enables Parity Checking. Again, that's the correct setting, so we leave it at default.

 Most drives ship with Termination Power and Parity Checking enabled, which is usually correct. If you have trouble accessing a tape drive, check the host adapter manual to determine if Termination Power and/or Parity Checking should be disabled.

Adaptec host adapters, which we use and recommend exclusively, by default automatically detect terminated SCSI devices on the bus and set their own termination status accordingly, so no further action is required to configure the drive properly. Note that a few internal SCSI cables have a built-in terminator at the end of the cable. If you use such a cable, make sure that termination is disabled on all drives connected to that cable.

- Once you have resolved SCSI ID and termination issues and have the drive physically installed, the next step is to connect the cables. Most adapters are supplied with a standard two-device cable. If you need to connect more than two drives, replace the cable before proceeding. Otherwise, connect the cable to each drive, making sure to align Pin 1 on the cable (indicated by a red stripe) with Pin 1 on each device (indicated by a small number, triangle, or dot on the connector). For SCSI IDs, it doesn't matter which drive connects to which cable position, so mix and match drives and cable positions in whatever way makes it easiest to route the cable. Just make sure that the physical last drive on the cable is the one that's terminated. Connect the power cable.

- After verifying all settings and connections, turn on any external SCSI device(s) first, and then turn on the PC. Ordinarily, the system should boot normally, but the SCSI tape drive may or may not be recognized, depending on the drive itself, your operating system, and other factors. Before you configure the operating system to use the drive, some systems may require one or both of the following steps:

CMOS Setup
> On most systems, the PCI bus assigns IRQs and port addresses automatically. If your system requires setting PCI bus parameters manually, do so during the first restart, using the system or motherboard documentation for guidance. (If your system BIOS is capable of assigning IRQs automatically, there will usually be a CMOS Setup option worded something like "Plug and Play OS?" If that option is set to No, the PC BIOS assigns IRQs. If it is set to Yes, the BIOS allows the Plug and Play capable OS [Windows 9X/2000/XP/Linux] to assign IRQs).

SCSI Setup

At boot time, the SCSI BIOS displays adapter and BIOS information and a list of installed SCSI devices. Ordinarily, the default settings are fine, but in some cases you may need to change settings to get the drive to work at all or to optimize its performance. If this is the case for your system, press whatever key sequence is needed to invoke the SCSI Setup routine and make the necessary changes, as recommended by the documentation for the host adapter and/or drive.

If either or both of these steps are needed, restart the system after completing each. After you complete these steps, the system should boot normally and physically recognize the tape drive.

Configuring Windows 9X/2000/XP to Support a Tape Drive

Windows 9X/2000/XP does not support *any* tape drives in the usual sense, although it may or may not recognize and display the name of an installed tape drive, depending on the drive and the version of Windows. Unlike most other devices, for which drivers are readily available and can be installed using the Add New Hardware Wizard, tape drives running under Windows depend on device support built into the backup application itself. This is why, for example, the Windows 98 Microsoft Backup applet—an OEM version of Veritas Backup Exec—can use some tape drives and not others: the program itself contains drivers for the supported tape drives. All this really means is that you can't use unsupported drives with the built-in backup applet. That's not usually a problem because most tape drives are bundled with backup software considerably superior to the Windows Backup applet.

Windows support for tape drives is analogous to Windows support for CD writers and DVD writers. Windows recognizes that the drive is present, but has no idea how to exploit its capabilities. Just as with CD/DVD writers, that functionality must be built into application software designed to support the drive, whether that application is supplied by a third party or comes as a Windows applet (as does the Windows Backup application or the limited CD burning application bundled with Windows XP). The backup software bundled with your tape drive will support it. If you buy a bare drive, you'll need to purchase backup software separately, unless the Windows Backup applet supports your drive and is sufficient for your needs.

Recent versions of third-party Windows backup applications include drivers for many recent-model tape drives. Most tape drives bundle a competent backup utility—often a special version of Backup Exec or ARCserve—that contains the necessary drivers to support that drive under the operating systems intended to run them. You may, however, need to download drivers for a new tape drive either from the tape drive manufacturer (most of which do not supply drivers) or from the backup software company, if one of the following is true:

- You have a previously purchased backup utility that does not contain drivers for the new drive.

- You have a backup utility you want to continue to use that was originally bundled with a drive you are replacing, and that backup utility has no support for the new drive.

- The backup application supplied with the new drive does not support the operating system you are using.

Before you purchase a tape drive for use with Windows, verify that the backup application you intend to use has drivers for that tape drive.

Configuring Linux to Support a Tape Drive

The ease of configuring Linux to support a tape drive depends on the Linux distribution and version, the type of drive, the interface it uses, and whether the drive is present when Linux is installed or is added later. If you use a modern, mainstream ATAPI or SCSI drive with a recent Linux distribution, installation will likely be straightforward. If you use an older distribution, an obsolescent or proprietary drive, or a drive that uses an interface other than ATAPI or SCSI, you may encounter significant problems getting the drive to work, if indeed you can get it working at all. You can use the following tape drives with Linux:

Travan, DDS, and AIT tape drives
Recent Linux releases natively support a wide variety of Travan, DDS, and AIT tape drives with ATAPI or SCSI interfaces. If you install and configure the drive and interface properly before you install Linux, the Linux installer will likely recognize the drive and automatically configure Linux to use it. In fact, Linux often does a better job than Windows 2000/XP of recognizing and configuring Travan, DDS, and AIT tape drives.

If you install a tape drive in a system with Linux already installed, log in as root and run the hardware detection utility (e.g., Kudzu in Redhat or Mandrake and Discover in Debian). If the drive is supported, the utility detects the drive, installs drivers, and automatically configures Linux to use the drive. If the drive is not recognized, check the web sites for the drive and your Linux distro to determine how to configure the drive manually.

 USB and FireWire (IEEE-1394) drives require a 2.4 or higher Linux kernel.

OnStream ADR tape drives
Linux support for OnStream tape drives differs according to the command set used by the drive. All second-generation (ADR2) drives and first-generation (ADR) ADR30, ADR50, and ADR50e SCSI drives use the standard SCSI command set, so the standard st (SCSI tape) driver suffices to interface the drive to the backup application (the ATAPI ADR2.60IDE drive requires both the ide-scsi and st drivers).

Most first-generation OnStream ADR drives—the DI30, DI30 FAST, DP30, USB30, SC30, SC30e, SC50, SC50e, and FW30—use a proprietary command set that optimizes those drives for storing streaming video. That command set differs significantly from the standard ATAPI and SCSI command sets, which means the standard st driver does not support these drives. Full (or even partial) Linux support requires a kernel rebuild or various workarounds. Fortunately, a modified version of the st driver, called the osst driver, is available. The osst driver interfaces standard backup applications to the proprietary command set of older ADR drives. For details about Linux support for first-generation OnStream tape drives, see *http://www.linux1onstream.nl/*.

Although the ide-tape driver supports the OnStream DI30 drive, we strongly recommend using the ide-scsi and osst drivers instead. The ide-tape driver writes tapes in LIN3 logical format, whereas osst writes tapes in LIN4 logical format. That means the osst driver reads tapes written with ide-tape, but the ide-tape driver cannot read tapes written with osst. Also, various problems have been reported using ide-tape with DI30 drives, ranging from inability to restore files to complete failure to recognize the drive.

FDC-based drives

Travan TR-3 and earlier QIC drives use the floppy drive controller (FDC) interface, either directly or in some cases via a parallel port connection. These drives are now so old that most have been retired, but if for some reason you must use an FDC-based tape drive on a Linux system, you may be able to get it running using ftape. The ftape driver supports QIC-40, QIC-80, QIC-3010 (TR-2), QIC-3020 (TR-3), Iomega Ditto 2GB, and Ditto Max drives. For more information about ftape, see *http://www.ibiblio.org/pub/Linux/docs/ HOWTO/other-formats/html_single/Ftape-HOWTO.html*.

We do not recommend using ftape in PCI-based systems, which is to say in any modern system at all. The ftape driver has known incompatibilities with some PCI motherboards. For details, view *README.PCI* in the ftape distribution.

Once Linux recognizes a tape drive, you can use bundled Linux applications such as tar, mt, mtx, dump, restore, and cpio to write and read tapes in the drive. You can also use full-featured backup applications such as BRU (*http://www.tolisgroup. com/*), Amanda (*http://www.amanda.org/*), and Arkeia (*http://www.arkeia.com/*) to implement a formal backup program.

Here are some useful sites that cover various aspects of using tape drives with Linux:

http://www.linuxtapecert.org
http://cdfpc2.mps.ohio-state.edu/linux/tape/
http://www.tldp.org/LDP/sag/index.html

Care and Feeding of a Tape Drive

Tape drives and tape cartridges are surprisingly durable, but getting the best results requires following a few simple rules:

Tape Drives

Clean the drive regularly!

The most frequent cause of tape drive problems is dirty read/write heads. Tape drive manufacturers typically recommend cleaning the drive monthly or after every 10 to 25 hours of use. It is also a good idea to clean the drive immediately after first using a new tape. Depending on how you use your drive and how clean your environment is, even that may be inadequate. Problems caused by dirty heads are not always immediately obvious because tape drives use industrial-strength ECC methods that allow them to recover from most read and write errors. The first sign of dirty heads may simply be that backups begin taking longer than they should. If your environment is typical, it's probably not excessive to clean the tape drive weekly or before each full backup. Some drives can be cleaned only by using the recommended cleaning cartridge. Other drives allow you to vacuum or blow out the dust and then use a foam swab moistened with rubbing alcohol to clean the heads and rollers (cotton swabs can leave debris on the heads, and should be avoided). Having once watched a cleaning cartridge destroy the heads on a tape drive, we prefer the second method if the drive manufacturer lists it as permissible.

 Some high-end tape drives keep track of how much the drive has been used since the last cleaning. For example, our Tecmar TS3900i DDS-3 drive generates a warning message in Backup Exec when it is time to clean the drive. Running a cleaning cartridge through the drive clears and resets the timer, and the message disappears until the next time cleaning is due. We've been told that some tape drives simply refuse to operate if you ignore the warning messages too long, but we've never experienced that, simply because we've never risked allowing an expensive drive to go too long without cleaning.

Avoid exposing tapes to magnetic fields

This should be obvious, but what may not be obvious is that stray magnetic fields from monitors and other peripherals can damage even tapes that are stored some distance from the source. We once found that tapes stored in a desk drawer had been damaged by the field from a monitor sitting on the desk surface above them. For DAT tapes, the only loss is the data stored on the tape because DAT drives format tapes on the fly as they write the data. For Travan and ADR tapes, any damage is fatal to the tape. These tapes are formatted at the factory, and cannot be reformatted by the user. If you expose a Travan or ADR tape to a magnetic field strong enough to damage the data on it, that tape can no longer be used.

Retension tapes frequently

Periodic retensioning is required with Travan and ADR tapes, but not with DDS or AIT tapes. Retensioning simply winds the tape out to the end and then back to the beginning. You should retension a tape before using it for the first time; if it has not been used for a month or more; if it has been shipped (or dropped); or if it has been exposed to a significant temperature change. As a rule of thumb, retension a tape used daily once a week, and one used weekly once a month. Note that you may need to retension a tape two or three times to eliminate all tape slack.

Store tapes safely
> Tapes are quite sensitive to their storage environment, and are happiest at the same levels of temperature and humidity that are comfortable for people. When a tape is not actually in the drive, always replace it in its sleeve or case to avoid dust. Never place a tape in direct sunlight. For safe storage onsite, use a fire safe. Make sure that the safe is rated to store magnetic media. Less expensive fire safes are designed to protect paper, and allow internal temperatures to exceed levels safe for tapes. If the temperature or humidity differ greatly between the storage and use locations, always allow the tape an hour or two to reach equilibrium before using it.

Replace tapes periodically
> Tapes do not last forever. Each time you use a tape, the magnetic medium becomes more abraded and the substrate stretches. For best results, replace tapes every two years or 50 uses, whichever comes first. That is, replace a tape that is used daily at least every two months. Replace a weekly tape at least once a year. Replace a monthly tape at least every two years. In addition to risking the data written to it, using an elderly, worn tape risks damaging the tape drive heads.

Troubleshooting Tape Drive Problems

Here, in rough order of frequency, are the most common tape drive problems and some things you can do to solve them:

Read/write errors
> If you experience numerous read/write errors, noticeably slower performance, excessive initialization time, or tapes that eject themselves immediately after they are inserted, first suspect a dirty drive. Cleaning the drive as described in the preceding section usually cures such problems immediately. Retensioning tapes periodically also helps avoid this problem.

Configuration problems or incompatibilities with backup software or drivers
> If the backup software doesn't recognize the drive, can't load the driver, or does not contain a driver for the drive, first make sure that the host adapter recognizes the drive as present at boot time. For SCSI, ensure the operating system recognizes the SCSI host adapter and download and install later drivers from the host adapter manufacturer's web site, if any are available. If you have recently installed a new version of your backup software, verify that it contains support for the tape drive, and download updated drivers for that drive if necessary. If your tape drive manufacturer provides downloadable firmware updates, download and install the latest recommended firmware for your drive.

SCSI communication problems
> If the controller does not recognize the tape drive or the controller or system hangs at boot, the most likely cause is physical damage to or a configuration problem with the SCSI chain. First verify that the data and power cables are undamaged and fully connected to the drive. Verify that there are no SCSI ID conflicts and check termination, particularly if you have just added a new SCSI device to the chain. If everything appears correct and the problem

persists, use the SCSI BIOS utility to make one or more of the following changes to the host adapter configuration: disable Sync Negotiation; disable Wide Negotiation; set the transfer rate to the lowest available value; enable Disconnect. In other words, slow things down until the drive functions properly. If none of this works, the most likely problem is a malfunctioning drive or controller. If other devices on that chain function properly, suspect the drive.

SCSI bus scan displays drive on all or most SCSI IDs
This is nearly always the result of assigning the tape drive the same SCSI ID as the host adapter. Reassigning the tape drive to an unused SCSI ID fixes the problem.

The Dirty Little Secret of Long Filenames

If you depend on your backup tapes to re-create a crashed hard drive, you need to know that a design flaw in Windows long filenames (LFN) means that your carefully made backup tapes may be nearly useless. This is a deficiency in Windows itself, a flaw in how long filenames and long directory names are implemented. Backup software can do nothing to work around the problem. Image backup is the only way to make a fully reliable backup under Windows.

 Read and heed these words: **It is impossible to make a reliable file-by-file backup under Windows if the volume uses long filenames or long directory names**.

The problem occurs because Windows assigns aliases to long directory names on the fly, as those directories are created, and then uses those generated aliases in the registry. For example, if you install Microsoft Office, it installs to the folder *C:\Program Files\Microsoft Office*. But when Windows creates the *Microsoft Office* subfolder in the *C:\Program Files* folder, it dynamically creates a short alias for the new folder. So, rather than the registry pointing to Word as *C:\Program Files\Microsoft Office\Office\Winword.exe*, as it appears in a directory listing, the registry might actually point to *C:\PROGRA~1\MICROS~3\ OFFICE\WINWORD.EXE*.

So far, so good. The problem is that Windows nowhere directly links that short directory name to the long directory name. As you use the system, you may create and delete other directories with long names that are assigned similar aliases. If you then back up that volume and subsequently restore it to an empty drive, Windows again creates short aliases on the fly, but *without any consistency in assigning short directory name aliases to the same long directory names to which they were originally assigned*. A concrete example makes all this clear.

We installed Windows NT 4 to an empty hard disk, using NTFS. It wouldn't have made any difference if we'd used Windows 9X or 2000/XP or the FAT file-system—all Windows versions have the same flaw. After installing the OS, we installed drivers for a Microsoft keyboard and mouse. Setup for those drivers created the subfolder *C:\Program Files\Microsoft Hardware*, which Windows assigned the alias *C:\PROGRA~1\MICROS~1*. We then installed Microsoft Office

2000. Setup installed that in two subfolders, *C:\Program Files\microsoft frontpage*, which Windows assigned the alias *C:\PROGRA~1\MICROS~2*, and *C:\Program Files\Microsoft Office*, which Windows assigned the alias *C:\PROGRA~1\MICROS~3*.

We then uninstalled the Microsoft keyboard and mouse drivers and deleted the folder that had contained them. This left *C:\PROGRA~1\MICROS~2* and *C:\PROGRA~1\MICROS~3* on disk, but *C:\PROGRA~1\MICROS~1* was no longer present. We did a backup to tape, formatted the hard disk, reinstalled Windows and the backup software, and restored from tape. The restore re-created the folders *C:\Program Files\microsoft frontpage* and *C:\Program Files\Microsoft Office*, but with aliases of *C:\PROGRA~1\MICROS~1* and *C:\PROGRA~1\MICROS~2* respectively. Unfortunately, the registry still thought FrontPage was in *C:\PROGRA~1\MICROS~2* and Office in *C:\PROGRA~1\MICROS~3*, which meant that Windows couldn't find either FrontPage or Office. In other words, Windows broke itself.

You might think that this is a convoluted series of steps that is unlikely to occur in the real world, but in fact this happens all the time. We frequently get messages from readers asking why their systems appear to have been completely corrupted after a disk failure and a restore from tape. This is invariably the reason.

If you've ever wondered while uninstalling a program why most uninstallers don't delete the empty folder, now you know the answer. If we hadn't deleted the empty folder in the preceding example, we might have avoided the problem. In particular, note that overly aggressive third-party uninstallers frequently contribute to this problem by deleting empty program folders by default.

In addition to implementing long file and directory names ineptly, Microsoft exacerbates the problem by using default folder names for most of its applications that start with *Microsoft*. In the preceding example, if Setup had simply named the directories *Hardware*, *FrontPage*, and *Office* (or even *MSHardware*, *MSFrontPage*, and *MSOffice*), there would have been no ambiguity in the aliases assigned to those folders, and the system would have worked properly after the restore. Note, however, that the problem isn't limited to Microsoft program folders. Any software that uses long file and directory names and also uses the registry to locate its program, data, or configuration files is subject to the same problem. To avoid this problem:

- When you install software, always install it to a folder with a short name if Setup offers that option. Most software installs to a long folder name by default, but the default installation location can usually be specified manually. Note that the option to specify the installation location manually may not be visible unless you choose "Advanced Setup Options" or something similar.

- When you create data directories, always use MS-DOS 8.3–compliant directory names. Some software allows you to "point" it toward a directory you have created yourself, but may then add entries to the registry to define that location.

Tape Drives

- Never delete a directory that may be subject to this problem, even if you've removed all of the files and subdirectories that the directory contained.

 Although you can disable 8.3 filename generation for NTFS volumes, doing so may cause compatibility problems with applications that expect 8.3 filename support. Nor are compatibility problems necessarily limited to older programs. For example, disabling 8.3 filename support may cause problems when burning ISO image files to CD.

Developing a Backup Strategy

This is a hardware book, so we don't spend much time on software. But, in our experience, many people who buy a tape drive have no idea how to use it effectively. We won't try to explain how to use your backup software because the specifics vary and nearly any software bundled with a tape drive is sufficient for the task, but we will devote some space to explaining how to get the most from your tape drive and backup software.

File Attributes and the Archive Bit

If you have a tape drive large enough to back up your entire hard disk and the time necessary to use only complete backups, the status of any particular file doesn't matter. Every file gets backed up every time, whether it was created that day or has been sitting unchanged for a year. But if you need to use some combination of complete and partial backups, the status of each file becomes critical. If a file is unchanged since the last complete backup, you want to ignore it when doing partial backups. If the file was created or changed since the last complete backup, it needs to be copied to the partial backup tape.

Windows maintains a file attribute for each file called the *archive bit*. When a file is created or changed, Windows toggles the archive bit on, indicating that that file is a candidate for backup. Backup software can manipulate the archive bit, either turning it off after it backs up the file, or leaving it on so that file will again be backed up the next time you do a partial backup.

The archive bit exists to provide a certain indication that a file requires archiving. Early Windows versions stored one timestamp for a file. In theory, that timestamp was changed when the file was created or modified. In practice, it was possible for an application to modify a file without changing the timestamp, which meant that a backup application that depended on the timestamp could fail to back up a file that had changed contents, which meant that the archive bit was the only reliable indicator of whether a file required archiving.

Linux stores more timestamp information about each file, including the date it was created, last accessed, and last modified, as does the Windows NT/2000/XP NTFS filesystem. In theory, that means such systems can be backed up reliably based on timestamp information. In practice, we still prefer using the archive bit as a flag because that bit always indicates the archive status of a file. If a backup is done based on timestamp, no indication remains with the file itself as to when (or whether) it was last backed up.

Understanding Backup Types

Backup software can use or ignore the archive bit in determining which files to back up, and can either turn the archive bit off or leave it unchanged when the backup is complete. How the archive bit is used and manipulated determines what type of backup is done, as follows:

Full backup

A *full backup*, which Microsoft calls a *normal backup*, backs up every selected file, regardless of the status of the archive bit. When the backup completes, the backup software turns off the archive bit for every file that was backed up. Note that "full" is a misnomer because a full backup backs up only the files you have *selected*, which may be as little as one directory or even a single file, so in that sense Microsoft's terminology is actually more accurate. Given the choice, full backup is the method to use because all files are on one tape, which makes it much easier to retrieve files from tape when necessary. Relative to partial backups, full backups also increase redundancy because all files are on all tapes. That means that if one tape fails, you may still be able to retrieve a given file from another tape.

Differential backup

A *differential backup* is a partial backup that copies a selected file to tape only if the archive bit for that file is turned on, indicating that it has changed since the last full backup. A differential backup leaves the archive bits unchanged on the files it copies. Accordingly, any differential backup set contains all files that have changed since the last full backup. A differential backup set run soon after a full backup will contain relatively few files. One run soon before the next full backup is due will contain many files, including those contained on all previous differential backup sets since the last full backup. When you use differential backup, a complete backup set comprises only two tapes or tape sets: the tape that contains the last full backup and the tape that contains the most recent differential backup.

Incremental backup

An *incremental backup* is another form of partial backup. Like differential backups, Incremental Backups copy a selected file to tape only if the archive bit for that file is turned on. Unlike the differential backup, however, the incremental backup clears the archive bits for the files it backs up. An incremental backup set therefore contains only files that have changed since the last full backup *or* the last incremental backup. If you run an incremental backup daily, files changed on Monday are on the Monday tape, files changed on Tuesday are on the Tuesday tape, and so forth. When you use an incremental backup scheme, a complete backup set comprises the tape that contains the last full backup and all of the tapes that contain every incremental backup done since the last normal backup. The only advantages of incremental backups are that they minimize backup time and keep multiple versions of files that change frequently. The disadvantages are that backed-up files are scattered across multiple tapes, making it difficult to locate any particular file you need to restore, and that there is no redundancy. That is, each file is stored only on one tape.

Full copy backup
A *full copy backup* (which Microsoft calls a *copy backup*) is identical to a full backup except for the last step. The full backup finishes by turning off the archive bit on all files that have been backed up. The full copy backup instead leaves the archive bits unchanged. The full copy backup is useful only if you are using a combination of full backups and incremental or differential partial backups. The full copy backup allows you to make a duplicate "full" backup—e.g., for storage offsite, without altering the state of the hard drive you are backing up, which would destroy the integrity of the partial backup rotation.

 Some Microsoft backup software provides a bizarre backup method Microsoft calls a *daily copy backup*. This method ignores the archive bit entirely and instead depends on the date- and timestamp of files to determine which files should be backed up. The problem is, it's quite possible for software to change a file without changing the date- and timestamp, or to change the date- and timestamp without changing the contents of the file. For this reason, we regard the daily copy backup as entirely unreliable and recommend you avoid using it.

Choosing a Tape Rotation Method

A *tape rotation method* is a procedure that specifies when each particular tape will be used, and what will be backed up to it. For example, for a simple tape rotation scheme, you might label five tapes Monday through Friday and then do a complete full backup to the corresponding tape each day. Some tape rotation methods are simple and use only a few tapes. Others are immensely complex and use many tapes. Choosing the most appropriate tape rotation method is a critical step in developing and implementing your backup plan.

On one extreme, you *could* use the same tape everyday, but that has obvious dangers, including the risk of that one tape being lost or damaged, the inability to retrieve a file that was deleted or corrupted more than a day previous, and the inability to keep an offsite copy. On the other extreme, Robert once did some consulting for a law firm that never reuses a backup tape. Every evening they do a complete backup and compare of their "active" volumes to a new tape, which is then stored indefinitely in their vault. They regard the small daily cost of a new backup tape as trivial relative to the benefit of being able to reconstruct their data exactly for any specified day.

Chances are, the best tape rotation method for you falls somewhere between those extremes. Here are some issues to think about when you choose a tape rotation method:

Availability
When you need to do a restore, whether of a single file accidentally deleted or of an entire volume whose hard drive crashed, time is often important. A proper tape rotation scheme ensures that the most recent backup data is immediately available to restore.

Archiving

The most recent version of your backup data may not be good enough. Perhaps a file was accidentally deleted or a database improperly modified some time ago, but that was only recently discovered. The most recent backup may, for various reasons, be missing the file you need. An ideal tape rotation method allows you to retrieve a version of a file from days, weeks, or months previous, before the file had been deleted or improperly modified. Tape sets created with the best and most powerful tape rotation methods allow you to select from multiple versions of the file so that you can retrieve the most recent good version. A good tape rotation method also makes provision for periodically removing a tape from the rotation and archiving it for historical reasons.

Redundancy

Tapes can break or be misplaced. Someone may overwrite the wrong tape. A good tape rotation scheme recognizes these facts, and uses redundancy to minimize the effect of such problems. If the file can't be retrieved from one tape, it should be retrievable from another.

Equalized tape wear

Ideally, you'd like all tapes in the set to be used equally often to distribute wear evenly across the set. The simpler tape rotation methods usually fall down in this regard. For example, the popular Grandfather-Father-Son rotation, described later in this section, requires writing to some tapes in the set once a week, to others once a month, and to still others only once a year. Although equalizing tape wear is a less important consideration for most users than the others described, doing so is desirable in that it minimizes the chance that a tape will break, stretch, or otherwise become unusable because it has been used too frequently.

Many standard tape rotation methods exist. Some are simple and use few tapes, but fail to meet some of the goals described earlier. Others meet each goal, or nearly so, but are difficult to manage and require many tapes. Some methods use only full backups, others use both full and partial backups, and still others may be modified to use either only full backups or a combination of full and partial backups.

 If you have a choice, use only full backups. Use partial backups only if you are forced to do so by limited tape drive capacity or a backup window that is too short to allow using all complete backups. When it comes time to restore, you will find that it makes your life much easier to have the entire data set in one place rather than distributed among multiple tapes.

Here are the most common backup rotations:

Daily full

The simplest rotation is to do a complete full backup each day, assuming you have both adequate tape drive capacity and a long enough backup window. Most sites that use this method use 10 tapes, labeled "Monday A" through "Friday A" and "Monday B" through "Friday B." Using this method offers the considerable advantages of simple administration and extreme data redundancy. It's always obvious which tape you should be backing up to. If you start a restore and your most recent backup tape breaks, you simply use the next most recent tape. All tapes receive equal wear, and can be replaced periodically as a set. You can cycle each backup tape offsite as it is replaced by today's backup, leaving your most recent backup available onsite for easy restores, while having an offsite tape that is only one day old. The sole disadvantage of this rotation is that it limits you to retrieving historical data from only two weeks prior, assuming that you use 10 tapes. This problem is easily addressed. Simply add four Quarterly tapes or 12 Monthly tapes to the rotation, and do a duplicate backup to the appropriate archive tape at the end of each quarter or month.

Weekly full with daily differential

This is probably the most commonly used rotation on PC-class systems. In its simplest form, it requires only three tapes: "Weekly A," "Weekly B," and "Daily." On "odd" Fridays, you do a full backup to Weekly A. On "even" Fridays, you do a full backup to Weekly B. Monday through Thursday, you do a differential backup to the Daily tape. This rotation is simple to manage and requires few tapes, but has the following disadvantages:

- Historical data can be retrieved for a period of at most two weeks. If you accidentally delete a file and don't realize it for a couple of weeks, that file is gone for good.

- If the Daily tape fails during a restore, your next most recent tape is the last Weekly tape, which means you may lose as much as four days worth of data.

- Only one current copy of the normal backup exists, so you must either keep it onsite for easy retrieval or offsite for safety.

- Tape wear is very uneven, since the Daily tape is used eight times more often than the Weekly tape.

Simply adding more tapes and making minor changes to the rotation solves most of these problems. For example, add a tape to do a second full backup each Friday, and store that tape offsite. Add a second Daily tape and alternate using them, or simply use a tape for each workday. To extend historical data, add four Quarterly tapes (or 12 Monthly tapes), do a full backup to the appropriate tape on the final day of the corresponding quarter (or month), and then store the tape.

The *weekly full with daily differential* rotation described earlier is an excellent choice for most people, but beware the similar-sounding *weekly full with daily incremental* rotation, which is the worst possible choice short of not backing up at all. For some reason, this rotation is recommended in many books and even in some tape drive manuals. **Don't use it if you value your data!** Its only advantage is that it minimizes backup times, but at the expense of data security. Because this rotation uses incremental backups, each Daily tape contains a different group of files. Restoring one file may require looking at multiple tapes to ensure that you are restoring the most recent version. Doing a complete restore requires that you be able to restore the most recent normal backup tape and all subsequent Daily tapes successfully. If any Daily tape fails during the restore, you must either revert to the last normal backup, losing all subsequent changes to files, or risk incoherent file versions caused by restoring only some of the Daily tapes.

The Grandfather-Father-Son rotation

The Grandfather-Father-Son (GFS) tape rotation method is more commonly used on servers than on personal systems, but it's worth considering if your data is very valuable and you think it's worth going to some trouble and expense to secure it. GFS is the easiest to manage of any of the "complex" tape rotations, requires relatively few tapes, and is supported directly by every backup program on the market. A typical GFS rotation tape set requires 21 tapes, as follows:

- Daily tapes. Label four tapes Monday through Thursday. Back up each day to the tape for the corresponding day, overwriting each tape once a week.

- Weekly tapes. Label five tapes Friday-1 through Friday-5. Back up each Friday to the corresponding weekly tape, using the Friday-5 tape only in months that have five Fridays. Weekly tapes 1 through 4 are overwritten once a month, with Friday-5 being overwritten less frequently.

- Monthly tapes. Label 12 tapes January through December. Back up the first (or last) of each month to the corresponding monthly tape. Monthly tapes are overwritten only once per year.

GFS meets most of the goals of an ideal tape rotation method. You can keep recent tape sets onsite, and migrate others offsite. GFS provides weekly granularity for the preceding month and monthly granularity for the preceding year. GFS provides numerous copies of both recent and older data. The disadvantage to GFS is that tape wear is uneven. Daily tapes are written once a week, weekly tapes once a month, and monthly tapes only once a year. Uneven tape wear is a small price to pay for the other advantages of GFS, however. Most GFS rotations use differential backup for daily tapes and full backup for weekly and monthly tapes, but nothing prevents you from using full backup for all tapes.

Our Picks

Although prices vary widely, buying any tape drive and tapes is a significant expense. Many people consider that expense unjustified, and so do not install a tape drive. If you find yourself thinking that way, we suggest you reconsider. Too often, we hear from readers who have lost their data. The cost of salvaging or re-creating that data may exceed the cost of a tape drive by orders of magnitude, assuming that it is possible to recover the data at all. Catastrophic data loss is a very common cause of small-business failures.

If you store your data on a network server that is properly backed up, you probably don't need a tape drive on your desktop PC. If you have a relatively small amount of data and are willing to rebuild your PC from scratch if the hard drive fails, you may be safe in backing up to a remote server or using a CD/DVD writer, removable hard drive, or similar product. But if you have a lot of valuable data on your system that is not otherwise backed up, you *need* a tape drive. Here are the tape drives we recommend:

Travan TR-5 tape drive
> **Seagate STT220000-series Travan TR-5.** For backing up small servers and desktop PCs, Seagate STT220000-series tape drives are a superb choice when drive cost is more important than tape cost. We consider the Seagate Travan tape drives to be the most reliable inexpensive drives available.
>
> Seagate produces multiple variants of this drive, including ATAPI and SCSI-2 versions, both of which are available as Hornet models (bare drives) or TapeStor models (bundled with BackupExec software). The more expensive Travan NS20 models support read-while-write and hardware compression, while the entry-level Travan 20 models do not. Otherwise, all use the same basic drive mechanism and have similar specifications. Barbara uses a SCSI Travan NS20 model on her main workstation, and typically gets 100 MB/min throughput with hardware compression enabled. Robert uses a Travan 20 ATAPI model without hardware compression on his primary test-bed system and gets 85 MB/min (*http://www.seagate.com*).

USB tape drive
> **Seagate STT6201U-R Portable 20.** If you need a tape drive that you can carry from machine to machine—either for backing up or for transferring huge amounts of data—a USB drive may be the best solution. We confess that we had reliability concerns about using a tape drive with a USB interface, but after using it extensively we conclude that the Seagate Portable 20 is as reliable as SCSI and ATAPI Seagate Travan drives, which is to say extremely so. At a rated 85 MB/min compressed throughput (versus 120 MB/min for the ATAPI and SCSI models), the USB version is a bit slower, but just as reliable. We typically get 60 MB/min throughput with this drive when backing up real-world data. Seagate also makes a 4/8 GB TR-4 version of this drive, which we have not tested. If you need a portable tape drive, the Seagate Portable 20 is the one to buy.

Either of the preceding drives is an excellent choice if drive cost is more important than tape cost. You can buy one of these drives and half a dozen $35 tapes and use them to back up a desktop system or small server adequately. If you back up frequently, you'll need to replace some or all of the tapes every year or two, but that's relatively inexpensive insurance for your data.

But there are situations in which tape cost is much more important than drive cost, and we suggest you determine carefully whether that is true for you. If you need many tapes, the difference between $35 tapes and $10 tapes adds up fast, and suddenly an "expensive" DDS tape drive that uses $10 tapes starts to look like a real bargain. You're a good candidate for a DDS tape drive if you back up daily or more often, if you need to archive data for past weeks or months, or if you need to back up more data than will fit on one tape. Here are the DDS tape drives we recommend:

DDS3 tape drive

Seagate STD224000-series. We've used DDS drives from Hewlett-Packard, Seagate, and Sony, and we think the Seagate STD224000-series DDS3 drives offer the best combination of price, performance, reliability, and robustness. This drive stores 12/24 GB, supports read-while-write and hardware data compression, and has rated throughput of 132 MB/min compressed. In our testing, we typically get 110 MB/min or so, which is closer to the rated performance than many drives we've tested.

Seagate sells the drive itself, called the Scorpion 24, or the TapeStor DAT 24 bundle that includes the Scorpion 24 and backup software. At $500 or so, not including the cost of a SCSI-2 host adapter, the Scorpion 24 is not an inexpensive drive, but then you need only buy fewer than a dozen $8 DDS-3 tapes versus the same number of $35 Travan TR-5 tapes to recover the additional cost of the drive relative to a Travan NS20 unit. We use the Seagate TapeStor DAT 24 on our main server, where it does yeoman service. If you need a fast, high-capacity tape drive that uses inexpensive tapes for a high-end desktop PC or a small server, the Seagate STD224000 is the one to buy.

DDS4 tape drive

Seagate STD2401LW-R. If even DDS3 isn't large enough or fast enough, the next step up is DDS4. DDS4 drives store 20/40 GB on a $17 tape, and are much faster than DDS3 drives as well. The best DDS4 drive on the market is the Seagate Scorpion 40, which is also available with backup software bundled as the TapeStor DAT 40. The Scorpion 40 is rated at 165 MB/min native and 330 MB/min compressed, and in our testing achieves throughput of more than 300 MB/min on compressible data. At $650 or so, the Scorpion 40 is definitely not cheap, but its large capacity, high performance, and use of relatively inexpensive large tapes make it an ideal drive for backing up workgroup/departmental servers and high-end workstations. Robert uses a Scorpion 40 tape drive on his main personal workstation, which has more than 200 GB of Ultra160 SCSI hard disk space. If you need to back up huge amounts of data, particularly if your backup window is short, we think you'll be delighted with the Seagate Scorpion 40 tape drive.

Seagate recently spun off its Removable Storage Solutions (RSS) tape drive business unit as a new affiliate called Certance. The drives themselves remain the same for now. Even the model numbers were unchanged when last we looked, although new models will have Certance CD numbers rather than Seagate ST numbers. Identical drives, some bearing Seagate labeling and others Certance labeling, will coexist in the channel for some time. Our endorsement of these Seagate-branded tape drives extends to the similar Certance models, although package contents (such as bundled software) may vary slightly from Seagate to Certance units.

Although we're advocates of using tape drives for backup, we recognize that not everyone needs or can afford a tape drive. If you're in that position, you're not completely out of luck. We've tested several alternatives to tape drives, including superfloppies, CD writers, DVD writers, removable hard drives, and so on. Each of them has disadvantages—expensive or unreliable media, slow throughput, or small capacity (or all of those)—but using any of them is better than not backing up at all. Even backing up to floppy disks is better than nothing. After considering and testing alternatives, here's our recommendation:

Tape drive alternative

Plextor PlexWriter Premium CD-RW drive or Plextor PX-504A DVD+R/RW drive. The PlexWriter Premium costs about $100. It writes at 52X and rewrites at 32X on $0.20 CD-R discs or $0.50 CD-RW discs, and stores about a gigabyte of data on a standard 700 MB disc (which can be read by nearly all standard CD and DVD drives). The PlexWriter Premium is nearly as fast as a slow hard drive, creates very reliable backups—although not as reliable as a tape backup—and is useful for other purposes such as copying audio and data CDs. The major limitation of the PlexWriter Premium is the approximately 1 GB capacity of its discs, which for many people is no real limitation at all. If you do need more capacity, the $225 Plextor PX-504A DVD+R/RW drive writes or rewrites about 4.7 GB of data to DVD+R or DVD+RW discs that sell for only a few dollars each. Like the PlexWriter Premium, the Plextor PX-504A DVD writer is fast, roughly matching the throughput of a DDS tape drive.

Like all optical writers, these drives have significantly poorer error detection and correction than a good tape drive. That's easy enough to get around, though. Simply make two copies of your backup. Even if a file is corrupted on one copy, which happens infrequently, that same file will almost certainly be accessible on the second copy.

In one sense, optical backup is more convenient than tape backup because you can access your backup data directly with an optical drive. We confess that, being belt-and-suspenders folks, we make CD-R and DVD+R backups of our current working data in addition to our tape backups of our entire database. More than once, we've reached for that optical disc backup to retrieve an accidentally deleted file without having to fire up the tape drive and restore it.

We recommend buying both a spindle of CD-R and DVD+R discs and a stack of highspeed CD-RW or DVD+RW discs. Do routine daily backups to an RW disc and then recycle the discs as necessary. For example, if you have 30 RW discs, you won't need to overwrite your daily backup disc until it's a month old. Once a week or once a month, pull a full archive set of your data to CD-R or DVD+R and store it somewhere safe.

For updated recommendations, visit: *http://www.hardwareguys.com/picks/tape. html.*

Tape Drives

10

CD-ROM Drives

CD-ROM drives are so standardized and ubiquitous that, excepting high-end SCSI models, they have become commoditized and are now obsolescent. Despite that, it's important to understand CD-ROM technology because it is the basis for current technologies including CD writers, DVD-ROM, and DVD writers.

If you use a CD-ROM drive only to play audio CDs, load software, and so on, nearly any recent CD-ROM drive suffices. If you need to replace a failed drive or buy a drive for a new PC, you can use an inexpensive ATAPI·CD-ROM drive— while they remain available—or you can substitute an ATAPI DVD-ROM drive, which also reads CDs. If you put more demands on a drive, such as accessing databases, playing games directly from CD, or using the drive as a source to duplicate CDs, it's worth learning about the differences between currently available drives.

This chapter and the following chapter cover standard CD-ROM drives and CD writers, both of which store data on optical discs. Most drive manufacturers other than Seagate use the spelling "disk" for drives that use magnetic storage. By convention, all manufacturers use the spelling "disc" for drives that accept optical media.

Many people are careful about the clear side of optical discs but take less care with the label side. In fact, the clear side is a tough, protective polycarbonate layer. Data actually resides on a thin aluminum substrate immediately beneath the label. Because the label is very fragile, it is the label side that deserves careful handling.

Commercially produced discs record data as a series of microscopic pits and lands physically embossed on an aluminum substrate. Optical drives use a low-power laser to read data from those discs without physical contact between the head and the disc, which contributes to the high reliability and permanence of optical storage. Write-capable optical drives use higher-power lasers to record data on special discs. CD-Recordable (CD-R) records data permanently to the disc, and is also called Write-Once. CD-Rewritable (CD-RW) allows data that has been written to be erased or overwritten, and is also called Write-Many.

Compact Disc Fundamentals

Unlike magnetic storage devices, which store data on multiple concentric tracks, all CD formats store data on one physical track, which spirals continuously from the center to the outer edge of the recording area. All CD formats use 3,234-byte physical sectors, which allocate 882 bytes to control and error correction data, leaving 2,352 bytes available. Different CD formats use this space differently: audio CDs use the entire 2,352 bytes to store audio data; computer CDs use only 2,048 bytes to store user data, and allocate the remaining 304 bytes to store additional ECC and control data, including header data and synchronization data. (Audio CDs are addressable to within one second; computer CDs must be addressable by sector, or 1/75 of a second.) Sectors are grouped as logical numbered tracks, which are listed in the Table of Contents (TOC) for the disc, a special unnumbered track that is analogous to the File Allocation Table and root directory on a computer disk.

All current CD formats derive from the original Compact Disc-Digital Audio (CD-DA) format introduced in 1974 as a replacement for vinyl record albums. The following standards define the formats used for compact discs:

Red Book
> The original CD standard that defines CD-DA (the audio CD), a method that allows digital recording of 74 minutes of audio separated into tracks. Red Book also defines CD infrastructure, including disc dimensions, optical stylus, modulation and error correction standards, subcode channels used for control and display, and the 16-bit Pulse Coded Modulation method used to store audio data. Red Book allows a CD to contain up to 99 tracks, each containing a single audio selection. Each sector contains 2,352 bytes of audio data, two 392-byte error detection code/error correction code (EDC/ECC) layers, and 98 bytes of control data, which is divided into subcodes (or subchannels) identified as P through W. Control data allows jumping to the beginning of each track, and stores such information as track number, track time, and total time. All computer CD drives support the Red Book standard.

Yellow Book
> Contains extensions to Red Book that define the Compact Disc - Read Only Memory (CD-ROM) standard, which allows CDs to store digital computer data. Yellow Book defines two sector structures for user data and the EDC and ECC used to ensure data integrity. Mode 1 is the common CD-ROM format, and segments the 2,352 available bytes as 12 bytes sync, 4 bytes header, 2,048 bytes user data, 4 bytes EDC, 8 bytes blank, and 276 bytes ECC. Mode 2, which is never used, segments the 2,352 bytes as 12 bytes sync, 4 bytes header, and 2,336 bytes user data. All computer CD drives support the Yellow Book standard.

> *CD-ROM XA*
> > The original Yellow Book standard defined a means to store computer data, but made no provision for audio or video data. CD-ROM XA

(Extended Architecture) extended Yellow Book with two new track types that allow a CD to store compressed audio and/or video data mixed with computer data. Mode 2, Form 1 is used for computer data, and segments the available 2,352 bytes as 12 bytes sync, 4 bytes header, 8 bytes subheader, 2,048 bytes user data, 4 bytes EDC, and 276 bytes ECC. Mode 2, Form 2 is used to store audio/video data, and uses 12 bytes sync, 4 bytes header, 2,324 bytes user data, and 4 bytes EDC. The subheader field describes sector contents, allowing Form 1 (data) sectors and Form 2 (audio/video) sectors to be interleaved within one track. CD-ROM XA-compliant drives can separate Form 1 computer data from Form 2 audio/video on the fly, delivering each to the appropriate destination for processing. The only CDs you are likely to find using CD-ROM XA formats are Kodak PhotoCD and VideoCD (both CD-i Bridge formats), the Karaoke-CD, and the Sony PlayStation CD.

Yellow Book defined the physical sector structure, but did not define logical file formats. This meant that early Yellow Book data CDs by necessity used proprietary file formats that were incompatible with each other. To address this problem, CD producers created the ad hoc High Sierra format, which was subsequently formalized almost without change by the ISO as ISO-9660. The strength of ISO-9660 was that it was universal—ISO-9660 discs are readable by nearly any operating system. The other side of that coin was that ISO-9660 achieved this universality by restricting choices to the least common denominator— e.g., filenames limited to 8.3, which was supported by all operating systems. The constraints imposed by ISO-9660 mean that it is seldom used anymore except where universal compatibility is more important than filesystem features—such things as huge tables of government data and other boring stuff. ISO-9660 is also still used occasionally to produce hybrid discs that are readable by both PCs and Macs. These discs use ISO-9660 formatting for the PC data and Mac HFS formatting for the Mac. But if the ISO-9660 format defined by CD-ROM XA is seldom used anymore, it was at least a start.

Green Book

An extension of Yellow Book that defines Compact Disc Interactive (CD-i). CD-i supports Mode 2, Form 2 audio, video, and picture data mixed with Mode 2, Form 1 computer data, which users can control interactively. CD-i CDs required a special CD-i player, which contained an embedded computer running a special operating system (OS/9, CD-RTOS), so CD-i tracks could not be played on normal CD-ROM drives. A hybrid format called CD Bridge defines a method for recording CD-i data on CD-ROM XA discs, allowing that data to be read by any CD-ROM XA drive. The only CD Bridge format still in common use is Kodak PhotoCD. The CD-i format achieved some popularity on dedicated CD-i players in the early to mid-'90s for games, educational programs, encyclopediae, and so on, but is now obsolete and has been replaced by various flavors of DVD.

Orange Book

Defines standards for recordable CDs. Part I defines Compact Disc-Magneto-Optical (CD-MO); Part II, Compact Disc-Write Once (CD-WO, usually called CD-Recordable or CD-R); and Part III, Compact Disc-Erasable (CD-E, usually called CD-Rewritable or CD-RW).

Orange Book defines both single-session (Disc-at-Once, DAO) recording, and incremental multisession (Track-at-Once, TAO) recording (explained in Chapter 11). Multisession allows recording an initial session that does not fill the disc, and subsequently adding one or more additional sessions until the capacity of the disc has been reached. Each new session contains a TOC that lists both the old and new information on the disc, so any CD-ROM drive or CD player used to read multisession discs must be capable of locating and using the last-recorded TOC. Any recent CD-ROM drive and most recent CD players can read multisession discs, but older drives and players usually cannot. Unless, that is, you use your CD burner to "finalize" the session, which closes the disc to further recording sessions and writes a final TOC that can be read by any CD drive or player. Even then, very old players may not be able to read the disc because their lasers and data pickups are incapable of dealing with the color and low reflectivity and contrast of recordable media.

White Book

Defines the Video CD format, also known as Digital Video (DV), developed and promoted by Matsushita, JVC, Sony, and Philips. Video CDs are a type of CD-ROM XA bridge disc based on the Karaoke CD standard. They use MPEG-1 compression to store up to 70 minutes of full-screen, full-motion video with CD-quality audio, using CD-ROM/XA Mode 2, Form 2. They can be played on a dedicated Video CD player, a CD-i player with a DV cartridge, or a PC with a CD-ROM XA drive, an MPEG-1 decoder, and the necessary software. White Book is now obsolete, and has been replaced by DVD.

Blue Book

Defines the Enhanced Music CD, also called CD-Extra or CD-Plus, which specifies a multisession format that stores mixed audio and data recorded as separate sessions to prevent standard CD players from attempting to "play" a data session. For compatibility with standard CD players, a Blue Book CD contains two sessions. The first session contains the audio tracks, and the second session a data track. A Blue Book CD stores a limited amount of data that is related to the audio, which comprises the major portion of the content on the CD. For example, a Blue Book CD of Johann Sebastian Bach's Brandenburg Concertos might include a historical background and the score, while a rock CD might include album notes and lyrics. Blue Book CDs can be played on any standard audio CD player (which sees a Blue Book CD as a standard CD-DA disc), on PCs with compliant CD-ROM drives, and on dedicated players.

CD-ROM Drive Performance

Although CD-ROM drives differ in reliability, the standards they support, and numerous other respects, the most important issue for most users is performance. But performance is not accurately described by the simple transfer rate number that most manufacturers use to characterize drive performance. There are actually two important performance metrics:

Data transfer rate

How fast the drive delivers sequential data to the interface. Data transfer rate (DTR) is determined by drive rotation speed, and is specified as a number followed by an X. All other things equal, a 32X drive delivers data at twice the speed of a 16X drive. But note that we have used 16X SCSI drives that transfer data faster than some 32X ATAPI drives, so it's a mistake to depend solely on X-rating. The specifications for some drives list only maximum burst transfer rate, which is always the advertised number, while others list sustained transfer rate, which is far more important to overall drive performance. Fast DTR is most important when you use the drive to transfer large files or many sequential smaller files—e.g., for gaming video.

Average access time

How fast the drive accesses random files located anywhere on the CD. Average access time is only loosely tied to DTR, is determined by the quality of the head actuator mechanism, and is rated in milliseconds (ms). Some inexpensive drives have very high nominal DTR ratings but relatively poor average access performance. To make matters more complicated, different manufacturers calculate average access using different methods, so you cannot necessarily compare figures from one manufacturer with those of another.

The following sections describe DTR and average access time in detail.

Data Transfer Rates

CD-DA discs record music as a digital data stream. The analog music is examined or *sampled* 44,100 times per second (the *sampling rate*) using 16-bit samples, for a data rate of 88,200 bytes/s. Multiplied by two channels for stereo, that means the CD stores 176,400 bytes for each second of music. Each second's data is stored as 75 physical sectors, each of 2,352 bytes.

Music data need not be completely error-free because an occasional flipped bit will be inaudible, which means the entire 2,352-byte capacity of each physical sector can be used to store actual music data. The same is not true for computer data, for which every bit must be correct. Accordingly, CDs store computer data using 2,048 bytes/sector, with the remaining 304 bytes in each physical sector allocated to error detection and correction data. This means that a computer CD running at the same speed as an audio CD delivers ($75 \times 2,048$ bytes) per second, or 150 KB/s. This data rate is called 1X, and was the transfer rate supported by early CD-ROM drives.

Later CD-ROM drives transfer data at some integer multiple of this basic 150 KB/s 1X rate. A 2X drive transfers (2×150 KB/s) or 300 KB/s, a 40X drive transfers data at 6000 KB/s, and so on.

CLV Versus CAV Versus P-CAV Versus Z-CLV

Unlike hard disks, which record data on a series of concentric tracks, CDs have only one track that spirals from the center of the CD out to the edge, much like a vinyl LP. Because the portions of the track toward the center are shorter than those toward the edge, moving data under the head at a constant rate requires spinning the disc faster as the head moves from the center, where there is less data per revolution, to the edge, where there is more. If an audio CD spun at some compromise constant rate, the audio would sound like the Addams Family's Lurch when the CD was playing the inner portion of the track, and like Alvin the chipmunk when it was playing the outer.

The solution is to change the disc rotation rate as the heads progress from the inner to the outer portions of the track. When you play an audio CD in a CD player (or in your computer's CD-ROM drive), the drive speeds up and slows down according to what portion of the track the heads are currently reading. This technology, shown in Figure 10-1, is called *Constant Linear Velocity (CLV)*.

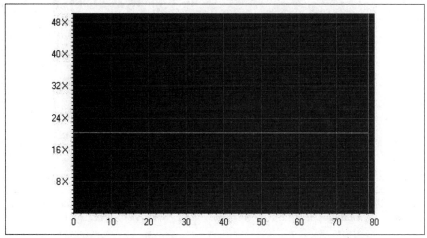

Figure 10-1. CLV technology, which spins a disc at a constantly varying speed to keep the data rate identical regardless of what part of the disc is being read (image courtesy of Ahead Software)

All audio CD players use CLV. CLV is a good choice for audio for two reasons. First, the drive only need spin fast enough to deliver 150 KB/s. Second, music is inherently sequential. That is, a music track is played from beginning to end, which requires only gradual changes in rotation speed. Early CD-ROM drives also used CLV, but it soon became apparent that CLV was not the best choice for data CDs, for two reasons. First, market demands meant that the speed of CD-ROM drives had to keep increasing, from 1X to 2X, 4X, 6X, 8X, and eventually to 12X or 16X. Delivering data at 16X requires spinning the disc much faster than for 1X audio. Second, data CDs are accessed randomly, which means that the head may have to move quickly from the inner to the outer portion of the track, or vice versa. In order to maintain CLV with such rapid head moves, the drive motor was required to make radical changes in speed. Motors capable of doing that are large, power-hungry, loud, and expensive. That meant 12X was the realistic limit for CLV CD-ROM drives, although a few 16X CLV CD-ROM drives were made.

The solution to this problem was to implement *Constant Angular Velocity (CAV)*, shown in Figure 10-2. CAV is a fancy term for simply spinning the CD at a constant speed, allowing the data rate to vary according to which portion of the track is being read. The advantage to CAV is that the drive can use a relatively simple, inexpensive motor because that motor runs at a constant rate. The disadvantage is that the data rate varies according to what portion of the disc is being read, which is really no disadvantage at all for data CDs. Actually, CAV drives are also capable of running in CLV mode, which is why you can play an audio CD in any CD-ROM drive. But that's slow CLV. For delivering data, which is their true purpose, CAV drives run at a much higher, but constant speed.

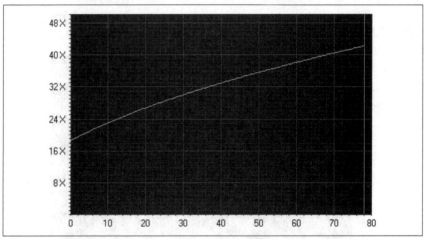

Figure 10-2. CAV technology, which spins a disc at a constant rate and the data rate varies according to what part of the disc is being read (image courtesy of Ahead Software)

Because the data rate on a CAV drive varies according to which portion of the track is being read, there's no single number that describes the drive's transfer rate. Accordingly, such drives are called *variable speed* or **-Max* (as in "48X Max") drives, and are rated using the fastest DTR (that on the outer portion of the track). The upshot is that a 40X Max drive may read the longer, outer portions of the track at 40X, but may read the shorter, inner portions of the track at only 17X, with an "average" speed for a full CD of 27X, and a somewhat lower rate for a partially full CD.

 48X Max CD-ROM drives are commonplace, and 56X drives are available. The maximum possible speed for optical drives of any sort is something near 60X because a disc spinning much faster than 60X may disintegrate catastrophically, very likely destroying the drive as well.

Some drives use *Partial CAV (P-CAV)*, shown in Figure 10-3, which combines CLV and CAV. For P-CAV, the transfer rate increases until the drive reaches maximum speed. At that point, the drive slows as necessary to maintain CLV. P-CAV drives reach maximum speed quicker than CAV drives, so their average transfer rate is typically higher.

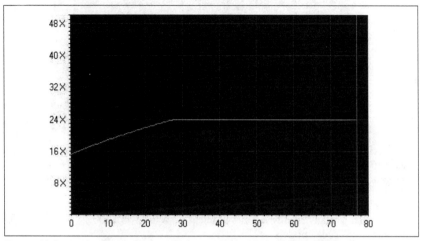

Figure 10-3. Using P-CAV, the disc reaches maximum CAV speed and then slows as needed to maintain CLV across the reminder of the disc (image courtesy of Ahead Software)

Finally, some drives use *Zoned CLV (Z-CLV)*, shown in Figure 10-4. A Z-CLV drive treats a disc as having a small number (usually three or four) of arbitrarily specified areas, and uses a different CLV rate for each area. Z-CLV is used primarily for CD writers, for which using CLV over the entire surface of a disc simplifies write parameters while maintaining high performance. Figure 10-4 shows the momentary troughs that occur when the drive motor changes from one CLV rate to the next as the heads move from section to section.

TrueX Drives

TrueX drives are no longer made, but were an interesting historical footnote. TrueX drives use CLV with a difference. Conventional CD-ROM drives read data with one weak LASER beam. TrueX drives split a stronger LASER beam into seven separate beams, which read seven sections of the track simultaneously. The drive combines those signals into one high-speed data stream, which allows a TrueX drive running at 9.5X CLV to provide DTR similar to a 52X CAV drive.

Because they spin discs slowly, TrueX drives are quieter than CAV drives with similar DTR. But TrueX drives have several drawbacks. TrueX drives sold for twice the price of comparable CAV drives, vibrate excessively, and have mediocre random access performance. They generate so much heat that the drive becomes quite warm during sustained operations, and discs may become uncomfortably

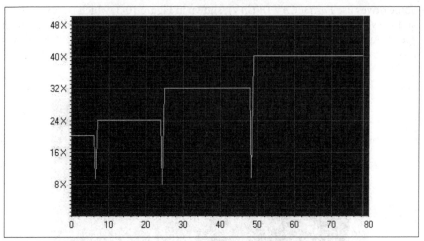

Figure 10-4. Z-CLV technology, which spins a disc at a constant rate, with the data rate varying according to what part of the drive is being read (image courtesy of Ahead Software)

hot to touch. Finally, Kenwood never released Windows 2000 or XP drivers for the following TrueX models:

- UCR415 and UCR416 (52X SCSI)
- UCR04010 (40X, 42X ATAPI)
- UCR411 and UCR412 (52X ATAPI)
- UCR420 (62X ATAPI)
- UCR421 (72X ATAPI)

We don't use TrueX drives at all. If we disassembled an old system with a TrueX drive, we'd toss it in the trash. New ATAPI CD-ROM drives cost less than $25, so attempting to recycle an old TrueX drive simply isn't worth it, even if the operating system supports it.

Average Access

Although it bears superficial resemblance to the hard drive rating with the same name, average access time for a CLV CD-ROM drive is much more complex to calculate, and is subject to manipulation by drive manufacturers who wish to boost their performance figures. Hard drives spin at a constant rate, and average access time is calculated as average seek time (the time required for the heads to move over the proper track) plus latency (the time required for the disk to spin the one-half revolution required on average to move the correct sector under the heads).

Average access for CLV CD-ROM drives was originally calculated using a similar 1/3 stroke method, assuming that the drive would be used mainly for reading large multimedia files. In about 1993, some manufacturers began substituting "random access" for 1/3 stroke testing. This method was subject to abuse because manufacturers could define the size of the zone they used for testing. Some chose very small zones to boost their average access ratings, with the result that some drives were advertised with average access times of less than 60 ms. Worse still, some makers began promoting seek time as a performance measure. Seek time is a useless performance measure for a CLV drive because it ignores the fact that a CLV drive needs to speed up or slow down the disc to the speed required for data to be read. The time required for this step—roughly analogous to latency, but subject to much wider variation—is determined by the quality of the motor used.

Newer drives, which use CAV, are less subject to these manipulation methods because the disc spins at a constant rate. However, manufacturers are still free to define the zone they use for random access testing, which means that you cannot safely compare different drives unless you know the testing method used to rate them. The upshot is that if you have an older CLV drive that has a very good average access rating, you should suspect that it is artificially inflated. A newer drive, even one with a substantially slower rated average access, will likely outperform the older drive by a significant margin. As a point of reference, the fastest CD-ROM drive we ever used, the recently discontinued Plextor UltraPlex Wide, is rated at 85 ms average access. Testing that drive against inexpensive ATAPI drives with faster published average access times revealed that the Plextor was in fact much faster at retrieving random data from a CD. Therefore, take any published average access rating with a grain of salt.

Choosing a CD-ROM Drive

The first consideration in choosing a CD-ROM drive is whether to buy a DVD-ROM drive instead. If price is important—as it may be if you are replacing a failed drive in an older system or building a new system on a tight budget—you can save $25 or so by using a CD-ROM drive. In those situations, consider the following issues:

DTR

> For most applications, DTR is the most important performance characteristic of a CD-ROM drive. DTR is most important if you use the drive mainly for sequential data transfer, such as playing games or loading software. Unless you have unusual needs, any name-brand $25 ATAPI 40X or faster drive is more than sufficient for anything you need to do.

Average access time

> Average access time is important if you use the drive mainly for random access, such as searching databases. Although access time and DTR are not inextricably related—it is possible to build a drive with a fast actuator and a slow motor or vice versa—there is a fair degree of correlation. Typical inexpensive ATAPI drives may provide true 100 to 200 ms average access (although they are often marketed with inflated average access performance numbers), while high-end drives, particularly SCSI drives, may provide true 85 ms access. If you use databases heavily, go with a high-end drive for its improved average access. Otherwise, a typical ATAPI drive will do the job.

Buffer size

> Currently available drives have buffers ranging from 64 KB to 512 KB or more. All other things being equal, the drive with the larger buffer will provide higher performance. But all other things are seldom equal, and a

drive with a smaller buffer from one manufacturer may outperform a drive from another manufacturer that has a larger buffer and otherwise identical specifications. We recommend treating buffer size as a minor issue when choosing a drive. If a drive is available in two models differing only in buffer size, and the price difference is minor, go with the larger buffer. Otherwise, ignore buffer size.

Interface

CD-ROM drives are readily available in ATAPI/IDE, SCSI, USB, and parallel interfaces. The vast majority of CD-ROM drives installed in systems or sold individually are ATAPI, which is inexpensive and adequate for nearly any application. Make sure any ATAPI drive you buy supports DMA (bus mastering) transfer mode, which improves performance and greatly reduces CPU utilization. SCSI drives typically cost $25 to $50 more than equivalent ATAPI drives (in addition to the cost of the SCSI host adapter, if your system is not already so equipped). Choose an ATAPI drive unless the faster average access and higher sustained throughput typical of SCSI drives is a factor (such as for high-speed CD duplication) or unless the internal-only limitation of ATAPI is an issue.

Internal versus external

ATAPI drives are internal-only. Parallel, USB, and FireWire drives are external-only. SCSI drives are available in either form. External drives typically sell at a $50 premium over similar internal models. Choose an internal drive unless you have a notebook, you have no externally accessible drive bays available in your desktop system, or you need to share the drive among multiple PCs.

Mounting method

Modern CD-ROM drives use tray mounting. Some older drives used caddy mounting, in which each CD is more or less permanently inserted in a protective cartridge called a caddy. In theory, tray mounting has two drawbacks: the tray mechanism is less reliable than the caddy mechanism, and the tray mechanism does not protect CDs from dust and physical damage. In practice, caddies are expensive and more trouble than they're worth. Some drives use a slot mounting mechanism such as that used by dash-mounted car CD players. This is in theory the best compromise, but few such drives are available, and we have had enough reports of problems with slot mounting mechanisms that we recommend avoiding them. Unless you have compelling reasons to do otherwise, choose a drive that uses tray mounting.

Formats and disc types supported

Format and disc type support were major issues when standards were still developing. Some drives, for example, could not read Kodak PhotoCD discs. Current drives support all formats and disc types you are likely to need to read. Any drive you buy should support the following:

Formats

CD-DA, CD-ROM Mode 1; CD-ROM XA Mode 2, Form 1 and Form 2; Multisession (PhotoCD, CD-Extra, CD-RW, CD-R) Mode 1 and 2; CD UDF (variable packets)

Disc type

ISO 9660-HFS; Rockridge; CD-I Bridge (PhotoCD, Video CD); CD-i; CD-i Ready, CD-Extra (CD-Plus); Enhanced CD; CD-R; CD-RW; CD+G; CD-Midi; CD-Text

Digital audio extraction (DAE)

If you will use the CD-ROM drive as a source drive for duplicating audio CDs to a CD-RW drive, make sure the drive supports DAE, which is required to copy audio digitally. All current CD-RW drives support DAE. Few CD-ROM drives shipped before mid-1998 fully support DAE, although some models offer partial DAE support.

A typical DAE-capable ATAPI CD-ROM drive supports DAE at only a small fraction of its rated speed. For example, our elderly Toshiba XM-6402B 32X ATAPI CD-ROM drive supports DAE at only about 6.8X. Many pre-1999 DAE-capable ATAPI 24X to 36X drives support DAE at only 1X or 2X. High-quality SCSI CD-ROM drives and ATAPI CD/DVD writers, such as the Plextor models, support DAE at or near their rated read speeds. Attempting to use DAE at a rate higher than the drive supports yields a "Rice Krispies" dupe—full of snaps, crackles, and pops (along with some hissing). If this occurs, the only solution short of replacing the CD-ROM drive is to set your CD-R drive to record at 2X or 1X.

In addition to DAE speed, the quality of DAE varies significantly among drive types and models. In general, older DVD-ROM drives provide mediocre DAE quality, although many recent models provide perfect DAE, or nearly so. ATAPI CD-ROM drives vary, but most recent name-brand models do a decent job of extracting audio. If you want the absolute best available DAE quality, use a SCSI Plextor CD-ROM drive.

The best way we know to test DAE speed and quality is the Nero CD Speed utility, shown in Figure 10-5, which is a free download from *http://www.cdspeed2000.com/*.

CD-ROM versus DVD-ROM

Although CD-ROM drives are still sold, the widespread availability of fast DVD-ROM drives at reasonable prices has greatly shrunk the market for CD-ROM drives. Before you buy a CD-ROM drive, consider buying a DVD-ROM drive instead. Modern DVD-ROM drives read all standard CD formats, provide very high performance, and can (of course) read DVD discs, something no CD-ROM drive can do. Although there is still a place for high-end CD-ROM drives, primarily for extracting digital audio and duplicating CDs, we think most people who are considering buying an ATAPI CD-ROM drive would be better served by spending $25 more for an equivalent DVD-ROM drive.

Installing and Configuring a CD-ROM Drive

External CD-ROM drives are "installed" simply by connecting them to the USB, parallel, or SCSI port, as appropriate, and connecting power, although SCSI models may require setting jumpers to configure SCSI ID and termination.

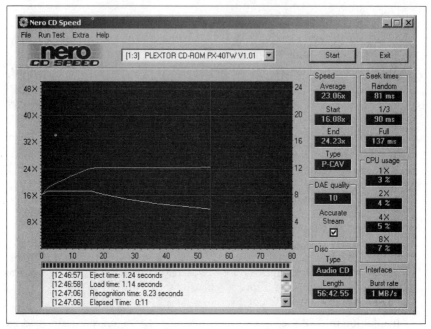

Figure 10-5. Using Nero CD Speed to test the speed and DAE quality of a CD-ROM drive (this drive shows average speed of 23.06X and perfect DAE)

Internal CD-ROM drives are 5.25-inch half-height devices, and require the same physical installation steps as any other 5.25-inch externally accessible drive. The exact configuration steps required differ between ATAPI and SCSI interfaces, as described in the following sections.

Installing and Configuring an ATAPI CD-ROM Drive

ATAPI CD-ROM drives are installed just like any other ATAPI/IDE device. Other than physical installation, the only decisions you need to make are whether to install the drive on the Primary or Secondary ATA interface and whether to jumper the drive as Sole, Master, or Slave. In general, use the following guidelines:

- On a system with one or two ATA hard drives and one ATAPI CD-ROM drive, install the first hard drive as Primary Master (PM), the second hard drive, if present, as Primary Slave (PS), and the CD-ROM drive as Secondary Master (SM).

- On a system with three ATA hard drives and a CD-ROM drive, install the first hard drive as PM, the second hard drive as PS, the third hard drive as SM, and the CD-ROM drive as Secondary Slave (SS).

- On a system with one or two ATA hard drives, an ATAPI CD-ROM drive, and an ATAPI tape drive, install the hard drives as explained previously, the CD-ROM drive as SM, and the tape drive as SS.

- On a system with an ATA hard drive, an ATAPI CD-ROM drive, and an ATAPI CD writer, jumper the hard drive PM, the CD-ROM drive PS, and the

CD writer SM. The goal is to have the CD writer on a different ATA channel than any drive that may be used as a source, including the CD-ROM drive and the hard drive.

- On a system with two ATA hard drives, an ATAPI CD-ROM drive, and an ATAPI CD writer, jumper the first hard drive PM, the CD-ROM drive PS, the second hard drive SM, and the CD writer SS. Recognize that attempting to create a CD from data on the second hard drive risks data corruption because the second hard drive and the CD writer are on the same ATA channel.

- On a system with an ATA hard drive, an ATAPI CD-ROM drive, an ATAPI CD writer, and an ATAPI tape drive, jumper the hard drive PM, the CD-ROM drive PS, the CD writer SM, and the tape drive SS.

ATAPI CD-ROM drives require no special configuration steps to function. All recent operating systems, including Windows 95/98, Windows NT/2000/XP, and Linux, load ATAPI drivers and recognize ATAPI drives automatically.

Master/Slave Problems with ATAPI CD-ROM Drives

We occasionally receive reports of ATAPI CD-ROM drives that work properly when configured as a Slave, but not when configured as a Sole or a Master drive, even when they are the only devices on the channel. We have never encountered this situation in working with hundreds of systems and CD-ROM drives over the years. However, it has been reported to us often enough that we believe a problem may exist, although we do not have adequate information to determine what combination of controller, drive, operating system, and so on causes the problem.

In theory, any ATAPI CD-ROM drive can function as a Master, Slave, or Sole drive on an ATA channel. That has been our experience. Many CD-ROM drives are designed to function properly as the only drive on a channel even when they're jumpered as a Slave. That's done as a matter of convenience and to avoid support calls when a user forgets to change the default jumpering, which is almost always Slave. Configuring an ATAPI device as a Master-less Slave is not officially supported in the ATA/ATAPI specification, though.

We speculate that one possible cause of the confusion is that an ATA channel may be set to use bus mastering (DMA). If that's the case, making a non-DMA capable CD-ROM drive the Master might indeed cause problems, although we have not tried this configuration. A channel must run both devices as either PIO or DMA, and the presence of a non-DMA device on the channel should make that channel revert to PIO, whatever the configuration settings happen to be. Most (but not all) currently shipping ATAPI CD-ROM drives are DMA-capable.

Enabling Bus Mastering (DMA) Support

By default, ATAPI CD-ROM drives may operate in Programmed I/O (PIO) mode rather than DMA mode, which is also called Bus Mastering mode. The fact that

PIO mode limits DTR to 16.7 MB/s versus the 33.3 or 66.7 MB/s DTR available with DMA is unimportant because no CD-ROM drive even approaches the DTR limit of PIO mode. What is important is that PIO mode causes much higher CPU utilization than DMA mode. A typical ATAPI CD-ROM drive operating in PIO mode may occupy 80% or more of the CPU when the drive is being accessed heavily, while the same drive operating under the same conditions in DMA mode may occupy only 1% to 5% of CPU time.

Accordingly, enabling DMA mode is usually a good idea, but doing so requires that the BIOS, operating system, chipset, and CD-ROM drive itself all support DMA mode. Most recent ATAPI CD-ROM drives support DMA mode. Most motherboards of late-model Pentium vintage or later also support DMA mode on their embedded ATAPI interfaces.

Enabling bus mastering (DMA) support with Linux

Linux DMA support differs significantly by distribution and version. Older Linux releases had limited support for UDMA, particularly for ATAPI devices. Recent releases generally recognize DMA-capable ATAPI devices and automatically configure the interface optimally. To determine the status of DMA, open a terminal window, change to the /proc/ide directory, and list the contents. That list displays the drivers for each IDE/ATAPI device and interface. It also contains a file, named for the chipset in use, that lists the current DMA status for each interface and drive.

Figure 10-6 shows the contents of the file /proc/ide/piix on an Intel system running Red Hat Linux 8.X. This system has two ATA interfaces. The primary ATA interface is IDE0 and the secondary is IDE1. Note that this file designates the Master on each interface as drive0 and the Slave as drive1, rather than naming each of the four devices uniquely as drive0 through drive3.

Two devices are connected, one to each interface. Device hda, an ATA-100 hard drive, is drive0 (Master) on the Primary Channel. Device hdc, a DMA-capable CD writer, is drive0 (Master) on the Secondary Channel. The list shows that DMA and UDMA are enabled for both devices. The second "DMA enabled:" line should really read "DMA level:". It shows that UDMA-5 (ATA-100) is enabled for hard drive hda and UDMA-2 for CD writer hdc.

For comparison, Figure 10-7 shows the contents of the file /proc/ide/via on an AMD system running Mandrake 9.X. The filename is via rather than piix because the system uses a VIA chipset rather than an Intel chipset. This file presents information similar to the piix file in the preceding example, but in more detail and arranged differently.

The first section lists details about the bus mastering configuration and capabilities of the system. The middle section describes the features, capabilities, and configuration of the primary and secondary IDE interfaces. The final section lists the transfer modes for drive0, an ATA-66 hard drive, and drive2, a UDMA-capable CD-ROM drive. Although drive1 and drive3 are listed as operating in PIO mode at 3.33 MB/s, that is simply the default value used when no drive is installed, as is the case here.

```
thompson@caldwell:/proc/ide                                       _ □ ✕
 File   Edit   View   Terminal   Go   Help
[thompson@caldwell /]$ cd /proc/ide
[thompson@caldwell ide]$ ls
drivers  hda  hdc  ide0  ide1  piix
[thompson@caldwell ide]$ cat piix

                        Intel PIIX4 Ultra 100 Chipset.

--------------- Primary Channel --------------- Secondary Channel -------------
                    enabled                          enabled
--------------- drive0 --------- drive1 -------- drive0 ---------- drive1 ------
DMA enabled:     yes            no             yes            no
UDMA enabled:    yes            no             yes            no
UDMA enabled:    5              X              2              X
UDMA
DMA
PIO
[thompson@caldwell ide]$
```

Figure 10-6. Displaying /proc/ide/piix, which lists DMA status on this Intel system

You can also use the hdparm command to view DMA settings, as shown in Figure 10-8. This system has a Plextor CD writer installed as hdc (the Secondary Master). Logging on as root and entering the command hdparm -i /dev/hdc lists information about the drive, including the transfer modes it supports. This drive supports PIO modes 0 through 4, all single-word (sdma) and double-word (mdma) DMA modes, and UDMA modes 0, 1, and 2. The asterisk next to udma2 indicates the drive is currently using UDMA Mode 2.

In most cases, as in these examples, a UDMA-aware kernel detects UDMA-capable devices and interfaces and automatically enables the highest level of UDMA common to the device and interface. If a UDMA-aware kernel does not enable UDMA for UDMA-capable hardware, that generally means either the kernel lacks the proper chipset driver or the kernel thinks enabling DMA isn't safe.

 If hdparm shows Linux is using a slower UDMA mode than the device and interface are capable of, check the cable. For example, if hdparm lists the current UDMA mode as udma2 (ATA-33), but you are certain the hardware supports ATA-100, verify that the device is connected with an 80-wire UDMA cable. ATA-66 and higher require an 80-wire cable to operate at full speed. Using a 40-wire cable forces the hardware to drop back to udma2 mode.

In the first situation—in which the Linux distribution doesn't fully support the UDMA features of the chipset—check the web site to see if a patch is available for that chipset. In the second situation, proceed with caution. Linux may not have enabled UDMA for a trivial reason, such as your BIOS not reporting the drive capabilities accurately. In that case, updating the main system BIOS may (or may not) solve the problem.

But it's also possible that Linux did not enable UDMA because it determined that doing so risked data corruption. Accordingly, although it is possible to do so, we

```
[thompson@meepmeep ide]$ cd /proc/ide
[thompson@meepmeep ide]$ ls
drivers   hda@   hdc@   ide0/   ide1/   via
[thompson@meepmeep ide]$ cat via
----------VIA BusMastering IDE Configuration----------------
Driver Version:                          3.34
South Bridge:                            VIA vt82c686a
Revision:                                ISA 0x22 IDE 0x10
Highest DMA rate:                        UDMA66
BM-DMA base:                             0xffa0
PCI clock:                               33.3MHz
Master Read  Cycle IRDY:                 0ws
Master Write Cycle IRDY:                 0ws
BM IDE Status Register Read Retry:       yes
Max DRDY Pulse Width:                    No limit
--------------------Primary IDE-------Secondary IDE------
Read DMA FIFO flush:          yes                 yes
End Sector FIFO flush:         no                  no
Prefetch Buffer:              yes                  no
Post Write Buffer:            yes                  no
Enabled:                      yes                 yes
Simplex only:                  no                  no
Cable Type:                    80w                 40w
-----------------drive0----drive1----drive2----drive3-----
Transfer Mode:       UDMA       PIO     UDMA       PIO
Address Setup:       30ns     120ns     30ns     120ns
Cmd Active:          90ns      90ns     90ns      90ns
Cmd Recovery:        30ns      30ns     30ns      30ns
Data Active:         90ns     330ns     90ns     330ns
Data Recovery:       30ns     270ns     30ns     270ns
Cycle Time:          30ns     600ns     60ns     600ns
Transfer Rate:   66.6MB/s   3.3MB/s  33.3MB/s  3.3MB/s
[thompson@meepmeep ide]$
```

Figure 10-7. Displaying /proc/ide/via, which lists DMA status on this AMD system

strongly recommend you not force Linux to use UDMA. If despite our advice you insist on forcing DMA, you can do so using either kernel boot parameters (for kernel 2.1.113 or higher) or the hdparm command. For details, see the manpage for hdparm.

Enabling bus mastering (DMA) support with Windows

All versions of Windows 98, 2000, and XP support DMA/UDMA modes. The exact steps required to enable DMA mode differ according to your chipset and the exact version of Windows you are using, as follows:

Windows 98/98 SE/Me

The original Windows 98 release and Windows 98 SE are both identified as 4.10.1998, and both are supplied with a native DMA driver, as is Windows Me. Use that driver rather than the driver supplied by Intel or another chipset manufacturer. The Microsoft drivers require DMA support in BIOS, so you may need to flash your system BIOS to the latest version before installing the

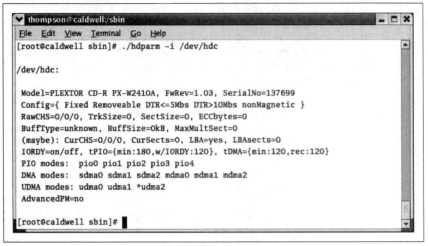

```
thompson@caldwell:/sbin                                          _ □ x

File   Edit   View   Terminal   Go   Help
[root@caldwell sbin]# ./hdparm -i /dev/hdc

/dev/hdc:

 Model=PLEXTOR CD-R PX-W2410A, FwRev=1.03, SerialNo=137699
 Config={ Fixed Removeable DTR<=5Mbs DTR>10Mbs nonMagnetic }
 RawCHS=0/0/0, TrkSize=0, SectSize=0, ECCbytes=0
 BuffType=unknown, BuffSize=0kB, MaxMultSect=0
 (maybe): CurCHS=0/0/0, CurSects=0, LBA=yes, LBAsects=0
 IORDY=on/off, tPIO={min:180,w/IORDY:120}, tDMA={min:120,rec:120}
 PIO modes:  pio0 pio1 pio2 pio3 pio4
 DMA modes:  sdma0 sdma1 sdma2 mdma0 mdma1 mdma2
 UDMA modes: udma0 udma1 *udma2
 AdvancedPM=no

[root@caldwell sbin]# █
```

Figure 10-8. Using hdparm to display the characteristics of an optical drive

driver. Before installing the Microsoft driver, remove the Intel BM-IDE driver (if present) by running the BM-IDE installation program and choosing deinstall. To install the Microsoft driver,

1. Right-click My Computer, choose Properties, and then click the Device Manager tab.

2. Locate the CD-ROM drive and double-click it to display the Properties sheet.

3. Click the Settings tab and mark the DMA checkbox in the Options section.

4. Close the dialog and reboot the system.

5. Redisplay the Properties sheet for the drive after rebooting to verify that the checkbox remains marked and that DMA is enabled.

Note the following considerations for Windows 98/98 SE/Me and DMA:

- On a clean install, we found that Windows 98/98 SE/Me automatically determines whether the chipset, drives, and BIOS support DMA. If so, DMA is automatically enabled by default.

- On an upgrade install to a system running Windows 95 OSR1 or earlier, we found that Windows 98/98 SE/Me Setup does not install DMA support, even if all required elements are present. If this occurs, you can enable DMA support by marking the DMA checkbox and restarting the system.

- On an upgrade install to a system running Windows 95 OSR2 or higher, we found that Windows 98/98 SE/Me Setup enables DMA only if Windows 95 had the Microsoft DMA drivers installed and enabled. If the drivers were not installed, or if they were installed but DMA was not enabled, Setup installs using PIO mode. Again, you can enable DMA support manually by marking the DMA checkbox and restarting the system.

- Installing Windows 98/98 SE/Me as an upgrade on a Windows 95 system running the Intel BM-IDE driver causes all sorts of IDE problems. The Intel BM-IDE driver version 3.01 has no uninstall option, but can be uninstalled using the version 3.02 or higher Setup program. Before upgrading to Windows 98/98 SE/Me, run BM-IDE version 3.02 or higher and choose the deinstall option.

Windows 2000/XP

Windows 2000 and Windows XP generally manage DMA properly and automatically. During a fresh install, Windows 2000/XP tests the ATA interface and the connected devices to determine DMA compatibility. If the interface and all connected devices are DMA-compatible, Windows 2000/XP enables DMA for that interface. A problem may arise during an upgrade installation, however. If the earlier OS version was not configured to use DMA, Windows 2000/XP may not enable DMA even though the interface and devices support it. To check DMA status on a Windows 2000/XP system, and to enable DMA if necessary, take the following steps:

1. If you're not sure how your CD-ROM drive is configured, restart the system and watch the BIOS boot screen to determine whether the drive is connected to the Primary or Secondary ATA channel and whether it is configured as Master or Slave.

2. Right-click the My Computer icon and choose Properties. Click the Hardware tab and then the Device Manager button to display the Device Manager.

3. Locate the IDE ATA/ATAPI Controllers entry and click the + icon to expand the listing. There should be three lines visible, assuming that both IDE channels are enabled. The first, which will be something such as Intel® 82801BA Bus Master IDE Controller, is for the ATA controller itself. The two remaining lines should be Primary IDE Channel and Secondary IDE Channel.

4. Right-click the channel to which your CD-ROM drive is connected, choose Properties, and then click the Advanced Settings tab to display the IDE Channel Properties dialog. This dialog, shown in Figure 10-9, has two sections, one for Device 0 (Master) and another for Device 1 (Slave). The listing for your CD-ROM drive should display the DMA mode currently in use in the Current Transfer Mode box. If it does, your drive is operating at peak efficiency, and you can exit the dialog. For example, Figure 10-9 shows that the CD-ROM drive installed as the master device on the secondary IDE channel is using Multi-Word DMA Mode 2, which is the highest DMA standard it supports.

5. If the Current Transfer Mode box for the CD-ROM drive lists *PIO Mode*, check the setting for that device in the Transfer Mode box. If the drop-down list in that box is set to DMA if available, that means that Windows has determined that either the interface or the drive (or both) do not support DMA. Exit the dialog and resign yourself to running in PIO mode. If the Transfer Mode box is set to PIO Only, use the drop-down list to change that setting to DMA if available, save your changes, restart the system, and redisplay that dialog. If the Current Transfer

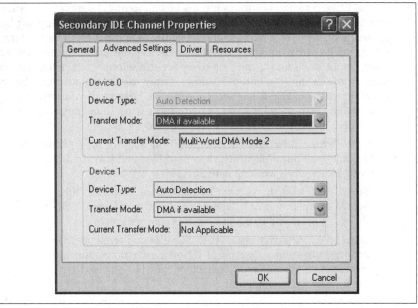

Figure 10-9. The Secondary IDE Channel Properties dialog, which shows that this drive is operating in Multi-Word DMA Mode 2

Mode box for the drive now displays a DMA mode, the drive is now using DMA. If the box still displays PIO Mode, Windows has determined that it is unsafe to use DMA mode.

Regardless of operating system, it's a bad idea to configure a PIO-mode device to share an ATA channel with a DMA-capable device. That's because ATA doesn't allow mixing DMA mode and PIO mode on one channel. If one device runs PIO mode, both must do so, which cripples the DMA-capable device. In particular, it's a horrible idea to put a PIO-only CD-ROM drive on the same channel as an Ultra-DMA hard drive because that means the hard drive will run in PIO mode, which cuts throughput by half or more and dramatically increases CPU utilization. Put the PIO-only drive on its own channel, alone or with another PIO-only device, or replace the drive with a DMA-capable drive.

Installing and Configuring a SCSI CD-ROM Drive

Installing and configuring a SCSI drive is somewhat more involved than installing and configuring an ATAPI CD-ROM drive. Rather than attempting to provide step-by-step instructions, which vary according to the specific drive and adapter, we've chosen to illustrate a typical installation using a Plextor UltraPlex 40Xmax drive and an Adaptec 2930 SCSI host adapter, noting potential pitfalls along the way:

1. If you have not already done so, the first step is to install the SCSI host adapter. To do so, power down the system, remove the cover, and locate an

unused PCI expansion slot that supports bus mastering. Many recent systems support bus mastering on all available slots. Older systems may support bus mastering on only some slots. In that case, the slots capable of bus mastering are normally white or ivory, and those not capable of bus mastering are brown or black. Remove the slot cover for the selected slot, align the bus connector with the slot, and press down firmly to seat the adapter. Use the screw that secured the slot cover to secure the adapter. If you have a spare drive activity indicator LED, you can connect it to J2 on the host adapter (Pins 1 and 2 if the cable has only two positions).

Both the Plextor drive and the Adaptec host adapter fully support *SCAM* (*SCSI Configured Auto-Magically*), a kind of Plug and Play for SCSI. Note the following issues when working with SCAM:

- *SCAM-compliant* drives such as the Plextor UltraPlex 40Xmax allow a SCAM-compliant host adapter such as the Adaptec 2930 to set the drive's SCSI ID and termination status automatically.

- *SCAM-tolerant* drives report their SCSI ID and termination status to the adapter, but cannot reset SCSI ID or termination status automatically. Instead, you must change jumpers or switches on the drive manually to set SCSI ID and termination.

- *Non-SCAM* drives do not even report their current settings to the adapter, let alone allow the adapter to reset them automatically. When using non-SCAM devices, you must manually verify settings and change them as necessary. Note that enabling SCAM on the host adapter may cause your computer to hang if you connect a non-SCAM drive because the adapter is unable to determine current settings for the non-SCAM device. If this occurs, use the Adaptec SCSISelect utility at boot time to disable SCAM on the adapter.

2. If you are installing a non-SCAM adapter and/or drive, you must set SCSI IDs manually using the jumpers or switches on the adapter and drive. If the adapter supports seven devices (plus the adapter itself), the adapter is normally configured as SCSI ID 7 (the highest-priority SCSI ID), leaving SCSI IDs 0 through 6 available for drives. ID 0 is normally reserved for the boot hard disk, and ID 1 for a secondary hard disk. A CD-ROM drive should normally be assigned to ID 2 or higher. If the host adapter is dedicated to devices other than hard drives, it is acceptable to assign ID 0 or ID 1 to the CD-ROM drive.

3. If you are installing a non-SCAM adapter and/or drive, you may also need to terminate the SCSI bus manually. Exactly two devices must be terminated on each SCSI bus, and these devices must be those at each end of the bus, as follows:

- If the SCSI adapter has only internal devices attached to it, the adapter itself and the final device on the internal SCSI chain must be terminated.

- If the SCSI adapter has only external devices attached to it, the adapter itself and the final device on the external SCSI chain must be terminated.

- If the SCSI adapter has both internal and external devices attached to it, *do not* terminate the SCSI adapter itself. Instead, terminate the final device attached to the internal chain and the final device attached to the external chain.

Note that most recent SCSI host adapters, including the Adaptec 2930, can automatically detect the presence of terminated SCSI devices on the bus and automatically set their own termination status accordingly. On Adaptec models, which we recommend exclusively, this option can be enabled or disabled by using SCSISelect to set Host Adapter Termination to AutoTerm, which is the default setting. Also note that a few internal SCSI cables have a built-in terminator at the end of the cable. If you use such a cable, make sure that termination is disabled on all drives connected to that cable.

4. Once you have resolved SCSI ID and termination issues and have the drive physically installed, the next step is to connect the cables. Most adapters are supplied with a standard two-device cable. If you need to connect more than two drives, replace the cable before proceeding. Otherwise, connect the cable to each drive, making sure to align Pin 1 on the cable (indicated by a red stripe) with Pin 1 on each device (indicated by a small number, triangle, or dot on the connector). It doesn't matter which drive connects to which cable position, so mix and match drives and cable positions in whatever way makes it easiest to route the cable. Also connect the power cable and the audio cable that links the CD-ROM drive to the appropriate connector on your sound card or motherboard.

5. After verifying all settings and connections, turn on any external SCSI device(s) first, and then turn on the PC. Ordinarily, the system should boot normally, but the SCSI CD-ROM drive may or may not be recognized, depending on your operating system and other factors. Before you configure the operating system to use the drive, however, some systems may require that you complete one or both of the following steps:

CMOS Setup

On most systems, the PCI bus assigns IRQs and port addresses automatically. If your system requires setting PCI bus parameters manually, do so during the first restart, using the system or motherboard documentation for guidance.

SCSI Setup

The SCSI BIOS displays its own splash screen while initializing, which normally displays adapter and BIOS information and a list of installed SCSI devices. Ordinarily, the default settings are fine, but in some cases you may need to change settings to get the drive to work at all or to optimize its performance. If this is the case for your system, press whatever key sequence is needed to invoke the SCSI Setup routine and make the necessary changes, as recommended by the documentation for the host adapter and/or drive.

If either or both of these steps are needed, restart the system after completing each.

General SCSI CD-ROM Troubleshooting

If you have installed your SCSI host adapter and drive properly and have installed the requisite drivers (described in the following sections) and your drive does not work, check the following items before proceeding to other troubleshooting steps:

- Is the host adapter installed in a bus-mastering PCI slot? Verify with the system or motherboard documentation that the chosen slot supports bus mastering, or try another slot.

- Are all SCSI devices turned on, and were they turned on when you booted the system? The SCSI adapter recognizes only devices that are active when the system boots. If necessary, power down all SCSI devices, turn off the computer, turn the SCSI devices back on, and then turn the PC back on.

- Are all SCSI cables and power cables connected properly? Verify that the Pin-1 orientation of all SCSI cables and devices is correct, and that the power cable is fully seated in each SCSI drive.

- Does each SCSI device on the bus, including the host adapter, have a unique SCSI ID, and is the bus terminated correctly? If not, correct the ID assignments and/or termination and restart the system.

- If SCAM is enabled on your host adapter, are you certain that all connected devices are SCAM-compliant (or at least SCAM-tolerant)? If not, either replace the non-SCAM device, or disable SCAM on the adapter and configure SCSI IDs and termination manually.

- Are you certain that you have installed all driver software that your adapter and/or devices require?

Windows 9X/2000/XP SCSI Driver Installation and Troubleshooting

Ordinarily, Windows 9X/2000/XP automatically detects installed SCSI host adapters and devices. If it does not, first verify that the hardware is installed and configured properly. If there is no apparent hardware problem, use the Add New Hardware Wizard to force installation of the necessary drivers for the new hardware.

To do so,

1. Open the Control Panel (Start → Settings → Control Panel) and double-click Add New Hardware. Accept the default selection to allow Windows to attempt to auto-detect the new hardware.

2. If Windows fails to detect the hardware, or locks up during the detection process, restart the system, reinvoke the Add New Hardware Wizard, and this time tell it that you want to select from a list.

    a. If you have a driver disk supplied by the manufacturer, choose the Have Disk option at the appropriate point in the process.

    b. Otherwise, use the lists of manufacturers and models displayed by the Add New Hardware Wizard to select the standard Windows drivers for the installed devices.

    c. If no listed device exactly matches what is installed, you can sometimes use the most closely similar device that is listed.

Ordinarily, the driver will load correctly and the device will be recognized. If problems occur, take the following steps to resolve them:

1. Open the Device Manager (Start → Settings → Control Panel → System → Device Manager). Locate the SCSI controller item in the list, and click the plus sign (+) to its left to expand the listing. Your SCSI host adapter should be listed. If it is not and you have not yet installed drivers manually, exit the Device Manager and install the drivers. If you have already attempted a manual installation and are certain that all hardware is properly installed and configured, contact the manufacturer or dealer for a replacement device.

2. If the device is listed, highlight it and click Properties to display the General page of the property sheet for the device. The Device Status section should state "This device is working properly." If it does not, the most likely causes are a resource conflict or a hardware problem. The Device usage section contains a list of stored hardware profiles. Make sure that the checkbox for current configuration (and any other configurations for which you want to use this device) is marked.

3. Click the Resources tab and examine the Conflicting Device list section at the bottom, which should state "No conflicts." If a conflicting device is listed, reconfigure one or both devices to eliminate the conflict.

4. After making any necessary changes to the General page and the Resources page, save your changes and restart the system. The device should be recognized properly. If it is not, contact the adapter manufacturer's technical support.

Changing CD-ROM Drive Letter Assignments

By default, all versions of Windows assign a CD-ROM drive the next available drive letter following those for any local volumes. If you subsequently install an additional hard disk or repartition your drive to create additional volumes, the letter assigned to the CD-ROM drive may change, which may confuse installed software that attempts to access the CD-ROM drive as the old letter. You can avoid this "musical chairs" reassignment of CD-ROM drive letters by manually assigning the CD-ROM drive a drive letter that is higher than the drive letter for any existing local or network volume. We use R: for the CD-ROM drive by long-standing habit, although there is something to be said for assigning it to Z. To assign a different drive letter to the CD-ROM drive, proceed as follows:

Windows 95/98/98 SE/Me
Right-click the My Computer icon, choose Properties, and then click the Device Manager tab. Double-click the CD-ROM drive to display its Properties sheet, and then click the Settings tab. Use the spinner to assign an unused drive letter to the CD-ROM drive and then restart the system.

Windows 2000/XP
If you have not already done so, right-click the Task Bar, choose Properties, click the Advanced tab, and mark the Display Administrative Tools checkbox in the Start Menu Settings pane. This adds Administrative Tools to the Programs (2000) or All Programs (XP) menu (it is also available in the Control Panel regardless of this setting). From the Control Panel, choose

Administrative Tools, and then Computer Management. In Computer Management, expand the tree if necessary to show items in the Storage branch. Click Disk Management, locate your CD-ROM drive in the lower-right pane, right-click its icon to display the context-sensitive menu, and choose the menu item Change Drive Letter and Path. Assign an available drive letter to the CD-ROM drive, save your changes, and exit. Once you accept the changes, the new drive letter takes effect immediately.

If you change the drive letter assignment for a CD-ROM drive, do so immediately after installing the drive or the operating system. If you use that drive under its original letter to install software, that software will later attempt to access the drive using the old drive letter.

Cleaning a CD-ROM Drive

The first symptom of a dirty drive is that you get read errors on a data CD or degraded sound from a music CD. If this happens, it is often because the CD itself is dirty or scratched, so try a different CD before assuming the drive is at fault. In theory, CD-ROM drives require little cleaning. They are reasonably well sealed against dust, and all recent drives incorporate a self-cleaning lens mechanism. That said, the fact is that CD-ROM drives accumulate dust and grime internally just like any other removable media drive. Caddy-load drives are less subject to this problem than tray-load drives, but all drives eventually become dirty.

For routine cleaning, simply wipe the external parts of the drive occasionally with a damp cloth. Many drive makers recommend using a drive cleaning kit every month or two, although we usually do so only when we begin getting read errors. To use these kits, which are available in wet and dry forms, simply insert the cleaning disc and access the drive to spin the cleaning disc for a few seconds. For a particularly dirty drive, you may need to repeat the cleaning process several times. Most CD-ROM drive manufacturers discourage taking more extreme measures, so if you go beyond these routine cleaning steps, you are on your own and may void your warranty.

Caddy-load drives can be cleaned more thoroughly by removing the drive from the chassis, vacuuming the interior gently (or using compressed air to blow it out), and then drenching it down with zero-residue cleaner. Tray-load drives may be more problematic because the tray on some drives blocks access to the interior whether it is open or closed. If that is not the case on your drive, you can clean it using the same procedure as for a caddy-load drive. If the tray does block access when it is open, the only alternative is to disassemble the drive, if that is possible.

Some drives use a crimped sheet metal enclosure that cannot be removed without damaging the drive. Other drives have a removable metal bottom plate, usually secured by four screws. Removing that plate may provide adequate access to the drive interior for cleaning purposes. If not, do not attempt to disassemble the drive any further. Unless your time is worth nothing an hour, it's easier and cheaper just to replace the drive.

If you experience errors reading some CD discs, the problem may be dirty discs rather than a dirty drive. We usually clean discs by spraying them lightly with Windex and gently drying them with a soft cloth. That method is frowned upon by some, but we've never damaged a disc by cleaning it that way. If you want to use an approved method, buy one of the commercial CD-ROM or CD Audio disc cleaners, which are readily available from computer and audio supply resellers.

Our Picks

The era of CD-ROM drives is rapidly drawing to a close. Many manufacturers have ceased production of CD-ROM drives, particularly ATAPI models, to concentrate instead on producing CD writers and DVD-ROM drives, although first-rate drives made by companies such as Hitachi, Panasonic, and Toshiba are likely to remain in limited distribution for some time. Most of the ATAPI CD-ROM drives still being produced are third-rate products made by Pacific Rim manufacturers, and should be avoided. DVD-ROM drives read CDs, so for most systems a DVD-ROM drive and/or a CD-RW drive is a better and more flexible choice than a CD-ROM drive. One stronghold of CD-ROM drives remains, however, because the best CD-ROM drives provide superior speed and quality for digital audio extraction and duplicating CDs. Here are the CD-ROM drives we recommend:

ATAPI CD-ROM drive

None. For entry-level systems and undemanding applications, use an ATAPI DVD-ROM drive. For mainstream systems, install an ATAPI DVD-ROM drive and an ATAPI CD-RW drive, or a combination ATAPI DVD-ROM/CD-RW drive. See Chapter 11 and Chapter 12 for more information.

SCSI CD-ROM drive

Plextor UltraPleX 40X. Plextor makes the best SCSI CD-ROM drives, bar none. In addition to being the fastest drives available, Plextor drives are built like tanks and provide faster and higher-quality DAE than any other drives we know of. The PX-40TSi UltraPleX 40max supports 20 MB/s burst-mode UltraSCSI transfers, provides true 24X DAE with bit-by-bit accuracy, and is a superb source drive for duplicating CDs. The Plextor PX-40TSUWi Ultra-PleX 40X Wide drive is the same drive, but with a Wide UltraSCSI (40 MB/s) interface. Both of these models are available in external versions at a slightly higher price. If extracting high-quality digital audio quickly or duplicating CDs perfectly is important to you, it's worth installing a SCSI host adapter and a Plextor SCSI CD-ROM drive (*http://www.plextor.com*).

For updated recommendations, visit: *http://www.hardwareguys.com/picks/ cdrom.html*.

11

CD Writers

CD Recordable (*CD-R*), CD Rewritable (*CD-RW*), and *CD-Mount Rainier Writable* (*CD-MRW*) drives—collectively called CD writers or CD burners—are CD-ROM drives with a difference: they have a more powerful LASER that, in addition to reading discs, can *record* (also called *write* or *burn*) data to special CD media. CD writers can be used for many purposes, including duplicating commercial data and music CDs, transferring large amounts of data to anyone who has a CD-ROM drive, and archiving or backing up data. The flexibility and low cost of CD writers, along with the low cost, reliability, and universal readability of the discs they produce, have made them one of the most popular PC peripherals. Any computer except perhaps an entry-level system should have a CD writer.

 Throughout this chapter, we use CD-(M)RW to refer collectively to CD-RW and CD-MRW drives. If the type matters, we use CD-RW or CD-MRW explicitly.

CD Writers and Media

CD writers use one or both of these media types:

CD-R discs

CD-R discs record data permanently. Data written to a CD-R disc cannot subsequently be deleted, which may be an advantage or a drawback, depending on how you use the drive. If you partially fill a CD-R disc, you can add more data to it during a later session, but once that disc is full, no more data can be written to it. CD-R discs are cheap—$0.20 each in bulk, and sometimes almost free after rebates—and are a cost-effective means to archive data or to transfer large amounts of data to someone else. CD-R discs can be read in all but the oldest CD-ROM drives, and in most consumer CD players made in the last few years. CD-R discs may be written to in audio or various data formats, and can be read by any CD-R, CD-(M)RW, or Multi-Read-compatible CD-ROM drive.

 MultiRead and *MultiRead2* are OSTA standards for CD-ROM and DVD-ROM drives and players. A MultiRead-compatible device can read pressed CDs (CD-DA and CD-ROM), CD-R discs, and CD-RW discs, and can read any disc written using fixed- or variable-length packets. MultiRead2 extends the specification to include DVD-ROM and 2.6 GB DVD-RAM devices. All MultiRead-compatible devices are also multisession-compatible, but the converse is not true. For more information, see *http://www.osta.org/specs/multiread.htm.*

CD-RW discs

CD-RW discs allow data to be erased. In fact, CD-RW was originally designated CD-Erasable (CD-E), but marketing folks decided that "erasable" had negative connotations. A CD-RW disc can be used repeatedly, deleting old data to make room for new. Current CD-RW discs can be written and re-written at least 1,000 or 10,000 times, depending on type. CD-RW discs are a bit more expensive than CD-R discs—$1 or so each as of June 2003—but their reusability makes this price difference trivial. Because CD-RW discs are less reflective than CD-R discs and much less reflective than standard pressed CDs, many CD-ROM drives and consumer CD players made in 1999 or earlier cannot read them.

CD writers have been made in three varieties:

CD-R drives

These drives can write CD-R discs but not CD-RW discs, and can read standard CDs, CD-R discs, and (usually) CD-RW discs. CD-R drives are usually used in "batch mode" to copy standard audio and data CDs. They can also be used with packet-writing software, although their lack of rewritability makes them better suited to archiving data than backing it up. CD-R drives remained popular through about mid-2000 because they cost less than CD-(M)RW drives. By late 2000, however, the price differential had all but disappeared, and with it CD-R drives. Nowadays, all new CD writers are CD-(M)RW drives.

CD-RW drives

These drives can write CD-R and CD-RW discs, and can read any CD disc. A common use for the RW functionality of CD-RW drives is packet-writing software, such as Ahead InCD or Roxio DirectCD, that allows the CD-RW drive to appear as a Windows drive letter and to function much like an enormous floppy diskette. For example, you can drag files over to the CD-RW drive icon and drop them to back up those files to the CD-RW disc, where they can also be readily retrieved using Explorer. When a disc is full, you can simply erase some or all existing files to make room for new ones.

CD-MRW drives

These drives are CD-RW drives with added hardware support for the Mount Rainier format described later in this chapter. Mount Rainier allows an optical drive to be accessed directly just like a floppy drive or hard drive, but requires explicit support from the operating system, BIOS, and drive. Unfortunately, most older CD-RW drives cannot be upgraded to add Mount Rainier support. Some 40X and many 48X CD-RW drives manufactured in mid-2002 or later are actually CD-MRW drives, although they may not be labeled as such and may require a firmware update to support Mount Rainier. Most CD-RW drives currently sold have Mount Rainier support.

CD-RW drives and CD-MRW drives both use CD-RW discs. There is no such thing as a CD-MRW disc, except in the sense that a standard CD-RW disc may be formatted to CD-MRW standards. That is, CD-RW discs and CD-MRW discs differ only in their logical formatting, not in any physical sense. A CD-RW disc formatted as CD-MRW can be written and read by a CD-MRW drive, but cannot be written by a CD-RW drive without first erasing the CD-MRW formatting. Any drive that can read a standard CD-RW disc can read a CD-MRW formatted disc, although it may require a helper application to make sense of the format.

Just as CD writers achieved critical mass in late 1996 and early 1997, it seemed that writable CD might be stillborn as a mainstream technology. DVD—in both read-only and writable forms—seemed poised to take over the optical market. But squabbling among DVD manufacturers and standards organizations led to a fragmenting of the writable DVD market, and the writable CD stepped into the breach. Even now, more than six years later, no writable DVD standard has yet emerged as an unquestioned market leader (although DVD+R/RW seems to be leading comfortably). DVD writers, although their prices are dropping fast and they are selling in increasing numbers, have not quiet yet become mainstream products.

Today, CD writers still offer an attractive combination of low price, reasonable performance, acceptable capacity, and good (although not perfect) compatibility between various media and readers. Their big advantage over such competing niche technologies as *Magneto-Optical (MO)*, *Phase Change Dual Optical (PD)*, and *Light Intensity Modulated Direct Overwrite (LIMDOW)* drives is simple: all of those drive technologies are proprietary, or have such limited market share that they might as well be. That means that few systems can read discs produced on those drives. CD writers, on the other hand, produce discs that can be read on hundreds of millions of ordinary PCs. Although each of the competing niche technologies has one or more advantages relative to CD writers, those advantages are seldom enough to outweigh the drawbacks.

CD writers will eventually be replaced by one of the writable DVD standards— DVD-R/RW, DVD-RAM, or DVD+RW—but it's still unclear which will prevail. When the marketplace sorts out a winner in the writable DVD competition, and when writable DVD discs approach the cost of CD-RW discs, then CD writers will fade away. But we don't expect DVD writers to become mainstream products for the next year or so. Until DVD writers and media fall to commodity price levels, CD writers will dominate the writable optical market. Even after writable DVD becomes common, CD writers will sell in reasonable numbers, and discs for them will remain available for years thereafter. You needn't worry about your new CD-MRW drive being obsoleted anytime soon.

CD-Recordable (CD-R) Drives and Media

Although CD-R drives are passé, CD-R technology itself, as implemented in CD-(M)RW drives, remains important. CD-R devolved in spirit from *Write Once/Read Many (WORM)* drives that were developed in the early 1980s and were popular in data centers from the mid-'80s until better means of permanent storage became available. WORM drives were so called because they used a relatively high-power writing LASER to make irreversible physical changes to the disc in write mode, and a low-power LASER (or the same LASER operating at lower power) to read the disc. CD-R works on the same principle.

CD-R technology is based on the Orange Book standard that was developed in the late 1980s and has since been updated, expanded, and split to standardize support for such functions as rewritability and other developing technologies. Philips released the first CD-R drive in 1993. It was extremely expensive, wrote at only 1X, and used $50 CD-R discs made by Taiyo Yuden.

Although they must function interchangeably with standard pressed CDs in CD-ROM drives and CD players, CD-R discs have a different structure. Like pressed CDs, the label side of a CD-R disc is typically printed on a scratch-resistant and/or printable coating that resides on a base of UV-cured lacquer. The next layer is a reflective backing against which the reading LASER impinges. This reflective layer may be gold, silver, or a silver alloy, depending on the brand and model of CD-R disc.

As with a pressed CD, a spiral groove is physically stamped into the backing layer at the factory. This groove makes 22,188 revolutions around a standard-length CD-R disc, with about 600 track revolutions per millimeter, and a total length of nearly 3.5 miles. Unlike the groove of a pressed CD, which has pits and lands embedded during pressing, the groove on a blank CD-R disc has no embedded pits, leaving the groove as one long, continuous land.

Whereas the next layer in a pressed CD is the protective polycarbonate layer, a CD-R disc has an extra layer between the reflective backing and the clear polycarbonate layer. This layer is an organic dye that is sensitive to light and heat, and is tuned to the 780 nm wavelength used by a CD writer LASER. Although various dyes are used, which vary in color in the visible spectrum, all of them are essentially transparent at the wavelength used by the reading LASER. In effect, then, a CD drive sees a blank CD-R disc as one long pristine groove—all land and no pits—with the dye layer providing no hindrance to light transmission and reflection.

 First-generation DVD-ROM drives use a 650 nm LASER that is so badly matched to the reflective characteristics of CD-R dyes that these drives may have trouble reading CD-R discs. Later DVD-ROM drives use a dual-wavelength LASER, which can read CD-R discs without difficulty.

When the CD-R is written to, the power of the writing LASER is modulated to literally burn pits into the dye layer. Write power typically ranges from 4 mW to 8 mW, compared to the ~0.5 mW used to read a disc. The LASER operating at write power heats the disc to 250° C, which causes a chemical reaction in the dye that renders it opaque at the wavelength used by a reading LASER. When the LASER of a CD reader strikes one of these burned pits, its light is absorbed and scattered, causing the reading LASER to recognize that area as a pit. In contrast, unburned areas allow the reading LASER to reflect cleanly from the pressed groove, which the reading LASER recognizes as a land. Burned and unburned areas on a CD-R disc thereby correspond to the pits and lands (respectively) on a pressed CD.

Although the method used to make pits and lands differs between pressed CDs and CD-R discs, most modern CD-ROM drives and CD players can read CD-R discs without problems. Some older drives and players cannot, however, and the reasons for that are simple. First, the overall reflectivity of CD-R discs is lower than that of pressed discs. That means a CD-R disc absorbs more of the light used by the reading LASER, which in turn requires a more sensitive optical pickup in the reader. Second, the contrast of CD-R discs is lower, which means that there is less relative difference in the amount of light reflected by pits and lands on a CD-R disc than on a pressed CD.

In combination, the general usefulness of CD-R, inexpensive drives and media, and increased performance and reliability mean that CD-R will remain a mainstream technology for several years to come. But CD-R is not a perfect technology.

Read compatibility of CD-R discs in older drives remains an issue, although such problems are decreasingly common as older, incompatible CD-ROM and DVD-ROM drives age and are retired from service. Unlike pressed CDs, whose aluminum backing layer has nearly level reflectivity across and beyond the visible light spectrum, the reflectivity of CD-R discs is optimized for the 780 nm wavelength used by standard CD-ROM drives. This increases the likelihood that any CD-ROM drive will be able to read the CD-R disc, which has much lower reflectivity than a standard CD. But it may cause problems when trying to read CD-R discs in very old CD-ROM drives, which were not calibrated to read CD-R discs, and in first-generation DVD-ROM drives.

The major advantage of CD-R, its write-once nature, is at the same time its major drawback. For some applications, such as archiving data, the immutability of CD-R is desirable. For others, such as doing daily backups or exchanging data between non-networked users, the permanence of CD-R and the requirement to close a disc before that disc can be read in ordinary CD-ROM drives wastes resources. With blank CD-R discs selling for less than $0.20 each in bulk, the cost in dollars and cents is minor, but juggling numerous partially full CD-R discs can be vexing.

For people who want to use a writable CD as though it were a gigantic floppy diskette, something else was needed. That something is called CD-Rewritable.

CD-(M)RW Drives and Media

CD-RW and CD-MRW drives are dual-purpose devices. When writing CD-R discs, they work just like ordinary CD-R drives. But if instead you use CD-RW discs and the proper software, a CD-(M)RW drive can erase an old file and write a new file in its place.

A CD-RW drive works almost like an enormous floppy drive. Almost because unlike the floppy drive, the CD-RW drive requires special software to provide drive-letter access (DLA). A CD-MRW drive works exactly like an enormous floppy drive. Exactly because the Mount Rainier specification defines the features necessary in the BIOS, operating system, and drive to allow the PC to recognize the CD-MRW drive natively and assign a drive letter to it in the same way that it assigns a drive letter to a floppy drive or hard drive.

CD-RW is an extension of CD-R technology, initially championed by Mitsubishi Chemical, a major maker of CD-R media, and a group of CD-R drive manufacturers including Hewlett-Packard, Sony, Philips, and Ricoh. CD-RW drives and discs started shipping in mid-1997, just as CD-R seemed poised to become a mainstream technology. Rewritability was considered such a huge advantage that for a time it appeared that CD-R would disappear, killed by CD-RW. That turned out not to be the case. Relative to CD-R, CD-RW had several problems initially, most of which are no longer an issue with the latest drives, media, and software:

Drive cost

When CD-RW drives began shipping, they sold at a substantial premium— $250 or more—over the price of CD-R drives with comparable speed and features. Nowadays, that premium has disappeared, and all CD writers support both CD-R and CD-RW. Most new drives support CD-MRW as well.

Media cost

CD-RW discs originally sold for 10 times the price of CD-R discs, which is to say $20 per disc at a time when CD-R discs were selling for $2 each. Although early CD-RW discs could be reused at least 1,000 times (and later versions 10,000 times), this relatively high cost per disc resulted in sticker shock for many potential users. Nowadays, CD-RW discs sell for a dollar or less each in bulk, not much more than CD-R discs.

Speed

The first CD-RW drives supported only 1X rewriting at a time when 4X CD-R drives were common, 6X CD-R drives were available, and 8X CD-R drives were on the near horizon. At those speeds, filling a CD-R disc took 10 or 20 minutes versus the 1.25 hours needed to fill a CD-RW disc, so CD-RW was used only by very patient people. The speed disparity remains, albeit in greatly reduced proportion. Current CD-(M)RW drives write at 52X and rewrite at 32X. With such a drive, writing a full CD-R disc takes 3 minutes or so, versus twice that to fill a CD-RW disc, a minor difference for most users.

Not all CD-RW discs are compatible with all CD-(M)RW drives. Four distinct types of CD-RW discs exist:

- Standard discs are the only type compatible with Standard (1X/2X/4X) drives, and can be written only at 1X, 2X, and 4X. Most High Speed and Ultra Speed CD-(M)RW drives can write to Standard discs. Standard discs can be read by any CD-RW drive.

- High Speed discs are identified by the High Speed CD-RW logo. These discs can be written at 4X, 8X, 10X, 12X, or CAV (4X through 10X variable or 4X through 12X variable) in High Speed and Ultra Speed CD-(M)RW drives, but cannot be written by Standard CD-RW drives. Most 1X and 2X drives and some 4X drives have trouble reading High Speed discs. High Speed discs and drives originally were limited to 10X, which was later increased to 12X. Most High Speed discs labeled as 10X can be written at 12X in most High Speed drives.

- Ultra Speed discs are identified by the Ultra Speed CD-RW logo. These discs can be written at 12X in High Speed drives, and at 12X, 16X, and 24X in Ultra Speed drives, but cannot be written by Standard drives. Any High Speed or Ultra Speed drive can read Ultra Speed discs, but many Standard drives cannot.

- The latest CD-(M)RW drives support 32X rewrites, but requires special 32X discs to achieve that speed. Using a standard Ultra Speed disc in a 32X drive limits rewrites to 24X. These 32X CD-RW discs were not yet available as of July 2003, but should become available later in 2003.

Buggy software

Although premastering software (such as EasyCD or Nero Burning ROM) works fine with CD-RW discs, it imposes batch-mode limitations. That is, you can use premastering software to dupe a CD to a CD-RW disc, or to batch-copy a selection of files from your hard drive to a CD-RW disc, but premastering software doesn't provide drive letter access. With drive letter access, the CD-RW disc appears as just another Windows volume, allowing you to use drag-and-drop to manipulate files. But drive letter access requires a different class of software, called packet-writing software. Until recently, all packet-writing software we tried caused compatibility problems and system crashes. In fact, Adaptec (now Roxio) DirectCD was so bad—particularly when running under Windows 2000—that we banished it permanently from our systems. Recent versions of InCD (from Ahead Software, the Nero Burning ROM folks) seem usable, although we've been burned so often by packet-writing software that we're still leery of it as a class. Don't let that discourage you if you want to use packet writing, though. Many of our readers report excellent results with InCD.

Convenience

To support packet writing, CD-RW discs must first be formatted, a process that took more than an hour on early CD-RW drives. That's less a problem now because modern CD-(M)RW drives require only a few minutes to do a full format on a CD-RW disc. In fact, preformatted CD-RW discs are available, but only for DirectCD, which we refuse to use. Formatting is a one-time operation and can be done in the background, so format times are seldom a problem.

There are three ways to prepare a CD-RW disc for use. For use with premastering software, it needn't be formatted at all. You can use it just as you would a CD-R disc. For use with packet-writing software, the CD-RW disc requires a full format before the first use (done either by you or by the factory). Finally, if the disc has already been formatted and had data written to it that you want to delete, you can do a quick format, which is analogous to a quick format on a floppy diskette. A quick format requires only a few seconds, and "zeros out" the disc without actually erasing the data previously written to it. As with quick-formatting a floppy, quick-formatting a CD-RW disc is insecure. Although the disc appears empty after the quick format, the data can still be retrieved by anyone with a sector editor. To do a secure erase on a CD-RW disc, choose the full-format option.

Confusion

Even knowledgeable people are confused about the relationship of premastering versus packet-writing software to CD-R versus CD-RW discs. Many people believe premastering software (such as Easy CD or Nero) can be used only with CD-R discs, and packet-writing software (such as DirectCD or InCD) only with CD-RW discs. That's simply not true. You can use premastering software with CD-RW discs (e.g., to duplicate a CD-ROM disc to a CD-RW disc), just as you can use packet-writing software for drive letter access to a CD-R disc. However, not all packet-writing applications support both media types. Roxio DirectCD and early versions of Ahead InCD, for example, can write either CD-R or CD-RW discs, but for patent reasons the current version of InCD can write only to CD-RW discs.

CD-(M)RW Technical Details

If you want to know more about the technical details of how CD-(M)RW drives and discs work, read on. Otherwise, you can safely skip to the next section.

CD-RW discs use *optical phase change* technology that is similar to that used by magneto-optical drives, but does not use magnetism to aid the phase change. CD-RW discs are constructed similarly to CD-R discs, except for the recording layer, which is dramatically different. Like CD-R discs, CD-RW discs include a preformed pristine spiral groove that provides servo (tracking) information, *absolute time in pregroove (ATIP)* timing data, and so on. But rather than the simple dye layer used by CD-R discs, CD-RW discs use a recording layer sandwiched between two dielectric layers that absorb and dissipate excess heat generated during writes.

The recording layer comprises a crystalline compound of silver (chemical symbol Ag), indium (In), antimony (Sb), and tellurium (Te), and so is often referred to as the AgInSbTe layer. Together, these chemical elements form an exotic mix with a very special characteristic: when heated to a specific temperature and then cooled, the compound forms a crystalline matrix, but when heated to a higher temperature and then cooled, the compound assumes an amorphous (disordered) form. The reflectivity of the crystalline form lands, at 25% or so, is much lower than the equivalent on a pressed CD or CD-R disc (>70%). The reflectivity of the amorphous form pits, at 15% or so, is also much lower than that on a pressed CD or CD-R disc (~25%). These lower reflectances, in combination with lower contrast (> 3:1 for pressed CDs and CD-R discs versus about 1.6:1 for CD-RW discs) means that CD-RW discs are much more likely to generate read errors or be unreadable in older CD-ROM drives and CD players.

CD-(M)RW drives use three LASER power settings to write and read data:

Write power

The highest power level. Heats the recording layer to high temperature (typically between 500° C and 700° C), called the *melting temperature*. When melted, the molecules that form the recording layer are extremely mobile, which allows them to assume an amorphous (noncrystalline) state as they cool. When amorphous, molecules are relatively nonreflective, and correspond to pits on a pressed CD. Write power is modulated during writing of a CD-RW disc to form pits as needed to represent data being written.

Erase power

A medium power level. Heats the recording layer to moderate temperature (typically 200° C), called the *crystallization temperature*. At this temperature, the molecules that form the recording layer have only limited mobility—insufficient to assume the fully unordered amorphous state, but sufficient to allow them to arrange themselves in a rigidly ordered crystalline state. When crystalline, molecules are relatively reflective, and correspond to lands on a pressed CD. Erase power may be applied unmodulated to return an entire CD-RW disc (or portions of it, such as a track or a file) to a formatted, blank state. Alternatively, erase power may be applied modulated to form lands as necessary to represent data being written.

Read power

A low power level. Does not significantly heat the recording layer, but provides sufficient illumination to allow the current state of each bit to be read. Read power is applied unmodulated. The resulting varying reflectance caused by the virtual pits and lands on the CD-RW disc surface modulate the light, which is then detected and decoded by the read circuitry of the drive.

CD-(M)RW does not use erasure in the traditional sense. Instead, new data is simply written over old data in one pass, which is called *direct over-write* (DOW). During a write, the LASER modulates between write power and erase power, selectively heating the small domains on the track that will become pits and lands. An area that is to be a pit has write power focused on it, heating it instantaneously to between 500° C and 700° C, from which the dielectric layers quickly cool it to the amorphous (nonreflective) state. An area that is to be a land has erase power focused on it, heating it to about 200° C, from which it cools to the crystalline (reflective) state. Once the disc has been written, the read LASER in a MultiRead-compatible device can discriminate between the less reflective amorphous areas (pits) and the more reflective crystalline areas (lands).

 When using a CD-RW disc with packet-writing software, which is described later in the chapter, how you can erase that disc depends on whether you have written to it using fixed-length packets or variable-length packets. In the former case, you can erase individual files, which is called *random erase*. In the latter case, the only option is to erase the entire disc, which is called *serial erase* or *sequential erase*, and in effect means reformatting the disc.

Writable CD Formats

The physical and logical format used by writable CDs is defined in the rainbow books described in Chapter 10. The following sections provide an overview of how data is physically and logically stored on writable CDs. For further detail, refer to the rainbow books.

CD-R discs are manufactured with a *pregroove* track that is 600 nanometers (nm) wide with a 1,600 nm pitch. The pregroove includes an impressed *timing wobble* of ±30nm radial excursion at 22.05 KHz, with an FM carrier modulated at 1 KHz superimposed on the pregroove. This modulation provides an absolute clock signal (called *absolute time in pregroove*, or ATIP) that provides an absolute location reference for any sector on the CD-R disc. Absolute addresses on the CD-R disc are specified in the form HH:MM:SS using ATIP information. Audio CDs are addressable in this manner with resolution of 1 second (75 sectors). Data CDs are addressable to the individual sector level.

Physical Formats

Because they must be readable in a standard CD-ROM drive or CD player, writable CDs use a physical format nearly identical to pressed CDs. The dimensions of a CD are 120.00mm in diameter (60.00mm radius) with a 15.00mm diameter central hole that accommodates the rotating center spindle of the drive. Beginning at the edge of the center hole (radius 7.50mm) and proceeding outward, a CD-R disc is divided into the following areas:

Clamping Area
> The *Clamping Area* is that portion of the disc that the drive spindle grasps to rotate the disc. On a pressed CD, this area extends from radius 7.50mm to 23.00mm. On a writable CD, this area occupies radius 7.50mm to 22.35mm.

System Use Area
> The *System Use Area (SUA)* is present only on writable discs, occupies radius 22.35mm to 23.00mm, and can be thought of as equivalent to the boot sector of a hard disk. The SUA contains data that tells a CD drive or player what kind of information is stored on the disc, where it is located, and what format it uses. The SUA is inside the radius readable by standard CD-ROM drives and CD players, so only CD recorders can read and write to this area. The SUA is divided into two subareas:

Optimal Power Calibration Area
> The *Optimal Power Calibration Area (OPCA)*, often called the *Power Calibration Area (PCA)* for short, is used by the CD writer as a testing area to decide the best *write schema* to use when writing to that disc. Each time you insert a disc into a CD-R drive, the drive fires its writing LASER at the PCA to calibrate that disc against the drive. Each such calibration uses one ATIP frame. Only 99 PCA ATIP frames are available, which limits a CD-R disc to 99 or fewer recording sessions.

> Many variables determine how the drive should best write to that disc—the type of dye and reflective backing material the disc uses, the proposed write speed, the firmware level of the drive, and so on. From this calibration testing, the drive decides the power level to use when writing, and whether to use a short write schema (typical for cyanine-based discs) or a long write schema (typical for pthalocyanine- and azo-based discs). The PCA begins at radius 22.35mm (ATIP -00:00:36 relative to the 23.00mm beginning of the Lead-in Area described later in this section).

CD Writers

Program Memory Area

The *Program Memory Area* (*PMA*) begins where the PCA ends, and extends to the beginning of the Lead-in Area at radius 23.00mm. The PMA is used to store a temporary TOC until the disc is *finalized* or *closed*. Closing a disc writes the temporary TOC stored in the PMA to the Lead-in Area. That makes the TOC (and therefore the disc) readable by a CD-ROM drive or CD player, but also means that the disc can no longer be written to by a CD recorder. The PMA can store location information for up to 99 track numbers, including the start and stop times for each track (for audio) or the sector addresses for data.

Information Area

The *Information Area* (*IA*) occupies a width of 35.00mm to 35.50mm, beginning at radius 23.00mm and ending between radius 58.00mm and 58.50mm. This area provides the general storage space to which user data is written. The IA is the only area of the CD that is visible to standard CD-ROM drives and CD players, and includes the following subareas:

Lead-in Area

The *Lead-in Area* occupies radius 23.0mm to 25.0mm on both pressed and writable CDs. This area contains digital silence in the main channel, as well as control information in various subcode channels that can be used to provide additional information to the drive or reader about the content of the disc. The most important of the subcode channel data is the TOC for the disc, which is stored in the Q-channel. The length of the Lead-in Area is determined by the space required to store up to 99 TOCs for the 99 tracks that may potentially be written to the Program Area.

A CD has a main data channel—which stores audio and/or computer data—and eight interleaved subcode channels, designated P through W, that can store supplemental control data that can be read by CD-ROM drives and CD players. When the CD format was originally designed, it was intended that the main channel would contain only data and that subcode channels would be used to store administrative information. Nowadays, such supplemental information is usually encoded within the main data channel, and the only subchannels that are generally used are the P channel, which specifies the start and end of each track, and the Q channel, which stores the TOC, the track type/catalog number, and the timecodes (in HH:MM:SS and frames) used to locate data on the disc. Subchannels R through W were formerly sometimes used to store graphics and other supplemental data, but are now seldom used. The DVD specification eliminates subchannel coding as superfluous.

If you've ever wondered why a CD-R disc that has been written to but not closed can be read in a CD recorder but not in a standard CD-ROM drive or CD player, this is why. Standard readers look for the TOC in the Lead-in Area, where it has not yet been written for a disc that is not yet closed. CD recorders can read the temporary TOC stored in the PMA, which allows them to read that disc. The PMA is invisible to standard CD-ROM drives and CD players, so as far as they're concerned, that disc has no TOC.

Program Area

> The *Program Area* (PA) occupies a width of 33.00mm to 33.50mm, beginning at radius 25.00mm and ending between radius 58.00mm and 58.50mm. The PA is where actual user data (audio or computer data) is stored. The PA varies in capacity according to the CD-R disc you use. Discs are available that store 63 minutes of audio (which corresponds to about 600 MB of data), 74 minutes (~650 MB), and 80 minutes (~700 MB). Different brands of discs also have minor variations from nominal capacity. Some nominally 74-minute discs, for example, can store as much as 76.5 minutes.

Lead-out Area

> The *Lead-out Area* occupies a radius of 0.50mm to 1.00mm, which begins between radius 58.00mm and 58.50mm, and ends between radius 59.00mm and 59.50mm. The Lead-out Area is created when the disc is closed, and defines the end of the Information Area.

Edge

> The remaining 0.50mm to 1.00mm at the outer edge of the disc is unused. This area has no formal name that we know of, and exists simply to protect the outer portion of the track from damage.

The preceding assumes that the data on the disc exists as one session, which is nearly always true for commercially-pressed CDs, as well as for writable CDs produced using Disc-at-Once recording (described in a later section). But Orange Book defines a concept called multisession for CD-R discs.

With multisession recording, the overall disc layout remains the same. As with a single-session disc, a multisession disc contains a Lead-in Area, a Program Area, and a Lead-out Area. The difference is that the Program Area on a multisession disc stores more than one session, each of which contains its own session-based Lead-in Area, Program Area, and Lead-out Area.

Like the disc itself, a session can be opened, written to, and closed. When a session is closed, that session can no longer be written to, but additional sessions can be added to the disc. In fact, closing a session on a multisession disc automatically opens a new session to which additional data can be written. Closing the session writes the session TOC to the PMA. This session TOC includes pointers to the start of the session Program Area for the new session and to the start time of the last-used (outermost) Lead-out Area.

Closing the session does not close the disc, however, which means that until the disc itself is closed, sessions on a multisession disc can be read only by a CD recorder (which can read the temporary TOC in the PMA) and by some recent CD-ROM drives. When the disc itself is closed, all sessions are closed and the temporary TOC is written to the Lead-in Area, allowing the disc to be read in any CD-ROM drive and most CD players.

Although the PMA makes provision for 99 tracks or sessions, in practice the number of sessions that can be recorded on a CD-R disc is much lower because of the overhead required for each session. When writing multiple sessions to a disc, the Lead-in Area for each session occupies 4,500 sectors (60 seconds or 9000 KB). The Lead-out Area for the first session occupies 6,750 sectors (90 seconds or 13,500 KB). The Lead-out Area for the second and subsequent sessions occupies 2,250 sectors (30 seconds or 4500 KB).

Logical Formats

The logical format of a CD specifies how data is arranged on the CD, and largely determines how data may be structured on the disc and what operating systems will be able to access it. CDs commonly use one of the logical formats described in the following sections.

ISO-9660

Most data CDs use the *ISO-9660 format* or one of its variants. ISO-9660 is based on the de facto standard High Sierra format that was developed by the CD-ROM industry as a cooperative effort because of the lack of formal standards that then existed for writing data to CDs. In the days before High Sierra came into use, it was quite common to find that you could not read the data on a particular CD-ROM because that CD was incompatible with your software.

The primary purpose of ISO-9660, which was adopted in 1984, was to standardize a common logical data format for data CDs and, at the same time, to facilitate data exchange among different computing platforms. As a least-common-denominator format, the original ISO-9660 format is feature-poor because it supports only features that are common across many platforms. For example, the MS-DOS 8.3 filenaming convention limited ISO-9660 to using 8.3 filenames.

At the time ISO-9660 was adopted, these limitations were not much of a problem. Most people ran either MS-DOS or a Mac using floppy disks or small hard disks, and the limitations of ISO-9660 were not onerous in those environments. But the world soon changed, and the strict limits enforced by ISO-9660 became a problem, particularly for those who wanted to use deeply nested directories and long filenames. Accordingly, the ISO-9660 specification was expanded to include three *ISO-9660 Interchange Levels* for naming files and directories on disc. From most to least restrictive, these include:

ISO-9660 Level 1
> *ISO-9660 Level 1* is the least-common-denominator level, developed to accommodate DOS filename limitations. Each file must be written to disc as a single, continuous stream of bytes, called an *extent*. Files may not be fragmented or interleaved. Filenames may contain from one to eight d-characters (see following section). Filename extensions may contain from zero to three d-characters. Directory names may contain from one to eight d-characters, and may not have an extension.

ISO-9660 Level 2

ISO-9660 Level 2 also requires that files be written to disc as a single extent, but filenames may be up to 255 d-characters long, with an extension from zero to three d-characters. ISO-9660 Level 2 discs are unreadable by some operating systems, notably DOS.

ISO-9660 Level 3

ISO-9660 Level 3 allows a file to be written in multiple extents, and so is used for packet writing. Filenames may be up to 255 characters long, with the same limitations as ISO-9660 Level 2.

Strictly interpreted, ISO-9660 filenames must end with a semicolon followed by the version number—e.g., *FILENAME.TXT;1*. Most operating systems ignore these final two characters when they access files or display directory listings. Versions of the Macintosh OS prior to 7.5 and some versions of Unix do not suppress the semicolon and version number, which causes problems if they attempt to access *FILENAME.TXT* rather than the actual filename of *FILENAME.TXT;1*.

The various ISO-9660 levels vary significantly in which characters are legal. In ISO-9660-speak, these characters are designated as follows:

d-characters

For strict compliance with ISO-9660 Level 1 file and directory naming conventions, only this character set may be used (and only in 8.3 format). d-characters include uppercase A through Z, digits 0 through 9, and the underscore character.

a-characters

The character set usable for ISO Volume Descriptors (discussed next). a-characters include all d-characters as well as the following symbols: space; comma; semicolon; colon; period; question mark; exclamation point; right and left parentheses; single and double quotes; greater-than and less-than symbols; percent; ampersand; equals; asterisk; plus and minus (hyphen) symbols; and forward slash.

ISO-9660 *Volume Descriptors* are optional information fields recorded at the beginning of the data area on the disc. Volume Descriptors were originally intended for use by CD publishers, but may be used by anyone who creates an ISO-9660 disc, assuming the mastering software supports assigning ISO Volume Descriptors (some don't, or support only some of the available volume descriptors). ISO-9660 Volume Descriptors include the following, with allowable sizes in parentheses:

System Name

The operating system for which the disc is intended (0 to 32 a-characters).

Volume Name

The disc name, displayed by the OS when the disc is mounted (0 to 32 a-characters).

Volume Set Name
> Used in multidisc sets to assign a common group name to each disc in the set (0 to 32 d-characters).

Publisher's Name
> The publisher of the disc (0 to 128 a-characters).

Data Preparer's Name
> The author of the disc content (0 to 128 a-characters).

Application Name
> .The name of the program, if any, needed to access data on the disc (0 to 128 a-characters).

Copyright File Name
> Points to a file (which, if present, must reside in the root directory of the disc) that contains copyright information (maximum 8.3 d-characters).

Abstract File Name
> Points to a file (which, if present, must reside in the root directory of the disc) that contains text describing the contents of the disc (maximum 8.3 d-characters).

Bibliographic File Name
> Points to a file (which, if present, may reside in any directory on the disc) that contains bibliographic information, such as ISBN number (maximum 8.3 d-characters).

Date Fields
> Four Volume Descriptor fields exist for dates: Creation Date; Modification Date; Expiration Date; and Effective Date. Each of these fields, if present, stores a date and time in the following format, with size given in bytes in parentheses: Year (4); Month (2); Day (2); Hour (2); Minute (2); Second (2); Hundredths of a second (2); Timezone (1 byte, signed integer; specifies the number of 15-minute increments from UCT from -48 West to +52 East).

ISO-9660 Variants

The very real limitations of ISO-9660 formatted discs gave rise to several alternative formats, all of which were based on ISO-9660:

Rock Ridge
> The *Rock Ridge format* is an extension of the ISO-9660 format, intended for use on Unix systems, which have much more liberal restrictions on the length of and characters used in filenames and directory names, as well as the depth of directories. Using Rock Ridge allows a CD to support long mixed-case filenames, symbolic links, and other conventions common to Unix systems. Although full Rock Ridge support is available only on Unix systems, a system running MS-DOS, Windows, or the Mac OS can still access the data on a Rock Ridge disc, but not the long filenames and other extended information. The Rock Ridge standard is available at *ftp://ftp.ymi.com/pub/rockridge* if you want to learn more about it.

Romeo

The *Romeo format* is an obsolete extension to ISO-9660, developed by Adaptec as a stopgap measure for early versions of its EasyCD premastering software. The *raison d'être* for the cutely named Romeo format was that Windows NT 3.5a did not support the proprietary Microsoft Joliet format, described next. Romeo supports filenames of up to 128 characters, including spaces. However, unlike Joliet, Romeo supports neither the Unicode character set nor associated short (MS-DOS 8.3) filenames. Romeo-formatted discs can be read under Windows NT 3.51 and 4.0, Windows 98/SE/Me, and Windows 2000/XP. Because there is no associated short filename, Romeo-formatted discs cannot be read under MS-DOS. Romeo-formatted discs can be read on a Macintosh to the extent that they do not use filenames that exceed 31 characters. The Romeo format was essentially overtaken by events, was seldom used even when current, and is almost never encountered today.

Joliet

Joliet is an extension of ISO-9660, developed by Microsoft to allow CDs to support long filenames, the Unicode character set, and associated short (MS-DOS 8.3) filenames. Joliet allows filenames up to 64 characters, including spaces. When read on a system running Windows 9X, Windows NT 4, Windows 2000/XP, or recent releases of Linux, a Joliet-formatted disc displays long file and directory names. When read on a system running an operating system that does not support Microsoft long filename standards, the Joliet-formatted disc is recognized as a standard ISO-9660 disc. Full information about the Joliet standard is available at *http://www-plateau.cs. berkeley.edu/people/chaffee/jolspec.html*.

Consider logical formatting issues carefully if you plan to use CD-R premastering software to back up a hard disk that uses Windows long filenames and long folder names. ISO formatting restrictions mean that it's quite possible to have multiple subdirectories in one directory (or multiple files in one directory) whose long names are unambiguous, but whose truncated names are not. That means you might be unable to copy all files to CD unless you are very careful about using filenames and directory names that will truncate to unambiguous short names.

Universal Disc Format (UDF)

ISO-9660 and its variants were designed for duplicating or premastering discs, but were never intended to allow incrementally adding small amounts of data to a disc. Although ISO-9660 allows adding data to a disc (until that disc has been closed), the only way to do so is by opening a new session on that disc. That means that writing even one new file incurs the overhead required for a new session, which ranges from 13 MB to 22 MB.

In part to address these ISO-9660 limitations, OSTA defined a new logical format for optical discs. The official designation of this format is *ISO 13346* but the common name is *Universal Disc Format (UDF)*. UDF is an operating system-independent logical formatting standard that defines how data is written to various types of optical discs, including CD-R, CD-(M)RW, DVD-ROM, DVD-Video, and DVD-Audio. UDF uses a redesigned directory structure that allows small amounts of data (called *packets*) to be written incrementally and individually to disc without incurring the large overhead associated with writing a new session under ISO-9660.

In effect, with UDF each packet is written as a subsession within a standard session, incurring the standard session overhead only when that standard session is closed. Packet-writing software typically closes the session automatically when the disc is ejected using the eject feature of the software. As with ISO-9660, an open session on a UDF-formatted disc can be read only by a CD recorder. Closing the session allows the disc to be read by a standard CD-ROM drive or CD player. It's possible, however, subsequently to open a new session and add additional packet data to the disc.

In addition to session overhead, UDF addresses another issue that makes ISO-9660 completely inappropriate for packet writing. ISO-9660 must know, in advance, exactly which files are to be written during a session. It uses this information to create and write the *Path Tables* and *Primary Volume Descriptors* that point to the physical locations of the files on disc. Because packet writing allows any arbitrarily selected file to be written to disc at any time, the information that ISO-9660 requires is not available before the write occurs.

UDF solves this problem by accumulating data about the physical locations of files as they are written. At the end of a packet-writing session, UDF consolidates these location pointers and writes them to disc as the *Virtual Allocation Table* (*VAT*). The VAT address of a file remains the same, even if it is overwritten. At the end of each packet-writing session, UDF creates a new VAT that includes not just the pointers for newly created or modified files, but also the pointers stored in the old VAT. That means the current VAT always includes pointers to every file that has been written to the disc since it was originally formatted.

 The advantages of packet writing come at the cost of reduced capacity. A typical CD-R/RW disc stores about 650 MB with ISO-9660 formatting, but stores only about 500 MB with UDF formatting. About 100 MB of that reduced capacity is accounted for by the complex UDF directory and control structures that allow data to be added and deleted incrementally. The remaining 50 MB or so is used to implement various measures to distribute wear evenly across the CD-RW disc, preventing some areas from being overused and thereby rendered unwritable while other areas remain lightly used.

Two versions of UDF are in common use:

UDF 1.02

UDF 1.02 was adopted in August 1996, and is the finalized version of the October 1995 UDF 1.0 specification. UDF 1.02 specifies standards for DVD and DVD-ROM, but does not support writable optical media. Windows NT 4, Windows 98/SE/Me, and Windows 2000/XP include native UDF 1.02 support that allows them to access DVD video and DVD-ROM discs natively.

UDF 1.5

> UDF 1.5 was adopted in February 1997, and addresses the requirements of sequential recorded media, including CD-R, CD-RW, and DVD-RAM. UDF 1.5 adds the VAT that is analogous to the DOS File Allocation Table, and, optionally, the *Sparing Table* that allows bad sectors to be marked as unusable and replaced by spare sectors. Windows 2000/XP includes native UDF 1.5 support, but Windows NT and Windows 9X do not. You can download UDF 1.5 reader software for these versions of Windows from *http://www.roxio.com*.

The UDF 2.0 and 2.01 specifications are available, but not yet commonly used in commercial products. For more information about UDF, see *http://www.osta.org*.

CD Recording Methods

There are several ways to write data to a CD-R or CD-RW disc. Not all CD writers support all of these methods, but any method that a drive does support can be used to write to either a CD-R or CD-RW disc in that drive:

Disc-at-Once (DAO)

> *Disc-at-Once (DAO)* recording writes the entire CD in one pass. The entire write must be completed without interruption. Once the write completes, no further data can be written to that disc. DAO recording can be used to write a single track (typical when creating a data disc) or multiple tracks (typical when creating an audio disc).

Track-at-Once (TAO)

> *Track-at-Once (TAO)* recording allows writing in multiple passes, as many as 99 tracks on a disc. Each track must be at least 300 blocks long, which translates to 600 KB for a typical data CD. TAO recording consumes 150 blocks in overhead for run-in, run-out, pregap, and linking. Also, because the LASER must be stopped and restarted for each track, there is at least one empty *run-out block* following each track and one empty *run-in block* preceding each new track. If the drive and burning software handle TAO recording properly, there will ordinarily be only one pair of run-out/run-in blocks between tracks. These blocks will be empty and therefore silent and ordinarily unnoticeable.
>
> Some combinations of drives and software handle TAO imperfectly, placing garbage data in the run-out/run-in interstices that results in audible pops on audio CDs. Also, some drive/software combinations enforce a fixed-length pause between audio tracks, introducing a 2-second pause between tracks even if that pause was not present on the source.

Session-at-Once (SAO)

> *Session-at-Once (SAO)* is a hybrid recording method that combines the advantages of DAO and TAO recording, allowing multiple sessions (as with TAO), but with DAO-like control over the interstitial track gaps.

Packet writing

> *Packet writing* is an alternative to DAO, TAO, or SAO recording that provides much finer granularity in session size. Packet writing supports multiple writes per track, requiring only seven overhead blocks per write—four for run-in, two

for run-out, and one for linking. Because an entire packet can fit in the writer's buffer, and because packets can be written independently, using packet writing effectively eliminates buffer underrun errors, which is one major reason for its popularity. Each packet is written independently, and can therefore be thought of as a very small session. But because each packet is written independently, there is a short break between packets, just as a small break exists between sessions on a multisession disc.

Packet writing is inherently slower than premastering because of the overhead required to create and manipulate the packets. A given group of files that requires five minutes to copy from hard disk to a CD-RW disc using premastering software may require twice that long to copy using packet-writing software. Because packet-writing software is normally used to provide DLA for drag-and-drop file manipulation, this speed differential is usually not an issue. However, if you need to copy large amounts of data, be aware that you will incur a significant performance penalty if you do so using packet-writing rather than premastering software.

Packet writing may use *fixed-length packets* or *variable-length packets*, each of which has some advantages.

Fixed-length packets
All packets written to any particular track are the same size (although packet size may differ between tracks). When using fixed-length packets, the CD writer waits until it has received enough data to fill a packet, assembles that packet, and writes it to disc. Buffer underruns are never an issue with fixed-length packets because packet size is always much smaller than the capacity of the CD writer's buffer. With fixed-length packets, the interpacket gap occurs at predictable locations, which makes discs written with fixed-length packets more likely to be readable by older CD-ROM drives, many of which are confused by the unpredictable locations of interpacket gaps on discs written with variable-length packets. Finally, a disc written with fixed-length packets allows file-by-file erase, whereas one written with variable-length packets can be erased only by reformatting it. Most current packet-writing software uses fixed-length packets.

Variable-length packets
The size of the packet varies according to the data stream. Small files may be written as a single packet, which reduces the number of write operations and increases both data storage efficiency and performance. Depending on the maximum packet length, any given packet may exceed the size of the CD writer's buffer, which again raises the specter of buffer underruns (although BURN-Proof and similar technologies used on recent CD writers eliminate the danger of buffer underruns). Discs written with variable-length packets are often unreadable on standard CD-ROM drives, and in CD writers that do not support variable-length packets (which includes quite a few older drives). Few current packet-writing software packages support variable-length packets, due to the inability of a disc written with variable-length packets to have individual files erased.

Any drive you buy should support all four of these modes. Sometimes DAO recording is the only usable method. For example, duplicating some CDs (particularly copy-protected games and so on) requires DAO. Also, DAO may be required to premaster a disc that will subsequently be pressed by a commercial duplicator because commercial pressing plants may recognize TAO gaps as errors, although that is less common today. TAO is useful when you are assembling a CD from various sources. Most (but not all) modern CD writers support both DAO and TAO mode. SAO is seldom absolutely required, but can be useful for special purposes, such as writing CD-Extra discs. Relatively few CD writers (notably Plextor models) support SAO. Packet writing is necessary if you want to use the drive as a logical volume within Windows. All CD-(M)RW drives and most (but not all) modern CD-R drives support packet writing. Not all, however, support both fixed- and variable-length packets.

In our experience, CD-R/RW packet writing as a technology is not quite ready for prime time because of the nagging compatibility issues that continue to plague it, including the following:

Writing software incompatibilities

Packet-writing software, such as Roxio DirectCD, functions by creating a virtual disc volume and assigning that drive letter to the CD-RW disc. For example, if your CD-(M)RW drive is D:, packet-writing software may assign the virtual volume E: to the CD-RW disc. When you drag and drop files between your hard disk and the CD-RW disc, you do so using E: rather than D:. In our experience, these virtual volumes often conflict on systems that use other software that creates virtual volumes, such as some tape drive software. Also, even when installed on a system without such other software, packet-writing software is often plagued by other incompatibilities, particularly on Windows 2000 and Windows XP systems.

Firmware problems

How well a drive supports packet writing is largely determined by the quality of its firmware, so just because a drive's specs claim that it supports packet writing doesn't necessarily mean that it does so well, or even adequately. We have found that the best drives for packet writing are those made by Plextor, which is no surprise. Plextor always does things right, and refuses to ship drives until it has all the issues worked out. That's probably why, for example, Plextor did not ship a DVD-ROM drive (let alone a DVD-recordable drive) until May 2002, more than three years after other manufacturers started shipping such drives in volume.

 Note that a simple firmware upgrade is insufficient to add packet-writing capability to a drive that does not support packet writing. Packet writing requires specific hardware that is not present on some CD-R drives, particularly older models.

The readability of packet-written discs in standard drives also varies. Older CD-ROM drives, particularly those that use read-ahead optimization, often generate read errors caused by the inter-packet gaps. Also, packet-writing software differs in how it closes discs. Some software closes the disc to UDF format, which means that disc can be read by a CD-ROM drive only if that drive is MultiRead-compatible and the system has UDF drivers installed. Other packet-writing software, notably Adaptec DirectCD 3.0, closes the disc to ISO-9660 format by putting what amounts to an ISO-9660 wrapper around the UDF contents. But DirectCD uses ISO-9660 Level 3 extents, which means the resulting disc may be impossible to read in systems running something other than Windows NT 4, Windows 98/SE/Me, or Windows 2000/XP.

 Although packet-writing software such as DirectCD and InCD has become associated in many people's minds with CD-RW media and premastering software such as Nero and EasyCD with CD-R media, there's really no such correlation. It's possible to premaster to a CD-RW disc, just as it's possible to use packet writing on a CD-R disc. We hate to risk any of our original audio CDs in our work area—they're likely to be sat upon or worse—so we frequently dupe an original audio CD to a CD-RW disc and play the copy. Similarly, we frequently keep a CD-R disc in a writer on a system with packet-writing software installed. That makes it trivially easy to back up by dragging and dropping our current working files onto the CD-R disc, which has the advantage relative to a CD-RW disc of being permanent.

So if you've gotten the idea that CD-R equals premastering and CD-RW equals packet writing, readjust your thinking. There are many advantages to using CD-RW discs for things generally thought of as being jobs for CD-R, just as there are many advantages to using CD-R discs for things usually considered to be CD-RW applications. The only difference between CD-R and CD-RW is that the latter is erasable. Period.

An emerging packet-writing technology called *Mount Rainier* (or *Mt. Rainier*; not even the sponsors have decided which form to use) addresses all of the problems common to earlier packet-writing methods. The Mount Rainier specification (*http://www.mt-rainier.org*) originated from a consortium founded by Compaq, Microsoft, Philips, and Sony, and now enjoys broad industry support. Mount Rainier drives, also called CD-MRW drives, are second-generation CD-RW drives that have hardware capabilities not present in older CD-RW drives.

A PC running a Mount Rainier-aware operating system natively recognizes a Mount Rainier drive and assigns it a drive letter at boot time, just as it would for a floppy drive or hard drive. The Mount Rainier drive appears as just another drive to the operating system and applications. You can create, copy, move, and delete files on the Mount Rainier drive just as you would on a floppy drive or hard drive. In effect, Mount Rainier replaces packet-writing applications such as Roxio DirectCD and Nero InCD by adding their functionality to the operating system itself. Mount Rainier has five key elements:

Hardware-based physical defect management
Existing packet-writing technologies use the software-based defect management provided by UDF 1.50, which requires a separate software layer running between the operating system and the CD writer hardware. CD-

MRW drives manage physical media defects in hardware, which means the operating system can treat a CD-MRW drive as it would any other drive—send data to it and allow the drive itself to be responsible for writing the data without errors. For increased reliability, Mount Rainier specifies two media defect tables, a main defect table in the lead-in area and a second copy in the lead-out area. During formatting, the drive identifies bad blocks and writes their addresses to both defect tables. Bad blocks are logically remapped to known-good blocks near the lead-out area, so data that would otherwise have been written to a bad block is instead written to a replacement block. In addition to being faster and more reliable, hardware-based defect management has the considerable advantage of isolating the operating system and applications from the underlying data integrity mechanism, which simplifies matters by presenting a standardized high-level interface to software that writes data to the CD-MRW drive.

2 KB logical write-addressing

Current CD-RW standards use a 64 KB block size, which is inefficient when storing small files and is a poor match for the 2 KB or 4 KB addressing used by hard disk drives and other standard storage devices. In particular, this mismatch in block sizes introduces filesystem inefficiencies and caching issues when transferring data between standard CD-RW drives and hard drives. Mount Rainier eliminates this performance bottleneck by adopting a 2 KB block size to allow efficient, transparent bidirectional transfers and caching between CD-MRW drives and hard drives.

Background formatting and fast eject

Standard CD-RW packet-writing applications can write only to a disc that has already been formatted. Unlike standard packet writing, in which formatting is a software function that must be complete before data can be written to the disc, Mount Rainier drives format discs transparently in the background as a function of the drive hardware, and can write data to a partially formatted disc. When you insert an unformatted disc in a Mt. Rainier drive, you can begin writing data to that disc within seconds after it spins up. The drive continues formatting the disc in the background until the process completes. If you eject a disc before formatting is complete, the data written to that disc is readable. When you reinsert the disc, the drive simply continues formatting from the point it stopped formatting. Because formatting is a low-priority background operation, the drive responds quickly to user read and write requests even while a disc is being formatted.

The Mount Rainier specification also incorporates a requirement for fast eject. With legacy CD writers, ejecting a disc may take several seconds to half a minute or more, depending on what the drive happens to be doing when you tell it to eject the disc. Mount Rainier drives eject discs very quickly, like a CD-ROM drive, because they give priority to write operations and do not require finalizing or other time-consuming operations before ejecting a disc.

Command set implementation

Older CD writers use hybrid command sets, sometimes including portions of the MMC-1 and MMC-2 command sets mixed with proprietary commands. That's why CD-burning software always lists supported drive models and may not work correctly or at all with a drive that is not on the supported list. To support a particular CD writer, the burning software must be coded to take all of the quirks of that model into account. Mount Rainier eliminates this hodgepodge of incompatible, incomplete, and proprietary command sets by mandating that all Mount Rainier drives be fully compliant with the MMC-2 command set. Because the command set is standardized and mandated, the operating system can assume that any Mount Rainier drive includes at least the minimum required feature set and will respond predictably to commands.

Compatibility and standards compliance

Backward compatibility and standards compliance are an important part of the Mount Rainier specification. Although only an MRW drive can write an MRW-formatted disc, any optical drive that can read CD-RW media can read an MRW-formatted disc. If the operating system has Mount Rainier support, nothing additional is needed for reading MRW discs in any optical drive, or for writing and reading MRW discs in a Mount Rainier drive. If the operating system does not have Mount Rainier support, MRW drives require a helper application to read or write MRW discs, and standard drives need a helper application to read MRW discs.

 Right now, there are no operating systems with Mount Rainier support, although that support is promised for Windows XP, Mac OS, and Linux.

Buffer Underrun Protection

In the past, anyone who used a CD writer sometimes made *coasters*, the common term for a ruined CD-R blank. Although packet writing and UDF effectively eliminated coasters, packet-writing software was useless for batch-mode tasks, such as duplicating CDs. Those tasks demanded premastering software, which unfortunately was by no means immune to generating coasters.

Originally, CD premastering was inherently an isochronous (time-dependent) process because data had to be delivered to the write head in a continuous stream from the time the write began until it completed. If that stream was interrupted long enough for the data stored in the writer's buffer to be exhausted—an accident called a *buffer underrun*—the blank was ruined. Buffer underruns were particularly common with IDE/ATAPI CD writers, although they were by no means rare even on SCSI burners.

Sanyo effectively made buffer underruns a thing of the past by developing a technology called *BURN-Proof* (*Buffer UnderRuN-Proof*) and licensing it to CD writer makers. In simple terms, BURN-Proof turns off the writing LASER when it runs out of data to write (duh), and then, when data is again available, restarts the burn exactly where it left off. In effect, BURN-Proof converts CD writing from an isochronous process to an asynchronous one.

BURN-Proof works by constantly monitoring the status of the CD writer's buffer to detect a potential buffer underrun condition. If the amount of buffered data falls to a critically low level, the BURN-Proof firmware finishes writing the current sector and then turns off the writing LASER until the amount of buffered data returns to an acceptably high level. When that occurs, the BURN-Proof firmware repositions the writing LASER to begin writing where it left off.

 If BURN-Proof kicks in, the resulting disc is not literally identical to a disc that was written without a buffer underrun occurring. Rather than restarting the write on the sector immediately following the last sector written before the buffer underrun, BURN-Proof must leave a short gap—the length of which varies with recording speed—between the last pre-underrun and the first post-underrun data sectors. Error correction circuitry on nearly all CD drives and players eliminates this minor hiccough, but very old CD drives and players may deal with it poorly—for example, by playing back an audible pop on an audio CD burned with BURN-Proof. Note that this condition applies only if BURN-Proof kicks in during the burn. If no buffer underrun occurs during the burn, discs produced on a BURN-Proof drive are indistinguishable from those produced on any other CD writer.

Our first experience with BURN-Proof was with the superb Plextor PlexWriter 12/10/32A IDE CD writer. With standard IDE CD writers we hesitated even to move the mouse while burning. We walked softly and worried about vibration from passing trucks. But the Plextor 12/10/32A and later PlexWriters eliminated those worries. Plextor CD writers with BURN-Proof are so robust that we successfully burned a disc from an image file on the hard drive *while we were defragging that hard drive*—a guaranteed way to ruin a disc with any CD writer that lacks buffer underrun protection.

The success of PlexWriter drives with BURN-Proof made buffer underrun protection a must-have feature, so other manufacturers soon followed with similar technologies. Nowadays, even inexpensive CD writers have some form of buffer underrun protection, whether the original BURN-Proof or a competing technology. Yamaha, for example, calls its method SAFEBURN. Sony calls it Power Burn, and LITE-ON calls it Buffer Underrun Free. The various technologies differ in minor respects, but all of them work.

It takes much longer to write a disc if the buffer underrun protection kicks in repeatedly, but the write does complete normally, and we have never had a problem reading the resulting discs. Unfortunately, buffer underrun protection cannot be retrofitted to an existing CD writer. If you want buffer underrun protection (and you should), the only way to get it is to buy a CD writer that supports it. Fortunately, CD writers are very inexpensive, and if your current writer is old enough to lack buffer underrun protection you probably need a new, faster writer anyway.

Buffer underrun protection works only if the burning software explicitly supports the specific buffer underrun technology used by the drive. For example, software that supports BURN-Proof for a Plextor drive may not support SAFEBURN on a similar Yamaha drive. If the software does not support the specific type of buffer underrun protection used by the drive, the feature is disabled, and you're as likely to burn coasters as if the drive had no buffer underrun protection. Most drives are bundled with burning software that fully supports their features, but you may not want to use the software provided with the drive. If you use third-party software, such as Nero Burning ROM, make sure your specific drive model appears on the compatibility list for the software.

Choosing a CD Writer

Use the following guidelines when choosing a CD writer:

Transfer rate

As with CD-ROM drives, throughput is rated in comparison to standard CD-DA, which transfers 150 KB/s, and is designated 1X. CD-(M)RW drives have three speeds. Usually, but not always, the first number refers to how fast data can be written to a CD-R disc, the second to how fast data can be written to a CD-RW disc, and the third to how fast the drive can read data. For example, a Plextor 48/24/48A writes CD-R discs at 48X, rewrites CD-RW discs at 24X, and reads discs at 48X. Note that fast CD writers use "max" ratings. For example, the PlexWriter 48/24/48A writes at 48Xmax, rather than writing at 48X across the entire disc surface. Also, fast CD writers sometimes have a lower maximum write speed for audio than for data. For example, a drive might write data at 40Xmax, but CD-DA audio at only 24X.

Average access

Most CD writers use heavier heads than CD-ROM drives, and so may have relatively slow average access times. For example, the Plextor 40/12/40A burner has an average access of 120 ms, much slower than the fastest CD-ROM drives. Some CD burners shipped in 2002 or later have greatly improved average access times. For example, the Plextor 48/24/48A has average access of only 65 ms. If you use a burner primarily for duping CDs, average access is relatively unimportant. If you use it heavily for reading CDs or for packet writing, average access time is more important. Current models range from about 65 ms to more than 300 ms average access. Buy a model with average access of 100 ms or less.

Interface

We used to tell readers that, all other things being equal, creating CDs was less trouble-prone with SCSI rather than ATAPI, and Windows 2000/XP rather than Windows 9X. The second part of that advice remains true. CD burning is more reliable under Windows 2000/XP than under Windows 98/SE/Me. But the first part of that advice is obsolete. The best modern ATAPI drives, such as the PlexWriter 48/24/48A, are at least as reliable as the best SCSI CD burners. Nowadays, we regard SCSI CD burners as a niche product.

About the only situation in which they are still superior to modern ATAPI burners is when you need to burn the same data to several CD writers simultaneously, as in commercial short-run duplication. If your needs are more typical, choose an ATAPI burner. Make sure that any drive you buy supports at least UDMA-2 (ATA-33).

Buffer size

Even on drives with BURN-Proof or similar technology, a large buffer is desirable because it helps prevent buffer underruns, whether or not those underruns are intercepted and corrected. For maximum reliability, a CD burner should have at least a 2 MB buffer, and 4 MB is better. Some current models have only 1 MB, and a few 512 KB or less.

Mt. Rainier support

Many drives do not support Mt. Rainier. Make sure the one you buy does.

Supported formats and methods

Any burner you buy should support at least the following:

Read-mode formats

CD-DA (Audio CD), CD-ROM, CD-ROM/XA, Audio-combined CD-ROM, CD-I, CD-I Ready, CD Bridge, Video CD, CD-Extra, CD-R (Orange Book Part II), and CD-RW (Orange Book Part III)

Write-mode formats

CD-DA (Audio CD), CD-ROM, CD-ROM/XA, Audio-combined CD-ROM, CD-I, CD-I Ready, CD Bridge, Video CD, CD-Extra, CD-RW, and CD-MRW

Writing methods

Disc-at-Once, Session-at-Once, Track-at-Once, multisession, fixed-length packet writing, variable-length packet writing, and Mount Rainier

Software

The software you use is as important as the CD-R hardware. Nearly all CD burners are bundled with various software, which is described in the following section. Despite the fact that it's "free," bundled software is not always the best choice.

CD Writer Software

A CD-R or CD-RW drive is a dumb device, which the operating system sees as just another CD-ROM drive. Using the drive to burn CDs requires special application software to enable writing, which may be bundled with the operating system or CD writer. Other than the drive itself and the discs you use, the most important element in obtaining fast, accurate burns is the software you use. Two major types of software are used with CD writers:

Premastering

Used to create a CD in a continuous batch mode operation. Premastering software allows you to duplicate entire discs, sessions, or tracks, and is most frequently used to replicate audio and data CDs or backup files from the hard drive. You can also use premastering software to assemble custom audio CDs that comprise individual tracks from several audio CDs or to create CDs that contain your own data with a layout that you define. Roxio Easy CD Creator is the most commonly bundled premastering software for Windows, but we much prefer Nero Burning ROM.

Packet writing

In addition to batch premastering, which all burners support, some burners support packet-writing mode. In simple terms, packet writing extends the Orange Book CD-R multisession specification. With early burners, you had to record the entire disc in one continuous operation. Orange Book Part II allowed keeping a volume open for multiple recording sessions. Packet writing goes further, allowing a session to remain open while adding discrete packets. Packet-writing software allows the drive to be addressed as just another Windows volume, much like a gigantic floppy disk. You can create, delete, and rename files and folders by using drag-and-drop or other standard Windows methods, including saving directly to the CD-R(W) disc from within programs such as Word. Roxio DirectCD is the most commonly bundled packet-writing software, but we much prefer InCD.

 Windows XP, the first Windows version to bundle a CD burning applet, includes a feature-reduced version of Roxio Easy CD Creator. Most Linux distributions include comprehensive premastering software, but have only limited support for packet writing.

Alas, the rapidly dropping price of CD burners has led some vendors to scrimp on the software bundle. Rather than include mainstream full-function packages, they instead supply simple, proprietary individual applets that perform basic functions. Although these applets are generally usable, you'll want one of the mainstream packages to get the most from your drive, so when comparing prices, include the cost of buying both a premastering application and a packet-writing application in the cost comparison. If your drive does come bundled with mainstream applications, always visit the software vendor's web site immediately to check for updates before you use the drive.

In addition to the third-party software that is supplied with the drive, do not overlook proprietary software. Some vendors, notably Plextor, supply a wide range of powerful and useful utilities with their drives. Although these utilities are Windows-only and typically support only that manufacturer's drive, they often provide enhanced capabilities not available in the third-party applications.

Recent Linux releases include all the tools you need to premaster discs, although this software takes the form of the "building block" utilities *cdrecord*, *mkisofs* and *cdrdao*, and GUI frontends such as X-CD-Roast, gcombust, KonCD, and Gnome Toaster rather than integrated applications such as Easy CD and Nero Burning ROM. Still, all the tools are present, and burning CDs under Linux is easy enough, albeit a bit Spartan for the taste of many Windows users. For all of that, our first attempt to burn a CD under Linux succeeded, which is something we can't say for Windows.

One of the most important and frequently overlooked aspects of CD burner software is firmware, which determines the capabilities and compatibility of the drive.

Good drives allow user-installable firmware updates. Good makers supply firmware updates as necessary to keep their drives current with changing conditions and standards. For example, a newly introduced disc type may require a different LASER power and write scheme than media supported by the existing firmware. If your drive's manufacturer makes the required update available, you can install it yourself and use that new media. If not, you're stuck with an increasingly obsolescent drive that may ultimately become unusable when the media it supports are no longer available. Note that most drives that do not support packet mode cannot be upgraded by a simple firmware update. Packet writing requires specific physical drive capabilities, and drives that do not have those capabilities will never support packet writing.

Installing and Configuring a CD Writer

In general, installing and configuring a CD writer requires the same steps detailed in the preceding chapter for CD-ROM drives. There are, however, some considerations peculiar to CD writers:

- For ATAPI writers, it is good practice to put the CD writer on a different channel from the source device(s). On a typical PC with a hard drive, a CD-ROM drive, and the CD writer, make the hard drive Primary Master (PM), the CD-ROM drive Primary Slave (PS), and the CD writer Secondary Master (SM). This allows you to record CDs directly from CD-ROM or from an image stored on your hard drive. If the PC has a second hard drive, set that drive to Secondary Slave (SS), and do not attempt to record CDs from it. If the PC has an ATAPI tape drive, set it to SS. Attempting to record from a source located on the same IDE channel as the writer generally works properly with recent systems and high-quality CD writers, but often leads to problems on older, slower systems and with inexpensive or older-model CD writers.

- If you have IDE bus mastering (DMA) drivers installed, remove them from the channel to which the writer connects, unless the drive manufacturer specifically recommends using DMA for its drive. We have frequently encountered problems with ATAPI writers on DMA-enabled channels, even when the writer was recognized by Windows as a DMA-capable device. Conversely, make sure DMA is enabled if your CD writer manual recommends doing so. Many CD writers faster than 16X require DMA mode for proper operation. If you are installing a CD writer that requires DMA mode and it shares a channel with another device, make sure the second device also supports DMA and is configured to use DMA. If the second device operates in PIO mode, that forces the channel to operate in PIO mode, which may render the CD writer unreliable or nonfunctional.

- SCSI writers coexist well on a host adapter shared with low-demand devices or those that will not be used while a CD is being burned, but you *may* have problems if you connect the burner to the same SCSI bus that supports hard drives. We have several SCSI systems with hard drives and CD writers connected to the same SCSI bus, and have never encountered a problem with that configuration. But we have received enough reports from readers who have had problems putting a hard drive and writer on the same SCSI channel that we believe this may sometimes be an issue. It's OK for a writer to share with scanners, tape drives, Zip drives, and similar devices. But if you encounter problems sharing the channel between your hard drive and writer, install a second inexpensive SCSI host adapter to support the writer and other non-hard disk SCSI peripherals.

- When you install a SCSI burner, never depend on the SCSI drivers supplied with the operating system. The bundled drivers are fine for hard disks and low-demand peripherals, but often have bugs and missing features that cause problems with CD writers. Download the latest drivers and ASPI files for your SCSI host adapter from the manufacturer's site.

- Writing CD-R discs—and more so writing CD-RW discs—generates considerable heat. Mounting the CD writer above other drives permits the heat to dissipate. If possible, mount the CD writer in a drive bay with unoccupied bays above and below it (particularly above it). If you frequently burn two or more CDs in quick sequence, install a drive cooler. PC Power & Cooling (*http://www.pcpowercooling.com/*) makes the best ones.

- Some CD writer manufacturers recommend specific registry tweaks or configuration changes to the operating system to support their drives optimally. Although we would never discourage anyone from following the manufacturer's advice, our experience is that these changes have little benefit on high-end (fast CPU, lots of memory, SCSI, Windows NT) systems, but are worth implementing on low-end (slow CPU, minimal memory, ATAPI, Windows 9X) systems.

Updating CD Writer Firmware

For most PC firmware, the cardinal rule is "if it ain't broke, don't fix it." It seldom makes sense, for example, to update your main PC BIOS unless you experience a BIOS-related problem or add new hardware that requires the BIOS update. But with CD writers, the rule is different: always install the latest available firmware for your CD writer.

Fortunately, updating CD writer firmware is usually remarkably trouble-free. If you screw up while updating your main system BIOS, you can render the system unusable. If you screw up while updating the firmware of your CD writer, you can simply run the firmware installation program again. We've updated many drives through many firmware revisions and have had very few problems doing so. There are two things to keep in mind, though:

Don't judge solely by make/model
Relatively few companies actually manufacture CD writers. Most companies, including some surprisingly large ones such as Hewlett-Packard, simply buy mechanisms from the actual maker and attach their name plates to the drives. Sometimes, companies sell different drives under the same model number. So if your friend has a Kamazuma CD-R523252 CD writer "just like" your Kamazuma CD-R523252, don't assume that you can use the same firmware update he did. Your drive may require a completely different firmware update file. Sometimes the only way to tell which firmware update you need is by comparing the serial number of your drive against the table posted by the manufacturer.

Don't assume that later firmware is necessarily better

In general, that's a safe assumption, but not always. We have (infrequently) encountered firmware updates that add functionality (such as support for 80-minute blanks) and fix some problems, but cause other problems. For example, in one case (we won't mention names because things like this happen to even the best manufacturers—and, no, it wasn't Plextor) we found that a CD writer with the new firmware would no longer use a particular type of blank that it had happily used before the update. Since we had a spindle of 100 of those blanks, we reverted to the older firmware version. So, when you visit the manufacturer's web site to download the latest firmware version for your CD writer, also download the earlier versions. They leave them posted there for a reason.

Determining the Firmware Revision of Your CD Writer

Before you update your CD writer firmware, it's a good idea to find out which version is already installed. That way, if you have problems under the new firmware, you can revert to a known configuration by reinstalling the older version. Most mainstream CD writer software can display detailed information about installed CD writers, including firmware revision level. If you run Windows, download a free copy of Nero InfoTool from *http://www.nero.com*. This utility, shown in Figure 11-1, is the best we've seen for viewing firmware level and other characteristics of a CD writer, and you can use it even if you don't have Nero Burning ROM.

You can also get some of this information directly from Windows, as described in the following sections.

Determining the firmware revision of your CD writer with Windows 9X

To determine which firmware revision your CD writer is using under Windows 9X, right-click My Computer and choose Properties to display the System Properties dialog. On the Device Manager page, locate the entry for CD-ROM and expand that entry to show installed CD-ROM devices. Double-click the entry for your CD writer to display Device Properties, and display the Settings page, shown in Figure 11-2.

Determining the firmware revision of your CD writer with Windows 2000

To determine which firmware revision your CD writer is using under Windows 2000, open the Control Panel, double-click Administrative Tools, then double-click Computer Management. Expand the tree to display the Storage → Removable Storage → Physical Locations branch, shown in Figure 11-3.

Locate the CD writer in the listing in the left pane. Right-click the name of the writer, choose Properties, and view the Device Info page, which includes the firmware revision number.

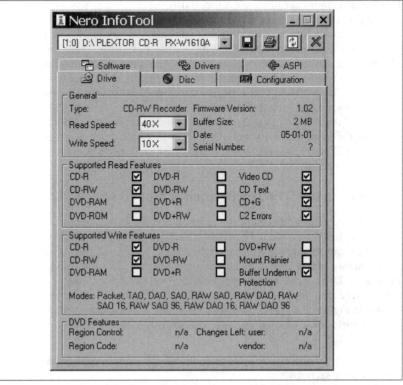

Figure 11-1. Nero InfoTool displaying the characteristics of this CD writer, showing the current firmware revision as 1.02

Determining the firmware revision of your CD writer with Windows XP

To determine which firmware revision your CD writer is using under Windows XP, open the Control Panel, double-click Administrative Tools, then double-click Computer Management. Expand the tree to display the Storage → Removable Storage → Libraries branch, shown in Figure 11-4.

Locate the CD writer in the listing in the left pane. Right-click the name of the writer, choose Properties, and view the Device Information page, which includes the firmware revision number.

Installing a Firmware Update

For Windows users, updating the firmware of a CD writer is normally just a matter of running a self-contained executable file or perhaps running an installer executable against a binary datafile. But read the directions before you proceed. For example, all firmware updates we've done require removing any disc from the drive before running the update. Also, firmware updates often specify that packet-writing software must not be running while the update is taking place. For safety's sake, we always disable all nonessential resident software and reboot the system before and after running the update.

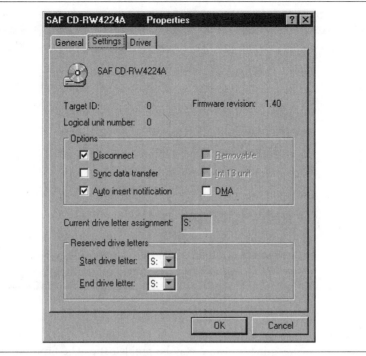

Figure 11-2. The Windows 98SE device Properties dialog, which shows that firmware revision 1.40 is installed on this CD writer

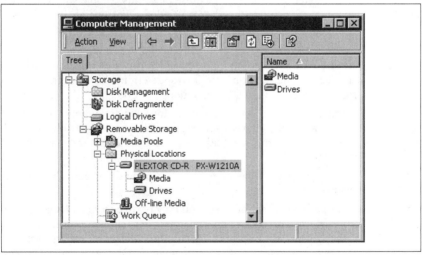

Figure 11-3. Using Windows 2000 Computer Management to view properties for the CD writer

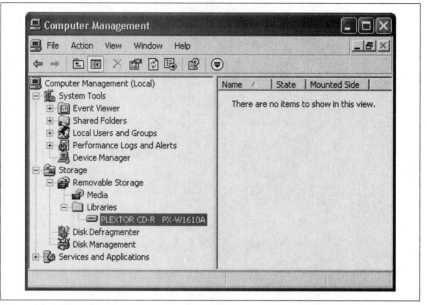

Figure 11-4. Using Windows XP Computer Management to view properties for the CD writer

For Linux users, updating firmware may be problematic. The firmware binaries themselves are almost never OS-specific, but the updater utility needed to flash them to the drive is. Most CD writer makers assume you run Windows or Mac OS and provide updater utilities only for those platforms. People who run Linux are out of luck, unless the system dual-boots Windows. Fortunately, there's more than one way to skin a cat. In decreasing order of ease and desirability, here are several ways to update your drive firmware under Linux:

- Ideally, choose a CD writer with Linux-friendly firmware updates available. If you must select among Linux-hostile drives, determine if one of those drives allows firmware updates via a DOS boot floppy or bootable CD.

- Search the Internet to find a Linux updater for your drive model. For example, the PXUpdate utility allows updating the firmware of some Plextor models using the binary firmware files supplied by Plextor for use with its Windows updater.

- If you have a spare drive or partition, install Windows long enough to update the firmware.

- Although we have not tried doing so, you may be able to run a DOS or Windows firmware updater under an emulator or virtual environment such as VMware (*http://www.vmware.com/*), Bochs (*http://bochs.sourceforge.net/*), or DOSEMU (*http://sourceforge.net/projects/dosemu/*). One of our editors notes, "Because most of the hardware is virtualized, this probably won't work. USB devices are a possible exception. I'm not certain that writers are even supported under VMWare; they may appear as regular CD-ROM drives."

- As a last resort, pull the drive from the Linux box and install it temporarily in a Windows system. Update the firmware and then move the drive back to the Linux system. This is one reason some people favor external CD writers for Linux systems.

- As a really last resort, allow yourself to be reassimilated by the borg. Strip your Linux box down to bare metal, install the latest version of Windows, and swear off using communistic free software. (No, we didn't choose this option, either...)

Although we update firmware regularly on Windows systems, we confess that we follow the "if it ain't broke, don't fix it" rule on Linux boxes. Perhaps hardware makers will eventually stop treating Linux users as second-class citizens, but until that day arrives we'll have to keep doing things the hard way. If you do buy a drive from a manufacturer that is clueless about Linux, it certainly can't hurt to complain to the company about its lack of Linux support.

Updating Drives with Foreign Firmware

Don't assume that you have to update your drive with firmware supplied by the drive maker. We know that sounds very strange. After all, installing, say, ASUS firmware on an ABIT motherboard is a fast way to render the motherboard useless. So who in his right mind would install, say, a Sony firmware update on an HP CD writer? Well, there are times when it may make sense to do exactly that.

For example, HP decided at one point not to issue updated firmware for its 8100i CD writer to support 80-minute CDs. As it happens, the HP-8100i drive is made by Sony, and is nearly identical to the Sony CRX100E drive. One of our readers decided to try updating his HP 8100i drive with the Sony CRX100E firmware, which did support 80-minute CDs. He ran the update. Sure enough, his drive accepted it and he was able to use 80-minute blanks. He now has a drive which is for all intents and purposes a Sony. The operating system says so, the CD writer software says so. The only thing HP about that drive now is the name on the bezel.

Such shenanigans are useful only for relabeled drives. For example, your new Brand-X CD-R522452 CD writer may actually be a relabeled Sony CRX220A1. But Brand-X may decide next month that Sony charges too much for its mechanisms and start buying Yamaha mechanisms instead. Most companies that sell relabeled drives are not very good about providing firmware updates for older models. When you visit the Brand-X web site, you may find that there are no firmware updates available, or that the most recent is a year or more old, which effectively means that your drive is orphaned. Don't despair, though. If you can find out who actually made the underlying mechanism, you *may* be able to get a recent firmware update for the drive under its real name (or from another OEM who uses the same mechanism).

For example, we own an antique Smart and Friendly SAF798 CD-R4224A CD Speedwriter Plus, which was the first CD writer we ever bought. That drive uses a JVC XR-W4080 mechanism, which is also used by the Creative Labs CD-R4224 drive. As an experiment, we downloaded the Creative Labs firmware update and installed it on the Smart and Friendly drive. That drive continued to work normally, although it reported itself as a Creative Labs drive until we reinstalled the Smart and Friendly firmware.

We would consider applying a foreign firmware update only in an emergency, such as the original vendor going bankrupt. If you try updating your CD writer with foreign firmware, you're on your own. **Don't blame us if it doesn't work, or even if your CD writer catches fire and burns down your computer.** Best case, the update will work. Worse case, it won't work, but will leave your drive in its original state. Worst case, the drive may cease functioning and you may not be able to return it to its original state. You have been warned.

Media Issues

There's been a lot of nonsense written about CD-R media. One person swears that gold/green discs are great and silver/blue discs worthless, and another says the opposite. The truth is that there are distinct differences in media, but no absolutes. Disc A may work perfectly in Drive A and not work at all in Drive B, and Disc B may work perfectly in Drive B and not at all in Drive A. That situation is less common with recent drives than it was with older models, but some drives still show a strong preference or dislike for particular disc types.

In general, newer drives, name-brand models, and those with current firmware are unlikely to have problems writing almost any brand of disc, except perhaps those you find on sale in the bargain bin. Older drives, no-name models, and those with outdated firmware may be very choosy indeed about which discs they'll use. Discs differ as follows.

CD-R blanks use one of these reflective layers:

Gold
> The metal used in early CD-R discs, and still used in some current discs. The advantage of gold is that it is stable. The disadvantage is that gold is expensive, even in the microscopically thin layers used in CD-R discs. As the price of CD-R discs plummeted, the cost of gold became an increasingly large part of the cost of the disc, which led some makers to substitute silver. By early 2002 many disc manufacturers had discontinued gold-based products or limited gold reflective layers to their premium or "professional" lines. Note that some CD-R discs that appear gold in fact use little or no gold in their formulations.

Silver alloy
> The advantages of silver alloy relative to gold are that it is relatively inexpensive and actually has better reflective characteristics across a wide spectrum. The chief disadvantage of silver is that it corrodes. Even a tiny crack in the label layer can allow airborne pollutants, particularly sulfur dioxide, to gain access to and react with the silver layer. If this occurs, the CD becomes unreadable.

Most current CD-R blanks use one of these dyes (although to avoid patent infringement, some disc manufacturers use similar but not identical dyes):

Cyanine
> As the name indicates, this dye is cyan (bluish-green) in color. Used with a gold reflective layer, cyanine-based discs appear green on the clear side and

gold on the label side (the so-called "green/gold" discs). Used with a silver reflective layer, cyanine discs appear light blue/silver. Cyanine was the first dye used to make CD-R discs, and quickly developed a reputation for stability problems. That has been overcome in current discs by using metal-stabilized cyanine. The advantage of cyanine is that it is more sensitive to light than other dyes, which means that cyanine discs tolerate a wider range of LASER power settings, making them more likely to be compatible with any given drive and firmware revision. For example, a typical cyanine disc can be written with a LASER power setting between 5.5 and 7.5 milliwatts, while a typical pthalocyanine disc requires 5.0 to 6.0 milliwatts. On the downside, accelerated aging tests show expected lifetimes for cyanine-based discs of "only" 50 years or so, significantly less than other dyes. In practical terms, no one 50 years from now will have a drive capable of reading any CD, so this matters little.

Pthalocyanine

This dye is a very pale yellow-green color, approaching colorless. With a gold reflective layer, discs appear gold/gold or greenish-gold/gold. With a silver layer, they appear light yellow-green/silver or even silver/silver. Because cyanine-based CD-R discs were protected by patent, other manufacturers developed alternative dyes, including pthalocyanine. The one thing to be said in favor of pthalocyanine is that its lower light sensitivity relative to cyanine gives it estimated archival stability of nearly 100 years. Lower light sensitivity also means that pthalocyanine-based CD-R discs are less likely to be compat-ible with any given CD-R drive, particularly an older model. All recent CD-R drives support pthalocyanine-based discs, and most older models can accom-modate them with a firmware upgrade.

Azo

This dye from Mitsubishi Chemical is a deep blue color. Azo discs use a silver reflective layer, which gives the data side a very deep blue color. Azo is even less sensitive to light than pthalocyanine, which gives azo-based discs expected archival stability of more than 100 years, and makes drive support even more problematic than with pthalocyanine. All recent CD-R drives support azo-based discs, and most older models can accommodate them with a firmware upgrade. Due to their insensitivity, some early azo-based discs did not support writing faster than 1X or 2X, but current azo-based discs such as the Verbatim Super Azo discs can be written at 48X or faster.

There is no single answer to the question, "Which is best?" There are numerous variables in the CD-R manufacturing process. The thickness and density of the dye layer vary, as does that of the reflective layer. Some manufacturers have begun using dyes that resemble those listed earlier, but have different characteristics. There is no way to tell by appearance alone which dye a disc uses. The physical groove structure of different CD-R blanks may differ, to optimize that disc for different LASER powers, writing speeds, and schemes. But the bottom line is that all CD-R blanks, including the no-name ones, are much better than they were a few years ago. The primary measure of CD-R disc quality, Block Error Rate (BLER), is much lower now than in the past. Even an average disc made in 2003 is as good or better than the best discs made a few years ago.

In the past, the problem was that, although most CD-R disc manufacturers made every effort to comply with strict Orange Book specifications, some CD writer manufacturers did not. The upshot was that different writers varied widely in which discs they could use successfully. In general, more compromises were made with inexpensive writers, which were typically much more media-sensitive than were more expensive models. A $175 Plextor burner would probably work with just about any media you chose. A $75 no-name ATAPI burner might have been very choosy indeed about which blanks it was willing to write.

Fortunately, those days are gone. Most current CD writers, even $50 ATAPI models, provide excellent compatibility with a wide range of disc blanks. Even so, it's important to keep your drive firmware up to date. As disc manufacturers change formulations and new disc types come on the market, you may need to update your firmware to enable your drive to use those new blanks.

When choosing discs, your sole criterion should be which media work properly in your recorder. The best starting point is one of the disc brands recommended by the drive manufacturer. Most manufacturers provide such a list on their web sites. Those lists are updated as new media types become available, and assume you have the latest firmware. At the price of blank CDs nowadays, there's little point to using bargain brands. We buy 48X-certified Taiyo Yuden blanks on spindles of 100 for something like $0.30 per disc and use them in all our burners. There's simply no point to risk using no-name blanks to save a few cents each.

Whichever blanks you settle on, recognize that any CD-R disc should be treated more carefully than a pressed CD. In particular, avoid exposing blank or recorded CD-R discs to sunlight or heat unnecessarily. Leaving an unprotected CD-R disc on the dashboard of your car is a quick way to destroy it.

Writable CD Capacities

Standard CD-R discs are available in 63-, 74-, and 80-minute lengths, which respectively store about 550, 650, and 700 MB of data in ISO-9660 format. For example, a nominal 74-minute CD-R disc stores (74 min×60 sec/min×150 KB/sec) = 681,984,000 bytes, 666,000 KB, or 650.390625 MB. CD data formats use 2 KB sectors, which means that a standard 74-minute disc contains (666,000 KB / 2 KB) = 333,000 sectors. Most blanks actually contain more than the required number of sectors. For example, a nominal 74-minute blank may contain 344,250 sectors, which translates to 76.5 minutes. This "extra" space permits *overburning* (writing more data to a disc than its nominal capacity) if the CD writer and software both support overburning.

Think twice before you try overburning. If your CD writer doesn't support it, attempting to overburn may physically damage the drive beyond repair and void the warranty. Many CD-ROM drives, even those that read ordinary CD-R discs, cannot read overburned CDs. Our advice about overburning is simple: unless there is no other way to do the job, don't use it.

Remember that when you write data to a CD recorder, the 2 KB logical sectors are actually written to 2,352 byte physical sectors, with the remaining space used for ECC code. That means that a standard 74-minute CD-R blank actually stores (333,000 sectors×2,352 bytes/sector) = 783,216,000 bytes or about 747 MB. Accordingly, you may find 74-minute discs with identical true capacities advertised as having nominal capacity from 650 to 780 MB, although something in the 650 to 680 MB range is most common.

When selecting CD-R discs, use the lowest-capacity discs big enough for your data. In practical terms, that means using 74-minute CD-R blanks rather than 80-minute blanks whenever possible. The 63-minute blanks have now all but disappeared from the market, and even the 74-minute blanks are becoming an endangered species. That's a pity because few burned CDs contain more than 63 minutes (550 MB), and CDs recorded on 63-minute blanks are in every respect superior to those recorded on 74-minute or 80-minute blanks. They are more likely to be readable on more CD-ROM drives and CD players, and are less likely to generate read errors. However, 63-minute blanks fell prey to the pervasive "more is better" way of thinking. Most people, given the choice of a 63- or 74-minute blank for the same price, chose the latter. The 63-minute blanks became harder and harder to find, and their increasingly limited distribution meant they eventually cost more than 74-minute blanks, and so disappeared from the retail channels. Alas.

You may not have the choice of 74- versus 80-minute blanks, depending on your CD writer. Not all CD writers can use 80-minute blanks, and even if the drive supports 80-minute blanks, your CD burning software may not.

In late 2001, some vendors began selling so-called 90-minute or 99-minute CD-R blanks. This increased capacity is achieved by tightening the spiral track and using overburning. Technically, these are not CD-R blanks at all because they are completely non-compliant with CD-R standards. Despite that, they work in some burners and some players, although both recording and playback problems are common with them.

Their actual capacity depends not just on the blank itself, but also on the burner, the software you use to write the blank, and the player or drive you use to read it. Not all burners can write these extended blanks, and not all drives and players can read them. If your burner writes them at all, it will likely limit writing to between 87:59 and 99:05. For example, our Plextor PlexWriter 24-10-40A writes, at most, 94:59, and our PlexWriter 8-2-20S, at most, 89:59. Also note that even burners that can write these oversized blanks cannot necessarily write them at all speeds the writer supports. For example, our PlexWriter 24-10-40A writes these discs only at 2X, 4X, and 8X, while the 8-2-20S writes at all supported speeds other than 1X.

If you want to play with these discs for recording music, fine, but we recommend you not count on them for anything that matters.

Before DVD writers became a mainstream technology, several manufacturers tried and failed to introduce higher-capacity replacements for CD-R. Most of these efforts were trial balloons that promised capacities of 1 GB to 1.5 GB, but disappeared without a trace before drives actually shipped. One exception was the Sony Spressa CRX200E-A1 Double Density drive, which shipped in limited numbers in 2001. This drive stored 1.3 GB on a CD-like disc, but had a fatal flaw. It required special double-density discs, which never achieved wide distribution, could not be used to record CD-Audio, and were incompatible with the Rainbow Book standards. Sony formalized its Double Density CD standard as the Purple Book, but that "standard" never caught on. Sony Double Density discs are now difficult to find.

Plextor took a different approach with the April 2003 introduction of PlexWriter Premium drives with GigaRec technology, which increases the storage capacity of standard CD-R discs by as much as 40%. Unlike earlier proposals to expand CD capacity, Plextor's solution is backward-compatible with existing drives and players. Although Plextor does not guarantee compatibility with every CD/DVD drive or player ever made—how could it?—discs recorded with GigaRec can be read by most CD-ROM, CD-R/RW, and DVD-ROM drives and players. Some old, low-quality, or inexpensive drives may generate read errors with GigaRec discs, but those errors are attributable to drive deficiencies rather than to the GigaRec disc.

Although we have not yet put a PlexWriter Premium drive through our usual rigorous testing, we expect that its ability to store about 1 GB on a 700 MB CD-R disc will appeal to those who want an economical backup solution. Security-conscious people will also like PlexWriter Premium drives because they can burn password-protected discs.

Archival Stability of CD-R(W) Media

So how long can you expect that CD-R disc you just burned to last? There's been a lot of nonsense written on that topic, but ultimately the answer is that no one knows. Projected lifetimes of 50, 100, and even 200 years are casually tossed around, as though they had any meaning.

Here's the truth. The only way to know for sure if a disc will last 100 years is to burn one, wait 100 years, and try to read it. Obviously, that's not a practical solution, so media manufacturers use various testing methods to estimate archival stability. All of those testing methods depend on accelerated aging, achieved by storing the disc at temperatures much higher than normal, often in conjunction with high humidity and high ultraviolet flux intended to simulate bright sunlight.

The rule of thumb in chemistry class says that the rate of most chemical reactions approximately doubles for each 10° C (18° F) increase in temperature. So, in theory, if one assumes that normal storage temperature for a CD-R disc is 20° C, a disc stored at 30° C ages twice as fast as normal, one stored at 40° C ages four times as fast, one stored at 50° C ages eight times as fast, and so on. The trouble is that that rule of thumb is just that—a rule of thumb—and the reaction rate slope is linear over only a limited range of temperatures.

The well-meaning chemist, being told that his Thanksgiving turkey should be cooked for 8 hours at 325° F, might reasonably conclude that he could decrease cooking time to four hours by setting his oven to 343° F, to two hours at 361° F, to one hour at 379° F, to 30 minutes at 397° F, and to 15 minutes at 415° F. We'll leave it to the reader to imagine the results of a turkey cooked 15 minutes at 415° F. (Robert was the well-meaning chemist, and he also didn't realize that he was supposed to remove the feathers. We are not making this up.)

So manufacturers project CD-R disc lifetimes based on testing them at high temperatures and in bright sunlight. But all that really determines is how long that CD-R disc is likely to last when stored at high temperatures in bright sunlight. Most people, of course, store their CD-R discs at room temperature and in the dark, or nearly so.

The real issue is not the archival stability of media, but the future availability of drives that can read the discs you're currently writing. Any CD you write today on a good-quality blank is almost certain to last at least 20 years, if not 100. But fast-forward to the year 2013. Finding a drive that can read a CD written in 2003 won't be a problem. In 2023, it may be a bit harder, but you should be able to find a drive that can read that CD written way back in 2003. But in 2103? Good luck. Try finding a drive today that can play back a wax cylinder audio recording made in 1900. Finding a drive to play a 100-year-old CD won't be any easier.

Labeling CD-R(W) Media

Finally, a few words about labeling. Drive and media manufacturers vary in what they recommend, and the best course is to follow those recommendations. However, some guidelines are nearly universal:

- *Never* use a standard sticky label on a CD-R disc. The adhesive may damage the label side of the disc, causing it to degenerate rapidly and become unreadable. Also, the small weight of that label is sufficient to imbalance the disc in high-speed players. At best, such an imbalance may cause read errors. At worst, it may destroy the disc or even the drive.

- The circular labels designed for CD-Rs are generally safe, but even they have been known to imbalance a disc if not applied perfectly centered. If you use such labels, never attempt to peel one off. Doing so may cause the top layer of the CD-R to separate, destroying the disc.

- Do not use a hard-tip marker, which may score the label layer. We usually label CD-R discs with a Sharpie soft-tip permanent marker. Some sources recommend not using a permanent solvent-based pen because it may etch the label layer. Other sources, including some CD-R manufacturers, *recommend* using a solvent-based permanent marker. Although we've never had a problem using the Sharpie, for maximum safety choose your marker according to the recommendations of the disc manufacturer.

When hand-labeling is not neat enough—e.g., for discs you plan to distribute outside your company—consider using printable discs, which have a surface that may be printed with an inkjet and/or thermal printer. These are available in various types and background colors, and generally work well if you follow the manufacturers' instructions carefully. Until recently, only expensive special printers could print on CDs. In June 2003, Epson began shipping the Stylus Photo 900, a sub-$200 inkjet printer that the Stylus Photo 900 even has a separate CD tray that feeds CDS automatically to the printer, so you don't have to feed them manually one-by-one. Although we have not yet had an opportunity to test this printer, it is reported to work well with printable CDs. We expect other printer manufacturers to follow Epson's lead, so the era of ugly, hand-labeled CDs and DVDs may be drawing to a close.

Burning CDs

The following sections condense our experience in burning a lot of CDs in various environments.

General CD Burning Guidelines

The process of burning CDs can be smooth and reliable or a complete nightmare. Which it is depends on the entire system you use to burn CDs—processor, memory, operating system, configuration settings, background processes, hard disk type and fragmentation level, source CD-ROM drive and the source CD itself, CD-R(W) drive, firmware revision, application software, and the blank discs themselves. In short, the process of burning CDs is a Black Art rather than a science.

That's less true now than it was even a couple of years ago because systems are faster, CD burners are better, and buffer underrun technologies have pretty much eliminated the danger of making coasters. But it still pays to keep in mind that what counts is not just the CD burner or the blanks, but the entire system. Once you have the system working reliably, making even a minor change to one element can break it. For example, we once added an apparently innocuous Windows NT service to our main CD-R burning system. Suddenly, a system that was formerly rock-solid for burning CDs was no longer reliable. Removing the service cured the problem.

On a properly configured system, you can burn hundreds of CDs uneventfully. On a marginal system with an older CD burner, even the slightest problem or anomaly can result in a ruined CD blank, called a "coaster." Making an occasional coaster is less aggravating now that blanks cost $0.30 each instead of $20 each, but it still wastes time. If your CD writer has buffer underrun protection, you're unlikely to have problems burning CDs regardless of what else the computer happens to be doing at the moment. If your CD writer does not have buffer underrun protection, use the following guidelines to burn CDs reliably:

- Regardless of the interface or operating system, take the following steps before recording a CD:
  - Disable power management, screen savers, schedulers, antivirus utilities, and any other software or service that may interrupt the recording process. In particular, if your PC is configured to answer phone or fax calls, disable that for the duration of the burning session.

- When recording from a disk image (writing the source data to the hard drive as an intermediate step rather than doing a direct CD-to-CD copy), defragment the disk drive before starting the burn.

- If your PC is on a network and is configured to share its disk or printer, disable sharing before attempting to burn a CD. If another user accesses your disk or printer while the CD is burning, the burn may fail.

- In the past, conventional wisdom was that making high-quality reproductions of audio CDs required that both source drive and CD burner be SCSI. That's no longer true in that some recent ATAPI CD-ROM drives are suitable as source drives for high-quality audio duping, but the ATAPI CD-ROM drives common in most PCs of 1998 or earlier vintage are likely not suitable source drives for doing high-quality audio dupes. If your CD-ROM drive is in the latter category, you can still do high-quality audio dupes by using your CD burner as both source drive and destination drive. Doing so requires that your CD copy utility support disc-to-image copying, whereby your burner reads the source CD, writes an image of that CD to your hard drive, and then uses that image as the source.

- If the data to be copied resides on a network drive, copy it to the local hard drive before attempting to burn the disc. Writing data from a network drive frequently yields a coaster, even on a 100BaseT network. Note that this caution applies only to writing CD-R discs, which is a synchronous (timing-critical) operation. We have frequently written CD-RW discs from data located on a network drive. Recording CD-RW discs in packet-writing mode is an asynchronous operation, so network delays have no effect on the integrity of the copy.

Burning On-the-Fly versus Burning Image Files

Broadly speaking, there are three ways to burn a CD-R disc, whether the source data is another CD or a random collection of files on your hard disk:

Burning on-the-fly
With this method, data is streamed from the source CD or hard drive, formatting and error-correction data is added in real time, and the resulting data stream is burned to the CD. The advantages of on-the-fly burning are that it is faster than other methods and it requires no extra disk space. The drawback is that on-the-fly burning is the method most likely to create coasters. Most recent systems are fast enough to dupe audio or data CDs on-the-fly successfully, but you may have problems if you attempt to write hundreds or thousands of relatively small files to a CD, as, for example, if you use your CD writer to back up your hard disk.

Burning true image files
This method uses a two-step process. Data to be written to the CD is first read and processed to add formatting and error-correction data. That formatted data is then written out to the hard disk as an ISO image file, which is an exact binary representation of the data as it will be written to the CD. The drawbacks to using true image files are that it takes longer and you must have enough free disk space to accommodate the image file, which can be 1 GB or more when you are copying audio data to an 80-minute blank.

Against these disadvantages, burning a true image file is by far the most reliable method, particularly on older, slower systems, and those that use an older model CD writer.

Burning virtual image files

This method is similar to using true image files, with the exception that an actual image file is not written to the hard disk. Instead, a virtual image file is created, which contains pointers to the locations of the files to be written to the CD. Because formatting, adding error correction, and all other preprocessing is done before the actual burn starts, using a virtual image file is more reliable than burning on-the-fly. Conversely, because the files to be written must be retrieved from random locations on the hard disk during the burn, using a virtual image file is less reliable than using a true image file. Using virtual image files is slower than burning on-the-fly but faster than using true image files.

If your CD writer has buffer underrun protection, you can use any of these methods successfully. On-the-fly burning is the fastest, so there's normally no reason to use anything else. If your CD writer does not have buffer underrun protection, the best method depends on the capabilities of your system, your CD writer, and your software, as well as the type of data you want to burn to CD. On-the-fly burns usually work well for duping audio or data CDs, and (assuming that you have enough free disk space) using a true image file is best for doing backups and similar operations that require writing many small files to disc. As always, the best way to judge is to try each method and use the fastest one that works reliably for you.

 If you are building a new system or installing a new hard disk on a system with an older CD writer, consider creating a dedicated hard disk partition to be used as a "staging area" for ISO image files. This partition needn't be large—a gigabyte or so is sufficient—but it should be on your fastest hard disk if there's a choice (and certainly on a hard disk that is on a different channel than the CD writer).

Configure your burning software to write the ISO image file to the dedicated partition. After you complete each burn, you can delete the ISO image file or move it elsewhere, freeing up the partition for the next burn. We've never had a problem just deleting the old ISO image file, but some belt-and-suspenders folks we know do a Quick Format of the partition each time to ensure the ISO image file is written sequentially to the partition.

Choosing the Optimum Burn Speed for Your Drive and Media

A recent CD burner generally works well at its maximum rated speed, at least if you use high-quality blank discs. If you have an older CD burner, don't assume that you can use its fastest speed, even if your burning software tests a disc and claims that it is writable at the highest speed. With older CD burners, burning at higher speeds is generally less reliable than burning at lower speeds, both because faster burning is more likely to generate errors while writing, particularly with marginal discs, and because the CD writer's buffer, whatever its size, empties faster at higher burning speeds. For example, when writing at 12X (1800 KB/s), a 512 KB buffer stores only about one-quarter of a second's worth of data. Any interruption in the data stream longer than that generates a coaster (unless the drive has BURN-Proof or a similar technology). Larger buffers and lower write speeds minimize the chance of buffer underruns and ruined discs.

But slow equals reliable is by no means a universal truth. Burning at a slower speed is sometimes *less* reliable. For example, we used one no-name 32X CD writer that wrote most discs reliably at 32X or 24X, some discs reliably at 16X, and very few discs reliably at slower than 16X. The optimal burning speed depends on numerous factors, particularly the combination of drive, firmware revision, and disc.

> With very few exceptions, discs certified for a higher speed can be burned reliably in a slower burner. For example, a 24X CD writer ordinarily works fine with discs certified for 32X, 40X, 48X, or higher. If you use several burners, it's worth doing some tests to determine one brand of fast disc that all of your burners can use. For example, we've standardized on Taiyo Yuden 48X blanks, which work properly in all of our burners, including some truly ancient models, which we have updated to the latest available firmware. Your mileage may vary.

In general, when we start with a new batch of media on a given CD writer, we first attempt burns at the highest speed the drive supports, regardless of the speed for which the disc is certified. For example, we had a spindle of Taiyo Yuden 24X certified blanks that burned without errors at 32X and 40X in several burners, although other burners generated errors at anything faster than 24X. In our experience, burning discs faster than their rated speed either works or it doesn't, depending on the particular CD writer and type of disc you're using. That is, if you try it and it works for one disc, it'll probably work for the rest of the spindle as well. If it's not going to work, you'll probably find out when you attempt to burn the first disc. As always, the best solution is to test in your own environment.

> Although CD burning software still offers the option, test burns are a holdover from the Bad Olde Days when CD blanks were very expensive. There's really no point to doing a test burn because even if the test succeeds, that doesn't guarantee that the actual burn will succeed. The way to do a test burn is to do a real burn instead. If it doesn't work, you've wasted only a little time and the $0.30 cost of the ruined blank.

Overburning

Overburning simply means writing more data to a CD-R blank than it is nominally designed to store, allowing you to fit more music or data on a standard CD-R disc. This is possible because most CD-R blanks contain more than the necessary number of writable sectors. For example, a 74-minute blank, which must have at least 333,000 sectors to yield 74 minutes of recording time, may actually contain 340,000 sectors, which allows it to record about 75.5 minutes. The number of "extra" sectors varies widely between different brands of CD-R blanks.

Some contain only a few extra sectors, while others contain enough extra sectors to allow recording up to 76, 77, or even 78 minutes on a nominal 74-minute blank.

To overburn successfully, the media, the CD recorder, and the software must all support overburning. If your software supports overburning, it is probably not configured to use it by default. You'll likely need to enable overburning manually, possibly for each disc you want to overburn.

In the days before 80-minute blanks became widely available, overburning was a popular way to defeat the ad hoc copy protection used by some game CD makers, who simply pressed CDs that contained more sectors than would fit on a standard 74-minute CD. The widespread availability of overburning-capable software and then 80-minute blanks has almost eliminated the use of this means of copy protection.

Do not overburn unless you are certain your CD writer supports it. Although we have never encountered the problem, we have numerous reports of CD writers which did not support overburning being physically damaged by attempting it. Even if your software allows overburning, do not assume that means it is safe to use overburning on your writer. Verify with the manufacturer that your writer supports overburning.

If for some reason you need to burn CDs larger than 650 MB/74 minutes, keep the following issues in mind:

- If your CD writer and/or CD mastering/duplication program does not support overburning 74-minute discs, you may be able to use 80-minute discs instead. Although 80-minute discs are marginally less reliable than 74-minute discs, they are more reliable than overburned 74-minute discs.

You *can* overburn 80-minute CDs, but it's probably not worth bothering. In the first place, most 80-minute blanks contain few extra sectors, often only enough for an extra minute or less. More important, even CD-ROM drives and CD players that can read 80-minute CDs may choke on overburned 80-minute CDs.

- Some CD writers and software support overburning 74-minute discs but do not support 80-minute discs, some support 80-minute discs but not overburning, some support both, and some support neither. If software is the limiting factor, check the maker's web site. The current versions of most CD-R software support 80-minute discs.
- Some CD writers can be upgraded to support 80-minute media by installing a firmware update. Others are physically incapable of writing more than 74 minutes or slightly more.

- The media most suitable for overburning, which is to say those with the greatest number of extra sectors, are often otherwise undesirable. If you buy some of these oversized discs for overburning, use them only when you need to overburn something.

- Most CD writers that do support overburning do so only in Disc-at-Once mode, which limits you to duplicating an audio or data CD (as opposed to premastering the data, as, for example, when you select a group of files and folders to copy). Some CD mastering software overcomes this problem by allowing you to create an ISO image of the data on your hard disk as a preliminary step, and then burning that image to the CD.

- Although it may seem possible to determine the maximum length of an overburn exactly, that is not the case. For example, a CD-R disc utility may report that a blank contains 351,000 sectors, which can be converted mathematically to a burn time of 78:00:00. In reality, though, limitations in your CD writer hardware or firmware will likely place a shorter absolute limit on the actual burn.

- Even if your CD burner and software support overburning, don't be surprised to see some pretty horrifying error messages during an overburn, such as *Fatal write error*, *Track following error*, or *Write emergency*. In fact, it's pretty common while doing a long overburn to have the software lock up at or just before the *Writing Table of Contents* phase. It may appear that you've made a coaster, but it's worth checking to see if the disc is readable. It often is, although by all rights it seems that it shouldn't be.

- Even if your CD burner and software support overburning and the process appears to complete normally, you may find that the material past the standard 74-minute length is degraded. Audio tracks may have various artifacts, including hisses, pops, and drop-outs. Datafiles may be corrupted. The more extensive the overburn, the more likely such problems are to occur.

- Overburning is a (rather dubious) art rather than a science. Actually, the same can be said in general for burning CDs, but this is particularly true when overburning. Just because you succeed once in overburning a disc doesn't mean that you'll succeed the next time, even with an identical disc and the same data.

- Some CD-ROM drives and CD players, particularly older models, cannot handle overburned and/or 80-minute discs. The usual symptom is that the drive or player refuses to accept the CD, simply ejecting it as soon as you insert it. Sometimes, a drive or player reads the first 650 MB/74 minutes and then simply stops reading in the midst of an audio track or file. In general, anytime you burn a CD larger than 650 MB/74 minutes by whatever method, be aware that read problems may result.

All of that said, our general advice is as follows:

- Stick to standard 74-minute CDs if at all possible, and don't try to record more than they are designed to hold. Otherwise, expect problems.

- If you absolutely, positively need to record more than 74 minutes on a CD, use an 80-minute blank in a CD writer designed to support it.

- If for some reason you must overburn a 74-minute blank, first make sure your CD burner supports overburning. Keep the overburn as short as possible, and test the resulting disc in the actual drive that will be used to read it before you assume that the disc will be readable.

Special Problems and Applications

Once you have your CD writer and software configured properly, burning CDs is usually a pretty straightforward process. There are, however, some special situations that deserve comment. The following sections detail some of the unusual situations you may encounter.

Copy-Protected CDs

This *was* a very nice section. We provided complete instructions for circumventing the various copy-protection methods that manufacturers use to make life difficult for honest users. But you'll never read that material. Why? Because we don't want to end up like Dmitri Sklyarov, who was imprisoned under the *Digital Millennium Copyright Act (DMCA)* simply because he exercised his First Amendment right to free speech. (And please don't ask us to email you the deleted text. We can't afford to take that risk.)

The sole purpose of the DMCA is to prevent all of us from doing things we have the right to do—such as making backup copies of the CDs and DVDs we buy—and saying things we have the right to say—such as how to make those backup copies. The DMCA was bought and paid for by the *RIAA (Recording Industry Association of America)* and *MPAA (Motion Picture Association of America)*, and benefits no one except the music and movie industries.

The definition of an honest politician is one who stays bought, but we nevertheless hope the monstrosity called the DMCA can be overturned. There are several things you can and should do to protect your own interests. Write or call your representatives and senators to complain about DMCA and demand it be repealed. Join the Electronic Frontier Foundation (*http://www.eff.org*) and support their efforts to preserve free speech. Hit the MPAA and RIAA where it hurts. Boycott their products, particularly those that are copy-protected. Make it clear to the MPAA and RIAA that their insane insistence on treating their customers as thieves is offensive, and that you won't put up with it.

Making Copies of Copies

Although it surprises many people—it certainly surprised us—the CDs you make in your burner are not necessarily exact copies of the source CD. For audio CDs, this usually isn't a problem. An occasional dropped or flipped bit will probably be inaudible. But for data CDs, it can be a major problem. We found this out while playing with a new burner. We duped the original FrontPage CD, and were able to install FrontPage from the dupe. But when we duped the dupe and then tried to install from the second-generation copy, Setup returned file read errors. Doing a binary compare on those files told the sad truth: the files were identical on the original CD and the first-generation copy, but differed on the second-generation copy.

Remember that CDs depend heavily on error-correction and detection code. All CD formats use 3,234-byte physical sectors, which allocate 2,352 bytes to data and the remainder to control and error correction data. Audio CDs use the entire 2,352 bytes for audio data. Yellow Book Mode 1 (data) CDs use only 2,048 bytes for data and allocate the remaining 304 bytes to another ECC layer. The problem arises because of the different ways that CD burners and software read and write Mode 1 data:

Raw mode

The drive reads the entire 2,352 byte sector as a raw bit stream and writes that raw data to the destination device. Any data read errors in either the data segment or the ECC segment are written literally to the destination. Working in this mode, generational degradation can overwhelm the ability of ECC to correct errors and result in a CD that returns read errors or contains corrupted files. This may occur as early as a second-generation copy, and almost certainly after several generations.

Cooked mode

The drive reads only the 2,048 byte data segment, using the ECC segment to verify the data and correct it if necessary. The drive then recalculates the proper ECC segment for that data segment and writes the original data segment with the new ECC segment to the destination disc.

This means it is impossible to ensure an exact copy of any CD that uses 2,352 byte data segments (audio CDs) or 2,336 byte data segments (Mode 2 data CDs) because those segments contain no sector-level ECC data. Fortunately, Mode 2 CDs are rare, and you can copy the common Mode 1 data CDs reliably by using cooked mode, assuming that your drive and software support it. To minimize copying problems, use the following guidelines:

- For Red Book (audio) CDs, use an original (pressed) CD as the source. There is no reliable way to make a copy of an audio CD that is itself a copy. When copying original source CDs, note that some drives disable some error-correcting features during digital audio extraction, or may use error correction only during DAE at 1X. Experiment to determine the optimum recording speed for best sound quality. Differences are subtle, particularly with recent drives and media, but they do exist. Some people swear you should always dupe audio CDs at 1X (or 2X or 4X), but the truth is that the optimum speed depends on the drive and media. Drive A may make the best dupes with Media A at 1X and with Media B at 4X, while Drive B may be exactly the opposite. Test with each drive and each time you change media.

- For Yellow Book Mode 2 data CDs, always use an original CD as the source. There is no reliable way to make a copy of a Mode 2 CD that is itself a copy. If you must copy a Mode 2 copy, do a file-by-file binary compare afterward to verify the copy.

- For Yellow Book Mode 1 data CDs, either use the original CD as the source (using either raw or cooked mode), or use cooked mode when copying from a source CD that is itself a dupe. Also note that problems may arise if the source dupe was made in raw mode rather than cooked mode.

Creating and Using a Bootable CD-R Disc

If your system and drive support the *El Torito Specification* (*http://www.phoenix.com/resources/specs-cdrom.pdf*), which allows booting from CD, a bootable CD can be a useful emergency fallback. The process required to create a bootable CD varies according to the mastering software package you use. See the documentation for details.

To boot from CD, the CD/DVD-ROM drive and system BIOS must support CD as a boot device, which nearly all recent models do. To set your system to boot from CD, run BIOS Setup and locate an option named "Boot Sequence" or something similar. That option will typically be set to something like "A:, C:, CD-ROM, SCSI" by default. Insert the bootable CD, change the boot sequence to make the CD-ROM the first boot device, and restart the system. The system will boot from the CD, which it will recognize as drive A:. (The actual FDD will become B:.)

Creating an AutoRun CD-R Disc

At times it's useful to create a CD that, when inserted in the drive, automatically loads and runs a specified program or document. For example, you can distribute HTML content on a CD that automatically invokes the user's browser and loads *index.html*. The only thing necessary to enable AutoRun for program files is to put a properly formatted *AutoRun.inf* file in the root directory of that CD. *AutoRun.inf* is a plain ASCII text file with the following syntax:

```
[autorun]
Open=CmdLine
```

Inserting a CD that contains *Notepad.exe* and *Index.html* in the root directory and the following *AutoRun.inf*:

```
[autorun]
Open=notepad.exe index.html
```

causes Windows to AutoRun *Notepad.exe* and load *Index.html* into it. You can optionally specify a path before the program or document name. *AutoRun.inf* supports many more options, which are documented at *http://www.microsoft.com/MSJ/0998/win320998top.htm*.

Unfortunately, AutoRun does not honor file associations, which makes it difficult to invoke the user's browser to run an HTML source file automatically. There are several workarounds for this problem, but the one we prefer is the small utility *Autohtml.exe*, developed by Mark Trescowthick and Ross Mack, which is available for download at *http://www.avdf.com/oct98/art_ot005.html*. That page includes full instructions for using the utility.

Repeatedly burning CDs while you are testing your custom *AutoRun.inf* is time-consuming and wasteful. One alternative is to modify the registry to allow AutoRun to work on a floppy disk. As always, back up before making changes to the registry, and proceed with caution. To make this change, which works on Windows NT/2000/XP and Windows 9X systems, run *Regedit.exe* and locate the value entry NoDriveTypeAutoRun, which resides in the key *HKEY_CURRENT_USER\Software\Microsoft\Windows\CurrentVersion\Policies\Explorer*. Double-click the value entry to edit the value.

Windows actually stores a 4-byte value, but only the following binary digits of the first byte are meaningful. Those digits are used as a binary bitmap, as follows:

```
Bit   Type
0     DRIVE_UNKNOWN
1     DRIVE_NO_ROOT_DIR
2     DRIVE_REMOVABLE
3     DRIVE_FIXED
4     DRIVE_REMOTE
5     DRIVE_CDROM
6     DRIVE_RAMDISK
```

By default, this bit mask is set to 10010101 (95H), which disables AutoRun for DRIVE_UNKNOWN, DRIVE_REMOVABLE, and DRIVE_REMOTE. The high-order bit is also set to disable AutoRun for reserved future devices. (1=disable Autorun; 0=enable it.) Change this bit mask to 10010001 (91H) to enable AutoRun for removable drives, including floppy diskette drives and Zip drives. Save the change and restart the computer. A floppy disk does not AutoRun when inserted because the floppy drive cannot notify Windows that the disk has been inserted. However, you can manually AutoRun that floppy by right-clicking the drive icon and choosing AutoPlay.

Packet Writing with Linux

Beginning with the 2.4 kernel, Linux offers limited packet-writing support. The 2.4 and 2.5 kernels have no native support for packet writing, but a kernel patch is available from the Linux UDF Project (*http://sourceforge.net/projects/linux-udf*) that adds basic packet-writing functions. The kernel patch should work with any CD-(M)RW drive that supports packet writing. As we write this, the major limitations of the patch are that it supports only CD-RW media and fixed-length packet writing.

To enable packet writing under Linux, take the following steps:

1. Download the latest version of the patch from kernel.org and apply it.

2. Configure the kernel by selecting packet support in the block device section and UDF support in the filesystem section.

3. Compile the kernel and modules, install the kernel, and reboot the system.

4. Download the latest version of cdrwtool, which is needed to format CD-RW discs.

5. Use the command make lib tools udf.o install to compile and install UDF support.

6. Format a new CD-RW disc using the command cdrwtool -d /dev/<device> -q.

7. Use the command ls /dev/pk* to verify that /dev/pktcdvd0 exists. If it doesn't, use the command mknod /dev/pktcdvd0 b 97 0 to create it.

8. Use the command pktsetup /dev/pktcdvd0 /dev/<device> to set up the CD writer.

9. Use the command mount /dev/pktcdvd0 to mount the device, at which point you should be able to read from and write to the drive.

Writable CD Troubleshooting

Troubleshooting writable CD problems is challenging. There are so many things that can go wrong, and so many variables you can change to try to fix the problem, that it may seem the only choice is to strip everything down to bare metal and start over. Usually such extreme measures are not called for, however. In the course of working with dozens of CD writers on many different systems, we've encountered an amazing variety of problems. The following sections describe how to cure those problems. If you're having a problem with your CD writer, chances are one of these fixes will cure it.

General Troubleshooting

Before you do anything else, take the following steps, which solve most writable CD problems:

- Read the manual. Sometimes the problem isn't really a problem at all. It's supposed to work that way.

- If you're writing to a new type (or even batch) of CD-R discs, try a different type of disc. Many problems are disc-related, particularly if you're using cheap discs. When we think the problem may be media-related, we generally try burning a Taiyo Yuden blank. If that fails, we look elsewhere for the problem.

- If the system is overclocked (or even just tweaked for maximum performance), try setting things back to standard values. Burning CDs is one of the most demanding things you can do with a system, and even minor stability problems are likely to manifest during the burn. If you're overclocking your processor, running PC100 memory at 133 MHz, running CL3 memory with CL2 timing, or something similar, set things back to standard and try the burn again.

- Check the manufacturer's web site for your CD writer to see if it has posted a firmware update. If so, install it. In addition to fixing bugs, firmware updates may add new capabilities (such as the ability to write 80-minute blanks) and add support for burning schema required by new types of media.

- Check the software manufacturer's web site to see if there's an update available. Most CD writer software makers update their software frequently, and patches often solve problems.

- For an ATAPI (IDE) writer, check the DMA status of the ATA channel that the writer connects to. Some writers, even those that theoretically support DMA, do not function properly if DMA is enabled. Others don't work properly unless DMA is enabled. If DMA is enabled on the channel, disable it, restart the system, and try again. If DMA is disabled on the channel, enable it, restart the system, and try again.

 On older systems, disabling DMA may not be enough. You may have to uninstall bus-mastering drivers. Also note that disabling DMA on any system may prevent you from burning CDs at 8X or higher.

- Under Windows 95/98, the file *\WINDOWS\SYSTEM\IOSUBSYS\Scsi1hlp.vxd* supports legacy SCSI devices but sometimes causes problems with CD writers. Rename or delete that file, restart the system to clear it from memory, and try burning again.

- Check the ASPI configuration. All CD writers, ATAPI and SCSI, use ASPI, either the generic ASPI driver formerly supplied by Adaptec or a proprietary ASPI driver supplied with the burning software. You want the latest version available. If you've installed new SCSI hardware and your CD writer suddenly stops working properly, it's possible that software setup for the new hardware installed an older version of ASPI on top of your later version. This occurs more often than it should. For example, we had a system with a CD writer that operated perfectly. We installed a SCSI HP scanner on that system, and suddenly the CD writer started producing coasters. When we checked the ASPI version, we found that the current version had been replaced with a 1997-vintage 1.X version of ASPI.

To check the ASPI configuration, use the Nero InfoTool utility described earlier in this chapter. You can also run Start → Find → Files or Folders and search for the file *wnaspi32.dll* on C: and all subdirectories. Ordinarily, there should be only one copy of the file on the system. If it is the Adaptec ASPI driver, it should reside in the *\WINDOWS\SYSTEM* folder (Windows 9X), the *\WINNT\system32* folder (Windows 2000), or the *\WINDOWS\system32* folder (Windows XP). If it is a proprietary ASPI driver supplied with the CD burning software, it generally resides in the home directory for that software (e.g., *C:\Program Files\ahead\Nero*). If you find other copies, delete them. Exception: if you have more than one operating system installed, it is proper for a copy of the file to reside in the system directory of each. If you suspect a problem caused by an ASPI conflict or an older version of ASPI, the best way to update ASPI is usually simply to reinstall the CD burning software.

If the preceding steps don't solve the problem, one of the following may:

- Try some other brand of software. For example, when we began testing Windows XP, a new burner arrived that included EasyCD and DirectCD, both of which were supposed to work with Windows XP. They didn't. We downloaded Nero Burning ROM and installed it. A few minutes later, we were happily burning CDs under Windows XP. Don't assume that the software that comes with the writer is necessarily the best software to use, or even that it will work properly. It seems that the choice of bundled software is sometimes made by the marketing department for reasons entirely unrelated to functionality or stability.

- Eliminate any software that creates virtual disk volumes. That includes not only packet-writing software (such as DirectCD), but such things as UDF drivers for DVD-RAM drives, the Onstream Echo backup software driver, and so on—anything that creates a virtual disk volume with an assigned drive letter. Unfortunately, when we say "eliminate" we mean a bit more than just uninstalling the software. In our experience, although uninstalling *may* work, it's more likely you'll need either to eradicate all references to the problem software from the registry, or else strip the disk down to bare metal and reinstall from scratch.

- If you're using an ATAPI CD writer, check the IDE configuration. Always install the writer on a different channel than the source drive(s) if at all possible. If you do on-the-fly (CD-ROM to CD-R) copies, install the CD writer and the CD-ROM drive on different channels. If you do indirect copies (writing the data first to the hard disk), install the CD writer and hard disk on different channels. The best configuration is generally to make the hard disk primary master, the CD-ROM drive primary slave, and the CD writer secondary master. This allows you to copy from either the CD-ROM drive or the hard disk without having both source and destination devices on the same channel.

> If your CD-ROM drive doesn't support DMA, putting it on the same channel as the hard disk may actually impair your ability to burn CDs successfully. This is true because ATA does not allow mixing DMA and non-DMA devices on a single channel. If you install a non-DMA CD-ROM drive on the same channel as the hard drive, that forces the hard drive to downshift from DMA mode to PIO mode. PIO mode slows throughput and greatly increases CPU utilization, both factors that contribute to coasters.
>
> In this situation, we recommend replacing the CD-ROM drive with a DMA-capable model or simply using the CD writer as the sole CD device in the system. If that's not possible for some reason, the best bet is probably to put both CD devices on the Secondary interface and always copy data to the hard disk before burning. Note, however, that that forces the CD writer to operate in PIO mode, which may limit the upper speed at which you can burn CDs. Typically, writing at 8X or higher requires DMA mode, some burners require DMA mode to do 4X copies reliably, and nearly all burners require DMA mode to do 16X copies.

- Most IDE CD writers are happiest as the master (or sole) device on the secondary ATA channel. If you have two devices on the secondary channel and the CD writer is set as slave, try switching the CD writer to master and the other device to slave. If that doesn't solve the problem, try disconnecting the other device temporarily. Some CD writers simply do not get along with some other devices on the same channel, typically older IDE tape drives, Zip drives, and similar devices.

Specific Problems and Issues

This section describes some specific problems and the fixes for them:

Test burn succeeds but real burn fails during TOC write
This is usually caused by *Auto Insert Notification* (*AIN*, Windows 9X) or *AutoRun* (Windows NT/2000) being enabled on the CD writer. The actual burn appears to proceed normally, but fails during the TOC write phase. This occurs because Windows periodically looks at CD drives. An unburned (or partially burned) disc contains no TOC, and so is of no interest to Windows. But when the burn process starts to write the TOC, Windows suddenly notices that a real disc is in the drive and attempts to read it, killing the burn. Of course, you really shouldn't bother doing test burns anyway.

Most CD writing software controls the status of AIN itself, turning AIN on or off as necessary. Generally, CD mastering software (e.g., EasyCD Creator) requires AIN be disabled for proper functioning, while packet-writing software (e.g., DirectCD) requires AIN be enabled. Properly behaved software generally handles this automatically, checking AIN status when you start the program, changing the status if necessary, and then returning AIN to the original status when you exit the program. However, not all software is properly behaved, and confusion can occur if you use a mastering package and a packet-writing package from different makers. For some CD writer software (e.g., Nero Burning ROM), AIN status doesn't matter.

To check or reset AIN status under Windows 95/98, start the Device Manager, expand the listing of CD-ROM devices, and double-click the entry for the CD writer to display the device Properties sheet. On the Settings page, shown in Figure 11-5, use the Auto insert notification checkbox to view or change the status of AIN.

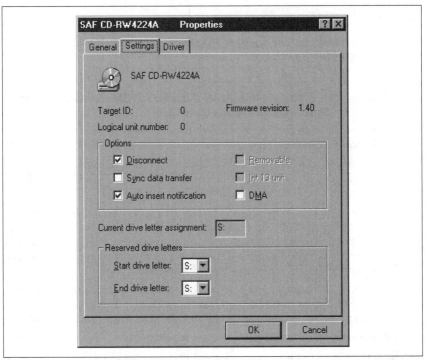

Figure 11-5. The device Properties sheet from within the Device Manager, where you can view or change the status of AIN under Windows 9x

Windows NT/2000/XP makes it a bit more difficult to view and change AutoRun status, requiring a direct change to the registry to do so, as shown in Figure 11-6.

If you frequently need to change AutoRun status in Windows NT/2000/XP, you can automate the process by creating two small registry files. Name them

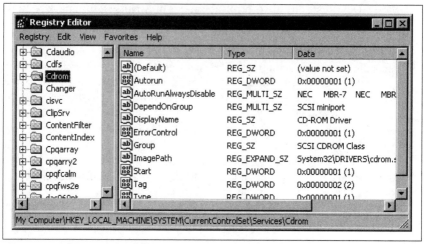

Figure 11-6. Using the Registry Editor to turn off AutoRun

descriptively, something such as *AutoRun-on.reg* and *AutoRun-off.reg*. To create these files, take the following steps:

1. Choose Start → Run, type regedit in the box, and click OK.

2. Highlight HKEY_LOCAL_MACHINE\SYSTEM\CurrentControlSet\ Services\Cdrom (as shown in Figure 11-6).

3. From the Registry menu, choose Export Registry File to display the Export Registry File dialog.

4. Verify that the Selected branch option button is selected in the Export range section and that the HKEY_LOCAL_MACHINE\SYSTEM\ CurrentControlSet\Services\Cdrom branch is selected.

5. Browse to the folder where you want to store the file, and type in a descriptive filename that corresponds to the current status of Autorun. For example, in the figure, Autorun is currently enabled (set to a value of 1), so we'd name this file Autorun-on. Click Save to write the file to disk, accepting the default Save as type of Registration Files.

6. Back in the Registry Editor, double-click the Autorun item in the right pane to display the Edit DWORD Value dialog. In the Value data box, change the value from 1 to 0 (or 0 to 1, as appropriate) and click OK.

7. Repeat steps 3 through 5 to save the second file.

Following these steps yields two files named *Autorun-on.reg* and *Autorun-off.reg*. To change the status of Autorun, simply double-click one or the other from Explorer. Windows NT/2000/XP prompts you that you are about to add the information in the file to the registry. Click Yes to change the setting for Autorun. Windows prompts you that the change has been made successfully. Click OK to clear the dialog. Autorun is now set to the value specified by the file. If you change Autorun status frequently, it's worth creating desktop shortcuts to each of these files.

It does no harm to reset Autorun from 0 to 0 or from 1 to 1, so you needn't check before running one or the other of these files. Simply double-click the one that sets Autorun to the value you need at the moment.

Test burn succeeds but real burn fails randomly during write

This problem is similar to the preceding one, but differs in that the burn process may die at any stage during the write, rather than just during the TOC write. Although there are many things that can cause this problem, if you have eliminated the more likely causes, consider the possibility of an inadequate power supply, particularly if you recently upgraded the system with a second hard disk, faster processor, more memory, or something else that places an additional burden on the power supply. CD writers require significantly more power during an actual write than during a test write, and an inadequate power supply may be able to provide the current required for a test write, but not an actual write.

CD writer rejects blanks

If the writer immediately ejects a blank disc, there may be a media, environmental, hardware, or software problem. To eliminate media, try inserting a different brand of blank. If that disc is accepted, it is likely the problem disc was defective or previously written (some drives and software reject coasters without a helpful error message). To eliminate environmental causes, verify the writer is not overheating and, if it is an external unit, that it is level. If you have recently added or changed hardware, verify that all cables and jumpers are correct and, if the writer is SCSI, that termination is set properly. Finally, if you have recently added software or hardware to the system, verify that AIN, DMA, and so on are configured properly and that ASPI is the correct version. If all of those seem correct, uninstall and reinstall the CD writer software. If all else fails, reinstall the operating system. If that doesn't work, chances are the CD writer needs to be repaired or replaced.

The CD writer reports a power calibration, PCA, or write schema error

Different types of discs require the writing LASER to use different power settings and methods of writing to the disc. Every CD-R blank includes a special area called the *Power Calibration Area* (*PCA*), which the writer uses to test LASER power and other write parameters before actually writing data to the disc. PCA errors occur when the writer can't determine how to write to a particular type of disc, or occasionally when the disc itself is defective. If you get a PCA error, try substituting a different type of disc. If that works, try another blank of the same type as the problem disc. If that works, the problem disc itself is defective. If other discs of the same type also return PCA errors, those discs are incompatible with your writer. Updating the writer firmware may allow it to use those discs, but some types of discs are simply incompatible with some types of writers. If the writer sporadically or reproducibly returns PCA errors with different types of discs, an inadequate power supply is the likely cause.

Additional CD-R(W) Source Material

You can find additional information about CD writers at the following web sites:

- *http://www.cdrfaq.org/*—The home of Andy McFadden's CD-Recordable FAQ. Good information about all aspects of CD-R(W).
- *http://www.cd-info.com/index.html*—The CD Information Center. Industry news, articles, bibliography, links to manufacturer sites, and various FAQs.

Our Picks

Here are the CD writers and related products we recommend:

ATAPI CD-(M)RW drive
> **Plextor ATAPI PlexWriter.** In the past, we preferred SCSI burners for their greater performance and reliability, and recommended ATAPI burners only when cost was the top priority. That changed when Plextor introduced the ATAPI 8/4/32A in early 2000, and followed it in July 2000 with the 12/10/32A. That drive was the first we'd used that had BURN-Proof technology. We found it impossible to burn coasters with that drive, even when we tried hard to do so. All recent Plextor ATAPI PlexWriters include BURN-Proof, and all are excellent products. If you want a reliable CD burner that will run for years, buy a midrange or high-end PlexWriter. Plextor PlexWriters are inexpensive, fast, and robust, and work flawlessly under Windows 98/98 SE/Me, NT/2000/XP, and Linux. You simply can't buy a better CD writer (*http://www.plextor.com*).

SCSI CD-(M)RW drive
> **Plextor PX-W4012TS PlexWriter 40/12/40S.** We still have several Plextor SCSI burners around here, but we haven't installed a new one recently. Plextor ATAPI burners are simply so good that there's seldom any point to installing a SCSI unit. The sole remaining bastion of SCSI CD burners is CD-R duplicators, who burn many identical CDs simultaneously. In that environment SCSI is a must-have, but for routine CD burning an ATAPI PlexWriter is actually a better solution. If we needed a SCSI burner, we'd buy the 40/12/40S.

USB CD-(M)RW drive
> **Plextor USB 2.0 PlexWriter.** If you need a portable CD burner to carry between machines or to use with a notebook computer, USB is generally a better choice than SCSI or FireWire, both because it costs less and because computers are more likely to have a USB port than a SCSI or FireWire port. The USB 2.0 PlexWriter model is the best USB burner on the market. In effect, it repackages the well-regarded ATAPI PlexWriter in an external enclosure. The USB 2.0 PlexWriter 24/10/40U and faster models require a USB 2.0 interface to achieve their rated performance. They also work properly with the ubiquitous USB 1.1 interface, although the slower interface limits writing and rewriting to 4X and reading to 6X. If you need a portable CD writer, the PlexWriter is the one to get.

FireWire CD-(M)RW drive
> **None.** Our first choice, Plextor, doesn't make a FireWire model. We formerly recommended a Yamaha model, but Yamaha has departed the CD writer market. Sony and others make FireWire CD writers and several vendors

bundle Plextor PlexWriter drives with external FireWire/USB 2.0 enclosures, but we have not tested any of those. If we had to choose a FireWire CD writer, we'd probably go with a PlexWriter in a third-party enclosure.

Mastering software

Ahead Software Nero Burning ROM. Roxio Easy CD Creator is bundled with most CD writers, including the Plextors, but just because it comes with a drive doesn't mean it's the best product to use. We and many others have experienced numerous problems using Easy CD under Windows 2000 and Windows XP, particularly when we also had DirectCD (Roxio's packet-writing program) loaded. Looking for better mastering software, we tried many competing products. The best we found was Nero, which is so much better than Easy CD that it's worth paying for separately. After burning a boatload of CDs with Nero on different systems with different CD writers under Windows 9X, NT, and 2000/XP, we've found that Nero is faster than Easy CD, much less likely to burn coasters when using a marginal configuration, and able to copy source discs that Easy CD chokes on (*http://www.nero.com*).

Packet-writing software

Ahead Software InCD. Packet-writing software provides drive-letter access to a CD burner, and allows you to move or copy files using drag-and-drop. For a long time, Adaptec/Roxio DirectCD was the dominant packet-writing software, but we had so many problems with it that we'd about given up on packet writing entirely. Ahead's InCD is a competing packet-writing program that actually works. Although we still don't use packet writing much—we prefer to burn CDs in batch mode with Nero—InCD is the product to use if you want packet-writing software.

CD-R discs

Taiyo-Yuden. We recognize that despite all we've said many people want a simple answer to the complex question of which CD-R discs to buy. If you don't have the time or patience to do your own testing, CD-R discs made by Taiyo Yuden are the best choice. They are sold under the Taiyo Yuden name and are relabeled by others.

CD-RW discs

Verbatim. We formerly recommended Ricoh CD-RW discs, but Ricoh no longer distributes CD-RW discs in the United States. Our original choice was a toss-up between Ricoh and Verbatim. We eventually chose Ricoh rather than Verbatim, but Verbatim, makes very good CD-RW discs that are readily available from online and local sources. There are four distinct types of CD-RW discs. Choose the type your CD-RW drive designed to accept. Older writers use Standard CD-RW discs that support 1X to 4X rewrites. MOre recent CD-RW drives use High Speed discs that support 4X to 12X rewrites. Most current CD-RW drives use Ultra Speed discs that support 12X, 16X, and 24X rewrites. The latest CD-RW drives support 32X rewrites, which require special 32X discs. As of July 2003, these 32X discs have not yet begun shipping in volume, so we are unable to recommend any specific brand for them. We expect Verbatim to introduce 32X CD-RW discs later in 2003, and those are what we're likely to try first.

For updated recommendations, visit: *http://www.hardwareguys.com/picks/cdrw.html*.

12

DVD Drives

DVD originally stood for *Digital Video Disc*, later for *Digital Versatile Disc* (yuck), and now officially stands for nothing at all. DVD is basically CD on steroids. Like a CD, a DVD stores data using tiny pits and lands embossed on a spiral track on an aluminized surface. But where CD-ROM uses a 780 nanometer (nm) infrared laser, DVD uses a 636 nm or 650 nm laser. Shorter wavelengths can resolve smaller pits, which enables pits (and tracks) to be spaced more closely. In conjunction with improved sector formatting, more efficient correction codes, tighter tolerances, and a somewhat larger recording area, this allows a standard DVD disc to store seven times as much data—about 700 MB for CD-ROM versus about 4.7 GB for DVD.

One significant enhancement of DVD over CD is that DVD does away with the plethora of incompatible CD formats. Every DVD disc uses the same physical file structure, promoted by the Optical Storage Technology Association (OSTA), and called *Universal Disc Format (UDF)*. This common physical format means that, in theory at least, any DVD drive or player can read any file on any DVD disc. Microsoft did not support UDF until Windows 98. This forced DVD content providers to adopt an interim standard called *UDF Bridge*, which combines UDF and the CD standard ISO-9660. Only Windows 95 OSR2 and later support UDF Bridge, which forced DVD hardware manufacturers to include UDF Bridge support with their hardware in order to support pre-OSR2 Windows 95 versions.

DVD-ROM

Two types of DVD discs are produced commercially: DVD-Video discs, which store movies, and DVD-ROM discs, which store games, databases, and other computer data. All DVD-Video discs are also DVD-ROM discs, but not all DVD-ROM discs are DVD-Video discs. In effect, DVD-ROM discs correspond to CD-ROM discs, and DVD-Video discs correspond to CD-DA audio discs. DVD-Video discs can be played in DVD-Video players, which are common in home theater setups, or in a computer's DVD-ROM drive. DVD-ROM discs can be played only in a DVD-ROM drive. Like CDs, DVDs are produced commercially by a mechanical pressing process. The DVD-ROM standard is specified by ECMA-267 (*http://www.ecma-international.org/publications/standards/ECMA-267.HTM*) and ECMA-268 (*http://www.ecma-international.org/publications/standards/ECMA-268.HTM*).

DVD-ROM Types and Capacities

DVD-ROM discs are (or will be) available in numerous standardized types, most of which are uncommon or not used at all. Discs may be of either of two physical sizes, and may have one or two sides, each of which may store data in a single or double layer. Like CDs, standard single-sided (SS) DVD-ROM discs are 1.2 mm thick. Double-sided (DS) discs are simply two thin (0.6 mm) discs glued back to back. Most DVD players and drives require manually flipping the disc to access the data on the other side. Each side may contain a single layer (SL) or a double layer (DL) of data. In the latter case, the top layer is semitransparent, allowing the laser to read the second layer underneath it, at the expense of sacrificing some capacity from each layer. Double-sided mixed-layer (DS/ML) discs use a single data layer on one side and a double layer on the other, a compromise made necessary by the limitations of current DVD production methods. DS/DL discs are still a laboratory curiosity, and are likely to remain so for some time. Table 12-1 lists the available DVD types and capacities. Capacities are always given in billions of bytes (10^9 bytes) rather than true gigabytes (2^{30} bytes), but are always advertised as "GB" nonetheless.

Table 12-1. DVD-ROM types and capacities

Type	Diameter	Layers	Actual GB	Stated GB	Video
DVD-1	80 mm	SS/SL	1.36	1.45	0.5 hr
DVD-2	80 mm	SS/DL	2.47	2.65	~1.3
DVD-3	80 mm	DS/SL	2.72	2.9	~1.4
DVD-4	80 mm	DS/DL	4.95	5.3	~2.5
DVD-5	120 mm	SS/SL	4.38	4.7	~2.0
DVD-9	120 mm	SS/DL	7.95	8.5	~4.0
DVD-10	120 mm	DS/SL	8.75	9.4	~4.5
DVD-14	120 mm	DS/SL+DL	12.33	13.24	~6.5
DVD-18	120 mm	DS/DL	15.90	17	~8.0

DVD-ROM Speed

Like CD drives, DVD drives use the "X-factor" to specify throughput. Confusingly, DVD "X" doesn't mean the same thing as CD "X". A 1X CD drive transfers data at 150 KB/s (0.146 MB/s), but a 1X DVD drive transfers data at 11.08 million bits/sec (1.321 MB/s), or about nine times the 1X CD rate. In theory, then, the X-rating for a DVD drive when playing a CD disc would be about nine times its DVD rating. In practice, that's not the case. Early-model DVD-ROM drives typically provide 20X to 32X max CD performance. Current DVD-ROM drives generally provide 40X to 48X max CD performance. DVD throughput faster than

1X is unimportant for DVD-Video, which always plays at 1X, but does provide faster and smoother searching. High throughput is more important if you use the drive to read DVD-ROM discs for playing games or for accessing DVD-ROM data.

Early DVD-ROM drives used CLV, spinning the disc more slowly on outer tracks and faster near the center, to maintain the constant data rate needed for DVD-Video. Current DVD-ROM drives use CAV, spinning the disc at a constant speed and using a buffer to maintain a constant data rate for sequential applications such as DVD-Video. A sure sign that a drive is CAV is if it lists "max" in its speed rating.

The actual throughput of a DVD-ROM drive depends on the type of disc it is reading. For example, a 16X drive may provide 16X max on single-layer discs, but only 10X max on double-layer discs.

As with CD drives, average access time is often not emphasized on DVD drives. The most common use of DVD drives is playing movies, which are sequential data, making both average access time and speeds higher than 1X unimportant. However, if you use a DVD drive to access databases or for other purposes where random access predominates, both average access time and throughput speed become more important.

Choosing a DVD-ROM Drive

In the past, DVD-ROM drives differed sharply in price and performance according to the generation to which they belonged. But DVD-ROM drives have rapidly become commoditized, much as CD-ROM drives did. Nowadays, even $60 entry-level ATAPI drives provide 16X read performance for DVDs and 40X or greater for CDs. You're unlikely to go wrong with a current-model DVD-ROM drive from any of the major Japanese producers including Hitachi, NEC, Panasonic, Sony, and Toshiba.

Use the following guidelines when choosing a DVD-ROM drive:

- Make certain the drive will read at least DVD-ROM (DVD-5, -9, -10, -18); DVD-R; and the following CD formats: CD-DA; CD-ROM; CD-ROM XA; CD+(E)G; CD-Midi; CD-Text; CD-I; CD-I Bridge (Photo-CD and Video-CD); CD-R; CD-RW; and multisession (Photo-CD; CD-Extra; CD-R; CD-RW). If possible, get a drive that will also read DVD-RAM (2.6 GB and 4.7 GB formats) and DVD+RW discs.

- In the past, we recommended getting a DVD hardware decoder card to watch DVD-Video on a PC. That advice is now obsolete. Even the slowest recent systems can display high-quality DVD-Video using the software decoders that are bundled with DVD drives and video cards. If for some reason you must watch DVD-Video on a slow system (< 400 MHz), rather than installing a dedicated DVD decoder card, we recommend installing an upgraded video card that supplies DVD acceleration in hardware. The video quality will likely be higher than with a DVD decoder card, and the newer video card benefits everything you do on the PC rather than just helping DVD-Video.

- DVD-ROM drives are available in ATAPI and SCSI interfaces. Early ATAPI drives had compatibility and performance problems, and so we recommended SCSI. Recent DMA-capable ATAPI drives are better in all respects than their predecessors, and in fact often provide better performance and more features than SCSI models. For that reason, we now recommend ATAPI DVD-ROM drives unless you are building an all-SCSI system.

DVD Writable and Rewritable

In addition to DVD-ROM, there are three writable DVD formats—*DVD-R(A)* for authoring, *DVD-R(G)* for general recording, and DVD+R—and three rewritable DVD formats—*DVD-RW, DVD-RAM,* and *DVD+RW.* All DVD writers and rewriters can read DVD-ROM discs, but each records to its own type of disc, none of which is fully compatible with any other or with existing standard DVD-ROM drives and players.

Incompatibility between the various standards has hindered the market acceptance of all of them, a problem that manufacturers have begun to address by introducing hybrid devices that read and write more than one format. For example, Pioneer produces a combination DVD-R and DVD-RW drive that also writes CD-R and CD-RW, and next-generation DVD-RAM drives will read and write DVD-RAM, DVD-R(W), and CD-R(W). As time passes, we expect this trend to continue.

 The DVD Forum has introduced a DVD Multi logo that certifies compatibility with DVD-R, DVD-RW, and DVD-RAM (although *not* with DVD+RW—the DVD Forum and the DVD+RW Alliance don't much like each other). A DVD Multi drive or player can play all three formats, and a DVD Multi writer can write all three formats.

The following sections describe the competing writable/rewritable DVD formats.

DVD-R

DVD-R (Recordable) was the first recordable DVD standard. DVD-R uses organic dye technology, and is similar conceptually to CD-R. DVD-R discs can be read by most DVD-ROM drives and DVD players. DVD-R 1.0 drives shipped in late 1997, cost $17,000, and stored 3.95 GB on a write-once DVD-R 1.0 disc, which at the time cost $80 each. *The DVD-R 1.0 standard is specified by ECMA-279 (http://www.ecma-international.org/publications/standards/ECMA-279.HTM).* DVD-R 1.9 drives shipped in mid-1999, cost $5,000, stored 4.7 GB on a write-once DVD-R 1.9 disc (which at the time cost $50 each), and could also write 3.95 GB 1.0 discs. DVD-R 2.0 drives shipped in late 2000, store 4.7 GB on write-once 2.0 discs (which are copy-protected), and can also write 1.0 and 1.9 discs. DVD-R branched into two subformats in early 2000:

DVD-R(A)
    DVD-R(A) (*DVD-R Authoring*) drives are for professional use, and use a 635 nm laser which can write DVD-R(A) discs, but not DVD-R(G) discs. DVD-R(A) drives can read either type of DVD-R disc, as can most DVD drives and

DVD players. DVD-R(A) drives sell for $1,500 to $5,000, and DVD-R(A) discs cost roughly twice what DVD-R(G) discs cost.

DVD-R(G)
> *DVD-R(G)* (*DVD-R General*) drives are for home use, are particularly suited to video recording, and use a 650 nm laser that can also write DVD-RAM discs, although as of July 2003 only Panasonic has shipped combination DVD-R(G)/DVD-RAM drives. DVD-R(G) drives can use double-sided discs and incorporate *CPRM* (*Content Protection for Removable Media*) copy protection, which means that DVD-R(G) drives cannot be used legally to duplicate DVD-Video discs.

According to various figures we have seen, DVD-R discs can be read by roughly 85% of older DVD-ROM drives and DVD players.

DVD-RW

DVD-RW (Rewritable) is a newer Pioneer technology, based on DVD-R but using phase-change erasable media similar conceptually to CD-RW. DVD-RW was formerly called DVD-ER and DVD-R/W before Pioneer settled on the DVD-RW designation. Like DVD-R, DVD-RW stores 4.7 GB per disc and produces discs readable by many DVD-ROM drives and players, although the lower reflectivity of DVD-RW discs fools some DVD-ROM players into thinking they're reading a dual-layer disc. DVD-RW discs can be read by about 65% of older DVD-ROM drives and DVD players. Recent DVD-ROM drives or players that have difficulty with DVD-RW discs can often be upgraded to support DVD-RW simply by installing updated firmware.

There are three distinct types of DVD-RW discs, all of which store 4.7 GB and can be rewritten about 1,000 times:

DVD-RW 1.0
> DVD-RW 1.0 discs were used with the first DVD-RW drives shipped in Japan, are seldom seen outside Japan, and have compatibility problems with some drives.

DVD-RW 1.1
> DVD-RW 1.1 discs do not support CPRM and so cannot be used for copying any CPRM-protected original DVDs.

DVD-RW 1.1B
> DVD-RW 1.1B discs support CPRM, and can be used to copy CPRM-protected original DVDs (but only if the producer of the original DVD has encoded the disc to permit copying, and only then by adhering to the restrictions enforced by the CPRM encoding on the original disc). In effect, this means that commercial DVD movies cannot be copied on a DVD-RW drive other than by using special software—the use or even possession of which is illegal in some jurisdictions—to bypass the copy protection.

In April 2001, Pioneer began shipping the sub-$1,000 DVR-A03 drive, which despite its name writes DVD-R(G) discs rather than DVD-R(A) discs. In addition to DVD-R(G) discs, the DVD-A03 writes DVD-RW, CD-R, and CD-RW, and by March 2002 had dropped to a street price of about $500. Apple and

Compaq bundled relabeled DVR-A03 drives with some Mac and Presario models, which greatly contributed to the popularity of DVD-R. Pioneer soon followed with the DVR-A04 drive and then the DVD-A05 drive, which doubled write speeds to 4X DVD-R, 2X DVD-RW.

 Using 4X DVD-R discs or 2X DVD-RW discs in an older recorder may destroy both the disc and the recorder unless you update the drive firmware before using the newer discs. This problem arises because older recorders do not recognize the newer high-speed discs. In attempting to determine media type, the drive turns on its laser and keeps it on in an endless loop, destroying the disc and burning out the laser. Updating the drive firmware prevents damage to your disc or drive. Pioneer DVR-A03, DVR-103, DVR-A04, and DVR-104 drives are affected, as well as relabeled OEM drives and some standalone recorders produced by Pioneer. Visit *http:// www.pioneerelectronics.com/hs/* for more details.

Excluding licensing costs, DVD-R(W) drives and discs are inherently no more costly to produce than CD-R(W), so it is possible that the broad-based support garnered by DVD-R(W) will reduce the price of drives and media dramatically, making DVD-R (and particularly DVD-RW) a viable competitor with other recordable DVD standards. As of July 2003, DVD-R(G) disks sold for $0.75 to $4 each, depending on disc quality and packaging, and DVD-RW discs for $1.25 to $5.50 each.

Pure DVD-R(W) drives remain the almost exclusive preserve of Pioneer, although repackagers such as QPS sell DVD-R(W) drives under their own labels and other manufacturers such as Sony produce hybrid DVD-RW/DVD+RW drives that can write DVD-R and DVD-RW discs. DVD-R(W) has the advantages of wide distribution, the best suitability for recording video, and the highest compatibility with older DVD-ROM drives and players. Against those advantages, it must be said that DVD-R(W) is the least suitable of the competing technologies for storing data, and therefore the least-appropriate choice for a general-purpose PC DVD writer.

DVD-RAM

The DVD-RAM standard is backed by Hitachi, Matsushita (Panasonic), and Toshiba, which until late 2001 had the writable DVD market all to themselves. Although DVD-RW and DVD+RW drives became widely available from several vendors by late 2001, relative to those writable DVD standards, DVD-RAM has several advantages for use in computers, including superior defect management, use of zoned CLV (PCAV) for faster access, and greater media protection via a cartridge. A DVD-RAM disc can be rewritten at least 100,000 times. Alas, only a tiny percentage of older DVD-ROM drives and almost no DVD players can read DVD-RAM discs.

First-generation (DVD-RAM Book 1.0) DVD-RAM drives began shipping in mid-1998, and used a mix of phase-change and magneto-optical technology to record 2.58 billion bytes per side on rewritable media. These discs are not readable by older DVD players and drives, although some recent DVD-ROM drives will read them. Second-generation (DVD-RAM Book 2.1) DVD-RAM drives, which began shipping in late 2000, read and write both original 2.6/5.2 GB DVD-RAM discs and 4.7/9.4 GB DVD-RAM discs.

Several DVD-RAM media types are available. Single-sided 2.6 GB discs are available in Type 1 (sealed) or Type 2 (removable) cartridges. Single-sided 4.7 GB discs are available in Type 2 cartridges. Double-sided 5.2 GB and 9.4 GB discs were originally available only in Type 1 cartridges, but are now available in Type 2 cartridges as well. In late 2002, noncartridge 4.7 GB and 9.4 GB DVD-RAM discs became widely available. These bare discs can be reliably written and rewritten in DVD-RAM drives designed to accept them, but many older DVD-RAM drives simply refuse to write them.

Although a cartridge is advantageous for computer use, a cartridge raises two issues. First, because standard DVD players and drives cannot physically accommodate a cartridge, DVD-RAM discs enclosed in cartridges cannot be read on these devices. Second, once removed from their cartridges, DVD-RAM discs may no longer be reliably recorded in some drives, particularly older models, so removing discs from their cartridges may effectively turn them into write-once media. Most older DVD-RAM drives will not write reliably (if at all) to a bare disc, but recent DVD-RAM drives generally write reliably to a noncartridge disc or to a disc that has been removed from and then reinstalled in its cartridge.

DVD-RAM 1.0 (2.6/5.2 GB) standards are specified by ECMA-272 (*http://www. ecma-international.org/publications/standards/ECMA-272.HTM*) and ECMA-273 (*http://www.ecma-international.org/publications/standards/ECMA-273.HTML,* released in June 1999 and February 1998, respectively. DVD-RAM 2.0 (4.7/9.4 GB) standards are specified by ECMA-330 (*http://www.ecma-international.org/ publications/standards/ECMA-330.HTM*) and ECMA-331 (*http://www.ecma-international.org/publications/standards/ECMA-331.HTM*), both released in December 2001.

Superior defect mapping and other technical considerations make DVD-RAM the best choice for recording data, but its limited compatibility with older DVD-ROM drives and players makes it a poor choice for recording video. If you need a DVD writer solely to back up or archive computer data, DVD-RAM may be the best choice, although DVD-RAM discs cost more than DVD-R(W) and DVD+R(W) discs, and the write speed of DVD-RAM drives is much lower than that of DVD-RW and DVD+RW drives. If you need to record video to be played back on standard DVD-ROM drives or players, choose another technology.

DVD+RW

Originally called DVD+RW, changed to +RW when the DVD Forum objected, and later changed back, DVD+RW is backed by Hewlett-Packard, Mitsubishi Chemical, Philips, Ricoh, Sony, Thomson Multimedia, and Yamaha. Although all are members of the DVD Forum, the DVD+RW standard is not recognized by that organization. First-generation DVD+RW drives were to use phase-change rewritable technology to store 2.8 GB per side. DVD+RW manufacturers formally abandoned the 2.8 GB DVD+RW 1.0 standard in late 1999, without ever having produced drives in commercial numbers. Second-generation DVD+RW drives, which finally shipped in volume in late 2001, expand capacity to 4.7 GB per side and support writing CD-R and CD-RW discs. DVD+RW discs are readable by most recent DVD players and DVD-ROM drives, although as with DVD-RW the lower reflectivity of DVD+RW discs causes some devices to mistake them for dual-layer DVD-ROM discs and therefore refuse to read them. A firmware update solves that problem in many drives and players that experience it. Roughly 65% of older DVD-ROM drives and DVD players can read DVD+RW discs.

DVD+RW backers claim two primary advantages for DVD+RW relative to DVD-RAM. First, like CDs, DVD+RW discs do not use a cartridge (although non-cartridge DVD-RAM discs are now available). This translates into lower costs for drives and media, and allows DVD+RW discs to physically fit standard drives. It also makes DVD+RW drives a viable alternative for laptop systems, which cartridge-based DVD-RAM drives are not. Second, DVD+RW drives use CLV access for sequential data (such as movies) and CAV access for random data, which allows higher performance. Balanced against this is the fact that DVD+RW discs can be rewritten only 1,000 times, versus 100,000 for DVD-RAM.

The obsolete and abandoned +RW standard is specified by ECMA-274 (*http:// www.ecma-international.org/publications/standards/ECMA-274.HTM*). The current DVD+RW standards are maintained by the DVD+RW Alliance (*http://www.dvdrw. com*) and as ECMA-337 (*http://www.ecma-international.org/publications/standards/ ECMA-337.HTM*). Another good (albeit unofficial) source for DVD+RW information is *http://www.dvdplusrw.org*.

DVD+R

The first DVD+RW drives could use only rewritable DVD+RW discs. CD-R remains popular despite the availability of rewritable CD-RW discs, and it was clear to DVD+RW supporters that a write-once version of DVD+RW would fill an important niche. The write-once version of DVD+RW, as you might expect, is called DVD+R. DVD+R provides the equivalent of a 4.7 GB CD-R disc. Roughly 85% of older DVD-ROM drives and DVD players read DVD+R discs, which is to say they have about the same level of compatibility as DVD-R discs.

DVD+R discs began shipping in mid-2002, and a firestorm erupted almost immediately. Some DVD+RW drive makers had preannounced the availability of DVD+R discs and had told buyers of first-generation DVD+RW drives that a simple firmware update would allow the drives to use DVD+R discs as well. That turned out not to be the case, and buyers of early DVD+RW drives learned that the only way to add DVD+R support was to replace their drives. Current DVD+RW drives support DVD+R and DVD+RW discs interchangeably. Like CD-R and DVD-R before it, DVD+R discs use organic dye technology, so nothing other than patent royalties prevents DVD+R (and DVD-R) discs from eventually falling to prices nearly as low as CD-R discs.

Writable DVD Formats Compared

It's clear that the competition to become the mass-market writable DVD standard is a three-horse race, but it is uncertain which will ultimately triumph. In the first edition of this book, we noted that the market had not yet determined a winner in the writable DVD format wars and that we hoped a single standard would prevail by the time the second edition was published. We said the same thing in the second edition, and now we're forced to say the same in the third.

Perhaps by the time the fourth edition is published we'll finally have a single standard. But we won't hold our breath. The issue is the huge amount of money at stake. If one standard prevails, DVD writers will become as commonplace as CD writers are now, and DVD blanks will sell by the billion. The company or consortium that holds the patents on the winning standard will rake in huge amounts in licensing fees for drives and discs. That means the companies involved aren't going to compromise, and the only hope for achieving a single standard is that the market will sort things out.

DVD-R and DVD-RW

These formats have the strong backing of Pioneer and Apple and the increasing popularity of home video editing to sustain them. DVD-R and DVD-RW discs are inexpensive (and getting cheaper every month) and readily available. Current drives write DVR-R discs at 4X, which matches DVD+R, and DVD-RW discs at 2X, versus the 4X write speed of DVD+RW. For the time being, DVD-R/RW discs are cheaper than DVD+R/RW discs, although we expect that to change as DVR+R/RW drives continue to gain market share.

DVD-R is an excellent choice for recording video because it offers very high compatibility with older DVD-ROM drives and DVD players. DVD-R(G) and DVD-RW are not the best choice for recording data because the DVD-R(W) format lacks defect mapping support (although new-generation drives may support Mt. Rainier, which implements defect mapping in drive hardware). DVD-RW is the least-desirable rewritable standard because its sequential access method prevents incremental rewrites.

 Because of the high price of drives and discs, DVD-R(A) is and is likely to remain a niche product, of interest primarily to professional video producers.

DVD-RAM

DVD-RAM has been shipping since 1998, is an official standard of the DVD Forum, is backed by Hitachi, Panasonic, and Toshiba, and has distinct advantages for recording data. Despite these advantages, various industry pundits including John Dvorak have declared DVD-RAM dead. We suspect that DVD-RAM, like Mark Twain, finds the rumors of its death to be greatly exaggerated. Without question, DVD-RAM suffers several disadvantages relative to DVD-RW and DVD+RW. DVD-RAM discs can be read by relatively few DVD-ROM drives and by almost no DVD players. DVD-RAM discs cost more than DVD-RW or DVD+RW discs. Finally, DVD-RAM is slow. Whereas DVD+RW rewrites at 4X and DVD-RW at 2X, DVD-RAM rewrites at just 1X, and that's with write verification turned off. Turning on write verification slows DVD-RAM writes to a snail-like 0.5X.

So why would anyone use DVD-RAM? Reliability, pure and simple. When we write 4.7 GB of data to an optical disc, we want some reasonable assurance that we will later be able to read every bit of that data without error. The defect mapping and robust error detection and correction of the DVD-RAM format provide a level of assurance that other rewritable formats do not.

DVD+RW and DVD+R

DVD+RW and DVD+R are not recognized by the DVD Forum, but are backed by the DVD+RW Alliance, which comprises, among others, Dell, HP, Mitsubishi/Verbatim, Philips, Ricoh, Sony, Thomson, and Yamaha. Second- and third-generation DVD+RW drives write DVD+R discs at 4X and rewrite DVD+RW discs at 2.4X or 4X. DVD+R discs are compatible with roughly 85% of older DVD-ROM drives and DVD players, which is comparable to DVD-R compatibility. DVD+RW discs are compatible with about 65% of older drives and players, which again is comparable to DVD-RW compatibility.

Relative to DVD-RAM drives, DVD+RW drives offer much higher speed at the expense of less-robust error detection and correction. Relative to DVD-RW drives, DVD+RW drives offer the following advantages:

Higher rewrite speeds

Current DVD+R and DVD+RW drives write high-speed discs at 4X, versus DVD-R 4X writes and DVD-RW 2X writes.

 Although 2.4X DVD+RW drives were not designed to use 4X discs, many such drives can use 4X discs if you upgrade the firmware.

Superior error detection and correction

Although DVD-RAM provides the best error detection and correction, current DVD+RW drives provide error detection and correction superior to DVD-RW drives, which do not support hardware defect management. The defect management used by DVD+RW drives is invisible to standard DVD-ROM drives and DVD players.

Lossless linking

DVD+RW drives support lossless linking, which means they can rewrite any individual sector of a DVD+RW disc directly, while maintaining compatibility with DVD-ROM drives and DVD players. Lossless linking also enables packet writing and Mt. Rainier (EasyWrite) support. Conversely, making a change to a DVD-RW disc requires rewriting the entire disc.

Background formatting

DVD-RW and DVD+RW discs must be formatted before they can be written to. The difference is that DVD-RW drives format discs in the foreground, which may take an hour to complete in a 1X drive. DVD+RW drives format discs in the background. After formatting the lead-in and a portion of the data area, which requires only a minute or so, a DVD+RW drive can immediately begin writing data to the disc as formatting continues in the background. A partially formatted disc can be ejected at any time and can be read by a standard DVD-ROM drive. When you reinsert the disc in the DVD+RW drive, formatting recommences and continues until completion.

DVD+VR support

DVD+RW drives support the DVD+VR video format, which allows editing a video disc while maintaining compatibility with DVD players. Conversely, the VR format used by DVD-RW drives requires rewriting the entire disc if you make even a minor change.

Here's our take on the competition. For backing up or archiving computer data, the best choice is a DVD-RAM drive. For general-purpose DVD writing, the best choice is a DVD+R/RW drive or a hybrid drive that can write DVD-R, DVD-RW, DVD+R, and DVD+RW. Such drives are often called DVD±RW drives (pronounced DVD-plus-or-minus-RW), an unofficial but useful designation that probably annoys both the DVD Forum and the DVD+RW Alliance. DVD±RW drives can write any DVD blank except DVD-RAM, which allows you to choose media type by price and suitability for the intended use. DVD+R and DVD-R blanks are fine for recording video, and DVD+RW blanks are usable (if not ideal) for backing up and archiving data.

 All these technologies are *legally* useless for duplicating DVD-Video discs (although very few technical hurdles exist and many people already do it on a regular basis). Laws such as the *Digital Millennium Copyright Act* (*DMCA*) and standards such as *CPRM* have effectively eliminated Fair Use provisions of traditional copyright. You can use these drives to store data or video that you have produced, but *not* as a digital VCR or to back up your DVD-Video discs, *at least without breaking the law*. Movie industry lobbyists are fighting desperately to make sure you don't have that option.

Read/Write Compatibility

Table 12-2 lists read/write compatibility between various types of DVD drives with CD and DVD media. Drives are in the heading row; media types are in the left column. The first circle indicates read compatibility and the second write compatibility. An asterisk on either or both sides of the slash means some but not all drive models of that type read and/or write the media type in question, possibly with limitations, which may be drive- or media-specific. For example, only some recent DVD-ROM drives can read DVD-RAM media, and some DVD-ROM drives cannot read DVD-RW media because they mistake them for dual-layer DVD-ROM discs.

Table 12-2. Drive and media read/write compatibility

	DVD-ROM	DVD-R(A)	DVD-R(G)	DVD-RW	DVD-RAM	DVD+RW
CD-DA	● / ○	● / ○	● / ○	● / ○	● / ○	● / ○
CD-ROM	● / ○	● / ○	● / ○	● / ○	● / ○	● / ○
CD-R	● / ○	● / ○	● / ○	● / ○	● / ○	● / ○

Table 12-2. Drive and media read/write compatibility (continued)

	DVD-ROM	DVD-R(A)	DVD-R(G)	DVD-RW	DVD-RAM	DVD+RW
CD-RW	●/○	●/○	●/○	●/○	●/○	●/○
DVD Video	●/○	●/○	●/○	●/○	●/○	●/○
DVD-ROM	●/○	●/○	●/○	●/○	●/○	●/○
DVD-R(A)	*/○	●/●	●/○	●/○	●/○	●/○
DVD-R(G)	*/○	●/○	●/●	●/*	●/○	●/○
DVD-RW	*/○	●/○	●/○	●/●	*/○	*/○
DVD-RAM	*/○	○/○	○/○	○/○	●/●	○/○
DVD+RW	*/○	*/○	*/○	*/○	*/○	●/●
DVD+R	*/○	*/○	*/○	*/○	*/○	●/●

Compatibility may vary by drive manufacturer. For example, a DVD-ROM drive made by a member of the DVD-RAM group may read DVD-RAM discs, but is unlikely to read DVD+RW discs. Conversely, a DVD-ROM drive made by a member of the DVD+RW group may read DVD+RW discs, but is unlikely to read DVD-RAM discs.

Choosing a Writable DVD Drive

You take a risk no matter which of the three competing technologies you choose. Whichever you buy, there's a chance it will be orphaned if the market chooses one of the others. So which of these drives should you buy?

- If you need reliable, high-capacity optical storage for data, get a DVD-RAM drive. A DVD-RAM drive is slower than the alternatives and won't write CD-R or CD-RW, but has very reliable error correction. DVD-RAM is suitable if the drive and the data it stores will be used on one computer, or if you need to transfer large amounts of data between computers that all have DVD-RAM drives. Other than performance and higher media cost, the chief drawback of DVD-RAM is that DVD-RAM discs are incompatible with many DVD-ROM drives and DVD players. In short, DVD-RAM is the most reliable of the competing formats for storing large amounts of data, but is the best choice only if high write speeds are unimportant and you will never need to read the DVD-RAM discs in a system without a DVD-RAM drive.

- If you need a general-purpose DVD writer, get a DVD+R/RW drive or a hybrid DVD+/-RW drive. These drives can write any DVD blank except a DVD-RAM disc, and most can write CD-R and CD-RW discs as well. DVD+/-RW drives offer the best combination of flexibility and reliability for most users. They produce discs that are readable by most DVD-ROM drives and DVD players, and write discs as fast or faster than competing single-standard drives. They are ideal for writing video discs, and a reasonable choice for backing up and archiving data.

- We consider single-standard DVD-R/RW drives undesirable because they limit your choice of media. In particular, we recommend against a DVD-RW drive no matter how low the price unless you are certain you will never use the drive for anything except recording video to DVD-R discs. In our opinion, DVD-RW

DVD Drives

compares poorly to DVD+RW for most purposes, so it makes little sense to saddle yourself with what amounts to a dedicated DVD-R video writer.

- A single-standard DVD+R/RW drive is a much better choice. It writes DVD+R discs, which are as useful for video as DVD-R discs, and also supports the superior DVD+RW rewritable format. Choosing a DVD+R/RW drive means you can't write DVD-R/RW discs, which for now cost a bit less than DVD+R/RW discs, but a single-standard DVD+R/RW drive costs $50 to $150 less than a hybrid drive of equal quality.

 Although it's still too soon to declare a winner in the writable DVD format wars, as of July 2003 we think DVD+R/RW is the leading candidate. DVD-RAM cannot compete as a mainstream writable DVD format, although it remains the safest format for archiving data. The only advantage that DVD-R/RW has relative to DVD+R/RW is somewhat lower media cost, and that disparity is disappearing quickly. We expect that discs for either format will soon sell at comparable prices. If that comes to pass, DVD-R/RW will simply fade away.

Installing and Configuring a DVD Drive

Installing and configuring a DVD-ROM drive or DVD writer requires the same steps detailed in Chapter 10, with the following exceptions:

- Windows 95B/98/Me and Windows 2000/XP support DVD-ROM drives natively, and see DVD writers as DVD-ROM drives. Windows can access DVD-ROM data discs directly, but it requires a player application to decode and display DVD-Video.
- Linux recognizes DVD-ROM drives and DVD writers only as standard CD-ROM drives. Although Linux can read ISO-9660-formatted DVD discs, reading UDF-formatted DVD discs (including standard DVD-Video and DVD-ROM discs) requires separate applications.
- Just as for writing CDs, Windows and Linux both require separate applications to write DVD discs in DVD-RAM, DVD-R/RW, or DVD+R/+RW drives. To write DVDs with an ATAPI DVD writer under Linux, you must configure the DVD writer to use the ide-scsi driver rather than the default ide driver.
- DVD drives use Region Coding, which restricts which DVD discs may be played in that drive. For example, a drive set to Region 1 (U.S. and Canada) can play only Region 1 discs, while a drive set to Region 2 (Europe) can play only Region 2 discs. By default, DVD Region is set to the installation location. The Region setting for the drive can be changed a limited number of times, typically five.

Configuring a DVD Drive Under Windows

The only configuration a DVD drive may require under Windows is resetting the Region Code using Device Manager. To do so, expand the listing for DVD/CD-ROM drives, double-click the entry for the DVD drive to display Properties, and then display the Advanced Settings page, shown in Figure 12-1. The line at the bottom of the dialog states how many more Region Code changes are allowed for this drive. Use the scrolling list to locate the country and click to highlight that country. Windows inserts the corresponding region in the New Region box. Click OK to confirm the warning dialog to reprogram the drive for the new region.

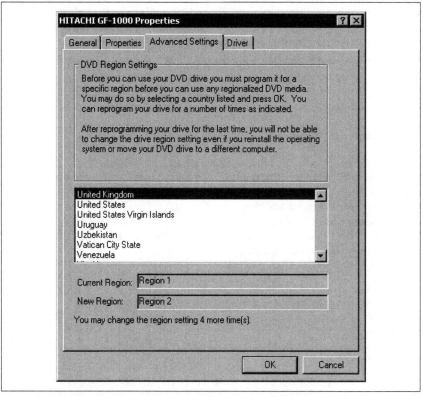

Figure 12-1. Using the Advanced Settings page of the Properties dialog to reset the DVD Region Code with Windows 2000 Professional

 Some DVD drives shipped before January 1, 2000 did not implement Region Code locking in hardware, instead using software and the registry to control the number of times the Region could be changed. If you have one of those drives and exceed the allowed number of Region changes, you can reset the counter by uninstalling the drive itself and the software that accesses it (e.g., a DVD player application), deleting all references to the drive and the software from the registry, and then reinstalling the drive and software. All DVD drives shipped on or after January 1, 2000 implement Region Code locking on a chip inside the drive itself, and in theory cannot be reset short of returning them to the manufacturer. Of course, many DVD manufacturers dislike region coding intensely, and have "accidentally" left ways by which a user can reset the region coding counter. We can't detail those here, but bypassing region coding is a popular topic on various Internet sites.

Configuring a DVD writer under Windows is no more difficult than configuring a DVD-ROM drive. Recent versions of Windows recognize a DVD writer natively as a DVD-ROM device, and can use it to read CD-ROM and DVD-ROM data discs. Because a DVD writer provides the read functions of a DVD-ROM drive, you can use it to watch DVD-Video discs simply by installing whatever player application you prefer and verifying that the Region Code is configured properly. Note, however, that DVD writers often have slow read speeds, so if you are ripping video, you may want to install a separate 16X DVD-ROM drive for that purpose.

Writing DVDs requires DVD writing software. Most DVD writers include software, although it may have limited functionality. Nero Burning ROM, our favorite software for burning CDs, also supports most popular DVD writers, and is an excellent choice if you need a full-featured writing package for Windows.

Configuring a DVD Drive Under Linux

Configuring a DVD drive under Linux requires a bit more work than doing so under Windows. In contrast to recent versions of Windows, which natively recognize a DVD-ROM drive as such, Linux by default sees a DVD-ROM drive as a CD-ROM drive. Without additional configuration, Linux can use a DVD-ROM drive to read a CD-ROM data disc and may be able to read a DVD-ROM data disc formatted as ISO-9660. That's where it ends, however. By itself, Linux cannot read UDF-formatted discs, which is to say standard DVD-ROM and DVD-Video discs, and it cannot play DVD movies.

In this respect, Linux is similar to Windows NT 4. Although neither understands DVD natively, that problem is not insurmountable. Either operating system can access data and video DVD discs with the help of player applications, many of which are available for Linux. Chances are your Linux distribution installed several player applications by default. If not, it's easy enough to locate, download, and install the player applications you need.

Configuring an ATA/ATAPI (not SCSI) DVD-ROM drive for optimum performance under Linux is straightforward. Add the following line to your startup script:

```
/usr/sbin/hdparm -c1d1k1 /dev/hdc
```

Substitute the appropriate device for */dev/hdc* if your DVD-ROM drive is other than Secondary Master (hdc). Our editor, Brian Jepson, notes, "As a general rule when working with *hdparm*, I usually leave it at -k0 for a couple of days, then check the logs for error messages and use *hdparm* to verify that it kept the settings. If all is well, I'll change the script to use -k1. If all is *not* well, I usually have to stop using –d1 unless I can figure out why it didn't keep."

You may also set up the DVD-ROM drive as a raw device for playback, which can increase read performance dramatically. To do so, add the following line, again substituting the appropriate device if your DVD-ROM drive is configured as something other than Secondary Master, and tell your DVD applications to read from */dev/raw/raw1* instead of */dev/hdc*:

```
/usr/bin/raw /dev/raw/raw1 /dev/hdc
```

Configuring a DVD writer under Linux may be more problematic. If your DVD writer uses a SCSI interface, most recent Linux versions automatically detect its capabilities and install it as a writable device. If your DVD writer uses the ATAPI interface, configuring it requires a few extra steps. By default, current versions of Linux recognize an ATAPI DVD writer as a CD-ROM drive and use the standard ide driver. To enable write support on an ATAPI DVD writer, you must configure the DVD writer to use the ide-scsi SCSI emulation driver rather than the standard ide driver. Once you do that, Linux recognizes the DVD writer as a writable SCSI device and you can write to the drive using applications such as dvdrtools (*http:// www.nongnu.org/dvdrtools/*) as well as standard Linux copy, archiving, and backup utilities.

In the following sections, we take you through the process we used to install, configure, and test an elderly Hitachi ATAPI DVD-RAM drive that we installed in an existing Linux system. That system initially had a Seagate hard drive as Primary Master and a Plextor CD writer as Secondary Master. We shut down the system, popped the lid, and installed the Hitachi DVD-RAM drive as Secondary Slave. We then put the system back together, connected all the cables, and fired it up. The following sections take it from there.

Viewing drive parameters

The first thing to verify is that Linux sees the new drive, and the easiest way to do that is to look at the list of the optical drives that Linux thinks are present. To view parameters for the installed drives, display */proc/sys/dev/cdrom/info*. This file lists the hardware capabilities of each optical drive and establishes that Linux recognizes that the drive is present. Example 12-1 shows the info file for a PC with two optical drives installed: a CD writer as Secondary Master and a DVD-RAM drive as Secondary Slave.

Example 12-1. The info file for a PC with a CD writer and a DVD-RAM drive installed

```
CD-ROM information, Id: cdrom.c 3.12 2000/10/18

drive name:             sr0     hdd
drive speed:            32      0
drive # of slots:       1       1
Can close tray:         1       1
Can open tray:          1       1
Can lock tray:          1       1
Can change speed:       1       1
Can select disk:        0       0
Can read multisession:  1       1
Can read MCN:           1       1
Reports media changed:  1       1
Can play audio:         1       1
Can write CD-R:         0       0
Can write CD-RW:        0       0
Can read DVD:           0       1
Can write DVD-R:        0       0
Can write DVD-RAM:      0       1
```

This example shows drive status immediately after the DVD-RAM drive was installed. The CD writer had already been configured to use the ide-scsi driver, which allows it to write discs as well as read them. Because the DVD-RAM drive is using the standard ide driver, it is shown as hdd rather than sr1.

Enabling the ide-scsi driver

Although Linux recognizes the DVD-RAM drive immediately after it is installed, it does so using the standard ide driver. By default the standard ide driver takes control of all IDE devices, including ATA hard drives and ATAPI optical drives. The standard ide driver is sufficient for hard drives and for read-only optical drives, but writable optical drives require SCSI emulation. The ide-scsi driver provides that emulation.

 Linux supports SCSI CD writers and DVD writers directly. The ide-scsi driver is necessary only to provide SCSI emulation to ATAPI CD/DVD writers. Some recent Linux releases recognize CD/DVD writers at install time and automatically enable ide-scsi support. If you are using an earlier release or adding an ATAPI CD or DVD writer to an existing system, you may need to enable ide-scsi support manually.

The easiest way to enable ide-scsi emulation is to add or edit a line in your boot configuration file. First, use the command grep ATAPI /var/log/dmesg to verify drive configuration. You should see output similar to that shown in Example 12-2. In this example, the DVD writer for which we want to enable SCSI emulation via the ide-scsi driver is currently recognized by the system as hdd, under the control of the standard ide driver.

Example 12-2. Using the grep command to verify drive configuration

```
[thompson@caldwell thompson]$ grep ATAPI /var/log/dmesg
hdc: PLEXTOR CD-R PX-W2410A, ATAPI CD/DVD-ROM drive
hdd: HITACHI GF-1000 B, ATAPI CD/DVD-ROM drive
hdd: ATAPI DVD-ROM DVD-RAM drive, 512kB Cache
scsi0 : SCSI host adapter emulation for IDE ATAPI devices
[thompson@caldwell thompson]$
```

To enable ide-scsi for hdd using the grub bootloader, log on as root and edit the file */boot/grub/grub.conf*. In the kernel line, add the text hdd=ide-scsi. Example 12-3 shows *grub.conf* with the added text in bold.

Example 12-3. The grub.conf file with ide-scsi emulation for hdd added

```
#boot=/dev/hda
default=1
timeout=10
splashimage=(hd0,0)/grub/splash.xpm.gz
title Red Hat Linux (2.4.18-18.8.0debug)
  root (hd0,0)
  kernel /vmlinuz-2.4.18-18.8.0debug ro root=LABEL=/ hdc=ide-scsi hdd=ide-scsi
  initrd /initrd-2.4.18-18.8.0debug.img
```

Example 12-3. The grub.conf file with ide-scsi emulation for hdd added (continued)

```
title Red Hat Linux (2.4.18-18.8.0)
  root (hd0,0)
  kernel /vmlinuz-2.4.18-18.8.0 ro root=LABEL=/ hdc=ide-scsi hdd=ide-scsi
  initrd /initrd-2.4.18-18.8.0.img
```

To enable ide-scsi for hdd using the lilo bootloader, log on as root and edit */etc/lilo.conf*. If there is an existing append line, simply add the text hdd=ide-scsi to that line. If there is no append line, add the line append="hdd=ide-scsi". Example 12-4 shows *lilo.conf* with the added text in bold.

Example 12-4. The lilo.conf file with ide-scsi emulation for hdd added

```
prompt
timeout=50
default=linux
boot=/dev/hda
map=/boot/map
install=/boot/boot.b
message=/boot/message
linear

image=/boot/vmlinuz-2.4.18-14
  label=linux
  initrd=/boot/initrd-2.4.18-14.img
  read-only
  append="hdc=ide-scsi hdd=ide-scsi root=LABEL=/"
```

After you restart the system, examine */proc/sys/dev/cdrom/info* to verify that the DVD writer is using the ide-scsi driver. In Example 12-5, the DVD-RAM drive now appears as sr1 rather than hdd, indicating that it is now controlled by the ide-scsi driver.

Example 12-5. /proc/sys/dev/cdrom/info showing that the DVD writer now uses the ide-scsi driver

```
CD-ROM information, Id: cdrom.c 3.12 2000/10/18
```

drive name:	sr1	sr0
drive speed:	0	40
drive # of slots:	1	1
Can close tray:	1	1
Can open tray:	1	1
Can lock tray:	1	1
Can change speed:	1	1
Can select disk:	0	0
Can read multisession:	1	1
Can read MCN:	1	1
Reports media changed:	1	1
Can play audio:	1	1
Can write CD-R:	0	1
Can write CD-RW:	0	1
Can read DVD:	1	0
Can write DVD-R:	0	0
Can write DVD-RAM:	1	0

DVD Drives

You can also examine the file */var/log/dmesg* to verify that the system is using the ide-scsi driver for the DVD writer, as well as to obtain other information. The two ide_setup lines in Example 12-6 indicates that the ide-scsi driver is being used for hdc and hdd. The hard drive (hda) is using DMA mode, as is the CD writer (hdc). Although hdb is shown as using PIO mode, in fact there is no device connected as Primary Slave.

Example 12-6. /var/log/dmesg showing that the DVD writer uses ide-scsi but operates in PIO mode

```
[thompson@caldwell var]$ grep ide /var/log/dmesg
BIOS-provided physical RAM map:
Kernel command line: ro root=LABEL=/ hdc=ide-scsi hdd=ide-scsi
ide_setup: hdc=ide-scsi
ide_setup: hdd=ide-scsi
ide: Assuming 33MHz system bus speed for PIO modes; override with idebus=xx
    ide0: BM-DMA at 0xffa0-0xffa7, BIOS settings: hda:DMA, hdb:pio
    ide1: BM-DMA at 0xffa8-0xffaf, BIOS settings: hdc:DMA, hdd:pio
ide0 at 0x1f0-0x1f7,0x3f6 on irq 14
ide1 at 0x170-0x177,0x376 on irq 15
ide-floppy driver 0.99.newide
ide-floppy driver 0.99.newide
EXT3 FS 2.4-0.9.18, 14 May 2002 on ide0(3,2), internal journal
EXT3 FS 2.4-0.9.18, 14 May 2002 on ide0(3,1), internal journal
[thompson@caldwell var]$
```

The status line for ide1 is cause for concern. That line indicates that the Secondary interface is operating in BM-DMA (bus mastering DMA) mode, but it also shows that the BIOS is reporting hdd (the DVD-RAM drive) as PIO mode. There's a possible conflict here, because both devices on an ATA interface must operate in either PIO mode or DMA mode. Interfaces don't support two devices operating in different modes, so this line is oxymoronical.

There is no reason the DVD-RAM drive should operate in PIO mode. The drive is DMA-capable, as are the interface and the cable. This may be just an initial status report and Linux may configure the DVD writer to use DMA later in the boot process. It's worth checking, though, because if this interface really is being forced to use PIO mode, the CD writer will no longer work properly.

When in doubt, use hdparm to verify the current operating status of drives. Example 12-7 shows the output of hdparm -i for both optical drives. Both use DMA, although the DVD writer is configured as an MDMA-2 device and the CD writer as UDMA-2. Because both devices on an interface must use the same DMA level, that means the CD writer will use MDMA-2 (16.7 MB/s), but that is more than fast enough to support 24X CD writing.

Example 12-7. hdparm showing that both optical drives are using DMA

```
[root@caldwell sbin]# ./hdparm -i /dev/hdd

/dev/hdd:

 Model=HITACHI GF-1000 B, FwRev=I0I0, SerialNo=
```

```
Config={ Fixed Removeable DTR<=5Mbs DTR>10Mbs nonMagnetic }
RawCHS=0/0/0, TrkSize=0, SectSize=0, ECCbytes=0
BuffType=unknown, BuffSize=0kB, MaxMultSect=0
(maybe): CurCHS=0/0/0, CurSects=0, LBA=yes, LBAsects=0
IORDY=on/off, tPIO={min:120,w/IORDY:120}, tDMA={min:120,rec:120}
PIO modes:  pio0 pio1 pio2 pio3 pio4
DMA modes:  sdma0 sdma1 sdma2 mdma0 mdma1 *mdma2
AdvancedPM=no

[root@caldwell sbin]# ./hdparm -i /dev/hdc

/dev/hdc:

Model=PLEXTOR CD-R PX-W2410A, FwRev=1.03, SerialNo=137699
Config={ Fixed Removeable DTR<=5Mbs DTR>10Mbs nonMagnetic }
RawCHS=0/0/0, TrkSize=0, SectSize=0, ECCbytes=0
BuffType=unknown, BuffSize=0kB, MaxMultSect=0
(maybe): CurCHS=0/0/0, CurSects=0, LBA=yes, LBAsects=0
IORDY=on/off, tPIO={min:180,w/IORDY:120}, tDMA={min:120,rec:120}
PIO modes:  pio0 pio1 pio2 pio3 pio4
DMA modes:  sdma0 sdma1 sdma2 mdma0 mdma1 mdma2
UDMA modes: udma0 udma1 *udma2
AdvancedPM=no

[root@caldwell sbin]#
```

Formatting a disc

After determining that the DVD-RAM drive is configured properly, the next step is to verify that the DVD writer can write to a disc. Formatting a disc is an easy test. To do that, we use the command mke2fs -c -v -b 2048 -m 0 /dev/scd1, where:

* mke2fs—creates a Linux second extended filesystem
* -c—checks for bad blocks
* -v—provides verbose output
* -b 2048—uses blocksize 2,048
* -m 0—reserves zero blocks for superuser
* /dev/scd1—the device to be formatted

After we issue that command, the DVD-RAM access light begins blinking, and the text shown in Example 12-8 appears.

Example 12-8. A verbose display when formatting a disc with mke2fs

```
[root@caldwell sbin]# ./mke2fs -c -v -b 2048 -m 0 /dev/scd1
mke2fs 1.27 (8-Mar-2002)
Filesystem label=
OS type: Linux
Block size=2048 (log=1)
Fragment size=2048 (log=1)
304800 inodes, 1218960 blocks
```

Example 12-8. A verbose display when formatting a disc with mke2fs (continued)

```
0 blocks (0.00%) reserved for the super user
First data block=0
75 block groups
16384 blocks per group, 16384 fragments per group
4064 inodes per group
Superblock backups stored on blocks:
        16384, 49152, 81920, 114688, 147456, 409600, 442368, 802816

Running command: badblocks -b 2048 -s /dev/scd1 1218960
Checking for bad blocks (read-only test): done
Writing inode tables: done
Writing superblocks and filesystem accounting information: done

This filesystem will be automatically checked every 35 mounts or
180 days, whichever comes first.  Use tune2fs -c or -i to override.
[root@caldwell sbin]#
```

After the format completes and you mount the device, you can read and write to the drive as you would to any other volume.

Troubleshooting DVD Problems

Any problem you encounter with a DVD-ROM drive or DVD writer is likely to have the same cause and solution as a similar problem with a CD-ROM drive or CD writer. Please refer to those chapters for detailed troubleshooting advice.

Our Picks

ATAPI DVD-ROM drives have largely replaced ATAPI CD-ROM drives, which are becoming increasingly difficult to find. Current DVD-ROM drives substitute well for a CD-ROM drive. They're a bit more expensive than CD-ROM drives, but you can buy a good DVD-ROM drive for less than $60. For a general-purpose system, we now recommend DVD-ROM rather than CD-ROM. Here are the DVD drives we recommend:

ATAPI DVD-ROM drive
> **Hitachi, Panasonic, Pioneer, or Toshiba.** All of these manufacturers produce first-rate DVD-ROM drives, although they vary in features, speed, and price. If all you need a DVD-ROM drive to do is read DVD-ROM and CD discs, nearly any model from a Japanese maker will suffice. If you need a drive that can read other formats, such as DVD-RAM or DVD-RW, or a drive that supports high-speed DMA modes, the details become more important. See our web site, listed at the end of this chapter, for current detailed recommendations.

SCSI DVD-ROM drive
> **Toshiba SD-M1401S.** DVD-ROM is primarily a consumer-oriented technology, so relatively few SCSI drives are available. Of those, the 10X SD-M1401S is the best we know of. SCSI is usually a step ahead of ATAPI in

performance, but the SD-M1401 SCSI drive is slower than its ATAPI cousin. Although we're SCSI advocates, when it comes to DVD-ROM, we use ATAPI. Unless you're building an all-SCSI system, we recommend you do the same (*http://www.toshiba.com*).

Combination DVD-ROM/CD-RW drive

Plextor 20/10/40-12A PlexCombo. In May 2002, Plextor shipped the Plex-Combo drive, which combines a 12X DVD-ROM drive with a CD burner that writes at 20X, rewrites at 10X, and reads at 40X. In the past, we gave combination DVD-ROM/CD-RW drives only a lukewarm recommendation. Although convenient, they were much slower than individual components, appeared more likely to fail, and lacked such niceties as BURN-Proof. Although the 20X writes and 10X rewrites of the PlexCombo are much slower than those of the fastest standalone CD burner models, they are more than fast enough for most purposes. The PlexCombo is solidly constructed, and after extensive testing we have concluded that it is as reliable as any other Plextor optical drive, which is to say extremely so. The PlexCombo is also the first combination DVD-ROM/CD-RW drive that supports BURN-Proof, which is a key factor in our recommendation. If you need both DVD-ROM and CD-RW functions and if 20X writes and 10X rewrites are fast enough for your needs, we recommend the Plextor PlexCombo 20/10/40-12A without reservation (*http://www.plextor.com*).

It's still not easy to choose among the competing writable DVD formats. Although it is slower and less compatible than the other standards, DVD-RAM remains an excellent choice for those who use a DVD writer to archive data. Conversely, for those who use a DVD writer to record video, DVD-R/RW drives are attractive because DVD-R/RW discs cost less than DVD+R/RW discs of comparable quality. DVD+R/RW drives have less robust error correction than DVD-RAM drives, and their discs cost a bit more than those for DVD-R/RW drives, but for many people DVD+R/RW is the best compromise. Hybrid DVD+/-R/RW drives can use -R/RW discs or +R/RW discs, but the drives themselves cost significantly more than single-standard drives. Accordingly, we recommend choosing one of the following drives, balancing your own priorities.

DVD-RAM drive

Toshiba or Hitachi. Both of these companies produce top-notch ATAPI DVD-RAM drives. Price, performance, and features vary between models, but if you need a high-capacity optical rewriter for archiving data, you're likely to be happy with a current model from either company. DVD-RAM is a poor choice for general-purpose DVD writing. But for storing data (as opposed to video), we think DVD-RAM is the best choice, and we believe that Toshiba and Hitachi make the best DVD-RAM drives available.

DVD-R/RW drive

Pioneer. Pioneer invented DVD-R, and its DVD-R/RW drives are first-rate. If you record primarily video, a Pioneer DVD-R/RW drive may be your best choice. Although for various technical reasons DVD-R/RW is inferior to DVD-RAM or DVD+R/RW for storing data, a DVD-R/RW drive unquestionably offers more flexibility than a DVD-RAM drive. If DVD-R/RW is right for you, we think you'll be happy with a current Pioneer model.

DVD+RW drive

Plextor. Plextor was very late to market with a DVD writer, finally shipping its PX-504A DVD+R/RW drive in March 2003. During a telephone conversation with a Plextor executive in 2000, Robert asked when Plextor would begin offering DVD writers. The response was that Plextor would not offer a DVD writer until it believed that one of the competing DVD standards had won. By shipping a DVD+R/RW drive, Plextor has come down firmly in the DVD+R/RW camp, and we can't argue with that judgment. Our experience with Plextor DVD writers has been uniformly excellent. DVD+R/RW writers have similar specifications and performance, but some other DVD writers are much more sensitive to media variations than Plextor writers. On that basis, and based on Plextor's traditional robustness and quality, we recommend (and use) Plextor DVD+R/RW drives as the best general-purpose DVD writers available.

To view our current specific recommendations by make and model, visit: *http://www.hardwareguys.com/picks/dvd.html.*

13

Hard Disk Interfaces

The hard disk interface defines the physical and logical means by which the hard disk connects to the PC. In the 1980s, the most popular disk interfaces were ST506/412 and ESDI, which are now obsolete. These old drives use two ribbon cables (a 20-pin data cable and a 34-pin control cable) versus the single-ribbon cable used by modern drives. Finding one of these old dual-cable drives in a PC by itself establishes that that computer is too old to be upgraded economically. A modern PC uses one or more of the following hard disk interfaces:

Integrated Drive Electronics (IDE)

IDE (pronounced as individual letters) was by far the most common hard disk interface used in PCs from the early 1990s through 2003. IDE is officially designated *ATA*, but is now often informally called *Parallel ATA* or *PATA*, to differentiate it from the new *Serial ATA (SATA)* interface. IDE is still used in new systems, although it is being superceded by *SATA*.

Serial ATA (SATA)

Serial ATA (SATA) is a new technology that will ultimately replace parallel IDE/ATA. SATA has several advantages over PATA, including superior cabling and connectors, higher bandwidth, and greater reliability. Although SATA and PATA are incompatible at the physical and electrical levels, adapters are readily available that allow SATA drives to be connected to PATA interfaces and vice versa. SATA is fully compatible with PATA at the software level, which means that the ATA drivers supplied with current operating systems work equally well with either SATA or PATA interfaces and drives.

SATA motherboards and hard drives began shipping in volume in late 2002 and had become readily available by July 2003. During the 2003/2004 transition period, most PCs and motherboards will include both SATA and PATA interfaces to ease the changeover. Manufacturers, loath to complicate inventory management and concerned about distribution issues, have been slow to introduce SATA versions of ATAPI devices such as optical drives, knowing that a PATA interface will almost certainly be available for connecting ATAPI devices. As SATA PCs and motherboards become more common, we expect most ATA/ATAPI devices will become available in SATA form.

Small Computer System Interface (SCSI)

Usually pronounced *scuzzy* (but sometimes *sexy*), SCSI hard disks are generally used in servers and high-end workstations, where they provide two major advantages: improved performance relative to IDE and SATA in multitasking, multiuser environments, and the ability to daisy-chain many drives on one computer. SCSI interfaces are available in various subtypes, which have different physical and electrical interfaces and transfer rates. Modern SCSI hard disks are the largest, fastest disks available, although recently IDE and SATA hard disks have begun to approach SCSI in size and speed. Within the different SCSI flavors, interfaces are well defined and standardized, but configuring SCSI to work on a standard PC can be complicated.

Modern ATA hard disks—whether PATA or SATA—are inexpensive, large, fast, standardized, and well-supported by PCs. SCSI disks are seldom used in desktop PCs because they cost more than ATA disks with similar capacity and performance. For example, if an ATA hard disk costs $90, a similar SCSI model may cost $175. In addition to the higher cost of SCSI drives, using a SCSI drive requires installing a SCSI host adapter, which may add $50 to $300 to system cost.

However, spending extra money on SCSI may increase overall system performance more than spending the same sum on a faster processor or a high-end video card, so don't rule SCSI out. The fastest hard drives, those that run at 15,000 RPM, are available only in SCSI versions. Also, in our experience, even midrange SCSI hard disks outperform fast ATA disks under heavy load, particularly under multitasking operating systems such as Windows NT/2000/XP and Linux.

IDE

Integrated Drive Electronics (IDE), formally called the *AT Attachment* (*ATA*) interface, is the means used by most computers to interface hard disks and other drives to the computer. Early hard disk interfaces used a separate hard disk and controller card, which limited throughput. In 1986, Compaq and Western Digital combined the hard disk and controller card into one unit, thereby inventing IDE. Early IDE drives used an expansion card called a paddle card, but this card was not really a disk controller. It simply provided an interface between the bus and the embedded disk controller on the hard drive itself. All modern systems have IDE interfaces embedded on the motherboard.

You may or may not need to understand much about IDE to install and configure a hard drive, depending on how old your hardware is. The most recent drives, motherboards, and BIOSs handle the hard parts for you, automatically detecting and configuring the drive, interface, and BIOS for optimum performance. So, if all you're doing is installing a new IDE hard drive in a recent PC, you can safely skip this entire section.

If, however, you're upgrading an older system with a new drive, installing an older drive in a new system, or installing an additional drive in a system more than a couple of years old, keep reading. If any of the components is more than a few years old, you need to understand quite a bit about IDE, not just to configure the PC for optimum performance, but also to ensure that your data is not corrupted by running data transfer rates higher than your hardware can safely support. Understanding the fundamentals of IDE also helps you make good decisions when you purchase drives, system boards, and add-on IDE interface cards.

IDE/ATA Standards and Implementations

Although IDE was originally proprietary, the cost and performance advantages of IDE quickly made it the standard hard disk interface. By 1990, most computer systems came with IDE hard disks. A slew of acronyms and standards has arisen as IDE proliferates, some meaningful and many that are just marketing hype. The formal ATA standards are maintained by *Technical Committee T13* of the *National Committee on Information Technology Standards* (*NCITS*), and may be viewed at *http://www.t13.org*. These standards include:

ATA-1

> The original IDE specification, ATA defines a standard 40-pin interface that supports two hard disk devices on one cable. ATA-1, adopted as *T13 0791M* and *ANSI X3.221-1994*, was withdrawn as a standard in 1999.

ATAPI (ATA Packet Interface)

> The first ATA standard supported only hard disks. Manufacturers soon realized that the ubiquity, high performance, and low cost of the IDE interface also made it ideal for nondisk devices such as CD-ROM and tape drives. The ATAPI standard was developed to allow these nondisk devices to be connected to a standard ATA port. ATAPI hardware connects to and works with any standard IDE or EIDE port (explained later in this section). Note that, although ATAPI devices connect to ATA ports, they are not ATA devices, and differ significantly from an ATA hard drive. This is not a problem with most motherboard IDE ports and IDE interface cards, but caching controllers and other intelligent interfaces must be explicitly ATAPI-compliant to support ATAPI devices.

ATA-2

> Advances in hard disk technology soon made it clear that the original ATA standard was too confining. Since the original standard was completed, several developments made it desirable to produce an updated version of the specification. That updated specification, ATA-2, adds faster PIO and DMA modes, improves Plug-and-Play support, and adds Logical Block Addressing (LBA). ATA-2, adopted as *T13 0948D* and *ANSI X3.279-1996*, was withdrawn as a standard in 2001.

ATA-3

> Provided several minor improvements to the ATA-2 standard, including enhanced reliability, especially for PIO-4, better power management, and the incorporation of *Self Monitoring Analysis and Reporting Technology* (*SMART*), which allows the drive to warn the operating system of impending problems. ATA-3 did not add any PIO or DMA modes faster than those defined in ATA-2. ATA-3 is officially known as *T13 2008D AT Attachment-3 Interface* and *ANSI X3.298-1997 AT Attachment-3 Interface*.

Hard Disk
Interfaces

ATA/ATAPI-4

Merges ATA-3 and ATAPI into a single integrated book-length standard and formalizes Ultra DMA 33 as a part of that standard. ATA-4 is officially known as *T13 1153D AT Attachment-4 with Packet Interface Extension* and *ANSI NCITS 317-1998 AT Attachment-4 with Packet Interface Extension*.

ATA/ATAPI-5

The current standard. ATA/ATAPI-5 formalizes Ultra DMA 66, but otherwise makes only relatively minor enhancements to ATA/ATAPI-4. ATA-5 is officially known as *T13 1321D AT Attachment-5 with Packet Interface* and *ANSI NCITS 340-2000 AT Attachment-5 with Packet Interface*.

ATA/ATAPI-6

The forthcoming ATA/ATAPI standard, which is already implemented in practice by drive makers. ATA/ATAPI-6 formalizes Ultra DMA 100 and 48-bit LBA, which expands the maximum disk size possible under ATA from 128 GB to 128 PB (i.e., a binary million times larger), but otherwise makes only relatively minor enhancements to ATA/ATAPI-5. As of July 2003, ATA-6 is still in development and is officially known as *T13 1410D AT Attachment-6 with Packet Interface*.

ATA/ATAPI-7

The next and likely final ATA/ATAPI standard, before SATA supersedes ATA/ATAPI. ATA/ATAPI-7 is expected to formalize Ultra DMA 133, but otherwise make only relatively minor enhancements to ATA/ATAPI-6. As with ATA/ATAPI-6, drive makers will incorporate the important parts of ATA/ATAPI-7 before it is formally standardized. As of July 2003, ATA/ATAPI-7 is still in development and is officially known as *T13 1532D AT Attachment-7 with Packet Interface*.

Although these formal standards define the ATA interface, the hard drives and interfaces you can actually buy are marketed using the following *ad hoc* standards:

Enhanced IDE (EIDE)

A Western Digital IDE implementation that incorporates and extends the ATA-2 and ATAPI standards. EIDE supports: two devices each on primary and secondary ATA interfaces, for a total of four devices; fast transfer modes (PIO-3 or better and multiword DMA-1 or better); Logical Block Addressing (LBA) mode; and connecting ATAPI devices such as CD-ROM and tape drives to the ATA interface. EIDE includes the Western Digital Enhanced BIOS, which eliminates the 504/528 MB limitation under DOS. Recent Western Digital hard drives and EIDE interfaces support some or all of the ATA/ATAPI-4 and proposed ATA/ATAPI-5 standards, including Ultra-DMA/16 and /33 (UDMA modes 0 and 1) and Ultra-DMA/66 modes 2, 3, and 4.

Fast ATA

A Seagate IDE implementation, later endorsed by Quantum, that counters the Western Digital EIDE initiative. Fast ATA and Fast ATA-2 are based on ATA and ATA-2, but not on ATAPI. Fast ATA supports: fast transfer modes (PIO-3 and multiword DMA-1); LBA mode; and Read/Write Multiple commands, also called Block Mode. Fast ATA-2 adds support for PIO-4 and multiword DMA-2. Recent Fast-ATA hard drives support Ultra ATA-33, -66, and -100.

Ultra ATA

> An extension to ATA-2, first proposed by Quantum and Intel, and now a part of the ATA/ATAPI-4 standard (as Ultra ATA-33 for UDMA modes 0 and 1), the ATA/ATAPI-5 standard (as Ultra ATA-66 for UDMA modes 2, 3, and 4), the proposed ATA/ATAPI-6 standard (as Ultra ATA-100 for UDMA mode 5), and the proposed ATA/ATAPI-7 standard (as Ultra ATA-133 for UDMA mode 6). Ultra-ATA enhances the earlier SDMA and MDMA modes by adding CRC error detection to prevent data corruption during fast DMA transfers.

To benefit from the increased data transfer rates provided by Ultra-DMA, the drive, the BIOS, the ATA interface, and the operating system must all support it. By late 1997 some PCs and motherboards included embedded Ultra ATA-33 support. Ultra ATA-66 drives and interfaces began shipping in early 1999. ATA-100 drives and interfaces first appeared in early 2001, and soon became standard on new systems and motherboards. ATA-133, championed by Maxtor, is unlikely to achieve critical mass. Only Maxtor makes ATA-133 drives, and Intel seems likely to transition its chipsets and motherboards directly from ATA-100 to SATA. It's easy to upgrade older systems to Ultra ATA simply by adding an inexpensive IDE interface card, such as those made by Promise, SIIG, and others.

IDE/ATA Data Transfer Modes

To understand ATA data transfer modes, it's necessary to understand something about how data is read from and written to the hard drive. Real-mode operating systems such as 16-bit Windows and DOS make read and write requests to the BIOS, which passes the command to the drive. Protected-mode operating systems such as Windows NT/2000/XP and Linux bypass the real-mode BIOS and use their own protected-mode I/O subsystems to accomplish the same purpose.

Data transfer commands are controlled by the BIOS or I/O subsystem, but execution speed—and therefore data transfer rate—is determined by the strobe frequency of the ATA interface hardware. The time needed to complete one full cycle, measured in nanoseconds (ns), is called the *cycle time* for the interface. A shorter cycle time allows more cycles to be completed in a given period, and therefore provides a higher data transfer rate. For example, a 600 ns cycle time yields 1.66 million cycles/second. Because each cycle transfers one word (16 bits or two bytes), a 600 ns cycle time translates to a data transfer rate of 3.33 MB/s.

ATA supports two data transfer modes, called *Programmed Input/Output (PIO) mode* and *Direct Memory Access (DMA) mode*. Both of these have several submodes that use different cycle times and have different data transfer rates. When an ATA interface interrogates a modern drive with the *Identify Drive* command, the drive returns its model, geometry, and a list of the PIO and DMA modes it supports, allowing the interface, given proper BIOS support, to automatically configure the best settings for optimum drive performance. With an older drive, an older BIOS, or both, it's up to you to configure these settings yourself, so it's important to understand what they mean to avoid either crippling drive performance by choosing too slow a mode or risking your data by choosing one that's too fast for your hardware.

Your operating system also determines whether an ATA hard disk is configured automatically for optimal performance. Windows 98/2000/XP and Linux (usually) detect DMA-capable interfaces and drives and configure them automatically to operate in the more efficient DMA mode. Windows 95 and Windows NT 4 use the less-efficient PIO mode by default, and must be configured manually to use DMA mode on hardware that supports it. Configuring DMA mode on ATA drives is described in Chapter 14.

Programmed Input/Output (PIO) Modes

PIO is a means of data transfer that requires the CPU to intermediate data exchanges between the drive and memory. This dependence on the CPU places unnecessary demands on it and slows CPU performance under multitasking operating systems. Accordingly, modern drives and interfaces substitute DMA modes, described later, to provide high-speed data transfer. PIO modes remain important, however, when connecting older drives to newer interfaces or vice versa. Table 13-1 lists PIO modes, not all of which are supported by all drives and all interfaces.

Table 13-1. ATA PIO modes

PIO mode	Cycle time	Transfer rate	Revision
PIO-0	600 ns	3.3 MB/s	ATA
PIO-1	383 ns	5.2 MB/s	ATA
PIO-2	330 ns	8.3 MB/s	ATA
PIO-3	180 ns	11.1 MB/s	ATA-2
PIO-4	120 ns	13.3 MB/s	ATA-2
PIO-5	90 ns	22.2 MB/s	Never implemented

PIO Modes 0, 1, and 2 are not used on recent systems except to support older drives. Using PIO Mode 3 or 4 provides reasonably fast transfer rates, but requires that the drive support the IORDY line for hardware flow control. If the interface delivers data faster than a PIO Mode 3 or 4 drive can accept it, the drive de-asserts IORDY to notify the interface to stop delivering data. Running a drive that does not support IORDY on an interface configured for PIO Mode 3 or 4 may appear to work, but risks corrupting data. If you are not certain that your drive supports PIO Mode 3 or 4, configure the interface to use PIO Mode 2.

Direct Memory Access (DMA) Modes

DMA is a data transfer mode that allows bidirectional transfer of data between drives and memory without intervention from the processor. If you use a multitasking operating system such as 32-bit Windows or Linux, using DMA mode increases performance by freeing the CPU to do other things while data is being transferred. DMA doesn't improve performance with single-tasking operating systems such as DOS or 16-bit Windows because the processor must wait until the transfer is complete before doing anything else. Table 13-2 lists DMA modes, not all of which are supported by all drives and all interfaces. Note that ATA-3 introduced no new modes.

Table 13-2. ATA DMA modes

DMA mode	Cycle time	Transfer rate	revision
Single Word Mode 0 (SDMA-0)	960 ns	2.1 MB/s	ATA
Single Word Mode 1 (SDMA-1)	480 ns	4.2 MB/s	ATA
Single Word Mode 2 (SDMA-2)	240 ns	8.3 MB/s	ATA
Multiword Mode 0 (MDMA-0)	480 ns	4.2 MB/s	ATA
Multiword Mode 1 (MDMA-1)	150 ns	13.3 MB/s	ATA-2
Multiword Mode 2 (MDMA-2)	120 ns	16.6 MB/s	ATA-2
Ultra-DMA Mode 0 (UDMA-0)	240 ns	16.6 MB/s	ATA-4
Ultra-DMA Mode 1 (UDMA-1)	160 ns	25.0 MB/s	ATA-4
Ultra-DMA Mode 2 (UDMA-2)	120 ns	33.3 MB/s	ATA-4
Ultra-DMA Mode 3 (UDMA-3)	90 ns	44.4 MB/s	ATA-5
Ultra-DMA Mode 4 (UDMA-4)	60 ns	66.7 MB/s	ATA-5
Ultra-DMA Mode 5 (UDMA-5)	40 ns	100.0 MB/s	ATA-6
Ultra-DMA Mode 6 (UDMA-6)	30 ns	133.3 MB/s	ATA-6/7

The SDMA modes were obsoleted by ATA-3, and are useful only for older drives and interfaces. MDMA modes provide reasonable transfer rates, and are useful for drive/interface configurations that are ATA-2 compliant, but where the drive and/or interface is not Ultra-ATA compliant. Using UDMA modes requires that the drive, interface, BIOS, and operating system be Ultra-ATA compliant. MDMA-2 and UDMA-0 provide identical transfer rates, but MDMA-2 does not use hardware flow control, while UDMA-0 uses CRC error detection to prevent data corruption.

Hardware that supports UDMA Modes 3 and 4, also called UDMA/66, began shipping in early 1999, and had become standard for new systems, motherboards, and hard drives by mid-2000. UDMA/100, also called Ultra ATA-100 or simply ATA-100, is an extension of UDMA/66 developed by Maxtor Corporation and since licensed by other drive makers. ATA-100 components began shipping in volume in early 2001, and are now standard.

ATA-100 provides 100 MB/s throughput for reads, but only 88 MB/s throughput for writes. ATA-100 uses the same 80-wire, 40-pin ATA cable as UDMA/66, which is sufficient to reduce reflections, noise, and inductive coupling to the level required by ATA-100, but reduces signaling voltages to 3.3V from the 5.0V used by all previous ATA standards. Installing a UDMA/66 or /100 drive on an older system requires adding a UDMA/66 or /100 interface card and using a special 80-wire, 40-pin ATA cable.

Ultra ATA-133, also called FastDrive/133, is another Maxtor initiative that has not been widely adopted by other manufacturers. It uses the same 80-wire, 40-pin cable as ATA-66 and ATA-100, and ATA-133 drives and interfaces are backward-compatible with earlier standards.

ATA-133 is a solution in search of a problem. As of July 2003, no ATA hard drive can saturate an ATA-100 interface. Even if that were possible, the ATA data would occupy the entire bandwidth of the PCI bus. Only one device on an ATA channel can be active at a time, which means that PATA will be replaced entirely by SATA before hard drives can saturate an ATA-100 interface. Contrast this with SCSI, which does allow multiple devices to use the channel simultaneously. The fastest SCSI hard drives exceed 60 MB/s throughput, which means that three drives on a channel can saturate even an Ultra160 SCSI interface. Our opinion is that ATA-100 will suffice for desktop systems until SATA replaces PATA, so we consider ATA-133 to be a marketing gimmick rather than a useful technology.

There are two ways to implement DMA. *First-party DMA*, also called *bus-mastering DMA*, uses a DMA controller embedded in the device itself to arbitrate possession of the bus and data transfer. *Third-party DMA* instead depends on the DMA controller that resides on the motherboard. If the motherboard is of recent vintage, either first-party or third-party DMA can be used for high-speed DMA transfer modes.

ATA Multichannel Support

The original ATA specification defined one dual-channel ATA interface that supported one or two ATA devices. ATA-2 defines a second interface, with the *primary interface* using standard ATA IRQ and base address, and the *secondary interface* using the alternate IRQ and base address that had always been set aside for that purpose. Any modern motherboard or interface card provides dual-ported ATA support.

Windows 9X/NT/2000/XP and Linux recognize and use the secondary interface automatically. DOS and 16-bit Windows are not dual-port ATA-aware, so installing more than two ATA drives with these operating systems requires either BIOS support for the secondary port or supplemental drivers. If BIOS Setup allows you to enter drive parameters for four drives, you already have the BIOS support you need. If BIOS Setup lists only two drives, you must (in order of desirability) install an updated system BIOS *or* use a dual-ported bus-mastering ATA adapter with an onboard dual-port BIOS *or* install dual-port device drivers.

In addition to the well-standardized primary and secondary ATA interfaces, some devices support semistandard tertiary and quaternary ATA interfaces. In theory, at least, you can support up to eight ATA devices on one computer by adding a dual-ported interface card that can be configured as tertiary/quaternary to a system that includes a standard dual-ported ATA interface, assuming that you have the four IRQs needed to support all four ports. We have not seen a BIOS that includes direct support for ATA Ports 3 and 4, although the current Phoenix BIOS specification allows ATA ports beyond 1 and 2 to be defined arbitrarily. Table 13-3 lists the IRQs and base addresses for ATA Ports 1 through 4.

Table 13-3. ATA port IRQ and base address assignments

ATA port	IRQ	Hex base addresses (Channel 0 / Channel 1)
Primary	14	0x1F0 – 0x1F7 and 0x3F6 – 0x3F7
Secondary	15 or 10	0x170 – 0x177 and 0x376 – 0x377
Tertiary	12 or 11	0x1E8 – 0x1EF and 0x3EE – 0x3EF
Quaternary	10 or 9	0x168 – 0x16F and 0x36E – 0x36F

The ATA Interface

Table 13-4 lists the pins and signal names for the ATA interface. Signal names that end with # are active-low. Signal names contained in square brackets are specific to the secondary ATA interface.

Table 13-4. ATA interface pinout and signal definitions

Pin	Signal	Pin	Signal
1	Reset IDE	2	Ground
3	Data 7	4	Data 8
5	Data 6	6	Data 9
7	Data 5	8	Data 10
9	Data 4	10	Data 11
11	Data 3	12	Data 12
13	Data 2	14	Data 13
15	Data 1	16	Data 14
17	Data 0	18	Data 15
19	Ground	20	Key (no pin)
21	DDRQ0 [DDRQ1]	22	Ground
23	I/O Write#	24	Ground
25	I/O Read#	26	Ground
27	IOCHRDY	28	P_ALE (CSEL pull-up)
29	DDACK0# [DDACK1#]	30	Ground
31	IRQ 14 [IRQ 15]	32	(reserved)
33	DAG1 (Address 1)	34	GPIO_DMA66_Detect_Pri [GPIO_DMA66_Detect_Sec]
35	DAG0 (Address 0)	36	DAG2 (Address 2)
37	Chip Select 1P# [Chip Select 1S#]	38	Chip Select 3P# [Chip Select 3S#]
39	Activity#	40	Ground
41	+5VDC (logic)	42	+5VDC (motor)
43	Ground	44	-TYPE (0=ATA)

The standard ATA interface used in desktop systems uses only pins 1 through 40. Pins 41 through 44 are implemented only in notebook ATA interfaces, for use with 2.5-inch and smaller drives. The additional four pins provide power and ground to the drives, which are not large enough to accept a standard power connector.

ATA interfaces are enabled or disabled in BIOS Setup. Disabling an unused interface frees the interrupt that would otherwise be used by that interface. If there are no devices connected to the secondary ATA interface, disable it in BIOS. If you are running an all-SCSI system, disable both the primary and secondary ATA interfaces. Conversely, if you install an ATA/ATAPI device as the first device on the secondary interface and find that it is not recognized, check BIOS Setup to verify that the interface is enabled. Although most recent systems automatically detect and configure PIO mode versus DMA mode, some systems require you to specify PIO mode versus DMA mode for each interface in Setup.

Configuring ATA Devices

Each ATA interface (often called a channel) can have zero, one, or two ATA and/or ATAPI devices connected to it. Every ATA and ATAPI device has an embedded controller, but ATA permits only one active controller per interface. Therefore, if only one device is attached to an interface, that device must have its embedded controller enabled. If two devices are attached to an ATA interface, one device must have its controller enabled and the other must have its controller disabled.

In ATA terminology, a device whose controller is enabled is called a *Master*; one whose controller is disabled is called a *Slave*. In a standard PC with two ATA interfaces, a device may therefore be configured in any one of four ways: *Primary Master*, *Primary Slave*, *Secondary Master*, or *Secondary Slave*.

Assigning masters and slaves

ATA/ATAPI devices are assigned as Master or Slave by setting jumpers on the device. ATA devices have the following jumper selections:

Master
> Connecting a jumper in the Master position enables the onboard controller. All ATA and ATAPI devices have this option. Select this jumper position if this is the only device connected to the interface, or if it is the first of two devices connected to the interface.

Slave
> Connecting a jumper in the Slave position disables the onboard controller. (One of our technical reviewers notes that he has taken advantage of this to retrieve data from a hard drive whose controller had failed, a very useful thing to keep in mind.) All ATA and ATAPI devices can be set as Slave. Select this jumper position if this is the second device connected to an interface that already has a Master device connected.

 When you jumper a device as Master or Slave, it assumes that role regardless of which position it connects to on the ATA cable. For example, if you jumper a device as Master, it functions as Master regardless of whether you connect it to the drive connector at the end of the ATA cable or the drive connector in the middle of the ATA cable.

Cable Select

All recent ATA/ATAPI devices have a third jumper position labeled *Cable Select*, *CS*, or *CSEL*. Connecting a jumper in the CSEL position instructs the device to configure itself as Master or Slave based on its position on the ATA cable. When you use CSEL, the device connected nearest the ATA interface is always configured as Master and the device on the end of the cable is always configured as Slave. CSEL has long been a part of the ATA Plug-and-Play standard and was first formalized in the Intel/Microsoft PC97 standard, but was little used until recently. If the CSEL jumper is connected, no other jumpers may be connected. For more information about CSEL, see the following section.

Sole/Only

When functioning as Master, a few older ATA/ATAPI devices need to know whether they are the only device on the channel, or if a Slave device is also connected. Such devices may have an additional jumper position labeled *Sole* or *Only*. For such devices, jumper as Master if it is the first of two devices on the interface, Slave if it is the second of two devices on the interface, and Sole/Only if it is the only device connected to the interface.

Slave Present

A few older drives have a jumper designated *Slave Present*, or *SP*. This jumper performs the inverse function of the Sole/Only jumper, by notifying a device jumpered as Master that there is also a Slave device on the channel. For such devices, jumper as Master if it is the only device on the interface, or Slave if it is the second of two devices on the interface. If it is the Master on a channel that also has a Slave installed, connect both the Master and Slave Present jumpers.

Using Cable Select

All recent ATA/ATAPI drives provide a Cable Select (CS or CSEL) jumper in addition to the standard Master/Slave jumpers. If you jumper a drive as Master (or Slave), that drive functions as Master (or Slave) regardless of which connector it is attached to on the ATA cable. If you jumper a drive as CSEL, the position of the drive on the cable determines whether the drive functions as a Master or a Slave.

CSEL was introduced in the ATA-2 and ATA-3 specifications as a means to simplify ATA configuration. The goal was that eventually all ATA/ATAPI devices would be configured to use CSEL. That would mean that drives could simply be installed and removed without changing jumpers, with no possibility of conflict due to improper jumper settings. Although CSEL has been around for years, it has only recently become popular with system makers. If you work on a PC built in the last year or two, you may encounter CSEL, so it's good to be aware of it.

Using CSEL requires the following:

- If one drive is installed on the interface, that drive must support and be configured to use CSEL. If two drives are installed, both must support and be configured to use CSEL.
- The ATA interface must support CSEL. For this to be true, the ATA interface must ground Pin 28. On many older ATA interfaces, Pin 28 is open or

high, and so cannot be used for CSEL. If Pin 28 is not grounded on the interface, any drive configured as CSEL that connects to that interface is configured as Slave.

- The ATA cable must be a special CSEL cable. Unfortunately, there are three types of CSEL cable:

  - A 40-wire CSEL cable differs from a standard 40-wire ATA cable in that Pin 28 is connected only between the ATA interface and the first drive position on the cable (the middle connector). Pin 28 is not connected between the interface and the second drive position (the end connector on the cable). With such a cable, the drive attached to the middle connector (with Pin 28 connected) is Master; the drive attached to the connector furthest from the interface (with Pin 28 not connected) is Slave.

  - All 80-wire (Ultra DMA) ATA cables support CSEL, but with exactly the opposite orientation of the 40-wire standard CSEL cable. With such a cable, the drive attached to the middle connector (with Pin 28 not connected) is Slave; the drive attached to the connector furthest from the interface (with Pin 28 connected) is Master. This is actually a better arrangement, if a bit nonintuitive—how can a wire be connected to the end connector but not to the one in the middle?—because the standard 40-wire CSEL cable puts the Master drive on the middle connector. If only one drive is installed on that cable, that leaves a long "stub" of cable hanging free with nothing connected to it. Electrically, that's a very poor idea because an unterminated cable allows standing waves to form, increasing noise on the line and impairing data integrity.

  - A 40-wire CSEL Y-cable puts the interface connector in the middle with a drive connector on each end, one labeled Master and one Slave. Although this is a good idea in theory, in practice it seldom works. The problem is that IDE cable length limits still apply, which means that the drive connectors don't have enough cable to get to the drives in all but the smallest cases. If you have a tower, you can forget it.

40-wire CSEL cables are supposed to be clearly labeled, but we have found that this is often not the case. It is not possible to identify such cables visually, although you can verify the type using a DVM or continuity tester between the two end connectors on Pin 28. If there is continuity, you have a standard ATA cable. If not, you have a CSEL cable.

 Keep unlabeled 40-wire CSEL cables segregated from standard cables. If you substitute a CSEL cable for a standard cable, drives that are jumpered as Master or Slave function properly. If you substitute a standard cable for a CSEL cable and connect one drive jumpered CSEL to that cable, it will function properly as Master. But if you connect two CSEL drives to a standard cable, both function as Master, which may result in anything from subtle problems to (more likely) the system being unable to access either drive.

Master/Slave guidelines

When deciding how to allocate devices between two interfaces and choose Master versus Slave status for each, use the following guidelines:

- Always assign the main hard drive as Primary Master. Particularly if your hard drive supports fast DMA modes (ATA-66 or ATA-100), do not connect another device to the primary ATA interface unless both positions on the secondary interface are occupied.

- ATA forbids simultaneous I/O on an interface, which means that only one device can be active at a time. If one device is reading or writing, the other device cannot read or write until the active device yields the channel. The implication of this is that if you have two devices that need to perform simultaneous I/O—e.g., a CD writer that you use to duplicate CDs from a CD-ROM drive—you should place those two devices on separate interfaces.

- If you are connecting an ATA device (a hard drive) and an ATAPI device (e.g., an optical drive or a tape drive) to the same interface, set the hard drive as Master and the ATAPI device as Slave.

- If you are connecting two similar devices (ATA or ATAPI) to an interface, it generally doesn't matter which device is Master and which Slave. There are exceptions to this, however, particularly with ATAPI devices, some of which really want to be Master (or Slave) depending on which other ATAPI device is connected to the channel.

- If you are connecting an older device and a newer device to the same ATA interface, it's generally better to configure the newer device as Master because it is likely to have a more capable controller than the older device.

- Try to avoid sharing one interface between a DMA-capable device and a PIO-only device. If both devices on an interface are DMA-capable, both use DMA. If only one device is DMA-capable, both devices are forced to use PIO, which reduces performance and increases CPU utilization dramatically. Similarly, if both devices are DMA-capable, but at different levels, the more capable device is forced to use the slower DMA mode.

ATA Cables

All desktop ATA cables have three 40-pin connectors, one that connects to the ATA interface and two that connect to ATA/ATAPI drives. All standards-compliant ATA cables—there are many that do not comply—share the following characteristics:

- An ATA cable must be at least 10 inches (0.254m) long, and no longer than 18 inches (0.457m).

- The center-to-center distance between one end connector and the middle connector must be 5 inches (0.127m) minimum to 12 inches (0.304m) maximum. The distance between the center connector and the other end connector must be 5 inches minimum to 6 inches (0.152m) maximum.

- Pin 1 is indicated by a colored stripe on the cable (usually a red stripe on a gray cable).

- ATA cables are keyed, either by blocking Pin 20, by using a keyed shroud, or both.

ATA cables come in three varieties:

Standard

A standard ATA cable uses a 40-wire ribbon cable and 40-pin connectors in all three positions. All 40 conductors connect to all three connectors. The only real variation, other than cable quality, is the positioning of the three connectors. A standard ATA cable requires using Master/Slave jumpering for connected devices. All connectors on a standard ATA cable are interchangeable, which is to say that any drive may be connected to any position, and the interface itself may be connected to any position, including the center connector. A standard ATA cable may be used with any ATA/ATAPI device through ATA-33. If a standard ATA cable is used to connect ATA-66/100 devices, those devices will function properly, but will fall back to operating at ATA-33.

Standard/CSEL

A standard/CSEL ATA cable is identical to a standard ATA cable except that Pin 28 is not connected between the middle drive connector and the end drive connector. A standard/CSEL ATA cable supports either Master/Slave jumpering or CSEL jumpering for connected devices. Connector position is significant on a standard/CSEL cable. The interface connector on a CSEL cable is either labeled or a different color than the drive connectors. The center connector is for the Master device, and the end connector opposite the interface connector is for the Slave device.

Ultra DMA (80-wire)

An Ultra DMA cable uses an 80-wire ribbon cable and 40-pin connectors in all three positions. The additional 40 wires are dedicated ground wires, each assigned to one of the standard 40 ATA pins. An Ultra DMA cable may be used with any ATA/ATAPI device—and should be for more reliable functioning—but is required for full performance with ATA-66 and ATA-100 devices. All Ultra DMA cables are CSEL cables, and may be used either with drives jumpered CSEL or those jumpered Master/Slave.

The following points about Ultra DMA cables are worth being aware of:

- The Ultra DMA cable was first defined for UDMA Modes 0 through 2, for transfer speeds up to 33 MB/s, but is optional for those modes. For UDMA Mode 3 and higher, the Ultra DMA cable is required.

- All Ultra DMA cables have Pin 28 wired to support CSEL mode, and so can be used to connect drives that use either CSEL or Master/Slave jumpering.

- Color-coded connectors were not specified for earlier ATA cables. The Ultra DMA cable specification requires the following connector colors:

Blue

One end connector is blue, which indicates that it attaches to the ATA interface.

Black

The opposite end connector is black, and is used to attach the Master drive (Device 0), or a single drive if only one is attached to the cable. If CSEL is used, the black connector configures the drive as Master. If standard Master/Slave jumpering is used, the Master drive must still be attached to the black connector. This is true because ATA-66, ATA-100, and ATA-133 do not allow a single drive to be connected to the middle connector, which results in standing waves that interfere with data communication.

Gray

The middle connector is gray, and is used to attach the Slave drive (Device 1), if present.

Note the difference between using a 40-wire CSEL cable and an 80-wire cable for CSEL operation. Although all Ultra DMA cables support drives jumpered either Master/Slave or CSEL, that does not mean you can freely substitute an 80-wire cable for a 40-wire cable. If the drives are jumpered Master/Slave, substituting an 80-wire cable works fine. However, if the drives are jumpered CSEL, replacing a 40-wire CSEL cable with an 80-wire cable causes the drives to exchange settings. That is, the drive that was Master on the 40-wire cable becomes Slave on the 80-wire cable, and *vice versa*.

- Because an Ultra DMA cable is required for ATA-66, ATA-100, or ATA-133 operation, the system must have a way to detect if such a cable is installed. This is done by grounding Pin 34 in the Blue connector, which attaches to the interface. Pin 34 carries the *GPIO_DMA66_Detect_Pri* signal (primary interface) or the *GPIO_DMA66_Detect_Sec* signal (secondary interface). These signals are also referred to as */PDIAG:/CBLID*. Because 40-wire ATA cables do not ground Pin 34, the system can detect at boot whether a 40-wire or 80-wire cable is installed. In some Ultra ATA cables, the grounding is done internally and is therefore invisible. In others, the signal conductor for Pin 34 is cut in the cable, as shown in Figure 13-1. Figure 13-2 shows a 40-wire standard ATA cable and an 80-wire UltraATA cable side by side for comparison. Note that the 80-wire cable uses a gray end connector, and so is not standards-compliant.

Compatibility Between Old and New IDE Devices

With only minor exceptions, there are no compatibility issues when using new ATA devices with old ATA interfaces or *vice versa*. Newer drives cannot yield their highest performance when connected to an ATA interface that does not support the fastest transfer modes the drive is capable of, just as a new interface can't improve the performance of an older drive. But you can connect any ATA drive to any ATA interface with reasonable assurance that it will function, although perhaps not optimally.

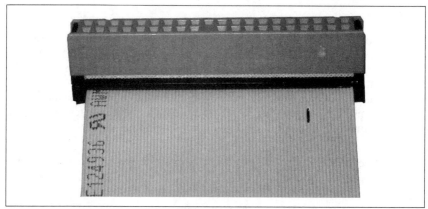

Figure 13-1. An Ultra DMA cable, showing Pin 34 cut

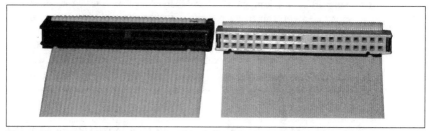

Figure 13-2. Standard 40-wire ATA cable (left) and Ultra DMA 80-wire cable

Nearly all modern ATA interfaces—including the ubiquitous Intel PIIX3 and PIIX4—support independent timing for Master and Slave devices. This means that you can safely put an old, slow ATA or ATAPI device on the same cable as a new, fast hard drive without concern that the older device will cripple the throughput of the newer one.

 Note that independent timing does not mean that you should mix DMA and PIO devices on the same interface. If an interface has one PIO-mode device connected, the other device must also run PIO. Also, independent timing does not mean that an interface supports multiple DMA modes simultaneously. For example, if you connect an ATA-66 drive and an ATA-33 drive to the same interface, both run as ATA-33 devices.

IDE Capacity Limits

Various IDE capacity limits exist, which depend on the BIOS, interface hardware, operating system, and other factors. There's a lot of information and misinformation about these limits, so it's worth getting the facts straight before you accept unnecessary limitations. Most of these limits are a result of interactions between the methods that the BIOS and the ATA interface use to address sectors on a hard disk. Even the oldest BIOS or ATA interface can address large hard disks. In combination, however, interactions between the BIOS and the interface may limit the number of addressable sectors to a fraction of the number either could address alone. Table 13-5 summarizes these limits.

Table 13-5. ATA addressing and BIOS addressing limitations

Maximum addressable	ATA limit	Int13 limit	Shared limit
Cylinders	65,536 (2^{16})	1,024 (2^{10})	1,024
Heads	16 (2^4)	256 (2^8)	16
Sectors per track	255 ($2^8 - 1$)	63 ($2^6 - 1$)	63
Disk size (bytes)	136,902,082,560	8,455,716,864	528,482,304

ATA addressing uses four registers that total 28 bits. ATA numbers cylinders starting at 0. The *cylinder address* is a 16-bit value, divided as a least-significant 8-bit *Cylinder Low* register and a most-significant 8-bit *Cylinder High* register, allowing up to 65,536 cylinders to be addressed. Each cylinder has a number of heads, also numbered starting at 0, which are addressed using a 4-bit value stored in the lowest four bits of the *Device/Head* register, allowing up to 16 heads to be addressed. Sectors are numbered starting at 1, and are addressed using an 8-bit value stored in the *Sector Number* register, allowing up to 255 sectors to be addressed. These capacities mean that ATA can address up to (65,536 × 16 × 255) 512-byte sectors, which equals 136,902,082,560 bytes.

BIOS Int13 API addressing uses three registers that total 24 bits. *Cylinder Low* is an 8-bit register that stores the least-significant eight bits of the 10-bit cylinder address. *Cylinder High/Sector Number* is an 8-bit register whose least-significant two bits store the most-significant two bits of the cylinder address and whose most-significant six bits store the sector number. In conjunction, these addresses allow up to 1,024 cylinders and 63 sectors/track to be addressed. *Head Number* is an 8-bit register, which allows up to 256 heads to be addressed. These capacities mean that Int13 can address up to (1,024 × 256 × 63) 512-byte sectors, which equals 8,455,716,864 bytes.

The impact of these limits depends entirely on the addressing method used by the BIOS. From the oldest to the newest, here are the methods used by various BIOSs:

Cylinder-Head-Sectors (CHS)
   Cylinder-Head-Sectors (CHS) is the access method used by early BIOSs to address individual sectors on a hard disk by identifying them directly by the cylinder, head, and sector where they reside. CHS in an ATA/Int13 environment is subject to the maximum common address register size supported for each element by ATA and Int13 addressing. This means that CHS can address at most 1,024 cylinders, 16 heads, and 63 sectors per track, which results in the 504/528 MB limit.

Extended Cylinder-Head-Sectors (ECHS)
   Extended Cylinder-Head-Sectors (ECHS) is the most popular of several access methods (others being *Large* and *Big IDE*) used by so-called *enhanced or translating BIOSs* to support hard disks larger than those supported by CHS. ECHS or *bit shift translation* works by lying about disk geometry, translating

an unsupported physical geometry to a supported logical geometry whose address will fit the available registers. For example, ECHS translation may represent a 1 GB drive whose physical geometry is 2,048 cylinders, 16 heads, and 63 sectors per track as having a logical geometry of 1,024 cylinders, 32 heads, and 63 sectors per track, allowing the full 1 GB to be recognized and used. The problem with ECHS translation is that it is nonstandard, and different BIOSs handle it differently.

Logical Block Addressing (LBA)

Logical Block Addressing (LBA) dispenses with CHS addressing entirely, and addresses each sector sequentially. With LBA addressing, all 28 address bits (16+4+8) are used as one LBA address, allowing up to 2^{28} (268,435,456) sectors or 137,438,953,472 bytes to be addressed. Note that, with LBA addressing, sector numbers start at 0. LBA assist translation can be used only with BIOSs and drives that support LBA. With LBA translation, the drive reports its actual geometry to the BIOS, which then multiplies the cylinders, heads, and sectors reported by the drive to determine the total number of sectors to be used for LBA translation. All modern BIOSs support LBA.

Various environments may enforce the following limits:

504/528 MB

Results from the interaction between ATA addressing and CHS Int13 addressing, which allows 1,024 cylinders, 16 heads, 63 sectors/track, limiting drive capacity to 528,482,304 bytes, or 504 MB. To get around this limit, you may upgrade the PC BIOS to one with LBA support, disable the embedded interface and replace it with one that has LBA support, or install a BIOS extender card that provides LBA support with the existing interface. If a hardware solution is not feasible, installing a third-party driver such as Ontrack Disk Manager allows using large disks, but with some limitations relative to the hardware solutions.

2.0/2.1 GB (hardware)

Various manufacturers attempted to solve the 504 MB limit by various methods, including modifications to the way registers were manipulated. One such method was to "steal" the two previously unused high-order bits assigned to the head register and assign them to the cylinder register, expanding it from 10 to 12 bits. This increased the number of addressable cylinders to 4,096, but in doing so limited the number of heads that could be addressed to 64. Because this translation method was not commonly used, the two high-order head bits cannot safely be assumed to be assigned to either the head count or the cylinder count, which allows 1,024 cylinders, 64 heads, and 63 sectors/track. Multiplying these numbers yields 2,113,929,216 bytes, usually stated as 2.0 or 2.1 GB. You've encountered this limit if the system hangs during POST when the BIOS attempts to translate the cylinders and heads. The solutions are the same as for the 504 MB limit.

2.0/2.1 GB (software)

This limit derives from how the FAT filesystem tracks hard disk space. FAT16 cannot use clusters larger than 32,768 bytes, or 64 512-byte sectors per cluster, and can track at most 65,536 clusters. Multiplying the numbers yields 2,147,483,648 bytes, or 2 GB. The only solution is use multiple partitions, each no larger than 2 GB. The FAT32 filesystem used by Windows 95B/98/2000 and the filesystems used by Windows NT/2000/XP and Linux are not subject to this limit.

3.27 GB

Some BIOSs do not properly handle cylinder counts higher than 6,322, enforcing a limit of about 3.27 GB. A BIOS has this limit if the PC hangs when you enter a value of 6,322 cylinders or more. The solutions are the same as those listed for the 504 MB limit.

4.2 GB

Some interfaces store the number of heads reported by the BIOS as an 8-bit number, calculated modulo-256. If the BIOS reports 256 heads, these interfaces fill the 8-bit register with zeros (the least significant eight bits), assume that the drive has zero heads, and refuse to allow it to be configured. This problem occurs if the drive reports 16 heads and 8,192 or more cylinders to the bit shift translation, effectively limiting drive size to 1,024 cylinders × 128 heads × 63 sectors/track × 512 bytes/sector = 4,227,858,432 bytes. Because LBA translation never reports more than 255 heads, this problem does not occur with BIOSs that use LBA translation. A BIOS has this limit if the computer hangs at boot after you create partitions on the drive. The solutions are the same as those listed for the 504 MB limit.

8.4 GB

LBA translation uses ID words 1, 3, and 6 of the *Identify Drive* command. These three 8-bit words allow maximum LBA values of 16,384 cylinders, 16 heads, and 63 sectors/track, for a total capacity of 8,455,716,864 bytes. Exceeding this limit requires BIOS support for Extended Int13 functions, which is available with recent BIOSs. Extended Int13 functions no longer transfer disk addresses via host registers. Instead, they pass the "address of an address" by placing a 64-bit LBA *Device Address* packet in host memory. The least-significant 28 bits of this packet contain a standard 28-bit LBA address. If the drive uses LBA, the least-significant 28 bits of this packet may be passed directly to the ATA registers. If the drive does not support LBA, the host translates the full LBA address to a CHS address, allowing the full capacity of the disk drive to be used, within overall ATA and LBA limitations.

The BIOS may have this limit if: (1) the PC hangs during POST when it tries to translate cylinders and heads; (2) the total disk capacity reported to the operating system is 8.4 GB or less; or (3) strange things happen when you partition or format the disk. For example, *fdisk* may refuse to partition the drive, claiming that it is read-only, or *format* may report a huge number of bad sectors. The solutions are the same as those listed for the 504 MB limit.

 The *atapi.sys* driver provided with Windows NT 4 does not recognize hard disks larger than 8 GB. To install Windows NT on a larger disk, follow the instructions in the Microsoft Knowledge Base article at *http://support.microsoft.com/support/kb/articles/q197/6/67.asp.*

32 GB

An Award BIOS dated earlier than June 1999 does not recognize drives larger than 32 GB. Current versions of the Award BIOS no longer have this limit. Many motherboard manufacturers have posted updates for their products that use an Award BIOS.

128 GB / 137 GB

This is an absolute limit that results from the 28-bit LBA used by ATA/ATAPI interfaces prior to ATA/ATAPI-6, which limits the total number of sectors to 268,435,456. Using standard 512-byte sectors, 137,438,953,472 bytes (128 GB) is the largest drive that can be supported by ATA/ATAPI-5.

128 PB / 144 PB

ATA/ATAPI-6 supports 48-bit LBA, which increases the maximum possible drive size using 512-byte sectors to 144,115,188,075,855,872 bytes (128 PB). It would require about 500,000 of the largest hard drives currently available to total 128 PB, so we don't expect this limit to become an issue anytime soon.

The Maxtor Big Drive Initiative

The 28-bit LBA used by ATA/ATAPI-5 and earlier interfaces limits hard drive sizes to 128 GB (binary, although drive makers use decimal, and so refer to 128 GB as 137 GB). Before 2001 this was not an issue, but during 2001 drive makers began shipping SCSI hard drives larger than 128 GB. They wanted to produce larger ATA drives as well, but 28-bit LBA made that impossible unless those drives used sector sizes larger than the standard 512 bytes. Using nonstandard sector sizes introduces severe compatibility problems, so there was no easy solution.

Maxtor Corporation solved the problem with its Big Drive initiative, which was subsequently adopted in ATA/ATAPI-6. Big Drive specifies a new ATA interface that uses 48-bit LBA. Those additional 20 bits allow the new interface to address a binary million (2^{20}) times more sectors than a 28-bit ATA interface, or ($2^{48} \times 512$ bytes/sector) = 144,115,188,075,855,872 bytes = 128 PB. Drive makers, of course, call that "144 PB."

 Don't bother telling us that binary values are actually kibibytes, mebibytes, and gibibytes, which use "bi" to indicate binary rather than decimal values. We're aware of this ill-considered initiative, and we don't know anyone who uses those words in real life. As an alternative, we propose everyone use the original definition of a kilobyte as 1,024 bytes, and substitute kidebyte, medebyte, or gidebyte when referring to decimal values. You heard it here first.

Compatibility between old and new drives and interfaces was a key issue, and Maxtor did an excellent job of maintaining that. 28-bit ATA/ATAPI drives can be used on a 48-bit interface, although doing so limits that interface to 28-bit LBA for all drives connected to it. Conversely, 48-bit hard drives can be installed on a 28-bit ATA interface, although doing so limits that drive to 128 GB usable capacity. SATA uses 48-bit LBA natively, and so has no realistic limit on drive capacity.

Working around ATA capacity limits

The cheapest and easiest workaround for ATA capacity limits is to update the system BIOS to a version that supports extended Int13. A BIOS update, if available, allows an older motherboard to support drives up to the 128 GB limit. The best (and possibly only) place to get an updated BIOS is from the computer or motherboard maker. This is true because, although many makers use BIOSs based on Phoenix, Award, or AMI core BIOS code, they may have made changes to it that render an updated generic BIOS unusable and may have also impacted the extended Int13 support present in the core BIOS code. That said, here are the BIOS levels necessary to eliminate the 8.4 and 32 GB limits:

American Megatrends, Inc. (AMI)
>AMI BIOSs dated January 1, 1998 or later include extended Int13 support. Contact AMI directly for update information (*http://www.ami.com* or 800-828-9264).

Award
>Award BIOSs dated after November 1997 include extended Int13 support and can be used with disks larger than 8.4 GB. Award recommends contacting Unicore for BIOS updates (*http://www.unicore.com* or 800-800-2467).

Phoenix
>All Phoenix BIOSs are Version 4. It's the revision level that counts. Phoenix BIOSs at Revision 6 or higher have extended Int13 support. Phoenix recommends contacting Micro Firmware for BIOS updates (*http://www.firmware.com* or 800-767-5465).

A BIOS update cannot eliminate the 128 GB ATA/ATAPI-5 limit because older ATA interface hardware supports only 28-bit LBA. If you require 48-bit LBA to support drives larger than 128 GB, install a PCI ATA interface card from Promise, SIIG, or another manufacturer, or replace the motherboard.

ATA RAID

RAID (Redundant Array of Inexpensive Disks) is a means by which data is distributed over two or more physical hard drives to improve performance and increase data safety. A RAID can survive the loss of any one drive without losing data. RAID was formerly a SCSI technology and was generally limited by cost to use on servers and professional workstations. That changed a few years ago when Promise Technology (*http://www.promise.com*) introduced a line of ATA-based RAID controllers that combine the benefits of RAID with the low cost of ATA, making RAID a realistic alternative for small servers and individual PCs.

ATA drives are so inexpensive that RAID is increasingly popular for protecting data on desktop systems. Do note, though, that using RAID isn't a substitute for backing up. RAID protects against drive failures, but does nothing to protect you against corrupted or accidentally deleted files. Never count on RAID to protect you against anything but drive failures.

For several years, we've used Promise ATA RAID cards on a couple of our servers and desktop systems. If you're building a small server, or even if you just want to protect the data on your PC, look into ATA RAID products. Many manufacturers now produce ATA RAID cards, and some premium motherboards include embedded ATA RAID support.

There are five defined levels of RAID, numbered RAID 1 through RAID 5, although not all of those levels are appropriate for PC environments. Some or all of the following RAID levels are supported by current ATA RAID adapters:

JBOD

JBOD, or *Just a Bunch Of Drives*, is a non-RAID operating mode that most RAID adapters support. With JBOD, two or more physical drives can be logically melded to appear to the operating system as one larger drive. Data is written to the first drive until it is full, then to the second drive until it is full, and so on. In the past, when drive capacities were smaller, JBOD arrays were used to create single volumes large enough to store huge databases. With 100+ GB drives now common, there is seldom a good reason to use JBOD. The downside of JBOD is that failure of any drive renders the entire array inaccessible. Because the likelihood of a drive failure is proportionate to the number of drives in the array, a JBOD is less reliable than one large drive. The performance of a JBOD is the same as that of the drives that make up the array.

RAID 0

RAID 0, also called *disk striping*, is not really RAID at all because it provides no redundancy. With RAID 0, data is written interleaved to two or more physical drives. Because writes and reads are split across two or more drives, RAID 0 provides the fastest reads and writes of any RAID level, with both write and read performance noticeably faster than that provided by a single drive. The downside of RAID 0 is that the failure of any drive in the array causes the loss of all data stored on all drives in the array, which means data stored on a RAID 0 array is actually more at risk than data stored on a single drive. RAID 0 is most appropriate for use as "scratchpad" storage—e.g., for temporary working files, or as part of a stacked RAID (covered later).

RAID 1

RAID 1, also called *disk mirroring*, duplicates all writes to two or more physical disk drives. Accordingly, RAID 1 offers the highest level of data redundancy at the expense of halving the amount of disk space visible to the operating system. The overhead required to write the same data to two drives means RAID 1 writes are typically a bit slower than writes to a single drive. Conversely, because the same data can be read from either drive, an intelligent RAID 1 adapter may improve read performance slightly relative to a single drive by queuing read requests for each drive separately, allowing it to read the data from whichever drive happens to have its heads nearest the requested data. It is also possible for a RAID 1 array to use two physical host adapters to eliminate the disk adapter as a single point of failure. In such an arrangement, called *disk duplexing*, the array can continue operating after the failure of one drive, one host adapter, or both (if they are on the same channel).

RAID 5

RAID 5, also called *disk striping with parity*, requires at least three physical disk drives. Data is written blockwise to alternating drives, with parity blocks interleaved. For example, in a RAID 5 array that comprises three physical drives, the first 64 KB data block may be written to the first drive, the second data block to the second drive, and a parity block to the third drive. Subsequent data blocks and parity blocks are written to the three drives in such a way that data blocks and parity blocks are distributed equally across all three drives. Parity blocks are calculated such that if either of their two data blocks is lost, it may be reconstructed using the parity block and the remaining data block. A failure of any one drive in the RAID 5 array causes no data loss because the lost data blocks can be reconstructed from the data and parity blocks on the remaining two drives.

A RAID 5 array with a failed drive (called a *degraded array*) can be read from and written to, although until the failed drive is replaced redundancy is lost and performance is snail-like because much of the data must be reconstructed on-the-fly using parity data. After the failed drive is replaced, the array must be rebuilt. This process takes a long time because each data and parity block from the failed drive must be reconstructed from the data and parity blocks on the good drives. During a rebuild, read and write performance of the RAID 5 is typically so slow that the array is for all practical purposes unusable until the rebuild completes. In normal operation, a RAID 5 provides somewhat better read performance than a single drive. RAID 5 write performance is typically a bit slower than that of a single drive because of the overhead involved in segmenting the data and calculating parity blocks. Because most PCs and small servers do more reads than writes, RAID 5 is often the best compromise between performance and data redundancy.

Stacked RAID

By using four or more drives, it is possible to combine the benefits of different RAID levels by using an array of arrays. For example, you can combine the speed of RAID 0 with the security of RAID 1 by creating two mirror sets (each of which has complete data redundancy) and then stripe those mirror sets for increased performance. Such a *stacked RAID* arrangement is informally referred to as *RAID 10, RAID 0+1*, or *RAID 1+0*. In a four-drive RAID 0+1 array, any one drive can fail without loss of data. Any two drives can fail without loss of data if the two drives are members of different mirror sets. Similarly, a workstation or server may use more complex stacked RAID arrangement, such as stacked RAID 5 and RAID 0, called *RAID 50, RAID 0+5*, or *RAID 5+0*.

RAID Levels 2 and 4 are seldom used in the PC environment. A few ATA RAID adapters, such as the Promise UltraTrack, support RAID 3, which is optimized for sequential reads of large files in applications such as streaming video.

Serial ATA

The *Serial ATA Working Group* (*http://www.serialata.org*) is a group of companies led by APT, Dell, Intel, Maxtor, and Seagate. In August 2001, this group released the *Serial ATA Specification 1.0*, which defines a replacement for the parallel ATA physical storage interface.

Serial ATA (SATA) drives and interfaces were originally expected to ship in volume in late 2001, but various technical and marketing reasons delayed deployment by a year or more. By late 2002, SATA motherboards and drives were in limited distribution. Maxtor and Western Digital had planned to ship SATA drives in 2002, but failed to do so, leaving Seagate as the only hard drive maker shipping SATA drives in significant quantities through early 2003.

Motherboards also lacked native SATA support until spring 2003. Beginning in fall 2002, a few premium motherboards such as the Intel D845PEBT2 and the ASUS A7N8X Deluxe incorporated SATA support, but those transition motherboards merely grafted on SATA support using third-party support chips. Native chipset-level SATA support had to wait for the arrival in spring 2003 of motherboards based on Intel Springdale- and Canterwood-series chipsets.

Despite the slow start, SATA is on track to replace PATA, particularly for hard drives. By late 2003, most mainstream hard drives and motherboards will be native SATA products. Although SATA will rapidly become the standard for hard drives, most new motherboards will also have PATA interfaces well into 2005. This is true because manufacturers of ATAPI devices, such as optical drives, will be slower to convert to SATA. PATA is good enough for ATAPI devices, and we suspect ATAPI device makers are concerned about complicating manufacturing, inventory, and distribution by producing both PATA and SATA models.

 You needn't worry about current PATA motherboards and drives being orphaned. During the transition, we expect most motherboards to have both PATA and SATA interfaces embedded. Also, inexpensive PCI SATA interface cards are available from Adaptec, Promise, SIIG, and others. We expect PATA drives to be available through 2006, and possibly into 2007 or later.

SATA can be used to connect internal storage devices such as hard drives, optical drives, and tape drives to the PC motherboard. *Serial ATA 1.0*, called *Ultra SATA/ 1500* or *SATA/150*, operates at 1.5 Gb/s, and provides 150 MB/s read/write performance for storage peripherals. *Serial ATA II* (*Ultra SATA/3000* or *SATA/ 300*) is already in the works, and will operate at 3.0 Gb/s. *Serial ATA III* (*Ultra SATA/4500* or *SATA/450*) is planned, and will operate at 4.5 Gb/s. Table 13-6 compares features of PATA, SATA, and other current high-speed bus standards.

Table 13-6. Serial ATA compared with other high-speed bus standards

Interface	PATA	SATA	SCSI	USB 2.0	IEEE-1394
Internal/External	●/○	●/○	●/●	○/●	●/●
Storage / I/O peripherals	●/○	●/○	●/●	●/●	●/●
2001 Speed (MB/s)	100	n/a	160	1.5	50
2002 Speed (MB/s)	100/133	150	160	60	50
2003 Speed (MB/s)	133	150	160/320	60	100
2004 Speed (MB/s)	133	300	320	60	200

Interface	PATA	SATA	SCSI	USB 2.0	IEEE-1394
Cable length (m)	0.45	1.0	12.0	5.0	4.5
Bootable?	Yes	Yes	Yes	No	No
Embedded interface?	Yes	Yes	Seldom	Yes	Seldom
Hot-pluggable?	No	Yes	Yes	Yes	Yes

SATA II is more than just a faster version of SATA 1.0. SATA II is to be introduced in two phases.

Phase 1 interfaces and drives, which we expect to ship in late 2003 or early 4003, target the small server and network storage markets. Phase 1 maintains the 150 MB/s data rate of SATA 1.0, but adds SCSI-like features such as command queuing, data scatter/gathering, and out-of-order execution and delivery. Phase I enhances manageability with features such as fan control, activity indicators, temperature control, and new device notification, and extends cabling lengths to allow rack-mounted hot-swappable arrays. Using these new features requires updated drivers and OS support (versus SATA 1.0, which is fully compatible with standard ATA drivers), but SATA II interfaces will be compatible with SATA 1.0 drives.

Phase 2 interfaces and drives, which we expect to ship during 2004, target the midrange server and network storage markets. Phase 2 increases the data rate to the second-generation 300 MB/s and includes various physical and topological improvements intended to support larger arrays of drives. As with Phase 1, Phase 2 requires updated drivers and OS support, but maintains backward compatibility with SATA 1.0 drives.

We don't expect to see SATA III products until at least 2005, so we'll reserve comment on them until we know a bit more about them.

SATA Features

SATA has the following important features:

Reduced voltage
> Current ATA standards use 5.0V or 3.3V (ATA-100/133). These relatively high voltages in conjunction with high pin densities make 100 MB/s the highest data rate that is realistically achievable. SATA uses 500 millivolt (0.5V) peak-to-peak signaling, which results in much lower interference and crosstalk between conductors.

Simplified cabling and connectors
> SATA replaces the 40-pin/80-wire parallel ATA ribbon cable with a seven-wire cable. In addition to reducing costs and increasing reliability, the smaller SATA cable eases cable routing and improves airflow and cooling. An SATA cable may be as long as 1 meter (39+ inches), versus the 0.45-meter (18 inch) limitation of standard ATA. This increased length contributes to improved ease of use and flexibility when installing drives, particularly in tower

systems. The smaller and less-expensive SATA connector replaces the large, cumbersome 40-pin connectors used by standard ATA.

Differential signaling

In addition to three ground wires, the seven-wire SATA cable uses a differential transmit pair (TX+ and TX-) and a differential receive pair (RX+ and RX-).

Improved data robustness

In addition to using differential signaling, SATA incorporates superior error detection and correction, which ensures the end-to-end integrity of command and data transfers at speeds greatly exceeding those available with standard ATA.

Operating system compatibility

SATA appears identical to PATA from the viewpoint of the operating system. This means that current operating systems can recognize and use SATA interfaces and devices using existing drivers.

Point-to-point topology

Unlike PATA, which permits connecting two devices to a single interface, SATA dedicates an interface to each device. This helps performance in three ways. First, each SATA device has a full 150 MB/s of bandwidth available to it. Although current drives are not bandwidth-constrained by PATA interfaces, as faster drives become available this will become an issue. Second, PATA allows only one device to use the channel at a time, which means a device may have to wait its turn before writing or reading data on a PATA channel. SATA devices can write or read at any time, without consideration for other devices. Third, if two devices are installed on a PATA channel, that channel always operates at the speed of the slower device. For example, installing a UDMA-6 hard drive and a UDMA-2 optical drive on the same channel means the hard drive must operate at UDMA-2. SATA devices always communicate at the highest data rate supported by the device and interface.

Forward and backward device compatibility

SATA backers appreciate that there will be a transition period during which PATA and SATA must coexist. Inexpensive dongles will adapt PATA devices to SATA interfaces, and SATA devices to PATA interfaces.

 SATA 1.0 drives are available in two types, and it's worth knowing the difference. *Native SATA* drives, such as the Seagate 7200 series, use SATA 1.0 protocols end to end, and support the full 150 MB/s data rate. *Bridged SATA* drives are actually PATA drives with interface circuitry that links interface-side SATA protocols to drive-side UDMA-6 or UDMA-7 protocols, using buffering to accommodate the differing data rates. The throughput of bridged SATA drives is limited to that of the underlying PATA UDMA protocol. In theory, that should make no difference because even the fastest ATA drives cannot saturate UDMA-6, but in practice a bridged drive may be slower than a native SATA drive.

SATA Connectors and Cables

SATA uses simplified connectors and cables. Connectors are keyed unambiguously. The 15-pin *SATA Power Connector*, shown in Table 13-7, and the seven-pin *SATA Signal Connector*, shown in Table 13-8, each use a single row of pins with 0.050 inch (1.27mm) spacing. SATA makes provision for hot-plugging using blind backplane connectors. The mating sequence for such connectors is shown in Tables 13-7 and 13-8 in the Mating column. Connections for ground pins P4 and P12 are made first, connections for the precharge power pins and the remaining ground pins are made second, and connections for the signal pins and remaining power pins are made third.

Table 13-7. SATA Power Connector pin definitions

Pin	Signal	Usage	Mating
P1	V33	3.3 V power	Third
P2	V33	3.3 V power	Third
P3	V33	3.3 V power, precharge	Second
P4	Gnd	Ground	First
P5	Gnd	Ground	Second
P6	Gnd	Ground	Second
P7	V5	5 V power, precharge	Second
P8	V5	5 V power	Third
P9	V5	5 V power	Third
P10	Gnd	Ground	Second
P11	Reserved		
P12	Gnd	Ground	First
P13	V12	12 V power, precharge	Second
P14	V12	12 V power	Third
P15	V12	12 V power	Third

Table 13-8. SATA Signal Connector pin definitions

Pin	Signal	Usage	Mating
S1	Gnd	Ground	Second
S2	A+	Differential signal pair A, positive	Third
S3	A-	Differential signal pair A, negative	Third
S4	Gnd	Ground	Second
S5	B-	Differential signal pair B, negative	Third
S6	B+	Differential signal pair B, positive	Third
S7	Gnd	Ground	Second

The two ends of an SATA signal cable assembly use identical receptacles. Either cable receptacle can mate to the signal segment of the device plug connector or to the host plug connector. The SATA specification defines the allowable length of

Hard Disk Interfaces

an SATA signal cable as 0 to 1 meter. As intriguing as it is to ponder the implications of a 0-meter cable, the real meaning of that part of the specification is that an SATA device can legally be connected directly to the host signal connector, without using a cable. Figure 13-3 shows two SATA signal connectors, with a motherboard mounting hole shown at the upper right for comparison. Note the seven contacts on the connector and the unambiguous keying. The 15-pin SATA power connector uses a similar physical connector, also with unambiguous keying.

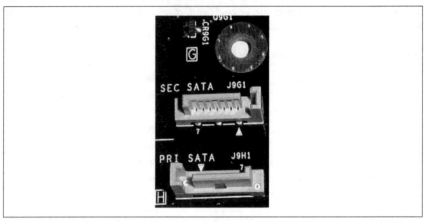

Figure 13-3. SATA interface ports

In addition to superior electrical characteristics and greater allowable length, one major advantage of SATA cabling is its smaller physical size, which contributes to neater cable runs and much improved airflow and cooling. Figure 13-4 shows an SATA signal cable on the left and a UDMA ATA cable on the right. Even allowing for the fact that an ATA cable supports two devices, it's clear that using SATA conserves motherboard real estate and greatly reduces cable clutter inside the case.

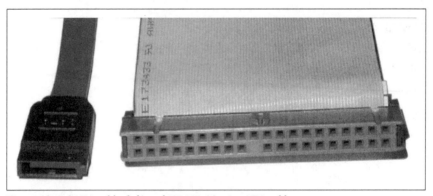

Figure 13-4. SATA cable (left) and UDMA 80-wire ATA cable

Configuring SATA devices

There's simply not much to say about configuring SATA devices. Unlike with PATA, with SATA you needn't set jumpers for Master or Slave (although SATA does support Master/Slave emulation). Each SATA device connects to a dedicated signal connector, and the signal and power cables are completely standard. Nor do you have to worry about configuring DMA, deciding which devices should share a channel, and so on. There are no concerns about capacity limits because all SATA devices and interfaces support 48-bit LBA. The BIOS, operating system, and drivers all recognize an SATA drive as just another ATA drive, so there's no configuration needed. You simply connect the signal cable to the drive and interface, connect the power cable to the drive, and start using the drive. Everything should be that simple.

SCSI

We'll devote less space to SCSI than IDE because IDE drives dominate the PC platform, but we will try to hit the high points of SCSI. SCSI (Small Computer Systems Interface) is a general-purpose I/O bus that is used in PCs primarily for connecting hard disks and other storage devices, and secondarily for connecting a variety of devices, including scanners, printers, and other external peripherals. Although common in the Apple Macintosh world, SCSI has remained a niche product in PCs, limited primarily to network servers, high-performance workstations, and other applications where the higher performance and flexibility of SCSI are enough to offset the lower cost of ATA.

SCSI Standards

SCSI is confusing because of the proliferation of terms, many of which refer to similar things in different ways or to different things in similar ways. There are actually three SCSI standards, each of which refers not to any particular implementation, but to the document that defines that level.

SCSI-1
> The *SCSI* standard was adopted in 1986 and is now obsolete. Originally called simply *SCSI*, but now officially *SCSI-1*, this standard defines a high-level method of communicating between devices, an *Initiator* (normally a computer), and a *Target* (normally a disk drive or other peripheral). SCSI-1 permits data to be transferred in *asynchronous mode* (*unclocked mode*) or *synchronous mode* (*clocked mode*), although commands and messages are always transferred in asynchronous mode. SCSI-1 uses the low-density 50-pin connector for both internal and external connections. The external low-density 50-pin connector is also referred to as the *Centronics SCSI connector*. SCSI-1 is a single comprehensive document that defines all physical and protocol layers, and is published as ANSI X3.131-1986.

SCSI-2
> SCSI-2 was adopted in 1994, and many current SCSI devices are SCSI-2 compliant. SCSI-2 updated the SCSI-1 standard to include faster data rates and to more tightly define message and command structures for improved

compatibility between SCSI devices. SCSI-2 devices use various connectors, depending on the width and speed of the implementation. SCSI-2 is a single comprehensive document that defines all physical and protocol layers, and is published as ANSI X3.131-1994.

SCSI-3

The monolithic documents that describe SCSI-1 and SCSI-2 became too unwieldy for the greatly expanded SCSI-3 specification, so beginning with the SCSI-3 specification the document was separated into multiple layered components, each defined by an individual standards document. Together, these individual documents comprise the *SCSI-3* standard, which is now officially referred to as simply SCSI.

For more information about SCSI standards, visit the SCSI Trade Association (*http://www.scsita.org*).

SCSI Implementations

SCSI implementations are characterized by their width (bits transferred per clock cycle), clock rate, and overall throughput, which is the product of those two figures. Bus width determines how much data is transferred per clock cycle, and may be either of the following:

Narrow SCSI

Narrow SCSI transfers one byte per clock cycle, using a one-byte wide data bus on a 50-pin parallel interface, which is defined by SCSI-1.

Wide SCSI

Wide SCSI transfers two bytes per clock cycle, using a two-byte wide data bus on a 68-pin parallel interface, which is defined by the SCSI-3 SPI document. Although SCSI-3 allows bus widths greater than two bytes, all current Wide SCSI implementations use two bytes.

The *signaling rate* (or *clock rate*), properly denominated in *MegaTransfers/Second (MT/s)* but more commonly stated in MHz, specifies how frequently transfers occur. Various SCSI implementations use signaling rates of 5 MHz, 10 MHz, 20 MHz, 40 MHz, and 80 MHz, which are given the following names:

SCSI

SCSI when used without qualification to describe a transfer rate refers to the 5 MT/s transfer rate defined in SCSI-1. Because SCSI-1 supports only narrow (8-bit) transfers, SCSI-1 transfers 5 MB/s (5 MT/s × 1 byte/transfer).

Fast SCSI

Fast SCSI describes the 10 MT/s transfer rate defined in SCSI-2. Used with a narrow interface (called *Fast Narrow SCSI* or simply *Fast SCSI*), transfers 10 MB/s (10 MT/s × 1 byte/transfer). Used with a wide interface, called *Fast Wide SCSI*, transfers 20 MB/s (10 MT/s × 2 bytes/transfer).

Ultra SCSI (Fast-20 SCSI)

Ultra SCSI, also called *Fast-20 SCSI*, describes the 20 MT/s transfer rate defined in an extension to the SCSI-3 SPI document (ANSI standard X3T10/ 1071D revision 6). Used with a narrow interface (called *Narrow Ultra SCSI* or simply *Ultra SCSI*), transfers 20 MB/s (20 MT/s × 1 byte/transfer). Used with a wide interface (called *Wide Ultra SCSI*), transfers 40 MB/s (20 MT/s × 2 bytes/transfer).

Ultra2 SCSI (Fast-40 SCSI)

Ultra2 SCSI, also called *Fast-40 SCSI*, describes the 40 MT/s transfer rate defined in SCSI-3 SPI-2. Used with a narrow interface (called *Narrow Ultra2 SCSI* or simply *Ultra2 SCSI*), transfers 40 MB/s (40 MT/s × 1 byte/transfer). Used with a wide interface (called *Wide Ultra2 SCSI* or *U2W SCSI*), transfers 80 MB/s (40 MT/s × 2 bytes/transfer).

Ultra3 SCSI (Fast-80DT SCSI)

Ultra3 SCSI, also called *Fast-80DT SCSI* or *Ultra160 SCSI*, describes the 80 MT/s transfer rate defined in SCSI-3 SPI-3. Fast-80DT actually uses a 40 MHz clock, but is double-pumped, which is to say that it makes two transfers during each clock cycle. Only wide interfaces are defined for speeds higher than Ultra2 SCSI, which means that Ultra3 SCSI transfers 160 MB/s (80 MT/s × 2 bytes/transfer).

Ultra320 SCSI (Fast-160DT SCSI)

Ultra320 SCSI, also called *Fast-160DT SCSI*, describes the 160 MT/s transfer rate defined in SCSI-3 SPI-4. Fast-160DT uses a double-pumped 80 MHz clock, and transfers 320 MB/s (160 MT/s × 2 bytes/transfer). The fastest current SCSI hard drives transfer less than 80 MB/s, which means that it requires at least two hard drives to saturate Ultra160 SCSI. Accordingly, few desktop systems or workstations require anything faster than Ultra160 SCSI. Ultra320 SCSI is used almost exclusively on midrange or larger servers.

In addition to being differentiated by bus width and signaling speed, SCSI devices may be one of two general types, which are incompatible with each other:

Single-ended

Single-ended SCSI (SE SCSI) devices use *unbalanced transmission* (one wire per signal), which minimizes the number of wires required in the connecting cable, but also limits maximum bus length and maximum data rates. Until recently, all PC-class SCSI devices were SE, but SE SCSI devices are now obsolescent.

Differential

Differential SCSI devices use *balanced transmission* (two wires per signal, plus and minus), which reduces the effects of noise on the SCSI channel. This requires a more expensive cable with additional wires, but extends the maximum allowable bus length and allows increased data rates. Originally, differential SCSI was used only on large computers, where the greater bus length of differential SCSI allows connecting mainframes and minicomputers to external disk farms. In modified form, differential SCSI is now commonplace on PCs. Two forms of differential SCSI exist:

High-Voltage Differential

High-Voltage Differential SCSI (HVD SCSI) was originally called simply *Differential SCSI* before the advent of Low-Voltage Differential SCSI, described next. HVD SCSI is very seldom used in the PC environment.

Low-Voltage Differential

Low-Voltage Differential SCSI (LVD SCSI) devices use differential transmission, but at lower voltage than HVD SCSI devices. LVD is where the action is in high-performance PC SCSI drives now, and where it is likely to remain for the foreseeable future. Although they are technically unrelated, LVD and U2W were often used as synonyms because most U2W hard drives use LVD transmission. However, Ultra160 devices have become common, and they also use LVD.

Table 13-9 summarizes implementations of SCSI you may encounter. For Narrow SCSI implementations, the word "Narrow" in the name is optional, and is assumed unless Wide is specified. The Clock column lists the signaling rate in MT/s. The DTR column lists the total data transfer rate, which is the product of the signaling rate and the bus width in bytes. The Devices column lists the maximum number of SCSI devices that may be connected to the SCSI bus, including the host adapter. The maximum number of devices supported on any Narrow SCSI bus is 8, and on a Wide SCSI bus is 16. Because a longer bus results in signal degradation, the number of devices supported is sometimes determined by the length of the bus. For example, Wide Ultra SCSI supports up to eight devices on a 1.5-meter (~ 4.9-foot) bus, but only four devices (host adapter plus three drives) on a bus twice that length.

Table 13-9. SCSI implementations

| Name | Clock | Width | DTR | Bus length (meters) | | | Devices |
				SE	LVD	HVD	
(Narrow) SCSI-1	5 MHz	8 bit	5 MB/s	6	-	25	8
Fast (Narrow) SCSI	10 MHz	8 bit	10 MB/s	3	-	25	8
Fast Wide SCSI	10 MHz	16 bit	20 MB/s	3	-	25	16
(Narrow) Ultra SCSI	20 MHz	8 bit	20 MB/s	1.5	-	25	8
(Narrow) Ultra SCSI	20 MHz	8 bit	20 MB/s	3	-	-	4
Wide Ultra SCSI	20 MHz	16 bit	40 MB/s	-	-	25	16
Wide Ultra SCSI	20 MHz	16 bit	40 MB/s	1.5	-	-	8
Wide Ultra SCSI	20 MHz	16 bit	40 MB/s	3	-	-	4
(Narrow) Ultra2 SCSI	40 MHz	8 bit	40 MB/s	-	12	25	8
Wide Ultra2 SCSI	40 MHz	16 bit	80 MB/s	-	12	25	16
Ultra3 SCSI (Ultra160)	80 MHz	16 bit	160 MB/s	-	12	-	16
Ultra320 SCSI	160 MHz	16 bit	320 MB/s	-	12	-	16

SCSI Cables and Connectors

SCSI devices use a variety of connectors. Until recently, there was little standardization, and no way to judge the SCSI standard of a device by looking at its connector. For example, current U2W devices use the 68-pin high-density connector, but that connector has also been used by old Digital Equipment Corporation (DEC) machines for single-ended devices. By convention, all SCSI devices have female connectors and all SCSI cables have male connectors. This rule is generally followed by modern SCSI devices intended for use on PCs, although it is frequently violated by very old PC devices and by devices intended for use outside the PC environment. Mainstream SCSI devices use the following cables and connectors:

DB25 SCSI connector

Some scanners, external Zip drives, and other Narrow SCSI devices use the *DB25 SCSI connector*, also called the *Apple-Style SCSI connector*. Unfortunately, this is the same connector used on PCs for parallel ports, which makes it easy to confuse the purpose of the connector on the PC. Devices are linked using a straight-through DB25M-to-DB25M cable.

 Avoid using DB25 SCSI connectors if possible. Connecting a SCSI device to a parallel port or a parallel device to a SCSI port may damage the device and/or the interface. If you must use DB25 SCSI, make sure all ports are clearly labeled.

50-pin Centronics SCSI connector

The *50-pin Centronics SCSI connector* is also called the *Low-density 50-pin SCSI connector* or the *SCSI-1 connector* and resembles a standard Centronics printer connector. Male SCSI-1 connectors are used on external cables for SCSI-1 devices, and by internal ribbon cables for both SCSI-1 and SCSI-2 devices.

Micro DB50 SCSI connector

The *Micro DB50 SCSI connector* is also called the *Mini DB50 SCSI connector*, the *50-pin High-density SCSI connector*, or the *SCSI-2 connector*. Male SCSI-2 connectors are used on external cables for SCSI-2 devices.

Micro DB68 SCSI connector

The *Micro DB68 SCSI connector* is also called the *Mini DB68 SCSI connector*, the *68-pin High-density SCSI connector*, or the *SCSI-3 connector*. Male SCSI-3 connectors are used on external cables and internal ribbon cables for SCSI-3 devices.

Ultra Micro DB68 SCSI connector

The *Ultra Micro DB68 SCSI connector* is also called the *Very high-density condensed 68-pin SCSI connector* or the *VHDCI SCSI connector*, and is also often incorrectly called the *SCSI-4 connector* or the *SCSI-5 connector*. The VHDCI SCSI connector is used by Ultra160 SCSI devices.

Single Connector Attachment (SCA)

The SCA interface, originally used primarily in large IBM computers, uses a standard 80-pin connector that provides power, configuration settings (such as SCSI ID), and termination of the SCSI bus. SCA was designed to allow hot-swappable drives to connect directly to the SCSI bus via an SCA backplane connector, without requiring separate power or interface cables. SCA interface drives can be connected to a standard 50- or 68-pin connector on a PC SCSI host adapter by using an SCA-to-SCSI adapter, which is readily available from most computer stores and mail-order sources. SCA devices are seldom used in PC-class hardware except in servers with hot-swappable drives.

Narrow single-ended SCSI cables, connectors, and signals

Narrow (8-bit) SCSI transfer modes use narrow (50-pin) cables. Officially, a narrow cable is called a *SCSI A cable*, but it may also be called a *SCSI-1 cable* or a *50-pin SCSI cable*. An A cable may use any of several connectors, including *standard-density 50-pin internal, high-density 50-pin internal, DD-50 50-pin external, Centronics 50-pin external, and high-density 50-pin external*. Narrow SCSI uses 50 signals, each carried on one of the 50 wires in the SCSI A cable, with the 50 wires organized into 25 pairs. For SE SCSI, each pair includes a signal wire and a signal return (ground) wire. Figure 13-5 shows a SCSI A cable with an internal 50-pin connector.

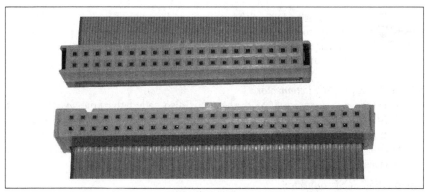

Figure 13-5. SCSI A cable (bottom) with IDE cable shown for comparison

Table 13-10 lists the pinouts for SCSI A cables and connectors. A "#" following a signal name indicates that signal is active-low. In an A cable SCSI bus, (reserved) lines should be left open in SCSI devices, may be grounded at any point, and are grounded in the terminator. All A cables use the same signals on the same conductor in the cable, but the pinouts to the connectors vary by connector type. In the table, "External" refers to a SCSI A cable that uses an external shielded connector. "Internal" refers to an unshielded internal header-pin connector.

Table 13-10. SCSI cable pinouts

	Connector pin #				Connector pin #		
Signal	External	Internal	Cable Conductor #		Internal	External	Signal
Signal return	1	1	1	2	2	26	Signal
Signal return	2	3	3	4	4	27	DB(0)#
Signal return	3	5	5	6	6	28	DB(1)#
Signal return	4	7	7	8	8	29	DB(2)#
Signal return	5	9	9	10	10	30	DB(3)#
Signal return	6	11	11	12	12	31	DB(4)#

Table 13-10. SCSI cable pinouts (continued)

Signal	Connector pin #		Cable Conductor #		Connector pin #		Signal
	External	Internal			Internal	External	
Signal return	7	13	13	14	14	32	DB(5)#
Signal return	8	15	15	16	16	33	DB(6)#
Signal return	9	17	17	18	18	34	DB(7)#
Ground	10	19	19	20	20	35	P_CRCA#
Ground	11	21	21	22	22	36	Ground
(reserved)	12	23	23	24	24	37	Ground
(no connection)	13	25	25	26	26	38	(reserved)
(reserved)	14	27	27	28	28	39	TERMPWR
Ground	15	29	29	30	30	40	(reserved)
Signal return	16	31	31	32	32	41	Ground
Ground	17	33	33	34	34	42	ATN#
Signal return	18	35	35	36	36	43	Ground
Signal return	19	37	37	38	38	44	BSY#
Signal return	20	39	39	40	40	45	ACK#
Signal return	21	41	41	42	42	46	RST#
Signal return	22	43	43	44	44	47	MSG#
Signal return	23	45	45	46	46	48	SEL#
Signal return	24	47	47	48	48	49	C/D#
Signal return	25	49	49	50	50	50	REQ#
							I/O#

Wide single-ended SCSI cables, connectors, and signals

Wide (16-bit) SCSI transfer modes use wide (68-pin) cables. Officially, a wide cable is called a *SCSI P cable*, but it may also be called a *SCSI-2 cable* or a *68-pin SCSI cable*. A P cable may use any of several connectors, most commonly *high-density 68-pin internal*, *high-density 68-pin external*, and *VHDCI 68-pin external*. Wide SCSI uses 68 signals, each carried on one of the 68 wires in the SCSI P cable, with the 68 wires organized into 34 pairs. For SE SCSI, each pair includes a signal wire and a signal return (ground) wire. Figure 13-6 shows a SCSI P cable with an internal 68-pin high-density connector. Note the twisted pairs in the cable segment at top.

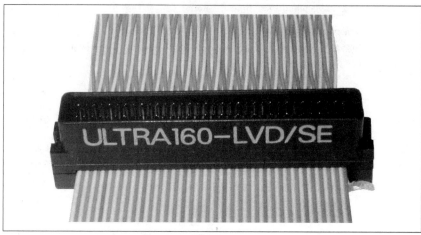

Figure 13-6. SCSI P cable with 68-pin high-density connector

 Early wide SCSI implementations used an awkward combination of two cables: a standard 50-pin A cable and a special 68-pin B cable. The B cable was never popular, and the combination A+B cabling was quickly replaced by the single 68-pin P cable.

Table 13-11 lists the pinouts for SCSI P cables and connectors. A "#" following a signal name indicates that signal is active-low. In a P cable, (reserved) lines are left open in SCSI devices and terminators. Although conductor numbers do not map directly to pin numbers, all P cable connectors use the same pinouts.

 A 32-bit SCSI Q cable was defined, but that cable was never implemented and so was dropped from the SCSI-3 specification.

Table 13-11. SCSI P cable pinouts

Signal	Pin #	Cable conductor #		Pin #	Signal
Signal return	1	1	2	35	DB(12)#
Signal return	2	3	4	36	DB(13)#
Signal return	3	5	6	37	DB(14)#
Signal return	4	7	8	38	DB(15)#
Signal return	5	9	10	39	DB(Parity1)#
Signal return	6	11	12	40	DB(0)#
Signal return	7	13	14	41	DB(1)#
Signal return	8	15	16	42	DB(2)#
Signal return	9	17	18	43	DB(3)#
Signal return	10	19	20	44	DB(4)#
Signal return	11	21	22	45	DB(5)#
Signal return	12	23	24	46	DB(6)#

Table 13-11. SCSI P cable pinouts (continued)

Signal	Pin #	Cable conductor #		Pin #	Signal
Signal return	13	25	26	47	DB(7)#
Signal return	14	27	28	48	P_CRCA#
Ground	15	29	30	49	Ground
Ground	16	31	32	50	Ground
TERMPWR	17	33	34	51	TERMPWR
TERMPWR	18	35	36	52	TERMPWR
(reserved)	19	37	38	53	(reserved)
Ground	20	39	40	54	Ground
Signal return	21	41	42	55	ATN#
Ground	22	43	44	56	Ground
Signal return	23	45	46	57	BSY#
Signal return	24	47	48	58	ACK#
Signal return	25	49	50	59	RST#
Signal return	26	51	52	60	MSG#
Signal return	27	53	54	61	SEL#
Signal return	28	55	56	62	C/D#
Signal return	29	57	58	63	REQ#
Signal return	30	59	60	64	I/O#
Signal return	31	61	62	65	DB(8)#
Signal return	32	63	64	66	DB(9)#
Signal return	33	65	66	67	DB(10)#
Signal return	34	67	68	68	DB(11)#

LVD SCSI cables, connectors, and signals

LVD SCSI transfer modes use a wide (68-pin) cable of special design and construction, which is labeled and referred to as a *SCSI LVD cable*. An LVD cable uses the same *high-density 68-pin* external and *VHDCI 68-pin* external connectors as a P cable. However, all LVD connectors, internal or external, must be shielded, so the *high-density 68-pin internal* connector is not supported for LVD.

Although a narrow (50-pin) LVD cable is defined by the SCSI standard, all actual LVD implementations are wide, so you will never encounter a narrow LVD cable.

Table 13-12 lists the pinouts for SCSI LVD cables and connectors. Because LVD uses differential signaling rather than the signal/ground method used by SE implementations, each LVD signal is actually a plus and minus signal pair, carried on a twisted pair within the cable. So, for example, whereas in SE SCSI conductors 2 and 1 carry the DB(12)# (active-low) signal and its "signal return" (ground), in LVD SCSI those same conductors carry the DB(12)- (negative) and DB(12)+ (positive) signal pair, respectively. LVD adds one signal not used by earlier variants. The DIFFSENS signal (conductor 31 in LVD Wide, and conductor 21 on LVD Narrow) is used to control differential signaling.

Hard Disk Interfaces

Table 13-12. SCSI LVD cable pinouts

Signal	Pin #	Cable conductor #		Pin #	Signal
DB(12)+	1	1	2	35	DB(12)-
DB(13)+	2	3	4	36	DB(13)-
DB(14)+	3	5	6	37	DB(14)-
DB(15)+	4	7	8	38	DB(15)-
DB(Parity1)+	5	9	10	39	DB(Parity1)-
DB(0)+	6	11	12	40	DB(0)-
DB(1)+	7	13	14	41	DB(1)-
DB(2)+	8	15	16	42	DB(2)-
DB(3)+	9	17	18	43	DB(3)-
DB(4)+	10	19	20	44	DB(4)-
DB(5)+	11	21	22	45	DB(5)-
DB(6)+	12	23	24	46	DB(6)-
DB(7)+	13	25	26	47	DB(7)-
P_CRCA+	14	27	28	48	P_CRCA-
Ground	15	29	30	49	Ground
DIFFSENS	16	31	32	50	Ground
TERMPWR	17	33	34	51	TERMPWR
TERMPWR	18	35	36	52	TERMPWR
(reserved)	19	37	38	53	(reserved)
Ground	20	39	40	54	Ground
ATN+	21	41	42	55	ATN-
Ground	22	43	44	56	Ground
BSY+	23	45	46	57	BSY-
ACK+	24	47	48	58	ACK-
RST+	25	49	50	59	RST-
MSG+	26	51	52	60	MSG-
SEL+	27	53	54	61	SEL-
C/D+	28	55	56	62	C/D-
REQ+	29	57	58	63	REQ-
I/O+	30	59	60	64	I/O-
DB(8)+	31	61	62	65	DB(8)-
DB(9)+	32	63	64	66	DB(9)-
DB(10)+	33	65	66	67	DB(10)-
DB(11)+	34	67	68	68	DB(11)-
DB(12)+	1	1	2	35	DB(12)-

You might think that because a wire neither knows nor cares what signal it carries, it would be possible to use a standard SCSI P cable with the appropriate connectors to link LVD devices. Physically, such a cable will fit, and electrically all the connections are correct, but the SCSI P cable will not work, or, if it works, it will not work reliably. LVD implementations, Ultra2 Wide and Ultra160, use higher signaling rates than a standard SCSI P cable is designed to support. LVD cables are of much higher quality than standard P cables, use twisted pairs rather than individual conductors, are always clearly marked as being LVD cables, and are required for LVD applications.

SCSI IDs and Termination

SCSI uses a logical bus topology, which means that all SCSI devices on a single SCSI bus connect to and share that bus. The logical bus is implemented with a *daisy-chain*, whereby the first device connects to the second device, which connects to the third device, and so on. The physical cabling used to implement this daisy-chain varies with the type of SCSI device, as follows:

- Many external SCSI devices and some older internal SCSI devices have two narrow SCSI connectors. To build the daisy-chain, you use a cable to connect the "out" SCSI connector on the first device to the "in" SCSI connector on the second device, the "out" SCSI connector on the second device to the "in" SCSI connector on the third device, and so on.

- Some external SCSI devices and most recent internal SCSI devices have only one SCSI connector. These devices connect to a cable that contains multiple device connectors, similar to a standard IDE cable. You can connect as many devices to these cables are there are positions. In effect, the daisy-chaining is done within the cable itself.

Each SCSI device on a bus is identified by a unique *SCSI ID*. On a Narrow SCSI bus, the SCSI ID must be in the range of 0 through 7, inclusive. By convention, the SCSI host adapter is assigned SCSI ID7, the primary hard disk (if present) is assigned SCSI ID0, and the secondary hard disk (if present) SCSI ID1. A Wide SCSI bus doubles the number of supported devices from 8 to 16, using SCSI IDs 0 through 15, with the same default assignments.

A SCSI bus must be *terminated* on both ends to prevent *Standing Wave Reflection* (*SWR*). When a SCSI signal on an unterminated bus reaches the end of the cable, it is reflected back toward the source, which causes errors because SCSI devices cannot differentiate between the reflected wave and the original signal. Two types of terminators exist:

Passive SCSI terminator
A *passive SCSI terminator* is simply a resistor pack that roughly matches the impedance of the SCSI bus. It is connected to the end of the bus, where it absorbs signals before they can be reflected, preventing SWR. A passive terminator relies on the SCSI host adapter to provide consistent voltage to the bus. If that voltage fluctuates, an impedance mismatch occurs between the cable and the terminator, which allows SWR and may cause errors on the bus. Passive terminators are used by SCSI-1 and some SCSI-2 devices.

Active SCSI terminator

An *active SCSI terminator* uses a live electronic circuit (a voltage regulator and associated circuitry) to maintain constant impedance at the end of the SCSI bus. Because active termination can regulate impedance much more accurately than a simple resistor, voltage fluctuations from the host adapter cannot cause the wide impedance swings that may occur with a passive terminator. More tightly controlled impedance translates into a more stable SCSI bus that allows higher speeds without errors. Many SCSI-2 and all SCSI-3 devices use active termination.

The method used to terminate the SCSI bus depends on the type of cable and devices used on the bus, as follows:

Standalone termination

Some external SCSI devices and a few internal SCSI devices have two SCSI connectors, which allow those devices to be physically daisy-chained by using separate cables to connect to the previous and next devices in the SCSI chain. Although some of these devices can be terminated by setting a switch or jumper to activate an internal terminator, many require instead using a separate SCSI terminator pack, which is connected to the unused SCSI connector on the last physical device in the chain.

Device-based termination

Most SCSI devices other than LVD/U2W drives contain internal SCSI terminators, which are activated by setting a switch or jumper. When connecting such devices, activate termination for the last physical devices on each end of the chain, and make sure that all intermediate devices have termination disabled. On most drives, disable termination by connecting the jumper labeled Terminator Disable (or similar) or disconnecting the jumper labeled Terminator Enable (or similar). On some older drives, the terminator is a resistor pack that you physically install or remove to enable or disable termination.

Cable-based termination

LVD/U2W drives make no provision for manual termination. If those devices are used as the last device on an SE SCSI bus, termination must be supplied by external means. For this reason, special cables are available that have built-in terminators. Figure 13-7 shows an LVD SCSI cable with a built-in active terminator.

Automatic termination

Some SCSI devices, particularly host adapters, sense whether they are the last device on the bus, and enable or disable termination automatically as appropriate.

 Technically, in addition to terminating the last physical device on the bus, you should also terminate the cable itself if unused positions exist beyond the last device. In practice, we have never bothered to do so and have never experienced problems attributable to not doing so. Usually, we just connect the last device to the last cable position, which sidesteps the problem.

Figure 13-7. LVD SCSI cable with a built-in active terminator

 When configuring SCSI devices, do not confuse *termination* with *termination power*. The former specifies which is the last device on the bus. The latter specifies the power source for termination, which may be the device or the SCSI bus. Configuring termination power incorrectly may cause various symptoms, including the system failing to boot or locking up immediately after boot.

A special case exists when you have both internal and external devices connected to a single SCSI bus. In this case, the host adapter, which is ordinarily on the end of the bus and therefore terminated, is instead in the middle of the bus and must not be terminated. In this situation, turn off termination for the host adapter, and terminate the last physical device on the internal chain and the last physical device on the external chain.

 Incorrect termination is one of the three most common causes of problems when installing SCSI devices (the others being assigning duplicate SCSI IDs and using poor-quality cables). Failing to terminate one or both ends of the SCSI bus may cause various symptoms, including one or more devices not being accessible, frequent errors and retries, slow throughput, or a complete failure of the SCSI bus. Another common error is terminating the bus at both ends *and* in the middle. This usually occurs when someone adds a terminated device to an existing bus and forgets to disable termination on one of the existing devices. If the new device is added to the end of the chain without disabling termination on the device that formerly ended the chain, the new device is not recognized. If the new device is added to the middle of the chain, the new device is recognized, but all existing devices downstream of the new device disappear.

On older SCSI devices, SCSI IDs and device termination are usually assigned manually by setting jumpers or switches on the devices, or, on external devices, by turning a small dial. Most newer SCSI devices support *SCSI Configured AutoMagically (SCAM)*, which is essentially Plug-N-Play for SCSI.

SCAM-compliant devices

    SCAM-compliant SCSI devices automatically report their current SCSI ID and termination status to the host adapter, and allow the host adapter to change those settings dynamically. In a system with a SCAM-compliant host adapter and all SCAM-compliant devices, you never need to set SCSI ID or termination manually.

SCAM-compatible devices

    SCAM-compatible SCSI devices automatically report their current SCSI ID and termination status to the host adapter, but do not allow the host adapter to change those settings. In a system with a SCAM-compliant host adapter and a mix of SCAM-compliant and SCAM-compatible devices, you ordinarily do not need to set SCSI IDs manually because the host adapter works around the IDs in use by SCAM-compatible devices by assigning unused IDs to the SCAM-compliant devices. You may, however, need to set termination manually because SCAM cannot reset an improperly terminated SCAM-compatible device.

Non-SCAM devices

    Non-SCAM SCSI devices neither report their current SCSI ID and termination status to the host adapter, nor allow the host adapter to change those settings. In a system with all non-SCAM devices, you must set SCSI ID and termination manually for each device. In a system with a SCAM-compliant host adapter and one or more non-SCAM devices, you must disable SCAM on the host adapter and configure all devices manually to avoid conflicts that may occur if SCAM unwittingly assigns the same SCSI ID to a SCAM-compliant device that is already being used by a non-SCAM device.

SCSI Interoperability

SCSI host adapters and drives used in PCs are in theory interoperable whatever their age and level of standards compliance. That is, if you have the proper cable, you can connect a new Ultra Wide SCSI hard drive to an old SCSI-1 host adapter and it will work, albeit at only the 5 MB/s transfer rate supported by the old host adapter. Similarly, you can connect an elderly SCSI-1 CD-ROM drive to a U2W host adapter and expect it to work. But just because you can do something doesn't mean you want to. Keep the following in mind if you mix SCSI device types:

- All devices on a SCSI bus communicate at the speed of the slowest device. For example, if you connect a U2W (80 MB/s) hard disk and a Fast SCSI (20 MB/s) CD-ROM drive to the same bus, the hard disk operates at 20 MB/s, which may significantly degrade hard disk performance. In general, assuming that your hard disks are all of the same type, the best practice is to place all hard drives on one host adapter or channel and put other SCSI devices (such as CD-ROM drives, tape drive, and scanners) on another, slower channel or host adapter.

- Although you *can* connect both wide and narrow devices to the same channel on a wide host adapter, you must install the wide devices physically closest to the host adapter, and use a cable converter that terminates the wide portion of the cable between the last wide device and the first narrow device.

- The presence of one SE device on the SCSI bus forces all other devices on the bus to operate in SE mode.

- Most LVD drives make no provision for setting termination on the drive and hardcode the termination power setting to *Drive Supplies the Bus*, both of which are standard practice for LVD host adapters, but may be incompatible with earlier host adapters. If you need to mix SE and LVD devices on one channel, construct the daisy-chain such that the final device is an SE device, which allows you to use its built-in terminator to terminate the channel. If for some reason the only choice is to put an LVD device as the final device on the cable, the only option is to use a cable with built-in termination.

ATA Versus SCSI

Relative to ATA, SCSI has the following advantages:

Performance
ATA drives, whether PATA or SATA, simply cannot compare to SCSI drives in performance under heavy load (although ATA drives may actually be a bit faster under light load because their simpler protocols impose minimum overhead). In our real-world testing, under very heavy disk access, the *slowest* SCSI drives we used were faster than the *fastest* ATA drives, particularly under Windows NT/2000/XP, Linux, and other multitasking operating systems. This held true across the board, even when we tested an elderly, midrange Seagate SCSI drive against the fastest of the current ATA drives. Although ATA may actually beat SCSI under light load, when disk activity starts to climb, SCSI is simply faster. Don't let anyone convince you otherwise.

To verify our impression of SCSI versus ATA, we did an experiment in mid-2002. At that time, Barbara's main workstation used a 7,200 RPM SCSI Seagate Barracuda drive. We built an identical system, but substituted a 7,200 RPM Seagate Barracuda ATA IV drive. During normal operation, performance of the two PCs was indistinguishable.

We then started an XCOPY operation that streamed gigabytes of data comprising hundreds of directories and thousands of files from a third system across our 100BaseT network to the hard drive of the ATA system. While that data was being copied, the ATA system was nearly unusable. Loading Word from the hard drive took literally a full minute, and opening a large document took even longer. We then repeated the experiment, but this time to Barbara's SCSI Barracuda. The drive banged away, certainly, but we were able to load programs and run things normally with very little performance degradation.

All this doesn't mean that the Seagate Barracuda ATA IV was a bad drive. It wasn't. In fact, it was one of the best ATA drives available at the time. But it does establish that ATA bogs down under load, whereas SCSI just keeps on ticking.

Bandwidth and concurrency

SCSI provides usable bandwidth at the nominal value stated. For example, a 160 MB/s Ultra160 SCSI channel in fact provides usable bandwidth of 160 MB/s, which may be shared among the devices on the channel. Given the actual 50 MB/s to 60 MB/s throughput of the fastest current hard disks, that means you can run two or three hard disks on an Ultra160 channel—all of which can read and/or write data simultaneously—without bandwidth becoming an issue. This is not true of ATA because ATA allows only one device to use the channel at a time, regardless of how much bandwidth may be going unused. For example, if you connect two ATA-133 drives to an ATA-133 interface, and each drive has actual throughput of 35 MB/s, the data rate on that channel will never exceed 35 MB/s.

Reliability

In our experience, SCSI devices are simply more reliable than equivalent ATA devices, both in terms of the robustness of the devices themselves and the reliability of communication on the channel. For example, with some effort, an inexpensive ATAPI CD burner without BURN-Proof can usually be configured to run reliably without generating excessive coasters, whereas an equivalent SCSI burner simply works. We also believe that most SCSI devices are better-built than many ATA devices, although we have no hard evidence to prove this speculation. One data point is that in late 2002 most hard drive makers reduced the warranty on many of their ATA models to one year, while most SCSI drives have warranties of three to five years.

Number of devices supported

A standard embedded dual-channel ATA interface supports at most four ATA/ATAPI devices, two per channel. A Narrow SCSI interface supports seven devices (besides the host adapter itself), and a Wide SCSI interface supports up to 15 devices. Many PCs now include a second hard disk, a tape drive, a CD burner, and so on. The ATAPI 4-device limit may force trade-offs that you'd prefer not to make, such as removing the CD-ROM drive when you install a CD burner, replacing a hard disk rather than adding a second hard disk, or adding a tertiary ATA adapter. SCSI avoids this problem.

Resource demands

ATA uses system resources relatively inefficiently. An ATA interface requires one interrupt per two-device channel, whereas a SCSI host adapter supports as many as 15 devices on one bus, using only one interrupt. On older systems with PIO hard drives, the difference in CPU utilization can be immense. PIO mode drives under load may demand 80% to 95% of the CPU, whereas SCSI drives (or ATA drives operating in DMA mode) may require from 0.5% to 2%.

Cable length and support for external devices

PATA is limited to 1.5-foot (0.46m) cables and SATA to 39.37 inch (1.0m) cables. Both officially support only internal devices (although various workarounds are available that allow using ATA devices outside the main system enclosure). Depending on the version, SCSI supports cable lengths from about 5 feet (1.5m) to 39.4 feet (12m) or more. Adding external SCSI devices is no harder than installing internal ones—less so, actually, because you don't even need to open the PC case.

New technologies ship first in SCSI

Interface issues aside, the simple fact is that manufacturers treat ATA products as mass-market items, whereas their SCSI products are premium items. That means new technologies always arrive first in SCSI. For example, 7,200 RPM hard disks were available in SCSI long before the first 7,200 RPM ATA drive shipped. Typical ATA hard drives run at 7,200 RPM, and the fastest at 10,000 RPM, whereas 7,200 RPM SCSI drives are entry-level, with 10,000 RPM drives the midrange, and 15,000 RPM drives readily available. The same is true for such things as very fast head actuator mechanisms. They ship first in SCSI, sell at a premium there for a while, and then gradually make their way into mass-market ATA drives.

SCSI has the following disadvantages:

Cost

More than any other factor, the cost of SCSI has kept it from becoming a mainstream PC technology. A few years ago, the premium was outrageous. Nearly identical drives might sell for $400 with an ATA interface versus $1,200 with a SCSI interface. SCSI hard disks still sell at a premium over similar ATA drives, but that premium is now much smaller. For example, in July 2003, we found 73 GB 7200 RPM Maxtor drives selling for about $75, while similar Ultra160 SCSI models sold for about $175. In addition to the higher drive cost, using SCSI also requires a SCSI host adapter, which costs $50 to $300.

Complex installation and configuration

ATA devices are simple to configure—set one jumper to specify Master or Slave, and connect the device to the primary or secondary ATA interface. Before the introduction of ATA-66 and ATA-100, which require a special 40-pin, 80-wire cable, ATA devices all used the same cables and connectors. Even with this change, installing and configuring ATA devices remains a straightforward task. SATA is even more straightforward. SCSI, conversely, can be quite complex. The diversity of SCSI standards, cables, and connectors, along with the need to specify SCSI IDs and to terminate the SCSI bus properly, mean there is more confusion and more room for errors when installing and configuring SCSI. For example, it is quite possible to buy a SCSI host adapter and a SCSI drive that are, if technically compatible, functionally mismatched. It is also possible to buy a SCSI cable that will not physically connect to the host adapter, the drive, or both. In practice, however, the widespread use of SCAM and the de facto standardization of cables and connectors have simplified installing and configuring SCSI to the level of ATA, at least for recent host adapters and devices.

Limited support by BIOSs and operating systems

Whereas the ATA interface is rigidly defined and supported natively by all BIOSs and operating systems, SCSI remains an add-on technology. In practice, this is a smaller problem than it might seem, as SCSI host adapter manufacturers provide loadable supplemental BIOSs, ROM-based configuration and diagnostics utilities, and solid drivers for all common operating systems.

On balance, the determining factors are how heavily you use your hard drive, the operating system you use, and whether you can afford the additional cost of SCSI. Under heavy use, SCSI stands up to much higher loads without bogging down, and provides much snappier response. If you use your hard drive lightly and/or you run Windows 9X, SCSI may be overkill. But if you use your hard drive heavily and run Windows 2000/XP or Linux, get SCSI if you can afford it. Before you spend an extra $400 buying the fastest processor available, consider spending that extra money on SCSI instead. If most of your work is processor-bound, get the faster processor and ATA drives. But if much of your work is disk-bound, you'll find that the system with the slower processor and SCSI drives will provide better performance.

One of our friends, who'd just spent a bundle on the fastest Pentium 4 system available at the time, made the mistake of sitting down in front of one of our systems that has a 15,000 RPM Seagate Cheetah X15 SCSI drive installed. He fired up Word, turned to Robert, and asked if this was a dual-processor system. Robert told him it wasn't and asked what made him think it was. He said everything just flew up onto the screen as soon as he double-clicked the icon, much faster than on his new system. When Robert told him that the system used a Celeron processor, the conversation became a bit strained. Robert finally stopped teasing him and explained that the system had an Adaptec Ultra160 SCSI host adapter and a 15,000 RPM Seagate Cheetah X15 drive. Kind of like one of those undercover police cars that looks like a junkyard reject but has a 500 HP engine.

Our Picks

Here are the ATA and SCSI host adapters we recommend:

ATA host adapter
> **Promise Technology.** An add-on IDE adapter is needed to upgrade systems with older motherboards or in which an embedded ATA adapter has failed. For example, we use an recent Promise ATA adapter to test ATA-133 hard drives in one of our testbed systems that supports only ATA-100 natively. Promise makes a variety of add-on IDE host adapters, one of which should suit your requirements (*http://www.promise.com*).

ATA RAID host adapter
> **Promise Technology FastTrak series.** RAID has historically been limited to SCSI servers or high-end workstations, but the Promise FastTrak adapters make RAID affordable by using inexpensive IDE drives. FastTrak adapters are available in for various UDMA levels, with two or four interfaces, and with support for varying RAID levels.

Serial ATA host adapter

SIIG. Serial ATA hard drives are now readily available, and will eventually replace parallel ATA drives entirely. If you upgrade older PATA systems and would prefer to use SATA drives, you can add SATA support by installing an inexpensive SATA adapter. Although SATA adapters are available from several companies, the only ones we've used are those made by SIIG. They're cheap, easy to find, and just work. What more could anyone ask for?

SCSI host adapter

Adaptec. For SCSI host adapters, we recommend Adaptec exclusively. Adaptec makes many models, from inexpensive models intended to support Zip drives and scanners to mainstream models for high-performance desktop systems, to high-end models for workstations and servers. We've used many of those variants, and have always been satisfied with their performance, reliability, and compatibility. Adaptec SCSI host adapters are universally supported and we never have problems with them. Every time we've been tempted to pay a bit less for another brand, we've later regretted that false economy. If you install SCSI in a system, use an Adaptec host adapter, period (*http://www.adaptec.com*).

Most people don't think much about cables, but high-quality cables are as important a part of your disk subsystem as the host adapter or the disk itself. We recommend the following cables:

ATA cables

The cables supplied with most high-quality motherboards, host adapters, and disk drives are good enough, if not the best available. We generally use those cables and have never had a problem with them. But cheap cables, such as those supplied with no-name motherboards or sold for $2 in the bargain bin at the computer store, are junk. The best ATA cable we know of is the Belkin F2N1107, but it costs $20, which seems expensive for an ATA cable. Computer stores and online vendors often carry two lines of ATA cables, a "value" series and a "premium" series. Our experience has been that "value" cables are a waste of money whereas the "premium" cables are usually perfectly acceptable.

SCSI cables

Adaptec. We have used Adaptec SCSI cables for years and have never had any problem with any of them. Adaptec sells a complete line of high-quality SCSI cables at reasonable prices, and we see no reason to spend more. Belkin (*http://www.belkin.com*) and Granite Digital (*http://www.granitedigital.com*) sell top-quality SCSI cables, which are priced accordingly. We've never had occasion to use them, although we know many people who swear by them.

For our current detailed recommendations by brand and model, visit: *http://www.hardwareguys.com/picks/hdinterface.html*.

14

Hard Disk Drives

Replacing the original hard disk or adding a hard disk is one of the most common upgrades. It's easy to do and a very cost-effective way to extend the life of a PC. This chapter explains what you need to know to choose, install, and configure hard disks and interfaces.

How Hard Disks Work

All hard disks are constructed similarly. A central *spindle* supports one or more *platters*, which are thin, flat, circular objects made of metal or glass, substances chosen because they are rigid and do not expand and contract much as the temperature changes. Each platter has two *surfaces*, and each surface is coated with a magnetic medium. Most drives have multiple platters mounted concentrically on the spindle, like layers of a cake. The central spindle rotates at several thousand revolutions per minute, rotating the platters in tandem with it.

A small gap separates each platter from its neighbors, which allows a *read-write head* mounted on an *actuator arm* to fit between the platters. Each surface has its own read-write head, and those heads "float" on the cushion of air caused by the Bernoulli Effect that results from the rapid rotation of the platter. When a disk is rotating, the heads fly above the surfaces at a distance of only millionths of an inch. The *head actuator assembly* resembles a comb with its teeth inserted between the platters, and moves all of the heads in tandem radially toward or away from the center of rotation.

 Platters are cheaper than heads. That means some drives have an odd number of heads, leaving one surface unused. For example, Seagate Barracuda 7200.7 series drives use 40 GB/surface technology and are available in 40, 80, 120, and 160 GB models. The 40 and 80 GB models use one platter with one and two heads, respectively. The 120 and 160 GB models use two platters with three and four heads, respectively.

The small separation between the heads and surfaces means that a tiny dust particle could cause a catastrophic head crash, so these components are sealed within a *head/disk assembly*, or *HDA*. The sealed HDA contains air filters that allow air pressure to equalize between the HDA and the surrounding environment. Opening an HDA other than in a factory clean room is a certain way to destroy a disk drive.

Each surface is divided into concentric *tracks* that can be read from or written to by that surface's head. Each surface on a modern disk drive contains thousands of tracks. Each track is divided into many *sectors*, each of which stores 512 bytes of data. Old drives used the same number of sectors on every track, typically 17 or 26. Modern drives take advantage of the fact that tracks near the outer edge of the platter are longer than those near the center by storing more sectors on the outer tracks.

All tracks that are immediately above and below each other form a *cylinder*. If a drive has eight surfaces, each with 16,383 tracks, that drive contains 16,383 cylinders, with eight tracks per cylinder. The concept of cylinders is important because it determines how data is written to and read from the drive. When a drive writes a file that is larger than one track, it fills the current track and then writes the remainder of the file sequentially to the next available track within that cylinder. Only if the capacity of the current cylinder is exceeded does the drive move the heads to the next available cylinder. The drive writes data in this fashion because selecting a different read-write head is an electronic operation that occurs quickly, while moving the heads to a different track is a mechanical operation that requires significantly more time.

The heads write data to the surfaces in exactly the same way that data is written to a floppy disk or magnetic tape. Each track contains myriad discrete positions, called *magnetic domains*, that can each store a single bit of information as a binary 0 or 1. When writing, the head exercises a magnetic flux to alter the state of a domain to a 0 or 1, as appropriate. When reading, the head simply determines the existing state of a domain.

Because they reside in such close proximity, it is nontrivial for a head to locate the correct track and sector. Early drives used a stepper-motor assembly similar to that still used on floppy drives. A stepper motor simply moves the heads to where the track is supposed to be, without reference to its actual location. On stepper-motor drives, thermal expansion and contraction gradually cause the expected locations of tracks to drift out of alignment with their actual physical location, which required frequent low-level formatting of the drives to return them to proper alignment. Stepper-motor hard drives were last produced in about 1990.

Later hard disk drives used a voice-coil actuator mechanism in conjunction with a dedicated servo surface. For example, a drive that had eight surfaces used only seven of these to store data, and dedicated the eighth surface to servo information that helped locate the correct track. A voice-coil drive does not seek to an absolute track position. Instead, the head actuator assembly seeks to the approximate position where it expects the track to be located. The servo head then fine-tunes the positioning by locating the servo track that corresponds to the desired track. Because all tracks in a cylinder must necessarily be aligned, locating the correct servo track automatically also locates the correct data cylinder. Early voice-coil drives were effective and not subject to thermal drift, but designers hated wasting an entire surface and head on servo data. All current drives use *embedded servo* information, which means that no surface is dedicated to servo information. Instead, servo data is interspersed with user data on normal data tracks, which allows every surface to be used to store data.

The hard disk drive connects to the PC via a controller interface. Early hard disk drives used a separate controller card that installed in an expansion slot and connected to the drive via ribbon cables. All modern disk drives, ATA and SCSI, have the controller embedded in the drive itself. A ribbon cable connects the drive to a connector located on the system board or to an expansion card that provides a connection point. Hard disk interface cards are not actually disk controllers, and are properly referred to as *host adapters*. They do not contain disk controller circuitry, but simply provide a connection point between the system bus and the disk controller embedded in the drive.

The disk controller serves as an intermediary between the system and the hard drive. When the system needs to read data from or write data to the drive, it issues commands to the controller, which translates those commands into a form understandable by the drive. The drive then supplies data to the controller during read operations, and accepts data from the controller during writes.

Choosing a Hard Disk

The good news about choosing a hard disk is that it's easy to choose a good one. Drive makers such as Maxtor and Seagate produce high-quality drives at similar price points for a given type and size drive. When you buy a hard disk in today's competitive market, you get what you pay for. That said, we will admit that we avoid IBM and Western Digital hard drives because we have experienced severe reliability problems with both makes.

Manufacturers often have two or more lines of drives that vary in several respects, all of which affect performance and price. Within a given grade of drive, however, drives from different manufacturers are usually closely comparable in features, performance, and price, if not necessarily in reliability. Neither is compatibility an issue, as it occasionally was in the early days of ATA. Any recent ATA hard disk coexists peacefully with any other recent ATA/ATAPI device, regardless of manufacturer. The same is generally true of SCSI drives. All of that said, we use Seagate and Maxtor ATA drives and Seagate SCSI drives when we have a choice.

Use the following guidelines when you choose a hard disk:

Choose the correct interface and standards
> The most important consideration in choosing a hard disk is whether to use PATA, SATA, or SCSI, based on the issues we described in the preceding chapter. Once you make that decision, choose a drive that supports the proper standards. For more about ATA versus SCSI, see the upcoming sidebar.

> *PATA*
>> Choose a PATA drive if you are building or upgrading a budget or mainstream PC that lacks SATA interfaces. Any drive you buy should support

UDMA Mode 5 (ATA-100) or UDMA Mode 6 (ATA-133). Only Maxtor produces ATA-133 drives. ATA-100 has more bandwidth than even the fastest current drives require, so ATA-133 has no real performance advantage. Choose a drive in the size, performance, and price range you want and don't worry about ATA-100 versus ATA-133.

SATA

Choose an SATA drive if you are building or upgrading a budget or mainstream PC that has SATA interfaces, and if an SATA drive is available for about the same price as the comparable PATA model. We listed the benefits of SATA relative to PATA in the preceding chapter, and although those benefits are real, they are seldom worth paying much extra for. If your system has SATA interfaces and the SATA drive you want costs only $5 or $10 more than the PATA model, it's worth choosing SATA. But if the price differential is much larger, or if you would have to buy a separate SATA interface card to use the SATA drive, stick with PATA.

Many hard drives are available with either PATA or SATA interfaces, often with nearly identical model numbers. The only obvious differences may be the data and power connectors, shown in Figure 14-1, but more significant differences between models may exist. For example, the top drive is a Seagate ST3120023A Barracuda ATA V, with a 2 MB buffer and average seek time of 9.4 ms. The bottom drive is a Seagate ST3120023AS Barracuda Serial ATA V, which has an 8 MB buffer and average seek time of 9.0 ms. The model numbers differ by only one character and the names are similar, but the SATA model is a faster drive.

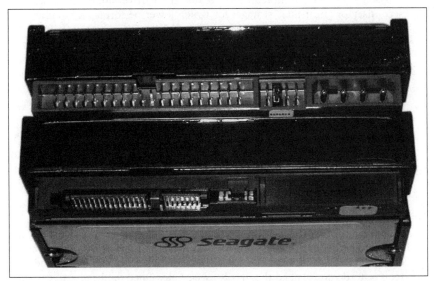

Figure 14-1. Two similar hard drives, with PATA (top) and SATA interfaces

SCSI

If disk performance is a major consideration, buy Ultra160 or Ultra320 SCSI drives. Even Ultra160 has sufficient bandwidth to support two 10,000 or 15,000 RPM SCSI drives, so Ultra320 provides no performance benefit for desktop systems. However, Ultra320 SCSI drives work properly on an Ultra160 interface and usually sell for little or no more than Ultra160 drives, so it makes sense to choose the faster interface. Purchase only SCAM-compliant drives.

It's tempting to buy the largest drive available, but that's not always the best decision. Very large drives often cost much more per gigabyte than mid-size drives, and the largest drives may have slower mechanisms than mid-size drives. So, in general, decide what performance level you need and are willing to pay for, and then buy a drive that meets those performance requirements, choosing the model based on its cost per gigabyte. All of that said, it may make sense to buy the largest drive available despite its high cost per gigabyte and slower performance, simply to conserve drive bays and ATA channels.

Choose the best rotation rate for your application

Rotation rate specifies how fast the drive spins. For years, all hard drives rotated at 3,600 RPM. Several years ago, drives that rotated at 5,400 or 7,200 RPM became available, initially for servers. This higher rotation speed has two benefits. First, a drive that rotates faster moves more data under the heads in a given amount of time, providing faster throughput. Second, the higher the rotation speed, the lower the latency.

Nowadays, 5,400 RPM ATA drives are used primarily in "appliance" applications such as set-top boxes and entry-level systems, where saving a few bucks in manufacturing cost is a major consideration. Some high-capacity ATA drives use 5,400 RPM mechanisms because these drives are typically used for secondary or "near-line" storage, for which lower performance is an acceptable trade-off for reduced cost. Mainstream ATA drives rotate at 7,200 RPM, and high-performance models at 10,000 RPM. Entry-level SCSI drives rotate at 7,200 RPM, mainstream models rotate at 10,000 RPM, and high-performance models at 15,000 RPM. All other things being equal, higher rotation speed provides faster data access and transfer rates, but with correspondingly higher noise and heat.

We recommend using 7,200 RPM or 10,000 RPM ATA and SCSI drives for mainstream applications. Choose a 5,400 RPM ATA model only when cost is an overriding concern, and even then you'll save only a few dollars by buying a 5,400 RPM drive rather than a 7,200 RPM unit. Choose a 15,000 RPM SCSI drive only if getting the highest possible disk performance outweighs the significant additional cost.

Give seek/access times heavy weight if you work mostly with many small files

Seek time is a measure of how quickly the head actuator can reposition the heads to a different track. Statistically, for a random access, the drive heads on average have to move across one-third of the disk surface. The time they require to do so is called the *average seek time*. Once the head arrives at the proper track, it must wait until the proper sector of that track arrives under the head before it can read or write data, which is called *latency*. Average

ATA Versus SCSI

The relative performance of ATA versus SCSI hard drives is hotly debated. Some argue that ATA and SCSI drives often use the same mechanisms, and the additional overhead of SCSI therefore means that ATA drives are faster. That's true as far as it goes, but it ignores some important issues:

Load

If you compare a 7,200 or 10,000 RPM ATA drive to an identical model with a SCSI interface under light loads, the ATA drive will probably benchmark as slightly faster, although not enough to be noticeable in a real working situation. But much of ATA's speed advantage is due to the simplicity of the ATA interface, and that simplicity incurs a penalty as load increases. Under moderate to heavy loads, particularly in multitasking environments, SCSI simply outperforms ATA. There's no question about that. That's why everyone uses SCSI drives on servers and workstations.

Multiple hard drives

If your system has two or more hard drives, SCSI has a big advantage. ATA does not permit simultaneous I/O on a channel, which means only one drive per channel can read or write at a time. With SCSI, you can have many hard drives on a channel, and all can read or write simultaneously at full bandwidth if the channel is fast enough.

Operating system

If you're running Windows 9X, the advantage of SCSI over ATA is minimal. Many benchmarks that are used to show that SCSI is no faster than ATA are run under Windows 9X. Under Windows 2000/XP, throughput and concurrency advantages of SCSI become apparent.

Faster mechanisms

The fastest ATA drives use the same head/disk assemblies as the slowest SCSI drives. If you need the highest possible performance, your only option is SCSI because the fastest HDAs are available only with SCSI interfaces.

We use ATA drives if cost is a major issue, if the system is likely to be CPU-bound rather than disk-bound, and if the system runs Windows 9X. If none of those three is true, we use SCSI. If one or two is true, we decide based on other issues, such as using SCSI if we need to install many peripherals and ATA if we don't. Buy the right size

Buy the right size

It's tempting to buy the largest drive available, but that's not always the best decision. Very large drives often cost much more per gigabyte than mid-size drives, and the largest drives may have slower mechanisms than mid-size drives. So, in general, decide what performance level you need and are willing to pay for, and then buy a drive that meets those performance requirements, choosing the model based on its cost per gigabyte. All of that said, it may make sense to buy the largest drive available despite its high cost per gigabyte and slower performance, simply to conserve drive bays and ATA channels.

—Continued—

Choose the best rotation for your application

Rotation rate specifies how fast the drive spins. For years, all hard drives rotated at 3,600 RPM. Several years ago, drives that rotated at 5,400 or 7,200 RPM became available, initially for servers. This higher rotation speed has two benefits. First, a drive that rotates faster moves more data under the heads in a given amount of time, providing faster throughput. Second, the higher the rotation speed, the lower the latency.

Nowadays, 5,400 RPM ATA drives are used primarily in "appliance" applications such as set top boxes and entry-level systems, where saving a few bucks in manufacturing cost is a major consideration. Some high capacity ATA drives use 5,400 RPM mechanisms, because these drives are typically used for secondary or "near-line" storage, for which lower performance is an acceptable trade-off for reduced costs. Mainstream ATA drives at 7,200 RPM and high-performance models at 10,000 RPM. Entry-level SCSI drives rotate at 7,200 RPM, mainstream models rotate at 10,000 RPM and high-performance models rotate at 15,000 RPM. All other things being equal, high rotation speed provides faster data access and transfer rates but with correspondingly higher noise and heat.

We recommend using 7,200 RPM or 10,000 RPM ATA and SCSI drives for mainstream applications. Choose a 5,400 RPM ATA model only when cost is an overriding concern, and even then you'll save only a few dollars by buying a 5,400 RPM drive rather than a 7,200 RPM unit. Choose a 15,000 RPM SCSI drive only if getting the highest possible disk performance outweighs the significant additional cost.

latency is one-half the time that the disk requires to perform a full revolution. A 7,200 RPM drive, for example, turns at 120 revolutions per second and requires 8.33 milliseconds (ms) for each full revolution. The *average latency* is one-half of that, or 4.17 ms. The sum of the average seek time and average latency is called *average access time*, and is the best measure of a drive's access performance. Do not compare average *seek* time of one drive to average *access* time of another. Because average latency is a fixed value that is determined solely by the drive's rotation speed, you can easily convert back and forth between average seek time and average access time to make sure you're comparing apples to apples. For a 5,400 RPM drive, look for an average access time of 19 milliseconds (ms) or less; for a 7,200 RPM ATA or SCSI drive, 14 ms; for a 10,000 RPM drive, 8 ms; and for a 15,000 RPM drive, 6 ms.

Even within a model series, average seek times may differ significantly by drive capacity, and may also differ for reads versus writes. For example, seek times for the 18.4 GB Seagate Barracuda ES2 are 6.9 ms for reads and 7.5 ms for writes, while seek times for the 36.9 GB Barracuda ES2 are 8.5 ms for reads and 9.25 ms for writes. Smaller drives are often noticeably faster than larger models from the same series. Accordingly, when we build a system for which disk performance is paramount, we configure it with a small, fast primary drive to store the operating system, applications, and primary data, and a larger, slower secondary drive to store everything else. For example, we've built several systems with 15,000 RPM 18.4 GB Seagate Cheetahs as the primary drive and 7,200 RPM 100+ GB Seagate Barracudas (SCSI or ATA) as the secondary drive. That achieves the goal of fast disk performance at a reasonable price. Of course, on a system for which price is no object, we would simply use an array of the fastest 15K drives available.

Give data transfer rate heavy weight if you work mostly with large files

In most applications, data transfer rate (DTR) is less important to overall performance than average access time. DTR does become crucial if you work primarily with relatively few large files (sequential access) rather than many smaller files (random access). DTR is determined by several factors, the most important of which are disk rotation speed, cache size, and the onboard circuitry. When comparing advertised DTRs, be aware that there are several possible ways to list them, including internal versus external and burst versus sustained. The various transfer rates of drives are normally well-documented on the detailed specification sheets available on their web sites, and less well-documented in typical marketing materials.

Overall, the most important basis for comparison is the sustained transfer rate. Note that on drives that use more sectors on the larger outer tracks, transfer rates can vary significantly between inner and outer tracks. For example, a Seagate Cheetah 15K.3 drive has transfer rates of 49 MB/s on inner tracks and 75 MB/s on outer tracks. The average of those numbers, called the *average formatted transfer rate*, is a good yardstick. For an entry-level ATA drive, look for an average formatted transfer rate of 14 MB/s or higher; for a mainstream ATA drive, 30 MB/s or higher; for a 7200 RPM SCSI drive, 35 MB/s or higher; for a 10,000 RPM SCSI drive, 50 MB/s or higher; and for a 15,000 RPM SCSI drive, 55 MB/s or higher. Note that none of these transfer rates is fast enough to saturate ATA-100, let alone SATA or Ultra160 SCSI.

Rotation rate, average access time, and DTR are all favored by drives with smaller form factors, and in particular those with smaller platters and higher data densities. This is true because it is easier and less expensive to run small platters at high speed than large platters, and because the smaller physical size of the platters means that heads need not move as far to access data on any portion of the platter.

Get a model with large cache if it doesn't cost much more

Disk drives contain cache memory, which in theory provides benefits similar to those provided by L2 cache on a CPU. Entry-level and mainstream drives typically have 2 MB, and high-performance drives may have 8 MB or more. Some manufacturers sell the same model drive with differing amounts of cache, often indicated by a different letter on the end of the model number. In our experience, larger caches have a relatively small impact on overall drive performance, and are not worth paying much for. For example, given two otherwise identical drive models, one with 2 MB cache and one with 8 MB cache, we might pay $5 or $10 more for the 8 MB model, but not more. Adding cache is cheap, but it doesn't provide the benefits of a fast head mechanism and a fast rotation rate, both of which are more expensive to implement.

Make sure the drive fits your computer

All drives use standard width/height dimensions and screw hole positions to allow them to fit standard mounting locations. Drives for standard PCs are available in two nominal widths, named for the size of the platters they use. Each width is available in different heights. Together, the width and height describe the *form factor* of the drive, as follows:

5.25-inch

Some drives, typically of large capacity, use the 5.25-inch form factor. These drives actually measure 6 inches wide and come in three heights. *Full-height* devices measure 3.25 inches vertically, and are relatively uncommon nowadays. About the only 5.25-inch full-height drives you may encounter are very large capacity SCSI hard disks intended for use in servers. *Half-height* drives measure 1.625 inches vertically, and are far more common. A few 5.25-inch drives have been made in *third-height* form, which measure 1 inch vertically. Any of these drives fits in standard 5.25-inch drive bays. All cases except some low-profile cases have at least one full-height 5.25-inch drive bay, which can also be used instead to hold two half-height 5.25-inch drives.

Relative to 3.5-inch hard drives, 5.25-inch drives typically have slower rotational speed, longer seek times, and higher latency, all of which translate to slower DTRs. These performance drawbacks are true regardless of the capacity or interface of the drive. The one advantage of 5.25-inch drives is that their larger physical size allows packing in more and larger platters, which in turn means that 5.25-inch drives, particularly full-height models, can have much larger capacities than 3.5-inch drives. Although many 5.25-inch SCSI drives indeed have very high capacities, this is not the case with 5.25-inch ATA drives. Such drives, notably the Quantum Bigfoot series, are low-end drives that are commonly found in consumer-grade PCs. These drives gain no advantage from their larger form factor. One of the best upgrades you can make to a system is to replace one of these 3,600 or 4,000 RPM 5.25-inch ATA hard drives with a modern 3.5-inch 7,200 or 10,000 RPM drive.

3.5-inch

Most hard drives use the 3.5-inch form factor. These drives actually measure 4 inches wide and come in two heights. Most drives are third-height, or 1-inch high. Some high-capacity 3.5-inch hard drives use the 1.625-inch high half-height form factor.

Pay attention to how much current the drive draws

Here's one that few people think about, but that can be critical. A drive that requires only a few watts at idle or during read/write operations can easily require 30 watts or more when it spins up. Spinning up three or four ATA drives (or even one high-performance SCSI drive) may draw more current than your power supply can comfortably provide. Nearly all modern drives and BIOSs automatically support staged spin-up, whereby the Primary Master ATA drive (or Drive 0 on the SCSI chain) spins up first, with other devices spinning up only after enough time has passed to allow each earlier device to complete spin-up. However, not all drives and not all systems stage spin-up, so note the startup current requirements of a drive before you add it to a heavily loaded system. The current requirements of a drive are normally detailed in the technical specification sheets available on the drive manufacturer's web site.

Consider length of warranty

In preceding editions, we didn't even mention warranty. Nearly all drives, at least retail-boxed models, had warranties of two years or longer, sometimes much longer. Length of warranty was a nonissue because most drives either failed right out of the box or lasted until they were too small to be useful. We frequently didn't return drives that had failed after a couple of years and were still under warranty because a replacement drive of the same capacity would have been too small to bother installing.

Things changed almost overnight in late 2002 when, following close on the heels of reported widespread problems with some Fujitsu drive models, every major drive maker except Samsung reduced their standard warranties from three or five years to one year. Conspiracy theorists had a field day, speculating that drive makers were cost-reducing their drives and shortening their warranties in the expectation that newer drives would have greatly increased failure rates. We don't believe that for a second.

Hard drive factories cost billions, and no manufacturer is going to risk that investment by producing failure-prone drives. We think it's more likely that drive makers were forced by plummeting hard drive prices, shrinking margins, and the hideously bad high-tech economy to cut costs. The administrative and other costs involved in replacing one drive returned under warranty probably exceeds the profit from selling 10 or even 100 new drives. We think drive makers reduced warranties to a year to minimize the infrequent but very costly need to replace older drives. We suspect that current hard drives are at least as reliable as the older models that had longer warranties, and we do not hesitate to use and recommend drives that have only one-year warranties.

That said, if length of warranty is important to you, some manufacturers do offer "premium" lines at somewhat higher prices. In addition to their longer warranties, these models may have a larger cache, typically 8 MB rather than 2 MB. We might be tempted to pay a few extra bucks for a longer warranty and larger cache, but for most purposes we regard the standard warranty as acceptable.

Here are some things that you can safely ignore when shopping for a drive:

MTBF

Mean Time Between Failures (MTBF) is a technical measure of the expected reliability of a device. All modern ATA drives have extremely large MTBF ratings, often 50 years or more. That doesn't mean that the drive you buy will last 50 years. It does mean that any drive you buy will probably run for years (although some drives fail the day they are installed). The truth is that most hard drives nowadays are replaced not because they fail, but because they are no longer large enough. Ignore MTBF when you're shopping for a drive.

MTTR

Mean Time to Repair (MTTR) is another measure that has little application in the real world. MTTR specifies the average time required to repair a drive. Since nobody except companies that salvage data from dead drives actually repairs drives nowadays, you can ignore MTTR.

Shock rating

Drives are rated in gravities (G) for the level of shock they can withstand in both operating and nonoperating modes. For drives used in desktop systems, at least, you can ignore shock rating. All modern drives are remarkably resistant to damage if dropped, but all of them break if you drop them hard enough.

Installing a PATA (Standard ATA) Hard Disk

To install a PATA hard disk, you physically install the drive in the PC, configure CMOS Setup to recognize the drive, and finally configure your operating system to use the proper transfer mode. Each of these steps is described in the following sections.

Physical Installation

The general procedures for installing any hard drive are similar, but the exact steps required vary according to the specific drive and case. Most cases contain *drive bays*, which form a part of the chassis structure designed to secure drives in place. Others use removable *drive cage* or *drive tray* arrangements, in which you first secure the drive to a removable carrier and then attach the carrier to the chassis. Whatever the arrangement, once you've removed the cover it will almost certainly be obvious how to physically secure the drive within the case. If it isn't, refer to the hardware documentation.

On a well-designed case, the screws that secure the drive will be readily accessible on both sides. Some cases are so badly designed that you may have to remove the drive bay assembly itself, or even the system board to access the screws on one side of the drive. Once you have removed the cover and decided where and how you will physically install the drive, take the following steps:

1. If you are also installing an enhanced PATA interface card, configure that card per the maker's instructions, attach the ATA cable(s) to it, and install the card in an available slot. If that card will replace one or both embedded system board ATA interfaces, restart the system and use CMOS Setup to disable the system board ATA interfaces before you install the card.

2. Ground yourself, open the antistatic bag that contains the drive, and place the drive flat on top of the antistatic bag. Recent systems automatically determine the proper drive parameters by querying the drive directly. However, if you are installing the drive in an older system, write down the drive parameters listed on the drive in case the BIOS fails to identify the drive.

 Most manufacturers print the drive geometry and jumper settings on the drive itself, but some drives are not labeled. The manufacturer's web site is usually the best source for this information. All ATA drives larger than 8.4 GB use the same CHS settings: 16,383 cylinders, 16 heads, and 63 sectors/track. The system determines actual drive capacity by using the LBA sector count.

3. If necessary, visually examine any existing drives to determine how they are jumpered and to which ATA interface they connect. On recent systems, there's an easier way. BIOS Setup identifies ATA-3 (or later) compliant ATA/ATAPI devices by name, the channel to which they connect, and whether they are configured as Master or Slave. Depending on the existing configuration, you may choose simply to add the new drive to a free channel, or you may need to rejumper existing drives and/or move them to another interface. Use the following guidelines to set Master/Slave jumpers when connecting ATA/ATAPI devices:

   • Make the hard disk from which the PC boots the Master on the primary ATA channel.

   • To connect only one device to an ATA channel, configure it as Master (or Only), whether it is an ATA hard disk or an ATAPI CD-ROM or tape drive. Note that most ATAPI CD-ROM drives and many ATAPI tape drives are jumpered as Slave by default on the assumption that they will be connected to an ATA channel that already has a Master hard drive on it. On most systems, an ATAPI Slave works properly as the only device on an ATA channel, and some BIOSes do not support ATAPI Masters, but the Master-less Slave configuration is technically not permitted. If an ATAPI device is not recognized after you change operating systems, suspect this as the cause.

   • To connect two ATA drives to an ATA channel, jumper one drive as Master and the other as Slave. The controller on the drive jumpered as Master controls both devices on the cable, so it usually makes sense to jumper the newer and presumably faster device as Master.

   • To connect two ATAPI devices to an ATA channel, jumper one drive as Master and the other as Slave. It generally doesn't matter which is which, but given the choice, set the newer device as Master.

- To connect an ATA hard drive and an ATAPI device to one ATA channel, jumper the ATA drive as Master and the ATAPI device as Slave. The reverse usually works, but is technically not permitted, and may cause problems if you later make changes to your system.

- On an ATA cable with two device connectors, it doesn't matter which device you connect to which connector, so long as you make sure that Pin 1 on the interface and each device is connected toward the red stripe on the cable. If you are connecting only one device to a cable with dual connectors, good practice suggests that you connect that one device to the end connector and leave the middle connector unused.

Note that this advice about jumpering drives assumes that you are using standard drives and cables, which is still by far the most common method. If you are using CSEL-compatible drives and cables, see "Using Cable Select" in Chapter 13 for information about configuring CSEL drives.

4. After you have jumpered the new drives (and rejumpered existing ones, if necessary), but before you mount the drive in the bay, connect the ATA cable to the new drive, making sure that the red stripe on the cable connects to Pin 1 on both the drive and the adapter. It may or may not be easier to connect the power cable as well at this point.

5. Slide the new drive into a drive bay, but don't secure it with screws just yet. If you've set a jumper incorrectly, you may need to remove the drive to correct the problem. If you didn't connect the power cable earlier, do so now, making sure that it seats fully.

6. Leaving the cover off for now, give the system a quick visual check to make sure everything is connected properly. Connect the keyboard, mouse, and monitor if you'd previously disconnected them, then flip the power on to start the smoke test. You should hear the new drive spin up. If it's difficult to tell (which it often is with newer drives), you can put your fingertip against the drive and feel it spinning up. Watch the screen as the system starts, and invoke CMOS setup.

CMOS Setup

After you've physically installed a new PATA hard drive, the next step is to get the PC to recognize it by configuring CMOS Setup. New BIOSs automatically detect and query-attached ATA devices during boot. If your system has such a BIOS, it will display installed ATA devices by type, name, and model during the normal boot sequence as it detects them. If this occurs, it's generally safe to assume that the PC has automatically configured BIOS settings for optimum performance. If you have an older BIOS, you have to configure it manually to recognize the new drive. The exact steps required to do so vary according to the BIOS type and revision level, but the following general guidelines should suffice:

1. Display the BIOS Setup screen that lists installed devices. Any modern BIOS should list four devices—Primary Master/Slave and Secondary Master/Slave.

If Setup has space for only two devices, you badly need a BIOS update. In fact, you need a new motherboard. With recent BIOSs, all ATA drives—including the one you just installed—should be listed by device name, size, and (perhaps) geometry, and ATAPI CD-ROM drives should be listed by name and type. If the drive you just installed is listed, the PC has configured that drive properly and you can use the operating system to partition and format the drive.

2. If the drive you just installed is not listed, try changing Drive Type for the channel where the new drive is installed from None or User to Auto, if that option is offered. The BIOS may or may not recognize the drive. If it doesn't do so immediately, try restarting the computer. If that doesn't work, but if the BIOS Setup main menu offers an option named IDE HDD Auto Detection (or something similar), invoke that option and then view BIOS Setup again to see if your new drive appears. If it does, you can use the operating system to partition and format the drive.

3. If the new drive still isn't listed, you'll have to configure it manually. To do so, examine the options available for Mode, enter the drive parameters recommended by the manufacturer for that mode, and choose one of the following modes:

Normal
> Configures the drive to operate in CHS addressing mode, which limits the drive to 504 MB.

Large
> Configures the drive to use ECHS translation mode. Select this mode, which may instead be labeled Large, ECHS, Translation, or something similar, only if the BIOS does not offer LBA mode, or if you are installing an older, non-LBA capable drive. Note that, because translation modes are not necessarily compatible between different BIOSs, you cannot safely move a hard drive configured to use translation mode on one machine to another machine, whose translation mode may be incompatible. If the two machines use compatible translation modes, everything may work properly. If not, the data will be scrambled beyond recovery when the second computer writes to the drive.

> If you need to move a drive that uses ECHS translation mode to another system, the only safe way to do so is to back up any data you care about, remove the drive from the old system, install it in the new system, and then repartition and reformat the drive. Of course, any drive in a system old enough to be using ECHS mode is probably too old and slow to be useful anyway, and with new drives available at such low cost you're better off just installing a new drive.

LBA
> Configures the drive to use LBA mode, which allows you to use the full capacity of the drive. Select this option unless you are installing an older, non-LBA drive. LBA mode is standardized, and it should be safe to move

Hard Disk Drives

a drive configured for LBA mode from one machine to another. We have done so many times, but your mileage may vary, so back up before you attempt this.

4. For BIOSs that require you to enter drive geometry manually, you should also examine the CMOS Setup screen that configures the embedded ATA interfaces, if available. Use this screen to configure the interface to use the fastest transfer mode common to the interface and the drive itself. For example, if you have just installed an Ultra-DMA/100 drive in a system with an older BIOS, you may find that the fastest mode supported by that interface is PIO-4 at 13.3 MB/s. If the embedded interface does not support modern high-speed transfer modes, consider replacing the interface. Enhanced ATA interfaces are relatively cheap, and allow you to take advantage of the faster throughput and greater safety of modern UDMA modes. If the drive is configured to use LBA, you can safely use the existing interface temporarily and replace it later with a faster interface. The drive will function properly as is with the upgraded interface, but will simply begin using the fastest transfer mode common to the drive and new controller.

5. Once the drive is installed, recognized by the system, and configured properly in CMOS Setup, turn off the system. Align the screw holes in the drive with those in the bay. If screws were supplied with the drive, use them. If not, you can use any standard drive screw, but first verify that it is not too long by using your fingers to tighten the screw into the bare drive, making sure that no resistance is felt before the screw is fully seated. Insert four screws to secure the drive, two on each side. Some drives and some bays also allow screws to be inserted from beneath. Once you have all four screws loosely secured, tighten each of them gently. Good practice (seldom seen nowadays) suggests using a lock washer or a small dab of fingernail polish to prevent the screws from vibrating loose.

6. With the drive secured, start the system again, and use the operating system to partition and format the drive.

Enabling PATA DMA Mode Transfers

Depending on what level UDMA your hard disk and interface support, enabling DMA transfers may or may not increase disk performance noticeably, but enabling DMA is always worthwhile because it greatly reduces the burden that PIO transfers place on the processor. If a computer has 75% CPU utilization using PIO transfers, that same computer using DMA transfers may provide the same or better disk performance at perhaps 1.5% CPU utilization. With multitasking operating systems, those extra free CPU ticks translate into faster system response.

To use DMA transfers, your drive, BIOS, and chipset must explicitly support DMA, and your operating system must have DMA drivers installed, loaded, and enabled. All versions of Windows 95, Windows 98, and Windows NT/2000/XP support DMA transfers, but DMA is disabled by default in some environments, as follows:

Windows 95B, Windows 98, and Windows 2000/XP
  A fresh install automatically installs DMA-capable drivers and tests the system for DMA support. Setup queries the chipset to determine if it supports DMA.

If it does, Setup queries the drive itself to determine what DMA level, if any, it supports. If the drive is also DMA-capable, Setup does a series of reads and writes to determine if the system reliably supports DMA. If any of these tests fail, DMA is disabled. If all three succeed, DMA is enabled automatically at the fastest DMA mode common to the drive and interface. Upgrading an existing system to Windows 95B, Windows 98, or Windows 2000/XP automatically enables DMA only if the DMA was previously enabled.

Francisco García Maceda, our technical reviewer, notes the following:

"This paragraph is correct as far as the theory goes. However, I have installed Windows 98 and 98SE dozens of times with DMA-compatible hardware and usually—perhaps 80% of the time—I have had to enable DMA manually. Once manually enabled, it works without a problem for months on end. I always verify that DMA is in fact enabled after any OS installation. This has happened to me with chipsets from Intel, VIA, SiS, ALi, etc., and with processors from Intel, VIA, Cyrix, AMD, etc., so I haven't been able to associate it with any particular hardware configuration.

I'm also amazed that large companies such as Dell, Compaq, IBM, and HP used to ship their computers without DMA enabled, even though those systems had full hardware support for DMA. Go figure! So I would add to always check DMA status after any install (whether an upgrade or a bare-metal install) or when you receive your fully assembled computer. With Windows 2000 I haven't had this problem."

Although we haven't the slightest doubt that Mr. Maceda has experienced exactly what he describes, our experience with Windows 98/98SE configuring itself automatically to use DMA mode has been better than his, albeit not perfect. The few times we recall a fresh installation of Windows 98/98SE failing to configure DMA properly were on systems with VIA chipsets. We have never encountered the problem on systems with Intel chipsets. The root of the problem seems to be that Microsoft (with some justification) did not fully trust DMA until recently, and so took the conservative approach when deciding whether to enable it.

Windows 95 and Windows 95A

These operating systems do not install DMA support automatically. If your ATA interface and drives are DMA-capable, you can install and enable DMA-capable drivers manually.

Windows NT 4.0

Does not install DMA support automatically, but SP2 and higher include DMA-capable drivers that you can install and enable manually. For detailed instructions, see Microsoft Knowledge Base Article 158873.

Enabling DMA transfers is always an adventure because the only way to determine if your system works properly with DMA is to try it. Therefore, before you enable DMA, make sure you can recover if it doesn't work as expected. Always do a full backup and verify, including the registry, before you attempt to enable DMA.

For Windows 9X, have a known-good Startup diskette available before you try to enable DMA. If DMA does not work properly, you can recover by booting with the floppy, starting Windows in Safe Mode, disabling DMA, and restarting the system.

For Windows NT, the process is more perilous. If problems are immediately obvious when you restart the Windows NT system after enabling DMA, you can restart the system and choose the Last Known Good configuration to revert to the earlier, non-DMA drivers. Just don't log on before you do this, or the non-DMA Last Known Good configuration will be overwritten by the flawed DMA configuration.

When you restart the PC, immediately check the current DMA status. All versions of Windows 9X and Windows NT 4 or later automatically disable DMA transfers at boot and revert to PIO transfers if they detect an obvious DMA problem. A DMA checkbox that won't stay checked when you restart the system is a good indication that your computer does not support DMA properly. Unfortunately, this is not foolproof. DMA may appear to install successfully, but may have intermittent problems anyway. Any of the following symptoms may (or may not) indicate a DMA problem:

- You cannot access the hard disk at all, or you notice corrupt or missing files.
- The drive sometimes hangs briefly or seems to speed up and slow down during file access.
- The keyboard or the foreground application sometimes stops responding for short periods, or the mouse becomes jerky or nonresponsive.
- Windows locks up during the Plug-and-Play detection phase of Setup.
- Windows will start only in Safe Mode.
- Windows shutdown takes a lot longer than before you enabled DMA.

If any of these problems occur, it does not necessarily mean that you cannot use DMA with your computer. The following are likely causes of the problems:

Cable
> According to the ATA standard, cables can be no longer than 18 inches (0. 45m), but we often see PATA cables of 24 inches and even 36 inches. These long cables simply will not work reliably, if at all, with high-speed DMA modes. Cables also vary greatly in quality. The ones you see for $1.99 in bins at the computer store are less likely to work reliably at high speeds than those that are supplied with a new DMA drive. When you're installing a DMA drive, always replace the old ATA cable with the cable that comes with the drive. If no cable came with the drive, buy a good-quality DMA cable separately. If you have problems with DMA, simply replacing the cable with a better cable may solve them.

Drive
> Any new drive should support DMA properly, but some early ATA-33 drives did not implement fast DMA modes correctly. If you reconfigure an older drive to use DMA, first check the manufacturer's web site for details on that model. Software patches for some models are available.

BIOS

Some early BIOS implementations that nominally provide DMA support do not do so correctly. If a more recent BIOS revision is available for your computer, downloading it and installing it may resolve intermittent DMA problems. If your current BIOS does not support DMA, you may find that a revised version is available to add that capability.

Determining if a drive supports DMA

The easiest way to determine if a drive supports DMA or Ultra DMA transfers is to check the specifications in the manual or on the web site. You can also use debug to query the drive directly to determine what level of DMA, if any, it supports. To do so, boot the PC using a DOS floppy that contains the debug utility. (Running debug under Windows NT/2000/XP does not allow you to access the registers needed to perform this test.) At the DOS prompt, type debug and press Enter. If the drive to be tested is connected to the primary ATA interface, type the following commands at the debug hyphen prompt, ending each line by pressing Enter. Note that the first character in each of the first four lines is the lowercase letter "o" rather than zero, and that all "1" characters are the numeral one rather than the lowercase letter "l".

```
o 1f6 a0
o 1f2 45
o 1f1 03
o 1f7 ef
i 1f1
```

The first line (o 1f6 a0) specifies the drive to be tested. The a0 argument specifies the Master drive. To test the Slave drive, substitute b0 (o 1f6 b0). The second line (o 1f2 45) specifies the DMA mode to be tested. Valid arguments are 40 through 46, inclusive, for Ultra DMA Modes 0 through 6, respectively. For DMA (*not* Ultra DMA) Modes 1 and 2, use 21 or 22, respectively. Start with the fastest mode you believe the drive supports. If the test fails for this mode, retest using the next-slower mode until you find a mode that the drive does support. The 03 argument on the third line (o 1f1 03) programs disk timing. The ef argument on the fourth line (o 1f7 ef) is the Set Feature command for the drive. Pressing Enter after the final line (i 1f1) reads the error status and returns either the value 00, which indicates that the drive supports the DMA mode being tested, or the value 04, which indicates that the drive does not support the DMA level being tested. If debug returns something other than 00 or 04, you've mistyped something. To exit debug, type the letter q at the hyphen prompt and press Enter.

If the drive to be tested is connected to the secondary ATA interface, use the following debug commands, which substitute "7" for "*f*" in the address string:

```
o 176 a0
o 172 45
o 171 03
o 177 ef
i 171
```

All other comments concerning the commands for the primary ATA interface also pertain to the secondary ATA interface.

With Linux, the best way to determine the DMA modes a drive supports and the DMA mode it is currently using is to run hdparm -i /dev/hd*, replacing the asterisk with the correct letter for the hard drive you want to test. Figure 14-2 shows that the drive we tested supports udma0 through udma5. The asterisk indicates that the drive is currently using udma5.

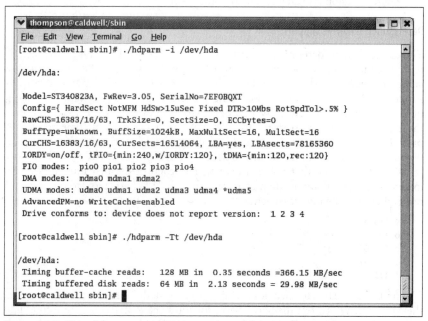

```
thompson@caldwell:/sbin                                          _ □ x
File  Edit  View  Terminal  Go  Help
[root@caldwell sbin]# ./hdparm -i /dev/hda

/dev/hda:

 Model=ST340823A, FwRev=3.05, SerialNo=7EFOBQXT
 Config={ HardSect NotMFM HdSw>15uSec Fixed DTR>10Mbs RotSpdTol>.5% }
 RawCHS=16383/16/63, TrkSize=0, SectSize=0, ECCbytes=0
 BuffType=unknown, BuffSize=1024kB, MaxMultSect=16, MultSect=16
 CurCHS=16383/16/63, CurSects=16514064, LBA=yes, LBAsects=78165360
 IORDY=on/off, tPIO={min:240,w/IORDY:120}, tDMA={min:120,rec:120}
 PIO modes:  pio0 pio1 pio2 pio3 pio4
 DMA modes:  mdma0 mdma1 mdma2
 UDMA modes: udma0 udma1 udma2 udma3 udma4 *udma5
 AdvancedPM=no WriteCache=enabled
 Drive conforms to: device does not report version:  1 2 3 4

[root@caldwell sbin]# ./hdparm -Tt /dev/hda

/dev/hda:
 Timing buffer-cache reads:   128 MB in  0.35 seconds =366.15 MB/sec
 Timing buffered disk reads:  64 MB in  2.13 seconds = 29.98 MB/sec
[root@caldwell sbin]# █
```

Figure 14-2. Using hdparm to test DMA support and drive performance

When you test DMA modes, you can also test drive performance. To do that, use the command hdparm -Tt /dev/hd*. In this example, the drive is doing buffered disk reads at nearly 30 MB/s, which is excellent performance for an ATA drive.

Enabling DMA mode transfers with Windows 9X

To determine if your system board and ATA interface support DMA, right-click the My Computer icon and choose Properties to display the System Properties dialog. Display the Device Manager and expand the Hard disk controllers item. You do not have DMA-capable hardware if you see only one or two entries that read Standard IDE/ESDI Hard Disk Controller. If the first entry is Intel 82371SB PCI Bus Master IDE Controller or similar, the system board and interface provide DMA support. The critical words are PCI Bus Master. The exact model number is less important.

Windows 98 and Windows 95B automatically load DMA-capable drivers if they detect DMA hardware. To install DMA support for the initial Windows 95 release, download and execute the file *http://support.microsoft.com/download/ support/mslfiles/remideup.exe* and follow the prompts.

After you restart the system, enable DMA transfers by right-clicking My Computer and choosing Properties to display the System Properties dialog. Display the Device Manager page and expand the Disk drives item. Double-click the drive in question to display its Properties sheet and display the Settings page, shown in Figure 14-3.

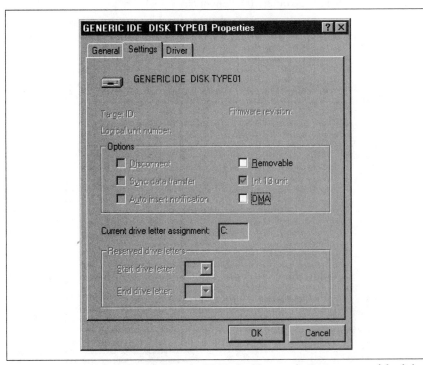

Figure 14-3. In Windows 9X, marking the DMA checkbox on the Settings page of the disk Properties dialog to enable DMA transfers

If a DMA-capable driver has been loaded, a DMA checkbox appears in the Options section. Mark that checkbox to enable DMA transfers for that drive. Exit the dialog, restart the system, and redisplay the dialog to verify that DMA remains enabled after the restart. If rebooting clears the checkbox, Windows has decided that some problem exists with DMA transfers, and has reverted to using PIO. If the checkbox remains marked, DMA transfers are enabled and should work, subject to the provisos listed earlier.

Enabling DMA mode transfers with Windows 2000 or Windows XP

To enable DMA under Windows 2000 or Windows XP, take the following steps:

1. Right-click the My Computer icon on the desktop and choose Properties to display System Properties.

2. Click the Hardware tab and then the Device Manager button to display the Device Manager.

3. Locate and expand the IDE ATA/ATAPI controllers item. On a standard system with both ATA controllers enabled, there should be three items listed, sorted alphabetically. One item describes the ATA controller itself (e.g., Intel(r) 82801BA Bus Master IDE Controller or VIA Bus Master PCI IDE Controller) and may be disregarded. The other two items should be Primary IDE Channel and Secondary IDE Channel.

4. Right-click the channel to which the device you want to enable DMA for is connected, choose Properties, and then click the Advanced Settings tab to display the dialog shown in Figure 14-4.

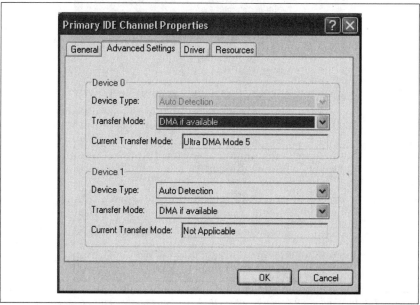

Figure 14-4. Windows XP showing this hard drive is using UDMA-5 (ATA-100) Transfer Mode

5. This dialog displays the Device Type and Current Transfer Mode for Device 0 (Master) and Device 1 (Slave) on the selected ATA channel. The Current Transfer Mode field shows the transfer mode currently in use, and may be changed as follows:

DMA Mode x or Ultra DMA Mode x

Windows is using the indicated MDA or UDMA mode, which is the fastest mode supported by the interface, cable, and device. For example, if the hard drive supports UDMA/100 and the embedded motherboard interface supports UDMA/66, but you use a standard 40-wire ATA cable, Windows configures the interface to use UDMA/33. If you replace that cable with an 80-wire UDMA cable and restart the system, Windows reconfigures the interface to use UDMA/66. You cannot explicitly choose the UDMA mode to be used.

PIO Mode or PIO Mode x

Windows is using the fastest PIO mode supported by the interface and device, typically PIO-4 (16.7 MB/s) unless the components are extremely old. If Transfer Mode is currently set to *PIO Only*, you may be able to enable DMA by setting Transfer Mode to DMA if available and restarting the system. If the Current Transfer Mode for the device still shows PIO Mode, that device cannot be used in DMA mode.

Not Applicable

No device is installed.

Enabling DMA mode transfers with Linux

Ordinarily, a UDMA-aware Linux kernel automatically enables UDMA for any UDMA-capable drives and interfaces it finds. If a recent Linux kernel does not automatically enable UDMA, it's usually because the kernel doesn't understand how to use the UDMA features of the chipset or it thinks UDMA is not safe to use. However, a BIOS glitch or similar minor problem may fool the kernel into believing falsely that DMA is not supported or is unsafe to use. If that happens, it may be useful to enable DMA manually.

With any kernel 2.1.113 or later, you can enable DMA manually by using kernel boot parameters. To do so, add the command ide0=dma or ide1=dma to your startup script, where ide0 is the primary ATA interface and ide1 the secondary ATA interface. We have never used this method for a tertiary or higher ATA interface, and we suspect that it would not work reliably, if at all, for anything except the primary and secondary interfaces. As always, enabling DMA for an interface means that all devices attached to that interface must support DMA. Using this command for an interface to which a PIO mode device is attached results in unpredictable operation at best, and may cause data corruption or boot failures.

The problem with using kernel boot parameters to enable DMA is that they merely ask the kernel to use DMA rather than ordering it to do so. Even after adding a DMA kernel boot parameter to your startup script, you may find the drive is not using DMA. If that occurs, you can force DMA with the command hdparm -d1 /dev/hd*, replacing the asterisk with the appropriate letter. Note that a kernel boot parameter sets DMA for the interface, while hdparm sets DMA only for a specified device. Accordingly, if you have two devices attached to the interface, use hdparm twice, once for each device. For example, if you have two hard drives connected to the primary ATA interface, use hdparm -d1 /dev/hda and hdparm -d1 /dev/hdb to enable DMA for both drives. Although we have never needed to do so, you can disable DMA for a device using the command hdparm -d0 /dev/hd*

Before you force DMA operation using hdparm, make absolutely, positively sure that the drive, interface, and cable really do support DMA, and that the kernel you use is compatible with the chipset's DMA features. Otherwise, you'll be forcing Linux to use DMA on hardware that doesn't support it, which *is certain* to corrupt data. If the kernel lacks support for your chipset, you may be able to locate a kernel patch to add the necessary support. Doing that means recompiling the kernel, however, so if a later kernel supports your chipset natively, it is generally easier to upgrade to a later Linux release.

Installing an SATA Hard Disk

Installing an SATA hard disk is much easier than installing a PATA model because there are no Master/Slave issues or DMA configuration steps to worry about. You simply secure the drive to the chassis and connect the signal and power cables. Most systems recognize an SATA drive and configure it automatically. If the system doesn't detect the drive automatically, you may need to use BIOS Setup to force detection. The following sections describe the steps necessary to install an SATA drive.

Physical Installation

In terms of physical installation, the only differences between PATA and SATA drives are that they use different cables and connectors, that you don't need to set Master/Slave jumpers on SATA drives, and that each SATA drive connects to a dedicated interface port. To install an SATA hard drive, take the following steps:

1. If the motherboard does not include an embedded SATA controller, install a PCI SATA host adapter card, such as those made by Promise Technology, Inc. (*http://www.promise.com*) and SIIG, Inc. (*http://www.siig.com*).

 A PCI SATA host adapter may require driver software supplied with the card.

2. Connect one end of the SATA data cable to the SATA connector on the motherboard or SATA host adapter. Remember that SATA uses a point-to-point topology, so each drive is connected to a dedicated interface connector using an individual data cable. The data cable connectors are identical on both ends, so it doesn't matter which end of the cable connects to the SATA interface. The data cable is keyed to make it impossible to attach incorrectly.

3. Secure the drive to the chassis using four mounting screws of the proper size (usually UNC 6-32), driving the screws through the side or bottom mounting holes. If the screws were not supplied with the drive, make sure they are not too long. Excessively long mounting screws can damage the drive. If you're unsure, test the screws by screwing them into the mounting holes using only your fingers. If the screws seat fully without resistance, they are short enough to be safe.

4. Connect the interface and power cables to the drive. The cable and drive connectors are both keyed to prevent installing the cable incorrectly. Depending on the physical arrangement of the drive and chassis, it may be easier to connect the cables to the drive before you secure the drive to the chassis.

The only problem you are likely to encounter when installing an SATA drive is that most power supplies do not have SATA power connectors. The solution is to use an SATA power adapter, one of which may be bundled with the SATA drive. If the drive did not come with an SATA power adapter, you can buy one at any well-stocked computer store or through an online vendor.

CMOS and OS Setup

After you physically install the SATA hard drive, restart the system and run BIOS Setup. If the SATA drive is not listed, use the BIOS Setup autodetect feature to force detection and restart the system again. Depending on the motherboard, the system may or may not recognize the new drive, as follows:

Motherboard without native SATA chipset support
Motherboards made before spring 2003 lack native (chipset-level) SATA support. Transition motherboards produced in late 2002 through July 2003—e.g., the Intel D845PEBT2 and the ASUS A7N8X Deluxe—use an embedded third-party controller chip such as the Sil 3112A to provide SATA support. Some systems add SATA support with a PCI SATA host adapter. Accessing the SATA drive on most such systems requires a driver.

For a new Windows 2000/XP system that is to boot from the SATA drive, insert the driver diskette when the operating system setup utility prompts you to install third-party storage drivers. For Windows 9X, follow the instructions provided by the motherboard or SATA interface manufacturer. If the SATA drive is a secondary drive on an existing system, use the OS driver update feature to load the SATA driver after the system boots to the original primary hard drive. If the SATA drive and interface don't appear on the list of IDE/ATA devices, which they probably won't, examine the list of SCSI devices.

Motherboard with native SATA chipset support
Recent motherboards, such as those that use Intel Springdale-family chipsets, recognize and use SATA interfaces and drives automatically. After you install the SATA drive, restart the system and run BIOS Setup. The new SATA drive should be listed as an installed device. If it is not, run autodetect, save the changes, and restart the system. The drive should then appear in the installed devices list unless the drive, cable, or interface is broken.

Some motherboards with embedded SATA interfaces offer SATA configuration options in BIOS Setup, and others do not. If you are adding an SATA drive to an existing system as a secondary drive, you should not have to alter BIOS settings. If you replace the boot drive, you may need to change boot order in BIOS Setup to allow the system to boot from the SATA drive. Depending on the BIOS, the boot order screen may list the SATA boot setting as SATA, the drive model number, or SCSI.

If the motherboard has embedded SATA interfaces, you are normally prompted to install any necessary drivers when you first start the system. If you didn't install these drivers during motherboard installation, you should be prompted for them during Plug-and-Play enumeration. Before you install an SATA motherboard, it is a good idea to visit the SATA controller manufacturer's web site to download the latest SATA drivers for that controller.

If a properly installed SATA drive is not recognized by the operating system, verify that BIOS Setup is configured properly and that you have loaded and enabled the latest driver for the SATA controller you are using.

Optimizing SATA Transfer Rate

Unlike PATA drives and interfaces, which may use various PIO and DMA modes, SATA drives and interfaces use only the 150 MB/s SATA transfer mode. You don't need to configure settings manually. If the SATA drive is running at all, you can be sure it's using optimum settings.

Installing a SCSI Hard Disk

When installing and configuring a SCSI hard disk, use the following guidelines:

- If possible, avoid mixing different types of SCSI devices on the same bus. For example, if your system has an Ultra160 SCSI hard disk and Ultra-SCSI CD-ROM, CD-RW, and tape drives installed, put the fast hard disk on its own SCSI bus and install the slower SCSI devices on a separate SCSI bus. If necessary, purchase and install an inexpensive SCSI host adapter to support the slower devices.

- For easiest installation and configuration, use all SCAM-compliant devices. *SCAM-compliant* drives allow a SCAM-compliant host adapter to set the drive's SCSI ID and termination status automatically. *SCAM-tolerant* drives report their SCSI ID and termination status to the adapter, but you must manually change settings on the drive if SCSI ID and/or termination need to be altered. *Non-SCAM* drives neither report their current settings to the adapter nor allow the adapter to reset them automatically. When using non-SCAM devices, you must manually verify settings and change them as necessary.

- Many SCSI problems are cable-related. The cables supplied with SCSI hard disks and host adapters are usually of decent quality, but we've seen some truly horrible ones. Good SCSI cables aren't cheap, and the $3 ones you find in the bin at computer stores should be avoided. We've always found Adaptec SCSI cables to be both reasonably priced and of high quality.

 If you plan to boot the system from a SCSI hard disk, that disk must connect to a *bootable SCSI host adapter*. Inexpensive SCSI host adapters, especially those bundled with CD burners and similar SCSI devices, are usually not bootable because they are intended merely to provide an inexpensive way to connect SCSI devices to a system that boots from an ATA hard disk.

Installing a SCSI drive may be more complicated than installing an ATA drive, particularly if your drive and/or adapter is not SCAM-compliant. The following steps illustrate the general procedure for installing a SCSI hard disk with a PCI SCSI host adapter. The exact steps vary depending on which components you use.

1. If you have not already done so, install the SCSI host adapter. To do so, turn off the system, remove the cover, and locate an available bus-mastering PCI slot. Recent systems support bus mastering on all slots. Some older systems support bus mastering on only some slots. In that case, bus-mastering slots are normally light-colored and nonbus-mastering slots are dark. Remove the

slot cover for the selected slot, align the bus connector with the slot, and press down firmly to seat the adapter. Use the screw that secured the slot cover to secure the adapter. If you have a spare drive-activity indicator LED, connect it to the appropriate pins on the host adapter.

2. If both the drive and host adapter are SCAM-compliant, proceed to Step 5. If the host adapter is SCAM-compliant but the drive is non-SCAM compliant, the system may hang if you leave SCAM enabled on the host adapter because the adapter is unable to determine current settings for the non-SCAM device. Disable SCAM on the host adapter by starting the system and running the ROM-based Setup utility for the adapter.

3. Set SCSI IDs manually using the jumpers or switches on the adapter and drive. If the host adapter supports seven devices (plus the adapter itself), the adapter is normally configured as SCSI ID 7, leaving SCSI IDs 0 through 6 available for drives. Higher-numbered IDs have priority. ID 0 is normally reserved for the boot hard disk and ID 1 for a second hard disk. Set the hard disk jumpers for the appropriate SCSI ID, according to whether the hard disk is the primary boot drive or a secondary drive.

4. Terminate the SCSI bus. Exactly two devices must be terminated on each SCSI bus, and these devices must be those at each end of the bus, as follows:

   - If the SCSI adapter has only internal devices attached to it, the adapter itself and the final device on the internal SCSI chain must be terminated.

   - If the SCSI adapter has only external devices attached to it, the adapter itself and the final device on the external SCSI chain must be terminated.

   - If the SCSI adapter has both internal and external devices attached to it, *do not* terminate the SCSI adapter itself. Instead, terminate the final device attached to the internal chain and the final device attached to the external chain.

 SCAM-compliant SCSI host adapters detect terminated SCSI devices on the bus and set their own termination status automatically. On Adaptec models, which we recommend exclusively, this option can be enabled or disabled by using SCSISelect to set Host Adapter Termination to AutoTerm, which is the default setting. Also note that some internal SCSI cables have a built-in terminator at the end of the cable. If you use such a cable, make sure that termination is disabled on all drives connected to that cable.

5. Once SCSI ID and termination are configured correctly, physically install the drive and connect the cables. Most adapters are supplied with a standard two-device cable. If you need to connect more than two drives, replace the cable before proceeding. Otherwise, connect the cable to each drive, making sure to align Pin 1 on the cable (indicated by a red stripe) with Pin 1 on each device (indicated by a small number, triangle, or dot on the connector). It doesn't matter which drive connects to which cable position, so mix and match drives and cable positions in whatever way makes it easiest to route the cable. Don't forget to connect the power cable.

6. After verifying all settings and connections, turn on any external SCSI devices first, and then turn on the PC. If the SCSI hard disk is to be the boot drive, run CMOS Setup and verify that the entry for ATA Primary Master is set to None or Not Installed. If necessary, change it, save the new entry, and restart the system. On most systems, the PCI bus assigns IRQs and port addresses automatically. If your system requires setting PCI bus parameters manually, do so during this restart, using the system or motherboard documentation for guidance. Save the new settings and restart the system again.

7. The SCSI BIOS displays its own splash screen while initializing, which normally displays adapter and BIOS information and a list of installed SCSI devices. Ordinarily, default settings are fine, but in some cases you may need to change settings to get the drive to work at all or to optimize its performance. If this is the case for your system, press whatever key sequence is needed to invoke the SCSI Setup routine and make the necessary changes, as recommended by the documentation for the host adapter and/or drive.

8. Once the drive is installed and recognized by the system, use the operating system to partition and format the drive.

Preparing a Hard Disk for Use

After you have physically installed the hard disk and configured CMOS Setup to recognize it, that drive must still be prepared before it can store data. This process requires three steps:

Low-level formatting
> *Low-level formatting*, also called *physical formatting*, records the tracks and sectors that are used to store data. Low-level formatting occurs at the hardware level, and is independent of the way that the disk will be divided and of the operating system that will use it. All ATA and most SCSI drives are low-level formatted at the factory, so you may not need to perform this step yourself.

Partitioning
> *Partitioning* divides the physical disk into one or more logical sections, each of which will contain one or more logical volumes identified by drive letter or a mount point under Linux. Any hard disk must contain at least one partition with at least one volume. Any new hard drive must be partitioned before it can be used.

Logical formatting
> *Logical formatting*, also called *high-level formatting* or *DOS formatting*, creates within the volume the logical disk structure (called the *filesystem*) needed by a particular operating system to store its data. Drives that will be accessed by DOS, Windows 3.X, and Windows 9X use the FAT filesystem (which comes in several variants). Windows NT/2000/XP uses either FAT or NTFS filesystems. Linux generally uses ext2, but ext3 is becoming more common.

The following sections examine each of these steps in turn.

Low-Level Formatting

Low-level formatting a hard drive lays down the tracks and sectors that will be used to store data and also embeds servo information that the drive head positioning mechanism uses to locate those tracks and sectors. Modern drives are low-level formatted at the factory, and cannot be low-level formatted by the user.

You sometimes need to low-level format a drive, or at least do something that resembles a low-level format. The three most common situations that require formatting a drive down to bare metal are the presence of a virus that cannot be eradicated by a logical format or by repartitioning the drive, a corrupted partition table that cannot be corrected by using a partitioning utility, and a drive that is beginning to develop bad sectors.

For all these situations, the solution is to pseudo-low-level format the drive with the maintenance utility provided by the drive manufacturer. Although these utilities do not do a true low-level format, they write binary zeros to every accessible bit on the drive, wiping all data and partitions from the drive. These utilities also typically have a sector-sparing function that allows them to detect bad sectors and swap them out for a spare sector, returning that drive to its factory-fresh, error-free state.

If you need to do a low-level format of your drive, download the latest version of the low-level format utility from the manufacturer's web site. Create a DOS-bootable diskette, and copy the low-level format program executable to that floppy. Boot the floppy and run the format program, carefully following all instructions supplied with the utility.

Most SCSI host adapters include a low-level format utility in ROM.

Partitioning

The next step required to prepare a disk for use is called *partitioning*. Partitioning logically divides a disk into segments, each of which can be logically formatted to store data in the format, or *filesystem*, used by a particular operating system.

Understanding partitioning

Each physical disk must have at least one partition, and may have as many as four. Creating the first partition on a physical disk drive creates the *Master Boot Record (MBR)* for that disk and writes the MBR to the first physical sector. Subsequent changes to the partitioning of that disk, no matter which operating system makes them, update that single MBR. The MBR on each physical disk contains a section called the *partition table*. The partition table tells the computer and the operating system how the hard disk is logically divided and how to access the information stored on that hard disk.

There are two types of partitions. A *primary partition* is one from which the computer may be booted. Each primary partition is logically formatted as a single volume for a particular operating system and is assigned one drive letter. A primary partition may occupy all or part of a physical hard drive, and a single hard drive may contain from zero to four primary partitions.

The second type of partition is called an *extended partition*. An extended partition is essentially a virtual physical disk, which may itself be subdivided into logical volumes. A disk may contain zero or one extended partition. The computer cannot be initialized from an extended partition, although the operating system files may reside on a volume located on an extended partition.

Extended partitions are neither formatted nor assigned drive letters. Instead, extended partitions are further divided, or subpartitioned, into logical volumes, each of which may be logically formatted and assigned its own drive letter under Windows or mount point under Linux. Each of these logical drives may be treated as an independent entity. You might, for example, create an extended partition, subdivide it into two logical drives, and then format one of these drives for FAT and the other for NTFS.

If a physical disk contains multiple primary partitions, you may format each primary partition for a different operating system, and mark one primary partition as *active*, which causes the computer to boot the operating system contained within that partition. Using multiple primary partitions is one way to install and boot multiple operating systems from the same hard disk. For the system to boot from the hard disk, at least one partition must be marked active. To change which operating system boots, you must use *fdisk* or another partitioning utility to change the active partition.

Windows NT/2000/XP refers to the active partition as the *system partition*. It contains the hardware-specific operating system bootstrap files needed to initialize the computer and begin the boot process. A disk may also contain a *boot partition*, which may be located on either a primary partition or a logical volume within an extended partition. The boot partition contains the remainder of the operating system files needed to load and run the operating system. The system partition and the boot partition may be (and often are) the same partition, or they may be located in different partitions, including those located on separate physical disk drives.

The system partition must be located on a primary partition, but the boot files of another operating system may share that primary partition. For example, one convenient way to dual-boot Windows 98 and Windows NT is to partition the disk with an active primary C: partition and a D: volume, which may be a primary partition or a logical drive in an extended partition. Installing Windows 98 to C: makes that volume bootable. Installing Windows NT to D: automatically installs the boot files to C:, making it the NT system partition, and installs the remainder of Windows NT to D:, making it the NT boot partition. Windows NT Setup also installs a boot manager, which allows you to choose between booting Windows 98 and Windows NT when you start the system. The advantage to implementing dual-boot this way is that you don't have to change the active partition to boot the other operating system.

To summarize:

- To be accessible to the operating system, each physical disk drive must contain at least one and at most four partitions. These partitions may be primary partitions or extended partitions.

- A physical disk drive may contain from zero to four primary partitions, each of which is formatted as a single unit and assigned its own drive letter. Each primary partition is formatted for a single type of filesystem. Different primary partitions on the same physical disk drive may be formatted for different operating systems. A primary partition may be any combination of (a) a system partition, which is used to start the operating system, (b) a boot partition, which contains operating system files, or (c) a general-purpose partition, which is used to store user files.

- A physical disk drive may contain zero or one extended partition. If the drive contains an extended partition, it may contain at most three primary partitions. An extended partition may be divided into one or more logical volumes, each of which may be formatted to contain a single type of filesystem. Different logical volumes within an extended partition may contain different filesystems.

- The system partition, also called the active partition, is a primary partition that contains the hardware-specific files needed to initialize the system and begin the boot process. Exactly one active partition must be present on the computer for it to boot.

- The boot partition contains the remaining files needed to run the operating system. The boot partition may be located on a primary partition, or on a logical volume within an extended partition. The boot partition may be and often is the same partition as the system partition.

How drive letters are assigned

Partitioning a disk with DOS or Windows assigns a drive letter to each primary partition and each logical volume created in an extended partition, a process called *dynamic drive letter assignment*. Adding and partitioning another hard disk or changing partitions on an existing hard disk may cause existing drive letters to change, which can confuse programs that expect themselves or their data to be on a particular volume and suddenly find that is no longer true. Modifying partitions under DOS or Windows 9X assigns drive letters as follows:

- Physical disks are numbered sequentially. The Primary Master is Disk 0, the Primary Slave is Disk 1, the Secondary Master is Disk 2, and the Secondary Slave is Disk 3. For SCSI disks, the drive with the lowest SCSI ID is Disk 0, the one with the next-higher SCSI ID is Disk 1, and so on.

- The first primary partition on each physical disk, beginning with Disk 0, is assigned a drive letter sequentially, beginning with C:. The first primary partition on each higher-numbered disk is then assigned the next drive letter in sequence. A disk that has no primary partition is skipped during this process.

- Starting with Disk 0, each logical volume is assigned a drive letter. All logical volumes on each disk are assigned drive letters before drive letters are assigned to any logical volumes on higher-numbered disks.

- Once all logical volumes on all disks have been assigned drive letters, the remaining primary partitions on each disk with unassigned partitions are each assigned a drive letter.

Assume, for example, that a computer has one physical disk, partitioned into one primary partition labeled C: and an extended partition that contains two logical volumes labeled D: and E:. If you then add a second disk and create on it a primary partition and an extended partition that contains two logical volumes, drive letters are reassigned as follows: the primary partition on Disk 0 remains C:; the primary partition on Disk 1 becomes D:; the two logical volumes on Disk 0, formerly D: and E:, are reassigned as E: and F: respectively; and the two new logical volumes on Disk 1 are assigned G: and H:.

To avoid this reassignment of drive letters, do not create a primary partition on the new hard disk. Instead, partition the entire disk as an extended partition and create three logical volumes within that partition. This leaves the original C:, D:, and E: drive letter assignments unchanged, and assigns F:, G:, and H: to the three new logical volumes. The only drawback to partitioning a disk without a primary partition is that the disk can never be made bootable without being repartitioned to contain a primary partition and then reformatted.

Windows 2000/XP partitioning works differently because it uses both dynamic drive letter assignment and *static drive letter assignment*. Before you run Windows 2000/XP Disk Management (Computer Management→Storage→Disk Management) the first time, Windows uses dynamic drive letter assignment to assign drive letters as described earlier. Running Disk Management converts these dynamic drive letter assignments to static drive letter assignments, which means that adding a new disk no longer causes drive letters to be updated automatically. You can, however, use Disk Management to reassign static drive letters manually to volumes. To do so, display a list of volumes within Disk Management, display the context-sensitive menu by right-clicking the volume label for the volume you want to change, and choose the Change Drive Letter and Path option. You can assign any drive letter that is not already being used by a local or network drive to any partition. Don't change the drive letter assignment for the system partition, though, because many applications and services assume that the system partition is C:.

Partitioning a hard disk

With only minor exceptions, partition tables and partitions are completely standard. This means, for example, that DOS can access a partition created by Windows NT and vice versa. You don't have to partition a disk using the native utility of the operating system that you plan to install on that partition. In broad terms, there are three ways to partition a disk: by using the Setup program provided by the operating system, which typically invokes its native partitioning utility; by using that partitioning utility manually; or by using a third-party partitioning utility such as PartitionMagic.

For better control, we partition disks manually rather than allowing the operating system Setup program to make partitions for us. Setup may make the same choices about partition sizes and types that we would have made ourselves, but then again it may not. You can use the fdisk utility from Windows 9X to partition a disk that will boot Windows 9X or Windows NT/2000/XP. To do so, boot a Windows Startup Disk that contains *fdisk.exe* (and *format.com*, which you'll need later) and take the following steps:

1. At the DOS prompt, type `fdisk` and press Enter to start the partitioning utility. If you are using the original Windows 95 `fdisk`, the main menu appears immediately. If you are using the Windows 95 OSR2 or Windows 98 `fdisk`, a preliminary screen appears to notify you that your disk is larger than 512 MB and that this version of `fdisk` has enhanced support for large hard disks, which is incompatible with Windows NT 4.0 and Windows 95 and earlier. Choose Yes to use this hard disk support, or No if you plan to install one of these earlier operating systems.

If you use the original Windows 95 *fdisk* (or choose not to enable large disk support with a later version of *fdisk*), the largest primary partition you can create is 2 GB. Although you can create an arbitrarily large extended partition, logical volumes within that extended partition can be no larger than 2 GB.

Later Windows 9X versions up to and including Windows 98SE include a version of *fdisk* that does not recognize the full capacity of disks larger than 64 GB. Windows Me *fdisk* does not have this limitation. For further information, see document Q263044 at *http://support.microsoft.com*. You can download an updated version of *fdisk* for Windows 98 and 98SE from *http://download.microsoft.com/download/Win98/Update/8266R/W98/EN-US/263044USA8.EXE*.

2. If there is only one physical disk installed, the main menu presents four choices. If more than one physical disk is installed, a fifth option appears that allows you to select the disk to be partitioned. Note that fdisk numbers the first physical disk as 1 rather than 0. If necessary, use option 5 to select the disk to be partitioned.

3. Use option 4, Display partition information, to view existing partitions, if any. If necessary, use option 3, Delete partition or Logical DOS Drive, to remove existing partitions and free up space for new partitions. Deleting a partition destroys all data on that partition, so be sure that's really what you want to do before you do it.

4. From the main menu, choose option 1, Create DOS partition or Logical DOS Drive, to begin partitioning the disk. fdisk displays the Create DOS Partition or Logical DOS Drive submenu with option 1, Create Primary DOS Partition; option 2, Create Extended DOS Partition; and option 3, Create Logical DOS Drive(s) in the Extended DOS Partition.

5. To create a primary partition, choose option 1. By default, fdisk creates the largest primary partition it can in the available space, and marks that partition Active (or bootable). Depending on the size of the disk and whether you enabled large disk support, that partition may or may not occupy all available disk space. If you override the default to create a smaller primary partition, note that fdisk does not automatically mark that partition active. Return to the main menu and choose option 2, Set active partition, if you want that primary partition to be bootable.

6. To create an extended partition for the remaining disk space (or for the entire disk if it has no primary partition), display the Create DOS Partition or Logical DOS Drive submenu and choose option 2, Create Extended DOS

Partition. Allocate some or all of the available disk space to the extended partition (remember that you can have at most one extended partition on the disk) and then return to the Create DOS Partition or Logical DOS Drive submenu.

7. Choose option 3, Create Logical DOS Drive(s) in the Extended DOS Partition, to create logical drives within the extended partition.

8. Restart the computer to put the partitioning changes you have just made into effect.

Different versions of fdisk support some or all of these undocumented command-line switches:

fdisk /mbr

Re-creates the master boot record. This process is nondestructive on Windows systems (it will wipe out lilo on a Linux system) and sometimes can salvage a disk that no longer boots. Using fdisk /mbr replaces the MBR executable code but does not change partitioning data. Most partition sector viruses replace or modify MBR code, so using fdisk /mbr is a fast, easy way to rid a system of a partition sector virus.

fdisk /partn

Saves partitioning information to the file *partsav.fil.*

fdisk /q

Prevents fdisk from rebooting the system automatically upon exit.

fdisk <#>/pri:*<size>*

Creates primary partition of <size> MB on disk number <#>.

fdisk <#>/ext:*<size>*

Creates extended partition of <size> MB on disk number <#>.

fdisk <#>/log:*<size>*

Creates logical volume of <size> MB on disk number <#>.

The partitioning tool we use is PartitionMagic from PowerQuest (*http://www. powerquest.com*). In addition to standard partitioning functions, PartitionMagic does things no other partition utility we know of can do, including changing the sizes of partitions and converting a partition from one filesystem to another on the fly. If you frequently install or repartition hard disks, you need a copy of this utility in your toolkit.

Logical Formatting

After you partition the disk to create logical volumes, the next step is to format each volume, which creates the filesystem structure that will organize the data stored on that volume. This *logical format* writes information to disk that is needed by the filesystem, including:

- A *partition boot sector* for the filesystem that occupies that partition. Don't confuse the partition boot sector with the MBR. Information contained in the MBR applies to the entire physical disk drive, while information contained in the partition boot sector applies only to the partition to which it is written.

- The *System ID Byte*, which identifies the partition type and the filesystem used to format it.
- Bad-sector mapping information.
- Various information specific to the filesystem, including disk-free and disk-used data and the location of files and folders within the partition.

In the DOS/Windows 9X environment, the filesystem you create will be one of the following.

FAT16

MS-DOS and the initial release of Windows 95 support only the FAT16 filesystem. FAT16 uses 16-bit addressing, which limits it to 65,536 discrete addresses. If FAT16 addressed individual sectors, it could access only (65,536 sectors × 512 bytes/sector = 33,554,432 bytes), or 32 MB. To get around this small limit, FAT addresses *clusters* rather than individual sectors. A cluster is a group of sectors. The number of sectors/cluster is always a power of two, is constant within a volume, and is determined automatically based on the size of that volume. Table 14-1 lists the cluster sizes that FAT16 uses for various partition sizes.

Table 14-1. The relationship of FAT16 partition size to cluster size

Partition size (MB)	Sectors / Cluster	Cluster size
0 – 32	1	512 bytes
33 – 64	2	1 KB
65 – 128	4	2 KB
129 – 255	8	4 KB
256 – 511	16	8 KB
512 – 1023	32	16 KB
1024 – 2047	64	32 KB

The downside to using clusters is that a cluster is the smallest addressable unit on the volume, so each file must occupy at least one cluster, and every file on average wastes half a cluster. This means, for example, that storing a 1-byte file on a FAT16 volume larger than 1 GB requires 32,768 bytes of disk space, and that storing a 32,769-byte file requires 65,536 bytes of disk space.

This allocated but unoccupied and unusable disk space is referred to as slack space. Large FAT16 volumes with many files have a lot of it. For example, a 1+ GB FAT16 volume with 15,000 files, each of which will average half a 32 KB cluster wasted, has (15,000 × 16,384), or 245,760,000 bytes of slack space.

FAT16 is the lingua franca of DOS/Windows operating systems. Any Microsoft operating system (and many non-Microsoft ones) can read and write FAT16 volumes. Windows 95 and later and Windows NT/2000 support slightly modified versions of FAT16 called VFAT, which support long filenames.

FAT32

The hard limit of 2 GB on FAT16 volume size and the huge waste on large volumes led Microsoft to introduce the FAT32 filesystem with Windows 95 OSR2. Microsoft really should have called it FAT28 because four of the 32 address bits are reserved. Using 28-bit addressing, FAT32 addresses up to 268,435,456 sectors or clusters. Addressing individual sectors, FAT32 can access (268,435,456 sectors × 512 bytes/sector = 137,438,953,472 bytes), or 128 GB. In fact, though, FAT32 does not use individual sector addressing, simply because the overhead involved in managing so many small disk space allocation units would significantly degrade performance. Instead, FAT32 continues to use cluster-based addressing, but with much smaller cluster sizes than FAT16. Table 14-2 lists the cluster sizes that FAT32 uses for various partition sizes.

Table 14-2. The relationship of FAT32 partition size to cluster size

Partition size	Sectors / Cluster	Cluster size
< 256 MB	1	512 bytes
256 MB – 8 GB	8	4 KB
8 GB – 16 GB	16	8 KB
16 GB – 32 GB	32	16 KB
> 32 GB	64	32 KB

The smallest FAT32 partition you can create with the fdisk and format utilities is 512MB, unless you use undocumented command-line switches, which are undocumented for good reasons. You can convert FAT16 volumes smaller than 512 MB to FAT32 by using the Windows 98 conversion utility or PartitionMagic, but there is little reason to do so because FAT32 benefits only large volumes.

FAT32 also eliminates the limitation on root directory entries, which allows you to store as many files and directories in root as you wish. Standard DOS applications are still limited to accessing files no larger than 2 GB, and Win32 applications to accessing files no larger than 4 GB.

There are some drawbacks to using FAT32. First, because FAT32 uses more but smaller clusters, file access on FAT32 volumes should theoretically be slower than on FAT16 volumes. We tested this by creating same-size volumes formatted for FAT16 and FAT32, restoring a standard file set, defragmenting the volume, and then running various disk benchmark programs. In each case, the performance of the FAT32 volume was 3% to 5% slower than that of the FAT16 volume. With equal volume and cluster sizes, there is little discernible difference between FAT16 and FAT32.

A more important consideration for many people is that FAT32 is supported only by Windows 95 OSR 2.X, Windows 98, Windows 2000/XP, and Linux. This means that on a system that dual-boots Windows 9X using FAT32 volumes and Windows NT 4 using NTFS volumes, neither operating system can access the other's volumes. The shareware product WinImage (*http://www.winimage.com*) allows Windows NT 4 to open FAT32 partitions directly, as does the Sysinternals utility FAT32 (*http://www.sysinternals.com/ntw2k/freeware/fat32.shtml*).

Windows 95 OSR 2.X and Windows 98 include FAT32-aware versions of the fdisk, format, defrag, and scandisk utilities, which can be used for either FAT16 or FAT32 partitions. Note, however, that DriveSpace3 compression does not support FAT32 partitions. The same is true of third-party disk utilities that predate FAT32. Attempting to use them on a FAT32 volume will at best not work, and may destroy your data. Most pre-FAT32 applications can reside on a FAT32 partition without difficulty, as can their data. Note that some pre-FAT32 device drivers, particularly DOS block-mode drivers such as aspidisk.sys (used to access SCSI drives without enabling BIOS support) do not work properly from FAT32 partitions.

To further complicate matters, Microsoft created an enhanced form of FAT32 called FAT32X to allow FAT32 partitions to extend beyond 1,024 translated cylinders, which means any drive larger than 8 GB. FAT32X partitions use a different filesystem flag in the partition table, and manipulating FAT32X partitions requires using methods that differ from those used for FAT32. The fdisk and format utilities included with Windows 95 OSR 2.X and Windows 98 automatically create FAT32X partitions on drives larger than 8 GB, and most computer vendors supply systems with large drives already formatted as FAT32X. Other than the bundled DOS/Windows utilities, the only utility we know of that can manipulate FAT32X partitions is PartitionMagic 4.0+.

NTFS

The native filesystem of Windows NT/2000/XP, NTFS places effectively no limits on the sizes of partitions, volumes, and files. NTFS is faster, more robust, and more secure than any FAT filesystem. If your computer runs Windows NT/2000/XP, there are only two reasons not to use NTFS. The first is that because only Windows NT/2000/XP (and, of course, Linux) can access NTFS volumes, using NTFS in a dual-boot environment means that the other operating system will not be able to access the NTFS volumes.

Second, there is a paucity of disk diagnosis and repair utilities available that are NTFS-aware. For a long time, Microsoft recommended creating a small FAT partition as the system partition from which NT would boot, and devoting the rest of the disk to one or more large NTFS partitions. Microsoft's thinking was that if there was a problem on the NTFS boot partition, you might still be able to get the system booted so that you could run a disk diagnostic utility. In practice, doing this doesn't accomplish much.

Although the Windows 2000/XP Recovery Console is a useful utility, it does not always allow you to recover from problems. For that reason, we generally configure our Windows 2000/XP systems to dual-boot two copies of the same operating system. By that, we mean that you should install your main Windows NT/2000/XP installation on one large NTFS volume, and install a second minimal Windows NT/2000/XP installation on another NTFS volume, ideally on a different physical drive. If the main installation fails to boot, you can boot to the other copy of Windows NT and use it to recover important data and configuration files from the main Windows NT installation before you attempt other recovery procedures. If all else fails, you can physically remove the unbootable drive from the problem system and install it as a secondary drive in a different

Windows 2000/XP system, which may allow you to recover critical datafiles from the problem drive.

 Three NTFS versions exist. NT 4 uses NTFS4. To add enhanced filesystem capabilities such as user quotas in Windows 2000, Microsoft upgraded NTFS4 to NTFS5. When XP was released, it included a minor variation of NTFS5, called NTFS5.1. As we found by sad experience when installing Windows 2000 in dual-boot mode on a system already running NT 4, Windows 2000 Setup converts any local NTFS4 volumes it finds to NTFS5, which means NT 4 can no longer read, write, or boot from those volumes unless SP4 or higher is installed. Even with SP4 or higher installed, NT 4 chkdsk cannot repair NTFS5 volumes. The only way we know to repair NTFS5 volumes under NT 4 is to use the third-party utility NTFSCHK (*http://www.sysinternals.com/ntw2k/ freeware/NTFSCHK.shtml*).

Formatting with Windows 9X

Windows 9X provides several ways to perform a logical format. You can use the fdisk and format utilities on a Windows 9X Startup Disk to partition and format a hard disk before installing Windows 9X. Once Windows 9X is installed, you can perform a logical format by right-clicking a volume in My Computer or Windows Explorer and choosing Format, or by using the command-line format utility. Command-line format uses the syntax format *<drive:>* /switches, where *<drive:>* is the drive letter assigned to that volume, and the available switches that pertain to hard disk formatting are as follows:

/v:*<label>*
> Specifies the volume label.

/q
> Specifies that format should perform a "quick" format, which reinitializes the filesystem but does not perform an actual format. Using this is a fast way to delete all data on a drive.

/c
> Tests clusters that are currently marked bad.

/s
> Copies system files to the disk being formatted, making it bootable.

Unlike the Windows NT command-line format utility, the Windows 9X utility does nothing that you can't do using the graphical utilities, so there is little reason to use it. For flexibility, we prefer to use PartitionMagic to partition and format a drive before installing Windows 9X.

Formatting with Windows 2000/XP

Windows 2000/XP provides several methods to perform a logical format. During Setup, Windows 2000/XP allows you to format existing or newly created volumes as either FAT or NTFS. Other than using a third-party utility such as PartitionMagic, this is the only method available to format an NTFS volume before Windows 2000/XP has been installed. The format process invoked during Setup is not very flexible, so we prefer to use PartitionMagic to create and format partitions before installing Windows 2000/XP.

Once a system is bootable under Windows 2000/XP, you can also perform a logical format on a disk by using the graphical Disk Management utility (Computer Management → Storage → Disk Management), by right-clicking a volume in My Computer or Windows Explorer and choosing Format, or by using the command-line format utility. The first two methods allow you to select all format options, but limit your choice of allocation unit (cluster) size. Command-line format provides complete flexibility in choosing cluster size, and uses the syntax format *<drive:>* /switches, where *<drive:>* is the drive letter assigned to that volume, and the available switches that pertain to hard disk formatting are as follows:

/fs:*<file-system>*
Where *<file-system>* specifies the type of the filesystem to be used, and may be FAT or NTFS.

/v:*<label>*
Specifies the volume label.

/q
Specifies that format should perform a "quick" format, which reinitializes the filesystem but does not perform an actual format. Using this is a fast way to delete all data on a drive.

/c
Specifies that files created on this volume will be compressed by default.

/a:*<cluster-size>*
Specifies the allocation unit size to be used for this volume:

- NFTS supports *<cluster-size>* 512, 1024, 2048, 4096, 8192, 16K, 32K, or 64K, but compression is supported only on volumes that use *<cluster-size>* 4096 or smaller.

- FAT supports *<cluster-size>* 8192, 16K, 32K, and 64K, all using 512-byte sectors, and 128K and 256K using nonstandard 1K and 2K sectors. FAT cluster sizes larger than 32K are unique to Windows NT and are not accessible by other operating systems that support FAT. FAT requires that the total number of clusters on a volume be less than 65,527. FAT32 requires that the total number of clusters on a volume be greater than 65,526 and less than 268,435,446.

In general, there are enough potential gotchas in using nonstandard cluster sizes that you should avoid using the command-line format utility to create nonstandard cluster sizes, and instead use the default cluster size proposed by one of the other Windows NT formatting methods.

Note that although Windows 2000 cannot format a partition greater than 30 GB using FAT32, it can *use* larger FAT32 partitions that were created with Windows 98/Me. Bizarrely, Microsoft states that this behavior is by design. For further information, see Knowledge Base articles Q277546 and Q184006. Windows XP also has some FAT32 limitations, which are discussed in articles Q314463 and Q310525. You can retrieve these articles from *http://support. microsoft.com.*

Converting a FAT16 volume to FAT32

There are few circumstances in which converting an existing FAT16 volume to FAT32 makes sense, but there are a couple of ways to do it if the need arises.

To use the bundled Windows 98 utility, choose Start → Programs → Accessories → System Tools → Drive Converter (FAT32). Drive Converter converts FAT16 to FAT32, but not the converse, so be absolutely sure you want to take this step before you start the program. If you change your mind later, you'll have to repartition and reformat the drive to revert to FAT16. Converting to FAT32 (or attempting to do so) may cause the following problems:

You can no longer dual-boot the system between Windows 98 and Windows NT 4
Although the bulk of the Windows NT 4 files may reside on a separate partition, Windows NT boots from the FAT16 partition. If you convert that partition to FAT32, Windows NT will not be able to access it and cannot boot.

You can no longer uninstall Windows 98
Because Windows 98 is the only current version of Windows that can access FAT32 partitions, converting a volume to FAT32 means that you can run only Windows 98 or higher on that partition.

Some of your programs may no longer run
Most applications do not care whether they are running on a FAT16 or FAT32 volume. A few, however—notably, disk utilities—do not operate or operate improperly on a FAT32 volume. Drive Converter attempts to detect incompatible applications, and notifies you before doing the conversion if it finds such programs, but this feature cannot be depended upon absolutely to identify problem applications.

FAT32 incompatibilities with hardware suspend or hibernate features
FAT32 does not play nice with some computers whose BIOSs support hardware hibernation. Usually, the worst that happens is that the hibernation feature is turned off, although we have received a couple of anecdotal reports of systems that, after going to sleep, refuse to access the hard disk when they awaken.

FAT32 incompatibilities with disk compression methods used by earlier Windows versions
Older Windows drive compression methods, including DriveSpace3, are incompatible with FAT32 volumes. If you convert a volume to FAT32, you

will no longer have the option of compressing it. A drive that is already compressed cannot be converted to FAT32.

PartitionMagic 4.0 or later can convert FAT16 to FAT32 and vice versa.

Our Picks

Over the years, we've used hard drives from many manufacturers, including Fujitsu, IBM, Maxtor, Quantum, Samsung, Seagate, Western Digital, and others. All of them have made some excellent drives and some mediocre ones, but over the last few years we've come to use Seagate (*http://www.seagate.com*) drives almost exclusively based on their performance and reliability. Maxtor (*http://www.maxtor.com*) also makes fast, reliable ATA drives and, like Seagate, has been an innovator in hard disk technology. We no longer use Western Digital hard drives because we experienced multiple premature drive failures with various Western Digital models. Although we have never had a premature drive failure with an IBM ATA hard drive, enough of our readers have reported severe problems with some IBM models that we avoid them as well. We don't have sufficient data to judge the reliability of Samsung models. Our experience is that Seagate and Maxtor ATA drives are fast, inexpensive, and reliable, so that's what we use and recommend, as follows.

ATA hard drive
> **Seagate or Maxtor.** If you need an ATA drive, choose a Seagate or Maxtor model of the appropriate size and speed. Both companies offer multiple lines of fast, reliable drives in both serial ATA and parallel ATA interfaces. One of them is almost certainly ideal for your needs. We normally use Seagate drives in our own systems, but Maxtor drives are also excellent.

SCSI hard disk
> **Seagate Barracuda and Cheetah series.** The 7,200 RPM Barracuda drives, formerly Seagate's midrange SCSI line, are now the company's entry-level SCSI drives. The Barracuda blows the doors off the fastest ATA drives, compares favorably in our testing to competing models from other makers, is incredibly reliable, and is remarkably inexpensive. When we need even higher disk performance, we install a 10,000 or 15,000 RPM Seagate Cheetah. We've used Seagate SCSI drives in our personal systems for years, as well as in workstations and servers owned by clients. Seagate SCSI drives are fast, quiet, and cool, have extremely low failure rates, and are competitively priced. There's not much more you can ask for in a SCSI drive.

For detailed current recommendations by brand and model, visit: *http://www.hardwareguys.com/picks/harddisk.html*.

15

Video Adapters

A *video adapter* accepts raw video data from the CPU, processes that data, and supplies it to the monitor in a form that the monitor can display. In DOS text-mode days, that wasn't a demanding job. Early video adapters simply interfaced the CPU to the monitor, did little or no manipulation of the raw data, and depended on the CPU itself to render the data into a form usable by the monitor. When Windows arrived, the emphasis shifted from text mode to graphics mode, which increased video processing demands dramatically.

That made it impractical to use the CPU to perform video processing, and a new generation of video adapters, called *graphics accelerators*, was born. A graphics accelerator offloads the video processing burden from the main CPU by serving as a dedicated video coprocessor. In doing so, it not only frees up the main CPU, but also reduces the amount of video data that crosses the system bus, which also contributes to faster system performance. All modern video adapters are also graphics accelerators.

Formerly, all video adapters were separate expansion cards, a form in which they are still readily available today. However, demand for reduced costs has resulted in motherboards with embedded video circuitry becoming much more common, a trend that is likely to continue. Although they are inexpensive and tightly integrated, the problem with embedded video adapters is that upgrading the video may require replacing the motherboard. But all current video adapters are so good that anyone other than a hardcore gamer is likely to find them more than good enough to get the job done.

Video Adapter Characteristics

The following sections describe the important characteristics of video adapters.

2D Versus 3D

The first graphics accelerators were 2D models, designed to provide hardware acceleration for common display tasks (drawing and moving windows, scaling fonts, and so on) when running standard business applications under Windows. 2D accelerators essentially treat your display as a flat, two-dimensional workspace. Although one window may overlay another window, the top or foreground window always has focus.

Conversely, 3D accelerators treat your display as though it has depth. For example, when you play a 3D computer game, an onscreen character may walk in front of a table. The video adapter must determine the relative positions of the character and the table as seen from the viewer's position and display that portion of the character that is in front of the table rather than the portion of the table that should be concealed by the character. 3D video cards also support a variety of supplemental functions to enhance realism—for example, adding textures to the surface of concrete or adding reflections to a pool of standing water. Adding these minor but visually important enhancements consumes a great deal of memory and processor power, so high-performance 3D video adapters are relatively expensive devices, with typical street prices of $125 to $300 or more.

 Midrange 3D video adapters, those that are 12 to 18 months behind the current generation, sell for $50 or so, and provide all the 3D performance most people need. For example, Robert built a replacement for his primary desktop system in April 2003. He used an Intel D875PBZ motherboard, an 800 MHz FSB Pentium 4/3.0G processor, a Plextor DVD+RW DVD writer, and two Seagate Serial ATA Barracuda V hard drives, all top-of-the-line products at the time. If this had been a gaming system, Robert would have installed a $400 ATI RADEON 9800 Pro. But because Robert doesn't play intensive 3D games on that system, he instead bought a $50 RADEON 7500 video adapter.

Note that 3D performance is merely a matter of degree. That is, even an elderly 2D-only adapter can be used to play 3D games, but because it does not incorporate 3D acceleration features in hardware, the main system CPU itself must do all of the calculations that would otherwise be done by a 3D adapter. The result is very high CPU utilization (with the associated system sluggishness) and jerky or poorly rendered 3D video without the modeling nuances provided in hardware by the 3D accelerator.

In fact, pure 2D accelerators haven't been manufactured for years. In the early 1990s, two distinct types of video adapters were available: moderately priced ($50 to $200) 2D accelerators intended for mainstream use with standard Windows programs, and very expensive ($500 to $2,000) 3D adapters intended for niche markets such as animation and video production. As 3D applications (particularly games) became more common, old-line 2D manufacturers such as Matrox and ATI incorporated a limited subset of 3D functions in their mainstream adapters. There it stood until a few years ago, when upstart companies such as 3dfx and *n*VIDIA caught the old-line makers napping by releasing graphics accelerators with a full range of 3D functionality.

That led to the current situation, where 3D performance is the only aspect of a graphics card that interests most people. Reviews talk of little but how video cards compare in various 3D benchmarks. That's unfortunate because in reality 3D performance is unimportant to most users. In fact, unless you are a serious gamer, 3D performance should probably be the last consideration when choosing a video card. Such factors as 2D display quality and availability of stable drivers are actually much more important for most users.

All video cards and embedded video chipsets currently available provide at least minimal 3D support. The important thing to remember is this: just as there is not much absolute performance difference between a $75 processor and a $300 processor, neither is there much real difference between a $75 video card and a $300 one. Benchmarks aside, the $75 card does everything that 99% of users are likely to need. Yes, there are differences, just as there are between processors, but unless you push your hardware to the limit you're not likely to notice much difference in day-to-day use.

Components

A video adapter comprises the following components:

Graphics processor
> Rather than depending on the main system CPU to create each video frame, a graphics accelerator contains a graphics processor, which is optimized to perform in hardware low-level video functions such as transferring bitmaps, doing color and pattern fills, scaling fonts, sizing and positioning windows, and drawing lines, polygons, and other graphics primitives. An accelerated video adapter also requires much less data to be transferred between the system bus and the video adapter. For example, to draw a circle with a frame grabber, the system CPU must create a bitmap of that circle and transfer it to the frame grabber. Conversely, given only the center and radius of the circle, a graphics accelerator can render the circle directly.

> Early accelerators were optimized for 2D graphics operations, which are still most important when running standard business and personal software such as word processors and web browsers. More recent accelerators, including all current models, provide 3D acceleration, which is primarily useful for playing 3D graphics-intensive games. Unfortunately, some recent 3D adapters, particularly *n*VIDIA models, are so heavily optimized for 3D that they provide mediocre 2D performance. We have several venerable Matrox video adapters, for example, that are useless for playing 3D games, but provide better 2D video quality than any current 3D accelerator.

Video memory
> Video adapters use memory for several purposes. A portion of video memory called the *frame buffer* stores the image as it is constructed by the graphics processor and before it is sent to the monitor. Available memory not occupied by the frame buffer caches fonts, icons, and other graphical elements to improve video performance. Some video adapters also allocate memory not being used by the main frame buffer as a second frame buffer, allowing the next frame to be created in the background while the current frame is being

displayed. The most important characteristics of video memory are its size, type, and speed. Video adapters use one of the following memory types:

DRAM (Dynamic Random Access Memory)
First- and some second-generation graphics accelerators used standard DRAM, which was not ideal for the purpose. DRAM is no longer used in video adapters because it is so slow, mainly because it is *single-ported*, which means that it does not allow data to be read and written simultaneously.

EDO DRAM (Extended Data Out DRAM)
EDO provides higher bandwidth than standard DRAM, can run at higher speeds, and manages read/write access more efficiently. EDO is single-ported, typically operates with 50 to 60 ns access times, is usually 64 bits wide, and yields overall bandwidth of 400 MB/s. EDO was commonly used in video adapters before the advent of SDRAM and the various specialized types of video memory described later in this list, and continued to be used until mid-2000 in some of the least-expensive video adapters. Nowadays, even the cheapest video adapters use something faster than EDO DRAM.

VRAM (Video RAM)
A special type of DRAM, VRAM is used only in video adapters and is designed to overcome the limitations of the single-ported arrangement used by DRAM and EDO. VRAM is *dual-ported*—which allows the next frame to be written while the last frame is being read—operates at 50 to 60 ns access times, is typically 64 bits wide, and yields overall bandwidth of 400 MB/s. Because it requires less-frequent refreshing than DRAM or EDO, it is much faster, and correspondingly more expensive. VRAM was commonly used in mid- to high-end video adapters through about 1997, but has been superseded by SDR-SDRAM and DDR-SDRAM, described later in this list.

WRAM (Windows RAM)
WRAM, first introduced by Matrox with its Millenium series of video adapters, is an enhanced version of VRAM that is somewhat less expensive to produce and provides about 20% higher performance than VRAM. Like VRAM, WRAM has been superseded by SDR-SDRAM and DDR-SDRAM.

SDRAM (Synchronous DRAM)
A step up from EDO, SDRAM runs the memory and graphics processor on a common clock reference, allowing faster access times and higher throughput. SDRAM is single-ported, operates at 8 to 15 ns access times, is typically 64 bits wide, and yields overall bandwidth of 800 MB/s at 100 MHz. SDRAM is now used only in inexpensive video adapters. SDRAM is now sometimes described as Single Data Rate SDRAM (SDR-SDRAM) to differentiate it from DDR-SDRAM.

SGRAM (Synchronous Graphics RAM)
SGRAM is an enhanced form of SDRAM, used only on video adapters, that supports write-per-bit and block writes, both of which improve performance over SDRAM when used with graphics accelerators that

explicitly support SGRAM. SGRAM video memory is single-ported, operates at 6 to 10 ns access times, is typically 64 bits wide, and yields overall bandwidth of 800 MB/s. SGRAM was formerly used on midrange and high-end video adapters, but has now largely been replaced by DDR-SDRAM, described next.

DDR-SDRAM (Double Data Rate SDRAM)

DDR-SDRAM differs from standard Single Data Rate SDRAM (SDR-SDRAM) in that it transfers data on both the rising and falling edge of the clock cycle, doubling transfer rate on a 64-bit bus to 1600 MB/s at 100 MHz or 2100+ MB/s at 133 MHz. As of July 2003, the fastest video DDR modules readily available run at 500 MHz and transfer 8000 MB/s on a 64-bit bus, 16,000 MB/s on a 128-bit bus, or 32,000 MB/s on a 256-bit bus.

DDR-SDRAM was first used only in expensive video adapters, but by early 2003 even many inexpensive video adapters used DDR-SDRAM. In addition to the speed of their graphics engines, video adapters are differentiated by the amount and speed of their onboard memory, as well as by the width of their memory interfaces. A low-end adapter may have 64 MB of DDR-SDRAM operating at 500 MHz on a 64-bit interface. A midrange adapter may have 128 MB of DDR-SDRAM operating at 750 MHz on a 128-bit interface. A high-end adapter may have 256 MB of DDR-SDRAM operating at 1,000 MHz on a 256-bit interface. Each jump in memory speed or interface width increases the bandwidth available for video operations.

GDDR-II and GDDR-III SDRAM (Graphics DDR-SDRAM)

As standard DDR-SDRAM approaches its performance limits, video adapter makers are designing chipsets for enhanced forms of DDR-SDRAM called Graphics DDR-SDRAM (GDDR-SDRAM). GDDR-II is a variant of the next-generation DDR-II memory, with point-to-point signaling support added for improved graphics performance. *n*VIDIA backs GDDR-II, which is regarded by many as a transitional standard. ATI favors GDDR-III, which is a graphics-specific variant of DDR-III, the follow-on to DDR-II. The price, performance, and scalability of GDDR-II and GDDR-III are uncertain, so most makers are trying to hedge their bets. Either standard might prevail, and it is quite possible that the two will coexist.

*n*VIDIA uses GDDR-II in the GeForce FX, and seems determined to force acceptance of that standard. Unfortunately, as of July 2003 JEDEC had not yet established a GDDR-II standard. Three slightly different and incompatible types of GDDR-II exist, which means chipset makers must design interfaces that are compatible with all three versions. ATI, on the other hand, is taking a wait-and-see approach. ATI has produced engineering samples using GDDR-II, but its production video cards use standard DDR memory. ATI hopes that using fast DDR-I memory with a 256-bit interface will provide sufficient bandwidth until GDDR-III chips are widely available at reasonable prices. 500 MHz DDR-I memory on a 256-bit interface yields 32 GB/s bandwidth, so we think that's a reasonable approach.

RAMDAC (Random Access Memory Digital-to-Analog Converter)

The RAMDAC examines video memory many times per second, using a look-up table to translate the digital values it finds in memory to the analog voltages that the monitor requires to display the corresponding colors. The RAMDAC contains three Digital-to-Analog converters (DACs), one each for the red, green, and blue signals that the monitor uses to display the full spectrum that it supports. The architecture and speed of the RAMDAC (along with the graphics processor itself) determine the combinations of resolutions, color depths, and refresh rates that the video adapter supports. All other things being equal, an adapter with a faster RAMDAC outperforms an adapter with a slower RAMDAC. Some video adapters are sold in two versions which differ only in the speeds of the RAMDAC and in the type and amount of memory installed. The faster versions, often described as "Ultra," "Max," or "Pro," usually sell at a substantial premium, run hotter, and provide no real benefit for most users.

Drivers

Drivers translate the display data generated by an application or operating system into the specific instructions needed by the graphics processor to create the image that will be displayed on the monitor. The driver decides how to present data to the graphics processor so as to optimize the hardware acceleration functions available on the graphics processor. That means that a mediocre graphics processor with an excellent driver may outperform an excellent graphics processor with a mediocre driver, so the availability of robust, well-optimized drivers for whatever operating system you run is a crucial factor in choosing a video adapter. Drivers are often optimized for particular combinations of resolution and color depth, so it's often worthwhile to experiment with different settings.

In the past, video drivers had to be written for a specific application running on a specific operating system using a specific video adapter. If you wanted to run UltraCAD 5.1 on a FastPix SuperVGA adapter with a 2.03 BIOS under ABC-DOS 3.3, you had to have a driver written specifically for that combination of hardware and software. The flood of 3D software titles and 3D accelerators made that situation untenable. The solution was to use an intermediate hardware abstraction layer (HAL) to isolate the graphics processor from the operating system and applications, and to develop standardized APIs to communicate with that HAL. Because applications need to understand only how to communicate with one or a few APIs rather than with every graphics processor available, they can run on any video adapter that supports an API that they understand how to communicate with. Two 3D APIs are dominant in the PC environment:

OpenGL

OpenGL was originally developed by Silicon Graphics Inc. (SGI) as a general-purpose 3D API. OpenGL found its first niche in high-end CAD systems running on Unix X-terminals, and was later implemented on PC workstations running CAD and other 3D graphics-intensive environments. With the release of a Windows version in 1996, support for OpenGL began to migrate downward to mainstream 3D applications, including games. OpenGL is widely supported by software developers because it offers better low-level control over 3D graphics operations and was perceived as being an easier API to write to than the competing Microsoft standard. OpenGL support can be implemented in two ways: *Mini Client Drivers (MCDs)* are relatively easy to write, but provide limited functionality. *Installable Client Drivers (ICDs)* are much more difficult to write, but provide additional functionality. The importance of OpenGL, particularly to the gaming community, is waning as Microsoft DirectX increasingly dominates 3D applications, but OpenGL remains important for professional graphics applications.

Direct3D (D3D)

D3D is the 3D acceleration part of DirectX, Microsoft's umbrella multimedia standard, which also includes DirectDraw (2D acceleration), DirectSound (audio), DirectInput (support for joysticks and similar input devices), and DirectPlay (Internet gaming). Versions through 5.0 were slow, buggy, and feature-poor when compared to OpenGL and proprietary 3D APIs. Microsoft refined and tuned D3D by reducing dependence on the main system CPU and incorporating OpenGL features. With version 6.0 D3D could finally compete on a reasonably equal basis with OpenGL and proprietary APIs, although it was still somewhat slower and less feature-laden. Although 3D software manufacturers had been burned by D3D 5.0, they recognized the improvements in 6.0, and most incorporated D3D 6.0 support immediately. The convergence between D3D and OpenGL continued with versions 7.0, 8.0, and 9.0, and applications that support only D3D are no longer at a significant disadvantage relative to those that support OpenGL and/or proprietary APIs.

For now, any 3D video card you choose should support the latest release of D3D, which is used by most current 3D games and other 3D applications. Many 3D applications, including some games, also support OpenGL for its higher performance and additional functionality, so ideally the card you choose should also have an OpenGL ICD. Support for the proprietary 3dfx Glide API, which dominated 3D gaming through about 1999, is no longer important because nearly all current games support D3D and/or OpenGL and because 3dfx has been subsumed by *n*VIDIA.

 In March 2003, Microsoft resigned from the OpenGL Architecture Review Board (ARB), the group that governs the OpenGL standard. Clearly, Microsoft intends to focus on its Direct3D standard, although OpenGL applications are so ubiquitous that we think it unlikely that Microsoft will abandon OpenGL in the near future.

Interface

Early video adapters, including the first generation of graphics accelerators, used the ISA bus, which soon proved inadequate to carry the high volume of video data required by graphics-based operating systems and applications. *VESA Local Bus (VLB)* adapters, shipped with many 486 systems and a few early Pentium systems, greatly improved throughput. ISA and VLB video adapters are obsolete but remain in limited distribution, although they are now difficult to find and use video chipsets that are several generations out of date. Any system so old that it accepts only an ISA or VLB video adapter is too old to be worth upgrading. Current video adapters use one of the following interfaces:

PCI

> The PCI bus is 32 bits wide and runs at 33.3 MHz, providing peak throughput of 133 MB/s. The fact that a PCI video card shares the bus with other PCI devices means that heavy transfers of video data reduce the bandwidth available to other PCI peripherals, such as hard disk controllers and network cards. This concern is still largely theoretical because PCI bus saturation is very rare with current systems and software.

AGP (Accelerated Graphics Port)

> Intel's concern about PCI throughput limitations and the increasing amount of data that new generations of 3D video adapters would demand led it to introduce AGP. Although AGP supports 2D operations, it provides no real benefit over PCI in 2D. As the name implies, AGP is a port rather than a bus, which means that it connects only two devices. AGP provides a direct unshared channel between the AGP video adapter and the system chipset, which allows the CPU to transfer data to the AGP card without the 133 MB/s limitation of the PCI bus.

AGP X1 transfers 32 bits per clock cycle at 66 MHz, for total peak base throughput of 264 MB/s. AGP X2 mode, called 2X AGP, transfers data on both rising and falling edges of the clock cycle to yield peak throughput of 528 MB/s. 4X AGP, introduced with the AGP 2.0 specification, doubles throughput again to just over 1 GB/s by transferring data four times per clock cycle. AGP 8X, the basis of the AGP 3.0 specification, doubles throughput again to just over 2 GB/s. Motherboards and video adapters with AGP 8X support began shipping in late 2002. The additional bandwidth of 8X AGP—or 4X AGP, for that matter, is of little practical importance because nearly all AGP adapters use local video memory rather than main system memory. Even the 2 GB/s bandwidth of 8X AGP pales compared to the 32 GB/s bandwidth of a 256-bit video memory interface using local DDR-SDRAM. AGP 8X is essentially just a marketing gimmick.

In theory, the AGP bus has two other throughput advantages relative to PCI. First, AGP uses pipelining, which allows it to sustain throughput at 80% of theoretical. Second, AGP uses *Sideband Addressing*, a process that allows queuing up to 32 commands and allows data and commands to be sent simultaneously. One highly touted benefit of AGP is *Direct Memory Execute* (*DIME*), which allows the AGP adapter to use system memory as though it were locally installed video memory. DIME is implemented with a device called a *Graphics Aperture Remapping Table* (*GART*), which can claim small, widely distributed areas of main memory and present them to the adapter as a large, contiguous area of virtual "local" video memory. In theory, DIME allows an AGP adapter with limited local memory to store large texture bitmaps and other graphical elements in main memory. In practice, DIME is of little real benefit because high-performance video adapters (PCI or AGP) have enough memory to store textures locally. Also, although DIME is faster than accessing main memory across the PCI bus, DIME is still slower than accessing local memory on the video card, particularly if that local memory is DDR-SDRAM memory, which high-performance video cards use. (See Figure 15-1 for a picture of AGP and PCI slots.)

Figure 15-1. An AGP slot (top) with two PCI slots below it

In short, AGP remains a solution in search of a problem, particularly for those who use primarily 2D applications. Windows NT users have no reason to prefer AGP because NT treats AGP cards as standard PCI cards, as do early releases of Windows 95. Windows 95 OSR2 or higher, Windows 98/98 SE/Me, Windows 2000/XP, and of course Linux have operating system support for AGP.

Despite its lack of real advantages over PCI, AGP is the best choice if your motherboard has an AGP slot. At the low end, AGP adapters cost less than comparable PCI adapters. At the midrange and high end, AGP is the only option. AGP is now the dominant interface, so manufacturers have ceased development of PCI adapters. That means the latest video chipsets are available only with AGP adapters, and any PCI adapter you can find is at least a couple of generations out of date.

1X AGP cards are no longer sold, and only obsolescent adapters use 2X AGP. Mainstream video adapters are now produced only in 4X and 8X AGP versions. Although there's nothing wrong with 8X AGP, neither does it make sense to pay extra for it if an otherwise suitable 4X AGP card is available. You may have little choice but to buy 8X AGP, however. Video card makers are abandoning 4X AGP in favor of 8X AGP as they introduce new models.

Embedded video adapters may be either PCI or AGP. If you buy a motherboard with embedded video, keep in mind that you may one day want to upgrade the video in that system. Doing that requires both that you can disable embedded video, which is not possible on all motherboards, and that you have an available slot for the new video card. Choose a motherboard with embedded AGP video circuitry that also contains an available AGP slot. Ideally, that AGP slot should be 4X or 8X. Note that some motherboards with embedded AGP video have no AGP slot. These can be upgraded only by installing a PCI video adapter. That wasn't a problem in the past, when PCI video adapters were still widely available, but high-performance video cards are no longer available with PCI interfaces.

AGP interfaces and signaling voltages

There are three versions of the AGP specification, as follows:

AGP1.0

AGP1.0 specifies an interface that supports 1X and 2X speeds with 3.3V signaling and a keyed 3.3V connector. AGP1.0 supports DIME, pipelined transactions, source-synchronous clocking, texturing, and sidebanding.

AGP2.0

AGP2.0 specifies an interface that supports 1X, 2X, and 4X speeds with 1.5V signaling. AGP2.0-compliant interfaces and adapters may use either a 1.5V keyed connector, which accepts only 1.5V devices, or a universal connector, which accepts 1.5V or 3.3V devices interchangeably. AGP2.0 adds Fast Writes to the protocols supported by AGP1.0.

AGP3.0

AGP3.0 specifies an interface that supports 4X and 8X speeds with 0.8V signaling. AGP3.0 uses the same 1.5V keyed connector or universal connector used by AGP2.0. AGP3.0 adds several protocol elements to those supported by AGP2.0, and removes support for some AGP2.0 features.

There are six types of AGP interfaces, and six corresponding types of AGP adapters, as follows:

AGP3.3V

AGP3.3V interfaces and adapters support 1X or 2X operation at 3.3V only, using a 3.3V connector. An AGP3.3V adapter can be installed in an AGP3.3V, UAGP, or UAGP3.0 interface. An AGP3.3V interface accepts an AGP3.3V, UAGP, or UAGP3.0 adapter.

AGP1.5V

AGP1.5V interfaces and adapters support 1X, 2X, or 4X operation at 1.5V only, using a 1.5V connector. An AGP1.5V adapter can be installed in an AGP1.5V, UAGP (described next), U1.5VAGP3.0, or UAGP3.0 interface (the latter two described later in this list). An AGP1.5V interface accepts an AGP1. 5V, UAGP, U1.5VAGP3.0, or UAGP3.0 adapter.

Universal AGP (UAGP)

Universal AGP (UAGP) interfaces and adapters support 1X, 2X, or 4X operation at 3.3V or 1.5V, using a universal connector. A UAGP adapter can be installed in an AGP3.3V, AGP1.5V, UAGP, U1.5VAGP3.0, or UAGP3.0 interface. A UAGP interface accepts an AGP3.3V, AGP1.5V, UAGP, U1.5VAGP3.0, or UAGP3.0 adapter.

AGP3.0

AGP3.0 interfaces and adapters support 4X or 8X operation at 0.8V only, using a 1.5V connector. An AGP3.0 adapter can be installed in an AGP3.0, U1.5VAGP3.0, or UAGP3.0 interface. An AGP3.0 interface accepts an AGP3.0, U1.5VAGP3.0, or UAGP3.0 adapter.

Universal 1.5V AGP3.0 (U1.5VAGP3.0)

Universal 1.5V AGP3.0 (U1.5VAGP3.0) interfaces and adapters support 1X, 2X, 4X, or 8X operation at 1.5V or 0.8V, using a universal connector. A

U1.5VAGP3.0 adapter can be installed in any AGP interface except the AGP3.3V interface. A U1.5VAGP3.0 interface accepts any AGP adapter except AGP3.3V adapters.

Universal AGP3.0 (UAGP3.0)

Universal AGP3.0 (UAGP3.0) interfaces and adapters support 1X, 2X, 4X, or 8X operation at 3.3V, 1.5V, or 0.8V, using a universal connector. A UAGP3.0 adapter can be used in any AGP interface. A UAGP3.0 interface supports any AGP adapter.

AGP3.3V interfaces and adapters are obsolete. Recent motherboards and adapters may use any of the other AGP types. Note that compatibility does not imply optimum operation. For example, although a recent 4X UAGP3.0 adapter functions when connected to an old AGP3.3V interface, the older interface limits the adapter to 2X performance.

AGP interfaces and adapters use specific determination pins to identify themselves and their capabilities. More specifically, the states of the MB_DET pin on the interface and the GC_DET and TYPEDET pins on the adapter identify the AGP level and voltage supported. Table 15-1 lists the compatibility of various AGP interfaces and adapters. It includes only those combinations that are physically compatible. For example, it does not list the AGP3.3V interface with an AGP1.5V adapter because that interface does not physically accept that adapter. A combination listed as Illegal/Not Supported means that the adapter physically fits the interface connector but does not function. If the interface and adapter are designed properly, no damage occurs.

Table 15-1. AGP compatibility by interface type and adapter type

Interface	Adapter	MB_DET	GC_DET	TYPEDET	Mode	Speed
AGP3.3V	AGP3.3V	Doesn't care	Open	Open	AGP3.3V	1X, 2X
AGP3.3V	UAGP	Doesn't care	Open	Ground	AGP3.3V	1X, 2X
AGP3.3V	UAGP3.0	Doesn't care	Open	Ground	AGP3.3V	1X, 2X
AGP1.5V	AGP1.5V	Open	Open	Ground	AGP1.5V	1X, 2X, 4X
AGP1.5V	UAGP	Open	Open	Ground	AGP1.5V	1X, 2X, 4X
AGP1.5V	AGP3.0	Open	Ground	Ground	Illegal	Not supported
AGP1.5V	U1.5VAGP3.0	Open	Ground	Ground	AGP1.5V	1X, 2X, 4X
AGP1.5V	UAGP3.0	Open	Ground	Ground	AGP1.5V	1X, 2X, 4X
UAGP	AGP3.3V	Doesn't care	Open	Open	AGP3.3V	1X, 2X
UAGP	AGP1.5V	Open	Open	Ground	AGP1.5V	1X, 2X, 4X
UAGP	UAGP	Open	Open	Ground	AGP1.5V	1X, 2X, 4X
UAGP	AGP3.0	Open	Ground	Ground	Illegal	Not supported
UAGP	U1.5VAGP3.0	Open	Ground	Ground	AGP1.5V	1X, 2X, 4X
UAGP	UAGP3.0	Open	Ground	Ground	AGP1.5V	1X, 2X, 4X
AGP3.0	AGP1.5V	Ground	Open	Ground	Illegal	Not supported
AGP3.0	UAGP	Ground	Open	Ground	Illegal	Not supported
AGP3.0	AGP3.0	Ground	Ground	Ground	AGP3.0	4X, 8X
AGP3.0	U1.5VAGP3.0	Ground	Ground	Ground	AGP3.0	4X, 8X

Table 15-1. AGP compatibility by interface type and adapter type (continued)

Interface	Adapter	MB_DET	GC_DET	TYPEDET	Mode	Speed
AGP3.0	UAGP3.0	Ground	Ground	Ground	AGP3.0	4X, 8X
U1.5VAGP3.0	AGP1.5V	Ground	Open	Ground	AGP1.5V	1X, 2X, 4X
U1.5VAGP3.0	UAGP	Ground	Open	Ground	AGP1.5V	1X, 2X, 4X
U1.5VAGP3.0	AGP3.0	Ground	Ground	Ground	AGP3.0	4X, 8X
U1.5VAGP3.0	U1.5VAGP3.0	Ground	Ground	Ground	AGP3.0	4X, 8X
U1.5VAGP3.0	UAGP3.0	Ground	Ground	Ground	AGP3.0	4X, 8X
UAGP3.0	AGP3.3V	Doesn't care	Open	Open	AGP3.3V	1X, 2X
UAGP3.0	AGP1.5V	Ground	Open	Ground	AGP1.5V	1X, 2X, 4X
UAGP3.0	UAGP	Ground	Open	Ground	AGP1.5V	1X, 2X, 4X
UAGP3.0	AGP3.0	Ground	Ground	Ground	AGP3.0	4X, 8X
UAGP3.0	U1.5VAGP3.0	Ground	Ground	Ground	AGP3.0	4X, 8X
UAGP3.0	UAGP3.0	Ground	Ground	Ground	AGP3.0	4X, 8X

Heed this warning. With modern PCs, there are very few cases in which installing a nondefective PC peripheral that physically fits can damage the peripheral or the system. One big exception is motherboards that use the Intel 845 or 850 chipset or the *n*VIDIA *n*FORCE chipset. Due to improper design and keying, a few AGP adapters that are actually 3.3V devices are keyed such that they can fit a 1.5V slot. Furthermore, they handle the A2 line incorrectly. The upshot is that installing one of these cards in an Intel 845, Intel 850, or *n*VIDIA *n*FORCE motherboard may destroy the AGP adapter and/or motherboard. The following AGP adapters have been reported to exhibit this problem:

- Some *n*VIDIA Riva TNT2 adapters
- All *n*VIDIA Vanta and Vanta LT adapters
- All SiS 6326 and SiS 305 adapters
- All S3 Savage4 adapters earlier than revision 3.0
- All 3dfx Voodoo3, Voodoo4, and Voodoo5 adapters
- Some *n*VIDIA GeForce2 GTS and GeForce2 Pro adapters

Note that this list may not be complete, and that the documentation that came with the adapter may have been printed before the problem came to light. Before you install any older AGP adapter in one of these motherboards, verify on the card and motherboard manufacturers' web sites that the card is compatible with the motherboard.

AGP Pro

The AGP 2.0 Specification introduced 4X mode, but had some deficiencies with regard to workstation graphics cards. In particular, AGP 2.0 allows a maximum of 25W of power, which is inadequate for high-end professional graphics cards. If AGP was to be usable for professional graphics adapters, Intel needed to make provision for the additional needs of such cards. To do so, Intel extended the AGP

2.0 Specification by adding the AGP Pro Addendum, which defines the following features:

AGP Pro connector

The AGP Pro connector expands the standard 132-pin AGP connector to 180 pins, by extending both ends of the standard AGP slot. A standard AGP 1X, 2X, or 4X card functions in an AGP Pro slot, but the converse is not true.

Increased power

A standard AGP 2.0 slot provides at most 25W of 3.3/5V power. An AGP Pro slot provides additional 3.3V power, adds 12V power, and can provide up to 110W of total power.

Multiple card/multiple slot support

AGP Pro permits using multiple cards in multiple slots. An AGP Pro solution can use the AGP Pro slot alone, or the AGP Pro slot and one or two adjacent PCI slots, which need be only standard 32-bit, 33 MHz, 133 MB/s PCI slots. Those adjacent slot positions can be used to supply additional electrical power, PCI bus functionality, mechanical support, or simply additional space. A 25W AGP Pro card may occupy only the AGP Pro slot. A 50W AGP Pro card (or cards) may occupy the AGP Pro slot and one PCI slot. A 110W AGP Pro card (or cards) may occupy the AGP Pro slot and two PCI slots. AGP Pro defines two pins, PRSNT1# and PRSNT2#, that are used to indicate the presence of an AGP Pro card, its type, and how much power it requires. Table 15-2 lists how those pins are used.

Table 15-2. AGP Pro slot configuration

PRSNT1#	PRSNT2#	AGP Pro Configuration
No connection	No connection	AGP Pro card not installed
Ground	No connection	50 W AGP Pro card installed
Ground	Ground	110 W AGP Pro card installed
No connection	Ground	Reserved

In addition to connection and power features, the AGP Pro Addendum specifies mechanical and thermal design criteria. AGP Pro is closely associated with the WTX workstation motherboard form factor intended for professional workstations, but a few ATX motherboards are available with AGP Pro support, most of which are targeted at serious gamers. Most AGP Pro video cards are intended for professional graphics, but some of the latest gaming video cards are or soon will be shipping in AGP Pro versions because they require more than the 25W that standard AGP can provide. AGP 3.0 includes AGP support, and AGP 3.0 Pro devices are backward-compatible with AGP 2.0 Pro devices.

See *http://developer.intel.com/technology/agp/agp_index.htm* for more detailed information about AGP, including AGP Pro and AGP 3.0.

AGP 8X is the last iteration of the AGP standard. The next generation of motherboards will replace AGP with an enhanced version of the PCI bus called *PCI Express*. This new bus standard will support very high data rates and other enhancements, including isochronous video support. We do not expect motherboards with PCI Express slots to begin appearing before mid-2004, and it may well be 2005 before PCI Express motherboards and expansion cards are common. For more information about PCI Express, see *http://www.intel.com/technology/ pciexpress/index.htm*.

Display Settings

The following display settings determine how much information a video adapter and driver display and how often that information is updated:

Resolution
> *Resolution*, also called *addressability*, refers to the maximum number of pixels that the video adapter can display, listed by vertical columns and horizontal rows. For example, a standard VGA adapter can display at most 640 columns by 480 rows of pixels, which is abbreviated as 640x480 resolution. Video cards do not support continuously variable resolution, but instead provide standard "prepackaged" combinations of vertical and horizontal resolution—e.g., 1280x1024. Using higher resolution permits more information to be displayed. Also, for any given size of an object onscreen, using higher resolution allocates more pixels to that object, avoiding "jaggies", "stair-stepping," and other video artifacts that degrade image quality. Conversely, using too high a resolution for the monitor size results in individual display elements becoming too small to be readable. The best resolution to use is determined by monitor size and quality, video adapter capabilities, and personal factors such as visual acuity.

Color depth
> A *pixel*, also called a *pel* or *picture element*, is the smallest individually addressable display element, and comprises three subunits, one each for red (R), green (G), and blue (B). *Color depth* refers to the number of discrete colors that can be displayed, and is determined by the number of bits allocated to each primary color, quantified as *bits-per-pixel* (*BPP*). Standard VGA allocates 4BPP, which allows at most 16 (2^4) colors to be displayed simultaneously from a total palette of 256 available colors. Current video adapters support 256-color mode (8BPP); High Color or 64K Color mode (16BPP, 65,536 colors, 5 bits each allocated to Red and Blue, and 6 bits to Green); and True Color or 16.7 Million Color mode (24BPP, 16,777,216 colors, 8 bits each allocated to R, G, and B). Note that, although True Color requires only 8 bits each on the Red, Green, and Blue channels (24 bits total), some adapters add a fourth "alpha" channel, and therefore require 32BPP. Although 256 colors are adequate for standard business applications, displaying continuous-tone High Color or True Color images with only 256 colors results in posterization effects that reduce realism. Any recent graphics accelerator can run True Color mode at commonly-used resolutions, and that is usually the best choice.

Refresh frequency
> A video card displays the screen image as a series of images that is replaced many times per second, even when the screen image is unchanging (e.g., your desktop). As with movies or television, a phenomenon known as *persistence*

of vision allows the human brain to recognize a rapid sequence of still images as continuous smooth motion. In order for this phenomenon to occur, screen updates must occur very frequently. The number of times per second that the video card replaces the current screen image with a new image is called the *refresh frequency*. The refresh frequency necessary to provide a stable image varies with the individual, monitor size, persistence of monitor phosphors, ambient lighting, the image being displayed, and other factors, but is typically somewhere between 60 and 90 images per second. Setting refresh frequency too low results in visible flicker. Setting it too high for any given combination of monitor and video adapter may limit you to using a lower resolution and/or color depth than you would prefer, so make sure that the monitor and video adapter you buy support reasonable refresh rates for the resolution and color depth you intend to run. We generally use a refresh rate of 75 Hz or higher on 15-inch monitors running 800x600; 75 to 85 Hz on 17-inch monitors running 1024x768; and 85 Hz or higher on 19-inch and larger monitors running 1280x1024 or higher. Most people find these settings suitable for running typical office productivity applications, web browsers, graphics packages, and so on. Note, however, that some special applications, such as medical imaging, may require very high refresh rates and accordingly expensive monitors.

Resolution and color depth settings together determine how much data must be stored for each image, and so the amount of video memory required. Refresh frequency determines only how often the image is updated, and so has nothing to do with the amount of video memory needed. Nearly all recent video cards have at least 8 MB of local video memory, which is sufficient to display 32-bit color at 1600x1200 resolution in 2D. 3D graphics accelerators have from 32 MB of local video memory to 128 MB or more, which is sufficient to display 3D games at high resolution.

Throughput

The overall throughput of a video adapter is constrained by the speed and architecture of its RAMDAC and video memory, and the number of bits that it processes per operation. The throughput required at any given combination of display settings is the product of four factors: resolution (how many pixels per frame), color depth (how much data per pixel), refresh rate (how many frames per second), and number of planes (one for 2D modes, and typically three or four for 3D modes). When a video adapter reaches its throughput limit, you can increase any of these factors only by reducing one or more of the others.

For example, a video adapter may have a RAMDAC that can process at most 225 million bytes/s. Operating in 2D mode, that adapter supports 1024x768 resolution at 24BPP and 85 Hz refresh. With those settings, the video adapter processes (1024 × 768 × 24BPP × 85 Hz = 200,540,160 bytes/s), well within the RAMDAC limits. Increasing resolution to 1152x864 requires (1152 × 864 × 24BPP × 85 Hz = 253,808,640 bytes/s), well beyond the capacity of this RAMDAC. To run 1152 × 864, you can either: (a) continue using 85 Hz refresh, but reduce the color depth from 24BPP to 16BPP (1152 × 864 × 16BPP × 85 Hz = 169,205,760 bytes/s), or (b) continue using 24BPP, but reduce the refresh rate from 85 Hz to 75 Hz (1152 × 864 × 24BPP × 75 Hz = 223,948,800 bytes/s).

Similarly, when the adapter runs in 3D mode, the requirement for three (or four) planes forces lower resolutions, color depths, and/or refresh rates. This RAMDAC, for example, is at its limit in 3D mode when running 800x600 resolution at 16BPP and 78 Hz (800 × 600 × 16BPP × 78 Hz × 3 planes = 224,640,000 bytes/s). This is why, relative to 2D cards, 3D video cards are equipped with a much faster RAMDAC (to process the additional data) and much more memory (to store the additional planes as well as supplementary information such as texturing data). In practice, you'll never need to calculate these numbers because video drivers support only those combinations of display settings that are within the ability of the video hardware.

Although conventional wisdom says increasing resolution and/or color depth slows performance because more information must be processed and transferred, this is not invariably true. Some video adapters run faster at 1024x768 than at 800x600, for example, or faster at 16.7 million colors than at 256 colors. Why? Because the driver is optimized for the higher resolution or color depth. Don't assume that increasing either resolution or color depth will slow down your video. Test each usable combination and pick the one that works for you.

Choosing a Video Adapter

Use the following guidelines when choosing a video adapter:

- Remember that video is just one part of your system. If your system has only a Pentium III/500 and 64 MB of memory, you're likely to be disappointed if you install a cutting-edge $400 graphics card. Buying a $150 midrange graphics card instead and spending the other $250 on a CPU, motherboard, and memory upgrade yields much better video performance, and increases general system performance as well.

- Unless you spend most of your computing time running resource-intensive 3D games, performance is probably the *least* important selection criterion. Current video adapters, and most older models, are more than fast enough to run standard 2D business applications at normal resolutions and refresh rates (e.g., 1024x768 at 85 Hz). Previous-generation 3D adapters are discounted deeply when their replacements ship, and are excellent choices for most users. These older video chipsets are often used for embedded video on integrated motherboards, and will suffice for nearly anyone. Don't forget that today's obsolescent chipset was the leading-edge barn burner not long ago. Don't get caught up in the horsepower race, and don't waste money buying performance that you'll never use.

- Buy only an AGP adapter, except in unusual circumstances. Check the motherboard manual to determine the type of AGP interface it uses, and then refer to Table 15-1 to determine the types of AGP card that are compatible. If you may later upgrade the motherboard, choose a U1.5VAGP3.0 or a UAGP3.0 adapter for maximum future compatibility.

Some older AGP motherboards have mechanical, electrical, or chipset limitations that prevent them from working properly with some AGP cards. Conversely, some older AGP cards do not function properly in some AGP motherboards. These problems were caused both by ambiguities in the AGP standard and by some manufacturers failing to adhere closely enough to the published standard. These problems were relatively common with motherboards and video adapters designed and sold until late 2000, and in particular with motherboards that use some older VIA chipsets. No current motherboards or AGP cards that we know of suffer these incompatibilities. If you're working with old components, check the maker's web site for details about possible conflicts.

If the motherboard has no AGP slot, the best option is usually to upgrade the motherboard. PCI video adapters are becoming hard to find, and by late 2003 will probably have entirely disappeared from the market.

- Display quality is subjective and very difficult to quantify, but a real issue nonetheless. The consensus, with which we agree, is that Matrox video adapters provide the highest 2D display quality, with ATI RADEON adapters close behind. We used to use Matrox adapters in many systems, but the 3D performance of mainstream Matrox adapters is so poor that we now use Matrox adapters only in systems that we're certain will never need to run 3D applications. For our own systems, we now use primarily ATI RADEON adapters, which combine superb 3D display quality and performance with 2D image quality that is only half a step behind Matrox. Although *n*VIDIA adapters provide excellent 3D performance, we have never cared for their 2D image quality, particularly at high resolution.

The other problem is that *n*VIDIA makes video chipsets, not video cards. *n*VIDIA sells video chipsets to other manufacturers that produce video cards. Some video cards based on *n*VIDIA chipsets are very good indeed, but some are quite poor. In other words, the presence of the *n*VIDIA name is no guarantee of quality.

ATI also sells RADEON chipsets to other manufacturers, such as SapphireTech and Crucial, differentiating ATI-branded products as "Built By ATI" and third-party RADEON adapters as "Powered By ATI." We have used RADEON video cards made by Crucial and SapphireTech and find their quality indistinguishable from ATI-branded products, although features and package contents may vary.

- If you buy a motherboard with embedded video, make sure the motherboard includes an AGP slot, ideally a UAGP3.0 slot. In a year or two, when even inexpensive video cards are faster than the embedded video, you can upgrade the video easily and inexpensively.

- Buy a card with enough memory. PCI video cards can use only memory that resides on the card itself. AGP video cards can also use main system memory, but for performance and other reasons it's always better to have the necessary memory on the video card itself.

- For running business software and other 2D applications, nearly any recent video card is adequate. Look for a card with at least 16 MB of video memory, but more than 32 MB is probably overkill.

- If you run 3D games or professional 3D applications, consider 32 MB of local video memory the absolute minimum. It is better to have 64 MB, and 128 MB or more is not excessive if you run hardware-intensive applications.

- Make sure that the adapter you choose has drivers available for the operating system you intend to use. This is particularly important if you run Linux or another OS with limited driver support. The best vendors, such as ATI, provide frequent driver updates for a broad range of operating systems and versions. Consider the manufacturer's history of providing frequent driver updates and supporting new operating system versions, which you can determine by examining the manufacturer's web site, checking the newsgroups, and cruising the hardware enthusiast web sites.

 Video driver availability may be an important consideration for Linux users. Most recent Linux distributions have basic 2D support for most popular video adapters, but may lack support for 3D acceleration, TV, dual-head, and other features. In the past, many Linux users chose Matrox for its excellent Linux support, but now *n*VIDIA is generally acknowledged to have the best Linux support. Although ATI ignored Linux for years, excellent 2D and 3D drivers are now available for ATI RADEON 8500 and later adapters, as well as some earlier models. Before you choose a video adapter for a Linux system, check the maker's web site and *http://www.xfree86. org/* to determine if acceptable drivers are available. You may also want to check the Linux distribution you are considering to make sure that the installer will detect and configure hardware 3D support without much hassle.

- Make sure the video card has a good warranty. Video cards used to be among the most reliable components of a PC. This is changing, not because manufacturers are cutting corners, but because new high-performance video cards are pushing hardware technology to the limit. Having a video card die after only six months or a year is now relatively common, particularly for those who push the card past its limit by overclocking it in pursuit of the highest possible performance. We've seen video cards with 90-day warranties, which is completely unacceptable. Regard one year as an absolute minimum, and longer is better.

Installing a Video Adapter

Physically installing most video cards is very straightforward. Simply choose an available expansion slot, seat the video card, and connect the monitor. Some combinations of AGP card and AGP slot are problematic, requiring extra care to make sure the card actually seats. You may think the card is fully seated, you may

Video Adapters

even have felt it snap into place, and yet when you fire up the system you have either no video or garbled video. If that occurs, turn off the system and make sure the video card really is seated.

 Many video adapters now come with heatsinks on the graphics chipset. Some whose chipsets run at very high speeds go further, adding a fan to the heatsink. If your adapter has a fan, make sure to connect power to that fan before you use the adapter. We received mail from a reader who didn't realize that connecting the fan was mandatory, and so overheated and damaged his expensive new video adapter.

Configuring Video Under Windows 98/Me/2000/XP

Windows 98/Me/2000/XP video is configured from the Display Properties → Settings dialog, shown in Figure 15-2, and the Display Properties → Settings → Advanced dialog, one page of which is shown in Figure 15-3. To view Display Properties, run the Display applet from the Control Panel or right-click a vacant area of the desktop and choose Properties. The following sections describe how to use Display Properties to configure Window 98/Me video settings. Windows 2000/XP is similar, with minor differences in the appearance, names, and functions of the dialogs.

Installing or Changing Video Drivers

Windows 98/Me does reasonably well at detecting common video adapters and installing the proper drivers for them. However, you may need to install a video driver manually in one of the following circumstances:

- Windows 98/Me does not have a driver for your adapter. This situation is more common than you might expect. For example, Windows 98/Me does not provide a driver for the ubiquitous Intel i740 video adapter. This situation may also arise if you install a new video adapter in an existing Windows 98/Me system.

- Windows 98/Me has a driver for your adapter and recognizes the hardware, but you have a more recent driver supplied by the adapter manufacturer. Manufacturers often provide enhanced drivers that are faster or support more features than the vanilla drivers included with Windows 98/Me.

- Windows 98/Me has a driver for your adapter, but fails to autodetect the presence of the adapter, or autodetects the adapter as a different model than is actually present. This situation also arises more often than it should.

To install a new or updated video adapter, first visit the video adapter manufacturer's web site and download the latest Windows 98/Me drivers for your adapter. Get the most recent release version of the driver, avoiding beta or unsupported versions. To install the driver, display the Settings page, click Advanced, choose the Adapter tab, and click Change to start the Update Device Driver Wizard.

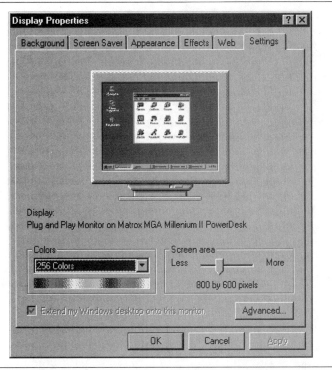

Figure 15-2. The Display Properties Settings page, where you configure hardware settings for your video adapter and monitor

Also use this dialog to set refresh rate. Available options depend on the combination of monitor, adapter, and driver being used. When using a Plug-and-Play monitor, the usual choices are *Optimal*—which selects the highest refresh rate supported by both the monitor and adapter at the current resolution—and *Adapter default*, which simply uses the (usually low) refresh rate that the adapter defaults to. Some configurations allow you to specify actual refresh rates—e.g., 60, 70, 72, 75, and 85 Hz. Before you specify a refresh rate manually, make sure your monitor supports that refresh rate at the resolution and color depth you have selected. Some configurations do not allow changing refresh rate, in which case the refresh rate drop-down list does not appear.

 Some manufacturers supply video drivers as executable files. Running the program installs the driver and may add a custom tab to the Display Properties dialog that allows you to set properties for that driver and adapter. Such drivers also often put a video management utility in the system tray, which you can use to change settings on the fly.

When you change resolution or refresh rate, some monitors automatically adjust to the new settings and display a properly centered image. Others require changing vertical and horizontal size and centering adjustments on the monitor to

Video Adapters

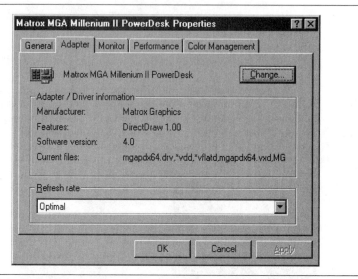

Figure 15-3. The Advanced Settings dialog, where you configure specific settings for the adapter and monitor, enable or disable video acceleration settings, and choose Color Management options (the exact pages in this dialog vary according to the video adapter and driver installed)

display the image properly. If you select a resolution and refresh rate that the monitor cannot display, the screen may be blank or filled with wavy lines. To correct this problem, restart the computer in Safe Mode by pressing F8 during boot and choosing Safe Mode. Choose the Standard VGA driver, restart the system normally, use Display Properties to select the proper driver and display settings that your monitor supports, and then restart the system normally.

Changing the Screen Area Setting

The screen area setting determines how much information is displayed on the screen by specifying the resolution of the image that the video adapter delivers to the monitor. The default resolution installed by Setup will be within the capabilities of your video adapter and monitor, but may not be optimum. Use the Screen area slider in Display Properties → Settings to change resolution. Note that the selection range is not continuous. If your monitor is Plug-N-Play-compliant and recognized by Windows 98/Me, Windows allows you to select only those discrete values that are supported by both the video adapter and monitor.

Although Windows 98/Me itself supports changing resolution on the fly, doing so requires that the video adapter and driver support that feature. Changing resolution with some older video adapters and drivers requires shutting down and restarting Windows. If this is the case with your system, Windows notifies you that a shutdown is required to put the change into effect and allows you to shutdown immediately or defer doing so. If you choose the latter, configuration changes do not take effect until you later restart the system manually.

Choosing a Video Driver

Deciding which video driver to use is nontrivial. If Windows 98/Me supplies a driver for your video card, you can assume that it is at least stable and provides the basic functions, although it may well be slower or have fewer features than the latest driver from the video card manufacturer. The alternative is using a driver from the adapter manufacturer, which may or may not be a good idea.

Some manufacturers have become famous for the "driver of the week." Each new release adds features, improves speed, kills old bugs, and (usually) introduces new bugs. Use such drivers at your own risk, and be prepared for a lot of crashes. Other manufacturers, notably Matrox and ATi, treat video drivers with the seriousness they deserve.

Our advice: choose a video card from a manufacturer that treats drivers with respect. For clients and standalone PCs, use the latest release driver certified by the adapter maker. For servers and other critical systems, use either the vanilla Microsoft driver or a later Microsoft-certified driver supplied by the adapter manufacturer. In either case, avoid subsequently upgrading video drivers unless there is a compelling reason to do so. Avoid beta and other bleeding-edge drivers unless you enjoy having your system crash unpredictably.

In particular, avoid using unreleased or beta *n*VIDIA video drivers, which *n*VIDIA itself says should be avoided. *n*VIDIA's business model requires it to provide early versions of drivers to its OEMs, and those drivers somehow always escape onto the Internet despite the efforts of *n*VIDIA to prevent that from happening. Gamers trying to wring the last drop of performance from their video cards download and install these unfinished drivers, and then wonder why their systems crash. Sometimes *n*VIDIA releases official drivers that aren't yet certified by Microsoft, and not all adapter vendors keep up with *n*VIDIA's release schedule. If you're using an *n*VIDIA-based card, never install anything other than the latest official drivers for it. The safest method is to wait until the adapter manufacturer has tested the drivers and released an installer. You have been warned.

If the monitor type is not recognized by Windows, be careful when changing resolution settings. Depending on the default monitor setting, Windows may allow you to select a resolution setting higher than the monitor actually supports. At best, this results in an unreadable display. At worst, it may overdrive and damage the monitor. A seriously overdriven monitor may begin whining like a Star Trek phaser about to self-destruct, with similarly catastrophic results likely. If this happens, turn off the monitor *immediately*. More than a few seconds of this abuse may turn a monitor into scrap.

If you find yourself with Windows set to a resolution that the monitor cannot display, shut down and restart Windows in Safe Mode. Use the procedure described at the end of the preceding section to reconfigure Windows to use a video driver and display settings that are supported by your hardware.

Enabling and Using QuickRes

If you frequently need to change resolution or color depths, the preceding procedure gets old fast. Enabling the Windows 98/Me QuickRes utility allows you to change resolution and color depth on the fly. To enable QuickRes, choose Display Properties → Settings → Advanced. On the General page of that dialog, mark the Show settings icon on task bar checkbox. With QuickRes enabled, clicking its icon in the system tray displays a menu that displays all combinations of resolution and color depth supported by the video adapter and monitor, and marks the active settings with a check mark. Change resolution or color depth by clicking the combination you want to use. The Adjust Display Properties menu item provides a one-click method for invoking Display Properties when you need to change properties other than those shown on the QuickRes menu.

 QuickRes was first released as one of the unsupported Windows 95 Power Toys utilities, but is integral to Windows 98/Me. If you installed QuickRes under Windows 95 and then upgraded to Windows 98/Me, the Windows 95 version of QuickRes may still appear in your system tray. If so, you can continue to use it. If you prefer to remove the older version and install the Windows 98/Me version, you'll have to edit the Registry. To do so, start the Registry Editor and open the key *HKEY_CURRENT_USER\Software\Microsoft\Windows\CurrentVersion\Run* Double-click the value entry Taskbar Display Controls to edit the entry. Change the value entry, which should be *RunDLL deskcp16.dll, QUICKRES_RUNDLLENTRY* to *RunDLL deskcp16.dll,* and save the change. You can then enable QuickRes 98 by marking the checkbox as described previously.

Changing Performance Setting

By default, Windows 98/Me configures the video driver it installs to use all accelerator functions. Ordinarily, this setting works properly and can be left as is. If you experience video problems, including a mouse pointer that is jerky (check that your mouse is clean first) or disappears entirely, odd video artifacts, or program crashes, Windows 98/Me permits you to selectively disable some video acceleration functions (Display Properties → Settings → Advanced → Performance). Before you use this feature, first attempt to locate and install an updated video driver. Otherwise, choose an accelerator setting as follows:

Full
> All accelerator functions enabled.

High
> Most accelerator functions enabled. Use this setting if you experience minor video or mouse problems. Performance will be degraded somewhat but may be acceptable, particularly for simple 2D applications such as word processing.

Low
> Most accelerator functions disabled. Use this setting if you experience severe video problems or have one or more programs that routinely hang. With this

setting enabled, performance may be marginally acceptable for text applications, but little else. Make getting a better video card a high priority.

None
> All accelerator functions disabled. Use this setting only if it is required to allow your system to run without crashing. When this setting is enabled, your video card is acting as a simple frame grabber, and its performance will almost certainly be unacceptable even for text applications. If you find this setting is required, replace your video card as soon as possible.

Windows 2000/XP uses a slider bar to offer similar performance settings in the Display Properties → Settings → Advanced → Troubleshooting dialog. The slider bar allows the following settings:

First position (None)
> Disables all accelerations. Use this setting only if your computer frequently stops responding or has other severe problems.

Second position
> Disables all but basic accelerations. Use this setting to connect more severe problems.

Third position
> Disables all DirectDraw and Direct3D accelerations, and all cursor and advanced drawing accelerations. Use this setting to correct severe problems with DirectX-accelerated applications.

Fourth position
> Disables all cursor and advanced drawing accelerations. Use this setting to correct drawing problems.

Fifth position
> Disables cursor and bitmap accelerations. Use this setting if you experience mouse problems (jerky or disappearing pointer) or image corruption.

Sixth position (Full)
> Enables all accelerations. This is the default setting for most recent Windows versions (Windows Server 2003 defaults to None) and the recommended setting unless you are experiencing video problems.

These descriptions of problems and recommended settings are based on Microsoft's advice. We recommend using settings other than Full only as temporary measures for troubleshooting. Your video adapter and driver should support Full acceleration. If they don't, something is wrong. Try updating the video driver to the latest stable version offered by the video adapter manufacturer. If that doesn't work, use a different video adapter.

Setting Font Size

Windows uses Small Fonts by default, but allows you to select predefined Large Fonts, or to specify a custom font size by choosing Other. The font size setting you select provides a "baseline" value from which the size of vector-based fonts used in applications is calculated. Choosing one of the predefined settings also installs a set of raster fonts that are used for such things as icon labels. A common reason for using Large Fonts is when you run higher than standard resolution—e.g., 1024x768 on a 15-inch monitor, where using Large Fonts or a custom font size allows you to make the text large enough to be readable. Be cautious, however. Many applications do not display properly using anything except Small Fonts. Note that instead of changing font size directly (Display Properties → Settings → Advanced → General), you can achieve similar results by selecting a different Scheme in the Appearance page of the Display Properties dialog.

Using Color Management

Getting consistent color across a wide range of peripherals, including monitors, scanners, and printers, is nontrivial, a task made more difficult by the diverse means used for producing color. Monitors produce color by illuminating phosphors. Printers may produce output that uses transmitted or reflected light to produce color by means of dyes or pigments. Scanners may capture either transmitted or reflected images. The color temperature of the lighting used to produce or view an image differs according to its source, and the gamma (in simple terms, contrast) varies with the device. With so many variables in play, the colors on your monitor are likely to be only an approximation of the original colors you scanned, and printed output is likely to differ substantially from both the original and the image on your monitor.

The different methods used to produce color mean that it is impossible to render color with complete consistency. A printed copy, for example, simply does not have the dynamic range that a transparency or monitor image has. But for those doing prepress work, some means of minimizing those differences is needed. To address this problem, Microsoft introduced *Image Color Management (ICM)* with Windows 95. ICM organizes the characteristics of each device (e.g., for a scanner, the color temperature of the light source and the gamma of the image sensor; for a printer, the reflectivity characteristics of its various inks) and uses those stored characteristics to make color reproduction as consistent as possible across different devices.

Windows 98/Me includes the ICM V 2.0 API, which improves on the limited capabilities of ICM V 1.0. Previously, you had to define color characteristics for each combination of application and device. Windows 98/Me allows you to define color management profiles which take into account the specific imaging color characteristics of each input and output device and allow all installed applications to use that shared profile to maintain color consistency. ICM characteristics for scanners and printers are set in the drivers for those applications. Those for monitors are set in Display Properties → Settings → Advanced → Color Management.

Color management is an extremely complex issue. For more information, search the Microsoft web site for "Integrated Color Management" or ICM.

Configuring Video under Linux

The setup utility in most recent Linux distributions automatically probes and configures the video adapter and display. Setup prompts you to confirm the hardware it detects and to choose display settings such as resolution and color depth. To reconfigure video settings under Linux, log on as root and run Xconfigurator or whatever equivalent utility your distribution provides. For example, Red Hat Linux 9 uses redhat-config-xfree86.

The Red Hat utility allows you to change resolution or color depth using the Display page of Display Settings, shown in Figure 15-4. Other GUI configuration utilities, such as the Mandrake Control Center, provide similar options. These GUI utilities are simply frontends. Each of them writes the necessary configuration information to the file */etc/X11/XF86Config*, which you can edit manually if you are certain you know what you are doing. After changing settings, you must log out and then log back in to restart the X server before the changes take effect.

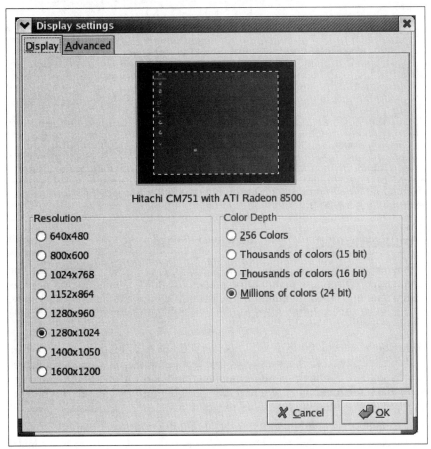

Figure 15-4. The Display page of Display Settings, where you configure resolution and color depth

The Advanced page of Display Settings, shown in Figure 15-5, allows you to configure the display type and video adapter type. If the video adapter and driver support 3D acceleration, the Enable Hardware 3D Acceleration checkbox appears and is enabled by default. If you run 3D applications, leave that checkbox enabled. If you run only 2D applications and experience video problems, disabling this checkbox may help.

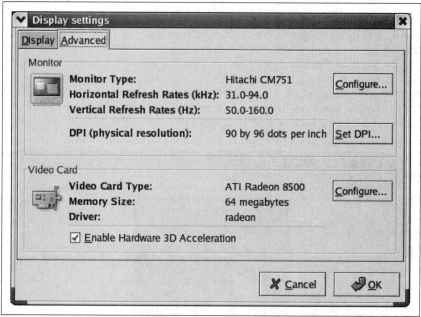

Figure 15-5. The Advanced page of Display Settings, where you configure display and video adapter settings

Troubleshooting Video Adapter Problems

If you experience video problems, first check the obvious things—that the monitor has power and is connected properly to the adapter, that no one has changed settings on the monitor, and so on. If you have another monitor handy, try connecting it to the problem system to eliminate the monitor as a possible cause.

Once you eliminate those possible causes, the next consideration is whether you've made any recent changes to your video hardware, software, or configuration. If so, that is a likely cause. Sometimes, problems caused by such a change don't manifest immediately. We have, for example, seen an updated driver function perfectly until one particular program was loaded or another piece of hardware was installed, which caused the system to crash and burn horribly.

That means the next step is to change video drivers. If a later driver is available, download and install it. If no later driver is available, try reinstalling the current driver. If problems manifest soon after installing an updated driver, try reinstalling the older driver.

Once they are installed and running properly, video adapters seldom fail, short of something like a lightning strike or abusing the adapter by overclocking it. In our more than 20 years of experience with hundreds of systems, we remember only a few instances when a functioning video adapter just died. Hardware failures are more likely today, not because newer video adapters are inferior to their parents, but because they're now pushed harder. High-end video adapters nowadays come with at least a heatsink for the graphics processor, and it's not unusual to see a video adapter on a gamer's system with a fan or even a Peltier cooler installed. If you install a high-performance adapter, make absolutely certain that the fan, if any, has power, and that there is free airflow to the heatsink. Many video problems on systems so equipped are due to simple overheating.

Here are some specific problems you may encounter, and how to remedy them:

Windows 9X displays only 640x480 with 16 colors, with no higher options available
Windows is using the standard VGA driver. If Windows 9X cannot detect the display adapter type when it is installed, it installs the vanilla VGA driver. Windows may have been installed or reinstalled improperly, or the display adapter may have been deleted in the Device Manager, and Windows did not successfully detect the video adapter the last time it was restarted. If the Color palette has options higher than 16, but the desktop area is fixed at 640x480, the monitor type may be incorrect or missing. To solve this problem, install the correct drivers for the video adapter and/or monitor.

The Windows 9X startup splash screen displays properly, but the desktop does not
This problem is also caused by incorrect video drivers or configuration errors. The startup screen is a low-resolution image that is displayed at standard VGA settings. To solve the problem, restart the system in Safe Mode, and reinstall or reconfigure the drivers for the video adapter and/or monitor.

Icons display incorrectly or as black squares
One likely cause is a corrupted ShellIconCache file, a problem that occurs frequently on systems running IE4 and TweakUI, but is by no means limited to those environments. To solve this problem under Windows 9X or NT, uninstall TweakUI (if it is installed), then delete or rename ShellIconCache (in the Windows directory) and restart the system, which automatically rebuilds the ShellIconCache file. Alternatively, view Display Properties → Appearance. In the Item drop-down list, select Icon. Use the Size spinner to change the icon size one step up or down and click Apply to save the change. Change the icon size back to its original value and click OK to save the change and exit the dialog. This process forces Windows to rebuild ShellIconCache. Icon display problems also occur sometimes on Windows NT 4 systems running early builds, a situation that is easily solved by installing the latest service pack. Finally, we have seen this behavior caused on one system by overheating. In that case, the icons displayed normally for some time after the system was started, but turned into black boxes after the system had been running for some time. Cleaning the dust out of the system and installing a supplemental cooling fan made the problem go away, and it has never returned.

The monitor displays random black or parti-colored blocks

These screen artifacts may appear only when using certain combinations of resolution and color depth, and are not affected by mouse movement or by running a different application. They may be persistent or may appear and disappear seemingly at random. This problem is a result of malfunctioning video memory. Possible causes include: upgrading an adapter with slow or mismatched memory; overclocking an adapter, improperly seated memory modules or corroded connectors; and the video adapter not being fully seated. If you are overclocking the adapter, stop doing so and see if the problem goes away. If the adapter is out of warranty and at least a year or two old, consider replacing it. Even inexpensive current adapters greatly outper-form anything of that vintage. If you decide to troubleshoot the problem, observe antistatic precautions. Remove and reseat the adapter in its original slot. If it is a PCI adapter, try moving it to another slot. Use your thumb to press gently on each chip or memory module to ensure it is fully seated. If the adapter uses memory modules, remove and reseat each of them, although this may be impractical if the modules require special tools. Use rubbing alcohol or a commercial contact cleaning product to clean accessible connec-tors and slots, both for memory and for the adapter itself. If you have recently installed a memory upgrade on the adapter, remove it temporarily to see if the problem disappears.

Text is scrambled, incomplete, or appears in an odd font

If this occurs when you build or upgrade a system, the most likely cause is incorrect video drivers. Download and install the most recent stable video drivers for your adapter. If it occurs on a system that had been working correctly, there are several possible causes. If text entered in an application appears in a strange font, but menus and other system fonts are correct, use preferences or options within the application to choose another font. If menus are scrambled only within one application, uninstall and then rein-stall that application. If the problem occurs in multiple applications and system applets, system font files may have been corrupted or replaced with older, incompatible versions. The easiest cure is to reinstall the operating system, using its repair option. If you run Windows 9X, the hardware acceler-ation setting may be too high. Decrease it, as described in the preceding section on Windows 98/Me. Although this problem usually is obvious when the system is first brought up, we have seen it occur on a system that had been running perfectly at the highest setting. In that case, installing a DVD drive broke the system. As it turned out, reducing hardware acceleration by one level allowed the video card and DVD drive to coexist, but we ultimately replaced the video card with a later model that would run with full hardware acceleration.

Under Windows NT 4, you replace a PCI video card with an AGP card, and another card stops working

Windows NT does not support AGP, but treats an AGP card as a PCI card. If the motherboard maps the IRQ assigned to the AGP slot to the same IRQ used by the first PCI slot, installing the AGP card creates an IRQ conflict. Move the affected PCI card to a different slot, or use BIOS Setup to remap IRQ assignments.

Video is usually fine, but becomes jerky during DVD playback

This is often caused by insufficient system resources (such as a slow processor, aging video adapter, or inadequate memory), by having too many other programs running, or by attempting to display DVD video at too high a resolution and/or color depth. If you use software MPEG decoding, instead of replacing the processor, consider upgrading to a video card that has DVD hardware support. If the DVD drive is ATAPI, configure it for DMA mode rather than PIO mode (see Chapter 12). Finally, Windows 9X IRQ Steering may configure the video card to share an IRQ with another card, such as a network card. Use the Device Manager to check IRQ assignments and verify that the video card is not sharing its IRQ. If it is, relocate the PCI card to a different slot.

When using an overlay DVD MPEG decoder card, one particular color (often magenta) doesn't display properly

This is an artifact of how some DVD MPEG decoder cards function, mapping the DVD video to one particular overlay color. As a temporary fix, connect the monitor directly to the video card except when you are displaying DVD video. The only real fix is to remove the DVD decoder and the current video card, and install a newer video card that provides hardware DVD acceleration.

Our Picks

State of the art for 3D video adapters changes more quickly than for any other PC technology. If you buy a $300 bleeding-edge 3D adapter that's the fastest on the market today, that adapter will have only midrange performance in six months, and entry-level performance within a year.

ATI and *n*VIDIA vie constantly for the title of world's fastest 3D adapter, one-upping each other frequently. In general, except when one or the other introduces an entirely new chipset, the fastest current ATI and *n*VIDIA 3D video adapters have performance within a few percent age points of each other. Which one is fastest depends on which benchmark you believe, which 3D applications and games you run, and what resolution you run them at. And the truth is that any reasonably recent ATI or *n*VIDIA 3D accelerator is more than fast enough for any but the most intense 3D games.

Of the two, we used to prefer *n*VIDIA because ATI drivers were often quite poor. In the last few years, we've come to prefer ATI overall. ATI has greatly improved its drivers, including its Linux drivers, its 3D performance matches or beats comparable *n*VIDIA cards, ATI 2D graphics and text are of noticeably better quality than that of *n*VIDIA, and ATI video capture functions are far superior to those of *n*VIDIA. In short, if all you want to do with a video adapter is play 3D games, it's probably a tossup between the fastest models from ATI and *n*VIDIA. But if you also want to use the video adapter for web browsing, email, and other typical productivity applications, we give ATI the nod for its superior display quality.

If you're building or upgrading a general-purpose system—one that will not be used for 3D games or professional graphics—we suggest you not worry much about which video adapter to choose. For undemanding 2D applications such as word processors and web browsers running at moderate resolution—in fact, for anything other than 3D graphics or other special requirements—nearly any reasonably recent embedded or standalone video adapter is sufficient. If you're buying a motherboard, buy one with embedded video if that is an option. Make sure the motherboard has an AGP slot and allows the embedded video to be disabled. That way, if your needs change later, you can install whatever video card seems best. If you're upgrading a system with an existing AGP-capable motherboard, buy an inexpensive AGP video adapter. If the existing motherboard is an older model without an AGP slot, that itself is good reason to install a motherboard that has an AGP slot and embedded video.

 We have recently come to prefer ATI RADEON video adapters made by Crucial Technology (the memory folks). Although Crucial manufactures a limited range of RADEON video adapters, one of them will probably be appropriate for your needs. For example, in July 2003, Crucial sold a $50 DX-7 RADEON 7500 to fill the need for an inexpensive adapter with excellent 2D image quality and reasonable 3D performance for casual gaming. For the midrange, Crucial sold the $83 DX-8.1 RADEON 9100, an excellent card for 3D gamers on a budget. For avid gamers who could afford a $400 video adapter, Crucial offered the DX-9 RADEON 9800 Pro. We trust Crucial's build quality, and Crucial offers the additional inducement of a lifetime warranty on their RADEON adapters.

For our most recent detailed recommendations by brand and model, visit: *http://www.hardwareguys.com/picks/video.html.*

16

Displays

PCs use one of two display technologies: a traditional "glass bottle" CRT monitor or a flat-panel display (FPD) that uses LCD technology. Although traditional CRTs remain dominant, FPDs are gaining ground fast. This chapter covers both technologies and tells you what you need to know to select and use the best display for your needs.

CRT Monitors

Like a television set, a monitor comprises a *cathode ray tube* (*CRT*) and supporting circuitry that processes the external video signal into a form that can be displayed by the CRT. Monitors use a different video interface than televisions, have much higher bandwidth, and can display much finer detail. In fact, with the proper adapter, computer video signals can be displayed on a standard television, but only at low resolution. Conversely, a monitor can be used to display television video at very high quality, although doing so requires using a video card with TV input, a tuner, and other electronics that are built into television sets but not monitors. The quality of the CRT and supporting circuitry determines the quality of the image a monitor can display. Because of their higher bandwidth and resolution, computer monitors cost much more than televisions with equal screen sizes.

Monitors comprise the following major elements:

CRT
> The CRT is essentially a large glass bottle, flat or nearly so on one end (the screen), tapering to a thin neck at the back, and with nearly all air exhausted. The inside of the screen end is covered with a matrix of millions of tiny *phosphor* dots (or stripes). A phosphor is a chemical compound that, when struck by electrons, emits visible light of a particular color. Phosphors are organized by groups of three, collectively called a *pixel*. Each pixel contains one phosphor dot that emits each of the additive primary colors red, green, and

blue. By choosing which dots to illuminate and how brightly to illuminate each, any pixel can be made to emit any one of thousands or millions of discrete colors. For example, 24-bit color allocates a full 8-bit byte to each of the three primary colors, allowing that pixel to be set to any of 256 levels of brightness. Three colors, each of which can be set to any of 256 brightness values, provides a total color palette of 256^3 colors, or about 16.7 million colors. The distance between nearest neighbors of the same phosphor color on adjacent rows is called the *dot pitch* or *stripe pitch*. A smaller pitch results in a sharper image and the ability to resolve finer detail.

Electron guns

The phosphor dots are excited by one or more electron emitters, called *electron guns*, located in the neck at the back of the monitor. A gun comprises a heated cathode, which emits electrons, and circuitry that focuses the free electrons into a thin beam. Most CRTs use three separate guns, one for each primary color. Sony Trinitron CRTs use only one gun. There has been much debate about the relative display quality of single-gun versus triple-gun CRTs, both of which have theoretical advantages and disadvantages. In practice, we find the images indistinguishable. The quality of the electronics used to control the shape and positioning of the electron beam is very important to image quality because the relative position of pixels to electron gun varies with the position of the pixel on screen. Pixels near the center of the screen are oriented at 90 degrees to the gun, and are struck dead-on by the beam. Conversely, pixels near the corners of the screen are struck by the beam at an angle, which, in the absence of correcting circuitry, causes the beam to assume an oval rather than circular shape. High-quality guns correct this problem by changing the shape of the beam according to the position of the pixel being illuminated. Lower-quality guns used in inexpensive monitors do a much poorer job of adjusting the beam, resulting in images blurring near the edges and corners of the tube.

Deflection yoke

The *deflection yoke* is located around the tapered portion of the CRT, between the guns and the screen. This yoke is actually a large electromagnet, which, under the control of the monitor circuitry, is used to steer the electron beam(s) to impinge on the correct phosphor dot at the correct time and with the correct intensity.

Mask

The *mask* sits between the electron guns and the phosphor layer, very close to the latter. This mask may be a sheet of metal with a matrix of fine perforations that correspond to the phosphor dot triads on the screen, or a series of fine vertical wires that correspond to phosphors laid down in uninterrupted vertical stripes. The perforations or stripes permit properly aimed electrons to impinge directly on the phosphors at which they are aimed, while blocking excess electrons. This blocking results in a cleaner image, but blocked electrons heat the mask. To prevent differential heating from distorting the mask, the mask is often constructed of Invar (an alloy with an extremely low coefficient of thermal expansion) or a similar material. Although the mask improves image sharpness, it also dims the image because areas blocked by the mask cannot emit light, so design efforts focus on minimizing the percentage of screen area blocked by the mask.

In practice, and despite the marketing efforts of manufacturers to convince us otherwise, we find that the mask type makes little real difference. Good (read expensive) monitors produce good images, regardless of their mask type. Inexpensive monitors produce inferior images, regardless of their mask type. Monitors from the best makers—Hitachi, NEC-Mitsubishi, and Sony— produce superb images using different masking methods. That said, however, there's no substitute for looking at the monitor yourself. You may have a strong preference for the type of picture produced by one of the following mask types:

Aperture grill

The Sony Trinitron television tube appeared in the 1960s as the first alternative to standard shadow mask tubes and has since been used in most Sony monitors. Rather than using the standard dot triads, aperture grill monitors use uninterrupted vertical stripes of phosphors, alternating red, green, and blue across the width of the screen. Masking is done by an aperture grill, which consists of a series of very fine vertical wires covering the full width of the tube, and corresponding to the phosphor stripes. In any given vertical phosphor stripe, no mask separates individual pixels vertically, so the top and bottom of each pixel must be delimited by the accuracy of the scanning electron beam. The advantages of the aperture grill are that it allows more electrons to pass than any other masking method, which makes for a brighter, saturated, high-contrast image on screen, and that the absence of hardcoded vertical boundaries on pixels allows using any arbitrary vertical resolution. A minor disadvantage is that the fine vertical wires that comprise the grill are easily disturbed by mechanical shock such as bumping the monitor, which results in a shimmering effect that may take a few seconds to stabilize. Also, the vertical wires are supported by one fine horizontal wire in 14-inch and smaller Sony monitors, or two such wires (which divide the screen roughly in thirds) on 15-inch and larger Sony monitors. These horizontal damper wires cast a shadow that some users find objectionable, particularly when they are visible on a light background. The Mitsubishi Diamondtron tube, used in Mitsubishi's midrange and high-end monitors, uses similar technology.

In early 2003, Sony announced its departure from the CRT monitor market and its intention to focus its efforts on flat-panel displays. As Sony winds down its CRT operations, it is unclear how much longer Sony will continue to produce Trinitron tubes for other monitor manufacturers. Existing orders and inventory already in the channel mean that new Trinitron-based monitors should remain available until late 2003, but if you want a Trinitron monitor, now is the time to get one.

Shadow mask

The *shadow mask* is a perforated sheet of metal whose holes correspond to *dot triads*, groups of three colored phosphors, which may be arranged in various ways. Three distinct variants of this masking technology are used.

The *standard shadow mask* is still used, particularly in inexpensive generic monitors and in the "value" models from name-brand manufacturers. The standard shadow mask is a perforated sheet of metal whose circular holes correspond to *dot triads*, groups of three circular colored phosphor dots arranged at the vertices of an equilateral triangle. The advantages of the standard shadow mask are that it is inexpensive and provides a reasonably sharp image. The disadvantage is that it blocks more screen real estate than other methods, resulting in a noticeably dimmer image, lower color saturation (muddy colors), and less contrast. Also, its triangular pixel arrangement means that vertical lines may show noticeable "jaggies." Standard shadow mask monitors are suitable for casual use, but are not the best choice for intensive use.

The *slotted mask*, developed by NEC, is a hybrid that combines the stability and sharpness of the standard shadow mask with most of the brightness, contrast, and color saturation of the aperture grill. The slotted mask is essentially a shadow mask in which the small round holes are replaced by larger rectangular slots. Like a standard shadow mask, the slotted mask uses discrete phosphor trios, although they are arranged as rectangular stripes and cover more of the screen surface. The slotted mask design is physically more stable than an aperture grill, while the larger slots allow many more electrons through than does a standard mask. The resulting picture is brighter than a standard shadow mask monitor, but less so than an aperture grill monitor.

The latest masking technology, *Enhanced Dot Pitch* (EDP) from Hitachi, improves on the standard shadow mask by increasing the size of the phosphor dots and changing their geometry from an equilateral triangle to an isosceles triangle. The larger phosphor dots result in a brighter image with more contrast and color saturation, and the changed geometry provides a better image that resolves finer detail. For example, a standard shadow mask monitor with a 0.28 mm diagonal dot pitch actually uses a 0.14 mm vertical pitch and a 0.24 mm horizontal pitch. A corresponding Hitachi EDP monitor uses a 0.27 mm diagonal dot pitch with a 0.14 mm vertical pitch and a 0.22 mm horizontal pitch. The smaller overall dot pitch renders finer detail, and the smaller difference between vertical and horizontal pitch results in subtle but very noticeable differences in image quality.

Monitor Characteristics

Here are the important characteristics of monitors:

Screen size

Screen size is specified in two ways. The *nominal size*—the size by which monitors are advertised and referred to—is the diagonal measurement of the tube itself. However, the front bezel of the monitor conceals part of the tube, making the usable size of the monitor less than stated. Various consumer lawsuits have resulted in monitor manufacturers also specifying the *Viewable Image Size (VIS)*, which is the portion of the tube that is actually visible. Typically, VIS is an inch or so less than nominal. For example, a nominal 17-inch monitor may have a 15.8-inch VIS. Small differences in VIS—e.g., 15.8-inch versus 16-inch make little practical difference. The smallest monitors commonly available are 15-inch, although ViewSonic still produces a 14-inch model in their economy OptiQuest line. 17-inch remains the most popular size, but 19-inch models are now so inexpensive that they may soon overtake 17-inch models in unit sales. 20-inch and larger monitors are still quite expensive, and are used primarily by graphic artists and others who require huge displays. Table 16-1 lists monitor size and resolution combinations that most people with 20/20 vision find optimum (++ is optimum; + is suitable; - is generally unsuitable; -- is completely unsuitable)

Table 16-1. Monitor size and resolution combinations

Resolution	Monitor Size (inches)			
	15	17	19	21
640 × 480	+	-	--	--
800 × 600	++	+	-	--
1024 × 768	-	++	+	-
1152 × 864	--	++	+	-
1280 × 1024	--	-	++	+
1600 × 1200	--	--	+	++

 People with less-than-perfect vision often use the next size larger monitor (e.g., running 800×600 on a 17-inch monitor or 1024×768 on a 19-inch monitor), but we recommend instead using the optimum settings listed and configuring Windows and applications to display larger-than-normal fonts (e.g., set Display Properties to use the "Windows Standard (large)" or "Windows Standard (extra large)" scheme; set Internet Explorer font size to "Larger" or "Largest"; set Word to display text at 150% or 200%, and so on). Using high resolution provides finer-grained images, which are easier on the eyes.

Dot/stripe pitch

Dot pitch or *stripe pitch* is measured in millimeters, and specifies the center-to-center distance between the nearest neighboring phosphor dots or stripes of the same color. Smaller pitch means a sharper image that resolves finer detail. Unfortunately, dot pitch, which is used to describe shadow mask monitors, cannot be compared directly to stripe pitch, which is used to describe aperture grill monitors. For equivalent resolution, stripe pitch must be about 90% of dot pitch. That is, a 0.28 mm dot pitch monitor has resolution similar to a 0.25 mm stripe pitch monitor.

Maximum resolution

> *Maximum resolution* specifies the maximum number of pixels that the monitor can display, which is determined by the physical number of pixels present on the face of the tube. The maximum resolution of many low-end monitors is identical to the optimum resolution for that monitor size. For example, 1024×768 is optimum for 17-inch monitors, so many low-end 17-inch monitors provide 1024×768 maximum resolution. Conversely, midrange and high-end monitors may have maximum resolutions higher than practically usable. For example, a high-end 17-inch monitor may support up to 1600×1200. There is no real benefit to such extreme resolutions, although it can be useful to have one step higher than optimum (e.g., 1280×1024 on a 17-inch monitor or 1600×1200 on a 19-inch monitor) available for occasional use for special purposes.

Synchronization range

> The *synchronization range* specifies the bandwidth of the monitor, which determines which combinations of resolution, refresh rate, and color depth can be displayed. Synchronization range is specified as two values:

Vertical Scanning Frequency (VSF)

> The inverse of the time the monitor requires to display one full screen. VSF (also called *refresh rate*) is measured in Hz and specifies the number of times per second the screen can be redrawn. To avoid screen flicker, the monitor should support at least 70 Hz refresh at the selected resolution. Within reason, higher refresh rates provide a more stable image, but rates beyond 85 or 90 Hz are necessary only for specialized applications such as medical imaging. Most monitors support a wide range of refresh rates, from very low (e.g., 50 Hz) to very high (e.g., 120 to 160 Hz).

Horizontal Scanning Frequency (HSF)

> The inverse of the time the monitor requires to display one full scan line. HSF is measured in KHz, and specifies the overall range of bandwidths supported by the monitor. For example, a monitor running 1280×1024 at 85 Hz must display 1024 lines 85 times per second, or 87,040 scan lines per second, or about 87 KHz. In fact, some overhead is involved, so the actual HSF for such a monitor might be 93.5 KHz.

Resolution and refresh rate are interrelated parts of the synchronization range of an analog monitor. For a given resolution, increasing the refresh rate increases the number of screens (and accordingly the amount of data) that must be transferred each second. Similarly, for a given refresh rate, increasing the resolution increases the amount of data that must be transferred for each screen. If you increase resolution or refresh rate, you may have to decrease the other to stay within the HSF limit on total bandwidth.

Note that manufacturers often specify maximum resolution and maximum refresh rate independently, without consideration for their interrelatedness. For example, specifications for a 19-inch monitor may promise 1600×1200 resolution and 160 Hz refresh. Don't assume that means you can run 1600×1200 at 160 Hz. 160 Hz refresh may be supported only at 640×480 resolution; at 1600×1200, the monitor may support only 70 Hz refresh.

Resolution and refresh rate alone determine the required bandwidth for an analog monitor. Color depth is immaterial because the color displayed for a given pixel is determined by the analog voltages present on the red, green, and blue lines at the time that pixel is processed. Therefore, at a given resolution and refresh rate, an analog monitor uses exactly the same bandwidth whether the color depth is set to 4, 8, 16, 24, or 32 bits because the video card converts the digital color data to analog signals before sending it to the monitor. For purely digital monitors, such as flat-panel units, greater color depth requires greater bandwidth because color information is conveyed to a digital monitor as a digital signal.

Tube geometry

Monitors use one of three geometries for the front viewing surface. *Spherical* tubes are used in older monitors and some inexpensive current models. The viewing surface is a section of a sphere, rounded both horizontally and vertically, which results in apparent distortion at normal viewing distances. This geometry keeps the center and corners of the screen close to the same distance from the electron guns, allowing the use of less-expensive shadow mask materials and less-sophisticated and cheaper electronics. *Cylindrical* tubes, first introduced with the Sony Trinitron, use a section of a cylinder as the viewing surface, and are vertically flat but horizontally rounded. This keeps the distance from gun-to-center and gun-to-corners similar, while reducing apparent distortion of the viewing area relative to a spherical tube. *Flat square tubes* (FSTs) are actually spherical in sections, but from a sphere with a radius so large that they appear nearly flat. The advantage to FST is that the image area is effectively flat, minimizing viewing distortion. The disadvantage is that the electron guns are much farther from the corners than the center, which in turn demands a relatively costly Invar mask and more expensive electronics to provide even coverage. Other than some "value" models, all current monitors, including Sony Trinitrons, use an FST. Don't consider buying a monitor that doesn't.

Controls and stored settings

All monitors provide basic controls—brightness, contrast, horizontal/vertical image size, and centering. Better monitors provide additional controls for such things as screen geometry (pincushion and barrel distortion adjustments), color temperature, and so on, as well as an onscreen display of settings. Changing display settings such as resolution and refresh rate may also change the size and position of the image. If you frequently change resolution, look for a monitor that can store multiple settings so that you will not have to readjust the monitor manually each time you change display settings.

Neck length

As 19-inch monitors become increasingly mainstream, monitor depth also becomes an increasing problem. Historically, most monitors were about as deep as their nominal screen size. With 15-inch monitors, depth was usually not a problem. With 17-inch monitors, depth began to be an issue, and with 19-inch monitors many people find that their desks are not deep enough to accommodate them. Manufacturers have responded by producing reduced-depth or "short-neck" monitors. A short-neck 17-inch monitor is about the depth of a standard 15-inch monitor, and a short-neck 19-inch monitor is about the depth of a standard 17-inch monitor. That shorter neck involves some trade-offs, however. Foremost is the fact that achieving that shorter depth requires changing the deflection angle from the standard 90 degrees to 100 or even 110 degrees. Increasing the deflection angle requires more expensive electronics to compensate and results in reduced image quality. In effect, you pay twice for a short-neck monitor because it costs more and provides an inferior image.

Choosing a CRT Monitor

Use the following guidelines when choosing a CRT monitor:

- Remember that a monitor is a long-term purchase. Even with heavy use, a high-quality monitor can be expected to last five years or more, whereas inexpensive monitors may fail within a year or two. We have several 17-inch monitors here that were purchased with one system and have been moved to two or three successor systems over the years. Good large monitors are inexpensive enough now that it makes sense to buy for the long term.

- Make sure the monitor is big enough, but not too big. Verify that your desk or workstation furniture can accommodate the new monitor. Many people have excitedly carried home a new 19-inch or 21-inch monitor only to find that it literally won't fit where it needs to. Check physical dimensions and weight carefully before you buy. Large monitors commonly weigh 50 lbs. or more, and some exceed 100 lbs. That said, if you find yourself debating between buying one monitor and another that's the next size up, go with the larger monitor. But note that if your decision is between a low-end larger monitor and a high-end smaller one for about the same price, you may well be happier with the smaller monitor. A $200 17-inch monitor beats a $200 19-inch monitor every time.

- Avoid reduced-depth monitors whenever possible. Space constraints may force you to choose a short-neck model. Just be aware that you will pay more for such a monitor, and its image quality will be lower.

- Stick with good name brands and buy a midrange or higher model from within that name brand. That doesn't guarantee that you'll get a good monitor, but it does greatly increase your chances. The monitor market is extremely competitive. If two similar models differ greatly in price, the cheaper one likely has significantly worse specs. If the specs appear similar, the maker of the cheaper model has cut corners somewhere, whether in component quality, construction quality, or warranty policies.

  Deciding which are the "good" name brands is a matter of spirited debate. Our opinion, which is shared by many, is that until its departure from the CRT market in early 2003, Sony made the best monitors available, although they sold at a premium. We now consider Hitachi, NEC-Mitsubishi, Samsung, and ViewSonic to be the "Big Four" monitor makers. Most of their monitors, particularly midrange and better models, provide excellent image quality and are quite reliable. Many people also think highly of EIZO/Nanao monitors. You're likely to be happy with a monitor from any of these manufacturers, although we confess that we use only Hitachi and NEC-Mitsubishi monitors on our own primary systems.

Further down the ladder are "value" brands such as Mag Innovision, Princeton, Optiquest, and others. Our own experience with value brands, albeit limited, has not been good. A Princeton monitor we bought died a month out of warranty, as did an OEM Mag Innovision model that we bought bundled with a PC. Two Mag Innovision monitors developed severe problems after less than two years of use. In our experience, which covers many hundreds of monitors purchased by employers and clients, the display quality of the value-brand monitors is mediocre, and they tend not to last long. The same is generally true of monitors bundled with systems. Although there are exceptions, bundled monitors tend to be low-end models from second- and third-tier makers. If you purchase a computer system from a direct vendor, we recommend you order it without a monitor and purchase a good monitor separately. You may be shocked by how little you are credited for the monitor, but that indicates just how inexpensive a monitor is typically bundled with systems. Also, make sure to request that the shipping cost be reduced accordingly. Although many direct vendors now offer free shipping, some still charge $100 or so to ship the system and monitor. If you order only the system unit, the shipping cost should be significantly lower, but some vendors do not reduce the shipping cost unless you ask them to do so.

- Buy the monitor locally if possible. You may pay a bit more than you would buying mail order, but, after shipping costs, not as much more as it first appears. Monitors vary more between examples than other computer components. Also, monitors are sometimes damaged in shipping, often without any external evidence on the monitor itself or even the box. Damaged monitors may arrive DOA, but more frequently they have been jolted severely enough to cause display problems and perhaps reduced service life, but not complete failure. That makes the next point very important.

- If possible, test the exact monitor you plan to buy (not a floor sample) before you buy it. If you have a notebook computer, install DisplayMate on it (the demo version is adequate and can be downloaded from *http://www. displaymate.com/demos.html*) and use it to test the monitor. If you don't have a notebook, take a copy of DisplayMate with you to the store and get permission to run it on one of their machines. In return for the higher price you're paying, ask the local store to endorse the manufacturer's warranty—that is, to agree that if the monitor fails, you can bring it back to the store for a replacement rather than dealing with the hassles of returning the monitor to the manufacturer. Mass merchandisers such as Best Buy usually won't do this (they try to sell you a service contract instead, which you shouldn't buy), but small local computer stores may agree to endorse the manufacturer's warranty. If the monitor has hidden damage from rough handling during shipping, that damage will ordinarily be apparent within a month or two of use, if not immediately.

- Most mainstream monitor manufacturers produce no 15-inch models (there's no profit in them), and usually three—Good, Better, and Best—models in 17, 19, and 21 inches. In general, the Good model from a first-tier maker corresponds roughly in features, specifications, and price to the Better or Best models from lower-tier makers. For casual use, choose a Good model from a first-tier maker, most of which are very good indeed. If you make heavier demands on your monitor—such as sitting in front of it eight hours a day—you may find that the Better model from a first-tier maker is the best choice. The Best models from first-tier makers are usually overkill, although they may be necessary if you use the monitor for CAD/CAM or other demanding tasks. Best models often have generally useless features such as extremely high resolutions and unnecessarily high refresh rates at moderate resolutions. It's nice that a Best 17-inch model can display 1600×1200 resolution, for example, but unless you can float on thermals and dive on rabbits from a mile in the air, that resolution is likely to be unusable. Similarly, a 17-inch monitor that supports 115 MHz refresh rates at 1024×768 is nice, but in practical terms offers no real advantage over one that supports 85 or 90 MHz refresh.

- Decide which makes and models to consider (but not the specific unit you buy) based on specifications. Any monitor you consider should provide at least the following:

Controls

Power; Degauss (if not automatic); Contrast; Brightness; Horizontal Size; Horizontal Position; Vertical Size; Vertical Position; Pincushion/Barrel Distortion Adjustment. Better monitors may add some or all of the following: On-Screen Display; Focus; Individual Red, Green, Blue Color Control (or Color Temperature); Tilt; Align; and Rotate.

Warranty

Inexpensive monitors often have a one-year parts and labor warranty (although 90-day warranties, particularly on labor, are not unheard of). Better monitors usually warrant the tube for two or three years (often excluding labor after the first year) with one-year parts and labor on the remaining components. Warranties on high-quality monitors may be for three years parts and labor. In reality, the value of a long warranty on a good monitor is less than it might seem. The few times we've seen a good monitor fail, it's either been soon after it was taken out of the box or after many years of use. Conversely, a two- or three-year warranty on an inexpensive monitor would be useful indeed because such monitors frequently fail after a couple of years. That's why you seldom find a good, long, comprehensive warranty on a cheap monitor.

Other specifications vary according to monitor size. Remember that shadow mask dot pitches are not directly comparable to aperture grill stripe pitches. A 0.28 mm diagonal dot pitch corresponds roughly to a 0.25 mm stripe pitch. Also, not all dot pitches are specified in the same manner. Some manufacturers specify the diagonal dot pitch. Others, such as Hitachi, specify individual horizontal dot pitch and vertical dot pitch. A monitor specified as having a 0.22 mm horizontal dot pitch and 0.13/0.15 mm vertical dot pitch corresponds roughly to a monitor with a 0.27 mm diagonal dot pitch. The minimum specifications follow, with preferable values in parentheses:

15 inches

13.8-inch viewable image size (VIS); flat square tube (FST); 0.28 mm diagonal dot pitch; maximum resolution 1024×768 (1280×1024); 75 Hz (85 Hz) refresh rate for standard 800×600 resolution. Automatically synchronize at 31 to 69 KHz (31—80 KHz) horizontally and 55 to 120 Hz (50—130 Hz) vertically. As of July 2003, a high-quality, brand-name 15-inch monitor can be purchased for $125.

17 inches

15.6-inch (15.8-inch) VIS; FST; 0.28 mm (0.27 mm) diagonal dot pitch; maximum resolution 1280×1024 (1600×1200); 85 Hz (100 Hz) refresh rate for standard 1024×768 resolution, and 75 Hz (85 Hz) refresh rate at 1280×1024. Automatically synchronize at 31 to 69 KHz (31—95 KHz) horizontally and 55 to 120 Hz (50—160 Hz) vertically. As of July 2003, a high-quality, brand-name 17-inch monitor can be purchased for $140, only $15 or so more than a comparable 15-inch model. That means buying a 15-inch model makes sense only if a 17-inch model is too large to fit the space available.

19 inches

17.8-inch (18.0-inch) VIS; FST; 0.28 mm (0.27 mm) diagonal dot pitch; maximum resolution 1600×1200 (1920×1440); 85 Hz (100 Hz) refresh rate for standard 1280×1024 resolution, and 75 Hz (85 Hz) refresh rate at 1600×1200. Automatically synchronize at 31 to 94 KHz (31—110 KHz) horizontally and 55 to 160 Hz (50—160 Hz) vertically. As of July 2003, a high-quality, brand-name 19-inch monitor can be purchased for $250.

21 inches

19.8-inch (20.0-inch) VIS; FST; 0.28 mm (0.27 mm) diagonal dot pitch; maximum resolution 1600×1200 (2048×1536); 85 Hz (100 Hz) refresh rate for standard 1600×1200 resolution, and 75 Hz (85 Hz) refresh rate at resolutions above 1600×1200. Automatically synchronize at 31 to 96 KHz (31—125 KHz) horizontally and 55 to 160 Hz (50—160 Hz) vertically. As of July 2003, a high-quality, brand-name 21-inch monitor can be purchased for $600.

- Choose the specific monitor you buy based on how it looks to you. Comparing specifications helps narrow the list of candidates, but nothing substitutes for actually looking at the image displayed by the monitor. For example, monitors with Sony Trinitron tubes have one or two fine horizontal internal wires whose shadows appear on screen. Most people don't even notice the shadow, but some find it intolerable.

- Make sure the monitor has sufficient reserve brightness. Monitors dim as they age, and one of the most common flaws in new monitors, particularly those from second- and third-tier manufacturers, is inadequate brightness. A monitor that is barely bright enough when new may dim enough to become unusable after a year or two. A new monitor should provide a good image with the brightness set no higher than 50%.

It's worth expanding a bit on what we consider "good" brand names because that's one of the most frequent questions we get from readers. When we talk to representatives of the various display manufacturers, we always ask them the

Displays

same question: "Other than your own company, which two or three companies make the best displays?" We hear the same names over and over, and our own experiences and reports from readers confirm which display makers are top-tier.

In the first edition of this book, the Big Four were (alphabetically) Hitachi, Mitsubishi, NEC, and Sony. NEC and Mitsubishi subsequently merged their monitor operations and two new names appeared on our list. In the second edition, we listed the Big Four for CRT displays as Hitachi, NEC/Mitsubishi, Sony, and ViewSonic, with Samsung close on their heels. In early 2003, Sony announced its departure from the CRT market. By that time, Samsung had demonstrated it was capable of consistently producing top-notch CRT monitors, so Samsung now joins Hitachi, NEC/Mitsubishi, and ViewSonic as a member of our Big Four.

Like all other component manufacturers, monitor makers have come under increasing margin pressures. A few years ago, we felt safe in recommending any monitor from a first-tier maker because those companies refused to put their names on anything but top-notch products. Alas, just as Gresham's Law says that bad money drives out the good, the same holds true for CRT monitors. To compete with cheap Pacific Rim monitors, first-tier makers have been forced to make manufacturing cost reductions and other compromises.

Accordingly, low-end models from first-tier makers may be of lower quality than they were in the past. The presence of a first-tier maker's name plate still means that monitor is likely to be of higher quality than a similar no-name monitor, but is no longer a guarantee of top quality. Many first-tier monitors are actually made in the same Pacific Rim plants that also produce no-name junk, but don't read too much into that. First-tier monitors are still differentiated by component quality and the level of quality control they undergo. There is no question in our minds that the first-tier monitors are easily worth the 10% to 20% price premium they command relative to lesser brands. In fact, we think it is worth the extra cost to buy not just a first-tier monitor, but a midrange first-tier monitor. We prefer Hitachi and NEC/Mitsubishi models, including their entry-level models, but the midrange and better Samsung and ViewSonic models are also excellent.

Flat-Panel Displays

CRT monitors have been the dominant PC display technology since PCs were invented, but that is beginning to change. Flat-panel displays (FPDs) are coming on fast. CRTs still outsell FPDs in retail channels. But in the distribution channel—those bundled with new PCs—FPDs exceeded CRTs in popularity by late 2002. Considering the high cost and relatively poor image quality of entry-level FPDs—and bundled FPDs are nearly always entry-level models—we are amazed that FPDs have become so popular so quickly.

FPDs are now common on high-end corporate systems, although FPDs are unlikely to displace CRTs on mainstream systems anytime soon. The cost and other advantages of CRTs ensure that they'll remain available for years to come, but the emphasis is definitely shifting to FPDs. During 2003 and 2004, we expect this trend to continue and indeed accelerate.

Flat-Panel Display Characteristics

Here are the important characteristics of FPDs:

Panel type
FPD panels are available in two broad types:

Passive-matrix panels
Passive-matrix panels generally use *Super Twisted Nematic (STN)* technology. These panels are commonly used on notebook systems, where they provide adequate display quality at a reasonably low price. Only the least-expensive desktop FPDs use passive-matrix technology, which should be avoided for its low display quality.

Active-matrix panels
Active-matrix panels generally use *Thin Film Transistor (TFT)* technology, and are superior to passive-matrix in every respect except price. Most entry-level FPDs and all premium FPDs use TFT technology, which we consider the minimum acceptable. TFT provides usable viewing angles of up to 170 degrees horizontally and vertically. TFT panels are made in what amounts to good, better, and best grades, with higher grades providing wider viewing angles and less color shift as the viewing angle moves off-axis. As of July 2003, the best TFT panels use *In-Plane Switching (IPS)* or *Multi-Domain Vertical Alignment (MDVA or MVA)*, which dramatically improve image quality when properly implemented. Unfortunately, the converse is not necessarily true. That an FPD uses IPS or MDVA does not guarantee a high-quality image, and unfortunately some very low-quality IPS FPDs are available. We expect IPS and MDVA technology to become a standard FPD technology later in 2003 and into 2004, with individual implementations, then as now, varying greatly in display quality.

 You will see references to *Enhanced Thin Film Transistor* technology. In fact, this is not a separate technology, but merely a marketing term used by display makers to differentiate quality levels among TFT panels.

Resolution
Unlike CRT monitors, which have a maximum resolution but can easily be run at lower resolutions, FPDs are designed to operate at one resolution, called the *native resolution*. You can run an FPD at lower than native resolution, but that results in either the image occupying only part of the screen at full image quality, or, via pixel extrapolation, the image occupying the full screen area but with greatly reduced image quality.

Interface
FPDs are available in analog-only, digital/analog hybrid, and digital-only interfaces. Using an analog interface requires converting the video signal from digital to analog inside the PC and then from analog to digital inside the monitor, which reduces image quality, particularly at higher resolutions. Synchronization problems occur frequently with analog interfaces, and can

cause various undesirable display problems. Finally, analog interfaces are inherently noisier than digital interfaces, which causes subtle variations in display quality that can be quite disconcerting. The following section presents FPD interfaces in more detail.

Refresh rate

Whereas CRT monitors require high vertical refresh rates to ensure stable images, FPDs, because of their differing display technology, can use much lower refresh rates. For example, at 1280×1024 resolution on a CRT monitor, you'll probably want to use an 85 Hz or higher refresh rate for good image quality. At the same resolution on an FPD, 60 Hz is a perfectly adequate refresh rate. In fact, on FPDs, a lower refresh rate often provides a better image than a higher refresh rate.

Rise time and fall time

Unlike CRT monitors, whose phosphor-based pixels respond essentially instantaneously to the electron beam, FPD panels use transistors, which require time to turn on or turn off. That means there is a measurable lag between when a transistor is switched on or off and when the associated pixel changes to the proper state. That lag, called *rise time* for when the transistor is switched on and *fall time* for when it is switched off, results in a corresponding lag in image display. On slow FPDs, even dragging a window can show noticeable smearing or stuttering as you move the image to its new location. Even the fastest current FPDs are too slow for the most demanding video, such as 3D games. The best FPDs have rise and fall times on the close order of 15 milliseconds (ms). Good FPDs have rise/fall times of about 30 ms. Inexpensive FPDs may have rise/fall times of 50 ms or more. We consider a rise/fall time of 30 ms acceptable for general use, but we're much happier with a rise/fall time of 15 ms.

Flat-Panel Interfaces

CRTs are an analog technology. The video data inside the PC is manipulated digitally, converted to an analog signal by the graphics adapter, and delivered to the CRT monitor, which can use the analog signal directly. Except for a few high-end models that can use discrete RGB connectors, CRT monitors universally use the standard 15-pin analog VGA connector.

Conversely, FPDs are inherently a digital technology. Although most FPDs can accept both analog and digital signals, using an analog signal requires converting that signal to digital before the FPD can display it. This double conversion— digital-to-analog inside the PC followed by analog-to-digital inside the FPD— reduces image quality and increases complexity and costs, but in a world of analog video adapters, FPD makers had no choice but to design their displays to accept analog inputs.

It would obviously be simpler to avoid the digital-to-analog-to-digital conversion and drive the FPD directly with the digital signal generated by the PC, and that's just what is done with new-generation display adapters and FPDs. But getting to that point was not simple.

The first efforts to standardize a digital interface for video began in 1996, but made little progress initially. Early efforts centered on adapting the well-established *Low Voltage Differential Signaling* (LVDS) standard in use for notebook systems to desktop systems. LVDS could not be used as is because it was designed for the short cable lengths used in notebook systems rather than the longer cable lengths required for desktop systems. National Semiconductor developed a modified LVDS it called FlatLink, and Texas Instruments developed a competing LVDS-based technology called FPD-Link, neither of which was compatible with the other and neither of which was widely adopted. Several other proposed standards also failed to achieve critical mass, including Compaq's Digital Flat-Panel (DFP), National Semiconductor's second-generation OpenLDI, and VESA's Plug-and-Display. Each of these technologies had some advantages relative to the others, but none was fully compatible with anything but itself.

By late 1998 it was clear that none of these technologies had achieved the market dominance needed to establish a de facto standard digital video interface. As is often the case, Intel stepped in, having decided that in its own best interests as well as those of the industry as a whole, a digital video interface standard had to be established, and sooner rather than later. Intel formed the Digital Display Working Group (DDWG), which initially included Compaq, Fujitsu, Hewlett-Packard, IBM, Intel, NEC, and Silicon Image.

That last name is important because in April 1999 the DDWG (*http://www.ddwg. org*) released the draft *Digital Visual Interface (DVI)* specification, which was largely based on the PanelLink *Transition Minimized Differential Signaling (TMDS)* technology developed by Silicon Image. Note that DVI does not stand for Digital *Video* Interface, although that is often mistakenly assumed. DVI is now effectively the main standard to which FPDs are designed. Because the earlier proprietary DFP and VESA Plug-and-Display interfaces are PanelLink-based, DVI-based displays can use these interfaces with only an adapter cable.

DVI provides 165 MHz of bandwidth per DVI link, and the DVI specification allows one or two TMDS links, for a combined bandwidth of 330 MHz. Single-link DVI supports up to 1600×1200 resolution at a 60 Hz refresh rate. (Although 60 Hz may seem an impossibly low refresh rate, particularly at 1600×1200 resolution, the characteristics of FPDs mean that lower refresh rates are quite usable, and in fact the image quality is often superior at lower refresh rates than at higher ones.)

Dual-link DVI is necessary to achieve higher resolutions, such as 1920×1080 (HDTV) and 2048×1536. Dual-link DVI devices use a single clock, which means that the two links remain synchronized, and bandwidth can be shared between them. The system uses one or both links transparently, depending on the bandwidth requirements of the connected display. DVI also implements various display standards that originated with earlier proprietary protocols, including standardized protocols that allow the computer, video adapter, and display to negotiate optimum settings.

DVI defines three types of connectors. The *DVI-Analog (DVI-A)* connector, shown in Figure 16-1, supports only analog displays. The *DVI-Digital (DVI-D)* connector, shown in Figure 16-2, supports only digital displays. The *DVI-Integrated (DVI-I)* connector, shown in Figure 16-3, supports digital displays, but also maintains backward compatibility with analog displays, although it does require an adapter that converts the standard 15-pin VGA analog plug to the DVI-I jack. The connectors are physically keyed so that a digital display cable fits a DVI-D or DVI-I connector but not a DVI-A connector, while an analog display cable fits a DVI-A or DVI-I connector but not a DVI-D connector. This prevents an analog monitor from being connected to a digital-only interface or vice versa, which could destroy the monitor, the interface, or both.

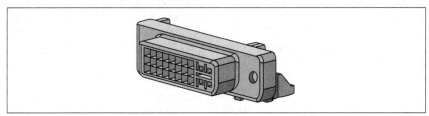

Figure 16-1. DVI-A analog-only connector

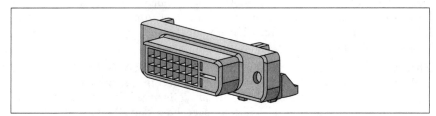

Figure 16-2. DVI-D digital-only connector

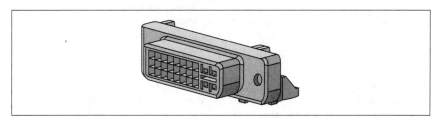

Figure 16-3. DVI-I hybrid digital/analog connector

The DVI-D and DVI-I connectors define 24 pins for digital connections, which can support two full TMDS channels. The DVI-I and DVI-A connectors also define four additional signal pins and a ground pin that add support for analog video. The DVI-D jack accepts a 12-pin (single-link) or 24-pin (dual-link) DVI plug, both of which are digital-only plugs. The DVI-I jack accepts those two plugs, and also accepts the new-style DVI analog plug, which has a protruding cross-shaped key that prevents it from being inserted in a DVI-D jack. The DVI-I jack has a corresponding hole that allows the DVI analog plug to seat. The DVI-A jack accepts only the DVI analog plug.

Of course, the ability of DVI to stream unprotected digital content is of great concern to the *Motion Picture Association of America (MPAA)* and the *Recording Industry Association of America (RIAA)*. The MPAA and RIAA want every cent they can suck out of consumers' pockets by means fair or foul. They are deathly afraid that people will steal their products rather than pay the inflated prices they demand, and so are willing to spend whatever it takes to buy enough legislators and judges to ensure passage and enforcement of such deplorable laws as the *Digital Millennium Copyright Act (DMCA)*, the real goal of which is to eliminate our Fair Use rights under copyright law.

To placate the MPAA, Intel developed the *High-Bandwidth Digital Content Protection (HDCP)* specification, which encrypts all data that travels across the DVI interface. Data is encrypted before being delivered to the DVI cable, and then decrypted by the DVI monitor prior to displaying it. A DVI monitor that does not support HDCP can still display protected content, but only in a degraded form of sufficiently low quality to pose no threat of providing an acceptable copy for distribution.

Even the MPAA doesn't really believe HDCP can prevent commercial piracy. The goal of HDCP is to prevent people from knocking off a copy of a DVD and giving it to a friend. Casual copying scares the MPAA and RIAA, particularly because many forms of it are protected under Fair Use and other provisions of copyright laws. Our sources tell us that HDCP has already been hacked, so it probably won't be long until casual HDCP exploits are commonplace.

FPD Versus CRT

Relative to CRT monitors, FPDs have the following advantages:

Brightness
> FPDs are, on average, brighter than CRTs. A typical CRT might have brightness of about 100 candelas/square meter, a unit of measurement referred to as a *nit*. (Some monitors are rated in foot Lamberts (fL), where one fL equals about 3.43 nits.) A high-quality 15-inch FPD might be rated at 300 nits, three times as bright as a typical CRT. This brightness disparity decreases a bit in larger sizes. For example, a high-quality 19-inch FPD might be rated at 235 nits. CRTs dim as they age, although a brightness control with enough range at the upper end can often be used to set an old CRT to near-original brightness. The *cold cathode ray tubes (CCRTs)* used to backlight FPDs also dim as they age, but generally fail completely before reduced brightness becomes a major issue.

Contrast
> Contrast measures the difference in luminance between the brightest and dimmest portions of an image, and is expressed as a ratio. The ability to display a high-contrast image is an important aspect of image quality, particularly for text. An average CRT monitor may have a contrast ratio of 200:1, and a superb CRT 250:1. An inexpensive FPD may have a contrast ratio of 200:1, and a superb FPD 500:1. In other words, even an inexpensive FPD may have a better contrast ratio than an excellent CRT monitor.

Usability in bright environments
> Even good flat-screen CRTs are subject to objectionable reflections when used in bright environments, such as having the screen facing a window. Good FPDs are much superior in this respect. Short of direct sunlight impinging on the screen, a good FPD provides excellent images under any lighting conditions.

Displays

Size and weight

A typical CRT is at least as deep as its nominal screen size. For example, a 17-inch CRT is often 17 inches or more from front to back. Large CRTs may be difficult to fit physically in the available space. Conversely, FPDs are quite shallow. The panel itself typically ranges from 1.5 to 3 inches deep, and even with the base most FPDs are no more than 7 to 8 inches deep. Also, where a large CRT may weigh 50 to 100 pounds or more, even large FPDs are quite light. A typical 15-inch FPD might weigh 12 pounds, a 17-inch unit 15 pounds, and even a 20-inch unit may weigh less than 25 pounds. That small size and weight means that it's possible to desk- or wall-mount an FPD with relatively inexpensive mounting hardware, compared to the large, heavy, expensive mounting hardware needed for CRTs.

 Stated FPD display sizes are accurate. For example, a 15-inch FPD has a display area that actually measures 15 inches diagonally. CRT sizes, on the other hand, are nominal because they specify the diagonal measurement of the entire CRT, part of which is covered by the bezel. For example, a nominal 17-inch CRT might have a display area that actually measures 16.0 inches diagonally. A couple of lawsuits several years ago convinced CRT makers to begin stating the usable size of their monitors. This is stated as *VIS* (*viewable image size* or *visible image size*), and is invariably an inch or so smaller than the nominal size.

This VIS issue has given rise to the belief that a 15-inch FPD is equivalent to a 17-inch CRT, a 17-inch FPD to a 19-inch CRT, and so on. In fact, that's not true. The image size of a typical 17-inch CRT is an inch or so larger than that of a 15-inch FPD, as is the image size of a 19-inch CRT relative to a 17-inch FPD.

Power consumption

A typical 17-inch or 19-inch CRT consumes 100 to 125 watts while operating. A typical 15-inch FPD consumes 35 watts, a typical 17-inch FPD 50 watts, and a typical 19-inch FPD 70 watts. At 20% to 60% the power consumption of a typical CRT, FPDs reduce electricity bills directly by consuming less power, and indirectly by reducing heating loads on air conditioning systems.

FPDs also have many drawbacks relative to CRT monitors. Note that not all FPDs suffer from all of these flaws, that newer models are less likely than older models to suffer from any particular flaw, and that inexpensive models are much more likely than premium models to suffer from these flaws, both in number and in degree.

Cost

The primary downside of FPDs is their hideously high cost. For example, for the $300 cost of a good entry-level 15-inch FPD, you could buy *two* good 17-inch CRT monitors or one excellent 19-inch CRT monitor, either of which provides both a larger display area and better display quality than the entry-level FPD. This is one area in which newer, better FPD models suffer much more than older, less-capable models because a good new FPD isn't cheap.

Don't expect the price of FPDs to drop anytime soon. Throughout 2002, display manufacturers and panel manufacturers sold FPDs near or even below cost to gain market share. In 2003, the need for better margins forced manufacturers to begin increasing prices. Accordingly, an FPD that sold for $400 in early 2003 was by July 2003 selling for $500 or thereabouts. We expect these higher prices to stabilize, but do not expect any significant price reductions in the next year or so.

Fixed resolution

FPDs are designed to operate at exactly one resolution, which is nearly always 1024×768 for a 14-inch or 15-inch FPD and 1280×1024 for a 17-inch or 19-inch FPD. Although you *can* run an FPD at a resolution lower than it was designed to use, you don't want to. Your choices are to have a sharp image that occupies only a portion of the FPD screen, or to use pixel extrapolation, which results in a full-screen image, but with significantly degraded image quality.

Backlight failure

A typical FPD uses an array of four CCRTs, which are similar to fluorescent tubes and provide the backlight without which the image cannot be seen. In early FPDs, the CCRTs often rated at as little as 10,000 hours of life. That sounds like a long time until you realize that if you leave such a display on 24 hours a day, the rated lifetime of the tubes is only about 417 days. And, of course, components do sometimes fail before their rated lifetime has expired, and the presence of four tubes quadruples the likelihood of an early failure. The upshot was that early FPDs were often warranted for three years, but with only a one-year warranty on the CCRTs. Many people found that these early models failed within that one-year period or shortly thereafter. That was disastrous because early 17-inch FPDs cost $2,000 or more and could not be repaired. Instead, for all practical purposes, they had to be remanufactured at a cost that was typically one-half to two-thirds the cost of a new display.

The situation is somewhat better with recent-model FPDs. Most manufacturers now use upgraded CCRTs that are rated for at least 25,000 hours, and better models use CCRTs rated for 50,000 hours. Also, although some current FPD models have been redesigned to allow the CCRTs to be replaced without remanufacturing the entire unit, replacing a backlight properly is a finicky job, even for the manufacturer. Accordingly, nearly all FDP manufacturers replace the entire unit rather than attempting to replace the CCRTs. However the job is done, replacing the CCRTs out of warranty is an expensive repair, even assuming that replacement parts are still available when your unit needs to be repaired. Be very conscious of the rated CCRT lifetime and warranty terms for any FPD you buy. Look for at least a three-year warranty that covers parts and labor on all components, specifically including the CCRTs.

Poor display of fast-motion video

Unlike phosphor pixels, which can be turned on or off almost instantly, transistorized FPD pixels have a rise time and fall time which may be noticeable when the screen displays fast-action video. On inexpensive FPDs, this may be noticeable as a "smearing" effect during operations as undemanding as dragging a window to another location. More expensive FPD units deal with this problem better, but even the best of the current FPD units are not fast enough to deal with demanding fast-motion video such as 3D gaming.

Limited viewing angle

CRTs present essentially the same image quality regardless of viewing angle. Conversely, FPDs present their best image quality only within a relatively small viewing angle, although better FPD units have larger viewing angles. When comparing viewing angles, make sure you're comparing apples to apples. Some manufacturers specify total angles, whereas others specify only half-angles from the perpendicular. For example, one manufacturer might specify a viewing angle of 80 degrees above and below the centerline, while another might specify a total angle of 120 degrees. The first display, of course, has a total viewing angle of 160 degrees—80 above and 80 below the centerline—which is 40 degrees greater than the second display, but that may not be clear. Note that some FPDs specify different horizontal and vertical viewing angles.

Color shifting

Most graphic artists we've spoken to refuse to use FPDs because the appearance of colors and the relationship between colors change depending on the viewing angle. This problem is particularly acute with inexpensive FPDs, although even premium units exhibit it at least to some extent. The newest, most-expensive FPD models, such as the Hitachi S-IPS units, minimize this problem to the extent that most people will not notice it, but those who insist on accurate color reproduction will likely still prefer high-end CRT monitors.

Pixel defects

An FPD panel is manufactured as a monolithic item that contains on the close order of 1 million pixels. Even though current manufacturing processes are quite good, many FPD panels have one or a few defective pixels. These defective pixels may be always-on (white), always-off (black), or, rarely, some color. People vary in their reaction to defective pixels. Many people won't even notice a few defective pixels, while others, once they notice a defective pixel, seem to be drawn to that pixel to the exclusion of everything else. Most manufacturer warranties specifically exclude some number of defective pixels, typically between five and 10, although the number may vary with display size and, sometimes, with the location of the defective pixels. As long as the display has that number or fewer defective pixels, the manufacturer considers the display to meet its standards. You may or may not find it acceptable.

Image persistence

Image persistence causes an image that has been displayed for a long time to remain as a ghost-like second image, similar to the burn-in problem on old monochrome monitors. This effect, although it is not permanent, can be quite disconcerting, particularly if you are working with images rather than text. This problem is much more common with older and inexpensive FPDs than with high-end current models.

Flat color rendering

Although the contrast and brightness of recent high-end FPDs are excellent, most FPDs provide subjectively less-vibrant color than a good CRT monitor. This is particularly evident in the darkest and lightest ranges, where the tones seem to be compressed, which limits subtle gradations between light tones or dark tones that are readily evident on a good CRT. Also, many FPDs seem to add a color cast to what should be neutral light or dark tones. For example, dark neutral tones may appear shifted toward the blue (cooler) or red (warmer) ranges. Again, this problem is less prevalent in high-quality, expensive FPDs than in entry-level units, and is also more likely to occur if you are using an analog interface versus a digital interface.

Choosing a Flat-Panel Display

If you have weighed the trade-offs carefully and decided that an FPD is right for you, use the following guidelines when choosing one:

- Regard TFT as a minimum. STN panels are not acceptable for desktop use.

- Current FPDs are available in analog-only, digital-only, and hybrid analog/digital models. Analog input is acceptable on 15-inch models running 1024×768, but on 17-inch models running 1280×1024, analog video noise becomes an issue. At that level of resolution, analog noise isn't immediately obvious to most users, but if you use the display for long periods the difference between using a display with a clean digital signal and one with a noisy analog signal will affect you on almost a subconscious level. At 1024×768, we regard an analog signal as acceptable. At 1280×1024, we regard a digital signal as very desirable but not essential for most users. Above 1280×1024, we regard digital signaling as essential.

- Insist on full 24-bit color support. Most current FPDs support true 24-bit color, allocating one full byte to each of the three primary colors, which allows 256 shades of each color and a total of 16.7 million colors to be displayed. Many early FPDs and some inexpensive current models support only 6 bits per color, for a total of 18-bit color. These models use extrapolation to simulate full 24-bit color support, which results in poor color quality. If a monitor is advertised as "24-bit compatible," that's probably good reason to look elsewhere. Bizarrely, many FPDs that do support true 24-bit color don't bother to mention it in their spec sheets, while many that support only 18-bit color trumpet the fact that they are "24-bit compatible."

- Most FPD makers produce two or three series of FPDs. Entry-level models are often analog-only and use standard TFT panels. Midrange models usually accept analog or digital inputs, and may use enhanced TFT panels. Professional models may be analog/digital hybrids or digital-only, and use enhanced TFT panels with IPS or MDVA. Choose an entry-level TFT model only if you are certain that you will never use the display for anything more than word processing, web browsing, and similarly undemanding tasks. If you need a true CRT-replacement display, choose a midrange or higher enhanced TFT model. For the highest possible image quality, choose a high-end model that supports IPS and is made by a top-tier manufacturer.

- Decide what panel size and resolution are right for you. Keep in mind that when you choose a specific FPD model, you are also effectively choosing the resolution that you will always use on that display.

- Verify the rated CCRT life. For an entry-level FPD that will not be used heavily, a 25,000-hour CCRT life is marginally acceptable. If you will use the FPD heavily, insist on CCRTs rated at 50,000 hours.

- Buy the FPD locally if possible. Regardless of whether you buy locally, insist on a no-questions-asked return policy. FPDs are more variable than CRT monitors, in terms of both unit-to-unit variation and usability with a particular graphics adapter. This is particularly important if you are using an analog interface. Some analog FPDs simply don't play nice with some analog graphics adapters. Also, FPDs vary from unit to unit in how many defective pixels they have and where they are located. You might prefer a unit with five defective pixels near the edges and corners rather than a unit with only one or two defective pixels located near the center of the screen.

- In return for the higher price you pay at a local store, ask them to endorse the manufacturer's warranty—that is, to agree that if the FPD fails, you can bring it back to the store for a replacement rather than dealing with the hassles of returning the FPD to the manufacturer.

- If possible, test the exact FPD you plan to buy (not a floor sample) before you buy it. Ideally, in particular, if you will use the analog interface, you should test the FPD with your own system, or at least with a system that has a graphics adapter identical to the one you plan to use. We'd go to some extremes to do this, including carrying our desktop system down to the local store. But if that isn't possible for some reason, still insist on seeing the actual FPD you plan to buy running. That way, you can at least determine if there are defective pixels in locations that bother you.

- Decide which models to consider (but not the specific unit you buy) based on specifications. Any FPD you consider should provide at least the following:

Controls
> Auto Adjust, Brightness, Contrast, Horizontal Position, Vertical Position, Phase, Clock, Color Temperature, RGB Color Adjustments, Saturation, Hue, Recall Default Settings, and Save Custom Settings.

Warranty
> Inexpensive FPDs may have a one-year parts and labor warranty, which is inadequate. Inexpensive models may instead have a three-year warranty on parts and labor, but warrant the CCRTs for only one year. In effect, that's just a one-year warranty with window dressing because the CCRTs are the one component that is by far the most likely to fail. Insist on a three-year parts and labor warranty that covers all parts, including CCRTs. If the manufacturer offers an extended warranty that covers all parts, consider buying that warranty.

Other specifications vary according to FPD size. For 15-inch models, the minimum specifications for an analog FPD are listed with preferable values for an analog/digital FPD in parentheses. For 17-inch and larger models, although analog-only models are available, we do not recommend those and so list only minimum specifications for a digital FPD:

15 inches

> TFT flat panel; 15-pin VGA analog connector (15-pin analog, DVI-D, S-video, and RGB composite connectors); pixel pitch, 0.297 mm; contrast ratio, 300:1 (500:1); brightness, 200 nit typical (300 nit typical); maximum resolution 1024×768 at 60 Hz or 75 Hz for analog (1024×768 at 60 Hz or 75Hz for analog and 1024×768 at 60 Hz for digital); viewing angle 120 degrees horizontal by 85 degrees vertical (130 degrees by 110 degrees); autosync range 31.5 to 60 KHz horizontal and 56 to 75 Hz vertical (same); video clock frequency 80 MHz (same); rise time 40 ms (25 ms); fall time 40 ms (25ms). As of July 2003, a 15-inch FPD meeting the minimum specifications can be purchased for about $350. One meeting the higher specifications costs about $475.

17 inches and larger

> TFT flat panel; DVI-D connector; pixel pitch, 0.264 mm; contrast ratio, 400:1; brightness, 250 nit typical; maximum resolution 1280×1024 at 60 Hz digital; viewing angle 150 degrees horizontal by 140 degrees vertical; autosync range 24 to 80 KHz horizontal and 56 to 75 Hz vertical; video clock frequency 135 MHz; rise time 25 ms; fall time 25ms. As of July 2003, a 17-inch FPD meeting these minimum specifications can be purchased for about $475, and a 19-inch unit for less than $800.

• Choose the specific FPD you buy based on how it looks to you. Comparing specifications helps narrow the list of candidates, but nothing substitutes for actually looking at the image displayed by the FPD. Some people like all FPDs, some dislike all FPDs, and some have strong preferences for one or another brand of FPD.

In FPDs, the best choices are more limited than for CRT monitors. We consider the first tier in FPDs to include only Hitachi and Fujitsu, with Samsung straddling the low first-tier/high second-tier boundary.

There is a distinct difference in image quality between entry-level and professional models, even those from top-tier makers. For example, the $325 Hitachi CML152 is one of the best entry-level 15-inch FPDs available, and yet we (and Hitachi) regard its image quality as suitable only for such undemanding tasks as word processing, web browsing, and similar general duties. Where image quality is critical, such as with desktop publishing, CAD/CAM, or imaging, a professional model is the minimum to consider, and you may well decide that a CRT monitor is preferable.

Installing and Configuring a Display

Physically installing a CRT monitor or FPD requires only connecting its video cable to the video adapter and plugging the monitor into the wall receptacle. The steps required to adjust the CRT monitor or FPD for best image quality vary according to the specific monitor you use. See the monitor manual for specific instructions.

We recommend using DisplayMate (see Chapter 2) when you install a new monitor or change video settings. In our experience, most monitors are not set for best image quality. Most people either use the default manufacturer settings or make a few arbitrary changes to brightness and contrast and let it go at that. Unless you've used DisplayMate to optimize it, chances are your monitor could be displaying a better picture than it is right now.

The steps required to configure the video adapter to use the monitor optimally vary by operating system, as described in the following sections.

Configuring a Display Under Linux

The setup utility in recent Linux distributions probes the video adapter and display to determine their capabilities and automatically configures optimum video settings. Setup prompts you to confirm the hardware it detects and to choose display settings such as resolution and color depth. To change the display type, log on as root and run Xconfigurator or whatever equivalent GUI utility your distribution provides. For example, the Mandrake Control Center, shown in Figure 16-4, allows you to select among hundreds of standard displays.

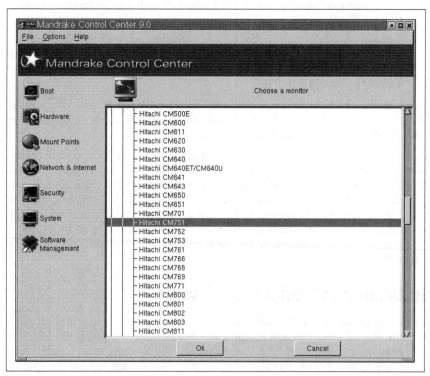

Figure 16-4. Using Mandrake Control Center to reconfigure display type

If your display is not listed, you can define a custom display type. Before you do that, check the manual to determine the combinations of resolution and refresh frequency that the monitor can support. For a digital FPD, also take color depth into account. Choose the optimum combination for your needs, define the display properly, and then configure the video adapter to use the settings you chose (see Chapter 15).

 If you define a custom display type, Linux assumes you have specified the correct parameters for the display, so you must be very careful to enter accurate values for horizontal and vertical synchronization frequencies. If you choose video settings that require more bandwidth than the display can handle, using those settings for even a few seconds may physically damage or destroy the display.

Configuring a Display Under Windows 9X/2000/XP

Windows 9X/2000/XP detects Plug-and-Play monitors and automatically configures the correct settings for them, both when that monitor was present during Setup and, at the next restart, when you install a new Plug-and-Play monitor. For non-Plug-and-Play monitors, Windows uses the Standard Monitor, which displays only standard VGA resolution. Monitor type is configured from Display Properties → Settings → Advanced → Monitor. Changing monitor type manually uses the same Update Device Driver Wizard described in Chapter 15, but the search options are less useful for monitors than adapters.

Windows enables Automatically detect Plug & Play monitors by default. With some display adapters, enabling this setting causes the monitor to flicker during detection each time the system starts. This is harmless, but some people find it disconcerting. If that's the case, once your monitor is installed properly you can safely clear this checkbox.

Windows also enables Reset display on suspend/resume by default. This setting causes Windows to send a reset to the monitor each time you resume from Suspend mode. This causes annoying flickering with most video adapters, but disabling it can cause problems with some monitors, including inability to resume because the monitor never "wakes up" from Suspend mode. If you decide to disable this function and this problem occurs, the only option is to restart the computer and re-enable this setting. Note that even with this setting enabled, some configurations fail to resume from Suspend mode. If that occurs, the only solution we know of is to disable power management for video functions.

If Windows does not detect the monitor model (or detects the wrong model), use the Update Device Driver Wizard to select the proper monitor model from among those supported by Windows or to install a driver provided by the monitor manufacturer.

Note that we refer to monitor "drivers" only for convenience. In fact, there is no such thing as a monitor driver in the same sense as a driver for a video adapter. The monitor "driver" is simply an information file that tells Windows the capabilities of that monitor—e.g., what refresh rates it supports at a given resolution—which allows Windows to choose optimal settings for that monitor for the video card in use.

Troubleshooting Display Problems

Troubleshooting CRT monitors versus FPDs begins with similar steps, but diverges due to the differing natures of the two display types. The first trouble-shooting steps are similar for either display type: power down the system and display and then power them back up; make sure the power cable is connected and that the outlet has power; verify that the signal cable is connected firmly to both video adapter and display and that there are no bent pins; verify that the video adapter is configured properly for the display; try the problem display on a known-good system, or try a known-good display on the problem system; and so on. Once you've tried the "obvious" troubleshooting steps, if the problem persists, the next steps you take depend on the type of display. The following sections cover basic troubleshooting for CRT monitors and FPDs.

Troubleshooting CRT Monitors

Monitors seldom fail outright without obvious signs, such as a loud snap or a strong odor of burning electrical components. Most monitor problems are really problems with the power, video adapter, cable, or hardware/software settings. To eliminate the monitor as a possible cause, connect the suspect monitor to a known-good system, or connect a known-good monitor to the suspect system.

If the monitor is the problem, it is often not worth repairing. If the monitor is out of warranty, parts and labor may cost more than buying a new monitor, which also gives you better specs and a warranty. About the only monitors we'd even consider repairing out of warranty are high-end 19-inch and 21-inch models, and even there the economics are dubious.

Even if the monitor is in warranty, the shipping costs may exceed the value of the monitor. For example, shipping a monitor both ways can easily cost $75 or more. If that monitor is a year-old 17-inch model, you're probably better off spending $150 on a new 17-inch monitor than paying $75 to fix the old one. Monitors have many components, all of which age together. Fixing one is no guarantee that another won't fail shortly. In fact, that happens more often than not in our experience.

Never disassemble a monitor. At best, you'll likely destroy the monitor. At worst, it may destroy you. Like televisions, monitors use extremely high voltages internally, and have large capacitors that store that energy for days or even weeks after the monitor is unplugged. Robert once literally burned a screwdriver in half when working inside a color television that had been unplugged for several days. Also, the large, fragile tube may implode, scattering glass fragments like a hand grenade. People who repair monitors and televisions for a living treat them with great respect, and so should you. If you must repair a monitor, take it to someone who knows what he is doing. You have been warned.

Here are some common monitor problems:

Monitor displays no image
Check the obvious things first. Verify the monitor is plugged in (and that the receptacle has power), the video cable is connected to the video card, the computer and monitor are turned on, and the brightness and contrast settings are set to the middle of their range. If none of these steps solves the problem, your monitor, video card, or video cable may be bad. Check the suspect monitor on a known-good system or a known-good monitor on the problem system.

If you have ACPI or APM power management enabled, it may be causing the problem. Some systems simply refuse to wake up once power management puts them to sleep. We have seen such systems survive a hardware reset without restoring power to the monitor. To verify this problem, turn off power to the system and monitor and then turn them back on. If the monitor then displays an image, check the power management settings in your BIOS and operating system and disable them if necessary.

Monitor displays only a thin horizontal line or a pinpoint at the center
This is a hardware problem. The flyback transformer or high-voltage circuitry is failing or has failed. Take the monitor to be repaired, or replace it.

Monitor flashes one color intermittently, even when the screen is blanked
This is a hardware problem with one of the electron guns. Take the monitor to be repaired, or replace it. This problem may also manifest as a strong color cast during normal operation that is not correctable using the normal color balance controls.

Monitor snaps, crackles, or pops when powered up, or emits a strong electrical odor
Catastrophic monitor failure is imminent. The noises are caused by high-voltage arcing, and the smell is caused by burning insulation. Unplug the monitor from the wall before it catches fire, literally.

Monitor emits a very high-pitched squeal
There are two likely causes. First, you may be driving the monitor beyond its design limits. Some monitors display a usable image at resolutions and/or refresh rates higher than they are designed to use, but under such abuse the

Displays

expected life of the monitor is shortened dramatically, perhaps to minutes. To correct this problem, change video settings to values that are within the monitor's design specifications. Second, the power receptacle may be supplying voltage lower than the monitor requires. To correct this problem, connect the monitor to a different circuit or to a UPS or power conditioner that supplies standard voltage regardless of input voltage.

Monitor displays some colors incorrectly or not at all

This is usually a minor hardware problem. The most likely cause is that the signal cable is not connected tightly to the monitor and/or video card, causing some pins to make contact intermittently or not at all. Verify that no pins are loose, bent, or missing on the cable or the connectors on the monitor and video card, and then tighten the cable at both ends. If that doesn't fix the problem, open the computer, remove the video card, and reseat it fully.

Another possible cause is that some hardware DVD decoder cards "steal" one color (usually magenta) and use it to map the DVD video signal onto the standard video signal. Short of replacing the DVD decoder card with another model that doesn't do this, the options are to live with the problem or to connect the monitor directly to the video card for normal operations and connect the monitor to the DVD decoder card only when you want to watch a DVD. Alternatively, consider removing the DVD decoder card. If your current video adapter includes hardware DVD support, or if you upgrade to such an adapter, you don't need a DVD decoder card.

Image rolls or a horizontal line scrolls constantly down the screen

The most likely cause is that the monitor is receiving inadequate power. Connect it to a different circuit or to a backup power supply that provides correct voltage regardless of fluctuations in main voltage.

Image flickers

The most likely cause is that the refresh rate is set too low. Change the refresh rate to at least 75 Hz. Flicker also results from interaction with fluorescent lights, which operate on 60 Hz AC and can heterodyne visually with the monitor. This can occur at 60 Hz (which is far too low a refresh rate anyway), but can also occur at 120 Hz. If you're running at 120 Hz refresh and experience flicker, either use incandescent lighting or reset the refresh rate to something other than 120 Hz.

Image is scrambled

The video card settings are likely outside the range supported by the monitor, particularly if you have just installed the monitor or have just changed video settings. To verify this, restart the system in VGA mode. If the system displays a VGA image properly, change your display settings to something supported by the monitor.

Image displays rectilinearly, but is incorrectly sized or aligned on screen

Most modern monitors can display signals at many different scan frequencies, but this doesn't mean that the monitor will necessarily automatically display different signals at full screen and properly aligned. Use the monitor controls to adjust the size and alignment of the image.

Image displays other than rectilinearly (trapezoid, parallelogram, barrel, or pincushion)

Depending on the monitor, video card, and video settings, this may be normal behavior, adjustable using the monitor controls. If the distortion is beyond the ability of the controls to correct, the problem may be with the video card, the monitor, or the driver. First try changing video settings. If the problem persists at several settings, move that monitor to a different system (or use a different video card) to determine whether the problem is caused by the monitor or video card. Repair or replace the faulty component.

Image wavers or shimmers periodically or constantly

This is usually caused by RF interference from another electrical or electronic device, particularly one that contains a motor. Make sure such devices are at least 3 feet from the monitor. Note that such interference can sometimes penetrate typical residential and office walls, so if the monitor is close to a wall, check the other side. Such image problems can also be caused by interference carried by the power line or by voltage variations in the AC power supply. To eliminate interference, plug the monitor into a surge protector. Better still, plug it into a UPS or power conditioner that supplies clean power at constant voltage.

Colors are "off" or smearing appears in some areas

The monitor may need to be degaussed. A monitor that sits in one position for months or years can be affected even by the Earth's very weak magnetic field, causing distortion and other display problems. Exposing a monitor to a strong magnetic field, such as unshielded speakers, can cause more-extreme image problems. Many modern monitors degauss themselves automatically each time you cycle the power, but some have a manual degauss button that you must remember to use. If your monitor has a manual degauss button, use it every month or two. The degaussing circuitry in some monitors has limited power. We have seen monitors that were accidentally exposed to strong magnetic fields, resulting in a badly distorted image. Built-in degaussing did little or nothing. In that case, you can sometimes fix the problem by using a separate degaussing coil, available at Radio Shack and similar stores for a few dollars. We have, however, seen monitors that were so badly "magnet-burned" that even a standalone degaussing coil could not completely eliminate the problem. The moral is, keep magnets away from your monitor, including those in speakers that are not video-shielded.

Troubleshooting Flat-Panel Displays

If you've tried the basic troubleshooting steps and your FPD still doesn't work properly, you may have one or more of the following problems:

No image

If your FPD displays no image at all and you are certain that it is receiving power and video signals, first adjust the brightness and contrast settings to higher values. If that doesn't work, turn off the system and FPD, disconnect the FPD signal cable from the computer, and turn on the FPD by itself. It should display some sort of initialization screen, if only perhaps a "No video signal" message. If nothing lights up and no message is displayed, contact technical support for your FPD manufacturer.

Screen flickers

Unlike CRTs, where increasing the refresh rate always reduces flicker, FPDs have an optimal refresh rate that may be lower than the highest refresh rate supported. For example, a 15-inch FPD operating in analog mode may support 60 Hz and 75 Hz refresh. Although it sounds counterintuitive to anyone whose experience has been with CRTs, reducing the refresh rate from 75 Hz to 60 Hz may improve image stability. Check the manual to determine the optimum refresh rate for your FPD, and set your video adapter to use that rate.

The screen is very unstable

First, try setting the optimal refresh rate as described earlier. If that doesn't solve the problem and you are using an analog interface, there are several possible causes, most of which are due to poor synchronization between the video adapter clock and the display clock, or to phase problems. If your FPD has an auto-adjust, auto-setup, or auto-synchronize option, try using that first. If it doesn't, try adjusting the phase and/or clock settings manually until you have a usable image. If you are using an extension or longer than standard video cable, try connecting the standard video cable that was supplied with the display. Long analog video cables exacerbate sync problems. Also, if you are using a (KVM) switch, particularly a manual model, try instead connecting the FPD directly to the video adapter. Many FPDs are difficult or impossible to synchronize if you use a KVM switch. If you are unable to achieve proper synchronization, try connecting the FPD to a different computer. If you are unable to achieve synchronization on the second computer, the FPD may be defective. Finally, note that some video adapter models simply don't function well with some FPD models.

Poor image

If the screen is displaying a full, stable image, but that image is of poor quality, first verify that the display is not connected through a KVM switch or using an extension cable. If it isn't, connect the display directly to the video adapter using the standard cable. If that is already the case, adjust the brightness, contrast, and focus controls. If you are unable to get a proper image using these controls, the problem is most likely a clock or phase mismatch, which you can cure by taking the steps described in the preceding item.

 The best way to adjust Clock and Phase is to use auto-adjust first. If this does not solve the problem, go to the Windows Start menu and select Shutdown. When the screen goes gray and the Windows Shutdown dialog appears, leave that dialog on screen, but ignore it. Use the gray screen to adjust Clock and Phase manually. Any problems with Clock and Phase and any changes you make to the Clock and Phase settings are very apparent on the gray screen. Although we have never run an FPD under Linux, our editor wonders if the unadorned X server (no window manager) might serve the same purpose. It displays a crosshatch pattern; if you are at the text console, you can generally start it just by running the command X and exit it with Ctrl-Alt-Backspace.

Always adjust Clock first. Clock is usually not a problem if you have used the auto-adjust feature of your monitor, but if you do have Clock problems, they will be evident as large vertical bars on your screen. Tweak the Clock setting until those bars disappear. Then adjust Phase. Phase problems are evident as thin black lines running horizontally across the screen. Adjust Phase until the lines disappear or are minimized.

Not all video cards synchronize perfectly with flat panels. The gray Shutdown screen exaggerates the problem, so do not worry if very tiny movements are visible after you've adjusted Clock and Phase as well as possible. After you've set the Clock and Phase controls for the best image possible on the gray screen, cancel the Shutdown and the image should be optimized.

Signal out of range message

Your video card is supplying a video signal at a bandwidth that is above or below the ability of your FPD to display. Reset your video parameters to be within the range supported by the FPD. If necessary, temporarily connect a different display or start Windows in Safe Mode and choose standard VGA in order to change video settings.

Text or lines are shadowed or blocky

This generally occurs when you run an FPD at other than its native resolution. For example, if you have a 15-inch 1024×768 FPD but have your display adapter set to 800×600, your FPD will attempt to display those 800×600 pixels at full screen size, which physically corresponds to 1024×768 pixels. The extrapolation necessary to fill the screen with the smaller image results in artifacts such as blocky or poorly rendered text, jaggy lines, and so on. Either set your video adapter to display the native resolution of the FPD, or set your FPD to display the lower-resolution image using less than the entire screen.

Some pixels are always on or always off

This is a characteristic of today's FPDs. Other than by pure chance, any FPD you buy will have some small number of defective pixels. Manufacturers set a threshold number below which they consider the display acceptable. That number varies with the manufacturer, the model, and the size of the display, but is typically in the range of five to 10 pixels. Nothing can be done to fix the problem. The manufacturer will not replace the FPD under warranty unless the number of defective pixels exceeds the threshold number. This is simply something you have to learn to live with if you want to use an FPD.

A persistent after-image exists

Again, this is a characteristic of current FPDs. The after-image occurs when the display has had the same image in one place for a long time. The after-image may persist even after you turn off the display. More-expensive models are less prone to this problem than entry-level models, but all FPDs exhibit the problem to some extent. It is simply another characteristic of FPDs that you must learn to live with.

Moving images blur, smear, or ghost

The transistor-based pixels in an FPD respond less quickly than the phosphors in a CRT. The least-expensive FPDs exhibit this problem even with

Displays

relatively slow image movement, as when you drag a window. Better FPDs handle moderately fast image movement without ghosting, but exhibit the problem on fast-motion video, such as DVD movies. The best FPDs can handle even fast-motion video reasonably well, although no FPD handles it as well as a CRT. The only real solution to this problem is to upgrade your FPD to a model with faster rise/fall times. The fastest currently available FPDs have 15 ms rise/fall times, which are adequate for anything short of 3D gaming.

Dim image

Use the brightness control to increase image brightness. If you have set brightness to maximum and the image is still too dim, contact the display manufacturer. The CCRTs used to backlight the screen have a finite lifetime and may begin to dim as they near the end of their life.

Image is only partially backlit

One or more of the CCRTs that provide the backlight have failed. Contact the display manufacturer.

Horizontal or vertical lines appear

If one or multiple horizontal and/or vertical lines appear on the display, first power-reset the computer and display. If the lines persist, run the auto-setup function of your display. If that does not solve the problem, power down the system and display, remove the video cable, and verify that the video plugs and jacks on both computer and display ends do not have broken or bent pins. Even if all appears correct, try a different video cable. If the problem persists, contact the display manufacturer.

Our Picks

Here are the displays we recommend. For our latest recommendations, detailed by brand and model, visit our web site, which is listed below.

15- and 17-inch budget CRT displays

NEC AccuSync. NEC is a first-tier maker that happens to have some very aggressively priced low-end models. Image quality and build quality are a step above monitors from second- and third-tier makers that sell for only a bit less. NEC provides a three-year warranty on its low-end models, which is a good indication in itself of their quality (*http://www.necmitsubishi.com*).

19-inch and larger CRT displays

Hitachi or NEC. We've used hundreds of first-tier monitors over the last 15 years, and of that group we generally prefer Hitachi monitors, with NEC a close second choice. Hitachi stopped producing its own CRTs in 2002 and now buys tubes from Samsung, but Hitachi quality control remains top-notch. Hitachi monitors are extremely reliable and competitively priced, and have simply superb image quality. NEC displays are also excellent, and some people prefer them to Hitachi models. Comparable Samsung and ViewSonic monitors are excellent products, but when we have a choice we specify Hitachi or NEC. If you want a rugged, reliable CRT with top-notch image quality, we recommend you do the same (*http://www.hitachidisplays.com* or *http://www.necmitsubishi.com*).

Flat-panel display

Hitachi or Fujitsu. We consider Hitachi and Fujitsu the first tier in FPD manufacturers, with Samsung a half step behind. Whether you're looking for an entry-level or professional FPD of any size, we think a Hitachi or Fujitsu model is the best bet. Fujitsu models are excellent, but they are more difficult to find at retail than Hitachi models. If you can't find a suitable Hitachi or Fujitsu model, you are likely to be happy with one of the better Samsung models (*http://www.hitachidisplays.com, http://www.fujitsu.com*, or *http:// www.samsung.com*).

In case you're wondering, neither Hitachi nor NEC/Mitsubishi has ever given us so much as a free mousepad or coffee cup. We just really like their displays.

If you work with multiple computers on your desk, buying a monitor for each is expensive and you soon run out of desktop real estate. Using a KVM switch allows you to share one keyboard, monitor, and mouse among multiple systems. For example, Robert works surrounded by nine computers. His main system has a dedicated 19-inch Hitachi monitor, but the other eight computers share two keyboards, two mice, and two monitors among them, in two groups of four. Here are the KVM switches we recommend:

Basic KVM switch

Belkin OmniCube. We've used a lot of KVM switches, both manual and electronic, and this is our favorite for home and small-business users. The Belkin OmniCube switch comes in two-port and four-port versions. Yes, you can buy a manual KVM switch for much less, but these provide very poor video quality, particularly when used with the cheap cables usually sold with them, and in some cases may actually damage the monitor. The Belkin OmniCube works well for us. Robert uses a Belkin OmniCube (with premium Belkin cables) on his desk to share his secondary monitor among four secondary computers (*http://www.belkin.com*).

 Like any electronic KVM switch, the OmniCube may be sensitive to the mouse you use (the Belkin didn't like our Microsoft Explorer oversized "red-light" mouse), so if you have problems, be sure to try a different mouse before concluding that the unit is at fault.

Enhanced KVM switch

Belkin OmniView. The OmniCube is perfect for homes and small businesses, but if you need more features or more ports look at the Belkin OmniView series. The OmniView SE is available in two-port and four-port models, which are expandable by stacking units to 8 ports and 16 ports, respectively. The OmniView Pro is available in four-port, eight-port, and 16-port models, which are expandable by stacking units to 64 ports, 128 ports, and 256 ports, respectively. The Pro models also add on-screen display and other features that are useful to someone who manages many computers from one console. Robert uses a four-port OmniView Pro on his test bench.

Whatever type of KVM switch you buy, plan to spend a fair amount on cables as well. You'll need one cable set for each connected computer. Those $8 "3-in-1" KVM cable sets sold by many computer stores almost guarantee poor performance, which is to say distorted, flickering, blurred images. Get name-brand cables. A basic Belkin set in a 10-foot length should cost $15 or so. A premium-grade Belkin set, with better shielding, gold-plated connectors, and so on, should cost $30 or so.

For updated recommendations, detailed by brand names and model numbers, visit *http://www.hardwareguys.com/picks/displays.html.*

17

Sound Adapters

Because no one envisioned sound as a business necessity, the only provision early PCs made for sound was a $0.29 speaker driven by a square-wave generator to produce beeps, boops, and clicks sufficient for prompts and warnings. Reproducing speech or music was out of the question. Doing that required an add-on sound card, and those were quick to arrive on the market as people began playing games on their PCs. The early AdLib and Creative Sound Blaster sound cards were primitive, expensive, difficult to install and configure, and poorly supported by the OS and applications. By the early 1990s, however, sound cards had become mainstream items that shipped with most PCs. By 2001 most motherboards included at least basic embedded audio, and by 2003 it was difficult to find a mainstream system or motherboard without good built-in audio.

 Properly, the term *sound card* applies to expansion cards, while *sound adapter* or *audio adapter* applies to any component used to provide PC audio, whether as an expansion card or as a device embedded on the motherboard. But like most people, we use these terms interchangeably.

With a sound adapter and appropriate software, a PC can perform various tasks, including:

- Playing audio CDs, either directly or from compressed digital copies of the CD soundtracks stored as MP3 or Ogg Vorbis files on your hard disk

- Playing stereo music, sound effects, and/or voice prompts in games, education, training, and presentation software, as well as for operating system prompts, warnings, and other events

- Capturing dictation to a document file, adding voice annotations to documents, or controlling applications using voice/speech recognition software

- Supporting audio conferencing and telephony across a LAN or the Internet

- Supporting text-to-speech software that allows the PC to "read" text aloud, aiding children who cannot read and people who are visually impaired
- Creating and playing back music using MIDI software and hardware

This chapter describes what you need to know to choose, install, configure, troubleshoot, and use a sound card effectively.

PC Audio Types

Sound cards support two categories of audio, which are detailed in the following sections:

Waveform audio
> *Waveform audio* files, also called simply *sound files*, store actual audio data. When you record waveform audio, the sound card encodes the analog audio data in digital format and stores it as a file. When you play waveform audio, the sound card reads the digital audio data contained in the file and converts it to analog audio, which is then reproduced on speakers or headphones. Waveform audio files can store any type of audio, including speech, singing, instrumental music, and sound effects. The playback quality of waveform audio depends primarily on how much detail was captured in the original recording and how much of that data, if any, was lost when compressing the data before storing it on disk. Uncompressed waveform audio files (such as .WAV files) are large, requiring as much as 10 MB per minute of audio stored. Compressed audio files may be 1/20 that size or smaller, although high compression generally results in lower sound quality.

MIDI audio
> Rather than storing actual audio data, *Musical Instrument Digital Interface* (*MIDI*) files store instructions that a sound card can use to create audio on the fly. MIDI audio files store only instrumental music and sound effects, not speech or singing. Originally used almost solely by professional musicians, MIDI is now commonly used by games and other applications for background music and sound effects, so MIDI support has become an important sound card issue. Because MIDI sound is created synthetically by the sound card, playback quality of MIDI files depends both on the quality of the MIDI file itself and on the features and quality of the MIDI support in the sound card. A MIDI file of an orchestral concert, for example, may sound like a child's toy when played by a cheap sound card, but may closely resemble a CD recording when played by a high-end sound card. MIDI audio files are small, requiring only a few KB per minute of audio stored.

Waveform Audio

Waveform audio files are created using a process called *sampling* or *digitizing* to convert analog sound to digital format. Sampling takes periodic snapshots, or samples, of the instantaneous state of the analog signal, encodes the data, and stores the audio in digital form. Just as digital images can be stored at different resolutions according to their intended use, audio data can be stored at different resolutions to trade off sound quality against file size. Five parameters determine the quality of digital sound files and how much space they occupy:

Sample size

Sample size specifies how much data is stored for each sample. A larger sample size stores more information about each sample, contributing to higher sound quality. Sample size is specified as the number of bits stored for each sample. CD audio, for example, uses 16-bit samples, which allow the waveform amplitude to be specified as one of 65,536 discrete values. All sound cards support at least 16-bit samples.

Sampling rate

Sampling rate specifies how often samples are taken. Sampling rate is specified in Hz (Hertz, or cycles/second) or kHz (kilohertz, 1000 Hertz). Higher-frequency data inherently changes more often. Changes that occur between samples are lost, so the sampling rate determines the highest-frequency sounds that can be sampled. Two samples are required to capture a change, so the highest frequency that can be sampled, called the *Nyquist frequency*, is half the sampling rate. For example, a 10,000 Hz sampling rate captures sounds no higher than 5,000 Hz. In practice, the danger is that higher frequencies will be improperly sampled, leading to distortion, so real-world implementations filter the analog signal to cut off audio frequencies higher than some arbitrary fraction of the Nyquist frequency—for example, by filtering all frequencies higher than 4,500 Hz when using a 10,000 Hz sampling rate. CD audio, for example, uses a 44,100 Hz sampling rate, which provides a Nyquist frequency of 22,050 Hz, allowing full-bandwidth response up to ~ 20,000 Hz after filtering. All sound cards support at least 44,100 Hz sampling, and many support the *Digital Audio Tape (DAT)* standard of 48,000 Hz.

Sampling method

Sampling method specifies how samples are taken and encoded. For example, Windows *WAV* files use either *Pulse Coded Modulation (PCM)*, a linear method that encodes the absolute value of each sample as an 8-bit or 16-bit value, or *Adaptive Delta PCM (ADPCM)*, which encodes 4-bit samples based on the differences (delta) between one sample and the preceding sample. ADPCM generates smaller files, but at the expense of reduced audio quality and the increased processor overhead needed to encode and decode the data.

Recording format

Recording format specifies how data is structured and encoded within the file and what means of compression, if any, is used. Common formats, indicated by filename extensions, include *WAV* (Windows audio); *AU* (Sun audio format, commonly used by Unix systems and on the Internet); *AIFF* or *AIF* (Audio Interchange File Format, used by Apple and SGI); *RA* (RealAudio, a proprietary streaming audio format); *MP3* (MPEG-1 Layer 3); and *OGG* (Ogg Vorbis). Some formats use *lossless compression*, which provides lower compression ratios, but allows all the original data to be recovered. Others use *lossy compression*, which sacrifices some less-important data in order to produce the smallest possible file sizes. Some, such as PCM WAV, do not compress the data at all.

Compressed formats, such as MP3 and OGG, may use *fixed bitrate (FBR)* compression (also called *constant bitrate [CBR]* compression), *variable bitrate (VBR)* compression, or both (although not at the same time). FBR compresses each second of source material to the same amount of disk space, regardless of the contents of that material. For example, after FBR compression, 10 seconds of silence occupies the same amount of disk space as 10 seconds of complex chamber music. VBR dynamically varies compression ratio according to the complexity of the material being compressed. For example, after VBR compression, 10 seconds of silence may occupy only a few bytes of disk space, while 10 seconds of chamber music may occupy many kilobytes. VBR typically provides better sound quality than FBR for a given file size because VBR uses space more efficiently.

Either compression type may use selectable compression ratios or a fixed ratio. For example, standard MP3 uses FBR compression, but most MP3 compressors allow you to select among various fixed bitrates, typically from 64 kilobits/second (kb/s) to 320 kb/s. FBR compression is exact. If you compress 100 seconds of audio at 256 kb/s, the resulting file always occupies 25,600 kilobits. Conversely, VBR compression is approximate because compression varies with the complexity of the source material. If you use VBR to compress 100 seconds of audio at a nominal 256 kb/s, the resulting file will probably occupy about 25,600 kilobits, but can be larger or smaller depending on how easily the source material could be compressed.

Some VBR applications use an arbitrary number to specify compression ratio. For example, Ogg Vorbis allows you to specify quality on a scale of 0 through 10, where 0-quality is roughly equivalent to 64 kb/s FBR, 5-quality to 160 kb/s FBR, and 10-quality to 400 kb/s FBR.

 The large size of uncompressed audio files means that most common waveform audio formats use some form of compression. An algorithm used to compress and decompress digital audio data is called a *codec*, short for coder/decoder. Windows 98, for example, includes the following codecs: CCITT G.711 A-Law and μ-Law; DSP Group TrueSpeech; GSM 6.10; IMA ADPCM; Microsoft ADPCM; and Microsoft PCM (which is technically not a codec). You needn't worry about which codec to use when playing audio; the player application automatically selects the codec appropriate for the file being played. When you record audio, the application you use allows you to select from the codecs supported by the format you choose.

Number of channels

Depending on the recording setup, one channel (*monaural* or *mono* sound), two channels (*stereo* sound), or more can be recorded. Additional channels provide audio separation, which increases the realism of the sound during playback. Various formats store one, two, four, or five audio channels. Some formats store only two channels, but with additional data that can be used to simulate additional channels.

Table 17-1 lists the three standard Windows recording modes for PCM WAV, which is the most common uncompressed waveform audio format, and representative MP3 and OGG modes. MP3 at 256 kb/s uses a little more storage than Windows' AM radio mode, but produces sound files that are nearly CD quality.

OGG-3 produces files that average about 17.5% smaller than 128 kb/s MP3 files, but provide superior sound quality. OGG-5 produces files that average about 40% smaller than 256 kb/s MP3 files, but provide comparable sound quality. OGG-10 produces files that average about one-third the size of uncompressed .WAV files, but provide sound quality that to our ears is indistinguishable from the original CD audio, even when played on a high-quality home audio system. MP3 and OGG bitrates are approximate.

Table 17-1. Uncompressed WAV modes versus compressed MP3 and OGG modes

Quality	Sample Size	Rate	Channels	Bytes/min	Compression
Telephone	8-bit	11,025 Hz	1 (mono)	661,500	PCM (1:1)
AM radio	8-bit	22,050 Hz	1 (mono)	1,323,000	PCM (1:1)
CD audio	16-bit	44,100 Hz	2 (stereo)	10,584,000	PCM (1:1)
MP3 (64 kb/s)	16-bit	44,100 Hz	2 (stereo)	~ 500,000	MP3 (~20:1)
MP3 (128 kb/s)	16-bit	44,100 Hz	2 (stereo)	~1,000,000	MP3 (~10:1)
MP3 (256 kb/s)	16-bit	44,100 Hz	2 (stereo)	~2,000,000	MP3 (~5:1)
OGG-0	16-bit	44,100 Hz	2 (stereo)	~ 500,000	OGG (~20:1)
OGG-3	16-bit	44,100 Hz	2 (stereo)	~ 825,000	OGG (~12:1)
OGG-5	16-bit	44,100 Hz	2 (stereo)	~ 1,200,000	OGG (~8:1)
OGG-10	16-bit	44,100 Hz	2 (stereo)	~ 3,000,000	OGG (~3:1)

MIDI Audio

A MIDI file is the digital equivalent of sheet music. Rather than containing actual audio data, a MIDI file contains detailed instructions for creating the sounds represented by that file. And, just as the same sheet music played by different musicians can sound different, the exact sounds produced by a MIDI file depend on which sound card you use to play it.

Three PC MIDI standards exist. The first, General MIDI, is the official standard, actually predates multimedia PCs, and is the oldest and most comprehensive standard. The other two standards are *Basic MIDI* and *Extended MIDI*. Both are Microsoft standards and, despite the name of the latter, both are subsets of the General MIDI standard. In the early days of sound cards, General MIDI support was an unrealistically high target, so many sound cards implemented only one of the Microsoft MIDI subsets. All current sound cards we know of support full General MIDI.

MIDI was developed about 20 years ago, originally as a method to provide a standard interface between electronic music keyboards and electronic sound generators such as Moog synthesizers. A MIDI interface supports 16 channels, allowing up to 16 instruments or groups of instruments (selected from a palette of 128 available instruments) to play simultaneously. MIDI interfaces can be stacked. Some MIDI devices support 16 or more interfaces simultaneously, allowing 256 or more channels.

The MIDI specification defines both a serial communication protocol and the formatting of the MIDI messages transferred via that protocol. MIDI transfers 8-bit data at 31,250 bps over a 5 mA current loop, using optoisolators to electrically isolate MIDI devices from each other. All MIDI devices use a standard 5-pin DIN connector, but the MIDI port on a sound card is simply a subset of the pins on the standard DB-15 gameport connector (see Chapter 21). That means a gameport-to-MIDI adapter is needed to connect a sound card to an external MIDI device such as a MIDI keyboard.

MIDI *messages* are simply a string of ASCII bytes encoded to represent the important characteristics of a musical score, including instrument to be used, note to be played, volume, and so on. MIDI messages usually comprise a status byte followed by one, two, or three data bytes, but a MIDI feature called *Running Status* allows any number of additional bytes received to be treated as data bytes until a second status byte is received. Here are the functions of those byte types:

Status byte

MIDI messages always begin with a *status byte*, which identifies the type of message and is flagged as a status byte by having the high-order bit set to 1. The most significant (high-order) four bits (nibble) of this byte define the action to be taken, such as a command to turn a note on or off or to modify the characteristics of a note that is already playing. The least significant nibble defines the channel to which the message is addressed, which in turn determines the instrument to be used to play the note. Although represented in binary as a 4-bit value between 0 and 15, channels are actually designated 1 through 16.

Data byte

A *data byte* is flagged as such by having its high-order bit set to zero, which limits it to communicating 128 states. What those states represent depends on the command type of the status byte. When it follows a Note On command, for example, the first data byte defines the pitch of the note. Assuming standard Western tuning (A=440 Hz), this byte can assume any of 128 values from C-sharp/D-flat (17.32 Hz) to G (25087.69 Hz). The second data byte specifies *velocity*, or how hard the key was pressed, which corresponds generally to volume, depending on the MIDI device and instrument. The note continues playing until a status byte with a Note Off command for that note is received, although it may, under programmatic control, decay to inaudibility in the interim.

MIDI Synthesis Methods

The process by which sounds cards produce audio output from MIDI input is called *synthesis*. There are three synthesis methods:

FM synthesis

FM synthesis combines multiple sine waves of differing frequency and amplitude to produce a composite wave that resembles the native waveform of the instrument being synthesized. How close that resemblance is depends on the instrument and the quality of the FM synthesizer circuitry, and may vary from reasonably close to only a distant approximation. Even the best FM synthesis sound cards produce artificial-sounding audio, particularly for "difficult" instruments. Until the mid-1990s, most consumer-grade sound cards used FM synthesis, but FM synthesis is now obsolete.

Wavetable synthesis

Wavetable synthesis uses stored waveform audio samples of actual instrument sounds to reproduce music. The sample may be used as is, or modified algorithmically to provide a sound for which no sample is stored. For example, the wavetable may contain a stored sample of an actual violin playing an A note at 1760 Hz. If the MIDI score calls for a violin playing that A note, the sample is used directly. If the MIDI score calls for a violin playing an A note one octave higher (3520 Hz) and that note is not available as a stored sample, the synthesizer creates the 3520 Hz A note based on the data it has stored for the 1760 Hz A note. The quality of wavetable synthesis depends on the number, quality, recording frequency, and compression used for stored samples, and on the quality of the synthesizer hardware. Early wavetable sound cards were limited to the samples stored on their onboard ROM, which was typically 512 KB to 4 MB. Many current wavetable sound cards have, in addition to samples residing on onboard ROM, the ability to use additional samples stored on disk and loaded into main system memory as needed.

Waveguide synthesis

Although good wavetable sound cards produce music quality an order of magnitude better than FM synthesis sound cards, they are still limited by the finite number of stored samples, and so still must simulate much of their output instead of using samples directly. For example, whereas most wavetable sound cards store a total of perhaps 4 MB of samples for all instruments, fully sampling just a piano would require 10 MB or more of samples. That means that some piano sounds must be interpolated from existing samples, which in turn means that the piano emulation is not as good as it might be because interpolated sounds are less realistic than sampled sounds. The latest synthesis method, *waveguide synthesis*, also called *physical modeling synthesis*, creates a virtual model of an instrument and produces sounds based on calculations made against that model. Full waveguide synthesis for all instruments is beyond the hardware capabilities of any current PC. Some current high-end sound cards, however, use waveguide synthesis in conjunction with wavetable synthesis to improve the realism of emulation for some instruments.

Downloadable Sounds

Downloadable sounds (DLS) is an extension to General MIDI that allows customizing the available MIDI sounds by temporarily replacing standard ROM-based MIDI wavetable instrumental sound samples with sound samples loaded from disk. DLS samples can be instrumental sounds, sound effects suitable for games (e.g., lion roars, tire squeals, or machine-gun fire), or even voice clips. In addition to customizing the available sounds, DLS allows software developers to ensure consistency across different sound cards and platforms—for example, by replacing ROM-based piano samples with DLS piano samples to make sure everyone hears the same piano. DLS Level 2 is supported by the DirectMusic component of Microsoft DirectX 7.0 and later running on Windows 95/98/2000/XP, and is used by an increasing number of games, education packages, multimedia encyclopediae, and similar software.

Sound Card Components

The key function of a sound card is playback—accepting a digital data stream or MIDI instructions from the PC and converting them to an analog audio signal that can be reproduced on speakers or headphones. Most sound cards can also do the converse—accept an analog audio signal and convert it to a digital data stream that can be stored on a PC. Sound cards use the following components to support these functions:

Converters
> Sound cards contain at least one *Digital-to-Analog Converter (DAC)* and one *Analog-to-Digital Converter (ADC)* for each of the two stereo channels, and some contain more. A DAC converts a digital audio stream into the analog audio delivered to the Line-out port. An ADC digitizes analog sound received from the Line-in or Microphone port. CD-Audio sound, generally the highest quality supported by sound cards, requires 16-bit resolution. The converters used in better-quality sound cards usually support higher resolution, typically 18- or 20-bit. Some expensive cards, such as the Sound Blaster Audigy 2, use 24-bit resolution for both recording and playback. Resolution sometimes differs between the DAC and ADC. For example, a card might use an 18-bit DAC and a 20-bit ADC. Internal resolution is often higher than that supported by the DAC/ADC, typically 24- or 32-bit.

Sample rate generator
> The *sample rate generator* provides the clock for the converters under the control of the PC. While nothing prevents using arbitrary or continuously variable sample rates, most sample rate generators instead support discrete sample rates, which are usually even fractions of 44,100 Hz and 48,000 Hz. A sample rate generator might support sample rates of 48,000, 44,100, 32,000, 24,000, 22,050, 12,000, 11,025, and 8,000 Hz. Many sound cards support differing rates for record versus playback. For example, a card may support playback rates of 48,000, 44,100, 22,050, 11,025, and 8,000 Hz, but record only at 44,100 Hz. High-end cards may support sampling rates as high as 96 KHz in Dolby Digital 5.1 mode and 192 KHz in stereo mode.

Processor
> The *processor* (also called the *sound generator* or *synthesis engine*) creates analog output from MIDI input by reading, interpolating, and combining wavetable samples into the composite audio waveform represented by the MIDI instructions. Most sound cards use a custom *digital signal processor (DSP)* such as the E-mu Systems EMU10K1 or EMU10K2, or the Crystal/Cirrus Logic CS4630 or CS8420. The processor used directly or indirectly determines several key capabilities of the sound card, including how many MIDI channels, voices, hardware-accelerated sound streams, and so on it supports. DSPs provide useful supplementary capabilities in hardware, such

as reverb and chorus effects, text-to-speech processing, and compression. Because a DSP is programmable, some DSP-based sound cards support related functions, such as faxmodem or telephone answering machine functions.

Connectors

Sound cards typically provide at least the following connectors:

Line-out

Line-out is a line-level (unamplified) stereo output intended to be connected to Line-in on amplified speakers, headphones, home audio equipment, or a tape or DAT recorder. Most sound cards provide one stereo Line-out port, but some provide two mono Line-out ports, designated Left and Right. Sound cards that support four speakers usually have two stereo Line-out ports, one each for front and rear speakers. The PC 99 standard color code for Line-out is lime, although for this and other color codes makers often pay scant attention to the exact hue. The standard icon usually stamped into the card bracket is three concentric circle segments (to represent audio vibrations) with an outward-pointing arrow anchored in the center.

Line-in

Line-in is a line-level stereo input intended to be connected to the Line-out of external analog audio sources such as a CD player or VCR. Some microphones can also be connected to Line-in. The standard color is light blue. The standard icon is the same as for Line-out, but with the arrow head pointing to the center.

Microphone-in

Microphone-in, sometimes labeled *Mic*, is a monaural input that supports inexpensive microphones for recording voice. The standard color is pink, although red is commonly used, and the standard icon resembles a microphone.

MIDI/gameport

MIDI/gameport is a DB-15 connector whose primary purpose is to connect a game controller. However, the standard gameport (see Chapter 21) also supports connecting external MIDI devices such as keyboards and synthesizers. Doing so requires a special octopus cable, available from the manufacturer, which extends the MIDI signals present on the gameport to MIDI-standard 5-pin DIN MIDI-in and MIDI-out connectors, which resemble standard AT keyboard connectors. The gameport should fully support analog and digital game controllers, including force feedback and DirectInput devices. Standard color is gold.

MPC-3 CD-in

Although some recent CD-ROM drives can deliver CD audio digitally across the bus to the sound card, listening to CD audio on most CD-ROM drives requires connecting the line-level Audio-out connector on the back of the CD-ROM drive to the Audio-in connector on the sound card. Older CD-ROM drives and sound cards used a chaotic mix of proprietary and nonstandard connectors, which sometimes made it very hard to find the right cable. Recent CD-ROM drives and sound cards all use a standard cable. The sound card uses a shrouded, keyed, four-contact header-pin MPC-3 connector, often called a Molex or ATAPI connector. The CD-ROM drive uses an unkeyed version of the same connector, sometimes called a Sony connector. *MPC-3 CD-in* is usually color-coded black to differentiate it from other connectors, described next, that use the same physical connector.

Some sound cards also provide some or all of the following connectors:

Speaker-out/Subwoofer
Speaker-out/Subwoofer is an amplified stereo output intended to be connected to unpowered speakers, or to some powered subwoofers that expect a high-level input. Do not use this output to connect to standard powered speakers. Although it will usually work without damaging the speakers or the sound card, sound quality will be noticeably inferior to that provided by the Line-out connector. Standard color is orange.

MPC-3 Aux-in
MPC-3 Aux-in uses the same physical connector as MPC-3 CD-in, described earlier, and is usually color-coded white to differentiate it. This connector accepts any line-level input, although it is most commonly used on systems that already have one CD-ROM drive to connect audio from a second CD-ROM, CD-R(W), or DVD drive.

MPC-3 Modem-in/out
MPC-3 Modem-in/out uses the same physical connector as MPC-3 CD-in and MPC-3 Aux-in, and is usually color-coded green to differentiate it. MPC-3 Modem-in is a line-level audio input/output intended to be connected to a line-level connector on a modem. This allows modem tones to be played through the speakers, and also supports such functions as Internet telephony and audio conferencing via the modem.

Daughtercard connector
Some sound cards include one or more daughtercard connectors, which usually take the form of a large header-pin connector similar to an IDE connector. Daughtercards, which are proprietary to the make and model of sound card, may be used to add wavetable support, to extend ROM-based wavetable samples, or for other similar purposes.

S/PDIF
Sony-Philips Digital InterFace (S/PDIF) is an RCA coax jack that provides a direct digital connection between the sound card and an external device with an S/PDIF jack (typically, a DAT deck). All S/PDIF ports support 48,000 Hz; most support 32,000 Hz; some support lower rates. S/PDIF is a standard feature on most high-end sound cards, and may be an option on midrange sound cards. Some sound cards have both S/PDIF input and output ports, but others have only an S/PDIF output. Because of limited room on the expansion bracket of the sound card, S/PDIF ports are often present as a header connector on the sound card, which uses an extender cable to a cliffhanger bracket where the S/PDIF connectors reside. Some sound cards use a proprietary connector that joins the sound card to a remote head, which often contains S/PDIF connector(s), line-in connector(s), and MIDI connector(s).

CD interface connector

Some older sound cards include interface connector(s) for a CD-ROM drive, which made it easier and cheaper to upgrade older systems to multimedia capability. These connectors may be any of five types: the three proprietary interfaces used by early-model Mitsumi, Panasonic, and Sony CD-ROM drives; a second ATA interface, intended for use on early ATA systems that had only one embedded ATA interface; and/or a SCSI interface. Using any of these interfaces is a bad idea. The proprietary interfaces are used only by CD-ROM drives too old to be usable. The IDE interface is normally slow and conflicts with the second ATA interface present on all modern motherboards. The SCSI interface is slow, probably supports only one SCSI device, and often causes conflicts. Indeed, the presence of any of these connectors indicates that the sound card is so old that it should be replaced.

Amplifier

Early sound cards were intended for use with unamplified speakers, and so included an onboard amplifier. Nearly all modern computer speakers have built-in amplifiers that require only line-level input. Sound card amplifiers usually produce inferior sound because they are inexpensive, underpowered, and poorly shielded, and must operate in the electrically noisy environment inside a PC. Some modern sound cards include an amplifier, primarily for use with devices (such as some powered subwoofers) that expect an amplified rather than line-level signal. A sound card that lacks an amplifier is not necessarily of low quality. In fact, the converse is often true. Many inexpensive sound cards include amplified outputs, and many high-end sound cards do not.

Sound Card Characteristics

Here are the important characteristics of sound cards:

Interface

Discrete sound cards have been made in ISA and PCI versions, but ISA cards are no longer available. All recent sound adapters, embedded or standalone, use PCI. The much smaller bandwidth of ISA limited ISA cards in many respects, including generally requiring that wavetable data be stored locally, placing an upper limit of about 16 on simultaneous sound streams, and making effective 3D audio support impossible. If you encounter an ISA sound card when stripping an older system for spares, pitch the ISA card. It's not worth keeping.

Synthesis type

FM synthesis is no longer used in current sound cards. All current midrange sound cards use wavetable synthesis, and some expensive sound cards use partial waveguide synthesis. The quality and features of wavetable synthesis vary depending on both the processor and the quality and size of the wavetable samples, with more-expensive cards producing better synthesis, as you might expect.

Channels

Each MIDI interface supports 16 channels, each corresponding to one instrument. Low-end sound cards have one MIDI interface, allowing up to 16 instruments to play simultaneously. Midrange and high-end sound cards usually have dual MIDI interfaces, allowing up to 32 simultaneous instruments. Some high-end sound cards, such as the Creative Labs Sound Blaster Live! Platinum, use a triple MIDI interface, which allows up to 48 simultaneous instruments. In general, 16-channel cards are suitable for most uses, 32-channel cards are useful for playing MIDI instrumentals realistically, and 48-channel cards are necessary only for the most complex MIDI environments. It's worth noting that Creative replaced its flagship 48-channel Sound Blaster Live! Platinum with the 32-channel Audigy 2.

Polyphony

Polyphony refers to the ability of a sound card to generate multiple simultaneous voices when playing MIDI. A *voice* corresponds to one note generated by one instrument. Do not confuse number of voices with number of channels. The 16 channels of a standard MIDI interface allow 16 instruments to play simultaneously. However, some instruments require multiple voices. For example, a piano occupies one MIDI channel, but if the musician is playing a single-note melody with one hand and three-note chords as accompaniment with the other hand, that channel requires four voices. A large number of voices is important for reproducing complex MIDI scores accurately. Voices may be hardware-based or software-based, and some sound cards use both types. A basic sound card might support 64-voice polyphony, 32 in hardware and 32 in software. High-end sound cards support 64 or more hardware voices, and may add software voices for a total of 256 to 1024 voices.

Frequency response

The range of human hearing is usually stated as 20 Hz to 20 kHz. All current sound cards nominally support this range or close to it, which is in fact required for PC99 compliance. However, few cards state dB for that range, which specifies how flat the frequency response curve is. A good card may have frequency response of 20 Hz to 20 kHz at 3 dB down. A professional-level card may have frequency response of 20 Hz to 20 kHz at 1 dB down. Inexpensive cards may claim frequency response of 20 Hz to 20 kHz, but that range may turn out to be stated at 10 dB down or some similarly absurd number, which in effect means that actual usable frequency response may be something like 100 Hz to 10 kHz.

Sampling rate

All current sound cards support waveform audio playback at 44,100, 22,050, 11,025, and 8,000 Hz. Many also support various intermediate playback rates and the DAT-standard 48,000 Hz. Some cards record only at 44,100 Hz, although most also offer other standard rates.

Signal-to-Noise ratio

Signal-to-Noise ratio (*S/N ratio*), stated in dB, measures the amount of signal (data) relative to noise, with higher numbers indicating better performance. A low S/N ratio translates to audible hiss. The best sound cards have 95 dB or greater S/N for analog audio; midrange cards about 90 dB; and inexpensive cards may have 85 dB or less. It's not unusual for a card to have somewhat lower S/N ratio for digital recording and digital playback. For example, an excellent consumer-grade sound card may specify an S/N ratio of 96 dB FS A-weighted for analog audio, 93 dB FS A-weighted for digital recording, and 90 dB FS A-weighted for digital playback. In a typical PC environment, noise level (both ambient external audible noise and the electrically noisy inside of the PC) and the typical use of low-quality speakers or headphones make it unlikely that anyone could differentiate between cards with S/N ratios of 80 dB or higher if that were the only difference. However, cards with higher S/N ratios are generally better shielded and use better components, which translates to better sound and less hiss.

Duplex mode

Half-duplex sound cards can either play sound or record sound, but not both at the same time. *Full-duplex* sound cards do both simultaneously. For simple tasks—listening to CDs or playing games—a half-duplex card is adequate. More advanced audio functions, such as Internet telephony and voice recognition, require a full-duplex card. Most midrange and all high-end sound cards are full-duplex.

Standards compatibility

In the past, software wrote directly to the sound card. That meant that compatibility with proprietary standards—initially AdLib and later Sound Blaster—was important because if your game or application didn't explicitly support your sound card, you simply couldn't use sound with that software. Microsoft took the initiative away from sound card manufacturers by incorporating standard sound APIs into Windows. Here are the standards you should be aware of:

Sound Blaster

Sound Blaster compatibility, formerly a *sine qua non* for any sound card, is now largely immaterial except to those who still use DOS software, including DOS games. True Sound Blaster compatibility requires fixed IRQ, I/O port, and DMA assignments, whereas PCI cards are assigned resources dynamically. Within those constraints, all Creative Labs sound cards and most competing cards boast (nearly) full Sound Blaster compatibility. If you still use DOS applications, though, it's worth verifying whether real-mode drivers are available for a sound card before you purchase it.

Microsoft DirectSound

Microsoft DirectSound (DS) is a component of DirectX. Developers can write to the DS API, rather than to the underlying hardware, with the assurance that their software will function with any DS-compatible sound card. DS compatibility has replaced Sound Blaster compatibility as an absolute requirement for any sound card.

Microsoft DirectSound3D

Microsoft DirectSound3D (DS3D) is an extension to DS that supports 3D positional audio, which is a technology that manipulates sound information to extend stereo imaging to full surround sound, allowing sounds to appear to come from any position around you. For example, when you're playing an air combat game and your missile hits a bandit in front of you, the sound of that explosion comes from the front. But if you didn't notice his wingman on your six, the sound of his missile blowing off your tail comes from behind. The realism of DS3D imaging in any given situation depends on the means used to reproduce the sound (two speakers, four speakers, or headphones) and the hardware capabilities of the sound card. But whatever the physical environment, DS3D provides noticeably better imaging than older 2D technologies. If you intend to use DS3D-enabled software, it's important to have hardware support for DS3D in your sound card because DS3D positional effects that cannot be processed in hardware are processed by the main CPU, which can bog down system performance.

Aureal A3D

Although Aureal went bankrupt in spring 2000, many cards with Aureal chipsets remain in use, and such cards were still available new as recently as late 2001. *Aureal A3D* is a proprietary 3D positional audio standard that is available only on sound cards based on the Aureal Vortex and Vortex2 chipsets, which have been made by Voyetra/Turtle Beach, Diamond Multimedia, Aureal itself, and others. A3D is available in two versions. A3D2.0 is supported only by the Vortex2 chipset, whereas the earlier and less-capable A3D1.0 is supported by both the Vortex and Vortex2 chipsets. A3D1.0 provides realistic 3D imaging even on dual-speaker systems or headphones. A3D2.0 provides extraordinary 3D effects, particularly on quad-speaker systems. A3D achieved broad support from game software manufacturers. For software without A3D support, A3D hardware drops back to using DS3D.

Creative Labs EAX

Creative Labs *EAX* (*Environmental Audio Extensions*) is basically a proprietary Creative Labs extension to DirectSound3D. EAX 1.0 is technically less ambitious than A3D2.0, but provides reasonable 3D imaging. EAX 2.0 and EAX Advanced HD Multi-Environment are significant enhancements that match A3D2.0 in most respects and exceed it in many. Given the dominance of Creative Labs, the various flavors of EAX are widely supported by game software.

Windows 9X and 2000/XP fully support DirectX, currently version 9.0. Windows NT supports only a subset of DirectX 3 functions, including DirectSound (but not DirectSound3D). That means that, although DirectSound-compatible sound cards can be installed and used under NT, 3D functions are not available.

Hardware acceleration

Midrange and high-end sound cards have an onboard DSP, which is a general-purpose CPU optimized for processing digital signals, such as audio. In 2D mode, the DSP provides enhanced audio effects such as chorus, reverb, and distortion. In 3D mode, it processes 3D-positional audio (e.g., DirectSound3D or EAX) algorithms locally, removing that burden from the main CPU. Inexpensive sound cards use the host CPU, which reduces performance significantly, particularly during complex operations such as 3D rendering. Any accelerated sound card should accelerate 32 or more DS and DS3D sound streams in hardware.

Choosing a Sound Card

Sound adapters fall into two broad categories. Consumer-grade sound adapters are made by companies such as Turtle Beach and Creative Labs and are widely available in retail channels. The better ones, such as the Turtle Beach Santa Cruz, suffice for any purpose for which you are likely to use a sound adapter. Professional-grade sound adapters—made by companies such as Aardvark, Digital Audio Labs, Event, Lucid, and Lynx—cost hundreds of dollars, are intended for professional audio production, have poor retail distribution, and are beyond the scope of this book. For a technical comparison of many models of sound adapters, see *http://www.pcavtech.com/soundcards/compare/index.htm*.

Use the following guidelines when choosing a sound card:

Choose embedded audio, if available, for general use
If you are building a new system or replacing a motherboard on an existing system, choose a motherboard with embedded audio, unless you need enhanced features that are available only with a standalone audio adapter. Recent embedded audio solutions support formerly high-end features such as 3D acceleration, enhanced MIDI functions, and surround sound, so the features you need are probably available with embedded audio. In addition to lower cost, embedded audio is well integrated, which minimizes installation and configuration problems. If you run Linux, check hardware compatibility carefully because Linux often provides limited or no support for recently introduced audio chipsets.

Embedded sound is often implemented as *soft audio*—e.g., the Analog Devices AD1980 chipset used in many Intel motherboards. Although soft audio solutions are inexpensive and may provide superior sound quality and features such as 3D positional audio, they depend on the main system CPU for processing. Using 3D audio features on a soft audio adapter may consume 10% or more of the CPU. We have never found this to be a problem, even when running CPU-intensive first-person-shooter games, but this additional burden on the CPU can cause jerkiness, hesitations, or other problems, particularly if the system has a slow CPU.

Don't buy too much sound card
When you add or replace a sound card, don't pay for features you won't use. Don't buy an expensive sound card if you'll use it only for playing CDs, listening to system prompts, light gaming, Internet telephony, voice recognition (on a fast system), and so on. High-quality sound cards available for $30 or so, such as the Philips Sonic Edge 5.1, include most of the features that more expensive cards provide, and are more than adequate for most purposes.

Don't buy too little sound card

If you use a sound card extensively for purposes such as 3D gaming, reproducing DVD sound, voice recognition (on a slow system), complex MIDI rendering, and so on, buy a sound card with hardware acceleration and other features that support what you use the card for. Capable consumer-grade high-end sound cards such as the Turtle Beach Santa Cruz sell for $65 or so, and are suitable for anything short of professional audio production.

Consider replacing an older sound card

If a sound card is more than two years old, consider replacing it if you are otherwise satisfied with the system. Even inexpensive current sound cards such as the $30 Philips Sonic Edge 5.1 provide better sound reproduction than high-end models that are a few years old, particularly for games and other MIDI applications. Note, however, that motherboards are now so cheap that it may be more cost-effective to replace the motherboard with a recent model that has the audio features you need and also provides other benefits such as a more recent chipset.

Avoid ISA sound cards

Don't even consider installing an ISA sound card. Even if you are upgrading a system that has an ISA slot and you happen to have a "free" ISA sound card languishing on your spares stack, do yourself a favor. Discard the ISA sound card and buy an inexpensive PCI card instead.

Avoid no-name sound cards

Stick to name-brand sound cards. We frequently hear horror stories from readers who have purchased house-brand sound cards—outdated drivers, missing or inadequate documentation, poor (or no) tech support, shoddy construction, incompatibilities with Windows 9X (let alone Windows 2000/XP and Linux), and on and on. What's particularly ironic is that you may pay more for a house-brand sound card than for a low-end name-brand card. You can buy decent name-brand sound cards for $30 from reputable companies. Don't buy anything less.

Make sure the sound card you choose has drivers available for your operating system

Nearly all sound cards are well supported under Windows 9X. Windows 2000 and Windows XP include drivers for most popular sound cards, but we have experienced conflicts and limited functionality with some of these drivers. Make sure any sound card you use with Windows 2000/XP has a certified driver supplied by the manufacturer. Linux now supports many sound cards, and both the number of models supported and the quality of that support seem to improve month to month. If you run Linux, however, verify that drivers are available for the exact model card you plan to use.

Bundled software

We admit it. We've never bothered to install any of the plethora of applications that are bundled with many sound cards, particularly high-end models, and we probably wouldn't know what to do with them if we did. But that's because we use sound cards only for playing MP3, Ogg Vorbis, and CD audio, recording audio from within other applications, Internet telephony, and similar applications. The software supplied with a sound card varies according to the market focus of that card. Cards targeted at gamers often include a game or two intended to show off the features of that card, although such games are often demos, feature-crippled, or older versions. Similarly, cards with high-end MIDI features often include a competent MIDI sequencer and editor, although again it's likely to be a "Lite" version, intended primarily to convince you to upgrade to (and pay for) the "Professional" version. But if you do need one of these functions and your needs are moderate, bundled software may do the job you need and allow you to avoid spending more money on individually purchased applications.

 Embedded audio has nearly destroyed the standalone sound card market, and this trend is accelerating. Originally, embedded audio sold well because it was cheap and adequate. Nowadays nearly all motherboards include embedded audio, and you can't get cheaper than free. Worse still for sound card makers, embedded audio is no longer merely adequate. Good embedded audio, such as that of Intel motherboards and the AMD-compatible nForce2 chipset, matches any but the best standalone audio for features and sound quality.

Installing a Sound Card

A sound card physically installs just as any other expansion card does. Some sound cards require many system resources, so keep the following guidelines in mind:

If you are building a new system

Install the PCI sound card before you install other components such as network adapters or SCSI host adapters, allowing the sound card to make first claim on system resources. Although Plug and Play usually does a good job of juggling resources, we have sometimes experienced resource conflicts when installing a sound card in a system that was already heavily loaded with other adapters. If that happens, the best course is to disable all adapters in the Device Manager (except essential ones such as the video card and IDE interface), physically remove those adapters, install and configure the sound card, and finally reinstall the other adapters one by one. If your CMOS Setup program allows you to assign an IRQ to a particular PCI slot, use that feature to assign IRQ 5 to the slot where you plan to install the sound card. If you experience conflicts or improper functioning, try installing the sound card in a different PCI slot.

If you are replacing an existing sound card

Before you remove the card, delete it in the Device Manager (if you are running Windows 9X) and delete all its drivers from the hard disk. Turn the PC off, take off the cover, physically remove the old sound card, and start the PC. Verify that all vestiges of the old sound card are gone. If the sound card is embedded, run CMOS Setup and disable it in BIOS. With all that done, turn off the PC again and physically install the new sound card. Start the system again and install the drivers for it.

Except for physically removing and replacing the sound card, we recommend following the same procedure when updating sound card drivers. That is, never upgrade sound card drivers. Instead, remove the old ones and install the new ones as a clean install. We have encountered problems more than once when attempting to upgrade existing drivers. A clean install avoids those problems.

If you are installing a sound card in a motherboard that has embedded sound

Before you install a sound card in a system with embedded sound, disable the embedded sound adapter either in CMOS Setup or by changing a jumper on the motherboard (or both). Every motherboard we know that includes embedded PCI sound allows you to disable sound in BIOS. Enabling or disabling sound usually has no effect on interrupts because embedded PCI sound uses one or two shareable PCI interrupts. Older motherboards, however, may have embedded ISA sound adapters, which may use fixed ISA interrupts. Such motherboards may or may not allow sound to be disabled and the interrupt made available for other adapters. If it is possible to disable the interrupt, doing so usually requires removing a physical jumper on the motherboard.

When installing a sound card, remember to connect the CD audio cable from the Audio Out jack on the back of the CD-ROM drive to the CD Audio jack on the sound card. If you have two CD or DVD drives installed, you can connect Audio Out from the second drive to the Aux In jack on the sound card, if present. We always forget to connect these cables, which is a good reason to test the system before putting the cover back on.

Configuring a Sound Card Under Windows 95/98/2000/XP

Configuring a sound card requires similar steps in Windows 95, 98, and 2000/XP, with minor differences in the names and sequence of dialogs. To configure a sound card under Windows 9X or 2000/XP, take the following steps:

1. After removing the existing sound card and drivers, if any, verifying that all vestiges of the old sound card drivers are gone, and physically installing the new sound card, restart the system. Note that the drivers supplied on CD-ROM with some sound cards must be present in the CD-ROM drive when you start the system.

2. Windows should recognize that the new sound card is present and display the Add New Hardware Wizard. Although Windows 9X includes drivers for many sound cards, you are usually better off using the Windows 9X drivers supplied by the sound card manufacturer. To do so, mark the Search for... option button and click Next.

Windows 2000 and Windows XP include drivers for relatively few sound cards. The drivers they do include often have limited functionality, such as supporting only two-channel sound on a four-channel card. We strongly recommend downloading Windows 2000/XP drivers from the sound card maker rather than using those provided with the operating system. Install Windows 2000/XP drivers in the same manner described for Windows 98 drivers.

3. When Windows displays the next dialog, either specify the location of the drivers or tell it which drives to search for them. Click Next to continue.

4. Windows should locate the proper drivers and load them. When the process completes, reboot the system. Most sound cards include an automated installation procedure for bundled applications, which usually autoruns immediately after the system restarts. Follow the prompts, and provide any necessary information to complete the installation.

5. For Windows 98, right-click the My Computer icon, choose Properties, and then click the Device Manager tab. For Windows 2000/XP, right-click My Computer, choose Properties, click the Hardware tab, and then click the Device Manager button. Then, for either version, expand the Sound, video and game controllers branch and verify that the sound card is installed properly and that no conflicts exist. Most sound cards also have a test utility that you should run to verify that all aspects of the sound card hardware and drivers are operating properly.

6. From the Control Panel, double-click Multimedia to display the Audio page of the Multimedia Properties dialog (Windows 9X) or the Sounds and Multimedia Properties dialog (Windows 2000/XP). If you have more than one audio device in your system, use the Preferred device drop-down lists in the Playback and Recording sections to select one of the installed audio devices as the default for each. Click the Advanced Properties buttons in the Playback and Recording sections to configure driver-specific options for such things as degree of hardware acceleration to be used, sample rate conversion settings, the type of speakers you are using, and so on.

Configuring a Sound Card Under Linux

Linux support of audio adapters is specific to the Linux distribution and audio adapter you are using. You can avoid most audio configuration problems by making sure your audio adapter is explicitly supported by the Linux distribution you intend to run. Before you install Linux, check the hardware compatibility list and support pages for the distribution, as well as the web site for the audio adapter manufacturer.

Using an outdated Linux distribution and an older audio adapter is a recipe for trouble. Recent Linux distributions automatically detect and configure nearly all recent audio adapters and most older models. If your audio adapter is not detected but is AC97-compliant, you may be able to use the i810_audio module, which allows many AC97 audio chipsets to provide at least basic audio functionality.

If you have an older audio adapter, or a recent adapter that is not supported by your Linux distribution, you may be able to use the adapter by installing the *Advanced Linux Sound Architecture (ALSA)* drivers (*http://www.alsa-project.org/*). Unfortunately, installing ALSA drivers may be difficult for inexperienced users because it requires either compiling the ALSA drivers into the kernel or building them separately as modules. The good news is that ALSA is being incorporated as a standard part of the Linux kernel. When the next major version of the Linux kernel is released, every Linux distribution will by default use this much more capable sound card driver architecture.

If you encounter compatibility problems with an older sound card or embedded audio adapter, by far the easiest solution is to remove or disable the adapter and install an inexpensive modern PCI sound card that is explicitly supported by your Linux distribution. Spending $25 may save you hours of recompiling kernels and tweaking arcane parameters, and the sound will probably be a lot better as well.

Choose something other than a Creative Labs Sound Blaster. Based on our own experience and that of others, we do not use or recommend Sound Blaster audio adapters. For example, well-known Open Source advocate Eric S. Raymond gave up in disgust, saying in part, "The Linux support for the SB Live! seems to be fragile and flaky. Troubleshooting it turned into a significant time sink and frustration source. In late January I finally got fed up and replaced it with a no-name PCI sound card. Later, the SB Live! went back in, but I'm now nervous about even upgrading my OS for fear the sound configuration will break again."

If ESR can't make a Sound Blaster work reliably under Linux, we're not even going to try.

The utilities used to configure a sound card vary by distribution. For example, Red Hat uses sndconfig, while for Slackware you must edit the Sound Support section of the file */etc/rc.d/rc.modules*. For more information, refer to the documentation for your distribution.

Troubleshooting Sound Card Problems

Most sound card problems are a result of improper, defective, or misconnected cables, incorrect drivers, or resource conflicts. Sound card problems that occur with a previously functioning sound card when you have made no changes to the system are usually caused by cable problems or operator error (such as accidentally turning the volume control down). Sound card problems that occur when you install a new sound card (or when you add or reconfigure other system components) are usually caused by resource conflicts or driver problems. Resource conflicts, although relatively rare under Windows 9X/2000/XP in a PCI/Plug-N-Play environment, are quite common on machines running Windows NT and/or ISA because sound cards are resource hogs.

To troubleshoot sound problems, always begin with the following steps:

---

1. Verify that all cables are connected, that the speakers have power and are switched on, that the volume control is set to an audible level, and so on. In particular, if the sound card has a volume wheel on the back, make sure it is set to an audible level. It's often unclear which direction increases volume, so we generally set the wheel to a middle position while troubleshooting.

2. Shut down and restart the system. Surprisingly often, this solves the problem.

3. Determine the scope of the problem. If the problem occurs with only one program, visit the web sites for Microsoft, the software company, and the sound card maker to determine if there is a known problem with that program and sound card combination. If the problem occurs globally, continue with the following steps.

4. Verify that the sound card is selected as the default playback device. If you have more than one sound card installed, verify that the default playback device is the sound card to which the speakers are connected.

5. If your sound card includes a testing utility, run it to verify that all components of the sound card are operating properly.

6. If you have another set of speakers and/or a spare audio cable, substitute them temporarily to eliminate the speakers as a possible cause. If you have a set of headphones, connect them directly to Line-out on the sound card to isolate the problem to the system itself.

If the problem is occurring on a new system, or one in which you have just added or replaced a sound card, take the following steps:

1. Verify that the speakers are connected to the Line-out or Speaker jack, as appropriate, rather than to the Line-in or Microphone jack. Connecting speakers to the wrong jack is one of the most common causes of sound problems. We do it ourselves from time to time.

2. Verify that the CMOS Setup settings are correct for OS type. If you are running Windows 95/98/2000, OS type should be set to PnP Compatible (or similar words); if you are running NT4, it should be set to Non-PnP OS.

3. Use the procedures described in Chapter 1 to verify that no resource conflicts exist. If conflicts exist, remedy them and restart the system.

4. Check the troubleshooting sections of the Microsoft web site and the web sites for your motherboard and sound card manufacturer. Some sound cards, for example, have problems with motherboards with certain Via chipsets, while other sound cards have problems with AMD K6-family CPUs when used with certain AGP video cards.

5. Remove the drivers, restart the system, and reinstall the drivers from scratch.

6. Remove the drivers, shut down the system, and relocate the sound card to a different PCI slot. When the system restarts, reinstall the drivers from scratch.

7. If none of that works, suspect either a defective sound card or a fundamental incompatibility between your sound card and the rest of your system. Remove the drivers, shut down the system, remove the sound card, install a different sound card, and reinstall the drivers for it. If the replacement sound card is the same model and exhibits the same symptoms, try installing a different model of sound card.

If the problem occurs on a previously working system, take the following steps:

1. If you have recently added or changed any hardware, use the procedures described in Chapter 1 to verify that no resource conflicts exist.

2. If you have recently installed or uninstalled any software, it's possible that Setup installed DLLs that are incompatible with your sound card, or removed DLLs that your sound card or applications require. Remove the sound card drivers and reinstall them from scratch.

3. If sound still does not function properly, suspect a sound card failure.

Here are some specific common sound problems and their solutions:

No sound

This is probably the most common sound problem, and can have many causes. Following the troubleshooting steps listed previously should resolve the problem.

Scratchy or intermittent sound

This problem can also have many causes. Perhaps the most common is the sound card itself. Older and inexpensive sound cards often have poor audio quality, particularly FM synthesis models. Other common causes include a defective or low-quality audio cable, speakers placed too close to the monitor or other source of electrical noise, and the placement of the sound card within the system. If you have a choice, locate a sound card as far as possible from other expansion cards. Another possible cause is that some video card drivers are optimized for benchmark tests by having them keep control of the bus. The result can be intermittent drop outs and scratchiness in the sound.

Computer sounds are audible but audio CDs are not

Computer sound is digital, and is delivered directly to the sound card via the bus. Audio CDs produce analog sound, and require a separate internal cable joining the audio out connector on the back of the CD-ROM drive to the CD Audio connector on the sound card. If you do not have the necessary cable, you can temporarily fix the problem by connecting a standard stereo audio cable from the headphone jack on the front of the CD-ROM drive to the Line-in jack on the sound card. Note that recent motherboards and CD-ROM drives can deliver CD audio as a digital signal directly to the sound card, obviating the need for a separate CD-Audio cable.

Only one channel is audible

If you have another set of speakers or headphones, connect them directly to the sound card Line-out port to isolate the problem to either the sound card or the speakers. Roughly in order of decreasing probability, the most likely causes and solutions are:

- The Windows audio balance control is set fully in one direction. Double-click the speaker icon in the System Tray and verify balance settings in the Volume Control dialog (or the replacement applet installed with your sound card drivers).

- The balance control on your speakers, if present, may be set fully in one direction. This happens commonly when someone blindly attempts to change volume or tone and turns the wrong knob. Center the speaker balance control.

- The audio cable is defective. Many audio cables, particularly those supplied with inexpensive speakers, are constructed poorly. Replace it with a high-quality, shielded audio cable, available for a few dollars from computer stores, audio specialty stores, and mass marketers such as Circuit City.

- The audio cable is not fully seated in either the sound card jack or the speaker jack. Verify that the cable is fully seated at both ends.

- You are using a mono rather than stereo audio cable to connect Line-out on the sound card to the speakers. Replace the cable.

- The sound card driver is not installed, is installed improperly, or is the wrong driver. Some sound cards may function partially under these conditions, and the most common symptom is single-channel audio. Uninstall any driver currently installed, and then reinstall the proper driver.

- Although it is rare, we once encountered a set of amplified speakers with one channel dead and the other working. Replace the speakers.

After installing a sound card, your PC speaker no longer works
This is by design in some sound cards. Installing the card and driver intentionally disables the PC speaker and routes sounds that would ordinarily go to the PC speaker to the sound card instead.

Windows suddenly loses sound
On Windows systems with properly configured and functioning sound cards, sound may disappear entirely for no apparent reason. This has happened to us on many different systems, using different motherboards and sound cards. The sound card still shows as installed, and everything appears perfectly normal, but the system simply stops sending audio to the speakers. This problem may or may not be accompanied by the speaker icon disappearing from the system tray. We have no idea what causes this, and we've never been able to get a satisfactory explanation from Microsoft. Restarting the system normally solves the problem, until next time. On systems in which "next time" is all too frequent, we have occasionally had some success by removing and then reinstalling the sound drivers.

The system locks up when you boot or bluescreens immediately after booting
This problem normally results from a severe resource conflict or an improperly installed card. Verify first that the card is seated fully. If it is, boot the system in Safe Mode (Windows 9X: press F8 during boot) or using the Last Known Good Configuration (Windows NT: press the spacebar when prompted). With the system booted, determine which devices and resources are conflicting, resolve the conflicts, and restart the system.

Our Picks

Here are the sound adapters we recommend:

General-purpose sound
Buy a motherboard with embedded audio. Nearly all recent motherboards have standard embedded audio. Even the basic embedded audio provided

with inexpensive motherboards is sufficient for most needs. Premium motherboards include better audio chipsets that provide top-notch sound and support such features as advanced 3D positional audio and Dolby Digital 5.1. The tight integration of embedded audio makes compatibility problems and resource conflicts much less likely. If you are building or upgrading a system, there is seldom reason to use anything other than the embedded audio supplied with the motherboard.

PCI sound card (budget)

Philips Sonic Edge 5.1. Although Creative Labs, SIIG, and others make good basic PCI sound cards, we think the Philips Sonic Edge 5.1 is the standout choice among PCI sound cards that sell for $30 or less. Sound quality is inferior to that of the Turtle Beach Santa Cruz or the Creative Labs Audigy 2, but the Sonic Edge is fine for playing DVDs, CD audio, or MP3/OGG files and for casual gaming (*http://www.pcsound.philips.com/_sonic605.html*).

PCI sound card (premium)

Voyetra Turtle Beach Santa Cruz. At $70 or so, this is the best consumer-grade sound card available. It supports six-speaker surround sound, including virtual 5.1 processing that emulates full surround sound from two-channel stereo sources. It supports all major PC audio standards, including A3D, EAX, DS3D, IA3D, and Sensaura, and provides DOS game compatibility under Windows 9X. Good drivers are available for all major operating systems, including Linux. We have experienced no compatibility problems with Intel, VIA, ALi, or SiS chipsets, which is more than we can say for some sound cards. Unless you work with PC audio for a living, the Santa Cruz is probably all the sound card you'll ever need. This is the sound card we install when features and sound quality matter (*http://www.turtlebeach.com/site/products/santacruz/*).

ISA sound card

None. ISA sound cards have always been trouble-prone, and are now obsolete. If a system has only ISA slots available, it's time to replace the motherboard. The embedded PCI audio on even inexpensive motherboards is a far superior solution.

For updated recommendations, visit: *http://www.hardwareguys.com/picks/soundcard.html*.

18

Speakers and Headphones

No matter how good your sound card is, it's useless unless you have speakers or headphones to listen to the audio it produces. Extreme high fidelity is usually unnecessary in PC speakers, both because system fans and other ambient noise tend to overwhelm minor differences in sound quality, and because most PC sound applications do not use or require high fidelity. That said, inexpensive PC speakers, with their 3-inch drivers and low-power amplifiers, often provide surprisingly satisfactory sound, and inexpensive headphones can produce sound rivaling the best consumer-grade audio equipment.

Speaker and Headphone Characteristics

Here are the important characteristics of speakers:

Number
> Computer speakers are sold in sets. Two-piece sets include two small speakers intended to sit on your desk or attach to your monitor. Three-piece sets add a subwoofer, which resides under the desk and provides enhanced bass response. Four-piece sets include four small speakers, and are useful primarily to gamers who have a 3D-capable sound card installed. Five-piece sets add a subwoofer to that arrangement. Six-piece sets include a subwoofer, a center-channel speaker, and four satellites, and are intended for PC-based home-theater applications. Most headphones use only two speakers, one per ear, but some use two horizontally offset speakers per ear to provide true four-channel support.

Frequency response
> *Frequency response* is the range of sound frequencies that the speaker can reproduce. The values provided for most speakers are meaningless because they do not specify how flat that response is. For example, professional studio-monitor speakers may provide 20 Hz to 20 kHz response at 1 dB. Expensive home-audio speakers may provide 20 Hz to 20 kHz response at 3

dB, and 40 Hz to 18 kHz response at 1 dB. Computer speakers may claim 20 Hz to 20 kHz response, but may rate that response at 10 dB or more, which makes the specification effectively meaningless. A reduction of about 3 dB halves volume, which means sounds lower than 100 Hz or higher than 10 kHz are nearly inaudible with many computer speakers. The only sure measure of adequate frequency response is that the speakers sound good to you, particularly for low bass and high treble sounds.

Amplifier power

Manufacturers use two means to specify output power. *Peak Power*, which specifies the maximum wattage the amplifier can deliver instantaneously, is deceptive and should be disregarded. *RMS Power* (*Root Mean Square*), a more accurate measure, specifies the wattage that the amplifier can deliver continually. Listening to music at normal volume levels requires less than a watt. Home audio systems usually provide 100 watts per channel or more, which allows them to respond instantaneously to transient high-amplitude peaks in the music, particularly in bass notes, extending the dynamic range of the sound. The range of computer speakers is hampered by their small amplifiers, but computer speakers also use small drivers that cannot move much air anyway, so their lack of power is not really important. Typical dual-speaker sets provide 4 to 8 watts of RMS Power per channel, which is adequate for normal sound reproduction. Typical subwoofers provide 15 to 40 watts, which, combined with the typical 5-inch driver, is adequate to provide flat bass response down to 60 Hz or so (although subwoofers often misleadingly claim response to 20 Hz). Headphones are not amplified, but use the line-level output of the sound card.

Connectors

Most computer speakers place the amplifier in one speaker, which has connections for Line-in (from the sound card), Speaker (to the other speaker), and DC Power (to a power brick). Many speakers also provide an output for a subwoofer. Some speakers also provide a second Line-in jack. This is quite useful if you want to connect both your PC and a separate line-level audio source, such as a CD player or another PC, to the amplified speakers, allowing you to listen to either source separately or both together. An increasing number of high-end speakers—particularly six-channel Dolby Digital 5.1 systems—provide direct digital inputs via a Digital DIN connector, an SP/DIF connector, or both.

 USB speakers were introduced several years ago, but never really caught on. USB speakers do not require an audio adapter, but the proliferation of embedded audio adapters eliminated that advantage. Sound quality of USB speakers is generally inferior to that of a good sound card and traditional speakers. USB speakers are still sold, primarily for travel applications, where low weight and simplicity are important concerns. We suggest you avoid USB speakers entirely.

Choosing Speakers and Headphones

Use the following guidelines when selecting computer speakers or headphones:

Choose speakers appropriate for your listening preferences and sound card capabilities

Picking suitable speakers requires considering what you listen to, how you listen to it, and the features of your sound card. For example, if you listen mostly to classical music at low to moderate volume, powerful bass is less important than flat, transparent frequency response in the midrange and highs. A high-quality set of dual speakers with frequency response from 90 to 18,000 Hz and 4 or 5 watts of RMS Power per channel will serve. Conversely, if you listen to rock or heavy metal, or if you play games and want to shake the walls, crystalline highs are less important, but bass is critical. You'll want speakers that include a powerful subwoofer. Similarly, if you have a 3D sound card, it makes little sense to couple it to a two-piece or three-piece speaker set. Buy a four-, five-, or six-piece speaker set to take advantage of the 3D capabilities of the card.

Avoid cheap speakers

The very cheapest speakers, those that sell for $5 or $8 or are bundled with inexpensive PCs, have sound quality noticeably inferior to speakers that sell for even a little more. Speakers in the $15 range and above use better (and more powerful) amplifiers, use better-quality drivers (typically separate midrange/woofers and tweeters), and provide additional features, such as the ability to connect more than one sound source or a separate subwoofer.

Stick with name brands

Altec-Lansing and Labtec are the best-known names in inexpensive computer speakers. Each produces a broad range of speaker models, one of which should be appropriate for almost any requirements. Creative Labs, Sony, Yamaha, and others also produce good computer speakers, although their range of models is smaller. Increasingly, well-known names in home audio—such as Bose, JBL, Klipsch, and Polk Audio—are entering the computer speaker market. Ironically, their background in high-quality home audio means they tend to publish realistic specifications for their computer speakers, which make them look inferior to lesser speakers for which the makers publish inflated specifications.

Make sure to buy speakers with the correct interface

Most computer speakers use an analog audio interface, which allows them to connect directly to the Line-out jack of your sound adapter. Some computer speakers—particularly high-end four-, five-, and six-speaker sets—instead use a direct digital connection via a Digital DIN connector, an SP/DIF connector, or both. If you are using a traditional sound adapter, make sure your sound adapter and speakers share a common interface method. Some computer speakers do not require a traditional sound adapter, but instead connect via USB.

Consider using headphones instead of speakers

Even inexpensive headphones often provide a better listening experience than good computer speakers, both because the cushions isolate you from ambient noise and because it's easier to render very high-fidelity sound with the small speakers and tiny power levels used by headphones. Headphones also allow you to work (or play) without disturbing others. If you're going to buy headphones, consider instead buying a headset, which adds a microphone to support such functions as voice/speech recognition, Internet telephony, and the ability to add voice annotations to documents. The only drawback to headphones is that most are not well suited for use with 3D sound cards, although some specialized four-channel headphones are available.

Get a no-questions-asked money-back guarantee

With speakers more so than any other computer component except perhaps input devices, personal preference must rule. Speakers that sound great to us may sound mediocre to you, and vice versa. The only way to know for sure is to listen to the speakers in your own environment. If they turn out to be unsuitable, you don't want to be stuck with them, so make sure you can return them without a hassle.

Our Picks

Which are the "best" speakers or headphones obviously varies according to the person using them and the use to which they are being put. In our opinion, most people will find a $25 set of Altec-Lansing or Labtec speakers or headphones perfectly sufficient for casual listening. As with home audio speakers and headphones, it's best to listen to PC speakers and headphones in your own environment before making a decision. That said, the area around a typical PC isn't a particularly good audio environment, so you may not appreciate the difference between good speakers and excellent ones.

New PC speaker models are introduced frequently, so rather than list specific brands and models here, we put that information on our web site. For our most recent detailed recommendations, visit: *http://www.hardwareguys.com/picks/ speakers.html.*

19

Keyboards

A *keyboard* is a matrix of individual switches, one per key. Pressing a key closes its switch, generating a signal that the dedicated *keyboard controller* built into the keyboard recognizes as the *make code* for that key. Releasing the key opens the switch, which the keyboard controller recognizes as the *break code* for that key. Using a firmware lookup table, the keyboard controller translates received make code signals to standard *scan codes*, which it sends via the *keyboard buffer* to a second keyboard controller located in the PC, which recognizes those scan codes as specific characters and control codes.

Because releasing a key generates a break code, the local keyboard controller can recognize when two keys are pressed together (e.g., Shift-A or Ctrl-C) and generate a unique scan code for each such defined key combination. For undefined key combinations (e.g., pressing "a" and then pressing "s" before releasing "a"), the keyboard controller recognizes that, even though a break code for "a" has not been received, the user's intent is to type "as", and so generates the scan code for "a" followed immediately by the scan code for "s".

Most people do not need to work with scan codes directly, but if you program you may need to use scan codes to control the behavior of a program when the user presses specific keys or key combinations. The *Microsoft Keyboard Scan Code Specification*, which includes the standard keyboard scan codes as well as alternative make and break PS/2 scan codes and USB code responses for the Windows Key, Application Keys, and ACPI power controls, is available from *http:// download.microsoft.com/download/whistler/hwdev3/1.0/WXP/EN-US/scancode.exe*. Microsoft also publishes the *USB HID to PS/2 Translation Table*, which provides mappings from the USB HID keyboard multimedia usages to PS/2. That file is available in PDF format from *http://www.microsoft.com/hwdev/download/tech/ input/translate.pdf* or in Excel format from *http://www.microsoft.com/hwdev/ download/tech/input/translate.xls*.

Communication between the two keyboard controllers is bidirectional and asynchronous, which allows the PC to illuminate and extinguish keyboard indicator lights and set Typematic parameters such as delay and repeat rate. The keyboard interface was standardized with the 1984 introduction of the IBM PC/AT, which means that any AT-class keyboard works with any 286 or higher PC, assuming that the physical connectors are compatible.

In addition to basic functions, the local keyboard controller may support various programmable functions, using either or both of these methods:

Keyboard-based

The local keyboard controller may support creating custom definitions for specific keys and key combinations and storing those definitions in the keyboard itself. When a key with a custom definition is pressed, the local keyboard controller generates the necessary scan codes directly and sends them to the PC. Because this method uses only standard scan codes, it has the advantage of not requiring a driver on the PC—which means the programmable functions can be used with any operating system—but the disadvantage of being limited to functions that can be performed using standard scan codes. This method was commonly used with early programmable keyboards, but is less common nowadays.

PC-based

Programmable functions may require a driver running on the PC. That driver recognizes nonstandard scan codes generated by the local keyboard controller and takes whatever action the driver defines for "hard-wired" special keys. For keys with custom definitions, the driver uses stored user configuration data to determine what action to take. This method has the advantage of supporting programmable functions that would be clumsy or impossible to implement using only standard scan codes (such as opening your web browser or email client), and is the method used by most current programmable keyboards. If the driver is not installed, such keyboards function as ordinary keyboards, with special-purpose keys and programmable features disabled.

 In our experience, fully programmable keyboards are suitable for "power users" but are likely to confuse casual users. We frequently receive calls from people using such keyboards who have accidentally enabled programming mode and have no idea how to get back into normal mode, or even that they'd done anything to cause the problem. A more subtle problem is that people often program their passwords into the keyboard, which both impairs security and causes support hassles if the password is cleared and the user has forgotten it, as often happens. Programmable keyboards should be reserved for people who are willing to learn to use their features and are aware of the potential security risks.

Keyboard Switch Types

Underneath each key is a switch. When the key is pressed, the switch closes. Three types of switches are used in keyboards:

Mechanical

These keyboards use standard spring-loaded momentary-on switches, most of which are made by Alps Electric. Pressing a key compresses a spring and causes a plunger on the bottom of the key to make physical contact to close the connection. When the key is released, the spring forces it back into rest position. These keyboards provide the clacky feel typical of the original IBM Selectric and PC keyboards, are quite durable, and are usually relatively expensive ($75 to $125).

Capacitive

These keyboards are unique in that pressing a key does not make electrical contact to complete the circuit. Instead, movement of the plunger on the bottom of a key alters the state of a capacitive circuit, which the keyboard controller recognizes as a key press. Keyboards with capacitive switches provide clacky feedback, are even more durable than mechanical keyboards, and are quite expensive ($100 to $200). As far as we know, only IBM and Lexmark have produced such keyboards.

Membrane

Most current keyboards use membrane switches. Unlike mechanical and capacitive keyboards, which use discrete physical switches for each key and are correspondingly expensive to produce, a membrane keyboard combines all key switches into one unit comprising three membrane layers. The bottom layer has printed conductive traces that correspond to the individual key switches. The middle layer is a spacer, with holes that expose each underlying switch. The top layer is an array of rubber domes, against each of which the bottom of a key impinges. When a key is pressed, it forces the conductive bottom of the rubber dome through the spacing layer and into contact with the switch traces on the bottom layer, completing the circuit. When the key is released, the rubber dome forces it back into rest position. Early membrane keyboards were known for mushy feel and lack of tactile feedback. Current production models are better in that respect, so much so that it is often difficult to tell by feel alone whether you are using a mechanical keyboard or a modern membrane keyboard. Membrane keyboards are also inexpensive ($15 to $50), and nearly as durable and reliable as the best of the mechanical and capacitive keyboards.

Switch type as it related to durability was an important factor when keyboards cost $200. With high-quality membrane keyboards now selling for $25 or so, that distinction is much less important.

Keyboard Styles

Keyboards are available in two distinct styles:

Traditional keyboard

A *traditional keyboard* is rectangular and has a constant slope, from highest at the rear to lowest at the front. These keyboards are available in various footprints, including standard (19x8 inches); midsize (18x7 inches); and space-saver (17x6.5 inches or less). Size is important to the extent that large keyboards occupy considerable desk space and may not fit some keyboard drawers.

Ergonomic keyboard

An *ergonomic keyboard* uses a split face and variable slopes, which allow for more natural and comfortable hand and wrist positions. Most ergonomic keyboards are as large as or larger than standard traditional keyboards, not least because they include a built-in wrist rest. Some claim that ergonomic keyboards help reduce *Repetitive Stress Injury (RSI)* problems such as *Carpal Tunnel Syndrome (CTS)*, but we have seen no credible evidence to support these claims. The secret to avoiding such problems, regardless of what keyboard style you use, is to take frequent breaks and to avoid using the keyboard continuously for more than an hour or so at a time.

Keyboard Interfaces

Keyboard interfaces are well standardized, and have been for years. This means that, with the exception of antique PC and PC/XT keyboards, you can plug any keyboard into any PC to which it can physically connect and expect it to work. The following sections detail the three keyboard interfaces currently in use.

AT Keyboard Interface

The AT keyboard interface was introduced with the IBM PC/AT in 1984, and is still used by the few AT and BAT motherboards still being produced. AT keyboards use the 5-pin DIN connector (female at the PC), shown in Figure 19-1 and whose pinouts are described in Table 19-1. On the PC side, the AT keyboard uses an Intel 8042 or equivalent interface chip, which is assigned IRQ1 and I/O base address 0060.

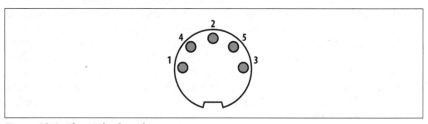

Figure 19-1. The AT keyboard connector

Table 19-1. AT keyboard interface signals and pinout

Pin	Signal name	Description
1	CLOCK	Keyboard clock; open collector CLK, CTS
2	DATA	Keyboard data; open collector RxD/TxD, RTS
3	RESERVED	Reset (usually not connected)
4	GROUND	Signal ground
5	VCC	+5VDC

The pin descriptions are self-explanatory, other than Pin 3. The 83-key IBM PC/XT keyboard and some 84-key IBM PC/AT keyboards used an early keyboard protocol that did not include a software reset command. For these keyboards, the PC uses Pin 3 to send a hardware reset to the keyboard. All systems and keyboards made in the last 15 years use a keyboard protocol that includes a software reset command, and nearly all recent keyboards leave Pin 3 unconnected.

PS/2 Keyboard Interface

The PS/2 keyboard interface was introduced with the IBM PS/2 series in 1986, and is now used by all ATX and ATX-variant motherboards. PS/2 keyboards use the 6-pin mini-DIN connector (female at the PC), shown in Figure 19-2 and whose pinouts are described in Table 19-2. On the PC side, the PS/2 keyboard uses the same Intel 8042 or equivalent interface chip as the AT keyboard, which is also assigned IRQ1 and I/O base address 0060.

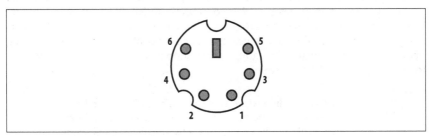

Figure 19-2. The PS/2 keyboard connector

Table 19-2. PS/2 keyboard interface signals and pinout

Pin	Signal name	Description
1	DATA	Keyboard data
2	RESERVED	No connection
3	GROUND	Signal ground
4	VCC	+5VDC
5	CLOCK	Keyboard clock
6	RESERVED	No connection
Shield	-	Ground

The AT and PS/2 keyboard interfaces use incompatible connectors, but are electrically and functionally identical. You can connect an AT keyboard to a PS/2 keyboard port or vice versa by building or buying an adapter that uses the pinouts listed in Table 19-3. Many new keyboards come with an adapter to allow their use with the other style connector. Such adapters can also be purchased at most computer stores.

Table 19-3. Pinouts for an AT-to-PS/2 or PS/2-to-AT adapter

PS/2 pin	AT pin	Description
1	2	Keyboard data
2	3	No connection
3	4	Signal ground

Table 19-3. Pinouts for an AT-to-PS/2 or PS/2-to-AT adapter (continued)

PS/2 pin	AT pin	Description
4	5	+5VDC
5	1	Keyboard clock
6	-	No connection

USB Keyboard Interface

Some keyboards can be connected to a USB port. Most USB-capable keyboards also provide a standard PS/2 connector, via either a split cable with both USB and PS/2 connectors or a separate adapter that converts the USB connector to PS/2. To use a USB keyboard, the PC BIOS must support USB keyboards, *and* you must run an operating system, such as Windows 9X/2000/XP or Linux, that supports USB. BIOS support is needed so that the keyboard can be used before the operating system loads to do such things as changing Setup parameters or choosing options from a boot menu. Operating system support is required for the keyboard to be accessible after the system boots.

> In previous editions, we concluded that USB-only keyboards were not ready for prime time. We experienced numerous lockups and other weirdities, including situations in which the PC continued to run normally but the keyboard was no longer recognized. Although such problems still occur with older hardware, and although we still prefer to use PS/2 keyboards for Linux systems, current USB keyboards are generally quite reliable with recent Windows systems.

Choosing a Keyboard

Use the following guidelines when choosing a keyboard:

Consider layout
> The position of the primary alphanumeric keys is standard on all keyboards other than those that use the oddball Dvorak layout. What varies, sometimes dramatically, is the placement, size, and shape of other keys, such as the shift keys (Shift, Ctrl, and Alt), the function keys (which may be arrayed across the top, down the left side, or both), and the cursor control and numeric keypad keys. If you are used to a particular layout, purchasing a keyboard with a similar layout makes it much easier to adapt to the new keyboard.

Give personal preference top priority
> Keyboards vary both in obvious ways—layout, size, and form—and in subtle ways—key spacing, angle, dishing, travel, pressure required, and tactile feedback. People's sensitivity to these differences varies. Some are keyboard agnostics who can sit down in front of a new keyboard and, regardless of layout or tactile response, be up to speed in a few minutes. Others have strong preferences about layout and feel. If you've never met a keyboard you didn't like, you can disregard these issues and choose a keyboard based on other factors. If love and hate are words you apply to keyboards, use an identical keyboard for at least an hour before you buy one for yourself.

Make sure your operating system supports extended keyboard functions

Some keyboards provide dedicated and/or programmable function keys to automate such things as firing up your browser or email client or to allow you to define custom macros that can be invoked with a single keystroke. These functions are typically not built into the keyboard itself, but require loading a driver. To take advantage of these functions, make sure a driver is available for the OS you use.

Consider weight

Although it sounds trivial, the weight of a keyboard can be a significant issue for some people. The lightest keyboard we've seen weighed just over 1 lb., and the heaviest was nearly 8 lbs. If your keyboard stays on your desktop, a heavy keyboard is less likely to slide around. Conversely, a very heavy keyboard may be uncomfortable for someone who works with the keyboard in his lap.

Avoid multifunction keyboards

Keyboards are low-margin products. As a means to differentiate their products and increase margins, some manufacturers produce keyboards with speakers, scanners, and other entirely unrelated functions built in. These functions are often clumsy to use, are fragile, and have limited features. If you want speakers or a scanner, buy speakers or a scanner. Don't get a keyboard with them built in.

Consider a wireless keyboard for special purposes

Various manufacturers make wireless keyboards, which are ideal for presentations and TV-based web browsing. Wireless keyboards include a separate receiver module that connects to a USB port or the PS/2 keyboard port on the PC. The keyboard and receiver communicate using either radio frequency (RF) or infrared (IR). IR keyboards require direct line-of-sight between the keyboard and receiver, while RF keyboards do not. Most IR keyboards and many RF keyboards provide very limited range—as little as 5 feet or so—which limits their utility to working around a desk without cables tangling. Some RF keyboards and a few IR keyboards use higher power to provide longer range, up to 50 feet or more. These are often quite expensive and provide relatively short battery life. Whichever type of wireless keyboard you get, make sure it uses standard (AA/AAA/9V) alkaline or NiMH batteries rather than a proprietary NiCd battery pack, which is subject to the infamous NiCd memory effect whereby NiCd batteries soon begin to lose the ability to hold a charge.

 The Northgate OmniKey keyboard, with its function keys down the left and a satisfyingly clacky feel, has attained nearly cult status among some users, although Northgate itself is long gone. Original OmniKey keyboards haven't been produced for years, so remaining working examples are sought after like Old Masters. Fortunately, there's an alternative. Creative Vision Technologies, Inc. (*http://www.cvtinc.com*) makes the Avant Stellar keyboard, which is more or less a clone of the Northgate OmniKey Plus. It isn't cheap, but it's as close as you'll find to the OmniKey in a current keyboard.

Configuring a Keyboard

Windows 9X/2000/XP allows you to customize some aspects of keyboard behavior. To do so, run the Keyboard applet (Start → Settings → Control Panel → Keyboard) to display the Keyboard Properties dialog, which includes the following pages:

Speed (Windows 9X/2000/XP)
> Includes settings for how long a key must be held down before it begins repeating and for how quickly it repeats. Also allows setting cursor blink rate, which controls how fast the virtual cursor blinks in Windows applications. Change any of these settings by dragging the associated slider. Changes take effect immediately when you click Apply or OK.

Language (Windows 9X) or Input Locales (Windows 2000/XP)
> These pages are nearly identical except for their names. They are used to install additional keyboard languages and layouts. Windows 9X allows specifying a key sequence (either Left Alt-Shift or Ctrl-Shift) to rotate through available languages from the keyboard. Windows 2000/XP provides the same choices, and adds an optional second key sequence to jump directly to the default language using the same key sequences listed for Windows 9X, with the addition of one character, 0 through 9, tilde, or grave accent. Windows 2000/XP also allows specifying the method used to turn off Caps Lock, either by pressing the Caps Lock key or by pressing the Shift key.

Hardware (Windows 2000/XP)
> This page displays the type of keyboard installed. It provides a Troubleshoot button, which invokes the Keyboard Troubleshooter Wizard, and a Properties button, which simply displays Device Manager properties for the keyboard.

Installing a programmable keyboard and driver may install a separate management application, or may simply add pages and options to the standard Keyboard Properties dialog. For example, Figure 19-3 shows the additional page of the extended Keyboard Properties dialog that results from installing the Microsoft IntelliType Pro driver under Windows 2000. If you install a programmable keyboard, make sure to locate and explore the options its driver provides. The default driver installation for some programmable keyboards leaves some very useful options disabled or set to less-than-optimum values.

Finally, do not overlook the Accessibility Options dialog, shown in Figure 19-4 (Start → Settings → Control Panel → Accessibility Options). This dialog is available in both Windows 9X and Windows 2000/XP. Although intended primarily to aid people with various disabilities, some options available here may be useful to anyone. In particular, anyone who has accidentally toggled Caps Lock on will appreciate the audible warning provided by ToggleKeys.

Linux also provides comprehensive keyboard configuration options via the configuration utilities included with the Gnome and KDE desktop environments. Figure 19-5, for example, shows the Red Hat 8.X Gnome Keyboard Accessibility Configuration dialog, which can be accessed by running gnome-keyboard-properties from the command line or by clicking Preferences → Keyboard → Accessibility from the Start menu.

Figure 19-3. The Windows 2000 Keyboard Properties dialog as modified by installing the Microsoft IntelliType Pro driver

Cleaning a Keyboard

Keyboards collect all manner of dirt, dust, and sticky spills, particularly if you smoke or drink near them. For routine cleaning, simply turn the keyboard upside down and shake it vigorously, which causes an incredible amount of stuff to fall out. Monthly, use your vacuum cleaner to do a thorough job. It's a good idea to shut down the system (or at least close all files) before you start vacuuming. Otherwise, the random series of keystrokes that vacuuming generates can have some unexpected results. In one case, we deleted a document. Formula 409 and similar commercial cleaners do a good job of removing grunge, but make sure the system is turned off while you use them, and try to avoid allowing too much to run down inside the keyboard. It's better to spray the cleaner on a paper towel and then wipe than to spray the cleaner directly on the keyboard.

All of that presupposes that your keyboard is just normally dirty. For cleaning seriously dirty keyboards (see Figure 19-6), we've been using the dishwasher method for more than 20 years. Most people think we're kidding when we recommend it, but it works for us. We've used it successfully with both mechanical and membrane-based keyboards. Proceed as follows.

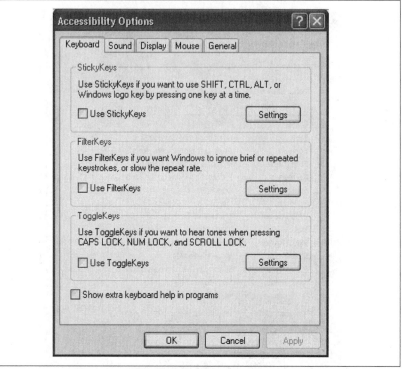

Figure 19-4. The Windows XP Accessibility Options dialog

1. Disconnect the keyboard from the computer. We probably shouldn't have to mention this step, but we don't want to get sued by someone who didn't realize it wasn't a good idea to run his system unit and monitor through the dishwasher.

2. Place the keyboard, keys down, in the top rack of the dishwasher. Secure the keyboard cable with a rubber band to keep it from becoming entangled in the moving parts of the dishwasher. Set the dishwasher for gentle cycle and coolest water temperature, if those options are available. Make sure to select the option for air-dry rather than a heated drying cycle.

3. Run the keyboard through an entire wash cycle, using dishwasher detergent. When the cycle finishes, remove the keyboard and douse it with at least a gallon of water, making sure to repeatedly flood the keys themselves. For safety's sake, we always recommend using distilled or deionized water, but in fact we always use ordinary tap water and have never had a problem. After rinsing, turn the keyboard this way and that and shake it to drain as much water as possible. Use a towel to dry the accessible parts. At this point, your keyboard should look like new (see Figure 19-7).

4. Set your oven to 150 degrees (or its lowest setting). We have no idea what the melting point of the plastic used in keyboards is, but we haven't melted one yet. Bake the keyboard until done, usually one to two hours. Let the keyboard cool, remove, and serve.

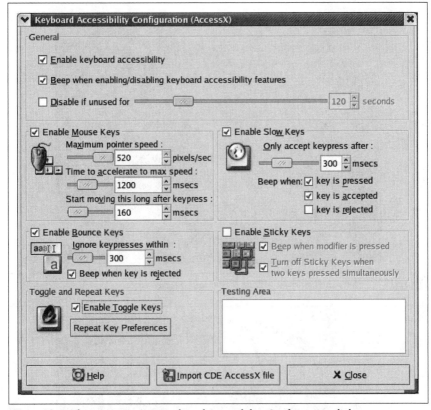

Figure 19-5. The Linux AccessX Keyboard Accessibility Configuration dialog

We generally put the clean keyboard back in our stock of spares, where it may have another month or three to air-dry naturally, but we've also reconnected a keyboard immediately after such treatment without any problems. We used to be concerned that puddles might still be lurking inside the keyboard, so we'd disassemble it and dry it thoroughly before reconnecting it. But we've found that a couple of hours inside a 150-degree oven does a pretty good job of evaporating any residual water. Your mileage may vary. If you hear a sloshing sound after drying, it's probably a good idea to disassemble the keyboard and check further.

Troubleshooting and Repairing Keyboards

Good keyboards are so cheap that spending much time troubleshooting or repairing them is counterproductive. Membrane keyboards are irreparable in practical terms. Mechanical and capacitive keyboards can be repaired, but with parts expensive and difficult to find and technicians charging $50+ per hour, it's cheaper just to buy a new one. The same goes for repairing a keyboard yourself, unless your time is worth nothing an hour.

Figure 19-6. A keyboard after more than a year without cleaning

Figure 19-7. The same keyboard after a trip through the dishwasher

If a keyboard stops working or behaves strangely, check to make sure the cables are connected properly. If everything appears to be correct, it's worth doing a simple swap to verify whether the problem is the keyboard or the PC. If a known-good keyboard also fails to work, the problem is most likely caused by a defective keyboard interface on the motherboard, for which the only realistic solutions are to substitute a USB keyboard or replace the motherboard. If the known-good keyboard works, replace the defective keyboard.

Our Picks

The choice of keyboard is, above all, a personal matter, but unless you have very strong preferences you'll probably find one of the following keyboards suitable. Here are the keyboards that we use and recommend:

Standard keyboard
> **Microsoft Internet Keyboard, Office Keyboard, or MultiMedia Keyboard.** If you want a standard straight keyboard, one of these models should suit you. The Internet Keyboard and MultiMedia Keyboard are PS/2-only. The Office Keyboard connects with PS/2 or USB. Barbara uses one or another of these standard keyboards on all of her systems (*http://www.microsoft.com/ hardware/keyboard*).

Ergonomic keyboard
> **Microsoft Natural Keyboard Elite or Natural MultiMedia Keyboard.** You'll either love or hate these "melted" keyboards. Robert loves them; Barbara hates them. The Natural MultiMedia Keyboard uses the PS/2 interface. The Natural Keyboard Elite uses the PS/2 or USB interface. Robert uses one or another of the Natural Keyboard models on his primary office systems.

> Some say that getting used to the Natural Keyboard layout takes a long time. That was not Robert's experience. He is a touch typist, and became completely comfortable with the Natural Keyboard in less than an hour. He uses Internet Keyboard models on some of his test-bed systems and switches back and forth without difficulty. The major adjustment is that the Natural Keyboard errs in putting the 6 key above and to the right of the T key, where it must be struck with the left index finger. Touch typists learn to strike the 6 key with the right index finger, and the change is a bit disconcerting at first.

Cordless keyboard (short-range)
> **Microsoft Wireless Optical series.** If your keyboard cord gets in the way, you like to work with the keyboard in your lap, or you need a cordless keyboard for your den or living room entertainment system, one of these Microsoft Wireless Optical keyboards may be just the thing. Microsoft makes various models in standard and ergonomic layouts, and either PS/2 or PS/2 and USB interfaces. Each includes a wireless optical mouse.

Keyboard-Video-Mouse (KVM) switches
> See Chapter 16.

For our most recent detailed recommendations by brand and model, visit: *http:// www.hardwareguys.com/picks/keyboards.html*.

20

Mice and Trackballs

Mice and trackballs are members of a class generically described as *pointing devices*. All pointing devices have the same purpose—allowing you to move the cursor (or pointer) around the screen and to click to select items or perform other functions. A great variety of fiendishly clever pointing devices are built into notebook computers, but nearly all desktop systems use mice. Those few that don't, use a trackball, which are essentially belly-up mice with their balls showing.

Mice Versus Trackballs

As with any input device, personal preference should rule choice. That said, relative to mice, trackballs have the following advantages:

- A trackball remains in place, and so requires less free desk space than a mouse.

- The trackball roller ball contacts your thumb rather than the desktop or mouse pad, which means it is less likely to require frequent cleaning. (However, "red-eye" optical mice do not require cleaning and so eliminate this advantage.)

- A trackball is often the better choice for 3D gaming and similar programs, where pointing and clicking are the most important functions.

- Some evidence suggests that using a trackball is less likely to cause RSI than using a mouse.

Trackballs have the following disadvantages:

- Most trackballs are designed such that you guide the pointer with your thumb, which is the least dexterous digit. Accordingly, many users find it harder to position the cursor exactly with a trackball than with a mouse.

- Most people find a trackball clumsier than a mouse for operations that depend heavily on click-and-drag, such as creating and editing documents.

- Some evidence suggests that using a trackball is more likely to cause RSI than using a mouse. (Yes, we know...)

Mice and trackballs are inexpensive enough that you should try both if you spend much time at a computer. If you have never used a trackball, doing so requires some adjustment. Many people find Microsoft optical trackballs—which look like a mouse with the red optical dome on the top or the side, depending on model— to be the easiest trackballs to adjust to.

Mouse Characteristics

Here are the important characteristics of mice and trackballs:

Mechanism
   Mice are available that use the following mechanisms:

   Mechanical
      Mechanical mice use a rubber-coated ball that contacts the mouse pad. Moving the mouse causes the ball to move, which in turn causes one or both of the internal cylindrical rollers with which the ball is in contact to move. These two internal rollers are oriented at 90° to each other, which allows one to respond to horizontal mouse movement and the other to vertical mouse movement. Connected to the end of each roller is a wheel with many small notches around its circumference. As the wheel rotates, these notches alternately pass or block light from an LED aimed to impinge on a sensor. The rate at and duration for which the sensors see the light flickering correspond to how fast, how far, and in what direction the ball is moving.

      Modern mechanical mice are inexpensive and reliable, but require frequent cleaning. The improvements in second-generation optical mice, described next, have largely relegated mechanical mice to bargain-basement systems.

   Optical
      Early mechanical mice provided limited resolution, were relatively unreliable, and required very frequent cleaning. Manufacturers addressed these problems by introducing optical mice, which substituted an optical sensor for the mouse ball. Reducing the number of moving parts increased reliability, and because the optical mouse was a sealed unit, cleaning was needed much less often. But first-generation optical mice had two drawbacks. First, their relatively primitive sensors required a special mouse pad that contained an embedded mesh of very fine wires and was easily damaged. Second, they were much more expensive than mechanical mice. As mechanical mice continued to improve, optical mice gradually became niche products and disappeared from the market for several years.

      A few years ago, Microsoft introduced second-generation optical mice that use enhanced sensors and more powerful laser diodes, which Microsoft calls IntelliEye technology. We call them red-eye mice. Because they are more sensitive and use a brighter light source, these mice can detect very minor variations in surface texture. That allows them to work on nearly any surface from a standard mouse pad to a bare desktop. In fact, they work on everything we've tried except a mirror. We've even used them successfully on featureless beige computer cases and unmarked sheets of white paper. Because they are sealed units, they do not require routine cleaning, which is a blessing for people who eat, drink, or smoke at their desks.

At first, IntelliEye mice were much more expensive than mechanical mice, but that price premium nearly disappeared as other manufacturers began shipping similar models. Basic red-eye mice now sell for $15, which has killed the market for mechanical mice. We now use only red-eye mice, and recommend them exclusively.

Because some red-eye mice draw more current than mechanical mice, they may be incompatible with some systems. In particular, some notebook computers have underpowered PS/2 ports that cannot drive some red-eye mice. Also, many KVM switches do not function properly or at all with red-eye mice.

Gyroscopic

At least one type of mouse doesn't require any mousing surface at all. Gyration's Ultra Cordless Optical Mouse can be used as a standard optical mouse when there is a mousing surface available. If there isn't, you can enable gyroscopic mode (at a substantial penalty in battery life) and simply wave the mouse around in midair. The built-in gyroscopes detect the mouse movements and translate them into pointer movements on screen. This capability doesn't come cheaply. A basic model with a 25-foot range sells for $70 or so, and models with longer ranges cost correspondingly more.

Number of buttons

Unlike the Macintosh world, where one-button mice are the rule, PC mice typically have two buttons, and some have three or more. In addition, many mice have a scroll wheel, which can function as another button. Using anything beyond the standard two buttons requires that both the driver and the application support the additional buttons. For example, the extended functions of the Microsoft Wheel Mouse are available only in applications that are specifically written to implement those extended functions, and only then if the enhanced mouse driver is installed to replace the standard mouse driver.

Interface

Mice have been produced in four interfaces. In relative order of current popularity, these interfaces include:

PS/2

The *PS/2 mouse* uses the same mini-DIN physical connector as the PS/2 keyboard, and interfaces to the PC using a second msi8042. But the mouse port uses IRQ12—versus IRQ1 for the keyboard port—which means that the mouse port and keyboard port are not interchangeable. All ATX motherboards provide a PS/2 mouse port on the I/O panel. Late model AT and Baby AT motherboards provide a PS/2 mouse port in the form of header pins on the motherboard, and use a port extender cable to jumper the header pins to a port connector on the back panel. The arrangement and pinouts of that header-pin connector are not standard. We have seen motherboards that use five-pin inline connectors, six-pin inline connectors, and 2x3 rectangular connectors. Even motherboards that use the same physical connector may use different pinouts. Most AT motherboards include a matching port extender. If yours does not, verify the pinouts in the motherboard manual before purchasing an extender.

*Mice &
Trackballs*

USB

A *USB mouse* uses no special resources beyond those claimed by the USB host controller itself. Unlike USB keyboards, USB mice do not require BIOS support because they need not be accessible until the operating system has loaded. They do require an operating system, such as Windows 9X/2000/XP or Linux, that supports USB. Many current mice offer the USB interface, and usually include an adapter to allow the mouse to be connected to a standard PS/2 mouse port.

Serial

Most AT and Baby AT motherboards from 1995 and earlier do not include a PS/2 mouse connector. With these systems, you normally use a *serial mouse*. A serial mouse uses a standard DB9F connector, and connects to a DB9M serial port connector on the PC. A serial mouse uses no special resources other than the standard serial port resources for the port to which it is connected (IRQ4 and base address 03F8-03FF for COM1, or IRQ3 and 02F8-02FF for COM2). You can connect a serial mouse to either serial port. When the mouse driver initializes, it detects which port the mouse is connected to and uses the appropriate IRQ and base address to access it. Serial mice are obsolete, although many remain in service on older systems.

Bus

A *bus mouse* (also called an *InPort mouse*) is so named because it connects to an adapter that plugs into the expansion bus. Bus mice were introduced to allow connecting a mouse to a PC that had no free serial ports. The adapter card is an 8-bit ISA card that provides selectable IRQ (usually 2, 3, 4, or 5) and base address settings. However, as an 8-bit card, it is limited to using 8-bit IRQs, most or all of which are already in use on a PC with two active serial ports, which is the reason for using a bus mouse in the first place. Ordinarily, the only available choice is IRQ5. If the system has an 8-bit sound card installed, IRQ5 is also occupied, which leaves no alternative unless you are willing to disable the IRQ for LPT1. Bus mice and InPort adapters are obsolete.

None of these interfaces is compatible with any of the others, although some mice are designed with autosensing circuitry to allow them to work with more than one interface. Dual compatibility is usually listed on the bottom of the mouse—e.g., "Serial and PS/2 compatible" or "USB and PS/2 compatible." In particular, be careful about interchanging PS/2 and bus mice, which use the same connector. Connecting a PS/2 mouse to a bus mouse port or vice versa can damage the mouse, the PC, or both.

Choosing a Mouse

Use the following guidelines when choosing a mouse or trackball:

Get the right size and shape

Mice are available in various sizes and shapes, including very small mice intended for children, the formerly standard "Dove bar" size, the mainstream ergonomic mouse, and some very large mice that have many buttons and extra features. Most people find nearly any standard-size mouse comfortable to use for short periods, but if you use a mouse for extended periods, small differences in size and shape often make a big difference in comfort. Although oversize mice such as the Microsoft IntelliMouse Explorer provide attractive features and functions, people with very small hands often find such mice too large to use comfortably. Pay particular attention to mouse shape if you are lefthanded. Although Microsoft claims that its asymmetric ergonomic mice are equally usable by left- and righthanders, many lefties find them uncomfortable and so resort to righthanded mousing. Other manufacturers, including Logitech, produce symmetric mice for which chirality is not an issue.

 Don't assume that hand size and mouse size are necessarily related. For example, Barbara, who has small hands, prefers the Microsoft IntelliMouse Explorer, which is an oversized mouse. She found that using a standard or small mouse for long periods caused her hand to hurt. Changing to a large mouse solved the problem.

Get a wheel mouse

Although some applications do not support the wheel, those that do are the ones most people are likely to use a great deal—Microsoft Office, Internet Explorer, Mozilla, and so on. Using the wheel greatly improves mouse functionality by reducing the amount of mouse movement needed to navigate web pages and documents.

Consider a mouse with extra buttons

Standard two-button mice (three, counting the wheel) are adequate for most purposes. However, five-button mice are ideally suited to some applications, such as games and web browsing. For example, the two extra buttons can be mapped to the Back and Forward browser icons, eliminating a great deal of extraneous mouse movement.

Make sure the cord is long enough

We have seen mice with cords ranging in length from less than 4 feet to about 9 feet. A short mouse cord may be too short to reach the system, particularly if it is on the floor. If you need a longer mouse cord, purchase a PS/2 keyboard extension cable, available in nearly any computer store.

Consider a cordless model

If your desktop is usually cluttered, consider buying a cordless mouse. The absence of a cord can make a surprising difference.

Buy an optical mouse

Old-style optical mice were a pain in the begonia. They required special mousing surfaces with fine embedded wires and frequently malfunctioned.

Red-eye mice changed that. They use a red LED light source and do not require any special mousing surface. We have used them on such featureless surfaces as a beige computer case and a plain sheet of paper. Basically, they work fine with anything other than a mirror or similarly reflective surface.

Because they are sealed units, red-eye mice do not require the frequent cleaning that mechanical mice do. Robert had to take his mechanical mice apart and clean them literally every few days, but red-eye mice can go for months at a time without any cleaning other than a quick wipe with a damp cloth. Good red-eye mice are very precise and extremely durable. Robert's den system had a Microsoft red-eye mouse, which he dropped to the hardwood floor several times a week. Finally, after more than two years of this abuse, the red-eye mouse died with a horrible rattle. The replacement continues to work perfectly, despite frequent falls.

Try a trackball

Trackballs have never really caught on, probably because most require using the thumb to move the pointer. At least one newer model, the red-eye Microsoft Trackball Explorer, resembles a mouse and allows using the index finger to point. In our experience, about one of every 10 people who try a trackball becomes a trackball convert. But trackballs sell probably only 1% the volume of mice, which says there are a lot of people who don't know what they're missing. Trackballs are also available in red-eye versions, and we prefer those to the mechanical versions for ease of maintenance.

Configuring a Mouse or Trackball

Windows 9X/2000/XP allows you to customize how your mouse behaves. To do so, run the Mouse applet (Start → Settings → Control Panel → Mouse) to display the Mouse Properties dialog, which for standard mice includes the following pages:

Buttons (Windows 9X/2000/XP)

The Buttons page in Windows 9X allows you to configure the mouse for right- or lefthanded use and specify the maximum duration between clicks that will still be recognized as a double-click. The Windows 2000/XP Buttons page has the same functions, and also allows you to specify whether a single click or a double click opens a file or folder. Changes in this dialog take effect immediately when you click Apply or OK. IntelliMouse 3.1 and later and recent Logitech mouse drivers allow or require you to specify the function of individual buttons, but don't allow you to switch between left- and right-handed configurations by clicking one option button.

Pointers (Windows 9X/2000/XP)

The Pointers page in Windows 9X allows you to change the appearance of the mouse cursor. If predefined mouse scheme(s) are installed, selecting one from the Schemes drop-down list defines all cursor types in one step. Double-clicking an individual pointer type displays a list of available cursor icons that can be assigned to that pointer type. Windows 2000/XP provides the same options, and adds a checkbox to enable pointer shadow.

Motion (Windows 9X/2000/XP)

The Motion page in Windows 9X allows you to set the speed of the mouse pointer using the Pointer speed slider. Depending on the mouse driver installed, other options may also appear on this page, including Snap-to (automatically move the pointer to the default option button in dialogs); Pointer trails (display a series of ghost pointers as the mouse is moved to prevent losing track of the pointer); and Vanish (hide the mouse pointer while typing). Windows 2000/XP provides the same options and adds standard Snap to default and Acceleration settings.

Hardware (Windows 2000/XP only)

These pages display the type of mouse installed. The Windows 2000/XP Hardware page provides a Troubleshoot button, which invokes the Mouse Troubleshooter Wizard, and a Properties button, which simply displays Device Manager properties for the mouse.

Installing a new mouse or an updated mouse driver may add pages and options to the standard Mouse Properties dialog. For example, Figure 20-1 shows one of the additional pages that result from installing the Microsoft IntelliPoint driver supplied with the Microsoft IntelliMouse with IntelliEye (where do they come up with these names?). If you install a new mouse driver, locate and explore the options it provides. The default settings for such things as wheel definition are probably useful, but one of the alternative options may better suit your work habits.

Recent Linux releases generally recognize and configure mice properly during installation, including support for extra features such as a scroll wheel or additional buttons. If you install a new mouse, run the mouse configuration utility supplied with your distro. Figure 20-2, for example, shows the Red Hat 8.X Mouse Configuration utility, which can be invoked by becoming root and running redhat-config-mouse from the command line or by clicking System Settings and then Mouse from the start menu. Because most Linux GUIs are optimized for a three-button mouse, Linux allows you to emulate a third button on a two-button mouse by depressing both buttons simultaneously.

The Gnome and KDE desktop environments also include utilities that allow you to change the configuration of the existing mouse. For example, Figure 20-3 shows the Red Hat 8.X Gnome Mouse Preferences dialog, which can be accessed by running gnome-mouse-properties from the command line or by clicking Preferences and then Mouse from the Start menu.

Cleaning a Mouse

No, we don't put mice through the dishwasher, although we may try that someday. Optical mice are sealed units, and so require little more than an occasional wipe with a damp cloth. How often you need to clean a mechanical mouse depends on your working environment. When we still used mechanical mice, Barbara, who is a true neatnik, needed to clean her mechanical mice only every few months. Robert, who smokes a pipe, needed to clean his mechanical mice every few days.

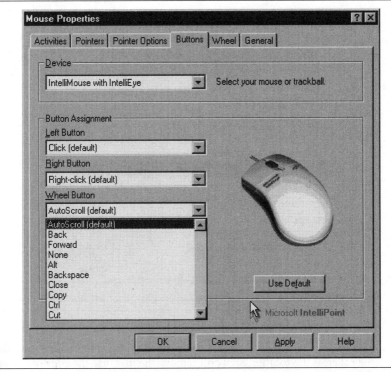

Figure 20-1. The Windows 2000 Mouse Properties dialog as modified by installing the Microsoft IntelliPoint mouse driver

The best sign that a mechanical mouse needs to be cleaned is when mouse movement suddenly becomes jerky or intermittent, particularly if the problem is limited to one direction. A mouse has two cylindrical rollers, one each to capture horizontal and vertical movement, and may also have one or more idler wheels designed to keep the ball in position. Dirt on these rollers and wheels is normally the cause of jerkiness and other movement problems. The best way we've found to clean a mouse requires only a soft cloth, an old toothbrush, and a bottle of rubbing alcohol. Take the following steps:

1. Dampen the cloth with alcohol and use it to wipe down the mouse cord and the exterior of the mouse.

2. Remove the plate that retains the ball and allow the ball to drop into your hand. Use the damp cloth to clean the ball and plate thoroughly and set them aside.

3. With the mouse upside down and using a strong light, look down into the hole normally occupied by the ball. Blow or shake out any large fluff balls or other accumulated trash.

4. Dip the toothbrush in alcohol and use it to scrub the rollers and wheels thoroughly, making sure to get them clean from end to end and all around their circumference. Because of the rolling action, hair and fibers can become

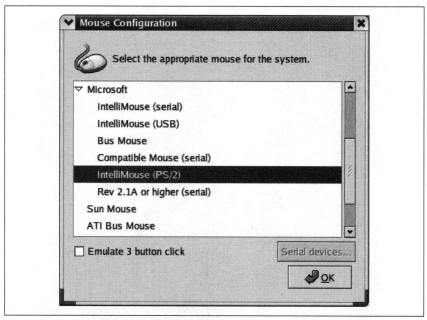

Figure 20-2. The Red Hat 8.X Mouse Configuration dialog

knitted in a mat around the rollers, to the point where they're almost welded to the roller. If the toothbrush won't remove the mat, use the edge of a sharp knife *gently* to break up the mat without scratching the roller and then use the toothbrush to remove the freed junk.

5. If the mouse has a wheel, the bottom of the wheel is probably accessible from within the mouse housing. Use your finger to press the dampened cloth against the bottom of the wheel while you rotate the wheel from the top to remove accumulated grunge.

6. While you're at it, use the damp cloth to clean the mouse pad and the desk immediately surrounding it.

But before you spend much time cleaning an old mechanical mouse, consider replacing it with a modern optical mouse. Good red-eye mice are available for less than $20. They're durable, provide more precise pointing than a mechanical mouse, and need only an occasional wipe with a damp cloth.

Troubleshooting a Mouse

If a mouse malfunctions, make sure the cable is connected properly and clean the mouse. If it still doesn't work, replace it.

Our Picks

In prior editions, we recommended Microsoft mice exclusively because they happened to be the best mice available. People sent us nastygrams accusing us of

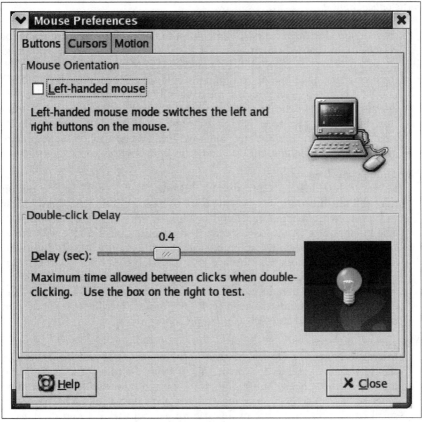

Figure 20-3. The Gnome Mouse Preferences dialog

being in the pay of the Borg. Well, we get as mad at Microsoft as anyone else does, so it's a pleasure to be able to recommend some non-Microsoft products in this edition.

Logitech mice are generally a bit less expensive than comparable Microsoft models, and some people actually prefer them, but whenever we try a competing model we invariably find ourselves coming back to Microsoft. Some also prefer tablets to mice or trackballs, but we have insufficient experience with tablets to have formed any valid opinions concerning them.

Here are the mice and trackballs we use and recommend:

Mechanical mouse

None. There is little reason to buy a mechanical mouse nowadays. Basic red-eye mice sell for as little as $10, and even the best red-eye mice cost little or no more than mechanical mice with similar features. The only reason to buy a mechanical mouse is if you have a notebook or KVM that doesn't work with red-eye mice. In that situation, we recommend an inexpensive Microsoft IntelliMouse.

Basic optical mouse

Samsung or Logitech Optical Wheel Mouse. At $12 or so each, these red-eye mice are good enough for nearly any purpose. Similar products are made (or relabeled) by Labtec, Keytronic, IOGEAR, and others. We haven't tried those, but we suspect any of them would suffice. Many models are available, most of which have two buttons and a scroll wheel. Most models have PS/2 and USB connectors, although some have only PS/2. These inexpensive red-eye mice don't have the best sensors or the most robust mechanical construction, but they're precise enough and durable enough to serve most people's needs well. Robert uses Samsung and Logitech red-eye mice on his secondary systems (*http://www.samsung.com* and *http://www.logitech.com*).

Five-button optical mouse

Microsoft IntelliMouse Optical or IntelliMouse Explorer. These five-button mice sell for three to four times the price of basic optical mice. They appear to be somewhat more durable and precise, but the difference is not large. The IntelliMouse Optical is a standard-size mouse that is usable with either hand. The IntelliMouse Explorer is an oversize mouse that is for right-handed use only. Both models have PS/2 and USB connectors. Barbara uses an IntelliMouse Explorer on her main system, despite her small hands, because she finds it reduces the frequency and severity of hand pain she experiences with standard-size mice. Robert uses an IntelliMouse Optical on his primary system (*http://www.microsoft.com*).

Miniature optical mouse

Microsoft Notebook Optical Mouse. This cute little USB-only rodent is just the thing when space is at a premium. At twice the price of a basic optical mouse, it's not cheap, but it does work on most notebooks, which some other red-eye mice do not. Many children and some adults who have very small hands prefer a mouse of this size for general use. We find it a bit too small for comfortable long-term use, but it is certainly superior to the built-in pointing devices used on most notebook computers.

Gyroscopic mouse

Gyration Ultra Cordless Optical Mouse. We haven't actually used this product, but we've received so many favorable comments about it from readers that we decided to include it in our recommendations. At $70 or so for the basic model, this is a very expensive mouse, but it is unique because it does not require a mousing surface at all. In optical mode, it works like any other red-eye mouse. But when you press the Bat-button, a miniature two-axis gyro spins up, which allows the mouse to function normally simply by being waved around in midair. One nice feature of the Gyration mice is their relatively long range. The range of the standard unit is rated at 25 feet, and the Pro unit at 100 feet. Frankly, we don't see a need for airborne mice, but many of our readers tell us they use this mouse (and the matched wireless keyboard) on home entertainment systems (*http://www.gyration.com/*).

Wireless optical mouse

Microsoft Wireless Optical Mouse or Wireless IntelliMouse Explorer. If you need a wireless mouse, either of these will do the job admirably. The Wireless Optical Mouse is an ambidextrous, standard-size wheel mouse that uses the PS/2 or USB interface. The Wireless IntelliMouse Explorer is an oversize five-button mouse that is USB-only. These units are intended for desktop use, and so have relatively short range. If you need longer range, use one of the Gyration units.

Trackball

Microsoft Trackballs. Microsoft produces two optical trackballs, which offer the same advantages as red-eye mice. These two models differ primarily in where the ball is placed. The **Trackball Optical** puts the ball on the left side near the middle, where it can be manipulated by the thumb. The **Trackball Explorer** puts the ball at the top front, where it can be manipulated by the index finger. We prefer the latter, but suggest you try both because some people prefer using their thumbs.

For our most recent detailed recommendations by brand name and model number, visit: *http://www.hardwareguys.com/picks/mice.html.*

21

Game Controllers

A *game controller* is a specialized input device optimized for use with games. Unlike mice and trackballs, which are relatively standardized in form and function, game controllers run the gamut in shape, size, features, and purpose. Some game controllers sit on the desktop. Others clamp to the desk, and still others are held in both hands and manipulated directly. Game controllers may have a joystick, a steering wheel, a flight yoke, or foot pedals, or may be what we call "grab, twist, and squeeze" controllers.

A particular game controller may be well-suited for one game and entirely inappropriate for another. For example, a game controller with a steering wheel may be perfect for playing NASCAR Winston Cup Racing, but unusable for a first-person shooter (FPS) game such as Quake. Serious gamers who play diverse games often own several game controllers and use the one most appropriate for the game they are playing at the moment.

Game controllers attach either to a game port, which most sound adapters provide as a combined game/MIDI port, or to a USB port. Although you may have only one game/MIDI port on a PC, that port can support two game controllers simultaneously by using a splitter, which is supplied with many game controllers or can be purchased at most computer stores. Also, some game controllers have ports on the controller itself, which allow additional controllers to be daisy-chained from the controller attached to the PC. As you might expect, it's possible to connect multiple USB game controllers, although not all combinations work properly and conflicts are common.

Game Controller Characteristics

Here are the important characteristics of game controllers:

Type

The first game controllers were *joystick controllers*, which are still popular and still most appropriate for playing flight simulator and air combat games. Some are marginally usable for some driving, racing, action/adventure, and sports games. *Steering wheel controllers*, many of which include foot pedals, are ideal for driving/racing games and some flight simulators, but ill-suited to other games. *Gamepad controllers* are suitable for action games, including first-person shooters, sports, and most arcade-style games.

Number of axes

An *axis* is a line drawn through the center of the joystick (or the D-pad on a gamepad) that defines the directions that one can move by manipulating the controls. All controllers have an *x-axis* (side-to-side movement) and a *y-axis* (front to back). Some controllers add a *z-axis* (up and down) and/or a *throttle axis*. Depending on the controller type, the third and/or fourth axes may also be called a *yoke control* or *rudder control*, for their intended function, or a *twist control*, for the method used to activate the axis.

Throttle

The *throttle* is a variable input, present on most joysticks and some gamepads, and normally assigned to the third or fourth axis on the controller. The throttle is usually used to control vehicle speed, and may be a slider, wheel, pedal, or variable-pull trigger, depending on the controller.

Response type

Motion along an axis can be tracked in two ways. *Proportional response* (common with joysticks) offers finer control because small stick movements result in small incremental movements on screen. *Nonproportional response* (common with gamepads) is all-or-nothing—any movement of the control along an axis results in full motion on that axis, offering faster response at the expense of fine control. Some controllers are programmable to allow choosing between proportional and nonproportional modes.

Number of buttons

All controllers have buttons, which are momentary-on switches used to fire weapons and perform similar on/off functions. Pure analog controllers are limited to two or four buttons by the gameport itself. Digital controllers and the Microsoft DirectInput API allow using any number of buttons.

Hat switch

A *hat switch*, sometimes called a *POV hat*, a *Point of View hat*, or just a *hat*, is so called because it usually resides on the head of the joystick, where it's easily manipulated by the thumb. The hat switch is a directional rocker switch (usually four-way, but sometimes eight-way) that allows you to rapidly change your POV to face front, rear, left, or right. Games that do not support POV may use the hat to provide four extra buttons.

Force feedback

Recent high-end game controllers have force-feedback technology, which uses small servo motors built into the game controller itself to provide physical feedback under the control of game software designed to use force feedback. For example, with a force-feedback joystick, as you pull a 7G turn you feel the joystick jerk and jitter as the aircraft control surfaces lose laminar flow, but as you extend to gain airspeed, the controls settle down again. When you come up on the six of a bandit and begin hosing him down with your 30mm rotary cannon, the joystick stutters as the gun recoils.

Well-implemented force feedback greatly enhances the ambiance of games that support it properly, but the quality of force-feedback hardware varies greatly between controllers. Even more important, games vary greatly in how well they integrate force feedback. Well-designed games use it elegantly to make the game more immersive. Many games, however, have simply grafted on minimal force-feedback support, and use it in only the most basic ways. This problem seems to be disappearing as new releases of such games usually make better use of force feedback. The only real drawback to force feedback is that it is expensive. A $50 controller without force feedback might cost $100 with it. Interestingly, this same technology (in much enhanced form) is used in current fly-by-wire combat aircraft.

Programmability

All current game controllers include DirectInput drivers or are compatible with standard Windows 9X drivers. A DirectInput-compliant controller can be programmed within any DirectInput-compliant game. However, Direct-Input provides only basic functionality, so many controllers come with their own programming software that provides extended functionality, including:

Cross-game commonality

By default, games may use different buttons for similar purposes. For example, one air combat game may use button 1 to fire guns, button 2 to launch a Sidewinder, and button 3 to launch a Sparrow. Another air combat game may offer similar weapons selection, but use different buttons. Programmable game controllers allow you to redefine button functions so that the same button performs similar actions in different games.

Stored profiles

Many modern game controllers are quite flexible and may be used with diverse games. Optimal controller configuration for one game, however, may be less desirable for another. Better game controllers can store multiple groups of configuration settings, called *macros* or *profiles*, that allow you to quickly load whichever settings are most appropriate for the game you're about to play, rather than having to reprogram the controller manually each time. Most such controllers come with predefined settings for various popular games.

Interface

Analog game controllers connect to the gameport. Digital game controllers connect to the gameport or to a USB port. Analog controllers are obsolete, although millions of them are still in service. Analog controllers provide limited functionality require frequent calibration, and using them degrades system performance. Digital game controllers provide greater functionality, seldom or never require calibration, and do not degrade system performance, so all game controller development now focuses on digital, and in particular on USB.

Gameport Interface

A standard PC gameport is actually a simple general-purpose analog data-acquisition port that supports four simple switched inputs and four variable-voltage inputs. A game controller connected to this interface uses one or more of the switched inputs to support buttons and one or more of the variable inputs to support a joystick, steering wheel, or similar device.

A *paddle* (originally used for Pong) is the simplest game controller. It uses only one switched input for a button and one variable input for a knob that controls movement in one direction. Accordingly, a gameport can support up to four paddles. A *joystick* uses one or two switched inputs for buttons and two variable inputs for a central stick that controls movement in both the horizontal (x-axis) and vertical (y-axis) directions. Accordingly, a gameport can support one or two joysticks. More complex game controllers use more of the switched inputs for additional buttons, and more of the variable inputs to control a third (z-axis) direction or for other purposes. This means that a gameport can support only one such controller.

Gameports do not require an IRQ, a DMA channel, or mapped memory, and occupy only one I/O base address. The downside of this small resource footprint is that gameports are not interrupt-driven, so the CPU must constantly poll the gameport to detect when a button is pressed or a stick is moved. Polling can require as much as 10% of the CPU, which degrades performance when you least want the performance hit—as you're playing a shoot-'em-up or trying to land a crippled fighter. The gameport connector on the PC is a DB-15F, shown in Figure 21-1.

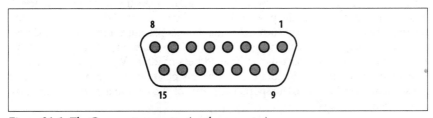

Figure 21-1. The Gameport connector (on the computer)

Table 21-1 describes the gameport interface and pinouts. On MIDI-capable gameports (usually those on sound cards), Pin 12 is MIDI data out and Pin 15 is MIDI data in.

Table 21-1. Gameport interface signals and pinout

Pin	Name	Joystick function	Paddle function	Direction
1	+5VDC	Joystick 1 power	Paddle A coordinate high	Out
2	Button 4	Joystick 1 button 1	Paddle A button high	In
3	Position 0	Joystick 1 x-coordinate	Paddle A coordinate wiper	In
4	Ground	Joystick 1 button 1 ground	Paddle A button ground	-
5	Ground	Joystick 1 button 2 ground	Paddle B button ground	-

Table 21-1. Gameport interface signals and pinout (continued)

Pin	Name	Joystick function	Paddle function	Direction
6	Position 1	Joystick 1 y-coordinate	Paddle B coordinate wiper	In
7	Button 5	Joystick 1 button 2	Paddle B button high	In
8	+5VDC	(unused)	Paddle B coordinate high	Out
9	+5VDC	Joystick 2 power	Paddle C coordinate high	Out
10	Button 6	Joystick 2 button 1	Paddle C button high	In
11	Position 2	Joystick 2 x-coordinate	Paddle C coordinate wiper	In
12	Ground	Joystick 2 button 1/2 ground	Paddle C/D button return	-
13	Position 3	Joystick 2 y-coordinate	Paddle D coordinate wiper	In
14	Button 7	Joystick 2 button 2	Paddle D button high	In
15	+5VDC	(unused)	Paddle D coordinate high	Out

There are two types of gameport, single- and dual-port. Table 21-1 describes the dual-port type. The single-port type uses the same connector, but does not support the Joystick 2 functions. In short, rather than supporting four switched inputs and four variable inputs, a single-port gameport supports only two of each, and can therefore support only one two-button, two-axis game controller. All current sound cards and most older sound cards provide dual-port gameports. Only a few very old models are single-port devices.

Joystick coordinate signals are analog inputs. Pins 3 and 6 report the x- and y-coordinates, respectively, for Joystick 1. Pins 11 and 13 do the same for Joystick 2. Moving the joystick alters the position of the slider on a 0 to 100 kΩ potentiometer, altering resistance, which in turn alters the voltage present on the pin. The gameport periodically samples the voltage on each coordinate pin using a monostable multivibrator. The gameport uses a base address of 201h. Writing to that address resets the monostable multivibrators and begins position measurement. Each byte subsequently read from 201h reports the status of the coordinate and button pins, as shown in Table 21-2.

Table 21-2. Gameport 201h byte

201h byte bitmask									
7	6	5	4	3	2	1	0	Description	Pin
1	0	0	0	0	0	0	0	Joystick 2, button 2 (0=closed, 1=open)	14
0	1	0	0	0	0	0	0	Joystick 2, button 1 (0=closed, 1=open)	10
0	0	1	0	0	0	0	0	Joystick 1, button 2 (0=closed, 1=open)	7
0	0	0	1	0	0	0	0	Joystick 1, button 1 (0=closed, 1=open)	2
0	0	0	0	1	0	0	0	Joystick 2, y-coordinate (0=timed-out, 1=timing)	13
0	0	0	0	0	1	0	0	Joystick 2, x-coordinate (0=timed-out, 1=timing)	11
0	0	0	0	0	0	1	0	Joystick 1, y-coordinate (0=timed-out, 1=timing)	6
0	0	0	0	0	0	0	1	Joystick 1, x-coordinate (0=timed-out, 1=timing)	3

Most game controllers introduced since mid-1999 use USB instead of or in addition to the legacy gameport interface. Because USB is a general-purpose digital interface, game controller designers can implement whatever custom functions they wish in the controller hardware and define support for those functions in the driver.

Choosing a Game Controller

More so than for any other input device, the "best" game controller is a matter of personal preference. If it feels right to you, it probably is right. If it feels wrong, it's probably wrong, no matter how much someone else may like it. Use the following guidelines when choosing a game controller:

Get the right type(s)
> Make sure the game controller type is appropriate for the games you play most often. If you frequently play two or more games that are ill-suited to using the same controller, buy two or more controllers, and use the type most suited to whatever game you play. We make some suggestions as to appropriate types on the web site listed in the "Our Picks" section.

Avoid analog game controllers
> All current game controllers worth having are digital models, although some analog models are still available. Note that some digital controllers use the analog gameport interface, including some high-end models. Digital gameport models are acceptable, but fully digital (USB) models are easier to swap in and out if you use multiple controllers. The only time it makes sense to use an analog controller is for games that run only under DOS or older Windows versions that do not support digital controllers, or if your system does not have USB ports and your gameport does not support digital controllers. Of course, you're unlikely to be playing games on such an antique system.

Check compatibility
> If you buy a model that connects to the gameport, verify that that controller is compatible with your gameport. Incompatibilities between PCI audio cards and digital game controllers are very common.

Buy a force-feedback model
> If an appropriate force-feedback model is available and is within your budget, buy it rather than the cheaper model. More and more games support force feedback every month, and that support is of a higher quality with each upgrade of many games.

Solicit advice from friends
> Friends are among the best sources of information about game controllers. You'll get a great deal of feedback from them, much of it conflicting, but valuable nonetheless. Not the least advantage of this method is that they'll probably let you play a few games with their controllers, giving you the opportunity to judge the merits for yourself in a realistic environment.

Installing a Game Controller

Physically installing a game controller is straightforward. Simply plug it into the gameport or a USB port, as appropriate. If the controller has both connectors, use the USB port unless the documentation suggests otherwise.

Before you connect the game controller, however, we suggest that you visit the Microsoft download site and update your copy of Windows to the latest drivers, particularly DirectX.

Troubleshooting Game Controllers

It's impossible to provide comprehensive information about troubleshooting game controllers because both the controllers themselves and the problems you may encounter are so diverse. A cheap game controller is probably going to physically break or otherwise fail sooner rather than later. There's not much we can say about that, except to suggest that you buy a better-quality game controller in the first place. If you experience problems with a good game controller, here are some actions to take:

Make sure the gameport is compatible with the game controller
> Not all gameport game controllers are compatible with all gameports. Gameport conflicts frequently cause problems, particularly with digital game controllers connected to some models of PCI sound cards. We have also had reports of conflicts between some game controllers and some AGP video cards on specific motherboards, although we have not personally experienced or verified these. Most game controller vendors have detailed FAQ pages that list known incompatibilities for each model they sell.

Install the latest release of DirectX
> DirectX is a work in progress. If you have problems with a game controller, particularly a new model or one you have just installed, download and install the latest version of DirectX from *http://www.microsoft.com/windows/directx/ downloads/default.asp*. Before you install the update, review the DirectX FAQ (*http://www.microsoft.com/windows/directx/default.aspx?url=/windows/directx/ productinfo/faq/default.htm*) carefully to discover issues pertinent to your own configuration. It's also a good idea to review the FAQs posted by the makers of your video card, sound card, game controller, and so on to discover any potential conflicts or interdependencies such as a need to update drivers for those devices.

 When you update DirectX, always check for supplementary updates, particularly if your system has a video capture card, an IEEE-1394 interface, or other video capture or digital video hardware or software. For example, after releasing DirectX 8.0, Microsoft released a patch called Digital Video Update for DirectX 8.0 (later renamed Video Capture Update for DirectX 8.0), which fixed various problems. Digital video is plagued by incompatibilities and nonstandardization, making such patches the norm.

If after you install a DirectX update your system seems sluggish or jerky, check the status of the *Poll with interrupts enabled* checkbox in the DirectX configuration applet. Beginning with DirectX 7.0, for some reason Microsoft enabled this checkbox by default. Clearing the checkbox should restore your system to normal operation.

Install the latest drivers

Some game controllers provide basic functionality using the default drivers provided with Windows. If your game controller appears to be only partially functional, you may need to install a driver to support its enhanced functions. Most game controller vendors frequently update drivers to fix bugs, add support for new games, and so on, so it's a good idea to check the vendor support page frequently.

Update your system BIOS

If you have problems with a game controller connected to an older system, update the system BIOS. For example, on one older system, we installed a joystick that the driver insisted on recognizing as a gamepad. We tried updating the driver software, DirectX, and so on, all to no avail. Then we noticed after updating the main system BIOS for unrelated reasons that the driver now recognized the joystick as a joystick. We reflashed the BIOS to its original level, and the problem recurred. We re-reflashed the BIOS to the updated level, and the problem went away again.

Make sure the game controller is configured for the game

If the game controller appears to work properly for one game but not others, make sure you've used the programmable functions of the game controller to configure it properly to support the other games. Most programmable game controllers include predefined profiles for popular games. If no profile is included for a game you purchase, check the vendor web site to see if an updated profile for that game is available.

Make sure the game is configured for the game controller

The default configuration settings for some games are inappropriate for some game controllers. For example, although many FPS games have freelook/mouselook disabled by default, the Microsoft SideWinder Dual Strike gamepad requires it to be enabled for proper functioning. Each time you install a new game, check the game controller manual or web site to see if there are specific instructions to configure the controller optimally for that game.

The following material describes some specific problems you may encounter and some possible solutions. As always, the best way to troubleshoot problems is to swap components. If you have another system and/or another game controller available, try swapping controllers back and forth between the system to determine if the problem is caused by the system or the controller.

No controller applet appears in the Control Panel

Install the software for your game controller. If you have already installed the controller software, install DirectX manually. Although most controller software installs DirectX, some requires you to install it yourself. Installing DirectX adds the Control Panel applet.

Installing a DirectX update causes problems

Reinstalling the latest version of your controller software after installing the DirectX update almost always fixes the problem. If that doesn't work, visit the controller maker's web site for additional information. If the web site offers no fix and you are using a gameport controller, try uninstalling your sound card drivers completely. Once you've eradicated all traces of the sound card drivers, shut down the system and physically remove the sound card. Then power the system back up (without the sound card) and shut it down again. Reinstall the sound card, restart the system, and reinstall the sound card drivers.

 Never try to downgrade DirectX by installing an earlier version over a later version. It just doesn't work, and attempting to do it causes worse problems than the one you're trying to solve. If you absolutely must revert to an earlier DirectX version, the only way we know to do so reliably is to strip the hard drive down to bare metal and reinstall Windows and all applications.

Installing a new sound card or updating sound drivers disables force feedback

Gameport DirectInput force-feedback controllers use MIDI signals to control feedback. If you didn't completely remove all vestiges of the old sound card drivers, the new card or drivers may not be configured to use MIDI correctly. Uninstall the sound card and drivers (as described earlier) and reinstall them.

Controller doesn't work on gameport switch or with extension cables

To make it easier to switch among controllers, some people install a gameport switchbox or extension cables. If you are having problems with a controller connected via a switchbox or extension cable, try connecting it directly to the system. Switches work with most analog controllers, but don't work with analog force-feedback controllers or any digital controller. Extension cables also often cause problems. The controller may not function at all, or it may function sporadically. Either dispense with the extension cables, or buy better-quality cables.

Y-cable doesn't work with two controllers

A Y-cable should allow you to share one gameport between two analog game controllers for head-to-head play. However, the pinouts of Y-cables are nonstandard and a given Y-cable may not work with a particular type of controller. If the controllers are different models, it may be impossible to find a Y-cable that allows you to use both. Even if the Y-cable works properly with the controllers, each controller will be limited to a subset of the functions that it supports when it is the only controller connected. The best solution is to use two identical controllers that have pass-through ports—which allows you to use the full feature set of both controllers—or to use USB controllers.

USB game controller does not work properly

Unfortunately, USB is not quite as Plug-and-Play as the industry would have us believe. If your USB controller is functioning improperly or not at all and installing the latest version of DirectX and the controller drivers doesn't solve the problem, you may experience one of the following hardware problems:

Defective USB port

If you're sure software isn't the problem, first try plugging the controller into a different USB port. We've encountered few bad root USB ports on motherboards, but bad ports are not uncommon on inexpensive USB hubs.

Incompatible USB controller, port, or device

In theory, USB is rigidly standardized, but in practice some implementations are plagued by incompatibilities. Early USB-capable motherboards—particularly Socket 7 and Slot 1 models based on pre-440BX Intel chipsets and all VIA chipsets—are USB-compliant in theory, but are buggy enough that the root hub ports may be useless. Nor is the fault always on the motherboard side. Some early USB devices, including game controllers, were not fully compliant and may or may not function properly when connected to a particular USB port. If the motherboard is at fault, you can solve the problem by replacing the motherboard or by disabling the motherboard USB ports and adding a PCI expansion card that provides two or more USB root ports. If the device itself is the problem, the only solution may be to connect it with an older USB port or to replace the device.

Inadequate USB power

Some USB game controllers draw more power than an unpowered USB hub can supply. If your game controller doesn't work when connected to an unpowered USB hub, try connecting it to a root hub port on the PC or to a powered USB hub port. Note that not all motherboard USB ports are fully powered. For example, some ASUS motherboards provide less current to the USB root hub ports than what some game controllers require. If your controller doesn't work when connected to a motherboard USB port but works when connected to a motherboard USB port on another system, using a powered USB hub will likely solve the problem.

Bad USB cable

Surprisingly often, USB cables are defective, particularly those you find for $3 in a bin at the computer store. But we've encountered defective USB cables of all sorts, including those bundled with motherboards and USB devices. We generally keep a couple of spare Belkin USB cables on hand for such eventualities (*http://www.belkin.com*).

Game controller fails to work when daisy-chained

The way USB is supposed to work and the way USB actually works are two entirely different things. Although you should in theory be able to daisy-chain USB devices freely, in practice it often doesn't work out that way. If your USB game controller doesn't work when daisy-chained, try connecting it to a root hub port or to a powered USB hub.

USB game controller doesn't work under Windows 95

First, make sure that you're using Windows 95 OSR2 or higher (Windows 95b). Early versions of Windows 95 had no USB support. Later versions had limited USB support, and any given USB game controller may or may not work with Windows 95b. Check the web site of the game controller manufacturer to verify whether the controller is supported under Windows 95b. Otherwise, upgrade to Windows 98SE (*not* Windows Me), Windows 2000, or Windows XP.

USB game controller doesn't work under Windows NT 4

Windows NT 4 has no direct OS support for USB, and only limited support for ActiveX (V 3.0a). Although it is possible for manufacturers to write custom USB drivers for their devices under NT 4 (e.g., the Iomega Zip Drive), we know of no game controllers for which current NT 4 drivers are available. Upgrade your OS to Windows 2000 or Windows XP.

Windows 98 doesn't shut down properly with a USB controller connected

The first release of Windows 98 had a bug that prevented some systems from shutting down with some USB game controllers connected. Physically disconnect the controller before shutting down or upgrade Windows to fix the problem.

Force-feedback controller does not center properly

With the game controller active, open the controller applet in the Control Panel. Disconnect the controller, recenter it while disconnected, and then reconnect it. Refresh or update the controller in the applet.

Older gameport controller fails on newer systems

Older gameport controllers were designed for the gameports on ISA sound adapters, which use 5V logic. Newer PCI adapters typically deliver only 3.3V to the gameport, which may be inadequate to drive the older controller. The only practical fix is to replace the controller.

Gameport controller works under Windows but fails under DOS

If your controller works properly with Windows games but doesn't work at all with DOS games, it's likely that you don't have DOS drivers installed in *autoexec.bat* and/or *config.sys*. Download and install DOS drivers for your sound card and gameport, assuming that they are available.

Our Picks

We play games infrequently (and aren't very good at them), so the game controllers we prefer are likely not the models a serious gamer would choose. But serious gamers don't need our advice, while beginners may appreciate being given a starting point. So, although we won't tell you how badly we play Quake because it's embarrassing, we do test new game controllers regularly and recommend specific models for people who are, like us, casual gamers. For our latest detailed game controller recommendations by brand name and model number, visit: *http://www.hardwareguys.com/picks/gamecont.html*.

Serial Communications

Despite the increasing popularity of USB, serial communications remain important to many PC users. PCs use serial communications to connect peripherals such as mice, modems, PDA cradles, barcode readers, and similar low-speed devices. In one sense, serial communications are straightforward. If you use the right cable and let Windows or Linux take care of configuring parameters, everything usually just works. When it doesn't, however, you need to understand quite a bit about the underlying plumbing to make things right. This chapter describes what you need to know about PC serial communications.

Serial Communications Overview

In serial communications, bits are transferred between devices one after the other in a series, whence the name. To communicate an eight-bit byte, the transmitting serial device breaks that byte into its component bits and then places those bits sequentially onto the serial communications interface. The receiving interface accepts the incoming bits, stores them temporarily in a buffer until all bits have been received, reassembles the bits into the original byte, and then delivers that byte to the receiving device.

Because any bit is indistinguishable from any other bit, serial interfaces must use some means to keep things synchronized between the transmitting and receiving interfaces. Otherwise, for example, if transmitted bit #4 were lost due to line noise or some other communication problem, the receiving interface would assume when it received bit #5 that that bit was bit #4, resulting in completely scrambled data. Two methods may be used to effect this synchronization:

Synchronous serial communication
> *Synchronous serial communication* is so called because the transmitting and receiving interfaces are synchronized to a common clock reference. Because both interfaces always "know what time it is," they are always in step, and always know which bit is on the wire at any particular time. Synchronous

serial communication methods are common in mainframe and minicomputer environments, but are little used in PC communications. Synchronous serial communications are normally used in the PC environment only to support specialized devices, which are usually bundled with the appropriate synchronous adapter and cable. Therefore, this book will have no more to say about synchronous serial communication.

Asynchronous serial communication

Asynchronous serial communication is the method commonly used in the PC environment. It is called asynchronous because the transmitting and receiving interfaces do not share a common clock reference. The transmitting interface may begin sending data at an arbitrary time, and the receiving interface is always "listening" for data. Because no shared time reference exists, the transmitting interface must embed markers into the data stream to alert the receiving interface that a block of data is about to arrive, and to indicate the beginning and end of the actual data block. These markers take the form of additional control bits sent before and after the actual data bits. Adding these control bits is called *framing* the data, and the control bits themselves are called *framing bits*.

Asynchronous Serial Framing

In asynchronous serial systems, data is broken into five- to eight-bit *words*, with seven- and eight-bit words by far most common. Seven-bit words are used for text-mode transfers because seven bits accommodate the entire low-order ASCII character set. Eight-bit words are used for binary-mode transfers (and may be used for text-mode transfers) because using eight bits allows the entire data byte to be transferred as a single unit.

When assembling the data to be transmitted, the serial interface adds control bits to the data block to create a *frame*. The frame begins with the *start bit*, a special double-length pulse that signals the receiving interface that transmitted data is about to begin arriving. Immediately following the start bit, the frame contains the data word, with the least-significant bit first. Immediately following the final data bit, the frame may contain a *parity bit*. The frame ends with one or more required *stop bits*, which signal the receiving interface that the frame is complete. When assembled, the start bit, data bits, parity bit, and stop bit together make up one frame.

Parity

Line noise and similar problems can "flip" bits, converting a zero bit to a one bit or vice versa and thereby corrupting the data word. Using a parity bit is a primitive means of detecting a flipped bit. If parity is used, the transmitting device calculates the value for the parity bit based on the values of the data bits in the word. The receiving device calculates the value of the parity bit based on the data bits it receives, and compares that calculated parity bit against the received parity bit. If the two do not match, the receiving device knows that a transmission error occurred and requests retransmission of that frame. Serial devices may use one of five types of parity settings, only two of which are useful for detecting transmission errors:

Even parity

Even parity (E) sets the parity bit to one or zero to force the total number of one-bits in the data word plus the parity bit to an even number. For example, if a byte contains the seven data bits 1-1-0-1-0-0-1 (four one-bits, which is an even number), the parity bit is set to zero for even parity, leaving the total number of one-bits in the eight-bit byte at four, an even number. Conversely, if a byte contains the seven data bits 1-1-0-1-0-1-1 (five one-bits, which is an odd number), the parity bit is set to one for even parity, forcing the total number of one-bits in the eight-bit byte to six, again an even number. Even parity with seven-bit data words was commonly used years ago for dial-up and direct serial connections to mainframes (including dial-up connections from PCs to CompuServe mainframes), but is otherwise little used.

Odd parity

Odd parity (O) sets the parity bit on or off to force the total number of one-bits in the data word plus the parity bit to an odd number. O parity is seldom used in PC communications.

Mark parity

Mark parity (M) always sets the parity bit to one (Mark). This setting provides no error detection, and simply uses the parity bit as a wasted "filler" bit. Some mainframe environments still use Mark parity.

Space parity

Space parity (S) always sets the parity bit to zero (Space). This setting provides no error detection, and simply uses the parity bit as a wasted "filler" bit. Some mainframe environments still use Space parity.

None

None, or no, parity (N) allocates all eight bits in the byte to data, leaving no space available for a parity bit. The N parity setting is used for nearly all PC serial communications.

Parity is such a primitive and unreliable means of detecting errors that using it simply wastes an otherwise valuable bit. Because it uses only one bit, parity can provide only limited error detection and no error correction. Parity detects single-bit errors, but cannot correct them because it doesn't know which data bit is wrong. Parity may also fail on multiple-bit errors. For example, if an even number of bits are flipped within one data word, parity cannot detect the error because calculated parity is identical for the original and corrupted data words. Finally, the parity bit itself may be flipped, resulting in a false error for a good data word.

In theory, you could correct the drawbacks of parity just by using more parity bits. For example, using three parity bits and a cyclic redundancy check (CRC) algorithm makes it possible both to detect and correct single- and multiple-bit errors in an eight-bit data word. In practice, no such CRC scheme is used in PC serial communications, primarily because of the additional overhead it would require. Instead, error detection and correction is performed in software by the serial devices, the device drivers, the operating system, and the application itself.

Asynchronous Frame Types

Many different asynchronous frame types can be created by using different combinations of data word length, parity type, and number of stop bits. Frame types are abbreviated using the number of data bits, the parity type, and the number of stop bits. For example, a frame that uses seven data bits, even parity, and one stop bit is abbreviated *7E1*, and one that uses eight data bits, no parity, and one stop bit is abbreviated *8N1*. These, incidentally, are the only two frame types commonly used in PC serial communications. The 7E1 frame type is still sometimes used for direct and dial-up serial connections to mainframes and for connections to old serial printers. The 8N1 frame type is used for nearly everything else.

 Because most asynchronous frame types use eight data bits (or seven data bits plus a parity bit) framed by one start bit and one stop bit, a serial link typically requires 10 bits to transfer each eight-bit byte, or 20% overhead. That means you can calculate the actual number of bytes per second transferred on an asynchronous serial connection as simply 1/10 of the bits/s rate. For example, a serial terminal connected to a Linux system at 38,400 bits/s transfers 3,840 bytes/s. This calculation does not hold for modern modems, which initially link asynchronously, but switch to synchronous mode once the connection is established. In synchronous mode, each byte requires only eight bits, plus the minor overhead required for framing and error correction data for each synchronous block, each of which contains many bytes.

Serial Data Transmission

A serial bit stream is actually placed on the wire as a rapidly changing series of voltages, with positive voltage used to represent logical zero, and negative voltage used to represent logical one. This serial bit stream is characterized by the nominal speed at which the bits are being sent, measured in bits per second, abbreviated bps and pronounced "bips." At higher data rates, the bit stream is specified in kilobits per second (Kbps or Kb/s) or megabits per second (Mbps or Mb/s).

 Capitalization is significant when referring to data rates. A lowercase "b" refers to bits, while an uppercase "B" refers to bytes. A lowercase "k" refers to decimal thousands (10^3 or 1,000), and an uppercase "K" to binary thousands (2^{10} or 1,024). Similarly, lowercase letters refer to decimal millions ("m") or billions ("g"), while uppercase letters refer to binary millions ("M") or billions ("G").

Serial data rates between devices cannot be set at just any arbitrary value. Instead, they are incremented into standard fixed rates that you select from. The lowest rate used is 50 bps. For historical reasons, the upward progression in data rates is somewhat odd. The next standard rate is 75 bps, followed by 110 bps and 150 bps. From there, the standard data rates double for a while, to 300 bps, 600 bps, 1,200 bps, 2,400 bps, 4,800 bps, 9,600 bps, 19,200 bps, and 38,400 bps. Beyond 38,400, speeds are less standardized. On a de facto basis, the next step up is usually 57,200 bps ("56K"), followed by 115,200 bps. Note that not all serial communications hardware supports every available data rate, particularly non-standard intermediate rates. For communications to take place, the serial interfaces on both ends of the connections must be set to the same data rate.

Although the term *baud* is sometimes used interchangeably with *bps* when discussing data rates, the two are not synonymous. Baud refers to the number of state changes per second, while bps refers to the data rate. Each state change may communicate one or more bits of information. If only one bit is encoded per state change, baud and bps are synonymous. In the PC environment, this occurs only at 300 bps, where a 300 bps modem is also a 300 baud modem. Conversely, a 2,400 bps modem actually operates at 600 baud, with four bits encoded per baud, and a 14.4 Kb/s v.32bis modem operates at 2,400 baud with six bits encoded per baud. Faster modems use various baud rates and encoding schemes to achieve higher bit rates. An ordinary telephone line can support a maximum baud rate of about 3,600 baud, which translates to a maximum data rate of about 56 Kb/s. Various FCC regulations reduce this theoretical maximum, so the actual maximum data rate achievable on a standard telephone line is about 53 Kb/s.

The original IBM PC and its clones implemented serial communications via software routines stored in BIOS. The slow performance of real-mode BIOS-based routines limited serial port speeds to 9,600 bps in early IBM PCs and to 19,200 bps in later PS/2 models. The bottleneck was the BIOS, however, and not the serial port hardware itself, so communications software vendors began to write software that ignored the BIOS and worked directly with the serial port hardware. By doing so, they were able to use the maximum data rate supported by the serial port hardware, typically 38.4 Kb/s in older PCs through 115.2 Kb/s or higher in recent computers.

Operating systems such as Windows 9X and Windows NT/2000/XP have formalized the process of working directly with serial hardware. They ignore the real-mode BIOS serial routines and provide their own high-efficiency drivers to allow serial communications to occur at the highest data rate supported by the serial hardware. This means that communications programs no longer need to incorporate direct serial access routines to ensure high performance. Instead, they simply use the routines provided by the operating system.

Flow Control

A serial interface may be configured as either *Data Terminal Equipment* (*DTE*) or *Data Communications Equipment* (*DCE*), which specifies which pins are used to transmit and receive data and control signals. Traditionally, serial ports are configured as DTE, and communications devices such as modems are configured as DCE. In practical terms, however, the DTE/DCE differentiation doesn't much matter. Any serial device, DTE or DCE, can communicate with any other serial device, DTE or DCE, so long as the proper cable is used to link them.

Ideally, a DCE would always be ready to receive data when the DTE was ready to send it. In the real world, that's not always the case. For example, a degraded telephone connection may render the local modem (DCE) incapable of sending data to the remote modem as fast as it is receiving data from the local DTE. DCE devices may be equipped with buffers to allow them to temporarily store a limited amount of data. This accommodates short-term mismatches between DTE-to-

DCE data rate and DCE-to-DCE data rate, but does nothing to accommodate mismatches of long or permanent duration.

The methods used to accommodate such mismatches are called *flow control*. Using flow control, the DCE device notifies the DTE device to stop sending data temporarily. When the DCE device has cut down on the backlog, it notifies the DTE that it is again ready to receive data. Flow control may be implemented in two ways.

Software flow control
> With *software flow control*, the DCE embeds special control characters into the data stream to notify the DTE to pause or resume sending data. The most common software flow control method is *XON/XOFF*. The resume character, ASCII 17 (0x11), is also called XON, DC1, or Ctrl-Q. The pause character, ASCII 19 (0x13), is also called XOFF, DC3, or Ctrl-S. A similar but less commonly used software flow control method is *ETX/ACK*, which uses ETX (ASCII 3, 0x03, or Ctrl-C) as the pause character and ACK (ASCII 6, 0x06, or Ctrl-F) as the resume character. Software flow control does not work well at speeds higher than about 9,600 bps, and so is seldom used for general-purpose communications nowadays.

Hardware flow control
> With *hardware flow control*, the DCE and DTE use signals asserted on standard EIA-232D pins (usually some combination of RTS, CTS, DSR, DTR, and CD) to control data flow. Because the need for flow control was not envisioned when RS-232 was designed, the standard does not define any hardware flow control method. This means that, in theory at least, all hardware flow control methods are proprietary. In practice, various ad hoc workarounds for hardware flow control have become so well established that they are considered de facto standards. Windows uses RTS/CTS, which it refers to simply as *hardware flow control*.

Serial Ports

PC *serial ports*, also known as *communications ports*, *comm ports*, *asynchronous ports*, or *async ports*, connect slow bit-oriented peripherals such as modems, mice, printers, and plotters to the fast, byte-oriented system bus. Serial ports may reside on motherboards or expansion cards, or be embedded on devices such as internal modems. PC serial ports haven't changed much over the years, although they're faster now and have larger buffers.

Serial ports were formerly used to connect almost anything to a PC—modems, mice, printers, plotters, etc. Nowadays, serial ports are used mostly to connect modems and other peripherals (such as the Palm cradle) that do not require high-speed communications. Serial ports have been replaced for most purposes by USB ports, but most current motherboards and PCs have one or two serial ports, although one or both may exist only as header pins on the motherboard, rather than as visible ports on the rear panel connector. Despite its obsolescence, though, using a serial port is sometimes the best (or only) way to get the job done. The following sections describe what you need to know to use serial ports effectively.

The so-called "legacy-reduced" motherboards and systems that began coming to market in late 1999 may or may not provide serial ports. "Legacy-free" systems and motherboards began shipping in volume in mid-2000, and do not provide serial ports (or many other formerly standard connections, such as parallel ports, PS/2 mouse and keyboard ports, a floppy diskette drive interface, etc.). These systems depend entirely on USB for external connectivity. If you need to connect a legacy serial device (e.g., a Palm cradle) to such a system, there are three options. First, you may be able to find a newer USB cradle or cable for your old device, especially if it's a PDA. You can buy a USB cable that works with models as old as the Palm III (it may work with earlier models, too), but you may need to upgrade to the latest Palm Desktop (a free download) for USB support. Second, you can install a PCI serial card, which typically supplies two high-speed serial ports and perhaps a parallel port. Third, you can buy a USB-to-serial converter, various models of which are available from Belkin and others.

Serial Port Standards

Because they transfer only one bit at a time, using serial communications interfaces to establish a unidirectional connection between two devices in theory requires only one data circuit. This circuit comprises one data (or signal) wire and a second wire (called the ground, return, or common) that completes the electrical circuit. In practice, most PC serial communications devices use additional wires to enable bidirectional communication, to provide control circuits between the devices, and so on.

Serial port interface and signaling specifications are defined by the Electronic Industries Association (EIA) standard *Interface Between Data Terminal Equipment and Data Communication Equipment Employing Serial Binary Data Interchange, Revision D*. This standard is properly abbreviated *EIA-232D*, but is usually called *RS-232C*, for the earlier and nearly identical revision C. The ITU (formerly CCITT) defines essentially identical standards as *V.24* (interface) and *V.28* (signaling).

DB25 pin definitions

EIA-232D defines pin assignments, but does not specify physical connectors. In the PC environment at least, a well-established de facto standard does exist for 25-pin serial connections. By convention, DTE devices (e.g., PC serial ports) use a 25-pin male D-sub plug connector, designated *DB25M*. DCE devices (e.g., modems) use a 25-hole *DB25F* female socket connector. There are exceptions. For example, some serial printers are DTE devices but use a DB25F connector. Figure 22-1 shows a DB25 connector.

Table 22-1 lists DB25 pin assignments. The column headings are self-explanatory, except the following:

I/O

> Signal direction, relative to the DTE. For example, a DCE (modem) asserts voltage onPin 5 (CTS) to notify the DTE (serial port) that it is ready to accept

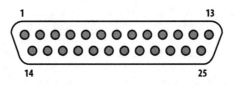

Figure 22-1. A DB9 connector

data from the serial port. We list this signal direction (from the DCE to the DTE) as In. Pins 1 and 7 are ground pins, and have no signal direction. Pin 11 is unassigned, and so has no signal direction.

CCITT, EIA, and RS

The circuit numbers/names used by CCITT, EIA, and RS standards documents, respectively. Circuits with a hyphen (-) are defined by the standard in question but not assigned a name. Circuits with a blank box are neither defined nor named.

Table 22-1. DB25 serial port pin assignments

Pin	I/O	CCITT	EIA	RS	Common name(s)	Abbreviations
1	-	101	-	AA	Chassis Ground	GND
2	Out	103	BA	BA	Transmit Data	TD, TxD, SOUT
3	In	104	BB	BB	Receive Data	RD, RxD, SIN
4	Out	105	CA	CA	Request To Send	RTS
5	In	106	CB	CB	Clear To Send	CTS
6	In	107	CC	CC	Data Set Ready	DSR
7	-	102	AB	AB	Signal Ground	SG
8	In	109	CF	CF	Data Carrier Detect, Carrier Detect, Receive Line Signal Detect	DCD, CD, RLSD
9	In		-	-	Test Voltage (+12V)	
10	In		-	-	Test Voltage (-12V)	
11					(unassigned)	
12	In	122	SCF/CI	SCF	Secondary Data Carrier Detect	SDCD
13	In	121	SCB	SCB	Secondary Clear To Send	SCTS
14	Out	118	SBA	SBA	Secondary Transmit Data	STD
15	In	114	DB	DB	Sync TX Timing DCE (Transmit Clock)	TC
16	In	119	SBB	SBB	Secondary Receive Data	SRD
17	In	115	DD		Sync RX Timing DCE (Receive Clock)	RC
18	In		LL		Local Loopback	LL
19	Out	120	SCA	SCA	Secondary Request To Send	SRTS
20	Out	108.2	CD	CD	Data Terminal Ready	DTR
21	In	110	CG	CG	Signal Quality	SQ
22	In	125	CE	CE	Ring Indicator	RI
23	In/Out	111/112	CH/CI	CH/CI	Data Signal Rate / Speed Indicator	DRS / SI
24	Out	113	DA	DA	Sync TX Timing DTE (Transmit Clock)	XTC
25	In		TM		Test Mode	

EIA-232D maps circuits, all of which are named from the point of view of the DTE device, to pin numbers. Placing a voltage signal on a circuit is called *asserting* or *raising* that circuit. For example, placing voltage on Pin 20 asserts (or raises) DTR. Although you probably don't need to understand these signals in detail, knowing something about their purposes will help you choose the right cable and troubleshoot connection problems. The signals asserted on the EIA-232D pins and pin pairs commonly used in PC serial communications have the following purposes:

Pin 1 (Protective Ground [GND]) and Pin 7 (Signal Ground [SG])
> Pin 1, if present, grounds one end of the cable shield to the equipment chassis to reduce interference. Pin 7 is the common ground reference for all signals on other pins. Pin 7 *must* be connected at both ends for communication to occur. It is a relatively common (although poor) practice for cables to connect the grounds together, forming a single circuit.

Pin 2 (Transmitted Data [TD]) and Pin 3 (Received Data [RD])
> These pins are used to communicate data. A DTE device transmits data on Pin 2 and receives on Pin 3. A DCE device transmits on Pin 3 and receives on Pin 2. Pin 7 is the common return and ground reference for both of these circuits.

Pin 4 (Request to Send [RTS]) and Pin 5 (Clear to Send [CTS])
> The DTE asserts RTS when it wants to send data to the DCE, and the DCE asserts CTS when it is ready to receive data. The DTE may not transmit data until the DCE asserts CTS. CTS may be linked to RTS, allowing the DTE to use RTS to assert CD, if the DCE is so configured.

Pin 6 (Data Set Ready [DSR]) and Pin 20 (Data Terminal Ready [DTR])
> The DCE device asserts DSR when it is powered on and not in test mode. The DTE asserts DTR when it is powered on. In modem applications, DTR may be used to emulate an off-hook condition. If the modem is in auto-answer mode, RI may be linked to DTR, causing DTR to be asserted and the modem to answer when an inbound ring is sensed.

Pin 8 (Received Line Signal Detector [DCD or CD])
> Although the proper name of this circuit is *Received Line Signal Detector (RLSD)*, nearly everyone calls it *Data Carrier Detect (DCD)* or simply *Carrier Detect (CD)*. The DCE asserts CD to tell the DTE that a carrier is present at the DCE. In modem applications, this means that the DCE is receiving a telephone line signal that meets its criteria for presence of a carrier. Many DTE devices will not transmit or receive data unless the DCE is asserting CD. Accordingly, in nonmodem (direct connect) applications, Pin 8 (CD) is normally tied to Pin 20 (DTR). Because the DTE normally asserts DTR as soon as it is turned on, this "spoofs" the DTE into believing that DCD has been asserted.

Pin 22 (Ring Indicator [RI])
> The DCE asserts RI to notify the DTE that the phone is ringing. When configured in auto-answer mode, the modem (DCE) asserts RI in step with the ring cadence. That is, when ring voltage is present, the DCE asserts RI; between rings, the DCE drops RI. The DTE instructs the DCE to answer the call by asserting DTR on Pin 20.

PCs commonly use nine of the preceding 10 pins and signals (excluding Pin 1, GND). Pins 12 through 17, 19, 21, 23, and 24 are not used for standard PC serial connections, but may be used in nonstandard ways by proprietary serial devices. Most commercial DB25 serial cables are labeled as "9-wire," "10-wire," or "25-wire." The first connects only the most commonly used pins. The second also connects GND. The third connects all 25 pins.

DB9 pin definitions

When IBM introduced the PC/AT in 1984, it used a nonstandard DB9M 9-pin serial connector that included only the commonly used pins. Because this connector is physically smaller, it allowed putting both a serial port and a DB25F parallel port on the same expansion card bracket. The market presence of IBM and the passage of years have combined to make this DB9M serial connector a de facto standard. Like the DB25, DB9 connectors are available in male and female versions, designated *DB9M* and *DB9F*, respectively. By convention, DTE devices use the DB9M. Few DCE devices use DB9 connectors. However, those that do usually use a DB9F. Figure 22-2 shows a DB9 connector.

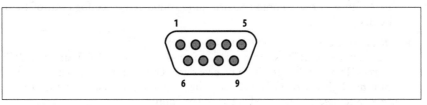

Figure 22-2. A DB9 connector

Although its pinouts don't map to either DTE or DCE, the DB9M serial connector is considered an "honorary" DTE device, with DTE-to-DCE interfacing accommodated by the cable. The DB9 connector includes the nine important signals, but the pinouts differ from DB25, as Table 22-2 shows.

Table 22-2. DB9 serial port pin assignments

Pin	I/O	CCITT	EIA	RS	Common name(s)	Abbreviations
1	In	109	CF	CF	Data Carrier Detect, Carrier Detect, Receive Line Signal Detect	DCD, CD, RLSD
2	In	104	BB	BB	Receive Data	RD, RxD, SIN
3	Out	103	BA	BA	Transmit Data	TD, TxD, SOUT
4	Out	108.2	CD	CD	Data Terminal Ready	DTR
5	-	102	AB	AB	Signal Ground	SG
6	In	107	CC	CC	Data Set Ready	DSR
7	Out	105	CA	CA	Request To Send	RTS
8	In	106	CB	CB	Clear To Send	CTS
9	In	125	CE	CE	Ring Indicator	RI

Universal Asynchronous Receiver-Transmitter (UART)

The *Universal Asynchronous Receiver-Transmitter (UART)* is the heart of a serial port. When transmitting, the UART receives the outbound byte stream from the system bus, converts the bytes into a bit stream, and places the bits onto the serial interface. When receiving, the UART receives an inbound bit stream from the serial interface, buffers the inbound bits, assembles them into bytes, and places those bytes onto the system bus. There are two types of UARTs.

A *dumb UART* generates an interrupt each time it sends or receives a byte. At low data rates this is acceptable, but at faster data rates these frequent interrupts put a heavy burden on the processor. Dumb UARTs have long been obsolete, but are often encountered in older systems such as 486s and Pentiums that have been converted to use as firewalls, fax servers, and other communications servers. Dumb UARTs can be used with Windows and Linux in applications for which data rates do not exceed 38.4 kb/s—e.g., 14.4 kb/s fax modems. The following are dumb UARTs:

8250

> The 8250 is an eight-bit UART used in original IBM PCs and compatibles, and occasionally encountered in newer PCs with secondhand serial cards installed. If you find an 8250, pull the card and throw it away.

16450

> The 16450 is a 16-bit UART used in PC/ATs and compatibles. It is common on 16-bit serial cards for 80286, 80386, and early 486 systems, and on the motherboards of such systems. It runs 19.2 Kb/s reliably, and may be usable at 38.4 Kb/s. It has only a one-byte buffer, making it unsuitable for multitasking operating systems such as Windows 9X/2000/XP and Linux. The 16450 may exist as a discrete chip on the system board or an expansion card, or as a part of a VLSI chipset. If the 16450 is socketed, you can replace it directly with a $5 16550AFN chip. If the 16450 cannot be replaced easily, disable it and install a modern serial card.

16550 (early models)

> The 16550 is a 16-bit UART used in late-model 486 systems, in Pentium and later systems, and in expansion cards intended for those systems. The 16550 has a 16-byte FIFO buffer, but early models have a bug that disables the FIFO buffer. This bug was fixed in later models of the 16550. Fixed versions are designated 16550A, but some chip makers did not change the labeling, making it difficult or impossible to discriminate visually between buggy models and fixed models. Windows (usually) reports an early 16550 as a 16450. Linux reports an early 16550 as a 16550, and a 16550A (regardless of labeling) as a 16550A. Early 16550 UARTs are unacceptable for multitasking use under Windows or Linux.

16650 (early models)

> The 16650 is a faster 16550-class UART that doubles buffer size to 32 bytes. Unfortunately, like early 16550 models, early 16650 models have a bug that disables FIFO buffering. Linux and Windows treat these early 16650 UARTs as 16450s, using only one byte of the buffer. Windows reports the 16650 as a 16550 or 16650, regardless of whether the 16650 is an older, buggy model or

a later, fixed model. However, Windows generally refuses to enable the FIFO buffer on an older 16650. Linux, as usual, reports the UART type accurately. If Linux reports the UART as 16650, it is an older model and should not be used for multitasking or high data rate applications. If Linux reports the UART as 16650V2, it is a fixed model and can be used.

A *FIFO UART* uses a first-in, first-out buffer to reduce the number of interrupts that occur when transferring data. The FIFO buffer may range from 16 bytes to 64 bytes or more. A FIFO UART buffers incoming data until the buffer reaches the *trigger level* (is nearly full). The UART generates an interrupt only when the trigger level is reached, which means a FIFO UART generates many fewer interrupts than a dumb UART and is much less likely to drop incoming data bytes. The following are FIFO UARTs:

16550 (late), 16550A, and 16C552
16550-family UARTs use a 16-byte FIFO buffer to support multitasking operating systems, which cannot always give immediate attention to interrupts generated by the serial port. Early 16550 models had a bug that prevented the FIFO buffer from being used. This bug was fixed in later models, which are officially designated 16550A. However, some chip makers produced fixed 16550s without changing the labeling, making it difficult or impossible to tell visually whether the UART is the buggy older model or the fixed newer model. Windows usually reports an early 16550 as a 16450, and uses it as though it were a 16450. Linux reports the buggy early model as a 16550, and the fixed newer model as a 16550 (regardless of how the chip is labeled). The 16550A functions properly under Windows and Linux, and supports 115 Kb/s throughput. The 16550A is the minimum acceptable UART for a modern system.

16650 (late)
The 16650 is essentially a faster 16550-class UART that doubles buffer size to 32 bytes and adds support for various modern BIOS features, including power management. Early 16650s suffer the same bug as early 16550s, and cannot be used reliably for multitasking or high data rates under Windows or Linux. It is usually impossible to tell visually whether a particular 16650 is the older, buggy model or the newer, fixed model. Windows generally disables the FIFO buffer on a buggy 16650, but enables the buffer for a fixed 16650. Linux reports an original 16650 as a 16650, and the fixed model as a 16650V2. The 16650 supports data rates up to 450 Kb/s, making it better suited than a 16550 for use with ISDN adapters and similar high-speed devices. Dual-16650 serial cards are available for less than $50.

16750 and later
The 16750 is an improved 16550-class UART that further expands the FIFO buffer to 64 bytes for transmit and 56 bytes for receive, and increases the maximum data rate to 900 Kb/s. The 16750, as well as similar enhanced versions such as the 16850 and 16950, are uncommon on PCs, and are used primarily on specialized, very high-speed devices such as T3 interface cards.

Determining UART type

Under DOS and Windows 9X, you can determine the UART type with Microsoft Diagnostics (MSD.EXE), with a general-purpose diagnostic utility such as SiSoft Sandra, or with a dedicated port diagnostics program such as PortMaster. Either of the latter two utilities can be downloaded from any of numerous Internet sites.

Figure 22-3 shows SiSoft Sandra displaying information about COM1 on an AMD Duron system, built on a Microstar motherboard that uses a VIA KT133 chipset, and running Windows 98. Sandra reports that COM1 uses a National Semiconductor 16550AN UART, which is not precisely true. The COM1 UART is actually just one of the functions provided by the Super I/O portion of the Southbridge of the VIA chipset. The UART is emulated rather than physically present, but as far as Windows and connected serial devices are concerned, this system might just as well have a real physical 16550AN UART.

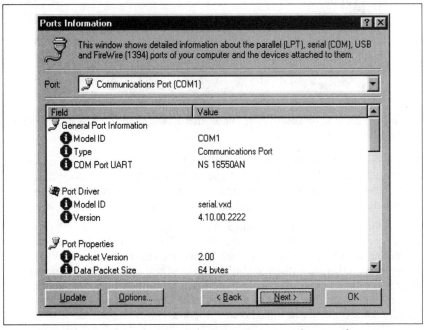

Figure 22-3. Using SiSoft Sandra Ports Information to view serial port configuration on a Windows 98 system

Utilities that run under Windows NT/2000/XP are limited in the amount and accuracy of the information they can provide because Windows masks the underlying hardware from the utility. For example, Figure 22-4 shows the results of running SiSoft Sandra Ports Information on a system running Windows NT 4. The Windows NT Hardware Abstraction Layer (HAL) prevents user-mode applications (such as Sandra) from accessing the underlying hardware, so Sandra can report only what Windows sees fit to tell it, which may be little or nothing.

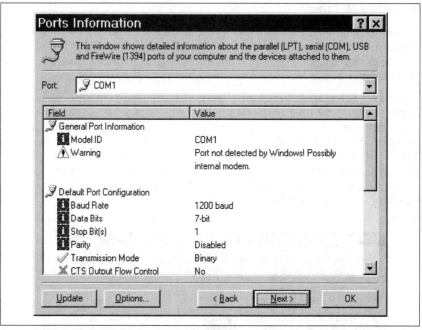

Figure 22-4. Using SiSoft Sandra Ports Information to view serial port configuration on a Windows NT 4 system

If your system boots Windows NT/2000/XP, the only way to obtain detailed information about the hardware is to boot DOS and run a DOS-mode diagnostic utility. You can use either a comprehensive commercial diagnostics program such as CheckIt for that purpose, or a dedicated small utility such as PortMaster.

If the device has not yet been installed in the computer (or if you're willing to pop the lid), you can sometimes determine the UART type by examining the chips on the device to locate a UART number. However, many devices use VLSI/ASIC components rather than discrete UART chips, making it difficult or impossible to identify the UART type visually. In these cases, if you don't have the documentation, the only convenient way to determine the UART type may be to install the board, boot DOS, and run a diagnostics program.

Some "enhanced" VLSI/ASIC-based 16450 serial ports with FIFO buffering added may falsely report themselves to the operating system and applications as 16550s, although PortMaster usually detects them properly. These UARTs are commonly found on early 486 motherboards and "high-speed" serial cards designed for 486 systems. These bumped-up 16450s may or may not function properly with any particular combination of operating system and application, and should be replaced with a serial port that uses a 16550AFN or higher UART.

Choosing UART type

Which UART you need to use for maximum throughput depends on three factors:

DCE-to-DCE rate

DCE-to-DCE rate specifies the actual link speed between the two communications devices. For example, V.90 "56K" modems actually talk to each other at a maximum of 53 Kb/s (rather than 56 Kb/s, due to FCC regulations limiting signal amplitude on a phone line). ISDN devices communicate with each other at 64 Kb/s when using one B channel, or 128 Kb/s when using two, and so forth.

Data compressibility

Data compressibility is the degree to which source data can be compressed by the communications device before being placed on the DCE-to-DCE link. Some data (e.g., text, web pages, and databases) contains a great deal of embedded slack space, and can be compressed as much as 4:1 by the communications hardware. Other data (e.g., images, executables, etc.) is much less compressible.

DTE-to-DCE rate

DTE-to-DCE rate specifies the actual link speed between the local serial port and the local communications device. Setting this speed faster than the DCE-to-DCE rate allows the serial port to provide compressible data to the communications device quickly enough that the DCE-to-DCE link never runs out of data to transfer. The compression algorithms used by most communications devices allow 4:1 compression in theory, although 1.5:1 or 2:1 is more common in practice. This means that the DTE-to-DCE data rate must be at least one and one-half or two times the DCE-to-DCE rate (and, ideally, four times) to make sure the DCE is never kept waiting for data.

After you determine the UART types used by your serial ports, use the following guidelines to decide if these ports are adequate for their intended purpose:

8250 and variants

Serial ports that use these UARTs are long obsolete, and are completely unsuitable for use in any modern system. 8250-class UARTs were used on original IBM PC- and XT- class systems, and 8250-class add-on cards were installed in some 486 and early Pentium-class systems. Replace any serial port that reports an 8250-class UART. If the UART is embedded in the motherboard, disable the motherboard serial port(s) in BIOS Setup, and install an add-on serial card with 16550AFN or higher UARTs.

16450 or higher

These ports are usually adequate for mice and similar low-speed devices, even on slow and/or heavily loaded computers.

16550A or higher

These ports are usually adequate for modems that use V.32bis (14.4 Kb/s), V.34 (28.8 Kb/s), or V.34+ (33.6 Kb/s). These ports are marginal for V.90 (56 Kb/s) modems, and single-channel (56/64 Kb/s) ISDN applications because they allow for only about 2:1 compression. A 16550A is unacceptable for dual-channel ISDN because it limits the DTE-to-DCE rate to 115.2 Kb/s, which is actually lower than the 128 Kb/s DCE-to-DCE rate. All other things being equal, 16550A ports are less likely to be a bottleneck on faster and lightly loaded computers. On midrange 486s and less, and on heavily loaded slow Pentiums, the 16550A may be a bottleneck, and should be replaced with a 16650.

16650 or higher

These ports are necessary to guarantee full throughput potential for any application that requires a DTE-to-DCE rate higher than the 115.2 Kb/s DTE limitation of the 16550A and slower UARTs. In other words, you really need a 16650 or better for anything above a 28.8 Kb/s V.34 DCE-to-DCE link. In practice, you probably won't notice much difference with anything up to a 56K modem, but you may notice a big difference with ISDN.

Resources Required by Serial Ports

Each standard serial port requires an IRQ and an I/O port. The serial port generates an interrupt on its assigned IRQ to get the processor's attention when it has data to transfer. The I/O port is a range of addresses, named for the first address in the range, that defines a "scratchpad" area that the serial port uses to exchange data with the computer. For example, I/O Port 0x3F8 includes the address range 0x3F8 through 0x3FF.

Serial ports are named *COM[xxx]:*, where *[xxx]* may be a number from 1 through 256. Although the serial port name technically includes the trailing colon, the colon is usually dropped for convenience, and that is the practice we follow. IBM originally defined only COM1 and COM2 for the PC BIOS, although it later defined standard values for COM3 and COM4 as well. Table 22-3 lists the standard COM port assignments for ISA/PCI systems. (Systems that use the EISA or MCA bus use additional COM ports with different settings, but these systems are obsolete and immaterial.) The values for COM1 and COM2 are invariant due to long usage. The values for COM3 and COM4 are semistandard, but may differ on some systems.

Table 22-3. Standard COM port assignments on ISA/PCI-based systems

Port Name	Base address	I/O port range	IRQ
COM1	0x3F8	0x3F8 – 0x3FF	4
COM2	0x2F8	0x2F8 – 0x2FF	3
COM3	0x3E8	0x3E8 – 0x3EF	4
COM4	0x2E8	0x2E8 – 0x2EF	3

Note that ports 1 and 3 and ports 2 and 4 share an IRQ. Although EISA and MCA systems permit IRQs to be shared gracefully, ISA/PCI systems do not. This means that, in effect, you can use only two serial ports safely on a system that uses standard COM port assignments. You may be able to get away with such sharing—say, by putting a serial printer on COM3 and a mouse on COM1—but you must make sure never to use both devices that share one IRQ at the same time.

Windows 95 went a long way toward solving this problem by adding support for up to 128 COM ports. Windows NT 4.0 goes further still, supporting up to 256 COM ports and allowing you to define custom values for IRQ and base address for each installed COM port. Because Windows applications use COM ports by name and are not concerned with underlying settings, it is relatively straight-forward to support multiple COM ports in the Windows environment.

A final note: PCs assign a priority to each IRQ, and process interrupts on the higher-priority IRQ first. The highest-priority IRQ is 0, followed by 1, 2 through 9, 10 through 15, and then 3 through 8. Put high-priority devices such as modems on a high-priority serial port (e.g., COM2/IRQ3) and low-priority devices such as mice on a lower-priority serial port (e.g., COM1/IRQ4). This is less important with recent UARTs than it used to be, but is still worth doing as a matter of good practice.

Enhanced Serial Ports

The proliferation of high-speed external serial devices, notably serial ISDN terminal adapters, made it obvious that something faster than the standard 16550 UART was needed. The standard serial ports on most PCs top out at 115 Kb/s or (rarely) 230 Kb/s. That's not fast enough to support the full throughput of a dual B-channel ISDN terminal adapter, which operates at 128 Kb/s natively and up to four times that fast when data compression is enabled.

To address that need, various manufacturers supply enhanced serial ports, which are add-on cards that include one or two serial ports. These use 16650, 16750, 16850, or 16C950 UARTs, which are essentially 16550 UARTs with additional buffering added and support for higher data rates. Some cards also include an embedded processor, typically an 80186 or 80286, which offloads interrupt handling from the main processor.

These adapters are overkill for normal serial port applications, may provide some benefit for 56K dial-up modems, and often provide a noticeable performance increase for ISDN applications. If you buy such a card, make sure that it includes any necessary drivers for your operating system.

Multiport Serial Adapters

Each standard serial port occupies one IRQ, which limits how many standard serial ports can be installed. Most computers need one or two serial ports at most, so this is seldom a problem. But there are applications—such as running a terminal server under Linux—for which it is desirable to have eight, 16, or more serial ports available. That's clearly impossible if each serial port requires one IRQ. The solution is a special board called a *multiport serial adapter*.

These adapters are available in ISA and PCI form, and are installed in the PC just like any other expansion card. They provide from four to 32 serial ports using only one IRQ. The serial port connectors reside in a separate external box that connects to the multiport serial adapter via multiple 8P8C ("RJ-45") connectors or a single proprietary octopus cable with many conductors.

Such adapters are available in two forms: "dumb" multiport serial adapters are little more than a collection of UARTs and connectors, use 8-bit transfers, generate an interrupt for each byte transferred, and depend on the host PC for processing power. "Smart" multiport serial adapters include a microprocessor (typically an 80286 or 386) that offloads serial interrupt processing tasks from the host PC. Smart adapters usually buffer 1 KB of data or more between transfers, greatly reducing the interrupt burden on the host system. Nowadays, most multiport serial adapters are of the smart variety.

Dumb terminals have become rare in most applications—LAN-connected PC clients are much more common nowadays, even on Linux systems—and so the need for multiport serial adapters is much less than formerly. If you do need one, for example, for process control, automation tasks, or building a terminal server for a modem pool—make sure that drivers are available for your operating system.

Serial Cables

If you have problems getting a serial port to talk to a peripheral, you're probably using the wrong cable. That's not surprising because there's no such thing as a standard serial cable. Serial cables differ in the connectors used on each end, the number and type of wires that are connected end to end, the *pinouts* (which pin on one connector is connected to which pin on the other), and the connections made internally within each local connector, if any. With permutations, there are literally millions of ways you *could* build a serial cable. Fortunately, only a handful are commonly used.

Common Serial Cable Types

Commonly used serial cables fall into one of the two following general categories:

Straight-through serial cables
> *Straight-through serial cables* are used to connect unlike devices (DTE to DCE). A straight-through cable is just what it sounds like—each pin on one connector connects to the corresponding pin on the other. On a DB25-to-DB25 or DB9-to-DB9 cable, this means that each pin on one connector connects to the same pin number on the other. On a DB9-to-DB25 cable, the wires connect different pin numbers, but the same signal. For example, DTR (Pin 20 on the DB25) is connected to DTR (Pin 4 on the DB9). Almost any cable with a DB9 connector connects all nine pins. DB25 cables may have all or only some pins connected, but the existing connections are straight-through.

Cross-over serial cables
> *Cross-over serial cables* are used to connect like devices (DTE to DTE, or DCE to DCE). Cross-over cables come in an amazing variety of pinouts, some reasonably standard and others specific to one particular type of connection—e.g., an HP LaserJet serial port to a DB25 PC serial port. The term *null-modem cable* is often misused to mean any cross-over cable, but a null-modem cable is really just one variety of cross-over cable.

PC serial ports are usually configured as DTE. Modems, mice, trackballs, digitizers, and scanners are usually DCE devices, and so connect to a PC with a straight-through cable. Serial printers and plotters are usually DTE devices, and so connect to a PC using some form of cross-over cable. Connecting two DTE PCs also requires a cross-over cable.

Any bidirectional serial cable must connect at least TD, RD, and SG (Pins 2, 3, and 7 on a DB25). Those to be used with hardware flow control require additional connections. Tables 22-4 through 22-6 show the pinouts for some common serial cables.

Table 22-4 shows the simplest possible bidirectional straight-through cables, which may be used to connect a DTE (e.g., a serial port) to a DCE (e.g., a modem). These cables are not commonly used because they make no provision for hardware flow control.

Table 22-4. Simple straight-through cables

DB9 to DB9	DB25 to DB25	DB9 to DB25	Connection description
Pin 2 to Pin 2	Pin 3 to Pin 3	Pin 2 to Pin 3	DTE RD to DCE TD
Pin 3 to Pin 3	Pin 2 to Pin 2	Pin 3 to Pin 2	DTE TD to DCE RD
Pin 5 to Pin 5	Pin 7 to Pin 7	Pin 5 to Pin 7	SG to SG

Table 22-5 shows the simplest possible bidirectional cross-over cables. These cables, which also make no provision for hardware flow control, are commonly used to attach DTE terminal server ports to DTE terminals in a host environment, but are uncommon in the PC environment.

Table 22-5. Simple cross-over cables

DB9 to DB9	DB25 to DB25	DB9 to DB25	Connection description
Pin 2 to Pin 3	Pin 3 to Pin 2	Pin 3 to Pin 3	RD to TD
Pin 3 to Pin 2	Pin 2 to Pin 3	Pin 2 to Pin 2	TD to RD
Pin 5 to Pin 5	Pin 7 to Pin 7	Pin 5 to Pin 7	SG to SG

Table 22-6 shows the connections for typical straight-through cables used to link DB25M and DB9M serial ports to a DB25F modem. Some programs, notably some bulletin board software, also require that Pins 12 and 23 be connected, which rules out using these programs with a DB9 serial port.

Table 22-6. Connections for typical straight-through modem cables

DB25F to DB25M	DB9F to DB25M	Connection description
Pin 1 to shield	n/a	Cable shield to ground
Pin 2 to Pin 2	Pin 3 to Pin 2	DTE TD to DCE RD
Pin 3 to Pin 3	Pin 2 to Pin 3	DTE RD to DCE TD
Pin 4 to Pin 4	Pin 7 to Pin 4	RTS to RTS
Pin 5 to Pin 5	Pin 8 to Pin 5	CTS to CTS
Pin 6 to Pin 6	Pin 6 to Pin 6	DSR to DSR
Pin 7 to Pin 7	Pin 5 to Pin 7	SG to SG
Pin 8 to Pin 8	Pin 1 to Pin 8	CD to CD
Pin 20 to Pin 20	Pin 4 to Pin 20	DTR to DTR
Pin 22 to Pin 22	Pin 9 to Pin 22	RI to RI

Table 22-7 lists the pinouts for a DB9-to-DB25 adapter cable, which allows a DB25 serial cable to connect to a DB9 serial port. We generally keep only straight-through, 25-wire, DB25-to-DB25 cables on hand, which can be used with such adapters to connect anything to anything.

Table 22-7. Pinouts for a DB9-to-DB25 adapter cable

DB9F	DB25M	Connection description (all straight through)
1	8	CD to CD
2	3	RD to RD
3	2	TD to TD
4	20	DTR to DTR
5	7	SG to SG
6	6	DSR to DSR
7	4	RTS to RTS
8	5	CTS to CTS
9	22	RI to RI

The following tables list the pinouts for serial cables that you can use with the MS-DOS InterLink or the Windows 9X Direct Cable Connection (DCC) utilities. Because a serial link is much slower (about 10 KB/s), use one of these serial cables to link the computers only if parallel ports are not available on both or if the operating system does not support direct parallel connections. The pinouts for parallel InterLink/DCC cables are provided later in this chapter.

Although Windows NT does not support InterLink, DCC, or direct parallel connection, you can also use these serial cables to connect a Windows NT computer and a Windows 9X computer via Windows NT RAS. For detailed instructions, see Microsoft article Q142065, *Connecting Windows NT to Windows 95 with a Null-Modem Cable*.

Table 22-8 shows a DB9F-to-DB9F serial cable for use with InterLink or DCC. Pins 1 and 6 are shown bridged because some motherboards cause a "Cable not connected" message to appear unless CD is asserted by being bridged to DSR (so that the voltage that appears on DSR anytime the modem is ready also appears on CD to spoof the DTE into believing that a carrier is always present). You can leave Pin 1 disconnected if this is not the case with your motherboard. However, it doesn't hurt to have Pin 1 connected, even if your motherboard does not require CD be forced high, so the pinouts shown result in a more generally useful cable. Table 22-9 shows a DB25F-to-DB25F serial cable and Table 22-10 a DB9F to DB25F serial cable, both for use with InterLink or Direct Cable Connection.

Table 22-8. DB9F-to-DB9F serial cable for use with InterLink or DCC

DB9F	DB9F	Connection description
1 & 6	4	CD and DSR to DTR
2	3	RD to TD
3	2	TD to RD

Table 22-8. DB9F-to-DB9F serial cable for use with InterLink or DCC (continued)

DB9F	DB9F	Connection description
4	1 & 6	DTR to CD and DSR
5	5	SG to SG
7	8	RTS to CTS
8	7	CTS to RTS

Table 22-9. DB25F-to-DB25F serial cable for use with InterLink or DCC

DB25F	DB25F	Connection description
2	3	TD to RD
3	2	RD to TD
4	5	RTS to CTS
5	4	CTS to RTS
6 and 8	20	DSR and CD to DTR
7	7	SG to SG
20	6 and 8	DTR to DSR and CD[a]

[a] Pins 6 and 8 are bridged per the explanation in the preceding text.

Table 22-10. DB9F to DB25F serial cable for use with InterLink or Direct Cable Connection

Table 22-10. DB9F to DB25F serial cable for use with InterLink or Direct Cable Connection

DB9F	DB25F	Connection description
1 and 6	20	CD and DSR to DTR
2	2	TD to RD
3	3	RD to TD
4	6 and 8	DTR to DSR and CD
5	7	SG to SG
7	5	RTS to CTS
8	4	CTS to RTS[a]

[a] Pins 6 and 8 are bridged per the explanation in the preceding text.

Cable Guidelines

Keep the following issues in mind when you need to buy or build a cable:

- Buy the cable if you can. Any cable you need is probably a standard item, and will be cheaper and better than one you build. If you need an unusual pinout, order a custom cable from Black Box, DataComm Warehouse, or another company that produces cables to order.

- Use the shortest cable possible for more reliable connections, particularly at high speeds. If you need a long cable, buy a high-grade one made with low-capacitance wire.

Serial Cables | 657

- Don't judge cables by appearance. Mass-produced cables appear similar, but vary in quality. Custom-built cables are usually of high quality, and priced accordingly. You'll get no more than you pay for, and sometimes less.

- Don't assume that a cable connects every pin that appears on the connector. Mass-produced cables usually have pins in each position, while custom-built cables often have pins only in the positions that are actually connected. Nearly any DB9 serial cable connects all nine pins, but cables with two DB25s may have anything from three to 25 pins connected, with nine and 25 wire connections most common. Any decent mass-produced cable lists the number of wires and how they are connected on the packaging, and sometimes on the connectors.

Making Cables

You'll probably never need to make a cable, but these guidelines will serve you well if you do:

- Create a grab bag of patch boxes, male-male and female-female 9- and 25-pin gender changers, 9-to-25 adapters, and so forth. You can get these things from Global, DataComm Warehouse, and similar places. They cost only a few dollars and occupy little space. Buy two of each, and add a straight-through 25-wire DB25-to-DB25 cable to the bag. The next time you desperately need a cable and all the stores are closed, you can use these parts to cobble together any cable you need.

- Use these parts to make a jerry-built cable that works, record the pinouts, order a custom cable made to those specifications, and leave the jerry-built cable in place until the new cable arrives to replace it.

- If you're running cables through walls to wall jacks, make those cables straight-through and label both ends accordingly. No one will remember the cable pinouts later, and testing pinouts on a cable when only one end at a time is accessible is almost impossible. Do the custom pinouts in the drop cable that connects the wall jack to the equipment, and label both ends of that cable, too. Note that a plain cable is a lot easier to run through walls and floors than one that already has connectors attached.

- To make semipermanent quick-and-dirty cables, keep a supply of RJ-to-DB connectors on hand. They are available from Global and other vendors in DB9 and DB25 male and female versions, and have a standard 6P6C ("RJ11") or 8P8C ("RJ45") jack on the back. The jack is prewired to loose pins, which you can insert as appropriate into the DB connector. You then use standard flat satin cable to link the two connectors. If six or eight wires are enough, you can make a custom cable with these connectors in about two minutes flat. We've made a lot of "temporary" cables this way that are still in use 10 years later.

Determining Pinouts on an Unknown Cable

At some point, you may find yourself looking at a cable with no idea how it's pinned out or whether it's usable for what you want to do. When that happens, proceed as follows:

Just try it

You can connect any RS-232 pin to any other pin without damaging anything. The worst that can happen is that nothing will work.

Look for a label

Labels may be unambiguous. One labeled "HP LaserJet" is probably just what you need to connect a serial HP LaserJet. Short labels may mislead. A cable labeled "null modem" may not have the pinouts you need for your "null modem" cable. Also, some cables are asymmetric—both ends may use the same connector, but the pinouts differ and the two ends are not interchangeable.

Identify the active pins visually

Custom-made cables often have pins only for active lines. By determining which pins are connected on each end, you can often make a reasonable guess about the actual pinouts. If the visible pins correspond to a "standard" cable type, chances are good that it is that type of cable.

Disassemble the connectors

Remove the connector hood and note the connections, including local loopbacks within the connector body. By noting which pin number is connected to which color wire, you can trace the pinouts end to end. Mass-produced cables ordinarily use molded connectors, making this method impossible to use.

Use a continuity tester or DVM

Assuming a male-to-female cable, insert one probe into hole 1 of the female connector, and then brush the other probe quickly against each of the pins on the male connector, noting the pin number each time the tester beeps to indicate continuity. Repeat this process for each hole of the female connector. On a female-to-female cable, it takes a bit longer because you cannot simply brush against the pins on the second connector. On a male-to-male cable, it may seem that you need three hands to keep everything lined up, but after some practice it takes only a couple of minutes to determine a pinout.

Loopback Plugs

In days of yore, every PC technician carried a set of loopback plugs for testing 9-pin serial ports, 25-pin serial ports, and parallel ports. Nowadays, it's pretty rare to see a loopback plug, but they can still be invaluable in diagnosing port problems.

In essence, a *loopback plug* (also called a *wrap plug*) is simply a connector of the appropriate type with internal wiring that connects paired pins such as TD and RD. When the loopback plug is connected to a serial port for testing, outbound signals from the serial port (e.g., TD) are looped back to the corresponding inbound pin (e.g., RD). If a signal does not appear as expected, either the outbound pin or the inbound pin is not doing its job.

High-end diagnostic software (such as CheckIt) often includes loopback plugs, either standard or as an option. You can also buy a combination DB25/DB9 loopback plug from most electronics distributors for $5 or so. If you have the components on hand to make cables, it's easy enough to make your own loopback plugs, using an empty D-shell connector and crimp-on, solder-on, or wirewrap pins. The exact pinouts required differ according to the diagnostic utility you are using, but most utilities can use a loopback plug which uses the following standard pinouts:

DB25F loopback plug

- 2 to 3 (TD to RD)
- 4 to 5 to 22 (RTS to CTS to RI)
- 6 to 8 to 20 (DSR to CD to DTR)

DB9F loopback plug

- 2 to 3 (RD to TD)
- 7 to 8 to 9 (RTS to CTS to RI)
- 6 to 1 to 4 (DSR to CD to DTR)

Installing and Configuring Serial Port Hardware

Before you buy a serial port, verify that you don't already have what you need. Serial ports are cheap, ubiquitous, and easily disabled, so you may already have one or more of them installed that you don't know about. Before you purchase a serial port expansion card, take the following steps:

1. Use the operating system or a diagnostics program to determine the number and configuration of installed serial ports.

   - For Windows NT 4.0, choose Start → Programs → Administrative Tools (Common) → Windows NT Diagnostics, click the Resources tab, and double-click the Serial item.

   - For Windows 2000/XP, right-click the My Computer icon and choose Properties. Click the Hardware tab and then the Device Manager button. Locate the Ports item in the Device Manager tree and double-click it to expand the listing to show individual ports. All installed COM ports (and LPT ports) are displayed. Double-click a port to display a tabbed dialog that provides information about that port, including details about General configuration, Port Settings, Driver details, and the Resources that port is using.

   - For Windows 9X, right-click the My Computer icon, click the Device Manager tab, expand the Ports (COM and LPT) item, highlight a port, click Properties, and finally click the Resources tab. Note the COM port number, IRQ, and I/O address assignments for each port present.

   - For Linux, open a terminal window. Display */proc/devices* and look for tty* devices in the Character devices section (use the cat command to display the file; if the file is so large that it scrolls off the screen, you can use the more or less command to display one screen at a time). The first column lists the interrupt assigned to the device and the second column the device name. Ordinarily, the primary serial port uses IRQ 3 and the secondary serial port (if present) uses IRQ 4. Display */proc/ioports* to view the base address and memory range assigned to each of the installed ports.

While you have this information displayed, record the details about each port (particularly which resources it is using), which you will need to avoid conflicts if you install another port. Also record unused IRQs that are available for use by another serial port. In addition to the minimal information supplied by Windows, diagnostic software may also report additional details. (Linux provides more details than you'll ever need to know about serial ports.)

2. Examine the rear of the PC case to locate an unused serial port connector. It may be a DB9M or a DB25M, and may reside on an expansion card bracket or on the chassis itself. If you find such a connector, it may or may not be connected to an unused serial port. If it is connected, that port may not be enabled. Conversely, active serial ports may not be represented by a back panel connector. For example, an internal modem uses a serial port, but does so internally, so no connector for that port appears on the back panel. Also, a port may be "orphaned"—installed and active, but not connected to a back panel connector. If that is the case, you can purchase a standard motherboard-to-back panel cable and connector at most computer stores for a couple of dollars.

3. Restart the computer, enter BIOS Setup, and locate the serial port settings section, if present. Determine if one or more serial ports are available on the motherboard but currently disabled. Such ports will not be reported by the BIOS, and so will not be recognized by Windows. The diagnostics program may or may not detect disabled ports. If BIOS Setup displays a disabled port, you can use Setup to enable and configure the port as described in the following section, assuming that the port uses a UART adequate for your intended purpose.

If you do need to buy a serial port card, get a dual-16650 card, which costs only $25 or so. Dual-16550 cards are still available, sometimes for less than $15, but having the 16650s is worth the small additional cost. Even if the system is old enough to have ISA slots, buy a PCI card rather than an ISA card. Serial ports are too slow to really need PCI, but you should avoid installing ISA cards in a PCI system whenever possible.

Once the port is physically installed and enabled, the next step is to configure the port hardware by assigning an IRQ and base address to the port. This is done differently according to the port being installed, as follows:

Motherboard ports

Most motherboards include two serial ports, typically designated Serial 1/2 or A/B. You map these physical serial ports to logical COM ports by setting jumpers on older motherboards or by using BIOS Setup on newer ones. Many motherboards restrict you to assigning Serial A and B to one of the four standard COM port settings for IRQ and base address. Some motherboards allow you to define custom IRQ and base address settings for each serial port, which you can use to configure unique settings that allow three or more serial ports to coexist. Any motherboard allows you to disable the embedded serial ports, which you may need to do if the embedded ports use less-capable UARTs and you are installing a serial expansion card to replace them.

Serial expansion cards

Simple serial expansion cards typically support two serial ports, although only one may be physically installed. If this is the case, empty sockets will exist to allow you to install an individual UART chip to add the second port. Each installed UART requires two UART support chips, designated 1488 and 1489. These chips may or may not be preinstalled for the empty UART socket. The chips necessary to add a second port are normally available from the same place you bought the card. Such simple cards are usually set by jumper to one of the four standard COM port settings. Newer cards, particularly those that use 16650 UARTs, may be set by jumper or by a setup utility bundled with the card. In the latter case, the utility may allow you to assign the serial port to any available IRQ and base address.

 If you are installing an add-on serial port card, don't install just any serial card you happen to find lying around. The best choice is a PCI card with 16650 UARTs, although 16550AFN UARTs will do in a pinch. Avoid ISA add-on cards in general, and in particular avoid 8-bit ISA serial port cards. These 8-bit cards have 8250-class UARTs and support only 8-bit IRQs, either of which renders them useless in a modern system.

If you need only one or two serial ports, configure them with standard settings for COM1 and/or COM2. If you need more than two, configure the least-flexible serial ports as COM1 and COM2 and use the ports that allow custom IRQ and base address settings for COM3 and above. Assign the standard ports 0x3E8 to COM3 and 0x2E8 to COM4, but assign unused IRQs to those ports. For example, you might configure COM3 for 0x3E8 and IRQ 10 (rather than the default IRQ 4). Doing so allows you to use all COM ports simultaneously with no risk of IRQ conflicts.

Configuring COM Port Settings

Once you have installed and configured the serial port hardware, the next step is to configure the operating system to use it. Windows automatically recognizes proper IRQ and base address values for serial ports reported by the BIOS that use standard BIOS settings—COM1 and COM2 in this example. Depending on the BIOS, nonstandard COM port assignments are often detected, but the hardware settings may not be reported correctly. For example, when we installed COM3 on an older system using 0x3E8 and IRQ 10, Windows 95 detected COM3 on 0x3E8, but assumed that it used IRQ 4.

Configuring COM port settings in Windows 9X

To configure COM port settings in Windows 9X, right-click the My Computer icon and choose Properties to display the Device Manager. If necessary, mark the View devices by type option button. Expand the Ports (COM and LPT) item, and double-click the port you are configuring to display the port Properties dialog, shown in Figure 22-5. The General page reports port status (in this case the port is working properly) and whether the port is available for use in the current profile.

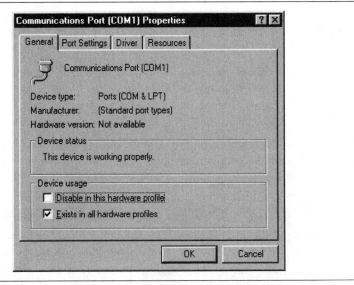

Figure 22-5. *The General page of Communications Port Properties displaying the operational status of the port*

Click the Port Settings tab to display the Port Settings page, shown in Figure 22-6, and use the drop-down lists to configure port defaults for speed, framing, and flow control.

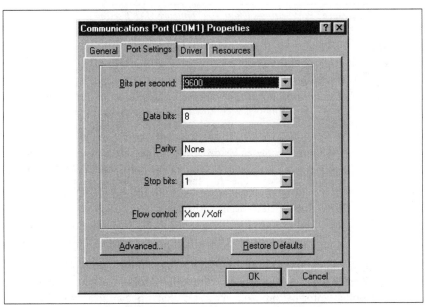

Figure 22-6. *The Port Settings page, where you configure communication parameters for the port*

The values you enter on the Port Settings page determine only the default settings for that port. Modem applications (such as Dial-Up Networking or fax software) change these settings programmatically to the values they require. The primary use of this page is to configure the correct settings for relatively simple devices such as a serial mouse or printer.

Windows automatically detects and enables 16550 FIFO buffering by default, but may use overly conservative settings. To optimize port performance, click the Advanced button in Port Properties to display the Advanced Port Settings dialog, shown in Figure 22-7. Move both slider bars to the far right for fastest performance, and leave them there unless you have problems with the port.

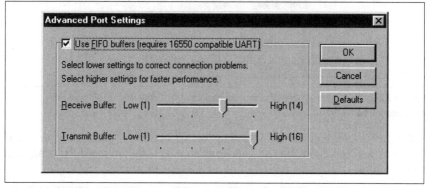

Figure 22-7. Advanced Port Settings, where you configure UART settings

 If a 16550-family UART is present, Windows nearly always detects it and enables the Use FIFO buffers checkbox automatically. If Windows does not enable FIFO buffers on your system, that means that the serial port has either a very old UART, or a FIFO-capable UART, but Windows is confused about the type of UART installed. That sometimes happens if the UART is embedded in a chipset rather than an actual standalone chip. For example, we have encountered some embedded UARTs that report themselves correctly as 16450s, but have supplementary buffering which emulates a 16550. In a case like this, the port may operate properly with FIFO buffering enabled. But be cautious about enabling buffering if Windows has left it disabled. There may be good reason.

To modify IRQ and/or I/O port settings, display the Resources page, shown in Figure 22-8. Clear the Use automatic settings checkbox, and select one of the Basic Configurations shown in Table 22-11. Highlight Input/Output Range or IRQ and click Change Setting. Select an available I/O port or IRQ, making sure that the Conflict information pane indicates that no conflicts exist. Save the changes and restart the system.

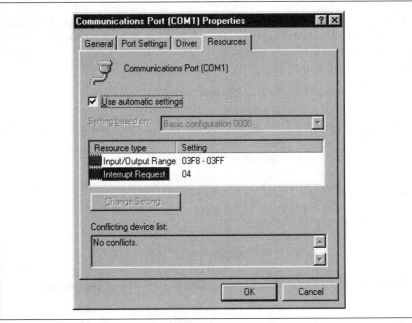

Figure 22-8. Windows 98SE displaying automatic settings for COM1

Table 22-11 lists Windows 98 (not Windows 98SE) Basic Configurations for COM ports. Basic Configurations 0, 2, 4, and 6 define standard uneditable values for COM1 through COM4, respectively. Basic Configurations 1, 3, 5, and 7 assign standard settings for I/O Port, but allow you to modify the IRQ. Choosing Basic Configuration 8 allows you to assign any IRQ and I/O port to a COM port.

Table 22-11. Windows 98 Basic Configurations for COM ports

Basic configuration	Comm port	Default IRQ	IRQ editable?	Default I/O port	I/O port editable?
0	1	4	No	0x3F8 – 0x3FF	No
1	1	4	Yes	0x3F8 – 0x3FF	No
2	2	3	No	0x2F8 – 0x2FF	No
3	2	3	Yes	0x2F8 – 0x2FF	No
4	3	4	No	0x3E8 – 0x3EF	No
5	3	4	Yes	0x3E8 – 0x3EF	No
6	4	3	No	0x2E8 – 0x2EF	No
7	4	3	Yes	0x2E8 – 0x2EF	No
8	Any	Variable	Yes	Variable	Yes

Table 22-12 and 22-13 list Windows 98SE (not Windows 98) Basic Configurations for COM ports 1 and 2, respectively. In each case, Basic Configuration 0000 uses the most common settings for that port, and allows editing neither IRQ nor I/O Port. Basic Configurations 0001 through 0004 allow you to choose a standard I/O Port address range and assign any available IRQ to that COM port. The Windows 98SE method differs from that of Windows 98 and Windows 2000 (described in the following section) in that it forces you to choose a predefined I/O Port address range, and allows editing only the IRQ assigned to that port.

Table 22-12. Windows 98SE Basic Configurations for COM1

Basic configuration	Default IRQ	IRQ editable?	Default I/O port	I/O port editable?
0000	4	No	0x3F8 – 0x3FF	No
0001	4	Yes	0x3F8 – 0x3FF	No
0002	4	Yes	0x2F8 – 0x2FF	No
0003	4	Yes	0x3E8 – 0x3EF	No
0004	4	Yes	0x2E8 – 0x2EF	No

Table 22-13. Windows 98SE Basic Configurations for COM2

Basic configuration	Default IRQ	IRQ editable?	Default I/O port	I/O port editable?
0000	3	No	0x2F8 – 0x2FF	No
0001	3	Yes	0x2F8 – 0x2FF	No
0002	3	Yes	0x3F8 – 0x3FF	No
0003	3	Yes	0x3E8 – 0x3EF	No
0004	3	Yes	0x2E8 – 0x2EF	No

Configuring COM port settings in Windows NT 4

To configure port settings in Windows NT, run the Control Panel Ports applet. The Ports dialog lists the COM ports that NT recognizes. Double-click the port to be configured and use the drop-down lists in the Settings dialog, shown in Figure 22-9, to configure default port settings for speed, framing, and flow control.

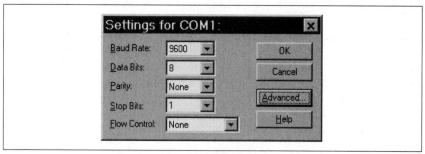

Figure 22-9. The Windows NT 4 Settings dialog, where you configure communication parameters for the port

To view or change settings for I/O port and IRQ, click the Advanced button in the Settings dialog, and use the drop-down lists to specify parameters for the port (see Figure 22-10). You can enable or disable FIFO buffering by marking or clearing the checkbox, but Windows NT 4 makes no provision for tuning FIFO performance from the GUI. Although it's probably not worth the time to do, you can modify FIFO buffering settings using the Registry Editor. FIFO settings are contained in the key *HKEY_LOCAL_MACHINE\SYSTEM\CurrentControlSet\Services\Serial*. The relevant value entries are:

RxFIFO

> The *RxFIFO* value entry specifies the number of bytes that must accumulate in the receive FIFO buffer before a COM port interrupt is triggered. RxFIFO is a REG_DWORD value. The default value for this entry is the value set for the Serial service, which is eight bytes.

TxFIFO

> The *TxFIFO* value entry specifies the number of bytes that must accumulate in the send FIFO buffer before a COM port interrupt is triggered. TxFIFO is a REG_DWORD value. The default value for this entry is the value set for the Serial service, which is one byte.

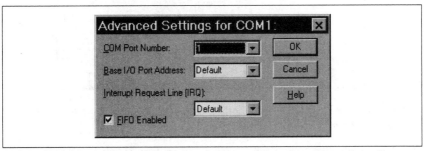

Figure 22-10. The Windows NT 4 Advanced Settings dialog, where you configure base address and IRQ for a selected COM port

Note the following when you are configuring COM ports under NT:

- NT may or may not recognize a newly installed port, depending on its settings. If the new port is not listed, click Add from the Ports dialog and use the drop-down lists to define port number, I/O port, and IRQ for the new port, as described earlier.

- You can enter a custom value for I/O port address instead of using one of those listed.

- NT does not prevent you from using settings that will cause port conflicts, so verify that the IRQ and I/O port address are available before configuring a port to use them.

Configuring COM port settings in Windows 2000/XP

To configure port settings in Windows 2000/XP, right-click the My Computer icon and choose Properties to display the System Properties dialog. Display the Hardware page and click the Device Manager button. If necessary, mark the View devices by type option button. Expand the Ports (COM and LPT) item, and double-click the port you are configuring to display the port Properties dialog, shown in Figure 22-11. The General page reports port status and whether or not the port is available for use in the current profile. The Port Settings page, shown in Figure 22-11, allows you to change the default speed and framing parameters for the port.

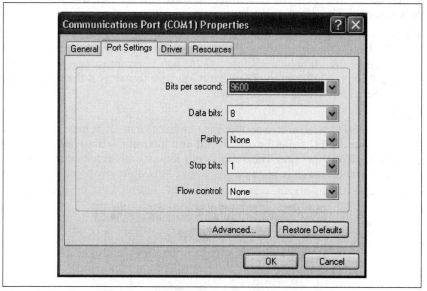

Figure 22-11. The Windows 2000/XP Port Settings, where you change default speed and framing parameters for the selected port

Windows 2000/XP automatically detects and enables 16550 FIFO buffering by default, but sets both Receive Buffer and Transmit Buffer to their fastest settings by default. On most systems, these settings work properly. If you encounter frequent retries or corrupted data on the serial port, try using these sliders on the Advanced Settings dialog, shown in Figure 22-12, to reduce the buffer settings in small increments.

To modify IRQ and/or I/O port settings, display the Resources page, shown in Figure 22-13. Clear the Use automatic settings checkbox, and select one of the Basic Configurations shown in Table 22-14 (for COM1) or Table 22-15 (for COM2). Highlight Input/Output Range or IRQ and click Change Setting. Select an available I/O port or IRQ, making sure that the Conflict information pane indicates that no conflicts exist. Save the changes and restart the system.

Tables 22-14 and 22-15 list Windows 2000/XP Basic Configurations for COM ports 1 and 2, respectively. In each case, Basic Configurations 0000 through 0003 define standard settings for the COM ports, with 0000 corresponding to the most common settings. For either port, choosing Basic Configuration 0004 allows you to assign any available IRQ and I/O port to that COM port. The Windows 2000 method is similar to that of Windows 98SE, except that Windows 2000 allows

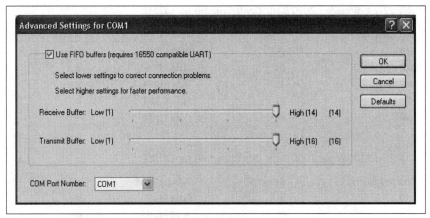

Figure 22-12. The Receive Buffer and Transmit Buffer sliders, which you can adjust for optimum performance

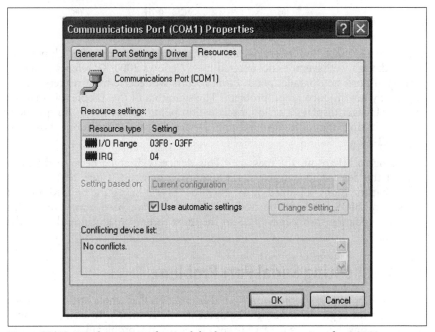

Serial Com-
munications

Figure 22-13. Windows XP Professional displaying automatic settings for COM1

editing both IRQ and I/O Port address range in Basic Configuration 0004, whereas Windows 98SE forces you to select from among the listed I/O Port address ranges, and allows editing only the IRQ assigned to the port.

Table 22-14. Windows 2000 Basic Configurations for COM1

Basic configuration	Default IRQ	Default I/O port	Editable?
0000	04	0x3F8 – 0x3FF	No
0001	04	0x3E8 – 0x3EF	No
0002	03	0x2F8 – 0x2FF	No
0003	03	0x2E8 – 0x2EF	No
0004	04	0x3F8 – 0x3FF	Yes

Table 22-15. Windows 2000 Basic Configurations for COM2

Basic configuration	Default IRQ	Default I/O port	Editable?
0000	03	0x2F8 – 0x2FF	No
0001	03	0x2E8 – 0x2EF	No
0002	04	0x3F8 – 0x3FF	No
0003	04	0x3E8 – 0x3EF	No
0004	03	0x2F8 – 0x2FF	Yes

On some i440BX-based systems—and perhaps systems with other chipsets as well, although we have not encountered it—Windows 2000/XP refuses to recognize serial ports and parallel ports. From reports we receive from readers, this is apparently not an uncommon problem. The symptom of this problem is that the Device Manager displays a yellow exclamation point for the port(s) in question. Double-clicking the port displays the Device status information shown in Figure 22-14.

According to Microsoft, the message "This device is disabled because the firmware of the device did not give it the required resources. (Code 29)" indicates either that the port is disabled in the BIOS but is still being enumerated, or that the system BIOS needs to be updated. Each time we have encountered this problem, updating the system BIOS to the most recent version indeed fixed the problem.

Troubleshooting Serial Port Problems

So many things can go wrong with a serial connection that whole books have been written on the topic. Without test equipment, you're limited to using common-sense solutions, but they will serve to resolve nearly any problem you are likely to encounter. Use the following guidelines to resolve serial port problems:

- If a newly installed serial connection doesn't work, it's almost always because the serial port is disabled or misconfigured, communications parameters are set wrong, or you're using the wrong cable. To resolve these problems, take the steps described in the preceding sections to verify that the port hardware is installed and configured properly, that the BIOS and Windows recognize the port, and that communications parameters are set properly.

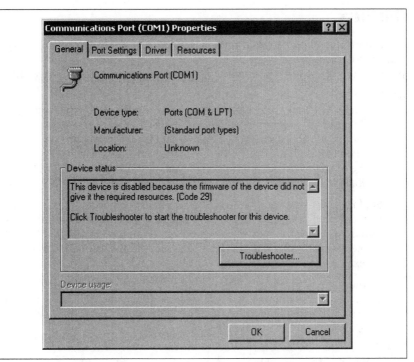

Figure 22-14. Windows displaying Device status as disabled when it does not recognize a port

- If the preceding steps don't solve the problem, try connecting the cable to a different serial port. If the device works when connected to another port, the new port may be defective. If the device doesn't work on the known-good port, suspect a problem with the cable or the device itself.

- If a working serial connection stops working, it's usually because someone or something changed port settings or communications parameters. Verify these first. If they appear correct, it's possible that Windows has munged its own configuration. Uninstall and reinstall the affected device (e.g., a modem) from within Windows. If that doesn't solve the problem, use the Device Manager to remove the port and restart the system. Windows will detect the "new" port and configure it automatically.

- If uninstalling and reinstalling doesn't solve the problem, the next likely cause is that the serial port, cable, or peripheral is bad. Determine which by swapping cables and/or connecting the peripheral to a different serial port.

- Note that some serial ports are very sensitive to voltage spikes and may be damaged during lightning storms by surges induced on inadequately protected phone lines without any other apparent damage to the PC. If a serial port suddenly stops working after an electrical storm, suspect physical port damage.

Our Picks

Serial ports are ubiquitous on modern systems. Other than the recent "legacy-free" motherboards and systems, nearly all modern computers have two serial ports, although one may exist only as a set of header pins on the motherboard.

Serial port

Nothing/Anything. Before you buy an add-on serial port card, make sure you really need it. Embarrassingly often, we've popped the lid on a system, intending to install a serial port, only to find that there was already a perfectly good one unused. In our defense, those little DB9 connectors are easy to miss in the tangle of cables on the back panel, and if the port is disabled in the BIOS, Windows doesn't report it as present.

So, first make sure you don't already have what you need. If it turns out that you do need to install one, think again. Serial ports consume a lot of resources for the functionality they provide. You may be better off installing an inexpensive A-B serial switch and sharing one port between two devices—for example, an external modem and a Palm cradle.

If you absolutely need to add a serial port, buy one of the inexpensive (~$20) serial port cards commonly sold by computer stores and mass marketers. We've used many different ones, all of which seem to work fine and none of which is noticeably better than any of the others.

Cables

Belkin Gold Series cables. Nowadays, the only serial cable you are likely to need is a standard, off-the-shelf modem cable. Belkin stocks a great variety of standard serial cables in various lengths, connector types, and pinouts. Although Belkin makes a less-expensive line of cables, its best grade is worth the few extra dollars it costs (*http://www.belkin.com*).

For updated recommendations, visit: *http://www.hardwareguys.com/picks/serial. html*.

23

Parallel Communications

While a serial interface communicates one bit at a time using one data line, a parallel interface communicates one byte at a time using eight data lines. This allows a parallel port to transfer data five or 10 times faster than a traditional serial port, but the additional complexity of keeping a full byte synchronized during each cycle also means that a traditional parallel cable cannot be longer than six to 10 feet, versus 50 feet or more for serial.

Nearly every PC has at least one parallel port, which may reside on the motherboard or on a video or I/O card. Some older computers have two or three parallel ports installed, usually because expansion cards were added that just happened to have parallel ports on them. Fortunately, PCs are pretty smart about detecting parallel ports at boot time and avoiding conflicts.

The so-called "legacy-reduced" motherboards and systems that began coming to market in late 1999 may or may not provide parallel ports. "Legacy-free" systems and motherboards began shipping in volume in mid-2000, and do not provide parallel ports (or many other formerly standard connections, such as serial ports, PS/2 mouse and keyboard ports, a floppy diskette drive interface, etc.). These systems depend entirely on USB for external connectivity. If you need to connect a legacy parallel device such as a printer to such a system, there are two options. First, you can install a PCI parallel card, which typically also includes one or two high-speed serial ports. Otherwise, you can buy a USB-to-parallel converter, various models of which are now widely available from Belkin and others.

Probably because it is so commonplace and so unlikely to cause problems, nearly everyone takes the lowly parallel port for granted. Unlike the serial port, the parallel port is so completely standardized that you can use it without thinking about it. In fact, a good argument could be made for the parallel port as the predecessor of Plug-and-Play. You can mix and match new and old ports, cables, and printers in any combination, and everything usually just works. Therein lies the problem.

The parallel port is a victim of its own standardization and backward compatibility. Parallel ports, peripherals, and even cables have undergone significant improvements over the years, but those improvements have been so low-key as to be almost invisible. Most people aren't even aware that they've taken place. So, although any old combination of parallel components will probably work, it may be doing so at a least-common-denominator level, crippling performance and functionality.

Something as simple as using an old printer cable to connect a new PC to a new printer may choke throughput. Even worse, you may use all new hardware and still get low performance or limited functionality just because you didn't know that you needed to make a minor change in the BIOS Setup for the parallel port. This chapter describes what you need to know to use parallel ports efficiently.

Mapping Parallel Ports to LPTs

The PC BIOS allocates three prioritized I/O port addresses to parallel printers. Port 0x3BC is the highest priority, followed by 0x378 and then 0x278. At boot time, the BIOS checks each of these addresses to detect parallel hardware. The highest-priority parallel port detected (which may be on any of the three I/O port addresses) is assigned as LPT1:. If a second parallel port is detected, it is assigned LPT2:. If a third port is detected, it is assigned LPT3:. Some BIOSes also make provision for LPT4:, but this is nonstandard and not widely supported.

This automatic detection of port hardware and assignment of LPT numbers means that installing another parallel port may change the LPT designation of existing ports. For example, the embedded parallel port on most motherboards is assigned port 0x378 (the second-priority address) by default. As long as it is the only port present, it will be mapped to LPT1: by the BIOS. If you add another parallel port configured for port address 0x3BC, that new port will be mapped to LPT1: and the existing port will be changed to LPT2:.

You set the I/O port address for most motherboard parallel ports in BIOS Setup, although older motherboards may require changing a jumper instead. You set addresses for parallel ports on most expansion cards by changing a jumper. Avoid changes in LPT mappings when installing parallel ports by verifying the port addresses for existing ports and setting the new port for a lower-priority address, if possible. Always make sure that the new port does not use the same address as an existing port, or results will be unpredictable.

Parallel Port Types

Parallel port hardware may be of five types, described next in the order of their appearance in PCs. A computer may contain any of these port types, and may include ports of more than one type. Earlier ports are limited in functionality and performance. Later ports provide increased functionality and performance, and may often be configured to emulate earlier port types when necessary to support older peripherals.

Unidirectional 4-bit parallel port

The *unidirectional 4-bit parallel port*, also called a *Standard Parallel Port* (*SPP*), is based on the de facto Centronics standard, and was the type of parallel port supplied with the original IBM PC and its clones. These ports are misnamed, as they are not unidirectional and are not limited to 4-bit transfers. An SPP does 8-bit output and can accept 4-bit (nibble) input.

In theory, these ports are limited to using a 2-meter (about 6 foot) cable, but this distance can be extended to 3 to 5 meters (10 to 16 feet) by using a high-grade parallel cable. Unidirectional 4-bit parallel ports are commonly found in older desktop and laptop systems, and are still supplied on some low-end I/O cards. These ports provide native throughput of 40 to 60 KB/s, although certain design tricks can push this to the 150 KB/s range.

Bidirectional 8-bit parallel port

When IBM introduced the PS/2 line in 1987, all but the two lowest-cost models (the Models 25 and 30) included a *bidirectional 8-bit parallel port*. Initially, these were *non-DMA ports*, called *Type 1 ports* by IBM. The parallel ports included with later PS/2 systems could also be configured as *Type 3 ports*, which use DMA. These ports support both 8-bit input and output, and provide about 75 KB/s to 300 KB/s throughput, depending on characteristics of the port itself, how it is configured, the speed of the external device, and the quality of the port driver.

Recent notebook and desktop systems often provide a bidirectional 8-bit mode for their parallel ports, as do some add-on port cards. Bidirectional 8-bit parallel ports provide better throughput than do 4-bit ports for connecting external devices such as tape drives and parallel port network adapters, if the device can take advantage of the 8-bit functionality. Note that some vendors also call 4-bit ports "bidirectional," so the terminology used to describe the port does not guarantee its level of functionality.

Enhanced Parallel Port (EPP)

The throughput limitations of even the Type 3 bidirectional 8-bit parallel ports soon became obvious as page printer technology improved. Manufacturers of scanners, storage devices, and other external peripherals were also starting to use the parallel port as an inexpensive alternative to expensive SCSI or proprietary interfaces. A superior parallel port technology was clearly needed. Xircom, Intel, and Zenith Data Systems got together and came up with the *Enhanced Parallel Port*, or *EPP*.

EPP offered performance and other advantages while maintaining backward SPP compatibility, so it quickly came into widespread use. There soon coalesced an informal confederation of manufacturers whose purpose was to promote and enhance the EPP standard. This group ultimately solidified as the EPP Committee, and successfully lobbied the IEEE-1284 committee to include EPP as an advanced mode in the IEEE-1284 specification described later in this section.

EPP supports 8-bit bidirectional communications at ISA bus speeds, providing throughput similar to that of 8-bit ISA bus cards. EPP provides theoretical maximum throughput of about 2 MB/s, and typical real-world throughput of more than 1 MB/s. Many 386 and 486 systems and most reasonably recent I/O expansion cards include EPP-capable parallel ports.

Extended Capabilities Port (ECP)

EPP was a reasonably satisfactory solution and was first to market, but Microsoft and Hewlett-Packard had been working on their own improved parallel port technology, which they named the *Extended Capabilities Port*, or *ECP*. Like EPP, ECP supports 8-bit bidirectional communications at ISA bus speeds. Unlike EPP, ECP uses DMA, provides a FIFO buffer of at least 16 bytes, and includes hardware data compression. These features allow ECP to provide better throughput than EPP—theoretically more than 2 MB/s, but typically about 2 MB/s actual. Some 486 systems, most Pentium and higher systems, and recent I/O expansion cards include ECP-capable parallel ports.

IEEE-1284 parallel port

The increasing diversity of parallel port hardware and the resulting potential for incompatibilities made it desirable to develop an umbrella standard that would combine and codify these earlier ad hoc standards into a single formal standard. The resulting document, *1284-1994 IEEE Standard Signaling Method for a Bidirectional Parallel Peripheral Interface for Personal Computers*, does so by defining five parallel transmission modes. IEEE-1284-compliant parallel port hardware, available on recent computers, motherboards, and expansion cards, can use one or more of the following modes to emulate earlier parallel port hardware, thereby ensuring both compatibility and optimum performance with almost any parallel peripheral:

Compatibility Mode

Compatibility Mode, also called *Centronics Mode* or *Standard Mode*, is a forward unidirectional mode that corresponds to the original SPP definition, and is included in the IEEE-1284 definition for backward compatibility with the installed base of SPP-only peripherals. Transferring a byte in Compatibility Mode requires four I/O instructions and additional overhead instructions, which limits throughput to about 150 KB/s. Pure IEEE-1284 Compatibility Mode is seldom seen in practice. Compatibility Mode as implemented by most integrated 1284-compliant controllers includes a FIFO buffer, which is used in conjunction with the Compatibility Mode protocol. This hybrid mode, which is not a part of the official IEEE-1284 standard, may be called *Buffered Mode*, *Fast Centronics Mode*, *FIFO Mode*, or *Parallel Port FIFO Mode*. It improves Compatibility Mode throughput to 500 KB/s or more by substituting hardware strobing for the software strobing used in true IEEE-1294 Compatibility Mode. The elimination of software handshaking nearly eliminates latency, and can increase throughput to 500 KB/s or more.

Nibble Mode

Nibble Mode is the slower of the two reverse channel modes defined by IEEE-1284. Nibble Mode may be combined with Compatibility Mode or a proprietary forward channel mode to yield full bidirectional capability. The advantage to Nibble Mode is that it can be used with any parallel cable and any parallel port hardware, including the original unidirectional 4-bit ports. The disadvantage to Nibble Mode is that it is the slowest way to send data from a peripheral to the PC. Like Compatibility Mode, Nibble Mode data transfer is managed by a software driver, which restricts throughput to about 50 KB/s. For printers, which use the reverse channel to transfer only small amounts of status information, this is not a significant limitation. For parallel interface disk and tape drives, network adapters, and similar devices that need full bidirectional bandwidth, Nibble Mode reverse channel throughput is wholly inadequate and should be used only as a last resort.

Byte Mode

Byte Mode is the faster of the two reverse channel modes defined by IEEE-1284. Byte Mode corresponds to the reverse channel mode of the 8-bit bidirectional parallel interface originally supplied with IBM PS/2 computers. In contrast to Nibble Mode, which transfers four bits at a time and requires two data transfer cycles to transfer one byte, Byte Mode transfers a full byte in one data cycle, using the eight data lines to do so. Byte Mode reverse channel throughput is comparable to forward channel throughput in unbuffered Compatibility Mode—about 150 KB/s. Using Compatibility Mode and Byte Mode together provides a half-duplex bidirectional connection that is comparable to the original IBM PS/2 bidirectional parallel interface.

EPP Mode

EPP Mode corresponds to the ad hoc Xircom/Intel/ZDS EPP definition. Intel first implemented EPP on the 82360 I/O chip that was part of the 386SL chipset. This pre-1284 EPP implementation is called EPP 1.7. The IEEE-1284-1994 EPP Mode definition formalizes EPP 1.7, but with some minor changes in signal definitions. As a result, not all EPP peripherals work reliably with all EPP ports. Any 1284-compliant EPP peripheral may be used with either an EPP 1.7 port or a 1284-compliant EPP port. An EPP 1.7 peripheral may be used with an EPP 1.7 port, but may or may not function properly with a 1284-compliant EPP port. EPP Mode can achieve data throughput comparable to an ISA bus card—on the close order of 0.5 to 2 MB/s.

ECP Mode

ECP Mode corresponds to the ad hoc Microsoft/HP ECP specification.

The original IEEE-1994 standard is supplemented by IEEE-P1284.3, *Standard for Interface and Protocol Extensions to IEEE-1284-1994 Compliant Peripherals and Host Adapters*. For our purposes, the only notable new feature of IEEE P1284.3 is that it defines additional protocols that allow daisy-chaining parallel-connected devices. Windows versions prior to Windows 2000 do not support IEEE-P1284.3 functions. Windows 2000/XP has partial IEEE-P1284.3 support, including the ability to select and operate more than one IEEE-1284. 3 daisy-chain device and an end-of-chain device, and basic support for the Datalink Layer. Windows 2000/XP does *not* support IEEE-1284.3 multiplexors or interrupts for IEEE-1284.3 daisy-chain devices.

Configuring Parallel Port Hardware

How you configure a parallel port may significantly impact performance and overall capabilities. Even on new systems that include capable parallel port hardware, the parallel port mode is often set to SPP by default. Many people unintentionally cripple the performance of their parallel ports simply because they don't know that better choices than the default are available.

The first step to configure a parallel port for optimum performance is to determine the capabilities of the port hardware. Examining the documentation may help, but documentation is often cursory, misleading, or missing entirely. Without detailed documentation, the easiest way to determine the capabilities of the parallel port hardware is to download and run *Parallel.exe*, which is available from many Internet file repository sites.

On older motherboards and expansion cards, you may have to set the mode by using a jumper. On newer systems, you can usually set the mode using the BIOS Setup program. The parallel port modes available are determined first by the capabilities of the port hardware itself. Even if the hardware supports all modes, however, the BIOS may not, so you may be limited in the choices you can make. In general, use the following guidelines when selecting a parallel port mode:

SPP Mode
> SPP Mode, which the BIOS may also call *Standard Mode, Basic Mode, 4-bit Mode, or Unidirectional Mode,* is the least-common-denominator choice, and corresponds to the original Centronics-compatible IBM parallel port. Use this mode only after determining that none of the more-capable modes works with your cable or peripheral.

Bidirectional Mode
> Bidirectional Mode, which the BIOS may also call *8-bit Mode* or *PS/2 Mode*, corresponds to the parallel modes introduced with the IBM PS/2 parallel ports. If you choose this mode, you may also be able to choose *Type 1 sub-mode* (also called *Non-DMA sub-mode*) or *Type 3 sub-mode* (also called *DMA sub-mode*). Choose Type 3 mode for better performance, as long as you don't mind consuming a DMA channel. Use this mode if only it and SPP work properly for your hardware. Also use this mode if you are using Windows NT, which does not support EPP and ECP modes.

EPP Mode
> EPP Mode, which the BIOS may instead call *Enhanced Mode*, is sometimes the best choice even if later modes are available. EPP includes some control features that are not provided by ECP, sometimes making EPP better suited for nonprinter peripherals such as parallel port storage devices and scanners. Also, you may need to choose EPP mode explicitly to support some early EPP-compliant devices that do not function properly with the updated EPP mode supported by IEEE-1284-1994 compliant ports. EPP uses IRQ channels for flow control. It does not use DMA or provide data compression, making it somewhat slower than the ECP mode described next.

ECP Mode
> ECP Mode, which the BIOS may call *Extended Mode*, is usually the best choice for transferring data to high-speed printers, although it does require a

DMA channel. Because it does not support some of the control features provided by EPP mode, ECP mode may not be the best choice to connect nonprinter peripherals.

IEEE 1284 Mode

IEEE-1284 Mode, which the BIOS may simply label *Auto*, is the most flexible choice. If the BIOS provides this option, choose it to allow the port to adjust automatically to the optimum mode for the device to which it is connected.

Parallel port support differs widely between Windows distributions, as described in the following sections.

Configuring parallel ports under Windows NT

Windows NT through V4.0 does not support EPP or ECP bidirectional communications ports. If a parallel port is configured as EPP or ECP, Windows NT 4.0 and prior will not detect the port.

Configuring parallel ports under Windows 2000/XP

Windows 2000/XP fully supports most parallel hardware, including standard parallel port devices, IEEE-1284-compatible and -compliant devices, and IEEE-1284.3 daisy-chain devices. Windows 2000/XP fully supports most parallel modes, including Centronics mode, IEEE-1284 modes, ECP mode, and EPP mode. Windows 2000/XP partially supports IEEE-1284.3 modes.

To configure a parallel port under Windows 2000/XP, right-click My Computer and choose Properties to display the System Properties dialog. Click the Hardware tab and then the Device Manager button. Locate and expand the Ports (COM & LPT) item within the Device Manager tree, and double-click the printer port you want to configure to display a dialog similar to that shown in Figure 23-1.

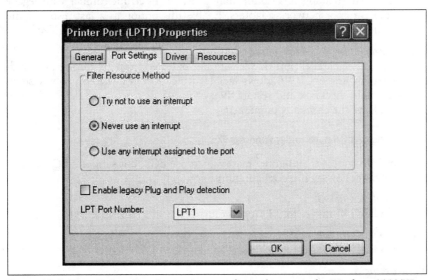

Figure 23-1. Using Printer Port Properties to configure the port under Windows 2000/XP

The Filter Resource Method determines how Windows 2000/XP manages the port, as follows:

Try not to use an interrupt
Marking this option causes the Windows parallel port driver to release any interrupt assigned to it if Plug-and-Play enumeration determines that the installed parallel port hardware does not require an interrupt to function properly. If the port hardware does require an interrupt for proper functioning, the Windows parallel port driver retains control of that interrupt. This setting works properly and automatically on most systems that use ACPI, and we can only suppose that Microsoft did not choose this as the default setting because the potential exists for conflicts on older hardware.

Never use an interrupt
This is the default setting for Windows 2000 and Windows XP. Marking this option causes the Windows parallel port driver to release any interrupt assigned to it for use by another device, even if Plug-and-Play enumeration determines that an installed parallel port requires an interrupt to function properly. This setting works properly on most modern systems that use a default configuration. However, if you reconfigure the parallel port in BIOS Setup to function as an EPP port, this setting may cause that parallel port to malfunction or not be recognized.

Use any interrupt assigned to the port
This option disables the Windows parallel port driver interrupt-filtering function, and allows the parallel port driver to accept and use any interrupt assigned to it. Enable this option only if (a) because of hardware, BIOS, or driver issues, the system does not operate properly unless an interrupt is available to the parallel port hardware, or (b) you have installed a high-speed parallel interface and driver that require an interrupt to function properly. Note that enabling this option may cause an interrupt conflict with legacy audio cards or network adapters. Enable this option as a last resort. Some parallel ports configured as EPP may require that this option be enabled.

Enable legacy Plug-and-Play detection
Some older parallel port devices are not detected properly during Plug-and-Play enumeration. If Windows fails to detect such a device on your system, mark this checkbox and restart the system. If all devices are detected properly, leave the checkbox unmarked.

Configuring parallel ports under Windows 9X

Windows 9X must be configured manually to use ECP, but supports ECP devices in any of the following five configurations:

Basic Configuration 0
Standard I/O ranges for LPT ports only

Basic Configuration 1
Standard I/O ranges for LPT ports and any IRQ

Basic Configuration 2
Standard I/O ranges for LPT ports, IRQ, and any DMA

Basic Configuration 3
Any I/O ranges for LPT ports only

Basic Configuration 4
Any I/O ranges for LPT ports and IRQ

To enable ECP support in Windows 9X, first use the system documentation, BIOS Setup, or a diagnostic utility to verify the IRQ and DMA settings assigned to the port you want to configure. In the Device Manager, expand the Ports (COM and LPT) item and display the Properties dialog for the port to be configured. On the Resources page, the Resource Settings pane shows the I/O port that was detected automatically and assigned to the device. Clear the Use automatic settings checkbox and use the Setting based on drop-down list to choose the appropriate Basic Configuration, according to whether the ECP port uses standard or custom settings. Change the Input/Output Range, IRQ, and/or DMA settings as needed to correspond to the port hardware configuration, save the changes, and restart Windows.

Configuring parallel ports under Linux

Linux has made great strides in adding support for various parallel modes. Linux 2.0 supported only Compatibility Mode and Nibble Mode. Beginning with 2.4, the Linux parallel port subsystem supports all standard IEEE-P1284.3 modes. For complete details on the Linux 2.4 parallel port subsystem, see *http://people.redhat.com/twaugh/parport/html/parportguide.html*.

Parallel Connectors and Cables

IEEE 1284-1994 defines both the electrical and physical interface for cables and connectors. Cable quality is critical for IEEE-1284, because various IEEE 1284 modes support much higher transmission speeds than SPP.

Parallel connectors

Traditional parallel cables use a DB25M connector for the PC end and a male, 36-pin, 0.085-inch centerline Champ connector with bale locks (commonly called a *Centronics C36M*) for the printer. The IEEE-1284-1994 specification allows these two traditional connectors to be used as before. It designates the DB25M the *IEEE-1284-1994 Type A Connector* and the C36M the *IEEE-1284-1994 Type B Connector*. IEEE-1284 also defines a new type of parallel connector, called the *1284-1994 Type C Connector*, which uses a 36-pin, 0.050-inch centerline mini-connector with clip latches, and is usually called a *mini-Centronics connector*. Printer cables are now available that use these connectors in many combinations.

PC-to-peripheral parallel cables

It used to be that a printer cable was a printer cable. Not anymore. Printer cables now come in a variety of types, which use different connectors and pinouts. The good news is that you can still use any printer cable to connect a PC to a printer—as long as the connectors physically fit—and that connection will work in some fashion. The bad news is that using an old printer cable may cripple the performance and functionality of the link.

When you buy a new parallel cable—which you should if you are now using an older cable to connect a recent port to a recent peripheral—make sure it's labeled "IEEE-1284-1994 Compliant." Tables 23-1 through 23-4 show the pin connections for the standard IEEE-1284 cables you are likely to need. To ensure optimum parallel performance, use an IEEE-1284 cable with connectors appropriate for your PC parallel port and the peripheral to be connected.

Table 23-1 shows the pinouts for a standard SPP 25-wire Centronics C36M-to-DB25M parallel printer cable, including signal polarities and directions. The missing C36M pins are not connected. The original IBM Parallel Cable and some inexpensive currently available cables use only 18 wires, using a single wire to tie DB25M pins 18 through 25 to C36M pins 19 through 30 and 33. These 18-wire cables may not work in all applications, notably with OS/2.

Table 23-1. The pinouts for a standard SPP 25-wire Centronics C36M-to-DB25M parallel printer cable

C36M	DB25M	Description	C36M	DB25M	Description
1	1	-nStrobe (out)	14	14	-nAutoFd (out)
2	2	+Data Bit 0 (out)	19	19	-Data Bit 1 Return (GND) (in)
3	3	+Data Bit 1 (out)	21	20	-Data Bit 2 Return (GND) (in)
4	4	+Data Bit 2 (out)	23	21	-Data Bit 3 Return (GND) (in)
5	5	+Data Bit 3 (out)	25	22	-Data Bit 4 Return (GND) (in)
6	6	+Data Bit 4 (out)	27	23	-Data Bit 5 Return (GND) (in)
7	7	+Data Bit 5 (out)	29	24	-Data Bit 6 Return (GND) (in)
8	8	+Data Bit 6 (out)	30	25	-Data Bit 7 Return (GND) (in)
9	9	+Data Bit 7 (out)	31	16	-nInit (out)
10	10	-nAck (in)	32	15	-nFault (in)
11	11	+Busy (in)	33	18	-Data Bit 0 Return (GND) (in)
12	12	+PE (in)	36	17	-nSelectIn (out)
13	13	+Select (in)			

Table 23-2 shows the pinouts for an IEEE 1284 A-to-B adapter cable, used to connect a DB25M, Type A EPP, ECP, or IEEE-1284-compliant PC parallel port to a peripheral with a Centronics, C36M Type B connector. Note that DB25M pins 1 through 17 carry the same signals as the preceding cable, and that DB25M pins 18 through 25 are similarly used for ground returns, although with slightly different definitions. Because it uses the same connectors as the SPP parallel cable described in the preceding table, the only way to differentiate this cable visually is to look for the "IEEE-1284-1994 Compliant" label.

Table 23-2. The pinouts for an IEEE-1284 A-to-B adapter cable

C36M	DB25M	Description	C36M	DB25M	Description
1	1	NStrobe	14	14	nAutoFd
2	2	Data Bit 0	19	18	nStrobe ground return
3	3	Data Bit 1	20, 21	19	Data Bits 0 & 1 ground return

C36M	DB25M	Description	C36M	DB25M	Description
4	4	Data Bit 2	22, 23	20	Data Bits 2 & 3 ground return
5	5	Data Bit 3	24, 25	21	Data Bits 4 & 5 ground return
6	6	Data Bit 4	26, 27	22	Data Bits 6 & 7 ground return
7	7	Data Bit 5	28	24	nAck, PE & Select ground return
8	8	Data Bit 6	29	23	Busy & nFault ground return
9	9	Data Bit 7	30	25	nAutoFd, nInit & nSelectIn ground return
10	10	NAck	31	16	nInit
11	11	Busy	32	15	nFault
12	12	PE	36	17	nSelectIn
13	13	Select			

Table 23-3 shows the pinouts for an IEEE-1284 A-to-C adapter cable, used to connect a DB25M, Type A EPP, ECP, or IEEE-1284-compliant PC parallel port to a peripheral with a mini-Centronics, Type C connector.

Table 23-3. The pinouts for an IEEE-1284 A-to-C adapter cable

Type C	Type A	Description	Type C	Type A	Description
1	11	Busy	14	16	nInit
2	13	Select	15	1	nStrobe
3	10	NAck	16	17	nSelectIn
4	15	NFault	17	14	nAutoFd
5	12	PE	19, 22	23	Busy & nFault ground return
6	2	Data Bit 0	20, 21 & 23	24	nAck, PE & Select ground return
7	3	Data Bit 1	24 & 25	19	Data Bits 0 & 1 ground return
8	4	Data Bit 2	26 & 27	20	Data Bits 2 & 3 ground return
9	5	Data Bit 3	28 & 29	21	Data Bits 4 & 5 ground return
10	6	Data Bit 4	30 & 31	22	Data Bits 6 & 7 ground return
11	7	Data Bit 5	32, 34 & 35	25	nAutoFd, nInit & nSelectIn ground return
12	8	Data Bit 6	33	18	nStrobe ground return
13	9	Data Bit 7			

Table 23-4 shows the pinouts for an IEEE-1284 C-to-B adapter cable, used to connect a mini-Centronics, Type C PC parallel port to a peripheral with a Centronics, Type B connector. This is an unusual cable for now, but will become more common if and when PC parallel ports with IEEE-1284 Type C connectors become more common. Because parallel ports are being deemphasized in new motherboards and PCs, that day may well never arrive.

Table 23-4. The pinouts for an IEEE 1284 C-to-B adapter cable

Type C	Type B	Description	Type C	Type B	Description
1	11	Busy	19	29	Busy ground return
2	13	Select	20	28	Select ground return
3	10	nAck	21	28	nAck ground return
4	32	nFault	22	29	nFault ground return
5	12	PE	23	28	PE ground return
6	2	Data Bit 0	24	20	Data Bit 0 ground return
7	3	Data Bit 1	25	21	Data Bit 1 ground return
8	4	Data Bit 2	26	22	Data Bit 2 ground return
9	5	Data Bit 3	27	23	Data Bit 3 ground return
10	6	Data Bit 4	28	24	Data Bit 4 ground return
11	7	Data Bit 5	29	25	Data Bit 5 ground return
12	8	Data Bit 6	30	26	Data Bit 6 ground return
13	9	Data Bit 7	31	27	Data Bit 7 ground return
14	31	nInit	32	30	nInit ground return
15	1	nStrobe	33	19	nStrobe ground return
16	36	nSelectIn	34	30	nSelectIn ground return
17	14	nAutoFd	35	30	nAutoFd ground return
18	-	Host Logic High	36	18	Peripheral Logic High

PC-to-PC parallel cables

Windows NT does not support direct parallel connections, but Windows 9X Direct Cable Connection can be used to establish a parallel-to-parallel link between two PCs. You can use three types of DB25M-to-DB25M cables for a DCC parallel connection, designated by Microsoft as follows:

Standard cable
> The *Standard cable*, shown in Table 23-5, is also called a *Basic 4-bit cable*, *LapLink cable*, or *InterLink cable*. This the slowest parallel DCC cable, but can be used to link computers with any types of parallel port, including dissimilar ports on the two computers. Expect throughput of 40 to 70 KB/s when using one of these cables—painfully slow, but still about 10 times the speed of DCC over a serial connection.

Table 23-5. Standard cable for use with InterLink or Direct Cable Connection

DB25M	DB25M	Connection description
2	15	Data bit 0 (active when high)
3	13	Data bit 1 (active when high)
4	12	Data bit 2 (active when high)
5	10	Data bit 3 (active when high)
6	11	Data bit 4 (active when high)
10	5	Acknowledge (active when low)

Table 23-5. Standard cable for use with InterLink or Direct Cable Connection

DB25M	DB25M	Connection description
11	6	Busy (active when high)
12	4	Out of Paper (active when high)
13	3	Select (active when high)
15	2	Error (active when low)
25	25	Ground to Ground

Extended Capabilities Port cable

The *Extended Capabilities Port cable*, shown in Table 23-6, is also called an *ECP cable*. This cable can be used to link computers that both have ECP parallel ports (including IEEE-1284 ports in ECP Mode) installed and enabled. It provides much faster throughput than the standard cable—500 KB/s or more, depending on the ports.

Table 23-6. ECP cable for use with InterLink or Direct Cable Connection

DB25F	DB25F	Connection description
1	10	nStrobe to nAck
2 – 9	2 – 9	Data to Data (straight-through)
10	1	nAck to nStrobe
11	14	Busy to nAutoFwd
12	16	pError to nInit
13	13, 17	Select to Select and nSelect
14	11	nAutoFwd to Busy
15	17	nFault to nSelectIn
16	12	nInit to pError
17	15	nSelectIn to nFault
18 – 25	18 – 25	Ground to Ground (straight-through)

Universal Cable Module cable

The *Universal Cable Module cable*, also called a *UCM cable*, can be used to link two computers that have different types of parallel ports. It's not really just a cable because it includes active electronic components that automatically optimize throughput between PCs with differing port types. This cable can be very useful when both PCs do not have ECP-capable parallel ports and you want to get the highest performance available for the combination of hardware being used—for example, duplicating a standard PC configuration to multiple PCs when those PCs do not have network cards, or backing up a notebook computer to a desktop system.

The only source we've found for this cable is Parallel Technologies (*http://www.lpt.com*). Its Universal Fast Cable costs $70, and includes monitoring software. When used to connect two ECP or two EPP ports, this cable can provide throughput of about 500 KB/s, within striking range of a 10 Mb/s Ethernet link. Note, however, that there is no real reason to buy this cable if all your parallel ports are ECP-capable—you can simply use the ECP cable described above. The benefit of this cable is that it automatically detects the port types in use and optimizes throughput for them.

Our Picks

Parallel ports are ubiquitous on modern systems. Any new computer or motherboard you can buy today (other than a legacy-free system) includes an IEEE-1284-compliant parallel port.

Parallel port

PC Parallel/Serial adapter. Very few systems require anything other than the embedded port. However, if you need to add a parallel port—either to replace an older, less-capable port or because you need a second parallel port to run a second printer—buy one of the inexpensive (~$20) parallel/serial port cards commonly sold by computer stores and mass marketers. We've used many different ones, all of which seem to work fine and none of which is noticeably better than any of the others.

Cables

Belkin Gold Series IEEE-1284 cables. Nowadays, the only parallel cable you are likely to need is a standard, off-the-shelf printer cable. Belkin stocks a great variety of standard IEEE-1284 printer cables in lengths up to 50 feet and various combinations of Type A, B, and C connectors. Although Belkin makes a less-expensive line of cables, its best grade is worth the few extra dollars it costs. Once you have one, you'll probably never need to buy a printer cable again (*http://www.belkin.com*).

For updated recommendations, visit: *http://www.hardwareguys.com/picks/parallel. html*.

24

USB Communications

The first PCs shipped in 1981 used serial ports and parallel ports to connect external peripherals. Although the RS-232 serial and Centronics parallel technologies had improved gradually over the years, by the mid-'90s those technologies had reached their limits. In terms of connectivity to external devices, the PC of 1995 differed very little from the PC of 1981; the ports were a bit faster, perhaps, but they were fundamentally similar.

In the interim, the bandwidth needs of external peripherals had increased greatly. Character-mode dot-matrix and daisy-wheel printers had given way to graphic-mode page printers. Modems were pushing the throughput limitations of RS-232. Also, it was obvious that emerging categories of external peripherals—such as digital cameras, CD writers, tape drives, and other external storage devices—would require much more bandwidth than standard serial or parallel connections could provide. Neither was bandwidth the only limitation. Serial and parallel ports have the following drawbacks for connecting external peripherals:

Low bandwidth
Standard serial ports top out at 115 Kb/s, and parallel ports at 500 Kb/s to 2 Mb/s. Although these speeds are adequate for low-speed peripherals, they are unacceptably slow for hi-speed peripherals.

Point-to-point connections
Standard serial and parallel ports dedicate a port to each device. Because there is a practical limit to the number of serial ports and parallel ports that can be installed in a PC, the number and type of external devices that can be connected are limited.

Resource demands
Each serial or parallel port occupies scarce system resources, in particular an IRQ. A PC has only 16 IRQ lines, most of which are already occupied. It is often impossible to install the required number of serial or parallel ports because insufficient interrupts are available.

Ease-of-use issues

Connecting devices to serial or parallel ports may be complex and trouble-prone because cable pinouts and port configurations are not well-standardized. Serial ports in particular accept a wide variety of different cables, none of which is likely to be interchangeable with any other. Parallel ports use more standardized cable pinouts, but various parallel devices may require different port configurations. In particular, attempting to daisy-chain parallel devices via pass-through ports often introduces incompatibilities. Also, serial and parallel ports are always located on the rear of the computer, which makes connecting and disconnecting them inconvenient.

What PCs really needed was a fast bus-based scheme that allowed multiple devices to be daisy-chained together from a single port on the PC. SCSI had the potential to fulfill this need, but its high cost and complexity made it a nonstarter for that purpose. *IEEE-1394*, also called *FireWire*, might have been suitable, but FireWire is a proprietary Apple technology with, at the time, high licensing costs that motherboard and peripheral makers refused to pay. The PC industry had long been aware of the need for better external peripheral connectivity, but it was not until 1996 that vendors finally began to address it. Their solution is called *Universal Serial Bus (USB)*.

USB is aptly named. It is *universal* because every modern PC or motherboard includes USB and because USB allows you to connect almost any type of peripheral, including modems, printers, speakers, keyboards, scanners, mice, joysticks, external drives, and digital cameras. It is *serial* in that it uses serial communication protocols on a single data pair. It is a logical *bus* (although the physical topology is a tiered star) that allows up to 127 devices to be daisy-chained on a single pair of conductors.

One convenient way to think about USB is as an outside-the-box Plug-and-Play bus. All connected USB devices are managed by the *USB Host Controller Interface (HCI)* in the PC, and all devices share the IRQ assigned to that HCI. Devices can (in theory, at least) be plugged or unplugged without rebooting the computer.

Although nearly all PCs and motherboards made since 1997 have USB ports, for a long time those ports were nearly useless, for three reasons:

- USB requires native operating system support to provide full functionality. Until Windows 98 and Windows 2000 began to proliferate, that support was lacking. Windows NT 4 and early Windows 95 releases have no USB support, although a few peripheral makers provided custom drivers to allow their devices to work under these operating systems. Windows 95 OSR 2.1 introduced limited support for a few USB devices, but using USB under Windows 95 is an exercise in frustration. Windows 98/98SE/Me/2000/XP support USB 1.1. Windows XP supports USB 2.0 natively if SP1 or later is applied, although you may need to download the latest release of the USB 2.0 driver from the Windows Update site. Even with the latest service pack installed, Windows 2000 does not support USB 2.0 directly, although you can download native Windows 2000 USB 2.0 drivers from the Windows Update site. For more information about USB 2.0 support under Windows 2000 and Windows XP, see Knowledge Base articles 319973 and 312370, respectively.

The Linux kernel has included USB support since 2.2.18. The Linux 2.4.20 or later kernel supports USB 2.0 directly.

 Only Windows 2000 and XP officially support USB 2.0, but many PCI USB 2.0 interface cards are available that include Windows 9X USB 2.0 drivers supplied by the hardware vendor. The only PCI USB 2.0 interface card we have used is the Adaptec USB2connect, which operates properly with the supplied drivers. But our readers report that many other brands of PCI USB 2.0 adapter cards provide fast, reliable USB 2.0 support under Windows 9X.

- USB peripherals were hard to find prior to 1999, and were often more expensive than versions that used legacy interfaces. By 2000, that situation had reversed itself, with USB peripherals readily available and often cheaper than peripherals with legacy interfaces. As of July 2003, nearly all mainstream external peripherals use the USB interface, and old-style serial and parallel peripherals are becoming hard to find.

- Early USB ports and peripherals often exhibited incompatibilities and other strange behavior. Removing a connected peripheral might crash your system, or a newly connected device might require a reboot to be recognized. Some peripherals demanded that their drivers be reinstalled every time they were disconnected and then reconnected. Some peripherals drew so much power that other devices on that USB port would cease operating or the system would refuse to boot until the offending device was disconnected. And so on. In fact, these conflicts and incompatibilities remain a problem with more recent USB interfaces and devices, although the problems are less severe. As of July 2003, it appears that the teething pains USB experienced during its early days have largely been overcome, although even some very recent motherboards and chipsets continue to cause problems.

Despite these problems, by mid-2000 USB had achieved critical mass. With Windows 98/SE/Me and Windows 2000 available and USB peripherals shipping in volume, USB transitioned from a developing standard with great potential into a real-world solution, albeit a flawed one. USB has now largely replaced the legacy connectors that clutter the back of recent PCs.

Legacy-reduced motherboards that began shipping in 2000 replaced or supplemented serial and parallel ports with additional USB ports—usually four rather than the previously standard two. *Legacy-free* motherboards provide nothing *but* USB ports for connecting external peripherals (other than perhaps video), and are usually equipped with six USB ports—four at the rear and two on the front panel. A few legacy-free motherboards also include IEEE-1394 (FireWire) ports. Most external peripherals now have *only* a USB interface, as serial and parallel peripherals now teeter on the edge between obsolescent and obsolete.

Despite its slow start and the nagging problems that still sometimes plague it, USB has moved from being the wave of the future to being the current standard. This chapter tells you what you need to know about USB.

USB Characteristics

All USB devices share several general characteristics. Among these are:

Hot swapping
> In theory, at least, USB peripherals can be connected to and disconnected from the bus at any time, without shutting down the computer or taking any action to inform applications or the OS that a device is being added or removed. In practice, this is not always the case, particularly with older interfaces and devices.

> USB mass-storage devices are an exception worth noting. Disconnecting the USB cable before the drive finishes writing may corrupt data. If you use a USB hard drive, tape drive, or CD/DVD writer, read and follow the directions carefully to avoid losing data.

Automatic configuration
> The USB host controller chipset installed on the PC motherboard or an add-on USB port card manages driver software and allocates bandwidth to each USB device attached to the bus. When a device is added or removed, the USB host controller automatically loads or unloads the driver for that device.

> Educate your USB drivers. When you connect a USB peripheral to a root hub port or external hub, the USB driver "learns" that device/port combination. If you connect and disconnect USB devices frequently, you can make things faster and easier by allowing the PC to learn all combinations of device and port. Rather than simply connecting a device to a port and leaving it connected, plug that device in turn into each available USB port. That way, you can connect any device to any port and have it recognized immediately.

Interrupt sharing
> A USB host controller occupies one interrupt, which is shared among all devices attached to the bus. This small resource footprint allows multiple USB host controllers to be installed in a system without undue demands on scarce IRQs. Although each USB host controller can in theory support as many as 127 devices, it's often better to distribute multiple USB devices among host controllers to avoid conflicts.

Bandwidth sharing and allocation
> A USB 1.1 bus provides 12 Mb/s of bandwidth and a USB 2.0 bus provides 480 Mb/s of bandwidth, which is shared among all devices attached to the bus. Many devices may communicate simultaneously on a USB, provided that adequate bandwidth is available to service all of them at the same time. Properly designed USB peripherals and drivers use bandwidth dynamically, releasing bandwidth they are not using so that it can be used by other devices. For isochronous (time-critical) tasks such as audio or video streams, USB permits dedicating bandwidth as needed to a particular peripheral, although that dedicated bandwidth then becomes permanently unavailable for use by other peripherals.

Embedded power connections

In addition to providing a data connection, USB provides electrical power to peripherals, allowing you to eliminate the tangle of power cables required by traditional peripherals. That power, however, is limited to 500 milliamps (mA), which must be shared by all unpowered devices connected to the USB port. In practice, that means that only low-power peripherals, such as keyboards and mice, can be powered directly by a USB connection. High-power peripherals, such as printers and scanners, usually (but not always) have their own power bricks and are powered directly from a standard AC receptacle. For example, the Canon Canoscan 1220U relies on the USB port for power. Despite the minimal amount of current available on the USB port, it is possible to connect multiple unpowered USB peripherals by connecting them to powered USB hubs, each port of which has its own 500 milliamp supply.

Multiple USB devices connected to an unpowered hub can collectively exceed the maximum power that hub can deliver, particularly if you have connected one or more high-draw hub-powered devices. Many unpowered hubs, particularly those embedded in keyboards and similar devices, do not supply the full 500 mA called for by the USB specification. For example, the USB hub embedded in Microsoft USB keyboards can supply at most 200 to 250 mA. Connecting too many devices or devices that draw too much current is one frequent cause of USB problems.

The following sections detail other important characteristics of USB interfaces and devices.

USB Versions

Three versions of USB exist:

USB 1.0

USB 1.0 was the original specification. Most systems produced from 1996 through mid-1998 have USB 1.0 ports. USB 1.0 supports data rates of 1.5 Mb/s and 12 Mb/s. Relatively few USB 1.0 peripherals were produced because by the time USB peripherals began shipping in volume, USB 1.0 had been superseded by USB 1.1. USB 1.0-compliant peripherals generally operate properly when connected to a USB 1.1 or USB 2.0 interface, but USB 1.1 or USB 2.0 peripherals may not function properly when connected to a USB 1.0 interface. USB 1.0 interfaces are primitive and buggy, so if your motherboard has USB 1.0 ports, we recommend you disable those ports in BIOS Setup and install an add-on PCI USB port card. The first release of Windows 98 included USB 1.0 support.

USB 1.1

USB 1.1 was formalized in September 1998, although many manufacturers produced USB 1.1-compliant motherboards and peripherals based on the proposed standard long before the formal standard was adopted. USB 1.1 also supports data rates of 1.5 Mb/s and 12 Mb/s, and was largely a clarification of ambiguities in the USB 1.0 specification. A few functional definitions were changed in USB 1.1, including minor changes to hub specifications, removing provision for battery-powered hubs, adding interrupt-out mode, and changes to recommended enumeration to eliminate the requirement for an 8-byte endpoint zero. Most changes, however, merely tightened up the existing requirements because experience had shown that there were enough ambiguities in the USB 1.0 specification to allow producing interfaces and devices that complied with the standard but were not interoperable. USB 1.1 interfaces and devices began shipping in mid-1998 and are still in production. Early USB 1.1 interfaces and devices suffered many incompatibilities, but current production models have relatively fewer such issues. You can download the Universal Serial Bus Revision 1.1 Specification from *http:// www.usb.org/developers/docs/usbspec.zip*.

USB 2.0

USB 2.0 was formalized in April 2000, with various errata and Engineering Change Notices later incorporated as supplements. USB 2.0 supports data rates of 1.5 Mb/s, 12 Mb/s, and 480 Mb/s, and provides full backward compatibility with USB 1.0 and USB 1.1 devices.

The uptake of USB 2.0 was slower than expected because USB 2.0 chipsets were slower in arriving than expected and because Microsoft initially did not provide USB 2.0 Windows drivers. Microsoft shipped native USB 2.0 drivers for Windows XP in early 2002 and for Windows 2000 in late 2002. Microsoft has no plans to provide Windows 9X USB 2.0 drivers. Using USB 2.0 under Windows 9X requires drivers supplied by the manufacturer of the motherboard (or PCI/USB card) and USB 2.0 peripherals.

With so many of the major players in the computer industry backing it, USB 2.0 saw a fast ramp-up during late 2002 and into 2003. Most motherboards introduced during fall 2002 and later have chipset-level USB 2.0 support, and by early 2003 USB 2.0 peripherals such as external hard drives and optical drives were readily available. Older systems can be upgraded to support USB 2.0 by adding an inexpensive adapter.

In addition to its much higher speed, the attraction of USB 2.0 is its standardization. Earlier USB versions had frequent compatibility problems, not the least because two different and slightly incompatible controller standards existed. USB 2.0 defines one controller interface, called the *Enhanced Host Controller Interface (EHCI)*, which eliminates many compatibility issues. You can download the most recent complete Universal Serial Bus Revision 2.0 Specification from *http://www.usb.org/developers/docs/usb_20.zip*.

USB Speeds

USB defines the following three speeds, all of which can coexist on one bus:

Low Speed

Low Speed USB peripherals operate at a data rate of 1.5 Mb/s, and are supported by USB 1.1 and USB 2.0 interfaces. Low Speed USB is intended for such low-bandwidth devices as mice and keyboards, and is designed to be inexpensive to implement. Low Speed USB devices use a captive cable that can be no longer than 3 meters. Actual throughput on Low Speed USB is typically limited by overhead and other factors to about 1.2 Mb/s, or 150 KB/s.

Full Speed

Full Speed USB peripherals operate at a data rate of 12.0 Mb/s, and are supported by USB 1.1 and USB 2.0 interfaces. Full Speed is the fastest speed supported by USB 1.0 and USB 1.1, and is intended for such moderate-bandwidth devices as printers and scanners. Full Speed USB devices use active components, which are more expensive to implement than the passive components used by Low Speed USB. Full Speed USB devices use a detachable cable that can be no longer than 5 meters. Full Speed USB seldom exceeds actual throughput of 900 KB/s or so.

Hi-Speed

Hi-Speed USB peripherals operate at a data rate of 480 Mb/s, and are supported only by USB 2.0 interfaces. Hi-Speed USB is intended for such high-bandwidth devices as external drives. Hi-Speed USB devices use active components that are more expensive than Full Speed USB components. Also, Hi-Speed USB hubs require additional circuitry to arbitrate between mixed Hi-Speed and Full Speed devices connected to that hub. Accordingly, Hi-Speed USB devices, particularly hubs, were initially more expensive than USB 1.1 devices, although that differential had largely disappeared by early 2003. Hi-Speed USB devices use the same detachable cable used by Full Speed USB devices, which can be no longer than 5 meters. Hi-Speed USB typically achieves actual maximum throughput of 35 to 40 MB/s, which is fast enough to keep up with all but the fastest hard drives.

In late June 2003, computer trade publications reported a brouhaha concerning the relabeling of USB components. Apparently, some component makers decided that labeling Low Speed and Full Speed USB components as USB 1.1 put them at a competitive disadvantage relative to USB 2.0 devices. With USB 2.0 the current standard, purchasers were avoiding USB 1.1 components in droves, even though such devices of course run properly with either a USB 1.1 or USB 2.0 interface. Accordingly, the manufacturers convinced the USB Forum to change labeling. Devices formerly known as "USB 1.1" (1.5 and 12 Mb/s) are now to be labeled simply "UBS". Hi-Speed USB 2.0 devices are now to be labeled simply "Hi-Speed USB" (without the 2.0 designation). The only change is semantic. The technology remains the same. We use the original terminology in this chapter for charity.

Also note that even official standards documents published by the USB Forum have inconsistent spelling and usages. Low Speed USB is referred to variously as Low Speed, low speed, Lo Speed, lo-speed, and other variants. Hi-Speed (the currently preferred form) may be referred to as High Speed, high speed, high-speed, hi-speed, and so on. As is the case with many standards documents, the authors appear to have gone to great lengths to get the important stuff right, but not paid much attention to consistent spellings and usages.

Note that USB bandwidth is shared among all devices connected to the bus, and that the system reserves some bandwidth (typically 10%) for control signals and other administrative purposes. Although many Hi-Speed USB devices require much less than 480 Mb/s, if you do connect more than one high-bandwidth Hi-Speed device to a single USB channel, you may throttle the bandwidth available to each when more than one are operating. In that situation, if your system has more than one USB 2.0 HCI, we recommend splitting your high-bandwidth devices among different host controllers.

USB Topology

USB uses a tiered-star topology, shown in Figure 24-1. At the center of the star is the *USB host*, which defines the USB, and only one of which is permitted per USB. (Note, however, that more than one USB host may be installed in a PC, and in fact most recent motherboards have multiple USB hosts installed.) The USB host resides inside the PC, and is implemented as a combination of hardware, firmware, and software. The USB host has one or more USB root hubs, which provide attachment points called *USB ports* to which *USB hubs* and *USB functions* may be connected. (Loosely speaking, a USB function is a peripheral such as a scanner, printer, mouse, digital camera, etc.)

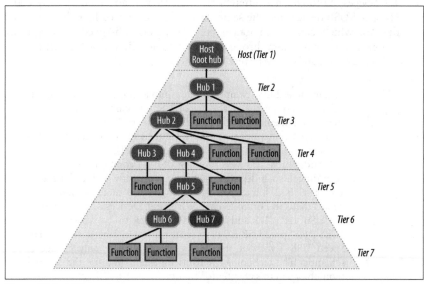

Figure 24-1. USB topology.

USB hubs use two types of connections. An *upstream connection* links the USB hub to another USB hub in the next-higher tier. A *downstream connection* links the USB hub to another USB hub or to a USB function located in the next-lower tier. Each USB hub has one upstream port, and may have as many as seven downstream ports. Via daisy-chaining, USB allows connecting a maximum of 127 devices (USB hubs and USB functions) in a maximum of seven tiers. The limitation on the number of tiers is required to ensure that the most distant USB device can communicate within the maximum allowable propagation delay defined in the USB specification.

In practical terms, you seldom need more than two or three USB tiers to connect a typical assortment of USB peripherals to a PC. However, it's worth noting that the USB limit of 5 meters on cable length applies between tiers. For example, if you need to locate a USB peripheral some distance away from a PC, you can extend the separation to as far as 30 meters by putting the USB peripheral in Tier 7 and installing USB hubs in Tiers 2 through 6. Note that Tier 7 can contain only USB functions. A USB hub that resides in Tier 7 is useless because any device connected to that hub resides in the nonexistent Tier 8.

If you mix USB 1.1 and USB 2.0 devices on a bus, it's important to understand the following points:

- USB 2.0 hubs support USB 1.0/1.1 and USB 2.0 devices, including downstream USB 1.0/1.1 hubs and USB 2.0 hubs, providing full bandwidth to each device according to its version.

- USB 1.0/1.1 hubs support USB 1.0/1.1 and USB 2.0 devices, but USB 2.0 devices connected to a USB 1.1 hub function as USB 1.1 Full Speed devices (i.e., at 12 Mb/s maximum), which means that it is pointless to connect a USB 2.0 hub downstream from a USB 1.1 hub.

- Although USB 2.0 hubs provide transparent support for Low Speed and Full Speed USB devices, that support incurs significant overhead on the USB 2.0 hub and is intended only for limited use, such as connecting a USB mouse and keyboard. Connecting multiple Low Speed or Full Speed USB devices to a USB 2.0 hub, either directly or downstream, degrades the ability of the USB 2.0 hub to support Hi-Speed USB 2.0 devices. If you have many Low Speed or Full Speed USB devices, connect them to a USB 1.1 root hub port and reserve your USB 2.0 ports for Hi-Speed devices.

USB Cables and Connectors

USB connectors and cables are simple and rigidly standardized. USB defines three plug/jack combinations, designated *Series A*, *Series B*, and *Series mini-B*.

Series mini-B connectors are smaller versions of the standard Series B connector, designed for devices such as digital cameras, for which a standard Series B connector is physically too large. Most devices that use Series mini-B connectors come with a Series-A to-Series-mini-B cable.

The narrow Series A jacks, shown in Figure 24-2, appear on the back of a PC or USB hub, and may be labeled "down" jacks. These provide connection points for USB peripherals, including USB hubs. Some USB peripherals have permanently connected cables that terminate in a Series A plug. Series A plugs always face upstream, toward the host system, and Series A jacks always face downstream, toward the device.

Figure 24-2. USB Series A connector

Peripherals that do not have a permanent cable instead have a Series B jack, shown in Figure 24-3. Series B plugs always face downstream, and Series B jacks always face upstream. Use a standard USB A-B device cable to connect these peripherals to the PC or hub.

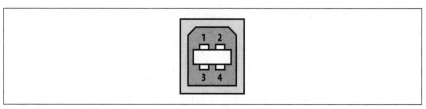

Figure 24-3. USB Series B connector

A USB cable uses four wires, two each for data and power. The data wires are a green/white twisted pair that carry +Data and –Data, respectively. USB uses differential digital signaling, which means that the same signal is present on each data wire, but with different polarity. This allows electrical noise to be eliminated from the circuit because induced voltages affect the + and – signals equally, netting to zero. The power wires may or may not be twisted. The red wire carries nominal +5V DC, and the black is a ground return for the power circuit. The USB specification permits cables as long as 5 meters (~16 feet), a limitation enforced by the allowable propagation delay between a port and a connected device.

The USB specification defines only three types of USB cable:

Low-speed captive cable
  Keyboards and similar low-speed devices use a *USB low-speed captive cable*. The maximum allowable length for a low-speed USB cable is 3 meters (9 feet, 10 inches). This limit is determined by the rise and fall times of low-speed USB signaling, which restricts low-speed USB cables to a maximum length only 60% that of standard full-speed/hi-speed cables. A USB standards-compliant low-speed cable must be *captive* or *hardwired,* which is to say that the cable either must be permanently connected to the device or must use a nonstandard or proprietary connector on the end that connects to the device. The concern is that if a low-speed USB device used a standard USB device connector, a standard detachable USB cable longer than acceptable for low-speed USB devices could be used to connect that device.

Standard detachable cable
  Most full-speed and hi-speed USB devices use a *USB standard detachable cable*. This cable is terminated on one end with a Series A plug and on the other with a Series B plug or Series mini-B plug. The maximum allowable length for a standard detachable cable is 5 meters (16 feet, 5 inches).

High-/full-speed captive cable

Some full-speed and hi-speed USB devices use a *USB hi-/full-speed captive cable*. This cable is terminated on one end with a Series A plug. The other end terminates either as a hard-wired connection to the device or with a vendor-proprietary connector. The maximum allowable length for a hi-/full-speed captive cable is also 5 meters.

Although the USB standard states that only these three cable assemblies are acceptable, it further emphasizes it by specifically prohibiting the following cable assemblies, all of which have been manufactured and sold despite their non-compliance:

Cable assembly that violates USB topology rules

Some vendors produce cables that terminate with two Series A plugs, two Series B receptacles, or two Series mini-B receptacles, which allow connecting USB ports and devices in prohibited combinations.

 Cables with two Series A plugs are particularly dangerous, because they can be used to link two powered ports with differing ground potentials, which may cause a fire. In theory, such a cable could be used to link two PCs directly via USB. In practice, this does not work and is dangerous. The only acceptable way to link two PCs via USB is to use a USB bridge. Note that some cables have USB bridge circuitry built into them, and so are in reality more than a simple cable. This prohibition does not apply to such USB bridge devices.

Extension cable assembly

A cable that terminates with a Series A plug and a Series A receptacle, a Series B plug and a Series B receptacle, or a Series mini-B plug and a Series mini-B receptacle is specifically prohibited by the USB specification. However, many vendors sell such cables, including some vendors who should know better. The purpose of these cables is to extend the distance between port and device by joining multiple cable segments. The risk is that the joined cables will exceed the maximum 5 meters permissible under the standard, which can cause problems, from sporadic operation to complete failure of the entire USB. Even if the joined cables total less than 5 meters, the electrical characteristics of the extended cable may fall outside specifications. Avoid using extension cables under any circumstances.

Standard detachable cable assembly for low-speed USB devices

The USB specification does not permit low-speed devices to use standard detachable cables. Standard detachable cables are used only to connect hi-speed/full-speed devices. Their capacitive load exceeds the maximum allowable for a low-speed device.

There is much confusion about which USB cables can be used at which speeds. Some vendors have confused the issue by producing so-called USB 2.0 cables. In fact, any detachable USB 1.1 cable is also a USB 2.0 cable, and can be used at 480 Mb/s. Note, however, that many of the cables supplied with USB 1.1 devices are technically not USB 1.1 cables because they don't meet USB requirements. These out-of-spec cables may work reliably with USB 1.1 devices, but are simply not good enough for the higher data rate of Hi-Speed USB 2.0 connections. By some estimates, 30% or more of the cables supplied with USB 1.1 devices do not meet USB specifications.

USB Data Transfer Modes

USB uses a set of unidirectional and bidirectional pipes to transfer user data and control information between the host and USB devices. Each device may support multiple pipes for different purposes, and data transferred in one pipe is independent from data transferred in other pipes. For example, a USB printer might have one pipe that it uses to receive page data from the host, and a second pipe that it uses to transfer status information to the host. USB defines the following data flow types:

Isochronous Data Transfers
> *Isochronous Data Transfers* are used for periodic, continuous communication between the host and a device, typically time-critical data such as audio or video streams. Isochronous Data Transfers are enabled by reserving the required amount of bandwidth for the isochronous device, which the USB host controller makes unavailable to other devices whether the isochronous device happens to be using that bandwidth at any given time. Isochronous Data Transfers have the highest priority for bandwidth. If all available bandwidth is reserved for Isochronous Data Transfers, no other device can use the USB.

Interrupt Data Transfers
> *Interrupt Data Transfers* are used for small, limited-latency transfers when timely, reliable delivery of data is required—for example, to receive coordinate changes from a mouse or status changes from a modem. Interrupt Data Transfers have lower priority for available bandwidth than do Isochronous Data Transfers.

Control Transfers
> *Control Transfers* are used to configure a device when it is connected to the USB, and may be used for other device-specific control, configuration, and status commands, including controlling other pipes on the device. Control Transfers usually comprise small amounts of data that are not time-critical, and have lower priority for available bandwidth than do Interrupt Data Transfers.

Bulk Data Transfers
> *Bulk Data Transfers* are used to communicate large amounts of nonperiodic, bursty data with relaxed timing constraints to a device—e.g., sending page data to a USB printer. Bulk Data Transfers are not time-critical, and have the lowest priority for available bandwidth. Some early HCIs implemented bulk

mode poorly, and so work properly with USB devices such as keyboards and mice but are unsuitable for use with devices such as scanners and printers.

USB Host Controller Interfaces

The intent of USB was to provide a standardized Plug-and-Play interface that would permit USB-compliant devices from any manufacturer to coexist peacefully with those from any other maker. The ball got rolling in September 1995, when 25 major PC companies announced the formation of a consortium to develop a nonproprietary, open Host Controller Interface (HCI) standard. This was necessary because the HCI was not defined in the USB specification itself. Although it would have been possible for each motherboard or chipset manufacturer to develop a proprietary USB HCI, that would have introduced serious compatibility issues between the multiple HCIs and USB peripherals. So, for the good of the industry and in the interests of interoperability, nearly all of the major players in the PC industry signed on to this initiative.

The HCI is the heart of USB, just as the chipset is the heart of a motherboard. In fact, the USB HCI is often referred to as the USB chipset. Just as the system chipset defines the functionality and capabilities of the motherboard, coordinates the working of other motherboard components, and arbitrates conflicting demands, a USB HCI chipset defines the USB and performs analogous services for connected USB peripherals.

The HCI may reside in any or all of the following three places:

Embedded in the motherboard chipset
All modern chipsets contain at least a USB 1.1 HCI embedded in the Southbridge. Most chipsets introduced after mid-2002 include a USB 2.0 HCI. The quality and compatibility of the embedded HCI depend on the maker of the chipset and its age, but even the best and most recent embedded USB 1.1 HCIs may have issues with some peripherals, particularly older models. If you use USB heavily, and especially if you use many peripherals, it's often a good idea to disable the embedded HCI in BIOS and substitute an add-on PCI USB controller of more recent vintage.

As a separate chip on the motherboard
A few motherboards implement the HCI as a discrete chip, separate from the main chipset Southbridge. This method is common in USB 2.0 transition motherboards. For example, early versions of Intel 845-family chipsets supported only USB 1.1. Some transition Intel motherboards, such as the D845BGSE, used a separate NEC mPD720100 USB 2.0 host controller as a stopgap to add USB 2.0 functionality until Intel chipsets with integrated USB 2.0 functionality became available. As with embedded USB HCIs, a discrete HCI can be disabled from BIOS Setup, should that become necessary.

On an add-on peripheral card
Add-on PCI USB adapters are available from numerous makers in both USB 1.1 and USB 2.0 variants. USB 2.0 adapters cost little more than USB 1.1 adapters, so we recommend only USB 2.0 models. All USB 2.0 adapters we are familiar with use the NEC mPD720100 host controller, which fortunately seems to be a good one.

If you buy a USB 2.0 adapter, make sure your operating system supports it *as a USB 2.0 device*. Otherwise, the operating system will recognize and use the USB 2.0 adapter as a USB 1.1 adapter. Microsoft supports USB 2.0 only with Windows XP and Windows 2000. USB 2.0 support under Windows 9X requires drivers supplied by the adapter maker. USB 2.0 support under Linux requires kernel 2.4.20 or higher.

It is becoming increasingly common for motherboards to include more than one HCI. Because each HCI defines a USB, motherboards with multiple HCIs actually have two or more USBs defined, each of which has its own root hub ports and operates independently from the others. The benefits to having multiple USBs are that you can segregate devices that conflict with each other by connecting them to separate USBs, that you can dedicate separate USBs to USB 1.1 versus USB 2.0 devices, and that multiple HCIs allow the system to have several USB ports available at both the front and rear of the case.

USB HCI Types

There are three types of USB host controller:

Open Host Controller Interface (OHCI)
    The *Open Host Controller Interface (OHCI)* is a USB 1.X interface that was developed by a consortium of PC makers led by Compaq, Microsoft, and National Semiconductor. OHCI places more of the burden for managing USB functions on hardware, and less on software. OHCI is most common in systems that use non-Intel chipsets, including those from ALi, SiS, and VIA. Windows 98/SE/Me and Windows 2000/XP include native OHCI drivers. You can download the full Open Host Controller Interface Specification from *http://h18000.www1.hp.com/productinfo/development/openhci.html.*

If you run Windows 98SE on a system with an OCHI, visit the Microsoft web site and read Knowledge Base article 253697. This combination of OS and HCI can cause some very odd behavior, such as unplugging a bulk-mode device from one root hub port causing a hub connected to a different root hub port to disconnect. One possible symptom, believe it or not, is your computer making a high-pitched whining noise, like a phaser about to self-destruct.

Universal Host Controller Interface (UHCI)
    The *Universal Host Controller Interface (UHCI)* is a USB 1.X interface that was developed by Intel. UHCI places more of the burden for managing USB functions on software, and less on hardware. UHCI is most common in systems with Intel chipsets, although many non-Intel chipsets also use UHCI. USB devices designed to use UHCI (e.g., the Intel USB camera) may not work properly with OHCI. Windows 98/SE/Me and Windows 2000/XP include native UHCI drivers. You can download the full Universal Host Controller Interface Design Guide from *http://developer.intel.com/design/USB/UHCI11D.htm.*

Enhanced Host Controller Interface (EHCI)

The *Enhanced Host Controller Interface (EHCI)* is the single USB 2.0 interface, used by all USB 2.0 devices. The simple fact that a single integrated HCI specification exists for USB 2.0 eliminates many of the problems that occurred with USB 1.1 because of competing HCI standards. Of Microsoft operating systems, only Windows XP and Windows 2000 have native EHCI drivers available. Microsoft has no plans to release EHCI drivers for any variant of Windows 9X. You can download the full Enhanced Host Controller Interface Specification from *http://www.intel.com/technology/usb/ehcispec.htm.*

USB HCI Issues

In addition to the standard they support—OHCI, UHCI, or EHCI—USB host controllers vary in how well they are implemented. Early host controllers from all manufacturers, including Intel, have numerous bugs and incompatibilities, which may manifest in various ways, from minor performance glitches to a complete failure of the USB to recognize devices.

It is important to be aware of the particular host controller your system uses. That information can save you trouble when you are attempting to connect various devices to your system, and may even help you avoid buying a new USB device that has known incompatibilities with your existing configuration. In general, HCI issues are independent of operating system. That is, an HCI that has problems under Windows 9X is likely to have the same or similar problems under Windows 2000/XP and Linux.

Here are details about some of the USB host controllers you are likely to encounter:

ALi chipsets

Although we do not have extensive experience with ALi chipsets, there have been enough reported problems that we consider USB support to be suspect. When configuring an ALi-based system to use USB, we recommend updating the main system BIOS to the most recent available, installing the latest chipset drivers, disabling ACPI and power management in BIOS, and setting the BIOS PnP OS? option to No. In Windows, replace the ALi USB Host Controller with the Windows Standard OpenHCI USB Host Controller, and disable USB error detection (for Win98 SE or later only). If your motherboard has an old ALi chipset and you encounter USB problems, often the most practical solution is to install a PCI/USB card.

AMD chipsets

The AMD-750 "Irongate" chipset has reasonably robust USB support for an older chipset. Microsoft Knowledge Base article Q241134 describes one known problem that occurs under Windows 98 and 98SE with low-speed devices such as mice and keyboards, and provides a patch for that problem. The AMD-760 and AMD-760MP provide generally reliable USB support, although we recommend running motherboards based on those chipsets with ACPI disabled. Although the first stepping of the AMD-760MPX chipset had a widely reported USB bug, we expect later steppings of that chipset to resolve the problem.

Intel PIIX3 (82371SB)

The *PIIX3*, used in the Intel 430HX Pentium chipset, is USB 1.0-compliant and does not function properly with many USB 1.1 devices. The PIIX3 supports one USB 1.0 UHCI and two root hub ports. This chipset (and the motherboards that use it) is so ancient that you should not even consider attempting to connect modern USB devices to it. If upgrading the motherboard is not an option, install an add-on USB card such as those sold by Adaptec. If for some reason you must use the 82371SB, you may be able to resolve some problems by substituting the 82317AB or 82371AB/EB driver.

> Technically, any USB 1.1-compliant peripheral should be compatible with any USB 1.0-compliant controller. The updates from the USB 1.0 Specification to USB 1.1 tightened up ambiguities on the peripheral side to eliminate conflicts, but made only minor changes to the host-side specification. Conflicts between USB 1.0 controllers and USB 1.1 peripherals are due less to the difference in USB specification level than to bugs in USB 1.0 controllers.

Intel PIIX4 (82371AB)

The *PIIX4*, used in the Intel 430TX chipset, is USB 1.1-compliant, despite the fact that its datasheet claims only USB 1.0 compliance. The PIIX4 supports one USB 1.1 UHCI and two root hub ports. Although this chipset should in theory support modern USB 1.1 devices, it is quite buggy and we therefore recommend not attempting to use it. Again, replace the motherboard or install a modern add-on USB adapter. If for some reason you must use the 82371AB, you may be able to resolve some problems by substituting the updated 82371AB/EB driver.

> For the Intel PIIX4 and later Intel chipsets, we suggest as a first step that you visit *http://developer.intel.com/design/software/drivers/platform/inf.htm* and download the most recent Intel Chipset Software Installation Utility. Heed all cautions listed.

Intel PIIX4E (82371EB)

The *PIIX4E* is used in the Intel 440BX, 400EX, 440LX, 440ZX, 440ZX66, 440GX, and 450NX chipsets, and is the oldest USB host controller that you should consider using in a production system. The PIIX4E supports one USB 1.1 UHCI and two root hub ports, and has many fewer compatibility problems than do earlier Intel USB controllers. The most common problem with the PIIX4E is a device not being recognized when you connect it. The PIIX4E also may become confused and lose connectivity if the screensaver kicks in or if the system enters standby, suspend, or hibernate mode. If that occurs, hot-plugging the device (disconnecting and then reconnecting the USB cable while the PC and device remain on) may resolve the problem. In our experience, the 82371EB seems reasonably well behaved with low-speed USB devices such as mice and keyboards, particularly under Windows 2000. It is more likely to have problems with hi-speed and bulk-mode USB devices, particularly scanners, printers, and digital cameras, and particularly under Windows 9X.

Intel I/O Controller Hub (ICH) (82801AA) and I/O Controller Hub (ICH0)
(82801AB)
The *82801AA I/O Controller Hub (ICH)* and *82801AB I/O Controller Hub*
(ICH0) are used in the Intel 810, 810E, 815, 815G, 815P, 820, and 840
chipsets. The 82801AA and 82801AB differ primarily in physical packaging,
although different drivers have been released for them. The 82801AA and
82801AB support one USB 1.1 UHCI and two root hub ports. Although the
82801AA and 82801AB have significantly fewer incompatibilities than earlier
Intel USB controllers, you may still experience intermittent connection problems. If you have problems with the 82801AA, try installing the 82801AB
driver, which is fully compatible with the 82801AA but has fewer issues.

Intel I/O Controller Hub 2 (ICH2) (82801BA/BAM)
The *82801BA/BAM I/O Controller Hub 2 (ICH2)* is used in the Intel 810E2,
815E, 815EG, 815EP, 820E, 845, 850, and 860 chipsets. The 82801BAM is
the mobile version of the 82801BA. The 82801BA/BAM supports two USB
1.1 UHCIs and four root hub ports. We have experienced no USB problems attributable to this chipset, and reported problems are relatively rare.
If you do experience problems, try substituting the 82801AB driver.

Intel I/O Controller Hub 3S (ICH3-S) (82801CA)
The *82801CA I/O Controller Hub 3-S (ICH3-S)* is used in the Intel E7500 and
E7501 chipsets. The 82801CA supports three USB 1.1 UHCIs, which provide
six USB 1.1 root hub ports. We have insufficient experience with this chipset
to judge its reliability with USB, although it is quite similar to the 82801BA/
BAM chipset. We would expect its features and compatibility to be similar to
that of the 82801BA/BAM.

Intel I/O Controller Hub 4 (ICH4) (82801DB)
The *82801DB I/O Controller Hub 4 (ICH4)* is used in the Intel 845E, 845G,
845GE, 845GL, 845GV, 845PE, E7205, and E7505 chipsets. The 82801DB
supports three USB 1.1 UHCIs, which provide six USB 1.1 root hub ports, as
well as one EHCI that provides six USB 2.0 root hub ports. We have experienced no USB problems attributable to this chipset.

Intel I/O Controller Hub 5/5R (ICH5/ICH5R) (82801EB/82801ER)
The *I/O Controller Hub 5 (ICH5)* and *I/O Controller Hub 5R (ICH5R)* are
used in the Intel 865- and 875-series chipsets. These two versions are functionally identical, except that the ICH5R version supports hardware Serial
ATA RAID. The ICH5/ICH5R supports one ECHI that supports eight USB
2.0 root hub ports. We have experienced no USB problems attributable to
this chipset.

nVIDIA nForce and nForce2 chipsets
Both of these chipsets are available in multiple versions, but USB features and
compatibility are similar for each of the chipsets. The first-generation *n*Force
chipset supports three USB 1.1 OHCIs, which provide up to six USB 1.1 root
hub ports. The second-generation *n*Force2 supports two USB 1.1 OHCIs,
which provide four USB 1.1 root hub ports, and one EHCI that provides up
to six USB 2.0 root hub ports. Our experience with *n*VIDIA chipsets is
limited, but we have never encountered a USB 1.1 or USB 2.0 problem attributable to the chipset.

If you are experiencing USB problems, the fix may be as simple as upgrading the main system BIOS, particularly if your USB controller is a recent model. Even if it is not, however, a BIOS upgrade may solve or minimize USB conflicts. For example, we have an elderly Intel SE440BX-2V motherboard with an 82371EB USB host controller.

Attempting to use an Epson inkjet printer and a UMAX scanner on that system was an exercise in frustration, with apparently random problems plaguing us. For no obvious reason, one or the other device would stop working. When both were working, powering off or disconnecting one device sometimes caused the other to fail to be recognized. Attempting to use the scanner while the printer was printing would sometimes lock up one or both devices. When we rebooted the system, sometimes only the printer would appear in the Device Manager; other times, only the scanner would appear. Sometimes there would be two copies of one or both devices in the Device Manager. And so on. In other words, a not-untypical USB 1.1 experience.

The camel-back-breaking straw happened one day when we connected a USB mouse. That worked fine, with one exception. Every time we moved the mouse, the printer ejected a sheet of paper. Arrghhh. Enough was enough. We finally installed a BIOS upgrade on the SE440BX-2V, and many of the problems became less severe. Then we stripped the hard drive down to bare metal and reinstalled the operating system. That pretty much cured the problem, although we still keep our fingers crossed.

SiS chipsets

In the past, we avoided SiS chipsets, as we have had numerous bad experiences with them, including what appeared to be irresolvable USB conflicts. We still avoid early SiS chipsets, but, as the old saying goes, even a blind pig finds an acorn occasionally. The SiS735 chipset for AMD processors is a solid chipset. It is inexpensive and fast, and appears to be robust in all respects, including USB support. We expect that the follow-on SiS745 chipset is just as good, although we haven't tested it. When configuring older SiS chipsets to use USB, we recommend updating the main system BIOS to the most recent available, installing the latest chipset drivers, disabling ACPI and power management in BIOS, and setting the BIOS PnP OS? option to No. In Windows, replace the SiS PCI to USB Open Host Controller with the Windows Standard OpenHCI USB Host Controller, and disable USB error detection (for Win98 SE or later only). If your motherboard has an old SiS chipset and you encounter USB problems, often the only real solution is to install a PCI/USB card.

VIA chipsets

We consider USB support in older VIA chipsets to be fundamentally flawed. Even recent VIA chipsets for both Intel and AMD processors have USB issues, although problems are most severe with VIA chipsets from 1999 and earlier. In our experience, system hangs, stop errors, and dropped connections are common with VIA chipsets, particularly if you use hi-speed bulk-mode USB peripherals. Unfortunately, the VIA web site is not forthcoming about USB issues, attributing problems primarily to operating system and power issues rather than to incompatibilities within the chipsets themselves. We recommend you avoid running USB on any VIA-based motherboard older than a year or two if at all possible, and also that you avoid VIA-based PCI/USB cards. If you run USB on any VIA chipset and experience USB problems, download and install the latest USB Filter Patch from *http://www.via.com.tw*. Better still, install a PCI/USB card and stop using the motherboard USB ports.

There is a severe USB bug in Windows 98SE (Windows 98, Me, and 2000/XP are not affected) running on systems with a VIA chipset and an AMD processor running faster than 350 MHz. See the Microsoft Knowledge Base article Q240075 for details and a patch file.

Windows 2000 and XP do not support VIA chipsets REV_04 or earlier. Windows 2000 explicitly does not support VIA chipsets with the VT83C572 or VT82C586 chips. Microsoft warns that these chipsets are irreparably flawed, that they cannot be fixed in software, and that using them may cause system instability or data loss.

Configuring USB

When you are installing new USB devices or troubleshooting existing USB devices, you may need to determine detailed configuration information about your USB interfaces, drivers, hubs, and ports, including the following:

USB HCI
It's frequently necessary to know which USB HCI your system uses. For example, the system requirements for a USB peripheral may state that it is incompatible with certain USB HCIs. Also, if you have occasion to trouble-shoot a USB problem, knowing which USB HCI your system uses may allow you to pinpoint the problem more quickly because various USB HCIs have known limitations and incompatibilities.

USB driver information
Although Windows generally installs a suitable USB driver, there are times when upgrading (or downgrading) the default driver is required to allow USB devices to function properly.

USB power information
A USB port provides 500 milliamps of current, which is shared by all devices connected to that port. Connecting several unpowered devices to a port can exceed the maximum allowable current, which may cause problems ranging from sporadic operation to complete failure of all connected devices. Windows allows you to view the total power consumption for each USB port as well as the power consumed by each device connected to that port.

The following sections detail the steps necessary to view and change USB configuration.

Identifying the USB HCI Under Windows 9X

To determine which USB HCI your system uses under Windows 9X, right-click My Computer, choose Properties, and click the Device Manager tab to display the Device Manager, shown in Figure 24-4. Double-click the Universal Serial Bus controllers item to expand it.

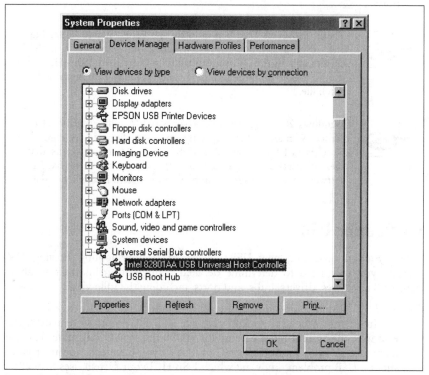

Figure 24-4. Windows 9X Device Manager showing this system uses an Intel 82801AA

Viewing USB HCI Properties Under Windows 9X

From the Device Manager, double-clicking the Host Controller Interface item displays the Properties dialog for the HCI, shown in Figure 24-5. This dialog includes detailed HCI information that may be useful in troubleshooting USB problems and resolving conflicts.

The HCI Properties dialog includes the following pages:

General page
   The General page displays summary information about the HCI type, manufacturer, and version. It also includes the Device status pane, which indicates when the HCI is working properly and may indicate the cause when the HCI

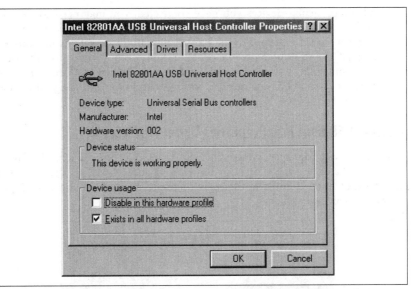

Figure 24-5. The Windows 9X HCI Properties dialog displaying detailed HCI information

is not working properly. You can also use the General page to disable the device in one or more hardware profiles.

Advanced page

The Advanced page includes the Disable USB error detection checkbox, which sounds like a dangerous thing to do. In fact, disabling USB error detection is sometimes necessary if USB is to run properly. If you are not experiencing USB conflicts or problems, leave USB error detection enabled. Otherwise, try disabling it. This page also includes the Bandwidth Usage button. Clicking that button displays the percentage of the available bandwidth consumed by each device connected to the port. This can be useful information when you troubleshoot USB problems because some USB devices, particularly early models, are "bandwidth hogs" that claim bandwidth regardless of whether they are using it and thereby prevent other devices connected to the same port from functioning correctly, if at all.

Driver page

The Driver page displays the HCI driver provider and version in use by the HCI. Click the Driver File Details button to display the paths and filenames of the USB driver files. Click the Update Driver button to invoke the Update Device Driver Wizard, which allows you to replace the current driver with a different version. Although the default driver generally works properly, depending on the HCI your system uses and the particular devices you have connected, you may need to replace the driver with a later (or earlier) version for full functionality.

Resources page

The Resources page displays the IRQ and I/O port being used by the HCI. By default, the Use automatic settings checkbox is marked, which is the proper setting for routine operation. But, depending on the HCI your system uses and the particular devices you have connected, you may need to clear that checkbox and assign settings manually. For example, Windows 9X typically assigns a shared interrupt to the HCI. Although this usually works properly, some HCIs and some hardware configurations do not work properly using a shared interrupt. If that occurs, use the Device Manager to locate an unused interrupt, clear the Use automatic settings checkbox, and assign the unused interrupt to the HCI.

Viewing USB Root Hub Properties Under Windows 9X

From the Device Manager, double-clicking the USB Root Hub item displays the Properties dialog for the root hub, shown in Figure 24-6. This dialog includes detailed root hub information that may be useful in troubleshooting USB problems and resolving conflicts.

Figure 24-6. The Windows 9X Root Hub Properties dialog displaying detailed root hub information

The USB Root Hub Properties dialog includes the following pages:

General page
> The General page displays summary information about the root hub type, manufacturer, and version. It also includes the Device status pane, which indicates when the root hub is working properly and may indicate the cause when the root hub is not working properly. You can also use the General page to disable the device in one or more hardware profiles.

Power page
> The Power page includes only the Power properties button. Clicking this button displays the Power dialog, shown in Figure 24-7. The Hub Information pane of this dialog lists the hub type and the maximum total power available per port. The Devices on this Hub pane lists the name and

description of each device connected to the hub and the power it requires. Connecting multiple unpowered USB devices to a hub is one of the most common causes of USB problems. If you experience USB problems, use this dialog to verify that the total power consumption of all connected devices does not exceed the maximum the port can deliver. Note that powered USB devices (those that connect to AC power directly) show very low power consumption, often only 0 mA to 5 mA. That is because this dialog shows only the power being drawn from the root hub, and not the power being supplied to the device by a wall outlet.

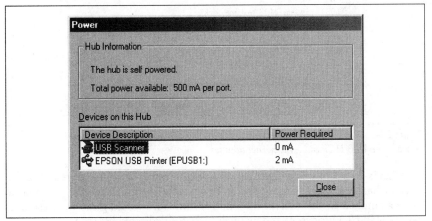

Figure 24-7. The Windows 9X Power dialog showing all devices connected to the hub and the amount of hub power required by each

Driver page

The Driver page displays the root hub driver provider and version in use by the root hub. Click the Driver File Details button to display the paths and filenames of the USB driver files. Click the Update Driver button to invoke the Update Device Driver Wizard, which allows you to replace the current driver with an updated version. Unlike the HCI driver, you will seldom have occasion to replace the root hub driver file.

Verifying USB Interrupt Sharing Under Windows 9X

Windows ordinarily assigns a shared interrupt to the USB HCI, which sometimes works properly. Often, however, USB works improperly unless the HCI has a dedicated interrupt. To verify USB interrupt sharing status under Windows 9X, from the main Device Manager dialog, click the Properties button to display the Computer Properties dialog shown in Figure 24-8.

In this instance, the Device Manager shows that USB HCI is sharing interrupt 09. You can safely disregard the ACPI IRQ Holder for PCI IRQ Steering entry; IRQ Steering entries are simply placeholders, and are unlikely to cause conflicts (at least on motherboards that have ACPI properly implemented, which essentially includes only recent motherboards that use recent Intel chipsets). Similarly, the SCI IRQ used by ACPI bus is a system-level entry, which is unlikely to cause a problem. The

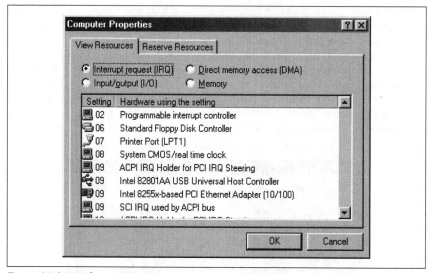

Figure 24-8. Windows 9X Device Manager showing this system shares an interrupt between the USB HCI and an Ethernet adapter

Intel 8255x-based PCI Ethernet Adapter (10/100) entry, however, represents a real piece of hardware that is using real interrupts and therefore has the potential to cause a conflict. In this case, it does not. If it did, we would go to the Resources page of USB HCI Properties and manually assign a dedicated IRQ to it.

Identifying the USB HCI Under Windows 2000/XP

To determine which USB HCI your system uses under Windows 2000 or Windows XP, right-click My Computer, choose Properties, display the Hardware page, and then click the Device Manager button to display the Device Manager. Double-click the Universal Serial Bus controllers item to expand it, as shown in Figure 24-9.

In this case, as is common on recent systems, the motherboard includes two distinct HCIs. These operate completely independently, and each HCI has a separate root hub associated with it. This doubles the number of root hub ports available, some of which may appear at the front of the case and some of which connect directly to the traditional location on the rear ATX I/O panel. Note that the secondary root hub ports often appear as a set of header pins on the motherboard, which may be extended to the front or the rear of the case, as necessary.

Viewing USB HCI Properties Under Windows 2000/XP

From the Device Manager, double-clicking the Host Controller Interface item displays the Properties dialog for the HCI, shown in Figure 24-10. This dialog includes detailed HCI information that may be useful in troubleshooting USB problems and resolving conflicts.

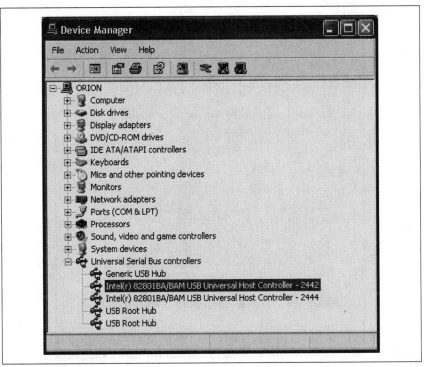

Figure 24-9. Windows XP Device Manager showing that this system uses two Intel 82801BA/BAM UHCIs

The HCI Properties dialog includes the following pages:

General page

The General page displays summary information about the HCI name, type, manufacturer, and location on the bus. It also includes the Device status pane, which indicates when the HCI is working properly and may indicate the cause when the HCI is not working properly. The Device usage drop-down list allows you to enable or disable the device. The Troubleshoot button (Troubleshooter in Windows 2000) invokes an automated dialog that attempts to resolve USB connectivity problems, although we must say that we seldom find the suggestions it offers very useful in solving an actual USB problem.

Advanced page

The Advanced page includes the Don't tell me about USB errors checkbox (Disable USB error detection in Windows 2000). Although error-detection sounds like a good thing, there are times when it must be disabled for USB to operate properly. During routine USB operation, leave USB error detection enabled unless you experience problems or conflicts. If that happens, try disabling error detection by marking this checkbox. This page also includes the Bandwidth-consuming device pane, which displays the percentage of the available bandwidth consumed by each device connected to the port. This

USB Com-munications

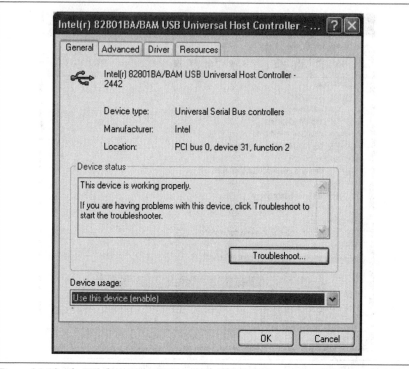

Figure 24-10. The Windows XP HCI Properties dialog displaying detailed HCI information

can be useful information when you troubleshoot USB problems because some USB devices, particularly early models, are "bandwidth hogs" that claim bandwidth regardless of whether they are using it and thereby prevent other devices connected to the same port from functioning correctly, if at all.

Driver page

The Driver page displays the HCI driver provider, date, and version in use by the HCI, as well as the name of the entity that digitally signed the driver. Click the Driver Details button to display the paths and filenames of the USB driver files. Click the Update Driver button to invoke the Hardware Update Wizard (Upgrade Device Driver Wizard in Windows 2000), which allows you to replace the current driver with a different version. Although the default driver generally works properly, depending on the HCI your system uses and the particular devices you have connected, you may need to replace the driver with a later (or earlier) version for full functionality. Windows XP includes a fourth button, Roll Back Driver, which allows you to easily revert to the previous driver version if the updated driver does not function properly.

Resources page

The Resources page displays the IRQ and I/O port being used by the HCI. By default, the Use automatic settings checkbox is marked, which is the proper setting for routine operation. But, depending on the HCI your system uses and the particular devices you have connected, you may need to clear that checkbox and assign settings manually, if that option is available.

Viewing USB Root Hub Properties Under Windows 2000/XP

From the Device Manager, double-clicking the USB Root Hub item displays the USB Root Hub Properties dialog, shown in Figure 24-11. This dialog includes detailed root hub information that may be useful in troubleshooting USB problems and resolving conflicts.

Figure 24-11. *The Windows XP Root Hub Properties dialog displaying detailed root hub information*

The USB Root Hub Properties dialog includes the following pages:

General page

The General page displays summary information about the root hub type, manufacturer, and location. It also includes the Device status pane, which indicates when the root hub is working properly and may indicate the cause when the root hub is not working properly. The Device usage drop-down list allows you to enable or disable the device. The Troubleshoot button (Troubleshooter in Windows 2000) invokes an automated dialog that attempts to resolve USB connectivity problems. The Windows 2000 version is rudimentary, but may be helpful in resolving simple problems. The Windows XP version is more polished, but is little more substantive than the Windows 2000 version.

Power page

The Power page Hub Information pane lists the hub type and maximum total power available per port. The Attached Devices pane (Devices on this hub in Windows 2000) lists the name and description of each device connected to the hub and the power it requires. If you have USB problems, use this dialog to verify that the total power consumption of all connected devices does not exceed the maximum the port can deliver.

Driver page

The Driver page displays the root hub driver provider, date, and version in use by the root hub, as well as the name of the entity that digitally signed the driver. Click the Driver Details button to display the paths and filenames of the USB driver files. Click the Update Driver button to invoke the Hardware Update Wizard (Upgrade Device Driver Wizard in Windows 2000), which allows you to replace the current driver with a different version. Windows XP includes a fourth button, Roll Back Driver, which allows you to easily revert to the previous driver version if the updated driver does not function properly. Unlike the HCI driver, you will seldom need to replace the root hub driver file.

Power Management page

This page, not present in Windows 2000, contains only two checkboxes:

Allow the computer to turn off this device to save power

Marking this checkbox, which is enabled by default, allows ACPI to power down the root hub port after a period of inactivity. We recommend disabling this option on desktop systems because USB peripherals frequently do not recover properly when coming out of standby mode. Problems range from connected peripherals no longer being recognized to two instances of the same peripheral appearing in the Device Manager to the peripheral appearing to be recognized properly but simply not working.

Allow this device to bring the computer out of standby

If you have one or more USB devices attached to the root hub that are capable of waking the system from standby, enabling this checkbox allows them to do so. For example, you might use a USB modem to receive incoming faxes. You may want your system available to receive faxes 24 hours a day but prefer that it not run constantly. If so, use the Screen Saver tab in Display Properties (or Control Panel → Power Options) to enable power management, shutting down power to the monitor and hard drive after a specified interval of inactivity, and enable this checkbox. When an inbound fax call arrives, your USB modem will wake the system and allow it to receive the fax. Note, however, that PCs do not awake instantaneously, and the time delay between the wake-up event and when the system actually becomes available may cause problems.

Verifying USB Interrupt Sharing Under Windows 2000/XP

To verify USB interrupt sharing status under Windows 2000 or Windows XP, from the Device Manager, choose View → Resources by Type, and expand the Interrupt request (IRQ) item, as shown in Figure 24-12.

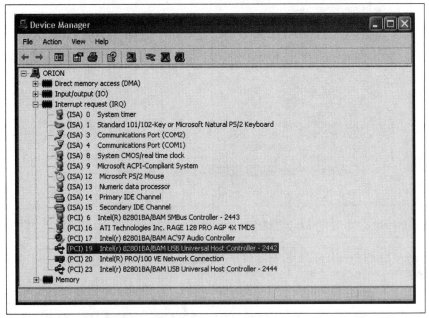

Figure 24-12. Windows XP Device Manager showing that this system dedicates PCI interrupts 19 and 23 to the two USB HCIs

On recent motherboards, Windows 2000 and Windows XP typically assign a dedicated PCI interrupt above 15 to each device. On older motherboards, Windows 2000 and Windows XP typically assign a shared PCI interrupt to the HCI, as shown in Figure 24-13. Despite all assurances by hardware manufacturers and Microsoft that USB operates properly with a shared interrupt, that is frequently not true. If Windows has assigned a shared interrupt to USB, use the Device Manager to locate an unused interrupt, clear the Use Automatic Settings checkbox, and assign the unused interrupt to the HCI.

On the system shown in Figure 24-13, Windows 2000 has assigned one shared PCI interrupt among the USB HCI, the SCSI host adapter, the video card, the network adapter, *and* the sound adapter. Surprisingly enough, all of these functions work properly. If a conflict did occur, we would use the Resources page of USB HCI Properties to manually assign a dedicated IRQ to it.

Configuring USB under Linux

The first draft of this section originally began, "USB under Linux is not ready for prime time." We eventually came to realize that USB under Linux "just works," and the reason for that change of heart is instructive.

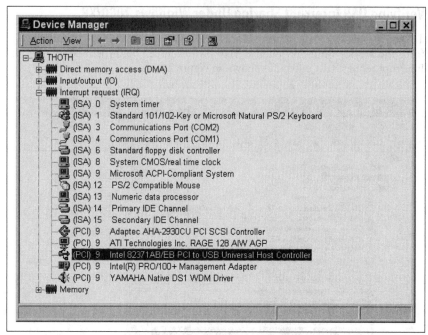

Figure 24-13. Windows 2000 Device Manager showing that this system shares one interrupt among the USB HCI and four other devices

In preparing to write this section, we installed current releases of Red Hat and Mandrake Linux on three representative test-bed systems—a Pentium III on an i815 motherboard, a Pentium 4 on an i845PE motherboard, and an Athlon on an nForce2 motherboard. We then connected diverse USB peripherals, from mice and keyboards to printers and scanners to external optical drives. Some of them weren't even recognized. Some of them worked, more or less. Some of them worked sometimes and not other times. Others didn't work at all. None of them worked reliably.

We had just about written off Linux as having poor USB support. Fortunately, we have a "back channel" mailing list of experienced Linux users to whom we turn when we have questions about Linux hardware issues. We told them about our problems with USB under Linux, and received many responses, all of which basically said, "USB works fine for me under Linux." Hmmm.

After much hair-pulling, we finally determined that the problem was ... a bad cable. Trying to make testing more convenient, we did something stupid. As often happens, cutting corners to save time actually ended up costing us time. We swapped systems and peripherals around during the failed initial testing, but we always used the same cables. One of the cables came with an HP scanner. It looked like a good cable, but it turned out to be a snake in the grass. If it had failed completely, we would have isolated the problem quickly. But it "almost worked," and that cost us days of frustration. If we'd followed our own troubleshooting advice we'd have solved the problem quickly. The moral is, if you're having USB problems, try using a known-good cable.

Although 2.2.18 and later kernels had partial USB support, the 2.4 Linux kernel was the first with full, robust USB support. USB 2.0 support arrived with the 2.4.19 Linux kernel. If you are running an earlier kernel and intend to use USB, we recommend upgrading to the most recent stable 2.4.X kernel or later.

In general, recent Linux releases require no USB configuration. If you run a recent Linux release on modern hardware, USB generally just works. The usual caveats apply, however. Recent Intel HCIs are much less likely to have compatibility problems than are older HCIs and those from some other manufacturers. VIA HCIs in particular seem to have as many USB problems under Linux as they do under Windows. Accordingly, it is important to determine the HCI your motherboard uses.

The KDE Control Center provides an easy way to identify the HCI. To use it for this purpose, start KDE Control Center, expand the Information branch in the left pane, double-click the PCI item, and scroll down in the right pane to locate the USB HCI items. Figure 24-14 shows dual 82801BA/BAM HCIs on an Intel ICH2 motherboard. The ICH2 HCIs are well-behaved in general, and function well under Linux. The HCI listing also provides other useful information, including the I/O port addresses and interrupts assigned to each HCI.

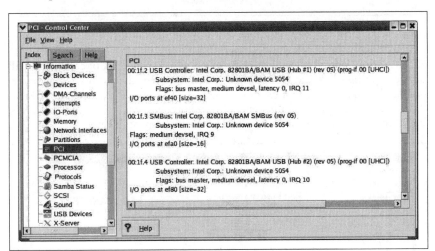

Figure 24-14. KDE Control Center displaying HCI type, I/O ports, and interrupts

From the command line, you can display HCI information using the command /sbin/lspci -v|grep HCI, the output from which is shown in the following example:

```
00:1f.2 USB Controller: Intel Corp. 82801BA/BAM USB (Hub #1) (rev 05) (prog-
if 00 [UHCI])
00:1f.4 USB Controller: Intel Corp. 82801BA/BAM USB (Hub #2) (rev 05) (prog-
if 00 [UHCI])
02:00.0 FireWire (IEEE-1394): Lucent Microelectronics FW323 (rev 04) (prog-
if 10 [OHCI])
```

You can also use KDE Control Center to determine interrupt-sharing status by double-clicking the Interrupts item. Figure 24-15 shows that the first usb-uhci has exclusive use of Interrupt 10, but that the second usb-uhci shares Interrupt 11 with ohci1394 (a FireWire interface) and eth0 (an Ethernet interface). Although shared interrupts may cause USB conflicts under Windows, we have never encountered any problems with a USB shared interrupt under Linux.

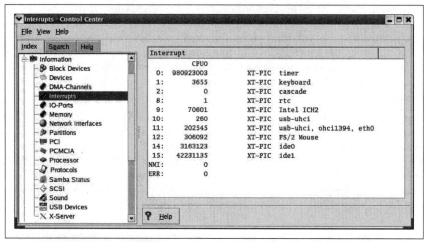

Figure 24-15. KDE Control Center displaying interrupt assignments

KDE Control Center can also list USB devices. To display a list of connected USB devices, double-click the USB Devices item. To view the details for a device, double-click that device. For example, Figure 24-16 shows the details for a UMAX Astra 3400U scanner. (We still haven't figured out what the "Unknown" device is, but it shows up regularly and doesn't seem to cause any problems.)

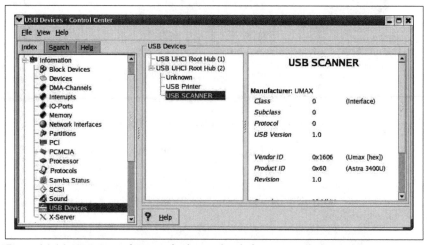

Figure 24-16. KDE Control Center displaying details for connected USB devices

If you don't have KDE installed or if you simply prefer the command line, use the command cat /proc/bus/usb/devices to display more USB configuration information than you'll know what to do with. The following example shows the USB configuration for the same system used for the previous GUI example:

```
T:  Bus=02 Lev=00 Prnt=00 Port=00 Cnt=00 Dev#=  1 Spd=12  MxCh= 2
B:  Alloc= 11/900 us ( 1%), #Int=  1, #Iso=  0
D:  Ver= 1.00 Cls=09(hub  ) Sub=00 Prot=00 MxPS= 8 #Cfgs=  1
P:  Vendor=0000 ProdID=0000 Rev= 0.00
S:  Product=USB UHCI Root Hub
S:  SerialNumber=ef80
C:* #Ifs= 1 Cfg#= 1 Atr=40 MxPwr=   0mA
I:  If#= 0 Alt= 0 #EPs= 1 Cls=09(hub  ) Sub=00 Prot=00 Driver=hub
E:  Ad=81(I) Atr=03(Int.) MxPS=   8 Ivl=255ms
T:  Bus=02 Lev=01 Prnt=01 Port=01 Cnt=01 Dev#=  2 Spd=12  MxCh= 4
D:  Ver= 1.10 Cls=09(hub  ) Sub=00 Prot=00 MxPS= 8 #Cfgs=  1
P:  Vendor=8086 ProdID=1122 Rev= 0.00
C:* #Ifs= 1 Cfg#= 1 Atr=e0 MxPwr=100mA
I:  If#= 0 Alt= 0 #EPs= 1 Cls=09(hub  ) Sub=00 Prot=00 Driver=hub
E:  Ad=81(I) Atr=03(Int.) MxPS=   1 Ivl=255ms
T:  Bus=02 Lev=02 Prnt=02 Port=00 Cnt=01 Dev#=  3 Spd=12  MxCh= 0
D:  Ver= 1.00 Cls=00(>ifc ) Sub=00 Prot=00 MxPS= 8 #Cfgs=  1
P:  Vendor=1606 ProdID=0060 Rev= 1.00
S:  Manufacturer=UMAX
S:  Product=USB SCANNER
C:* #Ifs= 1 Cfg#= 1 Atr=00 MxPwr=   0mA
I:  If#= 0 Alt= 0 #EPs= 3 Cls=ff(vend.) Sub=00 Prot=ff Driver=(none)
E:  Ad=81(I) Atr=03(Int.) MxPS=   1 Ivl=16ms
E:  Ad=82(I) Atr=02(Bulk) MxPS=  64 Ivl=0ms
E:  Ad=03(O) Atr=02(Bulk) MxPS=  64 Ivl=0ms
T:  Bus=02 Lev=02 Prnt=02 Port=01 Cnt=02 Dev#=  4 Spd=12  MxCh= 0
D:  Ver= 1.00 Cls=00(>ifc ) Sub=00 Prot=00 MxPS=64 #Cfgs=  1
P:  Vendor=04b8 ProdID=0005 Rev= 1.00
S:  Manufacturer=EPSON
S:  Product=USB Printer
S:  SerialNumber=W30169912131319590
C:* #Ifs= 1 Cfg#= 1 Atr=c0 MxPwr=  2mA
I:  If#= 0 Alt= 0 #EPs= 2 Cls=07(print) Sub=01 Prot=02 Driver=usblp
E:  Ad=01(O) Atr=02(Bulk) MxPS=  64 Ivl=0ms
E:  Ad=82(I) Atr=02(Bulk) MxPS=  64 Ivl=0ms
T:  Bus=01 Lev=00 Prnt=00 Port=00 Cnt=00 Dev#=  1 Spd=12  MxCh= 2
B:  Alloc=  0/900 us ( 0%), #Int=  0, #Iso=  0
D:  Ver= 1.00 Cls=09(hub  ) Sub=00 Prot=00 MxPS= 8 #Cfgs=  1
P:  Vendor=0000 ProdID=0000 Rev= 0.00
S:  Product=USB UHCI Root Hub
S:  SerialNumber=ef40
C:* #Ifs= 1 Cfg#= 1 Atr=40 MxPwr=   0mA
I:  If#= 0 Alt= 0 #EPs= 1 Cls=09(hub  ) Sub=00 Prot=00 Driver=hub
E:  Ad=81(I) Atr=03(Int.) MxPS=   8 Ivl=255ms
```

The default USB configuration is suitable for most purposes. However, if you need to tweak the USB configuration, you can rebuild the kernel with different USB support options. The KDE Linux Kernel Configurator, shown in Figure 24-17, provides an easy way to do that.

In the first draft of this section, we didn't give detailed instructions, on the theory that someone who couldn't figure out how to reconfigure, recompile, and install a kernel shouldn't be doing it in the first place. Our editor thought we should give a bit more detail, so we expanded the section. But do be careful.

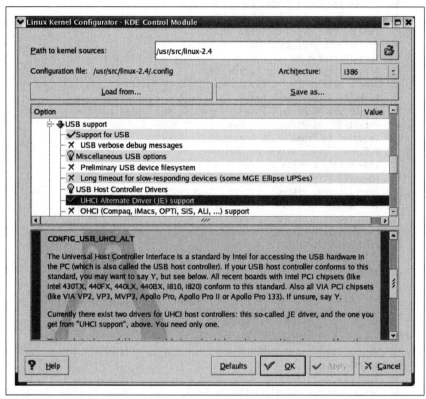

Figure 24-17. The Linux Kernel Configurator

Reconfiguring USB support options in the kernel is not for the faint of heart. Before you attempt it, make sure to read and understand the detailed technical documentation available on the Linux USB Project web site (*http://www.linux-usb.org/*).

To run the KDE Linux Kernel Configurator, log on as root, start KDE Control Center, expand the System item in the left menu pane, and choose Linux Kernel Configurator. Make any necessary changes, save those changes, compile and install the new kernel, and reboot the system. If you don't know how to compile and install a kernel, see the Linux Kernel HOWTO (*http://www.tldp.org/HOWTO/Kernel-HOWTO.html*).

Always save the new kernel under a different name. That way, if the new kernel won't boot, you can simply boot to the old kernel. If there's a problem with the new kernel and you saved it under the same name as the old kernel, your system may be unbootable.

Before you build a new kernel, check to see if kernel modules already exist for the alternate drivers. If they do, you may simply need to configure the kernel modules already present in the current kernel. For more information about configuring kernel modules, see the Linux Kernel HOWTO.

Troubleshooting USB

In an obvious Freudian slip, we accidentally named our first working draft of this entire chapter *Troubleshooting USB*. It's ridiculous, to be sure, but the simple fact is that working with USB often means spending lots of time troubleshooting it. In our experience and in that of many of our readers, USB can be the most trouble-prone technology you'll find in a PC.

The goal of USB is transparent, Plug-and-Play connectivity to diverse external peripherals. Alas, that goal is often unrealized other than by pure luck. USB is indeed wonderful when it works as it is supposed to. You simply plug in a device and it works. Unfortunately, the reality of living with USB is that you sometimes plug in a device and it *doesn't* work. Worse yet, not only does the new device not work. Also, your other USB peripherals may stop working. Arrrrghh.

In response to a reader query on our message board about troubleshooting USB, we said in part:

> "The problem with USB troubleshooting is that there are way too many degrees of freedom. Each device is a law unto itself. It's as though when troubleshooting an automobile, one possible answer to the problem was that you'd installed Shell gasoline and Mobil oil, which in combination with your Bosch ignition and Fram fuel filter had caused your right front headlight to work intermittently, but only if you were running four Michelin tires and had a Goodyear spare."

This pretty much sums up the frustrations of trying to troubleshoot USB using traditional methods. If you run only one or two USB peripherals, you may wonder what we're talking about. Millions of PCs happily use a couple of USB peripherals with no problem at all—until the day that you plug in a new USB peripheral or experience a minor communication problem with one of your peripherals, when suddenly the whole thing collapses like a house of cards.

Several factors determine the likelihood that any particular USB configuration will function properly. All other things being equal, you are less likely to have USB problems—and the ones you have are likely to be less severe—if your motherboard is recent and has a current BIOS, if you use recent, name-brand USB peripherals, if you use the latest release of your operating system, if you connect only a few USB peripherals (and leave them connected), and if you connect the peripherals to (preferably) root hub ports or to a powered USB hub. Conversely, if your motherboard is old or has an outdated BIOS, if you use old, off-brand USB peripherals, if you use an outdated version of your operating system, if you have many USB peripherals connected (and plug/unplug them frequently), and if you connect those peripherals to unpowered hubs, you are quite likely to have many USB problems, some of which may be quite severe.

Proactive USB Troubleshooting

At this point, most books and web sites that offer USB troubleshooting suggestions present a list of things to do when a USB problem occurs—connect the USB
device to a different port, reboot the PC, and so on. All good advice, and sometimes it even works. But the truth is that in order to avoid USB problems in the first
place and to solve those problems that do occur, it's important to start with a solid
foundation. Otherwise, you can troubleshoot until you're blue in the face and still
have problems—either the same boring old problems or exciting new problems.

The real secret to troubleshooting USB is to do everything possible to *prevent*
problems. Doing that requires optimizing the system for USB—configuring a new
system properly from the start, or reconfiguring an existing system to eliminate
things likely to cause USB problems. In order to build a stable, robust, reliable
USB system, do the following:

Verify your USB host controller
> The first step in building a stable USB system is determining which USB host
> controller your system uses, as described in the previous section. If it has a
> recent AMD, Intel, NEC, or nVIDIA host controller, you may be in luck. If it
> has an older AMD, Intel, or NEC host controller, or if it has any host
> controller made by ALi, SiS, VIA, or another company, you may need to
> install a PCI/USB card with a more recent USB HCI.

Check compatibility of each USB peripheral
> Before you proceed, take the time to visit the web site for each of your USB
> peripherals. Check the support section to determine if there are any known
> conflicts, incompatibilities, HCI issues, and so on. Many USB devices list
> conflicts with specific other USB devices, or with certain HCIs. Some USB
> devices work reliably with only one specific HCI—often the Intel 82371AB/
> EB—and have problems with older *or newer* USB HCIs. If any of your current
> devices conflict, you may need to run them on separate USBs. Also, search
> the Microsoft web site for details about your specific USB configuration. For
> example, if you have an ALi chipset, a search for "ali usb" turns up several
> interesting articles about problems and solutions that apply specifically to
> running USB with an ALi chipset under Windows.

Make sure device firmware and drivers are current
> Outdated device firmware or drivers can cause many USB problems, some
> subtle and some glaringly apparent. The most common symptom of outdated
> firmware or drivers is that a device does not "sign in" or "sign out" properly.
> That is, when you disconnect a USB peripheral, it should simply become
> unavailable, and when you reconnect it, it should simply become available
> again. If the device firmware or drivers are outdated, you may experience
> various problems, from having to reboot the system for the device to be
> recognized, to Windows loading a second instance of the driver, to Device
> Manager showing a second "ghost" instance of the same device, which is
> marked with a yellow exclamation point and cannot be removed short of
> removing the underlying device. This problem is most common with bulk-
> mode devices such as printers and scanners, although we have seen it occur
> with many different types of USB peripherals. To avoid this problem, ensure
> that the firmware and drivers for all of your USB devices are current.

Ensure that all USB hubs and cables are standards-compliant

USB 1.1 hubs are relatively simple devices, and so seldom cause problems. What problems we have experienced with USB 1.1 hubs, almost without exception, have been caused by hubs that do not supply the full 500 mA to their ports. Cables are a different story. Many cables supplied with USB 1.1 peripherals are not standards-compliant, and may cause problems ranging from sporadic communications glitches to outright failure of the entire USB. If your cables are of unknown provenance, replace them with certified USB cables. We are not aware of any issues with USB 2.0 hubs or the cables supplied with USB 2.0 devices.

Update your system BIOS to the most recent version

Many USB problems are caused by an outdated system BIOS. Before you connect USB peripherals to your system, update your system BIOS to the latest available version. If the latest BIOS update for your motherboard predates the release of Windows 98 in mid-1998, the likelihood that USB will function well on that motherboard is small.

 Be careful when updating the BIOS. A power failure during the update can render your motherboard unusable. For details about how to update your BIOS safely, see Chapter 3.

Configure your system BIOS to support USB properly

Strangely enough, default BIOS settings are not always appropriate for USB. For detailed information about configuring your BIOS to support USB properly, visit the manufacturer's web site and examine the support page for your specific motherboard model. In general, however, you should configure a motherboard to use the following settings:

Enable/Disable USB

Set to Enable. Note that many motherboards, particularly those from 1998 and prior, are set by default to disable USB. Also note that you may have to enable USB on the motherboard even if you have installed a PCI/USB card and are not using the motherboard USB ports.

Plug-and-Play OS?

This BIOS Setup option specifies whether interrupts and other system resources are under the control of the chipset or the operating system. For most USB chipsets, set to Yes for any version of Linux or Windows that supports USB, including Windows 9X/2000/XP. Note, however, that for some chipsets, particularly older models, the proper choice for this setting may depend on which processor is installed. For example, some ALi chipsets require setting this option to Yes if you have a Celeron or Pentium II, III, or 4 installed, but to No if you have a K6-2, K6-III, Pentium, or Pentium Pro installed.

IRQ Assignment

Set to Automatic or System for any version of Linux or Windows that supports USB, including Windows 9X or Windows 2000/XP.

Assign IRQ to USB?

The proper setting for this varies from motherboard to motherboard. In the absence of any specific recommendation from the motherboard manufacturer, we suggest disabling this setting for Windows 9X and enabling it for Windows 2000/XP. If you experience USB problems with one setting, try the other. Under Linux, the "device not accepting address" error message indicates that the HCI is unable to obtain a hardware interrupt. If this message occurs, use BIOS Setup to set "Assign IRQ to USB?" off.

Overclocking and memory timings

Overclocking a system almost guarantees USB problems. For stable USB operation, set your BIOS to use nominal FSB speed. Boosting the PCI bus above its default 33.3 MHz is one of the most common causes of USB problems. Also note that motherboards vary in how aggressively they set memory timings. Intel motherboards and other motherboards intended for OEM systems typically use relatively relaxed memory timings, which are consonant with reliable operation. Motherboards targeted at the "enthusiast" market often have very aggressive default memory timings, which may contribute to USB problems as well as to overall system instability.

BIOS power management

Disable this setting in BIOS. You want the operating system to control power management, if indeed you want to enable power management at all. We recommend against using power management in any form. Enabling ACPI (Advanced Configuration and Power Interface) in BIOS can cause a host of problems with USB. The fault lies not so much with ACPI itself as with poor ACPI implementations. Our rule of thumb is to disable ACPI on any motherboard that uses a chipset other than a very recent Intel model, such as the 845 series. Unfortunately, simply disabling ACPI in BIOS on an existing system doesn't solve the problems. The only practical way we know to eliminate ACPI conflicts is to disable ACPI in BIOS and then strip your hard drive down to bare metal and reinstall the operating system.

MPS level (multiprocessor systems only)

If you have a dual-processor system, it is probably set by default to use MPS 1.4. If you experience USB conflicts with this setting, reverting to MPS 1.1 may eliminate the problems.

Enable IRQ Steering in Windows 9X

Configuring IRQ Steering is described fully in Chapter 1. Under Windows 9X, having IRQ Steering enabled and properly configured is important to proper USB functioning. If IRQ Steering is disabled, it's nearly always because the BIOS settings are incorrect. Reboot the system, run BIOS Setup, and make sure that Plug-N-Play OS? is set to true and that IRQ Assignment is set to Automatic or System. When the system restarts, check IRQ Steering status as described in Chapter 1. Briefly, on the Settings page of the PCI Bus Properties dialog, make sure Device enumeration is set to Use hardware. On the IRQ Steering page of the PCI Bus Properties dialog, make sure the Use

IRQ Steering checkbox is marked. The IRQ Routing Status pane on the IRQ Steering page should include the following four lines: IRQ Steering Enabled; IRQ Table read from <source>; IRQ Miniport Data processed successfully; and IRQ Miniport loaded successfully.

Make sure USB has a dedicated IRQ

Despite what Microsoft and USB manufacturers claim, USB does not gracefully share an IRQ with other devices, especially under Windows 9X. Check the Device Manager to determine which IRQ is assigned to the USB HCI and whether that IRQ is shared with other devices. Under Windows 9X it is acceptable for an IRQ Holder for PCI Steering to share the HCI IRQ because that is simply a placeholder rather than a real device. But if the Device Manager shows that the IRQ assigned to the HCI is also being shared with a sound card, video adapter, network adapter, SCSI adapter, modem, or other device, the likelihood of USB problems occurring increases dramatically. For example, Figure 24-13 showed a USB disaster waiting to happen—an elderly Intel SE440BX-2V motherboard with ACPI enabled, using an old Intel 82371AB/EB HCI that shares IRQ 9 with a SCSI host adapter, a video adapter, a network adapter, *and* a sound adapter. When we tried plugging a USB printer into this system, it just whimpered.

The first step toward getting USB on a dedicated IRQ is to free up as many IRQs as possible. Begin by running BIOS Setup and disabling all unused devices. In many systems, COM1 and COM2 can safely be disabled, as can any printer port that uses an IRQ. If you use a USB mouse and/or keyboard, you may also be able to free up the interrupts assigned to the PS/2 mouse and keyboard ports. After you've freed up as many IRQs as possible, restart the system in Safe Mode, fire up the Device Manager, and delete all the corresponding devices. Note that you must do this in Safe Mode. If you attempt to remove devices while operating in Normal Mode, the next time you restart the system, Windows will restore the device and assign an IRQ to it.

At this point, you may have sufficient free IRQs that the USB HCI has been assigned a dedicated IRQ. If not, you may be able to force conflicting devices to other IRQs by juggling the arrangement of PCI cards in the system. Simply moving a card to a different PCI slot may remove the conflict. If none of these steps results in USB being assigned an unshared IRQ, the next step is to assign IRQs manually. To do so, start Windows in Safe Mode and follow the instructions given in Chapter 1.

Clean up the Device Manager in Safe Mode

A system with severe USB conflicts may display them in the Device Manager operating in Normal Mode. However, just because the Device Manager appears clean in Normal Mode does not mean that no USB problems exist. To view the true situation, restart your system in Safe Mode and run the Device Manager. Delete all instances of USB devices. Then delete the USB root hubs. Finally, delete the USB HCI. Restart your system and allow Windows to reinstall all devices and updated drivers.

Once you have done all of these things, you have established a firm foundation for USB. If you fail to do some or all of these things, you *may* be able to get USB running successfully, but don't be surprised if you encounter USB problems. Actually, you can do all of these things and still have problems, but at least having taken these steps you've done all you can to ensure reliable USB operation.

Reactive USB Troubleshooting

If you have a reasonably recent motherboard and have taken the steps described in the preceding section, your USB experience may well be trouble-free. Despite all efforts, however, you may one day be bitten by a USB conflict. If that happens, we suggest as a first step that you review the suggestions in the preceding section. For example, in the interval since you prepared the system, the motherboard maker may have released an updated BIOS, or later firmware versions may now be available for some or all of your USB peripherals. If so, download and install them.

Before you begin fiddling with your system, take a moment to visit the web sites for your computer or motherboard and your USB peripherals. You may find information there that will save a lot of useless mucking about. Most computer, motherboard, and USB peripheral vendors have detailed USB troubleshooting pages on their sites. You may find updated drivers, workarounds for specific problems, warnings about conflicts with specific devices, and so on.

Microsoft also provides some very useful information on its site about version-specific USB issues. We won't attempt to list specific pages because Microsoft frequently changes its site, but if you visit *http://www.microsoft.com*, choose the Search function, and search for the string "USB troubleshooting." You will find numerous useful pages.

If, having verified each of the preceeding items, you are still having problems with USB, there are several possible courses of action. Recognize, however, that not all USB problems can be resolved merely by tweaking and configuring your current hardware. Some USB problems are resolvable only by replacing hardware—either installing a PCI/USB card, replacing USB peripherals, or both.

Before attempting the following steps, check the Device Manager in Safe Mode. If anything odd appears there—such as two instances of the same peripheral or a peripheral flagged with a warning icon—delete all HID peripherals, USB peripherals, USB root hubs, and USB host controllers, in that order. Restart the system normally and allow it to reinstall all devices found. When a USB peripheral misbehaves, take the following steps:

1. If the USB peripheral is self-powered (uses a power brick), make sure the power brick is connected to an AC receptacle and that that receptacle has power. Self-powered USB peripherals may be recognized by the system even when they are not connected to AC power, but will be nonfunctional and may also cause other USB peripherals to malfunction.

2. Hot-plug the peripheral, which is to say disconnect the USB cable from the peripheral while the system and peripheral remain on, and then reconnect the cable. Many USB problems caused by momentary communications glitches are solved by this simple step.

If this is the first time you have connected the problem USB periph-eral and it is not self-powered (i.e., it depends on the USB for power), always use USB Properties in the Device Manager to verify that the total current draw does not exceed 500 mA, particularly if you are using an unpowered hub. If a device or a group of devices attempt to draw more than 500 mA, USB disables the port until the system is turned off and then on again. Note that inactive devices may draw less current than active devices, so it is possible for a group of devices on one USB to work properly until too many are activated at the same time, at which point the current draw exceeds the maximum allowable and the port shuts down.

3. Shut down the computer and turn off the computer and USB hub. Note that neither warm rebooting (Ctrl-Alt-Del etc.) nor even cold rebooting by pressing the reset switch are sufficient. You must actually remove power to the system using the main power switch to reset the USB controller registers. Although we have not encountered the problem ourselves, we have reports that some motherboards that remain powered even when the system is shut off (to support Wake-on-LAN and similar functions) must be physically disconnected from the AC power at the wall receptacle to clear the system entirely. After you have powered down completely, wait a minute or so before turning on the system. Verify that the problem peripheral is now func-tioning properly. If it is, also verify that your other USB peripherals are recognized and accessible.

4. If the problem persists, shut off power to the system, disconnect the USB peripheral, and then reconnect it to a different USB port. In order of prefer-ence, connect the peripheral to (a) a root hub port on a different USB controller, if your system has multiple USBs, (b) a powered hub port on a different USB controller, (c) a root hub port on the same USB controller, (d) a powered hub port on a different hub on the same USB controller, or (e) a different powered hub port on the same hub.

5. Try a different cable. Like any type of cable, USB cables vary from well-made to execrable. Those supplied with peripherals may or may not be of good quality. Those you find for a couple of bucks in computer stores are nearly always terrible. Also consider cable length. Although the USB specification allows cables as long as 5 meters, some peripherals function reliably only if you use a shorter cable. For example, some HP devices come with a 2-meter cable and a recommendation that longer cables not be used. We keep a short USB 2.0-certified cable available as a spare for troubleshooting purposes. Surprisingly often, replacing the cable solves the problem.

6. Connect the problem peripheral to another computer, ideally as the only connected USB device. If it does not function on the second computer, the device itself may be defective. Contact the manufacturer for assistance. If the problem peripheral functions on the second computer, the likely cause of the problem on the first computer is either a conflict between the problem peripheral and other peripherals, or an incompatibility between the problem peripheral and the host controller, which may be undocumented.

7. To eliminate conflict between peripherals as the cause, disconnect all USB peripherals from the first computer. Restart the computer in Safe Mode and, from the Device Manager, delete all USB devices, then all USB root hubs, and finally all USB host controllers. Shut down the system and turn the power off. Connect only the problem USB device and restart the system. If the problem was caused by a conflict between USB peripherals, the problem peripheral should now be recognized and accessible. You can try adding back the other USB devices until you find the one that conflicts with the device in question. Of course, it is possible to have compound-complex situations such as three- or four-way conflicts, but attempting to resolve those may land you in a mental institution. If you do find that the USB peripheral in question conflicts with another particular USB device, you may be able to use both on your system by installing them on (ideally) different USBs or at least on different root hub ports.

8. If, despite following these steps the problem peripheral continues to misbehave, the only workable solution may be to replace the peripheral with a comparable competing model or to install a PCI/USB card in your system.

We don't want to give you the impression that USB problems are inevitable, or to discourage you from using USB. If you use only one or a few USB devices, chances are you'll have no problems, particularly if your motherboard and devices are recent and you connect devices to root hub ports or powered hubs. Millions of people use USB successfully—yes, even on old VIA chipsets—but millions more have been discouraged by problems that can sometimes be resolved inexpensively and easily. USB problems can be among the most difficult and frustrating PC problems to fix, simply because there are so many possible causes and combinations of causes. However, if you build a solid foundation for USB and take our advice, the chances are excellent that your experience with USB will be pleasant.

Our Picks

USB 1.1 ports are ubiquitous on recent motherboards and systems. USB 2.0 ports are standard on chipsets, motherboards, and PCs designed after mid-2002, although low-end USB 1.1 PCs and motherboards were still being sold as of July 2003. Don't buy any new system or motherboard that does not provide native USB 2.0 ports.

The good news is that upgrading older systems to USB 2.0 is easy and inexpensive. We have used numerous USB port cards and hubs—everything from high-quality, name-brand components from Adaptec and ADS Technology to no-name Pacific Rim garbage. Our advice? Buying cheap USB port cards and hubs is a mistake. In our experience, name-brand components cost little more, are more reliable, and are much less likely to cause device conflicts.

For specific recommendations by brand and model, visit: *http://www.hardwareguys.com/picks/usb.html*.

25

Cases

Most people think of a case as merely the enclosure that holds a PC together. That view is reasonable for people who buy a PC and never open the case, but anyone who builds or upgrades PCs soon realizes that not all cases are created equal. This chapter describes what you need to know about cases.

Case Characteristics

PC cases are available in a bewildering array of sizes, shapes, and prices. *Form factor* is the most important thing about a case because it determines which motherboards and which power supplies fit that case. Cases are available in the following form factors:

AT

The 1984 IBM PC-AT introduced the *AT form factor*. AT cases accept full-size AT motherboards and reduced-size Baby AT motherboards. All AT-variant cases have a circular hole in the rear panel for the motherboard keyboard connector and knockouts for external DB connectors that mate to serial, parallel, and other ports present as header pins on AT motherboards. AT cases have been produced in two variants, which differ only in the power supply they accept. *Desktop/AT* cases use the original AT form factor power supply, with a paddle switch built into the power supply itself. *Tower/AT* cases use a modified AT power supply that instead has four main power leads that connect to a switch built into the case. Desktop/AT cases and power supplies are hard to find nowadays, but Tower/AT cases and power supplies are still readily available. AT cases of either type are a poor choice for building a new system.

Baby AT

AT motherboards require large cases. The demand for smaller systems resulted in *Baby AT (BAT)* motherboards and cases. A BAT motherboard is simply a reduced-size AT motherboard, and uses the same connectors and mounting hole positions. Like AT cases, BAT cases have been produced in *Desktop/BAT* and *Tower/BAT* form factors. Desktop/BAT cases accept only Desktop/BAT power supplies, which are smaller versions of the AT power supply, complete with paddle switch. Tower/BAT cases accept only Tower/BAT power supplies, which are smaller versions of Tower/AT power supplies. Confusingly, many recent BAT desktop cases and systems were designed to use Tower/BAT power supplies. Adding to the confusion, BAT has become such a catchall term that some so-called BAT cases can in fact accept full-AT motherboards and power supplies. Desktop/BAT cases and power supplies are difficult to find new now. New Tower/BAT systems were still being sold as recently as early 2000, so Tower/BAT cases (in both desktop and tower styles!) are still widely available to upgraders, although they are a poor choice for building new systems.

LPX

Corporate demand for low-profile systems and the desire to reduce manufacturing costs led to the creation of *LPX*, a variant of BAT. LPX cases accept only LPX power supplies and LPX motherboards, which use a riser card to arrange expansion cards horizontally rather than vertically. Although it was for a while popular for mass-market consumer systems and low-profile corporate systems, LPX failed as a standard for several reasons: many manufacturers implemented proprietary variations of LPX; expected cost savings did not materialize, largely because most LPX implementations required expensive supplementary cooling fans; and the riser card made it difficult to work on the motherboard, increasing support costs. LPX cases are still available, although their distribution is very limited. The only reason to purchase an LPX case would be to salvage components from an existing LPX system, but such systems are now so old that there's nothing worth salvaging.

The preceding three form factors are obsolete, although manufacturers continue to make them for the repair and upgrade market. The form factors of modern cases all derive from the *Intel ATX specification* (*http://www.formfactors.org/*). ATX includes the following variants, whose dimensions and motherboard/case compatibilities are detailed in Table 25-1.

ATX

Both the lack of a formal BAT standard and some increasingly troublesome problems with BAT component layouts led Intel to develop the *ATX form factor*, which it introduced with the Advanced/ML "Marl" motherboard in 1996. ATX redesigned component layouts for easier access, improved cooling, and other factors, but the important aspect of ATX for cases is that it dispenses with the AT keyboard hole and port knockouts on the rear panel, replacing them with a consolidated I/O panel of standard size and positioning. Also, ATX motherboards control the power supply directly, which means that the "power" switch on an ATX system actually just notifies the motherboard to turn power on or off rather than doing so itself. The original ATX specification is often loosely termed "full ATX" to differentiate it from smaller ATX variants, described next. A full-ATX case is usually the best choice for building a new PC.

Mini-ATX

As a part of the Intel ATX Specification, Intel also defines Mini-ATX, which is simply a reduced-size ATX motherboard. The primary motivation for Mini-ATX is manufacturing cost reductions because four Mini-ATX boards can be produced from a standard blank, which yields only two ATX boards. Mini-ATX cases accept Mini-ATX (or smaller) motherboards, but are too small for ATX motherboards. It costs nearly as much to make Mini-ATX cases as full-ATX cases, which accept both ATX and Mini-ATX motherboards, so Mini-ATX cases are very uncommon.

NLX

NLX, introduced in 1997, is the ATX version of LPX, and is intended for inexpensive, low-profile corporate and mass-market systems. NLX cases accept only NLX motherboards, which use riser cards similar to those used by LPX cases, and a full-length I/O panel rather than the standard ATX I/O panel. About the only reason to buy an NLX case is to salvage an NLX system whose case is damaged. NLX cases are readily available from numerous sources, but are a poor choice for building new systems.

microATX

Smaller translates to cheaper. Intel released the microATX Motherboard Interface Specification in 1998 in response to the demand for low-cost consumer systems, for which expandability is not an issue. microATX motherboards have only four expansion slots (versus seven for ATX), which allows using smaller and less-expensive cases. Some microATX cases accept only SFX power supplies (described in Chapter 26), which are smaller, cheaper, less powerful, and less functional than standard ATX power supplies. Because such cases are too small to accept a standard ATX power supply, upgrade options are severely limited. Although microATX cases are available from third-party manufacturers, their distribution is limited and they are a very poor choice for building new systems. microATX components are sometimes mistakenly designated μATX.

FlexATX

Just as microATX is a smaller version of ATX, FlexATX is a smaller version of microATX—picoATX as it were. FlexATX is an addendum to the microATX specification, intended for even smaller systems such as web devices, set-top boxes, and novelty PCs such as the Barbie PC and the Hot Wheels PC (we are not making this up). If for some reason you want to know more about FlexATX, download the *FlexATX Addendum Version 1.0 to microATX Specification Version 1.0* (*http://www.formfactors.org/developer/specs/atx/FlexATXaddn1_0.pdf*).

Mini-ITX

In December 2001, VIA Technologies introduced the Mini-ITX reference design, which uses a 170mm (6.7-inch) square motherboard form factor. Mini-ITX is a follow-on to ITX, for which reference designs existed that never went into production. Mini-ITX is essentially a smaller version of FlexATX and is backward-compatible with FlexATX and microATX. Micro-ITX focuses heavily on reducing PC size and power consumption. Mini-ITX systems accordingly use very small power supplies (less than 100 W) and slow, cool-running processors such as the VIA C3. Although Mini-ITX is theoretically an open standard, it is effectively proprietary because few manufacturers other than VIA support it. For more information about Mini-ITX, see *http://www.via.com.tw/en/VInternet/mini_itx_faq.jsp*.

WTX

Reversing the trend toward ever-smaller variants of ATX, the WTX Workstation System Specification Version 1.1 defines WTX as Intel's extension of the ATX standard to the requirements of midrange workstations, with explicit support for dual processors, large memory configurations, AGP Pro graphics, dual-fan power supplies, and other workstation-oriented features. WTX-compliant cases, power supplies, and motherboards began shipping in limited quantities in Q1 2000. For additional information about WTX, see *http://www.wtx.org*.

Table 25-1. Maximum motherboard dimensions and chassis compatibility for ATX form factor variants

Mother- board	Width$_{max}$	Depth$_{max}$	Fits ATX case style(s)					
			Full	Mini	micro	Flex	NLX	WTX
ATX	12.0"/305mm	9.6"/244mm	●	○	○	○	○	○
Mini-ATX	11.2"/284mm	8.2"/208mm	●	●	○	○	○	○
microATX	9.6"/244mm	9.6"/244mm	●	●	●	○	○	○
FlexATX	9.0"/229mm	7.5"/191mm	●	●	●	●	○	○
NLX	13.6"/346mm	9.0"/229mm	○	○	○	○	●	○
WTX	16.75"/425mm	14.0"/356mm	○	○	○	○	○	●

 Some hybrid cases are available that accept either BAT or ATX motherboards and power supplies, and include both the AT-specific keyboard connector hole and port knockouts and the ATX-specific I/O panel cutout. These cases may include a "universal" power supply that provides both AT and ATX motherboard main power connectors. These cases were formerly popular with some upgraders, as they allowed using an existing AT motherboard and upgrading to an ATX model later without replacing the case. Now that the AT form factor is nearly obsolete, such cases have become harder to find, although a few are still available.

Although form factor is the most important characteristic of a case, numerous other factors are worth considering:

Size and orientation

Cases are available in a variety of sizes and orientations, including *low-profile desktop, standard desktop, micro-tower* (for microATX boards), *mini-tower, mid-tower*, and *full-tower*. Low-profile cases are popular for mass-market and business-oriented PCs, but we see little purpose for them. They take up more desk space than towers, provide poor expandability, and are difficult to work on. Micro-tower cases take very little desk space, but otherwise share the drawbacks of low-profile cases. Mini/mid-tower styles—the dividing line between them is nebulous—are most popular because they consume little desktop space while providing good expandability. Full-tower cases are what we really prefer. They take up no desk space at all, and are tall enough that CD-ROM, tape, and other external drives are readily accessible. Their cavernous interiors make it very easy to work inside them, and they often provide better cooling than smaller cases. The drawbacks of full-tower cases are that they are more expensive than other cases, sometimes significantly so, and that they may require using extension cables for keyboard, video, and/or mouse.

 A proprietary PC style called *Small Form Factor (SFF)* is fast gaining popularity, primarily due to the efforts of Shuttle. Such systems are generally called "cubes," although they're really about the shape and size of a shoebox. Unlike Mini-ITX systems, which are low-performance "appliance" PCs, SFF systems use standard Pentium 4 or Athlon processors, and are designed to cram the power of a full-size PC into the smallest possible box.

SFF PCs have two important drawbacks. First, the form factor is nonstandard, which means you can use only motherboards that are designed to fit the specific case. Leading motherboard makers such as Intel, ASUS, Gigabyte, and MSI do not make SFF motherboards, so you are limited to motherboards from second- and third-tier makers such as Iwill, Jetway, Shuttle, Soltek, and Soyo. Second, cooling is critical when a high-performance processor, a fast hard drive, and a power supply of sufficient wattage are crammed into a shoebox-size enclosure. Although we do not have sufficient data to make an absolute prediction, we expect that the higher operating temperature of SFF PCs will lead to increased instability and a shorter life relative to similar components enclosed in a standard case. We recommend avoiding SFF PCs unless system size is the absolute highest priority.

Drive bay arrangement

The number and arrangement of drive bays may be unimportant if the system is unlikely to be upgraded later. All current cases provide at least one 3.5" external bay for a floppy drive, one 5.25-inch external bay for a CD-ROM, DVD-ROM, or CD-RW drive, and one 3.5-inch internal bay for a hard disk. That may change, however, as Microsoft and Intel strive to rid the world of "legacy" devices, including the venerable floppy drive. Table 25-2 shows typical arrangements for various case styles. Some cases can be configured as desktops or towers, and the number of drive bays may differ between configurations.

Table 25-2. Typical drive bay configuration in various case styles

	External bays		Internal bays		Total bays
Case style	3.5"	5.25"	3.5"	5.25"	
Low profile	1–2	1	1–2	0	3–4
Desktop	1–2	2–3	1–3	0–3	4–7

Table 25-2. Typical drive bay configuration in various case styles (continued)

| Case style | External bays | | Internal bays | | Total bays |
	3.5"	5.25"	3.5"	5.25"	
Micro-tower	1–2	1	1–2	0	3–4
Mini-tower	1–2	2–3	1–4	0–2	4–7
Mid-tower	1–2	3–4	1–5	0–3	5–8
Full-tower	0–2	3–12	0–8	0–8	8–14

Drive mounting method

Drives mount in most cases via screws driven directly through the chassis into the sides of the drives. This method is secure, provides good electrical grounding, and allows the drives to use the chassis as a heatsink. The drawback is that, for some chassis, it is difficult to access the screws on the right side of 3.5-inch drives. Some cases address this problem by using removable motherboard trays or removable drive bays. Others simply have access holes punched in the right side of the chassis. Some cases use mounting rails, which screw or snap onto the drive and fit slots in the drive bays. Rails are less likely to physically torque a drive, which can cause read/write problems, and make it easier to remove and replace drives. On the downside, rails provide inferior electrical and thermal contact compared to direct mounting, may rattle if they fit loosely, and sometimes cause vertical alignment problems where one drive that should fit an adjacent bay will not do so because the faceplate is a tiny bit too large. In practice, we've never much cared whether a case required securing drives directly or used rails. If you are building a system that you will seldom open, drive mounting method is relatively unimportant. If you are building a test-bed or other system in which you will frequently swap drives, either buy a case that uses rails or simply don't use screws to secure the drives.

Accessibility

Cases vary widely in how easy they are to work on. Some use thumb screws and pop-off panels that allow complete disassembly in seconds without tools, while disassembling others requires a screwdriver and more work. Similarly, some cases have removable motherboard trays or drive cages that make it easier to install and remove components. The flip side of easy access is that, unless they are properly engineered, easy-access cases are often less rigid than traditional cases. Years ago we worked on a system that experienced seemingly random disk errors. We replaced the hard disk, cables, disk controller, power supply, and other components, but errors persisted. As it turned out, the user kept a stack of heavy reference books on top of the case. As she added and removed books, the case was flexing enough to torque the hard disk in its mounting, causing disk errors. Rigid cases prevent such problems. The other aspect of accessibility is sheer size. It's easier to work inside a full-tower case than a smaller case simply because there's more room.

Provisions for supplemental cooling

For basic systems, the power supply fan and CPU fan normally suffice. More heavily loaded systems—those with dual processors, high-performance SCSI hard drives, lots of expansion cards, and so on—require adding supplemental fans. Some cases have no provision for adding fans, while others provide mounting positions for half a dozen or more fans. A few towers and hobbyist-oriented cases have supplemental fans as standard features, but most cases do not.

Construction quality

Cases run the gamut in construction quality. Cheap cases have flimsy frames, thin sheet metal, holes that don't line up, and razor-sharp burrs and edges that make them dangerous to work on. High-quality cases—such as those from PC Power & Cooling and Antec—have rigid frames, heavy sheet metal, properly aligned holes, and all edges rolled or deburred. One seldom-noticed specification is weight, which is largely determined by the thickness of the frame and panels, and can provide a good clue to case quality. Without power supply, for example, the PC Power & Cooling Personal Mid-Tower weighs 18 pounds (8.2 kg) and the similar Antec KS-288 weighs 23 pounds (10.5 kg). We have seen no-name cases of similar size that weigh as little as 12 pounds (5.5 kg). For cases, heavier is usually better.

Material

PC cases have traditionally been made of thin-sheet steel panels, with a rigid steel chassis to prevent flexing. Steel is inexpensive, durable, and strong, but it is also heavy. In the last few years, the popularity of "LAN parties" has increased, fueling a demand for lighter cases. A steel case light enough to be conveniently portable is insufficiently stiff, which has led case makers to produce aluminum cases for this specialty market. Although aluminum cases are indeed lighter than equivalent steel models, they are also much more expensive. For example, the steel PC Power & Cooling Personal Mid-Tower case weighs 18 pounds and sells for $49. The PC Power & Cooling Aluminum Mid-Tower case weighs 14 pounds and sells for $179. Such extreme price disparities are common for aluminum models, and "economy" aluminum models are so flimsy that they are not worth having. Unless saving a few pounds is a very high priority, we recommend you avoid aluminum models. Some specialty cases are made from such unusual materials as transparent plastic or wood. We suggest you avoid all such gimmick cases, and stick with a steel model from a good manufacturer such as PC Power & Cooling or Antec.

Choosing a Case

Use the following guidelines when choosing a case:

Choose the correct form factor

If you are migrating an existing motherboard, buy a case to fit that motherboard. If you are building a new system, buy a case that accepts full ATX motherboards, even if you're installing a Mini-ATX or microATX motherboard. A full-ATX case allows upgrading later to a full-ATX motherboard, and provides more working space even if the system will never have anything larger than a microATX motherboard installed.

Using a small motherboard (or one with poorly placed ATA connectors) in a full- or mid-tower case may require drive cables longer than the PATA maximum of 18 inches. Using ATA cables longer than 18 inches may corrupt data, particularly with Ultra-ATA hard drives. If an 18-inch cable is too short to reach a hard drive mounted in one of the top bays, you may be able to mount the drive in an internal bay that permits using the 18-inch cable. If not, consider substituting a SATA hard drive, which can use a 39-inch cable. Optical drives operate at lower data rates than Ultra-DMA hard drives, so there is less chance that data will be corrupted by a longer cable. Although we cannot recommend using P-ATA cables longer than 18 inches because they do not comply with the ATA specification, we have often used 24-inch cables for optical drives without experiencing data integrity problems.

Plan for expansion

Choose a case that leaves at least one or two bays—ideally 5.25-inch external bays—free for later expansion. As the price of tape drives, DVD-ROM drives, and CD/DVD burners continues to fall, you're likely to want to install one or more of them in the future. That's impossible without free drive bays. A mini/mid-tower case with three external 5.25-inchbays, two external 3.5-inch bays, and perhaps one or two internal 3.5-inch bays is usually the best compromise between size, cost, and available bays, although a full tower may be the best choice if your current configuration fills or nearly fills a mid-tower. Some cases can be ordered with two or three optional internal 3.5-inch bays for very little additional cost, typically $5 to $8. If in doubt, always buy the next size up.

Avoid cheap cases

It's always tempting to save money, but cases are one place where it's easy to spend too little. The cheapest cases ($30 or $40 with power supply) are often unusable due to misaligned holes and so on. Even midrange "name-brand" cases often have razor-sharp edges and burrs, which can cut you and short out wires. Expect to pay at least $35 (without power supply) for a decent mini/mid-tower case and $50 to $60 for a full tower. Paying 50% more than that usually gets you a much better case.

Buy case and power supply separately, if necessary

Many cheap and midrange cases include a "throw-away" power supply that's of poor quality and undersized. If you have such a case, do yourself a favor: discard the bundled power supply and install one of the power supplies we recommend in Chapter 26. At best, cheap power supplies cause reliability problems. At worst, we have seen cheap power supplies fail catastrophically, taking the motherboard and other system components with them. Better cases may be available with or without a power supply. If the standard power supply is appropriate, you may save a few bucks by buying the bundle. Otherwise, buy only the case and install a high-quality power supply sized appropriately for your needs. Standard power supplies fit standard cases interchangeably, so compatibility is not an issue.

Add supplemental cooling fans

Heat is the enemy of processors, memory, drives, and other system components. Cooler components last longer and run more reliably. A processor run at 50° C (122° F), for example, will last only half as long as one run at 40° C (104° F), but twice as long as one run at 60° C (140° F). The best way to minimize temperature inside the case is to move a lot of air through it. Although the power supply fan and processor fan may provide adequate cooling on lightly loaded systems, adding supplemental fans can reduce ambient case temperature by 20° C (36° F) or more on more heavily loaded systems. Many cases can be ordered with optional supplemental fans. If the case you order offers optional fans, order them. Otherwise, add the fans yourself. You can purchase supplemental fans for a few dollars from local computer stores and mail-order suppliers. They are available in various standard sizes from 60 mm to 120 mm, so make sure to purchase the correct size. Note that many cases that accept multiple fans use different sizes in different locations.

 Make sure supplemental fans blow the right way, including those that arrive installed in a case. Some power supplies have intake fans, and others have exhaust fans. The ATX specification recommends but does not require using an intake fan on the power supply. Many (including us) prefer power supplies that use exhaust fans, and many manufacturers now supply exhaust fans on ATX power supplies.

The danger arises when the power supply fan and supplemental fan(s) blow in the same direction in a tightly sealed case. When that happens, the fans work against each other, either pressurizing the case or creating a partial vacuum. In either event, airflow is reduced or eliminated, which causes the processor and other system components to overheat. Although most cases have enough vent holes and other gaps to prevent this from becoming a problem, we still generally attempt to "balance" airflow by configuring half the fans for intake and half for exhaust.

Supplemental fans can be mounted to blow in either direction. If your power supply uses an exhaust fan, configure supplemental fan(s) as intake fans. If your power supply uses an intake fan, configure supplemental fan(s) as exhaust fans. On a related issue, if your fans have foam air filters installed, check them periodically. Filters clog rapidly under dusty conditions, and a fan with a clogged filter is no better than no fan at all.

Consider accessibility

If you frequently add and remove components, consider purchasing a case with accessibility features such as a removable motherboard tray and drive bays. If you don't open your case from one month to the next, you may be better served by a case with fewer accessibility features, which is likely to be less expensive for equivalent quality and rigidity.

Cases

Consider shipping costs

When you compare case prices, remember that the cost to ship a case can be substantial. Cases you find at local stores already have that factored in. Mail-order companies may charge $20 to $40 to ship a case, or even more for heavy full-tower cases.

Our Picks

Although we certainly haven't used every case available, we have used a lot of them over the past 20 years. For our detailed current recommendations by brand name and model number, visit: *http://www.hardwareguys.com/picks/cases.html*.

26

Power Supplies

Power supplies lack glamour, so nearly everyone takes them for granted. That's a big mistake because the power supply performs two critical functions: it provides regulated power to every system component, and it cools the computer. Many people who complain that Windows crashes frequently understandably blame Microsoft. But, without apologizing for Microsoft, the truth is that many such crashes are caused by low-quality or overloaded power supplies.

If you want a reliable, crash-proof system, use a high-quality power supply. In fact, we have found that using a high-quality power supply allows even marginal motherboards, processors, and memory to operate with reasonable stability, whereas using a cheap power supply makes even top-notch components unstable.

The sad truth is that it is almost impossible to buy a computer with a top-notch power supply. Computer makers count pennies, literally. Good power supplies don't win marketing brownie points, so few manufacturers are willing to spend $30 to $75 extra for a better power supply. For their premium lines, first- and second-tier manufacturers generally use what we call midrange power supplies, better than the Pacific Rim junk used by some garage shops and low-end assemblers, but not nearly as good as what you can get on the aftermarket. For their mass-market lines—such as those sold at Circuit City, Best Buy, and Target— even name-brand manufacturers may compromise on the power supply to meet a price point, using what we consider marginal power supplies both in terms of output and construction quality.

This chapter details what you need to understand to choose a good power supply.

Power Supply Characteristics

Here are the important characteristics of power supplies:

Form factor
As with cases, the primary characteristic of a power supply is its form factor, which specifies dimensions and mounting hole locations, which in turn determine which case form factor(s) the power supply fits. Form factor also specifies the type of motherboard power connectors the power supply provides, which in turn determines the type(s) of motherboards the power supply supports. Table 26-1 lists compatibility of power supplies with cases.

Table 26-1. Power supply compatibility with case form factors

Case form factor	Accepts these power supply(s)								
	D/AT	T/AT	D/BAT	T/BAT	LPX	ATX	SFX	NLX	WTX
Desktop/AT (D/AT)	●	○	●	○	○	○	○	○	○
Tower/AT (T/AT)	○	●	○	●	○	○	○	○	○
Desktop/BAT (D/BAT)	○	○	●	○	○	○	○	○	○
Tower/BAT (T/BAT)	○	○	○	●	○	○	○	○	○
LPX	○	○	○	○	●	○	○	○	○
ATX	○	○	○	○	○	●	●	○	○
Mini-ATX	○	○	○	○	○	●	●	○	○
microATX	○	○	○	○	○	○	●	○	○
FlexATX	○	○	○	○	○	○	●	○	○
NLX	○	○	○	○	○	○	○	●	○
WTX	○	○	○	○	○	○	○	○	●

> AT-variant case/power supply issues are confusing because of the lack of standards. For example, many current BAT *desktop* cases use *Tower*/BAT power supplies *instead of* Desktop/BAT power supplies! See the preceding chapter for details on AT-variant cases.

Rated wattage
This is the nominal wattage that the power supply can deliver. Nominal wattage is a composite figure, determined by multiplying the amperages available at each of the several voltages supplied by a PC power supply by those voltages. Nominal wattage is mainly useful for general comparison of power supplies. What really matters are the individual wattages available at different voltages, and those vary significantly between nominally similar power supplies, as detailed later in this chapter.

Wattage ratings are meaningless unless they specify the temperature at which the rating was done. As temperature increases, the output capacity of a power supply decreases. For example, PC Power & Cooling rates wattage at 40° C, which is a realistic temperature for an operating power supply. Most power supplies are rated at only 25° C. That difference may seem minor, but a power supply rated at 450W at 25° C may deliver only 300W at 40° C. Voltage regulation may also suffer as temperature increases, which means that a power supply that nominally meets ATX voltage regulation specifications at 25° C may be well outside specifications during normal operation at 40° C or thereabouts.

Nominal voltage

Nearly all PC power supplies can use either 110/115V or 220/230V nominal. Some detect input voltage and adjust themselves automatically. Many, however, must be set manually for 110V or 220V, usually via a red sliding switch on the rear panel. Be very careful if your power supply is not autosensing. If the switch is set for 220V and you connect it to a 110V receptacle, no damage is done, although the system will not boot. But if the power supply is set for 110V and you connect it to a 220V receptacle, catastrophic damage to your motherboard and other system components is likely to occur.

Operating voltage range

This is the highest and lowest AC voltages that the power supply can accept while continuing to supply DC output voltages and currents within specifications. Typical high-quality power supplies function properly if the input voltage is within about 20% of the center of the range—i.e., 90V to 135V when set for nominal 110/115V input, and 180V to 270V when set for 220/230V nominal. Less-expensive, but still name-brand, power supplies may have a range of only about 10%—i.e., 100V to 125V when set for 110/115V nominal, or 200V to 250V when set for 220/230V nominal. Cheap, no-name power supplies often do not supply power to specification even when provided with nominal input voltages, if indeed they even list nominal output specifications. Having a broad operating voltage range is particularly important if you operate without a UPS or line conditioner to ensure that the voltage supplied to the power supply does not vary due to brownouts, sags, and surges. It is less important if you do have a line conditioner or line-interactive UPS, except as an indicator of overall quality of the power supply.

Input frequency range

This is the range of AC frequencies over which the power supply is designed to operate. Most power supplies function properly within the range of 47 Hz to 63 Hz, which is adequate for nominal 50 Hz or 60 Hz input. In practice, this means that the power supply will operate properly on any nominal 50 Hz input voltage so long as it does not drop below 47 Hz and any nominal 60 Hz input voltage so long as it does not rise above 63 Hz. This is seldom a problem, as utilities control the frequency of the power they supply very tightly. Inexpensive power supplies usually do not list input frequency range, although we have seen cheap Pacific Rim units that list their requirements as "50 Hz to 60 Hz AC," implying that they have no tolerance for frequency variations.

Efficiency

This is the ratio of output power to input power expressed as a percentage. For example, a power supply that produces 350W output but requires 500W input is 70% efficient. In general, a good power supply is 70% efficient. However, calculating this figure is difficult because PC power supplies are *switching power supplies* rather than *linear power supplies*. The easiest way to think about this is to imagine the switching power supply drawing high current for a fraction of the time it is running and no current the remainder of the time. The percentage of the time it draws current is called the *power factor*, which is typically 70% for PC power supplies. In other words, a 350W PC power supply actually requires 500W input 70% of the time and 0W 30% of the time. Combining power factor with efficiency yields some interesting numbers. The power supply supplies 350W, but the 70% power factor means that it requires 500W 70% of the time. However, the 70% efficiency means that rather than actually drawing 500W, it must draw more, in the ratio of 500W/0.7, or about 714W. If you examine the specifications plate for a 350W power supply, you may find that in order to supply 350W nominal, which is 350W/110V or about 3.18 amps, it must actually draw up to 714W/110V or about 6.5 amps. Other factors may increase that actual maximum amperage, so it's common to see 300W or 350W power supplies that actually draw as much as 8 or 10 amps maximum. That has planning implications, both for electrical circuits and for UPSs, which must be sized to accommodate the actual amperage draw rather than the rated output wattage.

Power factor is determined by dividing the true power (W) by the apparent power (Volts * Amps, or VA). Standard power supplies have power factors ranging from about 0.70 to 0.75. Some newer power supplies use active *power factor correction* (PFC), which increases the power factor to the 0.95 to 0.99 range, reducing peak current and harmonic current. In contrast to standard power supplies that alternate between drawing high current and no current, PFC power supplies draw moderate current all the time. Because electrical wiring, circuit breakers, transformers, and UPSs must be rated for maximum current draw rather than average current draw, using a PFC power supply reduces the stress on the electrical system to which the PFC power supply connects.

One of the chief differences between premium power supplies and less-expensive models is how well they are regulated. Ideally, a power supply accepts AC power, possibly noisy or outside specifications, and turns that AC power into smooth, stable DC power with no artifacts. In fact, no power supply meets the ideal, but good power supplies come much closer than cheap ones. Processors, memory, and other system components are designed to operate with pure, stable DC voltage. Any departure from that may reduce system stability and shorten component life. Here are the key regulation issues:

Ripple

A perfect power supply would accept the AC sine wave input and provide an utterly flat DC output. Real-world power supplies actually provide DC output with a small AC component superimposed upon it. That AC component is called *ripple*, and may be expressed as *peak-to-peak voltage* (p-p) in millivolts (mv) or as a percentage of the nominal output voltage. A high-quality power supply may have 1% ripple, which may be expressed as 1%, or as actual p-p voltage variation for each output voltage. For example, on a 5V output, a 1% ripple corresponds to 0.05V, usually expressed as 50mV. A midrange power supply may limit ripple to 1% on some output voltages, but soar as high as 2.5% on others, typically –5V, +3.3V, and +5V$_{SB}$. We have seen cheap power supplies with ripple of 10% or more, which makes running a PC a crapshoot. Low ripple is most important on +5V and +3.3V outputs, although 1.5% or lower ripple is desirable on all outputs.

Load regulation

The load on a PC power supply can vary significantly during routine operations—for example, as a DVD burner's laser kicks in or a DVD-ROM drive spins up and spins down. *Load regulation* expresses the ability of the power supply to supply nominal output power at each voltage as the load varies from maximum to minimum, expressed as the variation in voltage experienced during the load change, either as a percentage or in p-p voltage differences. A power supply with tight load regulation delivers near-nominal voltage on all outputs regardless of load (within its range, of course). A high-quality power supply regulates +3.3V to within 1%, and the 5V and 12V outputs to within 5% or less. A midrange power supply might regulate +3.3V to within 3% or 4%, and the other voltages to within 5% or 10%. Regulation of +3.3V is critical and should never exceed 4%, although many inexpensive power supplies allow it to vary 5% or even more.

 Load regulation on the +12V rail has become more important since Intel shipped the Pentium 4. In the past, +12V was used primarily to run drive motors. With the Pentium 4, Intel began using 12V VRMs on its motherboards to supply the higher currents that Pentium 4 processors require. ATX12V-compliant power supplies, typically advertised as "P4-compliant" or "P4-compatible," are designed with this requirement in mind. Older and/or inexpensive ATX power supplies, although they may be rated for sufficient amperage on the +12V rail to support a Pentium 4 motherboard, may not have adequate regulation to do so properly.

Line regulation

An ideal power supply would provide nominal output voltages while being fed any input AC voltage within its range. Real-world power supplies allow the DC output voltages to vary slightly as the AC input voltage changes. Just as load regulation describes the effect of internal loading, *line regulation* can be thought of as describing the effects of external loading—e.g., a sudden sag in delivered AC line voltage as an elevator motor kicks in. Line regulation is measured by holding all other variables constant and measuring the DC output voltages as the AC input voltage is varied across the input range. A power supply with tight line regulation delivers output voltages within specification as the input varies from maximum to minimum allowable. Line regulation is expressed in the same way as load regulation, and the acceptable percentages are the same.

Transient response

If the load on the power supply varies momentarily from the baseline and then returns to baseline, it takes a certain period for the output voltages to return to nominal. *Transient response* is characterized in three ways, all of which are interrelated: by the percent load change, by the amount of time required for output voltages to return to within a specified percentage of nominal, and by what that percentage is. These figures are difficult to compare because different manufacturers use different parameters that are not directly comparable. For example, a high-quality power supply may state that after an instantaneous 50% load change, the power supply requires 1 millisecond (ms) to return to within 1% of nominal on all outputs. A midrange power supply may specify the load change as only 20% and state that the 5V and 12V outputs return to within 5% of nominal within 1 ms. If the load change were 50% instead of 20%, that same midrange power supply might require 2 or 3 ms to return to within 5% of nominal and 10 ms to return to 1% of nominal (if in fact it could control voltages to within 1% under normal conditions, which it probably couldn't). In general, a power supply with excellent transient response will specify (a) a load change of 50% or thereabouts, (b) a return to at or near its standard regulation range, and (c) a time of 1 or 2 ms. A decrease in the first figure or an increase in either or both of the second two is indicative of relatively poorer transient response. The major benefit of good transient response is increased reliability in disk operations, both read and write. A power supply with poor transient response may cause frequent disk retries, which are visible to the user only as degraded disk performance. Many users who upgrade to a better power supply are surprised to find that their disk drives run faster. Hard to believe, but true.

Hold-up time

This is the period for which, during a loss of input power, the power supply continues to provide output voltages within specification. Hold-up time may be specified in ms or in cycles, where one cycle is 1/60 second, or about 16.7 ms. High-quality power supplies have hold-up times of 20 ms or higher (> 1.25 cycles). Lower-quality power supplies often have hold-up times of 10 ms or less, sometimes much less. There are two issues here. First, if you are running a standby power supply (commonly, if errone-ously, called a UPS) that has a switchover time, hold-up keeps the PC running until the UPS has time to kick in. This is less a problem with modern SPSs/UPSs, which commonly have transfer times of ~1 ms, compared to the 5 ms to 10 ms transfer times common with UPSs a few years ago. Hold-up time is even more important if you are not using a UPS because about 99% of all power outages are of one cycle or less, many so short that you aren't even aware they occurred because the lights don't have time to flicker. With such outages, a power supply with a long hold-up time will allow the PC to continue running normally, while one with a short hold-up time will cause the PC to lock up for no apparent reason. The first comment most people make who do not have a UPS and upgrade to a better power supply is that their systems don't lock up nearly as often. That's why.

Power Good signal

A power supply requires time to stabilize when power is first applied to it. When it stabilizes, the power supply asserts the Power Good (AT) or PWR_OK (ATX) signal to inform the motherboard that suitable power is now available, and continues to assert that signal so long as suitable power remains available. The time a power supply requires before asserting Power Good varies between models, between examples of the same model, and even between boots with the same power supply. Some motherboards are sensitive to Power Good timing, and may refuse entirely to boot or experience sporadic boot failures when used with a power supply that has lengthy or unpredictable Power Good timing. A superior power supply may raise Power Good within 300 ms plus or minus a few ms of receiving power. A midrange power supply may require from 100 to 500 ms before asserting Power Good. Another aspect of Power Good that is seldom specified is how long the power supply continues to supply good power after dropping the Power Good signal. A good power supply should continue to provide clean power for at least one ms after deasserting Power Good.

Noise and fan airflow rating

The power supply fan produces airflow that cools both the power supply itself and other PC components such as processors and drives. In general, doubling the airflow reduces system operating temperature by about 50%, which in turn increases the life of system components. The old chem lab rule says that increasing the temperature by 10° C (18° F) doubles the rate of reaction, and reducing it by 10° C halves the rate. That ratio holds roughly true for component life as well. A processor with a design operating temperature of 50° C, for example, will last twice as long if run at 40° C. But in the process of moving air, the fan generates noise. The amount and nature of that noise depend upon the number, design, size, pitch, and rotation speed of the fan blades; the size, design, and bearing type of the hub; the internal layout of power supply components; the depth and configuration of the venturi (air path); and other factors. In general, high cooling-efficiency power supplies are noisier than those that move less air, and power supplies that use sleeve bearings are quieter (albeit less durable) than those that use ball bearings. Noise is measured on the logarithmic dB(A) scale at a distance of 1 meter from the fan. On the dB(A) scale, each 3 dB change indicates a doubling or halving of sound energy. A very quiet power supply may be rated at 34 to 36 dB(A), which is almost inaudible in a typical work environment, and provide 20 to 30 cubic-feet-per-minute (CFM) airflow. A typical power supply may generate 40 to 44 dB(A), which is audible but not overly intrusive in most work environments, and provide 25 to 35 CFM. A high-performance power supply may generate 44 to 48 dB(A), which is distinctly noticeable, and provide 35 to 50 CFM.

Mean Time Between Failures (MTBF)

MTBF is a much-misunderstood way of specifying component reliability. MTBF for power supplies is a projected estimate based on a combination of operating data and calculated data as specified in MIL-HDBK-217. The MTBF projected failure curve for a particular model of power supply takes the form of a skewed bell curve, with a few power supplies of that model failing very early, the vast majority failing from a year to a few years out, and (at least in theory) a tiny number surviving for decades, with that number trailing off as time passes to almost (but never quite) zero. A good power supply has an MTBF of approximately 30,000 to 100,000 hours; a midrange power supply may have an MTBF of perhaps 15,000 to 35,000 hours; and a cheap power supply may have an MTBF of 10,000 hours or less. A 100,000-hour MTBF does not mean, however, that you can expect your power supply to last 100,000 hours, nor does it mean that that unit is "twice as reliable" as a unit with a 50,000-hour MTBF. Use MTBF only as a rough basis for comparison. It is safe to say that a unit with a 100,000-hour MTBF is probably more reliable than a unit with a 50,000-hour MTBF, which in turn is probably more reliable than a unit with a 10,000-hour MTBF, but don't attribute much more to it than that.

Another important characteristic of power supplies is the emissions and safety standards with which they comply. This information is useful both as it pertains specifically to the item being regulated and generally in the sense that power supplies that meet more and/or tighter regulatory approvals tend to be better built and more reliable.

Overvoltage protection, overcurrent protection, and leakage current

Properly designed power supplies include *overvoltage protection* circuitry that shuts down the power supply if output voltage exceeds specified limits, and *overcurrent protection* circuitry that protects the power supply (and the PC) from excessive current. At minimum, overvoltage protection should be provided for +3.3V (if present) and +5V and should cause the power supply to trip to reset if either of these voltages exceed nominal by 25% or more. Better power supplies also provide similar protection for +12V. Overcurrent protection should prevent any level of overcurrent, including a dead short, from damaging the power supply or PC. A good power supply might provide latching protection (a level-sensitive cutout) for +3.3V at 60 Amperes (A), +5V at 50A, and +12V at 20A. *Leakage current* specifies the maximum current that can leak to ground during normal operation, and should be less than one milliampere (ma) at 220/240V.

Emissions approvals

Electromagnetic interference (*EMI*) is noise generated by the switching action of the power supply, and comes in two varieties. *Conducted interference* is noise of any frequency that the power supply places on the AC source line. Conducted interference may cause problems for other devices connected to the same circuit, and is controlled by means of capacitive and/or inductive line filters to isolate the power supply from the AC source. *Radiated interference* is *radio frequency interference* (*RFI*) that may affect nearby electronic devices even if they are not connected to the same AC circuit (or any AC circuit at all). Radiated interference is controlled by physical shielding of the power supply, both by the power supply enclosure itself and by the shielding provided by the PC chassis. Both types of interference are regulated in the U.S. by the Federal Communications Commission (FCC), and in other countries by various regulatory agencies. A power supply should have FCC Class B approval (and/or the roughly equivalent CISPR22), although many inexpensive units have only the less-restrictive FCC Class A.

Safety approvals

Various safety standards are promulgated by standards organizations in the U.S. and elsewhere. Any power supply you use should have at least UL certification (UL 1950). Other standards to look for include: CSA Std. C22.2, TUV EN60950, IEC950, KS, SEMKO, NEMKO, DEMKO, SETI, and CCIB.

Volts, Amps, Watts, and Regulation

Power supplies are rated in watts, but that cumulative figure doesn't tell the real story. Watts (W) is calculated by multiplying Volts (V) and Amperes (A). A power supply must provide specific amperages (or currents) at numerous voltages—how many and which depend on the type of power supply. All PC power supplies provide at least +5VDC, +12VDC, and –12VDC. Some power supplies also provide +3.3VDC, –5VDC, and/or $5V_{SB}$.

Another important aspect of voltage—one that varies greatly between power supplies—is *regulation*, which specifies how tightly voltages are controlled. For example, a memory module that expects +3.3V may work at +3.2V or +3.4V, but will probably not work at +3.1V or +3.5V. Regulation may be specified as a maximum percentage variation or as a maximum variation in absolute voltage.

No standards body produced a formal specification for all aspects of the AT power supply or its BAT and LPX variants. However, the ATX power supply—along with its variants, the NLX and SFX power supplies—is completely defined in a group of documents, many of which are referenced in the following descriptions, and can be downloaded from *http://www.formfactors.org/developer/powersupply.htm*.

ATX/ATX12V Power Supply Specifications

ATX Specification Version 2.1 and associated documents define the ATX voltage rails and tolerances shown in Table 26-2. An ATX 2.1-compliant power supply must provide these voltages at these tolerances or better. High-quality power supplies provide tighter tolerances, sometimes much tighter, such as 1% across all positive voltages. Cheap power supplies often do not meet the required tolerances for one or more voltages, and are therefore technically not ATX power supplies. However, they look like ATX power supplies, quack like ATX power supplies, and are sold as ATX power supplies. Avoid any power supply that does not meet the following standard. V_{min} and V_{max} are calculated values, provided for the convenience of those testing power supplies with a DMM.

Table 26-2. ATX Specification Version 2.1 voltage rails and tolerances

Voltage Rail	Tolerance	V_{min}	V_{nom}	V_{max}
+3.3VDC	4%	+3.168V	+3.300V	+3.432V
+5VDC	5%	+4.750V	+5.000V	+5.250V
-5VDC	10%	-4.500V	-5.000V	-5.500V
+5V_{SB}	5%	+4.750V	+5.000V	+5.250V
+12VDC	5%	+11.400V	+12.000V	+12.600V
+12VDC (peak load)	10%	+10.800V	+12.000V	+13.200V
-12VDC	10%	-10.800V	-12.000V	-13.200V

The *ATX/ATX12V Power Supply Design Guide Version 1.2* defines two distinct types of power supply, the ATX power supply and the ATX12V power supply. An ATX12V power supply is a superset of an ATX power supply, and is backward-compatible with an ATX unit. ATX power supplies support motherboards that use +5VDC or +3.3VDC voltage regulator modules (VRMs). ATX12V power supplies support motherboards that use +5VDC, +3.3VDC, or +12VDC VRMs. The sole advantage of ATX relative to ATX12V is that ATX power supplies cost a bit less to produce, but that advantage is sufficient to ensure that the standard ATX power supply definition will be maintained in parallel with ATX12V. Standard ATX power supplies will continue to be produced for use in high-volume, low-end applications.

For ATX power supplies, the *ATX/ATX12V Power Supply Design Guide Version 1.2* recommends (but does not require) the power distribution levels listed in Table 26-3. A_{min} specifies the highest minimum amperage load the power supply should require to function. A_{max} specifies the lowest maximum amperages the power supply should provide continuously. A_{peak} describes startup surge current required to spin up disk drives. The 250W and 300W units include the ATX Auxiliary Power Supply Connector, and may or may not include the ATX Optional Power Supply Connector, both of which are described later in this chapter.

Table 26-3. Recommended power distribution for ATX power supplies

Voltage rail	160W ATX			200W ATX			250W ATX			300W ATX		
	A_{min}	A_{max}	A_{peak}	A_{min}	A_{max}	A_{peak}	A_{min}	A_{max}	A_{peak}	A_{min}	A_{max}	A_{peak}
+3.3VDC	0.3	14.0		0.3	14.0		0.3	16.0		0.3	20.0	
+5VDC	1.0	18.0		0.3	21.0		0.3	25.0		0.3	30.0	
-5VDC	0.0	0.3		0.0	0.3		0.0	0.3		0.0	0.3	
+5VSB	0.0	1.5	2.5	0.0	1.5	2.5	0.0	1.5	2.5	0.0	1.5	2.5
+12VDC	0.0	6.0	8.0	0.0	8.0	10.0	0.0	10.0	12.0	0.0	12.0	14.0
-12VDC	0.0	0.8		0.0	0.8		0.0	0.8		0.0	0.8	

The ATX12V power supply definition is a superset of the ATX power supply definition. An ATX12V power supply comprises an ATX power supply with the following changes:

Enhanced +12VDC output
ATX systems use +12V primarily for running drive motors, which do not require critical voltage regulation. The higher power requirements of fast modern processors have mandated a shift from 3.3V and 5V VRMs to 12V VRMs. Because such systems use +12V to power the processor, they require a power supply that provides higher current on the +12V voltage rail and that also addresses such issues as cable voltage drops, capacitive loading, cross-regulation, transient surge tolerance, and cooling. ATX12V power supplies meet these additional +12V requirements.

Additional power connector
ATX12V defines a new 4-pin power connector, described later in this chapter, that supports delivery of additional +12V current. The presence of this connector indicates that a power supply is an ATX12V unit. The absence of this connector indicates that a power supply is an ATX unit.

Removal of -5VDC requirement

Legacy support of ISA slots is the only reason for the presence of the -5VDC rail. The ATX specification requires the -5VDC rail, but the ATX12V specification omits it. Technically, that means an ATX12V-compliant power supply may not function with some older motherboards, but in practical terms most ATX12 power supplies provide the -5VDC rail.

ATX12V power supplies include additional 2X2 +12V and Aux power connectors and are intended for use with motherboards that require more than the 6A per contact supported by the ATX main power connector. For ATX12V power supplies, the *ATX/ATX12V Power Supply Design Guide Version 1.2* recommends (but does not require) the power distribution levels listed in Table 26-4. Although ATX12V does not specify -5VDC current requirements, most real-world ATX12V power supplies provide the minimum -5VDC current listed in Table 26-3. For more information about ATX12V, see *http://www.formfactors.org/developer/specs/atx/atx12vPSDGV1.pdf*.

Table 26-4. Recommended power distribution for ATX12V power supplies

Voltage rail	200W ATX12V			250W ATX12V			300W ATX12V		
	A_{min}	A_{max}	A_{peak}	A_{min}	A_{max}	A_{peak}	A_{min}	A_{max}	A_{peak}
+3.3VDC	0.3	14.0		0.3	20.0		0.3	28.0	
+5VDC	0.3	21.0		0.3	25.0		0.3	30.0	
+5V$_{SB}$	0.0	1.5	2.5	0.0	1.5	2.5	0.0	2.0	2.5
+12VDC	0.0	10.0	12.0	0.0	13.0	16.0	0.0	15.0	18.0
-12VDC	0.0	0.8		0.0	0.8		0.0	0.8	

NLX Power Supply Specifications

NLX Power Supply Recommendations Version 1.1 defines the NLX voltage rails and tolerances shown in Table 26-5. An NLX 1.1-compliant power supply must provide these voltages at these tolerances or better. Note that NLX has tighter requirements than ATX on some rails. This document also recommends (but does not require) the power distribution levels listed for a typical 145W sustained (160W peak) power supply. A_{min}, A_{max}, and A_{peak} are as described earlier. NLX power supplies may or may not include the NLX Optional Power Supply Connector described later in this section.

Table 26-5. NLX power supply voltage rails, tolerances, and power distribution

Voltage rail	Tolerance	V_{min}	V_{nom}	V_{max}	A_{min}	A_{max}	A_{peak}
+3.3VDC	4%	+3.168V	+3.300V	+3.432V	0.3	9.2	16.0
+5VDC	5%	+4.750V	+5.000V	+5.250V	1.0	16.0	18.0
-5VDC	5%	-4.750V	-5.000V	-5.250V	0.0	0.1	
+5V$_{SB}$	5%	+4.750V	+5.000V	+5.250V	0.0	0.72	
+12VDC	5%	+11.400V	+12.000V	+12.600V	0.0	1.4	4.0
-12VDC	5%	-10.800V	-12.000V	-13.200V	0.0	0.2	

Power
Supplies

For more information about NLX power supplies, see *http://www.formfactors.org/developer/specs/nlx/nlxps11.pdf.*

SFX/SFX12V Power Supply Specifications

Although it is derived from the ATX/ATX12V and NLX specifications, SFX/SFX12V makes compromises to permit lower-cost power supplies that meet the needs of inexpensive systems. SFX systems are designed to be low-cost, and the SFX specification reflects this with less-stringent requirements than the ATX and NLX specifications.

First-generation SFX 1.1 power supplies were designed to provide 90W maximum continuous power, with peak power of 135W for 15-second durations on a 5-minute duty cycle. Current SFX 2.1 power supplies provide higher currents to support the Pentium 4 and other power-hungry processors. The *SFX Power Supply Design Guide Version 2.1* defines the SFX voltage rails and tolerances shown in Table 26-6. An SFX 2.1-compliant power supply must provide these voltages with these tolerances or better.

Table 26-6. SFX/SFX12V power supply voltage rails and tolerances

Voltage rail	Tolerance	V_{min}	V_{nom}	V_{max}
+3.3VDC	5%	+3.14V	+3.30V	+3.47V
+5VDC	5%	+4.75V	+5.00V	+5.25V
+5V_{SB}	5%	+4.75V	+5.00V	5.25V
+12VDC	5%	+11.40V	+12.00V	+12.60V
+12VDC (peak load)	10%	+10.80V	+12.00V	+13.20V
-12VDC	10%	-10.80V	-12.00V	-13.20V

The *SFX Power Supply Design Guide Version 1.1* defined only one wattage for an SFX power supply. The *SFX Power Supply Design Guide Version 2.1* defines three SFX configurations, shown in Table 26-7.

Table 26-7. Typical power distribution for SFX power supplies

Voltage rail	90W SFX			120W SFX			150W SFX		
	A_{min}	A_{max}	A_{peak}	A_{min}	A_{max}	A_{peak}	A_{min}	A_{max}	A_{peak}
+3.3VDC	0.3	6.0		0.3	6.0		0.3	12.0	
+5VDC	1.0	11.0		1.0	12.0		1.0	14.0	
+5V_{SB}	0.0	1.0	1.5	0.0	1.0	2.0	0.0	1.5	2.0
+12VDC	0.0	1.5	4.8	0.2	3.0	6.0	0.2	5.0	8.0
-12VDC	0.0	0.2		0.0	0.2		0.0	0.3	

The *SFX Power Supply Design Guide Version 2.1* defines two SFX12V configurations, shown in Table 26-8. For both SFX12V power supplies, the combined output of the +3.3VDC and +5VDC rails is less than 61W.

Table 26-8. Typical power distribution for SFX12V power supplies

Voltage rail	160W SFX12V			180W SFX12V		
	A_{min}	A_{max}	A_{peak}	A_{min}	A_{max}	A_{peak}
+3.3VDC	0.5	16.7		0.5	16.7	
+5VDC	1.0	12.0		1.0	12.0	
+5V$_{SB}$	0.0	1.5	2.0	0.0	1.5	2.0
+12VDC	2.0	8.0	10.0	2.0	10.0	13.0
-12VDC	0.0	0.3		0.0	0.3	

For more information about SFX and SFX12V power supplies, see *http://www.formfactors.org/developer/specs/sfx/sfx12v2_1.pdf*.

TFX12V Power Supply Specifications

TFX12V is the newest standard power supply form factor. Like SFX/SFX12V, TFX12V is derived from ATX/ATX12V. TFX12V power supplies have a long, narrow physical shape that is optimized for small and low-profile microATX and FlexATX systems. TFX12V has an improved airflow design that allows the power supply fan to exhaust air from the area of the motherboard occupied by the processor, chipset, and other heat-generating components. TFX12V also uses fan speed control and other techniques for reduced noise relative to other power supply types. The *TFX12V Power Supply Design Guide Version 1.01* defines the TFX12V voltage rails and tolerances shown in Table 26-9. A TFX12V 1.01-compliant power supply must provide these voltages with these tolerances or better.

Table 26-9. TFX12V power supply voltage rails and tolerances

Voltage rail	Tolerance	V_{min}	V_{nom}	V_{max}
+3.3VDC	5%	+3.14V	+3.30V	+3.47V
+5VDC	5%	+4.75V	+5.00V	+5.25V
+5V$_{SB}$	5%	+4.75V	+5.00V	5.25V
+12VDC	5%	+11.40V	+12.00V	+12.60V
+12VDC (peak load)	10%	+10.80V	+12.00V	+13.20V
-12VDC	10%	-10.80V	-12.00V	-13.20V

The *TFX Power Supply Design Guide Version 1.01* defines two TFX12V configurations, shown in Table 26-10. For both TFX12V power supplies, the combined output of the +3.3VDC and +5VDC rails is less than 61W.

Table 26-10. Typical power distribution for TFX12V power supplies

Voltage rail	180W TFX12V			220W TFX12V		
	A_{min}	A_{max}	A_{peak}	A_{min}	A_{max}	A_{peak}
+3.3VDC	0.5	16.7		0.5	16.7	
+5VDC	0.3	12.0		0.3	12.0	

Table 26-10. Typical power distribution for TFX12V power supplies (continued)

| Voltage rail | 180W TFX12V | | | 220W TFX12V | | |
	A_{min}	A_{max}	A_{peak}	A_{min}	A_{max}	A_{peak}
$+5V_{SB}$	0.0	2.0	2.0	0.0	2.0	2.5
+12VDC	2.0	10.0	13.0	2.0	12.0	15.0
-12VDC	0.0	0.3		0.0	0.3	

For more information about TFX12V power supplies, see *http://www.formfactors. org/developer/specs/tfx12v/tfx12v_psdg_101.pdf*.

Power Connectors

All power supplies provide two types of power connectors. The first powers the motherboard and differs according to form factor. The second powers drives and other internal peripherals, and comes in two varieties, which are described in the following sections. Tower/AT and Tower/BAT power supplies include a third type of power connector—a high-voltage cable that connects the power supply to an external main power switch.

AT Main Power Connector

Table 26-11 lists the standard AT Main Power Connector pinouts used by all AT power supply variants, including Desktop/AT, Tower/AT, Desktop/BAT, Tower/ BAT, and LPX. PC/XT power supplies use the same pinouts, except that Pin P8-2 is unused. In addition to supplying various standard voltages, this connector includes a special-purpose pin. Pin P8-1, *PG*, carries the Power Good signal, which the power supply asserts once it has started and stabilized. The motherboard will not attempt to boot until the power supply asserts PG.

Table 26-11. Standard motherboard connector pinouts for an AT power supply

Pin	Color	Signal	Pin	Color	Signal
P8-1	orange (white)	PG	P9-1	black	ground
P8-2	red	+5V	P9-2	black	ground
P8-3	yellow	+12V	P9-3	white (blue)	-5V
P8-4	blue (brown)	-12V	P9-4	red	+5V
P8-5	black	ground	P9-5	red	+5V
P8-6	black	ground	P9-6	red	+5V

Note that P8 and P9 are separate connectors from the power supply, but mate to a combined connector on the motherboard.

 The P8 and P9 connectors are individually keyed, but it is possible to connect P8 from the power supply to the P9 connector on the motherboard and vice versa, with potentially catastrophic results.

P8 and P9 were IBM's original designation for these connectors. Not all power supplies or motherboards label these connectors, so you may have to determine which is P8 and which is P9 by examining wire colors. The colors shown are those most commonly used, but some AT power supplies use the alternative (ATX) color coding shown in parentheses. We have also seen AT power supplies that use completely nonstandard wire colors, such as green for ground wires.

When installing an AT power supply, the key factor is to ensure that, regardless of wire colors or connector labels, the connectors are aligned so as to place all four ground pins contiguously. It's safer still to examine the documents for the motherboard and power supply. We have seen a few proprietary motherboards and power supplies that used standard connectors but with completely nonstandard pinouts. This was clearly done to force customers to purchase replacement components from the original vendor, and is happily not something you're likely to encounter on any recent system.

ATX Main Power Connector

Table 26-12 lists the pinouts for the ATX Main Power Connector of an ATX or ATX12V power supply. This is a 2X10 connector with Pin 1 keyed. The motherboard connector is a Molex 39-29-9202 or equivalent. The power supply connector is a Molex 39-01-2200 or equivalent. All wires are 18 AWG, except Pin 11, which is specified as 22 AWG. For power supplies 300W or larger, the specification recommends using 16 AWG wires for +3.3VDC, +5VDC, and COM (ground). Note that wire colors are those recommended and commonly used, but may vary.

Table 26-12. ATX Main Power Connector configuration

Pin	Color	Signal	Pin	Color	Signal
1	orange	+3.3VDC	11	orange	3.3VDC
2	orange	+3.3VDC	12	blue	-12VDC
3	black	COM	13	black	COM
4	red	+5VDC	14	green	PS○ON
5	black	COM	15	black	COM
6	red	+5VDC	16	black	COM
7	black	COM	17	black	COM
8	gray	PW○OK	18	white	-5VDC
9	purple	5V$_{SB}$	19	red	5VDC
10	yellow	+12VDC	20	red	5VDC

In addition to supplying various standard voltages, this connector includes four special-purpose pins:

Pin 8 (PW_OK)
> PW_OK is the ATX equivalent of the AT Power Good signal, which the power supply asserts once it has stabilized. The motherboard will not attempt to boot until the power supply asserts PW_OK.

Pin 9 (5Vsb)

5V$_{sb}$ is the +5V standby circuit, which supplies +5V at low amperage to the motherboard even when the power supply is off. Any ATX power supply must provide at least 10 mA 5V$_{SB}$, but motherboards with the *Wake-on-LAN* (*WOL*) feature require 720 mA, which all ATX 2.1-compliant power supplies and most good ATX power supplies of earlier vintage also provide.

Pin 11 (Remote Sensing)

On the critical +3.3V rail, small loads can cause large percentage shifts in voltage. This pin provides a means for the power supply to detect the actual voltage present on the +3.3V rail at the main power connector and modify its output to compensate for up to 100 mV of drop due to cable, connectors, and PCB traces, thereby maintaining +3.3V within tolerance.

Pin 14 (PS_ON)

PS_ON is used by the motherboard to turn the power supply on and off.

 Dell has used nonstandard motherboards and power supplies since September 1998. Although recent Dell power supplies and motherboards use what looks like a standard ATX power connector, the pinouts are different.

Replacing a Dell power supply with a standard ATX power supply may destroy the motherboard and/or power supply as soon as you apply power to the system. Similarly, upgrading the motherboard in a Dell system with a standard ATX motherboard while continuing to use the standard Dell power supply destroys the motherboard and/or power supply as soon as you apply power to the system.

This situation is particularly insidious because Dell uses what appear to be standard components. For example, it buys Intel motherboards by the million, and those "Dell-version" motherboards resemble standard Intel motherboards in all respects except that the power supply connector is wired differently. For more information, see *http://www.hardwareguys.com/dellwarn.html*.

ATX/ATX12V Auxiliary Power Connector

The ATX/ATX12V Auxiliary Power Connector, shown in Table 26-13, is recommended for configurations that require more than 18A of +3.3VDC or more than 24A of +5VDC. This is an inline 6-pin connector with Pin 6 keyed. The motherboard connector is a Molex inline 6-pin 15-48-0412 header or equivalent. The power supply connector is a Molex 90331-0010 or equivalent. All wires are 16 AWG. Wire colors are standard. Few inexpensive power supplies provide this connector, but it is present on some better power supplies. With the shift to ATX12V and 12V VRMs, the importance of this connector is decreasing. Few motherboards include this connector.

Table 26-13. ATX Auxiliary Power Supply Connector

Pin	Color	Signal	Pin	Color	Signal
1	black	COM	4	orange	3.3V
2	black	COM	5	orange	3.3V
3	black	COM	6	red	5V

ATX Optional Power Supply Connector

In addition to the main and auxiliary power connectors, ATX 2.1 defines the ATX Optional Power Supply Connector, shown in Table 26-14. This connector is not required for ATX compliance, but provides various benefits, including fan monitoring and control, a remote 3.3V sense line (used to monitor and correct output on the 3.3VDC line), and a power source for IEEE-1394 (FireWire) devices. This is a 2X3 connector with Pin 1 keyed. The motherboard connector is a Molex 39-30-1060 or equivalent. The power supply connector is a Molex 39-01-2060 or equivalent. All wires are 22 AWG. Wire colors are standard. The first color indicates the base color, and the second the stripe color.

Table 26-14. ATX Optional Power Supply Connector

Pin	Color	Signal	Pin	Color	Signal
1	white	FanM	4	white/black	1394R
2	white/blue	FanC	5	white/red	1394V
3	white/brown	Sense	6	NC	Reserved

ATX Optional Power Supply Connector signals perform the following functions:

FanM

    FanM is a 2-pulse/revolution signal generated by the power supply fan that notifies the system of current fan speed. If this signal drops, the motherboard realizes immediately that the power supply fan has failed, and can shut down the system in an orderly manner.

FanC

    FanC is an optional signal generated by some motherboards to control fan speed for power supplies that are designed to allow this. The signal can range from 0VDC to +12VDC. A signal of +1V or less is recognized by the fan as an order to shut down, and a signal of +10.5V or more is recognized as an order to run at full speed. Intermediate voltage levels, which are supported by some motherboards and some fans, allow the system to instruct the fan to run at some intermediate speed. If this signal is left open (0VDC), properly designed fans run at full speed.

Sense

    This is a supplementary +3.3VDC remote sense line, which allows the power supply to monitor the actual voltage at the motherboard connector of the nominal +3.3VDC rail and adjust it to stay within specifications.

1394R

> *1394R* provides an isolated ground return path for the 1394V voltage rail, described next.

1394V

> *1394V* is a segregated voltage supply rail for powering IEEE-1394 devices. The voltage on this rail depends on the IEEE-1394 implementation, may range between +8VDC and +40VDC, and is typically unregulated. If implemented, this rail should deliver voltage only while PS_ON on the main connector is asserted low.

ATX12V Power Supply Connector

With the introduction of the Pentium 4 processor, Intel extended the ATX 2.03 specification to define a new type of power supply called *ATX12V*, which is a superset of ATX 2.03, and is now incorporated in the *ATX Specification 2.1* and the *ATX/ATX12V Power Supply Design Guide Version 1.2*. ATX12V power supplies include an additional 2X2 4-pin +12V power connector, shown in Table 26-15. The motherboard connector is a Molex 39-29-9042 or equivalent. The power supply connector is a Molex 39-01-2040 or equivalent. All wires are 20 AWG. Wire colors are standard. The purpose of this new connector is to deliver more +12V current to the motherboard than is available from the standard ATX main power connector. The presence of the 4-pin +12V connector indicates that a power supply is ATX12V. The absence of that connector indicates that it is a standard ATX power supply.

Table 26-15. ATX12V Power Supply Connector

Pin	Color	Signal	Pin	Color	Signal
1	black	COM	3	yellow	+12VDC
2	black	COM	4	yellow	+12VDC

According to Intel's policy, all Pentium 4 motherboards and all power supplies used with those motherboards must include the 4-pin +12V connector. Because installing such motherboards in existing systems may also require upgrading the power supply, some third-party motherboard makers have produced motherboards that lack the 4-pin +12V connector. This allows those motherboards to be installed in existing systems without a power supply upgrade, but we regard this as poor practice and suggest you avoid using such motherboards. In addition to the 4-pin +12V connector, ATX12V power supplies must also provide higher +5VDC standby voltage, required for systems that meet Intel's Instantly Available PC initiative.

If you already have a good high-capacity standard ATX 2.03 or higher power supply, you needn't replace it when you install a motherboard that requires ATX12V. Instead, buy an ATX12V adapter cable. These cables have a standard female drive power connector on one end and the 4-pin +12VDC connector on the other. We use the $8 PC Power & Cooling Pentium 4 12VATX Adapter, shown in Figure 26-1, for this purpose. Note, however, that many older or inexpensive ATX power supplies have inadequate amperage and/or very loose regulation on the +12V rail, and so may not be suitable for powering a Pentium 4 motherboard.

Figure 26-1. ATX12V adapter

The requirement for the new connector is due both to increased current draw by Pentium 4 processors and a shift in Intel's plans for future motherboards. Current ATX 2.03 or higher motherboards power components with DC/DC conversion from +5VDC and +3.3VDC sources. However, relative to +12VDC DC/DC conversion, +5VDC and +3.3VDC DC/DC conversion yields lower power transmission and conversion efficiencies. The change in emphasis to +12VDC DC/DC conversion provides increased efficiency and flexibility for forthcoming motherboards.

 Most but not all ATX12V-compliant power supplies are backward-compatible with ATX 2.03 or higher motherboards because they supply the same voltages and currents within the same specifications on the same rails as an ATX 2.03 or higher compliant power supply. However, some ATX12V power supplies do not provide the 3.3V rails required in the ATX 2.03 specification. Such power supplies are intended for special purposes, and cannot be used with standard ATX motherboards.

You can therefore use most ATX12V power supplies with any existing or future ATX-family motherboard, but you cannot use an old-style ATX 2.03 power supply with motherboards that have a 4-pin +12V connector, nor can you use an ATX12V power supply that lacks 3.3V rails with an ATX motherboard, regardless of whether that motherboard has the 4-pin +12VDC connector. For that reason, any new ATX power supply you buy should be an ATX 2.1 (ATX12V)-compliant unit that provides 3.3V rails, which will allow that power supply to be used with any modern motherboard.

NLX Power Connectors

The NLX Main Power Supply Connector uses the same pinouts, wire colors, and physical connectors as the ATX Main Power Supply Connector shown in Table 26-12. The NLX specification also defines the NLX Optional Power Supply Connector, shown in Table 26-16. This connector uses the same physical connectors and 22 AWG wire as the ATX Optional Power Supply Connector described in the preceding section, but uses different wire colors and a slightly different pinout. Wire colors are standard.

Table 26-16. NLX Optional Power Supply Connector

Pin	Color	Signal	Pin	Color	Signal
1	white	FanM	4	NC	Reserved
2	blue	FanC	5	grey	1394
3	brown	Sense	6	NC	Reserved

Pin 5 (1394) on this connector is analogous to Pin 5 (1394V) on the ATX connector, and also supplies voltage to unpowered 1394 devices. However, instead of using Pin 4 as a ground return path for 1394 voltage, this connector leaves Pin 4 unconnected. It appears unwise to share the main system ground return path with the ground return path for unregulated 1394 voltage from Pin 5, particularly with Pin 4 sitting there so obviously unused. If you understand the reason for this difference, please let us know.

SFX/SFX12V Power Connectors

The SFX Baseboard Connector uses the same pinouts, wire colors, and physical connectors as the ATX Main Power Supply Connector shown in Table 26-12, with one or two exceptions:

- Pin 9 ($+5V_{SB}$) is an optional signal for SFX power supplies. If present, it allows the motherboard to control the power supply, just as with ATX and NLX. If Pin 9 is not connected, the power supply must be controlled by a standard AC on/off switch.

- Pin 18 (-5VDC) is not connected on SFX power supplies because -5VDC is required only by ISA expansion slots, which are not supported by SFX systems.

SFX12V power supplies (but not SFX power supplies) also include the ATX12V connector described previously.

The SFX specification defines the required SFX Control Connector, shown in Table 26-17. This connector uses the same physical connectors and 22 AWG wire as the ATX and NLX Optional Power Supply Connectors described in the preceding sections, but has only one connection, FanON/OFF, which corresponds to FanC. Wire color is standard.

Table 26-17. SFX Control Connector

Pin	Color	Signal	Pin	Color	Signal
1	NC	Reserved	4	NC	Reserved
2	blue	FanON/OFF	5	NC	Reserved
3	NC	Reserved	6	NC	Reserved

TFX12V Power Connectors

The *TFX12V Main Power Connector* uses the same pinouts, wire colors and sizes, and physical connectors as the ATX Main Power Connector shown in Table 26-12, with one exception. Pin 18 (-5VDC) is not connected on TFX12V power supplies because -5VDC is required only by ISA expansion slots, which are not supported by TFX12V systems. TFX12V power supplies also include the ATX12V connector described previously.

Power-Supply-to-Device Connectors

Power supplies provide two types of connectors to power disk drives and other internal peripherals:

Peripheral Connector
> The *Peripheral Connector*, shown in Figure 26-2, is often called a *Molex Connector* by technicians. The cable uses a Molex PS-8981-04P or AMP 1-480424-0 connector or equivalent, and 18 AWG wires. Pin 1, at left as you view the connector face, carries +12V and uses a yellow wire. Pins 2 and 3 are COM (ground) and use black wires. Pin 4 is +5V and uses a red wire.

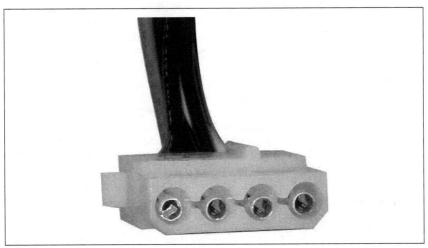

Figure 26-2. Peripheral Connector

Floppy Drive Connector
> The *Floppy Drive Connector*, shown in Figure 26-3, is often called a *Berg Connector*, and is also used by some other types of drives (5.25-inch floppy drives use the larger Molex connector also used by hard disks and other

drives). The cable uses an AMP 171822-4 connector or equivalent. The wires are 20 AWG. Pin 1, at left as you view the connector face, carries +5V and uses a red wire. Pins 2 and 3 are COM (ground) and use black wires. Pin 4 is +12V and uses a yellow wire.

Figure 26-3. Floppy Drive Connector

 Note that wire colors map to the same voltages on the Peripheral Connector and the Floppy Drive Connector, but the pinouts are exactly reversed. While building a home-made cable, we once toasted a drive by assuming the pinouts were identical, thereby putting +12V on a +5V device.

The number and type of device connectors provided are loosely linked to the form factor and power rating of the power supply. Generally, power supplies with low power ratings and those designed for smaller cases provide fewer device connectors, sometimes as few as three. Power supplies with higher power ratings and those intended to fit large tower cases provide more device connectors, sometimes as many as a dozen. So long as you do not exceed the power supply capacity, you can freely clone device connectors by adding Y-splitters, which are available for a couple of dollars at any computer store.

 Serial ATA hard drives use a different power connector. As of July 2003, few power supplies provide that connector, so the only option is to use an adapter cable to power Serial ATA drives from a standard Molex peripheral connector. We expect Serial ATA power connectors to become increasingly common on power supplies shipped after July 2003, and by early 2004, nearly all power supplies are likely to include Serial ATA power connectors.

Main Power Switch Power Connectors

Desktop/AT and Desktop/BAT power supplies have a built-in paddle switch to turn power on and off. ATX and ATX-variant power supplies seldom have a physical power switch because they are turned on and off by the motherboard. Some ATX power supplies have a rocker switch on the back of the power supply that disconnects the power supply entirely from mains power. This can be useful because the alternative is disconnecting the power cable when you need to kill all power to the system, including +5V$_{SB}$, which is ordinarily always present.

Tower/AT and Tower/BAT power supplies have no built-in main power switch. Instead, they have four power leads that connect to a push-button or toggle switch on the case, as shown in Figure 26-4. These leads, which are usually white, black, blue, and brown, carry AC mains voltage to the power supply.

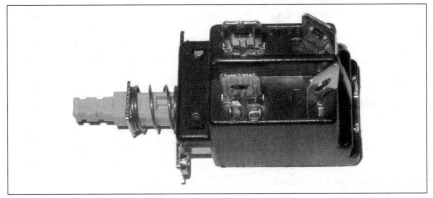

Figure 26-4. Typical connections for a Tower/AT or Tower/BAT power switch

 Although these four wire colors are relatively standard, different switches require connecting them differently. These wires carry full mains voltage, which can kill you, so *never work on them without first disconnecting the main power cable from the power supply*. Connecting them improperly can also damage the power supply and the computer, so never use trial and error or guess about which wire goes where. Contact the case and power supply manufacturers to verify it. Because these wires carry high voltage, we recommend using electrical tape to insulate the connections.

Real-World Power Supplies Compared

Table 26-18 lists the output by voltage of three nominally 350-watt ATX12V power supplies. The PC Power & Cooling Turbo Cool 350 ATX/ATX12V is a premium unit, with a street price of about $65; the Antec SL350 is a name-brand unit that sells for about $45; the Sparkle Power Inc. (SPI) FSP350-60BN is another name-brand unit that sells for about $50. We would like also to have compared a no-name Pacific Rim power supply, but finding technical specifications for such units is impossible, probably because they vary so much from one lot to another that no one bothers to test them.

The three key voltage rails are +3.3V, +5V, and +12V. Note that, although all the power supplies list individual maximum outputs for +3.3V and +5V, they also note maximum combined output of +3.3V and +5V—215W for the PC Power & Cooling unit, 230W for the Antec, and 220W for the SPI unit. Antec is alone, however, in specifying maximum combined output on the +3.3V, +5V, and +12V rails.

Power
Supplies

Table 26-18. Output comparison of three nominal 350 watt power supplies

Rail	PC Power & Cooling Turbo-Cool 350 ATX			Antec SL350			Sparkle Power Inc. FSP350-60BN		
	+/-	A_{max}	Watts	+/-	A_{max}	Watts	+/-	A_{max}	Watts
+3.3VDC	1%	28	92.4	5%	28	92.4	4%	28	92.4
+5VDC	5%	32	160	5%	35	175	5%	32	160
Maximum combined Wattage: 3.3 + 5			215			230			220
+12VDC	5%	15	180	5%	16	192	5%	15	180
Maximum combined Wattage: 3.3 + 5 + 12			n/a			330			n/a
-5VDC	5%	0.3	1.5	10%	0.5	2.5	5%	0.3	1.5
+5V$_{SB}$	5%	2	10	5%	2	10	5%	2	10
-12VDC	5%	0.8	9.6	10%	0.8	9.6	10%	0.8	9.6
Total nominal wattage			453.5			481.5			453.5
Total deliverable wattage			416.1			352.1			421.1

The main differences between these power supplies are as follows:

Total nominal wattage

The most obvious difference is in total nominal wattage. Simply adding the wattages on the individual rails tells us that the PC Power & Cooling and SPI units both total 453.5W, while the Antec is noticeably higher at 481.5W. That measure is meaningless, however, because the wattage deliverable on one rail may be constrained by the amount of wattage being drawn on another voltage rail.

Total deliverable wattage

For all three power supplies, the total deliverable combined wattage on the +3.3V and +5V rails is related. For example, the PC Power & Cooling unit can deliver up to 92.4W of +3.3V and 160W of +5V, but the combined total wattage on those two rails cannot exceed 215W. That means if you happen to be drawing 90W on the +3.3V rail, you can draw at most 125W on the +5V rail, even though that rail is rated for a maximum of 160W. In addition to limiting the combined +3.3V/+5V draw, the Antec unit also limits the combined +3.3V/+5V/+12V draw to at most 330W. Taking these combined limits into account, the PC Power & Cooling and SPI units can both theoretically deliver more than 400W, while the Antec unit is limited to at most 352.1W.

In effect, that means that the Antec is not really capable of delivering 350W unless you can load the +3.3V, +5V, and +12V rails in combination at or very near their maximum ratings. That may not happen with a real-world system. Instead, you may have one or two rails loaded to their individual limits, while another voltage rail has a great deal of reserve. Having a lot of unused +12V, for example, does you no good if what you really need is more +3.3V.

Conversely, the PC Power & Cooling and SPI units are more flexible because they place fewer constraints on combined wattages. Although each of them is capable of delivering more than 400W, they are of course still rated as only 350W power supplies. The difference between them and the Antec unit is that they place no limit on combined +3.3V/+5V/+12V wattage. That means that if a system has a very high draw on +12V (such as a fast Pentium 4 system), the power supply can still pump as much +3.3V and +5V as necessary, within its total 350W limit.

Remember that wattage rating depends heavily on the temperature at which the rating is done. We know that the PC Power & Cooling unit was rated at a realistic 40° C. We have no idea what temperature Antec or SPI used for their testing, but 25° C seems to be the industry standard. A nominal 350W power supply tested at 25° C actually delivers about the same wattage as a 230W power supply rated at 40° C.

Regulation

The PC Power & Cooling and SPI units are both within ATX/ATX12V specifications for regulation on all voltage rails. The Antec unit is not ATX-compliant because its 5% load regulation on +3.3VDC is less stringent than the ATX-required 4%. In practical terms, the Antec unit is likely to function adequately, but its poor +3.3V regulation is cause for concern. The SPI unit is regulated within ATX specifications. The PC Power & Cooling unit meets ATX requirements on every rail and greatly exceeds them on the critical +3.3V rail. Tight voltage regulation is key for system stability, so we know which of these power supplies we'd choose.

A more subtle aspect of nominal wattage is component loading. A premium power supply may deliver its rated wattage while driving its components at only 50% of their rated capacity; a midrange name-brand power supply may deliver near its rated wattage while driving its components at 70% of their rated capacity. A no-name power supply will likely deliver nowhere near its rated wattage, and will drive its components at 100% (or even more) of their rated capacity to do so.

Component loading has two important aspects. First, components driven at a fraction of their rated capacity are likely to exceed their design life significantly, while those driven at (or above) their designed limits are likely to be short-lived. Second, a component that is "loafing" is likely to perform much better than one that is being driven at or above its design capacity. For example, components designed to supply +3.3V and driven at 50% of capacity are likely to supply 3.3V bang-on; those driven at 100% of capacity may deliver 3.3V nominal, but the actual voltage may vary significantly. Unfortunately, short of disassembling the power supply (never a good idea) and checking the number, size, and quality of the components, about the only thing you can do to assure that the power supply you choose uses good components is to buy a good name-brand power supply.

Comparing the full spec sheets for these three power supplies turns up other differences not shown in the table, of varying significance. For example, the hold time of the PC Power & Cooling unit is 20 ms, which is the minimum required for

ATX compliance. The hold time of the SPI unit is specified as "16.6 ms minimum" and that of the Antec is unspecified, which means that technically neither of these units is ATX-compliant based on the listed specifications. Similarly, the PWR_OK delay times of the Antec and SPI units are listed as 100 – 500 milliseconds, which is technically within ATX requirements, but far inferior to the specific 300 millisecond PWR_OK delay specified for the PC Power & Cooling unit.

 Do not confuse hold time with PWR_OK delay. Hold time specifies the duration for which output power remains within specifications after input power is lost, as when the power flickers. PWR_OK delay time refers to when the power supply is turned on, and specifies the lag between the time all voltage rails begin supplying stable voltage and the time the power supply asserts the PWR_OK (Power Good) signal to the motherboard. Predictable PWR_OK delay is critical to the timing of the boot sequence.

In short, there are very real differences between power supplies, even if they have the same nominal rating. The PC Power & Cooling unit is a superb power supply, which will supply clean, closely regulated power even when driven at its rated wattage, and is unlikely to fail even if used 24X7 at its rated output power. The SPI unit is a very good power supply, likely to work reliably in less-demanding applications. The Antec unit is relatively poorly regulated, particularly relative to the PC Power & Cooling unit, and is an appropriate choice only when system cost is a very high priority. (In fairness, we should point out that the Antec SL350 is an economy power supply and that Antec does make better power supplies, including the superb TruePower series.) About the best you can say for no-name units is that power is likely to come out of them, although how much, how well-regulated, and for how long are in doubt.

Choosing a Power Supply

Use the following guidelines to choose a power supply appropriate for your system:

Choose the correct form factor
Above all, make sure the power supply you buy fits your case and has the proper connectors for your motherboard. If your motherboard includes the ATX Optional Power Supply Connector, buy a power supply that provides that connector. Consider buying such a power supply even if your current motherboard does not require that connector so that if you upgrade, the connector will be available.

Match power supply to system configuration
Some sources recommend adding up maximum current draws for all system components and sizing the power supply on that basis. The problem with that method is that it can be nearly impossible to determine those draws for all components, especially motherboards and expansion cards. We recommend using the KISS method instead, as follows:

Basic system

> For a desktop or mini-tower system with a low-end processor, 128 MB or less of RAM, one ATA hard disk, one ATAPI DVD/CD-ROM drive, and zero or one expansion card, install a 300W ATX12V power supply.

Mainstream system

> For a desktop or mini/mid-tower system with a midrange processor, 256 MB of RAM, one or two ATA hard disks, a DVD/CD-ROM drive, a DVD/CD writer, perhaps a tape drive, and one or two expansion cards, install a 350W power supply.

High-performance system

> For a mid- or full-tower system with a fast processor, 512 MB of RAM, one or two fast SCSI or ATA hard disks, a DVD/CD-ROM drive, a DVD/CD writer, a tape drive, and several expansion cards, install a 400W to 450W power supply.

Heavily loaded system

> For a full-tower system with fast dual processors, 1 GB or more of RAM, two or three fast SCSI or ATA hard disks, a CD/DVD-ROM drive, a DVD/CD writer, a tape drive, and all expansion slots filled, install a 450W to 600W power supply.

Obviously, individual configurations vary, but generally following these guidelines ensures that the power supply is adequate for the current configuration and has some room for growth if you add components. If in doubt, buy the next size up.

> If you build a dual-CPU system, make sure the power supply you choose is rated for dual-CPU motherboards. Even power supplies that have relatively high overall wattage ratings may not be adequate for dual-CPU motherboards. Dual processors may draw 150W or more, which may exceed the maximum allowable current at the required voltage. Our best advice for those building dual-CPU systems is to check the PC Power & Cooling web site (*http://www.pcpowercooling.com*) to locate a power supply appropriate for your configuration.

Match power supply capacity to case style

> Regardless of your current configuration, take case style into account. It is senseless, for example, to install a 200W power supply in a full-tower case. You might just as well buy a smaller case because that power supply will never support even a fraction of the number of devices the case can hold. Neither does it make sense to install a 600W power supply in a mini-tower case, which simply does not have room for enough drives to require all that power.

Avoid ATX power supplies that are not Pentium 4-compatible

> Any ATX power supply you buy should be ATX12V-compliant. Even if you're not using a Pentium 4 in that system, buying an ATX12V power supply protects your upgrade path if you decide later to install a newer motherboard. We expect that an increasing number of newly introduced

motherboards, both for Pentium 4 and other processors, will begin including the 4-pin +12VDC connector. If your power supply doesn't have this connector, you may need to replace the power supply when you upgrade the motherboard. (You can use an ATX12V adapter cable to pull +12VDC from a drive connector to the motherboard, but that doesn't guarantee that your original power supply will work with motherboards that require $+5V_{SB}$ current higher than required by ATX 2.03.) Buying an ATX12V unit now avoids that needless expense later.

Avoid cheap power supplies

Don't assume that the power supply bundled with an inexpensive case or a $20 unit you find on the sale table at the computer store is adequate. It probably isn't. A good power supply costs at least $35 for a basic system, $50 to $75 for a mainstream mini/mid-tower system, and $100 or more for heavily loaded, full-tower systems.

Avoid replacing proprietary power supplies

Some big-name computer makers (notably Compaq and Dell) have used proprietary power supplies in their systems, although this practice is fortunately less common nowadays. If a proprietary power supply fails, the only source for a replacement is the manufacturer, who may charge literally $500 for a power supply equivalent to a standard $50 unit. If you need to replace a proprietary power supply in a system that cannot physically accept a standard power supply, it may be cheaper to replace the PC than to buy a new power supply for it. Rather than pay proprietary prices, consider buying a new case and power supply and migrating the components from the failed unit to the new case. You may also have to buy a new motherboard, but you should be able to migrate the processor, memory, and other components.

A similar problem exists with some of the inexpensive systems sold by such retailers as Circuit City and Best Buy. Many of those use inexpensive, low-output SFX power supplies that are prone to fail quickly. For some of these systems, manufacturer policies make replacing a failed power supply quite expensive, even if the system is still under warranty.

 Instead of overpaying for a replacement power supply that's no better than the original, purchase a replacement power supply from PC Power & Cooling (*http://www.pcpowercooling.com*), which makes both a standard SFX power supply and a special SFX model for eMachines and HP 67XX models. Better still, replace the power supply *before* it fails. Doing so improves the system's reliability, stability, and life expectancy. Put the original, still-functioning power supply on the shelf as a spare, although you probably won't need it.

Installing a Power Supply

Standard power supplies are secured with four screws. To remove a power supply, disconnect the AC supply cord, the motherboard power cable(s), and all device power cables. Use one hand to hold the power supply in place while removing the four screws that secure it, and then lift it straight out. Some power supplies use a locking tab and slot arrangement, so you may have to slide the power supply a short distance to clear the tab before lifting it out. To install a power supply, reverse that process. Slide the power supply into place, as shown in Figure 26-5, making sure that the locking tab, if present, mates with the slot.

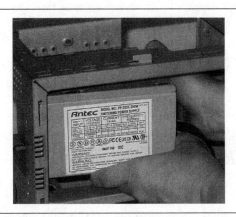

Figure 26-5. Sliding the power supply into position

Once the power supply is in place, align the screw holes and insert the screws, as shown in Figure 26-6. If necessary, support the power supply with one hand while you insert screws with the other. Most good cases (such as the Antec KS-288 shown) have a tray that supports the power supply, while other cases simply leave the power supply hanging in midair, secured only by the screws. In the latter situation, you may want to get someone to volunteer a second pair of hands to hold the power supply while you insert the screws, particularly if you're working in an awkward position. We've seen at least one motherboard damaged by a dropped power supply, which ripped the processor, heatsink/fan, and socket right out the motherboard on its way past.

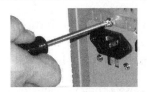

Figure 26-6. Securing the power supply by inserting the four screws (be sure to align it properly first)

Once the power supply is in place and secured, check the position of the voltage selection switch, shown in Figure 26-7, and reset it if necessary. Do not neglect this step. If the power supply voltage switch is set to 220/240V and you connect the system to 110/120V mains, nothing bad happens, though the system doesn't run. But if your mains voltage is 220/240V and you leave the power supply voltage switch set to 110/120V, you can expect your motherboard and connected components to literally burn to a crisp within a second of applying power to it.

Some power supplies are autosensing and so do not have a voltage selection switch. But if yours does have such a switch, make sure to set it properly before you connect any cables.

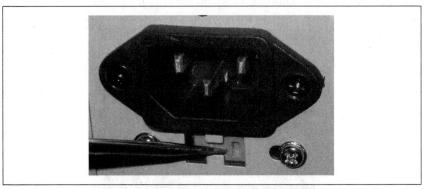

Figure 26-7. Setting the voltage selection switch for the correct local voltage

Once you have installed and secured the power supply and set the voltage selection switch, reconnect the motherboard power cables and all drive power cables. If your system has auxiliary fans that are powered from power supply connectors, reconnect those too. Once you've verified that everything is installed and connected correctly, reconnect the main power cable and apply power to the system.

Troubleshooting Power Supplies

Suspect a power supply problem if you experience any of the following symptoms, particularly in combination:

Parity check errors
Such errors may be caused by defective or poorly seated memory or by overheating, but insufficient or poorly regulated +3.3VDC or +5VDC (depending on memory type) from a failing or inadequate power supply is a likely cause.

Sporadic or regular boot failures
Obviously, such errors may instead be caused by hard disk, cable, or disk controller problems, but inadequate or poorly regulated +12VDC (less commonly, +5VDC) is also a common cause of this problem.

Spontaneous reboots or system lockups during routine operations, not attributable to running a particular program
Numerous other factors can cause this problem, but one common cause is insufficient or poorly regulated +3.3VDC and/or +5VDC being provided to the memory and/or processor.

Lockups after installing a new processor, memory, disk drive, or expansion card
Driver issues and resource conflicts aside, this problem commonly occurs when new components overload a marginal power supply. This is particularly likely to occur if you make dramatic changes to the system, such as

replacing a slow CPU with a fast, high-current CPU; if you expand memory significantly—e.g., from 128 MB to 512 MB; if you add a high-current expansion card such as a fast AGP video card or internal modem; or if you add a high-current drive such as a high-performance SCSI hard disk or a CD burner to the system. Note that the power supplies provided with commercial systems, particularly inexpensive ones, often have very little reserve.

Failure to function with a Wake-on-LAN (WOL) motherboard
The motherboard and power supply may both be operating properly but be incompatible. Many early ATX power supplies (and some current models) provide 100 mA or less of $+5V_{SB}$. Although that output met the ATX 2.01 requirements, WOL motherboards require $+5V_{SB}$ of at least 720 mA.

Slow disk performance
Although this may seem an odd symptom to be related to power supply problems, inadequate voltage and current can cause disk retries on both reads and writes. The error correction circuitry built into hard disks and controllers means that this problem often (usually) goes undiagnosed. People often say to us something like, "I replaced the power supply as you suggested, and now my hard disk seems a lot faster. Is that possible?" Yes, it is.

 A very common source of problems is using a noncompliant ATX-like power supply. We say "ATX-like" because many power supplies that fit ATX cases are not ATX-compliant. Motherboards vary in their tolerance for voltages that are slightly out of spec, and a marginal power supply that works fine with one motherboard may not work with another, even of the same model.

Troubleshooting power supplies is difficult for several reasons:

- Other than an outright power supply failure, problems caused by an inadequate or failing power supply are likely to be subtle—occasional memory errors, lockups, slow disk performance, and so on—and easily attributable to something other than the power supply.

- It is difficult to "bench test" a suspect power supply because PCs use switching power supplies rather than linear power supplies. Unlike linear power supplies, switching power supplies by design do not operate unless minimum loads exist on specific voltage rails. The minimum load required varies from model to model, but in practical terms you must connect at least a motherboard, processor, and hard drive to most power supplies before they function at all.

- Systems draw varying amounts of current at different voltages during routine operations. For example, a drive spinning up draws down +12VDC, which in turn may cause another voltage rail to fluctuate, causing problems that are not clearly linked to the +12VDC load. Even processors use varying amounts of current, depending on what they happen to be doing at the moment. This constant variation in draw and the interdependency of currents on different voltage rails make troubleshooting very difficult.

- Working inside a power supply is dangerous because high voltages are present, but testing only external connectors makes it difficult to trouble-shoot effectively. Despite this, *we do not recommend removing the cover from a power supply for any purpose.* If you do so and electrocute yourself, don't blame us.

With the high cost of labor, it is usually more cost-effective in a business environment simply to swap out a suspect power supply for a new or known-good unit, particularly if the suspect unit is old and/or was inexpensive to start with. Paying for an hour or two of technician time makes little sense when the alternative is installing a new $50 power supply.

If you're working on your own system, however, and if you have a DMM, you can do a few quick tests that may isolate the problem to the power supply. These steps involve testing voltages on specific wires of the main power supply connector while it is connected to the motherboard. Some connectors have built-in probe contact points that provide easy access to each signal. If yours does not, slide the probe down inside the body of the connector until it contacts the crimp-on connector to which the wire is secured. Ideally, use a DMM that permits logging maximum and minimum voltages over a period of time while you use the system. If you're using an inexpensive DMM, you'll have to settle for instantaneous readings, but those often suffice.

To test your power supply, have a list of pinouts and signals for your power supply type (AT or ATX) handy, and take the following steps:

1. With the black probe touching the power supply case, touch the red probe in turn to each Ground/Common (black) wire on the main power supply connector, on any subsidiary connectors, and on the Peripheral Connectors and Floppy Drive Connectors. The DMM should show 0.00V. Significant voltage present on any ground wire indicates a serious problem in the power supply.

2. If the system is completely dead when it is plugged in and turned on, the power supply may not be asserting Power Good. Even if the system runs, check the Power Good voltage because voltage variations on Power Good commonly cause subtle system problems. With the black probe of your DMM touching the power supply case or other grounding point, touch the red probe to the Power Good line. Power Good is nominally +5VDC. The DMM should indicate between +4.0V and +6.0V. Most motherboards trigger at from +2.0V to +2.5V, so a reading below +4.0V may allow the motherboard to boot, but indicates a possible power supply problem. If the DMM indicates less than +3.0V or more than +6.0V, replace the power supply. If no voltage is present, the power supply is not asserting Power Good, and is likely defective.

3. Test each voltage rail against ground to verify that they are within specifications. If a particular voltage appears on multiple pins, test that voltage at each pin.

4. For each Peripheral Connector and Floppy Drive Connector, test each of the two voltages present against ground. That is, touch the red probe to +12V (yellow wire), and then touch the black probe to the adjacent ground pin

(black wire). The DMM should read +12V within tolerance. Then touch the red probe to +5V (red wire) and the black probe to the adjacent ground pin. The DMM should read +5V within tolerance. Finally, touch each probe to one of the ground pins. The DMM should read 0.00V or something very near it.

If any of these tests fails, a defective or overloaded power supply is the most likely cause. In that event, replacing the power supply is usually the best choice. We have never attempted to repair a power supply ourselves, and do not recommend doing so. If the power supply is under warranty—good units often have three- to five-year warranties—call the vendor for an RMA number and ask if they are willing to cross-ship a replacement unit. If the power supply is not under warranty but is an expensive (high-wattage or redundant) and relatively new unit, contact the vendor about having it repaired. Some vendors quote a fixed price, while others charge time and materials. Be wary of the latter.

Our Picks

Although we certainly haven't used every power supply available, we have used a lot of them over the past 20 years. During that time, we have come to prefer power supplies from PC Power & Cooling (*http://www.pcpowerandcooling.com*). In every respect, PC Power & Cooling units are simply the best power supplies made. They are built like tanks, extremely reliable, and well regulated. In all the years we have used PC Power & Cooling power supplies, we have had exactly one unit fail. And that power supply failed gracefully, not taking the motherboard, processor, drives, and other components with it, as so often happens with lesser power supplies. PC Power & Cooling makes a variety of power supplies, including the Standard economy series, the TurboCool performance series, and the Silencer series of quiet power supplies. One of them is almost certainly right for your system.

In the past, we recommended PC Power & Cooling power supplies exclusively. Some readers balked at the higher cost of PC Power & Cooling units, however, so by popular request we began evaluating less expensive units. After looking at power supplies from Sparkle, Antec, Enermax, and others, we chose those made by Antec (*http:www.antec-inc.com*). The Antec TruePower units are the best power supplies we know of that are not made by PC Power & Cooling. They are well built, durable, tightly regulated, very quiet, and less expensive than similar PC Power & Cooling units. We regard Antec TruePower units as, if not quite equal to PC Power & Cooling units, at least the next best thing.

For what it's worth, Robert and Barbara use PC Power & Cooling or Antec True-Power power supplies in all of their personal systems and servers.

For our detailed current recommendations by brand name and model number, visit *http://www.hardwareguys.com/picks/power.html*.

27

Backup Power Supplies

There really is a difference between an *uninterruptable power supply* (*UPS*) and a *standby power supply* (*SPS*), but common usage now designates a unit properly termed an SPS as a UPS. We call a unit of either sort a *backup power supply* (*BPS*), which neatly sidesteps the terminology problem.

A BPS comprises a battery and some supporting circuitry, and is designed to supply power to your PC for a short period if the utility power fails. This temporary reprieve allows you to save your work and shut down the PC in an orderly fashion. BPSs differ in the quality of the power they supply, how much power they can supply, and for how long they can supply it. BPSs also condition the utility power to protect equipment against spikes, surges, drops, brownouts, and electrical noise.

What BPSs Protect Against

Most electric utilities supply consistent, well-regulated power. But as that power moves from the generating plant through the distribution grid to you, the power company gradually loses control of its quality. A good BPS protects against all of the following power problems:

Blackout
    A *blackout* is a sudden, complete loss of voltage, which may be accidental (a tree falling on a power line) or intentional (the power company shedding load during a power emergency). Blackouts are the reason most people consider buying a BPS, but they are the least-common power problem. Blackouts of very short duration, called *drops*, occur frequently and often pass unnoticed. Drops may be so short that the lights may not flicker. High-quality PC power supplies have enough inertia to continue supplying power to the PC during short drops. Lower-quality PC power supplies have much shorter hold-up times, so even very short drops may cause the PC to lock up. In fact, this is one of the most common causes of PC lockups, and installing a BPS eliminates them.

Brownout

A *brownout* is a significant reduction in voltage lasting from seconds to days. Short brownouts, called *sags*, are usually caused by a sudden load on the line, such as a high-amperage motor being turned on. Longer brownouts may be caused by the utility intentionally reducing voltage in response to demands heavier than they can meet. Utilities supply a nominal standard voltage, which in the U.S. normally ranges from 108V to 125V, with 110 to 115V most common. During a brownout, voltage may drop from nominal to 90V or less. Brownouts can damage equipment because as voltage drops, equipment draws more current to compensate, which increases heat production.

Surge

During a *surge*, delivered voltage is substantially (20% to 100%) higher than nominal. Surges may last from a fraction of a second to several seconds, and often result when a heavy load is suddenly removed from the circuit. Surges are relatively common, and all but the most extreme are relatively benign. Despite claims made by the manufacturers of so-called "surge protectors," most equipment takes normal surges in stride. A good BPS does, however, prevent them from reaching the equipment in the first place.

Spike

A *spike*, also called a *transient*, is an extreme overvoltage of very short duration. Spikes originate from various sources, including voltages induced by remote lightning strikes, transformer failures, and nonbrushless motors turning on and off. Although spikes may carry 50,000 V or more, most are of such short duration (milliseconds or less) that they deliver very little electrical energy. PC power supplies themselves protect against most spikes. A good PC power supply smothers typical short spikes of up to 5,000 V without affecting system operation. Spikes of higher voltage or longer duration are stopped by a good BPS. The worst spikes, those that result from a direct "bolt on copper" lighting strike nearby, cannot be stopped by any power protection equipment.

Most people don't realize that damage from electrical problems, particularly spikes, is incremental and cumulative. That is, a computer may absorb a severe spike and continue to operate normally. But that spike may have caused invisible damage to the chips, down almost at the quantum level. Computer chips, including memory and CPUs, typically use 12 V or less. A spike at even 10,000 times that voltage may simply lock up the system with no other obvious effects or apparent damage, but leave the system teetering on the edge. A subsequent spike, even a small one, may be the straw that breaks the camel's back. Little Spike finishes the job that Big Spike started, causing the system to fail for no apparent reason. A good BPS prevents such problems.

BPS Types

All BPSs have three common elements: a *battery*, which stores electrical energy against power failures; an *inverter*, which converts DC voltage supplied by the battery to the AC voltage required by the load; and *charging circuitry*, which converts AC mains power to the DC voltage required to charge the battery. IEEE recognizes three categories of BPS, which it terms UPS:

On-line

An on-line UPS (often called a *true UPS* to differentiate it from an SPS) connects the load directly to the inverter, which converts DC voltage supplied by the battery to standard AC voltage. The charging circuitry charges the battery constantly while the UPS is operating, and the equipment always runs from battery power supplied by the inverter. On-line UPSs are not often used on PCs because they cost substantially more than SPSs, described later in this list. An on-line UPS has two advantages. Because the PC runs on battery power all the time, there is no switch-over time, and no switch to fail. Also, because the PC does not connect to mains power, it is effectively isolated from AC line problems. Against this, an on-line UPS has three drawbacks. Foremost is cost, which may be 50% to 100% higher than an equivalent SPS. Also, because the system runs from battery constantly, UPS batteries typically require replacement more frequently than SPS batteries, and UPS batteries are not cheap. Finally, UPS efficiencies are relatively low. An SPS runs at nearly 100% efficiency during normal operations, and at lower efficiency only during power failures. A UPS runs its inverter all the time. That results in efficiency as low as 70%, which translates to higher electric bills. This is of little concern to most home and office PC users, but is a major issue for data centers. An on-line UPS may also be called a *dual-conversion on-line UPS*, to differentiate it from a line-interactive UPS, described next.

Line-interactive

A *line-interactive UPS*, also called a *single-conversion on-line UPS*, differs from an on-line UPS in that the load normally runs primarily from utility power as long as that power is available. Rather than convert utility power to DC, use it to charge the battery, and then reconvert it to AC for the load (the "dual-conversion" part), a line-interactive UPS feeds utility power directly to the load under normal conditions. Minor variations in utility power are smoothed out by the inverter using battery power. The defining characteristics of a line-interactive UPS are that the inverter runs at all times, and that the load is always dynamically shared between inverter and utility power. During routine operation, utility power may support 99% of the load and the inverter only 1%. During a brownout, the inverter may support 10% or more of the load. Only during a blackout does the inverter assume 100% of the load. A true line-interactive UPS has no switch-over time because the inverter and utility power dynamically share the load at all times, so a power failure simply means that the inverter instantaneously assumes 100% of the load. Although line-interactive units do not isolate the load from the AC line to the extent that an on-line UPS does, they are quite good at maintaining clean, steady AC to the load. Line-interactive UPSs are common in data centers, but uncommon in the PC environment.

Off-line

Any BPS used with a PC (or even a server) nowadays is almost certainly an *off-line power supply*, sometimes called a *standby power supply* (*SPS*). BPS marketers dislike "standby" and downright hate "off-line," so off-line power supplies are always described as "uninterruptable" power supplies, which they are not. The defining characteristics of an SPS are that it has a switch and that the inverter is not always running. During normal operation the switch routes utility power directly to the load. When utility power fails, that switch quickly disconnects the load from the utility power and reconnects it to the inverter, which continues to power the equipment from battery. SPSs are less expensive than on-line and line-interactive units because they can use a relatively inexpensive inverter, one rated for low duty cycle and short run time.

Unlike on-line and line-interactive units, SPSs do not condition or regenerate incoming AC before supplying it to the load. Instead, they pass utility AC power through a passive filter similar to an ordinary surge suppressor, which means that SPSs do not provide power as clean as that provided by on-line and line-interactive units. In theory, SPSs have another drawback relative to on-line and line-interactive units. Actual switching time may be considerably longer than nominal under extended low-voltage conditions and with partially depleted batteries. Because the hold-up time of a PC power supply decreases under marginal low-voltage conditions, in theory an SPS may require longer to switch than the hold-up time of the PC power supply, resulting in a system crash. In practice, good SPSs have typical switching times of 2 to 4 ms and maximum switching times of 10 ms or less, and good PC power supplies have hold-up times of 20 ms or longer at nominal voltage and 15 ms or longer during sustained marginal under-voltage conditions, which means this is seldom a problem. Several SPS variants exist:

Standard SPS

A *standard SPS* has only two modes—full utility power or full battery power. As long as utility power is within threshold voltage limits (which can be set on many units), the SPS simply passes utility power to the equipment. When utility power dips beneath threshold, the SPS transfers the load from using 100% utility power to using 100% battery power. Some standard SPSs also transfer to battery when utility voltage exceeds an upper threshold. That means that the SPS switches to battery every time a surge, sag, or brownout occurs, which may be quite frequently. This all-or-nothing approach cycles the battery frequently, which reduces battery life. More important, frequent alarms for minor power problems cause many people to turn off the alarm, which may delay recognition of an actual outage so long that the battery runs down and work is lost. Most entry-level SPS models are standard SPSs. The American Power Conversion (APC) Back-UPS series, for example, are standard SPSs.

Line-boost SPS

A *line-boost SPS* adds *line-boost* mode to the two modes of the standard SPS. Unlike line-interactive units, which use battery power to raise AC output voltage to nominal, line-boost units simply have an extra transformer tap, which they use to increase output voltage by a fixed percentage (typically, 12% to 15%) when input voltage falls below threshold. For example, when AC input falls to 100VAC, a line-interactive unit uses battery power to raise it 15V to 115VAC nominal. For

95VAC input, the line-interactive unit raises it 20V to 115VAC nominal. For 100VAC input, a line-boost unit uses the extra tap to raise output voltage by the fixed percentage (we'll assume 12%), yielding 112VAC output. For 95VAC input, the line-boost unit raises it by the same fixed percentage, in this case to 106.4VAC. That means that output voltage follows input voltage for line-boost units, with the resulting transients and current surges on the load side as the inverter kicks in and out. Most midrange and high-end PC SPS models are line-boost SPSs. The APC Back-UPS Pro and Smart-UPS series, for example, are line-boost SPSs.

Ferro-resonant SPS

A *ferro-resonant SPS* uses a *ferro-resonant transformer* rather than the tap-change transformer used by a line-boost unit. Its sole advantage relative to a line-boost unit is that it provides some power conditioning instead of allowing output voltage to vary with input voltage. Against that, ferro-resonant units have several serious drawbacks. First, as a high output-impedance source, ferro-resonant units are inherently unstable with some loads, including the power-factor-corrected (PFC) power supplies that are relatively common in PCs. Second, a ferro-resonant unit can introduce severe oscillation into output voltage even when input voltage is relatively clean and stable. Most important, although ferro-resonant units are often claimed to have zero transfer time, their actual transfer time can be greater than 25 ms, which is larger than the hold-up time of nearly any PC power supply. We believe ferro-resonant units are a poor choice for use with PCs.

BPS Characteristics

Here are the most important characteristics of a BPS:

Volt-Ampere (VA) rating

The *VA rating* of a BPS specifies the maximum power the UPS can supply, and is determined by the capacity of the inverter. VA rating is the product of nominal AC output voltage and the maximum amperage rating of the inverter. For example, Barbara's 120V APC Back-UPS Pro 650 can supply about 5.4A (650VA/120V). Connecting a load greater than the amperage rating of the inverter overloads the inverter and soon destroys it unless the BPS has current-limiting circuitry. Watts equal VA only for 100% resistive loads (e.g., a light bulb). If the load includes capacitive or inductive components, as do PC power supplies, the draw in VA is equal to Wattage divided by the *Power Factor* (PF) of the load. Most PC power supplies have Power Factors of 0.65 to 0.7. For example, Robert's APC Smart-UPS 1000 is rated at 1000VA but only 670 Watts, which means that APC assumes a PF of 0.67 when rating wattage for this unit.

Run time

The run time of a BPS is determined by many factors, including battery type and condition, Amp-hour capacity, and state of charge; ambient temperature; inverter efficiency; and percentage load. Of those, percentage load is most variable. The number of Amp-hours a battery can supply depends on how many amps you draw from it, which means the relationship between load and run time is not linear. For example, our APC Back-UPS 600 can supply 600VA for five minutes, but can supply 300VA (half the load) for 22 minutes (4.4 times longer). Doubling load cuts run time by much more than half; halving load extends run time by much more than twice.

 Many people believe VA rating and run time are somehow related. There is no such relationship, except that units with larger VA ratings typically also have a larger battery, which provides longer run time for a given load, both because the battery itself is larger and because the unit is supplying fewer amps than its rated maximum. It is, however, quite possible to build a BPS with a very high VA rating and a tiny battery or vice versa.

Output waveform

Utility AC voltage is nominally a pure sine waveform, which is what power supplies and other equipment are designed to use. The output waveform generated by BPSs varies. In order of increasing desirability (and price), output waveforms include: *square wave, sawtooth wave,* and *modified square wave* (often somewhat deceptively called *near sine wave, stepped approximation to sine wave, modified sine wave,* or *stepped sine wave*—marketers are desperate to get the word "sine" in there, especially for units that don't deserve it). The cheapest units generate square wave output, which is essentially bipolar DC voltage with near zero rise-time and fall-time, which allows it to masquerade as AC. Midrange units normally provide pseudo-sine wave output, which may be anything from a very close approximation to a sine wave to something not much better than an unmodified square wave. The output waveform is determined by the inverter. The inverter is the most expensive component of a BPS. Better inverters—those that generate a sine wave or a close approximation—are more expensive, so the quality of the output waveform generally correlates closely to unit price. Astonishingly, we once saw specifications for a no-name BPS that listed output waveform as "pure square wave," presumably intending to confound buyers with "pure" (a Good Thing) and "square wave" (a Bad Thing).

 We have heard reports of fires caused by connecting a surge suppressor between the BPS and the PC. Although we have not been able to verify the reports, it makes sense that feeding square wave power to a surge suppressor designed to accept sine wave input could cause it to overheat. On the other hand, there is nothing wrong with using a surge suppressor between the BPS and the wall receptacle. In fact, we recommend it, both to provide increased protection against spikes reaching the PC and to protect the BPS itself.

Battery replacement method

Although it sounds trivial, battery replacement method is one of the most important characteristics of a BPS. Batteries must be replaced periodically, perhaps as often as annually if you have frequent long power outages. Better units have user-replaceable batteries. Lesser units must be returned to the factory for servicing. It's both much less expensive and much more convenient to be able to replace batteries yourself.

 Before you buy a replacement battery from the UPS maker, check Graybar, W. W. Grainger, and similar industrial supply vendors. You may be able to find identical replacement batteries for half or less the price charged by the UPS maker.

Warranty

The length of warranty is a reasonably good indicator of the quality of the unit. Better units have a two-year parts and labor warranty, although the battery is usually excluded. Lesser units often carry a one-year warranty, and we have seen many of them fail not long past that time. The cheapest units may carry only a 90-day warranty.

Configuration options

Inexpensive BPSs may provide few or no configuration options. They may, for example, be permanently set to transfer to battery if the input voltage drops below 102VAC or rises above 130VAC. Better BPSs offer flexible options for setting such things as transfer voltage thresholds, warning type (audible, visual, email and/or pager notification, etc.), delay before warning, warning duration, and so on.

Status indicators

Inexpensive units provide few status indicators, typically only an LED that illuminates when the unit is operating on battery. Better units provide detailed LED or LCD status displays to indicate such things as load percentage, battery charge status, overload conditions, and battery replacement required.

Overload protection

All units include some form of overload protection. Less-expensive units often use a fuse, and may need to be returned to the factory if that fuse blows. Better units use a circuit breaker that can be reset by pressing a button.

Receptacle configuration

Most units include two types of receptacle, often differentiated by color. The first sort are backed up by the battery; the second sort are surge-protected only, and are useful for connecting items (such as laser printers) that you want surge-protected but do not want to run from the UPS. Also note that units vary greatly in how many receptacles they provide and how convenient they are to use. Inexpensive units mount a few receptacles on the back panel. Better units provide additional receptacles, and arrange them—either by spacing or by making the receptacle a female connector on a short extension cord—so that connecting a power brick or oversize plug does not block other receptacles.

Manageability

There are two aspects to BPS manageability:

Automatic shutdown

All but entry-level BPS units include a network interface port. By connecting that port to a serial port on the computer—which usually requires a nonstandard cable—and running automatic shutdown software supplied with the OS or the BPS, you can allow the BPS to shut down the computer in an orderly manner during a power failure before battery power runs out. If your computer runs unattended, automatic shutdown is a valuable feature. Some BPS models support automatic shutdown via a USB link. If yours does, make sure the unit also supports serial connection, or it will be unusable with Windows NT 4 and other OSs that don't support USB. Note that if you share one BPS among computers, you will be able to shut down only one of them automatically unless you purchase expensive hardware designed to distribute the automatic shutdown signal to multiple computers.

SNMP manageability

Simple Network Management Protocol (SNMP) can be used to centralize monitoring and control of a large network. In that environment, having SNMP-capable BPSs is important, but in typical home-office and small-business environments, SNMP support is a nonissue. Inexpensive BPSs do not support SNMP. Midrange and high-end SPSs may include it as a standard or optional feature. If SNMP is an issue for you, make sure that the BPS manufacturer supplies an MIB that is usable by your management package. If you don't know what an MIB is, don't worry about it.

Here are some BPS characteristics that are promoted by marketers but are largely meaningless:

Operating system certification

This item is pertinent only if you use shutdown software, either that bundled with the OS or that provided by the BPS manufacturer. The shutdown software provided with a modern OS recognizes most common BPS models, and can usually be configured to support oddball requirements from off-brand BPSs. Most people use the automatic shutdown software bundled with the BPS, as it is usually more functional and supports specific features of the BPS model. In that case, the only thing that matters is that it runs on your OS, which it is likely to do unless you're running something relatively uncommon such as OS/2. Linux support, formerly rare, is now common. OS certification should be at most a checklist item.

Switching time

Typical BPSs have nominal switching times of 2 to 4 ms. That's best case. Under adverse conditions, such as an extended period of low-voltage, partially discharged batteries, and so on, transfer time can be longer. A typical BPS might list worst-case transfer time of 8 ms, which should be within the hold-time of any decent power supply, even operating under adverse conditions. Shorter is obviously better here, but don't give nominal switching time too much weight.

Connected equipment warranty

Most BPS makers include a connected equipment warranty, typically for $25,000. In theory, if your equipment suffers damage attributable to a fault in the BPS, the BPS company pays to repair or replace it. That sounds good, but the truth is that few people ever collect on such warranties. There are so many exclusions and limitations, including the fact that the coverage is often subrogated to your home or business insurance, that such warranties are all sizzle and no steak.

Choosing a BPS

Use the following guidelines when choosing a BPS:

Select BPS type according to application
On-line and line-interactive units are too large and too expensive for most PC applications. Consider them only for enterprise/departmental servers and other critical systems. For standard PCs and workgroup servers, buy an off-line unit. If your location is subject to frequent power problems and you can afford to do so, choose a line-boost unit, which greatly extends run time under brownout conditions.

Pick a unit with adequate VA and run time
You can calculate VA requirements by checking the maximum amperage listed on the PC power supply and on each other component the UPS will power. Total these maximum amperages and multiply by the nominal AC voltage to determine VA requirements. The problems with this method are that it is time-consuming and results in a much higher VA than you actually need. For example, a typical 250W PC power supply that actually draws about 375 VA (250/0.67) when fully loaded may list 8A maximum draw, which translates to nearly 1000VA. A better method is to use one of the sizing tools that most BPS makers provide on their web sites. For example, the APC UPS Selector (*http://www.apc.com/sizing/selectors.cfm*) allows you to specify your system configuration, the run time you need, and an allowance for growth. From that information, it returns a list of suitable APC models, with the estimated run times for each. Or, for a quick-and-dirty selection, simply use the following guidelines:

Entry-level system
For a low-profile, desktop, or mini-tower system with a slow processor, 128 MB of RAM, one IDE hard disk, zero or one expansion cards, and a 15- or 17-inch monitor, choose a 280VA to 420VA unit.

Mainstream system
For a desktop or mini-tower system with a midrange processor, 256 MB of RAM, one or two IDE hard drives, one or two expansion cards, and a 17- or 19-inch monitor, choose a 350VA to 600VA unit.

High-performance system/small server
For a mini-tower or tower system with one processor, 256 MB to 512 MB of RAM, one or two fast ATA or SCSI hard drives, several expansion cards, and a 19-inch or larger monitor, choose a 500VA to 700VA unit.

Dual-CPU system
For a mini-tower or tower system with dual processors, 512 MB or more of RAM, two or three fast ATA or SCSI hard drives, several expansion cards, and a 19- to 21-inch monitor, choose a 650VA to 1000VA unit.

In each case, the smaller unit provides little reserve capacity for expansion, and may provide as little as five minutes of run time. The larger unit typically provides 30% to 50% reserve capacity for expansion, and run times of 15 to 25 minutes.

Consider buying one BPS for multiple PCs

If you need to protect multiple PCs in close proximity, consider buying one or a few larger units rather than many inexpensive smaller units. The larger unit will probably cost less for the same cumulative VA and run time, and will likely provide superior features (e.g., line-boost and a better waveform). The only drawback to one large unit versus multiple smaller ones is that the larger unit will be able to shut down only one connected system automatically unless you also buy shutdown-sharing hardware, which is quite expensive.

Get the best waveform you can afford

The very cheapest units provide square wave output, which PC power supplies can use for short periods without damage. However, running a computer on square wave power for extended periods stresses the power supply and may eventually damage it. Also, square wave units are entirely unsuitable for other electronic devices, which they can quickly damage. Buy a square wave unit only if the alternative is not being able to afford a BPS at all. For general use, buy a unit that provides simulated sine wave if you expect to run the PC for 10 minutes or less on backup power before shutting it down. Buy a true sine wave unit if you expect to run the PC for extended periods on backup power, or if you also plan to power equipment that is intolerant of pseudo-sine wave power (such as some monitors and external drives).

Make sure the BPS has user-replaceable batteries

BPS batteries are consumable items. Under normal conditions, a battery may be usable for between two and five years, but if you have frequent outages lasting long enough for the battery to undergo deep discharge, you may find that the battery needs to be replaced annually or more often. Many BPS units must be returned to the factory for battery replacement, which incurs very high shipping costs and leaves you without the BPS until it is returned. Better units have user-replaceable batteries, which allow you to stock a replacement battery, install it when necessary, and simply purchase another replacement. The advantage of user-replaceable batteries, both in cost and convenience, is difficult to overstate.

Our Picks

Over the last 15 years, we have bought scores of BPSs of every size and type for ourselves and our clients, nearly all of them from American Power Conversion (APC) (*http://www.apc.com*). We have had few problems with APC units, something we can't say for units we've used from some competitors.

For current recommendations by brand and model, visit: *http://www. hardwareguys.com/picks/bps.html*.

Backup Power Supplies

28

Building a PC

The first step in building a PC is to choose the components. In the first edition of this book, we included a chapter on designing a PC. As popular as that chapter was, it went out of date even before the book was published. For later editions, we decided to put such time-sensitive information on our web site, where it can be updated.

For the configurations we currently recommend, visit *http://www.hardwareguys. com/guides/guides.html*. There you'll find component lists, links to pricing information, and advice on choosing components for anything from a no-frills system to a high-performance system. We don't guarantee that these are the "best" system configurations possible (whatever that means), but they should at least provide a solid point of departure when you design your own system.

Purchasing Components

After you choose the components, the next step is to order them. Rather than shopping for the absolute lowest price for each component, we try to order everything from just one or two vendors. Ordering piecemeal incurs additional shipping costs that often nullify small price breaks on individual items. Although we try to order everything from one place, we usually have to place two or three orders because one or another vendor doesn't carry a particular item or is out of stock.

We're frequently asked to suggest which resellers are the best or cheapest or most reliable. We can't offer such advice because, although we buy a lot of stuff, we don't buy enough to have a statistically valid sample from one vendor, let alone from every vendor. All we can tell you is what we do, without representing that our choices are necessarily best for you. A reseller that treated us right may ship you the wrong items, and a reseller with whom we had problems may in fact be an excellent reseller overall.

Our first step is always to check Reseller Ratings (*http://www.resellerratings.com*), which offers detailed ratings of hundreds of resellers, including historical information. Because Reseller Ratings uses feedback from users, there's always the possibility that a reseller has stuffed the ballot box, so we look not just for a high overall rating, but a large number of votes. A reseller that has a perfect rating based on 10 votes may be an excellent company, or it may just have voted for itself. A reseller that has an excellent rating based on 1,500 votes is probably an excellent choice (although we suppose a particularly industrious dishonest reseller might have voted for itself 1,500 times).

Although the vendor ratings on Reseller Ratings may not be entirely reliable, we can say that ratings for those resellers from whom we have purchased generally correspond with our own experiences, good and bad. It's always worth your time to check a vendor's current rating, particularly if you haven't bought from that vendor for some time. Bad vendors almost never change their spots, but good vendors may take a sudden turn for the worse.

When evaluating vendors, pay particular attention to the following:

Shipping charges
> Make sure to factor the cost of shipping into your price comparisons. Some vendors advertise very low prices, but have ridiculously high shipping charges, particularly on monitors, cases, and other heavy or bulky items. We were once quoted $28 to ship a single hard drive by surface UPS, for example, and $63 to ship a 17-inch monitor. Many online vendors automatically calculate and display shipping charges, either per item or for your order as a whole. If a vendor doesn't mention shipping charges, regard that as a red flag.
>
> If a vendor offers "free shipping" (as an increasing number do), find out what limitations and conditions apply. Most vendors that offer free shipping require a minimum order amount. Many use slow shipping methods such as standard mail or UPS ground. Some even intentionally delay orders with free shipping, waiting several days after receipt of the order to actually ship it. In short, many vendors who offer free shipping do everything possible to encourage you to upgrade to a faster (and more costly) shipping method. If you need the items quickly, compare resellers according to the true costs including upgraded shipping charges, if any.

Return policy
> Read and understand the vendor's return policy. Vendors differ greatly in what they regard as an acceptable reason for a return and how they handle returns that turn out not to be defective. Also look carefully for any mention of a restocking fee, which may be 25% or more, and may be charged even if you are returning an item because it is incompatible with your system. Better vendors have a no-questions-asked return policy and do not charge restocking fees. Unless the product is defective, all vendors refuse returns of opened software (except in exchange for the same title) and printers that have had ink or toner installed.

Warranty policy
> Better resellers endorse the manufacturer's warranty. That is, if you buy a product from them and that product fails, you return the product to them and

they ship you a replacement. Most such vendors limit their endorsement of the manufacturer's warranty to 30 or 60 days. The very best vendors pay for shipping both ways, and will often cross-ship a replacement before they receive the failed product, although they will require you provide a credit card number to ensure that you actually return the defective product. Some vendors have no warranty policy at all. If a product from them arrives DOA, they require you to return that product to the manufacturer. Avoid those vendors.

To make it easy to compare total price and the price for each item, we create a spreadsheet with one column for the items to be ordered and other columns for two or three of our favorite vendors. After we determine which vendor has the lowest total price, we then compare individual item prices and ask that vendor to match any lower per-item prices quoted by their competitors. "NewEgg has this drive for $18 less than you guys are quoting. Will you match that?" Most vendors will, or will at least reduce the price somewhat.

If you want to take that a step further, use the price comparison services available on the Web to find really low prices. We use *http://www.pricegrabber.com*, supplemented by *http://www.pricescan.com* and *http://www.pricewatch.com*. Some of the prices you'll find are so low that they should raise a red flag. For example, when we checked tape drive prices, we found one vendor on PriceWatch.com that was advertising a particular Seagate tape drive model for $225. The least any other vendor was offering that drive for was $540, so we knew something was wrong with what that company was offering. It may have been selling a used, damaged, or nonfunctional drive, but if so you couldn't tell it from reading its web site. It claimed to be selling new, in-the-box units for that ridiculous price. Someone foolish enough to believe that company would doubtlessly have been badly burned when the product finally arrived (or didn't arrive).

Disreputable resellers change names as often as they change underwear. We once did a search on PriceWatch and found three different resellers offering a component we needed to buy. All of them had that part priced similarly, and all were far below the price offered by vendors we were familiar with. We did a whois lookup on the three domain names, and found that all three had similar registrant information. Apparently, disreputable resellers have caught on to the fact that a low-ball price may scare people off, and so have decided to give the appearance of safety by having several "different" companies offer similar prices. That's one very good reason to use the ResellerRatings site to check historical data for any company you plan to buy from.

We've learned not to buy from "bottom feeder" vendors. They may ship late or not at all, charge your credit card more than the price they quoted, add ridiculous shipping charges, sell OEM versions as retail-boxed versions, ship repackaged or otherwise inferior merchandise, and do other things to raise your blood pressure. Most stop short of outright fraud, but many tread near that line. It's just not worth the hassle to buy from them, but you can use their prices to beat down your preferred vendor. But recognize the TANSTAAFL principle: There Ain't No Such Thing As A Free Lunch. Reputable vendors can't match the prices offered by fly-by-night operations and still stay in business, but reputable resellers can usually do better than the prices they advertise.

When the items arrive, open the boxes immediately and verify their contents against both your original order and the packing list. Don't stop there, however. Open each individual component box and compare the actual contents against the proper contents as listed in the manual for that component. On one memorable occasion, we received a factory-sealed box that contained manuals, CD, and cables, but not the product itself! Check carefully.

Some vendors routinely ship used product but represent it as new. Regardless of who you buy from, make it absolutely clear that you will accept only new, factory-fresh product. Repackaged products are not acceptable. Someone returned them, perhaps for good reason. Vendors should ship returned products back to the manufacturer or distributor. Instead, many vendors simply put returned products back in inventory and ship them to the next buyer.

Don't accept the fact that a box is shrink-wrapped as evidence that it is factory-fresh. Many vendors have shrink-wrap machines, and use them to re-wrap returned products. Many manufacturers have taken to sealing the product box with a sticker or other means to make it obvious if that box has been opened.

If, despite insisting on new product, you receive a product that shows evidence of having been opened (e.g., broken box seal, broken CD seal, slightly bent header pins, expansion slot contacts that show burnishing from having been installed, etc.), contact the vendor immediately and demand to know why they shipped you a used product as new. Demand that they replace it with a factory-fresh product at their own expense, including issuing a pickup slip to have UPS come and get the original product. If the vendor is obstinate, threaten to request a charge-back from your credit card company and to make a complaint for wire fraud. That gets their attention.

Building the System

With all the components in hand, it's time to start building the system. If you've built systems before, you may be able to complete a simple system in a couple of hours, and even a complex system should take only an evening to build. If this is your first system, plan to assemble, configure, and test it over a weekend. Choose a well-lighted work area (the kitchen table is traditional) and lay out all of your components. We use old towels to protect the surface of the table. Observe anti-static precautions throughout.

 Many of the following steps may be done in whatever order is convenient. You may, for example, install the motherboard before the drives (although, having once dropped a drive on an installed motherboard, we prefer to install the drives first). Case design and motherboard layout determine the most logical order of steps, and may mandate doing things in a slightly different order than that listed here. Use your best judgment. Many of the complex steps—such as setting drive jumpers—are described in more detail in the relevant chapter.

Step 1: Prepare the Case

If you are recycling an old case, first remove all components and clean the case thoroughly, using a soft brush and vacuum cleaner to remove dust and a cleaner such as Fantastic or Formula 409 to remove grime. We sometimes take really filthy cases outside and literally hose them down (after first removing the power supply). If you do that, use a hair dryer to make sure the case is dry before you begin installing components. If you're not in a hurry, it's better still to let it sit a week or two and dry naturally. If the power supply has been in use for some time, it will likely have accumulated a lot of dust inside it. Do your best to remove dust using a brush and compressed air (the air hose at the gas station works well), but do not remove the cover from the power supply. Whether the case is new or old, check it thoroughly for sharp edges and burrs and file down any you find. That saves a lot of bloodshed later. Once the case is clean, dry, and defanged, proceed as follows:

1. Verify that all components are present, including the power cord and the package of small mounting hardware and other incidentals. If the case uses drive rails, there should be sufficient rails to mount a drive in each bay.

2. Remove the cover(s) and set them aside, as shown in Figure 28-1. If it is not obvious how to do so, see the manufacturer's instructions. You want the case wide open while you work on it. If the front bezel is removable, you may or may not need to remove it to mount drives. Most removable front bezels simply snap on and off bottom-first, but some are secured with screws. Some cases have a removable motherboard tray. If yours does, remove it also.

3. Remove all drive bezels from the front of the case to give you easy access later when you're installing drives. Depending on case design, you may have to remove the front case bezel before you can remove drive bezels. Most cases use plastic drive bay bezels, shown in Figure 28-2, which snap into place using a small hook on each side to secure them to the chassis. To remove these bezels, use a small flat-blade screwdriver to bow them slightly until the hooks are clear and then pull them out. Some cases use metal drive bay bezels, which are secured with a screw on each side.

   Most cases have metal plates at the front of each drive bay, immediately behind the bezel, to shield against RFI. On some cases, these plates are discrete pieces, mounted with screws or spring-clip retainers. On inexpensive cases, the plates are often stamped as a part of the chassis and may have to be twisted out, as shown in Figure 28-3, sometimes using pliers or a screwdriver. Doing that may leave a sharp barb. File it down now or it will cut you later. Make sure to vacuum up metal filings so that they can't short something out later. Cases often arrive with the plates already removed from one floppy drive bay and one externally accessible 5.25-inch drive bay (for a CD or DVD drive). You need not remove the metal plates from positions where you will not be mounting externally accessible drives. To make the system easier to work on, we sometimes remove all anti-RFI plates, risking the wrath of the FCC.

Figure 28-1. The Antec SX840 mid-tower case with side panel removed (note the two standard 80mm fans at rear and positions for two optional 80mm fans at front)

4. If you order a case and power supply together, the case usually arrives with the power supply installed. If so, verify that all screws securing the power supply to the case are tight and that the voltage selector (if present) is set to the proper input voltage. If you order a power supply separately, install it by aligning any locking tabs and slots, sliding the power supply into position, and securing the screws. Manufacturers often use cable ties to secure the wires coming from the power supply in a neat bundle. If yours did, carefully nip the cable ties with your diagonal cutters to free the wires. Better power supplies come with spare cable ties that you can use later to dress the wires. Electrical tape or the yellow plastic ties supplied with garbage bags work just as well. (See Figures 28-4 and 28-5.)

Figure 28-2. Removing a drive bay bezel with the main front bezel still in place (an anti-RFI plate is visible behind the bezel)

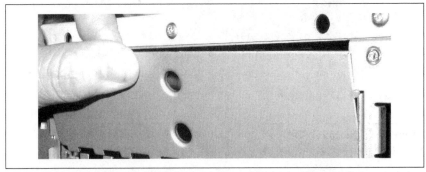

Figure 28-3. Removing an anti-RFI plate with the main front bezel removed

Many power supplies are adjustable for 110/115 volts or 220/230 volts. Make sure to set the power supply for the correct input voltage. If the voltage selection switch is set to 220/230V and your mains power is 110/115, the system won't boot but no damage occurs. But if the voltage selection switch is set to 110/115 and your mains power is 220/230, you will destroy your motherboard, processor, memory, and drives the moment you apply power to the system. Some power supplies automatically sense input voltage and adjust themselves accordingly. If there is no voltage selector switch on your power supply, check the manual rather than assuming that it is auto-sensing. (See Figure 28-6.)

Figure 28-4. Sliding the power supply into position, making sure to align locking slots and tabs

Figure 28-5. Inserting the screws (typically four) to secure the power supply

5. If it has not already been done, install the power switch and connect the main power cables.

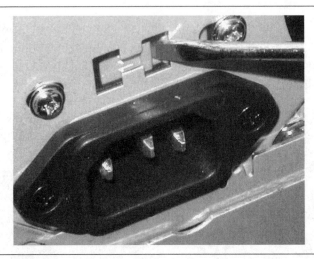

Figure 28-6. If the power supply has a voltage selector switch, make sure to set it correctly

a. Traditional AT power supplies for desktop cases have a built-in power switch (the "big red paddle switch"), and require no configuration.

b. Power supplies designed for AT mini-tower cases have four main power leads (usually blue, white, brown, and black) with spade lug connectors that attach to the power switch on the front of the case. If they are not already connected, connect them, being very careful to orient them properly. Note that these wires carry mains voltage; connecting them incorrectly may short the power supply and destroy it. Use electrical tape to insulate each of the four connections.

 Always disconnect the main power cord from the wall receptacle and/or the power supply before you work on the power switch.

c. In ATX cases, the power switch has only one light-gauge two-wire cable coming from it. You will connect this cable to the power switch header pins on the ATX motherboard during a later assembly step.

6. If the case has an LED to indicate CPU speed, change the jumpers on the back of the LED assembly to cause it to display the proper CPU speed. This step is entirely optional because the LED display is informational only, and has no effect on system operation. For years we had a Pentium III/550 system that displayed the CPU speed as 6 MHz, the default for that case, because we lost the instructions that told us how to change the display.

7. Install supplemental case fan(s), if necessary. Not all cases can accept supplemental fans, and not all systems require them. Minimally configured systems with basic processors ordinarily do not require supplemental fans. Heavily loaded systems—those with multiple hard drives, fast (or dual) processors, most or all expansion slots occupied, and so on—should have supplemental fans installed. Fans are available in several sizes, including 60, 70, 80, 90, and

120 mm. Some cases have multiple fan mounting positions which require different fan sizes.

Ensuring Proper Airflow

If you install supplemental fans, make certain they blow in the proper direction—aiding the main power supply fan rather than fighting it. We have seen processors destroyed by overheating in tightly sealed systems with supplemental fans blowing in the wrong direction.

- Standard AT power supplies and some ATX power supplies blow out from the power supply, exhausting air from within the case. For these systems, install supplemental fans to push air into the case.
- Some ATX power supplies suck air into the power supply, pressurizing the case. For these systems, install supplemental fans to draw air out of the case.

Most supplemental fans can be installed to push air in either direction, either by simply reversing the fan assembly or by throwing a small switch on the fan itself. Some cases are supplied with supplemental fan(s) installed. Do not assume that these fans are necessarily configured correctly. We have seen more than one such case with power supply and supplemental fans both configured to push air into the case, or both configured to draw air out of it. In a typical case, which has many openings for airflow, this may not be a problem. But in a well-sealed case, where the only airflow is through the fans, having the fans working against each other can result in rapid overheating.

---

8. Install the feet on the case. Feet are usually plastic devices an inch or so in diameter and a quarter-inch thick. They may be secured to the case bottom with a bolt and nut, with small plastic spreaders that are inserted from inside the case, or simply by peel-and-stick adhesive. In all cases, the feet are designed to prevent scarring of the surface that the case rests upon. Some cases have vents in the bottom of the case, and must have the feet installed for proper cooling.

9. Most ATX cases are supplied with a standard I/O template already in place, which may or may not be suitable for your motherboard. Remove the motherboard from its antistatic bag and compare the I/O panel on the back of the motherboard with the installed template, as shown in Figure 28-7. If the template that comes with the case is appropriate for the motherboard, proceed to the next step.

The Antec SX840 case comes with a standard I/O template installed, but the holes are in the wrong locations for the motherboard. That means we need to remove the I/O template that came with the case and install the I/O template that was supplied with the motherboard. To remove a template, press gently from the outside of the case until the template snaps out. Some templates seat very snugly, so you may need to use a small screwdriver to pry one edge loose before you can snap the template out, as shown in Figure 28-8. Be careful not

Figure 28-7. A motherboard I/O panel and matching I/O template

to bend the template as you remove it. They are made of thin metal that bends easily, and you may want to keep the standard template in case you ever want to install a different motherboard in this case.

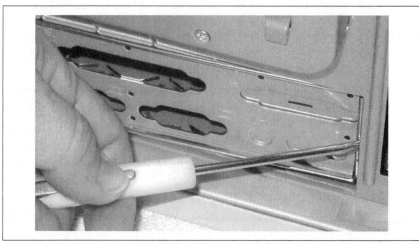

Figure 28-8. If necessary, use a small flat-blade screwdriver to pop the template

Install the new I/O template supplied with the motherboard from inside the case, and press gently toward the outside of the case until the template snaps into place, as shown in Figure 28-9. I/O templates can be difficult to install because they are made of easily bent metal and yet may require substantial pressure to seat. We generally get one edge aligned properly and then press gently until the template seats. If you are sure the template is aligned but cannot get it to seat, use the handle of a screwdriver on alternate corners until you feel the template snap into place, as shown in Figure 28-10. If you do not have the correct I/O template, contact the motherboard or case manufacturer to obtain one. Running the system without an I/O template installed risks disrupting airflow.

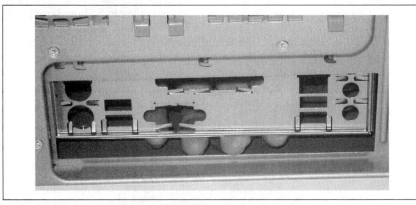

Figure 28-9. Inserting the I/O template from inside the case and pressing gently until it snaps into place

Figure 28-10. Using the handle of a screwdriver to gently press a template that refuses to seat

10. Lay the motherboard flat in the case to determine which positions in the motherboard tray require stand-offs. Screw brass stand-offs into those positions, as shown in Figure 28-11, and verify that each motherboard mounting hole has a corresponding stand-off installed. Also verify that no extra

standoffs are installed, which might short the motherboard. Some cases use all mounting holes; others use a combination of holes and slots. If yours uses slots, lay aside the proper number of white nylon stand-offs, which you will later snap into the bottom of the motherboard for each slotted position. Don't do that now, however, because it prevents the motherboard from lying flat while you install the CPU and RAM. If you need to remove a nylon stand-off from the motherboard, use your needlenose pliers to squeeze the prongs on the front side of the motherboard gently while pulling from the back side of the motherboard.

Figure 28-11. Installing a brass stand-off spacer for each motherboard mounting hole

After you have installed a brass stand-off spacer for each motherboard mounting hole, slide the motherboard into position and verify that all mounting holes line up with the stand-off spacers, as shown in Figure 28-12. Don't install any screws yet, though. We still need to install the processor and memory, and that's much easier to do with the motherboard outside the case.

Step 2: Configure the Motherboard

Motherboards differ greatly in how much configuration they require and exactly how it is done. Most recent motherboards use only one or two jumpers, or are configured through software during BIOS Setup. Older motherboards often have dozens of jumpers to set such things as CPU voltage, FSB speed, and CPU multiplier. Refer to your motherboard manual to determine the proper settings for your processor and memory, and make any required changes before proceeding. The Intel motherboard we're using has only one setup jumper, which we leave as is for the moment.

Step 3: Install the Processor

Before you begin processor installation, place the motherboard flat on a firm surface, padding it with the antistatic foam or bag supplied with it. Installing the CPU (and memory) may require substantial force, so it's important to ensure that the motherboard is fully supported to avoid cracking it.

Figure 28-12. Comparing motherboard mounting holes against chassis stand-off positions to make sure everything lines up

We're installing a Socket 478 Pentium 4 processor, so the instructions and illustrations in this section refer specifically to that processor. Even different models of the same processor may require slightly different installation steps. For example, a slower Pentium 4 uses a different heatsink than faster models, and the heatsink may use a thermal pad rather than the thermal "goop" used in this instance. If you're installing a different processor, see Chapter 4 for more detailed information.

To install the processor, ground yourself to dissipate any static charge, and then take the following steps:

1. Remove the processor from its packaging, and examine it closely to make sure that no pins are bent. A new processor should never have bent pins. If one or more pins are bent, that's certain proof that you were sold a used or repackaged processor. Do not attempt to straighten bent pins. Return the processor and insist on a replacement processor in original factory shrink-wrap.

2. The processor fits a Zero Insertion Force (ZIF) socket on the motherboard. To prepare the socket to receive the processor, lift the small lever on one side of the socket to the vertical position.

3. Examine the socket to determine which corner is Pin 1. Pin 1 may be indicated by a small diagonal cutout on the socket, by a dot or arrow, by a number 1 printed on the socket or motherboard itself, or by other similar means. Once you have located Pin 1 on the socket, locate Pin 1 on the processor, which is also marked clearly.

4. Carefully align the processor with the socket, making sure that Pin 1 on the processor corresponds to Pin 1 on the socket, and then drop the processor into place, as shown in Figure 28-13. We say "drop" rather than "press" because the processor should seat fully in the socket with little or no resistance (that's why it's called "Zero Insertion Force"). If you encounter resistance, either the pins are misaligned or the ZIF lever is not fully vertical. Don't force the processor into the socket because those tiny pins are very easy to bend, which effectively destroys the processor. When the processor is seated properly, its bottom should be flush against the top of the socket.

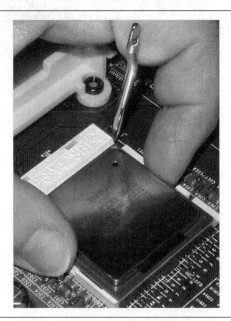

Figure 28-13. With the ZIF arm fully raised, carefully aligning the processor, making sure Pin 1 on the CPU corresponds to Pin 1 on the socket, and dropping the processor into place

5. With the processor fully seated, pivot the ZIF lever down until it is parallel to the motherboard to lock the processor into place, as shown in Figure 28-14. You may encounter resistance while closing the lever, which is normal. Continue pressing the level down until it snaps into place. Don't press too hard, though. If the lever seems not to want to seat, you may have the processor misaligned.

Figure 28-14. With the processor fully seated, lowering the ZIF socket arm until it snaps into place parallel to the motherboard and is secured by the plastic latch

6. Before installing the heatsink/fan unit, use a paper towel to polish the top of the processor to a mirror-like surface to remove fingerprints and other residue, as shown in Figure 28-15. Intimate contact between the processor and heatsink is critical to ensure proper cooling. Even a fingerprint can interfere with heat transfer.

Figure 28-15. Polishing the processor carefully before applying thermal compound

7. Most retail-boxed Intel Pentium 4 processors include a heatsink/fan unit and a premeasured amount of thermal compound in a syringe (some substitute a thermal pad on the heatsink base for the syringe of thermal compound). After you have polished the top of the processor, use the supplied syringe to

deposit the full amount of supplied thermal compound in a small pile at the center of the processor, as shown in Figure 28-16. Although it appears that using all of the supplied thermal compound will make a mess, you need to apply all of it to ensure proper cooling.

Figure 28-16. Applying the supplied thermal compound as a small pile at the center of the processor

8. Make sure the base of the heatsink (the part that comes in contact with the processor) is clean and polished. Lower the heatsink/fan unit gently into position, as shown in Figure 28-17. Keep the heatsink as level as possible as you lower it into contact with the processor. The goal is to press the heatsink gently into place, thereby spreading the thermal compound evenly over the surface of the processor to ensure good heat transfer. If you tilt the heatsink as you're moving it into place, most of the thermal compound may be shifted to one side of the processor. When the heatsink/fan unit is properly in place, it should be sitting level within the heatsink retention mechanism on the motherboard.

9. The heatsink/fan unit includes two spring-steel retaining brackets that clamp the heatsink into tight contact with the processor. Align each bracket so that the central hole fits over the corresponding tab on the heatsink/fan retention mechanism, and then use both thumbs to press the two ends of the retaining bracket until they snap into place against the heatsink retention mechanism, as shown in Figure 28-18. It may require substantial force to seat the bracket, so don't be afraid to press hard. With some brackets, it's easier to seat one side first while it's not under tension and then press down the opposite side until it snaps into place. Make certain that both ends of both brackets are secured, as shown in Figure 28-19. You don't want the heatsink/fan to come loose, particularly if the motherboard is mounted vertically.

Figure 28-17. *After applying thermal compound, aligning the heatsink squarely on top of the processor*

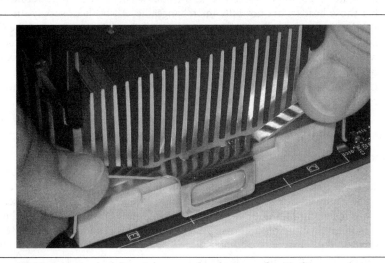

Figure 28-18. *Snapping both heatsink support brackets over the matching connectors on the heatsink retention mechanism*

Figure 28-19. When the retaining brackets are installed properly, the hole on each end snaps into the corresponding tab on the heatsink retention mechanism

10. The Pentium 4 CPU fan connects to a motherboard power header, as shown in Figure 28-20. Most motherboards include two or more such power headers, but those headers are not fully interchangeable. All of them supply the same voltage on the same pins, and any can be used to power any fan, but the CPU fan header is designed to report the speed of the CPU fan to the motherboard, where that information can be used by a hardware monitoring utility. Connect the CPU fan header to the specific motherboard power header intended for it. Other motherboard power headers can also report fan speeds to the motherboard, and are intended to power supplemental chassis fans.

Step 4: Install the Memory

Memory slots are always numbered, usually beginning with "0", but sometimes with "1". Always populate the memory slots from lowest to highest. That is, slot 0 should be occupied before you install a module in slot 1; both slots 0 and 1 should be occupied before you install a module in slot 2, and so on. This section illustrates installing PC133 SDR-SDRAM DIMMs in a D845WNL motherboard. Other modern memory modules—DDR-SDRAM DIMMs and Rambus RIMMs—are very similar physically and install the same way. For information about installing older-style memory, see Chapter 5.

To install the memory module, first pivot the plastic retaining arms on the DIMM socket away from the socket toward the motherboard. Align the keying notch(es) in the DIMM module with the corresponding keys in the memory slot, and the module itself with the slots in the side supports. These keying notches assure that

Figure 28-20. Connecting the heatsink fan power lead to the motherboard CPU fan header

you cannot install the proper module backward (because the keying notches are offset) and that you cannot install the wrong type of module (because SDR-SDRAM, DDR-SDRAM, and RDRAM all use different keying notch positions).

Once you have the module aligned with the slot, place one thumb on each end of the module and press straight down until the module seats in the slot, as shown in Figure 28-21. As the module seats, the retaining arms should be forced to the vertical position, as shown in Figure 28-22. If that doesn't happen, it usually means that the module isn't fully seated or that the retaining mechanism is defective. If you're sure the module is fully seated and the arms are still spread, move them inward yourself to lock the module in place.

Figure 28-21. Aligning the memory module and pressing down with both thumbs to seat it

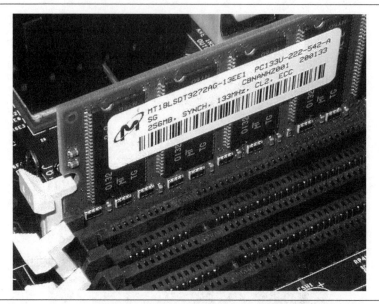

Figure 28-22. When the memory module is seated properly, the plastic retaining arm on each end automatically pivots into place, locking the module into the slot

If you have additional memory modules, install them in the same fashion. After you finish configuring the motherboard and installing processor and memory, lay the motherboard aside for the time being. Use the antistatic bag or foam packaging that came with the motherboard to prevent damage.

Step 5: Prepare Drives for Installation

Several steps may be required before installing some drives, including setting configuration jumpers, installing mounting hardware, and installing supplemental cooling. Some of those steps are difficult or impossible to perform after the drive is installed in the system, so plan ahead. If you are installing several drives, make a written plan of how each drive needs to be configured to ensure that there are no conflicts. As you configure each drive, check what you're doing against the list and mark off each drive as you finish it.

 Many find it helpful to label each drive with its function and settings—e.g., ID-0, ID-1, and so on for SCSI drives, and Primary Master, Primary Slave, Secondary Master, and Secondary Slave for ATA/ATAPI drives. If you later upgrade the system, visible labels eliminate the need to remove drives to examine their settings.

1. In turn, remove each drive from its packaging and set jumpers as necessary to configure it, as shown in Figure 28-23. Leave unused jumper blocks connected to only one pin, which has the same effect as removing the jumper block entirely, but leaves that block conveniently available for future use.

Figure 28-23. Using needlenose pliers to set the drive select jumper on the rear panel of the Plextor PlexWriter to Master

Standard (parallel) IDE/ATAPI drives

For each drive, set the jumper to designate the drive as Master, Slave, Only, or Cable Select, as appropriate. Some ATAPI drives, particularly tape drives, have jumpers to set other options, such as read-while-write or hardware compression. Set these jumpers as recommended by the documentation. A basic system uses one hard disk set as Primary Master and one CD-ROM, CD-RW, DVD-ROM, or writable DVD drive as Secondary Master. If your system has more IDE/ATAPI devices, see Chapter 14 for more information.

SATA drives

SATA drives require no master/slave jumpering. Each SATA drive connects to a dedicated SATA interface connector on the motherboard or an adapter card. In some circumstances, you may want your SATA drives to emulate a parallel master/slave arrangement. If so, see the manuals for the drives and SATA interface to determine how to configure the devices in emulation mode.

SCSI drives

Some SCSI drives require setting jumpers or DIP switches to specify a unique SCSI ID for that drive and whether it is terminated. By convention, the SCSI host adapter is assigned SCSI ID 7. ID 0 is reserved for the boot hard disk, and ID 1 for a secondary hard disk. IDs 2 through 6 are available for use by other devices such as tape and optical drives. Make sure that the last physical device on each SCSI bus (and only the last device) is terminated. For most drives, you enable termination by setting a jumper or DIP switch, but some drives use a small resistor pack instead. Many SCSI drives have numerous other settings—e.g., parity, termination power, and delayed motor start. Set jumpers for these options as recommended by the documentation. If the host adapter and drives are SCAM-compliant (SCSI Configured AutoMagically), SCAM sets ID and termination automatically, but it does no harm to set parameters manually even on a SCAM-compliant system.

Floppy disk drives
Standard floppy disk drives require no configuration.

2. Decide where to mount each drive, considering the following issues:

Convenient access
Place the externally accessible drives you use most often where it is easy to reach them. For example, for a tower unit that sits on the floor, place the CD/DVD drive in an upper drive bay.

Drive spacing
If you have more drive bays than drives, use that extra space to separate the drives, which improves cooling and makes it easier to connect cables or change jumpers.

Heat production
Some drives, such as CD/DVD writers and high-speed hard drives, generate a lot of heat—hard drives constantly and CD/DVD burners intermittently. Heat rises, so install heat-producing drives above other drives whenever possible. This system has only an IDE hard drive and a CD writer, so drive placement is not critical.

Cable routing
We've learned this one the hard way more than once. Make sure your cables will reach the positions where you install the drives. This is usually not an issue with desktop or mini/mid-tower cases, but with a full-tower case it's easy to install two drives that must share the same cable so far apart that the cable won't reach. It's also less a problem with SCSI or SATA cables than with standard ATA cables, which are limited to 18 inches. Take care even with SCSI, however. You may find that your SCSI cable is more than long enough, but the drive connectors are too close together to span two drives installed far apart.

Physical stability
If possible, avoid installing many heavy drives high in the case. The concern is not so much to prevent the case from tipping because most cases are very stable. But tower systems with many heavy hard drives (and the power supply) all installed near the top of the case are very awkward to manipulate because all of the weight is at one end.

3. If the drive is a 3.5-inch form factor and will be installed in a 5.25-inch bay, install the drive in a chassis adapter.

4. Attach any required mounting hardware, such as drive rails, to the drive. Note that some cases have multiple locations where drives can be installed that use different mounting methods, so it's important to decide where each drive will be mounted before you attach the mounting hardware to it. In some cases, drives are mounted directly to the chassis by driving screws through holes in the chassis and into the drive. Other cases, including the Antec SX840, use mounting rails, as shown in Figure 28-24. You will usually

find that the drive can be secured by four or more screws on each side. We normally use only two on each side—one front and one back—unless the system will be moved frequently or is subject to vibration. In that case, we use four screws on each side and secure them with a dab of nail polish to prevent them from vibrating loose. That's not necessary for this system, so we mount the rails with two screws per side. If your case uses plastic drive rails, make sure that at least one screw connects the drive itself to the metal grounding strap on the rail.

Figure 28-24. Securing the drive rails to the drive, making sure that the drive is electrically grounded to the chassis

5. For high-performance disk drives (some 7,200 RPM and all 10,000 and 15,000 RPM drives), install supplementary drive cooling to prevent over-heating. Small supplementary fans (so-called "drive coolers") are adequate for most 7,200 RPM drives. For 10,000 and 15,000 RPM drives, we recommend using a full bay cooling unit such as the PC Power & Cooling Bay-Cool, which integrates a 3.5- to 5.25-inch chassis adapter with two fans and a filtered inlet. The Seagate Barracuda ATA IV drive is a very cool-running drive, and requires no supplementary cooling.

6. If possible, connect the data cable to the drive while the drive is still outside the case, as shown in Figure 28-25. If you install the drive in the chassis first, it's much harder to make sure the cable is aligned properly. If more than one drive will connect to a cable, it's generally best to connect the cable to the "difficult" drive before you install it and make the connections to the more readily accessible drives after they're installed in the chassis. This system has only two drives, each of which has its own cable, so we can install both cables before installing the drives. When you install the cable, make sure the colored stripe on the cable corresponds to Pin 1 on the drive connector. Line the cable up, making sure that it is not offset by a row or column of pins, and then press it firmly into place. We'll connect the power cable later.

Use the proper ATA cable for the type of drive you are installing. Optical drives, tape drives, and similar lower-performance drives can use either a standard 40-pin, 40-wire ATA cable or a 40-pin, 80-wire Ultra ATA cable. For Ultra ATA hard drives, use only an Ultra ATA cable, as shown in Figure 28-26. If you use a standard ATA cable, the drive will operate, but will not provide its best performance. SATA cables are standardized and interchangeable.

Make sure to connect the drive to the proper connector on the cable. PATA cables have three connectors. Two are grouped together toward one end, and are used to connect drives. One end connector is widely separated from the other two, and connects to the motherboard ATA interface. If you're installing only one drive on the cable, connect it to the end connector, leaving the middle connector unused.

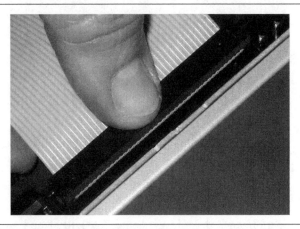

Figure 28-25. Connecting the data cable to the drive before installing the drive in the chassis (this drive, a Plextor PlexWriter, uses a standard ATA cable)

Step 6: Install the Floppy Disk Drive

Modern floppy disk drives (FDDs) have no user-configurable settings. All FDDs are set in hardware as B:. Whether the drive appears to the system as A: or B: depends upon which cable position you attach the FDD to and how the BIOS is configured. Install the FDD, noting the following:

- If the case has externally accessible 3.5-inch drive bay(s), use one of them for the floppy disk drive, saving the 5.25-inch bays for other purposes. If for some reason you must install the FDD in a 5.25-inch bay, you'll need to purchase an adapter for $5 or so.

- A standard FDD cable has three connector positions, one on each end and one in the middle. Between the middle and one end connector, a portion of the cable is twisted. The two connectors separated by the twisted portion are used to connect drives. The other end connector attaches to the motherboard FDD interface. Attaching the FDD to the connector on the far side of

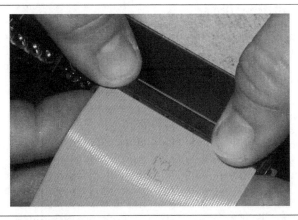

Figure 28-26. Connecting the data cable to the Seagate Barracuda ATA V hard drive (this drive uses an Ultra ATA cable, which is easily discernible from a standard ATA cable by the finer wires)

the twist makes that FDD A:. Connecting it to the middle connector (before the twist) makes it B:. Some cables have five connectors, with two connectors (one header-pin and one edge-card) at each drive position. These dual connectors can be used interchangeably, depending on which fits the drive. The edge-card connector was used by 5.25-inch FDDs, which are obsolete, but many adapters that allow a 3.5-inch FDD to be installed in a 5.25-inch drive bay use the edge-card connector.

- Most recent BIOSs support only one FDD, and have a BIOS setting that allows drives A: and B: to be swapped. This is important if the FDD cable supplied with your motherboard has only two connectors and no twist, as do some we have seen. In that situation, you can use the supplied cable to connect the drive, but make sure to use BIOS Setup to swap A: and B: so that the installed drive appears as A:.

Once you have determined where to install the drive and which connector you will use, slide the drive into the bay. Some drives and cases require that the FDD be installed from the front of the case, and others from the back. FDDs are inexpensive devices, and manufacturers don't spend much money on amenities such as shrouded connectors, so it's often easier to connect the data and power cables to the drive before you slide it into the bay.

Although power cables are keyed, it can be difficult to line up the connection after the drive is installed. If the power cable is too short to allow connecting it to the drive while the drive is outside the case, you will have to connect it after the drive is installed. Depending on where the drive is mounted, it may be difficult to see the connector with the drive in place. If that's true for your system, connect the power cable to the drive temporarily to determine how it should be oriented—e.g., "red wire toward the data cable."

Step 7: Install Other Drives

How you mount hard disk drives, tape drives, and optical drives varies from case to case, and may depend on the drive itself and whether the drive is to be mounted in an externally accessible bay. Some cases use multiple mounting methods, as follows:

Direct attachment

With typical mini- and mid-tower cases, slide the drive into the bay and secure it with screws to the bay itself. Depending on the particular case and drive, you may need to slide the drive into place from the front or from the back. Use the screws provided with the drive to secure the drive. If no screws were provided with the drive, make sure that the screws you use not only have the proper thread, but also are of the proper length. A too-long screw can project inside the drive enclosure and damage a circuit board or other component. Four screws—front and back on each side—are adequate, although there may be room to install as many as eight. Although it is not recommended practice, we have sometimes secured a drive with only two screws on the same side when the case design made it difficult to drive screws into the other side. We have never had any problems result from doing this, but if you do it, do so at your own risk.

Figure 28-27 shows a typical mini-tower arrangement. The drive in the top bay of this Antec KS288 case has all four screw holes aligned with the corresponding chassis holes, which automatically aligns the drive front to back to be flush with the front bezel. Cases built with sloppier tolerances use slots rather than holes to make up for the loose tolerances, although some well-built cases also use slots.

Ever wonder why stools have three legs? It's because three points define a plane, and a three-legged stool is therefore always stable, regardless of the unevenness of the surface it rests on. Our tech reviewer, Francisco García Maceda, called this to our attention. Francisco notes that when working with inexpensive cases he often uses only three screws to secure a drive because that minimizes the danger of the drive being torqued if the case flexes. He (and we) have seen this happen in cheap cases, and it can lead to anything from intermittent read and write problems to premature drive failure. So if you are installing a drive in a cheap case, consider using only three screws to do so. Better yet, replace the case.

Removable drive cages

Some cases use removable drive cages in which you install drives and then mount the cage with installed drives as a single unit. Drive cages are in all other respects similar to the arrangement described earlier. Figure 28-28 shows the removable drive cage being installed in the Antec SX840 case, with the hard drive already secured to the cage. This particular drive cage installs from the front and is secured by thumbscrews. Other removable drive cages install internally and are secured by standard screws or by a clamping arrangement.

Figure 28-27. A typical mini-tower arrangement, where drives secure directly to the chassis

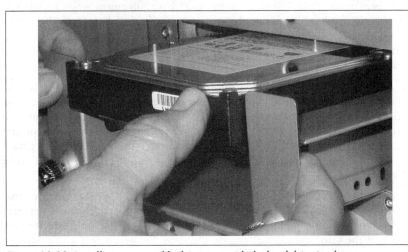

Figure 28-28. Installing a removable drive cage with the hard drive in place

Drive rails

Traditional desktop cases and some tower cases use drive rails, which are secured to the drives and fit slotted channels within the case. Rails are always mounted directly to the drive using screws. The rails may be secured to the case by a screw through the front of the rail into the front of the chassis, by a separate clip that screws into the front of the chassis to prevent the rail from sliding forward, or simply by snapping into place. Figure 28-29 shows the PlexWriter with attached rails being slid into place in the Antec SX840 case. These rails snap into place, which both secures the drive and aligns it properly front to back so that it is flush with the main front bezel once it is reinstalled.

Figure 28-29. The traditional arrangement, in which rails mounted to the drive slide into matching slots in the chassis, and are secured by a front screw or clips

Whichever mounting method(s) your case uses, verify that all externally accessible drives project the correct distance to ensure that they are flush with the front chassis bezel when it is installed. Some cases have alignment holes or snap-in drive rails that make this job trivial. Others require trial and error. In that situation, we usually mount one drive, temporarily mount the front chassis bezel to ensure proper alignment, and then install all other drives flush with the first drive we installed.

You may have to depart from your planned arrangement of drives if you encounter vertical alignment problems. Some externally accessible drives have front bezels that are just slightly too big or have a vertical offset that's slightly incorrect, preventing you from installing another externally accessible drive in the bay immediately above or below the problem drive. You can sometimes gently force such a drive to seat, but it's usually better to rearrange the drives to avoid such tight fits.

Before you install each drive, consider data cabling. If the drive is the only drive that will connect to a data cable, it's easier to attach the cable to the drive first and then feed the cable through the bay and into the chassis. If multiple drives will connect to the same data cable, choose the drive for which rear access will be most difficult after the drive is installed and connect the cable to that drive before you install the drive.

After you install and secure each drive, connect the data cable (if you have not done so previously) and then the power cable.

Step 8: Install the Motherboard

1. Slide the motherboard into position, verifying that each motherboard mounting hole aligns with its brass stand-off, that each nylon stand-off slides properly into the corresponding slot on the motherboard tray, and that the I/O connectors on the rear of the motherboard align properly with the I/O template (or the access holes in the chassis).

2. While maintaining continuous gentle pressure toward the rear of the chassis to keep the motherboard aligned with the mounting holes, insert one of the mounting screws, but don't tighten it fully. Continue inserting mounting screws loosely until all mounting holes are occupied. Finally, tighten each mounting screw gently, as shown in Figure 28-30. Finger-tight is adequate. We've seen people crack motherboards by applying too much torque to the mounting screws.

Figure 28-30. Tightening the motherboard mounting screws sufficiently to ensure good contact, but not so much as to risk cracking the motherboard

Make sure to install a motherboard mounting screw at every position. In addition to securing the motherboard physically, these screws also ground the motherboard to the chassis. Their positions are carefully calculated by motherboard designers with grounding in mind. Leaving one or more screw positions vacant can cause improper grounding, which may cause instability or high RFI emissions.

3. If you have not already done so, connect the CPU fan to the appropriate motherboard power header or to a spare drive power cable.

4. Connect the main power lead from the power supply to the motherboard. For ATX systems, the main power connector is a single 20-pin keyed connector, shown in Figure 28-31. The Main ATX Power Connector is keyed, which prevents misconnecting the main power lead.

Note to the upper right of the main ATX power connector the six solder points for the Auxiliary ATX Power Connector, shown in Figure 28-32. Although the Antec power supply provides this connector, this particular motherboard does not require it, so we leave it unused. If your motherboard

Figure 28-31. The main ATX power connector jack (the light object in the center)

has a connection point for the Auxiliary ATX Power Connector, make sure to connect it as well as the Main ATX Power Connector.

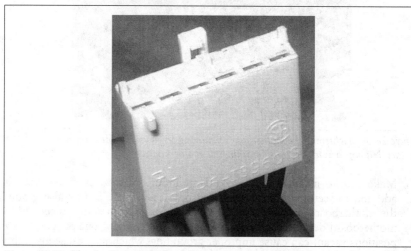

Figure 28-32. The Auxiliary ATX Power Connector plug

The motherboard we used requires the ATX12V Supplementary Power Connector, shown in Figure 28-33. This "P4 connector" supplies the additional 12V current required by Pentium 4 motherboards. It is keyed to prevent incorrect installation, and simply snaps into place, as shown in Figure 28-34. All Pentium 4 motherboards require this connector, and an increasing number of other motherboard have begun using it as well as the industry shifts to using 12V VRMs.

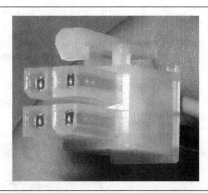

Figure 28-33. The ATX12V Supplementary Power Connector plug

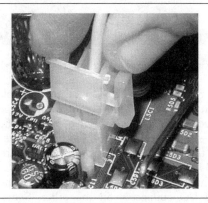

Figure 28-34. If you forget to insert the ATX12V Supplementary Power Connector, your Pentium 4 motherboard will not boot.

 The Antec power supply we're using for this project has a P4 connector. Older power supplies usually do not, even though they may otherwise be capable of powering a Pentium 4 system. If you're installing a Pentium 4 motherboard and the existing power supply is not P4-compliant, you may be able to save the cost of replacing the power supply by buying an adapter cable. These cost $5 or so, and are sold by PC Power & Cooling and most computer stores. They connect to a drive power cable on one end and have the connector shown in Figure 28-33 on the other. Pentium 4 motherboards don't care where they get the extra 12V current, as long as they do get it. Do note, though, that not all ATX power supplies are capable of supplying sufficient amperage on the 12V rail. Even those that are may not regulate the 12V rail closely enough.

If you're working on an older system, be careful. AT systems use two main power cables, each with a 6-pin keyed connector (often labeled P8 and P9), which connect to one 12-pin connector strip on the motherboard, shown in

Figure 28-35. It's possible to swap positions of these cables, which can destroy a motherboard, so be careful which you connect where. For nearly all AT power supplies, when both connectors are installed properly the black wires on each will be toward the center, but we have encountered AT power supplies with nonstandard wire colors. Verify connector orientation with the documentation for your power supply and motherboard instead of making assumptions. Note that some power supplies have both AT and ATX power connectors, as do some motherboards.

Figure 28-35. An AT power connector (the light object in the center)

5. ATX motherboards organize all I/O connectors in a block that matches the I/O template on the rear. AT motherboards use a permanently mounted keyboard connector that aligns with the keyboard hole in AT cases, but other I/O ports—serial, parallel, USB, and so on—exist only as groups of header pins on the motherboard. Those I/O ports are made accessible on the rear panel of the case by installing *port extenders*, shown in Figure 28-36, which are cables with a header-pin connector on one end and the appropriate I/O connector on the other. Some port extenders are normally supplied with the motherboard, but many AT motherboards do not include port extenders for all ports. For example, the extenders for Serial 2 and USB are often optional items. These port extenders are relatively standard items. If you're missing any, you can buy them for a few dollars at any well-stocked computer store.

To install a port extender, align the header-pin connector with the appropriate set of header pins on the motherboard, making sure that Pin 1 corresponds to the red stripe on the cable, and press down until the connector seats. Most port extenders have the external connector mounted on an expansion slot bracket. The case may have more expansion slot cutouts than the motherboard has expansion slots. If yours does, mounting the port extender in an expansion slot cutout costs nothing. If your system has the same number of expansion slots and cutouts, mounting the port extender in an expansion slot cutout wastes that expansion slot. Most AT cases contain several precut holes for DB9, DB25, and other connectors. On better cases, the covers for these holes are secured by screws. On inexpensive cases, the covers are die-cut and need to be twisted out with needlenose pliers. Remove the covers for the ports you need to extend. Remove the port extender connector from the slot bracket and mount it directly to a matching cutout in the rear panel of the chassis.

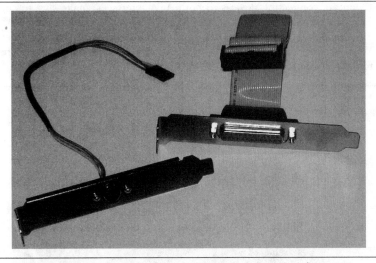

Figure 28-36. Typical port extenders for an AT motherboard (on the left is a PS/2 mouse connector, on the right is a DB25 serial port connector)

Step 9: Connect Cables to the Motherboard

All systems require connecting various cables to the motherboard. These include:

- Cables that connect floppy, hard, and optical drives to embedded motherboard interfaces
- Cables for miscellaneous functions, such as connecting audio out on the rear panel of a CD-ROM drive to the audio header on the motherboard, or connecting a CPU fan to a power header on the motherboard
- Cables that connect front panel switches (power, reset, keylock, etc.) and indicators (drive activity, power on, speaker, etc.)
- Supplementary case fans, which may connect to the motherboard or to power supply connectors

It's usually easier to connect these cables before you start installing expansion cards. Proceed as follows:

1. Connect the drive data cables from the back of each drive to the appropriate connector on the motherboard, making sure to align Pin 1 properly on both the drive and controller. Typical systems have at least two such cables: one 34-wire ribbon cable connecting the FDD to the FDD controller interface on the motherboard; and an IDE cable connecting the hard drive and CD- or DVD-ROM drive to the primary IDE interface connector on the motherboard. If the system has more than two IDE devices, or if you put the hard drive and optical drive on separate channels, you will also need to connect a second IDE cable from the additional device(s) to the secondary IDE interface connector on the motherboard. If the system has SCSI devices installed and the motherboard has an embedded SCSI host adapter, also connect cable(s) from the SCSI device(s) to the SCSI connector(s).

If you are connecting devices to both ATA interfaces, make sure to connect each cable to the proper interface. Figure 28-37 shows the Ultra ATA (40-pin, 80-wire) cable from the hard drive being connected to the primary interface. Visible behind that cable is a standard (40-pin, 40-wire) ATA cable connected to the secondary interface.

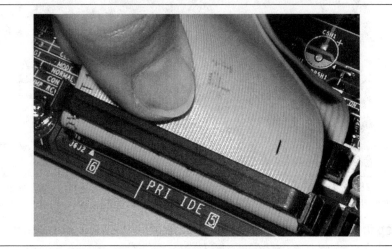

Figure 28-37. Connecting the drive data cables to the motherboard

2. If it has not already been done, connect a power cable from the power supply to the power connector on the rear of each drive, as shown in Figure 28-38. If you have more drives than power leads, use a splitter to allow two drives to share one power lead. Splitters may be provided with the case and power supply, or may be purchased inexpensively at any computer store. Although it's probably not a major issue, the power leads use relatively small gauge wires, so we try whenever possible to connect high-draw devices such as fast disk drives and CD burners to separate power leads. When you insert the power connector, press hard enough to make sure it seats fully. This sometimes requires substantial pressure, and we have seen systems with "failed" drives that were caused by the power connector falling out.

3. Connect any supplementary cables required, such as CD audio, CPU fan, hardware management, temperature sensors, Wake-on-LAN, chassis intrusion, video-source line-in, aux line-in, telephony, and so on. Refer to your motherboard manual for details.

4. Connect the front-panel cables to the header-pin connectors on the motherboard, which are usually arranged in a block near the front edge, as shown in Figure 28-39. Typically these connectors will include: power switch (ATX only); reset switch; hard disk activity LED; power-on LED; and speaker. Depending on the motherboard and case, you may also have connectors for keylock, Infrared port, and perhaps a secondary drive activity LED.

Connectors may or may not be labeled. If not, you will have to trace each wire back to the front panel to determine which connector is which. Most connectors are two-pin. For those that connect to switches, polarity is imma-

Figure 28-38. Connecting power cables to the drives

Figure 28-39. Connecting cables for front-panel switches and indicators to the motherboard

terial. For those that connect to LEDs, polarity may or may not matter. Best practice is to orient the connector for proper polarity. Most cases use the black wire of each pair for ground. The ground pin for each connector may or may not be marked on the motherboard. If not, refer to the manual.

One problem arises more often than it should. Sometimes, the pinouts on the motherboard do not match the pinout on the connector. Intel and other manufacturers are attempting to standardize the arrangement and pinouts for front-panel connectors, but many motherboards and cases still use their own arrangements. For example, we have encountered motherboards that have all four pins present for a standard four-position speaker connector (which actually needs only two wires anyway). If the four-position connector on the speaker wire has one position blocked, as is frequently the case, it is impossible to slide that connector onto the pins on the motherboard without some surgery. Sometimes you can penetrate the blocked position with a needle or sharp awl, or remove the plastic block with a small screwdriver or your needlenose pliers. If that doesn't work, you may be able to bend the extra pin far enough out of the way to slide the connector onto the three remaining pins. Other times, you must use your nippers to cut off the extra pin.

Even that's not the worst case. We have encountered some combinations of case and motherboard with oddball pinouts that are impossible to match up. For example, the case provides a single four-position connector that incorporates the Power LED and Reset Switch, whereas on the motherboard these functions are separated by several pins. In such cases, the only solution is to use a razor knife carefully to split the multiposition connector into separate one- or two-position connectors.

Some cases (oddly enough, usually the very inexpensive ones) avoid this problem entirely by using one-position connectors on all wires that lead to front-panel switches and indicators. That is, each wire is completely independent of every other wire, which allows you to connect individual wires in any fashion the motherboard requires. Dealing with individual connectors is clumsy and time-consuming, but it does provide complete flexibility.

The best way to avoid a situation like this is to verify ahead of time that the front-panel header pins on the motherboard match the connectors on the case.

5. If your case has a supplementary cooling fan or fans, connect the fan power lead(s) to the motherboard or to a spare power supply power connector, as appropriate.

Step 10: Install Expansion Cards

A modern motherboard includes some or all of the bus slot types shown in Figure 28-40. All motherboards provide PCI slots, most provide ISA slots (although the newest motherboards have no ISA slots), and many provide an AGP slot. You can install an expansion card only in a slot that is designed to accept it, either ISA, PCI, or AGP. The best rule to follow is to avoid installing any ISA cards if at all possible. If you have a choice between installing a PCI video card or an AGP video card, choose AGP. For everything else, use PCI.

Figure 28-40. An Intel SE440BX "Seattle" motherboard showing, from left to right, one ISA slot; one combined ISA/PCI slot (which can accept an ISA or a PCI card, but not both simultaneously); three PCI slots; and an AGP slot

To install expansion cards:

1. Decide where to install each expansion card. If you have more slots than cards, leave empty slots between cards to improve airflow and cooling. Video cards, particularly high-performance ones, generate significant heat, so always leave an unoccupied slot between the video card and adjacent cards if possible. Sound cards are also significant heat sources, so give them second priority when juggling empty slots.

2. If your case came with slot covers preinstalled, remove and set aside the slot covers and screws for each position where you will install a card. You may find that removing all slot covers makes it easier to install cards.

3. If internal cables connect to the card (e.g., a SCSI host adapter or a sound card), connect those cables before installing the card.

4. Install each card, as follows:

   a. Align the card bracket so that its bottom tab will slide into position between the case and the motherboard.

   b. Align the card-edge connector on the bottom of the card with the expansion slot. Before proceeding, make certain that the card aligns with the slot both side to side and front to back. Well-designed motherboards, cards, and cases are built to close tolerances, and nearly always align properly, as shown in Figure 28-41.

   Inexpensive components, particularly cases, are often built sloppily and may make it impossible to align the card with the slot front to back, as shown in Figure 28-42. We have seen cheap cases cause a misalignment of a quarter-inch (6.35 mm) or more. If you encounter this problem, the best solution is to replace the case with a better model. If for some reason you can't do that, use your needlenose pliers to bend the card bracket slightly to allow the connector to align with the slot.

Figure 28-41. With a high-quality case (this one a PC Power & Cooling mini-tower), expansion cards align properly front to back.

Figure 28-42. With a cheap case (this one a no-name Taiwanese product), it may be impossible to align expansion cards with the expansion slots

c. With the card aligned properly with the slot, use both thumbs to press straight down until the card seats fully in the slot, as shown in Figure 28-43. This may require significant pressure. You should be able to feel and hear the card seat. When the card is fully seated, the top of its bracket should be flush with the chassis and the screw slot in the card bracket should align with the screw hole in the chassis. When the card is fully seated and properly aligned, insert a screw to secure it.

5. Install a slot cover in each open slot position and secure it with a screw. Do not leave slot covers off unoccupied slots. Doing so damages cooling airflow.

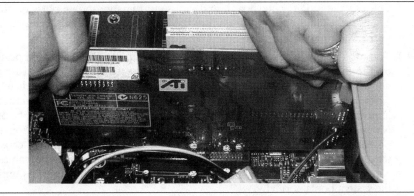

Figure 28-43. Using both thumbs to press the card straight down until it seats fully (be sure the card is aligned first)

We usually install all expansion cards first, and then install and configure the operating system. If you are building a heavily loaded Windows 9X/2000 system, it may be easier to configure if you install expansion cards incrementally. That is, install Windows with only essential cards (video and perhaps SCSI) in place. Once the system is configured properly, shut it down and install the sound card. Sound cards are notorious resource hogs, and should be installed immediately following video to give them first choice of available resources. Once video and sound work, install the other cards one by one. Using this piecemeal method sometimes allows Windows Plug and Play to configure the system properly when attempting to configure everything at once fails. Also note that some motherboards allow "locking down" specific IRQs to specific slots. If your motherboard supports this feature, you can use it to solve problems that may occur when Windows shares an IRQ with multiple devices. For example, slow video may be cured by making sure the video IRQ is not shared. Windows NT does not support Plug and Play, so there is no advantage to using this incremental method with it. Also be careful using this method with Windows XP because if you add or change the hardware environment significantly after activating Windows XP, you'll have to get a new activation code.

Step 11: Perform the "Smoke Test"

At this point, you're almost ready to turn on the PC for the first time. Don't replace the cover quite yet, though. You'll need to do a few more things inside the case before the system is complete. Proceed as follows:

1. Do a final check of the system, making sure that all cables are connected properly and that you haven't left any tools in the patient. Do not underestimate the importance of this final check. We have seen newly built systems shorted out and destroyed because a tool, screw, slot cover, or other conductive part was left where it shouldn't be. In fact, we always pick up the system and shake it gently to make sure no extraneous parts have been overlooked.

2. Connect the monitor, keyboard, and mouse to the appropriate ports on the computer. Connect the power cord to the PC power supply and then plug it into a wall receptacle. Turn on the monitor.

3. Turn on the PC. If all is well, the hard disk spins up, the BIOS screen appears on the monitor within a few seconds, and the system beeps to indicate a normal boot. If the system appears dead or beeps repeatedly, immediately disconnect the power and verify all cable connections and configuration jumpers. The most common problem is a floppy drive cable connected backward—which causes the floppy drive indicator to light and stay lit as soon as power is applied—or an IDE cable connected backward, which may cause the system to appear completely dead. In either case, check the cables, correct any problems you find, and reapply power. Repeat this process until the system boots normally.

4. Some motherboards require running BIOS Setup immediately to allow the system to self-configure. Doing that never hurts, so when the system prompts you with "Press <key-name> to run Setup" (or words to that effect), press the indicated key to run BIOS Setup. Don't make any changes to BIOS settings now. Simply save the default settings, exit, and allow the system to restart.

5. Check the BIOS boot screens to make sure that all installed components are recognized properly. In particular, the initial memory check should display the correct amount of memory, and the screen(s) that list installed devices should show all installed ports and IDE devices. IDE/ATAPI devices should be listed correctly by name or model number. Devices that require drivers are not recognized at this point, which is normal. On fast systems, screens often flash by too quickly to read. Press the Pause key to interrupt the boot process long enough to read each screen. To continue, press the space bar.

6. After you verify that all devices are recognized, restart the system and run BIOS Setup again. With most systems, you need to change only the time and date, and perhaps set the processor speed. Default values work perfectly well for other BIOS settings. Use the motherboard manual to determine which, if any, settings need to be changed. If you plan to delve deep into the BIOS settings to tune your PC for optimum performance, the motherboard manual may be of little use. Most provide only abbreviated descriptions of the most commonly changed BIOS settings. For detailed information about obscure settings, visit the web site of the BIOS manufacturer and download the full documentation for your BIOS version. Even with that information, however, you may find many BIOS options difficult to understand. We have found *The BIOS Companion* by Phil Croucher very helpful in deciphering obscure BIOS settings. You can order it directly from the author's web site at *http://www.electrocution.com/biosc.htm*.

7. If you have devices (such as a network card or SCSI host adapter) that have their own ROM-based setup programs, run those programs per the manufacturers' instructions.

8. When you complete BIOS Setup, save the changes and exit. Power the system down. Some motherboards, notably Intel models, have a configuration jumper that is set to one position for Configure and another position for Normal Operation. If your motherboard has such a jumper, move it to the position that sets the system for normal operation.

Step 12: Install Software

Install the operating system per the manufacturer's instructions. During installation or immediately thereafter, as appropriate, install any driver disks provided with hardware components. If possible, do this during installation to prevent problems. For example, when installing Windows NT 4, we first used the drivers provided on the NT CD for the Intel PRO/100+ Ethernet adapter. As it turns out, those drivers simply didn't support our more recent Intel adapter. We could have saved considerable time simply by supplying an updated drivers disk during installation rather than using the Microsoft-supplied drivers.

Don't assume that you should always install all motherboard utilities and drivers supplied by the manufacturer. After we finished building this system, we installed patches and drivers in the order recommended by Intel, which was to install Windows 2000, followed by SP1 (we actually used SP2), followed by the INF update, followed by DirectX 8, followed by the Intel Ultra ATA Storage Driver (which was subsequently incorporated in the Intel Application Accelerator utility).

After we installed the operating system and service pack, we benchmarked the system. SiSoft Sandra reported hard drive performance of 25,374. We then installed the INF update, DirectX 8, and the Intel Application Accelerator. When we benchmarked the system again, we found that hard drive performance had dropped to below 10,000. Thinking that perhaps there was a conflict of some sort with Sandra, we then tested the system using several other benchmarks, including *PC Magazine*'s WinBench 99 2.0. All reported much lower hard drive performance than expected.

We stripped the system down to bare metal, reinstalled Windows 2000 and SP2, tested again using all the benchmarks, and found that all reported very high performance. We then installed the INF update, DirectX 8, and the Intel Application accelerator again, and found that the hard driver performance benchmarks plummeted dramatically. Thinking that perhaps DirectX 8 was causing the problem, we stripped the system to bare metal again and installed Windows 2000, SP2, and DirectX 8. Running the benchmarks showed the same high performance as before we installed DirectX 8, so clearly the problem was somehow related to the Intel Ultra ATA Storage Driver.

After you complete the installation and restart the system, connect to the Web and check the manufacturer's web site to locate the latest production drivers for each hardware component you have installed, particularly motherboard, video, sound, and network. If you've installed a CD or DVD burner, be sure to look for the latest firmware version for it. Once you've updated all drivers, restart the system and install your applications.

Step 13: Finishing Touches

At this point, the system should be fully functional, but a few things remain to be done:

1. Dress the cables. Many OEMs and most individuals neglect this step, but it's an important one. The typical rats' nest of cables that results when you build a PC can impede airflow, causing sporadic problems due to overheating. One system we saw ran fine for a few minutes and then locked up. As it turned out, a loose wire had fouled the CPU cooling fan, causing the CPU to overheat and crash. If you have them, use cable ties to secure individual wires—like those on power connectors—into neat bundles, and then secure those bundles to the frame. If you don't have cable ties, the little yellow plastic ties that come with garbage bags work about as well. Tape ribbon cables in flat bunches, and secure them to the chassis, well away from the processor and fans. We've used everything from masking tape to duct tape with equal success, although the heat inside a PC can make some types of tape gummy and hard to remove. Fold over a quarter-inch or so at the end of the tape to provide a pull tab in case you need to remove the tape later.

2. If you have a tape drive or CD/DVD burner, run a full backup and stick it on the shelf. If your backup software allows you to make an emergency recovery disk, make one now.

3. If you have diagnostic software that provides a burn-in function, use it. Most hardware failures occur immediately. Those that don't are likely to occur within hours or days. When we're not in any hurry, we generally allow a system to burn in for a week or so before declaring it complete. Even when we are in a hurry, we generally insist on burning in the new system at least overnight. If you have hardware problems, it's better to find out now than later.

> We use and recommend BurnInTest from PassMark Software (*http://www.passmark.com*) for burning in new systems. BurnInTest and the other utilities from PassMark are not as well known as some, but we think they're among the best available.

4. Reinstall the cover on the case, and move the system to its permanent new location. Connect the monitor, keyboard, mouse, and any other external peripherals. Connect the power cord and start using the computer.

5. Enter a recurring to-do in your calendar to remind you to check every 30 to 60 days for updated drivers for the main system components, particularly video and sound. This is especially important if you've built the system using newly introduced components, or if you're using a relatively new release of your operating system.

Index

We'd like to hear your suggestions for improving our indexes. Send email to *index@oreilly.com*.

C

About the Authors

Robert Bruce Thompson is the author or co-author of numerous online training courses and computer books. Robert built his first computer in 1976 from discrete chips. It had 256 *bytes* of memory, used toggle switches and LEDs for I/O, ran at less than 1 MHz, and had no operating system. Since then, he has bought, built, upgraded, and repaired hundreds of PCs for himself, employers, customers, friends, and clients. Robert reads mysteries and non-fiction for relaxation, but only on cloudy nights. He spends most clear nights outdoors with his 10" Dobsonian reflector telescope, hunting down faint fuzzies, and is currently designing a larger truss-tube Dobsonian (computerized, of course) that he plans to build.

Barbara Fritchman Thompson worked for twenty years as a librarian before starting her own home-based consulting practice, Research Solutions (*http://www.researchsolutions.net*). Barbara, who has been a PC power user for more than fifteen years, researched and tested much of the hardware reviewed for this book. Barbara spends her working hours doing research for clients. During her leisure hours, she reads, works out, plays golf, and, like Robert, is an avid amateur astronomer.

Colophon

Our look is the result of reader comments, our own experimentation, and feedback from distribution channels. Distinctive covers complement our distinctive approach to technical topics, breathing personality and life into potentially dry subjects.

The animal on the cover of *PC Hardware in a Nutshell*, Third Edition, is a scallop. The scallop is part of the pecten family, which includes other bivalve mollusks such as clams and oysters. Also called the fan shell or comb shell, scallops can be found on the sandy bottoms of most oceans, in both deep and shallow water. Scallops do not usually stay attached to rocks. Instead, they either rest on the ocean bottom or swim by rapidly opening and closing their shells. The water ejected by the movement pushes them forward and allows them a freedom of movement unusual in bivalves.

The scallop's shell is made up of calcium carbonate and other minerals embedded in an organic matrix secreted from a layer of tissue called the mantle. The upper and lower halves of the shell connect at a straight hinge line that can measure from one to six inches. The shell's paired valves have sharp edges and undulating ridges that radiate out in the shape of a fan and range in color from red to purple, orange, yellow, or white.

Sarah Sherman was the production editor, and Audrey Doyle was the copyeditor for *PC Hardware in a Nutshell*, Third Edition. Matt Hutchinson and Claire Cloutier provided quality control. Reg Aubry, Derek Di Matteo, and Jamie Peppard provided production assistance. Nancy Crumpton wrote the index.

Hanna Dyer designed the cover of this book, based on a series design by Edie Freedman. The cover image is an 18th-century engraving from the *Dover Trea-*

sury of Animal Illustrations. Emma Colby produced the cover layout with QuarkXPress 4.1 using Adobe's ITC Garamond font.

David Futato designed the interior layout. This book was converted by Andrew Savikas to FrameMaker 5.5.6 with a format conversion tool created by Erik Ray, Jason McIntosh, Neil Walls, and Mike Sierra that uses Perl and XML technologies. The text font is Linotype Birka; the heading font is Adobe Myriad Condensed; and the code font is LucasFont's TheSans Mono Condensed. The illustrations that appear in the book were produced by Robert Romano and Jessamyn Read using Macromedia FreeHand 9 and Adobe Photoshop 6. The tip and warning icons were drawn by Christopher Bing. This colophon was written by Colleen Gorman.

Other Titles Available from O'Reilly

How to stay in touch with O'Reilly

1. Visit our award-winning web site

http://www.oreilly.com/

★ "Top 100 Sites on the Web"—PC Magazine
★ CIO Magazine's Web Business 50 Awards

Our web site contains a library of comprehensive product information (including book excerpts and tables of contents), downloadable software, background articles, interviews with technology leaders, links to relevant sites, book cover art, and more. File us in your bookmarks or favorites!

2. Join our email mailing lists

Sign up to get email announcements of new books and conferences, special offers, and O'Reilly Network technology newsletters at:

http://elists.oreilly.com

It's easy to customize your free elists subscription so you'll get exactly the O'Reilly news you want.

3. Get examples from our books

To find example files for a book, go to:

http://www.oreilly.com/catalog

select the book, and follow the "Examples" link.

4. Work with us

Check out our web site for current employment opportunites:

http://jobs.oreilly.com/

5. Register your book

Register your book at:
http://register.oreilly.com

6. Contact us

O'Reilly & Associates, Inc.
1005 Gravenstein Hwy North
Sebastopol, CA 95472 USA
TEL: 707-827-7000 or 800-998-9938
        (6am to 5pm PST)
FAX: 707-829-0104

order@oreilly.com
For answers to problems regarding your order or our products. To place a book order online visit:

http://www.oreilly.com/order_new/

catalog@oreilly.com
To request a copy of our latest catalog.

booktech@oreilly.com
For book content technical questions or corrections.

corporate@oreilly.com
For educational, library, government, and corporate sales.

proposals@oreilly.com
To submit new book proposals to our editors and product managers.

international@oreilly.com
For information about our international distributors or translation queries. For a list of our distributors outside of North America check out:

http://international.oreilly.com/distributors.html

adoption@oreilly.com
For information about academic use of O'Reilly books, visit:

http://academic.oreilly.com

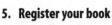

O'REILLY®

To order: *800-998-9938* • *order@oreilly.com* • *www.oreilly.com*
Online editions of most O'Reilly titles are available by subscription at *safari.oreilly.com*
Also available at most retail and online bookstores.